Contemporary
Literary Criticism

Guide to Gale Literary Criticism Series

For criticism on	Consult these Gale series
Authors now living or who died after December 31, 1999	*CONTEMPORARY LITERARY CRITICISM (CLC)*
Authors who died between 1900 and 1999	*TWENTIETH-CENTURY LITERARY CRITICISM (TCLC)*
Authors who died between 1800 and 1899	*NINETEENTH-CENTURY LITERATURE CRITICISM (NCLC)*
Authors who died between 1400 and 1799	*LITERATURE CRITICISM FROM 1400 TO 1800 (LC)* *SHAKESPEAREAN CRITICISM (SC)*
Authors who died before 1400	*CLASSICAL AND MEDIEVAL LITERATURE CRITICISM (CMLC)*
Authors of books for children and young adults	*CHILDREN'S LITERATURE REVIEW (CLR)*
Dramatists	*DRAMA CRITICISM (DC)*
Poets	*POETRY CRITICISM (PC)*
Short story writers	*SHORT STORY CRITICISM (SSC)*
Black writers of the past two hundred years	*BLACK LITERATURE CRITICISM (BLC)* *BLACK LITERATURE CRITICISM SUPPLEMENT (BLCS)*
Hispanic writers of the late nineteenth and twentieth centuries	*HISPANIC LITERATURE CRITICISM (HLC)* *HISPANIC LITERATURE CRITICISM SUPPLEMENT (HLCS)*
Native North American writers and orators of the eighteenth, nineteenth, and twentieth centuries	*NATIVE NORTH AMERICAN LITERATURE (NNAL)*
Major authors from the Renaissance to the present	*WORLD LITERATURE CRITICISM, 1500 TO THE PRESENT (WLC)* *WORLD LITERATURE CRITICISM SUPPLEMENT (WLCS)*

ISSN 0091-3421

Volume 145

Contemporary Literary Criticism

Criticism of the Works
of Today's Novelists, Poets, Playwrights,
Short Story Writers, Scriptwriters, and
Other Creative Writers

Jeffrey W. Hunter
SENIOR EDITOR

Tom Burns
ASSISTANT EDITOR

GALE GROUP

THOMSON LEARNING

*Detroit • New York • San Diego • San Francisco
Boston • New Haven, Conn. • Waterville, Maine
London • Munich*

STAFF

Lynn M. Spampinato, Janet Witalec, *Managing Editors, Literature Product*
Kathy D. Darrow, Ellen McGeagh, *Content-Product Liaisons*
Jeffrey W. Hunter, *Senior Editor*
Mark W. Scott, *Publisher, Literature Product*

Justin Karr, Linda Pavlovski, *Editors*
Rebecca J. Blanchard, Arlene Johnson, *Associate Editors*
Thomas Burns, *Assistant Editor*
Jenny Cromie, Mary Ruby, *Technical Training Specialists*
Deborah J. Morad, Joyce Nakamura, Kathleen Lopez Nolan, *Managing Editors*
Susan M. Trosky, *Director, Literature Content*

Maria L. Franklin, *Permissions Manager*
Margaret Chamberlain, *Permissions Specialist*
Debra Freitas, *Permissions IC Administrator*

Victoria B. Cariappa, *Research Manager*
Sarah Genik, *Project Coordinator*
Ron Morelli, Tamara C. Nott, Tracie A. Richardson, *Research Associates*
Nicodemus Ford, *Research Assistant*

Dorothy Maki, *Manufacturing Manager*
Stacy L. Melson, *Buyer*

Mary Beth Trimper, *Manager, Composition and Electronic Prepress*
Carolyn Roney, *Composition Specialist*

Michael Logusz, *Graphic Artist*
Randy Bassett, *Imaging Supervisor*
Robert Duncan, Dan Newell, Luke Rademacher, *Imaging Specialists*
Pamela A. Reed, *Imaging Coordinator*
Kelly A. Quin, *Editor, Image and Multimedia Content*

Library of Congress Catalog Card Number 76-46132
ISBN 0-7876-4634-2
ISSN 0091-3421
Printed in the United States of America

10 9 8 7 6 5 4 3 2 1

012302

Contents

Preface vii

Acknowledgments xi

Literary Criticism Series Advisory Board xv

Preface

Named "one of the twenty-five most distinguished reference titles published during the past twenty-five years" by *Reference Quarterly,* the *Contemporary Literary Criticism (CLC)* series provides readers with critical commentary and general information on more than 2,000 authors now living or who died after December 31, 1999. Volumes published from 1973 through 1999 include authors who died after December 31, 1959. Previous to the publication of the first volume of *CLC* in 1973, there was no ongoing digest monitoring scholarly and popular sources of critical opinion and explication of modern literature. *CLC,* therefore, has fulfilled an essential need, particularly since the complexity and variety of contemporary literature makes the function of criticism especially important to today's reader.

Scope of the Series

CLC provides significant passages from published criticism of works by creative writers. Since many of the authors covered in *CLC* inspire continual critical commentary, writers are often represented in more than one volume. There is, of course, no duplication of reprinted criticism.

Authors are selected for inclusion for a variety of reasons, among them the publication or dramatic production of a critically acclaimed new work, the reception of a major literary award, revival of interest in past writings, or the adaptation of a literary work to film or television.

Attention is also given to several other groups of writers—authors of considerable public interest—about whose work criticism is often difficult to locate. These include mystery and science fiction writers, literary and social critics, foreign authors, and authors who represent particular ethnic groups.

Each *CLC* volume contains individual essays and reviews taken from hundreds of book review periodicals, general magazines, scholarly journals, monographs, and books. Entries include critical evaluations spanning from the beginning of an author's career to the most current commentary. Interviews, feature articles, and other published writings that offer insight into the author's works are also presented. Students, teachers, librarians, and researchers will find that the general critical and biographical material in *CLC* provides them with vital information required to write a term paper, analyze a poem, or lead a book discussion group. In addition, complete biographical citations note the original source and all of the information necessary for a term paper footnote or bibliography.

Organization of the Book

A *CLC* entry consists of the following elements:

■ The **Author Heading** cites the name under which the author most commonly wrote, followed by birth and death dates. Also located here are any name variations under which an author wrote, including transliterated forms for authors whose native languages use nonroman alphabets. If the author wrote consistently under a pseudonym, the pseudonym will be listed in the author heading and the author's actual name given in parenthesis on the first line of the biographical and critical information. Uncertain birth or death dates are indicated by question marks. Single-work entries are preceded by a heading that consists of the most common form of the title in English translation (if applicable) and the original date of composition.

■ A **Portrait of the Author** is included when available.

■ The **Introduction** contains background information that introduces the reader to the author, work, or topic that is the subject of the entry.

- The list of **Principal Works** is ordered chronologically by date of first publication and lists the most important works by the author. The genre and publication date of each work is given. In the case of foreign authors whose works have been translated into English, the English-language version of the title follows in brackets. Unless otherwise indicated, dramas are dated by first performance, not first publication.

- Reprinted **Criticism** is arranged chronologically in each entry to provide a useful perspective on changes in critical evaluation over time. The critic's name and the date of composition or publication of the critical work are given at the beginning of each piece of criticism. Unsigned criticism is preceded by the title of the source in which it appeared. All titles by the author featured in the text are printed in boldface type. Footnotes are reprinted at the end of each essay or excerpt. In the case of excerpted criticism, only those footnotes that pertain to the excerpted texts are included.

- A complete **Bibliographical Citation** of the original essay or book precedes each piece of criticism.

- Critical essays are prefaced by brief **Annotations** explicating each piece.

- Whenever possible, a recent **Author Interview** accompanies each entry.

- An annotated bibliography of **Further Reading** appears at the end of each entry and suggests resources for additional study. In some cases, significant essays for which the editors could not obtain reprint rights are included here. Boxed material following the further reading list provides references to other biographical and critical sources on the author in series published by Gale.

Indexes

A **Cumulative Author Index** lists all of the authors that appear in a wide variety of reference sources published by the Gale Group, including *CLC*. A complete list of these sources is found facing the first page of the Author Index. The index also includes birth and death dates and cross references between pseudonyms and actual names.

A **Cumulative Nationality Index** lists all authors featured in *CLC* by nationality, followed by the number of the *CLC* volume in which their entry appears.

A **Cumulative Topic Index** lists the literary themes and topics treated in the series as well as in *Literature Criticism from 1400 to 1800, Nineteenth-Century Literature Criticism, Twentieth-Century Literary Criticism,* and the *Contemporary Literary Criticism* Yearbook, which was discontinued in 1998.

An alphabetical **Title Index** accompanies each volume of *CLC*. Listings of titles by authors covered in the given volume are followed by the author's name and the corresponding page numbers where the titles are discussed. English translations of foreign titles and variations of titles are cross-referenced to the title under which a work was originally published. Titles of novels, dramas, nonfiction books, and poetry, short story, or essay collections are printed in italics, while individual poems, short stories, and essays are printed in roman type within quotation marks.

In response to numerous suggestions from librarians, Gale also produces an annual cumulative title index that alphabetically lists all titles reviewed in *CLC* and is available to all customers. Additional copies of this index are available upon request. Librarians and patrons will welcome this separate index; it saves shelf space, is easy to use, and is recyclable upon receipt of the next edition.

Citing *Contemporary Literary Criticism*

When writing papers, students who quote directly from any volume in the Literary Criticism Series may use the following general format to footnote reprinted criticism. The first example pertains to material drawn from periodicals, the second to material reprinted from books.

Alfred Cismaru, "Making the Best of It," *The New Republic* 207, no. 24 (December 7, 1992): 30, 32; excerpted and reprinted in *Contemporary Literary Criticism,* vol. 85, ed. Christopher Giroux (Detroit: The Gale Group, 1995), 73-4.

Yvor Winters, *The Post-Symbolist Methods* (Allen Swallow, 1967), 211-51; excerpted and reprinted in *Contemporary Literary Criticism,* vol. 85, ed. Christopher Giroux (Detroit: The Gale Group, 1995), 223-26.

Suggestions are Welcome

Readers who wish to suggest new features, topics, or authors to appear in future volumes, or who have other suggestions or comments are cordially invited to call, write, or fax the Managing Editor:

Managing Editor, Literary Criticism Series
The Gale Group
27500 Drake Road
Farmington Hills, MI 48331-3535
1-800-347-4253 (GALE)
Fax: 248-699-8054

Acknowledgments

The editors wish to thank the copyright holders of the excerpted criticism included in this volume and the permissions managers of many book and magazine publishing companies for assisting us in securing reproduction rights. We are also grateful to the staffs of the Detroit Public Library, the Library of Congress, the University of Detroit Mercy Library, Wayne State University Purdy/Kresge Library Complex, and the University of Michigan Libraries for making their resources available to us. Following is a list of the copyright holders who have granted us permission to reproduce material in this volume of *CLC*. Every effort has been made to trace copyright, but if omissions have been made, please let us know.

COPYRIGHTED EXCERPTS IN *CLC*, VOLUME 145, WERE REPRODUCED FROM THE FOLLOWING PERIODICALS:

African American Review, v. 32, Fall, 1998 for a review of *Dear Future* by Heather Hathaway. © 1998 Heather Hathaway. Reproduced by permission of the author. —*America,* v. 180, January 2-9, 1999. Copyright 1999 America Press. Reproduced by permission. —*American Historical Review,* v. 100, June, 1995 for a review of *D-Day June 6, 1944: The Climatic Battle of World War II* by Alan F. Wilt. Reproduced by permission of the publisher and the author. —*American Literature,* v. 52, March, 1980. Copyright © 1980 by Duke University Press, Durham, NC. Reproduced by permission. —*Belles Lettres,* v. 7, Winter, 1991-92; v. 8, Spring, 1993; v. 9 Winter, 1993-94; v. 10, Spring, 1995. Reproduced by permission. —*Book World–The Washington Post,* v. 9, November 25, 1979 for "The Return of the Repressed" by Carolyn G. Heilbrun; March 27, 1988 for "A Death in India" by Martin Seymour-Smith; November 27, 1988 for "The Haunter and the Haunted" by Wendy Lesser; April 21, 1991 for "The Plight of Pedagogy" by Jonathan Yardley; August 13, 1995 for "Black Family Matters" by Angelyn Mitchell; October 20, 1996 for "This Is the Forest Primeval" by Tamsin Todd; v. 27, July 13, 1997 for "Minstrels and Their Masks" by Gayle Pemberton; September 18, 2000 for "Railroad History" by Patricia Nelson Limerick; May 3, 1987; July 16, 1989; February 11, 1996; July 2, 2000. © 1979, 1987, 1988, 1989, 1991, 1995, 1996, 1997, 2000 Washington Post Book World Service/Washington Post Writers Group. Reproduced by permission of the respective authors and the Washington Post Book World Service/Washington Post Writers Group. —*Boston Review,* v. XVI, October, 1991 for a review of *Isobars* by Edith Pearlman. Reprinted by permission of Russell & Volkening, Inc. as agents for the author. —*Chicago Tribune Books,* March 3, 1996 for "The Epic Journey of Capt. Lewis: A Young Man's Life on an Incredible Expedition," by Alexander Theroux; November 17, 1996 "Risky Business" by Michael Upchurch; September 3, 2000 for "Linking a Nation; Stephen Ambrose's Story of the Building of the Transcontinental Railroad" by Steve Weinberg. Reproduced by permission of the respective authors. —*Commentary,* v. 79, April, 1985; v. 84, August, 1987 for "The Vocation of Politics" by Richard John Newhaus. Copyright © 1985, 1987 by the American Jewish Committee. All rights reserved. Reproduced by permission of Commentary and Richard John Newhaus. —*Commonweal,* October 7, 1983. Copyright © 1983 Commonweal Publishing Co., Inc. Reproduced by permission of Commonweal Foundation. —*Contemporary Review,* July, 1989; v. 261, July, 1992. Reproduced by the permission of Contemporary Review Ltd. —*Contemporary Sociology,* v. 19, July, 1990 for "The Fate of Women Writers" by Chandra Mukerji. © 1990 American Sociological Association. Reproduced by permission of the publisher and author. —*Critical Texts,* v. 6, 1989. Reproduced by permission of Susan Gubar and Sandra M. Gilbert. —*Criticism,* v. XXXI, Fall, 1989. Copyright, 1989, Wayne State University Press. Reproduced by permission of the publisher. —*English Language Notes,* v. 28, September, 1990. © copyrighted 1990, Regents of the University of Colorado. Reproduced by permission. —*Esquire,* v. 110, November, 1988 for "Fifteen Minutes Over Soho," by Elizabeth Kaye. Reproduced by permission of Russell & Volkening, Inc. as an agent for the author. —*Essays on Canadian Writing,* n. 48, Winter, 1992-93. © 1992-93 Essays on Canadian Writing Ltd. Reproduced by permission. —*First Things,* November, 2000. Reproduced by permission. —*Georgia Review,* v. XLVII, Winter, 1993 for "Styles & Variations" by Erin McGraw. Reproduced by permission of the author. —*History,* v. 79, February, 1994. Copyright © 1994 Helen Dwight Reid Educational Foundation. Reproduced with permission of the Helen Dwight Reid Educational Foundation, published by Heldref Publications, 1319 18th Street, NW, Washington, DC 20036-1802. —*Insight on the News,* v. 16, July 3, 2000. Copyright 2000 News World Communications, Inc. Reproduced by permission. —*Journal of American Studies,* v. 33, 1999 for "Between Girls: Kay Gibbons' Ellen Foster and Friendship as a Monologic Formulation" by Sharon Monteith; v. 33, August, 1999 for a review of *Racechanges: Black Skin, White Face in American Culture* by Susan E. Rogers. © 1999 Cambridge University Press. Reproduced by permission of the publisher and the respective authors. —*Journal of English and Germanic Philology,* v. 88, July, 1989; v. 94, October, 1995; v. 95, April, 1996. Reproduced by permission of the University of Illinois Press. —*Journal of Modern Literature,* v. 17, Fall-Winter, 1990; v. XX, Summer, 1996. © Foundation for Modern Literature, 1990, 1996. Reproduced by permission. —*London Observer,* September 5, 1993; June 2, 1996. Reproduced by permission of The Observer Limited, London. —*London Review of Books,* Feb-

Literary Criticism Series Advisory Board

The members of the Gale Group Literary Criticism Series Advisory Board—reference librarians and subject specialists from public, academic, and school library systems—represent a cross-section of our customer base and offer a variety of informed perspectives on both the presentation and content of our literature criticism products. Advisory board members assess and define such quality issues as the relevance, currency, and usefulness of the author coverage, critical content, and literary topics included in our series; evaluate the layout, presentation, and general quality of our printed volumes; provide feedback on the criteria used for selecting authors and topics covered in our series; provide suggestions for potential enhancements to our series; identify any gaps in our coverage of authors or literary topics, recommending authors or topics for inclusion; analyze the appropriateness of our content and presentation for various user audiences, such as high school students, undergraduates, graduate students, librarians, and educators; and offer feedback on any proposed changes/enhancements to our series. We wish to thank the following advisors for their advice throughout the year.

Stephen Ambrose
1936-

(Full name Stephen Edward Ambrose) American historian, biographer, and editor.

The following entry presents an overview of Ambrose's career through 2000.

INTRODUCTION

For nearly forty years, Ambrose has been the author of several major historical and biographical works that focus on significant events in American history. He has written multivolume biographies of United States presidents Dwight D. Eisenhower and Richard Nixon, popular narrative studies of the Lewis and Clark expedition and the opening of the American West, and vivid accounts of World War II combat. Ambrose has also amassed the world's largest collection of oral histories related to a single battle, the D-Day invasion, which he used as source material to write *D-Day, June 6, 1944* (1994). Ambrose's military expertise came to the attention of director Steven Spielberg, who relied on Ambrose as a historical advisor for the acclaimed film *Saving Private Ryan,* the plot of which was partially drawn from Ambrose's writing about the Normandy invasion. Often praised for his balanced perspective and the narrative skill with which he presents individuals and historical events, Ambrose is among the most widely read professional historians in the United States.

BIOGRAPHICAL INFORMATION

Born in Decatur, Illinois, Ambrose was the son of family physician Stephen Hedges Ambrose and Rosepha Ambrose. Early in Ambrose's life, the family moved to Whitewater, Wisconsin, where he attended high school. He matriculated at the University of Wisconsin as a pre-med student, but after he enrolled in a history class, Ambrose became so enthralled with the subject matter that he changed his major. He received a B.A. from the University of Wisconsin in 1957, the same year that he married Judith Dorlester. Ambrose received a master's degree from Louisiana State University in 1958, but returned to the University of Wisconsin for his doctoral work, which he completed in 1963. From 1960 to 1964 he served as an assistant professor at Louisiana State University in New Orleans and wrote his first book, *Halleck* (1962). This admittedly minor work was to have great implications for Ambrose's career, as one of its few readers was former President Eisenhower, who was so impressed by Am-

brose's historical approach that he hired the then-28-year-old Ambrose to edit his papers. Ultimately, Ambrose became Eisenhower's official biographer. Ambrose has since spent thirty years researching the former president, leading to the completion of at least fifteen works about Eisenhower himself, his family, and events in which he played a pivotal role. Ambrose worked as an associate professor at Johns Hopkins University from 1964 through 1969. While at Johns Hopkins, he published three more works of history, *Upton and the Army* (1964), *Duty, Honor, and Country* (1966), and *Eisenhower and Berlin, 1945* (1967). In 1966, Ambrose's wife died and one year later, he married Moira Buckley. After leaving Johns Hopkins in 1969, he spent a year as the Ernest J. King Professor of Maritime History at the U.S. Naval War College and another year at Kansas State University as the Dwight D. Eisenhower Professor of War and Peace. During his career, Ambrose took advantage of several visiting professorships throughout the United States and Ireland. The bulk of his academic career, however, has centered around his alma mater, Louisiana State University (now known as the University of

New Orleans), where he taught from 1971 through 1995 and currently remains as a professor emeritus. He founded the Eisenhower Center at the University as well as the National D-Day Museum in New Orleans. In addition to authoring more than twenty-five books, Ambrose remains a frequent contributor to both scholarly and popular historical journals and newspapers. He currently lives in Helena, Montana.

MAJOR WORKS

Ambrose has spent the majority of his career concentrating on the history of the United States, with particular interests in World War II, Eisenhower and Nixon, and the exploration of the American West. His work has been heavily influenced by his strong personal belief in the merits of democratic society and his great respect for the individuals who defended the United States against totalitarian regimes. His World War II histories include *Pegasus Bridge* (1984), *Band of Brothers* (1992), *Eisenhower and the German POWs* (1992), *D-Day, June 6, 1944, Citizen Soldiers* (1997), and *The Victors* (1998). *Band of Brothers* is a personal story of war seen through the eyes of the men of E Company, 101st Airborne Division, who were responsible for holding Bastogne during the Battle of the Bulge and for capturing Berchtesgaden, Hitler's mountain hideaway. *Eisenhower and the German POWs,* co-edited with Gunter Bischof, cites abundant historical evidence to refute the assertions of author James Bacque that President Eisenhower was responsible for the deaths of perhaps one million German POWs in the waning days of World War II. *D-Day, June 6, 1944* approaches military history unconventionally, by focusing on the experiences of common Allied soldiers, non-commissioned officers, and second lieutenants rather than generals or political leaders. In Ambrose's opinion, the creativity of these foot soldiers and platoon commanders was essential to the Allies' victory over the Germans. The text of *D-Day* is drawn from more than 1,000 oral histories of soldiers present at Normandy on the day of the invasion. *Citizen Soldiers* also recounts the experiences of ordinary soldiers, from June 7, 1944, through the surrender of Germany. This work reiterates Ambrose's thesis that it was the basic decency, moral determination, and flexible thinking of young American men that led to the Allied victory.

Ambrose's acclaimed biographies include a two-volume work about Eisenhower—*Eisenhower: Soldier, General of the Army, President-Elect, 1890-1952* (1983) and *Eisenhower: The President* (1984)—and a three-volume work on Nixon—*Nixon: The Education of a Politician, 1913-1962* (1987), *Nixon: The Triumph of a Politician, 1962-1972* (1989), and *Nixon: Ruin and Recovery, 1973-1990* (1991). Ambrose portrays Eisenhower as one of the greatest figures of the twentieth century, a man born to lead and a chief executive who, contrary to some contemporary opinions, held his hand firmly at the helm throughout his two terms in office. While researching the Eisenhower administration, Ambrose also became fascinated with one of the most vilified political figures in American history—Richard Nixon, who served as Eisenhower's vice-president before ascending to the presidency himself. Ambrose was drawn to Nixon not out of admiration, but through curiosity about what went wrong during his presidential administration. The resulting three volumes constitute a perceptive portrait of a man who is considered one of the most complex political figures in U.S. history.

Ambrose's historical works about the American West—*Crazy Horse and Custer* (1975), *Undaunted Courage* (1996), and *Nothing Like It in the World* (2000)—are vivid narratives that portray the different kinds of personalities who overcame the many physical obstacles to America's westward expansion. *Undaunted Courage,* perhaps one of Ambrose's most highly regarded works, attempts to restore the reputation of Meriwether Lewis, co-leader of the Lewis and Clark expedition that was originally conceived by Thomas Jefferson. The work recounts the importance of Lewis's shared leadership with William Clark, the friendship between the two men, Lewis's excellence as a natural scientist, and his tragic demise. In *Nothing Like It in the World,* Ambrose celebrates the legions of anonymous workers who performed the backbreaking labor needed to build the transcontinental railway and describes the engineering, building, and financing decisions that occupied the men leading the effort. Ambrose's historical expertise has also drawn the attention of the producers and directors of various television documentaries and motion pictures. In 2001, the pay cable network HBO (Home Box Office) and director Steven Spielberg produced a ten-hour television mini-series adaptation of Ambrose's *Band of Brothers.*

CRITICAL RECEPTION

Ambrose's work has been hailed by many critics for its balance, its even-handed approach to men and events, and its engaging narrative presentation. Ambrose's biographies of Eisenhower and Nixon are widely regarded as definitive works on their subjects. Some reviewers have noted that Ambrose's willingness to criticize Eisenhower (his personal hero) and to express admiration for Nixon (a disgraced president) testifies to his judicious and objective historical approach. While his military histories of World War II, notably *D-Day* and *Citizen Soldiers,* have attracted considerable praise, some critics maintain that Ambrose tends to romanticize war, overlooking the reality of atrocity on all sides. Other reviewers have faulted Ambrose for not being sufficiently sensitive to political correctness. Also, because Ambrose is unabashedly patriotic and often reveres historical figures, some critics find his works long on adulation but short on analysis. However, it has been noted that Ambrose was unafraid to assail Eisenhower's handling of Joseph McCarthy and the growing civil rights struggle, despite his deep admiration for the man. Ambrose has been criticized for his failure to rely on primary sources, even when they are available, and for sometimes glossing over or omitting key points of history. Ambrose's books are written primarily for a popular audience rather than a scholarly one, and Ambrose has lamented the trend in contemporary historical writing toward focusing on theory rather than narrative.

PRINCIPAL WORKS

Halleck: Lincoln's Chief of Staff (history) 1962

Upton and the Army (history) 1964

Duty, Honor, and Country: A History of West Point (history) 1966

Eisenhower and Berlin, 1945: The Decision to Halt at the Elbe (history) 1967

The Supreme Commander: The War Years of General Dwight D. Eisenhower (history) 1970

Rise to Globalism: American Foreign Policy Since 1938 (history) 1971

Crazy Horse and Custer: The Parallel Lives of Two American Warriors (history) 1975

Ike's Spies: Eisenhower and the Espionage Establishment [with Richard H. Immerman] (nonfiction) 1981

Eisenhower: Soldier, General of the Army, President-Elect, 1890-1952 (biography) 1983

Milton S. Eisenhower: Educational Statesman [with Richard H. Immerman] (biography) 1983

Eisenhower: The President (biography) 1984

Pegasus Bridge: 6 June 1944 (history) 1984

Nixon: The Education of a Politician, 1913-1962 (biography) 1987

Nixon: The Triumph of a Politician, 1962-1972 (biography) 1989

Nixon: Ruin and Recovery, 1973-1990 (biography) 1991

Band of Brothers: E Company, 506th Regiment, 101st Airborne, from Normandy to Hitler's Eagle's Nest (history) 1992

Eisenhower and the German POWs: Facts against Falsehood [editor; with Gunter Bischof] (history) 1992

D-Day, June 6, 1944: The Climactic Battle of World War II (history) 1994

Undaunted Courage: Meriwether Lewis, Thomas Jefferson, and the Opening of the American West (history) 1996

Americans at War (essays) 1997

Citizen Soldiers: The U.S. Army from the Normandy Beaches to the Bulge to the Surrender of Germany (history) 1997

The Victors: Eisenhower and His Boys—The Men of World War II (history) 1998

Witness to America: An Illustrated Documentary History of the United States from the Revolution to Today [editor; with Douglas G. Brinkley] (history) 1999

Nothing Like It in the World: The Men Who Built the Transcontinental Railroad, 1863-1869 (history) 2000

CRITICISM

John Keegan (review date 22 October 1984)

SOURCE: "The Good General," in *New Republic,* October 22, 1984, pp. 43-6.

[*In the following review, Keegan offers positive evaluation of Ambrose's two-volume biography of Eisenhower.*]

"Eisenhower," this magnificent biography begins [*Eisenhower: Soldier, General of the Army, President-Elect, 1890-1952*], "was a great and good man," and with that no one of generous spirit would disagree. He was also, for more than half of his life, a poor man—in childhood dirt poor. It is from that fact in his background that a European reader would begin to assess his character. For the officer class in Europe, though often strapped for cash, has never been poor in the American sense. European officers are younger sons, clergymen's sons, sons of officers who have themselves had to scrimp and save. But the scrimping has always had to do with the keeping up of appearances which the haves and have-nots of their social order both accept at face value. Europeans accord their officer class the status of gentlemen, and thereby concede them a standing in society that automatically ensures them authority in their calling.

American officers, in the early days of the Republic, may have enjoyed a comparable head start. But by the time of Eisenhower's birth in 1890, when Manifest Destiny and open emigration had transformed the American class system out of all recognition to Europeans, the social certainties had gone. Some "southern gentlemen" continued to make West Point their goal. A few rich Americans allowed determined sons to go there; Patton, the most overrated of America's Second World War generals, was one of those. But the majority who arrived at the academy in Eisenhower's time were of the middling sort downwards. Marshall's family had fallen on hard times. Bradley had never known anything but the dawn-to-dusk deprivation of log cabin life. For both of them it was the free education West Point provided which drew them to the army. So it was with Eisenhower.

Eisenhower's father was a failed storekeeper (as, incidentally, Grant had also been). The town in which he sought to restore his fortunes, Abilene, Kansas, offered no bonanzas and few ways out for his six sons. But although he had lost his money, he retained two assets of inestimable value, family pride and a wife of character beyond price. The Eisenhowers were old Pennsylvania Dutch stock. So, too, were the Stovers, whose daughter Ida he married in 1885. They shared an upbringing in River Brethren fundamentalism and a veneration for education; indeed, it was the latter that brought them together when they prevailed on their families to let them attend a sort of college the Brethren ran in Lecompton, Kansas, in 1884. There he learned Greek well enough to read the Greek New Testament nightly for the rest of his life and she the Bible so thoroughly that she took pride in never needing to check any reference she chose to quote.

Stephen Ambrose's description of the upbringing this couple gave their sons, often done before but never more tellingly, prompts one to ponder the whole question of whether children got a better or worse start in their century than they get in ours. Neither Abilene High School nor the Eisenhower household could offer any of the Eisenhower boys a hundredth part of the athletic, library, laboratory, or computer facilities that modern suburban—even inner-city—parents regard as their offsprings' birthright. This did not stop three of the Eisenhowers from making immensely successful careers and a classmate of theirs from becoming president of Cornell. Had the Eisenhowers been Jewish and Abilene High School in Brooklyn, that might not prompt surprise. But neither was the case. Might it not be, however, that what family and school provided in nineteenth-century Kansas was something that few institutions, except perhaps the Jewish family and Bible class (and their power may be waning), do today? David Eisenhower's Greek Testament reading, Ida's mastery of the apt Bible reference, surely translated—linked as both were to an exigent moral code and, through their financial tumble, to an acute concern for social rehabilitation—into rigorous intellectual demands on their sons.

One way of explaining Jewish intellectual excellence is through the concern for textual precision, as a basis for an ethical synthesis, that the biblical tradition demands. The Afrikaners have it, too; so in their time did the Scots who, through the outlets provided by the British Empire, enjoyed career opportunities that the Transvaal could not provide and achieved fortunes, positions, and intellectual reputations as glittering, in a subfusc way, as anything that Vilna or Vienna could display. One effect of modern educators' devotion to the computer will be to ensure that its devotees will altogether lack that built-in facility for automatic switching and reprogramming of highly charged memory banks—a skill that all those children of the Book imbibed almost with their mother's milk.

Ida Eisenhower transmitted to her sons much more than sustenance, material or mental. She may already have found a biographer. If she has not, she would make a splendid subject for the burgeoning band of feminist historians, for she stands high in the ranks of remarkable Victorian mothers. Like the matriarch of the Buchan brood, she drove her children to great worldly success within a lively fear of the Lord; unlike John Buchan's mother, she did so with wit, fun, and good cheer. One of the most charming features of Stephen Ambrose's book is its reproductions of the family snapshots, in which the famous Ike grin stands forth unmistakably on her very un-Mennonite prettiness. Her husband had the inarticulate goodness of a John Ford itinerant preacher; she overflowed with a zest for life that, as her most famous son freely and gladly admitted, was a major force behind his rise to the White House.

West Point was the first step on the way. Not only was the education it gave free; it was also rooted in mathematics and engineering science. As a result, the West Point product, of which there were only a few hundred each year in Ike's day, was eminently fitted to succeed in his America. A cadet left the academy with a sharp practical intelligence and a personality which four years of subjection, succeeded by the demands of cadet-officer responsibility, had perfectly formed for a life of getting on with the other fellow. Throughout his career, Ike was to display to perfection the capacity to see the other fellow's point of view while working to get his own way—even, sometimes, when the other fellow was his constituted superior. If there is such a thing as the complete West Point product, Eisenhower was probably it.

Yet, though a great academy success, the pattern of American army life determined that his service, into middle age, would be routine almost to the point of inanity. One of the glories of American politics is that the United States is not an imperialistic power. The American officer of Eisenhower's vintage was therefore condemned to a round of posts in the American sticks. Their British contemporaries might, over twenty years, come to know the world from the Caribbean to the Himalayas. Eisenhower did not even see China, the only real overseas post open to an officer of the Old Army; his time in the Philippines was spent, as he later put it with uncharacteristic pith, "studying acting under General MacArthur"—to whom he acted as staff officer in Manila from 1936–39. Chance deprived him even of an assignment "over there"; by the time the tank unit of which he had been given command in 1918, as a temporary lieutenant colonel, was ready for action, the Great War was over.

He was therefore never to come under fire; and it would be eighteen years before he was a lieutenant colonel again. Mamie, the sweetheart whom he married in 1916—the author is less forthcoming than he might be about their life-long relationship—was uncomplaining about the straits to which his slow promotion through badly paid ranks consigned her. But narrow and constricting though the progression through Fort Leavenworth and Camp Meade was, Eisenhower inched ahead. And in the fall of 1941 he got his break. Appointed chief of staff of the Third Army for the Louisiana maneuvers (which were to be for American military reputation what the Italian campaign of 1796 was for the French), he scored a great success. Three months later, on the day after Pearl Harbor, Marshall's aide in Washington telephoned that "the Chief says for you to hop a plane and get up here right away." Eisenhower's career had begun.

It may be that Eisenhower's greatest achievement was to survive ordeal by fire at the hands of "the Chief"—George C. Marshall. For Marshall, who may have been one of the greatest of Americans, was certainly one of the most terrifying. Even Roosevelt seems to have held him in awe, perhaps because of Marshall's fixed habit of never allowing himself to laugh at any of the President's jokes. With lesser mortals he denied himself even a smile (there is only one photograph of a Marshall smile) and before subordinates he maintained the great stone face.

Eisenhower had therefore to win Marshall's approval by the only route the Chief of Staff recognized, mastery of grinding hard work. "Give me a few hours," was Ike's only counter when Marshall asked him, in effect, to map a war-winning strategy in the aftermath of Pearl Harbor. During the next months, in which he allowed himself a bare hour to mourn the news of his father's death, Eisenhower worked every minute God gave to design a scheme for American victory. In a few weeks he had thought through and rejected plans to concentrate American strength in the Pacific. By midsummer of 1942 he was wholly converted to the "Germany First" strategy and was established in a London headquarters where he was to translate principle into practice.

The meandering of Allied strategy, via North Africa and Italy, was to postpone his realization of the strategic concept he formed in the War Plans Division under Marshall. But it was to be the making of his future. Eisenhower may not have been a great field commander—though that could be argued. He was certainly a supreme military diplomat, and in the circumstances of coalition warfare that is a more important talent in a Supreme Commander, which he swiftly became. By the time of Normandy, he had established a masterly touch with the team—Montgomery, Bradley, Patton—that was to beat the German army, and could almost effortlessly defuse the squabbles that regularly arose among them.

Much has been made of Ike's failure to impose his own will on Montgomery and Patton after the break-out from Normandy, when it seemed (though less clearly in retrospect) that the war might have been won, given firmer direction, in 1944. The truth of the matter is that the Allies in France were overwhelmed by the extent of their own success, which was far greater than they had anticipated, and that the prospect of total victory that year was a chimera. Eisenhower saw that, kept his head, and did what was best under the circumstances. If he can be accused of a failure, it was in not insisting that Montgomery clear the Channel ports, rather than striking at Arnhem, a failure of omission rather than commission.

At the time no one, at his own level and above, considered that Ike had done anything less than he should. It was with that reputation that he returned from the war, and the only surprise about his postwar career is that it took one party or the other the time it did to capture him as a Presidential candidate. Stephen Ambrose's second volume, devoted to his Presidency, lacks something of the magisterial quality of the first. It has the appearance of having been written at greater speed and so with less reflection on Eisenhower the President's quality and achievements. Still, it is a superb piece of biography, a detailed and objective assessment of his management of government, spiced with fascinating revelations. Some of these (which carry over from

Volume I to II) concern his relations with the aspirant Vice President Nixon. Given the nature of Nixon's pleas for Ike's support during the Checkers affair—his language descended to the level of the latrine—it is astounding that his distinctly prim master kept him on the ticket.

One would have liked, perhaps, more of an assessment of the Presidency than the author supplies. With his broad conclusion, however, one would not disagree. Eisenhower, a man of war, had the balance and moderation in national security policy and foreign policy that perhaps only a man with prolonged exposure to casualty lists—and direct responsibility for them—can exercise. He was deeply skeptical about the efficacy of force and highly suspicious of the argument that security is a function of large defense budgets. He ended the Korean War. He squashed the Anglo-French efforts to bring Arab nationalism to heel by military means. He opposed single-handedly his own military establishment's inclination to settle affairs in Asia by the threat, perhaps even the use, of nuclear weapons. And he bowed out of his Presidency with a warning about the dangers of the growing military-industrial complex which would have fit better into the life of Gladstone than into the career of a man who self-proclaimed liberal opinion-makers characterized as the golf-playing companion of the common man's enemies.

Eisenhower was indeed a great and good man, because power did not deflect him from the values that his humble, high-minded, and God-fearing parents had given him in his Kansas childhood during the years of America's innocence. Those who continue to trust in the United States' unique capacity to do good in the world do so because they believe that there are still David and Ida Eisenhowers out in the great American heartland, rearing their broods on hope and on respect for the word.

Herbert S. Parmet (review date 29 October 1984)

SOURCE: "Unearthing the Real Ike," in *New Leader*, October 29, 1984, pp. 17-18.

[*In the following review of* Eisenhower: The President, *Parmet concludes that Ambrose's work is "by far the best and most authoritative Eisenhower biography available."*]

"Eisenhower gave the nation eight years of peace and prosperity," declares Stephen E. Ambrose near the end of his comprehensive and approving life of our 34th Commander-in-Chief [in *Eisenhower: The President.*] "No other President in the 20th century could make that claim. No wonder millions of Americans felt that the country was damned lucky to have him."

Ike's most outstanding quality, as Ambrose sees it, was his deft management of crises—from Dien Bien Phu to Little Rock to Sputnik. And contrary to a widespread impression, the White House was not run by assistants. Ike "kept all the power in his own hands," says the author, who confesses that even he—a scholar steeped in Ikeiana for most of two decades—was impressed by "how completely Eisenhower dominated events." American responses all over the world were his, "no one else's." Virtually nothing uncovered contradicts the President's claim that Secretary of State John Foster Dulles "never made a serious pronouncement, agreement, or proposal without complete and exhaustive consultation with me in advance and, of course, my approval."

En route to such conclusions, Ambrose has virtually guaranteed that it will be a very long time before anyone succeeds in climbing to the next plateau of biographical research on Dwight David Eisenhower. For his work is enriched by access to revealing sources, so that not the least of its virtues are gems of new information shaped by the talents of a judicious and meticulous historian into a smooth, essentially chronological narrative. (What better way to recall the poisonous atmosphere of the period than to point out that of the 221 Republican Representatives in the 83rd Congress, 185 sought membership on the House Un-American Activities Committee?)

Although Ambrose clearly thinks well of his subject, he delineates rather than celebrates Eisenhower's Presidency, thus preserving his credibility. On two issues, in particular—civil rights and Joe McCarthy—he confirms received opinion by admitting that Ike did not so much lead as attempt to reconcile his personal views with the demands of growing national sentiment and political expediency. The "sum total of Eisenhower's program" to help blacks consisted of appeals to Southern governors chosen by practically all-white electorates "for some sign of progress." When the U.S. Supreme Court handed down its 1954 *Brown v. Topeka* decision, Ike merely commented that the desegregation of public schools was now the law of the land.

His role in the McCarthy affair is equally familiar. Nonetheless, Ambrose manages to enlighten us by making an incisive point: It "was not the things Eisenhower did behind the scenes but rather his most public act"—the assertion of executive privilege during the Army-McCarthy hearings—"that was his major contribution to McCarthy's downfall." As with civil rights, the President's public stance consisted largely of ducking and weaving, hemming and hawing. Once more we are left to ruminate on the possible consequences had the junior Senator from Wisconsin been wise enough to avoid challenging the U.S. Army.

McCarthyism and race relations, however, did not evoke the real Eisenhower. Defense spending did. Ambrose explores in detail the path leading to the celebrated Farewell Address, which pointed to the dangers of the Military-Industrial Complex. He leaves no doubt that the President was not merely the innocent reader of a controversial script sneaked in by political scientist Malcolm Moos.

During the '50s Capitol Hill Republicans, riding the national mood, wanted to raise military outlays and to perform whatever budgetary surgery might be needed on foreign aid instead. To Eisenhower, though, cutting back defense spending was a prerequisite for all major goals: reducing the deficit, taxes and unemployment, as well as promoting trade and world peace. Consequently, Richard Nixon's attempt to match John Kennedy's call for a defense build-up during the 1960 campaign worsened Eisenhower's already frosty relationship with his Vice President. Nixon's defection, writes Ambrose, was "the deepest wound of all." Eisenhower felt it was a "cold rejection of everything he had stood for and fought for over the past seven and a half years."

These and other insights provide a clearer view of Eisenhower. The golfer not only read, he also wrote. He thought for himself, and was hardly the "captive hero" of liberal columnist Marquis Childs' imagination. Ike was a general, of course, but his refusal to bail out the French at Dien Bien Phu led opponents of the Vietnam War to cast him in retrospect as an "antimilitarist in the White House": He was a powerful force for peace and sanity guiding with a barely visible hand—while surrounded by would-be bomb-throwers like Nixon and Dulles, who began urging military intervention in Indochina as early as 1954.

In addition, this study of Eisenhower's Presidency is especially timely because there could be no more emphatic demonstration of how much the Republican Party has changed. The forces that would ultimately spawn the Reagan Revolution were admittedly flexing their muscles in the '50s, but the President worked to keep the Yahoos at bay. He sided with the conservatives seeking to prevent a takeover by the reactionaries. In fact, the threat from the GOP's Right-wing was one of the major reasons Eisenhower agreed to run in the first place, and its opposition grew steadily.

"Either this Republican Party will reflect progressivism or I won't be with them any more," was Ike's characteristic rejoinder. At a 1957 press conference he cautioned that "any modern political philosophy [has] to study carefully the needs of the people today, not of 1860." Furthermore, he said, "I believe that unless a modern political group does look these problems in the face and finds some reasonable solution . . . then in the long run we are sunk." Occasionally he was agitated enough to contemplate a realignment of our parties.

Ambrose reaffirms Eisenhower's stature. At least among academics, the recent revisionist trend has had its effect. Arthur Schlesinger Sr.'s 1962 survey asking historians to rank past Presidents placed Ike 22nd, saved from the very bottom of the "average" category by Andrew Johnson. Twenty years later, when Robert K. Murray and Tim Blessing tabulated the results of their own canvass, the man formerly best known for his golf landed in 11th place, high in the ranks of "above-average" Chief Executives. After almost two decades of research, Ambrose suggests that Ike deserves to be ranked among the greats—of those who served in this century, behind only Woodrow Wilson and Franklin Roosevelt.

That is a doubtful conclusion. Ambrose has written a substantial book that constitutes by far the best and most authoritative Eisenhower biography available, and others will draw upon his own evidence to challenge his lofty ranking. For one thing, it is rather hard to give such a high standing to someone who flunked the two great moral tests of his White House years: civil rights and Joe McCarthy.

Then too, his Administration bungled the diplomatic aftermath of the Cuban Revolution. Even more seriously, at the end of eight years in office, his cherished designs for détente lay in ruins, partly because one of our U-2 spy flights—a program he had personally authorized—was shot down over the Soviet Union in May 1960, prompting Nikita Khrushchev to cancel Ike's scheduled trip to Moscow. Finally, despite the author's comprehensiveness, he mysteriously skirts the question of Ngo Dinh Diem's coming to power in Vietnam, a legacy that surely weighed heavily on Kennedy.

These minor quibbles do not detract from the author's achievement. Readers can rank Ike themselves. Thanks to Ambrose, it will be easy to find the real Ike.

Spencer Warren (review date April 1985)

SOURCE: "The Real Ike," in *Commentary,* Vol. 79, No. 4, April, 1985, pp. 81-4.

[*In the following review, Warren offers favorable evaluation of* Eisenhower: The President, *but concludes that many questions concerning Eisenhower's complex personality remain unanswered.*]

As early impressions have given way to historical judgments, the reputation of Dwight D. Eisenhower as President has risen sharply. The release of a great mass of private papers in the past decade has inspired a number of accounts of the Eisenhower Presidency which have undermined the widely held view of Ike as a lazy, bland, uninvolved chief executive, one who remained above politics and let others run the government for him. The revisionists have established that Eisenhower most certainly was in control. He is now seen as a shrewd, even cunning, President, who, working through subordinates like John Foster Dulles and Sherman Adams, practiced a studied mode of indirect leadership that he believed made him most effective. As Richard Nixon, himself an object of Eisenhower's craft, observes in his inimitable style in *Six Crises,* Eisenhower "was a far more complex and devious man than most people realized, in the best sense of these words."

We now have what is likely to be the leading biography of Eisenhower for some time, by the historian Stephen Ambrose. The first volume [*Eisenhower: The President*] took Ike up to his election as President in 1952; this one recounts his Presidency and final years.

Describing Eisenhower as a "great and good man" who gave us eight years of peace and prosperity, Ambrose places him just below the top rank among Presidents. Eisenhower's reputation undoubtedly has improved by contrast with the failed Presidencies of the men who held the office in the twenty years after he left. This is particularly true in foreign affairs, where his leading claims can be made. He faced a series of crises during the tensest period of the cold war, more in number and more threatening than any (except for the Cuban crisis in 1962) faced by his successors. Eisenhower patiently resolved each crisis in a way favoring U.S. interests, without war and without losing a single American soldier. He ended the Korean war, kept the U.S. out of war in Indochina, twice prevented war with the Chinese Communists over Quemoy and Matsu, limited Western losses in the Suez crisis (though many would disagree here), and successfully diffused the 1958–59 Berlin crisis.

Ambrose recounts how, on repeated occasions, Eisenhower withstood strong pressure from the Joint Chiefs of Staff, Secretary of State Dulles, Vice President Nixon, and many in Congress, and decided against military intervention while still preserving the U.S. position. In meeting these challenges, Eisenhower demonstrated powers of incisive analysis, great coolness under pressure, independent judgment, confidence, and courage. And it was he alone who made the decisions; Dulles executed them. It is quite possible that without a man of Eisenhower's military judgment in the White House, we would have gone to war in the 50's, perhaps even nuclear war. Ambrose builds a persuasive case for the point advanced by Murray Kempton in his 1967 revisionist article on Eisenhower, namely, that, at least in the foreign arena, he was the "President most superbly equipped for truly consequential decisions we may ever have had."

Eisenhower succeeded in averting war while preserving America's worldwide position because he understood the proper relation of power to peace. In the great crises he faced, Eisenhower pulled off the difficult feat of maintaining U.S. credibility without resorting to force. His support for a strong defense, his military reputation, and the tough rhetoric he and Dulles employed enabled him to make credible threats—calculatedly ambiguous ones—that on several dangerous occasions helped to avert war and, in the case of Korea, to settle conflict. This masterly conduct of a policy of peace-through-strength, by a man who was not afraid to use force if need be, merits study by those today who are loudest in their professed desire for peace.

Yet during his second term, especially after the launching of Sputnik in October 1957, Eisenhower came under sharp attack for allegedly neglecting U.S. defenses. It seems a bit odd today to read the criticisms made by Democrats, *The New York Times,* and other liberal bastions about bomber- and missile-gaps and other supposed strategic deficiencies. In Ambrose's view, Eisenhower was at his finest in calmly opposing the national clamor for a crash build-up, including a $30-billion nationwide fallout-shelter program, during the near-panic that followed Sputnik. We now know that Ike was right and his critics wrong; there were no gaps in the strategic area, and under his defense program the U.S. enjoyed vast nuclear superiority over the Soviets in the 1950's and into the 1960's.

Eisenhower was the great general who struggled both to insure America's security and to slow the arms race. His supreme effort went into the search for nuclear disarmament; his greatest disappointment was probably the collapse of the 1960 summit following the U-2 incident. At the meeting with Khrushchev, he had hoped to reach a test-ban agreement as his final, crowning act of statesmanship. He had decided to accept a ban on all nuclear testing above and below ground, including a temporary moratorium on all underground tests below the verifiable level. The Pentagon, the CIA, and many atomic scientists were staunchly opposed, particularly to the moratorium, for which we would have had to rely on Soviet good faith. It is questionable whether agreement would ever have been reached on the details for on-site inspection, some form of which the Soviets had agreed to, and it is even more doubtful that the Soviets would have abided by the moratorium. But Eisenhower felt so strongly about the dangers of the arms race that, relying on his own military judgment, he overrode his advisers.

Any President must also be assessed on his economic policies, which, unfortunately, this book hardly touches upon. Eisenhower believed strongly that excessive government spending endangered the nation's economy. His tight-fisted budget policies were seen by many during the Keynesian heyday of the 1960's as hopelessly narrow-minded, but the rampant inflation and stagnating living standards of the 1970's, which followed the explosive growth of government after he left office, make them appear rather more far-sighted today. Yet Eisenhower's austerity policies—he opposed major tax reductions—and the two recessions that occurred during his Presidency, particularly the severe one of 1957–58, set the stage for the Republican debacle in the 1958 elections. This relegated the Republicans to the Depression-era minority status from which they had only just recovered in the 1940's, and from which they may only just be reemerging today more than twenty-five years later (though Watergate is perhaps equally responsible).

Alas, on the two most controversial domestic issues of his time, Eisenhower fell short. The confidence and command he displayed in facing our enemies abroad were missing at home when he confronted the problems of racial segregation and Senator Joseph McCarthy.

On the great moral issue of civil rights, Eisenhower failed, badly. Ambrose documents his callousness to the problem of racial segregation. He refused to endorse the Supreme Court's watershed 1954 *Brown* decision. He always said segregation was wrong, but just as often explained it was a problem that could be solved only by an evolution in attitudes, rather than by legal compulsion. In this he was proved wrong, as is demonstrated by the vast change in racial attitudes that followed the judicial and legislative reforms of the 1950's and 60's.

While paying lip-service to equality and proposing mild civil-rights legislation, Eisenhower often expressed as much or more sympathy for Southern segregationists as for their victims, who, he sometimes said, were too aggressive in pressing their claims. In 1957, when vacationing in Georgia, he refused to meet with Martin Luther King, Jr. His "moderation" and support for an "evolutionary" approach was in reality a policy of indifference that encouraged the South in its efforts to defy the Supreme Court and set the stage for the crises of the 1960's. Had he taken the lead, Republicans might, indeed, have regained much of the black vote they had lost in the 1930's.

Eisenhower has long been criticized for not challenging McCarthy, notably in the famous incident during the 1952 campaign when he excised from a speech he was to give in McCarthy's presence a paragraph praising General Marshall. (Marshall, who had largely made Ike's career in the war, had been viciously attacked by the Senator.) With new evidence, we now know that, true to his indirect style of leadership, Eisenhower surreptitiously maneuvered to help topple the Senator before and during the fateful Army-McCarthy hearings in 1954. Nevertheless his handling of McCarthy (and of civil rights) demonstrates the limitations of his mode of leadership.

Eisenhower recognized that the President must perform two functions, as sovereign head of state and as head of government. In the former, he is the embodiment of the people and must appear above politics and controversy. To be effective in the latter, he must do just the opposite. Eisenhower performed this second function in secret. He followed Machiavelli's advice to the Prince, "Everyone sees what you appear to be. Few experience what you really are." He was so successful at this that it took more than ten years after he left office for people to begin to learn the truth about his Presidency.

But in striving to separate his sovereign and prime-ministerial functions, Eisenhower often went too far. As the embodiment of the nation's ideals and principles, the President needs not only to enunciate them as generalities, but to apply them to matters at hand. Eisenhower's neutralist stance on civil rights demoralized millions of Americans, black and white, who looked to their President to bring reality to the nation's ideals.

With regard to McCarthy, Eisenhower's secretive campaign may have been the only way to deal with the popular Senator, as Fred Greenstein argues in his Eisenhower book, *The Hidden-Hand Presidency.* But it carried heavy costs. McCarthy intimidated thousands of Americans, many of them federal employees who looked to Eisenhower as their defender. These people, most of them innocent of wrongdoing, needed Ike's visible protection and support, but they did not get it until he moved to protect the Army against McCarthy's charges in 1954. Many were victimized by Ike's own loyalty program. While he was President, many careers were ruined, 830 employees of the Voice of America were dismissed, and books in its libraries were burned, all to appease McCarthy. How far above controversy must the chief of state stand?

Ambrose does not provide many details on what motivated Eisenhower's indirect mode of leadership; without these it is difficult to understand his character. Apparently his strategy was conscious and well thought-out. But was there more to it? The question needs to be asked because at times there is a pattern of inaction in Eisenhower's career that can be interpreted as indecisiveness rather than as evidence of a shrewd understanding of power. Often he appeared flabby and vacillating.

One example has to do with Eisenhower's relationship with Richard Nixon. Ambrose explains that while Eisenhower respected his lieutenant's intelligence, industry, and loyalty, he had outweighing reservations about him, and preferred to have another running mate in 1956. Indeed, in 1960 Eisenhower tried to persuade others to enter the race against Nixon. In 1956 he gave strong hints to Nixon, and used others, to try to persuade him to remove himself from the ticket. But Eisenhower would never act directly to remove Nixon. Ambrose concludes that he retained Nixon because he appreciated some of his qualities, the party wanted him, and because no one better could be found. But it is difficult to accept that this popular President was so limited in his choice of a likely successor, particularly given the strong misgivings he had about Nixon.

Dwight D. Eisenhower radiated honesty and sincerity, and he was a leader much loved by the American people. He was also an elusive man with a number of contradictions. He was the soldier-hero who often clashed with the Pentagon over policy and spending and at the end of his term denounced the "military-industrial complex." He was the supreme commander known for his empathy with his troops, who in a 1963 interview at the Omaha Beach cemetery movingly spoke not of the battle but of the parents whose sons lay buried there; but as President he was unable to summon imaginative sympathy for the millions of victims of segregation. He could be decisive in ordering the greatest amphibious invasion in history, or in turning back united pressure from his military advisers; but he often temporized and hesitated at home. He was a practical man, apparently not given to abstract thought, but also a Machiavellian figure shrewdly practicing an evidently elaborate theory of leadership.

Ambrose has performed an immense task, in what was obviously a labor of love, in mastering the Eisenhower papers. His manifest enthusiasm sometimes skews his judgments, but he is usually fair and always sound and comprehensive in recounting the Eisenhower Presidency. The complexities, however, remain; we need to know more in order better to understand Eisenhower and his Presidency.

Richard Harwood (review date 3 May 1987)

SOURCE: "The Man Who Would Be President," in *Washington Post Book World,* May 3, 1987, pp. 1, 14.

[*In the following review, Harwood offers positive assessment of* Nixon: The Education of a Politician, 1913-1962.]

Richard Nixon marked his 74th birthday on Jan. 9, one of those bittersweet occasions, I assume, in which laughter triumphs over tears. His life invokes both. He has been a major actor in many of the searing episodes of this bloody century and has been a witness to the rest. There was nothing trivial about his victories or defeats; they were on scales more grand than most of us would imagine (or could handle) in our own lives. By the age of 47, his new biographer, Stephen Ambrose argues, "he was the most hated and feared man in America—and next to [Dwight] Eisenhower himself, the most admired and wanted."

Today, almost 15 years after the dishonor and infamy of his resignation from the presidency, he is enjoying what one of his friends, Leonard Garment, has called "his astonishing final, final comeback." Writes Garment in a recent issue of *Commentary,* "It is [now] hard to find anyone who wants to kick Richard Nixon around." However that may be, it is doubtless true that the passage of time has made it possible to "reconsider" the man from a more detached perspective and to contemplate with less commitment and passion his obsessive quests for a place in the sun.

In that spirit, historian Ambrose has undertaken a two-volume Nixon biography, obviously determined to examine with a surgeon's neutrality all the clichés and stereotypical assumptions about the character of this strange and fascinating man. This first volume, covering the years 1913 through 1962, is subtitled *The Making of a Politician* but it is something more than that. It tries to explain how Nixon became Nixon and to explore that central question: "Why did so many people hate him so much?" Ambrose's answer to the question, offered as a series of clues and intuitions, seems to be this: that Nixon invented a political personality for himself—a stage role, as it were—and that he continued in the part (the humble, self-righteous character assassin) long after it played well in Peoria. The "real" Nixon, Ambrose believes, was never allowed to emerge, except fleetingly, for reasons that are not made clear. In any event it was the contrast between the artificial Nixon—the actor on the public stage—and the "real" person that produced throughout his career speculations about an "old" and a "new" Nixon.

Psychoanalytic explorations into his personality usually begin, as Garment has said, "in Nixon's boyhood, describing the early emotional impoverishment that produced an adult character based on resentment." Yet Ambrose provides little support for those kinds of speculations. His researches into Nixon's childhood are meticulous to a fault and lead him to conclude that the boy, far from being emotionally impoverished, "grew up in an atmosphere of security, surrounded by [the] love" of a large and extended family. But it was not a "fun" family. Its rhythms were defined by precepts of moral conduct—piety, thrift, hard work, self-sacrifice, self-improvement and prayer—which Nixon, even as a small child, took to heart. When he was 5 or 6, his mother said many years later," 'He always carried such a weight.' That's an expression we Quakers use for a person who doesn't take his responsibilities lightly."

In contemporary jargon, he was molded by this loving, pious family into a virtuous nerd; schoolmates called him "Gloomy Gus": "He went to great pains to brush his teeth. He would ask his mother to smell his breath to make sure he would not offend anyone on the bus. He insisted on a clean starched shirt every morning." He was bookish, argumentative, physically awkward and a poor athlete. He disliked hunting and fishing but loved music and reading. He had no close friends. He was clumsy and standoffish in his dealings with girls. And he was quite aware of his unpopularity. Years later, Ambrose reports, he told one of his White House assistants, "What starts the process [of character development], really, are laughs and slights and snubs when you are a kid. . . . If you are reasonably intelligent and if your anger is deep enough and strong enough, you learn that you can change those attitudes by excellence, personal gut performance while those who have everything are sitting on their fat butts."

He made A's in the classroom, was the grammar school valedictorian and the champion debater. It was the same in high school: he was an admired but virtually friendless scrub athlete, an honor student, a whiz on the debate team, a compulsive joiner and winner of a Harvard University scholarship (which he couldn't afford to accept) as the "best all-around student" at Whittier High School.

His capacity for hard work was remarkable. Even as a toddler he had regularly done family chores. When he entered Whittier College at the age of 17, his day began at 4 a.m. with a drive into Los Angeles to buy vegetables for the family store in Whittier. In the afternoons and on weekends he kept books for the store and, according to Ambrose, usually studied until midnight. And he managed in one way or another to carry on an active social and political life on campus: "president of his class, member of the Joint Council of Control, president of the newly formed men's club, reporter for the campus newspaper and sweater winner on the freshman football team." That was typical of his years at Whittier, as the human whirlwind—campus politician, academic grind, amateur thespian, fourth-string football player, public speaker, debater and dutiful son. "But one thing he never found there was friendship. . . . He was always lonely even though his frenetic life style meant that he was almost never alone."

The "Gloomy Gus" nickname followed him to Duke University law school where he was later remembered by one

classmate as "the hardest working man I ever met" and by another as "a very studious individual—almost fearfully so. I can see him sitting in the law library hunched over a book, seldom even looking up. . . . He never smiled. Even on Saturday nights he was in the library, studying." At one period during the Duke years Nixon lived alone in an abandoned, unheated tool shed lined with cardboard. But, Ambrose writes, "to Nixon there was no sacrifice involved in this Spartan style of life. He was indifferent to creature comforts. He really did not care what he ate, so long as it would sustain life, nor where he slept . . . nor what he wore . . . He got up each day at 5 a.m., studied until classes began, worked afternoons in the library at menial jobs paying thirty-five cents an hour, and studied again in the evening until midnight or later . . . He never had a single date at Duke."

Obsessive forms of self-denial and self-discipline are often associated with mysticism on the one hand and with materialistic greed on the other. But in Nixon's case the need, in Jesse Jackson's formulation, was to be "SOMEBODY!" Money, popularity and love meant little to Nixon. He was driven, Ambrose concludes, by a lust for "prestige, power . . . leadership," by "an insatiable hunger for success."

The campus years, especially at Whittier, were the apprenticeship for his true vocation—politics. He returned to Whittier from Duke, joined a law firm, married and served as a Naval supply officer in the Pacific when World War II came along. The Navy interlude was unusual for Nixon. It seems to have been the only time in his life when he was able to put aside ambition and compulsive behavior and allow a friendly, generous and uncalculating personality to emerge. His comrades, Ambrose writes, remembered him fondly as a sort of genial Mr. Roberts. But after the war those friendships, like other fleeting friendships in his life, were quickly forgotten. "It is noteworthy," says Ambrose, "that in his spectacularly successful postwar career, no one from the Navy, nor from Duke Law School, none of his classmates from Whittier High School or Whittier College, not even any member of his family, save only Pat, played a significant role, in public or private."

Nixon's emergence in politics as a Red-baiting Republican in the postwar years has been recounted in numbing detail by a variety of biographers and by Nixon himself in various memoirs. Ambrose attempts to bring to that subject a judicious perspective on the temper of the times. In a real sense, he argues, "anti-Communism" and the "Cold War" were bipartisan creations: "Except for the [Communist Party] itself, and its fellow travelers, everyone in politics . . . joined in the . . . anti-Communist crusades. [President Truman] led the way with his fire-breathing Truman Doctrine speech and his questionable executive order dismissing federal employees thought to be sympathetic to Communism."

This crusade became, for Nixon, a life-long preoccupation and a campaign tool to bludgeon the Democrats, including such cold warriors as Truman and Dean Acheson. Liberals especially resented his scurrilous campaign for the Senate against Helen Gahagan Douglas in 1950. He smeared her as the "Pink Lady." But, with a revisionist's touch, Ambrose reminds us that it was Douglas who initiated the Red-baiting by accusing Nixon of having "voted with [radical leftist] Representative [Vito] Marcantonio against aid to Korea." She also declared that, "On every key vote Nixon stood with party-liner Marcantonio against America in its fight to defeat Communism." Nixon, of course, responded in kind to the delight of Marcantonio who disliked Douglas intensely. She was also disliked by another congressman, John F. Kennedy of Massachusetts. Kennedy passed on to Nixon a $1,000 campaign contribution from his father with the comment, "I obviously can't endorse you but it isn't going to break my heart if you can turn the Senate's loss into Hollywood's gain."

Ambrose makes the interesting argument that it was not Nixon's policies as an elected official that enraged his enemies. As a lawmaker and vice president he was essentially a "mainstream" or "moderate" Republican, a supporter of the Marshall Plan, a defender of the embattled physicist, J. Robert Oppenheimer, and an early and consistent "progressive" on civil rights issues. He was an ally in the mid-1950s of Martin Luther King Jr. who supported the Republican ticket in 1956. But it was Nixon's unprincipled and vicious campaign style that defined his political personality in the public mind. On the stump, he was outrageous, a quality enhanced by his saccharine self-righteousness. The obsessive theme in his speeches was an implication that the Democrats—including Truman, Acheson and Adlai Stevenson—were treasonous in their "softness" toward Communism.

His patron, Eisenhower, deplored Nixon's campaign personality but recognized and exploited its political usefulness. It enabled him to take the high road while Nixon worked the gutters. But it also marked Nixon, in Eisenhower's mind, as "immature." He suggested repeatedly in his first term that Nixon withdraw from the ticket in 1956 and take a cabinet post in the second term to prepare himself for the presidency.

Their relationship, characteristically, was not based on friendship. Nixon remained the loner, a man who was comfortable haranguing a crowd and standing in the footlights (as he had learned as a debater and public speaker in school) but who was incapable of productive personal relationships outside his immediate family: "He disqualified himself for love by refusing to ever open himself and become vulnerable."

Nixon stepped off stage for a while after his defeat for the presidency in 1960 and his defeat for governor of California in 1962. His resurrection and return to politics, his fall into the lower depths and his final effort at vindication will be the subject of Ambrose' next volume. It should be a marvelously good read.

Herbert Parmet (review date 4-18 May 1987)

SOURCE: "Resurrecting Poor Richard," in *New Leader*, May 4-18, 1987, pp. 23-5.

[*In the following review, Parmet offers positive assessment of* Nixon: The Education of a Politician, 1913-1962.]

In the aftermath of his Presidency, the consensus view of Richard M. Nixon was nowhere more sharply put than in Jonathan Schell's *The Time of Illusion.* What characterized the Californian's politics, we were told, was the pursuit of a deliberate policy of "positive polarization." Now, a decade after Schell's analysis, we are reminded that this singular propensity was displayed well before Nixon became Chief Executive. By the time he reached the age of 47, he had "polarized the public more than any other man of his era." He was "the most hated and feared man in America—and next to Eisenhower himself, the most admired and wanted."

The first half of historian Stephen E. Ambrose's projected two-volume biography [*Nixon: The Education of a Politician, 1913-1962*], though, focuses on Nixon's personal ordeal, which is no less striking than the talent and political conditions that combined to produce the dominant figure of America's first three postwar decades. The account is a fascinating one, amply bolstered by factual details and shrewd insights. Ambrose is not discouraged by the familiarity of much of his material; he even manages to enliven the oft-told story of the Milhous and Nixon family backgrounds. But he also illumines many relatively little known incidents, such as the White House power struggle in the days following Dwight D. Eisenhower's 1955 heart attack.

The author is precise about Nixon's early work as a member of the House Committee on Un-American Activities (HUAC)—especially his successful pursuit of Alger Hiss—and makes it clear that Nixon was the Congressman responsible for giving the Committee what credibility it had. During the same period Nixon went abroad with the Herter Committee to assess Europe's postwar economic needs, only to find upon his return that California's 12th district was 3:1 against foreign aid. Undeterred, he voted for the Marshall Plan and waged a campaign to win over his constituents.

An uncompromising anti-Communist (without being a nationalist of the Robert A. Taft school), the young Nixon consistently supported President Truman's European containment program. However, he joined many in his party and some Democrats (including John F. Kennedy) in hitting the Truman Administration for the "loss" of China, and later protested the firing of General MacArthur. Eventually, he abandoned bipartisanship, together with most of the GOP; as Eisenhower's running-mate in 1952, he went along with John Foster Dulles' critique of containment.

The most important part of this volume deals with Nixon's vice presidency. One of his more visible roles in the office involved helping to lead his fellow Republicans away from their traditional isolationism. He was among those within the Administration who opposed the Korean armistice, and he favored military intervention to assist the French at Dienbienphu.

Unlike many Republican hardliners, Nixon was not what was termed in those years a "hard-shell" conservative. For all his opposition to unionism, he was not sufficiently anti-labor to support "right-to-work" laws. And as Ambrose shows, he was sympathetic to the struggle for racial equality, perhaps more so than anyone else high in the Administration (this has been noted by David Garrow, too, in his recent biography of Martin Luther King Jr.). Indeed, while for reasons of political necessity he adopted a "Southern strategy" that ruled out overt gestures of support for the civil rights movement, Nixon's personal conviction hurt him in the South during his first run for the Presidency.

The years under Ike were a period of almost unrelieved frustration for the young man from Whittier. Ambrose, who is also Eisenhower's principal biographer, gives us a fascinating description of the relationship between the two men, furnishing copious evidence for the claim that Ike "used Nixon in the most cynical fashion." He recounts how Nixon became completely infuriated at Eisenhower's conduct during the 1952 "secret fund" flap; how the President wavered before agreeing to retain the squirming Nixon as his running-mate in 1956; and how, after making that decision, Ike failed to lift a finger to stop Harold Stassen's campaign to dump Nixon in favor of Christian A. Herter. Yet Nixon's interest in expanding the constitutional responsibility of the vice presidency was fine with Eisenhower—as long as it did not involve giving too much leeway to this "immature" young man. As with Hubert H. Humphrey under Lyndon B. Johnson, Nixon suffered humiliations that almost seem built into the office.

Ambrose contends that, deep down, Ike "felt warmly toward Nixon, indeed regarded him almost as a son." The avuncular President simply "came out of one of those 19th century American families in which the son could never, not ever, live up to his father's expectations." The author adds that "Eisenhower treated his own son that way."

A further insight is gleaned from the diary of Ike's personal secretary, Ann Whitman, who watched the two during their eight years together from a privileged corner. The difference between them, Whitman wrote, is obvious: "The President is a man of integrity and sincere in his every action. . . . He radiates this, everybody knows it, everybody trusts and loves him. But the Vice President sometimes seems like a man who is acting like a nice man rather than being one."

Nixon's secretary, Rose Mary Woods, must have seen things differently, for she understood the difficulty of his position within the Administration. The Vice President was nonetheless loyal, dedicated and competent in every sense, observes Ambrose. Although undermined by Eisenhower,

he managed through diligence to be fairly effective, particularly at binding together discordant elements of the GOP. Repeating a pattern he exhibited at Whittier College and again at Duke law school, he was the thorough student, working overtime to master his job so that he would be ready, if necessary, to assume the Presidency. Party chairman Meade Alcorn thought him the best informed person in the Administration.

Still, as Ambrose demonstrates, many of Nixon's troubles were self-inflicted; his need to succeed created friction throughout his political career. During the 1946 House campaign against Jerry Voorhis, Nixon "made the transition from nice Quaker boy to ruthless politician without even noticing." His combativeness drew fire, and saddled him with the image later dubbed the "old" Nixon.

Helping to bring down Hiss hardly endeared the Congressman to liberal intellectuals, and Nixon knew this. Yet no matter how much the Eastern Establishment preferred to ignore what James Burnham called "the web of subversion," something had to be done about internal security. Whittaker Chambers' efforts and the Harry Dexter White case confirmed that those guilty of laxity were not rushing to assume responsibility. If the Republicans exploited the issue by Red-baiting and doing everything possible to fan hysteria, the Democrats made themselves vulnerable by denying not merely their own accountability but the very existence of a problem.

Nixon's performance during the HUAC hearings—especially his interrogation of witness Jack Warner on why Hollywood studios failed to show the same zeal against Communism that they had against Hitler—and his vitriolic Senate race against the wife of movie actor Melvyn Douglas led to unfair whispers of anti-Semitism. Actually, Helen Gahagan Douglas threw the first bit of mud by likening her opponent's record to that of fellow-traveling Congressman Vito Marcantonio and attempting to stick Nixon with the "soft-on-Communism" stigma; nevertheless, all that was remembered was "what Dick did to Helen."

In his first campaign with Eisenhower, Nixon did his job all too well, questioning the loyalty of such figures as Harry S. Truman, Adlai E. Stevenson and Dean Acheson. Ike admonished his young running-mate for being too partisan, even though he had sent him out to give the Democrats hell. Since childhood, Nixon had learned to use words instead of fists; now it was his extravagant campaign language that made him the favorite target of Democratic leaders.

The Eisenhower-Nixon tension persisted into Nixon's Presidential campaign against Kennedy. When asked at a news conference for an example of a decision Nixon had helped him make, Eisenhower replied: "If you give me a week, I might think of one." He called Nixon afterward to apologize, but the damage was done.

Despite additional frustrations caused by the White House and the lateness of Ike's campaign efforts in his behalf,

Nixon managed to push Kennedy to a photo-finish. Then, just two years later, his political life seemed to expire with his loss to Pat Brown in the California gubernatorial contest, made memorable by a parting shot at the press: "You won't have Nixon to kick around anymore, because, gentlemen, this is my last press conference. . . ." Ambrose concludes this volume by describing how Nixon "drove home from his last press conference . . . already discussing his future."

Today, nearly 13 years after he was forced to resign from the Presidency, Richard Nixon is again gaining prominence, his former Secretary of State has linked arms with him to issue foreign policy pronouncements, and the release of his White House papers by the National Archives has begun without causing any great stir. A third resurrection, if not a complete rehabilitation, is under way. A new set of judges apparently is ready to leave behind the old Herblock caricatures. And Ambrose has made an important contribution to advancing the remarkable turn of events.

Joan Hoff-Wilson (review date 21 June 1987)

SOURCE: A review of *Nixon: The Education of a Politician, 1913-1962*, in *Los Angeles Times Book Review*, June 21, 1987, p. 12.

[*In the following review of* Nixon: The Education of a Politician, 1913-1962, *Hoff-Wilson finds weaknesses in Ambrose's reliance on dubious primary sources and his lack of original analysis.*]

On the face of it, Stephen E. Ambrose has written a balanced, descriptive account [in *Nixon: The Education of a Politician, 1913-1962*] of the life of Richard Milhous Nixon from birth in 1913 to premature retirement from politics in 1962. Yet, underneath the polished prose and paced narrative, Ambrose's first volume of a projected two-volume biography of the 37th President of the United States makes perplexing reading, for two reasons.

First, instead of analysis, we are offered description or, worse, tantalizing one-liners. In connection with the death of Nixon's oldest brother, Ambrose asserts that Nixon "felt sorry for himself not Harold . . . [and] was to never again give his love and admiration . . . for fear of the pain of separation." Later, in reference to Nixon's close loss to John F. Kennedy in 1960 and win over Hubert Humphrey in 1968, we learn that his 1946 campaign against Rep. Jerry Voorhis in California "marked the beginning of what would become a lifelong obsession with percentages." Another one-liner occurs when Ambrose insists that Nixon's conduct in the Alger Hiss affair presaged that "in every future crisis of his life" he would "lash out in an uncontrollable fit of temper." (Of course, Nixon handled his last crisis—Watergate—with excessive calculation.) Finally, we learn that one of Nixon's "outstanding characteristics" was an ability to absorb facts. (Again, how about Watergate?)

The second perplexing aspect of the book is related to this inability to make historical sense out of Nixon's formative years and pre-presidential political career. It stems from both the sources Ambrose employs and his uncritical use of them. Unlike his best-selling and well-received biography of Dwight D. Eisenhower, which took 20 years, the gestation period for this present book has been three or four years at most.

It is to Ambrose's credit, let it be said, that he ignores the largely contradictory studies of Nixon's psyche. After rejecting psychoanalytical accounts, which rival those written about Adolf Hitler, he re-creates Nixon's early life and career, alas, primarily with an engaging synthesis of such books of dubious provenance as the Nixon biographies by Bela Kornitzer, Earl Mazo, and William Costello, together with some miscellaneous oral history interviews.

Ambrose thus portrays Nixon's formative years as not particularly traumatic for someone of his generation and background, growing up in two towns near Los Angeles. This most unloved of American politicians, he writes, was not unloved as a child. But he proves this point in part by relying on an even more questionable source, a still unpublished campaign biography by Charles Richard Gardner, created for the campaign of 1952. Freelancer Gardner hoped that this 262 pages of typescript, suitably printed, would advance his candidate, but it did not see the light of day (until now) even after he misrepresented himself to several publishers as a regular speech writer for Nixon. Ambrose's use of this partisan account hardly constitutes "thorough" or "meticulous" original research. Curiously, he has excised Gardner and Mazo's references to young Nixon's sense of humor and popularity. One can only assume that the purpose was to reinforce today's view of Nixon the friendless, frustrated outsider. As for oral history, Ambrose relies on interviews conducted by a group of undergraduates at Cal State Fullerton, who talked with officials of the Nixon Administration when they were still in office, in 1969–1972. These unsophisticated interviews hardly add scholarly cubits to the book under review.

Even when Ambrose begins to use Nixon's vice presidential papers—rather than a pastiche of unreliable biographies and oral histories—Nixon's personality and political significance do not come into focus. We learn late in the book that "Nixon was no demagogue" because he did not attack "Negroes, union men or Catholics," yet in early campaigns for the House and Senate and as Eisenhower's vice president and hatchet man, his "ruthless" (and strongly implied demagogic political behavior is described in detail.

Nor does Ambrose come to a conclusion about Nixon's 1952 "Checkers" speech. In his biography of Eisenhower, he concluded that there had been a serious effort to dump Nixon after the exposure of a slush fund, and that the Checkers talk not only saved his career but became "one of the great classics of American political folklore," giving Nixon "a solid power base of his own." Relying on many of the same sources, this biography relates that Nixon's position on the 1952 ticket had always been secure and that the entire incident amounted to a "charade."

Ambrose quotes extensively from Nixon's *Six Crises* to describe his political life, but in the final analysis, he suggests that they were all false crises, which is probably true. Still, one would never know it from the exciting narratives and extensive coverages. Equally ambiguous, he asserts that with respect to civil rights, Nixon "was well within the mainstream of the Republican party," only to belie that description with references to his unusually positive relationship with Martin Luther King Jr. in the 1950s.

Probably the most original interpretation is the account of Nixon's early California campaigns against Voorhis and Helen Gahagan Douglas. Despite anti-communist tactics, he was far from the McCarthy of California. Contrary to most liberal descriptions of Voorhis and Douglas, Ambrose leaves the impression that they were intellectual and political lightweights compared to Nixon and would have been defeated without the smear tactics attributed to him. There are also several insights into Nixon's significance as vice president. He differed with Eisenhower by supporting "lower taxes, a more action-oriented foreign policy, more social spending, more defense spending, and a willingness to live with debts." As for McCarthy's anti-administration attacks, anti-Communist reputation notwithstanding, Nixon "exerted all his considerable powers of persuasion on McCarthy to get him to back off."

Most of what we learn from this biography about Nixon's early life and career hence is in older biographies. And we are left with few clues about how experiences in Congress and as vice president may have formed or changed ideas. Ambrose has given a "mix and match" version of Nixon— not a "color-coordinated" foundation.

Ambrose's book will remain a graceful, if ambiguous, synthesis of what is well known about Nixon's life to 1962. [C. L.] Sulzberger's [*The World and Richard Nixon*] seems, sadly, a tired effort that accepts the standard paradoxical view of Nixon's career without adding any new insights into his foreign policies. Despite these new studies, we are left with the formidable task of divining for ourselves the purposes and procedures of this recent President of the United States.

John Charmley (review date 4 July 1987)

SOURCE: "A Classical Hero with Blue Jowls," in *Spectator,* July 4, 1987, pp. 32-3.

[*In the following review of* Nixon: The Education of a Politician, 1913-1962, *Charmley praises Ambrose's study of Nixon as "a superb biography which comes as near to explaining its subject as any biographer can hope for."*]

In an era when appearances count for so much in politics, especially the American brand, Richard Nixon was bound

to have a hard time of it; those blue jowls and that ski-slope nose ensured that whatever else he was, he was not telegenic. The famous 1960 debates between him and Kennedy saw a confrontation not between age and youth (the two men were almost of an age), but rather between the old politics, based upon hard work in the country, and the new politics, based upon meretricious performances on the television screen: Nixon's personality was always too complex to lend itself to successful exposure in that most transient medium. His own memoirs were a startlingly successful attempt to fix his character in print, and now, with the first volume of Professor Ambrose's *Nixon,* we have a superb biography which comes as near to explaining its subject as any biographer can hope for.

Aptly subtitled 'the education of a politician,' the book triumphantly succeeds in elucidating the mainsprings of Nixon's character and then in describing how it evolved during his early political career. From the very start young Richard was an unlovable outsider, but this fact fuelled his ambition; as he put it,

> What starts the process, really, are laughs and slights and snubs when you are a kid . . . [but] if you are reasonably intelligent and if your anger is deep enough and strong enough, you learn that you can change those attitudes by excellence, personal gut performance while those who have everything are sitting on their fat butts.

If he could not be loved, he would command respect.

Tragically, on the personal level, what he came to command was a mixture of respect and loathing. The immense effort which, even with intelligence and courage, was required to raise Nixon from Yorba Linda to a heart-beat from the White House, turned him ever more in on himself, emphasised his loneliness and did nothing to make him more lovable; this, in turn, spurred him on to yet greater efforts to win success. Within six years of entering politics he had won the Republican nomination for Vice-President and, after eight years in that office, he was poised to take the Presidency itself; but all this was, as Professor Ambrose brilliantly shows, at tremendous personal cost.

Never have the narrowing effects of a political career been better illustrated than they are here. If Nixon's emotionally crippled personality provided the motor for his political career, the demands of that career inflicted further blows upon it. At one level it denied him the happy family life which, with an adoring wife and two charming daughters, was available and which could have provided Nixon with all the love he could want; time would not permit him to have a private life. At another level the very lack of fastidiousness endemic in American political life encouraged the less desirable traits in his character: thus energy and ambition all too easily became a determination to win at any cost, whilst courage and patriotism deteriorated into bellicosity and flag-waving. The fruits of success turned out to be those of the Dead Sea.

Nixon is neither hagiography nor demonology. It is a magisterial biography by a superb historian whose command of his sources is equalled only by the compelling hold he quickly establishes over the reader. The final portrait is definitely of the school of 'warts and all' and the fact that he sets nothing down in extenuation nor condemnation makes Professor Ambrose's book all the more impressive. His pellucid account of the Alger Hiss case makes it plain that Nixon's instincts here were correct, and even if some of his methods were rough, his opponents were not playing by the Queensberry rules either. This was true throughout his career, but as the dog with the bad name suspicion was always directed at Nixon.

The formative period in the 'education of a politician' was the Vice-Presidency. As a biographer of Eisenhower, Ambrose is well-equipped to bring out the shabbiness with which the President treated Nixon. Desiring to remain above the arena of party strife, he sent Nixon down there to fight the battles and then condemned him in public for tactics which, in private, he condoned. Despite Nixon's long and loyal service, 'Ike' did nothing to help his political career, almost dropping him in 1956, and refusing to give him a clear endorsement in 1960 until it was too late. It is little wonder that 'Tricky Dick's' character was soured by the experience.

But with the tenacity which has always marked his career, Nixon persevered only to see, at the climactic moment, victory taken from his grasp by dubious methods by one of those who had 'everything' just by sitting on his 'fat butt'. For a man with the reputation of fighting dirty, Nixon's campaign against Kennedy was remarkably clean, making nothing of his reliance on drugs because of his injured back, nor of his compulsive (and to a man of Nixon's character, distasteful) womanising. To have lost so narrowly and in such a manner would have been galling to any one, especially to a man of Nixon's ambition, but to stand by and see your opponent then compared to King Arthur must have been unbearable—if Washington was Camelot then Kennedy was surely Launcelot.

This first volume ends in 1962 with what seemed to be Nixon's last campaign when he lost the Californian gubernatorial contest. But even if we did not know it, we could predict that he would return to politics. The story so superbly told is that of the hero of classical tragedy, the man who is brought low by defects in the very qualities which enabled him to rise. I shall wait impatiently for the next volume.

Sidney Blumenthal (review date 6 July 1987)

SOURCE: "He's the One," in *New Republic,* July 6, 1987, pp. 30-4.

[*In the following review of* Nixon: The Education of a Politician, 1913-1962, *Blumenthal writes that Ambrose's "old-fashioned sort of biography" serves as a "standard" point of reference for Nixon studies, but Ambrose's "professionally 'balanced' approach to an unbalanced subject does not penetrate deep enough."*]

The night of John F. Kennedy's inauguration, after the oratory about the torch being passed, the loser toured the mostly deserted Washington streets. Until the bewitching hour of midnight, Richard Nixon still commanded his official vice presidential car. He ordered his chauffeur at last to take him to the Capitol. He marched alone past the Senate chamber, down a corridor to the vast and empty Rotunda, and on to a balcony, where he gazed at the darkened horizon. Nixon had virtually willed himself to within a few thousand votes of the presidency. And in this portentous scene of departure, his will was almost palpable. Yet the story did not end here; his lonely leave-taking became the prelude to a return—and worse.

Stephen E. Ambrose's book [*Nixon: The Education of a Politician, 1913-1962*] is an old-fashioned sort of biography. The author, a historian at the University of New Orleans who has written the definitive two-volume biography of Eisenhower, seeks balance, not irony. Ambrose's facts are lined up in rows and made to march to a very measured judgment. His prudent interpretations do not stray from the accumulated details. There are no great themes, no theories of history, no analytical leaps. In short, Ambrose has written the standard, a middle point of reference, around which all Nixonia may be organized.

Ambrose's extension of the historian's empathy to his subject seems at first to make Nixon's motivation understandable. But the more we know, the more unknowable Nixon becomes. There is no searching point of view; and finally the professionally "balanced" approach to an unbalanced subject does not penetrate deep enough. Still, this sheer massing of material on Nixon cannot help but evoke a certain reaction. Ambrose's affectless prose is not without effect; this vanilla has an aftertaste.

The first of two volumes, the opening of an American tragedy, *Nixon* is utterly chilling in its inexorability. Even as we begin the first page the last terrible one is known. Nixon does not exactly drift toward his fate. Instead, his ambition builds into a juggernaut, driving him toward rule and ruin. Each of his passages was final, sealing him off from possibility. The more tightly Nixon coiled his ambition, the more he became entangled in forces outside himself. The biographer's piling up of facts seems almost heartless, because they are ultimately crushing; yet Ambrose's naturalistic style implicitly fits the amoral rise and fall of his subject. Richard Nixon's story belongs in Theodore Dreiser's world.

Nixon's trajectory has been described conventionally (and unconventionally in Garry Wills's *Nixon Agonistes*) as a parable of the Protestant ethic, according to which work and ambition produce virtue and success. Perversely, the worldly-wise Nixon twisted his success into failure: the self-made man unmade. *Nixon,* however, is at least as much about environment as it is about character, about a mechanical politician in a mechanistic universe, who was found by forces he eagerly rode.

Nixon, for his part, projected the impersonal as the enemy. Always he faced a faceless conspiracy that had to be brought under control. He was the individual against the crowd below and the elite above; the choice was always between order and chaos. Though his ascent to power was amazingly rapid—elected vice president at age 39—he believed he was constantly being thwarted. He sought to conquer a society with which he was radically at odds. And he never felt that he had arrived, that he could loosen his grip on himself. Thus his spirit was stunted by a fierce obsession with survival. "I had to win," he said, justifying his sordid first campaign. The situation was always desperate; he was always cornered by circumstance.

Nixon's most enduring piece of writing, *Six Crises,* about his struggle, is Benjamin Franklin's *Autobiography* with a paranoid subtext: half-banal, half-mad. Any self-revelation on Nixon's part was unintentional. He was certain that he risked destruction if he displayed authenticity; against his enemies, he carried insincerity as a shield. The political obliterated the personal. "In my job," he said in 1959 to Joseph Alsop, "you can't enjoy the luxury of intimate personal friendships. You can't confide absolutely in anyone. You can't talk too much about your personal plans, your personal feelings."

Nixon grew up, surrounded by a loving family, in a religious Quaker community. Like many Quakers, he was bred to be reserved in private but confident in public. The great mystery is his inability as an adult to trust. There is "nothing" to explain it, according to Ambrose. The death of his little brother, Arthur, made him strive harder to please his parents. He recited poetry, played the piano, debated like a champion, and rose every morning at 4 to pick up vegetables at a farmers market for the family store. In high school, he ran for class president, losing to an "athlete and personality boy." He had no close friends; but he was widely respected, and he had no enemies.

When he won a scholarship to Harvard, necessity demanded that he choose the hometown Whittier College. His family could not afford his living expenses elsewhere because his older brother, Harold, had contracted tuberculosis. Nixon, however, showed no discernible bitterness. Harold's death two-and-a-half years later apparently intensified his will to succeed. Nixon was the Big Man on Campus—class president, founder of a fraternity, rotten football player but good sport, and winner of the Reader's Digest Southern California Extemporaneous Speaking Contest of 1933. He was also the lead actor in the school play, so skilled that he could cry on cue. "Buckets of tears. I was amazed at his perfection," said the drama coach. The school yearbook recorded:

> After one of the most successful years the college has ever witnessed we stop to reminisce, and come to the realization that much of the success was due to the efforts of this very gentleman. Always progressive, and with a liberal attitude, he has led us through the year with flying colors.

Then on to Duke Law School, where he closed the library every night, including weekends, and lived in a small shed lined with cardboard, without heat. He graduated with honors, third in his class. "His life to date," says Ambrose, "had been an unbroken record of achievement and success."

Nixon's political career had its origins during the war, on a remote Pacific island, where the Navy man ran a small store, just like at home, and was an expert poker player, known for his disciplined bluffing. He carefully guarded his winnings, exhibiting the virtue of frugality, and saved the money for his first campaign. He came rushing out of the war, and almost immediately a goal for his energy materialized.

In his congressional district, a group of small businessmen called the Committee of 100 had formed, searching for a bright young man to support against the long-time incumbent, a New Dealer, Jerry Voorhis. "Like their counterparts throughout Southern California, and indeed through the nation," writes Ambrose, "these middle-class Old Guard Republicans were in a mood close to desperation." They believed they were true-blue Americans, but they had lost their rightful place in the world because of the unnatural Depression for which they had no explanation. Roosevelt's presidency was a warp in time. Yet again and again they had been frustrated. Liberalism was leading to socialism, which led to communism. What kept this un-Americanism in power was an unholy alliance of labor unions and minorities, Hollywood celebrities and federal bureaucrats. (This enemies list—cast as special interests, radical chic, and big government—has lasted for decades.) Two systems were in conflict, according to Nixon: "One advocated by the New Deal is government control in regulating our lives. The other calls for individual freedom and all that initiative can produce." With this formulation, Nixon convinced the Committee of 100 that he was the man to slate.

"Had enough?" was the Republican slogan of 1946. (These magic words were manufactured for the GOP by the Harry M. Frost advertising company.) Like the late 1970s, the late 1940s was a period of economic and foreign policy turmoil. And the right had ready answers. Communists and fellow travelers were "gaining positions of importance in virtually every federal department and bureau," Nixon told an American Legion crowd. "They are boring from within, striving to force private enterprise into bankruptcy, and thus bring about the socialization of America's basic institutions and industries." What's more, he elaborated at another campaign stop, "There are those walking in high official places . . . who would lead us into a disastrous foreign policy whereby we will be guilty of . . . depriving the people of smaller nations of their freedoms." Here was an anticipation of McCarthyism, and the prehistory of rollback and the Reagan Doctrine.

The symmetry between the right's frustration on the domestic scene and its frustration with the international scene was striking. At the war's end, communism, or more precisely the Red Army, was on the march. To conservatives, no explanation made so much sense as that President

Roosevelt had betrayed Eastern Europe at Yalta. For the right, the acceptance of the cold war, and of containment, and later of deterrence, meant reconciling itself to permanent frustration. The incumbent Democratic stewardship of this policy provided the opportunity to taint the Democrats as unpatriotic. By contrast, the right began to move away from the old isolationism toward an eschatological anticommunism—a program of simple vengeance that would result in an America once again untroubled by foreign problems. Nixon, in time, supported the Marshall Plan, the pillar of containment. Yet he cultivated the right's anxieties about a tense world; they were useful as a political instrument.

Nixon's campaign for Congress consisted of unalloyed lies, innuendos, and distortions. The words the judicious Ambrose uses to describe it are "vicious . . . snarling . . . dirty." Many of the neighbors and friends who had known Nixon since he was a boy were shocked by the apparent transformation of character. "To them, this was a 'new Nixon.'" Later, a group of them prevented the Whittier City Council from naming a street after their most famous son, then vice president. "I had to win," was Nixon's rationale—the Protestant ethic without ethics. *This* Nixon was the only "new Nixon" that ever really mattered.

But the emergence of the first "new Nixon" involved more than a question of character. From the beginning, Nixon's lack of principles was in the service of the principle of partisanship. He was very much a member of the resurgent Republican class of '46, and within that a creature of the embittered right wing. *U.S. News,* a purveyor of mostly uncritical Republicanism, immediately proclaimed 1946 as Year 1 in "a new cycle in American political history." This was wishful thinking, but it contained some truth, as Nixon's progress would bear out.

The realignment theory that emerged in the wake of Ronald Reagan's election has tended to overlook realignment's true origin in the old Republican minority and in its reaction against the New Deal, which brought it little but sorrow until the midterm elections of 1946. For the GOP, no greater gains have been recorded since: 56 House and 13 Senate seats. This shift was traumatic enough to inspire Senator J. William Fulbright to call for President Truman's acceptance of the electoral returns as a vote of no-confidence and, in the British way, to step down. Despite the shock, though, the general features of the old party system seemed stable, as the Truman victory two years later confirmed. Beneath the surface, however, there were deep cracks.

The 1946 results were a tremor, a premonition of the coming Republican strength in the Sunbelt and Mountain states. In Congress, the conservative Southern Democrats and the right-wing Republicans made an alliance of convenience that was not defeated until Lyndon Johnson assumed the civil rights cause as his own in 1964. The Democratic setback in 1946 also exposed the party's ideological confusion about the post-New Deal era, a confusion that is still to be resolved. But the right wing demonstrated its willingness to engage in a single-minded politics of desperation. This sentiment was later made into a complex formula by Kevin Phillips, an aide to Nixon's 1968 campaign manager, John Mitchell. In *The New Republican Majority,* Phillips proposed a polarization of the electorate along racial, ethnic, and regional lines. It was Nixon's historic mission to exploit these tensions to create a lasting GOP advantage.

Nixon's entrance onto the political scene was a sign to the old right of both hope and vengeance. He was loved for his enemies. His early Washington years illustrated the evil of the conspiracy that the Old Guard believed had been in power since 1933. "I was elected to smash the labor bosses," he declared upon arriving in the capital. He was tutored by Father John Cronin, one of the communism experts who attached themselves to the right, to expose Communists "in the State Department." So Nixon chose an assignment on the House Un-American Activities Committee.

That Alger Hiss turned out to have been almost certainly guilty was Nixon's great luck. He did not enter his first "crisis" as a disinterested party, but out of sheer partisan impulse. At a crucial juncture in the case, Nixon secretly met in a New York hotel room with the "senior brain trust of the Republican Party, and had this group decided to withhold its approval, Nixon would have had to drop the case." These men (John Foster Dulles, who was Thomas Dewey's chief foreign policy adviser; Allen Dulles; C. Douglas Dillon; Christian Herter) were the personifications of the GOP Eastern Establishment, held in contempt by the Old Guard. Yet Nixon's determination had made the case such a partisan cause that they were drawn into it. And Nixon convinced them to bless his continuing struggle.

Nixon had hit upon a theme that Republican candidates used with tremendous effect in the 1950 midterm elections. It was a theme that the GOP had been marketing at the lower frequencies for years, without much result. Now it worked: "Fear. Nixon knew that fear was the way to get to the public. Fear of Alger Hiss and his kind; fear of Stalin and his bombs and rockets; fear of change; fear of someone getting ahead in the arms race; fear."

When Hiss was convicted, Nixon immediately intensified his partisanship. "This conspiracy," he said, "would have come to light long since had there not been a definite . . . effort on the part of certain high officials in two administrations [Roosevelt's and Truman's] to keep the public from knowing the facts." Among the congratulatory notes he received was one he "cherished most," from the Old Guard icon-in-exile, Herbert Hoover: "At last the stream of treason that existed in our government has been exposed in a fashion that all may believe."

By now, Nixon was running for the Senate, attacking the Democrats as the blame-America-first party, a party that "has been captured and is completely controlled by a group of ruthless, cynical seekers after power—committed to policies and principles completely foreign to those of its founders." His campaign against Helen Gahagan Douglas was as noteworthy for its scurrilousness as his effort against Voorhis. Ambrose notes that Douglas herself was not entirely innocent of mudslinging. But once the campaign turned to mud, she was vastly outdone by the master.

Senator Nixon became Vice President Nixon in a thoroughly characteristic way: by becoming indispensable to the aspirations of a force larger than himself—those seeking the nomination of Dwight Eisenhower at the 1952 Republican convention. His role required nothing less than the betrayal of the Old Guard that had previously sustained him. Nixon had already been handpicked for the position by talent scout Dewey, who escorted him into a meeting with the Eisenhower political directorate months before the convention. Thus Nixon allied his ambition publicly with the force he had initially and privately encountered in the Hiss case.

The nomination turned on the outcome of a credentials fight between competing Southern delegations—one group pledged to Ike, the other to Senator Robert Taft, the Old Guard standard-bearer. And the key to the outcome of this issue was the vote of the big California delegation. Within the delegation, the central figure was Nixon, who, with great aplomb, fostered the notion that Taft was unelectable. Nixon then gave an eloquent speech on the convention floor swaying delegates to vote for the Eisenhower Southerners, who were then seated. Years later, in 1969, while swearing in Nixon as president, Chief Justice Earl Warren, who, as governor, had been the nominal leader of that California delegation, confided to Nixon aide Herb Klein "that but for Nixon he might have won a compromise nomination for president himself in 1952."

Two months after the convention, Nixon was revealed to have maintained an $18,000 "slush fund," set up by friendly businessmen, for his personal use. His famous defense in the "Checkers" speech commingled themes from Horatio Alger with themes from Alger Hiss. There was the paean to hard work—"every dime we've got is honestly ours"—and the resolve to root out the all-encompassing conspiracy—"I am going to campaign up and down America until we drive the crooks and communists and those that defend them out of Washington." Quickly, Eisenhower embraced him: "You're my boy!" Back home, his old drama coach at Whittier College, Professor Upton, watched his former student on television put his head on Senator William Knowland's shoulder and weep tears of joy. "That's my boy?" Upton shouted. "That's my actor!"

For Eisenhower, Nixon served as the partisan id. He spoke the unspeakable, earning him Adlai Stevenson's sobriquet as "McCarthy in a white collar." Ike kept his distance, while gaining the benefit. Nixon was his bridge to the Old Guard, his conduit to McCarthy, and generally a source of political information. The vice president's many suggestions for foreign intervention, including dropping atom bombs on Vietnam in 1954 when the French were besieged at Dien Bien Phu, were uniformly rejected by the commander in chief. But he learned a great deal, traveled widely, and ran for the White House in 1960 on his superior experience.

Within a year of his honorable defeat by Kennedy, he was thinking of running for governor of California, a base from which he could again venture forth to win the GOP presidential nomination. The party establishment, "from Eisenhower on down," feared that the California right would seize control of the state party. Since 1946 the Southern California right had grown more confident and virulent. Its motor, in the early 1960s, was a forerunner of the New Right, founded in the bitter aftermath of Taft's 1952 convention defeat: the John Birch Society. The shift from the time of Representative Nixon was apparent in the election as congressman of John Rousselot, the Birch regional director for Southern California and five Sunbelt states. Rousselot's 1962 fund-raising dinner featured the renowned toastmaster Ronald Reagan.

The suggestion that Reagan might be a candidate for governor quickened the pressure on Nixon. After he announced, his fund-raising lunch at the Bohemian Club was attended by the massed corporate titans of California—"quite a contrast to the Committee of 100 from the 1946 campaign," writes Ambrose. But Nixon was not anointed. Instead he endured a primary against a right-wing candidate, Joe Shell, a former college football star turned oilman. Nixon attempted to denounce the Birch Society while giving credence to its anti-communist passion; he also did not want to alienate its activists and the many Republican officeholders who were Birch members. In the meantime, liberal Republicans deserted him to support the incumbent Democrat, Edmund "Pat" Brown. Soon Nixon was giving his most memorable performance since the "Checkers" speech: "You won't have Nixon to kick around anymore, because, gentlemen, this is my last press conference." But he was wrong. There would be new Nixons; for them we must await Ambrose's concluding volume.

The Reagan years, filled with rhetoric about "a new cycle in American political history," have curiously obscured Nixon. After all, it was Nixon, the native Californian, who began what Reagan hopped aboard. Unlike Reagan, he was painfully self-conscious about what he was doing, and about the price that was being exacted from him and others. Nixon actually lived and bore the scars of the social Darwinism that to Reagan has always been romance.

Moreover, the achievements of what is called the "Reagan revolution" pale next to the transformations that Nixon accomplished at all levels. Nixon in China is still breathtaking. By contrast, the most celebrated Reagan accomplishment—the change in the national brain waves from worried to happy, partly intended to induce amnesia about Nixon—has been the most ephemeral. Reagan's current bouts of cheerfulness, while the special prosecutor prepares his briefs, are more detached from reality than ever. In retrospect, Reagan may be seen as the end of the era that Nixon inaugurated.

As Reagan's benumbing optimism wears off, many of those who had faith in its powers are returning to a primordial resentment. Conservative activists and placemen, columnists and policy-makers are getting themselves in the mood for a young Nixon. If he cannot be found in 1988, a reconstituted Committee of 100 undoubtedly will begin the search.

He's back.

Alan Brinkley (review date 16 July 1987)

SOURCE: "The Best Man," in *New York Review of Books,* July 16, 1987, pp. 10-3.

[*In the following review of* Nixon: The Education of a Politician, 1913-1962, *Brinkley finds shortcomings in Ambrose's unwillingness to offer speculative analysis of Nixon's psychological profile. However, Brinkley concludes that, while offering no new information, Ambrose's biography relates "a familiar story with uncommon balance, skill, and grace—and with a fullness and detail that no previous work can match."*]

Stephen Ambrose began his distinguished biography of Dwight D. Eisenhower with open admiration for his subject. Eisenhower, he writes, was "a great and good man . . . one of the outstanding leaders of the Western world of this century."[1] He offers no comparable evaluation of Richard Nixon in this first of two volumes on the life of the thirty-seventh president; indeed, there is no preface or foreword of any kind. Ambrose opens the book, almost abruptly, with a discussion of Nixon's ancestors. He ends, equally unceremoniously, with the defeated candidate driving home from his "last press conference" in 1962. Yet even without saying so, Ambrose has produced a study of Nixon [in *Nixon: The Education of a Politician, 1913-1962*] that is in many ways as powerfully "revisionist" as his earlier study of Eisenhower. Other biographers have scrutinized Nixon's youth and early career for the seeds of his later failures. This book makes it possible to understand why, through most of his life, Nixon was a great success.

Ambrose's reluctance to draw general conclusions from his work suggests that he may have surprised even himself with what he found. Like other liberal academics, he spent many years as a confirmed Nixon hater—so much so that in 1970 he helped lead a demonstration that disrupted a presidential visit to Kansas State University.[2] Ambrose retains a certain skepticism still; he makes no apologies for the many unsavory moments in Nixon's early career, and he takes his subject to task for his frequent distortions of his own past. But the Richard Nixon who emerges from

this thoroughly researched, impressively written, and remarkably balanced book is not, in the end, the dark, brooding, bitter figure whom so many hostile writers have described. He is a talented, successful, complicated man who at a very young age emerged as one of the most accomplished and admired public figures of his time.

Ambrose's challenge to the existing literature begins with his discussion of Nixon's childhood. Psychohistorians (and others) have pointed repeatedly to the difficulties of these years: the straitened circumstances that kept his family constantly moving from house to house and business to business; the deaths of two brothers from tuberculosis; the frequent separations from one or both parents; the severe father and the stern, miserly mother. In searching for explanations of Nixon's later problems, biographers have often pointed to the psychic scars he presumably absorbed in his youth. Fawn Brodie talks of an early "warping in his capacity to love" and a pattern of pathological lying "to bolster his ever-wavering identity."[3] Bruce Mazlish speaks of feelings of "betrayal," "guilt," and "anxiety" that remained forever unresolved.[4]

Ambrose has little patience with such speculation. Nixon's childhood, he argues, was not always comfortable and not always happy. But neither was it traumatic. Nixon grew up in a strict but stable home. His family's means were modest, but never desperate. In most respects, "his childhood was so normal as to be dull. No one abused him; there were no traumas, no betrayals, only love and trust." At Whittier College, he was a good student and a respected campus leader—"a human dynamo in student government, the man everyone counted on," "unanimously popular on and off the campus." At Duke Law School, he displayed an almost alarming diligence; a classmate called him "the hardest-working man I ever met." But he demonstrated as well both leadership and moral decency. As president of the Student Bar Association, he spoke frequently against racism and did volunteer work at a local legal clinic.

Nixon's young adulthood was, similarly, remarkable only for its relative normality. He became a successful lawyer in Whittier, California; began to make a name for himself as a civic leader; pursued and married an attractive and popular schoolteacher (Pat Ryan). He worked briefly in Washington for the Office of Price Administration in the first year of World War II, then served inconspicuously in the Navy as a supply officer in the Pacific. He was popular with his fellow officers during the war. They remembered him later as a warm and friendly man much like the movie character "Mister Roberts." (They remembered him, too, as a dedicated and talented poker player; his wartime winnings provided the stake for his first political campaign.)

In 1946, Nixon defied all predictions by defeating a popular incumbent, Jerry Voorhis, in a race for Congress. Four years later, he defeated the actress Helen Gahagan Douglas in a race for a vacant California seat in the United States Senate. Ambrose offers no defense of Nixon's harsh tactics in the race against Voorhis (other than to acknowledge that he was hardly alone that year in attacking Democrats for their ties to organized labor); the 1946 campaign was, he acknowledges, a "dirty" one, characterized by "a vicious, snarling approach that was full of half-truths, full lies, and innuendos." Indeed, Nixon anticipated almost all of the scurrilous charges and many of the vicious tactics that Joseph McCarthy would later employ. "REMEMBER," one Nixon advertisement proclaimed, "Voorhis is a former registered Socialist and his voting record in Congress is more Socialistic and Communistic than Democratic."

The campaign against Douglas in 1950 was another matter. Other biographers have seen in it the clearest evidence of Nixon's unscrupulousness and have cited his references to a "Douglas-Marcantonio Axis" (a link between Mrs. Douglas and the left-wing New York congressman Vito Marcantonio) as proof of his preference for the political low road.[5] Ambrose reveals that it was Douglas, not Nixon, who first raised the issue of "being soft on communism" in 1950; it was she who first tried to link her opponent to Marcantonio by making selective and dishonest use of voting records. Nixon responded in kind. Even the devastating, red-baiting (and vaguely sexist) nickname Nixon bestowed on Mrs. Douglas, the "Pink Lady," was in response to her use of a far more devastating (and more enduring) nickname for him—"Tricky Dick." Ambrose does not suggest that Mrs. Douglas's tactics excuse Nixon's own behavior; he does, however, help one to see the campaign in a different light.

Nixon was a highly respected young member of Congress. Ambrose describes him as the most adept and responsible member of the House Committee on Un-American Activities, "careful and exact with the facts," courteous toward witnesses, a "moderating influence" on that often reckless body. When Joseph McCarthy launched his crusade against Communists in government in 1950, Nixon at first denounced him for it. (Only the Communists were benefiting from McCarthy's charges, he said.) When J. Robert Oppenheimer came under attack that same year, Nixon publicly defended him. (I have complete confidence in Dr. Oppenheimer's loyalty," he declared.) His famous pursuit of Alger Hiss was relentless and effective; without Nixon, there would likely have been no Hiss case. But as Ambrose portrays it, Nixon's behavior throughout was honorable. His evidence was solid, and he allowed Hiss to ruin himself with his own lies and evasions.[6]

Nixon's later claims that the pursuit of Hiss proved a political liability were almost certainly disingenuous. In fact, the case transformed him into a major national figure almost overnight. By 1950, he was the most sought-after speaker and fund-raiser in the Republican party, a man already (at the age of thirty-seven) discussed as a future president. Yet Nixon profited from more than his reputation as an effective anticommunist in these years. He was also an important conciliatory force within his party, helping to nudge it toward the center on numerous issues. He opposed the powerful China Lobby and supported the Eurocentric foreign policy of the Truman Administration, including the initially controversial Marshall Plan. He avoided an open break with Joseph McCarthy, but he never endorsed McCarthy's tactics (and later, as vice president, participated quietly in the campaign to discredit him). "Thus," Ambrose notes, "both the Old Guard and the more moderate Republicans thought of Nixon as a friend and ally, as he indeed was." He even earned the admiration of the leaders of the party's eastern establishment. Thomas E. Dewey described him as being considered "an absolute star, a man of enormous capacity" and helped to persuade Eisenhower to offer him the vice-presidential nomination in 1952.

Nixon's experience in the campaign of 1952 was an ordeal few politicians could have survived. He was cut adrift by Eisenhower and forced to fight alone for his political life by denying spurious charges of financial impropriety; the result was the mawkish "Checkers" speech, which—effective as it was—so humiliated him that he was barely able to get through it without breaking down. On instructions from Eisenhower, Nixon became the "hatchet man" of the campaign, earning the contempt of the liberal press and making himself the butt of such attacks as Herblock's famous savage cartoons. The rigors of 1952, Fawn Brodie claims, "left him cynical, soured, and obsessively suspicious of political friendships."[7]

Yet whatever scars Nixon may have absorbed in 1952, they were seldom evident in his performance as vice president, which was, Ambrose claims, exemplary. He was, in fact, the most visible and successful vice president of this century. He endured frequent snubs and humiliations from Eisenhower without complaint and served the president faithfully and well. Eisenhower was reluctant to admit it (and in fact, in 1960, greatly damaged Nixon's presidential campaign by denying it), but he came to rely heavily on his vice president's advice on political matters and to respect (if not always to share) his views on international affairs. Nixon's many trips abroad won him the respect and admiration of even the most skeptical world leaders. Drew Middleton of *The New York Times* described the impact of a Nixon visit to London in 1958: The vice president "who arrived billed as an uncouth adventurer in the political jungles, departed trailing clouds of statesmanship and esteem." In 1955, when the president suffered a heart attack, Nixon behaved with grace and prudence. Emmet John Hughes, an Eisenhower speech writer and frequent Nixon critic, described him then as "poised and restrained . . . a man close to great power *not* being presumptuously or prematurely assertive."

Because Eisenhower chose to remain largely aloof from partisan politics, Nixon served as the Republicans' principal spokesman and most important leader throughout the 1950s. He campaigned strenuously in off-year elections; and while the party declined steadily in national strength during the Eisenhower years, Nixon's efforts probably prevented the hemorrhaging from growing even worse. By the end of the decade, moreover, he had emerged as one of the party's most dynamic and progressive figures. Long before it became politically profitable, he was an outspoken supporter of civil rights (and an important actor in the passage of the 1957 Civil Rights Act). Far more openly than Eisenhower (or, for that matter, John Kennedy), he supported the aims of the NAACP and spoke sharply against the rise of "massive resistance" by whites in the South. "I believe the issue is a moral one," he wrote southern editors in 1957, "and is of such transcendent importance that all Americans must face it."

Nixon began calling for a federal tax cut to stimulate economic growth well before John Kennedy seized on the issue and made it his own. Although as vice president he could not voice such feelings publicly, he complained in private of the "standpattism" of Eisenhower's leadership. "I am concerned," he wrote in 1958, "about the tendency in this Administration to be sort of a care-taker. . . . We must go out and look for new ideas." By 1960, he had, Ambrose claims, "identified himself with idealism and challenge every bit as much as Kennedy." Like Kennedy, he beckoned the nation to undertake great deeds, to work together "in a cause greater than ourselves, greater than our nation, as great as the whole world itself." (He was also, like Kennedy, a far more committed cold warrior than Eisenhower. He privately agreed with Kennedy's public criticisms of the administration in 1960: that it was spending too little on defense and that it was behaving too cautiously in resisting communism in the third world.)

Nixon made many mistakes in his campaign against Kennedy, but he did little to discredit himself. He steadfastly refused to raise the issue of Kennedy's Catholicism and repudiated those supporters who did so. He lost many black votes when Kennedy, not he, publicly intervened to have Martin Luther King, Jr., released from a Georgia jail. But while Nixon received no public credit for it, he too took action on behalf of King, appealing quietly to the attorney general to intercede—an appeal that came to naught because Eisenhower refused to get involved. The 1960 election was the closest in American history, so close that an investigation into vote-counting irregularities in several states might have reversed the outcome. Nixon refused to demand a recount, fearful that the result would be a protracted constitutional crisis. He accepted defeat with grace.

Had Nixon's public career ended more happily, had there been no Watergate and no Vietnam, it would be these features of his early life that historians would likely emphasize: his intelligence, talent, diligence, even decency; the traits that made him the most enduring and resilient political leader of his generation and, for a time, one of the most successful presidents of this century. But Nixon's public life did not, of course, end happily. And while it would be a mistake to examine his early career only for clues to his later problems, it is impossible to look at those years without asking how they help us to understand why things ultimately went so wrong.

Ambrose's otherwise impressive objectivity proves something of a handicap here, for he steadfastly refuses to speculate about the sources of Nixon's character. In fact, one might be tempted to conclude from the portrait here that Nixon's later problems emerged not from defects in his own character but simply from the extraordinary problems he encountered in the White House. Anyone elected president in 1968, Ambrose seems vaguely to imply, might have behaved similarly. Yet even if inadvertently, Ambrose provides ample evidence of several characteristics of Nixon's personality that almost certainly contributed to his eventual downfall.

One such characteristic was the burning resentment that seemed to settle on him in his youth and that he never managed to shed: the sense of himself as somehow an outsider, constantly at odds with the establishment. That was the source of the constant refrain, throughout his career, describing the hardships he had endured rising up through an unwelcoming world; and it was the source of the enduring bitterness toward those more "fortunate" than himself that seemed always to surface in moments of stress. Even when he became a man of wealth, fame, and power, part of him seemed always to remain the provincial boy from Whittier College who had been compelled to turn down a chance to attend Harvard because his family couldn't afford it; or the struggling scholarship student at Duke Law School who for a time lived in an unheated toolshed to save money.

Nixon's preoccupation with the Hiss case, for example, seemed at least in part a result of his personal resentment toward the elegant former diplomat whose manner he described as "condescending" and who, unlike Nixon himself, was constantly surrounded by what Ambrose calls "highly placed friends from the Washington social community." In the Checkers speech and throughout the 1952 campaign, he spoke frequently of the degree to which Adlai Stevenson ("who inherited a fortune from his father") had enjoyed "advantages" that Nixon himself had been denied. He liked to quote Abraham Lincoln: "God must love the common people—he made so many of them." In 1960, late in the campaign when things began going badly, he once again fell back on a vaguely pathetic appeal to the sympathy of the voters for his lack of the wealth and connections with which John Kennedy had been born. Murray Kempton later described him as "wandering limply and wetly about the American heartland begging votes on the excuse that he had been too poor to have a pony when he was a boy."[8] And in 1974, in his painful farewell to the White House staff after resigning the presidency, he talked again of his humble origins, as if they were somehow to blame for his predicament.[9]

What is perhaps equally striking about Nixon in his youth, just as it was striking in his maturity, was his inability to form close personal relationships. Even as a child, he was a conspicuous loner—dour, serious, known within his family as "Gloomy Gus." The pattern continued throughout his life. Nixon always had companions, but seldom real friends. "From grade school and then out into the world," Ambrose writes, "he left behind his old associates. . . .

When an acquaintance could only be called 'a friend from the old days,' Nixon lost interest in him."

Except for his warm and affectionate relationship with his two daughters, Nixon's adult life was, apparently, as emotionally barren as his youth. His marriage was stable and reasonably successful: but that was, Ambrose suggests, largely because Pat Nixon made so few demands of her husband, subordinated herself to his career, and became accustomed to a lack of intimacy. "I've given up everything I've ever loved," she once confided to a friend.[10] Only rarely, however, did she complain about what Ambrose calls an indifference from Nixon that "bordered on cruelty." In 1952, for example, she heard that her husband was to be nominated for the vice presidency not from him (he had promised her earlier he would not accept), but from a television news broadcast in a hotel restaurant in Chicago. She rushed to the convention hall, battled through the crowd to her husband's side on the podium, and kissed him on the cheek. He never looked at her. She never stopped smiling.

Outside his family, Nixon's most important (and most revealing) friendship throughout his adulthood was with the much-ridiculed Bebe Rebozo, a rich Florida real-estate magnate whom Nixon first met in 1950. Their relationship continued for three decades. It survived, however, not because of a close personal bond between them, but because of the absence of one. Rebozo subordinated himself to Nixon's solitary desires and asked nothing in return; he was as much a loyal servant as a friend, content to provide boats and vacation spots and, perhaps most important, silence to a man who had no interest in intimacy. "Bebe is like a sponge," Pat Nixon once said; "he soaks up whatever Dick says and never makes any comments. Dick loves that." Another mutual acquaintance remarked, more sardonically, "Nixon likes to be alone, and with Bebe along, he is."

Ambrose has no explanation for this intense, perhaps even pathological, personal isolation. "The inability to trust anyone is one of the principal personality traits of Nixon as an adult," he writes. The reason, he confesses, remains a "mystery." But he is almost certainly correct in seeing in this isolation a source of some of Nixon's later political problems. The absence of trusted friends and advisers, people in whom he could confide and on whose advice he felt he could rely, removed a critical check on his own, at times reckless, inclinations.

A second, and clearly related, characteristic was Nixon's literally obsessive preoccupation with politics. He worked compulsively, and the only work that interested him was political. He had no hobbies (other than a largely statistical interest in sports). He took vacations only at Pat's insistence and for nearly twenty years cut every vacation short to return to work. He saw his family seldom, ate dinner at home only once or twice a week, often spent the night on the couch in his office. He threw himself into every political campaign from 1946 through 1972, even when he was not himself a candidate, traveling widely and exhaustingly like a man possessed. He read and talked and apparently thought about almost nothing but politics; it was the only world that seemed to have any meaning to him.

After the 1960 election, Nixon moved to Los Angeles, established a lucrative legal practice, and prepared for life as a private citizen. Two years later, against the wishes of his wife (and, he later admitted, against his own better judgment), he launched an ill-fated campaign for governor of California, an office in which he had little interest and for which he had few qualifications. "Why," he asks in his memoir, *Six Crises,* "would anyone risk these advantages of private life and decide to re-enter the political arena?" Because, he replied, "once a man has been in public life for any period of time, his interests and ambitions change. . . . It just happened, because my fate sent me to Congress in 1946, that I became a primarily public man and must, therefore, remain in that channel."[11]

According to an epigram widely circulated in the 1950s, "when Nixon's public and private personalities meet, they shake hands." This missed the point. Nixon seemed to have no private personality. It was almost as if he ceased to exist once removed from the public stage. And like the lack of intimate friends, the lack of a private self—an internal balance wheel against which to measure one's actions—may help to explain why his judgment so frequently went awry.

Nixon is not alone among politicians in having these qualities. Franklin Roosevelt had similar difficulties forming intimate relationships. Lyndon Johnson was at least as obsessed with politics as Nixon. But Nixon possessed another characteristic that set him apart from most of his predecessors: his distinctively combative view of politics. Not for him LBJ's gregarious, backslapping, wheeling and dealing or FDR's artful manipulation of subordinates. His own instinct was for combat, crisis. Perhaps because he lacked close friendships or other interests, it was only in the midst of crisis that he could achieve emotional intensity, a sense of release. Perhaps, too, it was only through his combative political style that he was able to vent the deep grievances that at other times he felt obliged to repress.

Whatever the reasons, Nixon seems to have felt fully alive only when he could convince himself that he was engaged in battle. He wrote in *Six Crises* about "why men who have been in public life seldom leave it voluntarily" in extraordinarily, if perhaps unintentionally revealing, terms:

> Probably the greatest magnet of all is that those who have known great crisis—its challenge and tension, its victory and defeat—can never become adjusted to a more leisurely and orderly pace. They have drunk too deeply of the stuff which really makes life exciting and worth living to be satisfied with the froth.[12]

And so, throughout Nixon's public career, he felt a compulsion to approach every contest, every controversy as if his own (and the nation's) future depended on the outcome. If no crisis existed, he manufactured one and then used it to rationalize behavior that he might otherwise have abhorred. In his first campaign in 1946 against Jerry Voorhis, he developed a battlefield mentality that shocked many old acquaintances who had seen few signs of such combativeness in him in the past. Nixon himself apparently found nothing jarring about the "transition from nice Quaker boy to ruthless politician." According to Ambrose, "there is no evidence that there was any soul-searching involved. To him it was all of a piece—you did whatever you could to win." When every campaign was a crusade for the future of the Republic, when every opponent was a threat to peace and freedom, it was, as Ambrose notes, an easy step to believe that "any means were justified to reach the end." Thus, year after year, election after election,

> the basic message never changed. It was that a Democratic victory would lead to socialism at home and surrender to Communism abroad. . . . His sly use of innuendo, his denials that he had just said what everyone had just heard him say, . . . his trickiness with figures, his flights of hyperbole, his shameless hypocrisy—all these combined to make him hated, and admired.

His political tactics "were all directed toward deepening the political split rather than narrowing it." "He polarized the public more than any other man of his era." And as Jonathan Schell argues in his perceptive 1975 study of the Nixon presidency, he continued to do so throughout his public life, deliberately and apparently eagerly. Even after he claimed publicly to wish to "bring us together," as he did in 1968, when he finally captured the presidency, he embarked on a course that rested on the principle of "positive polarization"—a belief in the value of isolating and discrediting his enemies.[13] In 1972, after his landslide re-election victory and at a point when one might have expected him to feel some satisfaction and generosity, Nixon told an interviewer:

> I believe in the battle, whether it's the battle of a campaign or the battle of this office. . . . It's always there wherever you go. I, perhaps, carry it more than others because that's my way.[14]

So it had been throughout his long, often brilliant, and ultimately tragic public life.

Almost everyone believed Nixon's career had come to an end in 1962, when he lost his race for governor of California and lashed out at reporters in his celebrated "last press conference." (He was not, as some have claimed, drunk at the time—only exhausted and frustrated.) But he drove home from his "last" press conference, Ambrose concludes, "already discussing his future"—a future of which no reader of this book can possibly be unaware.

Ambrose has in this first volume added relatively little to the information available to us about Richard Nixon's intensively scrutinized life. Nor does he seem likely to do so in the volumes to come. He has uncovered no new cache

of manuscripts (and given the legal complications surrounding Nixon's presidential papers, scholars will probably have little access to them for years). He has conducted few interviews (and none at all with Nixon or his family). He has made no important discoveries. What he has done, however, is to tell a familiar story with uncommon balance, skill, and grace—and with a fullness and detail that no previous work can match; in doing so he recalls a man far more complex and accomplished than the caricature many have come to accept. And so one finishes this absorbing biography eager for Ambrose's account of the dramatic events to come.

Notes

1. *Eisenhower: Soldier, General of the Army, President-Elect* (Simon and Schuster, 1983), p. 9; *Eisenhower: The President,* the second and concluding volume of the biography, appeared in 1984.

2. An account of Ambrose's role in the demonstration appears in a letter from one of his former colleagues to *The New York Times Book Review,* May 31, 1987, p. 58. Ambrose subsequently survived an effort by the faculty senate at Kansas State to censure him for his loud and at times obscene heckling of the President; but the episode apparently helped precipitate his departure from the university. He now teaches at the University of New Orleans.

3. Fawn M. Brodie, *Richard Nixon: The Shaping of His Character* (Norton, 1981), pp. 25–26.

4. Bruce Mazlish, *In Search of Nixon: A Psychohistorical Inquiry* (Basic Books, 1972), pp. 22–26.

5. See, for example, Garry Wills, *Nixon Agonistes* (Houghton Mifflin, 1970), pp. 85–86.

6. Ambrose provides a withering picture of Hiss, portraying him as both dishonest and insufferably arrogant. He calls Allen Weinstein, author of *Perjury: The Hiss-Chambers Case* (Knopf, 1978), "much the closest and most careful student of the Hiss case" and implicitly endorses, Weinstein's conclusion that Hiss was guilty as charged.

7. *Richard Nixon,* p. 271.

8. *Nixon Agonistes,* pp. 144–145.

9. Richard Nixon, *Memoirs* (Grossett and Dunlap, 1978), pp. 1088–1089.

10. Lester David, *The Lonely Lady of San Clemente: The Story of Pat Nixon* (Crowell, 1978), p. 73.

11. *Six Crises* (Doubleday, 1962), pp. 424–435.

12. *Six Crises,* p. 426.

13. Jonathan Schell, *The Time of Illusion* (Knopf, 1975), pp. 73–74.

14. Quoted in Arthur M. Schlesinger, Jr., *The Imperial Presidency* (Houghton Mifflin, 1973), p. 217.

Richard John Neuhaus (review date August 1987)

SOURCE: "The Vocation of Politics," in *Commentary*, Vol. 84, No. 2, August, 1987, pp. 78-80.

[*In the following review of* Nixon: The Education of a Politician, 1913-1962, *Neuhaus commends Ambrose's "exhaustive" and even-handed scholarship, but contends that he is not successful in recasting Nixon as a more admirable figure.*]

During his 1962 bid for the California governorship, Richard Nixon was not helped by the remark of the master of ceremonies at one of his fund-raising dinners: "Too many people are saying, 'I don't like Nixon, but I don't know why.'"

People are still saying that. On the other hand, many say that they do not just not like Nixon, they hate him—and they think they know why. During the same 1962 race, the pollster Samuel Lubell found "an almost unbelievable personal bitterness toward Nixon among many California voters." Toward very few contemporary politicians (Senator Edward Kennedy comes to mind) is there a widespread animosity intense and nasty enough to warrant the word hatred. Richard Nixon has known what it means to be hated since his first, and successful, race for Congress against Jerry Voorhis in 1946.

Now, thirteen years after he resigned from the Presidency in disgrace, we are told that Nixon is back. His rehabilitation, if that is what it is, will likely be advanced by this first volume of Stephen Ambrose's biography [***Nixon: The Education of a Politician, 1913-1962***]. Ambrose, professor of history at the University of New Orleans, is given a large part of the credit for the enhanced standing of Eisenhower in recent years. It was no little achievement that Ambrose's two-volume biography helped rescue Eisenhower from the derision of his detractors. To rescue Nixon from the hatred of his enemies is much the more daunting task. Those who have a deep stake in despising Richard Nixon are almost certainly not going to be converted by this volume. But those who have disliked him for reasons they did not quite understand will have occasion to think again. They may not turn to actually liking Nixon, but they may leave this book sharing Ambrose's respect for the man.

As Gary Hart has recently discovered to his sorrow, Americans are not very good at separating personality (some call it character) from the issues. Unlike Hart, and despite several efforts to pin him with the charge of taking money on the side, Richard Nixon has been above reproach in his personal life. To put it differently, his personal life has been his political purpose.

The elusiveness of the private Nixon, which is presumably the real Nixon, is a constant theme in this book, as it has been in most writing about Nixon. The absence of evidence on this score is interpreted as an invitation to speculate and has been seized with enthusiasm by writers with an argument to make. Thus we have been favored with David Abrahamsen's *Nixon vs. Nixon: An Emotional Tragedy,* Bruce Mazlish's *In Search of Nixon: A Psychohistorical Inquiry,* Fawn Brodie's *Richard Nixon: The Shaping of His Character,* and Garry Wills's *Nixon Agonistes: The Crisis of the Self-Made Man.* The last, in sharp contrast to Wills's more recent fabulations regarding Ronald Reagan, has the merit of being an imaginative exercise of considerable force. But Ambrose departs from this genre altogether. He appears to be one of those historians who believe that in the absence of evidence you should not make it up.

What is known about the personal Nixon—and Ambrose's researches seem to be exhaustive—is told here with care and economy. Nixon's private life is, for the most part, his family life. In this connection, Ambrose's treatment of Pat Nixon is extensive and unstinting in its admiration. Far from her being "Plastic Pat," always playing whatever role her husband dictated for the moment, one gains the impression of a gracefully determined woman who had securely ordered her loves and loyalties, putting Richard Nixon and his public career at the top of the list.

It seems that Nixon was intimate with no one else. Those who, like Bebe Rebozo, were deemed to be close friends appear to have been useful sycophants, although Ambrose does not use the term. From his school days in Whittier, California, through his law-school years at Duke, and during his time in the Navy, many people respected and trusted Nixon, but almost to a person they say they never really knew him. In the early years, before he ran for political office, Ambrose reports that everyone agrees Richard Nixon was precisely the kind of man from whom one would *not* hesitate to buy a used car. But from the first campaign his politics was the politics of division, and then many began to dislike, distrust, and hate him, even as many others came to support and admire him, but seldom to like, never mind love, him.

Ambrose is telling a story more than he is making an argument. And yet the story is interspersed with judgments, and his judgments are frequently inconsistent. One consistent judgment, however, is that Richard Nixon was always much more at ease before a crowd than in person-to-person contacts, especially with his peers. We are told that Nixon was one of the great politicians of the century but he could never, like FDR or Lyndon Johnson, work personality and friendship to political purpose. To support Richard Nixon was to support his policies, and the career that advanced those policies. His life, we are led to conclude, is one of sweated earnestness, of competition without camaraderie. There were personal alliances but few personal bonds, and those alliances were always aimed at moving the crowds, which is to say, the voters. The goal was to get a majority by division. Ambrose observes: "He divided people along party lines, but he refused to use race, class, or religion as his issues. In these areas, where the American people were already sharply divided, Nixon tried to bring them together."

That observation comes in connection with the 1960 race against John F. Kennedy, which Ambrose thinks was Nixon's finest. Throughout the period covered by this first volume, however, Nixon refused to exploit some of the deepest fissures in the American public, especially that of race. Some readers may be surprised to learn how deep and consistent was Nixon's support for civil rights. He was much respected by key black leaders, although that respect was seldom translated into votes, and Nixon's position on race placed a severe strain on his relations with the right wing of the Republican party which was his core constituency.

Ambrose, who apparently started out not thinking very highly of Richard Nixon, says at several points that Nixon was a great man. What makes for greatness is a subject of interminable debate, but Ambrose's telling of the story fails to persuade at least this reader that the Nixon portrayed here is a great man. He is convincingly presented as a man relentless in the pursuit of his goals, possessed of a powerful sense of political responsibility, and unswervingly faithful to a few guiding ideas.

The word faithful has a religious ring, and that seems entirely appropriate to the Nixon portrayed. Formal religion, in his case Quaker religion, played little evident part in Nixon's life after his teen-age years. Presumably his many and long discussions with Billy Graham had something to do with religion (it is hard to imagine Mr. Graham discussing much else for very long). But one is led to believe that the religion to which Richard Nixon was faithful was the religion of political purpose.

This is to say something more than that politics—in the sense of the contest for power—was Nixon's religion. To make politics one's religion is, religiously speaking, idolatrous and, psychologically speaking, disastrous. Nixon's religion of political purpose was more elevated than that. Although Ambrose does not put it this way, the Nixon of this book had a calling, a vocation, to advance a great truth, and that truth was political freedom.

It was a truth well worth dividing people over. More precisely, Nixon's purpose was to bring to political expression the fact that people were already divided over the importance of freedom. Nixon, in short, was an anti-Communist. That was the most important political thing he was, and the most important thing he was was political.

In Alger Hiss the calling and the occasion converged to make Nixon a national figure of consequence. Alger Hiss was in his view neither eccentric nor deviant but a representative of the enemy. For Nixon, the nature and mission of the enemy were discovered in the Hiss case and diagnosed in Whittaker Chambers's *Witness.* This was the dark antithesis to freedom's truth and, in the opinion of many, the dark side of Richard Nixon. Behind Herblock's caricature of a sleazy and tricky Nixon they detected a sinister Nixon in the grips of a metaphysical obsession with the threat of Communism.

The argument might be made that Nixon would not have encountered such animosity had he been as musical in articulating freedom's cause as he was combative in opposing freedom's foes. But that would be to overlook the fact that there were, and are, enemies of the democratic proposition whose hatred of Nixon was eminently sensible from their viewpoint. No mere change of "style" would have won them over. As for those who were put off by Nixon's belligerent manner, Ambrose's account suggests that he rendered a service by tempering and bringing into the mainstream of democratic discourse whatever was legitimate in the screeds of the reckless and extreme, such as Joseph McCarthy and the John Birch Society.

The meaning of the subtitle of this first volume, *The Education of a Politician,* is not self-evident and is not explained. If education means growth and learning, there is little education here. There is no indication that Nixon read anything or talked with anyone about matters not directly related to the advancement of his political purpose. There is no evidence of intellectual curiosity ranging beyond the boundaries of the work that was his to do. By the end of his formal education Nixon knew that he had a remarkable capacity for leadership by virtue of hard work, combative engagement, and persuasive talent. By the end of his first term in Congress he knew that he had found his cause in anti-Communism. The rest is detail.

That is not to say that the rest is dull. In fact this telling of Nixon's story entails all the dramas, high and low, that shaped our political culture as we entered the night of the 60's. *Nixon* is competently, sometimes brightly, written, and one gets the impression that Ambrose is striving, above all, to be assiduously fair. In that he seems to have succeeded. As for the Richard Nixon we meet here, the subtitle might better have been "The Vocation of a Politician"—and to that vocation he was faithful. Of course this volume takes us only to 1962 and we are inclined to read the story through the lens of subsequent events. It is the notable achievement of Stephen Ambrose that he compels us to reread subsequent events through the lens of the story he tells.

Robert A. Strong (review date Summer 1988)

SOURCE: "Richard Nixon Revisited," in *Virginia Quarterly Review,* Vol. 64, No. 3, Summer, 1988, pp. 525-34.

[*In the following excerpted review essay, Strong offers positive evaluation of* Nixon: The Education of a Politician, 1913-1962, *but concludes that many questions about Nixon's personal motivations remain unanswerable.*]

Winston Churchill, in one of his many memorable observations, once described a Russian action on the international scene as "a riddle wrapped in a mystery inside an enigma." If you were to add a few more qualifying phrases and a few more synonyms suggesting bewilderment, you might come close to describing the problem Americans have in understanding our 37th president. There are multiple riddles, mysteries, and enigmas about Richard Milhous Nixon that his many biographers, critics, defenders, and political opponents have been unable fully to explain. Two new books—a biography of his pre-presidential career by the historian Stephen Ambrose [*Nixon: The Education of a Politician: 1913-1962*] and a collection of conversations with more than 20 of his closest associates and observers, edited by the director of the White Burkett Miller Center, Kenneth W. Thompson—go a long way to improving our public portrait of Nixon as a person and as a politician. These books do not provide a full-fledged revisionist account of Richard Nixon and are not intended to do so. They do, however, add much needed balance and detail to the existing accounts of his life and administration, and make it possible to see, not another "new" Richard Nixon, but the old one in a broader perspective.

Ambrose, in the first volume of his biography which covers the period from Nixon's birth to his "last" press conference in 1962, gives us an unusually objective account of Nixon's early years. Ambrose avoids the temptation to seek out some crucial traumatic event in Nixon's childhood which would explain the remainder of his life, a search that has preoccupied several of Nixon's psychobiographers. He discounts the importance often attributed to the death of Nixon's brother from tuberculosis and to the months that family members spent at the child's sickbed. There is, in Ambrose's view, no psychological "rosebud" which would unlock the mysteries of Nixon's personality; instead there is only the early and largely unexplained emergence of those mysteries.

For Ambrose, Richard Nixon's childhood was, in most respects, "so normal as to be dull." Frank Nixon, Richard's father, was a moderately successful businessman, who managed to miss out on the easy money that came to many in southern California, but was always able to provide for his wife and family. Nixon's later claims of "log cabin" origins and childhood poverty are, Ambrose notes, the product of exaggerated campaign rhetoric or understandable feelings of inferiority from a candidate who competed for national prominence with John Kennedy and Nelson Rockefeller. Compared to them, Richard Nixon was poor; compared to the rest of the American people, particularly during the depression years, he came from a comfortable household. Like his father, Nixon's mother was a hard worker who invested enormous energy in caring for her children and handling her share of the family enterprises. She was a strong and loving woman who encouraged her children to do well in school and to get as much education as they possibly could. The years of Richard Nixon's youth, other than those of his brother's illness, were happy ones with a large extended family in and around the small towns in which he grew up, regular religious training in the Quaker church, solid accomplishments in school, early responsibilities in the family store, and a healthy variety of childhood activities.

From this dull and normal background Nixon developed an unusual set of seemingly inconsistent qualities. The most important of these contradictory combinations, which is highlighted throughout the Ambrose book, involves the relationship between his public and private lives. From a very early age, Dick Nixon was shy in his personal dealings with individuals and small groups but at ease when performing in concerts, plays, and debates. On a stage, in front of a crowd, he had confidence and great success, easily winning high school debates, elections, and the acclaim of his schoolmates. At the same time, he seems to have had difficulty forming lasting friendships or intimate relationships of any kind outside his family. As a child he was both accomplished and awkward, widely popular and genuinely alone, combinations that would remain in evidence throughout his adult life. What accounts for these characteristics? Henry Kissinger, according to one of the transcripts in the Thompson book, is reported to have said that Nixon was never truly loved and could have been a far greater man and leader had even one person shown real affection for him. Ambrose disputes that claim and believes that Nixon came from a loving home. Later his own wife and daughters would provide him with the same sort of solid support he had received from his parents. Why then was he ill at ease outside his family circle but dynamic in the public arena? Ambrose suggests that it may have had something to do with his religious training. The Quaker church teaches modest individual behavior without public displays of affection at the same time that it encourages church members to speak out before the gathered congregation. But Ambrose offers that as only a partial explanation. In the final analysis, the dichotomy between the public and private Nixons, according to Ambrose, was "just the way he was."

Furthermore, Ambrose wonders whether Nixon really was all that comfortable with the public parts of his life. He was clearly good at acting, debating, public speaking, and almost anything that put him in a spotlight, but he was also extremely sensitive to criticism. Throughout his life he constantly placed himself in positions where criticism was virtually inevitable. Why did he choose to do this? Was his ambition so strong that he willingly opened himself to the likelihood of personal pain? And where did that ambition come from? Ambrose is not sure, concluding again that this, too, was part of the way he was.

In college and in law school Richard Nixon demonstrated considerable intelligence (a quality constantly mentioned by his former associates in the Thompson book), a moderately conservative set of political opinions, and an incredible determination to learn. Having turned down a scholarship to Harvard because the cost of cross-country transportation was prohibitive, he attended Whittier College, where he excelled in many of his classes and participated in the same kinds of activities he had enjoyed in high school—debates and student government. He also played college football with a gutsy enthusiasm that impressed his coach and teammates who were otherwise unimpressed by his ability to play the game. After graduation, he worked his way through Duke law school with a scholarship, a variety of part-time jobs, and an austere student life style that made it possible for rather short ends somehow to meet. When he finished law school and returned to southern California, Nixon was a typical, perhaps even an ideal, young professional. He was clean-cut, conscientious, honest, hard working, a serious young man widely respected by his colleagues. He was, Ambrose believes, precisely the sort of individual from whom you *would* have purchased a used car.

He was also bored with the practice of law. American entry into the Second World War, shortly after his marriage to Pat Ryan, ended that boredom, or at least gave him more exotic locations in which to be bored. After a stint in Washington as a lawyer for the federal government agencies that regulated the wartime economy, he enlisted in the Navy and served as a supply officer in the South Pacific. Once again he showed himself to be an industrious and efficient young man who carried out his rather mundane duties with notable success. He also became a first-rate poker player. In Ambrose's biography, poker serves as a minor metaphor, and Nixon's talent for the game becomes a clue to some of his behavior in his subsequent political career. The accomplished poker player, Ambrose reminds us, is a shrewd judge of character able to read an opponent's mood, degree of drunkenness, financial position, and skill while simultaneously hiding his own; he can quickly calculate the complicated odds that give clues as to whether a particular hand is likely to win; and, most importantly, he can bluff. "Bluffing is poker's great art form," and Nixon, Ambrose argues, was a master in its performance. When the war ended and Nixon returned to California, he had won enough money, perhaps as much as ten thousand dollars, to finance a campaign for congress.

Nixon's early political career, his meteoric rise to national importance and almost equally rapid fall, is a saga made up of familiar stories—the vicious campaigns against Jerry Voorhis and Helen Gahagan Douglas, the Alger Hiss investigation, the Checkers speech, the ambiguous relations between Eisenhower and his vice-president, the controversial trips to Latin America and Moscow, the crucial debates with John Kennedy, and the bitter and false farewell to the press after the unsuccessful gubernatorial campaign in California. Ambrose retells these stories with fairness and flair.

He does not excuse the redbaiting that Nixon used so effectively in his early political campaigns—campaigns that earned him the enduring nickname, "Tricky Dick"—but he does place those campaigns in the context of American political culture in the years following World War II when anti-communism was on the rise. Even before there was a McCarthy, there was McCarthyism and, as Ambrose points out, the "soft on communism" campaign label was such a tempting political weapon that even one of Nixon's opponents, briefly and rather foolishly, tried to use it against him. Nixon's anti-communism was, of course, unique among its many postwar practitioners because he not only

talked about the influence of Communists in American government, he also played a significant role in gathering evidence against the most notorious of the reputed Communist sympathizers in high places. As a congressman, Nixon worked hard to prove that Whitaker Chambers was telling the truth and that Alger Hiss was lying (or bluffing, in Ambrose's account). He also devoted considerable energy to supporting a moderate internationalist foreign policy. Nixon was an early and solid supporter of the Marshall Plan, despite the fact that it was generally unpopular in his conservative congressional district. He voted for European economic assistance and then made a concerted, and largely successful, effort to change public opinion in his district. His congressional career, in Ambrose's account, was not without substance and accomplishment.

As a senator, and shortly thereafter as vice-president, Nixon became embroiled in a nearly endless series of political campaigns. He ran for the Senate in 1950 and had the second position on the national ticket in 1952 and 1956; he represented the Republican Party as its most prominent spokesman in the off-year elections of 1954 and 1958; and he ran unsuccessfully for the presidency in 1960 and for governor of California in 1962. In the 1950's and early 1960's more votes were cast for Richard Nixon (and against him) than for any other American political figure. Much of Nixon's negative reputation comes from those years of campaigning when, particularly compared to Eisenhower, he became one of the most effective partisan politicians on the national scene. He did take time from his frequent campaigning to carry out his vice-presidential duties as well as the constraining circumstances of that office permit, showing particular grace and tact during Eisenhower's periods of serious illness, learning a great deal about foreign affairs during extensive travels, and preparing himself for the presidency more thoroughly than almost any candidate in recent decades. These accomplishments did not, however, impress a majority of the American voters. In 1960 he lost a close election to a young, handsome, and charismatic Democrat who promised a new frontier; in 1962 he lost by a larger margin to a middle-aged, burly, and traditional Democrat who promised to keep things in California very much as they were. For all intents and purposes, Richard Nixon's political career had ended, and his long-suppressed sensitivity to news media criticism exploded in a premature promise that Richard Nixon would, henceforth, no longer be available for newsmen to kick around.

At the end of Ambrose's book it is difficult to realize that much of Richard Nixon's career, including many of the most important episodes in that career, still lay ahead. The next volume of the biography will tell the story of Nixon's years in the "wilderness" (if New York City can be appropriately described by that term), his political comeback, his controversial presidency, and his final and dramatic fall from power in the aftermath of the Watergate break-in. Serious students of American politics and history will await that volume with genuine anticipation. . . .

Riddles, mysteries, and enigmas about Richard Nixon clearly remain. Even after 700 pages of Ambrose prose, important events in Nixon's youth and early career are largely unexplained. We do not fully know the forces that shaped his personality, and Ambrose is at his best when he warns us against believing that those forces are easy to find. We do not know enough about the character and the dimensions of Nixon's political ambitions, though it is clear that those ambitions were formidable factors in his adult life. We do know that there were evidently important dichotomies in Nixon's character and behavior, but it is sometimes difficult to explain their origins and trace their consequences. We know a great deal about the men who surrounded Richard Nixon during his presidency, but not nearly enough about the complicated relationships that existed among them. We cannot even say that we know all the facts about Watergate, the most exhaustively investigated presidential transgression of the 20th century. When Winston Churchill told the British public about the problems associated with the interpretation of Russian foreign policy, he meant to warn them against those who would suggest benign and superficial explanations of potentially dangerous events. That is good advice, not only for students of history coming to grips with complicated figures in our nation's past but also for citizens deciding how to cast their votes in years divisible by four.

Robert Dallek (review date 15 October 1989)

SOURCE: "Nixon Before the Fall," in *Los Angeles Times Book Review,* October 15, 1989, pp. 1, 9.

[*In the following excerpted review, Dallek concludes that* Nixon: The Triumph of a Politician, 1962-1972 *adds little to existing information about Nixon and, furthermore, includes contradictory assessment of Nixon's foreign policy skills.*]

Like the mythological Egyptian bird that consumed itself by fire and rose renewed from its ashes, Richard Nixon is a latter-day phoenix. Defeated by John F. Kennedy for the presidency in 1960 and by Pat Brown for the California governorship in 1962, Nixon told a press conference: "You won't have Dick Nixon to kick around any more."

As so often in his career, his words masked the reality of his actions. He at once began working toward the comeback that culminated in his two victorious campaigns for the White House in 1968 and 1972. Resigning the presidency in 1974 rather than face impeachment and conviction for Watergate crimes. Nixon began his final battle: the vindication by history. Making the case for himself in his 1978 memoirs, he has worked to convince Americans of his greatness as a foreign-policy leader and to obscure the truth of Watergate and other improprieties by blocking release of documents and tapes that might further blight his reputation.

His current campaign enjoys some success. A November, 1988, Louis Harris poll, asking a cross section of Ameri-

cans to rank the last nine Presidents from F.D.R. to Reagan in 11 categories, rated Nixon as "best in foreign affairs," well ahead of all the others, except Reagan, who was a close second.

Although a decisive plurality of the poll said that Nixon had set the lowest moral standards of all these Presidents, he scored better than Johnson, Ford, and Carter in several other categories. Having suffered the worst public humiliation of any President in U.S. history by resigning from office and having continued a spirited fight for vindication, Nixon has partly redeemed himself with some Americans who find considerable appeal in a man who doggedly struggles to overcome self-inflicted defeats.

Two new biographies by Roger Morris and Stephen Ambrose will undercut Nixon's efforts to create a positive historical image. . . .

Stephen Ambrose's biography [*Nixon: The Education of a Politician, 1913-1962*], the second of a three-volume work, begins in 1962 when, he says, Nixon launched his second drive for the presidential nomination, and ends with his reelection to the White House in 1972. Ambrose, a distinguished professor of history at the University of New Orleans and author of a fine two-volume biography of Eisenhower, has produced a study that is equally damning of Nixon but less convincing than Morris' book [*Richard Milhous Nixon: The Rise of an American Politician*].

Ambrose's biography rests on a more limited body of sources. Although he makes extensive use of Nixon's jottings on news summaries compiled during his first term and of some letters and memos in his presidential papers, the book largely rests on printed materials, memoirs and secondary accounts by journalists. Ambrose has also done some interviewing, but much less than Morris.

The result is a book that does not take us much beyond what we already knew about Nixon in the decade after 1962. Ambrose says that "It is not news that he [Nixon] was devious, manipulative . . . passionate in his hatreds, self-centered, untruthful, untrusting, and at times so despicable that one wants to avert one's eyes in shame and embarrassment. Nor is it news that this same man could be considerate, straightforward, sympathetic and helpful, or that he was blessed with great talent, a superb intellect, an awesome memory, and a remarkable ability to see things whole, especially on a global scale and with regard to the world balance of power. If he was the ultimate cynic, a President without principle in domestic politics, he was also the ultimate realist, a President without peer in foreign affairs."

The most interesting feature of Ambrose's book is the extent to which he contradicts his own assertion about Nixon's matchless leadership in world affairs. Ambrose has warm praise for Nixon as a President with a world view who understood the need for a "new era of negotiations" with the Russians and the Chinese. Indeed, Nixon had the imagination and foresight to do what no other post-1945 President had done—seek detente with the Soviets and normal relations with China that became essential steps in the developing end to the Cold War. Yet Ambrose is sharply critical of Nixon's slow withdrawal from Vietnam, which cost so many additional lives for no productive end. He also faults Nixon's policies toward Cambodia, Chile, India and Pakistan, describing them as leaving a legacy of serious unresolved problems.

In time, Ralph Waldo Emerson said, every scoundrel becomes a hero. Richard Nixon is not there yet.

John Edward Wilz (review date Summer 1990)

SOURCE: A review of *Eisenhower: Soldier, General of the Army, President-Elect, 1890-1952,* and *Eisenhower: The President,* in *Presidential Studies Quarterly,* Vol. XX, No. 3, Summer, 1990, pp. 623-26.

[*In the following review, Wilz offers positive evaluation of* Eisenhower: Soldier, General of the Army, President-Elect, 1890-1952 *and* Eisenhower: The President.]

Three years after leaving the White House, in 1964, former-President Eisenhower put through a phone call to Stephen Ambrose, a twenty-eight-year-old assistant professor of history at Louisiana State University. Impressed by Ambrose's recent biography of the Civil War general Henry Halleck, Ike wanted Ambrose to assist in the project, just getting under way at Johns Hopkins University, of publishing Eisenhower's private papers. Flabbergasted, Ambrose acceded to the great man's wishes, and over the next five years, during which he had numerous private conversations with Eisenhower, assisted in editing the first five volumes of the Eisenhower papers. He also began to assemble information for a full-dress biography of the onetime general and president, and in 1983–1984 his enterprise came to fruition. The result was the two-volume biography that is the subject of the present review.

Ambrose is an unabashed admirer of Eisenhower. He sets out the overarching theme of his work on the opening page of Chapter One [in *Eisenhower: Soldier, General of the Army, President-Elect, 1890-1952*] when he writes that "Dwight Eisenhower was born to command and became one of the great captains of military history. He also was born to lead, and . . . became one of the most successful Presidents of the twentieth century." Still, he does not refrain from criticizing the subject of his biography. Most importantly, he questions various decisions made by Eisenhower during the North African and Mediterranean campaigns of 1942–1943, and (during the White House years) his cautious approach in the matter of the demagogic communist-hunter from Wisconsin, Senator Joseph R. McCarthy, and his manifest absence of enthusiasm for the crusade to eliminate the scandal of second-class citizenship for Americans of African descent.

Relentlessly chronological, Ambrose's biography traces the life of Eisenhower from the cradle to the grave. The author describes the life of the future general and president in the onetime cow town of Abilene. The Ike of the Abilene years emerges from Ambrose's pages as an athletic and hot-tempered youth who, by the time (at age twenty) he departed Abilene for West Point, was endowed with a curious and active mind, remarkable self-confidence, and an engaging personality whose hallmark even at the early stage of life was an infectious grin. Ambrose relates Eisenhower's years at West Point, his courtship of Mary Geneva "Mamie" Doud, and his frustration during the time of United States belligerency in World War I, when he failed to secure an overseas assignment. During an interesting stint at Camp Meade, Maryland, in the aftermath of the Great War, Ambrose observes, Eisenhower and his fellow officer George S. Patton, Jr., each commanded a battalion of tanks. No less than Patton, Eisenhower became an enthusiastic advocate of tanks operating independently of the infantry—only to abandon such advocacy when so ordered by superior officers. Of larger personal moment during that period of his life and career, Eisenhower suffered the loss of his three-year-old son "Icky," a victim of scarlet fever.

Ambrose describes the 1920s and 1930s as a time of frustration for Eisenhower, inasmuch as advancement in the minuscule Army of that period was almost impossible. Still, senior officers recognized Ike to be a man of rare ability, and various of them actively sought to have him assigned to their commands. One such senior officer was Douglas MacArthur, and, as is well known, Eisenhower spent much of the 1930s toiling under MacArthur, first in Washington, then in the Philippines. Toiling under the grandiloquent MacArthur was rewarding, but the relationship between the two men was often tense. Another senior officer who recognized Eisenhower's talents was General George C. Marshall, who became chief of staff of the Army in 1939, and as the United States edged toward the general war that had broken in that same year, Marshall advanced Eisenhower to positions of high responsibility. Then, in 1942, Marshall arranged for Eisenhower to be appointed the commander of the newly organized European Theater of Operations.

There are no surprises in the author's account of Eisenhower's performance as the commander of the ETO. Ambrose provides a fairly standard account of a commander who had a unique gift for reconciling differences among leaders of a multinational army and keeping such prima donnas as George Patton and the insufferable Bernard Montgomery functioning in accord with the general strategy worked out at ETO headquarters—a commander who had a sure grasp of the political verities of coalition warfare (as when he turned aside a move by British commanders to relegate American troops to a secondary roll after GI's performed poorly in early operations in North Africa, a relegation that would have touched off a popular outburst in the United States—also when assorted advisers proposed that he sack Montgomery, a sacking that would have infuriated the people of Britain).

Otherwise, Ambrose's General Ike was no Napoleon, that is, he displayed little flair for strategic or tactical innovation. He made mistakes. He was unduly cautious in the Torch operation in North Africa and laggard in pressing Montgomery to move against the port of Antwerp in late summer and autumn of 1944. (The opening of Antwerp was essential to any thrust by the Western Allies into the heart of Germany.) He consented to Montgomery's inane operation aimed at seizing a bridge across the Rhine at Arnhem in the Netherlands. Still, Eisenhower, like Ulysses S. Grant in the Civil War of 1864–1865, determined to bring to bear the superiority of the Anglo-Americans in men and firepower and simply wear down the enemy. And that was precisely what he did. Certain British commanders may have derided him as one who lacked imagination and boldness. But, as Ike later noted, only eleven months elapsed between the D-Day landings on the Normandy coast in June of 1944 and the unconditional surrender of the Germans in May of 1945.

Ambrose offers a conventional but richly detailed account of Eisenhower's life and career from the end of the global war through his election to the presidency. He intimates that Ike's stewardship as president of Columbia University was more fruitful than critics have thought. But his case for that proposition is not persuasive. He shows how during those years Eisenhower became an intimate friend of a coterie of millionaire businessmen—Ike's "gang"—whose passions were playing golf and bridge and talking politics. The gang lavished gifts, free trips, and the like on the general, and for his part Eisenhower spent as much time with members of the gang as possible. "With them," Ambrose writes [on p. 476], "he could relax as he could with no one else."

The second volume of Ambrose's biography—the one that centers on the presidential years—makes larger demands on the reader than the first volume. Because Eisenhower tended to confront only one problem at a time during the pre-presidential years, Ambrose's rigidly chronological account of unfolding events in Volume One is easy to follow. But during the presidential years, Ike was invariably dealing with a variety of diverse and nettlesome problems, foreign and domestic, at any given moment, and as a consequence of Ambrose's determination to keep his account chronological, the reader encounters Eisenhower's handling of the McCarthy problem and his approach to such questions as civil rights and policy regarding China and the Middle East in a variety of scattered sections. The reader who has little or no prior knowledge and understanding of the main currents of the Eisenhower presidency might find it hard to keep the various threads of the narrative in mind as the author moves, chronologically, from one topic to the next.

The organization aside, Ambrose has written a splendid account of Eisenhower's White House years—and the eight years that followed (to his death in 1969). It offers abundant detail, but is not weighted down with detail. The balance is precisely what it should be. Otherwise, Am-

brose, like many other scholars who have come to take a warm view of the Eisenhower presidency, is decidedly generous in his assessment of the thirty-fourth occupant of the presidential office. (A graduate student in my colloquium in contemporary American history recently wrote in a summary critique of Ambrose's second volume that the author had obviously "fallen in love with his subject.") Like Arthur Larson, Fred I. Greenstein, and others, he dismisses the contention of Eisenhower's critics in the 1950s that Ike was a figurehead chief executive who was not in command of his own administration—for example, that John Foster Dulles rather than the president was the architect of the administration's foreign policy. Ambrose's argument appears beyond dispute. The author believes that, overall, Ike the president provided sensible and effective leadership for the North American superpower during a dangerous period. Ike clearly was a man of peace who strove mightily to resolve the problem of the Cold War and find a formula for achieving genuine disarmament. And during his watch, the national economy remained stable and prosperous.

The reader of Ambrose's splendid account may very well arrive at a somewhat less generous assessment than the author regarding Eisenhower the president, the more so when she or he ponders Ike's lackluster record in civil rights, his endorsement of Joe McCarthy's goals if not his methods, his use of the CIA to overthrow existing regimes in Iran and Guatemala, his blunderbuss policy of massive retaliation in the matter of national defense, his seemingly reckless behavior during the crises in the Formosa Strait (although Ambrose appears to view Ike's handling of those crises as a veritable triumph), his tolerance of the dubious methods employed by J. Edgar Hoover and the FBI in the quest for domestic subversives. Still, it is hard to quarrel with Ambrose's essential point that Dwight D. Eisenhower was one of the great Americans of our century, a good and decent man, one who was bright and resourceful, a man of good judgment and strong will, one who could confront difficult problems and make difficult decisions—a man who served his country honorably and effectively for a half-century, one who made a deep and laudable imprint on the history of our times.

Kevin P. Phillips (review date 24 November 1991)

SOURCE: "The Rediscovery of Richard Nixon," in *Los Angeles Times Book Review,* November 24, 1991, pp. 4, 11.

[*In the following review of* Nixon: Ruin and Recovery, 1973-1990, *Phillips commends Ambrose's "thorough and even-handed" approach, but finds fault in the book's inaccurate political history and lack of comparative analysis between Nixon and other U.S. presidents accused of unethical dealings.*]

In both tenacity and perspicacity, Richard Nixon's political re-emergence over the last 14 years has proven as extraordinary as his earlier success at hauling himself back from defeat in the 1962 California gubernatorial race and going on to win the presidency (on his second try) in 1968. Historians and journalists are only just beginning to deal with the forces and circumstances involved.

In "Why Americans Hate Politics," political writer E.J. Dionne calls Nixon the man who could have made a more moderate Republicanism work. In "One of Us," *New York Times* columnist Tom Wicker writes that Nixon's strength emerged from a political communion with middle-class values and Middle America, a communion that inspired many voters to support him as "one of us."

The other Republican President who began a watershed, Abraham Lincoln, shared this appeal. But the Republicans lost it in the Gilded Age and again in the late 1920s—and may be doing so again under George Bush—by getting caught up in an elite politics of Wall Street and tax breaks for the richest small minority of Americans. Some key Democrats recognize that these old "cloth coat" Republican loyalties have begun to move Nixon beyond his old partisanship. When Mario Cuomo told a Washington Post reporter that Nixon's common-man origins, loyalties and persistence were somewhat like Lincoln's—for which Nixon sent him a thank-you note—the New York governor was acting on a sage realization that cloth-coat Republican hearts are not necessarily with George Bush in 1992.

Indeed, in Nixon's own most recent book, he noted that his father Frank had voted for third-party Progressive presidential candidate Robert LaFollette in 1924, during the Roaring Twenties boom, because the GOP incumbent in the White House, Calvin Coolidge, was too much for the rich. This is another aspect of the rediscovery of Richard Nixon by liberals and centrists: the realization that maybe he meant what he said two decades ago about being for all those Middle Americans, Joe Six-packs and Peoria residents.

It is becoming increasingly clear that Nixon, back in 1968, was the founding father of the Republican era that went on to claim the White House for five of six terms, interrupted only by Jimmy Carter in the reaction against Watergate. Presidents who fill this era-launching role stand out historically, which is already forcing renewed attention to Nixon in the supra-Watergate sense.

Thus it is somewhat disappointing that while Stephen Ambrose's subtitle [of ***Nixon: Ruin and Recovery, 1973-1990***] is evenly split between ruin and recovery, his book's contents aren't. Nixon's ruination in Watergate takes up at least two-thirds of these pages, with only a fifth or so devoted to his recovery over the last 15 years. That allocation could be a mistake. The book itself has more than a few hints that historians may find themselves shifting emphasis.

Take the accompanying blurb from the publisher, Simon & Schuster. It remarks of Nixon that "Within a decade and a half of his resignation, not only had he become America's elder statesman, but he was threatening to become America's beloved elder statesman." Ambrose's own television appearances discussing the book have conveyed an impressed-with-Nixon quality that presumably would have surprised him when he began his three-volume project a decade ago. This may be telling us something the author's actual words don't.

Most of the book is his usual, well-done arrangement of history. Unluckily for Ambrose, however, the Watergate chapters are already partially dated by the new analyses and revelations in *Silent Coup: The Removal of a President,* the best-seller by Len Colodny and Robert Gettlin, which appeared this spring. That was too late for Ambrose to note its powerful arguments that Nixon knew less about Watergate than was previously thought, and while hardly innocent, was significantly misled by his White House counsel, John Dean, who was deeply involved. Future historians will not be able to discuss Watergate without taking *Silent Coup* into account.

Interestingly, Ambrose himself notes that in 1977, when broadcaster Diane Sawyer, then a Nixon aide, prepared a Watergate "flow chart" tracing day by day the events of June, 1972, to August, 1974, Nixon told her, "You know, this is the first time I've really understood everything that happened." The Colodny-Gettlin revelations, however, suggest he was premature. Facts and relationships are still emerging. Indeed, *Silent Coup* should be amplified by other new reexaminations from ex-Nixon aides, principally from former Chief of Staff Bob Haldeman.

Fortunately, partly obsolescent approaches to the scandal's origins don't matter to the bulk of the volume, which ranges from the unraveling of Watergate in the Spring of 1973 to the painful days of 1974–75, after Nixon had left office. Besides being readable, Ambrose is thorough and even-handed.

His principal weakness is politics. In fact, the first paragraph of his first chapter begins with two errors: that in the 1972 election, Nixon beat Democrat George McGovern by 60%-40% (it was 61% to 38%) and that the Democrats made gains in both houses of Congress (they actually lost a dozen seats in the House). After beginning so inauspiciously, the limitations of Ambrose's political knowledge don't matter so much for the rest of the book—1972, after all, was Richard Nixon's last election—until the author comes to the Nixon "recovery" years of the 1980s.

Even so, the hundred or so pages Ambrose devotes to Nixon's political and historical comeback between 1977 and the summer of 1990 represent a trailblazer of sorts. This is the first major Nixon chronicle to award the "recovery" label, and others are sure to follow.

In 1992 or 1996, Nixon, as the first GOP President of the post-1968 Republicans era, may face another interesting "first"—in contrast to the other Presidents who presided over the beginning of electoral watersheds. Jefferson, Lincoln, Jackson and Franklin Roosevelt died well before their parties' cycles in office came to an end. As a result, they did not have to face the ungluing of their old voting coalitions in favor of something new, along with the strain in loyalties that might involve.

Richard Nixon, despite his ongoing Republican fidelities, may be the first President to have presided over one watershed and then lived to confront the shifts and questions of the next one. Cloth-coat Nixon Republicans may be a pivotal swing group in the 1990s, like Jacksonian Democrats were in the pre-Civil War North.

Nixon's re-emergence in U.S. political history has been additionally greased by the increasing disrepute and scandals overtaking other Presidents. John F. Kennedy's reputation was sinking even before the autumn, 1991, revelations by his girlfriend, Judith Exner, that she had to carry money to mobster Sam Giancana, some of which apparently paid for mob help in making Illinois go narrowly Democratic in 1960. That was the election Nixon lost by a very small margin, but declined to contest for fraud because of the divisiveness of such an action.

Lyndon Johnson's integrity also has been tarnished in new biographies; Oliver North, in turn, suggests that Ronald Reagan must have known all about Iran-Contra and thereby participated in a major cover-up of his own. George Bush remains to be seen. Small wonder that the Watergate-era attempt to portray Nixon as a uniquely immoral President has all but imploded as the evidence about other recent Presidents unfolds.

Stephen Ambrose did not deal with any of these points, but I think future biographers will have to. It is unrealistic to call Richard Nixon "America's beloved elder statesman," as the book blurb does. Beloved, Nixon will never be. However, with a record 60 appearances on the cover of Time magazine to his credit, and with the 50th anniversary of his election to Congress approaching in 1996, Nixon is well on his way to being the most important U.S. politician of the second half of the 20th Century. And with Ambrose's book as one launching pad, new generations of historians will find themselves trying to explain why.

William L. O'Neill (review date 30 December 1991)

SOURCE: "The High Cost of Watergate," in *New Leader,* December 30, 1991, pp. 16-17.

[*In the following review, O'Neill offers praise for* Nixon: Ruin and Recovery, 1973-1990.]

The first line of Stephen E. Ambrose's smashing conclusion to his biography of Richard M. Nixon [***Nixon: Ruin and Recovery, 1973-1990***] says it all: "This is the political story of the century."

In volume one Ambrose described Nixon's rapid rise from small-town lawyer to the Vice Presidency, his narrow loss to John F. Kennedy, and then his humiliating defeat by Edmund G. "Pat" Brown for the governorship of California in 1962. That would have finished any other politician, and at the time everyone except Nixon believed he was through. But no sooner was his "final" press conference at an end than he began planning his future.

In volume two Ambrose showed how over the next few years Nixon positioned himself to become the inevitable GOP candidate for President in 1968, how he narrowly scraped by that year, and how he went on to win re-election with 60.7 per cent of the vote in 1972—the third widest margin in history. Yet Nixon derived no pleasure from his triumph because the Democrats still controlled both houses of Congress and he knew they were out to get him. They would succeed, too, as a result of the crimes and deceptions that we know collectively as Watergate, though not until Nixon had put up a tremendous fight.

Two thirds of ***Ruin and Recovery***'s 597 pages of text concerns that fight, and, while many books have already been written about Nixon's fall, none is so absorbing. The tight focus helps, for it is easy to get lost in the telling of the huge and complex Watergate saga. Ambrose relates as much of the story as he needs to, always keeping Nixon at the center. It also helps that the author is a seasoned interviewer and mines the infamous Nixon tapes with skills gained from long experience as an oral as well as a document historian.

Ambrose thinks Nixon could have held on to the Presidency in any number of ways—most obviously by burning the tapes—but mistakenly "chose to try to save all by risking all." The tapes were important to his strategy, not because they enabled Nixon to keep track of who knew what and what he had said to whom—a major concern, for he was weaving an intricate web of deceit—but because he thought that they would be his salvation.

On June 4, 1973, after listening to hours of recorded conversation between himself and White House Counsel John Dean, Nixon told Chief Adviser H. R. Haldeman that the tapes established his innocence. This will astonish anyone who heard Dean's testimony before Congress, which amounted to a damning indictment of the President and was supported by the tapes. Nixon, however, was buried by then in a tangle of lies and coverups that confused even him. Moreover, as Ambrose points out, he was convinced that if he handled the public relations side of a problem well he had solved the problem itself. Thus he considered using edited versions of the tapes on his own behalf, since they contained exculpatory remarks he had made for that very purpose.

Although Watergate turned out well in that the guilty paid for their crimes, the cost was high. Part of that cost was blowing an outside chance to end the Arab-Israeli struggle. On the morning of October 20, 1973, during the Yom Kippur War and just hours before the Saturday Night Massacre of Special Prosecutor Archibald Cox, Attorney General Elliot L. Richardson, and his deputy William Ruckelshaus, the President sent a long cablegram to Henry Kissinger in Moscow. It instructed the Secretary of State to accept an informal offer made by Soviet leader Leonid I. Brezhnev prior to the outbreak of fighting to cooperate with the United States in a superpower resolution of the Arab-Israeli conflict. Nixon had not been interested when Brezhnev initially brought up the idea, but the Yom Kippur War persuaded him that a long-term solution had to be imposed upon the participants. The cable, Ambrose says, showed the President at the top of his form and offered the first real hope for a lasting peace in the Middle East.

Kissinger, who wanted only a simple cease-fire, was furious. He called Alexander M. Haig, the new White House Chief of Staff, to rail against Nixon's change of course. Haig replied angrily that he had problems of his own and could not worry about the Secretary's. Sarcastically Kissinger asked what kind of trouble could there be in Washington on a Saturday night. Haig then told him of the impending confrontation between the President and the Justice Department. Kissinger realized at once that Nixon would be too busy to follow through on the superpower initiative so he could safely ignore it. Perhaps it would have failed, but the fact remains that a potential settlement of the Middle East problem could be torpedoed by Kissinger because Watergate kept Nixon from doing his job.

As this suggests, Ambrose is not a Kissinger fan. Indeed, he represents the Secretary as the one successful liar in Nixon's official family. The principal lie concerned the role he played in the illegal wiretapping of reporters' and National Security Council staff members' telephones between 1969 and 1971. Despite his active participation in the scheme, Kissinger blew up when newspapers began reporting the story in June 1974. He went so far as to hold a special press conference to falsely proclaim his innocence, and he threatened to resign if people did not stop questioning his honor. Aghast at the thought of losing the only senior member of Nixon's government who still commanded respect, the media did not call his bluff.

Of the scholars who have subjected Nixon to critical study, and few have examined him in any other way, Ambrose is the fairest. Even so, he concludes that Nixon was unfit to govern, and that he would have been impeached had he not resigned. But Ambrose regrets that much of Nixon's foreign policy and the last hopes for domestic reform went with him.

Everyone remembers the disgraced President's big strokes: détente with the Soviets, the strategic arms limitation talks, the opening to China—all, as Ambrose said in volume two, uniquely Nixonian. Because the new turn in foreign policy was so personal, it depended on Nixon staying in office. After he left détente collapsed and SALT II was never ratified. Another decade of arms races and superpower competitions passed before relations with the Soviet Union improved.

Except for expanding some Great Society programs, Nixon did not accomplish much at home. The choicest idea of his first term, the Family Assistance Program, was sabotaged by Congressional Democrats to prevent Republicans from getting credit for reforming the welfare system. In his second term Nixon tossed out various proposals, including an expanded student loan program, health insurance for all Americans, energy independence, and mass transit improvements. Whether or not he would have gotten any of these through Congress, he meant to try, which is more than his successors have done. And without him to protect it revenue sharing died, a major reason why so many cities and states are in financial distress today.

With Nixon's departure the Republican middle ground collapsed: The GOP fell into conservative hands, Ronald Reagan became President, spending for armaments surged upward, domestic programs were slashed, the income tax was reduced, and a mountain of debt accumulated that has paralyzed government. Almost everything is worse now than when Nixon was President, not solely because he left office too soon, yet that is part of the reason. We lost more than we gained when Nixon resigned, Ambrose finds. This will be resisted by liberals who still refuse to give Nixon credit for anything, and by conservatives who never felt he was one of them and have a vested interest in representing the Reagan years as America's finest. No matter, Ambrose is right.

The last third of volume three describes Nixon's climb back from oblivion. With his usual doggedness he worked hard to rehabilitate himself, continuing to meet with world leaders and to write books. When the Richard Nixon Library and Birthplace was dedicated on July 19, 1990, everyone showed up—the three other living Presidents, four secretaries of state, Bob Hope, and Barbara Walters. He is an elder statesman now, a venerable presence at official occasions and a pompous font of obsolete wisdom on foreign policy issues. He remains as mendacious as ever, as self-serving and as self-righteous, but he is in the game again—forever it appears.

Ruin and Recovery is biography at its best, a fabulous story told with great zest and drive, as fair to its subject as it can be, yet strongly opinionated. Ambrose says he loved writing this book. Readers will love it too.

Anthony Howard (review date 1 February 1992)

SOURCE: "By Hook or By Crook," in *Spectator,* February 1, 1992, p. 32.

[*In the following review, Howard offers positive assessment of* Nixon: Ruin and Recovery, 1973-1990.]

'He went out the same way he came in, no class'—that was John Kennedy's comment on his rival the day after Richard Nixon lost the presidential election to him in 1960. Many would say the same about Nixon's last demeaning exit from the White House 14 years later. For most of this third volume of his epic biography of the only US President ever to be forced to resign, Stephen E. Ambrose seems to belong to their company. The story of Nixon's deceit and dissimulation over Watergate has not lost its ability to chill and, although Ambrose tries hard to tell it dispassionately, the meticulously researched case he builds up ensures that the final result is totally devastating. When, beleaguered and embattled, the 37th President eventually announces at a Florida press conference, 'People have got to know whether or not their President is a crook—well, I am not a crook', it is hard to resist the conclusion that he was at least being consistent. He was lying to the end.

In that sense, Ambrose's book [*Nixon: Ruin and Recovery, 1973-1990*] certainly does nothing to restore Nixon's reputation. But by devoting the last quarter of his narrative to his subject's pertinacious climb-back to respectability, the author does at least add something new to the Nixon canon. This part of the story is told with something approaching admiration, and, while not every reader will share that feeling, it is hard to withhold a certain grudging respect for the truly remarkable stamina that Nixon displayed in adversity.

There were moments, of course, of abject self-pity. Nixon always had his maudlin side—and as late as April 1990 he thought nothing of telling *Time* magazine that 'no one had ever been so high and fallen so low' (conveniently ignoring the fact that, unlike his erstwhile Attorney General, John Mitchell, he at least had escaped going to prison). But mostly, it was his sheer determination to fight back from disgrace that prevailed and Ambrose is at his best in describing the various staging-posts on that journey.

At first, there was simply exile. The former Western White House at San Clemente became Nixon's Elba; and Ambrose is right to emphasise that the five years he spent there—'the paying of penance', as he slightly sententiously puts it—were critical to the whole rehabilitation process. Even then, as in the David Frost 1977 TV interviews, he broke cover occasionally—never, however, by taking the easy way out of offering the American people the forthright apology for which they yearned. Stubbornness was consistently an essential part of Nixon's character and, while he was willing to admit to mistakes, he was determined not to confess to any actual wrong-doing. That was why Gerald Ford's presidential pardon hurt him most of all, since it necessarily implied that somewhere there was guilt.

Yet as early as 1976, with his trip to China, Nixon had even put that behind him. If he was without honour in his own country, he was an idol in the nation to which in his years of power he had arranged the famous 'opening'. After that, the ice had been broken and by the autumn of 1978 he was being fêted in Paris and even being cheered by students in the Oxford Union. He still had problems with domestic opinion, but Anwar Sadat's death three years later brought him back for the first time to the White

House, flying off from there to Egypt in the company of the three other living ex-Presidents (to the Shah's funeral a year earlier he had gone, defiantly, alone). For a President who had always prided himself on his command of foreign policy, it was perhaps only appropriate that the road to recovery should have lain through international globetrotting.

By the beginning of 1980, when he moved from California to New York, Nixon had even begun to restore his fortunes at home. He had started giving newspaper interviews to carefully selected correspondents and in the presidential campaign of 1980, which brought Ronald Reagan to the White House, found himself employed by the NBC network as a commentator on the electoral process. If he had not wholly wiped the slate clean—it was not until 1990 that he got his own presidential library (and then without any input of federal funds)—he had at least achieved a measure of acceptability.

Given what he had to live down, it was—as James Reston originally wrote of Nixon when he won his party's nomination in 1968—'the greatest comeback since Lazarus'. Ambrose is particularly perceptive on the qualities possessed by this strange, lonely autodidact—the total opposite of the normal extrovert politician—that made the miracle possible. He is a bit given to being portentous—there is far too much about 'this author' feeling or doing this or that—but he has crowned the edifice of his impressive trilogy with an admirably fair-minded last volume covering easily the most controversial aspect of what was already a singularly resilient political career.

Esmond Wright (review date July 1992)

SOURCE: "The Man Who Came Back," in *Contemporary Review*, Vol. 261, No. 1518, July, 1992, pp. 45-6.

[*In the following review, Wright offers praise for* Nixon: Ruin and Recovery, 1973-1990.]

Despite the high drama of a now-familiar story, and despite the daunting detail, this is a remarkably fair study. Indeed, Ambrose comes gradually to like Nixon [in *Nixon: Ruin and Recovery, 1973-1990*]. 'That is not easy to do, as he doesn't really want to be liked.' What he admires—and what he conveys—is that Nixon never gives up, and is always true to himself.

The main strength of the book lies in its variety: beginning in the triumph in the Presidential election of November 1972 to the slow two-year agony, from the (foolish, unnecessary and unauthorised) Watergate break-in until the resignation of August 1974; the roll-call of the now near-fictional characters, Haldeman, Ehrlichman, Dean and Mitchell, Colson and the Cubans; Nixon's awareness that 'It will be each man for himself, and one will not be afraid to rat on the others'; and, afterwards, the long and solitary anguish of his own night of the soul, in retirement in California. He was aware that he had made bitter enemies over his twenty-five years in Federal politics, and that they had been unforgiving. Hatred of Nixon became and long remained a national obsession. But the qualities that had ministered to his own undoing—his own lack of trust in others, and his own conspicuous lack of friends—became now his bedrock. He set out deliberately to maximise his strengths, notably his special expertise in foreign policy—in the opening to China, in ending the American involvement in Vietnam, in warning Israel not to go too far, in establishing détente in Europe. The few men he had come to trust were, in fact, the leaders of other countries—De Gaulle and Churchill, Mao and Chou—and they now became his models and his inspiration; they too had fought back, and went on fighting. He became not only a foreign policy expert but an Elder Statesman, listened to with a new, reluctant and hard-won respect at home and abroad. So that Ambrose can conclude that 'when Nixon resigned, we lost more than we gained.'

Ambrose adds, in his epilogue, his own psychological analysis; he sees much that explained Nixon in the early poverty, the struggle for recognition, the total self-containedness. His verdict is admirably balanced. Nixon was 'heroic, admirable and inspiring, while simultaneously being dishonourable, despicable and a horrible example.' As the years pass, he grows in stature. Perhaps Kissinger's view is the shrewdest of all: 'He would have been a great, great man had somebody loved him.'

This is a superb, readable and scholarly biography of a remarkable and fascinating man.

James N. Giglio (review date Winter 1993)

SOURCE: A review of *Nixon: Ruin and Recovery, 1973-1990*, in *Historian*, Vol. 55, No. 2, Winter, 1993, pp. 372-73.

[*In the following review, Giglio offers positive assessment of* Nixon: Ruin and Recovery, 1973-1990.]

Bryce Harlow once compared Richard Nixon to a cork: "Push him down and he pops right back up" (583). The enduring resiliency of Nixon is one of the central themes of *Ruin and Recovery*, the concluding segment of Stephen E. Ambrose's three-volume biography. He covers the "peace with honor" settlement in Vietnam, the Yom Kippur War, Nixon's fascination with China, détente with the Soviet Union, the Watergate crisis, Nixon's exile, and his recovery.

On domestic matters, Ambrose rightly focuses on the national obsession with Watergate, which, of course, cost Nixon his presidency. Largely through the use of White House tapes, Ambrose documents Nixon's complicity in the cover-up and his abuse of power. Like other scholars, he portrays Nixon as a flawed personality who deceived his colleagues, his family, and himself. Yet he argues that

other contemporary presidents also relied on dirty tricks, used the IRS to punish political enemies, wiretapped, taped conversations in the Oval Office, and other assorted abuses of power, including using the presidency for personal gain. More than anything, the forced disclosures of the White House tapes contributed to Nixon's demise. Ambrose addresses the key question of why Nixon failed to destroy the tapes by explaining that the president thought that they "constituted his best defense, if used selectively, and because he was certain he could command complete control of them" (197). Nixon had underestimated the persistence of Archibald Cox, John Sirica, and Sam Ervin.

The resignation nearly killed Nixon. Hounded by subsequent suits and possible trials, he not only faced cardiovascular shock following surgery for phlebitis, but he also supposedly verged on suicide. What saved him was his loving family, a few friends, and his own determination not to be thought a quitter: "A man is not finished when he is defeated; he is finished [only] when he quits" (522). Ambrose chronicles his recovery, beginning with the television interviews with David Frost, his speeches in Middle America, his visits abroad, and his published books. Though Ambrose refers to Nixon as an elder statesman, he recognizes the limitations of Nixon's return, for the Republican party has failed to recognize his existence. Moreover, there is no evidence that Reagan or Bush ever adopted his extensive recommendations.

In his final assessment, Ambrose portrays Nixon as a consummate actor, a risk taker, extremely self-disciplined and proud, one who failed to see the limits of power, and as a leader who despised virtue. He labels Nixon as the angriest president, one who found it difficult to trust and love others. In discussing Nixon's weaknesses, Ambrose, without providing alternative explanations, discounts the impact of early relationships, particularly the harshness of Nixon's father. He sees Nixon's resignation as bad for the country for it destroyed his foreign policy initiatives and his domestic commitments. (Didn't Watergate devastate both?) Moreover, the resignation paved the way for the Reagan Revolution, which Ambrose views as a major setback.

Ambrose's study is thoughtful, critical, and empathetic. It seeks to humanize Nixon. It is weak in its sources, for much of Nixon's correspondence and tapes remain unavailable, forcing Ambrose to rely on memoirs, Nixon's writings, and newspapers.

John Kentleton (review date February 1994)

SOURCE: A review of *Eisenhower and the German POWs*, in *History*, Vol. 79, No. 255, February, 1994, p. 186.

[*In the following review, Kentleton offers positive assessment of* Eisenhower and the German POWs.]

In 1989 James Bacque in *Other Losses: An Investigation into the Mass Deaths of German Prisoners of War at the*

Hands of the French and Americans after World War II alleged that Eisenhower as commander of the American army of occupation deliberately withheld food and shelter from captured German forces, causing the death of between 800,000 and one million prisoners of war through starvation and disease. Furthermore, this crime, carried out by the American and French armies, had been subsequently covered up with the connivance of professional historians. To investigate these grave charges, the Eisenhower Center at the University of New Orleans organized a conference in 1990; this volume records its proceedings. In the turmoil of war-torn Europe, with food scarce, transport disrupted, shipping needed for the Pacific and a huge influx of refugees, POWs became DEFs ('disarmed enemy forces'), thereby avoiding the obligations of the Geneva Convention which the allies simply could not honour, if required to feed five million German prisoners a ration equal to their own soldiers. The camps were rudimentary, often a field with no shelter, a string of barbed-wire and a handful of guards. The Rhine meadow ones were the worst. A small percentage of prisoners died unnecessarily. This much is made clear by the editors in their introduction and the eight papers covering the issue's context, the situation of Germany in 1945, the POW question in German historiography and the problems posed by 'conspiratorial history'. On Bacque's wilder assertions, the various contributors do an expert demolition job. Indeed, they are at their most effective when most restrained. Just occasionally one or two allow themselves to be provoked into *ad hominem* rejoinders: 'Those parts of Other Losses that might rise above a failing grade in an undergraduate term paper are not new' (p. 53); Bacque's 'amateur's cookie cutter' (p. 55); 'this ex-publisher' (p. 56). No doubt it is galling that sensational charges against prominent individuals attract undue notice; Nikolai Tolstoy's *The Minister and the Massacres* is cited as a comparable example; but that Tolstoy's relationship with the great Russian writer may be remote, or that his title of count may have no legal basis, is an unworthy irrelevance (p. 184). The best antidote to bad history is good history. This volume is an example. Moreover, the plethora of essential footnotes are mercifully where they should be in a well-produced book. The publishers, too, deserve credit.

Earl F. Ziemke (review date March 1994)

SOURCE: A review of *Eisenhower and the German POWs,* in *Journal of American History,* Vol. 80, No. 4, March, 1994, p. 1526.

[*In the following review, Ziemke concludes that* Eisenhower and the German POWs *does not adequately explain the deaths of German POWs in Allied prison camps.*]

World War II as specialty has an occupational hazard: It attracts the attention of persons who create sensational hypotheses for which they lack validating evidence. In 1987, I received a call from a James Bacque, who said he be-

lieved Gen. Dwight D. Eisenhower had been responsible for the deaths of hundreds of thousands, possibly a million, German POWs in American hands after the German surrender. Had I come across information that would substantiate such a charge? If not, did I know where it was to be found? I told him I had none and most seriously doubted that any existed.

In 1989, a book appeared bearing the title *Other Losses: An Investigation into the Mass Deaths of German Prisoners at the Hands of the French and Americans after World War II.* The author, James Bacque, accused Eisenhower of having surreptitiously—by means of "winks and nods"—created a "lethal" DEF (disarmed enemy forces) status that denied the Germans their POW rights and subjected a million of them to death by starvation and neglect. To prove his case, Bacque assumed that "other losses," a term military personnel officers routinely used in their bookkeeping, was a euphemism invented to conceal the deaths. *Other Losses* drew little attention in the United States, some in Canada and England, and more in Germany, where it was simultaneously published in German.

On February 24, 1991, in an article in the *New York Times Book Review,* Stephen E. Ambrose, director of the Eisenhower Center at the University of New Orleans, summarized Bacque's most egregious falsifications and distortions and announced that the Eisenhower Center had assembled an international committee of historians "to get at the full truth." The present volume is the result: eight essays by two German, one Austrian, one Canadian, and four American scholars.

To let the "facts," as the subtitle indicates, confute Bacque, the committee assembled a mass of German and American evidence against his contention that a million prisoners died—or could have died—because they were denied adequate rations even though no actual food shortage existed. Regrettably, in doing so it has all but lost sight of the alleged perpetrator, Eisenhower. Bacque's sole objective, despite his protestations of sympathy for the POWs, was to enroll Eisenhower in the ranks of mass murderers alongside Adolf Hitler and Joseph Stalin. The DEF category was his "smoking gun," and to it the committee has given a bare nine pages.

Bacque understandably does not look beyond Eisenhower for the origins of the DEF category. The committee rightly ascribes it to the London-based, American-British-Soviet European Advisory Committee (EAC) but draws an astounding conclusion: "the decisions that fated hundreds of thousands of German soldiers to languish for months and even years in Allied camps were not Eisenhower's but Allied occupation policy forged in a spirit of severity toward those who had plunged Europe into unfathomable misery." In short, the DEFs were victims, not of Eisenhower, but of his superiors' vengeful policy.

Had the committee given the EAC decision somewhat closer attention it could have ascertained that the Americans in the EAC harbored no desire to see German soldiers "languishing" in camps (as those whom the Soviet Union declared POWs in fact did) but regarded the DEF category as a means of assuring an early and rapid disbandment of the German forces. Having made that observation, the committee might have been able as well to deal more coherently with events after the surrender and to achieve a decisive judgment on the Bacque volume. As the matter stands, however, the prospective reader will find this search for "truth" as much perplexing as enlightening.

Scott Jaschik (essay date 18 May 1994)

SOURCE: "D-Day: New Book Pays Tribute to the Heroism of Individual Soldiers," in *Chronicle of Higher Education,* May 18, 1994, pp. A8-9, A14.

[*In the following essay, Jaschik discusses Ambrose's scholarly interests, his use of oral history to compose* D-Day, June 6, 1944, *and critical reaction to his portrayal of the Normandy invasion in this work.*]

Stephen E. Ambrose has revered the veterans of World War II since he was 10 years old. The war had just ended, and former GI's who lived in his neighborhood in Whitewater, Wis., played basketball on his family's driveway.

"I just thought they were giants, both physically and because I knew enough of what they had done during the war," says Mr. Ambrose. "There would be guys out there with terrible scars, terrible stories. I thought they were giants then and I still do."

Mr. Ambrose, professor of history at the University of New Orleans, pays tribute to some of his heroes in ***D-Day, June 6, 1944: The Climactic Battle of World War II.***

The book will be released next month to mark the 50th anniversary of the Allied invasion of France. It argues that the victories in Normandy were less a result of good planning and military superiority than of American values of independent thought and the heroism of individual soldiers. Because the Allied, and particularly American, soldiers were able to think on their feet and respond to changing conditions, Mr. Ambrose says, they overcame tremendous setbacks to win the crucial battles of D-Day.

On D-Day, the Allies landed on a series of French beaches in Normandy and started the drive to Germany to defeat Hitler. The landing came after two years of intense planning for a way to retake France and push the German forces out of Western Europe.

The book is based on interviews with 1,400 participants in on both sides of the battles. According to Mr. Ambrose, those are more first-person accounts than have ever been collected about any battle. He says that he gathered the interviews out of the conviction that, taken together, they would change the way D-Day is viewed.

'FROZEN WITH FEAR'

Mr. Ambrose sees his book as revisionist, in that it gives credit for the victory to common soldiers, not to the commanders. "What's clear now is that this was a second lieutenant's battle, not a general's battle." he says. "The Germans were frozen with fear about instituting an action on their own, and the American soldiers were the exact opposite."

Mr. Ambrose begins his book by reviewing the German and Allied preparations for the invasion and then walks the reader through each phase of D-Day: the air bombardments that preceded the landings, the journey across the English Channel, and the landings themselves. Frequent quotations from the combatants recall how they fought and what they saw.

Some of the vignettes are funny, as in how condoms were used to protect the muzzles of rifles from sand and water. Many others are tragic, particularly the descriptions of the first landings at Omaha Beach, where miscalculations led to terrible Allied casualties.

Sgt. Thomas Valance describes being shot five times and collapsing against a sea wall: "The bodies of my buddies were washing ashore, and I was the one live body in amongst so many of my friends, all of whom were dead, in many cases very severely blown to pieces."

While most of the stories come from Americans, the book also includes accounts from British and Canadian soldiers, and from men in the German forces as well.

Already, some historians have said that Mr. Ambrose's book will be the definitive account of a battle that was a turning point in World War II and, some say, the 20th century in establishing American leadership of the world's democracies.

Theodore A. Wilson, a professor of history at the University of Kansas and the editor of a collection of essays on D-Day, says Mr. Ambrose's book fills a void. Much has been written about the leaders, he says, and a good deal of popular writing has been done on individual soldiers. But those accounts have been "choppy and without context." Mr. Wilson says.

"What Steve Ambrose has done is to integrate all of those stories with the larger context."

Others, however, say that Mr. Ambrose's acknowledged admiration for his research subjects has clouded his objectivity.

"I think he has met all of these people and come to like them. So he ends up praising them more than assessing what they did," says Russell F. Weigley," professor of history at Temple University and author of *Eisenhower's Lieutenants: The Campaign of France and Germany, 1944-45* (Indiana University Press). "He veers away from a historian's real job of writing history to erecting a kind of monument," Mr. Weigley says.

30 Years of Research

For Mr. Ambrose, the D-Day book is the culmination of 30 years of research on the career of Dwight D. Eisenhower, who planned and led the invasion.

Mr. Ambrose was a 28-year-old freshly minted Ph.D. in 1964 when the former President called to ask if he would help edit his papers. Eisenhower had read Mr. Ambrose's first book, **Halleck: Lincoln's Chief of Staff,** published by the Louisiana State University Press in 1962. "I suspect that maybe 300 people read that book, but I was lucky, that he was one of them," Mr. Ambrose says.

That led to a job as assistant editor for five volumes of Eisenhower papers that were published by the Johns Hopkins University Press in the 1960's, Mr. Ambrose's fascination with Ike never dimmed.

He has written six scholarly books about Eisenhower. That figure doesn't count a children's book about the man, a biography of Eisenhower's brother Milton, or a three-volume biography of President Nixon that grew out of research on Nixon's role as Eisenhower's Vice-President.

Spending a career studying Eisenhower "was the best decision I ever made," says Mr. Ambrose. He says Eisenhower—in contrast to many of the politicians who followed him—was honest, straightforward, and concerned foremost with the national interest. "You can't have a better life than living with Dwight Eisenhower. I hero-worship—unabashedly."

The mistakes at D-Day that Mr. Ambrose writes about in his new book do not diminish his view of Eisenhower, he adds. "Eisenhower set up the situation where these second lieutenants could do the things they did to win."

Mr. Ambrose credits Eisenhower for giving him the idea of collecting oral histories about D-Day. When talking to Eisenhower, Mr. Ambrose says, he noticed that he could remember "every single detail" about D-Day, even though "he couldn't remember for the life of him" other important events of his military or political career.

"I started to figure that it might be that way for every man who went in on D-Day," he says. So in 1983, Mr. Ambrose founded the Eisenhower Center at the University of New Orleans to collect oral histories of D-Day veterans. The center took out advertisements in newspapers seeking the names of people who went through the battle, and researchers visited reunions of military units looking for willing interviewees.

The aging of D-Day participants, most of whom are in their 70's, gave the project urgency.

Veterans of D-Day were sent tapes and instructions to tell their stories "minute by minute." Transcripts of those tapes run anywhere from 5 to 100 pages.

A small team of students helped Mr. Ambrose. In addition, the Eisenhower Center's associate director, Günter Bischof, interviewed German participants. Mr. Bischof is an Austrian native whose father was a soldier in the Wehrmacht.

Starting three years ago, Mr. Ambrose read all of the transcripts, checking the accounts against each other, and preparing his manuscript. He says it is "sort of an art form" to figure out which stories to use and which ones to discard. Some of the transcripts appeared to be a mix of actual memories combined unintentionally with events described in movies or books, and some just did not ring true, he says. In the end, he adds, he made his choices based on whether accounts were confirmed by others or the historical record.

"It becomes probability. It's 'I know that so-and-so was there and he didn't see this,'" Mr. Ambrose says.

A common theme of the oral histories, he adds, was that the American soldiers were willing to do whatever was necessary to win. They had the gumption to carry off a constantly evolving battle plan—even under a barrage of enemy fire.

Mr. Ambrose is quick to add that using oral history worked only because of the basic honesty of the interviewees. "These guys downplay rather than exaggerate what they have done," he says. He would never attempt an oral political history, he says, "because politicians lie so much."

Mr. Ambrose suggests that historians who want to study the Vietnam or Persian Gulf wars should employ similar techniques. "You can study documents and they will tell you how generals came to decide this or that. But if you are writing about war, you've got to get to the men who fought it. You've got to get to the grunts."

Real Experiences

Where historians come down on Mr. Ambrose's new work depends in part on their views of oral history. To those who have been pushing for military history to shift away from battle plans and weapons and pay more attention to the lives of common people, the D-Day book is a welcome reinforcement.

"What is most significant about this book is that he is able to tell a traditional military story with the experiences of enlisted men," says Judy Barrett Litoff, a professor of history at Bryant College and author of the forthcoming *We're in This War Too: World War II Letters of American Women in Uniform* (Oxford University Press).

Ms. Litoff says Mr. Ambrose's reputation as Eisenhower's biographer will force more-conventional military historians to take note of oral history. "If anyone's going to bridge that gap, it's Stephen Ambrose," she says.

Gerhard L. Weinberg, a professor of history at the University of North Carolina at Chapel Hill, says he is writing a generally positive review of Mr. Ambrose's book for a publication he declines to name. Mr. Weinberg, author of *A World at Arms: A Global History of World War II* (Cambridge University Press), says Mr. Ambrose's book will help clarify the world's understanding of D-Day. First, he says, Mr. Ambrose's analysis makes clear that the invasion was "an enormous gamble," not the "sure thing" many have come to believe it was.

In addition, he says Mr. Ambrose's portrayals of German soldiers help correct the false image of them as "supermen." In actuality, Mr. Weinberg says, "the Germans goofed frequently, and the German leadership, far from being very sound, was confused and venal."

At the same time, however, Mr. Weinberg notes that the genre Mr. Ambrose chose—a focus on a single day—placed limits on what he could include, just as Mr. Weinberg's recent book faced different constraints. "There was not room in my book for discussions of combat operations, but if you write about a specific battle, there is not room for a nuanced discussion of the broader picture," he says.

Other scholars are more critical, Allan R. Millett, professor of military history at the Ohio State University, says Mr. Ambrose's thesis relies on the incorrect belief that a loss for the Allies at Omaha beach would have doomed D-Day as a whole. "I think that the critical thing that Allied planners did was to prevent German reinforcements from getting to the beach quickly," says Mr. Millett, co-author of *For the Common Defense: A Military History of the United States* (Free Press).

If the Allies hadn't salvaged the landing at Omaha Beach on the first day, Mr. Millett says, other options were available. "Either troops would have been moved from the other beaches or there would have been another landing."

THE 'COMMEMORATIVE' TRAP

Mr. Weigley of Temple says that Mr. Ambrose has fallen into a trap common with "anniversary" books. "There comes with them a strong temptation to write commemorative volumes rather than critical history. The historian somewhat compromises his role," he says.

The book provides a useful "worm's-eye view" of the action on D-Day, Mr. Weigley says. But Mr. Ambrose's patriotic fervor clouds the story, he adds. "I think he is critical of the military plans to excess, and, conversely, he may emphasize the heroism to excess."

Mr. Weigley has written a critical review of the book for *Parameters,* a journal of the U.S. Army War College. "I am a friend of Stephen Ambrose's and this book disappoints me," he says.

Such criticism doesn't surprise Mr. Ambrose. "This book is triumphalism, and that is the scorn of the academic community," he says, predicting that the major history associations will ignore his work at their scholarly meetings.

"History departments today aren't interested in politics or war or heroes, but that's what *people* are interested in," he says. He adds that the disdain with which he expects many academics to view his book reflects the way they are out of touch with their students. "Young people don't want to know what labor unions were doing about women's rights in 1830. They want to know about Andrew Jackson."

For his part, Mr. Ambrose is doing his best to tell the story of D-Day. In addition to publishing his book, he is organizing the National D-Day Museum, scheduled to open at the University of New Orleans in 1996.

For next month's anniversary, Mr. Ambrose will travel to France. Asked which site of the invasion he would visit on June 6, Mr. Ambrose says the choice was easy: He will spend the day with a group of veterans at the American cemetery in Normandy.

William L. O'Neill (review date 6-20 June 1994)

SOURCE: "Operation Overlord from the Inside," in *New Leader,* June 6-20, 1994, pp. 12-13.

[*In the following review, O'Neill offers praise for* D-Day, June 6, 1944.]

Cornelius Ryan's classic *The Longest Day,* though still a wonderful read, came out in 1959 when much vital information about Operation Overlord remained classified or was otherwise unavailable. Thus a need existed that many historians were eager to fill, and early this spring books began pouring off the presses to coincide with the 50th anniversary of the momentous event.

There are at least two reasons why ***D-Day, June 6, 1944*** stands out in what is now a crowded field. Its first advantage is the author himself, Stephen Ambrose, one of the best and most widely read of contemporary military historians and biographers. He brings to his new work the narrative drive, thorough research and muscular prose he is justly famous for. Second, as the director of the Eisenhower Center at the University of New Orleans, Ambrose has been able to draw on some 1,400 oral histories and written memoirs contributed by D-Day veterans. This important collection, the largest number of firsthand accounts of a single battle in existence, has made it possible for him to fill his story with details and observations that could only come from men who had been there.

Ambrose begins by setting the stage in 10 chapters that describe the rival armies and commanders and the problems facing each side. The sequence ends with Eisenhower's decision, one of the most critical of the War, to move out on June 6 despite a heavy rain. Ike staked Overlord on his belief that the 36 hours of decent weather his chief meteorologist was predicting would arrive on schedule. Had he taken the safer course the attack would not have been mounted until two weeks later, when, as it happened, one of the worst storms in many years struck the English Channel. Either it would have wrecked the invasion or forced another delay, jeopardizing the element of surprise on which everything depended. And an Allied failure would have dragged out the War in Europe for another year at the minimum.

The next 21 chapters establish that, if posterity owes much to Eisenhower, it owes even more to those who were called upon to carry out the operation. There is a good deal of exciting battle narrative here, but Ambrose never loses control of the argument he is making virtually from the first page to the last: American productivity alone is not what won the War; American democracy was no less a factor, for it had produced men whose spirit and initiative could not be matched by opponents serving a dictatorship.

At the top, Eisenhower had complete charge of every aspect of the offensive, while the defense of Normandy was conducted by two field marshals, Erwin Rommel and Gerd von Runsted. They had contradictory defense plans, uncertain writs of authority, and were subject to constant interference from Hitler—who personally retained control of the all-important Panzer (armored) divisions. Indeed, a coherent response was impossible under these circumstances.

In contrast, the best American commanders knew that in battle flexibility is everything, and they had the freedom to act accordingly. Nobody demonstrated this better than Colonel Paul Good, who led the 175th Infantry Regiment. At the conclusion of a briefing he picked up the operation plan for D-Day, which was thicker than a big phone book, tossed it over his shoulder and told his officers: "Forget this goddamned thing. You get your ass on the beach. I'll be there waiting for you and I'll tell you what to do. There ain't anything in this plan that is going to go right." He was correct, especially about Omaha Beach, the most difficult of the five invasion sites, where almost everything did go wrong. Nevertheless, determined men in small uncoordinated groups, relying largely on their own ingenuity, managed to prevail. Only Americans, Ambrose believes, could have done this.

Yet if plans meant little after the attack started, they were critical before. Brilliantly executed deception moves—including a superb air campaign that virtually isolated Normandy from the rest of France while doing damage elsewhere—kept the Germans from knowing where the assault would take place and prevented Hitler from marshaling his numerically superior forces to repel it. The Allies did make a few mistakes. In particular, dropping two airborne divisions at night behind the Atlantic Wall—the chain of fortifications defending France's coast—caused immense confusion and needless casualties that a dawn drop would have avoided.

But the Germans, Ambrose notes, committed far more numerous and costly errors than the Allies. Moreover, Hitler's insistence on directing the battle himself paralyzed his officers at every level. To cite one instance, the vitally important Panzer divisions deployed close to the beaches achieved full readiness by 2:00 a.m. on D-Day, but they were not authorized to counterattack until early afternoon when it was easy for naval gunners to turn them back. The German Navy and Air Force failed utterly to interfere with Allied movements.

Ambrose is scornful of the Atlantic Wall. Rommel reasoned that once ashore the Allies could not be driven off because supporting naval gunfire would break up his counterattacks, and therefore the invaders had to be stopped on the beaches. Runsted, Rommel's nominal superior as Commander in Chief West, disagreed. He wanted to concede the beaches and mass his forces inland beyond the range of the naval guns. Hitler split the difference, giving Rommel three Panzer divisions and Runsted four—although none of them could move without the Führer's authorization.

As Ambrose sees it, Runsted was right. He dismisses Rommel's argument that counterattacks well inland would still fail because of Allied air power. Had Runsted's strategy been followed, Ambrose speculates, the Allied advance would have stalled at the Somme-Seine barrier. Yet when the Germans launched a Panzer counterattack on August 6 against the Americans who had broken out of Normandy, it was destroyed by rampaging tank-killers of the American tactical air arm. The subsequent rout was so complete that one terrified German unit actually surrendered to the U.S. 405th Fighter-Bomber Group.

This suggests that Rommel was right. If the Allies could be stopped at all, it had to be on the beaches. But Rommel lacked the means to do so, and probably still would not have succeeded with all seven Panzer divisions at his disposal. There seem to have been only two things that could have caused D-Day to go wrong: bad weather or German foreknowledge of the Allied landing sites. Absent either of those conditions, the Allies' overwhelming air and naval superiority, together with the vast stretch of coast to be defended, assured Germany's ruin. On D-Day the Atlantic Wall was pierced at all five points of attack, mostly within the first hour. The best the Germans could do was buy time; the outcome of the invasion was never in doubt.

Historians will of course always disagree on one or another point. It is unlikely, though, that any will produce a book like *D-Day, June 6, 1944,* with its wealth of detail, absorbing vignettes and rich anecdotal material. Take the following observation by a former ranger who survived the landing and 11 more months of combat. The Allied

High Command, he remarked in his oral history, was right to ensure that "there be no experienced troops in the initial waves that hit the beach, because an experienced infantry-man is a terrified infantryman, and they wanted guys like me who were more amazed than they were frozen with fear, because the longer you fight a war the more you fig-ure your number's coming up tomorrow, and it really gets to be God-awful."

By the time darkness fell on June 6 some 175,000 men had gone ashore, of whom about 5,000 became casualties. This was a smaller number than many had expected, but D-Day was only the beginning of America's crusade in Europe. By the time it ended, General Omar N. Bradley recorded in his memoirs, "586,628 American soldiers had fallen—135,576 to rise no more. The grim figures haunted me. I could hear the cries of the wounded, smell the stench of death. I could not sleep: I closed my eyes and thanked God for victory."

The 50th anniversaries of many famous World War II events—the Battle of Midway, Guadalcanal, victory in North Africa, even Pearl Harbor—have passed practically unnoticed in the last two and a half years. The anniversa-ries yet to come, it appears, will be similarly neglected. D-Day alone holds a place in our collective memory of America's role in World War II. And Stephen Ambrose's compelling book reminds us very graphically of the great things this country once accomplished.

But in remembering D-Day we should not forget the cost of victory. During the War American families who lost loved ones overseas displayed gold stars in their windows. After D-Day, and because the fighting in the Pacific had gotten fiercer too, entire constellations of such stars came out all across America.

Carlo d'Este (review date 30 December 1994)

SOURCE: "The Culprits of Market-Garden," in *Times Lit-erary Supplement,* December 30, 1994, p. 27.

[*In the following excerpt, d'Este concludes that* D-Day, June 6, 1944 *is "enormously readable and will undoubt-edly become a standard work of its genre," despite its overemphasis on the American role in the Normandy inva-sion.*]

The summer of 1994 marked the commemoration of the fiftieth anniversaries of two famous and very different battles of the Second World War. On June 6, the world's attention was focused on Normandy, where in 1944 the turning point of the war occurred when Allied forces launched their long-awaited cross-Channel invasion on Sword, Juno, Gold, Omaha, and Utah beaches.

There is a dramatic contrast between D-Day and Septem-ber 17, 1944, the date the Allies launched Operation Market-Garden, the greatest airborne and glider operation

in history, and a bold strategic gamble aimed at ending the war in the same year by gaining an Allied bridgehead north of the Rhine. D-Day was characterized in these pages (*TLS,* June 10) as "a necessary day", a prerequisite that had to be successfully carried out if the Allies were to de-feat Nazi Germany and end the war. Arnhem may best be remembered as "a tragic day", which began so promis-ingly but ended, as Martin Middlebrook, the author of *Arnhem 1944,* writes, as "the last major battle lost by the British Army, lost not by the men who fought there but by the overconfidence of generals, faulty planning and the failure of a relieving force given too great a task."

Whereas D-Day was the result of months of rigorous plan-ning, Market-Garden was a military disaster thanks largely to the blunders of its architects, who planned it in haste, and in the process not only violated established principles of offensive warfare, but failed to heed the valuable (and costly) lessons learned from earlier airborne operations, including Normandy. In Normandy, bravery and good lead-ership were rewarded by victory; at Arnhem, valiant men were ill served and died needlessly. Although the stand of Lieutenant-Colonel John Frost's 2nd Parachute Battalion at Arnhem bridge is widely considered one of the most he-roic episodes of the Second World War, Market-Garden failed to establish the vital bridgehead north of the Rhine, a strategic objective which has come to be popularly known as "a bridge too far."

Stephen E. Ambrose's **D-Day, June 6, 1944** and Martin Middlebrook's *Arnhem 1944* are as different as the battles they chronicle. As both Eisenhower's official biographer and a historian of the Second World War, Ambrose brings impressive credentials to the writing of a fiftieth-anniversary account of D-Day, which he appropriately subtitles *The Climactic Battle of World War II.* Ambrose's book draws on a vast archive of 1,400 oral histories col-lected at the Eisenhower Center of the University of New Orleans, of which he is the director, to retell the dramatic tale of the first twenty-four hours of the great invasion.

Unfortunately, readers interested in a full account of the Anglo-Canadian landings are certain to be disappointed. Ambrose's account is unbalanced: twenty chapters (more than 300 pages) are devoted to the American airborne and amphibious landings, while five short chapters (sixty-six pages) detail the Anglo-Canadian landings. The primary focus of the book is bloody Omaha beach, where for a precarious time the landings seemed destined to fail. Am-brose attributes the Allied triumph on D-Day to the valour of the officers and men who snatched victory from what might have been a disaster on Omaha. However, in his zeal to pay tribute to the heroics of the participants, he of-fers simply too many first-person accounts and too little objective analysis of the decisions and events of that mo-mentous day, which ought to be part of any fifty-year ret-rospective. For example, the landings and operations of the British 3rd Division in the Sword sector are not even mentioned, despite the fact that what transpired there was the object of later controversy concerning the early capture of Caen, which Montgomery had promised. Despite these shortcomings, however, **D-Day, June 6, 1944** is enormously readable and will undoubtedly become a standard work of its genre.

Alan F. Wilt (review date June 1995)

SOURCE: A review of *D-Day, June 6, 1944,* in *American Historical Review,* Vol. 100, No. 3, June, 1995, pp. 872-73.

[*In the following review, Wilt offers positive evaluation of* D-Day, June 6, 1944, *though finds shortcomings in Ambrose's overstated comparison of Eisenhower and Erwin Rommel, his generalizations about the Atlantic Wall debacle, and his predominant focus on the American role in the battle.*]

Stephen E. Ambrose's book on D-Day [**D-Day, June 6, 1944**] has scaled the heights: a selection of the Book-of-the-Month and History Book clubs, nine weeks on the best-seller list, the most heralded of the works commemorating the fiftieth anniversary of that fateful day. A well-known historian in his own right, Ambrose acknowledges his many debts in writing the book, from Forrest Pogue, the noted American military historian, who was actually interviewing wounded men offshore on June 6, 1944, to Cornelius Ryan, whose *The Longest Day* (1959) became a classic in the use of first-hand accounts to depict the Normandy assault. Ambrose's outstanding work continues that tradition, for at its heart are 1,380 oral histories that, as director, he and others at the Eisenhower Center in New Orleans undertook and gathered from other sources to describe the battle.

Ambrose's intent is to provide a popular, up-to-date version of the invasion and to have it serve as an inspiring reminder of what democracies, when roused, can accomplish. He succeeds on both counts, and even the most knowledgeable historian will gain new insights into the background and execution of the operation.

The book's most noteworthy feature is its gripping narrative. Ambrose writes exceedingly well, and his use of the oral accounts to illustrate the horror and valor of war makes for compelling reading. Ambrose's centerpiece is the American landings at Omaha Beach, to which he devotes nearly one-third of his 583-page narrative. One of the soldiers, Sergeant Harry Bare, described getting ashore as follows: "We waded to the sand and threw ourselves down and the men were frozen, unable to move. My radio man had his head blown off three yards from me. The beach was covered with 'bodies,' men with no legs, no arms—God it was awful" (p. 331). As for getting off the beaches in the face of enemy fire, Private Raymond Howell explained his thought process. He remembers thinking, "If I am going to die, to hell with it, I'm not going to die here. The next bunch of guys that go over that . . . wall,

I'm going with them. So I don't know who else, I guess all of us, decided, well it's time to start" (p. 345). Of course, others besides Howell also made it up the bluffs to the commanding heights above, so that "bloody" Omaha could be held.

Ambrose covers not only the combat side of the battle but also delves into seldom discussed aspects, such as telling vignettes about the reactions of individual French citizens in the Calvados landing area, the role of American women doing factory work, and the involvement of the 320th Barrage Balloon Battalion, one of the few African-American formations to take part in the invasion. He also describes the broadcasts of Axis Sally, the Ohio native but longtime Berlin resident who mesmerized numerous GIs and British soldiers with her "sweet, sexy voice," but who frightened them on occasion with her knowledge about specific allied units.

Ambrose also discusses technological features of the operation in understandable terms. For instance, his description of the German defenses from foreshore obstacles to reinforced concrete fortifications are graphic as well as accurate, and he further gives proper due to a number of British "inventions," including midget submarines that were to guide DDs ("swimming tanks") to shore and tanks with flails to detonate land mines. Neither does he neglect the often overlooked American B-26 medium bombers and P-47 fighters, whose pilots and crews played extremely important roles in the successful campaign to gain air superiority over the beachhead and beyond.

Moreover, Ambrose rightly emphasizes allied landing craft, that precious commodity, and its intrepid, civilian developer, Andrew Higgins. Not by chance did the U.S. Congress in 1992 authorize the building of the National D-Day Museum in New Orleans, on the site where Higgins and his employees built and tested his boats.

Besides Higgins, Ambrose fills his book with other heroes, from the lowest in rank to the highest. He is particularly impressed by the airborne and infantry troops, and, as one might expect from a biographer of Dwight Eisenhower, Ambrose accords the American supreme commander a prominent part in the book. The author's attempt to compare Ike with Field Marshal Erwin Rommel, the German tactical commander, however, is overdrawn. It would have been more appropriate to compare Eisenhower with his German counterpart, Field Marshal Gerd von Rundstedt, and Rommel with either of the Allies' ground commanders, the American General Omar Bradley, or the British General Sir Bernard Montgomery. But neither Rundstedt nor Bradley adequately fits the heroic mold, and although the flamboyant Montgomery might have been appropriate, his abrasive egocentrism eliminated him as a possibility. Ambrose carries the Eisenhower-Rommel comparison, despite its being insightful and masterfully etched, too far.

The book also contains other disputable points. Among them is Ambrose's generalization that the Atlantic Wall was "one of the greatest blunders in military history" (p. 577), a statement that ignores the fact that Germany's holding of numerous harbors and their approaches helped cause an allied logistic crisis in the late summer and fall of 1944, which, in turn, helped prolong the European war into 1945. In addition, even though Ambrose dispels the myth that British and American troops did not train sufficiently for the assault, his contention that the Axis soldiers spent their time primarily building defensive barriers is wide of the mark. They both constructed and trained, and their performance on D-Day was not as deficient as alleged. Also, try as Ambrose might to be fair to each of the allied nations, the Americans emerge as the true heroes, and the other partners—the Canadians, the French, the Poles, the Dutch, even the British—at best become supporting members of the cast.

Nevertheless, although Ambrose's traditional approach will bother some historians, none will deny his ability to combine a first-rate narrative with a significant theme. He also does not gloss over what he considers allied military mistakes, such as the dropping of the U.S. airborne troops at night and the unreadiness of ground forces for hedgerow combat. But over and over his main point is that, although the allied soldiers, sailors, and airmen fought well, they would have much preferred not to have been fighting at all. In this sense, ***D-Day*** forms an appropriate link with the democratic tradition Ambrose extols.

Blaine Harden (review date 11 February 1996)

SOURCE: "Where the Wild Things Were," in *Washington Post Book World,* February 11, 1996, pp. 3, 7.

[*In the following review, Harden offers positive assessment of* Undaunted Courage.]

Feeling unmoved? Sensing perhaps that you live in uninteresting times? Weary of politicians who define vision as kicking AIDS victims out of the military? If so, historian Stephen Ambrose has a tonic for you.

Undaunted Courage is about a time when America was young, the federal government was bold and the president knew what he was doing. President Thomas Jefferson executed the Louisiana Purchase for a song, doubled the territory of the country overnight and in 1803 dispatched a handsome 30-year-old Virginian to do nothing less than fill in the blanks of our collective future.

Meriwether Lewis, a tobacco grower with an indifferent education, could not remember how to spell his widowed mother's married name. But he could command men, sweet-talk Indians and put a bullet on the mark at a distance of 220 yards. Most important for history, he could, after 12 hours in a canoe, sit down by the campfire and write closely observed and movingly poetic notes about a world that white men had never seen. He explored rivers, mapped mountains and sewed up the West between the

Mississippi and the Pacific—and, on his way back home to a hero's welcome in Washington, managed to get himself shot in the butt by one of his own men.

Ambrose, whose 17 previous books include one on D-Day and a highly regarded trilogy on Richard Nixon, showcases himself in this book as an exceptionally shrewd storyteller. In his introduction, Ambrose explains that he and his family have been obsessed with the Lewis and Clark Expedition for 20 years. They have repeatedly followed the explorers' footsteps across the Great Plains and through the Rockies. That obsession has paid off handsomely. For by digging beneath schoolbook sermons about the expedition, Ambrose has uncovered an extraordinary American character.

Ambrose's Lewis is a tender and tormented soul. Like the West that he conquered, his natural blessings seemed without limit. He was exceptionally good-looking, a kind and loyal friend, an instinctive naturalist and a gifted writer (whose stream-of-consciousness style Ambrose compares to those of Faulkner and Joyce). On meeting the Shoshone, Lewis wrote, "We wer [sic] all carresed [sic] and besmeared with their grease and paint till I was heartily tired of the national hug."

But he drank too much and he peaked too early.

He was paralyzed after the expedition by what was probably the most significant case of writer's block in this nation's history. The entire world was waiting to read his journals. They would have been a cinch to edit. Yet, for reasons known only to himself, the explorer never turned his journals into a book.

Lewis found it impossible to hold on to greatness. After his grateful friend the president named him governor of the Territory of Louisiana, he did not report to work in St. Louis for nearly two years. He was gamboling in Philadelphia, Ambrose explains, enjoying "too many balls with too many toasts." When he did take the governor's job, he attempted—and failed—to use his influence to make himself rich. Ambrose believes Lewis was probably a manic-depressive.

In 1809, just three years after his glorious return from the West, his performance as governor came under attack in Washington. While traveling east to explain himself, Lewis surrendered to depression. He was just 35 years old and famous beyond his imagining, and he shot himself in the head. When he did not die, he shot himself in the chest. When he did not die, he cut himself from head to foot with a razor. "I am no coward," he said as he bled to death, "but I am so strong, [it is] so hard to die."

With this spectacular young man, then, as the sympathetic heart of his book, Ambrose goes to work as a historian. It's a job he performs with impressive economy and insight. He tells us how Jefferson, "the greatest champion of human rights in American history," blended paternalism and genocide in his dealings with the Indians. As their "new Father," Ambrose explains, Jefferson had a nonnegotiable Indian policy—"get out of the way or get killed."

Ambrose neatly captures the primitiveness of Jefferson's era, a time when no means of transport moved faster than a galloping horse, when the learned president himself believed the Mandan Indians to be a lost tribe of Welshmen, when the cure for the flu was frequent bleeding and massive doses of laxatives.

If this book has a weakness, it's the relative paucity of detail about the Columbia, the great western river that Jefferson had hoped would be the Northwest Passage across the continent. Lewis and Clark disappointed their president by finding that the Columbia did not link up with the Missouri. In seeming sympathy with that disappointment, Ambrose gives short shrift to a river that Lewis and Clark called "inconceivable" and "incredible" and "horrid." But that, perhaps, is a parochial quibble from a reviewer who was born near the Columbia.

This is a fine and important book, intelligently conceived and splendidly written. It explains how the continental nation was made, flushes out human beings who did the making and reminds us of the magnificent things that government can do when it does have a vision.

Alexander Theroux (review date 3 March 1996)

SOURCE: "The Epic Journey of Capt. Lewis: A Young Man's Life on an Incredible Expedition," in *Chicago Tribune Books*, March 3, 1996, p. 1.

[*In the following review, Theroux offers positive assessment of* Undaunted Courage.]

On July 4, 1803, the nation's 27th birthday, the very same day Napoleon sold Louisiana to the United States, Capt. Meriwether Lewis was making final preparations for the greatest exploring expedition in the history of this country. President Thomas Jefferson had selected his personal secretary and fellow Virginian to travel up the Mississippi and Missouri, cross over the Rockies, go down the Columbia and reach the sky-blue Pacific. "The object of your mission is single," stated the president, "the direct water communication from sea to sea formed by the bed of the Missouri & perhaps the Oregon." Jefferson also wanted Lewis and his party to explore the new land, as well as extend commerce, collect specimens for science and establish an American claim on Idaho, Oregon and Washington.

It was to be a legendary 2 1/2-year trek, and although at the end Lewis' partner, Capt. William Clark, would write, "Ocian in view! O! the joy," it fell out that no Northwest Passage existed—there was no all-water route across country, or anything remotely resembling it. Ultimately, the complicated Lewis considered the expedition a failure, fell into depression and in 1809 took his life.

Using previously untapped materials and journals, Stephen E. Ambrose in *Undaunted Courage* superbly updates Richard Dillon's 1965 biography of Lewis and with as much passion as scholarship takes us again through the details of this epic journey. The 19 men went through hell. They were often exhausted. Although they commonly ate hominy and lard one day, salt pork and flour the next, and sometimes caught fish (or had beaver tail and buffalo tongue as delicacies), they were often badly starved, especially crossing the Rockies. Floggings were not infrequent for sleeping at sentry, insubordination and drunkenness. They often hazarded drowning as they crossed raging rivers, including the Salmon. Needle grass, noted Lewis, penetrated "our mockersons and leather legings and (gave) us great pain." Ticks and gnats drove them mad. Mosquitoes and the malaria they spread were a plague. Storms, blizzards, lost boats, dysentery, VD all awaited them. They were scorched in the plains by the merciless sun and frostbitten in the mountains, with their keelboat locked rigidly into the ice during the winter of 1804–05.

Much was terra incognita. Indians were everywhere. It was mostly territory where no white man had ever entered. Sioux, Arikara, Crows, Assiniboines, Cheyennes, Kiowas, Arapahoes, Otos and Omahas, Flatheads, Salish, Nez Perce, Osage and Clatsops surrounded them, tribes that were civil, peaceable, at times even distinguished. The men mostly feared the Blackfeet, with good reason, and in one confrontation Lewis shot one dead. Going over the Continental Divide, they met a Shoshone war party, which was quickly pacified by blue beads and mirrors, which they described, artfully, as "things like solid water." It was thanks to a Shoshone interpreter/translator whom they met at Ft. Mandan that the explorers managed to overcome apprehensions when encountering that people.

Sacagawea, nicknamed "Janey," was the only Indian, the only mother, the only woman and the only teenage person on the trip, a 15-year-old who was six months pregnant when they met her—one of the wives of a Toussaint Charbonneau, a French Canadian of middle age living among the Hidatsas as a trader. A slave, one of only two in the party—York, Clark's indentured black servant and lifelong companion, was the other—Sacagawea gave birth to her first child, Jean Baptiste, on Feb. 11, 1805. This was the source of some apprehension, as they didn't want to lose her, for, as Lewis noted, she was their "only dependence for a friendly negociation with the Snake Indians on whom we depend for horses to assist us in our portage from the Missouri to the Columbia River."

With insight and compassionate understanding, Ambrose, a historian very much interested in following the footsteps of his subject, takes us into the world of Meriwether Lewis and, where possible, by way of journals and jottings and note-takings, into the workings of his mind.

Undaunted Courage is, as much as anything, the personal drama of Lewis, for whom Jefferson, 31 years older, was something of a father. Jefferson had opened the president's house (not called the White House then) to the young man as an ideal finishing school, probably taught him how to write and over the course of two years gave his energetic protege "a college undergraduate's introduction to the liberal arts, North American geography, botany, mineralogy, astronomy, and ethnology."

Lewis was only 29 when he captained the expedition. Self-control, Ambrose tells us, was "not his strongest character trait." He was a better zoologist than a botanist, more of a scientist than Clark, who was the better waterman and so more often manned the keelboat. Clark was also the better mapmaker. Neither was a trained naturalist. Lewis was a drinker and could be headstrong. (Lewis and Clark, however, got on famously and during the whole expedition supposedly had only one minor disagreement about an overloaded boat).

It is Ambrose's considered judgment that Lewis was a manic-depressive, which, as Jefferson well knew, was a family disorder—he had not only seen the melancholy of Lewis' father, William, but also witnessed the same in Meriwether in 1801, when they had lived together and Meriwether was given to strange silences. During the expedition, whole months went by without diary entries, and, astonishingly, there isn't a single recorded word from Lewis about their arrival at the Pacific. "We don't have his description of what he saw and how he felt in this moment of triumph," observes Ambrose, who attributes it to lassitude.

Indisposition or vice, that mood seemed to characterize the last, lost years of this brave American hero, when, sadly, inexplicably, his drinking began to increase as his self-esteem waned. He began taking medicine laced with opium or morphine. (Lewis had been shot and badly wounded during his travels.) Even his snuff-taking became inordinate.

He was luckless in love and couldn't cope, unlike the stronger and more predictable Clark. Lewis never married. Worst of all, especially to Jefferson, he never got around to organizing the valuable journals that the president impatiently wanted to see in print. On top of it all, his finances were in a sorry state. Soon he began telling lies and talking wildly and late one afternoon in Tennessee on his way to Washington, in a poorly built log-cabin inn that took in overnight customers, he shot himself.

With wonderful attention to detail, compiling previously unknown information about weather, terrain, science, food, flora and fauna, native peoples, even the devious political situation Jefferson was facing, Ambrose takes us into the interior of an adventure filled with high romance and personal tragedy, involving, all at once, the greatest of all American explorers, surely one of the greatest presidents and easily the greatest expedition ever undertaken in the history of this country. His vivid portrait of America as the background for this undertaking—forested and wild, vast and mountainous, rich and abundant—brings back the kind

of dreams these men actually found, breathlessly stared upon, and awakens them again.

Gordon S. Wood (review date 4 April 1996)

SOURCE: "The Writingest Explorers," in *New York Review of Books,* April 4, 1996, pp. 18-21.

[*In the following review, Wood offers favorable evaluation of* Undaunted Courage.]

The Lewis and Clark expedition of 1804–1806 is the greatest adventure of exploration in American history. The astronauts of the 1960s knew more about the surface of the moon they were to land on than Lewis and Clark knew about the northwest part of the Louisiana territory they were sent to explore by President Thomas Jefferson. And Lewis and Clark and their party were out of touch with their fellow Americans back home for long periods of time—weeks, months, years—longer certainly than the minutes when the astronauts were unable to communicate with Earth. Besides, the Lewis and Clark expedition had little of the technology that makes even space travel today seem routine. The members of the expedition had only boats, horses, and their legs—all of which makes the expedition seem within the capacity of ordinary campers and hikers in our own time.

Indeed, Lewis and Clark's exploit is more alive for us at the end of the twentieth century than it was for Henry Adams a century ago. Whereas Adams could write nine volumes on the history of the Jefferson and Madison administrations and scarcely mention Lewis and Clark, we today cannot reexperience the adventure often enough. Maybe it is because we have now thoroughly mapped the territory the expedition explored and crisscrossed it with modern highways that the exploit has become all the more fascinating for us—the kind of extended camping trip we might read about in the travel section of our newspapers. We all cannot go to the moon, but Lewis and Clark's expedition seems to be an experience of exploration that ordinary backpackers and hikers can actually attempt to share in or duplicate, complete with L.L. Bean gear, white-water rafting, and extended nature walks.

At any rate, every year dozens of enthusiasts retrace the trail of the expedition. Scholars and laymen have formed an organization exclusively devoted to studying and celebrating the venture. New sites and monuments commemorating the expedition are still being dedicated. And we cannot read enough about it. In the 1970s Donald Jackson edited a superb two-volume edition of the *Letters of the Lewis and Clark Expedition,* and in the early 1990s Gary Moulton and the University of Nebraska Press completed their modern eight-volume scholarly edition of the journals of Lewis and Clark. Over the past several decades we have had numerous monographs on one aspect or another of the expedition—on Jefferson's plans for exploration, on the Indians the expedition met, on the flora and fauna it found, on the medicine it practiced, on the geography it explored. And finally there have been many narrative accounts, stirring accounts, of the whole expedition. This one by Stephen Ambrose is the most recent and it is one of the best.

Although Ambrose has written occasionally on some nineteenth-century events, he is best known for his work on modern America. He has written multi-volume biographies of Eisenhower and Nixon, and most recently an exciting account of D-Day in World War II. But this book is different: it not only deals with events of nearly two centuries ago, but it is, he says, "a labor of love." Ambrose, it seems, is one of those Lewis and Clark enthusiasts. He has followed the expedition's trail many times; indeed, every summer since 1976 he and his family have journeyed to Montana. He has crossed the Lolo Trail on horseback or foot five times. He has canoed the Missouri River Breaks in northern Montana ten times. He has camped at the Lemhi Pass almost every year since 1976. He and his family, he says, "have been obsessed with Lewis and Clark for twenty years."

Ambrose has written a very readable narrative [in *Undaunted Courage*], made for brief attention spans. He has divided his book into thirty-eight chapters; each chapter is about twelve pages long and is headed by the dates of the narrative it covers. Within these short chapters the paragraphs are numerous, many containing no more than a sentence or two. Sometimes there are not even sentences, just short phrases, as if Ambrose were duplicating diary entries: e.g., "Another day on the river. Making about eighteen miles per day. Endless. Exhausting."

Ambrose brings his experience with military history and military affairs to bear on the story, judging Captain Lewis's and Captain Clark's decisions and actions from the point of view of commanders in charge of a military company, which is exactly what they were. Ambrose's judgments are shrewd and balanced: he makes some harsh criticisms of the leaders at times, but on the whole he supports their decisions and actions. If a reader knows little of the expedition and wants a solid, readable account of it, then this book is a good place to begin.

Lewis is the central character of the book, not Clark. Jefferson, too, is an important character in the story but only insofar as he relates to Lewis and the expedition across the continent. Clark, the former army officer chosen by Lewis to accompany him, remains throughout a somewhat shadowy figure, even though one senses that Clark's solidity, common sense, and way with people were crucial to the success of the mission.

The book opens with several chapters on the youth and early life of Meriwether Lewis. Born in 1774 in the western part of Virginia, not far from Monticello, Lewis grew up expecting to become a member of the minor gentry of Virginia heading a plantation with about two dozen slaves.

But he had what he called a "passion for rambling"; and once he joined the army to help put down the Whiskey Rebellion in Pennsylvania in 1794, he never looked back. "Seldom," writes Ambrose, "would he spend more than a winter at one place for the rest of his life."

When Jefferson became president in 1801 he wanted a secretary, not only to handle the private affairs of the household but also to advise him on the Ohio Valley and military matters. He especially wanted to know which Federalist officers should be dismissed from service, since he planned to cut the size of the army by half. Who was better for the post than his twenty-six-year-old Virginia neighbor Captain Lewis, who knew the West and the army and was a good Jeffersonian Republican to boot?

Although Jefferson was apparently not thinking of Lewis's leading a western expedition when he appointed him secretary, he certainly had been thinking for decades about supporting some sort of exploration of the far western territory beyond the Mississippi—even though that territory belonged to the Spanish. Jefferson was the greatest expansionist in American history. "[He] wanted land. He wanted empire," declares Ambrose. Jefferson felt that sooner or later the entire continent would become American—because the Spanish hold on their territory was so weak and the exploding population of the United States would spread everywhere. In 1783 he asked the Revolutionary War hero George Rogers Clark (the older brother of William Clark) to lead a privately sponsored expedition to explore the West, but Clark declined. When Jefferson was minister to France he encouraged the extravagant and ill-fated hopes of John Ledyard to cross Siberia and reach the western coast of North America. Later, as secretary of state, Jefferson supported several plans for expeditions up the Missouri.

In the meantime, in 1792 an American sea trader, Captain Robert Gray, had discovered and named the Columbia River, and Captain George Vancouver of the British Navy and the Canadian trader Alexander Mackenzie were staking British claims to the northwest portion of the continent and threatening to take complete control of the fur trade around the Columbia River. In 1792–1793 Mackenzie in fact made the first crossing of the continent north of Mexico, at least by a white man. Mackenzie's account of his expedition, published in 1801, was apparently what jogged Jefferson into action.

Sometime in 1802 Jefferson offered Lewis the command of a military expedition that the US government would undertake to explore the trans-Mississippi West. Lewis had volunteered for an expedition, planned by Jefferson, that was to take place in 1793 and never came off; he undoubtedly had conveyed to Jefferson in numerous conversations his desire to explore the West. It was an excellent choice. As Jefferson explained to Dr. Benjamin Rush, "Capt. Lewis is brave, prudent, habituated to the woods, & familiar with Indian manners & character." Although Lewis was "not regularly educated," he knew enough about nature to select and describe flora and fauna that were new. And what he did not know he could learn. Jefferson sent Lewis off to Philadelphia for crash courses in astronomy, natural history, medicine, and ethnology with several scientific experts.

Yet so much about the land beyond the Mississippi remained unknown or wrongly understood that no one could prepare fully for what lay ahead. Although Jefferson had the most extensive library in the world on the geography, cartography, natural history, and ethnology of the American West, he nevertheless assumed in 1800 that the Rockies were no higher than the Blue Ridge Mountains, that mammoths and other prehistoric creatures still roamed along the upper Missouri among active volcanoes, that a huge mile-long mountain of pure salt lay somewhere on the Great Plains, that the western Indians may have been the lost tribes of Israel or wandering Welshmen, and, most important, that there was a water route, linked by a low portage across the mountains, that led to the Pacific.

Lewis wanted a co-commander and selected his old army friend William Clark. Clark was four years older than Lewis and had been Lewis's immediate superior for a time, but in 1796 he had resigned his captain's commission and was engaged in family business in the Ohio Valley when he received Lewis's invitation. Since the army regulations for the expedition provided for only a lieutenant as the second officer, Clark did not get his captain's commission back. But Lewis was determined that Clark be treated as his equal and kept his status as a lieutenant a secret from the men of the expedition. Having co-commanders was an extraordinary experiment in cooperation, in violation of all army ideas of chain of command, but it worked. Lewis and Clark seem never to have quarreled and only rarely disagreed with each other. They complemented each other beautifully. Clark had been a company commander and had explored the Mississippi. He knew how to handle enlisted men and was a better surveyor, mapmaker, and waterman than Lewis. Where Lewis was apt to be moody and sometimes wander off alone, Clark was always tough, steady, and reliable. The two men trusted each other completely; they had, writes Ambrose, "one of the great friendships of all time."

Lewis left Pittsburgh and started down the Ohio River on August 31, 1803, and made the first entry in what became the journals of the expedition. The journals, says Ambrose, "have a driving narrative that is compelling, yet they pause for little asides and anecdotes that make them a delight to read." Donald Jackson, editor of the *Letters of Lewis and Clark,* describes the two captains as "the writingest explorers of their time," men who "wrote constantly and abundantly, afloat and ashore, legibly and illegibly, and always with an urgent sense of purpose." In often vivid and sharp prose they described much of what they encountered—plants, animals, people, weather, geography, and unusual experiences. In reading the journals we experience the journey as the two captains experienced it. Ambrose is not exaggerating in calling the journals "one of America's literary treasures."

In October 1803 Lewis picked up Clark in Indiana, and gathered some of the recruits for what was called the Corps of Discovery. The party spent a long winter at River Dubois, across from St. Louis, waiting for the formal transfer of the Louisiana territory from Spain and France to the United States and enlisting more men for the expedition. The group set out on May 14, 1804, with forty-odd men, including Clark's black slave, York. The explorers traveled up the Missouri, and by October reached the villages of the Mandan Indians, in present-day North Dakota, where they decided to spend the winter of 1804–1805.

Since traders had penetrated this far up the Missouri, the expedition had not yet covered completely unknown ground. Lewis and Clark spent time during this first stage of the journey dealing with some disciplinary problems and the death of a sergeant—the only member of the Corps to die on the journey. Although they had a nearly violent confrontation with the Teton Sioux in present-day South Dakota, most of the time the captains left the Indians they met more bewildered than angry. The translation problems were immense. The Indians would speak to an Indian in the expedition, who then spoke in another Indian tongue to someone who understood that tongue but could only speak French, who then passed on what he heard to someone who understood French but also spoke English. Only then could Lewis and Clark finally find out what the Indians had originally said. Their reply, of course, had to repeat the process in reverse. Tedious as conversation with the Indians was, Lewis and Clark worked out an elaborate ceremony for all the Indian tribes they encountered, informing them that the United States had taken over the territory and that their new father, "the great Chief the President," was "the only friend to whom you can now look for protection, or from whom you can ask favours, or receive good councies, and he will take care to serve you, & not deceive you." After what became the standard speech to the Indians, the captains distributed some presents—from the large store of beads, brass buttons, tomahawks, axes, moccasin awls, scissors, mirrors, as well as US flags and medals with Jefferson's visage, that they carried with them.

The Corps of Discovery spent the winter of 1804–1805 in a fort it constructed near the Mandan villages. In April 1805 Lewis and Clark sent back their heavy keelboat and some enlisted men to St. Louis along with a written report, a map, and some botanical, mineral, and animal specimens to be delivered to President Jefferson. Joining the party now was the Shoshone woman Sacagawea with her husband and their infant son; she was to prove invaluable as a translator during the next stages of the journey.

In six canoes and two pirogues the group of thirty-three set out on April 7, 1805, to proceed up the Missouri to the Rockies. Even though Lewis, as he wrote in his journal, was about "to penetrate a country at least two thousand miles in width, on which the foot of civilized man had never trodden; the good or evil it had in store for us was for experiment yet to determine," he could not have been happier. "This little fleet," he said, "'altho' not quite so rispectable as those of Columbus or Capt. Cook, were still viewed by us with as much pleasure as those deservedly famed adventurers ever beheld theirs; and I dare say with quite as much anxiety for their safety and preservation."

At this point in the narrative Ambrose really begins indulging in what earlier had been only occasional references to the "first" this and the "first" that. So in addition to having "the first collection of weather data" and "the first election" west of the Mississippi and "the first" American descriptions of the tepees and ceremonial dress of the Plains Indians, we have either the "first Americans" or the "first white men" to see a Sioux scalp dance, view the Rockies, kill a grizzly, confront a Shoshone war party, hear of the Nez Percé Indians, enter present-day Idaho, Washington, and Oregon by land, journey on the Columbia River east of the Cascades, and make the first transcontinental linking of what would become the United States. Even the decision of where to spend the winter of 1805–1806, which Lewis and Clark put to a vote of their party, becomes an occasion for Ambrose's listing of firsts: "the first vote ever held in the Pacific Northwest . . . the first time in American history that a black slave had voted, the first time a woman had voted." (This last is incorrect.)

Despite his happiness in getting his expedition going once again in April 1805. Lewis scarcely realized how arduous the rest of the journey to the Pacific would be. It took the party four months just to get to the Rockies, including a month-long portage of the Great Falls of the Missouri. The men suffered badly from their virtually all-meat diet. Most of the time Lewis gave the ailing soldiers some of the fifty dozen pills that Dr. Rush had prescribed for the journey. Generally referred to as "Thunderclappers," the pills were composed of a variety of drugs, each of which, says Ambrose, was "a purgative of explosive power; the combination was awesome."

By the time the party reached the Continental Divide, on the present Montana-Idaho border, in August 1805, Lewis (who turned thirty-one on August 18) realized that there would be no simple portage to the waters of the Columbia. Although the commanders did not know it, they could scarcely have picked a more difficult place to cross the Rockies. From the Shoshone Indians the expedition got guides and horses for the journey across what one sergeant called "the most terrible mountains I ever beheld." The crossing of Lolo Pass in the Bitterroots was the expedition's worst experience. Beset by snow and hail, exhausted and half-starved, the men killed their horses and drank melted snow for nourishment. Yet the expedition made 160 miles in eleven days: "It was," writes Ambrose, "one of the great forced marches in American history."

On September 22, 1805, the party finally reached the country of the Nez Percé Indians on the Clearwater River in Idaho, where it built canoes for the trip down the Clearwater, the Snake, and the Columbia to the Pacific. On November 7, 1805, though the group was still in the estuary of the Columbia, Clark described what he saw: "*Ocian in*

view! O! the joy! . . . Ocian 4142 Miles from the Mouth of *Missouri* R." The men built a fort, Fort Clatsop, on the Oregon side of the Columbia estuary and spent a long wet winter there, with the captains writing descriptions of nature and the Indians and making a map. In March they began their return, spending a month with the Nez Percé waiting for the snow to melt in the Rockies. After crossing the mountains Lewis and Clark separated, Lewis exploring the Marias River in present Montana and Clark traveling down the Yellowstone River. On their trip Lewis and his men ran into a party of Blackfoot Indians who tried to steal their horses. In the only real violence of the expedition Lewis and his men killed two of the Indians and were lucky to escape with their lives. In view of all the trouble it caused, Ambrose rightly judges Lewis's entire Marias side trip a big mistake.

Reunited in North Dakota, the captains revisited the Mandan villages where they had wintered in 1804–1805. They left Sacagawea and her husband and child with the Mandans, and moved rapidly down the Missouri to St. Louis, which they reached on September 23, 1806. From the time they had originally set out from St. Louis, they had been gone two years and four months. Nearly everyone had given them up for lost—except Jefferson.

The completion of this "epic voyage," writes Ambrose, was by itself enough to place Lewis and "his partner-friend" in "the pantheon of explorers." But he and Clark had done more. In addition to opening up a "fur-trading empire" in the West, the explorers had brought back "a treasure of scientific information." Their "discoveries in the fields of zoology, botany, ethnology, and geography were beyond any value." They had discovered and described 178 new plants and 122 species and subspecies of animals. By systematically recording all they had seen—"from weather to rocks to people," says Ambrose—they introduced new approaches to exploration that affected all future expeditions. Their marvelous journals, which one historian has called "perhaps the most important account of discovery and exploration ever written," became "the model for all subsequent writing on the American West."

Without a photographer or an artist present Lewis and Clark had only words to record what they saw. Here, for example, is Lewis's description of the bighorn sheep in the upper parts of the Missouri:

> The head and horns of the male . . . weighed 27 lbs. it was somewhat larger than the male of the common deer, the boddy reather thicker deeper and not so long in proportion to it's hight as the common deer; the head and horns are remarkably large compared with the other part of the anamal; the whole form is much more delicate than that of the common goat, and there is a greater disparity in the size of the male and female than between those of either the deer or the goat. the eye is large and prominant, the puple of a deep sea green and small, the iris of a silvery colour much like the common sheep; the bone above the eye is remarkably prominant; the head nostrils and division of the upper lip are precisely in form like the sheep. . . .

These were just the opening lines. Lewis went on for another seven hundred or so words detailing the characteristics of this creature.

But the public knew none of these descriptions. It was delighted just to see the explorers, who were cheered and fêted everywhere they went. Jefferson secured Lewis's election to the American Philosophical Society and appointed him governor of the Territory of Louisiana. Although both explorers received double back pay and land bonuses, they expected that publication of their journals would make their fortune. But, alas, Lewis seemed unable to get the manuscript ready for publication. After returning to St. Louis to take up the governorship, Lewis became involved in establishing a fur company and other get-rich schemes and apparently began drinking heavily and taking drugs and running up debts. He had no practical experience in politics or government and, says Ambrose, "had more success than was good for him." Jefferson pleaded with him to get the manuscript of the journals to a printer, but Lewis never even answered Jefferson's letters. With the War Department on his back over his policies as governor and refusing to honor his drafts of money, Lewis in the late summer of 1809 decided to return to Washington to clear his name. He took the journals with him, intending, he told Clark, to see to their publication.

As he traveled eastward he behaved strangely, drinking heavily and taking pills; twice he tried to kill himself, and on September 11, 1809, he wrote out his last will and testament. At Fort Pickering (present site of Memphis, Tennessee) Major James Neelly, the army's agent to the Chickasaws, agreed to accompany Lewis to Washington. But on October 10, 1809, Lewis with two servants went on ahead of Neelly and that evening stopped at an inn seventy miles west of Nashville. Sometime later that night he shot himself twice, and, failing to kill himself, cut himself with a razor. Lewis begged the servants to shoot him, but they refused and shortly after sunrise on October 11, 1809, he died of his wounds. He was thirty-five.

This strange end has sparked a great deal of historical controversy and a number of charges of conspiracy and murder. The most recent is a 1994 book by the late David Leon Chandler, *The Jefferson Conspiracies: A President's Role in the Assassination of Meriwether Lewis,* whose descriptions of hidden designs involving Jefferson and General James Wilkinson put even the elaborate concoctions of Oliver Stone to shame.[1] Ambrose quite rightly dismisses these imagined murder plots (neither Clark nor Jefferson doubted that Lewis had killed himself), and concludes that the really "great mystery of Lewis's life" is why he did not prepare the journals for publication.

Clark tried to pick up the pieces, and he persuaded young Nicholas Biddle to edit the journals. In 1814 Biddle published a narrative account of the journey that omitted most of the material on the flora and fauna. Because Biddle's *History of the Expedition Under the Commands of Captains Lewis and Clark* was for the next ninety years the only printed account of the expedition based on the journals, Lewis and Clark received no credit for most of their discoveries in nature.[2] Others renamed the plants, animals, birds, and rivers that they had discovered and named, and these later names, not Lewis's and Clark's, were the ones that survived. By failing to publish the journals, says Ambrose, in a bit of hyperbole, "Lewis had cheated himself out of a rank not far below Darwin as a naturalist." But he remains, in Ambrose's opinion, "the greatest of all American explorers, and in the top rank of world explorers." This may not be true, but Ambrose's book has at least made it seem so.

Notes

1. William Morrow, 1994.

2. In 1893 Dr. Elliott Coues published a new annotated edition of Biddle's *History* in which he identified many of the plants and animals mentioned in the text. But it was not until Reuben Gold Thwaites, director of the State Historical Society of Wisconsin and an experienced documentary editor, published in 1904–1905 his multi-volume edition of the *Original Journals of the Lewis and Clark Expedition* that the world discovered what Lewis and Clark and their subordinates had actually written.

Patricia Nelson Limerick (review date 7 April 1996)

SOURCE: "The Blank Page, the Final Frontier," in *Los Angeles Times Book Review,* April 7, 1996, p. 3.

[*In the following review of* Undaunted Courage, *Limerick finds shortcomings in Ambrose's military perspective and uncritical admiration of Lewis and Clark.*]

Imagine that you are a student and that the registrar's computer has been playing tricks with your course enrollment. You thought you were signed up to take the standard American history course, but the computer has placed you instead in a history class for ROTC cadets.

Things become puzzling when your instructor's lively stories keep returning to the same theme: the proper behavior and philosophy of a good company commander. Although unexpected and often quite interesting, this preoccupation does not strike you as doing full justice to the rich meanings of American history.

In similar ways, Stephen E. Ambrose's **Undaunted Courage** is a story on a big scale with meanings squeezed into a framework built on a considerably smaller scale.

There is no question that this is a good and readable story. Meriwether Lewis was an extremely interesting man and writer, and any book with the license to quote him at length carries a competitive advantage. Born on Aug. 18, 1774, on a Virginia plantation neighboring that of Thomas Jefferson, Lewis hunted, learned nature lore and served in the militia. Soon after Jefferson became president. Lewis moved into the White House as his private secretary. The two often discussed exploring a land route to the Pacific Ocean, and in 1803, Jefferson successfully persuaded Congress to fund the mission.

Lewis invited his friend, Lt. William Clark, to help him lead 26 men into a vast terrain, much of which had just become, with the Louisiana Purchase, America's own.

After devoting five opening chapters to Lewis' origins and relationship with Jefferson, Ambrose's next 25 chapters take their shape from the story of the expedition: the trip up the Missouri River in a 55-foot covered keelboat and two small craft; the cold winter in what is now North Dakota, where they acquired the help of a captive Shoshone woman, Sacagawea; the move from keelboat to canoes before crossing the Great Falls of the Missouri: the strenuous crossing of the Rockies; the wet winter at Ft. Clatsop on the Pacific Coast; the rushed, anticlimactic return to St. Louis.

Repeatedly, Ambrose, a historian best known for his three-volume biography of Richard Nixon and a recent oral history of D-Day, locates the meaning of these stories in lessons of universal military practice. At the Pacific camp, Lewis' goals in maintaining order and discipline, Ambrose says, were "the goals of every company commander from the time of the Roman Legions to today." Meanings reaching so far over time can stretch themselves pretty thin. "A good company commander looks after his men," Ambrose writes, adding that Lewis was like "the head of a family," evincing concern for his men matching "that of a father for his son."

A family composed of men accompanied by one Indian woman, however, would seem to be a social unit calling for an awareness of the various meanings and workings of masculinity, especially when a Virginia gentleman undertook to lead a party composed largely of French Canadians. But the call for an analysis of culture and gender is one of several calls from the 1990s that Ambrose has decided not to answer.

In truth, if you concealed the title page and asked readers to guess the publication date of this book, estimates might vary considerably. The subtitle's reference to the "opening" of a presumably locked-up West, the celebration of the "discovery" of lands long occupied by Native Americans and the use of the terms "braves," "red men" and "squaws" suggest a publication date in the 1950s.

Other phrasings sound very much more like the '90s: rivers were "free of any pollutants"; Lewis was most likely "manic-depressive"; beyond the Platte River, the expedition entered "a new ecosystem"; Lewis was "sensitive and caring" toward his mother. Ambrose is, moreover, very much a celebrant of hindsight—in his phrasing, "after-action analysis"—and an enthusiast for the identification of "mistakes."

And mistakes accumulated badly at the end. For those taken by human nature and its weird ways, the final seven chapters of the book, covering Lewis' last three years of life, may well be the most intriguing.

When the explorers returned after a two-year journey of 6,000 miles, there was much celebration, for they had been presumed dead. But Lewis—the man who rose to every challenge in his crossing of a continent—was laid out flat by the conditions of his return. Preying on his apparent predisposition to mental illness, three prosaic elements of early 19th century American social and cultural life knocked the triumphal explorer off his feet: the difficulty of courtship, the irritations of administering a territorial government and, perhaps worst of all, the problems of preparing a manuscript for publication.

Upon their return, Lewis and Clark both went looking for wives and jobs. Clark got a wife; Lewis didn't. Clark became the capable superintendent of Indian affairs for the Louisiana Territory; Lewis became governor of the same territory, trying to use his office to profit from the fur trade. An extraordinary degree of bureaucratic and factional cat-fighting circled around Lewis' tour. As Ambrose puts it, "if he was a near-perfect Army officer, Lewis was a lousy politician."

And then there was the problem of manuscript preparation. After signing up a publisher and illustrators and consulting experts in a burst of activity in Philadelphia, Lewis did absolutely nothing with the journals. Despite big expectations and big promises, Lewis-as-author went into major-league default and denial.

For any writer who has ever missed a deadline, this episode in non-publication shows Lewis at his most human and most in range of empathy. It cannot be a comfort, then, to know that Lewis, in mid-writer's block, went mad. To rescue himself from financial ruin partly caused by the Madison administration's refusal to pay some of his official expenditures, Lewis set off to Washington. He made it only to the hills of Tennessee, however, where he was found dead in an inn. While schoolbooks told us that he was murdered. Ambrose argues that he committed suicide.

By his failure to prepare the journals for publication, Ambrose asserts, "Lewis cheated himself out of a rank not far below Darwin as a naturalist." In the observation of nature and the describing of specimens, Lewis was a remarkable fellow, alert and observant to beat the band. But if Lewis came up with an organizing idea, a concept anywhere near as powerful as evolution, the record of this breakthrough does not survive. The comparison of Lewis to Darwin tells us, instead, that we are reading a biographer who had become very fond of his subject.

Acknowledging that Lewis is one of his "heroes," Ambrose argues that the explorer needs to be better appreciated. Lewis' suicide "hurt his reputation" and deprived him, for instance, of the honor of having a river or another major geographical feature named after him. Those with more of an enthusiasm for word play and puns may notice what Ambrose did not: with a minor twist of misspelling, "Louisiana" Territory stands ready for transformation.

In the interior West today, we are doing considerably better than Lewis did in courtship and marriage and, as the current renaissance in western literature indicates, we are dealing very well with the challenges of preparing manuscripts for publication.

But in matters of governance, the tangled, factional, profiteering, rumor-filled and contentious politics of Lewis' territory in 1809 seem entirely too familiar. Stymied to find a way to reconcile public interest with personal profit and locked in a struggle over the question of who will benefit from the region's great resources and magnificent scenery, we are indeed residents of Lewisiana Territory.

Ambrose tells us that Lewis, in the spring of 1805, "turned his face west. He would not turn it around until he reached the Pacific Ocean." The turning around, the looking back, the return to life in one's own contentious home country, proved and proves to be the hardest part. The "after-action analysis" necessarily remains incomplete.

Peter G. Boyle (review date June 1996)

SOURCE: A review of *Eisenhower: A Centenary Assessment,* in *Journal of American History,* Vol. 83, No. 1, June, 1996, pp. 277-78.

[*In the following review, Boyle concludes that* Eisenhower: A Centenary Assessment *is "a useful addition to scholarship on Eisenhower."*]

In 1990, on the occasion of the one hundredth anniversary of Dwight D. Eisenhower's birth, the Eisenhower Center at the University of New Orleans, which is dedicated to the study of the life and times of General and President Eisenhower, sponsored a year-long series of lectures on his career. The lectures, revised for publication and edited by the center's director and associate director, Stephen E. Ambrose and Günter Bischof, constitute the volume under review. Publication of a centenary assessment five years after the centenary suggests an undue lapse of time between the delivery of the lectures and their publication. Nevertheless, the book is a useful contribution to the ongoing reassessment of Eisenhower.

Andrew J. Goodpaster, Eisenhower's staff secretary during most of his presidency, offers a judicious foreword, which is, not surprisingly, very favorable to Eisenhower. Goodpaster argues that the absence of apocalyptic events in the 1950s and the achievement of solid economic growth and social cohesion for the majority of Americans were largely due to Eisenhower's leadership style of good preparation, joint effort, and the deflation of issues. Ambrose and Bis-

chof's introduction is an excellent summary of the trends in historiography on Eisenhower, with a succinct discussion of the most significant works that offered the traditional view of Eisenhower as an ineffective president, the revisionist accounts since the late 1960s that viewed Eisenhower very positively, and postrevisionist accounts since the late 1980s that have added reservations to the revisionist interpretation. The remainder of the volume consists of contributions by both established scholars and younger historians. None of the contributors would accept the traditional jaundiced views of Eisenhower offered by intellectuals of the 1950s and 1960s, but they divide between the revisionist and postrevisionist view.

There are only two contributions on Eisenhower in World War II, by Forrest C. Pogue and M. R. D. Foot. There is a very good contribution by Thomas M. Sisk on a neglected period of Eisenhower's career, his time as the North Atlantic Treaty Organization's (NATO) Supreme Allied Commander, Europe, in 1950–1952. For the most part, however, this centenary assessment is an appraisal of Eisenhower as president.

Some of the contributors summarize the familiar views of authorities, while others break new ground with original research. Fred Greenstein, for example, offers a convenient, brief summary of his well-known conclusions on Eisenhower's "hidden-hand" leadership style; William L. O'Neill summarizes the favorable aspects of the domestic history of the United States in the 1950s in a spirited, vigorously argued piece. Stanley I. Kutler offers an innovative interpretation of Eisenhower and desegregation, suggesting that Eisenhower's choice of judges quietly shaped a judiciary that pushed the South toward the inclusion of blacks as equal citizens.

On foreign policy issues, several contributions are more innovative. Thomas A. Schwartz offers a stimulating analysis of Eisenhower and the Germans, discussing Eisenhower's roots as a German American and his relations with Germans as a general and president. Anna K. Nelson makes good use of the very full minutes from National Security Council meetings in the 1950s to discuss Eisenhower and the foreign policy process. Steven F. Grover makes an interesting comparison between Eisenhower's liberal policy over the issue of Cuban sugar prices in 1954–1956 and his rigid policy toward Fidel Castro in 1959–1960. The essays by Bischof on the Austrian Peace Treaty and Robert A. Wampler on NATO and nuclear weapons are based on detailed research, while Gordon H. Chang largely repeats previously published views on Eisenhower and China, with the exception of some general reflections on the comparative leadership styles of Eisenhower and Mao Zedong. H. W. Brands presents some general reflections on Eisenhower's style in foreign policy. The volume concludes with an overall appraisal of Eisenhower by Ambrose.

A centenary assessment by its nature tends to the laudatory, and this volume is no exception. Moreover, there are significant differences between the contributions addressed to a general audience and the more specialized essays. Foot, for example, recounts familiar material on Eisenhower and the British in World War II and offers a very thin analysis of Eisenhower's relations with British leaders in the 1950s, while Schwartz presents a sophisticated, wide-ranging study of Eisenhower and the Germans. Nevertheless, the combination of the contributions that summarize recent work on Eisenhower, such as the one by Greenstein, and the more specialized original contributions, such as those by Kutler and Grover, make this a useful addition to scholarship on Eisenhower.

Albert Furtwangler (review date December 1996)

SOURCE: A review of *Undaunted Courage,* in *Journal of American History,* Vol. 83, No. 3, December, 1996, pp. 1007-8.

[*In the following review of* Undaunted Courage, *Furtwangler concludes that Ambrose fails to capture the literary and larger philosophical dimensions of the book's subject.*]

This book has had widespread success, including weeks as a national best seller. For thousands of new readers, it may ease the way into the great Lewis and Clark expedition of 1803–1806. It consolidates dozens of studies from the past thirty years to tell the story in short, accessible chapters with full explication.

Nevertheless, the overarching design of this study leaves much to be desired. The full title promises to unite three difficult subjects, but they remain separate and baffling. Meriwether Lewis remains an enigmatic figure, a brilliant explorer on the trail but an inexplicably shattered man after his return who finally took his own life. Thomas Jefferson remains the inscrutable American scholar-statesman, a patron and mentor to Lewis in one mood, a cold and official taskmaster in another. The American West has long been a meeting place and battleground for people from every continent. Its "opening" exploration involves dozens of ill-assorted characters and plenty of bitter conflict. But here that event emerges as a triumph of Jeffersonian intelligence and determination.

Stephen E. Ambrose admits some conflicting aims in his introductory pages [in *Undaunted Courage*]. He claims to be writing a new biography of Lewis, but that is mainly because he learned in 1992 that James Ronda was already at work on William Clark. In fact, the thick core of this book is a straight chronology based on both explorers' records, fleshed out with information from recent expert publications in many fields.

More frankly yet, Ambrose offers this book to mark years of happy family life in Montana and along the Lewis and Clark Trail. And Montana as a happy hunting ground is at the dead center of his tale. When Lewis invades from the

East, Ambrose says he "stepped forward, into paradise," and he means it. He goes on to describe a summer-lit world abounding in game, with no threatening Indians in sight. (None appear until desperately needed—for crossing Idaho.) It is in Montana that Lewis reaches the height of his talents and his bliss. Once he drops back east into the world of others' maps, he becomes entangled in drink, drugs, writer's block, and political corruption. He can never return up the Missouri River. He sinks into despondency and dies.

Ambrose thus rewrites a very bleak *Paradise Lost.* No Satan, no serpent, no Eve, no heaven, no hell. For God the Father, read Jefferson the mastermind—creating an American Adam and setting him going, then retiring to Monticello like a properly Enlightened First Cause. Wilderness to the west and bureaucracy to the east do all the rest. Ambrose ignores such literary patterns; many historians will feel that he rightly sticks to explaining the facts of diplomacy, science, courage, adventure, and scenery. But the life of Meriwether Lewis embodies a westering motif that begins with Odysseus and presses on to Vietnam. To see it only in Enlightenment terms is to slight its depths of tragedy and transcendence.

Lisa E. Emmerich (review date Fall 1997)

SOURCE: A review of *Undaunted Courage,* in *Historian,* Vol. 60, No. 1, Fall, 1997, pp. 123-24.

[*In the following review, Emmerich offers generally positive assessment of* Undaunted Courage.]

This work is the story of two magnificent obsessions. The first, as is obvious from the title, is the epic of love of exploration that drew Meriwether Lewis and Thomas Jefferson into the partnership that ultimately opened the trans-Mississippi West to European American settlement. The other obsession, revealed more clearly with the turn of each page, is that of the author. Captivated by Lewis and his remarkable journey, Ambrose has spent the last twenty years leading family, friends, and students down most of the same paths and waterways that the expedition followed. Every mile walked along the Lolo Trail, every riffle canoed on the Missouri River, and every starry night spent deep in the Bitteroot Mountains brought the author that much closer to the heart and the spirit of the man he reveres as "the greatest of all American explorers" (475).

Ambrose blends natural history, political history, and biography in *Undaunted Courage,* giving readers a sophisticated narrative that references every extant source on Lewis and Clark. As well as any biographer can know a subject, the author *knows* Meriwether Lewis, and he wants his readers to share his appreciation of this remarkable man. Ambrose recounts Lewis's childhood and youth and highlights the evolution of his relationship with Thomas Jefferson. From there, the narrative focus shifts to the expedition, and the reader follows Captain Lewis and his company from the earliest planning stages (1801–1803), through the actual journey (1803–1806), to the triumphant return (1806–1807). En route, the author enumerates the innumerable "firsts" of the trek, including the first Euro-American sightings of buffalo, grouse, condors, prairie dogs, the Rocky Mountains, the Columbia Gorge, the Lakota, Shoshones, Nez Percé, and Blackfeet. The author is, at times, less careful in noticing the native people whom Lewis and Clark encounter along the way and in acknowledging that they knew these "firsts" as familiar components of their cultural landscapes. His account concludes with the sorry denouement of the grand adventure, Lewis's failures as governor of the Louisiana Territory, his deepening melancholy, and his ultimate suicide in 1809.

Undaunted Courage is biographical history writ large by an author who is well accustomed to storytelling on a grand scale. But, in this instance, the effect is less magisterial and much more intimate. Ambrose knows and loves the country traveled by Lewis and Clark. He fully understands and carefully explains the scientific, diplomatic, and ethnographic importance of their undertaking. Ambrose clearly respects and admires Lewis, his indispensable partner, Captain William Clark, and the rest of the group of explorers who accompanied them. Enthusiastic esteem permeates the narrative but does not blunt the occasional criticism of Lewis as an expedition leader and later as a "man-about-politics." Only once, at the end of the saga, does the narrative distance slip. There, with the spectre of the suicidal Lewis haunting the narrative, Ambrose, the biographer/historian, gives way to Ambrose the fellow explorer, nearly two centuries removed, who cannot fully understand why Meriwether Lewis, this man "of courage undaunted," would end his life in a backwoods inn on the Natchez Trace, so far away from the western lands that he loved.

Howard Lamar (review date October 1997)

SOURCE: "The Search for American Heroes," in *Yale Review,* Vol. 85, No. 4, October, 1997, pp. 146-50.

[*In the following review, Lamar offers favorable evaluation of* Undaunted Courage, *praising Ambrose's narrative skill and successful effort to humanize Meriwether Lewis.*]

Stephen E. Ambrose, the author of *The New York Times* bestseller *D-Day* and the biographer of Dwight D. Eisenhower and Richard Nixon, has always been in search of American heroes. In *Undaunted Courage* he goes back in time to write about one of the country's first official explorer-heroes, Meriwether Lewis of the famous Lewis and Clark Overland Expedition of 1804–6. Unlike other accounts of Lewis and Clark, however, Ambrose with good reason not only rescues Meriwether Lewis from two centuries of obscurity but presents him as a fascinating, complex, strong, contradictory individual. He also portrays

Thomas Jefferson as a more shrewd, highly political, and tough figure than we usually encounter in American texts. For Ambrose, Jefferson was a practical politician standing midway between the opposite categories of dreamer and schemer.

It could almost be said that Ambrose has rescued Lewis from a conspiracy of silence imposed by several generations of historians. Henry Adams more or less dismissed both Lewis and Clark as frontier types who could not have been any good as scientific explorers since they were not formally trained or educated.

Because Lewis died early and Clark lived a long time as a key Indian superintendent in Saint Louis and produced a remarkably accurate and detailed map of their western trip, Clark became the dominant figure in the usual Lewis and Clark accounts. But as Ambrose points out repeatedly, Lewis was the single planner, the quartermaster, and the senior officer who headed the expedition. Even so, Clark, the brave frontiersman who had drawn a superb map, became the hero everyone wanted to write about.

Other historians, almost studiously avoiding what Lewis and Clark had achieved, fastened on the story of the Shoshone woman Sacagawea and called her not only a guide but the savior of the expedition when she persuaded her Shoshone people to furnish the explorers with horses that allowed them to travel through the Rockies on their way to the Pacific. Indian tribes and historians alike have fought verbal battles as to whether Sacagawea was a Shoshone or from another tribe and whether she lived to a great age or died of a "putrid fever" in 1809. Besides getting horses from her brother Cameahwait, as the journals acknowledge, the presence of a woman in the Lewis and Clark party "reconciles all Indians that we are not a war party." It should be said that Lewis and Clark appreciated her but that she was not their savior.

More recently, the psychological historians have had a go at Lewis and Clark by asking such questions as did Lewis have a crush on Clark and/or did Clark have an affair with Sacagawea? Both tantalizing speculations die from lack of evidence. Now medical historians have gotten into the act by arguing that Lewis was depressed and later committed suicide because he had contracted syphilis from the Indians and died when the disease began to affect his brain.

Fortunately for the reader, Ambrose keeps these questions in perspective. But even more fortunate is that all the known papers and correspondences relating to the Lewis and Clark Expedition have been edited by Professor Gary Moulton of the University of Nebraska in an exhaustive ten-volume edition. With Moulton's edition, Stephen Ambrose had most of his materials right at hand. *The Journals of the Lewis and Clark Expedition* put to rest all questions about Lewis's competence as a scientific observer and demonstrate conclusively what an incredible treasure trove of information the two men gathered. Aided by the work of such other scholars as Donald Jackson,

James Ronda, and Paul Russell Cutright, Ambrose has synthesized Lewis and Clark's findings brilliantly.

Even so, the real secret of the powerful impact of *Undaunted Courage* on hundreds of thousands of readers is Stephen Ambrose's contagious enthusiasm for reliving the Lewis and Clark trail over the Rockies, the Lolo Pass Trail, by hiking and riding it on horseback each fall with his wife, children, and grandchildren. There is even an Ambrose grandson named Meriwether.

The question still remains what has Ambrose told us about Lewis himself that could be called new. Besides being the first full biography of Lewis, this is the first book to describe his childhood and life in the context of a Virginia plantation society and economy. Ambrose argues persuasively that Lewis got his sense of authority and command because he and his family were plantation aristocracy and slaveowners.

Ambrose also demonstrates that Lewis was obsessed with getting an education. He left his widowed mother and a brother in Georgia to return to Virginia to be tutored. He fought for what little formal education he got and urged his brother Reuben and a stepbrother to attend school. It quickly becomes clear why Jefferson liked Lewis so much: he was the perfect willing pupil whom Jefferson deliberately trained for the western expedition he had been planning for twenty years.

Ambrose gives us yet other valuable clues to Lewis's character by tracing his early years in the army on the frontiers of the Old Northwest. Army life was rough, crude, and punctuated by violence and hard drinking. What Ambrose has done, however, has been to explain why Lewis was so attracted to the wilderness. He finds that Lewis was always curious about trees, wild plants, birds, and animals. He was almost a John Muir, but with a shotgun. In effect, Jefferson could hardly have found another army officer who had such an overwhelming curiosity about nature.

When Jefferson finally decided to send Lewis west, he packed him off to Philadelphia for crash courses in astronomy, medicine, and scientific descriptions of plants with Dr. Benjamin Rush, Benjamin Smith Barton, and others. Early historians have made fun of this superficial training, but Ambrose argues that Lewis was such an avid pupil that what he learned was substantial.

Moreover, Lewis was in charge of getting boats built to go down the Ohio, buying supplies and guns, and purchasing medicines. In short, this was Lewis's expedition. Clark came on at the last minute and had no role in the planning. Yet Lewis and Clark, both army men and frontiersmen, admired and respected each other. Lewis made Clark co-commander and called him captain even though that rank was formally denied Clark throughout the expedition.

Lewis and Clark's epic journey to the Pacific and back is a familiar story to many but is so well told by Ambrose that it seems a fresh, new saga. After they returned to Saint Louis in September 1806, the country learned of their two-year successful journey and declared them heroes.

We come now to what is the first weakness or troubling part of Ambrose's biography of Lewis. Lewis came home a national hero. He was wined and dined everywhere from Saint Louis to Philadelphia. He had one big task ahead of him: to write up and publish his and Clark's extensive journals. But after writing Jefferson a wonderful summarizing letter from Saint Louis he wrote no more. He never asked for scientific help or chose an editor or a publisher. Ambrose tries to excuse Lewis by saying he was disappointed that he could not report to Jefferson that the West was a future agrarian empire and so felt that he had failed Jefferson. By this time Lewis was drinking heavily and may have been taking drugs. An inebriated Lewis, though handsome and charming, appears to have scared off the women he found attractive and wished to marry.

The next episode we might blame partly on Jefferson himself. He named Lewis governor of Louisiana Territory, but Lewis proved to be no politician and soon came to grief dealing with sophisticated French merchants and aggressive American frontier politicians. Jefferson should have kept him in the East to edit the journals. But Lewis was at fault, too, because he was anxious to get rich in the fur trade and gave friends special deals. Ambrose freely acknowledges this venal side of Lewis's character.

Lewis's periods of drinking and depression became more pronounced as he got deeper into trouble as governor. When he decided to return to Washington via the Natchez Trace, he demanded whiskey and a gun at a frontier home in Tennessee and shot himself not once but several times. Neither Clark nor Jefferson were surprised, and Jefferson himself wrote a kind of a obituary that brilliantly analyzed Lewis and the problem of depression in the Lewis family. It is there that Jefferson described his erstwhile secretary as possessing "undaunted courage"—hence the book's title.

What Ambrose has done is to make Lewis a real person, a hero who was at once a frontiersman and a near poet. Lewis's description of the Great Falls of the Missouri is a beautiful example of his occasional eloquent prose. His excitement over the discovery of a new plant or bird echoes John James Audubon. His being at home in the wilderness and appreciating nature for itself reminds one of Daniel Boone.

Lewis, then, should be listed as a westering nature lover, not quite in the category of Muir, Audubon, Thomas Nuttall, or Henry David Thoreau, but a near relative. Similarly, he was fascinated by the West as the mysterious unknown, as were Jefferson, Jedidiah Smith, John Colter, and John C. Frémont. Ambrose's accomplishment has been not only to rehabilitate Lewis as a person and frontier hero but to point to a new way of seeing other intelligent frontiersmen whom historians have previously made into unthinking macho types. In this context one awaits with anticipation a forthcoming biography of William Clark by historian James Ronda. Meanwhile, **Undaunted Courage** may well remain the most effectively narrated American adventure story to appear in this decade.

Josiah Bunting III (review date 21 December 1998)

SOURCE: "Fighting Words," in *National Review*, December 21, 1998, pp. 60-2.

[*In the following review, Bunting offers positive assessment of* The Victors *and Ambrose's focus on the military experiences of individual soldiers.*]

For whom is serious history written? The American academy has long answered: for other university scholars. On occasion, works of academic scholarship become popular: one can think of any number of such books. But in the eyes of university colleagues, their authors as a consequence soon become suspect—quietly derided, yet envied. Historians vulgarly praised as "good writers" are similarly fretted over. Propulsive narrative, pellucid prose, epigrammatical assertion or conclusion, vivid exemplification: such things virtually guarantee the wary regard of other professional historians.

There is a sub-species of history writing that particularly excites academic contempt. This is the history of men at war: not of ministers of war or defense secretaries, but of military leaders and ordinary soldiers. That military history should occupy the lowest caste in the history profession is unsurprising. The fact of organized slaughter in the service of state policy is deeply offensive to the liberal dream of human perfectibility, a reminder that mankind at the close of the twentieth century remains in the end no more advanced, as Richard Eberhardt wrote, than in our ancient furies. And since the end of the military draft in 1972, not many are those men and women, one day to become scholars and writers of history, who have voluntarily served in uniform. Few historians have any feel for the grit and heft and horror, for the enduring attraction for some, of "making war."

For these reasons, military history is usually written by historians without either academic credentials or academic appointments. One thinks of the great historian of the British army, Sir John Fortescue; of John Wheeler-Bennett, of Douglas Southall Freeman (who continued to edit a large daily newspaper while he wrote his magnificent histories of Lee and his lieutenants), of Barbara Tuchman, Elizabeth Longford, Brian Farwell, and John Keegan—all of whom wrote or are writing for large audiences.

Writers like these grip hands with the great historians of an earlier century—Macaulay, Parkman, Bancroft, Henry Adams. Their concern is fundamentally with human character and intelligence under the grossest and most unremitting stresses life furnishes: those of sustained military campaigning.

Among such historians, no American now writing is read more widely than Stephen Ambrose. The popularity of his recent books is reminiscent of G. M. Trevelyan's comment about Lord Macaulay's *Lays of Ancient Rome*—that their sales might be said to vary directly with the price of coal. Ambrose is an academic historian and brilliant classroom teacher who may be said, using a naval metaphor, to have slipped his moorings.

In his books and lectures Ambrose often concludes by describing small units of young soldiers, walking through towns in the great theaters of war in 1945. Almost alone among such groups, squads of American GIs evoked smiles of delight, reassurance, gratitude, and confidence among those who saw them pass by. They were a soldiery whose military training had not effaced the essential goodness of the people and culture that had bred them. They were instinctively trusted by people who saw them—who perhaps a week earlier had watched enemy armies pass along the same streets, armies whose military men had been instructed that they represented superior races and cultures, with a destiny to conquer and subdue.

The picture is of course somewhat idealized. It reminds us of *Saving Private Ryan* (for which Ambrose was the principal technical advisor) and dozens of older war movies in which American squads are microcosmic melting pots of citizenship and ethnicity. And it reminds us also—which explains much of Ambrose's popularity—of the degree to which we yearn for the emotional adhesion of a country united in a just and mighty purpose.

His newest book—the author's fifth since 1994—**The Victors**, bears the subtitle *Eisenhower and His Boys—The Men of World War II.* It is an integration of several earlier works, including the enormously popular **Citizen Soldiers** and its various predecessors. Among these are **Band of Brothers: E Company, 506th Regiment, 101st Airborne**, and **D-Day, June 6, 1944.** The titles suggest the continuing focus of most of this historian's work: young Americans brought to their country's service by a variety of motives—pure patriotism, the desire to prove something and earn distinction, the felt obligation to serve. But the soldiers Ambrose writes about were sustained in their combat service above all by an irreducible unwillingness to break faith with those of their own small units.

Thus while Ambrose has been criticized for reducing history to an immense series of episodes and anecdotes, strung together loosely in a narrative making few moral judgments, but allowing the facts to speak for themselves, this critique misses the point altogether. Ambrose is determined to show, as Thucydides did in the *The History of the Peloponnesian War,* and as Lincoln pronounced in the Gettysburg Address, that the essential goodness of a moral, democratic society makes of its citizens military defenders who will triumph over enemies whose soldiers are the products of totalitarian, racist, and authoritarian regimes. Someone once wrote: Churchill speaks of the soft underbelly of Europe, and a private crawls forward three feet in the rain. Ambrose is the recorder of the private's progress. To fasten upon multiple, unregarded lives and tiny incidents is to illuminate the larger thesis by accretion. Ambrose accomplishes this with great power.

So while *The Victors* summarizes and reconsiders Ambrose's earlier World War II themes, it does so for the declared purpose of making a narrative history of "the Supreme Commander and the junior officers, NCOs, and enlisted men carrying out his orders—generally ignoring the ranks in between."

Like Emerson's Lincoln, Ambrose's wartime Eisenhower seems in some sense—however ironic the word in 1998—an aboriginal American, the very embodiment of American leadership in war: slow to anger, vast in wrath, yet boyish, bumptious, always able to get a kick out of things, understanding that no crisis, however distended and destructive, can be allowed to register in the persona he presents to those he leads, his soldiers, and those he represents, his countrymen. Ambrose writes: "He spoke with great earnestness, a perfect expression of the devotion to duty that he felt deeply . . . but all followed by that big grin and a verbal expression of bouncy enthusiasm . . . he was so big, so generous, so optimistic, so intelligent, so outspoken, so energetic—so American."

But the soldiers he led are the real subjects of *The Victors.* Ambrose's mission throughout is not unlike that of Joseph Conrad. The novelist said he wanted to take his audience by the lapels and demand:

> Don't you see? Can't you understand? This is what your countrymen are *like,* in their best selves, in the hearts of their hearts, when once the blast of some mighty and worthy crusade has blown in their ears. Once they were this, and you must be worthy as their heirs, and nothing can make you worthy that does not lift you beyond the petty dreams and ambitions of your contracted lives.

Near the end of *The Victors,* a representative GI remembers: "We did our duty because our country asked us to, and our comrades depended on our doing it." That was all. Or as Churchill said of Eisenhower's own hero, George Marshall: Succeeding generations must not be allowed to forget his example.

Eric T. Dean Jr. (review date June 1999)

SOURCE: A review of *Citizen Soldiers,* in *Journal of American History,* Vol. 86, No. 1, June, 1999, pp. 295-6.

[*In the following review excerpt of* Citizen Soldiers, *Dean takes issue with Ambrose's tendency to conflate heroism and cruelty in his portrayal of World War II as a "good war."*]

World War II, despite the fact that it left over four hundred thousand Americans dead and hundreds of thousands of other veterans maimed in body or mind, has until recently persisted in the American imagination as a "good war," one that was fought for a necessary and noble cause, and one in which American fighting men did their duty overseas and then came home to appreciative civilians and jubilant parades, which eased their reentry into civilian life. However, in the wake of the Vietnam War, we have become acutely aware of the physical and psychological travails of American veterans, and historians have begun to take a closer look at the life of the common soldier and have thereby reexamined the idea of World War II as the classic "good war." Stephen E. Ambrose's *Citizen Soldiers* and Gerald F. Linderman's *The World within War* are part of this reevaluative process.

In *Citizen Soldiers,* Ambrose takes a broad look at the American campaign in western Europe by considering every level of the war effort, from the strategy discussions of generals to the tactics employed by junior officers and the life of the combat soldiers "on the ground." The dominant theme is that the "citizen soldiers" of the United States were called from the peaceful pursuits of civilian life and were matched up against the fanaticism of Adolf Hitler's Third Reich; America's men met this test successfully, and through a mixture of effective leadership, courage, and innovation, primarily by junior officers and NCOs (noncommissioned officers), saw the cause through to victory.

America's fighting men were unprepared for much that they encountered, but reacting with resourcefulness and persistence, they devised methods to deal with each problem as it emerged, such as converting tanks to bulldozers to plow through the hedgerows of Normandy or coordinating infantry, tanks, and tank-busting aircraft into a highly effective machine of destruction and doom, which was then deployed against German defenders. Ambrose's thesis that it was the junior officers ("middle management") who should be credited with victory finds an analogue in John Kenneth Galbraith's *The New Industrial State* (1978). Indeed, it is Ambrose's assertion that American World War II veterans, all too often dismissed as "men in gray suits," went on in the 1950s to make this country into an industrial giant and success story and to spread democracy throughout the world.

While Ambrose presents an abundance of evidence for the grisly and awful nature of combat—the noise, shock, and feelings of total helplessness and bewilderment that it could induce ("I dreaded going into combat again")—his read on the American war effort is that it was heroic, spectacular, and magnificent. In that sense, his narrative sometimes seems to drift into a form of cheerleading that disconnects from the evidence. For instance, he recounts an incident when infuriated American infantrymen took German tankers prisoner and proceeded to execute them by shooting them in the back of the head. The last German was a young man who was sobbing and rocking back and forth on his knees, pleading for mercy with pictures of his family on the ground in front of him. The unmoved GIs shot and killed the German. That is not heroic or magnificent. That is the cruel and ugly face of war.

Steve Weinberg (review date 3 September 2000)

SOURCE: "Linking a Nation: Stephen Ambrose's Story of the Building of the Transcontinental Railroad," in *Chicago Tribune Books,* September 3, 2000, p. 5.

[*In the following review, Weinberg offers favorable assessment of* Nothing Like It in the World.]

When I was young, the building of the interstate highway system transformed the U.S. The obstacles were huge, but road crews working heavy machinery got the job done. The time spent driving between major cities was cut in half.

Amazing as the building of the interstate highway system was, something far more amazing had occurred a century earlier—the building of a transcontinental railroad, with no heavy machinery to do the heavy lifting. How tens of thousands of laborers managed to build a serviceable railroad across rivers, through mountains and into deserts with little more than shovels, axes and dynamite boggles the mind.

Stephen Ambrose's new book makes the how of it understandable, but no less mind-boggling. With publication of this book, a lot of minds will be boggled, because when Ambrose writes, a lot of people read. Perhaps no Ph.D. historian has ever reached so many readers. ***Nothing Like It in the World,*** about the building of a railroad that made the U.S. accessible from east to west, deserves to be a best seller, much like Ambrose's books about the Lewis and Clark expedition (***Undaunted Courage***) and the Army during the final year of World War II (***Citizen Soldiers***), to name just two of his 22 previous works.

Early in the book, Ambrose admits that despite his training as a historian specializing in 19th Century American culture, he balked when his editor suggested the topic. He had stereotyped the men behind the building of the transcontinental railroad as corrupt. "I wanted nothing to do with those railroad thieves," Ambrose writes. But he and his editor agreed on a compromise: He would spend six months reading "the major items in the literature, so I could see if there was a reason for a new . . . book on the subject."

Ambrose found many previously published books to admire, including Maury Klein's 1987 work *Union Pacific: Birth of a Railroad, 1862–1893* and George Kraus' *High Road to Promontory: Building the Central Pacific Across the High Sierra* (1969). Ambrose decided to go ahead by focusing on a question that previous authors had for the most part ignored: How did they build the railroad? rather than, How did they profit from it?

As it turns out, David Haward Bain, a teacher at Middlebury College, was researching a similar book. Bain's *Empire Express: Building the First Transcontinental Railroad,* reached stores in late 1999. It is equally well-written and, at almost 800 pages, nearly twice as long as Ambrose's book.

Bain covers a longer time period. For instance, he opens with a scene from 1844, as Asa Whitney, who has been scheming about how to finance a transcontinental railroad for many years, is on a ship that has to travel halfway around the world to get from the Atlantic Ocean to the Pacific Ocean. The journey steels Whitney's resolve when he returns to the East Coast to lobby Congress for a railroad. Another key railroad promoter, Grenville Dodge, does not appear in Bain's book until Page 157.

Ambrose, on the other hand, opens his book with a chance 1859 meeting in Council Bluffs, Iowa, between Dodge and soon-to-be president Abraham Lincoln. Lincoln, on the campaign trail in his quest for the White House, hears from his host that Dodge, in the audience, knows more about railroads than anybody in the nation.

At this juncture, Ambrose's skill at setting scenes, using dialogue and building suspense takes over. In Ambrose's telling, Lincoln "studied Dodge intently for a moment and then said, 'Let's go meet.'" Lincoln and his host strolled to a bench where Dodge was sitting. "Lincoln sat down beside Dodge, crossed his long legs, swung his foot for a moment, put his big hand on Dodge's forearm, and went straight to the point: 'Dodge, what's the best route for a Pacific railroad to the West?'

"Dodge instantly replied, 'From this town out the Platte Valley.'

"Lincoln thought that over for a moment or two, then asked, 'Why do you think so?'"

After hearing the answer, Lincoln "went on with his questions, until he had gathered from Dodge all the information Dodge had reaped privately doing surveys for the Rock Island Railroad Company on the best route to the West. Or, as Dodge later put it, 'He shelled my woods completely and got all the information I'd collected.'"

Despite Ambrose's storytelling skills, I would recommend Bain's book over Ambrose's for its comprehensiveness. But Ambrose fans, as well as readers who want a shorter version than Bain's, will not be wasting their money or time with ***Nothing Like It in the World.***

The cast of characters is unforgettable. The stars of Ambrose's drama include Dodge, a Civil War Union general who became the chief engineer of the Union Pacific as thousands of workers laid track after the war's end; Theodore Judah, the professional surveyor who conceived the

Central Pacific, the second line that met up with the Union Pacific in the Utah wilderness; Mormon religious leader Brigham Young, whose power in Utah made him a key player automatically; financiers who contributed unimaginable amounts of money to the project, especially Thomas Durant, Oakes Ames, Oliver Ames, Leland Stanford, Collis Huntington, Charles Crocker and Mark Hopkins; Lincoln; Union Gen. Ulysses S. Grant, who would later become president; and Gen. William T. Sherman, who probably could have been elected president if he had chosen to run.

Of all those men he admires, Ambrose seems to have a special relationship with Judah, who started his labors as an 18-year-old railroad construction manager. Judah possessed great vision, setting out to explore the Sierra Nevada range because there might be a mountain pass that would make railroading from coast to coast possible. How he returned from that arduous, dangerous adventure to team up with his wife, Anna, as Washington lobbyists in favor of railroad construction is a tale of optimism and persistence. There was no choice in Judah's mind: Government funding had to be involved, because only the government possessed the resources to pay for it.

To Ambrose's credit, he does not spend all of his precious space on the tycoons and professional engineers. He also devotes considerable attention to the laborers who sweated day in, day out for years under conditions so harsh that words almost fail. Those laborers, mostly of Chinese and Irish descent, are the mostly unnamed heroes of the saga.

The obstacles that had to be overcome—and the questions that arose because of them—provide the book with endless drama. What route should the tracks follow? There were so many choices, each one tied up in questions of geography, politics and finance. Once started, would the project really be completed given the obstacles? How many lives would be lost during construction? How many individuals and institutions would go bankrupt trying to profit?

Ambrose has the answers, some of them surprising, for his legion of readers.

Patricia Nelson Limerick (review date 18 September 2000)

SOURCE: "Railroaded History," in *Washington Post Book World,* September 18, 2000, p. C3.

[*In the following review of* Nothing Like It in the World, *Limerick criticizes Ambrose's uncritical generalizations about the American transcontinental railroad and his sentimental view of its construction.*]

Stephen Ambrose has grown weary of negativity. Finding in the first transcontinental railroad a prime opportunity to reroute U.S. history back to its proper track of pride, he offers Americans a journey to an appealing destination. *Nothing Like It in the World* gives readers a ride back to an era when people felt good about American history, inspired by the nation's leaders and proud of their triumphs.

Unity is the point and punch line of this book: Just as the Civil War united North and South, the building of the Union Pacific and Central Pacific railroads united East and West. "Next to winning the Civil War and abolishing slavery," Ambrose declares in his opening sentence, "building the first transcontinental railroad . . . was the greatest achievement of the American people in the nineteenth century." "Most of all," he says, "it could not have been done without teamwork."

In repeated declarations, Ambrose casts the fighting of the Civil War and the building of the railroad as parallel and similar enterprises in the cementing of national unity. In truth, the analogy may be uncomfortably close. Like soldiers in an army, the workers on the railroads were subordinates in a hierarchy; rather than acting as democratic citizens freely expressing their support of a project for the national good, they followed orders, and if they did not, they soon sought employment elsewhere. As the Chinese men who attempted a strike in the Sierra Nevada certainly learned when construction boss Charles Crocker simply withheld their food supplies, the railroads' practice of "teamwork" could be enforced with assertions of power that other historians would be hard-pressed to interpret as expressions of democratic unity.

Not once but many times, Ambrose reminds readers that this railroad was an enormous and unique accomplishment, that it resembled the Civil War in spirit and outcome, that it demonstrated American enterprise, toughness and determination at their best. Along with repetition, he makes a full surrender to the necessity of the "meanwhile" mode of narrative construction: The fighting of the Civil War, the building of the Union Pacific, the building of the Central Pacific, the lobbying in Washington are linked by "meanwhiles" deployed in a manner not always notable for its grace (Theodore Judah, engineer of the Central Pacific, "spent the early fall working on his annual report. Meanwhile the Battle of Antietam had been won by the Union . . .").

The men in charge of the railroad repeatedly faced the choice between building it "fast" or building it "well." The companies, under great financial pressure to win the race and claim as much trackage as possible, chose "fast," and it sometimes seems that Ambrose has modeled his own choices on theirs.

But his willingness to trust nostalgic memory over established scholarship poses even more of a puzzle. In 1965, historian Wallace Farnham published an article in the *Journal of American History* establishing that stories about Grenville Dodge, chief engineer for the Union Pacific, cannot be verified by any evidence from the time. Written into his published memoirs, Dodge's tales—discovering a crucial mountain pass while being chased by Indians, meeting with Abraham Lincoln in Council Bluffs, Iowa, and Washington to influence Lincoln's choice of railroad routes—give every sign of being apocryphal, imagined into being years later. On the day in which legend has him escaping hostile Indians, for instance, Dodge's diary records no word about heroic escapes; on the contrary, as he described his journey to his wife, "The trip would have suited you, if it had not been for the tediousness of it." (Ambrose in a footnote responds to Farnham's conclusion that this story is false: "For my part, the story rings true; besides, there were plenty of other eyewitnesses." He does not cite those witnesses.) Nearly all the stories that Farnham found to be poorly supported, if not actively discredited by documentary evidence, appear in Ambrose's book, presented as fact. (In a footnote, Ambrose acknowledges that Farnham concluded that Dodge's story of chatting with Lincoln in Council Bluffs in 1859 was probably false. Ambrose then declares that the story "strikes me as true, even down to the details." He does not offer an explanation for this impression, or cite counter-evidence.)

Ambrose is, after all, a writer entirely at home and at ease with sweeping generalizations. The race for construction between the two companies, he declares, "was democracy at work." If so, it shows that democracy is an enormously complicated political animal, capable of working congenially with organizations characterized to their core by elitism and hierarchy. And, by all the evidence, this kind of democracy has proved both resilient and highly exportable.

The omnipresence of railroads around the globe makes the book's repeated claims for American uniqueness difficult to understand. The title, ***Nothing Like It in the World,*** certainly describes the transcontinental railroad's position at a particular historical moment. But the proliferation of railroads—throughout home countries, empires and colonies—was a feature of late-19th-century and early-20th-century life virtually everywhere on the planet.

If uniquely American virtues and strengths of character made possible the building of this particular railroad, how was it that railroads involving comparably strenuous engineering and financing have appeared all over the world, in places where these singular American qualities did not prevail?

"The truth," Farnham wrote in 1965, in an era when historians were much more comfortable using absolute terms like truth, accuracy and fact, "is too complex for romantic legend." "The species of legend fashioned out of magic, heroism, and vanity still prospers," Farnham said, and "nowhere more vigorously" than in the story of the transcontinental railroad. As Stephen Ambrose himself observes, "Exaggeration is endemic to railroad historians."

FURTHER READING

Criticism

Apple, R. W. "Beyond Damnation or Defense." *New York Times Book Review* (12 November 1989): 1.
    Review of *Nixon: The Triumph of a Politician, 1962-1972.*

Barrett, Laurence I. "Martyr or Machiavelli?" *Time* (6 November 1989): 100.
    Review of *Nixon: The Triumph of a Politician, 1962-1972.*

Betty, Mary Lou. "The Fifties and Ike." *Humanities* 18, No. 5 (September-October 1997): 8.
    Ambrose discusses the Eisenhower era and his relationship with the former president.

Bliven, Naomi. "Ike." *New Yorker* (1 July 1985): 95-7.
    Bliven offers a favorable evaluation of *Eisenhower: The President.*

Blumenthal, Sidney. "The Primal Republican." *New York Times Book Review* (24 November 1991): 3.
    Review of *Nixon: Ruin and Recovery, 1973-1990.*

d'Este, Carlo. "Put Out More Flags." *New York Times Book Review* (21 December 1997): 10.
    Review of *Citizen Soldiers.*

Hymel, Kevin. Review of *Comrades,* by Stephen Ambrose. *Military History* 17, No. 1 (April 2000): 68.
    Offers positive assessment of *Comrades.*

Jones, Malcolm Jr. "From Sea to Shining Sea." *Newsweek* (19 February 1996): 70.
    Review of *Undaunted Courage.*

Josephy, Alvin M. Jr. "Giants in the Earth." *New York Times Book Review* (10 March 1996): p. 9.
    Review of *Undaunted Courage.*

Kisor, Henry. "Working on the Railroad." *New York Times Book Review* (17 September 2000): 8.
    Review of *Nothing Like It in the World.*

Patterson, James T. "The World of Richard Nixon." *Reviews in American History* 18, No. 3 (September 1990): 414-8.
    Review of *Nixon: The Triumph of a Politician, 1962-1972.*

Reardon, Patrick. "'Pegasus Bridge' Tells the Human Side of War." *Chicago Tribune* (24 March 1985): C36.

Reardon offers a positive assessment of *Pegasus Bridge.*

Sheppard, R. Z. "Blood, Sweat, and Guile." *Time* (2 October 2000): 95.
   Review of *Nothing Like It in the World.*

———. "Profiles in Courage." *Time* (24 November 1997): 108.
   Review of *Citizen Soldiers.*

Sherrill, Robert. "The Strange Career of Richard Nixon." *Washington Post Book World* (12 November 1989): 1, 13.
   Review of *Nixon: The Triumph of a Politician, 1962-1972.*

Summers, Harry G., Jr. "The Men of Company E." *New York Times Book Review* (6 September 1992): 11.
   Review of *Band of Brothers.*

Trevelyan, Raleigh. "Telling It Like It Is." *New York Times Book Review* (29 May 1994): 1.
   Review of *D-Day, June 6, 1944.*

Tripp, Nathaniel. "The Men Who Beat Hitler." *New York Times Book Review* (22 November 1998): 14.
   Review of *The Victors.*

Walton, David. "Byrds Out, Chippewas In." *New York Times Book Review* (14 November 1999): 24.
   Review of *Witness to America.*

Additional coverage of Ambrose's life and career is contained in the following sources published by the Gale Group: *Contemporary Authors,* **Vols. 1-4R;** *Contemporary Authors New Revision Series,* **Vols. 3, 43, 57, 83;** *Something About the Author,* **Vol. 40; and** *Literature Resource Center.*

Jacques Barzun
1907-

French-born American historian, nonfiction writer, essayist, critic, and editor.

The following entry presents an overview of Barzun's career through 2000. For further information on his life and works, see *CLC,* Volume 51.

INTRODUCTION

A renowned cultural historian, educator, and critic, Barzun is the author of more than thirty books on wide-ranging subjects encompassing music, art, education, and European intellectual history and literature. Upholding traditional views about language and pedagogy throughout his life, Barzun has been recognized as an erudite and independent-minded critic of contemporary academic trends and the deterioration of shared cultural heritage in the United States. His critique of higher education in *The American University* (1968) remains a prescient analysis of slipping standards, overspecialization, and an imperiled tenure system. At age ninety-two, Barzun published *From Dawn to Decadence* (2000), a magisterial survey of Western cultural and intellectual history, which is regarded as the capstone of his distinguished career.

BIOGRAPHICAL INFORMATION

Born in Creteil, France, Barzun was the son of Anna-Rose and Henri Barzun, a respected author. It was with his parents that Barzun experienced the turbulent and exciting artistic world of early twentieth century Paris. Frequent visitors in the Barzun home included avant-garde artists such as Fernan Léger, Wassily Kandinsky, Marcel Duchamp, and Jean Cocteau, and the poets Ezra Pound and Guillaume Apollinaire. Barzun received his early education at the Lycee Janson de Suilly in Paris, and taught for the first time at the school when he was only nine years old. Because of the devastation throughout Europe following World War I, his father encouraged him to pursue his education in the United States. In 1920, Barzun arrived in New York City, where he would spend most of his life. Barzun settled at Columbia University, from which he received a bachelor of arts degree in 1927, a master of arts degree in 1928, and a doctorate in 1932—the same year he published his first book, *The French Race* (1932). He taught history at Columbia from 1929 to 1975, earning distinction as the Seth Low Professor of History and University Professor of History. Barzun also served as an administrator at Columbia, holding the positions of dean of graduate faculties from 1955 through 1958 and dean of faculties and provost from 1958 to 1967. With his colleagues at Columbia (including Lionel Trilling), Barzun reshaped and expanded the humanities curriculum. His strong belief in the efficacy of the traditional teacher-student relationship positively influenced several generations of students. Barzun joined the board of editors for *Encyclopedia Britannica* in 1962 and was a member of the board of directors for the Macmillan publishing house from 1965 until 1975. He then became a literary advisor at the Charles Scribner's Sons publishing company from 1975 to 1993. Barzun married Mariana Lowell in 1936; the couple had three children. Following Mariana's death in 1979, Barzun married Marguerite Davenport in 1980. Barzun has received many awards, including the prestigious French Legion of Honor and the Silver Medal of the Royal Society of Arts (1972). In honor of his high scholarly achievement, Barzun received the Gold Medal for Belles Lettres and Criticism from the American Academy and Institute of Arts and Letters in 1987.

MAJOR WORKS

Though an eminent academician, Barzun has written the majority of his books not for other scholars, but for the educated public. His primary field of interest is nineteenth-century European culture, particularly Romanticism, a movement that he is credited with helping to resurrect from disrepute with *Romanticism and the Modern Ego* (1943) and *Classic, Romantic, and Modern* (1961). Throughout his career Barzun has advocated open discourse in all areas of culture, contending that when theories are accepted unquestioningly, lively inquiry into history, science, art, music, and other areas becomes stifled. Barzun's most important early works that expound these ideals include *Darwin, Marx, Wagner* (1941) and *The House of Intellect* (1959). His works published since the early 1980s—especially *A Stroll with William James* (1983), *The Culture We Deserve* (1989), *Begin Here* (1991), and most notably *From Dawn to Decadence*—continue to augment Barzun's astute cultural commentary. *A Stroll with William James,* which Barzun calls an "appreciation" rather than a biography, conveys his enthusiasm for James's originality and intellectual contributions to American thought. Moreover, the work establishes a strong argument for placing the philosopher near the top of the hierarchy of great American scholars. In Barzun's opinion, James—who coined the phrase "stream of consciousness," extolled the virtues of pragmatism, and virtually invented the discipline of psychology—could only flourish in an atmosphere where even the most universally accepted ideas were open to lively dispute.

The Culture We Deserve, a collection of twelve essays originally published between 1972 and 1989, defines culture as the enduring contributions a society passes on to posterity, made possible through the free exercise of ideas within a disciplined atmosphere. Barzun uses the essays to debunk the ideas of the so-called "grand unifiers" of history, including Karl Marx. *The Culture We Deserve* maintains that art has been shackled by the willingness of critics, the public, and artists themselves to call everything "interesting," whether or not it has artistic merit. The final chapter of *The Culture We Deserve,* titled "Toward the Twenty-First Century," outlines areas of cultural decline that Barzun believes will result through the rejection of manners and ideas that have been part the Western world's heritage for five hundred years. Though he criticizes events, acts, and beliefs antithetical to his own stance of liberal humanism, Barzun's work is not a jeremiad against events in the present day. Rather, he views current cultural upheaval as the dawning of an age as momentous as the Renaissance.

An Essay on French Verse (1991)—addressed to readers of English poetry—explains the rules of French prosody and then, beginning with the eleventh-century epic *La Chanson de Roland,* demonstrates how each century brought changes in the forms of French poetry. Barzun has also written about music as an integral component of cultural history, notably in *Berlioz and the Romantic Century* (1950), which combines two of his favorite topics—Romanticism and the nineteenth-century French composer Hector Berlioz. *Begin Here* builds on arguments made in Barzun's earlier *The American University,* in which he discusses the importance of reevaluating the tenure tradition and the damage that the "publish or perish" mentality has done not only to the university but also to scholarship as a whole. Barzun skewers the "new math" and "whole" language movements, insisting that they are responsible for turning out millions of functionally illiterate students in the United States. He also maintains that "education" (a term that he eschews) is not synonymous with teaching and learning; rather, it is an accrual of intellectual experiences over a lifetime.

From Dawn to Decadence, written nearly sixty years into his scholarly career, is a synthesis of Barzun's thoughts about the past five hundred years of Western civilization. Barzun uses the term "decadence" to refer to the dissolution of established thought and tradition occasioned by the full societal integration of ideas that were once new but have become stagnant. For example, he contends that the movement in the United States to "reinvent government" is a signal that representative political systems as we know them no longer meet the needs of the culture. *From Dawn to Decadence* dates the modern era from the Protestant Reformation and notes four great revolutions that have shaped the modern world—the religious, the monarchical, the liberal, and the social. At the end of the book, Barzun despairs that the Western canon will not be transmitted to future generations; in fact, he believes the transmission has already largely ceased. Barzun's deep concern over

education—including the subjects taught and the process and purpose of teaching itself—extends back to his earliest work, including *The Teacher in America* (1945) and *The Tyranny of Idealism in Education* (1959). Barzun has also authored several works on such diverse subjects as Abraham Lincoln, crime detection, and rhetoric and research methods. *The Modern Researcher* (1957), which Barzun co-edited with Henry F. Graff, appeared in a fifth edition in 1992 and remains a respected introduction to the study of history.

CRITICAL RECEPTION

Barzun's erudite prose has held a well-regarded place in American letters for more than sixty years, occasionally sparking controversy but always inspiring respect. Reviewers have greatly admired his skill at structuring rhetorical arguments—he makes a general statement and then supports it with copious and well-reasoned specifics so the concept under discussion can be seen clearly or implemented unambiguously. Barzun's *From Dawn to Decadence* was widely praised as the climax of his literary career. Although some critics object to his low opinion of twentieth-century Western culture after the First World War, most reviewers comment favorably on Barzun's insights and the illuminating anecdotes in the work. In this and other volumes such as *A Stroll with William James,* Barzun is credited with bringing his subjects to life in a rich tapestry of serious learning and reflection. Critics have posited that with his scholarly roots buried so deeply in the nineteenth century, Barzun's opinions are often old-fashioned or dated. However, other reviewers have applauded Barzun for dismissing the theoretical approaches of deconstruction, postmodernism, and narrow academic preoccupations with race, class, and gender, and instead favoring well-structured, detached narrative histories that speak to the larger public. Despite his conservative view of education and culture, Barzun is regarded by many as a judicious critic whose common sense and broad-mindedness enable him to argue forcefully in defense of classical curricula and higher standards—in *The American University, The Culture We Deserve,* and *Begin Here,* for example—without appearing shrill. An honored elder statesman of American letters, Barzun continues to garner esteem for his lifelong commitment to scholarship and learning.

PRINCIPAL WORKS

The French Race: Theories of Its Origins and Their Social and Political Implications Prior to the Revolution (nonfiction) 1932

Race: A Study in Modern Superstition (nonfiction) 1937

Of Human Freedom (nonfiction) 1939

Darwin, Marx, Wagner: Critique of a Heritage (nonfiction) 1941

Romanticism and the Modern Ego (nonfiction) 1943

The Teacher in America [published in England as *We Who Teach*, 1946] (nonfiction) 1945

Berlioz and the Romantic Century [republished as *Berlioz and His Century: An Introduction to the Age of Romanticism*] (nonfiction) 1950

Pleasures of Music: A Reader's Choice of Great Writing About Music and Musicians from Cellini to Bernard Shaw [editor] (nonfiction) 1951

God's Country and Mine: A Declaration of Love Spiced with a Few Harsh Words (nonfiction) 1954

Music in American Life (nonfiction) 1956

The Energies of Art: Studies of Authors Classic and Modern (nonfiction) 1956

The Modern Researcher [with Henry F. Graff] (nonfiction) 1957

Lincoln, the Literary Genius (nonfiction) 1959

The House of Intellect (nonfiction) 1959

The Tyranny of Idealism in Education (nonfiction) 1959

Classic, Romantic, and Modern (nonfiction) 1961

The Delights of Detection [editor] (fiction) 1961

Science: The Glorious Entertainment (nonfiction) 1964

The American University: How It Runs, Where It Is Going (nonfiction) 1968

On Writing, Editing, and Publishing: Essays Explicative and Hortatory (essays) 1971

A Catalogue of Crime [with Wendell Hertig Taylor] (nonfiction) 1971

The Use and Abuse of Art (nonfiction) 1974

Clio and the Doctors: Psycho-History, Quanto-History, and History (nonfiction) 1974

Simple and Direct: A Rhetoric for Writers (nonfiction) 1975

Book of Prefaces to Fifty Classics of Crime Fiction, 1900-1950 [with Wendell Hertig Taylor] (nonfiction) 1976

Critical Questions on Music and Letters, Culture and Biography, 1940-1980 [edited by Bea Friedland] (nonfiction) 1982

Lincoln's Philosophic Vision (nonfiction) 1982

Classic Short Stories of Crime and Detection [editor, with Wendell Hertig Taylor] (short stories) 1983

A Stroll with William James (nonfiction) 1983

A Word or Two Before You Go . . . (essays) 1986

Scholarship Today: The Humanities and Social Sciences [with Jaroslav Pelikan and John Hope Franklin] (nonfiction) 1987

The Culture We Deserve: A Critique of Disenlightenment [edited by Arthur Krystal] (nonfiction) 1989

Begin Here: The Forgotten Conditions of Teaching and Learning [edited by Morris Philipson] (nonfiction) 1991

An Essay on French Verse: For Readers of English Poetry (criticism) 1991

From Dawn to Decadence: 500 Years of Western Cultural Life, 1500 to the Present (nonfiction) 2000

CRITICISM

Richard Rorty (review date 9 May 1983)

SOURCE: "The Pragmatist," in *New Republic*, May 9, 1983, pp. 32-4.

[*In the following review of* A Stroll with William James, *Rorty discusses contradictions in James's philosophical positions and Barzun's inability to reconcile such fundamental oppositions.*]

Everybody who reads William James's letters falls in love with the man. He seems the companion nobody ever had: the one who never gets depressed or angry or bored, is always honest and open, always thinks you interesting. Somehow James, in his early thirties, managed to shuck off all his neuroses, all those fantasies that lead the rest of us to distort and manipulate other people for our own self-protection. After frightening bouts of melancholia during his twenties, accompanied by an inability to harness his own energies, suddenly he changes into Whitehead's "adorable genius"—fluent, focused, and indefatigable. Barzun once asked Whitehead what he had meant by that much-quoted phrase. Whitehead replied, "Greatness with simplicity; I mean by greatness the absence of smallness in *any* respect." This sort of greatness brought its reward. James seems to have spent the rest of his life, as Barzun says, "among a perfect galaxy of long, unbroken friendships." Even his marriage was happy; even his children liked him. His letter to his dying father is the one everyone wishes he or she had had, or will have, the charity and the courage to write. The lifelong pleasure he and his brother Henry took in one another (*pace* Leon Edel) seems little short of a miracle.

Sheer envy of such a life has helped make frequent the sneer, cited by Barzun, that James "was greater as a man than as a philosopher." Barzun argues [in ***A Stroll with William James***] that he was about as great as a philosopher gets. What Barzun likes best is James's "radical empiricism"—the insistence, which runs from *The Principles of Psychology* through *Varieties of Religious Experience,* that experience reveals more than natural science knows. For Barzun, James's great virtue is his resistance to "reductionism"—the claim, common to T.H. Huxley in James's day and to B.F. Skinner in ours, that everything ought to be made as "scientific" as possible. Barzun rightly says that such attempts dehumanize and distort science along with everything else. He places James, very helpfully, against the background of the various movements of the 1890s that spoke for art against science, for "life" against mechanism. He associates James with Nietzsche and Shaw as well as with Bergson and Whitehead. He thinks that much that has happened since James's day has reinforced James's attempt to put science in its place, to resist what Whitehead called "the fallacy of misplaced concreteness." This is the fallacy of thinking that the vocabulary of the natural sciences is somehow in closer touch with reality than the vocabulary of poetry, mystical theology, or common sense.

The trouble with this defense of James, however, is that it is ambiguous between two philosophical positions, just as James's own writings were ambiguous. The first position says that the whole notion of "being in touch with reality" is silly. Truth is not "correspondence with reality," it is simply the property of beliefs that work. The virtue of a vocabulary is not its ability to represent reality accurately, but rather its ability to get us what we want. This is the position James called "pragmatism." The second position—"radical empiricism"—says that some vocabularies are deeper, truer to "experience" than others, and that the vocabulary of the physical sciences is a lot less deep than some others. James said that pragmatism and radical empiricism were independent theses, but he did not see that they point in opposite directions. The reason James's reputation as a philosopher has suffered is not, as Barzun says, the persistence of "the Idealist tradition." Rather it is that, as the century has worn on, philosophical opposition to scientism has taken the form of opposition to any form of metaphysics—physicalistic, vitalist, idealist, or whatever. The radical empiricist side of James, the line of thought he shared with Bergson and Whitehead, began to look less attractive, because it seemed a futile attempt to beat science at its own game, to find a way of speaking that more accurately represented how things were than did physics. For Heidegger, for example, scientism came to seem merely one variant of the true enemy, which was the metaphysical urge itself. Process philosophy seemed merely scientism turned on its head. From another angle, Wittgenstein challenged the idea that there was anything called "experience" to express—anything that mediated between our vocabularies and the referents of those vocabularies. For the later Wittgenstein, equations and emotional states are equally concrete or equally abstract, and so the concrete-abstract distinction loses its point.

The pragmatist side of James can be quoted in support of this Wittgensteinian view, but the radical empiricist side is full of Bergsonian nostalgia for the rich, whooshy, sensuous flux we bathed in before conceptual thought started to dry us out. If one wants to defend James as a philosopher, one has either to rehabilitate the metaphysical urge—the urge to get in direct contact with something called "reality" or "experience"—or else drop the radical empiricism and stick to the pragmatism. Barzun gives a sympathetic account of James's pragmatism—defending it yet again against the hackneyed charge that it is an apology for American hucksterism—but he does not see how deeply it cuts. He still takes seriously the sort of philosophical problem pragmatism is supposed to dissolve, as when he says that "the mystery remains why concepts and their equations happen to fit observed relations among things." This remains a mystery only on a correspondence theory of truth.

James wanted to defend his father's right to be a Swedenborgian as on all fours with Huxley's right to be an agnos-

tic, but his treatment of religion is as ambiguous as the rest of his thought. Sometimes, as in certain parts of "The Will to Believe" (an essay that is not really as "simple, straightforward and carefully qualified" as Barzun says it is), he claims that belief in God is a live and forced option. Elsewhere he suggests that belief in God cashes out as the adoption of a certain moral attitude (e.g., willingness to take "moral holidays"). Sometimes, as Barzun says, he seems to sidestep the need for fideism by appealing to "the perfectly natural experience of 'spirit,'" where "spirit" describes "a quality perceived as other than physical or strictly intellectual." At other times he eschews appeals to "perceived qualities of experience" and treats the physical-spiritual distinction as a misleadingly metaphysical way of expressing a difference between styles of life. Philosophers who try to teach "The Will to Believe" together with *Pragmatism* are always asked by their students to resolve these ambiguities, but there is no easy way to do so. When James is disparaged as a philosopher, it is mostly by philosophers who have realized that he can be quoted to excellent effect on both sides of many of the issues he discusses.

There are, however, philosophical virtues other than consistency and argumentative rigor. Neither Nietzsche nor James were strong in either respect, but they were the most original philosophers of their time, and the ones of whom we can still make the most use. Of the two, James was the less obsessive and the more generous, Nietzsche the more powerful and more resentful. Neither could quite make up his mind whether to offer a new metaphysics or to abjure metaphysics, but such waffling does not greatly matter. Between the two of them, they sketched out the possibility of a freer, more romantic, more playful, form of philosophical life—a possibility that our century is still exploring.

Barzun's book is, as its title suggests, an appreciation rather than a biography, a philosophical analysis, or a commentary. Sometimes, when Barzun finds just the right turn of phrase to express James's attitude on a certain issue, it is splendidly illuminating. At other times, when Barzun turns away from James to take pot shots at contemporary intellectual fashions that he despises, it loses focus. But Barzun is the sort of person James liked to stroll with. Of the dozens of books about him that have appeared in the last seventy years, James might have liked this one the best.

Michael Kellogg (review date 7 October 1983)

SOURCE: "Home-grown, Full-bodied Philosophy," in *Commonweal*, October 7, 1983, pp. 541-2.

[*In the following review of* A Stroll with William James, *Kellogg concludes that Barzun's enthusiasm and erudition inspires renewed respect for James, though Barzun's "wide-ranging" digressions cause his book to lack focus.*]

"American philosopher," like "English wine," is close to a contradiction in terms. Despite the label, one expects little more than a watered-down import. All the more reason, then, to cherish those few products, like the philosophical writings of William James, that are both home-grown and full-bodied. Unfortunately, James, who died in 1910, is still known largely for his pioneering work in psychology. His philosophical writings, despite their range, subtlety, and concreteness, are little read, even by academics.

This neglect is due in part to the unfortunate label with which he saddled his thought. "Pragmatism" seems to imply in the crudest sense that what works is good and true. As Professor Barzun puts it [in **A Stroll with William James**] "James and Pragmatism have been branded as typically American, a mind and a doctrine to be expected from a nation of hucksters."

A deeper reason for the oversight, however, lies precisely in James's virtue of concreteness. He had an artist's love for the jumbled details of life and refused to take refuge in generalities that would "house and hide the chaos." As a consequence, he left no set of easily digestible doctrines upon which students and scholars alike could feast. In fact, his most persistent theme is the need to resist the tyranny of abstract thought.

Such a refrain may sound curious when intoned by a philosopher. Abstractions, senseless or not, are his stock in trade and, as the saying goes, "It's a poor carpenter who criticizes his tools." But James's point is simply that, as we move from one level of generality to a higher one, we must ensure that no details crucial to the point at hand are left behind. Abstractions are not eschewed, merely refined and used with care. Hence, James's writings overflow with illustrations and qualifying examples. What he says of *The Principles of Psychology* could be applied to any of his works: "There is no closed system in this book." James is open to all that experience has to teach us.

This concreteness makes James a delight to read, but difficult to teach. Hence the neglect. Students read what professors assign. Professors assign what they can summarize and impart in a lecture. James is simply too untidy to be packaged so. (I fear my own experience is indicative. In six years of a steady and eclectic diet of philosophy courses at two universities, nothing by William James was ever assigned reading.)

Jacques Barzun's new book may go some way toward curbing this waste. Through half a century of reading and meditating upon James, his enthusiasm for the nuances and refinements is undiminished. More important, he has the gift of imparting that enthusiasm. Professor Barzun makes one burn to read William James.

The book is aptly titled. There is no hint of the scholar's forced march or the biographer's field trip. We are introduced to James as to an intimate friend of the author's, and the conversation is lively and wide-ranging. Too wide-ranging, perhaps. In keeping with the stroll motif, Barzun loves to wander off, applying Jamesian ideas and insights to contemporary issues. He decries the lack of concreteness in modern discourse and the prevalence of colorless psycho-biographies. He discusses the death penalty, current research on the inheritance of acquired characteristics (a neo-Lamarckian doctrine to which James, Freud, and Nietzsche subscribed), and the deplorable state of our schools.

Professor Barzun has opinions on everything and expresses them regardless of any real or imagined connection with James. Yet the book merits the persistence it requires. Despite the digressions, Barzun manages to convey not only the richness of James's writings on psychology and philosophy, but also their unifying theme: man's creative role in fashioning truth.

James coined the phrase "stream of consciousness" to capture the flowing, variable nature of experience. He was reacting against British empiricism, which taught that the mind is merely a collection of ideas that passively mirror objects. James thought this static conception missed the crucial step wherein the mind imposes order on the flux of creating concepts. Objects are not merely presented to the mind for labeling. We, in effect, "create" the objects by settling upon a particular scheme of concepts. In other words, concepts are not predetermined by experience. Rather, they are creatively imposed on experience as "the mind's act of self-defense against universal drift and decay."

James's theory of truth is tied to this psychological insight. Truth resides in the creative interplay of autonomous concepts and given experience. Truth is what works in the sense that true propositions constitute a workable ordering of experience. They permit us to cope with the flux.

This neo-Kantian theory of truth informs James's thought on every topic, including ethics, aesthetics, and religion. With it, he continually avoids both the dominant idealism of his day (which treated concepts as themselves objects) and the logical positivism that followed him (treating concepts as strictly reducible to bundles of experiences). He also anticipates Wittgenstein's work on language and T.S. Kuhn's on the philosophy of science by half a century.

Professor Barzun's book is frustrating in many respects. It cries out for judicious trimming and a more orderly presentation. But it still conveys a profound understanding of all aspects of James's thought. And it stakes out, in convincing fashion, James's claim to greatness and originality as an American philosopher.

Alfred Kazin (review date 10 November 1983)

SOURCE: "The Exceptional William James," in *New York Review of Books,* November 10, 1983, pp. 3-4, 6.

[*In the following review of* A Stroll with William James, *Kazin discusses the development and distinctive qualities of James's philosophical thought.*]

William James, dead these seventy-three years, is a living and much-cherished figure to Jacques Barzun, whose sparkling appreciation [in *A Stroll with William James*] honors his "mentor," a man and thinker without a describable lapse who "knows better than anyone else the material and spiritual country I am traveling through." Unlike all other philosophers Barzun likes to "read in," James's

> ideas, his words, his temperament speak to me with intimacy as well as force. Communication is direct; . . . he "does me good." I find him visibly and testably right—right in intuition, range of considerations, sequence of reasons, and fully rounded power of expression. He is for me the most inclusive mind I can listen to, the most concrete and the least hampered by trifles.

Barzun does not have to say that his love and homage owe much to one overriding fact. William James is a figure impossible to imagine in contemporary America. With James as his herald and shield, Barzun makes a point of this whenever he comes anywhere near today's "half-educated" citizens, our age that "cries out for all the freedoms," our "politics, which after all is only hasty management under stress." He notes with pursed lips that nowadays "*all* deficiencies from idleness to cheating invite interested care—so much, that none is left to bestow on those who perversely perform and stay out of trouble."

One can see why Barzun has taken this "stroll" not only with William James but out of the hateful 1960s—and 1970s and 1980s—into the nineteenth-century Cambridge where the stroll begins. The most memorable chapter in his book, stirring in its way as Freud's account of the stroll with James in 1909, when James asked Freud to walk on ahead while he lay on the ground recovering from an angina attack, is Barzun's account of the founding of modernism in the cultural rebellion of the 1890s. James appears here as a modernist with the élan of Barzun's other culture heroes Shaw and Nietzsche. But, Barzun goes on to lament, modernism, so often mistakenly relegated to the 1920s, was (as we can see now) done in by World War I.

Whether or not James was a "modernist," he is certainly not our contemporary. Years ago I started collecting reminiscences of James by his last surviving Harvard students, old neighbors in Cambridge, auditors at Columbia and Stanford. What most stood out in the memories of these very old people was James's dependable unconventionality, his freshness and love of novelty in all things. Even in 1890 and 1904 he had nothing in common with "the age." The iconoclastic educator and libertarian Alexander Meiklejohn, a man always in trouble with authority and the established, remembered with astonishment James (in the frock coat of the period) lecturing at Teachers College while perched on the edge of the stage.

Without seeming unworldly, James appeared to family, friends, and even detractors (such as Santayana) wholly removed from the commonplaces of society, the pettiness of academe, the grasping, at another's expense, which

James in a famous letter to H.G. Wells called "the bitch goddess." I shall later argue, in discussing James's subjective and salvational use of religion, that he was indeed unworldly. In any event, as Barzun proudly demonstrates, he was unlike anyone else. A famous philosopher whose academic degree was an MD, a founder of modern laboratory psychology who confessed that the first lecture he heard in psychology was the first lecture he himself gave, a clinician of the "varieties of religious experience" whom ridicule could not swerve from psychic research, a founder of the minuscule, powerless Anti-Imperialist League after the US crushed the Filipino insurrection, a scornful opponent of the "strenuous life" exhorted by his sometime student Theodore Roosevelt, William James was in no way a conventional American, a conventional professor, or even the typical humanitarian liberal in New England who replaced the man of faith.

He was above all—a favorite point with Barzun—not a "pragmatist" in the "practical" style supposed to be an American habit and ideal. Quite apart from being one of the great American writers—even in the formal argument of philosophy—and leaving behind him a body of superlative letters (the inexhaustible vividness of his personality turns these into one of the great autobiographies), James was a naturalist who argued against positivism, a psychologist who called psychology "trivial," a philosopher whose most famous works were given as popular lectures, a passionate defender of any man's "will to believe" who never for a moment testified to an existent God. What he said of his brother Henry can begin to explain William himself. "He is a native of the James family, and has no other country."

Although Bernard Shaw is another of Barzun's heroes, it is surprising that he does not cite Shaw's admiration for the genius of Henry James, Sr. With his usual Irish bravado, Shaw proclaimed this son of an Irish Protestant greater than his famous sons. Although only William and Henry matched and enlarged their father's intellectual vitality, even the untalented were aware of the family as exceptional, which may be why the two youngest sons, "Wilky" and "Bob," and the lone girl, Alice, suffered so much—not least from condescension by William and Henry. When the Civil War came, the father easily sent off his nongenius sons; he was neither sorry nor surprised to hear from William and Henry that they were not fit to fight.

The "James country" was made possible by the private wealth passed on by the first William, the Irish immigrant; the spasmodic schooling in several European countries and America; the elder James's contempt for commerce; the despotic, perhaps unbearable, love that the crippled father, always at home, imposed on children who could escape him only in Europe. The father's intellectual vehemence, oddly mixed with his innocent removal from worldly cares, left its stamp on future generations. Not long before his death just a few years ago, "Billy" James, the philosopher's charming son, rose at a family party to tell the guests: "Alice and I have decided to accept the twentieth century." (It was like the Jameses for the philosopher to have a sister and a wife named Alice, and to have a son William who married an Alice.)

I am sure that wonderfully clever and sophisticated as William James was, *he* never quite accepted "modern times" despite his pioneering as a laboratory psychologist and his founding of "pragmatism." Barzun finds this removal lovable and infinitely valuable, and it is. Barzun's homage is ultimately directed to James's pluralism in every sense, his detestation of system making, of "bigness" in every form. He especially prizes James's ability to indicate the actual movement within his thought, his genius for locating the concrete and the particular. These are literary proficiencies, as well as a "lifelike" inclination, on every philosophical issue, to show ideas *becoming* truths as a validation of every corner we turn in experience. James's psychology was most unlike the psychologies that dominate our age in its gift of conviction. Our *ideas,* in his view, are our values, our values our real personality. To the extent that we know our values, we are human; to the extent that we live them, we are free.

This, by current notions, is nonsense, unrealistic, and certainly "elitist." James recognized that only a few people could possibly share his values in the style, the complete psychic sense, in which he literally embodied them. These few were likely to be the "sick souls," the intellectual saints, whose personal crises and conversion to the faith they had long resisted he sympathetically reported in *The Varieties of Religious Experience.* He was so much in tune with the "sick" that he slipped in an account of his own nervous breakdown as reported by a "French correspondent."

To believe that values—active, unresting, insatiable—are one's personality, that such values, no matter where and how learned, are the genesis of behavior and relationships, is to accept and to endure personality that is antinomian, "religious," necessarily solitary. Alfred North Whitehead said at Harvard in the 1920s that religion is what we do with our solitariness. If James had lived to hear that, he would have linked "solitariness" positively with the state of being "exceptional" that the Jameses saw as their role, their mission, their fate. Henry James in a remarkable letter near the end of his life said that loneliness was the starting point of all his work and the harbor to which it returned. Alice James, who had a more acute mind than her unfortunate younger brothers, accepted a terrible life racked with illness only when she began her now famous diary. She became happy when she developed cancer; only the proximity of death provided her with occasion for metaphysics:

> It is the most supremely interesting moment in life, the only one in fact when living seems life. . . . It is as simple in one's own person as any fact of nature . . . and I have a delicious consciousness, ever present, of wide spaces close at hand, and whisperings of release in the air.

William, learning of her terminal illness, wrote her that

> . . . life and death seem singularly close together in all of us—and life a mere farce of frustration in all, so far as the realization of the innermost ideals go to which we are made respectively capable of feeling an affinity and responding. . . . Father would find in me today a much more receptive listener. . . .

"Father" explains some of William's propensities, not what the children wearily called "Father's ideas." The ideas are in fact now unrecoverable. The elder James was preoccupied with tracing his liberation from the omniscient God-tyrant of Calvinism into his personal transaction with Swedenborg's "spiritual worlds" which exist only *through* us. His throbbing, teeming, overcrowded, altogether personal theology records a private journey that he never completed in a conception of God himself; he was too busy itemizing every step of the way. William Dean Howells said in a review, "Mr. James has written a book called *The Secret of Swedenborg* and has kept it."

William, born into a positivist age, trained in medicine, a naturalist on Agassiz's scientific expedition to Brazil, could not have copied "Father's ideas"; like his own to the very end of his life, they were provisional, personal, a way to keep oneself going "in the battle of life." What his father had, as William was to have it overwhelmingly, was temperament, the energetic sense of his own abysmal want. In *Society the Redeemed Form of Man,* the elder James described how in England in 1844, lingering at the dinner table, "suddenly, and for no apparent reason, his composure abruptly abandoned him and he found himself face to face with an invisible terror." He was redeemed by learning from Swedenborg that a person lost to himself can be reborn in his "Divine Natural Humanity." The incorporation of God in man, Swedenborg explained, is the sole purpose and destiny of creation. James, Sr., was to fuse this with the Fourierist deliverance of man in society. None of these projections is as vivid as the elder James's sense of his suffering, his liberation from other people's God:

> . . . imagine a subject of some petty despotism condemned to die, and with—what more and worse—a sentiment of death pervading all his consciousness, lifted by a sudden miracle into felt harmony with universal man, and filled to the brim with the sentiment of indestructible life instead, and you will have a true picture of my emancipated condition.

William was to credit his recovery from depression to his belief that he could prove the freedom of the will by exercising his freedom. The father attested—cloudily—to the divine partnership, the son to the freedom we actually use. Different idols of the mind, but this ability to transpose absolute depression and intellectual recovery, bondage and freedom in the religious sense, seems almost hereditary.

The gift of "perspectivism," as Barzun calls it, was William's genius for locating the unexpected in any context. He scintillated in the art of transposition. It explains why his life and career are so fortifying, for his way of thinking is that of a man arguing himself out of one difficulty after another. James said that the "axis of reality" runs through our personal lives and nowhere else. "Our civilization is founded on the shambles, and every individual existence goes out in a lonely spasm of helpless agony. If you protest, my friend, wait till you arrive there yourself!" But terror forces salvation upon us—a salvation found in "accumulated acts of thought," not maxims, that should win the external unfriendly universe to ourselves. Publicly—James functioned more through popular lectures than any other first-class American intellectual except Emerson—he told his relatively innocent and provincial contemporaries that everything was working out. What runs through his letters is his admission that his own battle had to be won over and over again.

Barzun's James is equable on all occasions, too merely intelligent to have had such a desperate want as James repeatedly acknowledged. Barzun himself is of course too intelligent and informed to ignore James's inner despairs. But I don't think Barzun's condescension to the uprooted, ill-educated, morally abandoned people in our society prepares him to appreciate James's interest in the abnormal and the marginal as clues to all that is hidden and perhaps universal. James the physician was certainly "motivated" to heal himself. His seeking of another's reality makes his letters wonderful in their loving playfulness—and candor. In finding himself over and over again in others, he recalled the extraordinary relationship that his father tried to find with God. William was a primary naturalist of souls, Henry the master novelist of interlocked personalities.

As Barzun admiringly notes, only William James, staring at an octopus in an English aquarium, would have remarked on such "flexible intensity of life in a form so inaccessible to our sympathy." Only this talent for the unexpected, for seizing upon any moment as an "occasion" of truth, explains his critical need to realize oneself in *acts* of thought. The real meaning of pragmatism is surely this freedom of the overburdened consciousness to make itself actual. But while pragmatism is not "practical" in the common sense, it does give us a sense of thought as necessarily and perhaps inherently provisional. And since we live in a world more and more closed off from what used to be called the "moral sciences"—the physical sciences alone now suggest the infinity within which we live—I do not see in James what Barzun does: an example we can follow, a guide beyond compare.

James was a phenomenon, not a model; an astonishing exception to everything we know, not—despite a lifetime of teaching—someone whose teaching can still be followed through his writing. It is his charm, his relative purity, his eloquence that win us—not a body of thought that we can turn to as we do to Nietzsche's. James in his last years, struggling with a bad heart, regretted that he had given so much of himself to lectures and articles, felt that he owed himself one big book that would explain and justify his philosophy. It is surprising to see how many of his most famous works, after the one systematic treatise of the great *Psychology,* are collections of essays and lectures. Even if he had lived to attempt it, I do not think he could have given his philosophy ultimate form, for the whole direction of his thought and its catch-as-catch-can style were against this.

Nietzsche, seemingly a counterpart to James for literary genius and a sense of himself as exceptional, also wrote more and more in personal, spasmodic form. But if the axis of reality runs through personal lives, it wholly occupied Nietzsche. What we get from Nietzsche is a counter-philosophy to Platonic-Christian stasis, a constant rebuttal of the historic illusion that the world stands upon or in any way represents a moral tradition. Nietzsche is a poet-philosopher like the pre-Socratics, one who not only locates the primordial elements as truth but identifies himself with them in the audacity of his style. For all his opposition to system building, his love of *apercu* comes across to his readers as a quest for truth, because Nietzsche cannot bear to represent to himself anything that is not truth. James is experimental, "personal" in the American way; he is forever asking the world what it can do for him and how it may save him.

Thought was indeed serious to William James just to the extent that it enabled him to save himself. Maybe it did. Nietzsche could not save himself at all. He went crazy in his thought, and in a sense fell victim to his thought: it was so much bigger and more hallowed than himself. His own sense was not the ultimate issue. He did not want to use thought, and he did not expect thought to release him from anything. Truth really existed, although Nietzsche, in this respect just another modern philosopher, could not prove this.

Louis Menand (review date 16 February 1987)

SOURCE: "Talk Talk," in *New Republic,* February 16, 1987, pp. 28-33.

[*In the following excerpt, Menand offers unfavorable assessment of* A Word or Two Before You Go.]

Jacques Barzun, former dean, provost, and university professor at Columbia, is an authority often cited by [William] Safire when he wants to throw cold water on a usage but needs someone else to look like a pedant for doing it. For where Safire fiddles, Barzun burns. His brief pieces on language, [in **A Word or Two Before You Go**] written over many years and to meet a variety of occasions, attack, but with the prescriptive and proscriptive fervor missing from the "On Language" columns, the same kind of stock villains that Safire's do—psychiatrists, sociologists, advertising copywriters—along with a few real pigeons: Esperanto, Basic English, and the advocates of phonetic spelling. But Barzun reserves a special fury for the depredations of copy editors.

Barzun's diatribe against copy editors, drawn from a longer screed he published two years ago in the *American Scholar,* is a piece of work—though it does perform the useful service of exploding the assumption that punctiliousness about language is the token of a civil nature. Like many writers, Barzun has been frustrated at times by having to undo changes made in his copy by editors who missed an allusion, or who followed some rigid requirement of house style beyond the bounds of good sense, or who sought counterproductively to improve clarity with a new word or a different phrasing. The frustrations of editing (which, he can be sure, run in both directions) are part of the business of writing for publication. This is the style of generosity in which Barzun reflects on the situation: "It is a paradox that when language at large is being roughly treated by the heedless, a set of rigid notions and worthless rules are being enforced by the unliterary and ill-educated." And he accuses copy editors of "error, confusion, arrogance, and coercion, all doing damage to style and intellectual independence."

"Perhaps nervous fiddling becomes an uncontrollable habit when one earns one's bread by striking, slashing, changing," Barzun muses. The sentence sums up exactly the social context the piece pretends does not exist. Most copy editors are young and earn perhaps a tenth of the income Barzun earns. Their job is to render uniform and unambiguous material generally written by people who make far less of a fetish of correctness than Barzun does. The task is often difficult, since it is in the nature of even the most careless writers to be wounded when their copy is changed. And it is in the nature of the business of writing that when the editor improves the story, the writer gets the credit. The notion that the people who, without prospect of greater reward, attempt to enhance that credit are really engaged in sabotage smacks of superciliousness. When Barzun writes that "current jargon and vulgarisms . . . [are] perhaps the copy editor's native tongue," he is guilty of basing a personal and social judgment on merely literary evidence. When he writes that "many an editor is determined to furnish thoughts out of her own stock to eke out the author's poor supply," he is guilty of something worse. For it is the only sentence in the entire book in which the feminine pronoun is used when the gender is unspecified.

Barzun does offer a few hints about the social vision that informs his critique of other people's usage:

> Two of the causes of decline in *all* modern European languages have been: the doctrines of linguistic "science" and the example of "experimental" art. They come together on the principle of Anything Goes—not in so many words, usually, but in unmistakable effect.

And elsewhere he attributes the decay of the language to "the poets and novelists of the last hundred years. It was they who taught us to reassign meanings to words—not occasionally but steadily—at the same time as they showed for syntax a disregard all too easy to imitate." This analysis has the advantage of all reductive generalizations: by

explaining everything, it makes more thoughtful discriminations seem supererogatory. Having identified the villain, the author feels free to spend the rest of the time railing at the victims.

The obvious difficulty with Barzun's larger picture is one that often undermines prescriptive talk about talk: If language abuse is simply the outer sign of some profound social disease, why should we waste time curing the symptom? But in fact writers like Barzun do have a reason for naming and rooting out language deviants. It is to identify those members of the group who are not to be trusted in the larger matter of curing the disease. If this is so, then surely we have a right to turn the tables. Should we trust someone who writes, as Barzun does in his final essay, "On the Necessity of a Common Tongue," that blacks are among the groups in our society who "speak . . . English unwillingly or with difficulty"? The characterization reveals a sensibility of astonishing impercipience. What does Barzun think American blacks are speaking—African?

Michael Dirda (review date 16 July 1989)

SOURCE: "The Battle of the Books," in *Washington Post Book World,* July 16, 1989, p. 5.

[*In the following excerpt, Dirda discusses Barzun's disillusionment and contempt for contemporary culture in* The Culture We Deserve.]

Books, like marriages, are rewarding in direct proportion to the passion we put into them. A critic like Roland Barthes could get more out of a half-baked Balzac novel than most of us will get out of a lifetime studying *Madame Bovary.* Better enthrallment to an adventure story than a bored skim through a masterpiece.

Still, for more than a hundred years humanists such as Matthew Arnold, Irving Babbitt, T.S. Eliot and Russell Kirk have called for a focused canon of works as a means of preserving or reestablishing a common culture. Each has spoken eloquently for the traditional, as do Jacques Barzun, Peter Shaw and Robert Proctor now, but all of them betray the desperation of men fighting for a lost cause.

Barzun's *The Culture We Deserve* is the most dispassionate of these three recent cultural critiques, though his tone betrays a magisterial sadness: He looks out on the world and sees only darkness. Fragmentation, the analytical method, overproduction, specialization and permissiveness have wrecked civilization.

His well-crafted essays—from various periodicals—elaborate these old-fashioned, rather familiar views. The cult of the analytical leads to sterility and narrowness; in its place Barzun exalts Pascal's *esprit de finesse,* or "intuitive understanding," which "seizes upon the character of the whole altogether, by inspection." Modern scholarship's canons and terminology, wryly notes this distinguished historian, "stimulate ingenuity and foster disputation, which together give a pleasant sense of mastery and comradeship, whereas original intuition is solitary and unsure." Shoptalk has driven out conversation "which is the principle of the good society and the good life." Ours is a world of know-how rather than cultivation.

According to Barzun, we can even have too much of a good thing: "Great works too often seen or performed, too readily available in bits and pieces, become objects of consumption instead of objects of contemplation." At the same time, in fiction and history we have turned away from plot and narrative, preferring "states of mind . . . , strange detail, analytic depth." And we have consequently lost the true benefits of reading history:

"It exercises the imagination and furnishes it, discloses the nuances of the familiar within the unfamiliar, brings out the heroic in mankind side by side with the vile, tempers absolute partisanship by showing how few monsters of error there have been, and in all these ways induces a relative serenity."

Barzun needs that serenity. For the most part, he doesn't see any solution to our resulting "decay of public hope"; we will simply have to weather this period of alexandrianism and trust that a renaissance and not a dark age is in the offing.

Edmund Fuller (review date Spring 1990)

SOURCE: "Exeunt the Humanities?" in *Sewanee Review,* Vol. XCVIII, No. 2, Spring, 1990, pp. xxxviii, xl-xli.

[*In the following review, Fuller offers a positive assessment of Barzun's "provocative, challenging, and occasionally startling assertions" in* The Culture We Deserve.]

"Right now . . . one can ask whether all over the world the idea of a university has not been battered beyond hope of recovery for a long time."

Those blunt words were not written by an outsider hostile to universities, or by an ideological disrupter from within, but by a man of impeccable credentials for appraising what passes currently as higher education. Their author is Jacques Barzun who, in his long association with Columbia University, has worn the titles of Seth Low professor of history, dean of faculties, and provost. He is also an extraordinary fellow at Churchill College, Cambridge.

If you seek a model of the classically educated, broadly cultured man, in this time when there is a dearth of such attributes, you cannot find a better than Professor Barzun, though happily he is not without peers. He was born in France but has lived in the United States since he was thirteen years old. He is now over eighty. His writings have dealt with history, literature, language, music, art, and

manners. Of his many books two of the finest are *Teacher in America* (1945) and *The House of Intellect* (1959).

To the list now is added *The Culture We Deserve,* a selection of twelve essays from various periodicals. One was written in 1972, but the others all derive from the 80s. A few have been revised and renamed since their first appearance. Their range over a variety of cultural subjects fully justifies the book's collective title.

Rather than attempt a short summary of the densely packed thoughts in these essays, I will interweave a sampling of Barzun's most provocative, challenging, occasionally startling assertions without always designating the specific essays from which they are culled. Tracking them down will be one of the pleasures for readers of the slender book. The seeming randomness of this method also will demonstrate the unity of theme that underlies the approaches to various aspects of it: they overlap, or interlock, as you prefer.

Mr. Barzun has a gift for terse vivid images. Decrying the vogue for introducing the currently topical into college curricula, he says: "As things stand now, the new is brought on campus and dissected before the body has time to cool."

Apropos the current vogue for Marxist analysis, in American universities with a boundless appetite for discredited notions, he sums up the spirit "which informs the literature of Marx and his disciples, the spirit of exposure and revelation, the animus of a war against appearances, the search for a reality made up of conspirators and their victims."

Under the heading "Where is History Now?" he examines the latest quests for a "scientific" history, as initiated in France by the *"Annales* group" who have turned from narrative history of great events, and of men and women who have influenced them, to statistical scrutiny of, say, the rural economy of a French province at the time of the revolution. The resulting product, still in fashion in many quarters, is what Barzun calls not history but "retrospective sociology."

"Exeunt the Humanities" reminds us of an almost forgotten aspect of Woodrow Wilson, not as president of the U.S., but as eminent historian and as president of Princeton University. Wilson called it the "business of a college to re-generalize each generation," to strive for "a general orientation, the creation in the mind of a vision of the field of knowledge . . . the development of a power of comprehension."

The most challenging of Barzun's positions on higher education, though he is not entirely alone in holding it, is this assertion: "The very nature of the humanistic purpose excludes the elective system. The humanistically unprepared can have only hearsay opinions—or none at all—about what to elect and what to leave untouched."

Of criticism, in any field of the arts, Mr. Barzun again is blunt: "Criticism will need an injection of humility—that is, a recognition of its role as ancillary to the arts, needed only occasionally in a temporary capacity. . . . Pedantry and pretentiousness must be driven out of the republic of letters."

Shifting attention, finally, to the behavioral rather than the cultural, he is concerned about the decline of respect for basic civil authority. Today "intellectual opinion leans automatically toward the objector, supports local passion against any central authority, and denounces all sanctions." As a corollary "the odd new idea is that authority exists to ratify the decisions of its declared enemies."

With such paradoxes in the closing essay (ironically the earliest written) he looks toward the twenty-first century. Barzun, whose mood clearly is grim, makes a valiant effort to see encouraging prospects and paths toward improvement. In spite of that, his tone essentially is prophetic, not in the foretelling, but in the darker diagnostic sense of that term, in the midst of this culture we deserve.

John P. Sisk (review date Spring 1990)

SOURCE: "Culture in the Eighties," in *Salmagundi*, No. 87, Spring, 1990, pp. 360-68.

[*In the following positive review of* The Culture We Deserve, *Sisk examines the philosophical and aesthetic perspective that informs Barzun's critique of intellectual laxity, relativism, and reductionism in contemporary art and thought.*]

I began my long acquaintance with the work of Jacques Barzun in the fall of 1945 at West Palm Beach, an idyllic change from a previous assignment in the jungles of British Guiana. In the public library I found **Romanticism and the Modern Ego** and **Darwin, Marx, Wagner.** They were exactly what I needed after a four year sabbatical in the Air Force, especially since I expected to return to the classroom and teach Romanticism. In both books I found reasons to update some of my opinions about the Romantics, my reading of Paul Elmer More, Irving Babbitt and T.S. Eliot not having prepared me to see the Romantics as humane pragmatists and having left me ill-equipped to argue against those who wanted to dismiss the Romantics as escapists or inspirers of fascism.

I discovered in time that one of the pedagogically most useful features of **Romanticism and the Modern Ego** was a seventeen-page section that gave a sampling of the term "romantic" in modern usage. Here was the semantic underbrush through which the author had to work his way if he wanted to make his point that his subject was very much alive. I was happy to see that this section had remained intact when the second and revised edition appeared in 1961 as **Classic, Romantic, and Modern.** I am happy now to see that Barzun remains a champion of the

Romantics in **The Culture We Deserve,** essays written in the eighties by a man who is himself in his eighties.

Nothing is more characteristic of Barzun than his practice of clearing away the semantic underbrush as a way of getting into a subject. He does this memorably in an exchange with Donald J. Lloyd in *The American Scholar* (Spring 1951) as he opposes Lloyd's go-with-the-flow approach to usage, which makes much of the analogy between language change and inevitable natural processes. For Barzun the analogy is wrong "because language is an artificial product of social life." Then (in a remark that can take us back to his treatment of determinism in **Darwin, Marx, Wagner**) he adds this: we cannot "know what is inevitable until we have tried good and hard to stop it." But the debate with Lloyd also looks ahead thirty years to **"License to Corrupt"** in the new book. Here, after opposing the dogma that language is simply a live creature endlessly evolving about which one had best take a laissez faire attitude, Barzun launches into a brilliant seven-page answer to the question, "What is language?" Chief among his adversaries are those linguists "who urge upon the hoi polloi corruption unlimited." Unable to see that language "is a work of art, a collective work of art, a work of collective art," the corrupters are not likely to think of language as a rich estate the stewardship of which imposes a moral burden.

As one might expect, **The Culture We Deserve** opens with Barzun clearing away the common misuses of the word "culture" that make it so easy to apply it to "any chunk of social reality you like or dislike." Indeed, the book can be seen as an extended definition of "culture" just as the earlier **A Stroll with William James** can be seen as an extended definition of "pragmatism." Culture, cultivation of the self, is declining in a time of cultural glut. The causes are self-consciousness, the fragmentations of specialism, and the magical spell of science that lead to a confusion of the pedantic minutiae of "analytic methodism" with that intuitive understanding that Pascal called the *esprit de finesse*. The impulse of culture is a love that leads to communion of two kinds: "with the living, by the discovery of kindred through conversation, and with the dead, by the intimacy of admiration for greatness."

"The essence of culture," Barzun says in his introductory note to the book, "is interpenetration. From any part of it the searching eye will discover connections with another part seemingly remote." This searching eye (call it the metaphoric imagination) is everywhere at work in the essays that follow. Its opposite is the pedantic impulse that delights in a "miserlike heaping up of factual knowledge." The danger, he says in **"Exeunt the Humanities,"** is "our present combination of specialist and halfbaked humanist education" that threatens to leave us a nation of pedants. But a nation of pedants in which the natural passion for unity is not structured by the proper definitions and distinctions will be especially susceptible to grand unifiers like Spengler, Marx, and Toynbee (Isaiah Berlin in his great essay on Tolstoy called them hedgehogs) who practice what Barzun calls, in an essay so titled, "the fallacy of the single cause."

Those who have been following Barzun over the years are aware of his continuing concern with this passion for unity. In **Darwin, Marx, Wagner** (1941), for instance, this passion appears as a thirst for an invincible absolute which envisages progress in terms of one final solution. In **The House of Intellect** (1959) it is "the desire to embrace the whole world in some benevolent imperium of love, science, or art." In **Science: The Glorious Entertainment** (1964) "the cause of our pain when we examine the burden of modernity is the imposition of one intellectual purpose upon all experience." In **Clio and the Doctors** (1974) this passion is behind the claim "that 'at last' history is going to be made whole by the adjunction of the science of mind or the science of society." Barzun's sympathies, and James's as well, have all along been with romantic diversatarianism and pluralism, with Berlin's foxes rather than the single-valued hedgehogs. Not that foxes automatically escape his searching eye; he makes us aware that many an apparent fox is only a compulsive antinomian in disguise, inspired with the rage for absolute freedom that, in the concluding essay, is one of the marks of our dissolving time.

Indeed, one finds this critical alertness to the fallacy of the single cause everywhere in **The Culture We Deserve,** so that the reviewer is in a position to make a standard remark about a collection of essays: that inevitably there is a good deal of repetition in it. So there is; in fact, taking Barzun's work as a whole there is a good deal of repetition: significant themes, events, key historical figures and events, and characteristic rhetorical practices keep recurring. In other words, Barzun, like Montaigne or Pascal or Swift, tends to sound like himself wherever you pick him up. He never sounds more like himself than in a brief essay, **"The Great Switch,"** that appeared in the Summer 1989 issue of *Columbia,* the Columbia University magazine. In about a thousand words, and beginning as he so often does "with a little history," he relates the growing appeal of single-issue politics to the jumble we have made of the terms "liberal," "conservative," and "socialist." Here he is repeating his function as refiner of the language of the tribe, at the risk, of course, of offending those who prefer not to see their own single issues so historically relativized.

The problem with the term "repetition" (and the Romantics have had a hand in this) is that it has become thoroughly pejorative, as if repetition were not one of the omnipresent facts of human existence. The indiscriminate fear of repetition is a fear of life since it is a fear of the recurring processes and patterns that make life possible and intelligible. Certainly, in literature and the arts one must distinguish between a repetition that is static (see the recurrences of plot and theme in the Barbara Cartland romances, for instance) and a repetition that is dynamic and always open to revitalizing new contexts (see Shakespeare's romances, for instance). It is the hedgehogs, not the diversatarian foxes, who tend to be the static repeaters.

The fear of repetition has a good deal to do with the definition of the artist and the "glut of art" that is the subject of "A Surfeit of Art" in the new book. Deeply buried in the collective mind, says Barzun, is the nineteenth century's glorification of the artist as hero, seer, and genius. This glorification is enhanced and complicated by our own post World War II myth of the self, believed to be most authentic when it is most original, and most original when producing aesthetic objects the very originality of which is the chief criterion of value. Art thus having become a cult, having replaced religion as a means of personal salvation, the aspiring artist is morally entitled to foundation and government support, as if "the pursuit of happiness" in The Declaration of Independence clearly implied the pursuit of aesthetic self-actualization. To borrow Roger Shattuck's useful term from *The Innocent Eye,* we are in thrall to the Demon of Originality, a thralldom that has political as well as religious and aesthetic consequences.

Because art generates excitement and the life of the artist appears to be so wonderfully free, "more and more people in each generation decide that they want to be artists." The resulting glut of art "has made us into gluttons, who gorge and do not digest" and who "find everything wonderful in an absent-minded way." The merely shocking or odd is "suddenly interesting enough to gain a month's celebrity" and to reinforce a policy that tends "to reward cleverness, not art, and to put one more hurdle in the path of the truly original artist." As Barzun puts it in **"The Paradoxes of Creativity"** that appeared subsequently in the Summer 1989 *American Scholar,* "Nowadays, originality, the cult of the new, and plain shock power have such a hold on our judgement that we pay humble attention to a great deal of nonsense and charlatanism." It is safe to guess that it was no surprise to him when the National Endowment for the Arts, that current patron of creative originality, began to draw the outraged attention of people like Senator Jesse Helms because of the obscene form of some of the creative originality it was sponsoring. Certainly here was one kind of reductive and protective reaction to the glut of art that might have been predicted. Here too was another consequence of "the conversion of culture into industry," as he puts it in **"Culture High and Dry,"** where the point is made that an equally formidable glut has followed the university's emphasis on publish or perish.

These three essays are splendid examples of the extent to which a Barzun essay is grounded on and nourished by historical and quotidian particulars. The searching eye is panoramic in its reach yet always focused on the immediate project. The reader gets the impression that he is seeing only the tip of an iceberg about which vastly more could be said if the occasion of the saying were different. This marshalling of detail must not be confused with that miserlike heaping up of factual knowledge produced by "analytic methodism." Barzun is on the side of Pascal's *esprit de finesse* so that the result is a high form of entertainment: not only do you get a lot of interesting information but you get the aesthetic pleasure of seeing it gracefully and wittily controlled. This is at the same time good arguing strategy. Not that it will persuade everyone. In these post-modernist and anti-rhetorical times good writing in whatever genre is often enough suspected of being seductively escapist rather than truth-revealing simply by virtue of being good writing: doomed to being merely self-referential in proportion as it qualifies as literature.

Barzun's position with respect to such skepticism has always been clear. In **"Look it Up! Check it Out!"** he remarks that "information theory, not interested in message, but in the chances of getting its 'shape' across, tries to dominate psychology, linguistics, and anything else in which meaning still lurks untouched by abstraction." Because he has no confidence in a disjunction of message and shape, the very shape of his essays is both argument for and demonstration of the kind of pragmatic humanism he espouses. That kind of humanism is always inclined to specify the general and the abstract. When in *The Modern Researcher* (written with Henry F. Graff) the researcher-turned-writer is advised to use plain words and avoid jargon and clichés he gets a still useful list of "forbidden words." When in *Teacher in America* Barzun says that the entire faculty must cooperate in improving the decadent condition of student writing, he shows that faculty in eight very detailed pages how to be the demanding and pains-taking critics of student papers they must be if they are to have any effect. And when in *God's Country and Mine* (1954) we read: "Whoever wants to know the heart and mind of America had better learn baseball, the rules and realities of the game," we are not surprised when the generalization is supported with four pages of specifics behind which is the searching eye of a very knowledgeable fan.

With this wealth of supporting detail (see it also in the Romantics) goes the effective structuring, easiest to appreciate in the essays. I know of no better place to see these characteristics at work than in **"Thoreau the Thorough Impressionist,"** published in the Winter 1987 *American Scholar* but delivered as an address to the Thoreau Society in Concord the previous summer. Given its occasion (the anniversary of Thoreau's birth) it is a rather daring enterprise, beginning as it does by disqualifying "Civil Disobedience" and *Walden* as responsible and coherent political statements. As a political thinker Thoreau is childlike, solipsistic, prone to verbal trickery and other devices of rabblerousing. Along with his "rather conventional denunciation of the shams and hypocrisies of men in towns and in trades" goes his inability to see that he was free to live as he did "only by the bounty of a large, well-established state."

Then comes the dramatic reversal, even more effective from having been hinted at early on. Thoreau must not be praised for qualities he does not possess, but should be seen as a poet, "the earliest and greatest of American imagists" for whom inconsistency, diversity and contradiction are the true measure of his poetic experience. If we see him as the Impressionist he is, we can appreciate him for his rare "sense of the immensity of the cosmos, the minuteness of its parts, and the simultaneity of its motions."

Thus we end up not with a classic author debunked but disentangled from a reputation he does not deserve so that he can be properly valued.

In this essay Barzun is being the historical relativist, which is to say that he is "reckoning with time and place" (also the title of one of the essays). As he shows us now in the **"The Bugbear of Relativism,"** the failure to do this is largely responsible for the equation of relativism "with general looseness, with unanchored judgment and unpredictable behavior" when it should mean "the practice of *relating,* of linking." Relating and linking are, of course, what the author has promised in his introductory note, and what he has abundantly delivered. Now it is as necessary to dispose of the pejorative sense of the word as it is elsewhere necessary to dispose of an all too popular image of Thoreau. This is especially necessary since the definition of relativism he rejects can drive one into the arms of those inflexible anti-pluralists who, as the logic of the fallacy of the single cause works its way with them, are all too likely to become committed one-worlders. Against such wistful hedgehogs he quotes one of his favorite pragmatists, Cardinal Newman: "Not to know the relative disposition of things is the state of slaves or children."

At this point an unwary reader may think that Barzun is about to come down solidly on the state of a creative release from all traditional restrictions, as if he were a latter-day countercultural guru disguised as an emeritus college professor with a seductive prose style. Such a reader might be quickly and perhaps profitably disillusioned as he is asked to see the relation between a relaxing or changing of standards and the undesirable moral, social, and political side effects: the cultish irreverence, the incapacity for self-discipline, the subordination of the needs of community to individual conscience. He will be told that "Place and proportion make up the difficult relativism of fitness." When the sense of place and proportion breaks down the fundamental decencies break down too. When the spirit of "anything goes" affects the arts, the Demon of Originality walks tall in the land and "much spiritless contriving masquerades as innovation." In the meantime, linguistics in a state of liberation is loathe to recognize a right and wrong in language. Ironically, then, the spirit of "anything goes" multiplies rather than reduces absolutes, since "the partisans of the various liberations seldom adjust their demands relative to the other, conflicting social needs." Clearly, Barzun's kind of relativist will not hesitate to take a determined stand against facile conceptions of inevitable processes. It is an exhilarating yet sobering essay, one that places on us something like the burden that F. Scott Fitzgerald in his famous "Crack-Up" essay places on his first rate intelligence: the necessity of having to function while entertaining two opposing ideas.

In his introductory note Barzun refers to these eleven essays as chapters, as if whatever their original places and occasions of publication they should now be thought of as thematically interrelated parts of a single structure. This is indeed their effect as they build toward the concluding chapter, **"Toward the Twenty-First Century,"** and its concern with "the plausible signs that civilization is in decline." Here he is not competing with hedgehogs like Toynbee, Spengler, or Teilhard in the business of prediction. What we get is a judicious consideration of the futures our culture now makes it possible to contemplate. "Like representative government, like capitalism, like traditional religion," he writes, "the culture that the West has been painstakingly fashioning since Columbus has ceased to serve and satisfy." We have come to an epoch, a time of *turning,* the distinguishing marks of which confront us wherever we look: the contempt for law and order; the antinomian suspicion of all counsels of restraint that undermines the authority of morality and religion; the certainly centrifugal and potentially anarchic cult of originality; the bankruptcy of the very bourgeois values that have funded our utopian expectations; the dissolving effect in the humanities of what Paul Ricoeur has called the hermeneutics of suspicion inherited from Marx, Nietzsche, and Freud and now being exploited exuberantly by the post-structuralists; the pervasive disgust with the project of civilization among artists and intellectuals; the "Samson complex" among the young and not so young that expresses itself in a yearning "to bring down the whole edifice on one's head and the heads of its retarded upholders."

If in these conditions Barzun is no more willing than William Butler Yeats to specify what rough beast might be slouching toward Bethlehem to be born, he does offer us a pragmatist's consolation. "As long as man exists," he says, "civilization and all its works exist in germ. . . . Civilization is not identical with *our* civilization, and the rebuilding of states and cultures, now or at any time, is integral to our nature and more becoming than longing and lamentation." And the worst lamenters are those who, having lost faith in one or another inevitable process, are all too likely to be enlisted in the fallacious single cause of the next rough slouching beast that comes their way.

So having come this far with Jacques Barzun, we are in effect back strolling with his beloved William James and with the necessity of the will to believe. With the will to believe goes the tragic sense of life that led James to scorn all utopian blandishments as attempts to flinch away from the "wild element" that is a permanent feature of this world and which our natures are adapted to wrestle with. The will to believe and the tragic sense of life are in Barzun too—here as in earlier work. This is why *The Culture We Deserve* is such a bracing stroll with a critic we need, and never more than when his searching eye is most unflinching.

Virginia Quarterly Review (review date Spring 1990)

SOURCE: A review of *The Culture We Deserve,* in *Virginia Quarterly Review,* Vol. 66, No. 2, Spring, 1990, p. 64.

[*In the following review of* The Culture We Deserve, *the critic characterizes Barzun's essays "breezy" but "refreshing."*]

Biting the hand that feeds one has become a favorite sport of several American scholars, who collect handsome royalty checks from the very mass marketing industry that they decry in their best sellers. Jacques Barzun, who engaged in the culture battles long before it became fashionable and lucrative, has joined the fray with his own collection of stimulating but ultimately frustrating essays. These pieces from the last decade offer his complaints regarding everything from scholarship (overspecialization and theorizing) to relativism (its abuse) to the humanities (poorly served by academia) to high art (its overabundance) to linguistics and rhetoric (their silly scientism). The parts are greater than the whole, as a compelling, overarching perspective on our current plight only peeks through on occasion. Nonetheless, two of Barzun's recurring themes are the most important: the self-consciousness of modern culture and its calculated self-hatred. Professionalization, overemphasis on method and theory, the cult of the expert, and parochialism have drained criticism of usable substance. Ultimately, he concludes in a compelling final chapter, Western civilization is realizing its own self-destructive impulse. A distrust of judgment or order of any kind causes "the urge to flee the octopus organization and the distant rule of unseen hands, so as to huddle with a few friends and bemoan our lot or demonstrate against it." Quite rightly, he denies to the self-styled "deconstructionists" and youthful "post-modernists" the claim of being revolutionary. Until they dare to remake the university, rather than participate cynically in its careerist game, they have no real claim to newness. Despite a breezy tone, which tends to speak more to the already-converted than argue effectively, Barzun's essays are a refreshing contribution to the noisy and suspect market in culture-whining.

Sanford Pinsker (review date Fall-Winter 1990)

SOURCE: A review of *The Culture We Deserve,* in *Journal of Modern Literature,* Vol. 17, Nos. 2-3, Fall-Winter, 1990, pp. 211-12.

[*In the following review of* The Culture We Deserve, *Pinsker expresses sympathy for "Barzun's heartfelt, uncompromisingly idealist pronouncements," though finds little evidence that Barzun's hopes will be realized.*]

The dozen essays collected here [in *The Culture We Deserve*] explore the gap between claim and performance in contemporary culture: art and literature, education and scholarship, philosophy and history. Not surprisingly, Barzun has sobering things to say about our current state of cultural affairs. For Barzun, culture is not "any chunk of social reality you like or dislike" but, rather, what used to be called "cultivation—cultivation of the self." And it is within that Arnoldian sense of "cultivation" that Barzun finds ample evidence for evasions of thought and for flights from common sense. Thus, "professional historians no longer write for the public but for one another"—and the same charges can be laid at the doorstep of literary critics and philosophers. The effect, of course, is that scholars tend to know more and more about less and less.

Nor is Barzun amused at the concern for "relevance"; and if there are moments when he makes common cause with the relevancy-blasting Allan Bloom, there are others when he seems ready to cast his vote with Jesse Helms.

But as Barzun goes on to argue, his title cuts two ways: if "the culture we deserve" reflects our current overproduction of art and the equally calculated obscurity by too many of our critics, it also suggests that a reaction—indeed, a renaissance—may be within reach:

> What is wanted is an open conspiracy of genuine young Turks who will turn their backs on analysis and criticism and reinvent—say—the idea of the university, and show what it can do; who, seeing that bureaucracy is inevitable, will rethink the art of administration and make it work. And when the energies of reconstruction revivify the landscape, the fine arts will spontaneously mirror the change, show a new face, and the public, enheartened, will rejoice in the new life.

Faced with Barzun's heartfelt, uncompromisingly idealistic pronouncements, one does not want to respond by paraphrasing Hemingway's bitterly ironic, "Isn't it pretty to think so?"—but nothing on the horizon suggests that such a cadre of young Turks is at hand.

Jonathan Yardley (review date 21 April 1991)

SOURCE: "The Plight of Pedagogy," in *Washington Post Book World,* April 21, 1991, p. 3.

[*In the following review, Yardley offers a positive assessment of* Begin Here.]

It is difficult to imagine a more pungent, perceptive or eloquent commentary on contemporary American education than this collection of 15 pieces [**Begin Here**] by Jacques Barzun. Written over the past four decades, but mostly of fairly recent vintage, these essays and speeches all boil down to the book's opening words: "Forget EDUCATION. Education is a result, a slow growth, and hard to judge. Let us talk rather about Teaching and Learning, a joint activity that can be provided for, though as a nation we have lost the knack of it." Or, as Barzun puts it many pages later:

"The error began with the replacement of the word *pedagogy* with the word *education*. Pedagogy is not a beautiful word, but it sticks to the point of teaching. It denotes the art of leading a child to knowledge, whereas education properly refers to a completed development, or the whole tendency of the mind toward it. A person is taught by a teacher but educates him- or herself, partly by will, partly by assimilating experience. The educator's egotistical urge to blur this distinction is at the root of our present predica-

ment. Thinking that we can '*give* an education,' we make wild claims and promises and forget to teach what is teachable. Babbling incessantly, we grope toward the remote, ill-defined, unattainable goals that fill our blatant advertising."

Which is to say that there is little in **Begin Here** to give comfort to the establishment, the educationists whose behavior Barzun penetratingly characterizes as "exaggeration of goals and results; seeing the student not as an individual but as an example of some psychological generality; taking any indirect means in place of the straight one; and finally: mistaking words for facts, and intentions for hard work." By contrast with these practitioners of bureaucratic obfuscation and evasion, Barzun is a passionate advocate of the basics: not in the sense of "Back to Basics" sloganeering favored by certain pitchmen for pedagogical fundamentalism, but in the deeper sense of teaching and learning as basic activities we no longer understand.

Begin Here is, like everything else Barzun has written in his very long career, civil and restrained in its language, but for all of that it is—as it should be—an angry book. It grieves and infuriates Barzun that "the once proud and efficient public school system of the United States—especially its unique free high school for all—has turned into a wasteland where violence and vice share the time with ignorance and idleness, besides serving as a background for vested interests, social, political and economic." It appalls him that "the arts have simply given universal warrant for the offbeat, the unintelligible, the defiant without purpose," and that "the schools have soaked up this heady brew." It enrages him that the "main business" of higher education is not "the mental life" but "socialization, entertainment, political activism, and the struggle to get high grades so as to qualify for future employment."

Yes, Barzun is an old-fashioned man, one to whom much if not indeed most of what now occurs in classrooms from kindergarten to graduate school is merely chic, trendy and self-indulgent. But his are the words not of a political opportunist or newspaper fulminator; he has been a teacher all his adult life, has written about teaching with intimate knowledge and understanding, and therefore has earned the position of dissent he now occupies. He's a man of advanced years with no agendas to pursue or axes to grind; he merely wants us, for our own good, to re-examine what we expect our schools to do and to ask ourselves whether that is indeed their proper purpose.

He writes of "the manifest decline" in our schools as "heartbreakingly sad," and puts his finger right on the problem: "Instead of trying to develop native intelligence and give it good techniques in the basic arts of man, we professed to make ideal citizens, supertolerant neighbors, agents of world peace and happy family folk, at once sexually adept and flawless drivers of cars." We expect the schools to impart not knowledge but attitudes, or, as Barzun puts it, "not an idea but a mere notion." He writes:

"Some years ago, a new school superintendent in the Southwest calculated that by state authority he must find room in the curriculum for about 200 subjects. They included: driver education, sex education, kindness to animals, shopping and local resources, care for endangered species, family living, global understanding, and *no* sex education. Legislatures are ever ready to add requirements that sound worthy or useful. Few survive in practice, but enough are attempted to make a mockery of the idea of schooling."

That idea, quite simply, is that schools exist, to quote once more Barzun's felicitous phrase, to teach "the basic arts of man." Those arts grow ever more difficult and complex as we take each step along the ladder from grammar school to university, but in a proper system of schooling they are always the focus of our efforts—not socialization, not attitudinizing, not entertainment, but learning. The problem is that learning is hard while these various "playthings" are easy, and it is a central argument of ***Begin Here*** that for a number of reasons—not the least of them sheer laziness—we have chosen the easy over the difficult, in the process abandoning the most basic obligations of the schools.

"It is a great mistake," Barzun writes, "to implant the idea that learning can be steadily exciting, or that excitement is a good frame of mind for acquiring knowledge. Developing a genuine interest in a subject comes only after some drudgery, and only when the learner gets to the point of seeing its order and continuity, not its intermittent peaks of excitement." Thus the grammar schooler must master the basics of arithmetic before being permitted the excitement of calculators and computers; the college student must understand Chaucer and Milton before being granted the fun of Alice Walker and Louis L'Amour.

These assumptions would seem so obvious as to require no elaboration, yet they have been abandoned by American education at all levels, not so much by teachers themselves as by the educationists who shape the policies of the schools. What they have given us is a nation in which 60 million people are to some degree functionally illiterate, in which reading and writing are in steady decline, in which the "bits and pieces" principle of television has become the national fixation. We talk a lot about excellence, but "excellence is for sloganeering exclusively"; in the schools, as in government and most other institutions, our "muddled feelings about brainwork" have led us to hold true intellectual excellence in contempt and to honor both the glib and the inarticulate.

Whether there is any real prospect of changing this is at best problematical, for it is a matter of deep cultural bias that is not susceptible to economic or legislative remedy. But if there's anyone out there who'd like to try, there couldn't be a better primer than ***Begin Here.***

Paul Shore (review date November-December 1991)

SOURCE: A review of *The Culture We Deserve*, in *The Humanist*, Vol. 51, No. 6, November-December, 1991, pp. 46-7.

[*In the following positive review of* The Culture We Deserve, *Shore clarifies and defends Barzun's pessimistic view of contemporary thought, education, and art.*]

A superficial family resemblance exists among a number of the educational documents to appear during the 1980s, among them the U.S. government study *A Nation at Risk,* Allan Bloom's *The Closing of the American Mind,* Mortimer Adler's *The Paideia Proposal,* and E.D. Hirsch's *Cultural Literacy.* Although each of these works differs significantly in emphasis, all share a mood of urgency— almost despair—toward the knowledge and skills students possess and argue for a rediscovery of some common body of knowledge which can serve as a unifying element for both formal education and society as a whole.

The Culture We Deserve seems at first glance to be a close cousin of these other critiques of American culture and education, but it is, in fact, something quite different from either a Spenglerian forecast of doom or an airtight proposal for sweeping reform. Barzun, a prominent figure in American education for many decades and an emeritus professor of history at Columbia University, offers here a collection of related cultural essays, some of which were written as long ago as 1972. Barzun understands culture not in the sense that social scientists now use the term but in the earlier sense that emphasizes the lasting contributions of a social entity rather than its more ephemeral accomplishments and activities.

Barzun's targets are numerous and at times surprising. In "Where Is History Now?" he faults the *Annales* school of historians, the product of his native France, because they have abandoned telling a story of consecutive events and replaced it with the microscopic examination of quantitative facts or literary words. Barzun notes that not only are diplomacy, dynastic change, and the other mainstays of pre-*Annales* historians missing from the new history but so is a wider audience for historical writing. In the nineteenth century, the writing of history was an art form, evaluated on aesthetic as well as other criteria, and educated general readers devoured the historical writings of Macauley, Guizot, and Prescott. Barzun argues that the decline of the relationship between the educated general reader and the trained historian is part of a larger set of transformations that our culture is undergoing—transformations that fragment, isolate, and obscure the significance of individual and collective human experience.

Surprisingly, Barzun also takes aim at reference books (of all things) and publicly supported art. Most of us would consider the appearance of a new reference work as at least a potentially positive development, but Barzun sees in the contemporary cataloguing of facts an unattractive parallel with the Alexandrian lexicographers of late antiquity, who served a senescent culture by recording the meanings of forgotten words. As for publicly supported art, Barzun argues in the essay, **"The Insoluble Problem: Supporting Art"**:

> The religion of art has so many adherents that every unit in society longs to join in artistic expression; school, church and town, businesses, hospitals, and cruise vessels—all want to be art centers.

The result is a glut of art and artists and a revolution of endlessly rising expectations that result in the "overproduction" of art as well as the creation of a star system that saves would-be connoisseurs from the trouble of thinking and deciding what art is of most value. Abundance has not brought satisfaction, Barzun believes, but only the pressure to produce even more.

By the time the reader has absorbed several of Barzun's essays, it becomes clear that the book's title is not merely a sarcastic putdown but an accurate summary of the position presented in each of the chapters. Any society—ours included—gets the culture it deserves. The tendency of the twentieth century toward specialization, on the one hand, and intercommunication, on the other, has produced an overly busy society in which competing ideas and a lack of a sense of unity and direction leave the average citizen unsure what his culture consists of. Barzun's largest and most saturnine piece, **"Toward the Twenty-First Century,"** suggests that we are facing a change in the culture of the West as momentous as that which occurred at the end of the ancient world. For Barzun, the apparent decline of liberalism, the inability of science to provide comprehensive and comprehensible answers, and the elevation of terrorism to some level of political legitimacy as a means of bringing about change all point to the final breakdown which has been predicted by many writers for most of this century.

But it is here that Barzun parts company most dramatically from Bloom and many of the other Jeremiahs, as well as from an earlier generation of prognosticators. Commentators of the early 1970s—such as Charles Reich (*The Greening of America*) and Marilyn Ferguson (*The Aquarian Conspiracy*)—saw big, positive changes ahead for Western culture, while the writers of the 1980s tended toward a decidedly more pessimistic view of the future. Barzun, with a prudence that is both admirable and at times frustrating, refuses to pretend that he knows the answer. He recognizes that prophecies of the end of civilization have been made for centuries, and that, even when such writers as Augustine have been correct in predicting the end of their own eras, they have fared less well in predicting what would come next. Instead, Barzun holds out the possibility of a new civilization emerging from the declining forms of our own, and he reminds us:

> Civilization is not identical with *our* civilization, and the rebuilding of states and cultures, now or at any

time, is integral to our nature and more becoming than longing and lamentations.

But if lamentations of the fall of civilization are not appropriate, criticism of specific aspects of our culture are, and Barzun offers critiques that are valid—whether or not one accepts the idea that our culture is reaching a crisis point. Barzun perceives a connection between the plague of illiteracy and the scramble of linguists to focus on the spoken word and reduce the importance of the written word. He is worried about the misplaced egalitarianism that applies the word *language* to every form of communication, no matter how limited its repertoire or function. He is for the return of the humanities—not as a vehicle for the training of competent members of capitalist society or the production of an elite corps of specialists but as a basis for a common language available to every element of any society.

None of these positions should be dismissed lightly as the reactionary arguments of an antiquarian who was born when Freud and Tolstoy were still alive. Barzun wants our current culture to be less crowded with events, less focused on fragmentary rather than whole experience, and, most significantly, less *easy*. The American tradition of maximizing options and minimizing effort has, in Barzun's view, blunted the influence of culture on all of us.

The implications of this view for education, however, do not inevitably point toward a Great Books curriculum or even the streamlined "Back to Basics" program found in *A Nation at Risk*. Barzun's message is more subtle and potentially more powerful. He calls for an end to the nonserious view of culture perpetuated by not only the quantitatively minded and the narrow specialist but by every "educated" expert who has invested too heavily in a particular ideology or an arbitrarily defined discipline. He despises the unrigorous "casualness and hatred of limits" which has masqueraded as broadmindedness in many educational settings. And Barzun sets an extremely high educational ideal for every intelligent member of our society. Although he avoids the word so often overused by educators, Barzun is talking about excellence—or, perhaps more precisely, the Greek concept of *arete,* a unique state fostered by self-discipline, talent, passion, and (very often) sacrifice. We must care about substance while redesigning theory, he argues. And we must revere those attempts which have succeeded in some ways to bring into view a larger portion of human experience.

Barzun's call to excellence is worth heeding. If enough of those who call themselves our intellectual and creative leaders would strive for the ideals Barzun sets forth, we would be able to say without shame that we have the culture we deserve.

Wallace Fowlie (review date Winter 1992)

SOURCE: "From Apollinaire's Knee," in *American Scholar,* Vol. 61, No. 1, Winter, 1992, pp. 138, 140-41.

[In the following review, Fowlie offers a favorable evaluation of An Essay on French Verse.]

No one title would be adequate to describe the contents of this small book [*An Essay on French Verse*]. Its author first carefully explains the rules of French prosody, and then he explores the changes it underwent in each century. The ten-syllable line of *La Chanson de Roland* in the eleventh century was recast into the twelve-syllable line, the alexandrine, in the thirteenth century. These two major types of lines remain the favorites in the nineteenth and twentieth centuries. Professor Barzun contrasts the classical alexandrine line with the iambic pentameter used by Shakespeare. The history of France and the political systems have affected the lives of the poets and influenced the development of French poetry from century to century. All of these topics—aesthetics, theory, history, biography, social change—are included in this "essay on French verse," because the central preoccupation of the critic is language.

France grew into a nation from the ruins of the Roman civilization in Gaul, and at the same time a new language evolved. The language had a simple origin. With few exceptions French comes directly from Latin. The pre-Roman Celts left almost no traces in the new language. There were a few hundred words introduced by the Frankish conquerors. Whereas the English language has a double origin from the Roman occupation and the Saxon invaders, the literature of France, like its language, is homogeneous. The more complex origin of English has enabled English writers to reach effects of diversity and strangeness and richness. Such traits characterize English literature. The genius of French, coming from its sole origin in Latin, is still today characterized by simplicity and clarity.

English critics of French poetry have pointed out in their attacks this simplicity of the French language and the strict rules of versification. They claimed that the rhyming alexandrines and the preference for abstractions turned what should be poetry into oratory. Often they have claimed there is no French poetry before Baudelaire, with the possible exception of Villon, in the fifteenth century. This attack diminished in the twentieth century when Eliot and Pound recognized Mallarmé, Rimbaud, and Laforgue as genuine poets and models for their own writing.

Mr. Barzun discusses the French language ("a vowel language with difficult nasals"), the mute *e,* and the irrational spelling. Then, with admirable skill, he analyzes the rules of rhythm and rhyme. These three early chapters are justifiably based on the theory that the first major achievement of French verse was the neo-classical theater: the tragedies of Racine and the comedies of Molière.

When Louis XIV took over the government in the seventeenth century, France reached her maturity. The king centralized society around his palace at Versailles, and the theater became a permanent institution in France. The youthfulness and romantic idealism of Corneille's *Le Cid* (1636) and his tragedies of power were soon replaced by Racine's tragedies of the heart. Racine's alexandrines are both dramatic and harmonious. Mr. Barzun names him

"the most obedient of the neo-classicists" and seems to agree with Robert Lowell who, when he translated *Phèdre,* called Racine "perhaps the greatest of French poets."

Some of the most brilliant pages in *An Essay* are on Molière and La Fontaine, the two masters of comedy. Their vocabulary is the richest of their century. Remorseless in his ridicule of *Les Femmes savantes,* lucidly analytical in *Le Misanthrope,* Molière paints a world of vain ideals, of cold hearts, and futile consolations. Englishmen usually love Molière and detest Racine. The liberties taken by Molière are also in La Fontaine whose *Fables* are miniature plays. He was not a naturalist but a poet, and he made of a humble literary genre one of the most finished examples of French classical art.

The eighteenth was a great century for prose (Voltaire, Diderot, Rousseau) but a poor century for poetry. Mr. Barzun devotes few pages to it and passes quickly to the long spell of romanticism, and to its leader, Victor Hugo. From this point on—it is the mid-point of the book—the critic analyzes the theories and art of French poets during one hundred years, from approximately 1830 to 1930. Hugo, with his mastery of every form of verse (except the sonnet) was, according to Jacques Barzun, the liberator of democratic France and the greatest French poet. He did for poetry in France what Wordsworth did for it in England. Both poets brought changes to diction and subject matter. In the succeeding schools of Parnassian, symbolist, and surrealist poetry, there are traces of romanticism. These pages on Hugo and the information in the pages that follow will be valuable for today's students of French poetry. To illustrate Hugo's mastery of French versification, Mr. Barzun appended to *An Essay* the text and his translation of Hugo's *Les Djinns* (Evil spirits), taken from *Les Orientales.*

Musset, who is not favored by critics today, is treated generously by Mr. Barzun, who believes that the fluidity of Musset's lines and their ease and elegance are deceptive. Despair is the prevailing mood of the poems, which the critic sees as continuing the tradition of Marot in the sixteenth century, and even of Molière and La Fontaine in the seventeenth. Vigny, more solemn than Musset, was the stoic who in his strong poem, *La Mort du Loup,* believes man's duty is silent resignation in a world of evil.

Balzac died in 1850. About that time romanticism as a literary movement came to an end. It is true that Hugo continued to live and produce for more than thirty years longer. The school of romanticism had re-created French poetry. Its spirit was one of progress and change. It was therefore inevitable that the romantic ideal would be the stepping-stone for a first advance. This advance, whether it is called *le Parnasse,* or *le symbolisme,* or *le surréalisme,* is the subject of the last forty pages of the *Essay.*

For each of these changes or metamorphoses, Mr. Barzun finds admirable formulas and makes useful critical observations. Baudelaire's *Les fleurs du mal* (1857) was outrageous by nineteenth-century standards, but today he is usually the first French poet the English and Americans read after Villon. His fifty prose poems, without meter or rhyme, describe an urban world. He translated the stories of Poe and called attention to the poetic theories of Poe, which the symbolists Mallarmé and Valéry drew upon. Rimbaud's *Illuminations* was the new contribution to the new genre of the prose poem, initiated by Aloysius Bertrand and Baudelaire.

Second in importance, after Hugo, is Mallarmé, who taught that a poem does not tell but suggests. Since his death in 1898, Mallarmé has influenced each generation of poets in England and America. His art is very exact and at the same time ambiguous. The precise meaning of a word in a Mallarmé sonnet is often to be found in the root or etymology of the word. Jacques Barzun reveals several examples of this practice, dear to Mallarmé and to his principal disciple, Paul Valéry.

Rimbaud, the most precocious and perhaps the most rebellious French poet, wrote his poems (such as *Le Bateau Ivre*), his prose poems (*Les Illuminations*), and *Une Saison en enfer* (a spiritual autobiography) between the ages of sixteen and twenty. These writings are today considered as an important source of what is called "modernism."

One of the last-mentioned poets in *An Essay* is Guillaume Apollinaire who came midway between the two generations of the symbolists and the surrealists. The case of Rimbaud had somewhat fixed the portrait of the youthful poet as a vindictive, sullen, and even persecuted adolescent, hostile to family and state and religion. Apollinaire changed this portrait to that of a young man without family and country (he was born of a Polish mother and an Italian father), and without a sentiment of vindictiveness. His attitude was one of gratitude to France for receiving him (an attitude similar to that of many artists: Picasso, Picabia, Chagall, Giacometti), of constant gratitude to his family of friends.

L'Esprit nouveau, a lecture given by Apollinaire shortly before his death (1918) and published a month later in *Le Mercure de France*, is the synthesis of his major theories on poetry and the modern spirit in art. A sense of exuberance must preside over the new spirit, as well as a desire to explore everything, regions of the world and regions of the heart, to bring to every experience that critical sense and that common sense which the Frenchman believes he inherits at birth. The artist must never neglect the new popular forms of art—the cinema, for example, of which Apollinaire was a prophet.

Mr. Barzun's book makes it clear that modern poetry owes almost everything to Baudelaire. Mallarmé, as an admirer of Baudelaire, became the most studied symbolist of modern poetry. Rimbaud was the dazzled initiate and rebel. Apollinaire, without possessing the poetic genius of Mallarmé or Rimbaud, was able to bring poetry back from its Mallarmean hermeticism and Rimbaldian violence to tenderness and nostalgia, to the gentleness of the clown.

As a child Jacques Barzun knew Apollinaire. He sat on the poet's knee as Apollinaire talked with him and amused him. It is a delightful autobiographical remembrance that serves as a conclusion to a book written by a man who throughout his very active life as teacher, scholar, and critic has read and studied and loved French poetry.

William H. Pritchard (review date Spring 1992)

SOURCE: "Art of the Difficult," in *American Scholar,* Vol. 61, No. 2, Spring, 1992, pp. 312-15.

[*In the following review of* Begin Here, *Pritchard commends Barzun's pedagogic ideals and concurs with his negative critique of contemporary American education, though notes that Barzun's recommendations contain "an element of Old Codgerism."*]

It is almost half a century since Jacques Barzun published his wise and witty *Teacher in America* (1945). I was, briefly, a graduate student in philosophy at Columbia University when the book was republished eight years later (as one of the first paperback titles in Doubleday-Anchor's memorable venture), and although I had read some of what William James and John Dewey had to say about teaching, Mr. Barzun's book was the first I encountered that took on the subject in a wholly contemporary, wholly pertinent way. From time to time I sat in on Jacques Barzun's course in eighteenth- and nineteenth-century European history, where he lectured with elegance to an attentive audience. My assumption at the time was that small classrooms filled with discussion were preferable to large lecture rooms, but Barzun, along with John Herman Randall of the philosophy department, gave lectures that— though quite different in manner—were equally filled with informative judgments and mischievous critical wit. By contrast, Lionel Trilling seemed unhappy lecturing to students and was most himself in the give and take of classroom argument.

Teacher in America describes the lecture room as

> the place where drama may properly become theater. This usually means a fluent speaker, no notes, and no shyness about "effects." In some teachers a large class filling a sloped-up amphitheater brings out a wonderful power of emphasis, timing, and organization. The speaker projects himself and the subject. The "effects" are not laid on, they are the meaningful stress which constitutes, most literally, the truth of the matter. This meaning—as against fact—is the one thing to be indelibly stamped on the mind, and it is this that the printed book cannot give.

And yet Barzun's fluency and the "meaningful stress" with which he treats a subject come across remarkably in the books he has written. *Teacher in America* has a vibrancy and confidence that suited the postwar surge in college and university enrollments, with a concomitant ambitiousness about pedagogical possibilities. But no one, including Mr. Barzun, knew just what we were in for.

Begin Here, a collection of writings from the past four decades about school, teaching, curriculum, is subtitled (rather somberly) *The Forgotten Conditions of Teaching and Learning.* There is a pervading sense, in the essays taken together, of things having gone off the track in disheartening ways—of wrong choices made, wrong roads taken. In one of the essays, **"Teacher in 1980 America: What He Found,"** we are directed to what "the once proud and efficient public-school system of the United States—especially its unique free high school for all" has turned into: "a wasteland where violence and vice share the time with ignorance and idleness." School is now the place that turns out functional illiterates numbering in the millions, a place where incompetent students are passed anyway, where any course is as good as any other one, and where "bilingual education" undercuts the teaching of English. Barzun is not concerned to explore the sociological fact of the United States as a multicultured society, members of which no longer inevitably melt down in the melting pot and turn into good democratic citizens who sometimes read books. His sharp eye and sharp tongue are inclined toward a more detached view of things, often ironic or satiric—and, as Wyndham Lewis once reminded us, satire is deliberately "unfair." These essays (many of them originally lectures) operate in bold, simplified strokes, and their formulations are correspondingly unambiguous. This doesn't mean that Barzun is less than wholly serious in his analysis but that his seriousness is not leavened with sympathetic understanding of the enormous problems of current-day American society. He may know all, but he doesn't forgive all.

If he's critical of bilingual education, he's completely unforgiving about "education" talk generally. The first two words of his book are strong ones: "Forget EDUCATION." He would have us talk instead about schooling and teaching; "educational nonsense" he defines as "any plan or proposal *or critique* which plainly disregards the known limits of schooling or teaching." It follows then that he has little sympathy with the monstrous courses "in" education and with the schools "of" education that have alienated so many prospective teachers by wasting their time, and wasting it in the terms of a vicious and pretentious vocabulary. Barzun characterizes the language in which educationists talk and think as one of "abstraction instead of direct naming; exaggeration of goals and results; seeing the student not as an individual but as an example of some psychological generality; taking any indirect means in place of the straight one." The substitution of words and intentions for facts and hard work is at the core of the educationist boondoggle.

Teaching, insists Barzun, is not problem solving (as the educationists claim) but rather "a series of *difficulties.*" To deal with these difficulties is an art, and teaching is an art of difficulty. Recalling us to conditions of teaching and learning frequently forgotten, he reminds us that "it will

always be difficult to teach well, to learn accurately; to read, write, and count readily and competently; to acquire a sense of history and develop a taste for literature and the arts—in short, to instruct and start one's education or another's." He even suggests that, when you think of it, the life of teaching is an "unnatural" life—invading the privacy of another to tell him or her how to think, how to behave. Yet given the ease with which Barzun is quite willing, in this book (as in his previous ones) to tell us how to think and behave, it's hard to credit his claim that teaching is unnatural. Say instead, as one of the most felicitous phrases in a book filled with them says, that it is "a blessing thoroughly disguised."

One of the most interesting chapters in *Begin Here* is titled **"History is Past and Present Life,"** where Mr. Barzun describes in some detail what a curriculum of courses in history might look like from the seventh grade through high school. Since as a historian he believes that his subject is "the best remover of provincialism and egotism," he sets out to imagine how that removing might be done, beginning at around the age of thirteen or fourteen. As he does with "education," he scorns and deftly satirizes "research" when applied—and it was applied to the "research" papers my own children were assigned—to seventh and eighth graders: "The word should not even occur, for at that level the thing is non-existent." Call it what it is, a report on reading, instead of pretending that "Egyptian religion" is first "researched" then "acted out by the whole class." (Barzun reserves special contempt for such activities when performed by separate groups of students, lounging on the floor: he is all for desks and chairs—no "running about" on separate projects.) His notion of a desirable sequence of history courses is one that, over six years, would survey the bases of Western Civilization in the following order: American History, History of England, Europe Since 1500, Ancient Greece and Rome, The Middle Ages, American History Since 1865. Such "basic" courses would be conducted in an equally basic style, one that emphasizes nothing more or less than the centrality of reading:

> Read first and last. History is for reading, and developing a taste for reading history ensures lifelong pleasure. Let some striking portion of Prescott's *Conquest of Mexico* be assigned to a few students, to be read and turned into a précis, the best summary to be read aloud in class. Other small groups can read and write something on the same subject, or a similar one. Teach the students to be good critics of what they read—which means, to know how to praise as well as to criticize— and not to moralize.

Recalling my junior high and high school experiences in social studies (as it was called), I note that it was the history part that stimulated me; that when we were given a narrative of events—a story, with the implied question, always, "What happens next?"—those events usually became engrossing. Unfortunately all too much time was spent on the social studies aspect: learning the principal products of various cities in New York State (Troy manufactured shirts, I remember), or fussing with questions of voting and politics by putting on our own make-believe election. This sort of learning to be a Good Democratic Citizen was treated by the clever ones among us with little respect (no doubt to our discredit). We should have been reading Prescott instead, or H.G. Wells's *Outline of History*—or any well-written narrative, however popularized.

Of course such a program as Barzun suggests has a lot less chance of getting put into place today than it had even in the 1940s, since it would immediately be dubbed elitist and hierarchical and thrown out the window. The "forgotten conditions of teaching and learning" these essays engage with so eloquently are not about to be remembered by administrators or educationists, Democrats or Republicans, nor by the Education President (remember him?). A stir of interest and indignation may occur briefly when statistics show we're running well behind the Asians and the Europeans in science subjects (a recent study has us ranking between eighth and thirteenth in achievement levels at various grades), but no one will worry overmuch about how, or even whether, history or literature or music get represented.

Barzun talks a lot about the importance of teaching "rudiments" and how learning them isn't "fun": "Sight-reading [of musical notation], taking dictation of intervals and rhythm, learning to sing and play in tune . . . learning to draw in perspective, to copy in various mediums, and use colors in the light of theory is nothing but hard work . . . some of it learning by rote." In the factory town where I went to public schools, almost nobody was headed for college; but we learned such things, those rudiments (even though I never could draw in perspective, hard as they tried to teach me), along with diagramming sentences, memorizing poetry, and too much gymnasium work on the tumbling mats and parallel bars. There is doubtless an element of Old Codgerism in the belief that these activities, or most of them, somehow did us good—but I confess to believing it.

In the book's last section (titled "Advanced Work") Barzun takes up life in the contemporary college and university, pointing out, in his introduction to the section, that college used to be—to the incoming freshman—a "revelation." Here is a place where you were called "Mr. or Miss in class without irony" (it's now Ted or Susie, and you would be politically correct to use "first year student" rather than "fresh*man*"), where "friendly but not chummy" faculty members taught "certain definite things of agreed importance," and, above all, where you spent "many hours of reading in real books, written by adults for adults." Fifty years later there is no comparable step up from high school, since colleges and universities

> have been transformed into a motley social organism dedicated to the full life. It does include the mental life, but certainly makes no fetish of it. Rather, intellect weaves in and out of the main business, which is socialization, entertainment, political activism, and the struggle to get high grades so as to qualify for future employment.

The incoming freshmen have already been told that they are mature and entitled to endless options; their last two years of high school have offered courses similar to the ones they encounter as first-year college students, and—as Barzun points out mordantly—"'research' holds no mystery: they have been expert at it since the seventh grade." Instead of a place apart, the college "re-creates the whole of society: unions and strikes, protests, insults, violence, madness, and the agencies needed to cope with these diversions." Those agencies include "a small army of security guards, a corps of psychiatrists and counselors, facilities for free artistic productions, a supply of contraceptive information and devices, and housing and subsidies for political and ethnic separatism." In 1949, when I was a freshman, my college's "security guards" consisted of a single slow-moving individual who was called exactly what he was—"Mack the Cop."

Can it be that in the changed circumstances of today's college or university much good work still gets accomplished by students and teachers just as devoted as ever they were to the life of the mind? I hope that Barzun would say yes, and agree that even though the college is now less a place apart than a re-creation of the larger society, there are still lots of students reading difficult books while managing to ignore counselors, security guards, and even contraceptive information. The sentiment from a Randall Jarrell poem has it that "in those days everything was better." If we hesitate to make that pronouncement about yesterday's college or secondary school compared with today's, we can at least agree that everything was . . . well, *different*. And Barzun's own assumptions about human psychology are so different from the going (and knowing) ones that he can claim, in a delightful commencement address given a couple of years ago to the New England Conservatory of Music, that it's important to find "a Self" . . . "a solid entity that you can trust, because you have made it yourself and made it well." This "ordered set of reflections, conclusions, and convictions" should be the aim of teaching, and nothing is more difficult than the process of shaping that Self, making it well. The stimulus and discipline from outside that contributes most to this shaping is—once again—reading: reading "thick" books, books you want and need to reread. These are what provide the conditions for teaching and learning, just in case we forgot.

Dudley Barlow (review date November 1992)

SOURCE: "Perennial Difficulties," in *Education Digest*, Vol. 58, No. 2, November, 1992, pp. 39-40.

[*In the following review, Barlow offers a positive assessment of* Begin Here.]

I have just spent a few very enjoyable weeks in the company of a remarkable mind; I have been reading Jacques Barzun's ***Begin Here: The Forgotten Conditions of Teaching and Learning.*** This is a collection of 15 essays written over a number of years and published in this collection this year by The University of Chicago Press. I have been reading little sections to my car pool, to my departmental colleagues, and to my wife.

I admit freely that one reason I enjoyed Barzun's book so much is that he and I share some of the same prejudices. For example, machine-scored tests.

Barzun says, "I think its use harmful to teaching and learning, both. I know all the arguments in favor of these so-called objective tests. They are easy to grade. Uniformity and unmistakable answers secure fairness. With such tests one can compare performance over time and space and gauge the results of programs and devices." His chief complaint against machine-scored tests is that they test "nothing but recognition knowledge."

"The worst feature of this game of choosing the ready-made instead of producing the fresh idea," he says, "is that it breaks up the unity of what has been learned and isolates the pieces. In going through the 50 or 100 questions nothing follows on anything else. It is the negation of the normal pattern-making of the mind. True testing issues a call for patterns, and this is the virtue of the essay examination."

Barzun thinks machine-scored tests are useful for quizzes, but not as assessments of what students really know. As he puts it, "Knowing something—really knowing it—means being able to summon it up out of the blue; the facts must be produced in their right relations and with their correct significance. When you know something, you can tell it to somebody else." Hurrah!

One of the chief virtues of this book is Barzun's ability to spot educational sophistry. "A sure sign of nonsense in the offing is the emergence of new names for well-known things. Under the educationist regime, English became 'language arts'; the school library, 'general information resource'; the school period, a 'module.'" Each of us could add to this brief list of puffed-up educational labels. At the school where I teach, the "learning resource center" is run by the "media specialist." I don't know about you, but I want my librarian back. . . .

Some of you will remember all the talk a few years ago about teaching the "affective domain." While Barzun does not use that term, he discusses the notion. "One great source of nonsense . . . is trying to teach the virtues verbally. A second is engineering human traits. The aim is to reach certain results head on. For example, it is true that students are hampered if they think poorly of themselves; they need a certain amount of self-esteem. Why not *give* it to them? Eighty-three percent of teachers in a recent inquiry considered this their 'top role.' Two states have added to their education departments a 'Bureau of Self-Esteem.' All this as if self-esteem were a definite commodity that one has or hasn't and that can be produced and injected when lacking.

"What a bureau can certainly produce is more bureaucracy, with paperwork and jargon to burden and bewilder teachers still more. Self-esteem comes from work done, from new power over difficulty, which in school means knowing more and more and coping easily with serious tasks. Boredom disappears with progress, with perceived advance toward completion and mastery."

In the first essay in the book, Barzun gives us the best antidote I have ever read for all of the nonsense that constantly assails our schools. "To rediscover its true purpose is always in order for an institution or any other being, and doing so entails scraping away all pointless accretions. It is always a painful act. . . ."

"There is unfortunately no method or gimmick that will replace teaching. We have seen the failure of one touted method after another. Teaching will not change; it is a hand-to-hand, face-to-face encounter. There is no help for it—we must teach and we must learn, each for himself and herself, using words and working at the perennial Difficulties."

I loved some of the things Barzun said at a meeting of the National Art Education Association in 1978. ". . . Tell yourself what you know about art, about teaching, about people young and old. Trust your common sense, keeping away from the old grooves of educational piety, and you will make some interesting discoveries, reach conclusions you can rely on, because they come out of your whole experience and not your slogans and shoptalk."

Teachers grouse a good deal when a new fad sweeps over education, but we generally succumb to the political pressures around us and fall in line to wait it out until the current vision is replaced by a revision. We need to take Barzun's advice about sitting down and telling ourselves what we know. And then we need to tell others. Inherent in this is our professional obligation to stand up and make our voices heard when nonsense gets in the way of what we know we should be doing.

Herbert I. London (essay date May-June 1993)

SOURCE: "Jacques Barzun's American University," in *Society,* Vol. 30, No. 4, May-June, 1993, pp. 71-82.

[*In the following essay, London reconsiders the decline of contemporary university education a quarter century after the publication of Barzun's* The American University.]

Jacques Barzun's work ***The American University,*** published in 1968, still stands as one of the most lucid, informative statements on the subject of the university ever written. With keen insights, he describes the university and its quintessential features, demarcating the ancestral, perhaps more congenial, university from the one that emerged in his day as teacher and administrator in the 1960s. Presciently he walks the reader through the mine fields of sixties "reform," ever hopeful for the future of an institution to which he has devoted his professional life. But despite his admirable vision and power of analysis, even Barzun did not fully foresee then the extremes that emerged from the noisy radicalism of the 1960s. Even he could not imagine the corrosive influence of an all-embracing orthodoxy on campus.

Nevertheless, *The American University* is still essential reading for anybody who wishes to understand the essence of Barzun's role and the nuances of university life. The book is a primer on the atavistic yearning of youthful rabble rousers. He displays a wisdom in these pages that can guide college administrators and embolden presidents even today. Most evident is Jacques Barzun's wonder and excitement over the teaching and learning process. To read these pages is to understand why former students, now in their fifties and sixties, still wax lyrical when talking about his classes—for lyrical they were and lyrical his observations remain.

There is in Barzun's treatment of university life a clear demarcation of an era when interests were simpler and gentler than ours, a less fanatical era, when errors in judgment could be corrected without heroic effort. The university in that less complex era was not saddled with affirmative action policy and redressing the wrongs of the past, nor was it entwined with government interests, refashioning the curriculum in order to satisfy politically active groups, settling community concerns, nor was it conceived of as a problem-solving institution of first resort. How prosaic it now seems to describe the university as a purposeful sanctuary from the "real world."

The university president in that innocent period could, as Barzun notes, "deal off-hand with seventy or seven hundred people and take care of their infrequent wants, easily knowing what had gone before and what he was doing now, to use or not as a precedent the next time." Now the president, by virtue of his reconstituted role, has become a negotiator who deals with committees, with bargaining agents, and legal counsel. His faculty's demands are limitless and are often put forward discommodiously as "nonnegotiable"—a feature first introduced into university life by student radicals. The president's primary role now is to maintain campus equilibrium between competing interests, and his success is often determined by an ability to avoid trouble on his watch. It is hardly surprising, therefore, that there are no Nicholas Murray Butlers on campus today.

While Barzun quite appropriately separates the old from the new, the ironic publication date of 1968 (the year of the student riots at Columbia University) militates against any analysis of the "postmodern" period in university life. This is the era in which the trends Barzun describes became entrenched and a mood of despair and irrationality observed in inchoate form became manifest in curriculum organization and university-wide practices.

While war and depression, government intrusiveness, and advanced technology played their part in changing the face of the university and in introducing "a new mode of administration," systemic changes in the university occurred as society changed. An inability to cope with the vicissitudes of bureaucratic complexity compelled university officials to alter quotidian affairs from a gemeinschaft of personal contact and understanding to a gesellschaft of contracts and regulation. Mr. Chips was replaced by Perry Mason. The university was caught in the vortex of fundamental social change which it reflected until roughly 1968 and then promoted from 1968 to the present.

This reshaping of the university to accommodate the winds of change is an essential point acknowledged but, due to timing and the rush of events, is only partially explored by Barzun. For most of this century, even going back to the origin of the university at Johns Hopkins and Stanford in the nineteenth century, purpose and goals were well articulated by the founders. Knowledge was an end worth pursuing. The foundations of knowledge were largely unshaken by fashionable trends. And, despite occasional controversies over curriculum and academic freedom, the pace of change was slow.

The reason for the slow pace of change until the sixties was the singularly focused purpose of university life. Teaching and research, learning and study, constituted the faculty-student equation. The utopian effort to refashion society through university reformism was not yet on the horizon. Nor was the university yet in thralldom of adjudication of real and perceived social injustice. Administrators had not yet fallen into a rabbit's hole where symbols were deciphering tools and words were deconstructed like soap bubbles. Not yet had ideas once evaluated on their merit been filtered through the net of race, class, gender, and third-world ideology. Not yet had students' rights been inserted into the Fourteenth Amendment, *loco parentis* was not yet abandoned. Not yet did researchers do Washington's bidding in an effort to obtain government subventions for their pet projects. Not yet were large numbers of students persuaded that rational discourse itself was little more than a plot to keep them subordinate.

In the "new age" the possibility of economic mobility through a university education has been converted into the right to a university education as part of equal opportunity. The university has become Plato's paradigm for democracy: available to everyone without the necessity of accepting responsibility or meeting prerequisites. In the nineteenth century, Charles Eliot, a president of Harvard, once said that the reason why Harvard has so much knowledge was that freshmen bring so much in and seniors take so little out. Today most scholarly studies and SAT scores reflect a different reality. Freshmen know very little, yet think they know a lot, and seniors know a lot about very little and do not know whether to take what they know with them or discard it.

There is, indeed, a college for everyone. But few ask if there should be a college for everyone. With standards reduced to the lowest common denominator, universities have vitiated the pursuit of excellence. One obvious manifestation of this trend is undifferentiated grades. In 1976 I gave up using the Dean's List, since it had become little more than a student roster. The pursuit of political objectives in the academy goes on unabated. The byzantine contortions university administrators exhibited in an effort to address the representation of blacks, Hispanics, Native Americans, and other designated minorities has forced colleges and universities to reduce admissions decisions to the very considerations of race they allegedly deplore. Hoisted by the petard of fairness, justice, and equal opportunity, university leaders are obliged to administer by category, arbitrariness, and inequality. Rather than apply a blind standard of need for financial aid, university administrators are forced to consider race in their calculus in order to satisfy political expectations. It is therefore not unusual for a student with wealthy black parents to be given a scholarship that would be denied to a middle-class white student.

The consequence of such decisions is to drive perpetual litigation and to pit group against group. Ironically, the efforts to integrate the campus have led to segregation. With race as a central criterion for all decisions, black students are unjustifiably clannish, demanding, and sometimes permitted to have their own dormitory space and separate eating facilities. At the 1991 Vassar College graduation there was a separate graduation ceremony for black students. Black students wore on their hoods the tri-colors of African liberation (red, green and black) instead of the Vassar colors. These specially decorated hoods were paid out of general student funds.

In order to accommodate the many interests on campus and the various talents and aptitudes of students, the university has created a metaphorical supermarket of courses. There are courses that are hard and courses that are soft; some pander to race and gender and others are bereft of any meaning; some have value and others are translations of "Sesame Street" for immature adolescents. As the university's purpose becomes increasingly ambiguous, catalogues get thicker. Not only is there a college for everyone, now there is a course for everyone. Instead of reading texts that liberate the individual from a narrow, provincial, limited perspective, avatars of a new culture argue for texts that reinforce the study of what is familiar or what passes for politically acceptable.

It is almost a cliché to contend that most college students have not read the great works of Western civilization, or of any civilization for that matter, are science and math illiterates, and cannot construct logical arguments in a debate or written statement. It is hardly surprising that, buffeted by the ethos of total egalitarianism, the indiscriminate supermarket of ideas and a radical agenda, most students graduate from college "trained in incapacity," to borrow a phrase from Thorstein Veblen. Perplexed by the success of his book *The Closing of the American Mind,* Allan Bloom once asked me whether I had an explanation for the book's phenomenal sales. Granted that most people do not read

Nietzsche (discussion of whose writings takes up the second half of the book), and granted that serious philosophy does not a bestseller make, I suggested that parents, confounded by the psychobabble of their college-educated children and tired of being called bourgeois and philistine, were willing to invest $20 to find out why they were wasting $25,000 a year. Bloom nodded knowingly.

The proliferation of scholarship with specialties now so arcane that the average person cannot possibly know what is meant by academic terminology has reduced knowledge to a form of mysticism or revealed truth. A faculty member at the New School for Social Research describes himself as a "post-modern semiotics instructor." After having listened to him lecture, I am convinced he is a witch doctor enamored with obfuscation of language and meaning. Yet, he is not alone. I have observed two kinds of modern instructors. First, there is the Pied Piper, eager for recognition, for whom teaching is synonymous with sermonizing. Then there is the instructor who is eager to get teaching over with in order to spend time doing research. The former is a frustrated preacher; the latter often an opportunist for whom teaching is little more than a means to an end.

As teaching has been downgraded and the curriculum made into a political football, the rhetoric of self-praise employed by academics to describe their craft has risen dramatically. Words like excellent, profound, life-enhancing are pegged into the vernacular of a university life manipulated by advertising techniques. It is as if adolescents were being told "be all you can be in the university." How, in that case, can parents possibly tell John or Mary "college is not for you"? The college experience has gone from a rite of passage to a right of passage. All the while, the educational experience has been transmogrified into a world rescue experience. Students are now asked to solve problems that even experts cannot control.

At commencement exercises, university presidents, in acts of collective conceit and deceit, tell assembled family members that this class is prepared to fight hunger, nuclear proliferation, homelessness, environmental contamination, disease, despair, urban decay. There is virtually no limit, it is suggested, to what these youngsters can do. Of course, most students neither believe nor act out such exaggerated rhetoric. It would be a refreshing change if these same presidents were saying, "I can assert that these graduates have read classic texts, can write a coherent paper, make logical judgments, understand the essential principles of science, speak a foreign language, and recognize themes in history." But no, such assertions would be far too commonplace for the by now conventional hyperbole. It is the illusion that counts.

Such illusions have taken universities down a path where every opportunity for a new program is seized. What Barzun calls the "Babel index" is the temptation to do what rewards of money and glory demand. In the face of these blandishments the university is helpless to steer an independent course. It is often defined by the parameters of community involvement and external rewards. The lure of money and recognition is not only a blandishment for the university as a corporate body, it is also an almost irresistible attraction for the professor. Scarcely a full professor in the Western world is without opportunities to consult, advise, and write in return for money. Every presidential candidate travels with his coterie of hired academic hands. The compromise an academic makes with a world external to the university has fundamentally altered the expectations, commitment, and loyalty of the professorate. A flight from teaching that has reached epidemic proportions is in large part a function of divided loyalty.

Behind divided loyalty and obedience to several masters lurks a pervasive ambiguity about good teaching and scholarship. Is good teaching necessarily the art of stimulating students? Does it fit into the Procrustean bed established by those expressing a political or social orthodoxy? Is good teaching related to popularity? Is scholarship measured by the number of articles and the stature of the journals in which they are published? Most importantly, who is to judge? In a setting where celebrity status is in the ascendancy, far too often a superficial evaluation is made while the less obvious contribution of well-crafted lectures, concern for students, and careful grading is overlooked. It is, therefore, hardly surprising that the shared bonds of collegiality have retreated before the attractions of money, released time, and recognition.

Foremost on the faculty agenda is tenure—an institution deeply ensconced in higher education "to make professors independent of thought control." While tenure offers a charter of freedom for the professor, it is an institutional gamble in which the university bets that "the young genius," as Barzun puts it, will not "ripen into a dull old man, who has to be supported for years even when insupportable." The financial vicissitudes in higher education are forcing a careful review of this once sacrosanct institution. But there are other reasons for the reexamination of tenure that Barzun's illuminating analysis of this question could not anticipate.

In the traditional vision, the university perpetuated the idea of Western civilization in two separate but related ways. First, it imparted an intellectual method that rejected the dogmatic, orthodox, and conspiratorial in favor of a broad-minded empiricism and a regard for the world's complexity. Second, it conveyed an underlying appreciation for the values of free societies, most notably a respect for the individual and for the ideals of personal liberty and constitutional democracy which emanated from it. As a result, the university experience had a dual character, in part a process of intellectual training and in part a process of socialization.

This view of the academy, however, is alien to the spirit of what aspires to become the new, activist vision, protected by the same institution of tenure and academic freedom as the traditional version, yet fundamentally at odds with it

methodologically and substantively. Armed with totalistic visions and millennial expectations, its partisans have little sympathy for open discourse or analytic procedures that fail to guarantee desired conclusions. As Howard Zinn, erstwhile professor of history at Boston University, once put it, "In a world where justice is maldistributed, there is no such thing as a 'neutral' or representative recapitulation of the facts." In such a view, objective truth is only what the present dictates or the future requires.

The organizing principle of the new scholarship inheres in its purpose rather than in its methods or theories. Its purpose is unremitting attack on cultural as well as political and economic institutions. This is a scholarship which sets out to prove what is already known; in short, the direct antithesis of what scholarship is. Yet, the ally in this systematic campaign to "capture the culture" (to borrow a phrase from Antonio Gramsci) is tenure and academic freedom. The classroom now frequently becomes the setting for ethnic and class antagonism. Until recently the university served as an important means of assimilating the upwardly mobile and integrating future leaders of American society. A significant portion of the professorate now strives to do the reverse, fostering political estrangement and cultural segmentation. Tenure and academic freedom in the febrile minds of would-be revolutionaries have been transformed from institutions that militate against external pressure and manipulation into institutions that promote them.

I disagree, however, with Barzun's assertion that "the loss of intellectual revelation [among students] is partly due to the improvement of the high school and its adoption of much of the contents of general education." Many colleges, he says, are giving freshmen the sense of repetition of what has already been learned. This claim does not square with my experience. Not only am I convinced that high schools are not improving, based on my assessment of incoming freshmen, but the number in the highest quintile of SAT scores—as one superficial symptom of the secondary school malaise—has been declining ever since 1963. The agitation organized by students during the overheated period from 1967 to 1973 was prompted by rootlessness. The combination of war, the draft, a desire for social experimentation, spiralling divorce rates promoted activism instead of thought, problem solving instead of evidence gathering, doing instead of reflecting. The university as a center of learning was converted into a Paris Commune of sorts.

As I look back to that period, the high-school education students received did not help matters. It was an era of curriculum experimentation that produced a generation that was out of touch with basic cultural cues and unfamiliar with even the rudimentary facts about government and history. When Chester Finn Jr. and Diane Ravitch asked in their book *What Do Seventeen Year Olds Know?,* their answer, after much testing, was, not very much. Thrust into a college setting, enthralled with a utopian vision, these naive seventeen-year-olds, who do not know that the American Revolution came before the French Revolution, turned into right-thinking revolutionaries. Rather than arriving at opinion through a process of learning, reasoning and concluding, these products of American high schools made judgments *parti pris,* as if it were in the air they breathe or the coaxial cable that brought them visual images.

Where Jacques Barzun is unquestionably right is in his contention that students are "caught in the mandarin system" that makes a degree indispensable to a professional career. Therefore students are obliged to endure bad teaching and other manifestations of neglect. In a sense not well-understood by student radicals of bygone days and certainly not understood by students today, they are often victimized. Yet, this was not and rarely is the reason for campus agitation. The prototypical student radical of the late sixties has been replaced by a different complacent prototype today, albeit rootlessness is a feature common to both generations. In the past, rootlessness manifested itself as rebellion, now it is manifest as a search for orthodoxy, whether it takes the form of symbols, deconstruction, or obsession with third world authors. Students, as befits their age and idealism, have been in search of facile answers to complex questions, but it is—or should I say was—the responsibility of faculty members to lead them to a path in which the search is for truth rather than for slogans. But truth is elusive.

Barzun brings great insight to the student orientation as it evolved in the sixties and beyond, but perhaps the clearest demonstration of his perspicacity is in his description of university administrations as "above and below." As an administrator for twenty years, I understand full well that I work for a faculty and that whatever limited influence I possess stems from my artful use of persuasion. I cannot pull rank since rank as an ascribed state does not exist in the increasingly egalitarianized university. I am after all only one member of a team consisting of president, vice presidents, and other deans who in synchronous devotion to a well understood and accepted goal can move the university community along haltingly and who, under normal circumstances, may only debate, consider, review, and disagree.

Today's decanal duties include nourishing a faculty with grant money, foundation support, concessions from the central administration, and a filtered assessment of how government regulations and the latest administrative missives influence its work, what Barzun calls "intelligent facilitation." A dean is part mountebank, part manager, part executive, part interpreter, part fund raiser, and part alchemist. He must keep his school intact by orchestrating natural antipathies among faculty members, students, and alumni groups, and he must do so with sufficient good cheer so that confidence in his management ability is maintained.

Perhaps the most notable shift in higher education is that a professor who once focused on his students and his pension and did almost everything for himself, is now thrust into a setting where, as a result of specialization, regula-

tions, and diverse and clashing interests, he is obliged to rely on others, most especially his dean. At bottom, a faculty does not want to administer the college, except when it believes the administrative decisions impinge on the prerogatives of teaching and scholarship. As Barzun noted: "It is his [dean's] business to serve *them* [faculty members], not his likes and dislikes." [emphasis in the original]

The most glaring moment of recognition, in a book filled with echoes of the past, struck me in the chapter about the budget. A mystical air surrounds this item called the budget. Although prepared with a precision that reifies numbers, it also charts priorities and standards. The budget measures nothing tangible, yet whatever is tangible in the university cannot exist without it. It is a document of compromise, deliberation, and assumptions; it is a distillation of views about the future, yet firmly anchored in the past. Departments, individual faculty members, and other constituents brandish knives to get their "fair" slice of this metaphorical "pie."

At the center of all bickering and compromises there is an objective reality composed of debits and credits and the fear of a deficit. The word education, however, is rarely mentioned and the budgeting process is informed by a decided tilt toward retention of programs already in place. Rarely does anyone apply "zero budgeting" methods, in which each program director is obliged to make a case for his budget each year. Should such a policy be introduced, the university would probably not be the same again. Whatever animosity exists among faculties would be exacerbated by a stated justification for their existence. Recognition of this likelihood is what greases the budget-resolution wheel. Most constituents would rather have partial rewards than a Hobbesian world of each against all.

Leading the charge for university budget reform are those who wish to change the university to reflect their political principles. These are the neo-libertarians, who, through a prism of dissatisfaction with the status quo, wish to convert the university into their version of utopia. Utopia, for them, is related to curriculum reform, which often includes eagerness to erase the distinction between teacher and student, authority and constituent. That a university cannot directly serve social ends is a point overwhelmed by the flood-tide of political discontent. Even normally sober academics now engage in the hyperbole of some brave new world led by recent college graduates who have the wisdom to solve social problems their elders are unable to remedy. Mercifully, the era of "relevance" has come to an end. But it has been replaced by an age of irrelevance, though not perceived as such, since many academics assert, on the contrary, that they are curing present ills.

It is, of course, customary for university presidents to proclaim that graduates are being prepared to face the demands of modern life. Yet, the meaning of these words "prepare for life" is ambiguous. Recently a colleague tried to address this problem by proposing that students should learn problem-solving techniques as undergraduates. When pressed, he had to admit that problem solving without knowledge was impossible. On another occasion I heard a distinguished scholar refer to the need for student "experience." Again the claim had a spurious ring to it. If experience is the essence of education, then my grandfather quite obviously deserved a PhD.

Barzun advances the notion of "preposterism" to make the point that since knowledge is valuable, every aspiring college teacher shall produce research. The resultant knowledge explosion has had its fallout in every sector of society. There is more work published to little purpose than ever before. And the more that is published, the less we understand about our nation, our individual roles, our principles, our beliefs, and ourselves. So much of this so-called research is produced at the expense of teaching. Barzun contends that the best liberal arts colleges have "a strong grip on solid subject matter and trust to its broadening, deepening and thickening effect." If this claim was true once, it is most certainly less true now. Universities compete for scholars judged mainly by reputation. Despite lip service given to teaching, it is much less valued than research, as both the allocation of chairs and salary determination amply demonstrate.

The explosion of research has also trivialized the curriculum through the proliferation of courses which pay obeisance to what is fashionable. One critic of higher education refers to the course guidebook as the "Chinese menu for dilettantes." What the extensive listing of courses actually represents is the abdication of faculty responsibility. In an atmosphere in which the purpose of higher education has been obscured by a reformist agenda and the curriculum has been turned into a battlefield for departmental scrimmage, the number of courses grows in proportion to designated self-interest and the effort to accommodate "new" disciplines.

The by-product of this change is an undergraduate program often devoid of commitment to teaching and often lacking any coherent purpose. The ambiguity of most college curricula is deeply embedded in the general ambiguity of what a university should be. Barzun notes the two oft-repeated contradictory messages in higher education: this is a public institution capable of participating in the affairs of state—at New York University we say "a private university in the public service"—and this is an elite institution, an ivory tower, if you will, whose majesty should not be compromised by the affairs of state. Retaining the dignity of the university, specifically its devotion to research, is increasingly difficult when the desire to merge and blur all roles and all purposes dominates university life. As more and more demands were imposed on universities—demands universities could not fulfill and would not resist—the rhetoric of higher education changed. Literature describing the institution invariably refers to saving neighborhoods and even saving nations, having world-class athletic programs and world-class laboratories; rarely do these descriptions mention the value of simple exchange between mentor and student that may inspire a thirst for knowledge.

Alfred North Whitehead maintains in *Science and the Modern World* that the twentieth-century research university is constructed in accordance with the principles of seventeenth-century physics. He argues that the revolutionary physics of our century, with its reconceiving self and world and its integration of fields of study, came too late to be incorporated into a Newtonian structure of mechanical parts separated by function. The "new" university is in fact old at heart. It fractures science and the humanities and reduces truth, goodness, and beauty to mere expressions of subjective judgment. Moral virtue, an essential component of education before the Enlightenment, has been relegated to the archaic as professional and technical study are in the ascendant.

William James's discussion of this "scientific nightmare" did not prevent the evolution of the modern university, nor did the emergence of revolutionary ideas in physics and philosophy. These ideas offered a conception of an integrated world of freedom, responsibility, and moral vitality. But the university was already well on its way to becoming a Cartesian world of departments and bureaucracies. I may be day dreaming, but I am persuaded that many people outside the academy believe that the university has failed to address the common concern for meaning, the humane, and the ethical.

Each university department guards its private domain of expert knowledge with jealousy—a subject matter base underwritten by professional associations. Hence, willy-nilly, the university has become a gatekeeper for professional power and academic identity. In its attempt to assemble the disparate parts into a whole, the university community presupposes an experiential sense of the world, a sense contradicted by the very compartmentalization of knowledge the university promotes. Moreover, as technology is increasingly focused and as professionals are increasingly specialized, judgments about the world that emerge from the study of disciplines are construed solely in technical terms, often imperiling a sense of broadly defined human significance. It is hardly surprising that a new breed of humanities professor has similarly relegated all subject matter to the realm of ideology, on the principle that truth is transitory. Universals are repudiated by this new-age professor, nurtured by an environment that is narrowly specialized. Professionalizing the humanities should be seen as an essential contradiction. It is worth recalling the subtitle of Allan Bloom's *The Closing of the American Mind*, namely, *How Higher Education Has Failed Democracy and Impoverished the Souls of Today's Students*.

The failure of the modern university is its unwillingness to consider "holistic" thinking, a way of thinking that cuts across disciplinary barriers. To conceive of a mind separate from a body is to misunderstand the interdependence of all the elements within the self. At the same time, an obsessive concern with the self, with the ego's interests, has converted much learning into the pursuit of the I. I have lost patience with colleagues who start every discussion with the words, "How do you feel about . . . ?" Since the meaning of personal feeling cannot be dissociated from the meaning of the world, the question is ultimately foolish unless clearly related to a reasoned conception of life.

The story is told about a conversation between Ludwig Wittgenstein and Sigmund Freud, in which the would-be master of the mind asserted that through protracted and undirected talk one could ultimately decipher the mystery of the unconscious. Wittgenstein, however, remained unpersuaded. "Sigmund," he reportedly said, "the reason I believe your assumption is wrong is that talk without limit or purpose ends in futility." Wittgenstein was not only making a point about psychotherapy, but also about education. Pedagogy demands limits and purpose. We cannot study everything or know anything without some idea of what is to be learned.

With cynicism about higher education on the rise at a rate only slightly slower than the rate of increase in tuition, I believe it is time to consider the end of the university as we have known it. I should hasten to note that I do not welcome this development; my observations are little more than logical extrapolations from my own experiences and from what I have seen happening since Jacques Barzun wrote the *American University* a quarter of a century ago.

In her book *The Case Against College,* Caroline Bird counsels that in calculating the costs and benefits of a college education, middle-class parents should not automatically rule in favor of college for their children. Whether a college degree provides the economic rewards that are widely promised relative to the investment is, however, less significant than the fact that the university is a likely casualty in a changing climate of opinion.

The inevitable lockstep of the high-school-to-college odyssey is waning, because the economic conditions, the cost of tuition cost for university studies, and the politicization of the academy militate against the expectation of business as usual. Tuition costs, as everyone knows, have soared beyond the reach of even many well-to-do parents. In the past four years, with inflation hovering around 3.5 percent annually, tuition increases at private colleges have averaged 9 percent. The typical salaried parent sending a child to a private college (let us say someone earning $50,000 a year) is in a vise, because it is presumed by admissions officers that the parent is earning enough to pay the tuition tab. But if this parent were to send a son or daughter to, say, Princeton, it would be inviting bankruptcy. After covering tuition, room and board, books, and other expenses totalling more than $25,000, the wage earner would, after paying taxes, be driven into the ranks of the poor. College presidents routinely descend on Washington with their lobbyists seeking succor for financial problems; and to an extraordinary degree they have been successful. Aid to higher education—after the so-called cuts of the Reagan-Bush years—is in the $12 billion range.

We are now, however, in the era of budget cutting. The halcyon days of guaranteed assistance, minimally at the inflation rate, are over. The once sacred cow of educational spending is now simply another budget item. If government is no longer a savior, neither are continued tuition increases. Raising tuition expense above inflation only exacerbates market conditions, since the pool of potential applicants for admission is reduced. Scarcely a university administrator in the country fails to lament a condition in which universities price themselves out of a middle-class market. Is it any wonder that admissions standards have eased in most colleges and that the search has begun in earnest for the "new" student, a person older than the typical eighteen-year-old freshman?

Demographic characteristics of the nation are affecting college enrollment. The baby boom has become a distant memory and the recent baby "boomlet" will not have a profound effect on the percentage of adolescents in the population. In fact, the over-sixty population group will soon be growing faster than the under-nineteen population. Thus the 1960s are not likely to be repeated. We will not see anytime soon—and probably not again—an American population with one out of three people attending a college or university. If anything, the "birth-dearth"—a decline in the number of children per family—is likely to characterize the population of the United States for some time to come. With the present birth rate of 1.8 children per family, there is little doubt that there will not be enough adolescents by the year 2020 to sustain the present number of colleges and universities, unless a larger than characteristic portion of the nation's high-school graduates are encouraged and subsidized to attend colleges and the number of colleges is reduced.

Both of these changes are already evident. Many colleges have closed their doors and other closings are imminent. Some colleges have joined with others in a confederation of necessity. Some have engaged in a systematic reduction of faculty members and enrolled students. Still others are seeking adult students to replace the diminishing adolescent pool, and yet others dip deeper into the cohort of high-school graduates to secure enrollment.

At Hampshire College, for example, officials argued in 1982 that in order to retain an enrollment of 1200 students they would be obliged to lower admission standards. After an unsatisfactory experiment with marginal students, they switched gears and reduced enrollment from 1200 to 1000—at the same time reducing the faculty by 10 percent. Such decisions to retrench are becoming commonplace. If not retrenchment, then merger. In this vein Barrington College of Rhode Island merged in 1985 with Gordon College of Massachusetts. However, when merger does not seem to be the answer, coeducation sometimes is. Vassar College strengthened its precarious financial situation by becoming a coeducational institution. Even one of the last holdouts, Goucher College, a women's school since its founding in 1885, decided to become coeducational in 1987.

Reinforcing this enrollment trend is the growth of corporate-based alternatives to a college degree, including conferring of degrees by corporations. One no longer has to go to college for a diploma. I.B.M., to give one illustration, now operates the largest "university" in the world from its Armonk facility. Bell and Howell offers a degree program for its present employees and as a lure for potential employees. Corporations can attract some of the brightest graduates with a promise of free tuition, a secure job, and training appropriate to the workplace. While university officials contend that this kind of corporate education is narrowly specialized and often does not include liberal arts courses, these programs must be seen against a backdrop of increasing cynicism about the value of a liberal arts education and toward what is regarded as its often fraudulent character. Despite the claim that the university is a guardian and custodian of culture, an assumption shared by Barzun and others, the conflation of fiscal demands and a reduction in university standards make the corporate BA competitive with the conventional college degree.

Very few academics who have thought about the subject would contend that the manner in which college degrees are presently offered will prevail in the next century. Fiber optic technology and the marriage of computer and television permit a high quality, customized, and inexpensive degree accessible at home to everyone. The capital investment in university buildings and equipment, the investment in tenured faculties, and the cost of recruiting students militate against the continuation of the present university system. If the university has gone through two phases in this century—the time of innocence and dominant leaders and the era of bureaucracy—a third phase, dominated by technology, is looming over the near horizon.

If the legitimacy of higher education were not in question, perhaps the tide of technological change could be slowed. But since the 1960s, in fact since the publication of the **American University,** the university as the broker of ideas has been converted into the university as the would-be molder of history. In the process, the authority of the institution has suffered in public word and deed. In the decade roughly from 1964 to 1974, the university was at the center of a political maelstrom of anti-Vietnam sentiment and of demands for free speech and participatory democracy.

As the sanctuary for all unpopular opinion, the university was being converted into a hothouse for a succession of fashionable views. Academic freedom became an apparatus for protection from criticism. When opponents disapproved of the propagandizing, the flag of academic freedom was raised along with vague references to McCarthyism.

If the academic responsibility of the past was to nurture youthful minds and provide a context for judgment, however questionable some of the methods may have been, the febrile members of the academic community now see their job as conversion, that is, excoriating "naïveté" and exposing the "corrosive" elements in the nation and in the cul-

ture. Not that this effort has been entirely successful. Students today are like students of the past: skeptical of their professors' views. But despite student skepticism, a conventional wisdom on campus has emerged. Feminism is a given, invariably accepted without question. Affirmative action is part of the academic catechism. Investment in South Africa is *verboten.* The Strategic Defense Initiative is the wrong policy. Rich people are by definition exploitive. Businessmen are avaricious. These views are not hypotheses that can be subjected to rigorous analysis. They are incantations accepted without even a nod to rational investigation, as "sensitivity training" and its resultant bureaucracy on many campuses would seem to suggest.

Partly as a consequence of this development, there have been a staggering number of federal and state reports about the university in the last ten years, all concluding in one way or another that something is wrong. William Bennett, the former Secretary of Education, writes in *To Reclaim a Legacy* that the liberal arts have become so "diluted" that college graduates know little of the "culture and civilization of which they are members."

Knowledge of American history or European civilization is not a prerequisite for graduation from most colleges. Frederick Rudolf, coauthor of *Integrity in the College Curriculum,* points to "the accelerating decline of the undergraduate degree." He contends that in "what passes for a college curriculum, almost anything goes." Even where efforts are made to restore quality to the undergraduate program, they are often subverted by a university pork barrel in which the retention of one course in French, for example, is secured by like consideration for a course in philosophy within the so-called core curriculum.

While administrators invariably claim devotion to high standards, tuition dependency cannot help but affect them adversely. The National Education Association, notably charitable to student opinion, notes in a report on colleges that students are "increasingly reluctant to undertake courses of study in colleges that challenge their academic skills." This condition, by the way, is not likely to change in a "buyer's market" unless all universities institute the same requirements—a highly implausible scenario. Bennett has pointed out that fewer than half of the nation's colleges demand the study of a foreign language as a degree requirement, compared with 90 percent a scant twenty-five years ago. Rudolf describes higher education as "a supermarket where students are shoppers and professors are merchants."

As the liberal arts have been faring badly, career programs have grown in stature and importance. They also pay the university's bills. Business and engineering, to cite "hot" fields, often require nothing more than a rudimentary brush with the humanities. At many universities, Master of Liberal Arts programs have been introduced for college graduates without liberal arts training. These ploys are not altogether the fault of universities. Desire to make higher education into an instrument for democratizing placed the university squarely in the middle of an obligation it could not shirk. Many students, lacking adequate preparation for college study, were "dumped" into the academy with the expectation that in four years small miracles could be performed. However, faculty members, trained in a narrow area of specialization and often not equipped with pedagogical skill, were poor operatives for the task of remedial teaching.

The answer to this dilemma was a variety of reforms, including undifferentiated grades (pass/fail), that blurred differences in ability and contaminated the meaning of a degree. Between 1963 and 1992 the share of the student population majoring in traditional arts and science disciplines declined precipitously. Philosophy lost 60 percent of its students, and English 72 percent, while psychology, arguably the softest of the social sciences, gained 56 percent. Journalism is the fastest growing undergraduate program. At New York University it enrolls the highest number of undergraduate students. Of course, part of this general trend away from the arts and sciences can be attributed to the economic recession and to poor instruction, but some portion of the shift is clearly related to a virtual abandonment of the much-touted goal of excellence.

How serious can the university's mission be when "freshman" is eschewed from the language as an offense to first-year female students; when Crispus Attucks, an obscure mulatto who was inadvertently killed in the Boston Massacre, is exalted as an American hero in history courses, and when "peace studies" are introduced as a discipline in order to decry the existence of nuclear weapons? It is the attention given to such issues and the media coverage of campus turmoil that have altered the once rubber-stamp public support for higher education.

The baby boom of the post-war era accelerated public and private spending on colleges and universities to levels grossly out of proportion to any future demographic realities. Higher education was deemed an unqualified good; therefore, the more you have of it, the better it is for the body politic. One cannot travel for more than three miles on the San Diego Freeway without seeing a sign pointing to a community college. That these colleges may be superfluous with the declining pool of adolescents in the nation seems obvious.

What is not so obvious is the continuing misguided faith in education as a anodyne for all that ails us. As evidence from the past three decades illustrates, most of the social reforms imposed on universities in order to relieve perceived social problems had a greater effect on the university than on the social problems themselves. For example, affirmative action policy has had a profound effect on the proliferation of university bureaucrats and on admissions policy, but it has not had any influence on relieving racial tension. Some academics argue, validly I believe, that this policy has exacerbated racial tension.

Many communities with a population over 50,000 considered it a disgrace if the town did not have a community college. After all, if it is good for the big cities, why should it not be good for the towns and the suburbs? Community status got entangled with the presence of a college. The late Nelson Rockefeller once described the state-supported college system as his greatest accomplishment as governor of New York. He neglected to point out, however, the enormous cost of this system to the taxpayers of the state: $4.5 billion a year, equal to a $17,000 subvention per student. In our own era of austerity, taxpayers have a valid reason to voice their concern about the way in which their money is spent. A taxpayer revolt on aid to higher education—public and private—is not yet manifest, but the context for legislative decisions on education has changed to such an extent that higher education is no longer shielded from disapprobation.

Much of the money on campus is being spent on an activity that is increasingly subject to careful scrutiny research. As is attested by the vast majority of Nobel laureates, most researchers have a university appointment. A symbiosis between the university and basic research has evolved over the past half century. It was in large part fostered by government, since this was a relatively inexpensive way for the state to support universities and simultaneously to support research. It saved an enormous investment in government-sponsored research centers. This convenience for government and benefit for the university has been criticized by some academics as obliging the university to do the government's bidding. Recent controversy over the research for the Strategic Defense Initiative (SDI) demonstrates the point. If one is truly concerned about securing the autonomy of the curriculum and protecting it against ideological assault, then one should also be concerned about the intrusion of government projects into university life, an intrusion that may jeopardize the independence of researchers.

At this writing, it appears that government is gradually, but perceptibly, disengaging itself from university research programs. At the same time, a host of think tanks have been organized to fill the gaps universities have left in basic research. Scientists are just as likely to do research at Bell Laboratories as they are at a university. It can also be shown that the majority of college and university facilities are not used for serious research. A recent National Science Foundation report, after reviewing faculty contributions, indicates that only about fifty universities constitute serious science-research centers. If the paucity of research at most colleges were recognized, the transition to alternative research facilities and the corresponding budget retrenchment may not seem so formidable.

Professors are in a "declining industry" where salaries have not kept pace with inflation. As a result, many moonlight in order to keep pace. The moonlighting usually takes the form of consulting, which diminishes loyalty to the university and dedication to teaching, particularly the teaching of general undergraduate courses. In report after report on university instruction, whether from the National Endowment for the Humanities or the Carnegie Council on Teaching, reference is made to unsatisfactory college teaching. But where will future teachers come from when the liberal arts have fallen from grace, when serious scholarship is not encouraged and only rarely found, and when salaries cannot compete with those in comparable fields? The college classroom may once have been the arena for vigorous intellectual discourse, but a report of student complacency in the *Chronicle of Higher Education* indicates that this condition is no longer all pervasive. In most student polls, undergraduates can rarely name one professor who inspired them. Where, for a contemporary generation of students, is the inspiration that students at Columbia enjoyed in the period from 1940 to 1970, when they were taught by Jacques Barzun, Lionel Trilling, and Mark Van Doren?

To an extraordinary degree, college education has become, in the bad sense of the word, personal—too intensely personal, another example of solipsism in our society. William Bennett has pointed out how success in school is frequently unrelated to success outside of school and how academic subjects tend to be "of limited consequence in the real world." If he is right or even partially right, then the university's legitimacy has ceased to exist. A National Institute of Education report concludes with the plea that "all bachelor's degree recipients should have at least two years of liberal education." If they are not getting it, what are they getting? Visibly, young people are scrambling to get jobs, which they think requires only training, not education. At a time when colleges are trying to lure students, the wise offer of an education is not likely to find many takers.

In his article "The Case against Credentialism" in the *Atlantic Monthly,* James Fallows noted, "What is rewarded is excellence in school, which is related to excellence on the job only indirectly and sometimes not at all." If college work has so little application to employment, why should parents invest thousands of dollars in it? And if the argument for higher education is not utilitarian (which it is only indirectly) then a case must be made for learning as the edification of soul and character. Even the remaining ardent defenders of the university are incapable of making this claim effectively. What we are left with is college as an adolescent rite of passage that provides a remote chance youngsters will discover an area of vocational interest which may prove to have a lasting effect on their lives.

Thirty years ago, the university was put on a pedestal as the place where "the whole man" was developed (it was a time when the word man still had its full, genderless meaning of "human being"). So confident were they about this assertion that, as far as I know, very few of my classmates questioned that claim. The university could be exalted because it stood for something worthy and intelligible. That is no longer true. I could argue that the fate of the university is not related to the future of education; the two are not necessarily synonymous. But reflecting on what I have noted in these pages and Barzun's observations, I am convinced that we are entering a new phase in the evolution

of the university. It is already the case that learning and research are being fostered elsewhere, chiefly by business corporations acting in self-defense against ill-prepared college graduates. Once parents are persuaded that this less costly alternative can confer the same advantages as the elite institutions, the university we have recently known will be obsolete.

There is much to be lamented about the passing of the university even in its most recent incarnation. At its best, the university can promote the exchange of ideas and develop an appreciation of our common humanity. It can usher in moments of enlightenment that for young minds can be intoxicating. It can inspire vocations and arouse devotion to public service. There must be dozens of men and women today so inspired by the Barzun-Trilling seminars at Columbia of decades ago that they decided to follow the path of their mentors into teaching. If the university is destined for decline and demise, the present moment is not one for rejoicing.

Jacques Barzun with Sarah F. Golo (interview date 3 April 2000)

SOURCE: *"PW* Talks with Jacques Barzun," in *Publishers Weekly,* Vol. 247, No. 4, April 3, 2000, p. 69.

[In the following interview, Barzun discusses his notion of "culture" and "decadence" and the general thesis of From Dawn to Decadence.]

[Golo:] Your book **From Dawn to Decadence: 500 Years of Western Cultural Life** *is so wide-ranging, it covers everything from the literary to the culinary. How do you define "Culture"?*

[Barzun:] Cultural history cannot be defined, because it really has no limits. "Culture" can be seen as high culture, the arts—generally. But anthropologists have changed all that. . . . When they went to see primitive peoples, they covered absolutely everything those peoples were doing—from how they cooked to how they worshiped.

In the book, you say that the Bible used to be the common culture of the West, but no longer is. Do we have a common culture today?

It used to be that colleges and universities provided for a certain group of people—not the whole country, but a good many—a common culture. But now that has been attacked. Now everyone has his own little specialty and enjoys it more than exploring outside it and grasping other things. So we really have no common intellectual background. I notice in the press, for example, that many familiar allusions to the Greek gods are steadily misused. Everything is a little diluted, a little off-key, and it's a sign that we haven't got anything like a common culture.

Is your book an attempt to establish one?

It can't done as a program; it has to exist as tradition. You can't say, 'I'm going to reestablish culture,' though I think there are some people who are hopeful. . . . Someone has recently written a volume of several hundred cultural facts that people are supposed to know, I don't think it works that way. You can't just memorize facts—it must enter your mind as part of a story. It must be part of the books you've read, the things your friends refer to casually in conversation.

What do you mean when you say our era is "decadent"?

Decadence is the falling apart of ideas and received tradition. I think it's something that happens inevitably when the leading ideas of a particular era—400 or 500 years—are all worked out. That is true of the arts and literature, and it is true also, not always at the same time, of institutions, And I suggest that all the talk today about reinventing government is an admission that the parliamentary system—that representative government—has gotten into a jam. It's impossible to reform even when people do agree about the reform. Another important institution, the nation-state, is now breaking up into separate units that people can defend against other units. All that is decadence. It's not unusual; it happens over and over again. It can last a long or short time depending on circumstances.

Did your feeling that our era was decadent prompt you to do this 500-year study, or did the study come first and then the assessment of our time?

The latter. After linking a number of studies of separate periods and movements, I decided that if I lived long enough, I would try to make a synthesis, fill in the gaps, and see whether any kind of coherent picture came out of the effort. In studying to do this filling in and organization, I came to the conclusion that I have just discussed with you.

Karl E. Meyer (review date May-June 2000)

SOURCE: "Venturing Provocative Judgments," in *New Leader,* Vol. LXXXIII, No. 2, May-June, 2000, pp. 42-3.

[*In the following review, Meyer offers a positive assessment of* From Dawn to Decadence.]

My spontaneous response upon learning of Jacques Barzun's hefty new work was delight and surprise that he is still with us and still scribbling. Born in France in 1907, formerly a professor of history and provost at Columbia University, author of *Berlioz and the Romantic Century* (1950) and other important books, Barzun is seemingly the sole survivor of that once celebrated constellation on Morningside Heights: Lionel Trilling and Meyer Schapiro, Richard Hofstadter and Margaret Mead, C. Wright Mills and Ivan Morris, among others. At 92, on the evidence of this bravura performance, Barzun remembers more than most of us have learned.

From Dawn to Decadence: 500 Years of Western Cultural Life might at quick glance appear to be that soporific thing, a professorial "survey," an eye-glazing assemblage of names and dates plastered in place with platitudes. But wait. Barzun wakes us up with the first of his 30-odd sketches of the West's geniuses and troublemakers. About Martin Luther, he begins: "When the miner's son from Saxony, Luther, Lhuder, Lutter, or Lotharius as he was variously known, posted his 95 propositions on the door of All Saints' Church at Wittenberg on October 31, 1517, the last thing he wanted to do was to break up his church, the Catholic (= 'universal'), and divide his world into warring camps."

That sentence is typical of the graceful concision the author sustains for 800-plus pages. There follows a summary, seasoned with aphorisms, of the unreformed Church of Rome, its gluttonous monks, its corrupt but art-loving Popes, its practice of ordaining boys of 12 as bishops, their wealthy families having provided early for their future happiness. "The system was rotten," the author asserts in a passage that helps explain his title. "This had been said over and over, yet the old bulk was immovable. When people accept futility and the absurd as normal, the culture is decadent. The term is not a slur; it is a technical label. A decadent culture offers opportunities chiefly to the satirist, and the turn of the 15C had a good many, one of them a great one: Erasmus." That introduces us to Luther's counterpoise in the battle of ideas, a tolerant Christian reformer who did not experience faith as a passion. And who lost out.

Impressively, Barzun keeps a complex narrative flowing as it moves from century to century, from the arts and sciences to politics and plumbing, its themes encapsulated in the lives of the famous, the infamous or the scarcely known (e.g. the feminist Christine di Pisan, the medical innovators Paracelsus and Thomas Beddoes, the military engineer Vauban, the financial adventurer John Law, the gifted educator Marsilio Ficino, the English critic James Agate).

The book is also leavened with apt boldface inserts—crisp snippets from songs, speeches and books, many unfamiliar, such as the astute prophecy of the British ambassador to Austria in 1913: "Serbia will someday set Europe by the ears and bring about a universal war on the Continent." Another strategy is the use of "cross-sections" to suggest how the world looked from Madrid in 1540, Venice in 1650, London in 1715, Weimar in 1790, Paris in 1830, and Chicago in 1895—altogether a nice flourish, with a suitable cadenza: New York around 1995.

But what truly confounds narcolepsy is Barzun's unfashionable willingness to venture provocative judgments. "Taken in all," he writes, "Venice [in 1650] was the nearest approach ever made to Plato's system of rulers by duty and dedication who govern soberly." Or:

"It is a notable feature of 20C culture that for the first time in over a thousand years its educated class is not expected to be at least bilingual."

"Louis XIV was much too clever to have said, 'The State? I am the State.'"

"A movement in thought or art produces its best work during the uphill fight to oust the enemy, that is previous thought or art. Victory brings on imitation and ultimately Boredom."

"The great advantage for science of an aimless universe is that it frees the imagination. Since there are no preconceived 'ends' that things must 'reach,' anything is possible."

"Kipling is too often regarded as a jingo imperialist. On more than one occasion he was a severe judge of his country . . . evidently aware of portents of change, of some risen wind that could overturn and destroy. His uttering that perception while the queen was being glorified was apt. The Victorian institutions, and their counterparts outside England, no longer commanded allegiance or respect. The thoughtful knew that a certain view of life must be given up, but not by revolution in the heroic mood—that had bred its own evils. The ethos could be overturned in the literal sense—turned upside down—by ridicule, by doing in all things the exact opposite. Gilbert and Sullivan's topsy-turvydom was to be enacted in social thought and real life."

Barzun's erudition and enormous range have earned him the right to plunge his oars into the deepest seas. He is old-fashioned in the best sense of that phrase, irradiating *From Dawn to Decadence* with the scholarship of figures whose names one rarely sees nowadays, like Preserved Smith, Alfred Jay Nock, José Ortega y Gasset, Joseph Wood Krutch, and Sir Norman Angell, a reminder of the untapped riches in forgotten volumes.

In any such Moby Dick of a book there is the risk that the great white whale will take over and run amok. Barzun maintains control, on the whole I think successfully, by defining what he is about and sticking to his design. His focus is on the modern era, which he dates from the Reformation, and the great revolutions that have shaped our minds and behavior—the monarchical, liberal and social, roughly a century apart.

Within each, he traces thematic currents, identified as Emancipation, "the modern theme par excellence"; Individualism, or the irrepressible urge to develop one's talents; Secularism, stemming from classic works that depict the world in a man-centered way; and Primitivism, or the restless quest for a simpler, fairer natural order. These themes mingle and jostle, inspiring visions of Utopia, religious insurrections, demands for social and economic equality, but also contending brands of political extremism, Right and Left.

Mercifully, Barzun is not captive to any historical System. He freely acknowledges what common sense tells us, that history offers a vision and not a transcript of the past, but

that good visions "are not merely plausible; they rest on a solid base of facts that nobody disputes"—something common sense also tells us. (Not all "facts," however, are what they seem. Despite the near-universal belief that Marx was the first to refer to "the dustbin of history," the coiner of the phrase was the British politician and writer Augustine Birrell.) Barzun is content to describe the contents of our overarching culture, noting with fastidious care the West's endless series of persisting opposites, in religion and art, politics and morals.

And what is the final reckoning? On this Barzun is calmly categorical. Our age is Decadent, though not in the sense of total ruin, or the loss of energy and talent. "On the contrary," he writes, "it is a very active time, full of deep concerns, but peculiarly restless, for it sees no clear line of advance. The forms of life as of art seem exhausted, the stages of development have been run through. Institutions function painfully. Repetition and frustration are the intolerable result." Boredom and fatigue are unavoidable, hence the proliferation of religious cults and the impulse of primitivism. The upshot is floating hostility to things as they are: "The hope is that getting rid of what is will by itself generate the new life."

On the living canvas of experience we have indeed explored the outer limits of extremism: nationalist, militarist, Marxist, capitalist, theocratic and racist. In the West at least, victory has seemingly gone to a flawed system of welfare capitalism that gives us wealth at the expense of fairness, and to a consensual democracy that enthrones focus groups. Yet of human skills, the predictive is perhaps the most fallible; who in 1900 got the 20th century right? Can there be, one wonders, another Luther waiting at the door?

Jacques Barzun with Arthur M. Schlesinger Jr. and Mark LaFlaur (interview date 21 May 2000)

SOURCE: "The Writing Life: A Talk Between Arthur M. Schlesinger Jr. and Jacques Barzun," in *Los Angeles Times Book Review,* May 21, 2000, pp. 3-4.

[*In the following interview, Barzun comments on his definition of "decadence," as elaborated in* From Dawn to Decadence, *and his view of current religious, geopolitical, literary, and historical trends that characterize the "boredom" and fragmentation of cultural decline.*]

[The following introduction was written by Mark LaFlaur.]

It is difficult now to imagine an age when a weekly newsmagazine would print a cover story on "America and the Intellectual," illustrated with 13 commissioned photographs by Alfred Eisenstaedt. The magazine was *Time,* the date was June 11, 1956, and the cover illustration was of a handsome, dignified man of 48 looking toward a lighted lamp of learning, the kind seen on college rings. Although more famous men (alas, they were all men) discussed in the article could have been shown on the cover (J. Robert Oppenheimer, for instance, or Frank Lloyd Wright), it was Jacques Barzun of Columbia University whom the editors chose to lead the piece, subtitled "The Reconciliation." Education editor Bruce Barton Jr. found in Barzun an affectionate (though not uncritical) relationship between a thinker and his adopted country—indeed, one of Barzun's best-selling books, published in 1954, was titled *God's Country and Mine*—and, no less important in those days, an intellectual who had never been much interested in communism.

The publication 44 years later of Barzun's *From Dawn to Decadence* is a remarkable occasion on several counts, among the most noteworthy of which is that, although it is the crowning work of a 92-year-old author with more than 30 titles in print, it has been taking shape in his mind for more than six decades. A cultural history of the last 500 years, a historical era from its birth to its dissolution—published in the closing months of a millennium might strike some as conveniently timed.

From Dawn to Decadence has been long in coming; indeed, this work has passed through probably one of the longest gestations ever, for in the early 1930s Barzun (in his 20s) was already planning a large cultural history of the West, but he didn't begin writing it until 1992. As a Columbia doctoral candidate, he was in Paris for research on his dissertation when an elderly librarian at the Bibliothèque Nationale, a friend of Barzun's father and an accomplished author, advised the young historian that a great survey must be done not at the beginning of one's career but toward the end. The reason is that when a writer is young, his ideas tend to be derivative and half-baked, and his head half-empty, compared to the learning he will have acquired by his later years.

Barzun put off writing the big book until later and looked upon his other books as "preliminary studies, like sketches for a great mural." The preliminary studies include such highly regarded works as *Romanticism and the Modern Ego* (1943), his best-selling *Teacher in America* (1945), *The House of Intellect* (1959) and *The American University* (1968). He oversaw the completion of Wilson Follett's "Modern American Usage" (1966), has translated numerous works from the French and has written, edited and collaborated on such varied subjects as romanticism, music, teaching, language, science, race and crime fiction.

Born in the artistic community of L'Abbaye de Créteil near Paris in 1907, Jacques Martin Barzun is the son of Henri Martin Barzun, a writer and diplomat, and Anna-Rose Barzun. He was educated at the Lycée Janson de Suilly, Paris, and taught his first class at the age of 9, when the trench warfare of the Great War was taking all available young men. ("All I remember about it," he recalls in *Teacher in America,* "is that it had to do with arithmetic and that the room seemed filled with thousands of very small children in black aprons.") Before the war, Barzun had enjoyed a happy childhood in the company of

some of the greatest artists of the Cubist Decade. Growing up in a "nursery of living culture," he sat in the studio while Albert Gleizes painted his mother's portrait, played in the garden while his father discussed modern art with Marcel Duchamp, Raymond Duchamp-Villon and Jacques Villon and was bounced on the knee of Guillaume Apollinaire while the poet amused him with stories. "Every Saturday and sometimes oftener," Barzun writes in *The Energies of Art* (1956), "the stage [at home] was full: Marinetti acting and shouting, Archipenko making Léger roar with laughter, Delaunay and Ozenfant debating, Paul Fort declaiming his ballads. Varèse or Florent Schmitt surrounded at the piano. . . . On view at close range were also: Ezra Pound, Cocteau . . . Kandinsky . . . Brancusi. . . ." As he has written elsewhere, growing up in that artistic milieu, it was his early impression that "making works of art by exerting genius was the usual occupation of adults. . . . The joy of being was the joy of being *there*; the zest for life was tied to the spectacle of good things being done with confident energy." This was before August 1914.

After World War I he came to the United States to study at Columbia, which he entered at 15. (His father advised against the European universities, decimated and demoralized by the war.) He studied history at Columbia College and graduated at the head of his class in 1927, half a year before his 20th birthday. He had hoped to enter the French diplomatic service, but the war and his American education derailed him from that calling. He considered the law, but his advisors at Columbia persuaded him that he had a knack for narrative history. Barzun is widely known from teaching at Columbia for nearly five decades (1927 to 1975), where he and Lionel Trilling taught the famous colloquium on great books from the 1930s into the mid-1960s. In the 1950s and '60s, he served as dean of graduate faculties, then as dean of faculties and provost and as university professor before his retirement in 1975.

We caught up with Jacques Barzun recently at the New York Historical Society, where we found him in a public conversation with Arthur M. Schlesinger Jr. The following is an edited transcript of their talk.

[*Schlesinger:*] **From Dawn to Decadence** *is a remarkable book. Jacques Barzun seems to have read everything, remembered everything, and woven the history of the Western mind and sensibility together in a relatively seamless whole. Barzun is essentially a historian, but a most unusual historian because he is such a master of so many diverse forms of human expression—music, painting, philosophy, politics, war, statecraft, religion, science, morals, manners—and he understands them all, as a historian must, as revelations of the society that produced them.*

I think we might begin by asking you what you have in mind by this word "decadence."

[Barzun:] Decadence means "falling away, falling apart," and it is something that happens over and over again in history. It may do so in a part of a culture, or in more than half, or pretty much in the whole of a culture at a given time. It comes when the idea of every activity begins to lose its force and its appeal because everything it contains has been worked out, and the more rapid the falling away, the happier the prospect because it levels the ground and enables the newcomers, the youth with bright new ideas, to get started and to establish the next phase of history, to which we give the name of another culture. The very beginning of the history that I undertake to tell in this book was an age of decadence. The 15th century found all sorts of institutions, and particularly the Catholic Church, in a sorry plight. Even the officials of the church said it needed reform from top to bottom. But one of the characteristics of decadence is that although many people see what ought to be done to move on, the institutions are so arthritic that they cannot.

Is decadence irreversible?

Irreversible on the same track, yes. The engine cannot go back. Although very often the next phase—and this is also characteristic of the age of the Protestant Revolution in the 16th century—claims that it is a return. The Protestants wanted to go back to the primitive church, which had no pope and no bishops, no elaborate ritual, just believers huddling together and hoping for grace from on high. That phase is a recurring theme in the 500 years that I treat of, and I give it the name of primitivism: the desire to simplify civilization when it gets too complicated and, being too complicated, has reached a state of stagnation.

You disclaim in the book any cyclical theory of the pretensions of Oswald Spengler or Arnold Toynbee. Yet is there not a cyclical element in your waves of recurrence?

No. I wouldn't call it cyclical because that implies a return to the identical beginning, and the beginnings are all different. If you start looking at civilizations from Egypt through Greece through the Roman empire through the various stages of the medieval, you see that history doesn't repeat except at a level of abstraction. That is to say, the acts of people are all different and all new, but you can say political action is very much the same now as it was in the time of Andrew Jackson, or you can find similarities. Just as you can find similarities in the faces of people you know, but each is individual, and I think each culture is individual.

I well remember Alfred North Whitehead giving his last lecture at Harvard in 1936. His last words of his last lecture were, "Civilizations die of boredom."

Oh yes, I'm a great believer in boredom. I've seen it and I've felt it. And it comes over a people when certain great important ideas are worked out. For example, I think that the resistance of many young people to European culture, saying that dead white European males and their books and their works ought to be thrown into the wastebasket, that is a rationalization of a feeling of boredom. We've heard it, we've seen it. Isn't there a phrase, "Been there. Done that"? That is historical boredom.

Would you relate the rise of fundamentalism around the world today—Protestant fundamentalism, Islamic fundamentalism, Hindu fundamentalism, Jewish fundamentalism—to the same impulse?

Yes. It reminds me of what was happening in 15th century Europe when the disaffection from the church began to intensify. There were all sorts of groups forming little cults. New schools were open to teach what was felt to be the true faith and so on. People look for something to believe in, and not only believe in the religious sense but believe in the institutional sense. Feeling that one belongs to a going concern and not to a dead old corporation that is static in routines. That is the situation of decay, decadence, demand for the new and the necessary destruction before the new can really arise.

On this question of fundamentalism, there is a kind of urgent fanatic quality about it. Is this fanaticism a necessary accompaniment of boredom or an escape from boredom?

No. I don't think that fanaticism arises from boredom, but it arises from despair. Despair about the particular concerns or the particular situation that a group feels is a threat or a failure to perform the right things that this new urge demands.

But people in this state of exhaustion of old forms, old ideas, old institutions are searching for something new, and they find it perhaps in a kind of revelation.

Yes, and they have a sense—perhaps not put into words, but they feel it strongly—that the old cohesive forces have given way. For example, the great creation of the Western world in the last 500 years has been the nation-state. And the nation everywhere is falling apart. It's extraordinary to think, for example, that England, which isn't so big that it can afford to come into pieces again, has given Scotland and Wales parliaments. We take it for granted because we read it in the paper and hear it on television, but that's an extraordinary fact. In France, after years of very tight nationhood and national feeling, the government is now subsidizing the revival of local dialects, of which there turn out to be many more than anyone thought.

Isn't this partly a consequence of globalization? The nation-state as you say is fading away. Daniel Bell once said that the nation-state is too big for the small problems and too small for the big problems. So it's no longer the institutional unit of adaptation. At the same time, nationalism remains the most potent of political emotions.

The desire to be a nation often is accompanied by no notion of what it entails. For example, all these little states which dot the South Pacific are dependent on the old big powers, which used to own them. They can't defend themselves, their economy needs continual injections. The Comoros Islands off the east coast of Africa are a wonderful example. The total area is nearly 840 square miles, and there are four islands, and for the last 15 years, at least one of them—the smallest, Ahjouan Island—has fought the federal government of those four, and now it has achieved its independence. And the neighboring nations from Africa, and to the east also, celebrated that as a great feat of liberation.

Globalization is upon us in the sense that the new technologies, the electronic and cybernetic technologies, elude national sovereignty. Cyberspace is beyond the control of individual states. Nations no longer have the power to decide their own economic destiny. But the people are plunged into this vast anonymous sea which they don't like, they don't fully comprehend, they can't control, and they feel a great need for belonging. This need for belonging results in a return to smaller units of some kind, whether defined religiously or ethnically. So in a certain sense, the more the world integrates, the more it disintegrates.

Yes. Everywhere, everybody wants to belong to a small cozy group for protection which has a language of its own, traditions, religion, cookery, everything. "We ourselves alone"—Sinn Fein—is the phrase that describes that. And it is going forward in this country to a far greater extent than anyone realizes. It doesn't mean that national government will fall apart and leave only a checkerboard of small regions, but it does show the mood and the tendency, and it is heightened, I think, by the fact that the modern world of technology makes the individual feel oppressed, badgered, unhappy, and it's perfectly natural then to try to form a little family circle. And the family circle means the ethnic group, large or small.

You say in your book that the novel was the characteristic genre of the 19th century. What was the characteristic genre of the 20th century?

The novel suited the 19th century peculiarly well because the 19th century was aware of something it called "Progress." Science and industry seemed to prove the reality of progress, and progress was a historical fact. The 19th century was the century of history; people lapped up history the way they did novels. And the novel is a fictional history. It adopts all the tricks of narrative history—description of incidents, psychology of movers and shakers—and very often among the early masterpieces of the novel, the setting is actual. It happens here, there or the other place. And by the end of the century the novel has gone to such a pitch of historicity that the author is attacked if he misrepresents a particular detail, whether it's important or not.

J.B. Priestley told me once that he would receive insulting letters if he had a character wandering about London and taking the wrong street from one place to another. That's an extreme example of the feeling that the 19th century created about the novel form. It is also a very democratic form in two ways. First, it's about ordinary people, every kind of person. Unlike the tragedy in verse, which is about princes and kings and warriors, it's about you and me. In

another way, the novel is democratic in being an incitement to envy on the one hand—you read about so-and-so and you wish you were situated the way they are, lucky as they are—and also it's very snobbish. If you think back to any of the novels that you have enjoyed, care to reread, and look at the characters who are badly treated, you find that they have red hair, or a loud voice, or too much chin, or poor table manners—it's pure snobbery that a novel distinguishes the people you are supposed to like from those you don't like.

If I were someone else. I'd probably say the characteristic genre of the 20th century is the film. But I don't think the film is a literary genre, so I can't give the proper answer. It's difficult to say what strictly literary work is characteristic of the 20th century. Perhaps the kind of popular philosophy that is expressed in aphorisms, in sayings, in names and nicknames. For example, the term "highbrow and lowbrow," that seems to me a characteristic form of thought and expression. You can gather from that that I think the characteristic genres today are very popular indeed in the sense of representing the thought of the people much more than the thought of unusual persons, highly gifted and also highly biased in one way or another. Perhaps we arrive through this fumbling of mine at the possible choice of the comics as the characteristic genre.

You raise one question in your book which has always baffled me, and that is the way in which writers like Dickens could produce such a constant body of work without benefit of typewriters, without benefit of computers, and at the same time conducted extensive correspondence. How do you figure they did that?

I attribute it to the presence of a group of people who have been totally forgotten: servants. It's perfectly true that we have no notion of the extent to which the world up to, say, 1920, to take a year at random, depended on the servant class. And of course they were well or badly treated—mostly badly, I suppose—but they helped the world's work. For example, when Leigh Hunt, an early 19th century English poet, was at his lowest financially and was begging money from Byron and Shelley and other people, he and his wife and two children had two servants. Later on, I read somewhere, the admirals in the British navy were being cut back from an allowance of 20 to 14 servants. Now, in Dickens' household or George Eliot's, or any other writer's, there would be four or five servants, and they did all sorts of things that now we do for ourselves, which liberated Dickens or Bulwer-Lytton or George Eliot from drudgery to write, to give lectures. Dickens was an amateur actor and he indulged in theatricals. He did a million things that we are prevented from doing because we have to go through the chores we all know.

Your book is a brilliant example of analytical history. What do you make of the current school of younger historians who think everything is a social construct?

They have no sense of history. They are rotten with abstraction, which is a great disease of the modern world and another sign of decadence. When abstraction which of course is indispensable, gets to be to the third or fourth degree, the world recedes, and everything looks as if it had been made by the process of abstraction itself.

William H. McNeill (review date 21 May 2000)

SOURCE: "What It All Means: Why Jacques Barzun Is America's Greatest Teacher," in *Los Angeles Times Book Review*, May 21, 2000, pp. 1-3.

[*In the following review of* From Dawn to Decadence, *Mc-Neill praises Barzun's treatment of Western cultural history from the Reformation to the First World War, but opposes Barzun's disdain for twentieth-century culture and his bleak view of the future.*]

"The bulk of the book . . . is a delight because it presents a strong character full of surprises. He is learned but practical, unmistakably of his time . . . conservative but unconventional. His genius is in common sense . . . unusual judgments made by clear-eyed observation and couched in lapidary words." Jacques Barzun, distinguished historian, critic and academic administrator, uses these words to characterize Boswell's "Life of Johnson." They also constitute an apt appraisal of Barzun's own, and truly amazing, new book [*From Dawn to Decadence*].

Like Samuel Johnson, Barzun is impressively learned, conservative and unconventional in many of his judgments, writes with an acute sense of the fuzzy and changeable meanings of words and treats his reader to innumerable lapidary bon mots. On top of that, he offers an admirably coherent and comprehensive portrait of the cultural achievements—"art and thought, manners, morals and religion"—of what we once confidently called "Modern" and more recently and accurately label "Western" civilization.

The deposit of a lifetime, this book is sui generis: likely—I am tempted to say certain—to become a classic. But, as Barzun is at pains to point out, taste changes, reputations rise and fall (even, or especially, Shakespeare's); and, because Barzun is thoroughly out of tune with the "decadence" he sees in European and American cultural accomplishment since 1920, this delightful and monumental book may, I suppose, be cast aside by contemporary arbiters of taste with the same deaf ear he turns to them.

Barzun's history is organized around "four great revolutions—the religious, monarchial, liberal, and social roughly a hundred years apart—whose aims and passions still govern our minds and behavior." Or, more exactly, "Three spans, each of approximately 125 years, take us, roughly speaking, from Luther to Newton, from Louis XIV to the guillotine, and from Goethe to the New York Armory Show. The fourth and last span deals with the rest of our century. If this periodization had to be justified, it could be said that the first period—1500 to 1600—was dominated by the issue of what to believe in religion; the second—1661 to 1789—by what to do about the status of the individual and the mode of government; the third—1790 to 1920—by what means to achieve social and economic equality. The rest is the mixed consequences of all these efforts. What then marks a new age? The appearance or disappearance of particular embodiments of a given purpose."

Cultural history, in short, is a matter of human consciousness and desires; and individuals who are able to express perennial human wishes in new ways are the agents of change, the shapers of styles and the molders of culture. Barzun accordingly decorates his pages with numerous, often brilliant, pen portraits and summary judgments of individual writers, musicians, artists, philosophers and the like. Some are surprising choices, being all but unknown—Finlay Peter Dunne or James Agate, for example; while others, like Luther, Voltaire, Goethe and T.S. Eliot, are utterly familiar and expected.

Barzun resorts to other unusual devices. One is to capitalize a dozen or so words that symbolize recurring themes in his history. Thus EMANCIPATION, PRIMITIVISM, INDIVIDUALISM, ANALYSIS and half a dozen other abstract nouns appear in full dress whenever Barzun resorts to them. He thus exploits typography to show how the same (or almost the same?) themes recur in surprisingly different guises across the entire span of the modern era.

A second device is to punctuate chapters treating more or less coherent cultural changes, like "The West Torn Apart" for Luther and the Reformation, "The Reign of Etiquette" for 19th century romanticism with what Barzun calls "Cross Sections." These are chapter-length miscellanies, only partially held together by sketches of "The View from Madrid Around 1540" or, as the case may be, from some other city at some subsequent time with which each "Cross Section" begins.

Then there are the boldface insets decorating many of his pages. They produce others' remarks, more or less relevant to the discourse on the rest of the page. Taken together, these insets constitute an extraordinary chrestomathy of unfamiliar quotations. A few samples must suffice:

> The public, the public—how many fools does it take to make a public?
>
> —Chamfort (an almost forgotten moralist "who committed suicide in prison to foil the guillotine").

> On John D. Rockefeller. He is a kind of Society f'r th' Prevention of Cruelty to Money. If he finds a man misusin his money, he takes it away fr'm him and adopts it.
>
> —Mr. Dooley.

And angry, impudent verse from Ernest Hemingway:

> The age demanded that we sing
> and cut away our tongue.

> The age demanded that we flow
> and hammered in the bung.
> The age demanded that we dance
> and jammed us into iron pants.
> And in the end the age was handed
> the sort of shit the age demanded.

Yet another unusual trait: Every so often Barzun pauses to explain how a particularly contentious word got entangled in its present confusion of meanings, usually concluding that there is nothing to do but use it anyway. Sometimes, however, he coins anew, as "church hierarchy thoroughly humanistified" or uses rare words that drove me to the dictionary, for example, "rugosities" that is, wrinkles or "rutilant," that is, shining. But as a thoroughly self-conscious literary stylist, "with only a touch of pedantry here and there to show that I understand modern tastes," Barzun's prose is in fact easy to read and delightfully witty, loaded, as it is, with fresh and surprising judgments and an enormous freight of miscellaneous, unfamiliar information.

Nor are his pithy observations restricted to traditionally defined high culture. Consider, for example, "Three other cultural by-products date from early in railway history. One is the ticket. . . . The second is artificial time. . . . A third, more readily acceptable innovation, was the new taste for whiskey . . . brought into gin-soaked England by the Irish navvies. . . . [T]heir nickname . . . is the diminutive of 'navigator,' so-called because originally they were recruited to build canals but diverted to the swifter carrier." This vignette is supplemented further down the track by another aside, explaining that the "science" of phrenology "was facilitated, unexpectedly, by the building of railroads. The land taken for them often included disused cemeteries, and the exhumed skulls went to those most eager to exploit them."

Overall, I judge that Barzun's exploration of past cultural epochs, each masterly in itself, reaches an apogee with his anatomy of the extraordinary fertility of the 19th century. This is where most of his specialized scholarship concentrated, and this is clearly where he is most thoroughly at home. Nonetheless he is master of all he surveys. In the first era, for example, I found his appraisal of Luther and Rabelais especially afresh, sympathetic and persuasive. In his next section, his organizing concept of a "monarch's revolution" is unfamiliar—yet obvious, once juxtaposed with the time-worn array of other European revolutions; and Barzun's portraits of Louis XIV's court and of such diverse figures as Mme. de Montespan, Cromwell, Fenelon, Rubens, Bayle, Bach, Diderot, Rousseau and others offer much curious information and always present his own, often idiosyncratic, appraisals of their achievements. And, as I said before, when he gets to the Romantic era and its sequels down to 1920, the diapason of his learning and the range of his provocative observations reach a climax worthy of Beethoven himself.

But World War I somehow deafened him. Born in France in 1907 (he tells us how as a child he took refuge from Big Bertha in a Parisian cellar), Barzun came to New York in 1920, studied at Columbia University and remained there as teacher and administrator until retirement. That a man of 92 could complete this massive work is itself a minor miracle, which he attributes to "insomnia and longevity—sheer accidents." That he finds himself radically out of sympathy with recent cultural changes is not surprising, given his age. Yet, as always, he is self-aware, saying in his preface, "I have not consulted current prejudices. My own are enough to keep me busy as I aim at historical detachment. . . ."

Yet, though I am only 10 years his junior, my own pattern of experience leads me to quite opposite conclusions about the cultural accomplishments of the Western world since 1920. Barzun sees only decadence: the breakdown of a rich tradition that now must somehow be thrown away for something fresh and new to arise. Decadence is not a pejorative for him but a description of this sad and somehow inexorable condition. For, according to Barzun, all the potentialities of Western culture have now been worked out and pushed to such extremes as to defy further elaboration. Only rejection, mockery, caricature remain. Deconstruction on a vast scale everywhere and in all dimensions of consciousness is the wasteland he sees around him, with only a hope of some eventual renaissance, perhaps 300 years hence, when, after centuries of "deschooling," he imagines how "[s]ome among the untutored group taught themselves to read, compiled digests, and by adapting great stories and diluting great ideas provided the common people with a culture over and above the televised fare. . . . This compost of longing, images, and information resembled that which medieval monks, poets and troubadours fashioned out of the Greco-Roman heritage." And, Barzun implies, yet another civilization, with its own future eras of styles and sensibilities, may thus arise and flourish just as the Western culture he treasures once did. Frankly, such forebodings about a coming Dark Age of deliberate "deschooling" and future renaissance strike me as absurd.

Perhaps the fundamental problem is that Barzun sees only the repudiation of common sense and the dematerialization of physical reality in the amazing flux of modern physics and cosmology. I, on the contrary, think I detect the emergence of a new, compelling and fundamentally historical world view—cosmological, physical, terrestrial, biological and semiotic—that ought to have as many fertile consequences for art, literature, music and all the other manifestations of the human spirit as did the emergence of the Newtonian world machine in the 17th century that Barzun recognizes as a distinctive chapter of the Western past. What I see is not decadence, therefore, but the dawn of a new era, featuring a novel evolutionary vision of physical as well as of cultural realities and building upon a predominantly Western matrix of inherited ideas and sensibilities. This surely is an enormous accomplishment that almost exactly coincides with Barzun's own lifetime and fits neatly into the arbitrary chronological limits of the century immediately behind us.

And ahead? Visions of catastrophe are easy to conjure up, but none resembling Barzun's closing reverie. Two shaping circumstances come to my mind instead. One is the break-up of village communities and the corresponding emancipation (and psychological-social exile) of the world's peasantries. This profoundly alters the lopsided pattern of urban-rural relations that sustained civilizations of every stripe across the last 5,000 years. Its consequences are yet to be experienced but are sure to be profound.

This dimension of the past entirely escapes Barzun's purview because his concerns are wholly and exclusively urban. Yet the modern disruption of village life in Europe was fundamental, with roots going back to the 14th century, and it was only accomplished in most of the Western world (not yet everywhere in Europe, though; consider Albania) after World War II. But the breakup of village communities is now a global tidal wave, engulfing peasants everywhere on the strength of instantaneous communications, mechanized transport and commercialized farming.

A second fundamental factor on the world scene is demographic surge and collapse, unevenly distributed among the Earth's peoples and sure to provoke massive migration and chronic political instability in the near future. For most of the modern age, demographic growth prevailed among civilized societies while radical decay prevailed among all the populations newly brought into contact with the human majority of disease-experienced Eurasians. Now it is urban dwellers everywhere who, by and large, fail to reproduce themselves. How disrupted village communities and restless urban masses (each today numbering about half of humankind) will interact and perhaps collide looms as the principal social, political and cultural question at the start of the new millennium.

As a cultural historian, Barzun completely disregards demography, assuming that biological and cultural reproduction is, so to speak, automatic. Yet in a larger historical frame, demographic increase and decrease most certainly played a fundamental role in cultural as in all other aspects of human history. And more specifically, Europe's general pattern of demographic growth since 1500 and the extraordinary swarming of European peoples between 1750 and 1920 was surely what sustained the efflorescence of European high culture that Barzun so admires.

As for the future of that culture, it seems to me that what is most likely to happen is accelerated intermingling with elements from other cultural traditions. This has been happening throughout Western history, though Barzun pays almost no attention to such phenomena as the vogue for chinoiserie in the 18th century or to the ensuing attraction first to Indian transcendentalism and then, after the "opening" of Japan in 1854, to Japanese styles of art. Similarly, he barely refers to African roots of new styles of French art in the first decade of the last century but does recognize the African heritage behind jazz.

In general, Barzun views the Western tradition as self-contained and impervious—or perhaps merely indiffer-

ent—to the outside world. Before 1800, when communications were weak, and after that date, when European power and technology easily dominated everyone else, this was partly—but only partly—true. In time to come, however, neither of these insulating circumstances is likely to prevail. Accordingly, a rich, cosmopolitan mingling will probably ensue, opening who knows what new paths of sensibility and understanding for artists and thinkers of the new millennium who can be expected to explore them as vigorously and as diversely as their European and American predecessors, whom Barzun celebrates so fondly, did in their own more limited universe of discourse.

So not decay but growth is what I see around me: growth so tumultuous that it is impossible to foresee its course; and growth that, as always, destroys or discards what others hold dear. By Barzun's own account, this was what happened time and again within the Western tradition. So more of the same, and on a widening geographical scale, is what I anticipate—with ever-present possibilities of abrupt catastrophe—ecological, nuclear or demographic—lurking in the background. But that, too, is perennial. From the very beginning, increasing human skills and knowledge assured the conservation of catastrophe, making breakdown rarer (thanks to human foresight and concerted efforts at prevention) and more costly whenever foresight and prevention failed. Yet humankind has, so far, always survived and continued to thrive. Not decadence, then, but continued cultural efflorescence is what the future probably holds. Or so I, an observer 10 years younger and wholly rooted on this side of the Atlantic, prefer to believe.

Roger Shattuck (review date 29 June 2000)

SOURCE: "Decline and Fall?" in *New York Review of Books,* June 29, 2000, pp. 55-8.

[*In the following review of* From Dawn to Decadence, *Shattuck finds flaws in Barzun's historical periodization and takes issue with his underestimation of developments in twentieth-century art and history.*]

1.

"All is true." In the original edition of *Le père Goriot,* Balzac left this terse epigraph in English. It is the subtitle or alternate title of *Henry VIII,* an unfinished play uncertainly attributed to Shakespeare. The epigraph acknowledges Balzac's profound admiration of the Bard. At the same time, it affirms the cumulative and competitive veracity of Balzac's immense fictional universe. But I believe that these three childishly simple words also imply a dilemma.

Artists and writers constantly confront the teeming plenitude of the natural world that surrounds us on all sides, temporal and spatial. Both the novelist and the historian, if they lower their guard for an instant, can feel overwhelmed, obliterated, not so much by nothingness and emptiness as by the superfluity of existing things and creatures and events. A flood of sensations and of material reality can destroy our hold on life and self. "All is true" can be better interpreted as a cry of desperation than as the purr of serene contemplation. Can we hold our ground in the face of the world's sheer profusion?

Balzac, like a great gladiator in his long bathrobe, brooding over a coffee urn, created a proliferating anti-universe called *The Human Comedy.* A less pugnacious mind—say a historian's—will try to hold on against the profusion of life by finding shapes and patterns in that swarm of events. Stories, both historical and fictional, represent our principal means of staying sane, of weathering the typhoon of consciousness. "All is true" does not so much assent to the undifferentiated existence of everything as recognize the need to simplify, to reduce the world to livable dimensions, to choose out of the plenitude some terrain on which to build our settlement.

It is history that concerns us here, as a source of stories and as an evolving discipline. In an era when the culture is organized to support a great number of scholars producing a wide variety of historical works, what kind of history do we need most? Is the question even pertinent? For we seem to have everything already: a tendentious five-volume history of everybody's private life from antiquity to the present; a corrective multivolume treatment of the bourgeoisie in the nineteenth century; a thousand pages of anecdotes to argue that our modern world was born between 1815 and 1830; a jovial volume to recall how the Irish saved civilization from extinction during "the Dark Ages." The newest history titles freely mix fact and fiction for jaded palates. Enterprising biographers obtain passkeys that open all archives and brush aside all remnants of privacy. Could we possibly wish for anything more from historians?

Despite its freedoms in the past half-century, history has been squeezed from many directions. In our schools, progressive reforms swept up history and geography into a shapeless container called Social Studies tending constantly toward the contemporary. In higher education, history cannot be made to fit into the Procrustean bed of the tripartite division of disciplines into humanities, sciences, and social sciences. A pack of more recent fields—sociology, cultural studies, interdisciplinary studies, women's studies—trample on traditional history in order to establish their own courses in the undergraduate curriculum. On all levels, from grade school to college programs, the value of the history survey course has been questioned. The textbook containing a lively narrative account of, say, European history or US history has lost ground. Microprobes of local history and seminars on changing gender roles and the survival of racism increasingly crowd out the survey.

In schools, teachers are both inclined and encouraged to teach without a textbook. They believe that photocopied materials allow greater flexibility and circumvent the "cookie-cutter curriculum." Everyone acknowledges how essential the knowledge of history is to the citizens of a democracy with their responsibility to vote. But considering the shift today toward avoiding any sequential narrative account of history, I wonder just how the coming generations will learn enough history to understand the present and not be overwhelmed by the growing challenge of "All is true."

The subtitle of Jacques Barzun's new book, *From Dawn to Decadence: 500 Years of Western Cultural Life, 1500 to the Present,* informs us that it honors in some fashion the conventions of the survey. Is it then suitable for adoption as the textbook in the few surviving survey courses in Western history? Not easily, because it presupposes a basic knowledge of political and military history. Barzun has written the summa of a practitioner of cultural history who at the age of ninety-two wishes both to assemble the essential elements of his extensive writings and to surpass them in a final statement.

2.

Son of a spirited avant-garde poet who was a rival of Apollinaire in pre-World War I Paris, Jacques Barzun grew up in a household frequented by artists. They were all hatching new movements in a great burst of productivity on all fronts. Some, including Barzun *fils,* refer to those pre-war years as the Cubist decade. In 1920, at age thirteen, he came to the United States, attended high school, and moved on to Columbia University. After an AB and a Ph.D., he accepted a position in the history department and published a series of distinguished writings. Today, he could be called the dean of American historians and not simply on grounds of seniority.

For over sixty years, Barzun has pursued three interlocking careers. As an influential and successful teacher-scholar at Columbia, he worked closely with his contemporary Lionel Trilling to reinvigorate the teaching of the humanities and to establish an important program of required courses in general education. A similar program flourishes today and attracts a large number of qualified undergraduates seeking an integrated set of courses in several disciplines prior to the specialization of a major. The Festschrift volume *From Parnassus* (1976), which appeared on Barzun's retirement at sixty-eight, conveys the impression of a lively lecturer and discussion leader who earned the respect of his colleagues and favored undergraduate over graduate teaching.

Endowed with a powerful synthesizing mind and large resources of energy, Barzun undertook a second and parallel career as an administrator. In the office of provost at Columbia, he both attended to the scut work that sustains any institution and wrestled with the postwar surge in graduate education which caused serious financial imbalances. He left the provost's job not long before Columbia's crisis in 1968 when students attempted to close down the campus.

He also found time, along with Trilling and Auden, to help start up and run the Readers' Subscription book club.

This administrative work never seemed to slow Barzun down in his third career as a critic and historian whose writings met high standards for scholarship and at the same time reached a large general readership. Most of his books were published by trade houses rather than university presses. Because he avoided political statements and did not engage in the polemics surrounding *Partisan Review*, Barzun did not fit the description of a public intellectual. But his voice was listened to when he spoke. Two books, which appeared in close succession fifty years ago, made his reputation. ***Darwin, Marx, Wagner: Critique of a Heritage*** (1941) identified these three powerful cult figures as false Romantics who espoused a science of "mechanistic materialism" that separates man from his soul. ***Romanticism and the Modern Ego*** (1943; an expanded and widely read new edition retitled ***Classic, Romantic, and Modern*** was published by Anchor in 1961) defends the "cultural renovation" of the Romantic era against its many enemies, from Irving Babbitt on:

> [Romanticism] treasured fact and respected the individual as a source of fact. Accordingly, its political philosophy was an attempt to reconcile personal freedom with the inescapable need of collective action. Rousseau, Burke, Kant, Hegel, agreeing on the nature of the problem, differed only in lesser particulars. They were not anarchists or imperialists, but theorists of equilibrium in motion.

After this reaffirmation of a scorned tradition, Barzun capped and illustrated his extended argument on Romanticism with a wide-ranging study on music and history, ***Berlioz and the Romantic Century*** (1950). There was enough genius and histrionic bluster in Berlioz to make this a popular book. In the Great Conversation of Western culture, I believe that Barzun's vigorous defense of Romanticism helped to ignite a countermovement: it took the shape of a revival of eighteenth-century thought and the emergence of Enlightenment studies in the 1960s and 1970s.

When Barzun retired from teaching in 1975, some of his most productive years were still ahead of him. But several shifts had taken place in his outlook that influenced the direction of his writing. For one thing, his wonderfully informed discussion of music had attracted him to a field distinct from intellectual history and social history: namely, cultural history, with particular emphasis on the arts. In 1954 the European section of the American Historical Association asked Barzun to address their annual meeting. What he chose to say represents the manifesto of a newly pertinent discipline: **"Cultural History as a Synthesis."**[1]

In his eloquent defense of the close association of the arts with history, Barzun hopes to avoid one lurking professional danger. "Since we cannot believe in a *Zeitgeist* invisibly at work like Ariel on Prospero's Isle, I submit that style . . . is an answer to a common want." But period styles soon come to sound little different from a refried

Zeitgeist. "Style is the solvent in which incompatibles are meant to merge." In any case, I believe that in this essay on cultural history Barzun took an important step toward his latest book, which falls into that category.

I detect two further points at which Barzun changed course in a way that contributes to ***From Dawn to Decadence.*** The fifteen-page epilogue he wrote in 1960 for ***Classic, Romantic, and Modern*** turns its attention to the contemporary scene. He argues that the "annihilation" of art by Action painters and by poets such as Allen Ginsberg, plus the dilution of art into populism, have brought about a "Carthaginian end" for the arts after their new beginning in the early nineteenth century. "The Romantic purpose, in other words, has come by the severest logic to end what it began, destroying in its last effort all the romantic and classical forms that took their rise in the Renaissance."

This discouragement with the cultural history that was taking place around him did not fade with the passage of time. The editors of the multivolume *Columbia History of the World* (1972) commissioned Barzun to write the closing essay, entitled **"Toward the Twenty-First Century."** The twelve-page commentary he wrote opens with the cautionary tale of the German scholar Schedel, who in 1493 predicted the close of history rather than the new surge of discovery, commerce, learning, and the nation-state that soon opened one of the great eras of history. Self-forewarned yet undismayed, Barzun cites the loss of faith in ideals and traditions that doomed Greece and Rome, considers the political and civil woes that beset the 1960s, and concludes: "What Western civilization is witnessing, in short, is the last phase of the great emancipation promoted in the eighteenth century."

This short essay presents in outline form the sequence of events and interpretations that will be filled out to eight hundred pages in ***From Dawn to Decadence.*** Consciously or not, Barzun has devoted the last decade to a comprehensive history that begins where Gibbon left off—with the fall of Constantinople in 1453 and the end of the extended Roman empire in the East. Barzun constructs a readjusted version of Gibbon's accounting for a decline and fall. The word "emancipation" employed in the above quotation becomes the leitmotif of Barzun's full-length book. Many of his previously published writings contribute to this final opus. It has grown like a fertile delta at the mouth of a long career.

3.

In his "Author's Note" for ***From Dawn to Decadence,*** Barzun tells us that he strives for objectivity without giving up reactions of sympathy and antipathy. In the loose entity of the West, he sees a "single" as well as a "mongrel" culture. The last paragraph of the prologue declares, "Our distinctive attitude toward history, our habit of arguing from it, turns events into ideas charged with power." But even though he prints in small capitals a number of recurrent themes, Barzun is not writing a history of ideas.

He devotes his attention alternately to events, to ideas, and to people, an amalgam presented primarily through stories. And the people are true agents, great men and great women who have initiated and pursued events and ideas. His treatment of Christine de Pisan, Mme. de Staël, and Florence Nightingale places them in full perspective as historical actors.

Barzun's basic thesis about the shape of the modern era since 1500 provides the division of the book into four parts following four chronological periods. Part One (1500–1660) deals with the "religious revolution" of the Reformation. Part Two (1660–1789) concerns the rise of monarchy as an institution and the development of the nation-state. Part Three (1789–1920) takes up the political and cultural consequences of the French Revolution. And Part Four (1920–the present) includes the aftershocks of World War I, the Soviet experiment, and the decline of the "demotic" culture of the United States.

In the last four pages, Barzun abruptly changes costume from historian to prophet and writes an imaginary "Prologue" dated 2300 "as our own era reaches an end." Our end is described not as Apocalypse but as Boredom, in which the culture of the past is rediscovered and treasured. "The parallel with the Middle Ages is plain." I find this short coda distracting. It neither reinforces nor extends the argument of the book; rather it turns aside into obscure mutterings about a new beginning for culture.

What then does Barzun's net catch for us out of the vast sea of facts to form this volume of cultural history? Let's look at a chapter in Part Three called "Things Ride Mankind," which deals with the mid-nineteenth century. Following a chapter mostly on British political thought, this one demonstrates that a period often called "Victorian" and associated with a narrow moralism is far better characterized by varieties of materialism: the Crystal Palace exhibits, realism in the novel and in painting, the shock of evolutionary theory, photography's summons to pure appearances, and Marx's dialectical materialism. Into this flea market of topics Barzun introduces enthusiastic semi-asides on his favorite neglected figures of the period, including Walter Bagehot and Oliver Wendell Holmes (*père*).

In order to hold his vast array of cultural materials together, Barzun relies on a strong sense of periodization, the articulation of chronology into an ordered sequence of periods. The four periods he chooses, which I described above, roughly follow national, military, and political developments. Barzun takes little time to explain that he begins with the Reformation because he believes that the phenomenon we call the Renaissance does not belong primarily to fifteenth-century Italy as the proud humanists proclaimed. "So if any renaissance ever did occur, it was in the 12C, leading to the high medieval civilization of the 13th." He cites Henry Adams, J.J. Walsh, and J. Huizinga as authorities. This blurring of the Renaissance two centuries backward in time disturbs me less than Barzun's failure to deal with another major thesis about periodization.

The strong formulation of it appears in an appendix Ernst Robert Curtius added to the English-language edition of *European Literature and the Latin Middle Ages* (1953):

> A great English historian, G. M. Trevelyan, is of the opinion that the real break in modern history is not the sixteenth century, but the eighteenth. The Industrial Revolution has meant a much more radical change than the Renaissance or the Reformation. Medieval forms of life subsist until about 1750, to put it roughly. When we consider on the other hand that medieval thought and expression become creative only around 1050, we get a period of about seven hundred years which manifests a unity of structure. We need not bother to find a name for this period. But if we try to consider it as a cultural unit, we may get a better understanding of our past.

> The middle of the eighteenth century witnessed not only the beginnings of that great economic change which is termed the Industrial Revolution. It saw also the first powerful revolt against cultural tradition, which is marked by Rousseau.

Barzun missed an opportunity to reformulate the case for 1500 as the break, standing for both the Renaissance and the Reformation, as against the juncture affirmed by Curtius. We now fluently call that juncture the Enlightenment.

As is entirely natural and understandable, the problems of periodization in dealing with the recent past are even more challenging than those reaching back several hundred years. How Barzun divides up the twentieth century forms—as we shall see—an integral part of his thesis about decadence.

What audience will this book reach? It does not advance a single strong revisionist thesis to rearrange our understanding of events. It does not just tell the old story over again with new material added. Barzun takes the old story for granted and emphasizes the contribution of the arts and of intellectual currents. Comparison is difficult. Today, historians feel considerable pressure, intellectual and commercial, to abandon the West and Europe as proper subjects of history in favor of the world, the globe. One of the few good history surveys that remains in print is William McNeill's *A World History* (fourth edition, 1999). Its five hundred pages provide the basic knowledge needed to follow Barzun's cultural history with full comprehension and appreciation. There is always H.G. Wells's *The Outline of History* (1920), whose 1,200 pages remain highly readable. (A revised and annotated *Outline* would make a worth-while publishing project.)

Barzun mentions Spengler's *The Decline of the West* (1918–1922), but the book left little mark on his thinking. Paul Johnson's understanding in *The Birth of the Modern* (1991) of what makes up the content of cultural history and of the importance of periodization overlaps Barzun's to a considerable degree. But Johnson chooses to concentrate his 1,100 pages on the interval between 1815 and 1830 in order to bring one period to life in its particulars. Barzun's book belongs to no ready category.

My hunch is that historians will not pay much attention to *From Dawn to Decadence* on the assumption that it contains nothing new. History teachers will see it as too long and unsystematic and old-fashioned for adoption in courses. Serious readers of biography and history, who know what to expect from Barzun, will find here a welcome synthesis of his career and of his major methods and views. He has gone to considerable lengths to tell a story with clear transitions, frequent cross-references, and a strong forward movement. The analogy used earlier of netting a catch of fish does justice to the glistening variety of people and events and works he sets before us. Barzun is rarely dull.

4.

I have two substantial criticisms to make of his ambitiously conceived and unevenly executed book. Both refer to the final two hundred pages. The first concerns the shape and meaning Barzun gives to the twentieth century. The second criticism concerns his treatment of the arts in the same period.

Barzun refers to the period between 1885 and 1905 in France both as the Nineties and as the turn of the century. It was an effervescent moment that combined the voluptuous aesthetics of Decadents and Symbolists with the strong reformist and scientific impulse of Naturalism in the novel. "A Summit of Energies" he calls the chapter on the turn of the century. However, the following chapter, "The Cubist Decade," reveals that we had not yet reached the summit in the earlier period. The years 1905–1914 changed the "negative" energies of the Nineties into "affirmative" accomplishments and became "the fountainhead in every department of culture." Diaghilev and the Ballets Russes brought new energies from the East. The 1913 Armory Show carried the excitement to the United States.

Here begins Book Four of Barzun's account. "The Great Illusion" of European alliances, the cult of violence and war, "the Great Switch" from liberalism to the welfare state and communism, and the unspeakable massacres of trench warfare—all these factors and more halted the long forward march of history since 1500. They reveal, Barzun argues, the loss of faith, loss of nerve, and destruction of culture caused by "the Great War." Parody, the Absurd, popular consumerism, boredom, and irreverence invade all aspects of culture. In the closing pages, Barzun confesses to feeling "some hesitation . . . about applying the word *Decadence* to the whole West and the whole era." Yet he has done so "without tremor." For Barzun, the great unexplained disaster of the twentieth century, the turning point of modern history to which all other events, cultural included, must be related, is the Great War of 1914–1918.

I believe that the last fifty years have gradually shown us the error of that dark opinion. World War I with all its horror did not interrupt the cultural and political continuities that linked pre-war to postwar in Europe and America. Even the 1917 Soviet takeover in Russia did not immediately appear to threaten the rest of the world. Not until the years between 1929 and 1934 did the great shift occur in a sequence often overlooked. First the stock market crash and the spread of economic hardship throughout the West caused political instability, with Hitler taking power in Germany, and a growing distrust of unbridled capitalism as a functioning economic system. During that crisis of vulnerability among capitalist democracies, the third Communist International shifted policy drastically in May 1934. Moscow changed from a refusal to associate with the non-Communist left to a great welcoming of all sympathizers into front organizations, peace congresses, and anti-fascist manifestations. "The Hand Outstretched" was the motto circulated in all countries to encourage a popular front. Faced by the partial collapse of capitalism, by the impending threat of the Nazis, and by the naive idealism and powerful propaganda that worked in favor of the Soviet Union, the "Red Decade" of the 1930s was a period of crisis and a turning point for the entire Western world more serious than that of World War I.

Barzun holds onto 1914 as the turning point and thus, I believe, misplaces the periodization of cultural history in the twentieth century. He also remains oblivious to the historic importance of the West's multiple responses to the crisis of the Thirties. World War II addressed the most immediate danger of Nazi Germany and Japan. It was followed swiftly by the cold war of atomic terror and attrition that lasted forty years and finally ended in the downfall of the totalitarian Soviet regime. And gradually a set of political initiatives and compromises in Europe and the United States have partly tamed the free market and introduced the modified socialist reforms embodied in the welfare state.

Can one come to a balanced judgment about the "decadence" of the West in the twentieth century without considering World War II, the cold war, and the efforts of democracy and capitalism to meet the challenges that emerged in the Thirties? These were cultural events as well as military and political events. The leadership of Churchill, Roosevelt, De Gaulle, and Marshall, and, yes, in a different style, of Thatcher and Reagan is part of a saga that does not deserve the word "decadence." Other horrors have occurred and continue to occur. But Barzun's treatment of twentieth-century history leaves the impression that nothing positive, nothing heroic, no major effort to defend civilization has occurred since the Great War abruptly cut off the creative energies of the Cubist decade. For the overall thesis of this book about the trajectory of a five-hundred-year era, and about the last century in particular, I find this omission disabling.

Barzun chose part of a chapter from Part Four—entitled "The Artist Prophet and Jester"—to publish in advance of the book in *The American Scholar* (Winter 2000). Here Barzun accepts the term "Modernism" to designate the most significant directions in the arts "from the time of this final victory won by the religion of art in the early 1920s." No two critics ever seem to agree about the dating of Modernism, and the plausible analogy of modern art to a religious movement has appeared several times in earlier chapters without adequate discussion and evidence. Barzun traces Modernism through the standard reference points of Eliot, Joyce, and Proust, and omits mention of the crisis of abstract art that goes back to the Cubist decade. These choppy pages discuss the Dada and Surrealist movements and overlook their close continuity with prewar escapades by Jarry, Apollinaire, and Duchamp. And both movements put up a sturdy resistance—for as long as they could hold out against the culture—to the very category of art as a description of what they were doing. They called art "an alibi" and "a lamentable expedient." For Barzun, Modernism has become "at once the mirror of disintegration and an incitement to extending it." After this inept chapter, Barzun descends, or rises, increasingly into the tones of a jeremiad directed against contemporary culture as a whole. The book ends with the West irretrievably on the skids, its institutions in decline, lacking leadership and self-understanding. It is a very limited view of our time.

Barzun or his copy editor should have repaired a number of solecisms that mar his generally workmanlike prose. For example: "Gluck had declined composing Beaumarchais' text." "She also practiced the right to be as sexually free and initiative as men." "The next instant, emotions varied—appall for some, joy for others." ". . . She found later in life a congenial husband, though his latter days darkened hers by becoming ill, alcoholic, and of uncharacteristic bad temper." Painting sometimes lures Barzun beyond his depth. "Perspective is based on the fact that we have two eyes." He's thinking of depth perception, not perspective. When he refers later to an exhibition in 1874 of paintings by Manet and others rejected by the annual Salon, he is confusing the Salon des Refusés with the first show of the Société Anonyme (or Impressionists).

Barzun entitles a chapter in Part One "The Eutopians" to suggest that More, Campanella, Bacon, Rabelais, and others were writing not about "no place," but about "a good place." Eutopias contributed much to social thought. Then he writes as follows:

> Eutopian morals show how mistaken are modern critics who keep complaining that science has made great progress in improving material life but has lagged in doing the same for the ethical. There was no progress to make. Men have known the principles of justice, decency, tolerance, magnanimity from an early date. Acting on them is another matter—nor does it seem easier for us to act on our best scientific conclusions when we deal with bodily matters: an age that has made war on smoking and given up the use of the common towel and the common cup should prohibit shaking hands.

Is this a major pronouncement by a cultural historian? If so, he never investigates the "early date" to which we can trace the origin of our moral principles. And the entire design of *From Dawn to Decadence* suggests a movement of progress and regress unlike that of science and charac-

teristic of culture—including justice, decency, and the like. Is there "no progress to make" in ethics in order to deal with nuclear weapons and genetics? Barzun can hardly mean it. He is the first to acknowledge cultural and ethical accomplishments. A few pages later in the same chapter, Barzun makes much of Shakespeare's "invention of 'character'" out of mere types. The sympathy with which Barzun presents the sensibilities and intelligences of Pascal, Hazlitt, and William James recognizes a gradual growth of consciousness, a changing perception both of interior life and of the lives of others. Everything Barzun writes declares that we are still engaged in winning (or losing) our way toward moral principles, whose gradual discovery is in part the creation of that very search. The exploration of the major category of the disinterested in ethics, aesthetics, and science belongs to the era surveyed by this book. Barzun does not mention it. The pirouette at the end of the above paragraph about smoking and handshaking trivializes the significant question raised by the opening sentences of the paragraph and reveals Barzun at his most captious.

5.

Particularly for the reader who is exploring both the highways and the byways of history, *From Dawn to Decadence* overflows with rewards. It fills its eight hundred pages the way a natural history museum seems always to need more space for its specimens. Barzun has a restless magpie mind that revels in details. He gives us fine portraits of Luther, Emperor Charles V, Cromwell, Diderot, and others. Despite the antibourgeois pronouncements and gestures that emanate from his favorite nineteenth-century figures, Barzun knows and states the importance of a strong middle class to give stability to a vital culture. And he does not hesitate to give free rein to his love of language. An incorrigible philologist, he conjures up revelations from words we use every day. Why do judges sit in "chambers"? How have we all come to have a surname or last name, whereas for centuries one given name was enough for ordinary people? What does "encyclopedia" say about the shape of knowledge? Why is "experimental" an inappropriate term to apply to a work of art? Barzun seeks out such questions and they lead to some of his juiciest asides.

Near the end of Part Three, Barzun decides to write a five-page excursus on the state of history as written today:

> When Lord Acton, dean of the profession and editor of the *Cambridge Modern History,* told his juniors: "Take up a problem not a period," he was directing them to a social situation in place of a series of events. In France, a group headed by Lucien Febvre had a similar idea: no more events but "collective mentalities."

Pressed by such tendencies, "narrative gives way to description" and "the historian turns into a sociologist." Barzun refuses to be browbeaten and brandishes his sarcasm:

> Now individuals were deemed unimportant. Neither great men nor medium-size ones had influence; only

the crowd had power, and what it affected was not events, which matter little, but the broad conditions of life. This motionless history defied a tradition of 2,500 years.

Well, history too must change—if not progress. Barzun's own history in *From Dawn to Decadence* relies as much on "social situations" as on narrated events. I believe that his book could have been shorter and stronger if he had stopped his account of culture with the enthusiastic chapter on the Cubist decade without trying to find the underlying shape of the twentieth century. That way, we would read many illuminating views of culture and fewer philippics. Barzun's sense of an ending does not make good history.

Note

1. It appeared in *The Varieties of History: From Voltaire to the Present*, edited by Fritz Stern (Meridian, 1956).

Sebastian Mallaby (review date 2 July 2000)

SOURCE: "Look Back in Wonder," in *Washington Post Book World,* July 2, 2000, p. 8.

[*In the following review, Mallaby offers a positive assessment of* From Dawn to Decadence.]

At 92, Jacques Barzun has earned the right to be eccentric. He serves up a book [*From Dawn to Decadence*] 800 pages long but proudly saves space by writing "16C" instead of "sixteenth century." He has spent most of his working life in New York, that center of hard-selling self-promotion; but he begins his opus by stating grimly, "I do not expect the reader to be steadily grateful." His focus on Western civilization is almost gratuitously dismissive of other cultures; at one point he labels Buddhism and Islam "cults," to be bracketed along with yoga and transcendental meditation. As he says himself, "I have not consulted current prejudices. My own are enough to keep me busy."

And yet grateful is precisely how this reader felt after taking Barzun's guided tour through the past half-millennium. Barzun is conversational, wise and rich in entertaining detail; he restores color to faded memories of history and paints in the mural where bits were missing. Yes, there is prejudice; but it is too frankly stated to be insidious and too intelligent to be dull. Over a life of research begun in the 1920s, Barzun has been marinating his idiosyncratic sense of history. The result is deliciously exotic.

Barzun passes judgment on obscure figures of the past as though they were his intimates. There is the Archbishop of Mainz, "a gross and greedy young man," and Pope Leo X, "the esthetic voluptuary." When he comes to more famous characters, Barzun tosses off unnervingly bold verdicts. Referring to the literary output of Erasmus, he assures us that "Nothing like his sway over the minds of his contemporaries has been seen since; not even Voltaire or Bernard Shaw approached it." He thinks nothing of quoting St. Augustine and Hemingway in the same paragraph. Describing Luther's antipathy to festivals grafted on to Christianity from pagan origins, Barzun breaks off to tell us that it was in the same spirit that, in 1982, the Truth Tabernacle in South Carolina (125 members) hanged a Santa Claus.

These cross-century comparisons are not just intended to dazzle. Barzun is promoting a particular brand of history, one that emphasizes the similarities across the ages rather than the differences. Other cultural historians, perhaps straining too hard, have claimed to discern the distinctive spirit of an era. Then they have presented this Zeitgeist as the explanation for some grand turn of events: Max Weber and R.H. Tawney each suggested that Protestantism sparked capitalism.

Barzun is generally impatient with such claims. He protests that capitalism predates Protestantism; the Medici banking empire thrived in pre-Reformation Italy, and Catholic abbots lent surplus funds at interest. He adds that Protestantism was sometimes hostile to capitalist instincts; Luther and Calvin both decried materialism. For Barzun, no single spirit dominates an age; rather, common themes coexist and compete across the centuries.

What is the use of cultural history if it cannot explain anything? It provides an enriching canon, and a reminder that things we take to be unique today have their repeated precursors. We may think we live in a confusingly globalized world, but 16th-century French and Spanish kings fought each other on Italian soil with German and Swiss armies. We may presume that the fight against tobacco is a purely modern crusade, but James I of England complained of that "custom loathsome to the eye, hateful to the nose, harmful to the brain, dangerous to the lungs" at the start of the 17th century. We may suppose that fluid sexual relations arrived with the Pill, but in 1534 an Anabaptist sect led by John of Leyden created a commune that, as Barzun puts it, "satisfied one of the recurrent dreams of the occidental mind: community of goods and of women."

Yet Barzun is not completely free of explanatory ambition. He hopes his book may shed light on "where in the past our present merits and troubles come from"; and it turns out that the troubles most preoccupy him. Toward the end of his book, he fumes against the century through which he has lived, complaining that the Western canon is under attack from people who know nothing of its content; that educated people have ceased to be bilingual; that the welfare state serves to dehumanize; that casual dress is slovenly, as is "the curious use of first names soon after acquaintance." Most passionately of all, Barzun objects to the forward-looking impulse, the dogma that the new is better than the old. In science, each new gizmo is greeted with breathless enthusiasm. In art, a mind-twisting avant-garde no longer shocks; it is taken for granted.

And how did we come to this? Barzun appears to believe in a version of the "ratchet theorem," which animates conservative declinists from Robert Bork to Marvin Olasky. This theorem holds that impulses that were constructive in the past have finally advanced too far, producing a kind of decadence. The urge to rebel against stifling standards has advanced freedom; but when refrigerator doors are shown as art, standard-busting has outlived its usefulness. The urge to satirize absurd aspects of life was once healthy; but modern writers declare that life itself is Absurd, and counsel submission to the resulting nihilism. The forward-looking spirit has driven much progress; but a society in which "you're history" has become a choice insult merely celebrates ignorance.

An historian may be forgiven for saying this. But, in one of his endlessly engaging asides, Barzun acknowledges the case for ignorance of the past; the illusion that one is breaking new ground lends energy to human endeavor. If Americans did not suspect that history is bunk, they might be less dynamic than they are. If they had less faith in technology, and were less inclined to expect the best from the future, the wild and creative New Economy bubble might never have been inflated. Perhaps it ought to worry those denizens of dot-com land that Barzun's backward-looking book is on the bestseller list.

Suzanne Fields (review date 3 July 2000)

SOURCE: "A Turning Point for Moral Decay?" in *Insight on the News,* Vol. 16, No. 25, July 3, 2000, p. 48.

[*In the following review, Fields offers a positive assessment of* From Dawn to Decadence.]

When a book criticizing our current culture runs to more than 800 pages, with 798 footnotes, and would break bones if you dropped it on your foot, it's more than a little surprising to find it on the *New York Times* best-seller list.

In fact, the popularity of such a book may be enough to refute its central thesis—that the last century began a steep and irrevocable decline in what we've honored as Western cultural life for the past 500 years.

From Dawn to Decadence: 1500 to the Present, by Jacques Barzun, nevertheless touches a nerve in the culture wars that could just be one of those "tipping points" to turn things around. Mr. Barzun, 92 years old with a strong sense of history, is so erudite and witty about intellectual life for the past 500 years that you almost believe he lived in each of the centuries he writes about.

In this high-tech teletubby age of short attention spans, the printed word as written by Mr. Barzun revives a love and respect for literature and philosophy that defies the contemporary Philistines of deconstruction. On reading the book, I was reminded of a scene in the science-fiction novel *Fahrenheit 451,* by Kurt Vonnegut, in which a literate culture has been destroyed. But hidden in a forest, a small group of renegades spends each day memorizing a great book so that the books will be available to the next generation.

We are not that far gone. Not yet. But it's not news that in the second half of the last century the Western canon took a devastating hit. For a cultural critic who bemoans the trivialization and political correctness that pervades contemporary academic life, Jacques Barzun offers the best window of hope I've encountered since the dreary debunking of great ideas got under way.

The popularity of Mr. Barzun's book suggests that there's a large public that craves the discipline of discriminating thought. Despite the dismal education many readers have received at some of our finest colleges, they nevertheless are reading this book. Maybe they've reached the stage to want something better than junk and trash.

A clue for optimism also resides in the author's definition of decadence. All that it means is "falling off." As Mr. Barzun writes, "It implies in those who live in such a time no loss of energy or talent or moral sense. On the contrary, it is a very active time, full of deep concerns, but peculiarly restless, for it sees no clear lines of advance. The loss it faces is that of Possibility."

I agree that such an analysis is true for many young men and women trapped in the tyranny of "women's studies," "gay studies," "black studies." They have spent their time and their restless energy actively reading propaganda rather than about great ideas and have wasted opportunities for illuminating intellectual debate. For them, possibility is foreshortened. But Mr. Barzun and a number of conservative critics and scholars offer a loud and serious voice in the culture wars—and that could begin to make a difference.

David Gress (review date November 2000)

SOURCE: "A Rich and Tangled Web," in *World and I,* Vol. 15, No. 11, November, 2000, p. 235.

[*In the following review, Gress offers a positive evaluation of* From Dawn to Decadence.]

Seven decades of life, reading, learning, and experience has gone into ***From Dawn to Decadence,*** an impressively energetic, exhilarating, and spirited work of a wise man and great scholar, Jacques Barzun. Seven adult decades, that is; Barzun is in his nineties and presents this latest and largest of his works as the fruit of a lifetime. And it is no monument to crusty pedantry or grab bag of unconnected anecdotes. It is a vigorous chronicle full of strong and convincing themes, an account of how the West was made and how it is now unmaking itself.

The modern West was shaped, Barzun argues, by four revolutions and the ideas, themes, and aspirations that inspired them. They are the religious, monarchical, liberal, and social revolutions. Barzun defines revolution precisely, as the "the violent transfer of power and property in the name of an idea." Each of the four took classic form in one or more Western countries; thus, the religious revolution in Germany in the 1520s, when Martin Luther broke with the Catholic Church; the monarchical revolution in the 1660s in France, when Louis XIV and his minister Colbert centralized power and ritualized kingship; the liberal revolution in France in 1789; and the social revolution in Russia in 1917.

These classic cases then reverberated throughout the West, stimulating social, cultural, political, and technological change in response to the leading ideas of each revolution. Thus, for example, the concept of equality and the idea that government should promote it were not unique to Russia in 1917 but were of growing influence and popularity throughout the West. Russia was the classic and most extreme case of a political movement trying to put them into practice.

Barzun's book explains how these revolutions and associated ideas came about and how their repercussions interacted to produce the modern West, which swears allegiance to all these ideas put together. The five most important of them are emancipation, individualism, primitivism (that is, the notion that original and natural is better than later and artificial), analysis or scientific method, and self-consciousness. All made their first appearance in the era of the religious revolution and the new humanism, the movement that recovered classical civilization and rejected theological tutelage of the individual conscience, scholarship, and social values, customs, and laws. They were then taken up and developed by statesmen, scientists, inventors, scholars, administrators, warriors, and poets until the tangled web that is the modern West gradually emerged.

The book is full of gems. Some are anecdotes about people, others are brilliant capsule explanations of common conundrums. In a few deft strokes, Barzun solves them. For example the distinction between reason and rationalism, which he explains while discussing René Descartes, one of the founding figures of the scientific outlook and the scientific method:

> A less obvious cultural influence of the Cartesian philosophy and its method has been to promote faith in Reason. Mankind has always used reasoning—argument went on in cave, tent, or prairie hut—but the Cartesian or scientific reason is of a particular kind. Like geometry, it starts from clear and distinct ideas that are abstract and assumed to be true. Faith in this type of reason is a creed, often passionate, called Rationalism. It differs from the workaday use of our wits by its claim that analytical reasoning is the sole avenue to truth.

> This conviction is one that is being questioned today, and not for the first time. Unfortunately, the combatants on both sides keep arguing whether the modern mind is harmed—some say victimized—by "too much reason,"

the attackers holding that science and numbers are not the only truth; the defenders retorting that if reason is given up, intellectual anarchy and wild superstition will reign. The latter are right about reason as an activity—reasoning; the former are right about Rationalism, the dominance of a particular form of reason and its encroachment where it does not belong.

THE REFORMATION

We know the religious revolution of the sixteenth century as the Protestant Reformation. By this revolution, the power and property of the Catholic Church in large parts of Europe were transferred to the secular princes. When Barzun says transfer of power, he means it in the full sense, as power over ideas and souls as well as economic and political power.

The reformers, Martin Luther, John Calvin, and their followers, took Christianity out of the institutional church and rested it firmly on the Bible itself, the property of all believers. To them, being Christian meant knowing the Bible. Therefore, everyone should be able to read. Putting a Bible in every home and expecting every Christian to be able to read it gave Protestant Europe and gradually the whole West "a common background of knowledge, a common culture in the high sense of the term." This culture rested on an intimate knowledge of the Bible and its stories that is now fading, a symptom of the decadence of the West as a whole. Barzun provides a striking illustration of the force of this common culture in its heyday in the early nineteenth century:

> When Coleridge was lecturing in London on the great English writers, he happened to mention Dr. Johnson's finding on his way home one night a woman of the streets ill or drunk in a gutter. Johnson carried her on his broad back to his own poor lodging for food and shelter. Coleridge's fashionable audience tittered and murmured, the men sneering, the women shocked. Coleridge paused and said: "I remind you of the parable of the Good Samaritan" and all were hushed. No amount of moralizing could have done the work of rebuke and edification with such speed and finality.

The religious revolution ended in a dying fall. By the end of the sixteenth century, many thinkers and writers of Europe were rejecting the religious enthusiasm of their elders and recommending sober moralism and an attitude of stern detachment from worldly passions. Some were prefiguring the next, monarchical revolution by defending centralized administration; others were laying the foundations of modern science. In Barzun's view, the beginning of modern science and the scientific outlook in the seventeenth century is the last act of the religious revolution. It was a revolution not only in theology and public morality but in epistemology as well, replacing, as another scholar once put it, the knowledge of authority with the authority of knowledge.

EMANCIPATION AND PRIMITIVISM

Barzun has taken trouble to make his ample and generous book user-friendly, something to be grateful for, given its range and scope. The four revolutions launch and help to define three great periods of Western history of about 125–150 years each and one shorter period, the last, in which we live. Its end, though perhaps near, is not yet visible.

The first period runs from the Reformation to the scientific discoveries of the young Isaac Newton in the 1660s, the second from the origins of the Versailles court of Louis XIV, the Sun King, to the beginning of the French Revolution in 1789. The third ends in 1914, when the great European war put an end to the peaceful, progressive, and liberal world of the late nineteenth century and modern art arrived at the heart of the culture, an event encapsulated in a famous exhibition at the New York Armory. The fourth period, finally, is the century of the social revolution, that of equality. The concept has turned out to be both universally accepted—no government, however conservative, proposes to return to the social discrimination and the minimal state of the nineteenth century—and problematic. For what is equality? Is it equality of income and assets, social condition, or that most intangible and characteristic of late Western ideals, self-esteem?

Barzun devotes a section to each of the four epochs. The chapters blend analysis and explanation of the major themes with accounts of figures, some famous, others known mainly to scholars, who in various ways represented, developed, lived, or argued about the ideas of the era. The result is not, as one might fear, an accumulation of anecdotes and fragmented chunks of narrative but a tapestry in which the continuing, underlying themes are ever present but never intrusive or boring.

Two pervasive themes of Western culture are what Barzun calls emancipation and primitivism. Emancipation is the idea of releasing human beings from bondage to institutions or powers seen as unjust or evil. Barzun traces the earliest form of this concept to the religious revolution. Primitivism, often closely linked to emancipation, is the idea of returning to origins and seeing higher value in an earlier, purer, better state of one's culture, religion, or personality. In Lutheranism, the dominant form of reformed Christianity in northern Europe, primitivism meant the idea that true Christianity was that of the apostles or of Jesus Christ himself, a religion without a hierarchical church and in which every man could, and must, be his own priest, where everyone was equal to God and no one needed a mediator—priest or pope—to manage relations with the divine.

Primitivism has cropped up again and again in Western literature and politics. It appears as the cult of natural man and natural human virtue, as in the idea of the noble savage, devised by the French Renaissance writer Michel de Montaigne, who can justly be called the father of modern anthropology. One has only to study the writings of ancient, Indian, or Chinese cultures to see how bizarre the idea of the noble savage is, the idea that people of primitive habits, without cities and literature, are more virtuous than civilized and literate people. Yet it is an idea that is

alive and well in America today, as the multiculturalist worship of non-Western cultures on campuses across the land illustrates.

THE WESTERN PERSONALITY

Of all the major Western ideas, perhaps the most crucial, or at least the most fascinating and peculiarly Western, is the idea of self-consciousness. Its roots are in ancient Greece—recall that the Delphic oracle commanded visitors to "know thyself"—and in ancient Israel, in the Bible's teaching on human nature and its call to constant self-examination and self-judgment. It became a dominant theme in the sixteenth century, when Montaigne, who is perhaps the most archetypally Western man of all, took it in a new direction that was to have vast repercussions throughout all later Western thought and action, whether literary, political, religious, or scientific.

Most people who have heard of Montaigne think of him as a skeptic, as someone who undermined the bloody certitudes of the theologians and warriors who were tearing Europe apart in wars of religion that were also wars of plunder, conquest, and aggrandizement. But this is to see only one side of him. Montaigne had many positive ideas and principles, but he arrived at them in a new way, the way of self-consciousness. In doing so, Barzun explains, he made self-consciousness the principle of knowledge and action. What we know, want, and believe comes from inside us, and that inside is neither simple nor unidimensional:

"Montaigne, then, is not 'a skeptic' in the sense of a shoulder-shrugging philosopher who looks at the world with tolerant amusement; he is skeptical in the sense of the reader who does not believe without evidence and the scholar who does not take any particular truth as final. This outlook in no way prevents having rooted convictions. To name only one, Montaigne is sure that people ought not to be burnt for their beliefs. . . ."

> So things stood with Montaigne when he began his exploration. Gradually, without any upheaval of feeling such as accompanies sudden conversion, he came to see that to philosophize is to learn how to live. One can only speculate about what brought on the change: it seems reasonable to suppose that the turn came from the increasingly vivid sense of the inmost self and its frequent independence from the intellect. To learn to die is a mental project born of worldly observation; to learn to live is also a project, but it takes in that "depth and variety," that "weakness" to which Montaigne attributes the temper of his opinions, and indeed of his experience as a whole.
>
> The theme of self-consciousness can never be more manifest than here, and its embodiment in the *Essays* has a cultural import that has hardly been recognized: Montaigne discovered Character. I mean by this that when he calls Man *ondoyant et divers,* a phrase so precise that it is difficult to translate—"wavelike and varying" will have to do—he replaced one conception of the individual by another, deeper and richer.

The fate of self-consciousness encapsulates the whole history of the West. In Barzun's view, the four revolutions and their associated ideas erupted in particular times and places and then entered the common stream of the culture. But it is human nature, or at least Western human nature, to pursue all themes and ideas to their extreme, to the point that they risk becoming debilitating rather than fertile. It has been a trait of the most inventive minds of the West, in whatever field of activity, to push ideas to the limit to see what new insight or stimulus they might provide. In men and women of genius, this can lead to further breakthroughs in culture, art, politics, and society. But it can also lead to decadence, and that is the problem of the West today.

In the case of self-consciousness, the critical change happened in the beginning of the Romantic era, around the turn of the eighteenth century. At that time, a group of French thinkers and writers developed a refined form of psychology of the passions and feelings. Unlike the psychology of Montaigne, this version was not guided by a strong positive morality but tended to become an exploration of feelings for their own sake, leading to a sort of emotional wheel-spinning or narcissistic indulgence in emotion rather than to fruitful self-discovery.

Among these French thinkers were the so-called Ideologues and the philosopher and essayist Germaine de Sta'l. These writers

> all bear witness through their work to the growing scope of self-consciousness. Goethe, also of their time, was alarmed by its spread and wondered how far it would go and do damage to spontaneity in art and human relations. The conscious mind is not always self-conscious. . . . The medieval church, requiring confession of sins, made frequent self-survey unavoidable, and from the Reformation onward a new intensity of religious feeling imposed the question "is my soul destined for salvation?" The search for an answer could be excruciating and take years, as Luther and [John] Bunyan told the world. But the effort had a definite range and purpose, whereas secular self-consciousness knows no limits and rarely has a stated goal; it is exploration without end and can become paralyzing.

Which is where we are today, in the age of anxiety and the identity crisis, which has been going on much longer than many think. In recent decades it has become public and accepted to have low self-esteem, to wonder who one is, to waver between defensive apology and arrogant assertion of rights, and to indulge in endless searches for oneself. But, as Barzun notes, "a self is not found but made." The failure to take that point and act on it is the precise measure of the decadence of the West in an age that, as the *New York Times* writer Maureen Dowd put it, sets "publicity over achievement, revelation over restraint, honesty over decency, victimhood over personal responsibility, confrontation over civility, psychology over morality." No one in our time, Barzun says, would understand or repeat the English poet William Wordsworth's cry during the French Revolution, "Oh, what a joy to be alive!"

HISTORY IS NOT FATE

The final chapters are "a sketch of a culture at its close," something that Barzun notes with the detachment of the sage and with minimal regret. Nor is he forecasting social or political catastrophe; he is no doomsayer but an observer. Decadence, in his view, is the natural condition of a society that has explored its native options and tendencies—the ideas and themes I have mentioned—to and beyond their natural limits. What we have today is a society characterized above all by separatism, which is what happens when sundry groups and people pursue different interests and deny or neglect what they have in common.

Separatism is promoted by the egalitarian or, as Barzun calls it, the demotic temper of the times. Everyone and every group has a right to be different. At the same time, all these groups and people want help to achieve their goals. This promotes a self-nourishing circle of political and social ambitions to make the world ever better, ever safer, and ever more uniform; but these goals can never be met, partly because they are illusory and infantile, and partly because the very dissatisfaction symbolized by the prevailing separatism means that no one is ever content. The exaggerated emphasis on self-consciousness feeds discontent and produces the sickly fear of responsibility and refusal of maturity that also seem characteristic of the demotic age.

Yet history is not fate. Niches of Western culture may and probably will survive, though forgotten by the MTV and Internet people and all those who hold to the Bill Gates thesis: the idea that computers and cyberspace are making everything better and better all the time. Neither is history fate in the sense that all that went before was part of a logical progression to what is now. History is not a single story, nor does it mainly consist of rational progress but of events and passions that sometimes produce results we in hindsight see as forming a logic of development; not so, usually, for the participants. An example: "The century that laid down the fundamentals of science"—the seventeenth—"is the one that got rid of public baths and of the very idea of regular bathing."

In a final, whimsical chapter posing as a future historian's analysis of what happened to the West after our own time, Barzun guesses that the Gatesian idea of endless, computerized prosperity without culture and history will finally generate an attack of boredom:

> The attack was so severe that the over-entertained people, led by a handful of restless men and women from the upper orders, demanded Reform and finally imposed it in the usual way, by repeating one idea. These radicals had begun to study the old neglected literary and photographic texts and maintained that they were the record of a fuller life. . . . They distinguished styles and the different ages of their emergence—in short, they found a past and used it to create a new present. Fortunately, they were bad imitators . . . and their twisted view of their sources laid the foundations

of our nascent—or perhaps one should say, renascent—culture. It has resurrected enthusiasm in the young and talented, who keep exclaiming what a joy it is to be alive.

Another kind of comfort—bracing and from the age that was already losing the old Western commitment to the whole life—is that of Alfred Tennyson in his poem "Ulysses." These are the words of a man who, unlike Wordsworth in the 1790s, is not young but who nevertheless cannot stop seeking beyond the sunset. At the end of such a road lies not self-doubt or anxiety but the endless discovery of history, world, self, and life that Montaigne recommended and enjoyed and that Barzun, that latter-day Montaigne, provides for our enrichment:

> Come, my friends,
> 'Tis not too late to seek a newer world.
> Push off, and sitting well in order smite
> The sounding furrows, for my purpose holds
> To sail beyond the sunset, and the baths
> Of all the western stars, until I die. . . .
> Tho' much is taken, much abides; and tho'
> We are not now that strength which in old days
> Moved earth and heaven; that which we are, we are;
> One equal temper of heroic hearts,
> Made weak by time and fate, but strong in will
> To strive, to seek, to find, and not to yield.

John J. Reilly (review date November 2000)

SOURCE: "The End of History?" in *First Things*, No. 107, November, 2000, pp. 43-4.

[*In the following review, Reilly offers a favorable assessment of* From Dawn to Decadence.]

From Dawn to Decadence is one of those wonderful books that cannot be categorized. Some reviewers have compared it to *The Education of Henry Adams*, the great intellectual autobiography that seemed to sum up the last fin-de-siècle. The comparison does no injustice to either work. Jacques Barzun was born in 1907, and so has lived through a not insignificant slice of the period he covers, but even he did not know Descartes personally. And yet in some ways *From Dawn to Decadence* reads less like a history than it does like a personal memoir of the last half-millennium, with people and topics selected chiefly because the author is interested in them. The effect is delightful, though sometimes a little disorienting. Perhaps the one thing you can say for sure about *From Dawn to Decadence* is that it provides the most cheerful explanation you are ever likely to get for why Western culture is ending.

Jacques Barzun really needs no introduction. Anyone interested in William James, the great Romantic composers, the role of race in historical writing, or a dozen other subjects has already encountered him somewhere. (A book he coauthored with Henry Graff, *The Modern Researcher,*

sticks in my mind after twenty-five years as a philosophy of historiography disguised as a reference guide.) In *From Dawn to Decadence,* he manages to touch on just about all his lifelong interests, and without turning the book into a mere anthology.

The format is loosely chronological, with the great era of the post-medieval, "modern" West divided into several lesser ages. The whole text is broken up into digestible chunks of commentary and biography. We get assessments, sometimes quite idiosyncratic ones, of almost all the great names of the modern era, but many of the biographies are of persons the author deems worthy-but-obscure. Some of these subjects really are virtually forgotten, such as the ingenious eighteenth-century polymath, Dr. Georg Lichtenberg. Others are just a bit neglected, such as the senior Oliver Wendell Holmes. (Barzun manages to praise this physician and essayist while barely mentioning his jurist son.) A particularly entertaining feature of the book is the brief, apt quotations set into the margins. Had it not been for *From Dawn to Decadence,* I would never have known that Thursday was bear-baiting day at the court of Elizabeth I.

From Dawn to Decadence has only a minimal amount of political and military narrative, which is something of a drawback since the author routinely makes unexplained allusions to people and events that may no longer be common knowledge. (Do undergraduates today know what Stanley said to Livingston? I'm afraid to ask.) And then there are the fact-checking lapses inevitable in a work of this scope. These will allow readers to entertain themselves by looking for mistakes. More than one reviewer has noted that modern calculus does not use Newton's notation, as Barzun says, but that of Leibniz. However, this review may be the only place you will read that those long-range shells the Germans fired at Paris (and Barzun) during the First World War did not come from Big Berthas, but from Krupp's *Pariskanone.*

Parlor games aside, the author corrects errors that are far more important than the ones he makes. He points out, for instance, that, no, M. Jourdain did not speak prose, and that Molière knew this as well as anyone. It is anachronistic, he reminds us, to suppose that Galileo was tried because the Inquisition believed the Copernican model threatened man's place in the universe. Rousseau's works cannot be made to say, he observes with a note of exasperation, that Rousseau was a revolutionary who wished mankind to return to a state of nature. Intellectual superstitions of this sort are probably immortal, but it is a good idea to try to correct them at least once every five hundred years.

While a book as genial as this one can hardly be accused of promoting anything as crudely Germanic as a theory of history, it does present a sketch of the last half-millennium. According to Barzun, the West has been working out a cultural impulse that it received in the Renaissance, an impulse that had become exhausted by the end of the twentieth century. This impulse was not an ideology or an agenda but an expandable list of desires, particular forms of which can be detected throughout all the cultural and political controversies of the great era. The names of these desires are helpfully capitalized wherever they are mentioned, so that Emancipation is graphically shown to play a role in every major controversy from the Reformation to the women's suffrage movement. Another example is Primitivism, the perennial impulse to return to the original text, to the early constitution, to the uncluttered state of the beginning. Other trends of the modern era have been informed by the desires for Abstraction, Reductivism, and Self-consciousness. Ideas like these can hardly be said to have been the motor of Western history, but looking for their various incarnations over the centuries does make it much easier to view the era as a whole.

Barzun laconically informs us that late medieval Europe was a "decadent" society. I myself had thought that Richard Gilman had permanently retired that word with his study *Decadence: The Strange Life of an Epithet,* but Barzun may persuade readers that "decadence" is neither a moral category nor a bit of implicit vitalism. Rather, Barzun says, the term "decadent" may properly be used of any social situation that is blocked, where people entertain goals for which they will not tolerate the means. Decadent societies tend to become labyrinthine in both their cultures and their styles of government, as people create small accommodations within a larger unsatisfactory context. Decadent periods can be sweet, as Talleyrand remarked of pre-Revolutionary France, but partly because they are obviously ephemeral.

Decadence may end in the explosion of a revolution, by which Barzun means the violent transfer of power and property in the name of an idea. Revolutions are great simplifiers that pave over the labyrinths and open up possibilities that were unimaginable just a few years previously. There have been four of these revolutions during the modern era, each more or less defining an age. There was the religious revolution of the Reformation, which first stated themes that would recur through the rest of the era. There was the monarch's revolution of the seventeenth century, in which the aristocracy was tamed and large, centralized states began to appear. The monarchs, of course, got their comeuppance in the liberal revolution at the end of the eighteenth century. Most recently, every throne, power, and dominion was shaken by the social revolution at the beginning of the twentieth.

Barzun seems to believe that the twentieth century was so traumatized by the First World War that it was never able to fully exploit the positive possibilities in what he calls the "Cubist Decade" that preceded the war's outbreak. Rather, the Age of Modernism (not to be confused with the modern era) largely confined itself to analysis and destruction. Thanks to the First World War, the more distant past became unusable: the sense of living in a completely new age left the past with nothing to say. No restraints remained on the expression of the desires that had characterized the whole modern era. The result was that, by centu-

ry's end, the chief remaining impulses in Western culture had developed to a theoretical maximum. So ends an age.

This conclusion would be depressing, were it not so reminiscent of similar conclusions in earlier eras. Barzun notes that at the end of the fifteenth century, some people held that the sixth millennium of the world was about to end—and history along with it. As is often the case with this kind of sentiment, the people who shared it were on to something, if the end of history is taken to mean the end of history as they knew it. Barzun ends the book on a note of hopeful speculation. He looks back from a more distant time on our immediate future, which he supposes will be an age when history will wholly disappear from even the minds of the educated. Indeed, so completely will the modern age be forgotten that its rediscovery will have an impact quite as revolutionary as the impact that classical culture had on the late medieval world. The result, Barzun hopes, will be another renaissance, when the young and talented will again exclaim what joy it is to be alive.

FURTHER READING

Criticism

Allen, Gay Wilson. "An American Philosopher." *Washington Post Book World* (29 May 1983): 6.

> In this review of *A Stroll with William James,* Allen discusses James's philosophical approach and path-breaking contribution to psychology.

Birnbaum, Milton. "Teaching and Learning Revisited." *Modern Age* 35, No. 1 (September 1992): 73.

> A review of *Begin Here.*

Casement, William. "Traditionalism Well Spoken." *College Teaching* 39, No. 4 (Fall 1991): 161-2.

> A review of *Begin Here.*

Everdell, William R. "Idea Man." *New York Times Book Review* (21 May 2000): 11.

> A review of *From Dawn to Decadence.*

Gates, David. "A Real-Life Renaissance Man." *Newsweek* (22 May 2000): 76.

> Provides an overview of Barzun's career and thought, as well as a discussion of *From Dawn to Decadence.*

Gross, John. "So Much Greatness Worth Remembering." *Wall Street Journal* (18 May 2000): A24.

> A review of *From Dawn to Decadence.*

Hart, Jeffrey. "Barzun's Summa." *National Review* (22 May 2000): 56.

> A review of *From Dawn to Decadence.*

Kimball, Roger. "Closing Time: Jacques Barzun on Western Culture." *New Criterion* 18, No. 10 (June 2000): 5.

Provides an overview of Barzun's life and thought, as well as a discussion of *From Dawn to Decadence.*

Lawlor, Sheila. "Educating the Educators." *Times Literary Supplement* (17 May 1991): 23.

Lawlor offers a positive assessment of *Begin Here.*

Martines, Lauro. "Picture All This." *Times Literary Supplement* (2 March 2001): 26-7.

A review of *From Dawn to Decadence.*

Rothstein, Edward. "A Sojourner of the Past Retraces His Steps." *New York Times* (15 April 2000): B7.

Profiles Barzun's life, career, and historical perspective.

Smith, Ralph A. "Culture in a Bind: Barzun on the Decline of the West." *Arts Education Policy Review* 102, No. 3 (January-February 2001): 37.

A review of *From Dawn to Decadence.*

Tonsor, S. J. "A Wanderer in No Man's Land." *National Review* (4 August 1989): 41.

A review of *The Culture We Deserve.*

Weeks, Linton. "500 Years of Attitude." *Washington Post* (14 June 2000): C1, C12.

In this following essay, based on an interview with Barzun, Weeks discusses the central themes of *From Dawn to Decadence* and reports Barzun's views on historical change, cultural decline and renewal, and contemporary society.

Additional coverage of Barzun's life and career is contained in the following sources published by the Gale Group: *Contemporary Authors,* **Vols. 61-64;** *Contemporary Authors New Revision Series,* **Vols. 22 and 95; and** *Literature Resource Center.*

Fred D'Aguiar
1960-

English poet, novelist, and playwright.

The following entry presents an overview of D'Aguiar's career through 2000.

INTRODUCTION

With the publication of his debut poetry volume, *Mama Dot* (1985), D'Aguiar emerged as a prominent figure among a young generation of writers of Caribbean descent who have broadened the scope of contemporary British literature. Because D'Aguiar was born in London but reared in Guyana, his childhood experiences play a distinctive role in his writings. Concerned primarily with themes of colonial marginalization and racial identity, he has striven to present a perspective that takes into account both public and private concerns. Historical developments play an essential role in his work, particularly those of the slave trade between Africa and the Americas, the economic and political troubles of postcolonial Guyana, and the post-World War II influx of Caribbean immigrants to Britain. D'Aguiar began his writing career as a poet, and his poetic sensibility continues to inform his work in other genres, notably the novels *The Longest Memory* (1994) and *Dear Future* (1996).

BIOGRAPHICAL INFORMATION

D'Aguiar was born in London in 1960, the second child of immigrants from the Caribbean nation of British Guyana. His parents both worked for London Transport, and their schedules made it difficult to care for their two sons. When he was two years old, D'Aguiar and his older brother were sent to Guyana to live with their paternal grandparents, who lived in a house at Airy Hall, about forty miles from the capital of Georgetown. The house belonging to D'Aguiar's grandparents, "Mama Dot" and "Papa T," was a large one, made up of family members African, Asian, and European in origin. D'Aguiar spent the majority of his time in Guyana at Airy Hall, which was removed from the racial problems and political warfare of the capital. He spent the final four years of his Guyanese youth in Georgetown, where he lived with his maternal grandparents. At age twelve, D'Aguiar and his brother moved back to London (and a country increasingly antagonistic toward immigration by nonwhite members of the Commonwealth), where they lived with their newly divorced mother. D'Aguiar attended the Charlton Boys Secondary School, where he was, if only briefly, exposed to Caribbean litera-

ture. He then trained and worked for a period as a psychiatric nurse. During this time, D'Aguiar attended a series of writing workshops at the University of London. He began a three-year course in English literature at the University of Kent, graduating in 1985. (He had been exposed to English poetry during his boyhood in Guyana by his grandfather, Papa T.) In 1985, D'Aguiar published his first book of poetry, *Mama Dot*. He then released two more collections of poetry before the production of his first play, *A Jamaican Airman Foresees His Death* (1991). Three years later he published *The Longest Memory,* his first novel.

MAJOR WORKS

The most significant part of D'Aguiar's oeuvre consists of his poetry and fiction. His first book, *Mama Dot,* grew out of a series of poems about a composite character based on both his grandmothers. The book is divided into three parts, with the first section devoted to the multifaceted metaphor of Mama Dot. With the image of Mama Dot, D'Aguiar combines the everyday and mythic qualities of the grandmother figure, and in the process creates a practical, no-nonsense Caribbean woman who provides a link to an African past. The second section of the book, "Roots Broadcast," deals with experiences of metropolitan alienation. A long poem called "Guyana Days" makes up the book's third section and deals with the poet's return as an adult to the country of his youth. D'Aguiar's second poetry collection, *Airy Hall* (1989), is also divided into three sections, with the first two dealing extensively with the author's experiences in Guyana. While the first part takes a rather nostalgic look at the past, the second grimly reflects Guyana's postcolonial deprivation and corrupt politics. The author again closes the book with a single long poem, "The Kitchen Bitch." This poem (whose title refers to a kind of kerosene lamp traditionally used in rural Jamaica) is based on an annual walk that the author takes at Hebden Bridge, where Sylvia Plath is buried. Superimposed on this walk is the drama of an expedition leader who loses his sanity as his fellow walkers die one by one. Metaphor plays an important role in *Mama Dot* and *Airy Hall,* serving as representations for personalities and places in D'Aguiar's early life in Guyana. In D'Aguiar's poetry the choice of language also occupies a significant position. He often uses for effect what has been called "nation language," namely, the varieties of Creole spoken in the Caribbean and spread elsewhere via immigration. *British Subjects* (1992), the author's next poetry collection, more closely depicts the dilemma of the immigrant. The book's poems illustrate the tension felt by immigrants' children, who are alienated by the nation into which they are born.

Bloodlines (2000) is an epic verse novel dealing with slavery in the American South during and after the Civil War. Rendered in the ottava rima meter, the story centers upon a slave, Faith, who falls in love with the plantation owner's son, Christy, after he rapes her. The two elope and are later separated. Christy eventually learns that Faith has died while giving birth to their child, a son who is presumed dead but has lived and narrates the story. In the stage play *A Jamaican Airman Foresees His Death,* D'Aguiar confronts British attitudes toward nonwhite colonial immigrants following the collapse of the empire in the 1940s. In the play four young men in Jamaica enlist in the Royal Air Force. At the training base in Scotland, they are confronted with demeaning treatment, culminating in the racially-motivated assault of Alvin, the leader of the group. Alvin is rescued by a Scottish woman named Kathleen, and the two fall in love. Alvin's and Kathleen's happiness, however, is destroyed when he accidentally shoots down an Allied plane, is dishonorably discharged, and declines into insanity. While making sure not to sacrifice the play's narrative clarity, D'Aguiar emphasizes metaphor and language in such a way that the poet's voice is readily apparent. D'Aguiar's experience as a poet also seems to have encouraged experimentation with the traditional form of the novel. His first novel, *The Longest Memory,* directly addresses the issue of slavery in the Americas. The unconventional narrative consists of a series of monologues spoken by slaves and masters on an early-nineteenth-century Virginia plantation. The story centers upon Whitechapel, a slave who seeks to lead a dignified life by working hard and cultivating the master's respect. Even after his wife is raped by the overseer, Whitechapel treats the resulting child as his own son. When this son eventually tries to escape from the plantation, Whitechapel tells his master, unintentionally contributing to the boy's violent death. The novel's monologues, reflecting D'Aguiar's poetic sensibility, work to create multiple voices, a chorus of sorts that evokes not only a variety of emotional and intellectual responses to the novel's events but also subjective time shifts. *Dear Future* also involves a search to remember, a task aided by the evocation of symbolic images and the rejection of a direct, chronological narrative. In this novel, D'Aguiar considers the politics of postcolonial Guyana from a child's viewpoint. Consisting of a series of episodes in the life of the young Red Head, the novel demonstrates how global capitalism and corruption among the local elite have betrayed the promise of the nation's independence. D'Aguiar's novel *Feeding the Ghosts* (1999) likewise features a quest for memory, with symbolism used to unite the different physical and temporal spaces of the story. The novel centers upon Mintah, a slave who has survived the seaboard murders of her fellow slaves. Through Mintah's severed connection to her family and community, the novel explores the creation of cultural identity.

CRITICAL RECEPTION

D'Aguiar's *Mama Dot* attracted considerable critical appreciation and immediately established the writer as a tal-

ented new voice in poetry. These early poems were commended for their clarity, humor, and sense of irony. Though his subsequent poetry collections received mixed assessments, reviewers have continued to appreciate the originality and wit of D'Aguiar's verse. In his writings about the hardships of life in postcolonial Guyana and the problems of nonwhite immigrants in Britain, D'Aguiar has demonstrated a keen awareness of aesthetic, cultural, literary, as well as political issues. His focus on the legacy of slavery, notably in *The Longest Memory* and *Feeding the Ghosts,* is recognized for his exploration of power, identity, history and memory. Reviewers are quick to note the overriding influence of poetry in his novels, which focus on memory to examine bonds of kinship. *The Longest Memory* and *Dear Future* have been well received for their intensity and intelligence, though some critics contend that D'Aguiar's experimentation with narrative form causes these works to suffer from a lack of focus and depth. His verse novel, *Bloodlines,* was deemed an ambitious experiment but was generally unfavorably reviewed. Despite such criticism, D'Aguiar is esteemed for his distinctive poetic sensibility and his provocative explorations of racism and postcolonial identity.

PRINCIPAL WORKS

Mama Dot (poetry) 1985
The New British Poetry [editor, with others] (poetry) 1988
Airy Hall (poetry) 1989
A Jamaican Airman Foresees His Death (play) 1991
British Subjects (poetry) 1992
The Longest Memory (novel) 1994
Dear Future (novel) 1996
Feeding the Ghosts (novel) 1999
Bloodlines (verse novel) 2000

CRITICISM

Sean O'Brien (review date 7-13 July 1989)

SOURCE: "Towards a Revelation," in *Times Literary Supplement,* July 7-13, 1989, p. 737.

[*In the following review, O'Brien concludes that* Airy Hall *is a mixture of "disappointment" and "refreshing ambition."*]

The title sequence of Fred D'Aguiar's second collection, **Airy Hall,** consists of eighteen poems about the Guyanan village where his boyhood was spent. It expands and enriches the prose account D'Aguiar gave in *Poetry Review*

(Volume 75, Number 2, August 1985), and emphasizes his gifts in handling the evidence of the senses. Dry washing is heard "chattering" on a line; leaves "describe a slowed, / ziggurat fall"; a whole section of **"Airy Hall at Night"** brilliantly evokes the horrible toadness of a trodden-on toad. According to D'Aguiar, Airy Hall is a place you could drive or sprint through without noticing it, and he convincingly re-creates its remoteness, its heat, its stillness, its seemingly uneventful secrecy. At a barely explicit level, though, he seems to want to push the poems further, towards a revelation for which the speaking picture is inadequate.

Exactly how this squares with the observation in **"Airy Hall Barrier"** that "Many deny what we see / Has anything to do with anything" is not made clear in the sequence, but at times the effort to signify afflicts the verse with hyperaesthesia, and the result is cramped and overwritten. The most striking example is **"Airy Hall's Feathered Glories."** Describing the capture of songbirds, it staggers towards its conclusion under the burden of its setpiece role:

> After an absence hard to string
> A sentence in, ambition itself,
> Nursed from crawl, to walk, to run,
> Enters the brashest of suns, cages
> Held high as lamps, mirrors or trophies
> Brimming a tongue-tied, granite dark.

Faced with such grammatical discomfort and insistent symbolism the unsympathetic reader might be put in mind of 1940s Apocalyptic impatience with clarity: "a tongue-tied, granite dark"? Come again? Yet while these lines deflect rather than convince, D'Aguiar is surely right to keep hammering away at the effort to fuse private imaginings with cultural and political realities.

In this context, **"Frontline Chronicle,"** from the book's second section, takes on special importance. It records, first D'Aguiar's quarrel (at the time of the Brixton insurrection?) with a man who insisted that writing must be bare and direct—a view the poet could neither share nor, at the time, effectively dispute—and second his opponent's violent death, apparently in police custody. It is a "direct" and painful poem, but part of its point is that D'Aguiar has sacrificed none of his attachment to art to achieve it. The very fact that he remains unconverted to populism may account for the deforming strain and uncertain progress of some of the poems, for his methods remain based in English traditions which have rarely been called on to serve the purposes he has in mind. **"Only the President's Eggs Are Yellow"** applies satire with surreal affiliations to a stalled Third World economy but ends up infected by the mixture of inertia and febrility it records, while **"El Dorado Update,"** the most nearly oral poem in the book, similarly amasses detail without acquiring momentum.

If the suspicion grows that D'Aguiar has yet to satisfy himself as to his technical intentions—his cadences veer from memorable to inaudible—he proves willing to take this and other matters on in the lengthy closing poem **"The Kitchen Bitch."** Narrating an ill-starred journey through mountain and jungle, seemingly from the viewpoint of a former guerrilla, it is a work whose Gordian unfriendliness is likely to gain it more acknowledgements than readers. The combination of disappointment with refreshing ambition is typical of the book: better this, perhaps, than some easier successes.

Maya Jaggi (review date 19 April 1991)

SOURCE: "Four Rum Jamaicans," in *Times Literary Supplement,* April 19, 1991, p. 19.

[*In the following review of* A Jamaican Airman Foresees His Death, *Jaggi commends the play's powerful symbolism and humor, though finds shortcomings in its uneven pacing and underdeveloped contemporary parallels.*]

The title of Fred D'Aguiar's play sounds an echo of W. B. Yeats's poem "An Irish Airman Foresees His Death." Through an episodic, exuberant juxtaposition of dialogue, verse and song, D'Aguiar transfers the poem's ambivalence about fighting another country's battles to the experience of a Jamaican airman in the Second World War.

Set initially in Jamaica in the 1940s, the play satirizes the cynical appeal made to the dominions, to fight for King and country. Kojo, an eccentric creole seer, parodies Churchill's broadcasts with scatological relish, while mocking the gullibility of the young, rum-soaked Jamaicans who enthusiastically queue to join up. D'Aguiar humorously reveals the mixed motives of a naive foursome (played with engaging fervour by Clarence Smith, Sidney Cole, Maynard Eziashi and Fraser James) who enlist more in a spirit of fortune-hunting and sexual bravado than of patriotism. Yet it also exposes their illusions about the metropolitan power ("Britain is the father, Jamaica mother to me", the boys chant), which others warn against.

As the scene shifts to an airbase in Scotland, disillusionment sets in, with the Jamaican recruits relegated to menial tasks: one cleans the toilets, "flushing out the enemy" in "germ warfare"; others end up in the canteen or the barber-shop. Meanwhile, the locals' idea of hospitality is to ambush Clarence Smith's Alvin, "to see if he has a tail." Only Alvin's rescue at the hands of a Yeats-quoting Scottish lass helps thaw the coldness of the welcome. But Alvin, a rear-gunner of prowess, is grounded for accidentally shooting down an Allied plane. In a twist to the title, the Jamaican airman succumbs not to extinction, but to the slower death of insanity, after being labelled a murderer, and dishonourably discharged.

The poet D'Aguiar's gift for metaphor, and the affective power of his language, combine with a quirkily wry humour to propel a drama which sometimes threatens to lose sight of its narrative threads. Through metaphors of flight, or drowning, the play powerfully captures the hopes, bewilderment, vulnerability and blindness of the young volunteers.

Hettie Macdonald's adventurously informal promenade production lends itself to the play's oscillations of mood. Though a little chaotic at the outset, and tending at times to lose paces it settles into an exciting unpredictability, as the roving audience (offered rum punch and peanuts at the door) literally pursues the action into the various corners of the theatre. The only drawback to the production is its resolute rootedness in the Second World War years, which muffles resonances for the present. Neither simply about the war years, nor about racial bias within the armed forces, the play also serves to dramatize the hopes and disillusionment of all those who have been lured to the metropolis. Urgent parallels with the present are hinted at in Alvin's fateful encounter with British justice which condemns him not for his actions but for his colour. His consequent decline into mental illness also mirrors a grim sociological reality.

D'Aguiar's play sparks important issues which he has the demonstrable talent to develop further and more boldly. In this production, energetic and engaging as it is, they run the risk of being comfortingly relegated to a distant past.

Paula Burnett (review date 12 November 1993)

SOURCE: "Thames Barriers," in *New Statesman & Society,* November 12, 1993, pp. 37-8.

[*In the following excerpt, Burnett offers a generally positive assessment of* British Subjects, *though she notes that some of poems in the volume "do not earn their place."*]

The peculiarly British ambivalence about black cultural expression is well summed up by topical events. On the one hand, the South Bank Centre and the Arts Council are staging *Out of the Margins,* a celebration of British black and Asian writing. On the other, the government has announced that it is to close down the Commonwealth Institute by turning off the funding tap from 1996. With funds already reduced to little more than a trickle, the Foreign Office policy has starved all areas of the institute's work over the past decade. Yet that work has heroically continued to nurture the cultural climate in which such events as the South Bank festival can blossom.

So many of the black and Asian writers taking part have been fostered by the institute's encouragement. So many British citizens, both black and white, children and adults, have begun to appreciate a multicultural society through visits to the galleries and its special events. So many writers and students have been able to share the literature of the Commonwealth through the library, unique in this country. If all that goes, Britain will be the poorer, and the coming generations of writers may never materialise.

E A Markham and Fred D'Aguiar are examples of writers who are, at the moment, British. They engage creatively with their experience of living here, but the riches they offer are very much shaped by their identity as black citizens of the Commonwealth. We lose either the institute, or them, at our peril . . . .

There are coruscating moments, too, in Fred D'Aguiar's third collection of poems, *British Subjects.* The title signals a digging into British identity for a young writer born in Britain of Caribbean parentage, then raised in Guyana, and until recently resident in Britain. His earlier work was more firmly placed in Guyanese life and language, particularly the first book, *Mama Dot.* Now his Guyanese sense of a water-bound landscape is naturalised to the tidal reaches of the Thames. A night flight over London and "my neck of the woods" reveals "The Thames ribbed and corseted / by traffic despite its peregrinations / in a black wetsuit."

Later the river is "sanskrit in black ink / scribbling away into the dark." Building on his conjuring of Columbus as a Triton figure rising from the river in **"1492,"** he now imagines that Bob Marley's locks break the plaited tide. The Thames Barrier becomes a grand metaphor of racial exclusion.

Guyana is now a place with museums to be visited like a tourist, although he is accompanied by his mentor—the novelist Wilson Harris—who expounds their shared history. D'Aguiar is of the next generation after Harris, but needs to guard against assuming an august mantle too easily. Some of the poems here do not earn their place. His editors at Bloodaxe should have been sterner, helping him to complete the shift from a promising narrative skill to a richer metaphoric texture while retaining his ear.

That said, there are some strikingly original poems here; particularly fables such as **"A Gift of a Rose,"** in which relationships between the black community and the police are poignantly allegorised. D'Aguiar has begun to speak authoritatively of a British experience, but he is now in the US. Britain risks losing him and other talents such as Caryl Phillips.

It was at the Commonwealth Institute that a remarkable epic poem, written in London by the Jamaican Jean Binta Breeze, recently had its first reading. A national commitment to such writers and the institute is vital if the English language—enriched for centuries by different cultures—is to continue to thrive.

Ian Sansom (review date 7 January 1994)

SOURCE: "Sincere Despair," in *Times Literary Supplement,* January 7, 1994, p. 18.

[*In the following review, Sansom offers an unfavorable evaluation of* British Subjects.]

The astonishing output of Bloodaxe Books over the past fifteen years is a testament to editor Neil Astley's enthusiasm and hard work. Unfortunately, Astley has worked so hard that he now sometimes seems to be asleep on the job—this, at least, would help to explain why *British Subjects,* Fred D'Aguiar's third collection, and his first from Bloodaxe, is not as good as it should be.

For D'Aguiar excites high expectations. His short but brilliant first collection, *Mama Dot,* was published in 1985, when he was twenty-five years old. In 1988, he was joint editor of the ground-breaking Paladin anthology, *The New British Poetry,* and 1989 saw his second collection, *Airy Hall,* win the Guyana Prize for Poetry. Since then he has written plays, held the prestigious Judith E. Wilson Fellowship at Cambridge University and now teaches at Amherst College, Massachusetts. E. A. Markham included him as the youngest poet in *Hinterland,* the excellent (Bloodaxe) anthology of Caribbean poetry, where D'Aguiar's tough, fluent poems with their distinctive conceits (in **"Mama Dot's Treatise"** mosquitoes "suck our blood / From the cradle / And flaunt it / Like a fat wallet") did not look out of place alongside work by stalwarts like Edward Kamau Brathwaite and James Berry. It is D'Aguiar's obvious talent that makes *British Subjects* such a disappointment and makes one wish for some severe editorial blue-pencilling.

British Subjects is true to its title—apart from two short poem-sequences set in Guyana and Germany, the collection concerns itself with life in Britain's cities and towns, from Whitley Bay to Greenwich. D'Aguiar's focus is sharp but the poetry is sluggish: in the poems dealing directly with issues of race and racism his usual gusto is replaced by a laboured sincerity. When, in **"A Gift of a Rose,"** for example, two policemen "stopped me and gave me a bunch of red, red roses" the immediate effect is dizzying, provoking, but over the next four stanzas the image collapses under its own weight. **"Colour,"** on the other hand, in which the narrator's colour seeps away, is intriguing but half-baked.

Some of D'Aguiar's old interests and skills are still apparent. His earlier collections explored and celebrated the geography of people's lives in Guyana; the new British-based poems are still fascinated by the complex interaction between individuals and their environment, though now the observations are voiced with an eloquent despair, as in the opening to **"Inner City"**:

> The way a man lets his dog
> strip the bark off a young tree
> and the children of that man
> break branch after branch
> till the naked trunk of the thing
> stands, a dead stump.

There are occasional flashes, too, of D'Aguiar's highly wrought intelligence, in **"Honest Souls,"** and of his smart-arse wit in the gnomic obscenities of **"Thirteen Views of a Penis"**:

> A Buddhist demonstration of faith:
> how much drinking water (uncarbonated)
> can a monk draw up his untumid penis.

But there has undoubtedly been a diminishing and a slackening in his style. Where he once drew widely on effects of repetition and dialect to produce his linguistic melodies, his tunes are now cheap and cheerless, as in the opening poem **"Ballad of the Throwaway People"**: "we are the throwaway people / The problem that won't go away / people." And where his imagination once thrived in the luxuriant atmosphere of the poem sequence (the *Mama Dot* and *Airy Hall* poems, the long, magnificent **"The Kitchen Bitch"**), the sequences in *British Subjects* are shorter and seem half-hearted—most of the poems in the sequence **"The Body in Question,"** for example, are weightless, brittle, rather silly: "Buttocks are a source of worry for those who look over / their shoulder at a full-length mirror."

Fred D'Aguiar is a good poet, but this is a poor collection. It makes one wonder, despairingly, whether in fact the insufficiencies of *British Subjects* have something to do with the insufficiencies of its British subjects.

Abdulrazak Gurnah (review date 15 July 1994)

SOURCE: "Resisting Ignorance," in *Times Literary Supplement,* July 15, 1994, p. 22.

[*In the following review, Gurnah offers a positive assessment of* The Longest Memory.]

In the mythology of defiance to racial slavery in the United States, no act has quite the resonance as that of learning to read and write. There were practical reasons for the prohibition of literacy by the slave-holders, but among them was also a desire to have their assumption of the African's degraded humanity fulfilled. For the slave, overcoming the prohibition was a form of resistance to this assumption and a step towards liberation. In *The Longest Memory,* it is insurgent acts like these which indicate to the overseer that Chapel is bound to run one day.

The events in the novel take place on a Virginia plantation owned by Mr Whitechapel about the turn of the nineteenth century. An old slave, called Whitechapel after his master, betrays the route of his son's escape to the planter. The son is also called Whitechapel, shortened to Chapel to distinguish him from his father. Whitechapel's betrayal leads to Chapel's capture, horrific whipping and death. This is the central memory of the novel, but through it are revealed other memories which construct the degraded world of the slave plantation. "Remembering" is the novel's method, as different voices take up the narrative at various points. Fred D'Aguiar makes good use of Whitechapel, an Uncle Tom figure who personifies the debate about what is a responsible act under slavery. He is the oldest man on the plantation, the only one born in Africa, father and grandfather and great-grandfather to nearly two-thirds of the slaves. He has acquired some credit from the planter and the overseer because he has accommodated himself to slavery but, above all, he has survived. He betrays not because he is abject, but to teach his son that resistance is useless, to school him "in the idea of obedience."

Chapel is not really his son. He is the son of Saunders the former overseer, who was the father of the current overseer, also called Saunders. He had raped Chapel's mother a few days before she married Whitechapel. The overseer and Chapel are half-brothers, though neither knows it. It is because Whitechapel thinks Saunders knows that he does not expect him to whip his half-brother to death. That is the "prodigious carpet" of intimate interweavings which display the finer cruelties of slavery. Chapel's immediate reason for running away is Lydia, the planter's daughter. It is she who teaches Chapel to read—his mother is the cook at the big house and he hangs around while Lydia is reading to herself. When they are discovered, long after Chapel has mastered the skill, it is *Romeo and Juliet* they are found reading together. Their own story has some parallels with the star-crossed lovers. Their love is a secret. They are young; Lydia is sixteen and Chapel is thirteen. The secret conversations they hold on clear nights are reminiscent of the anguished dialogue of the young lovers. Their plan to run away together ends in tragedy and misunderstanding. The *Romeo and Juliet* motif, and Chapel's absorbing interest in English classical texts—Shakespeare, Spenser, Donne—figure his desire to be a poet as well the tradition he belongs to. It is, then, as someone who belongs to that tradition that he makes his bid for freedom and happiness.

The Longest Memory is written in a form which is both fluid and complex, using language of some intensity. The "memories" are given to different participants—Whitechapel, Mr Whitechapel, Lydia, Cook, and so on—and this results in some unevenness of both voice and pace. The pace slackens when the different voices go over events that we already know about without adding anything; Mr Whitechapel's visit to the club is an example of this, as are Cook's two sentimental monologues. These sections stand out in an otherwise tense and tightly constructed narrative. Whitechapel, though, is wonderfully effective, bewildered and heroic, overcome by his action yet stoical in his acceptance of ostracism by his children and grandchildren. In his figure, *The Longest Memory* effectively demonstrates the inevitable intimacies between oppressor and oppressed.

Paula Burnett (review date 2 September 1994)

SOURCE: "Ocean Views," in *New Statesman & Society*, September 2, 1994, pp. 36-7.

[*In the following excerpt, Burnett offers a positive assessment of* The Longest Memory.]

Two years on from the 1492 quincentenary, the Euro-American past still haunts British minds. Not only has the

infant 23rd in line for the throne improbably been named Columbus, but London publishing has delivered four new novels addressing the shared transatlantic experience. Three of them have voyages at their heart. All revisit the guilt and suffering of the past, and all hold up to the light the racial encounters and moral conflicts of Atlantic history. . . .

Liberalism is taken apart in the poet Fred D'Aguiar's first novel, *The Longest Memory*. D'Aguiar, a British-born Guyanese, tackles the myth of the benign slave owner with a cleverly constructed tale set on a Virginia plantation, which exposes liberalism as self-interested and skin-deep. It tells the history of an Uncle Tom's betrayal of his runaway son, because he trusts his liberal master. The enigmatic story is unfolded through a series of separate narrations spoken by those involved, beginning with the disillusioned father, now ostracised as guilty by his own community, although he was the betrayed.

As speaker after speaker uses the same neutral language—eloquent, rational, ethical, low-key—impatience sets in, until it dawns that the apartheid of the fragmented narrations is cunningly transcended by this common idiom. The separate testimonies unravel, in all its tragic poignancy, a story of interracial rape in one generation balanced by doomed interracial love in the next. The black father's misplaced faith in liberalism is inverted in his son's resistance.

This deceptively simple book resonates long after it is finished; it addresses not only the dilemmas of the past but also today's generation gap in racial attitudes. D'Aguiar brings off the difficult feat of embracing, sincerely, both black militancy and a forgiving pluralism. "Memory is pain trying to resurrect itself," concludes his old man. . . .

Andrew Salkey (review date Autumn 1994)

SOURCE: A review of *British Subjects*, in *World Literature Today*, Vol. 68, No. 4, Autumn, 1994, pp. 864-5.

[*In the following review, Salkey compares* British Subjects *to the verse of W. H. Auden and Phillip Larkin.*]

The primary thematic thrusts of Fred D'Aguiar's spirited verse [in *British Subjects*] support subjects that readily yield themselves up to satire and irony. Of course, this is not to say that he writes down to levels of sarcasm, cynicism, or ridicule. Indeed, he does the very opposite; he achieves peaks of exuberant phrase-making, punning, humor, paraphrase, and fancy.

In one of D'Aguiar's most ironically layered narrative poems, the persona, an authentic citizen of Britain and the Commonwealth, lands at Heathrow, approaches Customs, and gives himself over "to the usual inquisition"; but he discovers after handing over his passport "the stamp, British Citizen, not bold enough / for my liking and too much for theirs" (from **"Home"**). Then there is the Cockney cab driver "who won't steer clear of race, / so rounds on Asians. I lock eyes with him / in the rearview when I say I live with one." And now, see how the poet resolves that confrontation, with the wryest of witty strophes: "I have legal tender burning in my pocket / to move on, like a cross in Transylvania."

One example of D'Aguiar's splendid, irreverent wit, aptly imagized, is his debunking of the young, angelic faces on the headstone over the grave of an unknown African slave, in Bristol, described as "Those cherubs with puffed cheeks, as if chewing gum" (from **"At the Grave of the Unknown African"**). Quiet wordplay, fused with accurately patterned, figurative phrasing, resulted in this piquant, panoramic vista as seen at night three thousand feet above the lights of London: "The pearl necklaces of traffic / break, trying to get round / my neck of the woods" (from **"Domestic Flight"**).

Fred D'Aguiar certainly might regard the following comparison with scant favor, but I am inclined to seize on it and so close my comments, in spite of the opposition it will be met with from the poet himself and from his many admirers throughout the Caribbean: *his barbed, clever and playful manner reminds me of W. H. Auden's and even Philip Larkin's.* The following six-line stanza from **"Notting Hill"** is, I think, a fair corroboration of that remark:

> Never mind street names, they're postal
> conveniences. Life is a honeycomb
> made to eat; just sort out the sting
> from the honey and the choreography
> comes with ease, grace, so rock on,
> but mind that island in the road!

Angelyn Mitchell (review date 13 August 1995)

SOURCE: "Black Family Matters," in *Washington Post Book World,* August 13, 1995, p. 8.

[*In the following excerpt, Mitchell offers a positive assessment of* The Longest Memory.]

Many contemporary black writers exhibit a preoccupation with history—both public and personal—in their work. Because blacks have not always had the opportunity to engage in self-representation, they understand the importance of being able to tell one's own story. Toni Morrison, Charles Johnson and Maryse Conde have situated their most critically acclaimed novels—*Beloved, Middle Passage,* and *I Tituba, Black Witch of Salem,* respectively—within the historical context of American slavery. By presenting slavery from the slaves' perspective they not only record and preserve the slaves history and culture but also provide a look at the interior lives of black men and women. Younger black writers such as A. J. Verdelle, Fred D'Aguiar and Lionel Newton also situate their recently re-

leased novels within a particular historical context in order to illuminate the interior lives of black people. . . .

In *The Longest Memory,* his first novel, Guyanese writer Fred D'Aguiar examines the legacies of American slavery. D'Aguiar uses the memories of his characters to tell his story by means of various techniques and mediums: first-person narrations, stream of consciousness, shifting narrative voices, newspapers, diaries, and poetry. He also explores a multitude of themes, including miscegenation and fatherhood.

In his meditation on memory and history, D'Aguiar also examines the familial and romantic relations between blacks and whites. Set in 19th-century Virginia, the narrative centers on the plight of an elderly slave father who tries to save his escaped son's life by revealing his whereabouts. After he is returned to the plantation, the son is whipped to death by his half-brother, the overseer. In this ironic situation, D'Aguiar juxtaposes the contrasting beliefs of the father, who believes in the "safety" of slavocracy's status quo, and the son, who is educated and in love with the master's daughter and wants to emancipate himself from slavery. The father then is left feeling responsible for his only son's death. Of his selfish act, he concludes, "I killed my son because I wanted him next to me when I died."

D'Aguiar creates "the longest memory" through a mosaic of events that allows all of the characters to recount their respective recollections of the events. This is primarily a story of fathers and sons; the women of this novel are flat characters who serve only to help define the male characters. Overall, the novel's strengths are in its illumination of slavery's devastating psychological effects on all of its participants, black and white, and of the often unexamined psychology of the slave community. . . .

A. L. McLeod (review date Autumn 1995)

SOURCE: A review of *The Longest Memory,* in *World Literature Today,* Vol. 69, No. 4, Autumn, 1995, pp. 851-2.

[*In the following review, McLeod offers an unfavorable assessment of* The Longest Memory.]

Although the publisher describes ***The Longest Memory*** as a novel, it is at best a novella; and if we subscribe to Poe's view that a story is a work than can be read conveniently at one sitting, then this work (under 25,000 words) belongs to the shortest of the genres of prose fiction. But is not merely length that allows this categorization: there is no substantial development of character, no complexity of interaction among characters, no feeling that a major statement about life (or any of its aspects) has been explored adequately. As a result, Fred D'Aguiar (whose poetry has been acclaimed) cannot be said to have created, in this his first fiction, a work comparable to any of the fictions of his celebrated Guyanese countrymen such as Wilson Harris, Jan Carew, or Edgar Mittelholtzer. Perhaps the explanation is to be found in his choice of subject and location.

The story presents in several forms (newspaper editorials, confessionals, reminiscences, conversations, even rhymed couplets) the recollections of a group of plantation family members, neighbors, and slaves, of the death by whipping of a young slave, the product of miscegenation, and the ramifications of the established mores and morality of late-eighteenth- and early-nineteenth-century Virginia slave-holding society. However, because of the brevity of the story, the author has not been able to develop any persuasive case on issues such as cruelty, ameliorative administration, Southern policy, Abolition, or interpersonal relationships. Cases are stated and abandoned; people mouth platitudes and commonplaces; even Sourface, the patriarch and centenarian central character, who suddenly decides that he has no name, remains little more than a cipher. (The other characters hardly become individuals at all.)

While the subject matter might have been appealing to the author, one wonders whether he fully realized the difficulties of trying to replicate the spoken and written style of Tidewater Virginia: it seems that he has been influenced by other writers' attempts at antebellum speech and language—or else by film versions. "North, here we come!" seems a most improbable exclamation from a Great House teenager of the era. And one wonders whether a longtime resident of Virginia would observe in his diary for 2 May that he is "late for the cotton harvest." Those who have read recent works on slavery (especially in Virginia) and discipline in the Royal Navy circa 1800—or even in Australia, a penal colony, at the same time—will not be as shocked as the author apparently is about such matters.

It would seem that D'Aguiar could have produced a far more affective and effective work had he written at greater length, in greater detail, and with tighter focus on one or two characters or incidents only. Further, had the style of the several narrators been reflective of their educational and social levels, greater realism would have produced more differentiation of characters.

Paula Burnett (review date 22 March 1996)

SOURCE: "The Nightmare Republic," in *New Statesman & Society,* March 22, 1996, pp. 39-40.

[*In the following review, Burnett offers a positive assessment of* Dear Future.]

A megalomaniac leader whose dentist has planted a micro-transmitter in his rotten tooth to broadcast his secrets to the opposition takes an early-morning canter on the beach with his bodyguard. He ends up shooting the horse because the animal shies at the high-frequency noise. The country is recognisable as Guyana, where Fred D'Aguiar

grew up, but it could be any state where politics has degenerated into a game of naked power.

Reminding us that he was a poet before he was a novelist, and that magic realism is as much at home in the Anglophone world as in the Latin countries, D'Aguiar is playing with the figure of the Guyanese bone flute. He updates it with a macabre humour that permeates this new book [*Dear Future*]. His first novel was about slavery; this one traces the fortunes of a contemporary Caribbean "sea-split family" (to use a phrase of Andrew Salkey's).

The story becomes a song of innocence and experience. The harmless family at its centre—which manifests the Guyanese ideal of cultural and racial pluralism, symbolised by the colour red—is sucked into the vortex of degeneracy that passes for public life. It is a world where "progress", as seen in the replacing of the old red sand road with the creeping black ribbon of tarmac, is heavily ironised.

D'Aguiar creates a powerful sense of the vulnerability of innocence, right from the opening scene in which a child is accidently struck on the head by a good-natured wood-chopping uncle. It is this boy, Red Head, whose consciousness dominates the book. He and his brother, part of an extended family in rural Guyana, dream of the return of their mother, who lives in London with three younger sons.

Doing her bit to oust the corrupt leader, she falsifies postal voters' lists and struggles to survive in a mixed immigrant community rife with the double rip-off of capitalism and patriarchy. But at least the sons growing up in the sordid city (which she longs to clean) are left with a future. Time runs out for those in Guyana, in a memorable scene at the book's centre.

Political power-play is examined through the magnifying glass of trivial pursuits—the games ordinary people play. There are sports and small-town contests here, children's amusements and friendly rivalries. They give the book a foreground intricately embroidered with small figures at recreation, as in a Breughel marketplace. It is ingeniously constructed around the dynamic of the contest, with the domestic version placed in ever more urgent counterpoint with the wider power struggle. As it provokes questions about the power of the powerless, the novel's last hope is the sensitivity and imagination of ordinary folk.

Red Head narrates the final section. He addresses his future in spare language that makes the more decorative style of the rest (which has seemed irritatingly lax at times) resonate in retrospect with the pace of old-fashioned courtesies. D'Aguiar is shaping into a crafty storyteller who challenges his reader to think. His bone flute plays a haunting tune.

Sean O'Brien (review date 6 June 1996)

SOURCE: "A Necessary Gospel," in *London Review of Books,* June 6, 1996, pp. 24-5.

[*In the following review, O'Brien offers a generally positive evaluation of* Dear Future, *but concludes that the novel contains unresolved underlying concerns.*]

It was as a poet that Fred D'Aguiar first won recognition, with his 1985 collection **Mama Dot,** set in the Guyanese village where the English-born D'Aguiar was sent to be educated. The place is dominated by Mama Dot, the archetypal grandmother, source of wisdom, comfort and discipline, a woman so important that when she falls ill nature itself goes to pieces.

> Bees abandon their queens to red ants and bury
> Their stings in every moving thing: and the sun
> Sticks like the hands of a clock at noon.
> Drying the very milk in coconuts to powder.

This vivid, funny, uncluttered work, moving between standard and Nation language, was immediately attractive. D'Aguiar, however, had other subjects and formal challenges in mind. Apart from its title sequence, his second book, *Airy Hall* (1989), was a much more troublesome affair, showing the pressure of a more discursive and politically complex area of his imagination, at some cost to clarity and impetus. **"The Kitchen Bitch,"** an ambitious but clotted narrative, seemed strongly influenced by the Guyanese novels of Wilson Harris, whose hallucinatory, half-abstract, outrageously bejewelled manner is as dangerous in its idiosyncrasy as that of Hopkins or Dylan Thomas. Problems persisted into D'Aguiar's most recent collection, *British Subjects* (1993), and it comes as no surprise that he should recently have turned to fiction: the loose baggy monster offers more room than poetry for certain kinds of manoeuvre. What is interesting, though, is that with his second novel, *Dear Future,* D'Aguiar has once more put village life in the foreground: the author's disclaimer notwithstanding, for the Co-Operative Village of Ariel read Airy Hall.

In a brief, charming, slightly mysterious Preface to a selection of his poems in E. A. Markham's anthology *Hinterland: Caribbean Poetry from the West Indies and Britain* (1989), D'Aguiar wrote:

> As children we used to try and catch fireflies by locking onto their zigzag, lights-on, lights-off flight in the dark, the same zigzag uncles told us to run if chased by an alligator. When the light of a firefly came on we dashed to it, in the brief dark that followed we slowed then stood still, momentarily, lost in directionless night, left only with an afterglow. Then it would spark again forming an imaginary necklace of light that folded on itself.

Both the alligator and the zigzag path recur in *Dear Future,* as does the tale, recounted later in the essay, of an uncle stepping onto a log to cross a trench, only to find it

sprouting legs and teeth. The pursuit of the firefly seems to speak for the blend of persistence and luck needed for writing to happen, while the delicacy of the quarry suggests the unencumbered naturalness the writer wants to attain—a condition D'Aguiar remembers from his earliest poems, where 'the images *felt* as much as *meant* something; meaning and feeling occupied the same space.' In his imaginative return to Airy Hall/Ariel in *Dear Future,* D'Aguiar achieves, in the idyllic opening from which the novel gradually darkens, a lightness and élan capable of supporting a substantial shipment of personal and social history.

The Longest Memory (1994), D'Aguiar's fictional debut, moved deliberately away from home ground. It was a tentative but at times effectively lyrical novella set in Virginia in the early 19th century. It told of the murder by flogging of a young slave, Whitechapel. Having fallen in love with the plantation-owner's daughter during forbidden meetings in the library (literacy here is the instrument of a gentle eroticism), Whitechapel plans an escape and elopement. He is betrayed by his father Old Whitechapel, a pragmatic survivor who believes he is acting for the best and that the young man will be punished but not killed; the son's executioner is, we learn, his white half-brother. Diaries, newspaper editorials, monologues and Whitechapel's own rhyming couplets are woven together to create the sense of a communal tragedy. The book's themes—race, family division, memory, loss, betrayal and power—recur in a transfigured form and to much greater effect in *Dear Future.*

The precocious Red Head, aged nine, is accidentally smashed in the forehead with an axe by his uncle Beanstalk while chopping wood. In his stunned condition he is visited by dreams: one of playing draughts with the President while on horseback; another of a man crippled by polio riding a bicycle off the end of the pier; a third involving a strangely decorated kite (an image harking back to *Mama Dot*). During this bravura passage, an imp of prophecy also appears, insisting that there were four dreams, not three, and leaving the sinister refrain, 'There will be red, then there will be black.' Although some of the dream-elements are encountered later in the book, D'Aguiar's use of visions and prophecies has less to do with narrative outcomes than with the description of feelings and states of mind. The initial patterning is allowed to unravel: the fulfilment of one part of the dream-prophecy prevents the fulfilment of another, so that Red Head's future belongs to the realm of might or should-have-been. At the same time, his unusually adult intelligence is assured of its innocence by the limited experience to which he can apply it. The portents, meanwhile, are offset by the sudden introduction of Red Head's vast extended family—26 relatives, including his magnificent grandparents, Bash Man Goady (his older, more matter-of-fact brother)—and his Asian girlfriend Sten, all of whom D'Aguiar is able to animate in a comedy of ordinary happiness where there appears to be all the time in the world. In Ariel nothing may have quite happened yet, but no aspiration seems implausible, whether it is Uncle Wheels's ambition to win a national bike race, or Red Head's to be a draughts champion. In Wheels's case the family have already decided that he's the victor, while Red Head's success is a foregone conclusion. Somewhere in Red Head is a feeling that everything—including the absence of his parents—will come to make sense. Confined to bed by his grandmother after the axe accident he asks when he can get up:

'All I want is to know.'

'Soon, soon.'

His mother had gone abroad with his three younger brothers and left him in Ariel . . . she too had told him soon. She would return soon. That was six months ago. He missed her. She was bony but her skin was soft. She was sweeter than any fruit or flower, whereas Granny carried the odour of soap, and, when she'd just brought clothes in off the line, of the sun. At his age every desire was soon. And his father had gone away. Just like that, he'd dived into the hot afternoon, his eyes hidden with a nod just in time to avoid the sun. The last time Red Head had talked with Bash Man Goady about missing their mother, father and brothers, they were having a walk-race to school. His brother was breathless but he'd paused to draw hard on the air and had spoken as if they had been swinging in the hammock at the bottom of the house.

'If you don't think about it, it won't hurt.'

He had taken his brother's advice as a necessary gospel. So far it seemed to work when he was awake.

If Ariel is a fragile enclave, it is also a richly mixed society (hence Red Head's hair). Red Head and his family keep faith with this complexity, and D'Aguiar allows Ariel its brief utopian moment. 'Grandad spoke of men who'd married women they'd fallen in love with regardless of race and who had themselves been the products of various unions between the races. He pointed to the fact that he was Portuguese, his wife African, one daughter-in-law half-Amer/indian, another Indian. Let them try and separate us. Let them try.'

But the politics of the big city, in which Red Head's parents are implicated, begin to press in on Red Head and the rest of the family. With the approach of elections, the party of government, bent and in hock to the IMF, seizes on a national tour by the great wrestler Singh to represent its own prowess and symbolise its forthcoming triumph at the polls. Singh, wooed away from the Opposition, has never been known to lose: indeed his attraction lies in the fact that his victory is only ever a formality, as the Government wishes its own to be. The distribution of blank election leaflets, the President remarks, 'was an act of genius . . . if what was meant by it was that the people should write their own campaign promises since their wish was the Government's command.' As for Singh, the Government and its fixers have reckoned without the intervention of Red Head's family, which naturally boasts a wrestling uncle, Bounce. Cunningly trained by Grandad in the psychology of the ring, Bounce wins with a combination of kidology and a strategic headbutt. The transition from

comedy to catastrophe is effected with great skill, leaving Red Head's family and Sten barricaded in the house, besieged by a murderous crowd.

The following section is less successful. Satirising the venal 'them' who rule the wholehearted 'us' of Ariel, it opens with an evocation of one of Red Head's dreams, as a civil servant, Brukup, 'the capital's best known polio victim', rides his bike off the end of a pier. He is killing two birds with one stone, disposing of some papers bearing evidence of vote-rigging, while also emptying his bowels. On emerging from the water, he proceeds along the half-made roads of the capital for a relaxing visit to the brothel. D'Aguiar handles this perfectly efficiently, but like his grotesquely fat and sweaty colleague and rival Gamediser, Brukup has no secrets for the reader to uncover. These figures of Jonsonian appetite only half-engage D'Aguiar's interest—and ours. Others in this grim episode of city comedy, such as the President's secretary-cum-whore, or the dentist paid by the Opposition to bug the President's teeth, seem to have been recruited from a Tom Sharpe novel. The President himself is vain enough, a nasty piece of work, posing on horseback, threatening his staff with knocking their false teeth out, but that's all there is to him.

The action moves to Britain for the penultimate section, which recovers the strength of the opening. With three of her sons, Red Head's mother is in London on behalf of the Government, in theory to mobilise, but in fact to invent, the overseas vote in the forthcoming general election. She is a believer in the President's work, ripe for exploitation and gradual abandonment by her political masters. When the money runs out, she is forced to move to a grim bedsit and takes on sewing work for Mr Ahmad, who becomes her lover as well as her employer: 'The children called out one night, thinking perhaps the two adults they adored were choking in the fine dust shed by the fabrics which had taken over the room.' Ahmad already has a wife, although this is only revealed when Red Head's mother and the three boys have converted to Islam. As the boys recover from circumcision, Ahmad arrives with a box of Swiss chocolates and announces: 'You can be wife number two.' The end of the relationship is a good example of D'Aguiar's readiness to include mess and complication, to have his characters follow the zigzag path which leaves this courageous woman even further away from home. The tone of the writing reflects her own determined calm, so that when she is beaten up while using a telephone box, the random horror of this (not wholly unpredictable) incident must be juxtaposed with the boys' outing on their new bikes (gifts from the still-hopeful Ahmad) over the landscaped hills of a rubbish dump. When Ahmad's eldest son Shaheen falls off and breaks his arm, one of the boys remarks:

'You fell off your bike, not a tower block.'

This was a new word in his vocabulary, acquired when he accompanied his mother to view a flat the council had allocated to her, on the 12th floor of an estate made up entirely of several towers. She wanted to take the flat for all the rooms it offered, but when she looked down from the window at the people below, she said they resembled ants and made her feel dirty, since she couldn't grab a broom and sweep them out of sight.

The London episodes lead back to the theme of time, felt in the whole section as an inescapable inertia, an exile that has still not been admitted. The bedsit itself is a 'clock', for whose smooth running she is endlessly responsible; she is also the time-keeper of her own loss, acknowledged in her recognition and accommodation of a monotonous suffering. She thinks of her two sons 'with such regularity it was more like an occupation, so that the instances when she felt nothing were rare'. The section ends with her lying sleepless at dawn in grey and white London: 'Soon she would force herself to get up and attack those cuffs and collars, breaking her meticulous stitch in two places and pulling the entire thread clear of the cloth like a bird pulling a worm from a lawn.'

The final section back in Ariel, from which the book takes its title, is a series of letters addressed to the future by Red Head from an imaginative Limbo-state, the simplified landscape of soil and vegetation where he and Bash Man Goady are learning to die:

> Dear Future,
>
> I am considering calling off this whole arrangement on account of your stubborn silence. Don't imagine that I am not aware that this may be a test of my stoicism. I am not a fool. I was hit with the back of an axe and death stepped up to carry me away and I fought him off single-handed.
>
> Life took my mother and three brothers from me and I put up with what I had left, my elder brother, and lived that life. You should know, dear future, that I laboured on in the belief that I would see them again.

The reader may well feel manipulated by Red Head's speculations and enquiries and by his general reasonableness as he comes to realise that this is where things end, that he and Bash Man Goady will never see the family again, that his future cannot exist because he doesn't. These doubts about the ending of the novel give rise to other questions about the construction of *Dear Future.* There is a suspicion that the tale may have taken over from the teller, which may account for the feeling that this bold, funny and sensuous book is shadowed at several points (notably in the city-political passages) by a larger, as yet unwritten and probably more conventionally realistic work.

Michael Upchurch (review date 17 November 1996)

SOURCE: "Risky Business: Fred D'Aguiar Continues to Take Chances in His Second Novel," in *Chicago Tribune Books,* November 17, 1996, p. 4.

[*In the following review, Upchurch offers a favorable assessment of* Dear Future.]

When Guyana-born poet Fred D'Aguiar turned to fiction last year with his debut novel, *The Longest Memory,* he proved to be a writer who likes taking chances on both topic and technique.

His subject: the fatal whipping of a runaway slave on the plantation of a "liberal" but absentee Virginia slave-owner. His approach: a nimble inhabiting of all the parties involved, giving each protagonist—black, white and shades in between—a vivid voice and presence on the page.

Though the book's central incident was horrific, D'Aguiar's explorations of the background prejudices, desires, appeasements and rationalizations leading up to it were so subtle and precise that the book felt less like a history lesson than a canny illumination of a distant era. His control of his volatile subject matter, too, was so dexterous that at times it resembled a kind of steely, rueful wit.

In his second novel, *Dear Future,* a gentler but still rueful wit is at work, and although the book is set closer to home—in a South American country much like D'Aguiar's native Guyana—it takes as many technical risks as *The Longest Memory.*

The initial focus of *Dear Future* is a young boy named Red Head, not for the color of his hair, but for an accidental blow delivered to him on the forehead with the back of an axe. This prompts him literally to see red: "Red in the earth and clouds and sky, a red dye making visible the air he could only feel until now. . . ."

In other words, he bleeds profusely before passing out. When he comes to, he finds himself blessed (or cursed?) with visionary powers in the form of an impish voice that won't leave him alone. Its constant refrain—"There will be red, then there will be black"—makes little sense to him. Could it refer to the dusty red road of his village, soon to be paved? Or does it foretell bloodshed with the approaching presidential election in the unstable Cooperative Republic where Red Head lives?

The four sections of the novel unveil the meaning of the prophecy from the vantage points of village life, palace life, exile and—talk about risks!—the afterlife.

The opening section—a picaresque account of Red Head's family activities—appears at first to be meandering. But a closer look reveals that its loose, anecdotal feel disguises some careful groundwork. Besides, the family portrait is enjoyable in itself as it gathers together a clamorous crew of multiethnic grandparents, uncles, aunts and cousins, all with various talents.

Red Head's particular talent is for draughts (the British word for the game of checkers), and he dreams of winning the National Draughts Championships. But his uncle's entry in a government-sponsored wrestling tournament comes up first, and it has perilous consequences for D'Aguiar's young hero.

The book's second section follows a difficult day in the life of a comically dictatorial president whose connection with Red Head's family is unclear at first. Again the tone is picaresque, though with menacing undercurrents.

In the two closing sections, the rest of the story falls cleverly into place, including the fate of Red Head's mother, who had to abandon her two eldest sons (their dad disappeared long ago) in order to earn a living overseas. All of it is as unpredictable and strange as life itself—and not just because of D'Aguiar's fondness for magic-realist flourishes.

What is most surprising about *Dear Future* is its lightness of touch, given that its topics are family diaspora, government tyranny and crushed human potential. One senses that D'Aguiar unconditionally admires an adventurous spirit—especially when that spirit knowingly takes on merciless odds.

D'Aguiar's gift with language is generous as well, even if his echoes of other writers—Ben Okri, Henry Green—suggest he hasn't entirely settled into his own style. Still, there are numerous details to delight here, such as his description of Red Head wading into a village pond: "A cool stocking rode up his legs."

Throughout the book, D'Aguiar is a deft juxtaposer of unlikely sights and sounds, sometimes poignant and sometimes humorous. Red Head's mother's romance with a devout Muslim, for instance, has nervous-making ramifications for her three young sons who accompany her into exile: "Over crisps, popcorn, Smarties and Pepsi, Uncle Ahmad explained circumcision."

Filled with surprising story twists and rich with visions that span fantasy and reality, *Dear Future* is good news indeed from a writer whose own future couldn't look brighter.

Bruce King (review date Winter 1997)

SOURCE: A review of *Dear Future,* in *World Literature Today,* Vol. 71, No. 1, Winter, 1997, p. 206.

[*In the following review of* Dear Future, *King faults the novel's complexity, lack of narrative development, and weak conclusion.*]

I have followed Fred D'Aguiar's work with interest ever since I read *Mama Dot,* his first volume of poetry, and attended the Royal Court production of *A Jamaican Airman Foresees His Death.* The success of *The Longest Memory,* a novel in which the prose has the sensitivity of verse, confirmed D'Aguiar's ability to treat black history with complexity. Each work contributed to a new canon of literature written by West Indians born or long resident in England. *Dear Future,* however, may be his first book without such a future. The curse of magic realism has in-

fected a highly poetical yet realistic writer; the new novel is difficult to get into, the technical complexity is greater than the story, its narrative movement fragments rather than builds, and the conclusion is thin and sentimental.

The novel shows how politics and exile can destroy family; themes include the role of the West Indian woman as family head, the fragmentation of family as a result of the West Indian diaspora, and the creation of the "black" Briton from a variety of nationalities, religions, skin shades, and cultures. As in the novels of Wilson Harris, who appears the model for D'Aguiar's version of magic realism, history is retold in new forms and fantastic stories to permit renewal and avoid the burden of the past. The corruption, racial divisions, and violence that characterized Guyanese politics are neutralized by fantasy, humor, and grotesque caricatures. But this remains a story of people damaged by history, hope, poverty, and politics. The mother in the story is herself a true believer of the nationalist leader; to survive, she becomes corrupt and a victim of his tyranny. Her husband, a diamond prospector, hides in England with the money of others. Raymond, a dentist for whom she worked in Guyana, fears for his life after having placed a transistor pickup in the filling of the dictator's teeth. The mother earlier left Raymond to become a government agent, as he had no future. Her current man in London is a Moslem who tricks her Hindu-Indian Portuguese children into being circumcised by a Jewish rabbi, a trick to which she consents as she hopes to marry, until she learns that the Pakistani is already married and wants her as a second wife. She does not even love him but needs the sex and companionship.

The Longest Memory concerned a father's brutal treatment of his son supposedly to help him survive as a slave but also to hide the father's sins. The new novel also reveals the guilt of parents, especially fathers, and the struggle to survive in a harsh world. In British Guyana different groups of the world's populations were brought together to develop a colony, then were left with one another at independence. The resulting violence was made worse by American and British interference and by ideologies. In *Dear Future* D'Aguiar gives imaginative form to how this history separated children from parents, how some offspring became British while others died in Guyana, and what being a British West Indian or a black Briton means beyond the simplicities of race relationships. The themes and prose are good, but not the story line or its treatment; this novel is more likely to be discussed than read with pleasure.

Gary Amdahl (review date 13-20 January 1997)

SOURCE: "Fabulous Red Head," *The Nation,* January 13-20, 1997, pp. 32-4.

[*In the following review, Amdahl offers a positive evaluation of* Dear Future.]

Fred D'Aguiar begins his second novel, *Dear Future* (the first, *The Longest Memory,* won the Whitbread and the

Higham awards in England), with the bright violence and not-quite singsong meter of a fairy tale: "Red Head got his name and visionary capacity at age nine when he ran behind an uncle chopping wood and caught the back of the axe on his forehead. His uncle, Beanstalk, feeling the reverberations of a soft wood as it yielded to the blade he'd swung back, looked over his shoulder and saw his favourite nephew half-run, half-walk in a wobbly line, do an about-turn, then flop to the ground in a heap." The next sentences are distinctly in the tall-tale mode, detailing Beanstalk's ability to walk upon and lasso alligators before anyone else can so much as shout the word, making the first paragraph a promise that the book will be easily and pleasantly consumable—which, fortunately, turns out not to be the case.

Set in an unnamed Caribbean country whose "Cooperative Republic Village[s]," border dispute and ties to Great Britain suggest D'Aguiar's native Guyana, and peopled with characters whose nicknames are descriptive and/or meaningful and bestowed upon them by the community (Red Head, Beanstalk, Wheels, Bounce and the melodious but faintly malevolent Bash Man Goady, for instance), *Dear Future* is a novel that manages to be part of the relatively new but rigorous (and vigorous) tradition of the Caribbean novel, and yet wonderfully itself.

This is no mean feat. Stories, because there are so few of them, tend to be predictable, and categories, genres, even traditions, masking the tyranny of mediocrity as necessary discipline or enjoyable convention, enhance that predictability—mainly with an eye toward assuaging the consumer's pre-purchase doubts and hesitations. If the Caribbean novel is, as George Lamming (whose *In the Castle of My Skin* is considered one of the principal texts in a tradition he helped articulate) has it, a work "crowded with names and people" but "rarely concerned with the prolonged exploration of an individual consciousness," a work in which it is "the collective human substance of the Village" that "commands our attention," it is equally true that the door is thus thrown open to cardboard functionaries. If it is true that (Lamming again) in novels where "community, and not person, is the central character. . . . There is often no discernible plot, no coherent line of events with a clear, causal connection," it is also true that the narrative freedom can slight a reader's need to feel that what has happened will affect what is to happen, that characters live in an economic, political and biological web peculiar to postcolonial culture. Finally, if the postcolonial novel is perforce concerned with the wretchedness of poor people, the means by which they endure and their restoration to humanity, its writers must beware the cartoon dialectic of good guys and bad guys: rich native religions versus a corrupt and empty Christianity; authentic creoles and pidgins versus artificial English; black versus white.

There are, in other words, a number of traps that D'Aguiar skirts perilously but manages to avoid. His success must be traced almost paragraph by paragraph: The struggle against predictability, against what in the end is simple facility and "ease of use" (in the belief that "ease" promotes not satisfaction but deterioration, of language, muscle, dignity—whatever), is here, in *Dear Future,* as subtle as it is sweet.

To pick up where we left off, at the close of paragraph one: After fairy tale and tall tale, D'Aguiar goes deeper and stranger.

> Something made the uncle stare at the boy's forehead as if he were watching a miniature screen. The ruptured screen resembled a door blown off its hinges. Out stepped a white body of fluid in one boneless move. As if surprised by the sudden recognition that it was naked, the nubile body gathered about itself a flowing red gown which ran in ceaseless yards, covering all of the boy's face in seconds.

This is prose not, perhaps, as impenetrably and surreally lush as Wilson Harris's in *The Palace of the Peacock,* nor as richly poetic and thorough in its recovery of detail as Lamming's, but it does require its own kind of attention. As D'Aguiar slips soundlessly from fairy to tall to strange and tells the stories that compose "Dreams from the Republic of Nightmares"—Red Head's visions; the slow and grotesque progress of a main road being paved as it approaches Ariel, Red Head's village, which does not want it; a bicycle race and the preparation of Red Head for a draughts tournament; a wrestling match between a government-backed professional touring the country as part of an election campaign and one of the uncles; and the consequences of that astounding match—it's easy to be lulled by the easygoing fabulosity of it all. There is, however, a disturbing murmur to be heard, faintly but at all times, and just when you think you've got the hang of it, the bright violence erupts again, this time growing darker and darker by the sentence, as a mob of the President's men bears down, with torches and cutlasses, on the homes of the village. Chapter and section end; we move on to "Nightmares from the Republic of Dreams."

This simple transposition is alarming in the quiet D'Aguiarian way: What can the difference possibly mean? The subject matter is certainly different: The four stories here deal mainly with the knavery of the President's factotums, but the tone is comic, as witness this description of "the heaviest person on the presidential payroll," named Gamediser, at a whorehouse: "She would take his little dead meat, as he called it, into her mouth, switch to milking it with both hands heavily lubricated, sit on it and rodeo until she was out of breath and bored, tie him up and beat him until he got scared and wept and eventually released the tiny, unhemmed white flag that signalled his surrender." Another episode shows the President's dentist gone over to the opposition, implanting a bug in a presidential cavity. But suddenly the fun and games are all over, as suddenly as the tall tales were, and the President's eccentricities have turned lethal. In the light of that particular muzzle flash, one begins to see how D'Aguiar moves back and forth in time, telling a story in one place and exposing it in another, concealing terror in pleasant melodies and slapstick.

"Homing" flips the colonial coin; landing London side up, we get a whole new cast of characters and another shift in tone, to something like "dirty realism"—the story of a poor working mother and her three small boys, who turn out to be none other than Red Head and Bash Man Goady's younger brothers. Snatched up by the President from her job as a dental assistant and made a "campaign secretary" ("She's a fine campaign secretary for twenty-five and stunning-looking, but her pussy hang down to her knee from dropping pickney every year since she seventeen"), she is sent to London to fabricate a sizable overseas-absentee vote, but paid so poorly she cannot save enough money to return home (and what sentimental perversity makes her wish to? her employers implicitly ask). There's a good deal of drudgery and despair in "Homing," but the dirt is sweet. When she's assaulted by xenophobes at a telephone booth, the longer-lasting memory is of the way her children console her, and the way she refuses to poison them with hatred and fear.

If the play of D'Aguiar's prose in these first three sections, and the reach between subtext and text, has made for a refreshing unpredictability, it fails to prepare the reader for the sorrow and the power of "Dear Future," twenty-six very short sections in the form of letters from Red Head to an idea. He and Bash Man Goady are still boys, and the letters refer to boyish pursuits like mudballs and slingshots, but it becomes clear they are in some way terribly alone and in some place terribly strange. All the images that have been gone over lightly—Granddad's refusal to allow Gamediser into his home; the spittle dripping off the boys' wrestling uncle, Bounce, spat from a score of angry mouths; the spittle hanging threadlike from the mother's threadbare coat, spat from the tiny pursed mouths of two or three tiny weak minds; the children huddled in a room making dolls and a toy car from a matchbox and matches while in another room a door is being battered down—these images all flash again in a much harsher light, and D'Aguiar's novel emerges as not at all the book the reader seemed to be reading, a much angrier and despairing novel than the light hand has let on, warmhearted but disturbing, straightforward but off-center, all the happiness on a slight incline that has not seemed steep until the attempt to climb back up to it is attempted. "Dear Future," writes Red Head the visionary, "You don't know me. We won't meet."

Bharat Tandon (review 22 August 1997)

SOURCE: "Marine Motifs," in *Times Literary Supplement,* August 22, 1997, p. 22.

[*In the following review of* Feeding the Ghosts, *Tandon praises D'Aguiar's evocative description and plotting, but concludes that the work lacks an underlying element of coherence.*]

Sea-water and wood, with their capacities simultaneously to preserve and obscure, figure strongly in Fred D'Aguiar's long historical novella. While the suggestive conjunction of natural materials in sea-stories is hardly innovative (*Moby-Dick,* for one, makes much of the *Pequod*'s cannibalized shipwork), here it allows the author a base for what turns out to be an extended meditation—often harrowing, sometimes a little self-regarding—on the persistence, necessity and attendant costs of remembering. After all, one reason why ghosts are such fertile subjects for novelists is that they share with novels a particular way of combining different temporal dimensions; and *Feeding the Ghosts,* as its title suggests, punctuates its main narrative with flashbacks, not only as stylistic effects but as central motifs.

Taking his cue from Derek Walcott's "The Sea is History"—adapted here into "The sea is slavery"—D'Aguiar tells of a disease-ridden slave-ship returning from its dirty work in Africa. Captain Cunningham, his own motives all too manifest, strong-arms his crew into summarily dumping all the sick slaves overboard:

> "We have surrendered seven good men to these waters and lost thirty-six of our holdings. I do not intend to bury another. One-twelfth of our holdings lost? With each loss our commission dwindles. These three months of hard work, sacrifice and suffering will come to nothing. We must act decisively or return to our families and friend and investors empty-handed. Which is it to be, gentlemen?"

Of 132 slaves thrown overboard, one miraculously survives: Mintah, an English-speaker, punished not for sickness but for insubordination toward Kelsal, the first mate, whom she disturbs to an extent initially unexplained. Climbing back up the side of the ship, she takes refuge with the cook's assistant, and begins to "haunt" below decks, becoming a talisman of strength for those left alive, as one who has come back from the dead ("the men touched her for some of her magic to rub off on them and to check that she wasn't an apparition"). But after an abortive rebellion leads to her recapture, a long, hallucinatory reverie uncovers her past, and specifically how she once nursed Kelsal back to health in Africa—indeed, it was she who reminded him of his name, which is all the more ironic given that it is Kelsal who is engaged in obliterating the identity of the slaves, their lives reduced to ink:

> Both slaves were presented to the captain, who opened a ledger which he shielded against the light rain that had just begun and made two strokes in it.

Nor is this Mintah's last action from the past. Back in England, Cunningham's insurance claim on the slaves appears to be going smoothly until Simon, the cook's assistant, produces Mintah's written testimony in a book: a direct opposite to Cunningham's ledger in which lives are lost. The Dickensian vigour of this episode is one of the highlights of the novel, as D'Aguiar intertwines the rhetoric of litigation with more selfish concerns:

> An unexceptional crowd for what should be a conventional hearing: a party of avaricious investors pitted

against a parsimonious insurer. Lord Mansfield was sure he'd be out of court in time to dine at The King's Head, a cured pheasant, his favourite.

But Mintah's ghostly intercession is not enough, and she is last seen as an old freed slave in Jamaica, working in wood, having taken it on herself to become a collective memory for the dead slaves ("There are 131 of them. A veritable army").

This is clearly a poet's novella, less interested in the sheer number of incidents than in the weight they carry; consequently, the most satisfying aspects of the story are D'Aguiar's precise observations of the resonances of language, and its capacity to transform what it describes—most chilling is the contrast between the unceremonious dumping of the nameless slaves and the burial of a member of the crew: "The plank holding the carapaced body was angled out over the side and tilted and William Pelling slid off it and the sea swallowed." Nevertheless, there is something that doesn't quite cohere in D'Aguiar's rich prose (Lord Mansfield, with his "pleasant pheasant", isn't the only devotee of internal rhyme in this novel). Perhaps it is to do with the novel's status as an historical reconstruction, in that it shares with other forms of restaging a way of being meticulous and disturbing, but finally lacking a degree of interiority.

Heather Hathaway (review date Fall 1998)

SOURCE: A review of *Dear Future,* in *African-American Review,* Vol. 32, No. 3, Fall, 1998, pp. 506-8.

[*In the following review, Hathaway provides a positive evaluation of* Dear Future.]

In a 1992 interview (*Ariel* 24.1 [1993]), Guyanese author and editor Frank Birbalsingh discussed with his countryman Fred D'Aguiar the relationship between art and politics in D'Aguiar's first two volumes of poetry, *Mama Dot* (1985) and *Airy Hall* (1989). Birbalsingh remarked on D'Aguiar's ability to "record the continuing suffering and deprivation of the Guyanese" people, but he was particularly struck by "the absence of any instinct to blame. Your quiet recording of the human toll of Guyanese politics suggests deep and genuine affection for the victims—a firm bond of unspoken solidarity with them. But you don't cry out." D'Aguiar replied that, "in writing about politics, I felt I should try and step back from any emotional attempt to lay blame or responsibility. I felt there are other forms of writing where that could be done more properly." His most recent novel, *Dear Future,* appears to embody that form. This prose work does indeed record the human toll of Guyanese politics as it chronicles the activities of one extended family suffering under the reign of a corrupt government, but it also "cries out" against such oppression, particularly in the final section of the novel, which consists of a series of letters addressed to "Dear Future" by the child protagonist, Red Head. Although some critics

have dismissed this conclusion as trite and unconvincing, it is precisely through these letters that D'Aguiar's political commentary is most strongly, if subtly, articulated.

The novel consists of four parts, the first two of which are set in a fictional space closely resembling Guyana. (D'Aguiar's decision not to mention a specific location universalizes the plot, thus making the novel's political commentary applicable to a number of post-colonial Caribbean nations.) Part one, "Dreams from the Republic of Nightmares," introduces the main character, Red Head, a boy who becomes clairvoyant after being accidentally struck on the head with an axe by his uncle. In the seven chapters that comprise this section, D'Aguiar paints Red Head's extended family, using intensely melodic prose that is underscored by a magical realism recalling the work of Wilson Harris or Gabriel García Marquez. These chapters reveal the source of the family's tensions with the government and describe their frightening, confrontational culmination. Both the strength and weakness of this section lie in its lyricism. While D'Aguiar's widely acclaimed first novel *The Longest Memory* (1994) is marked by a successful interweaving of a highly developed sense of poetic imagery with an analysis of North American slavery, *Dear Future* occasionally suffers from a lack of rhetorical restraint that detracts from the more biting political critique the author seeks to offer. D'Aguiar is clearly aware of this potential liability in his writing. As he explained to Birbalsingh, he considers both "nostalgia" and "an over-lyrical way of writing that romanticizes one's material" to be significant "pitfalls" to aesthetic achievement: "I try to avoid those two problems," D'Aguiar stated in 1992, "by giving my writing a hard edge all the time. Whenever I find myself being over-lyrical, I introduce political observation, or something that is slightly harder."

Not surprisingly, following the magical if also somewhat muting language of part one comes a section that focuses directly on the political scheming surrounding an upcoming election in the region. As suggested by its inverted title, "Nightmares from the Republic of Dreams," part two reverses our perspective on the relationship between the ruling elite and the populace by contrasting the noble (if somewhat fantasized) peasant group depicted in part one with the ignominy of the nation's "democratically" elected officials. D'Aguiar seems to use these first two sections (which could rightfully constitute a novella in themselves) as a unit to consider the impact of political corruption on all segments of Guyanese society. Echoing some of his earlier poetry, he exposes how the transition from colonialism to independence—and the violence, class divisions, and economic crises that accompanied this passage—left many questioning the promise implicit in that move. "What people, what nation, what destiny?" D'Aguiar demands in his poem **"El Dorado Update."** The cultural disunity at the heart of these questions becomes graphically personified in *Dear Future* by the demise of Red Head's clan at the hands of the government and its supporters.

But while D'Aguiar depicts a nation hobbled by a legacy of colonialism which has fostered greed, deception, and despair, he also implies that the potential panacea to these larger social ills may be found within the microcosm of the family. While the first part of **Dear Future** portrays the deep loyalty of Red Head's extended kin to one another in Guyana, part three, significantly titled "Homing," shifts tone and location altogether to explore what happens when familial connections become strained by diasporic migrations. Revisiting a subject he probed in his third collection of poetry, **British Subjects** (1993), D'Aguiar considers how one small portion of the diaspora, the protagonist's mother and his two younger brothers, fare as black Caribbean immigrants in Britain. "Homing" chronicles the activities of Red Head's mother in London as she generates fake ballots for the incumbent government by creating a list of non-existent, absentee voters; in the process, it shows how the hybridizing forces of the metropole both break down and yet strengthen the ties of immigrants to the homeland. While on one level the children are detached from their native roots by the forces of urbanization, television, and intercultural contact (their mother has an affair with a Pakistani who converts the family to Islam), on another level both Red Head's siblings and his mother remain intimately linked by what D'Aguiar refers to in a different context as an "emotional map" of home, to the family and geography across the ocean.

The connection, of course, goes both ways. The final section of the novel, "Dear Future," is comprised of multiple brief letters directed to the Future by Red Head, now living in a netherworld he describes as an "ever-present past," where he awaits the return of his family. Just as his estranged mother in England longs for the two children she left behind, so too do Red Head and his older brother cling to memories of their mother and siblings: "I miss them because I perished missing them. My brother is the same. But he speaks as little about those things as he did when we thrived." Red Head's quest for a reunion of his family becomes a nearly constant preoccupation, but it is greeted by the Future only with "stubborn silence." Although this section of the novel is admittedly difficult to decipher, it becomes clear over the course of these epistles that the plight of the child is in some ways parallel to that of the fictionalized Guyana itself. "Grant me this simple thing," Red Head pleads. "You don't even do me the honour of saying 'No.' Instead you do what everyone with power over me (because I love them) has done to me up to now: kept me waiting in silence. This is not me about to give up. No way. You owe me this one thing since you are a right that has been denied to me. You know that. Work this one little thing for me. Let me know that you have given my people a sign of my continued existence." Like most colonial enterprises, British Guyana was originally settled by several different racial and ethnic groups whose descendants were positioned, upon independence, to forge a new nation in the face of internal dissension and external interference. But on the way to making a future, D'Aguiar seems to imply, the nation risked and continues to risk getting stuck in the present. Not until Guyana, like

Red Head, realizes that its "present *is* [its] future" and that its "future is there, will always be there, to be lived" can it free itself from a state of hopeless despair rooted in an "ever-present past." Far from being trite and unconvincing, the last section of **Dear Future** brings closure to the many strands that have been introduced throughout the course of this provocative novel, and links them through an abstract but important commentary on the history and prospects of a nation.

Ervin Beck (review date Autumn 1999)

SOURCE: A review of *Feeding the Ghosts,* in *World Literature Today,* Vol. 73, No. 4, Autumn, 1999, p. 796.

[*In the following review of* Feeding the Ghosts, *Beck finds D'Aguiar's evocation of the slave trade interesting but unexceptional.*]

In 1781 a fatal malady broke out on the slave ship *Zong,* killing seven crew members and many of the slaves. Fearing that sick slaves would lose all their value in Jamaica, Captain Cunningham commanded very ill slaves to be thrown overboard, in order to collect insurance on their deaths and to prevent the plague from spreading further on the ship. In a court trial in Liverpool, brought by the insurers against the investors, the judge sided with the investors, confirming once more the law that Africans are only "stock" to be bought and sold.

The main character in Fred D'Aguiar's latest novel is Mintah, a young African woman who had been taught English in a Danish Christian mission. When she is thrown overboard, for insubordination rather than for ill health, she almost miraculously climbs back on board, unnoticed, and, while in hiding, begins writing the story of her experience on the *Zong*. Based on a historical event, **Feeding the Ghosts** is a kind of documentary fiction, which recreates one version of the Middle Passage. It may find its widest audience among young readers in schools, since its hero and heroine are young, its content is sensational without being salacious, and its style and structure are in the plain, straightforward mode.

Most of the book seems concerned with proving that Africans are human beings, not merely animals. The only white character who believes this is the homeless, blond cook's boy, who befriends Mintah in her hiding and presents the written account of her experience as evidence against the shipowners in the courtroom. Although the court in 1781 reaffirmed the slaves' status as "livestock," the book concludes with the victory of abolitionist sentiments in 1833, when the aged Mintah observes the celebrations for the end of slavery in Jamaica. Either because the story is perfunctorily told, or because such an issue is no longer high drama, this major part of the narrative is interesting but not compelling.

Part 3 builds upon the metaphor in the title, with "feeding the ghosts" referring to Mintah's attempts to keep alive and appease the spirits and memories of the 131 slaves cast overboard. She does so by helping twice that many slaves escape to freedom from Maryland to the North, by planting 131 trees, and by carving 131 figures out of wood, inspired by the African god of wood who also guided the hands of her wood-sculptor father in Africa. The novel itself both "feeds the ghosts" and, according to a universalizing voice in the epilogue, implicates all readers in the lives and deaths of the drowned slaves.

These metaphors, although apt, seem overwrought and come too late to raise the novel much above the ordinary. For the rich possibilities latent in Middle Passage narratives, one must still return to the allusive novel *Middle Passage* by Charles Johnson (1991; see *WLT* 65:4, p. 707) or to the fruitfully ambiguous long poem *Turner* by David Dabydeen (1994; see *WLT* 69:3, p. 629).

William Scammell (review date 2 September 2000)

SOURCE: "Poetry Gets the Last Laugh," in *Spectator*, September 2, 2000, pp. 34-5.

[*In the following review, Scammell offers a negative assessment of* Bloodlines.]

The last big poem on black history was Derek Walcott's *Omeros*, which mixed up Homer with the textures of Caribbean life, and probably helped him to clinch the Nobel Prize in 1992. Some people thought it wonderful; others never got past the pomp and circumstance of the opening chapters. Fred D'Aguiar's *Bloodlines* takes its formal inspiration not from the epic but from the verse-novels of Byron and Pushkin, or so at least the blurb assures us: 'Read this book fast like a novel, savour every word like a poem.'

It begins with the rape of a slave, Faith, by her white owner's son, Christy. This brutal act results, paradoxically, in true love, more passionate lovemaking, and in the pair's banishment by the outraged father:

> 'My son, the very thing I feared you'd do
> you've gone and done. You've fallen in love
> with one when all you were supposed to do
> was fuck as many as you liked, not love.'
> 'Father, everything you say is true,
> except the dirty part. Negroes love
> like us and fuss like us and wash the same
> as us. That's why I'm proud to take the blame.'
>
> 'How dare you stand in front of me and say
> such things. I will not allow you to blacken
> this family's name. Leave my house today
> and take her with you. And never come back.'
> His father turned on his heels and stormed away.
> Christy's head spun, he felt faint and fell flat
> on his face on a persian rug that cushioned
> his fall and saved his face from being crushed.

In the first verse 'love' rhymes inertly with itself three times, and 'do' twice; in the second the rhymes are so far-flung and hopeless ('blacken / back / flat'; 'cushioned crushed') that bathos hangs its head in shame, or perhaps goes bounding off in search of Pope and Swift's *The Art of Sinking in Poetry*.

This level of dismal ineptitude is sustained throughout 160 pages of high-flown and sententious nonsense, which is frankly an insult to the history of persecution it tries to evoke. The American civil war slides by, and a brutal boxing match, but the several characters who undergo these tragedies never come to life, nor does the dream of a paradisal state where 'the races love one another' and Africa is a 'land at the rainbow's / end'. Whatever skills informed D'Aguiar's previous collections, such as *Mama Dot*, seem to have been overwhelmed by the enormity of his subject. 'My train is death but the engine is my craft. / Death wins but poetry gets the last laugh.' It does indeed.

John Greening (review date 22 December 2000)

SOURCE: "Fast Like a Novel," in *Times Literary Supplement*, December 22, 2000, p. 22.

[*In the following review, Greening offers an unfavorable assessment of* Bloodlines.]

The verse novel is becoming a popular genre. From Vikram Seth's *The Golden Gate* to Craig Raine's *History: The Home Movie* to Les Murray's *Fredy Neptune*, publishers have had to find ingenious ways of marketing what has generally been considered unmarketable—the Long Poem. Some have kept the v-word well clear of the front cover; others blazon it like a health warning. And so it is with Fred D'Aguiar's new "novel-in-verse": we are advised to "Read this book fast like a novel, savour every word like a poem." But by the end of *Bloodlines*, I had still not found a satisfactory way of reading it. D'Aguiar writes in ottava rima, which can certainly be used to tell a story, but it is a tricky form to control, makes a heavy demand on rhyme words and is most effective when the writer is as witty as Byron or Auden. D'Aguiar is not a witty writer (although he tries once or twice), nor is his subject funny.

Bloodlines is set in the American South of 1861 and narrated by the child of Faith and Christy. Faith is a slave, who after being viciously raped by the plantation owner's son, falls in love with him. They elope and are helped by a mysterious, idealistic old man, Tom, who deliberately tells them nothing of himself, but (we find out later) had once been a slave, and had "entered the history of folk-talk" by scalping his overseer. His story (and the healing power of his relationship with Stella) makes up the middle section. Tom has been taught by Stella "to ferry runaways to the next safe residence" as part of the so-called "Underground Railroad", but during this run there is an ambush. The three are separated for ever. Faith (already pregnant) is gang-raped, but finds refuge in the service of Mrs Mason, a relatively sympathetic mistress, with whom she forges a bond. Christy makes a new life as an itinerant pugilist, dehumanized, ever searching for Faith, fighting like a demon for her sake. Tom at first appears to have drowned, but emerges to carry with Stella ("my mate, / saviour") the slaves' inexpressible burden through the Civil War and on into years of lyrical fantasizing about Africa. Later, Christy tracks down Mrs Mason and learns that Faith died giving birth to their son, who is himself "presumed dead, / missing at sea." So this child, our narrator, brings the novel to a close, speaking to our own age from a kind of immortality, a permanent state of decay, a limbo of parentlessness and dislocation:

> So history greeted me. I am condemned
> to live an eternity, unless all the conditions
> that brought me into being somehow mend:
> I mean Slavery and all its ramifications
> marching unfazed into the new millennium.
> Everything that I see in countries and nations
> tells me this is true: Slavery may be buried,
> but it's not dead, its offspring, Racism, still
> breeds.

Read **Bloodlines** "fast like a novel", and you follow an occasionally moving, often bold and shocking tale of slavery, involving simple archetypal characters, told in something which might have been a prose style, were it not continually wrenched aside by the wilfulness of the form: "Yes, pregnant. She doesn't know it yet, / that inside is not quite what it used to be, / though from her demeanour she suspects. / Call it female intuition and you would be / warm." Savour every word, and we can enjoy many beautiful passages and absorbing set pieces: on the river with Tom ("The river knew, / as the keel made its cut, that it would heal . . ."); Faith's impassioned monologue of love and need; Christy's boxing ordeal; the evocation of Civil War battlefields. But soon we begin to wish that the poet himself had done more of the savouring: "He told them to hide under a tarpaulin: / 'Listen all you like but do not show / your faces, no matter how appalling'. . . ." Such frequently painful rhymes, uneasy line-breaks and generally vague metre deaden whatever dramatic or poetic life this might have had. **Bloodlines** is ambitious and occasionally shimmers with a symbolic resonance, but it has neither the fascinating nightmare imagery of, say, Dave Smith's poems of the American South, nor the metrical momentum of a truly readable long poem such as John Gurney's epic *War.*

FURTHER READING

Criticism

Atamian, Christopher. Review of *Dear Future*, by Fred D'Aguiar. *New York Times Book Review* (10 November 1996): 56.

A mixed review of *Dear Future.* Atamian compliments D'Aguiar's prose, but faults the author's character development.

D'Aguiar, Fred with Frank Birbalsingh. "An Interview with Fred D'Aguiar." *Ariel* 24, No. 1 (January 1993) 133-45.

An interview originally conducted on April 11, 1992, in which D'Aguiar discusses his Guyanese background, English education, literary influences, and cultural, political, and aesthetic concerns in *Mama Dot, Airy Hall,* and *British Subjects.*

Dwyer, Janet Ingraham. Review of *Feeding the Ghosts,* by Fred D'Aguiar. *Library Journal* 124, No. 1 (January 1999): 147.

A positive review of *Feeding the Ghosts.* Dwyer calls the novel "gripping" and "poetic."

Review of *Feeding the Ghosts,* by Fred D'Aguiar. *Publishers Weekly* (23 November 1998): 58.

A positive review of *Feeding the Ghosts,* in which the reviewer calls the novel "a unique work of fiction."

Hooper, Brad. Review of *Dear Future,* by Fred D'Aguiar. *Booklist* 92, No. 22 (August 1996): 1880.

In this review, Hooper offers a positive assessment of *Dear Future,* although he argues that the novel is "less cohesive and compelling" than D'Aguiar's *Longest Journey.*

———. Review of *Feeding the Ghosts,* by Fred D'Aguiar. *Booklist* (1 December 1998): 650.

In this review, Hooper offers a positive assessment of *Feeding the Ghosts,* calling the novel "haunting."

———. Review of *The Longest Memory,* by Fred D'Aguiar. *Booklist* (15 December 1994): 735.

In this positive review, Hooper praises *The Longest Memory* for its "evocative" and "spare" language.

"Open Book." *Village Voice* (16 February 1999): 79.

Review essay including discussion of *Feeding the Ghosts.*

Reardon, Patrick T. "Painful Lesson: *Longest Memory* Recalls Slavery's Physical and Psychological Horrors." *Chicago Tribune Books* (20 March 1995): 5.

Reardon offers a positive assessment of *The Longest Memory.*

Ross, Michael E. Review of *The Longest Memory,* by Fred D'Aguiar. *New York Times Book Review* (7 May 1995): 26.

In this review, Ross offers a positive assessment of *The Longest Memory.*

Scott, Whitney. Review of *British Subjects,* by Fred D'Aguiar. *Booklist* (15 March 1994): 1322.

In this review, Scott summarizes the concerns of D'Aguiar's poems in *British Subjects.*

Sowd, David. Review of *The Longest Memory,* by Fred D'Aguiar. *Library Journal* 119, No. 21 (December 1994): 132.

    In this review, Sowd offers a positive assessment of *The Longest Memory.*

Wormald, Mark. "Visions in the Village." *Times Literary Supplement* (15 March 1996): 25.

    Wormald faults what he perceives as narrative inconsistency and lack of focus in *Dear Future.*

Additional coverage of D'Aguiar's life and career is contained in the following sources published by the Gale Group: *Contemporary Authors,* **Vol. 148;** *Contemporary Authors New Revision Series,* **Vol. 83;** *Contemporary Poets*; *Dictionary of Literary Biography,* **Vol. 157; and** *Literature Resource Center.*

Kaye Gibbons
1960-

American novelist.

The following entry provides an overview of Gibbons's career through 1999. For further information on her life and works, see *CLC*, Volumes 50 and 88.

INTRODUCTION

Gibbons is best known for novels that focus on self-reliant southern women and the challenges they face in their lives. Typically set in her native rural North Carolina, Gibbons's stories are told in the dialects of first-person narrators. Her characters are often guided by shared virtues, such as an innate common sense or a refusal to suffer from self-pity. Common themes in her work include the vicissitudes of love and marriage, sickness, death, racism, poverty, and the horrors of child abuse.

BIOGRAPHICAL INFORMATION

Gibbons was born to Charles and Alice Butts in Wilson, North Carolina, on May 5, 1960. Her father was a tobacco farmer, and the family lived on a farm in rural Nash County. Gibbons was very close to her mother, who committed suicide at the age of forty-seven. Gibbons later wrote about this painful childhood event in her semi-autobiographical work *Ellen Foster* (1987). She lived with her father before moving to live with her aunt. This was a brief arrangement, however, and after her father's death in 1972, Gibbons stayed with a foster family until she was able to live with her brother in 1973. She lived there until fall 1978 when she started attending North Carolina State University in Raleigh. In 1980, the summer before transferring to the University of North Carolina at Chapel Hill, Gibbons discovered that she suffered from manic depression and was eventually hospitalized several times for treatment. In 1984, she married Michael Gibbons, with whom she had three children, but later divorced. While at the University of North Carolina, Gibbons studied southern literature under Louis Rubin, who had a profound influence on her writing and her career. Rubin encouraged her to finish the manuscript for *Ellen Foster,* and to publish the novel through the university's Algonquin Press. Gibbons has won numerous awards, including the Sue Kaufman Prize for First Fiction from the American Academy and Institute of Arts and Letters for *Ellen Foster*; a fellowship from the National Endowment for the Arts; and the PEN/Revson Foundation Fiction Fellowship for a

writer thirty-five years old or younger in 1990. Gibbons continues to write and lives in Raleigh with her second husband and their five children.

MAJOR WORKS

Gibbons's first novel, *Ellen Foster,* is about a displaced young girl who watches her mother die as the result of a self-induced overdose. After suffering sexual and psychological abuse at the hands of her father, state authorities eventually intervene and remove Ellen from the house. Ellen then experiences a series of difficult situations and suffers various forms of abuse from her biological family. Only when Ellen joins a "foster" family is she able to find nurturing and acceptance. Along her journey, Ellen undergoes profound changes, including abandoning her inherited prejudices against African Americans and learning to accept her best friend, Starletta, as her equal. *A Virtuous Woman* (1989) tells the story of Jack and Ruby Stokes, who reminisce about their unlikely relationship, while they deal with Ruby's imminent death from cancer at the age of 45. *A Cure for Dreams* (1991) follows four generations of women as they live through hardships and learn from each other's stories. The novel is narrated by Marjorie, the great-granddaughter in a large southern family. *Charms for the Easy Life* (1993) revolves around Charlie Kate, a folk healer in North Carolina whose husband left her to raise their daughter, Sophia. Years later, Sophia discovers that her own marriage is dissolving, and that she will have to raise her daughter alone. When Sophia's husband dies, Charlie Kate moves in, and the three women form a feminine collective. *Sights Unseen* (1995) relates the effects that a mother's manic depression has on her daughter and is based on Gibbons's own experiences with depression. In *On the Occasion of My Last Afternoon* (1998), Emma Garnet Tate, a nineteenth-century daughter of a Virginia plantation owner, seeks to escape her father's tyrannical rule. Her escape is ultimately achieved by a marriage to Quincy Lowell, a well-to-do doctor, who takes her away to a new life in Raleigh, North Carolina.

CRITICAL RECEPTION

While reviewers have compared Gibbons to Eudora Welty and other southern writers, most have recognized Gibbons as a unique voice in southern literature. Kathryn McKee has stated, "In focusing her novel on female discourse, Gibbons distinguishes her work both from the fiction written by the forefathers of the southern renascence and from the writing produced by her southern literary contemporaries." Many critics have applauded Gibbons's realistic portrayal of contemporary southern life. They also have commended her deft use of dialogue, because it generally avoids the contrivances of southern colloquialisms and skillfully arranges a cadence to give the characters' voices their southern flavor. Nancy Lewis has stated, "With a vernacular authenticity that leads us to believe she didn't need to do her homework, she has presented us with stories and characters most definitely real, uncontrived, and of their time." While well-received by critics and readers alike, one of the criticisms voiced against *Ellen Foster* has been that the anti-racism message is somewhat dulled by the characterization of Starletta as a voiceless cog in the machinery of Ellen's life. Earlier in her career, some critics accused Gibbons of drawing one-dimensional male characters who act as mere foils for her female heroines. However, Gibbons has been frequently praised for the economy of her writing style. Lewis has surmised, "Perhaps it is the southern storyteller's inherited practice of honing and editing to please the listener's ear that has given Kaye Gibbons her skill in economy and structure." Throughout her career, Gibbons has found a loyal audience of readers and largely appreciative critics. Jane Fisher has summed up her popularity stating, "This wide acclaim stems from her ability to find comedy in tragedy and moral beauty in ugliness."

PRINCIPAL WORKS

Ellen Foster (novel) 1987
A Virtuous Woman (novel) 1989
A Cure for Dreams (novel) 1991
Charms for the Easy Life (novel) 1993
Sights Unseen (novel) 1995
On the Occasion of My Last Afternoon (novel) 1998

CRITICISM

Veronica Makowsky (essay date Winter 1992)

SOURCE: "'The Only Hard Part Was the Food': Recipes for Self-Nurture in Kaye Gibbons's Novels," in *Southern Quarterly,* Vol. 30, Nos. 2-3, Winter, 1992, pp. 103-12.

[*In the following essay, Makowsky discusses the relationship between food and nurturing in Gibbons's* Ellen Foster *and* A Virtuous Woman.]

In an article on Katherine Anne Porter's Miranda stories, Kaye Gibbons observes that "Porter's language, for all its superficial simplicity, pulls the reader vertically towards submerged meanings and horizontally backward through time and memories" (**"Planes of Language"** 74). The same could be said of Gibbons's own novels. The narrators of *Ellen Foster* and *A Virtuous Woman* are relatively uneducated, but their apparently unsophisticated commentary is actually a palimpsest of meanings, drawing the reader through past, present and future. Food, Gibbons's major metaphor for these levels of significance, is as basic and instinctive as the voices of her narrators. In their preoccupation with meals, Gibbons's narrators are all seeking the perfect recipe for happiness: how to provide nurturance for others, how to receive it for themselves and, most importantly, how to nurture themselves.

Gibbons is well-versed in the southern female *bildungsroman* and, in addition to Porter's Miranda, has commented appreciatively on Eudora Welty's Laura McRaven in *Delta Wedding* and the various girls of Welty's "Moon Lake" (**"Planes of Language"** 76, 77). Of Miranda, Gibbons remarks, "Viewed superficially, her struggles are neither extraordinary nor metaphoric" (76). In her first novel, *Ellen Foster,* Gibbons provides us with a heroine whose "struggles" are indeed "extraordinary" and "metaphoric" as signaled by a line from the epigraph for the novel, taken from Ralph Waldo Emerson's epigraph to "Self-Reliance": "Suckle him with the she-wolf's teat." *Ellen Foster* is Gibbons's attempt to rewrite the saga of the American hero by changing "him" to "her" and to rewrite the southern female *bildungsroman* by changing its privileged, sheltered, upper-class heroine to a poor, abused outcast. Like Porter and Welty's protagonists, Ellen faces the psychological and spiritual problems of growing up, but she must also confront sexual abuse, homelessness and, above all, hunger. The "she-wolf's teat" would seem like ambrosia to Ellen.

The novel opens with ten-year-old Ellen trying to shield her sick mother from her father's abuse. Ellen's mother has just returned from the hospital for treatment of the chronic heart condition she acquired in her youth from rheumatic fever, which Ellen calls "romantic fever" (3). Ellen's malapropism is actually quite accurate since her mother married beneath her class in what she must have believed to be a romantic escape from her own overbearing mother. Her mistake is glaringly obvious as Ellen's boorish father insists that her invalid mother make dinner, though she is plainly incapable of feeding anyone. Ellen comments that her mother "would prop herself up by the refrigerator" (2) and "looks like she could crawl under the table" (5). Because these props of domesticity—the refrigerator and kitchen table—are inadequate, Ellen herself must act as substitute homemaker. Her thoughts turn more to contamination, however, than to nurture: "What can I do but go and reach the tall things for her? I set that dinner table and like to take a notion to spit on his fork" (4).

With Ellen's help, her mother gets dinner on the table and fulfills her physical role as nurturer, but she never learns to nurture herself. All she wants to ingest is an overdose of her medication in order to escape her unbearable marriage. Again, Ellen takes on the parental role as she implores: "Vomit them up, mama. I'll stick my finger down your throat and you can vomit them up. She looks at me and I see she will not vomit. She will not move" (9). Ellen's mother is so debilitated physically and mentally that she poisons herself and can look at, but not nurture, her only child. Her father refuses to allow Ellen to call for help and later, as Ellen rests in bed beside her dying mother, she asserts, "And I will crawl in and make room for myself. My heart can be the one that beats" (10). Ellen is expressing contradictory desires: to return to the womb's safety where she was fed and to take over the life-sustaining role of the mother's heartbeat and nourishing bloodstream.

Although Ellen's mother is totally unable to nurture her child at the beginning of the novel, in her earlier seasons of relatively good health she taught Ellen the lessons about life to which Ellen clings after her death. Ellen's favorite memory is of gardening with her mother.

> She nursed all the plants and put even the weeds she pulled up in little piles along the rows. My job was to pick the piles up and dispose of them. I was small my own self and did not have the sense to tell between weeds and plants.
>
> I just worked in the trail my mama left.
>
> When the beans were grown ready to eat she would let me help pick. Weeds do not bear fruit. She would give me a example of a bean that is grown good to hold in

one hand while I picked with the other. If I was not sure if a particular bean was at the right stage I could hold up my example of a bean to that bean in question and know.

(49)

Once again, through the production of food, Gibbons suggests that from her mother Ellen learned not only right from wrong, beans from weeds, but also what an exemplary adult is, a model who has grown "to the right stage." After her mother's death, Ellen desperately needs these lessons as she confronts a series of caretakers who cannot or will not feed her, physically or mentally.

Ellen's father has plainly not grown to the "right stage"—he still expects others to nurture him. When her mother was in the hospital, Ellen had to supply her place as nurturer: "If I did not feed us both we had to go into town and get take-out chicken" (3). After her mother's death, he expects ten-year-old Ellen to replace her mother sexually as well. The perverse immaturity of his sexuality is evident in his focus on Ellen's body as baby food, milk and candy. "You got girl ninnies he might say. . . . Somebody else calling out sugar blossom britches might sound sweet but it was nasty from him" (43, 44). Although we might like to believe Ellen's father is a rare monster, Gibbons evidently intends him to represent a socially pervasive view of women as objects for consumption. His black drinking buddies advise him, again in eating imagery, on the night that he rapes her: "Yours is just about ripe. You gots to git em when they is still soff when you mashum" (37).

While her father is attempting to consume her, Ellen is trying to feed herself.

> The only hard part was the food. The whole time I stayed with him he either ate at the Dinette in town or did without. I would not go to the restaurant with him because I did not want to be seen with him. That is all.
>
> I fed myself OK. I tried to make what we had at school but I found the best deal was the plate froze with food already on it. A meat, two vegetables, and a dab of dessert.

(25)

Ellen is not just putting food in her stomach; she is attempting to maintain her standards. She will not eat with her father, especially in public, but she still manages to fulfill the nutritional requirements she learned in school. Although she may be keeping her dignity before the outside world, eating the proper food groups, and physically starving, the "froze food" indicates spiritually cold comfort.

Not all the standards she retains from her past help nurture her. Ellen's refuge is the house of her black friend Starletta which "always smells like fried meat" and where Starletta's "mama is at the stove boiling and frying" (29). Starletta's parents welcome Ellen, assure her of a haven against her father's abuse and even take her shopping for clothes, but Ellen cannot accept them as a substitute family because, as she says, "I would not even eat in a colored house" (33). The tenacity with which Ellen clings to her standards betrays her in this instance because she cannot differentiate between the content of nourishing love and the packaging of color: "No matter how good it looks to you it is still a colored biscuit" (32).

By court order Ellen is sent to live with her maternal grandmother who, unfortunately, is not a sweet, white-haired old lady ready to feed the poor child milk and cookies, as Ellen quickly perceives: "My mama's mama picked me up in her long car that was like the undertaking car only hers was cream" (61). Ellen's recognition of her grandmother's poisonous propensities is evident in her association of her grandmother's car with a hearse and food ("cream"), as well as her refusal to use the word "grandmother." Ellen's intuitions are accurate since her grandmother is taking Ellen not to nurture her, but to punish her for her mother's death, persisting in the belief that a ten-year-old child could and would connive with her father to poison her mother. Ellen's grandmother will not acknowledge that her mistreatment of her daughter helped precipitate her fatal marriage but projects the blame on Ellen and makes the small girl work in the fields in the intense heat of summer.

Ellen's grandmother provides her with sufficient food "just because she did not have it in her to starve a girl" (75) but does not mind starving her for affection. "We ate right many miniature chickens or turkeys. I do not know the difference. But they were baked and not crunchy the way I most enjoy chicken. When we both ate at the same Sunday table we both picked at our little individual chickens and turkeys and did not talk. And still it was OK by me" (66).

Her grandmother upholds class distinctions at the expense of pleasure and communion as they eat baked chicken, instead of the satisfyingly vulgar fried, and "individual chickens and turkeys" instead of food from a common serving dish. Ellen's insistence that she was glad they did not talk shows how much she has lost hope in her grandmother as nurturer. She had early decided that "she might be a witch but she has the dough"; later, "I called her the damn witch to myself and all the money she had did not matter anymore. That is something when you consider how greedy I am" (61). Ellen has learned that there is more to a meal than food on the table and that society's substitution of money for "dough" produces an inedible mess.

Once again Ellen is placed in a situation in which she must nurture an adult, first mentally and then physically. Her grandmother feeds her hate on the sight of Ellen. "Her power was the sucking kind that takes your good sense and leaves you limp like a old zombie. . . . She would take all the feeling she needed from somebody and then stir it up with some money and turn the recipe back on you" (68). Ellen is force-fed her grandmother's hate, but is

unable to regurgitate it because she cannot separate the hatred from her identity. "It is like when you are sick and you know all the things you ever ate or just wanted to eat are churning in you now and you will be sick to relieve yourself but the relief is a dream you let yourself believe because you know the churning is all there is to you" (72).

Although she recognizes her grandmother's hatred, Ellen takes care of her in her final illness and follows the doctor's advice to "feed her particular foods" (72). Ellen does not feed her grandmother out of love but because her grandmother has perversely fed Ellen's feelings of irrational guilt over her mother's death, consuming Ellen's "good sense" in knowing that a ten-year-old child could not prevail against her father.

Despite Ellen's care, her grandmother dies, and she is reluctantly taken in by her mother's widowed sister Nadine, who has a daughter about Ellen's age. As Ellen expects, Nadine is solely concerned with nurturing Dora and regards Ellen as an intruder on their relationship, much as her late husband must have been. Ellen comments, "I stayed in the spare bedroom Nadine's old husband lived in. He did not die flat out but he had a stroke of something and wasted away in here" (95). Ellen foresees a similar starvation for herself but tries to avert it. "I thought about taking my meals in my room but I did not like the picture of me eating off a tray slid to me like I was on death row. So I would eat at the table like normal" (95). "Like normal" appears to be a false simulacrum because Nadine rids herself of the indigestible intruder by throwing Ellen out of the house on Christmas day.

Having learned that blood ties do not necessarily nurture, Ellen tries a nontraditional family. She throws herself on the mercy of a woman who takes foster children. Naively, she believes that "foster" is the family's name and renames herself accordingly, but once again her linguistic error points to truth since "to foster" means to further growth, or, in other words, to nurture. The reader knows Ellen's hunch about this woman is correct when Ellen smells fried chicken as she enters the house, picking up a three-day-old scent that she, in her desperation, apprehends.

Ellen repeatedly refers to her new home in terms of gratified hunger. "There is a plenty to eat here and if we run out of something we just go to the store and get some more" (2). Cooking becomes associated with the rituals of community and love as the children and their foster mother cook their week's lunches on Sunday and receive individual cooking lessons during the week. The kitchen is no longer a place of conflict or empty routines, but is filled with affection. Ellen says of her foster mother that "she is there each day in the kitchen and that is something when you consider she does not have to be there but she is there so I can squeeze her and be glad" (86).

Although Ellen is certainly much happier, her continuing obsession with food shows how deeply traumatized she is from years without nourishing affection.

If I am very hungry my dress comes off of me in a heartbeat. Sometimes I hurry too fast and I forget to unzip my back. It is helpless to smell lunch through a dress that is hung on your face. I have busted a zipper and ripped two neck collars trying to strip and my new mama told me some things about patience.

I stay starved though.

(58)

This comment comes approximately midway through the novel, which is narrated in a series of contrasting flashbacks to Ellen's life at her foster home. As the novel continues, Ellen's references to food decline dramatically, as if she begins to feel secure about food and affection.

By the end of the novel Ellen has learned the folly of social distinctions according to class and race, in addition to those she had learned about "blood" kin. She can assert that if Starletta "tells me to I will lick the glass she uses just to show that I love her and being colored is just the way she is" (85). When her foster mother allows her to invite Starletta to spend the weekend and to request her favorite dishes, Ellen remarks that Starletta "could see how I enjoy staying laid up in my bed waiting for supper to cook. And you can guess what all is on the menu" (123). Since Ellen is now nurtured by an adult, she can share that nurturing with someone younger and less privileged than herself, as evidenced in the last lines of the novel. "And all this time I thought I had the hardest row to hoe. That will always amaze me." The imagery recalls Ellen's favorite memory of growing beans with her mother and indicates that she sees woman's lot as hard, "work[ing] in the trail [her] mama left" (49), but she can lend a hand to the next woman down the trail, so that all will be fed.

Ellen has certainly mastered Emerson's lesson of self-reliance, but that is not an end in itself, and although her gutsy, vernacular voice recalls Huck Finn, she does not light out for the territories in an attempt to maintain that autonomy. She is also a more successful heroine than Porter's Miranda, of whom Gibbons writes, "She does not yet know that she cannot reorder the past nor order her future by an act of will. She needs something closer to an act of faith" (**"Planes of Language"** 75). Through Ellen, Gibbons redefines self-reliance, not as a willed and threatened isolation, but as the maturity that enables an act of faith in others and, in turn, that allows a girl to contribute to, as well as receive from, the female tradition of community and nurturance.

In her second novel, Gibbons goes back in time to a protagonist of the same generation as Ellen Foster's mother, as if to ask why such virtuous women seem fated to suffer in the past. Although the food imagery is not overwhelming in *A Virtuous Woman,* as it is in *Ellen Foster,* it remains a major element, as indicated by lines from the epigraph.

> She bringeth her food from afar
> She riseth also while it is yet night,
> And giveth meat to her household.
>
> (*Proverbs* 31: 19–21)

Significantly, the virtuous woman of *Proverbs* is portrayed as feeding others, not receiving nurture from others, or, most importantly, nourishing herself.

Ruby Woodrow Stokes, like Ellen Foster's mother, has married beneath her class, but unlike Ellen's mother, who marries to escape a hostile, emotionally starved mother, Ruby seems to be fleeing a surfeit of nurturing. Of her father and brothers, she recalls: "If I had a tough piece of meat on my plate, the minute one of them saw me struggling they'd lean over, take my knife and fork from me and cut the meat up for me. I never rebelled against it, snatched my knife back and said, 'I'll cut my own meat up, thank you'" (25–26).

Predictably, Ruby's mother is a woman so sheltered from reality that she cannot cope with it. When Ruby's father hires migrant workers, her mother decides to invite them inside for a meal served on her best china. She cannot comprehend the dirt and destruction left behind by the untaught and hostile workers and deals with the situation by ignoring it, retreating to her room and refusing to talk about it.

Ruby repeats her mother's experience with migrant workers by marrying one, John Woodrow, and finds him not only unappreciative but unfaithful and abusive. He even criticizes her higher-caste slenderness, ordering her to "put some meat on them bones!" (68). Their marriage cannot feed her, but rather chokes her: Ruby calls herself "a good country girl who'd married this man and bitten off way, way more than she could chew" (34). Since her family's food was prepared by a servant, Ruby does not know how to cook. She realizes that she is incapable of nurturing herself physically or spiritually and knows that John Woodrow will not do it for her. She sarcastically remarks, "I'd have come nearer thriving on John Woodrow's love than the food we had" (35). Instead of learning to feed herself, she learns to poison herself from John Woodrow's example. In response to his taunts about what a "little Miss Vanderbilt" (37) she is, Ruby begins the smoking that will lead to her death from cancer years later.

Ruby, though, is not a total masochist who will continue to swallow more than she can chew. She decides to regurgitate it by planning to kill John Woodrow when he makes her "sick to [her] stomach" (46), lying in bed with another woman. She is spared the trouble of murdering him herself when she learns he is hospitalized after a knife fight. Instead of rushing to the hospital to resume her role as victim, Ruby stays away, despite the admonitory example of one of the migrant women. "She said the man's face was sliced this way and that and his wife stayed right by him, feeding him through a straw, picking glass slivers from his lips. The woman told the story like it was a privilege for the man's wife to pick at his lips" (69). Ruby refuses her gender role as the nurturer of her abuser, someone who would cut herself by removing glass from his lips, but she does not have to put her conviction to the test since John Woodrow dies of his injuries.

Ruby also learns to rebel against the class and race systems, as Gibbons indicates in a scene about serving food. Ruby is working as a house servant to the Hoovers, the family that hired John Woodrow and the other migrants for the field. They gloat over having so refined a servant, someone who seems from a higher social class than themselves. Ruby can now identify with her family's black servant, Whistle Dick, who was fired by the cook for eating food intended for guests: "the more I thought of Whistle Dick, the more I wanted to. Then I'd have been out, just like he was when Sudie Bee caught him sneaking the pineapple slices off a ham" (49). When Frances Hoover tries to show Ruby how to arrange sandwiches on a platter, a genteel female art which Ruby knows well, Ruby fantasizes: "Whew! I just thought of Frances tasting one of those little ladyfingers her sister brought and commenting on how she put in way, way too much salt. Then I say maybe she ought to have something to wash it down, how it's the rat poison I sprinkled on top that brings out the salty flavor" (79). By the time of John Woodrow's death, Ruby can recognize the poisonous nature of southern gender, race and class systems.

Recognition cannot save Ruby, for in the pre-feminist South she believes herself to be anomalous and alone. Although she sees the degraded condition of the Hoover women, she cannot bond with them, nor would they allow her to since the male-dominated culture sets woman against woman in competition for masculine approval. Frances must prove with a platter of sandwiches that she is a better hostess than Ruby. Her obese daughter, cruelly nicknamed Tiny Fran, turns on both Frances and Ruby, who comments: "My God! That girl just hit her mama! Then she went to the refrigerator and poured herself a big glass of chocolate milk, saw me standing there by the pantry and said to me, 'Hand me a box of soda crackers in there'" (39). Tiny Fran is pregnant out of wedlock and her father has basically paid one of his workers, Burr, to marry her by giving him land. Suffering with morning sickness and with disgust at this patriarchal barter, Tiny Fran can only hurt herself, not the system. Ruby observes that she is "settling her stomach with soda crackers and undoing all the good that was doing with a quart of chocolate milk, then sick and frustrated and not understanding why" (40).

"Not understanding why," Tiny Fran perpetuates the cycle of domination by indulging her son Roland with all the chocolate milk he can drink so that he would "grow up and give her more attention than her daddy did and Burr did" (106). Unsurprisingly, he grows up to be incarcerated for his brutal beating of a young woman. Tiny Fran also continues the tradition of woman against woman by failing to nurture her daughter June. Tiny Fran and Roland would "sit down and split a chocolate cake but she wouldn't have given June air if she was in a jug" (90).

Ruby realizes she cannot go back to her parents since her experiences have deprived her of the sheltered innocence that they would value and continue to nourish. All those years of having her meat cut up for her, however, had made her incapable of moving forward alone and nourishing herself. She literally marries the next man who comes along, the Hoovers' tenant farmer Jack Stokes, and allows herself to be consumed like a nut fallen into his hands from the pecan tree under which Jack sees her "sitting . . . like a prize" (18).

Unlike John Woodrow, though, Jack has the grace to recognize that he is feeding off Ruby. "And then I see me, the biggest buzzard of them all, circling too, circling Ruby, waiting" (16). Throughout their marriage, he continues to associate Ruby with food. After her death he likes to remember her on a trip to the beach "riding the whole way with a pineapple cake between her feet and holding a pound cake" (93). He fears that her cancer will spoil her for his consumption and for her role as a status object for him: "Ruby has the creamiest soft skin and I hated to have brown spots ruin her for people" (2). To Jack, her disease is the buzzard who got there first: "Ruby's cancer ate up most of everything we had saved" (58–59).

As John Woodrow had wanted Ruby to play one culturally assigned role, that of sex object, so Jack Stokes wanted her to play another, that of the nurturing mother who would compensate for his own mother's refusal to act the way her gender seemed to dictate. Jack recalls:

> I'd always have to think of my mama whenever Ruby made a pie, which was every Sunday morning until she got so weak she couldn't hardly crawl out of the bed. . . . Mama would've been put off by Ruby's pies, too much, too good. . . . sometimes I want to ask mama why she couldn't ever have made I and daddy just one pie, just a plain one. But I guess a hard woman like my mama didn't think about dessert. . . . I excuse the pies I didn't have because I was satisfied by Ruby's so many times.
>
> (15)

Jack's mother did provide food for the family: "she used not to flinch when she'd scald a chicken, dip it in the cast-iron pot outside and it steaming, and pluck it faster than you could yell" (15). Jack, however, cannot accept the nurture without subserviently feminine sweetening, "dessert." His mother appears to have been killed by the indigestibility of her gender roles and her husband and son's blindness to them. Jack remembers: "She passed when I was fourteen, food poison. Turned out to be a bad piece of meat, but we thought first it was just the stomach flu" (14).

Ruby, unprepared for self-reliance, is willing to depend on Jack for her survival since she can earn her keep and her dignity by playing nurturing mother to him. She knows "he's just like a child" (7) and decides to master the skills she needs to tend him, primarily culinary ones. She muses:

> Cooking's not like cleaning. You don't just know what good is and then cook it. You need a touch that comes with time and patience, especially if you grew up playing the piano while meals were being prepared and then coming into the kitchen just in time to put parsley

on the plates. But you ought to see the way I've kept this house and cooked for Jack. I'm sorry to say that I might not have much in my life to be proud of, but I'm surely pleased with myself every time I see bread rise, and it rises every time.

(73)

She is so proud of her one accomplishment that she even wants to provide for Jack after her death. The woman who makes a pie every Sunday as long as she can stand up spends the last months of her life cooking for her husband. In the novel's opening passage, she announces: "By Thanksgiving I'll have everything organized. I tie a package of pork with some corn, beef with some beans, and so forth, so all Jack should have to do is reach into the freezer and take out a good, easy meal" (5). She continues her cooking despite her recognition of its ultimate futility: "somehow, when I see him a year, two years from now, he's letting himself in Burr's house, hungry, lonesome" (6). As Ellen Foster also learned, frozen food is a cold, rapidly consumed comfort.

Although their marriage might be considered a decent one, in that both partners lived up to their parts of the bargain without conflict or violence, neither Ruby nor Jack was really nourished enough for growth. Ruby cannot ask for Jack's reassurance and sympathy as she fights her cancer because she knows the topic distresses him and sends him to drink. She must confront her final feelings alone. Jack remains a child who lives on the level of appetites. Jack's questions after Ruby's death are not what we usually consider existential ones: "I had three big questions every day I needed a answer to, What's for breakfast? What's for lunch? What's for supper?" (123). He continues his search for a mother-substitute: "Isn't it every man's dream that when his wife dies he has somebody to step in and do for him?" (134). In the last scene of the novel, he is rescued by a woman, Burr's daughter June, who finds him in bed sucking on a bottle, the alcoholic kind.

A Virtuous Woman ends ambiguously. June has been "fostered" by Ruby since she could get no attention from Tiny Fran, and she may be replacing Ruby as a mother-figure in the final scene of the novel.

> June told her father that when she finished cleaning Jack's house she'd like to go back into town and buy some things for supper and they could all eat together. *Something Jack would like, the way Ruby would've made it. She showed me how to make the dough, and we sat at the table, rolled it out and cut it into long strips. Then she held me over the pot and let me drop them in.*

(147)

June could be regarded as continuing the tradition of female subservience that she learned from Ruby, yet the care, the craft, the nurturing in June's memory of Ruby have the same positive connotations as Ellen Foster's memory of picking beans with her mother.

In *A Virtuous Woman,* Gibbons redefines the virtuous woman, but not by discarding female crafts and traditions, particularly cooking, with their connotations of nurturance. She is not suggesting that the nurturing of others indicates servility. Instead, she suggests that the truly virtuous woman can nurture herself as well as others, not sacrifice herself for the good of others since that "good" turns out to be the evil of John Woodrow or Ellen Foster's father's abuse or Jack Stokes's childishness. June embodies both old and new values. She has not only learned to cook, but, with Ruby's encouragement, has become an architect in a nearby town. Although she has lost Ruby, she still has female support and another kind of female example. We learn that June has a friend named Ellen who is one of the orphans Ruth Hartley is raising. When Ellen's foster sister Stella is beaten up by Tiny Fran's son Roland, Ellen reports him to the police and rides with Stella and Ruth in the ambulance (104–05). Ellen and June may be the new virtuous women who know that in order to nourish others they must first nurture themselves or all will ultimately go hungry.

Works Cited

Gibbons, Kaye. *Ellen Foster.* 1987. New York: Random, 1988.

———. "Planes of Language and Time: The Surface of the Miranda Stories." *Kenyon Review* 10.1 (1988): 74–79.

———. *A Virtuous Woman.* Chapel Hill: Algonquin, 1989.

Stephen Souris (essay date Summer 1992)

SOURCE: "Kaye Gibbons's *A Virtuous Woman*: A Bakhtinian/Iserian Analysis of Conspicuous Agreement," in *Southern Studies,* Vol. 3, No. 2, Summer, 1992, pp. 99-115.

[*In the following essay, Souris uses the narrative theories of Mikhail Bakhtin and Wolfgang Iser to analyze the multiple narration of Gibbons's* A Virtuous Woman.]

> And after it all, after it's all said and done, I'll still have to say, Bless you, Ruby. You were a fine partner, and I miss you.
>
> —Jack Stokes

The bare story of Kaye Gibbons's *A Virtuous Woman* (1989) is simple enough. When we stand back from the moment-to-moment experience of this multiple-narrator novel, it settles in our memory as the story of the relationship between a man named Jack and a woman named Ruby who lived together for a quarter of a century in rural North Carolina. The novel details how they met and fulfilled each other's basic existential need for the attention and love of another. It also portrays their disappointment over not being able to have children, Ruby's death from lung cancer, and Jack's desperation, after his wife's death, from not knowing how to cook for himself and keep house.

Such a summary of the novel, however, cannot do justice to the narratological uniqueness of *A Virtuous Woman*. As a multiple-narrator novel in the tradition of Faulkner's *As I Lay Dying,* the decentered narrative mode sets up interesting dynamics and raises various aesthetic issues. By drawing from the theories of Mikhail Bakhtin and Wolfgang Iser—two theorists of novelness who are especially relevant to multiple-monologue novels—we can assess the complexities of Gibbons's book. Bakhtin's theory of dialogized heteroglossia, applied to a multiple-narrator novel, leads one to look at the nature, extent, and genuineness of the multiple voices; the degree to which the commitment to a variety of different voices results in centrifugal or disorderly tendencies; the way in which intermingling of perspectives within single monologues (what I call "intra-monologue dialogicity") functions as a counter-centrifugal, ordering force; and the way in which relationship across monologues (what I call "inter-monologue dialogicity") also serves to provide structure and cohesion in multiple first-person monologue novels. Iser picks up where Bakhtin leaves off (both in their respective articulations and in my use of them) because although Bakhtin suggests he would consider the dialogic potential of utterances such as monologues set side-by-side (especially in *Speech Genres and Other Late Essays*), he devotes most of his attention instead to the examination of dialogicity within single utterances. Iser's phenomenologically rigorous examination of the way a reader constructs a text by making connections between sections during a moment-by-moment processing of the narrative is perfectly suited to the task of examining the dialogic potential across monologues in multiple-narrator novels. This unique hybrid of narratological models can uncover features of *A Virtuous Woman*—or any other multiple-narrator novel—that would not be as apparent without the special rigor of Bakhtin's and Iser's theories.

Before drawing on Bakhtin and Iser to get at the dynamics of this multiple-narrator novel, it will be useful to touch upon the salient features of *A Virtuous Woman* when it is considered in the context of other multiple-narrator novels so that an overall sense of its uniqueness can be given at the outset. Like Louise Erdrich's *Tracks,* it limits the multi-perspectivalism to just two voices, and, like *Tracks,* it alternates between the two, without non-monologue interchapter material. Through this turn taking, the story of Jack and Ruby's life together is conveyed. With each monologue consisting of an installment of the story, the narrative progresses in a fairly linear and chronological manner. The two voices are very distinct, in personality as well as language. Each is presented as if talking casually to a listener, even though no audience is present.[1] At the end of her first monologue, Ruby asks, "Don't you believe it to be so?" (14). And Jack, at one point, says, "Listen and let me tell what else I think about it" (95). At another point he says, "Listen and tell me if you don't hear something that won't turn your stomach" (109). The audience is none other than the reader, as is often the case with contemporary multiple-narrator novels: when it becomes clear

that the monologists are not speaking to anyone in particular, readers realize that *they* are the audience.

The presentation of the story is actually more complicated than I have suggested, as will usually be the case when one attempts to extract a story from the discourse of a multiple-narrator novel. First, the narrative begins after Ruby's death and then circles back to show us what led up to it—much like Peter Matthiessen's *Killing Mister Watson* begins with the gunning down of Watson and then shows us what led up to it. Another complicating factor is that although the "story" of their life together is presented chronologically, with each monologist sharing in the linear presentation, Ruby is presented talking shortly before her death about their life together as she tries to cook enough food to keep Jack fed for several months after her death (one review of the novel is entitled "As Ruby Lay Dying" [Powell]); he, on the other hand, is presented reminiscing after her death, apparently after he has eaten his way to the bottom of the freezer full of food she prepared.[2] It is only through the careful pacing and editing by the author as arranger that their accounts are synchronized.

One of the most salient features of this novel is the agreement it foregrounds between the two narrators. As we shall see, the nature of their agreement is remarkable, given the tendency for narratives that work by way of multiple narrators to flaunt disagreement. *A Virtuous Woman* thus belongs at the opposite end of the spectrum from Matthiessen's *Killing Mister Watson* and Auchincloss's *The House of the Prophet* regarding the use to which the multiple narrator mode is put.

Another remarkable feature of this novel, when it is considered in the context of contemporary multiple-narrator fiction, is its switch in the final chapter to traditional omniscient third-person narration. I can imagine only two possible reactions to this radical deviation from the series of alternating first-person monologues: either relief or disappointment. A reader like Robert Towers, who, writing about Erdrich's *Tracks,* declares, "[T]he narration of events is kept at such a pitch that finally one wishes to stop one's ears" (40), would probably experience relief.

Finally, any discussion of this novel's salient features should mention the epigraph. An excerpt from Proverbs 31: 10–25, "The Good Wife," it presents a highly idealized notion of what an ideal wife in Biblical times would do. The passage from which the epigraph is taken also refers to the ideal wife's children and her fear of the Lord. The following story presents us with a very contemporary woman who is not ideal in the Biblical sense. She had neither children nor fear of the Lord. An interesting tension is thus established between the epigraph and the narrative, drawing our attention to the completely unidealized nature of the characters constituting this story. Epigraphs to novels are, of course, always important; but when an author of a multiple-narrator novel includes an epigraph, it plays an especially important role given the author's inability—usually—to provide the kind of commentary that is possible in third-person narratives.

Having considered the salient features of this multiple-monologue novel, we can now approach it from the perspective of Bakhtin's interest in multiple voices and Iser's emphasis on reader participation in the construction of the text.

A Bakhtinian/Iserian analysis of *A Virtuous Woman* requires first taking up the issue of heteroglossia. We need to ask how Bakhtin's definition of heteroglossia as "a plurality of independent and unmerged voices and consciousnesses, a genuine polyphony of fully valid voices," and his description of it as "the unification of highly heterogeneous and incompatible material . . . with the plurality of consciousness-centers not reduced to a single ideological common denominator" (*Problems*, 6, 17) helps us assess the multi-voicedness of this multiple-narrator novel.

A Virtuous Woman, while restricting itself to only two voices, does present us with a compelling variety in the two consciousnesses depicted and it presents each personality as a fully valid entity. The title is therefore misleading because the novel is as much about Jack as it is about Ruby; it is about their relationship. They are both fully realized and given equal time.

Jack is a simple, down-to-earth fellow, as we see on the very first page: "My wife's name was Ruby Pitt Woodrow Stokes. She was a real pretty woman. Used to I used to lay up in bed and say, 'Don't take it off in the dark! I want to see it all!'" (3). He has alcoholic tendencies, although he won't admit it: "I'm not really what I would call a drinking man. I hardly ever take a drink except when I need one" (4). Ruby cooks and cleans for him. He doesn't like intellectuals: when Roland, the son of Jack and Ruby's neighbors, ends up in jail and sociological explanations are offered for how Roland could have gone wrong, Jack says, "I think folks in town in general try to think too goddamn much" (112). Ruby offers this assessment of Jack's simplicity: "[T]here's something raw and right there on the surface with him. Sometimes, I swear, he's just like a child. You have to be so careful" (9).

Gibbons exploits the opportunity to further characterize Jack through the language he uses. The son of a tenant farmer and a poor tenant farmer himself, Jack's grammar is what one would expect. Characteristic of his speech are the constructions, "Used to I used to" (as we've seen), "it won't so much like I feel like" (60), and "trying to shove Jesus down I and mama's throats" (16). Furthermore, his language is relatively simple. There are no sophisticated words or constructions, and thus—since the language we use both reflects and determines our perceptions—his observations about himself, Ruby, and life in general tend to be simplistic. For example, his way of summing up Ruby's childhood is to say it was "too good" and his way of summing up her life with Woodrow, her abusive first husband, is to say it was "too bad" (5). Although these simple labels are accurate enough, his unsophisticated language does not allow him to get at subtleties. Gibbons's use of unsophisticated and "grammatically incorrect" language to

further characterize Jack is significant in the context of other multiple-narrator novels: frequently such narratives, while being committed through the very narrative mode to a heteroglot variety of viewpoints, do not fully exploit the opportunity to differentiate one character from another through the kind of language used.

Gibbons also makes a contribution to the body of contemporary multiple-narrator novels through her decision to include this relatively simple-minded fellow. Faulkner would take that idea to a compelling extreme and make poetry out of it (e.g., Benjy in *The Sound and the Fury*), but using such a character is risky for most writers of multiple-narrator novels because the reader may lose interest. Gibbons handles this situation very well.

Ruby's voice is very different from Jack's. The daughter of genteel landowners, she has led a protected life without hardship or difficult choices. Indeed, her attraction to the rogue Woodrow is explained—through her own sophisticated self-analysis—as the result of that over-protected, privileged childhood: she saw him as a victim and he thus took on heroic proportions for her. In contrast to Jack, she loves to think. She can even spend an entire day at it, meditating all by herself. The page after Jack denounces folks in town for thinking too much, she tells us: "All yesterday, all day yesterday all I did was think, and then I waited for Jack, waited for him twice to come home and spell me from all my thoughts" (113). Her meditative monologues are full of sensitive observations about life. Both her thoughts and her language are more sophisticated than Jack's.

One of the triumphs of this novel is the rendition through specific and idiosyncratic details of two very different personalities. With this marked difference between the two and the fact that the first-person mode is used to characterize each from within, the novel, while restricting itself to only two voices, is impressively heteroglot and "highly heterogeneous." Approaching it from the context of Bakhtin's theory of novelness helps us gain an appreciation of the multi-perspectivalism of *A Virtuous Woman.*

The next question to ask about a multiple-narrator novel when approaching it from a Bakhtinian perspective is whether or not its commitment to heteroglossia results in a certain relativism and, if so, what the epistemological implications of that are. Bakhtin's definition of heteroglossia quoted above—including the reference to "the unification of . . . incompatible material"—already implies a certain relativism. His oft-quoted declaration that the heteroglot, Galilean novel "is a perception that has been made conscious of the vast plenitude of . . . languages—all of which are equally capable of being 'languages of truth,' but, since such is the case, all of which are equally relative, reified and limited" (*Dialogic,* 366–67) is an important declaration to keep in mind when approaching a multiple-narrator novel from a Bakhtinian perspective. Related to the inquiry into whether a multi-perspectival novel offers a relativized view of reality is the question about the degree of centrifugality that results from an insistence on multiple perspectives without a single, monologizing correct perspective. To what extent, we can ask, does each narrator's perspective function as a centripetal force with the sum total of the various centripetal forces being a centrifugal one?

Jack and Ruby are different enough—as my brief summaries of their personalities should suggest—to tempt a reader to expect and look for such relativism and centrifugality. Approaching *A Virtuous Woman* from the vantage point of other multiple-narrator novels that emphasize difference and disagreement between narrators, like *As I Lay Dying* and *Killing Mister Watson* (and many others), one is ready with the slightest hint of difference and disagreement to read *A Virtuous Woman* as a radically relativized, and therefore centrifugal, narrative. The novel's opening seems to set us up for precisely such a novel, suggesting an uneasy tension between husband and wife. Jack, in the novel-opening monologue, tells us about the time Ruby, dying of cancer in the hospital, asked for a cigarette. Propped up in an oxygen tent, all she could do was motion to him. He thought she was blowing him a kiss and was annoyed to discover she was gesturing for a cigarette. Ruby's first section likewise contains some hints of tension. She complains that Jack is incorrigibly forgetful, and she tells of the ugly scene between them when he heard she had terminal cancer: she wanted to be comforted and all he could do was declare, "Anybody mean as the old squaw'll outlive everybody" (8–9). She then launches into what appears to be a feminist diatribe against men in general, arguing that they are dependent on women to keep life going and that they fall apart when their women become incapacitated. She declares,

> If you want to see a man afraid just put him in a room with a sick woman who was once strong. See, I know now that this world is built up on strong women. Built up and kept up by them too, them kneeling, stooping, pulling, bending, and rising up when they need to go and do what needs to get done. And when a man sees a woman like that sick and hurt, especially the kind of man who knows a woman's strength but can't confess it, when he sees her sick or hurt it terrifies him, like he's witnessing a chunk of the universe coming loose and he knows he doesn't have what it takes to stick it back together.
>
> (13)

Two monologues into the novel, we might think we're in for an up-close look at a sensitive woman who is unhappy with her insensitive husband. By presenting these hints of conflict right at the outset through a narrative strategy that encourages the reader to look for differences between narrators, Gibbons prepares us for a very imperfect relationship—indeed, she tempts us into thinking that it was a terribly compromised one.

There are other disagreements and differences between these two that could be exploited for effect in order to establish the radically relative way two human beings can

perceive things. We've already seen that they are two very different personality types, pointed up by the juxtaposing of Chapter 11, in which Jack asserts that people tend to "think too goddamn much" (112), with Chapter 12, in which Ruby tells us how she can spend the entire day thinking to herself. Other examples of how this narrative has the potential for being a highly relativized multiple-narrator novel are Ruby's telling Jack she doesn't like him shooting target practice because it takes him away from her, when the truth is that it reminds her of her former husband; and Ruby's telling Jack when they met for the first time that she was a researcher (to prevent him from thinking she was just a tenant farmer's wife). Much mileage could be gotten from such lies to show two people who are caught up in their own subjective realities.

In spite of ample opportunity to suggest the gulf between consciousnesses (even to the point of portraying subjectivity to a solipsistic extreme), however, Gibbons conspicuously exploits the multiple-narrator mode to emphasize the shared reality that defined this relationship. This is one of the most interesting aspects of *A Virtuous Woman* when it is compared with other multiple first-person monologue novels. It is also the most important way in which the narrative counters the relativistic and centrifugal tendencies inherent in the narrative mode. Repeatedly, the narrative sets up an event, subject, or person that functions as a common denominator between the two narrators (a technique called triangulation), and, sometimes through juxtaposing monologues in which the common denominator appears in each one, insists on agreement.

One example of Gibbons's radically different use of the technique of triangulation (when her novel is compared with other multiple-narrator novels) is Jack's and Ruby's attitude toward religion. Neither one believes in God in a conventional way. She does believe in a spirit that lives on after the body dies (117), but, she explains, "I don't believe I had a maker. I don't believe anybody did. . . . It's just not the way Jack and I think things are organized, if you can call everything that goes on organization. We'd just rather stay amazed at how it all happens, I mean this world bumping right along with no plan at all" (116). We have no reason to doubt her claim to be speaking for the two of them—"this heathen couple" (118) she calls Jack and herself—because we have previously heard Jack's harsh thoughts about Christianity.

> Listen to how God up there is supposed to make everything and everybody and everything's due to turn out according to his will and all. And we get the wars and the people starving and people hurting people and animals the way Roland did [he hung Ruby's mule], and I'm supposed to go down there to Ephesus on Sunday morning and say, 'Thank you, Jesus, thank you for the sunshine and the food on my table and all the birds singing and the likes of Adolf Hitler and Roland Stanley.' No thank you! I'll have no part of it! Beats the hell out of me why somebody'd want to sit up somewhere and think up harm. . . .
>
> (95–96)

While their disbelief takes on a different cast with each (his is a Job-like resistance and hers is more out of a preference for a spiritual alternative), their essential agreement contributes to Gibbons's unusual agenda of using the multiple-narrator mode to show the possibilities of understanding, communication, and union between people.

Another example of how Gibbons uses triangulation to establish agreement is seen with the subject of Jack's reluctance to accept the land Ruby inherited from her parents. Jack explains: "I just didn't want a place I didn't know" (60); Ruby reports, in the very next monologue, that Jack simply "couldn't take a strange place" (75).

Yet another example of conspicuous agreement occurs at the outset of the novel. Jack tells us:

> God, you ought to've seen her in the hospital, weak, trying to sit up, limp as a dishrag. She'd lost down so much, looked like she'd literally almost shook the meat off, all that coughing and spewing up she'd done. If you want to feel helpless as a baby sometime, you go somewhere and watch such as that. Seemed like every time she'd cough a cold shudder'd run up and down me.
>
> (4–5)

Men who feel "helpless as a baby" when their women are out of commission are just what Ruby rails against in her monologue immediately following this opening monologue. The narrative does nothing to suggest that her forcefully articulated position needs to be counterbalanced with a different perspective.

The most interesting example of radical agreement between the two monologists has to do with the moment they met. The accounts agree in all details. There is no need to quote from their respective accounts: a summary will do justice to each version. She was sitting under a tree smoking and he came by hauling manure. A skinny, unattractive man, he sauntered up to her as if she were just another female to flirt with; however, they had a free and casual conversation devoid of the usual exaggerated dynamic between man and woman in such circumstances precisely because he was no Romeo. She lied about doing research on migrant workers, not wanting him to think she was the wife of just such a worker; he knew she was lying, and she knew he knew it. After hearing Woodrow was her husband, he then told her what he knew about Woodrow's altercation, and he offered his help if she ever needed it. The only thing Gibbons doesn't do here to enhance the conspicuousness of the agreement is juxtapose the two accounts through contiguous monologues (his account occurs in Chapter 5, pp. 45–48, and her account is found in Chapter 8, pp. 68–72).

Gibbons's refusal to show radically different reactions to common events, subjects, or people acting as intersections between monologues in order to suggest the subjectivity of perception is a radical departure from the norm in the multiple-narrator novel, and is one reason why the novel coheres as much as it does in spite of the centrifugal tendencies of such decentered, multi-perspectival narratives.

In addition to taunting us, as it were, with a refusal to establish difference between narrators through the technique of triangulation, this narrative counters the centrifugal potential inherent in the form by showing how simple existential need is behind Jack's interest in Ruby and Ruby's interest in Jack. Although very different in personality, they are united at a level that is deeper than their differences. As an abused woman who did not realize what she was getting into when she left her genteel background to elope with Woodrow, Ruby turned to Jack for security. Jack tells us, "All she said was she wanted somebody to take care of her, and if I promised to, she'd marry me" (46). But Jack also got something out of the arrangement: her love for him made him feel like a man. He declares, "[B]efore I married Ruby I'd felt like a boy on the outside looking in, but Ruby, when she loved me, I said, This is what is must feel like to be a man" (46). It is the similar desire and need for another that overcomes their differences and overcomes the potential of this narrative form to overwhelm us with epistemological confusion from a chorus of competing subjectivities.

Although Jack and Ruby are united at this deeper level and agree on the fundamental details of their life together, they are very different people, which in itself contributes to the coherence of a potentially disconcerting decentered narrative: through the regular alternation between the two voices—the one a sensitive, meditative, "feminine" voice (Gibbons works with conventional gender differences in this novel)—a rhythm is set up which confers a certain order upon the narrative. (It is this rhythm between the two voices, ultimately, that prevents Jack's simple-mindedness from ever becoming boring.)[3]

Another way in which *A Virtuous Woman* counters the centrifugality inherent in the multiple-narrator mode is through a strictly linear story line that threads its way through the monologues. This points up the highly artificial nature of the narrative: separated by time and death, Jack and Ruby tell the story of their life together as if they were seated side by side, taking turns in offering installments that advance the story with each change of speaker. Many contemporary American multiple-narrator novels opt for this kind of coherence through a linear story line advancing through the monologues (as opposed to the alternative strategy, which *The Sound and the Fury* best exemplifies); but Gibbons's novel is unique in separating the voices so radically in space and time. This distinct separation between the moment of speaking for the monologists is a source of confusion until one reads far enough to understand what Gibbons is doing. The ultimate effect of creating the narrative from carefully synchronized voices, however, is more than the imposition of order upon the narrative: it suggests a bond between the two that transcends death. Gibbons thus has more of an excuse for and artistic purpose in constructing the narrative via strictly chronological installments than is usually the case in multiple-narrator novels with a forward-moving story line.

The next Bakhtinian issue to consider in analyzing this multiple-narrator novel is the question of intra-monologue dialogicity—that is, the intermingling and interpenetration of perspectives *within* single utterances. This would be another way to counter the centrifugal tendencies of such a narrative. Assuming that his analysis of Dostoevsky's epistolary novel *Poor Folk* is an indication of what he would do with any multiple-narrator novel, Bakhtin would probably look for evidence of one monologist's awareness of and grappling with the ideas of the other monologist, such that, in his formulation, utterances that externally resemble monologues take the form of "microdialogues." It is my contention that Bakhtin would see "dialogized monologues" (*Problems,* 248), or monologists speaking with an "intense sideward glance at someone else's word" (*Problems,* 203) as a primary counter-centrifugal force in multiple-narrator novels. *A Virtuous Woman,* like other recent American multiple-narrator novels, is not noteworthy for the way it portrays individual consciousness consisting of an active confrontation with other viewpoints—where "[t]he hero's attitude toward himself is inseparably bound up with his attitude toward another, and with the attitude of another toward him" (*Problems,* 207)—or an "infiltration of anticipated responses" (*Problems,* 246) into the monologists' talk. No double-voiced discourse can be said to exist in the monologues of Gibbons's novel like Bakhtin illustrates is the case in the letters between Makar and Varvara in *Poor Folk.* Approaching contemporary multiple-narrator novels from Bakhtin's extraordinary sensitivity to and fondness for such double-voiced discourse within single utterances points up the absence of such sophisticated depictions of consciousness in novels that do not feature it. Without Bakhtin, the absence of this might go unnoticed. In any case, given the extraordinary degree of agreement, and thus coherence, that Gibbons's novel has, the lack of intra-monologue dialogicity does not make it a more scattered novel: it coheres well enough without such intermingling of perspectives at the site of individual consciousness.[4]

Wolfgang Iser can be profitably added to our analysis of *A Virtuous Woman* because of the way his phenomenological model of the process of reading provides the concepts and the terminology for articulating how what I am calling inter-monologue dialogicity can be said to exist in multiple-narrator novels. Iser offers a more complete account of how the centrifugal potential of a multiple-narrator novel can be countered. Padgett Powell's analysis of *A Virtuous Woman* in the *New York Times Book Review* is pertinent at this point because of his observation about the separation by time and death of the voices: "There is considerable risk in separating these two voices by time and death, for the alternating monologues are sufficiently out of phase that their constructive union is the work of the reader . . ." (12). My argument about this novel, which Iser's model helps articulate, is that a willing and non-resisting reader will gladly create the dialogue between the voices that confers order upon this seemingly fragmented narrative. Such active work on the part of the reader is in the service of exploring the inter-monologue dialogicity

that Bakhtin implies would exist in a multiple-narrator novel. A reader enters into a "dyadic interaction" (*Act,* 66) with the elements of the text, where the text is seen as consisting of "instructions for the production of the signified" (*Act,* 65). Meaning for Iser is "text guided, but reader produced" ("Interview," 71). If intra-monologue dialogicity is merely uncovered through careful scrutiny of a reader (such as Bakhtin analyzing passages in Dostoevsky), inter-monologue dialogicity exists only in the mind of the reader, with the reader functioning as the very site of the dialogicity.

What all this amounts to with most multiple-narrator novels is the Iserian reader's embarking upon the relativizing task suggested by Bakhtin's cryptic assertion in "The Problem of the Text" that "[a]ny live, competent, and dispassionate observation from any position, from any viewpoint, always retains its value and its meaning . . . [because] [t]he one-sided and limited nature of a viewpoint . . . can always be corrected, augmented, transformed . . . with the help of like observations from others' viewpoints" (124): the balancing of one perspective against another in many multiple-narrator novels is through the active involvement of the reader. In *A Virtuous Woman,* what the active reader attempting to get the monologues to enter into a dialogue with each other does—to his or her surprise, perhaps—is not balance one report with the conflicting information of another account; rather, s/he establishes the very agreement of the monologists through entering the *Unbestimmtheitsstellen,* or gaps, between the monologues and actively juxtaposing one account against another where they converge. The reader of Gibbons's novel is not pressed into service to relativize the narrative through careful juxtapositions and comparisons of accounts as the reader looks backwards and forwards at each moment of the reading process. Instead, the reader is pressed into service to establish the similarity between monologists, as we saw with our earlier analysis of Jack and Ruby's meeting under the tree. That example is especially noteworthy because the two accounts of the incident are not juxtaposed through contiguous placement of monologues: the reader must actively look backwards from Ruby's account to link it up with Jack's account a few monologues earlier. The theme horizon or foreground/background *Gestalten,* then, of *A Virtuous Woman*—the structures that a reader creates, in Iser's scheme, through juxtaposition of passages—consist of the reader's actively yoking together separate moments. But instead of a gestalt defined by difference, the gestalt is one of similarity. Perhaps an image consisting of tuning forks can explain what occurs in Gibbons's novel: what the Iserian reader does with a text like *A Virtuous Woman* is bring together accounts spanning monologues and speakers so that they resonate just as two tuning forks can resonate with each other if one is made to sound and is brought close enough to the other.

Iser's phenomenologically rigorous model of the reading process is thus custom made to help us articulate the nature and mechanism of the intermonologue dialogicity of

A Virtuous Woman, as well as other multiple-narrator novels. The reader responds to the gaps, or conceptual spaces, between monologues to effect the links between narrative installments—the links in Gibbons's novel being essentially links of agreement suggesting that an unusual degree of harmony existed between Jack and Ruby. This meaning of the text is thus produced by the reader, responding to and governed by the prompts of the text. Iser would not allow for free-association or the free play of the reader's subjective predispositions: the inter-monologue dialogicity perceived and effected by the reader as the site of that dialogicity must lend itself to "intersubjective analysis" (*Act,* 49–50).

Another way Iser's theory helps uncover and explain inter-monologue dialogicity, or what Bakhtin calls "[d]ialogical relations among utterances" ("Problem," 114), in *A Virtuous Woman* has to do with feedback loops. Part of his theory of the reading process consists of the proposition that a reader makes provisional judgments as the text is encountered that will be modified as the reader encounters new information. The unit defined by Chapters 13 and 14 of Gibbons's novel provides us with an opportunity to demonstrate the usefulness of this subtlety of Iser's theory. Chapter 13 opens with Jack describing how Ruby's death has affected him:

> I'm sick of being by myself, sick of myself, sick all the way around of looking around and not seeing a damn thing but the four walls and my old ugly self looking back out of dirty, smeared up mirrors. Ruby'd be ashamed. This place looks like the pigs slept in it, and I walk around all day looking like the witches rode me all night, raggedy, messy. I know it but I haven't been able to do anything about it. You just can't expect a man to take and do without a woman when he's done with one long as I did.
>
> (125)

While the description that follows of the pathetically ineffectual would-be maid, Mavis Washington, is humorous, we are nevertheless left with a sense of disgust, especially when Jack says at the end of this monologue: "Isn't it every man's dream that when his wife dies he has somebody to step in and do for him?" (139). We have to wonder at this point in the novel if the narrative isn't arguing against Jack because he seems only concerned about the loss of a housekeeper in Ruby.

When we encounter Chapter 14, however, our harsh assessment of Jack is modified by the way this monologue reminds us that Ruby had her own needs fulfilled through Jack. She says, "I did want somebody to take care of me. I needed it. And when I felt all that goodness coming from Jack, it didn't matter what the person looked like that sent it out to me. Maybe I did want a daddy, but that's okay, too" (143). Ruby tells us that her family's maid was perceptive when she declared, after hearing that Ruby married a man twenty years her senior: "Shame the law don't allow Miss Ruby to marry her daddy. All she wanting is to marry her daddy" (143). What she says here makes us re-

call Jack's reporting that "(a)ll she said was she wanted somebody to take care of her, and if I promised to, she'd marry me. I said then, I say now, 'That's the best thing in the world for me, for the both of us, best thing for anybody to do for somebody'" (46). It is as if the narrative were playing games with us here, tempting us into dismissing Jack as a selfish, insensitive man who only needed a wife to take care of him, but then rescuing him from dismissal by reminding us with the next monologue that Ruby got something out of the deal, too. The fact that Gibbons departs from the chronological pattern established throughout the novel in bringing Ruby back from the dead, so to speak (in Chapter 14), makes this strategy more transparent. Thus, an interesting kind of inter-monologue dialogicity is established through the active role of the reader who pairs up the two monologues. The result of our momentarily harsh judgment of Jack in Chapter 13 and our revised, more tolerant judgment after Chapter 14 is that our tolerance of him is surer because it has been challenged but reaffirmed. Being told by a conventional omniscient third-person narrative voice that Jack and Ruby each got something out of the relationship would have a radically different effect because it would not require as active an engagement from the reader.

The final aspect of *A Virtuous Woman* I'd like to discuss in the context of a Bakhtinian/Iserian analysis is its concluding chapter. Gibbons's novel stands out in the context of other multiple-narrator narratives for the fact that it ends with a section narrated from an omniscient third-person perspective, bringing to a close the rhythm between voices that has defined the novel up to this point. The opening paragraph of Chapter 16 is remarkable for the complete abandonment it signals of the multiple first-person mode. It presents and comments on Jack's struggle to adjust to Ruby's death, and his hoping her spirit would visit him at night. Because of the significance of this strategy in the context of other recent American multiple-narrator novels, I will present the opening paragraph in full.

> For every minute Jack slept that night he was awake for two. Every branch scraping the roof was Ruby descending, every dog scrambling underneath the porch was Ruby rising. Only when he woke up at daylight and released himself from his damp, tangled sheets did he realize that his own body had fooled his heart the night before, just as trees and dogs had caused him to lie and wait. And sleeping and awake he had dreamt of Ruby. He needed relief from his night, but holding her pillow and crying as he'd done other nights would not help him. His frustration and anger had rooted in and taken hold well below the place where tears start, and so would not be washed up nor out by them. His pain was the sort that burrows in and tortures until the source of the struggle is understood, reconciled, and removed.
>
> (151–152)

This is in the best 19th-century omniscient mode, where the narrative freely comments on and analyzes characters. The last two sentences are especially noteworthy for the subtle psychologizing they attempt. For the first time in this novel, we are offered "objective" commentary that sums up in an interpretive fashion what we have seen in Jack from his own perspective.

Not only does the final chapter comment on Jack, it also presents the perspectives of Burr and his daughter June through italicized interior monologues. (Jack is also allowed to speak in interior monologues.) We thus get a variety of outside voices in this final chapter, in addition to the third-person narrative in which they are embedded, which provides us with additional perspectives on Jack and Ruby.

The chapter ends with an interior monologue showing Jack's thoughts. It concludes with, "And now, let me try to live" (165). This confers significant closure on the narrative because of its attempt to suggest everything would be fine, especially with Jack's receiving some land from Burr. Jack's struggle to adjust to Ruby's death is effectively over. The novel thus ends on an optimistic note.

My reaction to this final chapter is entirely negative, and while I usually focus on what *is* accomplished with any particular narrative strategy, I cannot resist commenting on what is sacrificed through this concluding chapter. The falling off is especially apparent when *A Virtuous Woman* is read in the context of other multiple-narrator novels. I believe the final sentence compromises the novel because, in Bakhtinian terms, it is a betrayal of the openendedness and "unfinalizability" that the multiple first-person mode allows for so well. It is also an artificially imposed order: after we see Jack distraught, the resolution to carry on is too facilely asserted. As for incorporating the additional voices of Burr and June and opening with a full-blown omniscient narrative voice, we do not need the additional perspectives offered by the omniscient voice and the voices of Burr and June. What we learn from Burr and June doesn't really amount to much, anyway. The entire chapter represents an abdication of the commitment to a rhythm established by the voices of Jack and Ruby, dialogized by the reader. This chapter seems to come out of a nostalgia for an orderly narrative conclusion that artificially ties up the loose ends. I wonder if Gibbons didn't originally end with Jack in the previous chapter (which would have framed the narrative nicely), only to have been told by an editor that she couldn't leave her readers dangling with an ending that did not resolve things. But ending with Jack in Chapter 15, preparing for another visitation of his wife's spirit by washing the sheets and sprinkling them with her favorite powder, would have been perfect: it would allow the novel to end on a convincing and authentic note of imbalance, entirely consistent with what the loss of Ruby means to Jack. *A Virtuous Woman* would make an even more remarkable contribution to the array of contemporary multiple-narrator novels by ending with the final paragraph of its penultimate chapter, where we find Jack trying to "woo" (147) Ruby's spirit into visiting him:

> And I'll tell you, having your dead wife haint you [during the night] can really tip your day off to a fine start.

> Outside I've got the sheets flapping in the wind, I had the coffee turn out this morning, and I got a free sample of gargle in the mailbox. I think about all I've got left to do is fix up for her and say, "Ruby Pitt Woodrow Stokes! Come on down!"

> (149)

* * *

Writing about *A Virtuous Woman* in the *Women's Review of Books,* Marilyn Chandler, titling her piece "Limited Partnership," asserts that Jack and Ruby's marriage was a "sturdy but unfilling compromise reached through a tacit negotiation over the terms of each other's needs." As she reads the novel, the marriage is more about "survival" than "satisfaction" (21). My sense of this book is very different: although I would not exactly call it an "ode to joy," as one of the novel's advertising blurbs puts it (inside the front cover), I do experience it as a tribute to the understanding and togetherness that is possible between two human beings—even if, as the back cover announces, Jack and Ruby "didn't fall in love so much as they simply found each other and held on for dear life." This special bond between Jack and Ruby is epitomized by the passage in which Jack describes the time Ruby asked him, without offering an explanation, "to hold her real tight from the back" and then cried for a long time:

> I knew Ruby. I knew she was crying for babies she wished had been born to us, ones I couldn't give her. And as ignorant a man as I am, I knew what I was hearing. I knew the sound of Ruby crying for babies the way I know a robin's call, the same way I know the sparrow's.

> (103)

Gibbons makes the novel's tribute to the bond between Jack and Ruby more palpable by not making her portrait of this couple overly idealized. Instead, she grounds it in concrete and sometimes unattractive particulars (which the book's epigraph from Proverbs helps us realize).

One might wonder why Gibbons uses the multiple-narrator mode if she wants to insist on and pay tribute to the togetherness of Jack and Ruby, since the multiple-narrator novel is usually used to exploit the opportunity to suggest a relativized and subjective epistemology. By employing a narrative mode that tempts us to look for difference and disagreement, we are the more impressed with and moved by the agreement we discover between Jack and Ruby. Using a narratological model that consists of a Bakhtin/Iser pairing allows us to raise questions about such a narrative that contributes to a definition and appreciation of the unusual degree of togetherness portrayed by the novel: Bakhtin's theory of novelness helps us raise questions about such a narrative's multi-perspectival nature and the consequences of it; and Iser's phenomenological theory of the reading process helps articulate how intermonologue dialogicity can be said to exist in such a narrative with the help—and through the agency—of the reader.

Notes

1. Marilyn Chandler fails to appreciate the highly oral quality to the first-person narration by referring to the chapters as "interior monologues" (21).

2. The difficulty of reading this novel created by the highly unusual strategy of having Jack and Ruby speak from different points in time is suggested by the fact that a reviewer can erroneously write, "In alternating interior monologues, Jack and Ruby remember and reflect upon their past *in the weeks of Ruby's dying*" (Chandler, 21; emphasis added).

3. A similar rhythmical phenomenon can be said to exist in Erdrich's *Tracks,* where the regular alternation between the refreshing normalcy of Nanapush and the discomforting disturbance of Pauline defines the central dynamic of that novel, conferring a kind of order upon the potentially centrifugal narrative. *A Virtuous Woman,* however, while setting up a rhythm through the difference between two voices, does not play upon our emotions as much as *Tracks* does: we are not confronted with the same extremes in Gibbons's novel with which Erdrich's novel confronts us.

4. There are a few moments in this novel where Gibbons seems to play with the possibilities of enriching a speaker's utterance and the quality of the consciousness portrayed through having that speaker imagine and respond to criticism. The first example occurs in the monologue where Jack is describing his need for a woman twenty years his junior. In this passage, he imagines a disapproving reaction from his audience:

> Think what you will! Shock, shock! I don't give a damn. If I gave a damn, I would've kept it to myself. I had to do what I had to do. See, a man like me does what he needs to do more often than he wants to, and I saw Ruby and I had to have her, needed her. She was the most gorgeous thing I'd ever seen in my life, sitting under Lonnie Hoover's big pecan tree that morning like a prize, and the thought of me going long as I had without one made me think, started me to think that I might could try for this girl. [. . .]
>
> She wasn't but twenty then, and me forty, and it was almost five months from the day I met her that I married her. I know what it sounds like, like a old lecher got him a child-bride when her first husband wasn't even cold yet. Go ahead and think it. It just shows how much you don't know me, or Ruby.

(20–21)

The second example comes from a monologue by Ruby in which she is describing the hell she went through with Woodrow: "Somebody could say, 'If she loved her family so much, why didn't she run away and call someone to come get her?' I thought

about it a hundred times a day, believe you me" (37). She then explains why that was not possible.

These two examples are the only passages in the novel where Gibbons attempts something approaching intra-monologue dialogicity, though the anticipation is of responses from the reader, not another character. Given the paucity of such examples in recent American multiple-narrator novels, the fact that Gibbons gives us two examples of it is very significant, even if she does not fully exploit in her novel the opportunity for enriching a monologue by having speakers anticipate responses from listeners or actively imagine and respond to the perspective of another speaker in the novel.

Works Cited

Bakhtin, Mikhail. *The Dialogic Imagination.* Ed. Michael Holquist. Trans. Caryl Emerson and Michael Holquist. Austin: University of Texas Press, 1981.

———. "The Problem of the Text in Linguistics, Philosophy, and the Human Sciences: An Experiment in Philosophical Analysis." Bakhtin, *Speech Genres,* 103–131.

———. *Problems of Dostoevsky's Poetics.* Trans. Caryl Emerson. Minneapolis: University of Minnesota Press, 1984.

———. *Speech Genres and Other Late Essays.* Trans. Vern McGee. Austin: University of Texas Press, 1986.

Chandler, Marilyn. "Limited Partnership." *Women's Review of Books,* July, 1989: 21.

Gibbons, Kaye. *A Virtuous Woman.* New York: Random House, 1989.

Iser, Wolfgang. *The Act of Reading: A Theory of Aesthetic Response.* Baltimore: Johns Hopkins University Press, 1978.

———. "Interview: Wolfgang Iser." *Diacritics* 10 (1980): 57–74.

Powell, Padgett. "As Ruby Lay Dying." *New York Times Book Review,* April 30, 1989: 12.

Towers, Robert. "Roughing It." *The New York Review of Books,* November 19, 1988: 40–41.

Julian Mason (essay date 1993)

SOURCE: "Kaye Gibbons (1960-)," in *Contemporary Fiction Writers of the South,* edited by Joseph M. Flora and Robert Bain, Greenwood Press, 1993, pp. 156-68.

[*In the following essay, Mason provides an overview of Gibbons's life and career.*]

Kaye Gibbons has now published two more novels since she burst upon the public's awareness with her 1987 novel, ***Ellen Foster,*** to acclaim and awards. She has shown herself to be a skillful, imaginative, sensitive, and interesting novelist, who has taken the perseverance of the human spirit and Nash County, North Carolina, where she grew up, for her continuing literary domain, as she explores its people, ways, and past. Her work is bold and experimental, but easily accessible, winning for her a large body of readers. She is young, but already established, and not breaking stride as she continues to produce challenging and satisfying fiction at a steady pace.

BIOGRAPHY

The daughter of a tobacco farmer, Charles Batts, and his wife, Alice, who lived in the rural Nash County community of Bend of the River (near the Tar River), about seven miles south of Rocky Mount, North Carolina, Kaye Batts was born on May 5, 1960, in a hospital in Wilson, North Carolina. She has a brother 13 years older than she, and a sister 9 years older. They are related to Nathaniel Batts, the first-known permanent white settler in North Carolina, who built a home in coastal North Carolina in 1655. She grew up on the family's farm in Nash County, which is in the upper center of the coastal plain of eastern North Carolina, experiencing the agricultural seasons and hot summers and being relatively poor.

Gibbons greatly admired her mother, who was called Shine and who provided order and stability through perseverance and hard work. After her mother killed herself at age 47 with an overdose of pills in March 1970, Gibbons stayed on with her father until she went to live with her mother's sister near Bailey, North Carolina, in 1971. This was not a satisfactory arrangement, and after Gibbons' alcoholic father died in May 1972 she moved to a foster home, also near Bailey, which she had chosen partly on the basis of observing at church the woman whose home it was. During 1972–73 she also had extended visits with various other relatives. In June 1973 her brother married, and she moved into his home in Rocky Mount and benefited from the interest in her shown by his wife. She lived there until she entered North Carolina State University, in Raleigh, in fall 1978, having graduated from Rocky Mount High School.

While growing up, Gibbons had watched television and read as much as possible, early becoming fascinated with both oral and written language and what could be done with it. In the fourth grade she discovered both the fiction and poetry of Poe, and later Shakespeare's sonnets and the works of numerous other writers. At one stage she wanted to be a lab technician, then later a lawyer; and she became more and more interested in the world beyond her immediate environs, and in reading. She also began writing and publishing poetry. She loved school and the discipline, order, stimulation, and opportunities for learning that it provided. In the rather chaotic year after her mother's death, school kept her going. In high school she was somewhat bookish and an outsider, though she also participated in some extracurricular activities. She went to North Carolina State University with a scholarship from the Veterans Administration, and she also worked at the university library. At the university she decided to major in political science, then switched to history, and finally to English, because in it more writing and analyzing of writing were required.

In the summer before she transferred to the University of North Carolina at Chapel Hill in fall 1980, Gibbons had manic-depressive problems, and in August 1981 she entered a hospital in Raleigh, staying there till March 1982, meanwhile again attending classes at North Carolina State. In 1983 she had another attack and remained out of school for some time. During this period she worked at various jobs, including as a waitress and in a bookstore. In 1984 she met Michael Gibbons, 12 years her senior, originally from Queens, New York, then a graduate student in landscape architecture at North Carolina State; and on May 12, 1984, they were married. They have three daughters— Mary (1984), Leslie (1987), and Louise (1989).

In summer 1985 she returned to classes at Chapel Hill, and in the fall she enrolled in Louis Rubin's course in Southern literature. During the course, in Rubin's lectures and in the writings of James Weldon Johnson, Mark Twain, and others, she encountered various emphases on the use of and validity for everyday speech in literature and on the relationships of language and place. Also, a voice came to her which led to her writing the poem **"June Bug,"** which was eventually published in the *Carolina Quarterly,* but more immediately was the stimulus for the thirty pages of fiction she began in November 1985 and showed to Rubin. He recognized her talent and at the end of November encouraged her to finish the work. In early January, Rubin had her first novel, *Ellen Foster* (1987). With little revision, it was published by Algonquin Books of Chapel Hill. Then, in 1986, while Gibbons was taking a seminar in the Southern novel with Rubin, she wrote an essay on the Miranda stories of Katherine Anne Porter; it was soon published in the *Kenyon Review.*

Her second novel went through four drafts, the first of which was poor, but which yielded the principal male character for the final version, published by Algonquin as *A Virtuous Woman* (1989). For each of the first two novels her imagination had depended primarily on her memories and experiences and on those of her family. The third novel, *A Cure for Dreams,* which went through four drafts before being published by Algonquin (1991), required a good bit of research, the results of which were blended with memories or what Gibbons had heard from relatives and others, as the novel deals with decades before she was born.

In the early stages of work on it she had read *Such as Us: Southern Voices of the Thirties* (edited by Tom Terrill and Jerrold Hirsch, University of North Carolina Press, 1978), based on oral histories collected by the Federal Writers' Project under the direction of W. T. Couch. This led her to the hundreds of such personal histories transcribed by the project from interviews and available at the university library in Chapel Hill. Gibbons read these extensively, gathering not so much characters or actions but mostly metaphors, terms, language patterns, customs, and general ambience. She was impressed with the respect that the project's interviewers had for their subjects, how they helped the person's own voice come through. She also read printed collections of North Carolina folklore. However, while she used in the novel much that she found in her reading, if she needed a term that she did not have, she sometimes made up one of the same type as those she had encountered.

Gibbons' first two novels had been composed on a typewriter. For the third she used a computer. Although she had a study at the North Carolina State University library during 1989 and 1990, as its first (and then reappointed) Writer of the Year, most of her writing is done at home, often at night, sometimes in the wee hours of the morning. This schedule helps keep her close to her children, who also are a high priority for her. The obligation has become more important following her recent divorce.

Although she does not plan to read, Gibbons has been a success on the reading circuit, and she makes appearances on radio and television. In October 1989 she shared the platform with Eudora Welty as the two invited speakers to inaugurate the annual Eudora Welty Writers' Symposium as part of the activities for the inauguration of the first woman president of Welty's alma mater, Mississippi University for Women. Gibbons spoke on the influence of Welty in her finding her own self as a writer. Gibbons also occasionally writes book reviews for the *New York Times Book Review* and other periodicals.

Gibbons cherishes the order and stability that her children and her writing provide. She has said that only after writing ***Ellen Foster*** could she really be herself and feel good about that. In ***How I Became a Writer*** she wrote:

> My mother's death both freed me and marked me. . . .
> If she was still living, I would still be bound to my old home, and I know I would not have turned to literature and used it as I have.
>
> (5)

> I write novels to set order to what memories my mind has allowed me and to create something of lasting value in all those gaps I seem to have.
>
> (4)

> My life changed with the marriage and the birth [of my daughter], and the memory of my mother escorted me through the transition from a girl who loved literature better than her life to a woman who overcame her past and got at the business of living.
>
> (5)

As she said to one interviewer: "Between good genes and a harsh environment, I think I turned out OK"; and so have her books, the first two already having sold over 25,000 copies each in hardback and over 40,000 each in paperback.

MAJOR THEMES

Most of the themes that one finds in Gibbons' works fit well what in other contexts she has said are her primary beliefs and concerns as a writer and as a person. She has definite ideas about what she believes she should try to do as a writer, what her concerns are, and how she hopes to present them to the reader. She writes about the "commonplace" things of the everyday lives of her characters in order to show the tensions, passions, opportunities, and effects on the human spirit of this aspect of living (as opposed to, but related to, the larger, more dramatic occurrences), both on the surface and below it. This larger aspect of the experiences of most people also has important value for understanding a character and what that character is, thinks, and does. One reviewer wrote that Gibbons "recounts mundane details of everyday life in such a compelling and innovative way that we are left both stunned and wiser." She wants the reader to listen to and look at closely this particular richness and how it can lead to art and to fulfilling life, even in its many disguises.

Gibbons emphasizes the quiet, strong heroism of survivors, especially women, who persevere to bring order and peace out of chaos, good and joy out of difficulty, getting through the day, the years, a life, and making the best one can of it all, in spite of mistakes, catastrophes, misunderstandings, threats, injury, inadequate resources, sorrow, grief, disappointment, pain, death, disillusionment, and weariness. She finds hope in the strong, self-reliant individual coping with the quiet dramas and firm challenges of every day's journey and what that requires not only to survive but also to triumph, at least to the point of having inner peace, or even joy in the soul, from taking hold and doing what needs to be done, from bouncing back and going on. In this hope she reflects various aspects of her own experience and the admiration she has for her mother, and the epigraphs for her novels come from Emerson, the Bible, and a statement of belief in the validity of each person's own experience and voice.

She wants her characters to speak to us directly, for themselves, in truth and honesty, about life without illusions. Not only are her principal characters well drawn and memorable, but many of her lesser ones are vividly and well drawn, too, though they tend to pale in the shadows of her dominant first-person central characters. She explores experience in relation to family, in relation to interactions between people who should be close because of birth or because of choice, as through such relationships they try to effect order, stability, happiness, love, and validity for themselves and their existence. Gibbons explores the difficulty of knowing and shaping the self, particularly in relation to others and to one's past, both personal and collective. In doing this, she helps us see the universal in the particular and the magic amidst the mundane.

Gibbons finds it most pertinent to focus her concerns and interests through women characters and to explore the "phenomenon of being female" and the burdens of women, particularly as wives and mothers, and especially among less affluent women in the South. In doing this she has made good use of her memories of her own experiences and those of her family, as she attempts to give them order and meaning, to understand, control, shape, and accept.

She has written in *How I Became a Writer*: "So I believe that it is under the incredible burden of memory that I write, and I cannot trade my memory, as much as I've often wanted to do so. My past is what it is. All that memory will allow me or any other writer to do is order it through language" (5).

With each of her three novels she has gone further back in time for settings, characters, and other material—into her own past and into the past that impinges on her past. Though the format differs, each book quickly establishes a chronological and developmental position at which the central characters have arrived and then, retrospectively and with a first-person point of view, explores how they arrived at that point, with almost no concern in the particular novel for what might come later than, or because of, its beginning point. It is likely that through research and her imagination she will continue to explore further and further back. In this regard, her fourth novel will really be part two of *A Cure for Dreams,* bringing that focus even further toward our time. One result of this movement back into the past is a lessening of intensity with each novel, resulting in more clarity and in changes of format and tone as she is forced into even more distance from her material than she has cultivated in her earlier work. Also, with each book she covers more time, as she continues to develop her portrayal of interactions between the old South and the more modern South and their ways and traditions.

Students of Southern writing often point to concerns with place (and land), family (and history), and religion (and sin and guilt) as primary themes or concerns in the body of Southern literature. Gibbons does little with the last, but she certainly emphasizes the other two. With each novel she has become more specific about both time and place as her literary imagination has been accepted and praised and as she has become more comfortable with being a writer and with using material from the locale she came from. Also, books that cover more time require more specificity, for both writer and reader. Most reviewers understood her first two novels to be set in the South, and North Carolina reviewers understood them to be in set in North Carolina; but others mistakenly have written of her settings as "deep South," "backwoods," or even Georgia, which is not as likely to happen again.

She has pointed out that all three novels are set in the same "landscape," and some readers have noticed that some of the characters and places in one novel appear also elsewhere in her fiction, though we see them somewhat differently in each novel or story because of time differences, narrator differences, familial and geographical angle differences in focusing and vantage points, and different emphases—as in the works of William Faulkner, Wendell Berry, and others who write extensively about one particular locale.

One reviewer has suggested that Gibbons intends a series of interlocking novels. Certainly she is mining the rich artistic possibilities of human experience (history, mores, and language) in the rural Nash County, North Carolina, area in which she was raised and near which she lived even after moving into town; and she has found it a fertile and worthy locale for her explorations, which helps with the reality of her details (that ring true to one who knows that area). However, in much less-effective, less-important, and less-developed uses, she does deal briefly with western and coastal North Carolina in *A Virtuous Woman,* and with Kentucky and Ireland in *A Cure for Dreams.* She has said that in each of her novels she hopes to convey an accurate impression of a place and time and a respect for their traditions.

Language and voice are important components of Gibbons' art—important to her realistic intentions and her faithfulness to time and place, and important to the effectiveness and success of what she is trying to accomplish in the reader's experience. She wants the reader to sense the worth and uniqueness of the character through that person's distinctive voice, usually as she or he speaks directly to the reader, thus better enabling sharing of feeling. Like James Weldon Johnson, she has chosen to avoid dialect, but to strive for an awareness of idiom characteristic of and appropriate for that particular individual and time and place. This depends more on metaphors, word choice, and syntax than on pronunciation and grammar.

Some of her characters are not formally well educated, but are intelligent, highly aware of their world, and often wise; they are not caricatures, nor condescended to, but are presented with respect. She begins her conceptualization of a work with character and voice, not with plot or abstract ideas. She strives for a direct, concrete experience—not of exaggerated local color, but of regional realism and the universal therein. Through a focus on the area she knows best, she wants to emphasize for the reader not oddities or peculiarities or differences, but universal and eternal verities and some sense of their flavor in that time and place. She uses rural anecdotes and sayings because her characters would use them, to help them understand, control, and go on as these are adapted and applied to current circumstances. They are not clichés, but pregnant and versatile significations from a body of wise tradition and custom, which she respects, parts of a commonly held and available rich treasure trove of shared community experience. One reviewer wrote that she "makes the colloquial compelling." In her writing, interior experience is more important than surface experience, and language is the important interpretive mechanism for bringing that to the reader, even concerning memories of surface experience.

Gibbons has shown herself to be unafraid of writing from inside characters of various ages, complexities, and backgrounds, male or female, and in varied circumstances and times, many of which she herself has not experienced— and in doing so well and interestingly, and with verisimilitude, insight, and understanding. She is good at using contrast, humor (which she feels is essential), and folk and popular culture, without their being inappropriately intrusive. Each of her novels has been less directly autobiographical than the one before it, and structurally more complex (though quite different in tone) as she has continued to adapt and experiment with a first-person point of view and layerings of structure in her attempt for directness of experience for the reader and the fullness of awareness that comes from multiple focuses and the depth, irony, perspective, counterpoint, and understanding made possible therein—which is how we know and experience life ourselves, not primarily in a linear way.

In *Ellen Foster* she shifts back and forth between past and present as Ellen speaks to us, using her good present to intersperse assurance, and also to provide relief from her persistently bad past, for author, character, and reader. In *A Virtuous Woman* she uses disjointed time as Jack speaks to us of his wife, Ruby, who is already dead, and in alternating chapters, as she approaches death, Ruby speaks to us of Jack. In *A Cure for Dreams,* the layering is more complex but not more difficult, even if one does experience less directness of speech because of the form and tone of the book. In it Gibbons has a contemporary (1989) woman briefly introduce and close the book, in between letting that woman's recently dead mother (1920–89) speak to us directly about her own self and even more so about her own mother (who in italics occasionally speaks for herself) and about her own grandmother and the impact of both of them on her, up to the 1942 birth of the introducer. (*Ellen Foster* had covered only a little over a year, focusing primarily on one character, and *A Virtuous Woman* over two and one-half decades, focusing primarily on two characters.)

Such forms require an alert and attentive reader, whose experience is enriched by them. Gibbons has not found the short story to be her genre, saying that she has good ideas for short stories but doesn't find it easy to develop them for that form. The short stories she has published are clearly inferior to her novels and were produced under pressure to do so, the one in *The Quarterly* a rearranged extracting from *Ellen Foster* and the other, **"The Headache,"** a more interesting but flat and somewhat inept story also set in Nash County.

Gibbons is serious about both the art and the craft of writing, though in *How I Became a Writer* she wrote: "I've never believed anyone can will the mind to create a thing of beauty. I like to think artistic creation starts in a more mysterious place, somewhere deep within, probably somewhere way far back in one's past" (5). In addition to writing fiction, she enjoys reading widely and analyzing and writing about literature. This is evident in her book reviews and in her essay on Katherine Anne Porter's Miranda stories (where she finds purpose in fiction in some ways not unlike her own purpose). She respects and enjoys, and has been influenced by, a variety of literature from across the ages, from Geoffrey Chaucer to Flannery O'Connor, William Faulkner, and Eudora Welty. Clearly, as a writer she also has been influenced by the teaching and editorial advice and encouragement of Louis Rubin; and she plans

to follow Welty's example and remain with the South as both residence and primary subject.

She is not a writer who writes according to a rigid daily schedule; she does not force her writing. She writes first for herself and is not very self-conscious or audience-conscious while doing so. She writes with great economy and efficiency of style and with control of her material and no wasting of words, which results in novels that are not long, but are compact, yet fully realized; as one reviewer said, they are "all a novel should be and more than most ever are," and as another put it, they are "stunning in their power and grace." This economy of literary means is not a result of her having little to say, but of her having so much to say and with such belief and purpose that she does not wish to lead herself or the reader away from the book's main thrust in any way, resulting in significant accomplishment and no wasted effort for writer or reader, which is but one sign of her well-focused skill.

SURVEY OF CRITICISM

One of the obvious indications of how Gibbons' novels have been received is the awards and editions they have produced. For *Ellen Foster* she received the Sue Kaufman Prize for First Fiction from the American Academy and Institute of Arts and Letters. (The Academy's literary awards committee included Irving Howe, Donald Barthelme, James Dickey, Allen Ginsberg, Anthony Hecht, Elizabeth Spencer, and Anne Tyler.) *Ellen Foster* also received a special citation from the Ernest Hemingway Foundation, and was chosen by the American Library Association as one of the Best Books for Young Adults in 1987. In 1988 *Ellen Foster* was fifth on France's best-seller list, and in 1989 *A Virtuous Woman* led the *Atlanta Journal and Constitution*'s list of best-sellers in the Southeast. That same year Gibbons received from the National Endowment for the Arts a fellowship to aid her in writing a third novel, and for that work-in-progress she received in 1990 the first PEN/Revson Foundation Fiction Fellowship for a writer 35 years old or younger.

The paperback editions of the first two novels are in Random House's Vintage Contemporaries series (for *Ellen Foster* Random House outbid Dell, Viking Penguin, and Washington Square), and Paramount optioned the movie rights for *Ellen Foster.* Editions of both of the first two novels appeared in England, France, Germany, Italy, Spain, and Sweden. *A Virtuous Woman* also was published in Denmark. Both of them were both reviewed and discussed with her widely in the United States and abroad, mostly enthusiastically and favorably, in newspapers and magazines and on radio and television, and led to various interviews in both print and nonprint media. (Anyone using the interviews should consult a chronological spread of them because of how her responses to some things changed over time.)

Many reviewers immediately compared 11-year-old Ellen Foster with some other child of fiction, usually also an orphan, created by a well-known writer—for example, Twain's Huck Finn, Cinderella, Charles Dickens' Oliver Twist or David Copperfield, or J. D. Salinger's Holden Caulfield. That this occurred so often might be seen as demeaning; but upon reading the full reviews, one realizes that this impulse was the result not of a sense of imitation on her part nor even of influence on her, but rather a recognition of Ellen's uniqueness and the book's quality, which let Gibbons seem deserving of consideration alongside such literary predecessors. Most reviewers emphasized Ellen's pluck, perseverance in the face of great and various difficulties, endearing straightforwardness, boldness, wit, spontaneity, resilience, practicality, wisdom, and tough stoicism, along with her coming to grips with friendship with her young black friend, Starletta, and the search for love and familial stability. Generally they found Ellen's voice (the matrix of this first-person narrative) to be matter-of-fact, detached, clear, simple, honest, controlled by the author, convincingly that of a child (even when talking of death, murder, eternity, race, etc.), and, while of course limited in its information, reliable. Unfortunately, several reviewers misinterpreted Ellen's use of "old" when speaking of herself and thought it referred to either or both chronological or experiential age instead of understanding Gibbons' intended use of it as a Southern term of acceptance and endearment (as in: "I like old John there").

A number of reviewers mentioned how close *Ellen Foster* comes to melodrama, yet avoids it by focusing not so much on Ellen's multitude of difficulties themselves, but on her resourcefulness and her belief in herself as she deals with these difficulties. They found the result of Ellen's voice and its speaking directly to us, and of Gibbons' focusing, to be a book not sentimental, but human, humorous, and compassionate, with a believable survivor as its heroine. A number mentioned not only the skill of the characterization in the book, but also how this is enhanced by the book's moving back and forth between Ellen's past and present experience, giving the reader a meaningful counterpoint of awareness and perspective, and greatly assisting the possibility for humor even when things are quite grim and desperate—which is often. A few reviewers who also interviewed Gibbons began to see some parallel between her book and her own life, but they did not explore it very far and usually did not deal with it in their reviews, leaving it to comments within the published interviews.

Even before *Ellen Foster* was published, there was remarkable praise for it, which Algonquin understandably used in its publicity, advertising, and dust jacket for the book. Eudora Welty wrote: "What a marvelous writer she seems to be on almost every page. . . . A stunning new writer. . . . The life in it, the honesty of thought and eye and feeling and word!" Walker Percy wrote: "It's the real thing. Which is to say: a lovely, breathtaking, sometimes heart-wrenching first novel." Alfred Kazin wrote: "A captivating, often hilarious mix of Victorian fairy tale and fresh American lingo . . . [with] the wickedest relatives in literature since *King Lear* . . . in a style primitive, saucy,

and exhilarating." Elizabeth Spencer wrote: "Original, compelling, and frighteningly real, the voice of Ellen Foster makes the reader know her story in her own terms. I was absorbed and moved. Kaye Gibbons is a new writer of great force. She knows how to speak to our hearts." Most reviewers agreed that the author of *Ellen Foster* was one to watch, and in his review Jonathan Yardley wrote: "a work of considerable subtlety and intellectual sophistication. . . . a sly, funny book about a sly, funny girl. . . . Yet it is a mark of Kaye Gibbons' accomplishment that in no way is Ellen a moral or intellectual prodigy; she is simply a good little girl who makes her way out of trouble through the stubborn belief that life can be better than what it's been for her thus far. She is a terrific kid, and *Ellen Foster* is a terrific book."

When Gibbons' second novel appeared, readers and reviewers were wondering if she had been able to sustain the level of accomplishment that had been so widely praised for *Ellen Foster.* Though *A Virtuous Woman* is in a number of ways quite different from *Ellen Foster,* most who reviewed it believed that she had produced another successful work and a worthy follower of her first book. The approaches of the reviewers of this second novel seem, however, more varied. Padgett Powell wrote of it in comparison and contrast with Faulkner's *As I Lay Dying* and *The Wild Palms,* emphasizing how "banged up" its characters are, calling it a complex novel, and emphasizing its structure and "balances and counterbalances, symmetries and their neat absence that shore up the book, creating a sturdier vessel. . . . there is also some 'moral structure.'" He concluded that the novel is worthy of its interesting characters and its dangerous but somewhat ingenious alternation of first-person point of view chapters, with Ruby talking to us as she approaches death and Jack talking to us after she has died, and together giving us their past, while at first apart and then together. A French reviewer emphasized the book's honesty and integrity, dignity and humility, its themes both simple and deep, its treatment of the daily emotions of the heart. Marilyn Chandler approached the novel in response to its impressive explorations of what love and marriage are and can be, what the relations can be between good and well-intentioned man and woman, which she finds expressed in "a simplicity of language and childlike emotional honesty touching and even gripping" to the readers of today's world. She found a skillful sustaining of tension between the language of the characters and "the depth and magnitude of the feelings and questions they manage to evoke."

Various reviewers praised the language of *A Virtuous Woman,* including its images and metaphors, its rural Southern cadences, and the matter-of-fact power in its storytelling, as its two principal characters speak directly to the reader. Several wrote of it as a deceptively simple and quiet book without much action, yet a deep book as it unsentimentally explores how love comes to be and grows, even with pain. An English reviewer said the book has the simplicity of good country music's focusing on the bare bones of life and traditional values, while a Kansas re-

viewer compared it to "good fiddle music," and one in
Florida wrote of Gibbons' lines as having "the tensile
strength of wire; pluck one and it snaps right back." Some
reviewers found the ending of the book, with its noticeable
change to omniscient point of view, flawed or weak; others found it strong, necessary, or helpful. Most found the
novel's two major characters admirable and very real, persons who learn a lot about life, love, and sorrow, and
whom the reader is glad to have met and to have learned
from. One said that Gibbons clearly loves her characters
for who they are. Often there was an emphasis on the
compelling aspect of the narrative and a declaration that
this novel, with its wisdom and art, is far above much of
what now passes "as fine literature." Various reviews spoke
of grace, joy, decency, gentleness. A North Carolina reviewer called Gibbons an "exceptional writer who relies
on the simplest words to convey the deepest emotions and
conditions of the human spirit," and Fredric Koeppel
wrote: "The human spirit is a wonderful thing, and it's a
rare author who can believably depict its simple grandeur
and dignity. That ability is the chief attribute of Kaye Gibbons."

The reviews of **A Cure for Dreams** appeared widely and
were generally praising, but were not as many or usually
as long as those for her first two novels, and as a whole
they were more muted. Often reviewers tried to focus on
this book in relation to her other two and to try to discern
themes, concerns, and intentions in all three together, both
comparing and contrasting, and making attempts to deal
with what was now clearly a writer with a developing career, no longer just a talented beginner. Of course they focused on plot and characterization, and they also usually
particularly noticed form and ambience and how these, in
their estimations, were or were not more effective than
those in her first two books. Although there were emphases on the three novels together, this book also was allowed integrity of its own. Lee Smith called it "lyrical and
lovely, shot through with moments of recognition." Valerie
Sayers compared its structure to easygoing, meandering
Sunday rides in the country, "willing to take detours if the
landscape looks promising, willing to sit awhile if the
vista is curious, willing to backtrack" if something had
been missed. She also called attention to "a highly stylized
and charming narrative voice, one that mixes 19th-century
formality (and chapter headings) with 20th-century directness." Josephine Humphreys wrote of Gibbons' "delicate
hand," which keeps the distinctive characteristics of her
characters from seeming exaggerated. She said that the
story's telling is "economical and quick," with scenes and
characters "drawn surely and sharply," and it "sounds spoken, its language often stranger and stronger than literary
language . . . [its] style both simple and baroque." For
her, "this is a novel of vision and grace. It shines." Stacey
D'Erasmo also called attention to a nineteenth-century aspect in Gibbons' novels, and found the three of them together to be "like a feminist *Spoon River Anthology* for
mothers and daughters, full of methods for surviving, escaping, and outliving brutality." Most reviewers called attention to the strong, dominant female central characters in

this book and in its two predecessors, a focus on the "eternal feminine," and some to the corresponding weakness of
the male characters; but Jerry Mills also stated that it is a
book for anyone who "values subtlety and craft and the
nuances of feeling that language in skillful hands can
evoke. And it is a book for anyone who wants to know
what makes the South such fertile literary ground." Sayers
called attention to the language of the book also: "What a
good ear Kaye Gibbons has . . . [taking us] down the
back roads . . . [pointing] out what incredible lives are
lived in those ordinary places." Dannye Romine's *Charlotte Observer* review concluded: "Four years ago, we
knew nothing of Kaye Gibbons. Then boom! This Nash
County native swooped down upon us with fearsome talent . . . giving us music that, in Flaubert's words, will
melt the stars."

Bibliography

WORKS BY KAYE GIBBONS

"June Bug." *Carolina Quarterly* 38 (Winter 1986): 55.

Ellen Foster. Chapel Hill, N.C.: Algonquin, 1987.

"The Headache." *St. Andrews Review* 32 (Spring/Summer
1987): 3–8.

"The Proof." *Quarterly* 1 (Spring 1987): 60–72.

*How I Became a Writer. My Mother, Literature, and a Life
Split Neatly into Two Halves.* Chapel Hill, N.C.: Algon-
quin, 1988. Without the first five words of this title, the
contents of this pamphlet also has appeared in the *Leader*
(November 10, 1988): 22–27; and in *The Writer on Her
Work, Volume II: New Essays in New Territory,* ed. Janet
Sternburg, New York: W. W. Norton, 1991.

"Planes of Language and Time: The Surface of the
Miranda Stories." *Kenyon Review* n.s. 10 (Winter 1988):
74–79.

"A Nash County Girl's Tribute." *News and Observer*
(Raleigh, N.C.) (November 5, 1989): 5D.

A Virtuous Woman. Chapel Hill, N.C.: Algonquin, 1989.

Family Life. Rocky Mount, N.C.: North Carolina Wes-
leyan College Press, 1990. Three chapters from *A Cure for
Dreams.* "To Be Published by Algonquin Books." Limited
to 500 numbered and signed copies.

A Cure for Dreams. Chapel Hill, N.C.: Algonquin, 1991.

STUDIES OF KAYE GIBBONS

Bell, Mae Woods. "Writing Is Part of Life for Kaye Gibbons." *Rocky Mount* (N.C.) *Telegram* (April 26, 1987): 41.

Brinson, Linda. "It's OK: Novelist Writes on after a Difficult Revelation." *Winston-Salem Journal* (June 18, 1989):
H10.

Chandler, Marilyn. "Limited Partnership" (Rev. of *A Virtuous Woman*). *Women's Review of Books* 6 (July 1989): 21.

D'Erasmo, Stacey. Rev. of *A Cure for Dreams*. *Voice Literary Supplement* (April 1991): 5.

Earle, Ralph. "Vices and Virtues" (Rev. of *A Virtuous Woman*). *Spectator* (Raleigh, N.C.) (April 27, 1989): 25.

Fleischer, Leonore. "Is It Art Yet?" *Publishers Weekly* (May 8, 1987): 34.

Hoffman, Alice. "Shopping for a New Family" (Rev. of *Ellen Foster*). *New York Times Book Review* (May 31, 1987): 13.

Humphreys, Josephine. "Within Marriage, A Secret Life," (Rev. of *A Cure for Dreams*). *Los Angeles Times Book Review* (May 19, 1991): 13.

Johnson, Maria C. "Speaking from Experience: At 29, Writer Has Lived Many of Life's Stories." *Greensboro News and Record* (August 31, 1989): B1-B2.

"Kaye Gibbons," 46–50 in *Contemporary Literary Yearbook, 1987* vol. 50. Detroit: Gale Research, 1988.

"Kaye Gibbons." Television interview by William Friday on *North Carolina People,* University of North Carolina Center for Public Television (July 24, 1989).

Koeppel, Fredric. "Household Labels Rile New Novelist Gibbons." *Commercial Appeal* (Memphis) (July 8, 1990): G1—G2.

———. "Novels Feature Southern Setting, Characters without Caricatures" (Rev. of *Ellen Foster* and *A Virtuous Woman*). *Commercial Appeal* (Memphis) (July 8, 1990): G4.

Manuel, John. "Clear Vision: Raleigh Novelist Discusses Fame, Fortune and Her Forthcoming Book." *Spectator* (Raleigh, N.C.) (July 19, 1990): 5–6.

Mills, Jerry Leath. "Kaye Gibbons: 'The Eternal Feminine' in Fiction" (Rev. of *A Cure for Dreams*). *News and Observer* (Raleigh, N.C.) (March 10, 1991): 5J.

Powell, Padgett. "As Ruby Lay Dying" (Rev. of *A Virtuous Woman*). *New York Times Book Review* (April 30, 1989): 12–13.

Romine, Dannye. "Literature Liberates: Raleigh's Kaye Gibbons Finds Freedom, Affirmation in 1st Novel." *Charlotte Observer* (April 26, 1987): 1F, 13F.

Rosenheim, Andrew. "Voices of the New South" (Rev. of *Ellen Foster*). *Times Literary Supplement* (London) (November 25, 1988): 1306.

Sayers, Valerie. "Back Roads, Strong Women" (Rev. of *A Cure for Dreams*). *Washington Post* (April 8, 1991): C3.

Sill, Melanie. "This Perfect Story Has a Happy Ending." *News and Observer* (Raleigh, N.C.) (April 27, 1987): 8A-9A.

Slater, Joyce. "*A Virtuous Woman* Grabs Reader from Start" (Rev. of *A Virtuous Woman*). *Atlanta Journal-Constitution* (May 28, 1989): N8.

Tyler, Phyllis. "Kaye Gibbons: 'To Be a Writer You Have to Eat Literature.'" *Independent* (Durham, N.C.) (April 23, 1987): 24–25.

Yardley, Jonathan. "Child of Adversity: A Young Heroine Finds Happiness Overcoming Prejudice" (Rev. of *Ellen Foster*). *Washington Post* (April 22, 1987): C2.

Kaye Gibbons with Bob Summer (interview date 8 February 1993)

SOURCE: "Kaye Gibbons," in *Publishers Weekly,* Vol. 240, No. 6, February 8, 1993, pp. 60-1.

[*In the following interview, Summer and Gibbons discuss Gibbons's change of publishers and the development of her fourth novel,* Charms for the Easy Life.]

In the decade during which she published her first three novels, Kaye Gibbons won critical acclaim, a legion of readers and literary prizes. Yet when she approached her fourth novel, the 32-year-old writer momentarily lost her voice. Gibbons had recently weathered some difficult times: a reluctant but pragmatic move to Putnam from Algonquin Books of Chapel Hill, the publisher of **Ellen Foster, A Virtuous Woman** and **A Cure for Dreams**; a divorce; a brief move from North Carolina to California; and a return to Raleigh, N.C.

With the help of Putnam editor Faith Sale, however, Gibbons found her voice again. Late last year she concluded the project that had first daunted her and rushed the last manuscript pages to Putnam. The novel, which *PW* called "a touching picture of female bonding and solidarity" (Fiction Forecasts, Jan. 11), will be published next month as **Charms for the Easy Life.**

All of Gibbons's novels to date concern Southern women who shoulder the burdens of their ordinary lives with extraordinary courage. Much of the uncanny wisdom these heroines display has grown out of Gibbons's own philosophy of life and approach to her craft. "Nobody ever told me it was going to be easy," she says about the writing life. "If I weren't a writer, I'd probably be a lawyer or an architect. I wouldn't want to do anything easy, and I *chose* to be a writer." Then, slipping into the self-mocking humor that softens her frank, beyond-her-years maturity, she adds, "Maybe somebody should give *me* a charm for the easy life."

Between finishing **Charms,** hunting for a larger house, and getting organized to leave her three young daughters (eight, five and three years old) next month for a 20-city promotional tour, Gibbons has not found much time to relax. She says her home is "kind of a zoo," and suggests lunch with *PW* at a Raleigh restaurant with her significant other, Frank Ward, continuing afterward in a conference room at Maupin, Taylor, Ellis and Adams, the law firm in which Ward is a partner (and Armistead Maupin's father a senior partner). "Frank knows more about my books than I do," she says airily, "so if you have any deep questions, ask him."

Speaking with an often startling directness, Gibbons confesses that she is always at a loss when she gets inquiries about the symbolism in her novels. "I worked hard to put into the book everything a reader needs to know," Gibbons says. "The deadliest question to ask me is what this novel is about. All I can say is that it's about three women—a grandmother, mother and daughter—and what they give to and take from each other."

Some of her resistance to discussing the book's background comes from her experiences with her first novel, *Ellen Foster.* That stark and affecting story is brought to vivid life by the voice of a young country girl upon whom tragic circumstances force an uncanny wisdom. Some interviewers, noting that Gibbons herself was born and raised in rural Nash County, asked about similarities between Ellen and the author. "*Ellen Foster* is emotionally autobiographical," Gibbons now confirms without qualms. "My mother *did* commit suicide when I was 10"—as does Ellen's mother in the book—and her father, a tobacco farmer, "really did drink himself to death. But I didn't go to live with my grandmother, as Ellen does, although I did live with a couple of aunts before moving in with my older brother, which was fortunate for me. But the years between 10 and 13 were pretty hard," she says, with typical understatement.

Still, she insists, *Ellen Foster* was not written to provide "an emotional catharsis, but as an artistic exercise." Gibbons—who grew up an avid reader, thanks to a local library, since there were few books at home other than a Bible and the World Book Encyclopedia—began the novel in 1985 when she was taking a course taught by Louis Rubin at the University of North Carolina at Chapel Hill. (She had attended North Carolina State University on a scholarship, with plans to become a teacher, then switched to U.N.C. She never "quite completed" requirements for a degree from either school, however.)

During her studies, Gibbons had become fascinated by the work of James Weldon Johnson, a turn-of-the-century African American poet. "He seemed to me to be the first poet in the South—not the first writer, since Twain had already done it—to make art out of everyday language. Inspired by him, I wanted to see if I could have a child use her voice to talk about life, death, art, eternity—big things from a little person."

She began writing a poem from the viewpoint of the black girl who becomes Ellen's best friend, but the story gradually metamorphosed into a novel. She sensed that finishing the book marked a turning point in her life. "I knew in a spiritual, inward way that it was going to make a difference to me and my family, although I didn't know what that would be." Rubin, who had founded Algonquin two years earlier, read the book and asked to publish it. "Then he asked several of his fellow writers, people like Miss Welty, Walker Percy and Elizabeth Spencer, to read it. I'll always be grateful to him."

Despite that validation, Gibbons had so little self-confidence that she faced post-publication interviews "terrified that I would be found out" as a literary pretender. Though she claimed the book was "a complete fabrication," the fact that her mother had died when she was a child led people to focus on the issue of its autobiographical elements. Gibbons began "making up ailments she could have died from" rather than admit the parallels to her own life. "I had read enough Thomas Wolfe to know what would happen if that occurred. I didn't want the publicity hook to be my miserable childhood."

But honesty finally surfaced when she sat down to talk with *Atlanta Journal-Constitution* book editor Don O'Briant, whom she describes as "a wonderful gentleman. He asked me how much Ellen Foster resembled me. I had intended to lie, but I couldn't; I decided then and there to tell the truth. Besides, I was pretty much out of made-up ways my mother could have died."

Interview difficulties didn't end there, however. When she was touring for the Vintage paperback edition of *A Virtuous Woman*—in which the male character's bravado renders him insensitive to his late wife's devotion—"without fail, I was asked why I hate men. I hope that, with *Charms,* the dogs will be called off on the matter of my fictional male characters," Gibbons says, referring to the sympathetic characterization, in *Charms,* of Tom Hawkings, whom she calls "a fully drawn, compassionate, good-looking and romantic man."

She insists, however, that Hawkings was not modeled on Ward, the key man in her life now. Nor did Hawkings emerge until the novel was well under way. Although Gibbons had planned to continue the story of the black midwife introduced in *A Cure for Dreams,* early drafts were "flat." Gradually it dawned on her that she needn't commit herself to a sequel. "Perhaps I watched *Ghostbusters II,*" speculates Gibbons, an avid movie fan who says she learns about structuring fiction from films. "Something told me to rewrite the book and make it stand on its own."

She agrees with those who think writing is a mysterious process. "As a writer, it's my job to come up with 300 pages or so every two years. Each time I begin, I know it's going to happen, but I'm scared it won't. It's working with that element of fear that keeps a book going." This remains true even though her work to date has received many rewards and much recognition. *Ellen Foster* was awarded the Sue Kaufman Prize for First Fiction by the American Academy of Arts and Letters and a special citation from the Ernest Hemingway Foundation; *A Virtuous Woman* earned her an NEA fellowship; *A Cure for Dreams* garnered the PEN/Revson Foundation Fellowship and the *Chicago Tribune*'s Heartland Prize; and Gibbons was a breakfast speaker at the 1991 ABA, with Jeffrey Archer and Alice Walker. Despite these honors, Gibbons claims that she approaches each book with "a fear of looking over an abyss and knowing I have to jump."

In the case of *Charms,* Gibbons made her leap after "hearing" the voice of indomitable Charlie Kate. She felt it obvious that the midwife should be white, not black, as originally conceived. "She was just wild, and I've felt feisty ever since she came into my life. I really liked the pithy way she spoke, although I had to struggle to control her." To prevent the strong character from taking over, Gibbons chose another character for the first-person narrator, a device she says she "can't seem to get away from."

Gibbons was determined to make Charlie Kate intellectually up-to-date, although her origins were simple and rural. "Now, there's a difference between being intellectually sophisticated and educated in a sophisticated manner," the novelist argues. "I wanted her to possess all the knowledge of a Yale graduate, but she could not have gone to Yale. So I had her educate herself. I gave her a subscription to the *Saturday Review of Literature,* which someone like her would have read in the '40s, and had her read James Thurber in the *New Yorker.* I wanted her medically sophisticated, so I gave her a subscription to the *New England Journal of Medicine.* And I made her an admirer of Winston Churchill; they would have gotten along famously."

Gabriel García Márquez figured in Gibbons's rewrite. "The first draft was top-heavy with period detail, since I didn't know how to incorporate historical information into a novel. But rereading *A Hundred Years of Solitude* taught me how to do it."

Other books that influenced Gibbons were *The Frank C. Brown Collection of North Carolina Folklore* (Duke University Press), where she found the "magical" rabbit's foot tale from which she chose *Charms*'s title. She also digested 53 books about the WW II period. "Maybe 10 of those were top-down histories, like John Keegan's *The Second World War.* Then I went to 'the people' and let them tell me history from the bottom up. That's a lot more fun. I like to watch historical events trickle down." She credits oral histories, including Studs Terkel's *The Good War* and the WPA's Depression-era interviews, as "primary sources of information."

But the rewrite was still troublesome. And when she thought the novel was finally finished, "I found I had killed off the wrong people! I called Bob Furnam [the Raleigh doctor who gave medical guidance for *Charms*], and he worked backward with me on the death that had to occur in the last 30 pages."

Faith Sale both steadied *Charms* and helped bring it to life. Gibbons believed that "she would be a firm hand to guide me," as did Liz Darhansoff, the agent who has been "a rudder" to Gibbons since *Ellen Foster.* "I came to Faith through Amy Tan, whose *Joy Luck Club* she edited. She

was at the forefront of my thinking when I decided to leave Algonquin." The departure, she stresses, was entirely without acrimony.

"Faith understood the first 30 or 40 pages of *Charms* intimately, and she could see its possibilities," Gibbons says, but the editing process was "arduous. We went at it unrelentingly, determined to make it the best it could be. I think that two lesser women would have shot themselves—and/or each other—during the editing of this book."

Gibbons stresses that the novel honed by that writer/editor partnership is no more "commercial" for being published by a large trade house than were her previous works. "I wondered while I was writing if there would be people who would flip through the book to see if I had put sex into it, or a car chase—anything that smacks of commercialism. But they won't find anything like that. Maybe it's more opened up than my previous books, but that could reflect my getting older and having more life experiences, having read Márquez and getting the courage to expand, or being a single mother who has a better relationship with my children. But really, if the book appeals to a wider audience, it's because the story is more appealing."

Judith Beth Cohen (review date October 1993)

SOURCE: "Daughters of the South," in *Women's Review of Books,* Vol. 11, No. 1, October, 1993, p. 24.

[*In the following review, Cohen discusses the Southern women in Gibbons's* Charms for the Easy Life, *Pam Durban's* The Laughing Place, *and Elizabeth Berg's* Durable Goods.]

Sensitive daughters and powerful parents are the focus of these three recent Southern novels. Charlie Kate, part folk-healer, part-scientist, the North Carolina grandmother in Kaye Gibbons' fourth novel, *Charms for the Easy Life,* defies labels as she rises off the page. Louise Vess, the mother in Pam Durban's first novel, *The Laughing Place,* is a formidable figure with upper-class aspirations and stiff upper lip, thwarted by the small universe of Timmons, South Carolina. In *Durable Goods,* Elizabeth Berg's first novel, set on a Texas military base, it's an abusive father who looms large. Though all three daughter-narrators are both blessed and cursed by these powerful parent figures, Gibbons' medic/grandmother Charlie Kate might well become the most memorable older woman in twentieth-century literature.

In a deadpan, matter-of-fact voice, Gibbons' narrator Margaret invites us to enter Pasquotank County, where Charlie Kate becomes a legend after saving a black man from a lynching. From the grateful survivor, she receives an "easy life charm . . . the hindfoot of a white graveyard rabbit caught at midnight, under the full moon, by a cross-eyed Negro woman who had been married seven times." In the pre-World War Two countryside around Raleigh, Charlie

Kate's deeds are both practical and magical: she provides sex education for every child, sends a deserving boy to medical school, frees a woman's hand from a wringer, forces a bumbling doctor to retire, and heals the hermit son of a witch and a warlock. She's also "the first woman anybody knew with the courage not only to possess a toilet but to use it." With this perfect balance of the outrageous and the mundane, Gibbons suspends our disbelief and we accept Charlie Kate's remarkable gifts.

When her husband doesn't show up for supper, Charlie Kate wastes no time; she breaks his dishes, yelling "To hell with him!" Her daughter Sophia claims she didn't have time to miss her father, for she "was highly involved in the life of the second grade." Sophia does learn that men will leave you: when her own cad of a husband cheats on her, she begs her mother to "do something," but Charlie Kate won't cross the line from natural medicine to black magic. Unemotionally, Sophia's daughter Margaret describes her own father's early death: "One evening my mother called God to the house and he came."

There's no mourning on Margaret's part, for she knows they'll have a better time without him, and indeed they do. Charlie Kate—who wouldn't cross their threshold while he lived—moves in, and daughter, mother and grandmother form an enduring female household as the world explodes into war.

Literature, medicine and the progress of the war are what matter to them. Though they eat like bachelors, they manage so well that soaking blood from their laundry garments is their toughest challenge. Margaret falls asleep listening to Charlie Kate reading aloud from medical journals. She becomes "fascinated with her mind, enamoured of her muscular soul." When debates break out about men or literature (what did become, they wonder, of the disappearing narrator in *Madame Bovary*?), Margaret sides with her grandmother. She's so attached to their household that, contrary to Sophia's wishes, she puts college off, confident that reading and learning happen best inside their threesome.

Gibbons challenges our common operating assumptions: here children do not suffer when fathers disappear, neither do men offer solace and completion. She imagines a feminist alternative to the patriarchal myth of man as rescuer or savior. Her characters don't accept the reality they are given, they alter it. Just as Charlie Kate revises the letters wounded soldiers dictate to Margaret, Gibbons uses her delightful wit to rewrite the dominant narrative about rural Southern women. Though Margaret knows her grandmother would have populated the world entirely with women just like herself, men are not absent from these lives. With Charlie Kate's help, Sophia wins her married lover, and Margaret finds her own beau; but these couplings are reluctantly made, as if Gibbons' women know their collective power is bound to be diluted when they leave the female circle.

Annie Vess in *The Laughing Place* longs for a new language with which to speak to her mother, yet it is separa-

tion rather than bonding that marks this narrative. Recently widowed herself, Annie returns to tradition-bound Timmons, South Carolina, after her father's sudden death. She sees a world of "taboos of color, line and proportion . . . arcane as that of an ancient religion . . . to which women must conform." Durban's realistic prose is slow-moving and reflective, her imagery characterized by opposites: low country/high country, private/public, dark/light. The grieving mother and daughter live as "spies in each others' lives, leaving messages in a code to which neither . . . held the key." Gradually Annie uncovers her father's sexual betrayal, grows up and moves beyond her mother's crushing orbit. Her accomplice is Legree Black, a self-proclaimed redneck-naturalist, a sort of primeval man with a visionary gift. Annie falls in love with this sometime photographer who had once "let in the light and made a picture of [her] father's darkness."

Durban is a sharp chronicler of the contemporary Southern landscape, where crass schemes for selling condos to wealthy retirees coexist with yearly ceremonies for the Confederate dead. Annie understands her mother: she "should have been a diplomat, architect, designer of monumental buildings," and the confines of marriage made her "vehement and fierce." When Mrs. Vess finds solace in born-again Christianity, Annie wryly rejects her Jesus as another romance novel hero, yet her own answer is no less conventional.

Ultimately Durban's tale is one more gloss on the oedipal myth: a daughter searches for a man to replace her father. Though Annie claims she "could never again disappear or dissolve into another," it is Legree, "the rescuer of turtles blinded by artificial light," who helps her see the truth about her idealized marriage and her dead father.

Katie, the twelve-year-old narrator of Elizabeth Berg's slim novel *Durable Goods,* gets her period and learns she is to relocate once again. Her widowed father, a military officer, follows protocol precisely but can't control his own rage. "I do not believe the army is a good idea for people with regular human hearts," is Katie's diagnosis.

Berg takes us inside Katie's experiences as they unfold—we're with her as she disappears under her bed to hide from her father's blows; we listen as she holds conversations with her dead mother or watches her sister being beaten. "Remember," she asks her sister later on, "when we used to pull down our pants to look at our butts in the mirror to see his handprints, see whose was darker?" Remarkably, she's able to see her father's pain as well, how "he can only go so far in a good direction. Then something happens. He is all broken apart."

Berg has enriched our literature by giving us a young girl able to transcend abuse, and she helps us understand the flawed father as well as his victims. *Durable Goods* can be compared to Kaye Gibbons' debut novel, ***Ellen Foster*** (1987). Like Katie, eleven-year-old Ellen loses her mother and is abused by both her father and grandmother, yet she retains her spirit and wit, outsmarting the therapist assigned to her. Ellen managed to find herself a new mama and a new name. But comfort wasn't enough for her; she insisted upon justice, bringing her black girlfriend home, amazed that "all this time I thought I had the hardest row to hoe."

Like *Charms for the Easy Life, Ellen Foster* includes dimensions of class and color that reveal a whole social structure. Gibbons' novels encompass more than the private lives Durban and Berg depict so well. She goes beyond predictable realism to give us a deeper imaginative truth in her subversive vision of women's possibilities. The mythic grandmother Charlie Kate, her finest achievement thus far, allows us to dream in a new vocabulary.

Gale Harris (essay date Winter 1993/1994)

SOURCE: "Beyond the *Scarlett* Image: Women Writing about the South," in *Belles Lettres,* Vol. 9, No. 2, Winter, 1993/1994, pp. 16-8.

[In the following essay, Harris asserts that the heroines of several contemporary Southern novels, including Gibbons's Charms for the Easy Life, *go beyond the image of Scarlett O'Hara in portraying life for women in the South.]*

Whether presented in the context of tragic, humorous, or almost mythic circumstances, the southern women portrayed in five recent works do more than rebuild their lives and nurture their offspring. They create an environment in which truth can come to light, intimacy can be undertaken and maintained, and hope can arise from disillusionment and betrayal. Although Scarlett's last words may ring false to some observers of human nature, the women in the books reviewed here clearly have found diverse but unmistakable paths to more promising tomorrows.

Like Scarlett, Georgie in Louise Shivers's *A Whistling Woman,* is a survivor of the Civil War. She always has assumed that her father died like so many others in that conflict. Georgie is only eight when, in 1867, her mother, Chaney, finds work on a virtually abandoned plantation. When she is 14, Georgie is lured into a confused and passionate affair that leaves her pregnant and abandoned by the son of the plantation's owner. Chaney forbids Georgie to name the son of "that fine family" as the child's father. Instead, Chaney pretends she is pregnant and raises Wilkes as if he were her own child. In time, Chaney begins to deny the true circumstances of Wilkes's birth even to his own mother.

Although Georgie's later, happy marriage to another man is a "honey cure," she is still plagued by nightmares that have haunted her since childhood, and she keeps waiting for something to pounce. Eventually, Georgie comes to terms with the deception surrounding Wilkes's birth and learns the terrible secret of her father's death and the source of her nightmares. By then, she has forged her own

alternative to Chaney's warning that "a whistling woman and a crowing hen is no good either to gods or men." Georgie concludes that this adage means more than that men want women to be quiet. She believes that "most women *know* so much that they never tell, know so many secret things, which sometimes they're just making a little, slow, low whistling sound of warning. Don't mess with a whistling woman."

Shivers grew up in the tobacco country of eastern North Carolina, and her novel bears the authentic voices of rural women in that region. Georgie's narrative reflects the simplicity of life and daily contact with elemental things that add richness and profundity to the lives of ordinary but gifted women.

When Georgie feels she is ready to slap her husband's face "just to break the routine," she rises early and walks out in the backyard "where I could have the air to breathe myself, just the air without anybody else breathing it." Her last images are of mother and daughter husking peas and watching the dried hulls being taken by a fall wind, blown "like ghosts of fireflies down the street of the town." Shivers could not have added a single page to this slim novel that could have conveyed more completely the quiet triumph of a woman who attains her powers the moment she learns what stories to tell and what secrets to keep.

Kaye Gibbons's *Charms for the Easy Life* is another deceptively simple novel that presents three generations of whistling women. Like Shivers's story, it is set in rural North Carolina. Already a midwife at the age of 20, Clarissa—or Charlie—Kate marries the ferryman who has transported her across the river to visit her patients. As Charlie's talents, confidence, and practice increase, her husband grows more frustrated with his life and leaves "the way sad men leave: he did not come home from work." With no friends or acquaintances other than her patients, Charlie and her daughter, Sophia, are too busy and involved in life to miss him.

Sophia makes an equally unfortunate choice for a husband, but her daughter and narrator of the story, Margaret, completes the trio, which creates a new order in which women are the intrepid doers, the smart financial investors, and the savvy judges of character. The bond among these women as well as the individual strengths they have developed enable Sophia and Margaret to forge new relationships and separate lives when promising opportunities arise.

In Charlie Kate, Gibbons has created a mythic persona that rivals other monolithic heroes such as Paul Bunyan. Charlie's campaigns for social reform are always successful; her interventions in the personal lives of her patients are nearly always supremely gratifying; and her authority, when questioned, is always upheld to the extreme regret of the skeptics. Contemplating Charlie's eventual death, Margaret realizes "how intimidating [her] grandmother would be to all those trillions of dead people who'd never met her."

Margaret's narrative reinforces the legend by interweaving the known facts of Charlie's life with tales that her granddaughter has had to "half invent by dream." It is indicative of Gibbon's invisible mastery of the storytelling form as well as the truth of her vision that one tall tale only whets the appetite for another. Together these anecdotes create a detailed and believable portrait of three strong and loving women whose lives are enriched by what they give. Like all viable myths, Gibbons's story of Charlie Kate and her descendants imparts hope and guidance for an easy life, "depending on your definition of easy."

Resourceful, indomitable women apparently abound in south Georgia, where Bailey White lives with her mother. *Mama Makes Up Her Mind and Other Dangers of Southern Living* opens with White's warning that when her mother "starts to move across a room, people pay attention. You can never be sure she's not going to grab you by the top of the head to steady herself. And she's pretty free with that walking stick, too." Thus are we introduced to Mama, who lets ornithologists use her daughter's fevered body to hatch wild turkey eggs, camps on the edge of a meadow when she gets tired of her family's demands, and serves feasts made from fresh road kill. Mama bathes on the back porch even in the dead of winter and sleeps there through a hurricane that destroys the roof of her niece's house.

White's Aunt Belle is fond of junkets in search of ferry boats, thunderstorms, and unexplained mysteries. She also tames wild alligators and teaches them to bellow on command. Bailey is no slouch herself, braving nightmares and oversized gear to become a volunteer fireperson, resourcefully maintaining an antique used car, and wrestling an old Underwood typewriter from an attic in Virginia to her mother's kitchen table, where Mama is writing *her* memoirs.

If Mama's recollections are anything like her daughter's, they will be full of eccentrics who are intent on their idiosyncratic purposes and oblivious to the stares and opinions that deter most of us. White balances these quixotic personalities with her own sensitivity and reflections on the heart beneath the quirks. Although the urge to impart a moral or revelation in every brief story leads to forced endings, White's craftsmanship and insight meld beautifully in several pieces. In one, she is appalled to find herself reading to her pupils a classic children's book that she realizes extols the virtue of war. Another story describes how she and a cousin overcome their initial disinterest to explore each other's hobbies, a process that leads to a brief, aromatic unity.

Not all relationships between generations of southern women are as harmonious as Charlie Kate's or Bailey White's families. But even the most troubled connections have a power that can transform lives. In Pam Durban's *The Laughing Place,* a mother and daughter find different and often conflicting ways to cope with a man's betrayal of his family. The mother, who tolerated her husband's de-

ceit, swiftly expunges his belongings from their house after his death. His daughter, Annie, also recently widowed, discovers her father's secret life only after she returns home for his funeral.

As Annie tries to cope with her father's legacy of broken promises and shattered loyalties, her disillusionment threatens to engulf her remaining relationships. She breaks with her new lover, Legree Black, because she is afraid she can no longer care deeply enough. Annie's sharpest battles are reserved for her mother, whom she can no longer believe possesses "a set of special senses tuned forever to the world and to [her] children, made for making one known to the other." Although her mother's religious conversion increases this sense of loss, Annie eventually sees "with what will and what grief [her mother] has claimed her life." Her mother's triumph and her own renewed closeness with Legree help Annie to forgive the people she loves and to cherish her life, "so broken and so full of promise," above any paradise or the "beauty of anyone's dreams."

Durban's first novel surpasses the promise of her previous work of short stories, *All Set About With Fever Trees.* The almost mystical insights that characterized her stories illuminate nearly every page of *The Laughing Place.* The women in her novel overcome loss, disillusionment, and anger not merely through action and an instinct for survival. They also recognize and eventually embrace inner forces that endlessly seek to grow and change, to open and allow for more of life's possibilities, and to "hold all darkness and still remain a harvest." Durban shows us the strength, intelligence, and awareness that allow two women to "live on this earth as though [they] belong here."

In Christina Baker Kline's *Sweet Water,* the relationship between a grandmother and her granddaughter leads to revelation and forgiveness. Cassie Simon lost her mother at the age of three and never knew the grandfather who died and left her his house in Sweetwater, Tennessee. When she moves from New York to the town where she was born, Cassie begins to hear and tries to unravel stories about the accident that killed her mother and the possibly related drowning of her grandmother's closest friend.

Cassie senses the hostility in her grandmother but does not understand that she wants something still hidden in the inherited house. When the older woman's desperate efforts to recover her secrets lead to a confrontation with her granddaughter, Cassie helps her family face the past and begin a healing process.

Kline unfolds the secrets of Sweetwater in alternating accounts by Cassie and her grandmother, Clyde. Cassie's passages are longer and more expository, but despite descriptions of her artistic growth and a passionate affair, they fail to provoke much interest in their narrator. Clyde's stories, although much briefer, are more revealing and constitute the true heart and voice of the novel. Clyde is a complex character whose initial submission to her unfaithful husband is transformed into a bitter dominance that not even death can relieve. The unquenchable taste for revenge, however, is not the result of an inherent desire for supremacy but rather the heart's effort to control pain that it can neither tolerate nor understand. Although Kline's development of Cassie lacks definition, her portrait of Clyde brims with the fire, relentlessness, and fallibility we find in the most memorable southern women.

What distinguishes these new southern women from their predecessor, Scarlett O'Hara? Evenly matched in gumption and in the will to survive, the new heroines surpass the old in an awareness that may be succinctly called heart. Having heart is not merely possessing courage, tenacity, or the belief that things will be better tomorrow. Having heart is deliberately probing one's fate and misfortune for signs of grace, for glimpses that encourage one to embrace rather than reject life. Taking heart can mean that a woman rejects submission and carves her own path in the world. It also can mean that she finds and links with what Durban calls other messengers, "passing in and out, over and through each other's days and nights, carrying news from one place to another." Women writing about the South today are bearing heartening messages: life may not always be easy, but it can sustain the dream as well as reality, the flight as well as the journey taken step by step.

Tonita Branan (essay date Spring 1994)

SOURCE: "Women and 'The Gift for Gab': Revisionary Strategies in *A Cure for Dreams*," in *Southern Literary Journal*, Vol. 26, No. 2, Spring, 1994, pp. 91-101.

[*In the following essay, Branan describes how language empowers the women in Gibbons's* A Cure for Dreams.]

Several months before her third novel appeared, Kaye Gibbons voiced anxiety over "the recent dispersal and watering down of language, the lost language in the South" (Wallace 8). With her (then) forthcoming work, *A Cure for Dreams,* she intended to "take the language back to a very pure time . . . the Depression," noting that "the hardest part of writing . . . has been trying to create a whole community with everything intact" (8, 9). Create a community Gibbons does—a community of talkers in *Dreams,* and not of least importance, a community whose talk is largely represented through and controlled by women. The book's principal narrators, Lottie Davies, the matriarch, her daughter, Betty Davies Randolph, and Betty's daughter, Marjorie Polly Randolph, share the telling of their familial history, which ranges from Ireland's Great Potato Famine to December 15, 1989, and which extends also to the experiences of friends in the Davies' circle. Chronicling the incessant, overlapping conversations of these three generations of females who live on Milk Farm Road, an anonymous farming borough in North Carolina, *A Cure for Dreams* projects women who talk to each other, talk about each other, gloss old phrases, name their children,

weave fictitious accounts of "what really happened," write poems, critique men's letters, and read one another's bodies.

Of the three narrators, Lottie in particular uses words time and again to effect communal change: through elision she outsmarts Deputy Carroll in an unsolved murder case, by subverting racist labels she includes her black friend, Polly, at white folks' gatherings, and through tacit euphemism she "explained betting to women so they could have a little thrill on a Saturday afternoon" (64). Far from lingering in marginal spaces or shutting up when men speak, Lottie turns tricks with her talk to get things done, a feature also notably exemplified in her friend, Sade Duplin, the figure through whom Gibbons modifies Susan Glaspell's 1917 short story, "A Jury of Her Peers." *A Cure for Dreams* replaces Glaspell's crazy, speechless, victimized Minnie Wright with Sade, a woman equally victimized, but one who maintains her wits and agile tongue even as she strikes back against a brutal husband. Simply put, Lottie Davies and Sadie Duplin contradict feminist theories which cast language as a pernicious, ultra-patriarchal mechanism that, at best, renders women aphasic and, at worst, strips them of their sanity.[1] Since Lottie and Sadie talk with intent and talk well, any discussion of *A Cure for Dreams* must attend to the productive relation Kaye Gibbons establishes between female characters and discourse.

In *Honey-Mad Women* Patricia Yaeger departs from usual feminist positions by downplaying women's speechlessness, addressing instead the ways female writers have created gaps in male discourse to insert meanings and revisions distinctly feminine. Opting for Hannah Arendt's philosophy of the "infinitely improbable" in language instead of Foucault's notion that the word/logos fundamentally restrains, Yaeger asserts:

> Speech has [the] capacity to initiate, to interrupt and start things anew because speech is more than a function of the social order: the word can always be said or seized differently, can operate as a form of action. . . . To be able to act is to enter the flux and influence its direction.
>
> (94–95)

Yaeger further argues that females possess both the aptitude and the tools to "rewrite [our] culture" and identifies "our need, as women, to invent language games that challenge and change linguistic codes" (29, 15). Most importantly, her theory of emancipatory strategies offers means for analyzing Lottie Davies's oral tactics in *A Cure for Dreams.* In terms of Yaeger's concepts and classifications, Lottie "wrench[es] . . . syntactic patterns" "into new shapes" and recognizes the double-life of speech by allowing her own and others' words more than one meaning (98, 103). Quintessentially "honey-mad"—a woman who "appropriates the language 'racked up' in her own body" and dares to shout—Gibbons's Lottie Davies exemplifies the type of female artist whom Yaeger commends for "writ[ing] new possibilities" (28, 15).

By and large Mrs. Davies ignores orthodox rules of grammar. Much to her daughter's dismay, Lottie fashions syntactic patterns to her own liking, declaring that punctuation constrains expression and therefore "[doesn't] matter" (26). Because Betty's narrative packages her mother's speech in correct grammar, Gibbons jars readers with passages of Lottie's jumbled-up writing; besides "renounc-[ing] the apostrophe and comma," Mrs. Davies characteristically clumps four or five clauses together before offering a period for rest (27). Consider, for instance, an example of Lottie's correspondence toward the end of *A Cure for Dreams.* As Betty angrily writes a letter to Herman Randolph, a beau who has joined the navy without consulting her, Lottie criticizes her daughter's note and "snatch[es]" the pencil to do a "better" job (147). Since we literally watch Lottie write what we read, the moment is highly ironic; in effect, Gibbons allows a character to assume the author's role, and, as author, Lottie crosses the borders of genre in a metafictional moment by writing in epistolary form. While Betty "just watch[es]," Mrs. Davies drafts the weighty document:

> Dear Herman,
>
> Just a note. I have heard this morning that you have joined the navy Swell Is this true? I'm telling you if you signed up to go to the navy you are going to hate it. You may not now sonny boy but you will later on I wouldn't think you would join the navy. My mother is very surprised and she thought I'd been going with somebody with better sense than to join the navy to be shot at in the water. Its not so smart to me either since everybody in the world knows you cant swim three feet. Although you may be mad about something you did not have to join the navy to get pleased. This is just what I have heard today so if you have not joined please do not pay attention to it.
>
> Love
>
> Betty
>
> (147–48)

As in a former letter to Betty, Lottie opens casually with "just a note" before firing a series of arguments, managing to highlight her own opinions concerning Betty and Herman's misunderstanding ("My mother is very surprised and she thought I'd been going with somebody with better sense"). Lottie's second sentence, a run-on, establishes her sarcasm; she debunks the statement, "you have joined the navy," by moving immediately to a judgment ("Swell") and then to a question ("Is this true?"). The prevalence of S's and T's toward the end of the sentence generates a spitting alliteration, the sounds of which Lottie sustains by rapidly piling monosyllable upon monosyllable. Mrs. Davies uses this rushed, alliterative tactic throughout: of the letter's one hundred and forty words, only twenty-five are polysyllables, and phrases such as "hate it," "not now sonny boy but," "somebody with better sense," and "to be shot at in the water," maintain Lottie's precedent of harsh noises.

As part of her persuasive strategy, Mrs. Davies assumes a condescending tone toward Herman. Except for the letter's salutation, she never addresses him by name, instead calling the young man "you," "sonny boy," and "somebody with better sense." And though initially Lottie doubts Herman's judgment, prophesying his regret over joining the navy ("you are going to hate it"), she later insults both his intellect ("Its not so smart to me") and his physical competence ("you cant swim three feet"). Finally, Lottie seizes the opportunity to define Betty and Herman's argument as neatly as she defines navy (i.e., "be[ing] shot at in the water"), in that she interprets the young man's actions as a response to Betty, a response to some hypothetical fight over which he must be "mad," and thereby ignores the possibility that Herman may have joined the military of his own accord. We find, then, that Lottie's letter denies Herman Randolph any dignity; she writes to intimidate her daughter's beau, to reverse his decision or at least convince him of his stupidity. However cruel, Lottie fulfills her goal of outcomposing Betty. After reading her mother's note and feeling slightly appeased by its bitter wit, Betty imparts, "[the] letter was as good as anything I could've written, and I'd forgotten he couldn't swim" (148). The written words that "refuse to be constrained by literary form" obtain for Lottie the results she desires (Benstock 88).

If Lottie Davies gets what she wants with a pen, her manipulation of speech is even more effective, perhaps because *A Cure for Dreams* resounds with conversations. Through talk Lottie avoids victimization at the hands of a husband whose "gristmill served as church," directs Bridget O'Cadhain's stolen passage from Ireland to Kentucky, obtains the material goods she desires, salvages Charles Davies's reputation among her kin, and secures Milk Farm Road's acceptance of the impudent foreigner, Trudy Woodlief (18). Yet Mrs. Davies's communicative expertise rests as much with her ears as with her tongue. In listening to what others say, Lottie recognizes that speech may well carry more than one meaning, and she often responds with non-literal interpretations. When Betty lies to her mother, for instance, insisting that Trudy Woodlief "expressed . . . warm appreciation" for Lottie's donations of furniture, the matriarch shouts, "Phooey," confident that an ingrate like Trudy would never "appreciate" gifts, much less appreciate them warmly (97). In short, Lottie Davies acknowledges that her own and others' words can lead what Patricia Yaeger calls "a double life," that the letter at once "upholds the law" and "offers a path for wandering away" (103).

Gibbons's fifth chapter, "An account of things which heretofore were unsaid, or a lesson for the tardy," traces the murder of Roy Duplin, a man generally despised as "a sonofabitch" who "treat[ed] his wife . . . nastily in public" (46, 40). While the deputy sheriff searches Duplin's yard for "bullet casings and footprints and all the other kinds of things a man would naturally look for," Lottie comforts Roy's wife, Sade, who croons and cries at the kitchen table (42). As Mrs. Davies prepares chamomile tea and tidies several rooms in the house, she "reads" Sade's lamentations more loosely than had Sheriff Carroll:

[Lottie] had been to her share of funerals and knew the varying pitches of wives' wails, the sounds made for husbands corrupted with cancer, knocked down by strokes and heart attacks, bitten by water moccasins, or gored by crazy bulls. . . . When she heard Sade's very peculiar cry, she said to herself, This is neither the cry of a woman startled by death or relieved that it has finally come.

(43)

Considering various motives for Sade Duplin's outbursts, Lottie at last hears "a woman being afraid, in the main, of being caught" (43). The narrative continues, "Then [Lottie] knew exactly what had happened," and methodically recounts Mrs. Davies's re-creation of Roy's murder, step by step. In Lottie's thinking, a pie with only one piece cut and unkempt stitching attest to a wife's fury with her husband; no woman eats a prized pie alone, the matriarch contends, until "pushed past her point," nor does she sew "wild and uneven" stitches unless "distracted out of her mind" (43, 42). Deciphering Sade's behavior with non-literalist eyes and ears, Mrs. Davies constructs a possible chain of events that led to shotgun blasts and a dead man. Whether or not we endorse Lottie's style of logic, we must acknowledge that she reasons along broader lines than Sheriff Carroll, that she welcomes clues ignored by the law and opens up—rather than restricts—the meanings of "trivial" evidence.

Milk Farm Road's "Queen Bee" also grants multiplicity to her own words and actions (100). Quizzed over the travesty of her marriage, Lottie steps into Charles's shoes and explains how easily he could have misinterpreted his young bride. When Betty asks, "Do you think you ever said or did anything . . . [to make him] believe he'd found a girl who'd knock herself out working on a farm?" Lottie replies, "No. Absolutely not," but then imagines her husband's point of view:

[Charles] knew I trusted him and would more than likely yearn for things to do in his favor. He also knew that I knew how to work because Pop drank like he did and left work to the women. He had ridden by our fields and seen me getting up fodder. . . . Charles rolled all these ideas and sights of me together in his hands and opened them again and saw me there helping him break field boulders with a pickax. . . .

(12–13)

Willing to admit more than one interpretation of words she uttered as a sixteen-year-old, of deeds she thought denoted, "I'm marrying you for love and rest," Lottie allows her husband a degree of leeway (13). In fact, not only does Mrs. Davies accept words' double-edge, but she at times purposefully tampers with meaning. Determined, for instance, to buy expensive fabrics for herself and her child, Lottie "educates" Charles, misrepresenting her shopping sprees as self-sacrificing, economical outings:

Charles, the gingham was through the roof. Through the roof! So I did you a favor and bought this. I know it seems incredible that a simple cotton runs more than

chintz. I could hardly believe it myself. . . . I'm not thrilled with it, but the gingham was high as a cat's back. . . . I don't mind going about gaudy to save you money, and neither does [Betty]. We're both glad to do it.

(16–17)

Hence Lottie lies if truth becomes an inconvenience or obstacle. On another occasion, visiting her kin in Kentucky, she twists tales of Charles's death to such extremes that the family regrets their loathing of the man (106). Betty remembers, "[my mother] told [her sisters] a very moving account of how my father pulled a rover from in front of a train, thus sparing the hobo's life and losing his own," a version far different from Lottie's earlier description to Louise Miracle: "Charles was discovered upside down, straight upside down on his head with the river rocks on either side, like bookends" (106, 83). Lottie Davies uses words, splits them up and recombines them, to perpetuate the reality she wants perpetuated.

A counterpart of the speechless woman metaphor that Gibbons revises is the woman gone insane, a literary phenomenon exhaustively treated in Gilbert and Gubar's *The Madwoman in the Attic*. Summarizing these authors' position, Mary Eagleton notes that in the British and American literary traditions, a woman writer must accommodate criticism which labels her "unfeminine" and "presumptuous" for attempting the act of authorship; accordingly, she "is involved in a complex balancing act between apparent conformity to certain patriarchal literary norms and a trenchant critique of those same standards" (41). Gilbert and Gubar theorize that the "authorial rage and desire and antagonism" driving that critique are displaced in the image of the madwoman (Eagleton 41). But other feminists, such as Yaeger, question the ease with which women's studies has accepted Gilbert and Gubar's trope as "the" trope to characterize women's writing. In her introduction to *Honey-Mad Women* Yaeger charges that American feminists have "focused on women's discursive limitations," and that we need, instead, "to establish a matrix of images that will emphasize women writers' empowerment" (18, 32). No doubt Kaye Gibbons agrees. In a novel that deals so forthrightly with women's relation to language, not a single madwoman haunts *A Cure for Dreams*; in fact, the only character to lose his mind is Charles Davies, Lottie's husband, a workaholic who commits suicide when business slows during the Depression.

That Sade Duplin escapes life in an insane asylum surprises both Lottie and Betty Davies, both of whom know "all the details of exactly how Roy [Sade's husband] was imposed upon," or rather, how Roy was murdered in cold blood (41). For the plot of Sade's crime Gibbons borrows from and brilliantly recasts Susan Glaspell's "A Jury of Her Peers," a short story adaptation of Glaspell's famous one-act play, *Trifles* (1916). "A Jury of Her Peers" traces the investigation of John Wright's strangling, a deed for which Mrs. Wright is jailed and awaiting trial. The story opens with the sheriff and county attorney escorting Lewis

Hale, who discovered Wright's body, to the Wright home-place in search of evidence for a motive. Two women, Mrs. Hale and Sheriff Peters's wife, accompany the group to gather clothes for the incarcerated Minnie Wright. While the men inspect Wright's bedroom, barn, and yard, Mrs. Hale and Mrs. Peters uncover proof of domestic violence in the kitchen and sitting room. Among other items, the women find an unfinished quilt with a single block stitched crookedly ("the difference [from the other pieces] was startling" [335]) and a strangled canary, Minnie's pet. As Elaine Showalter observes, Mrs. Hale and Mrs. Peters "recognize their own bonds within a cultural system meaningless to men. . . . In a moment of silent conspiracy, they resew the pieces and destroy the other evidence" that might implicate Minnie Wright in her husband's homicide (242).

Similarities between Glaspell's story and Gibbons's fifth chapter are striking. Much of the evidence in these accounts is identical (kitchen wares, food, shoddy stitching) and the suspect wife in each is covertly defended by female neighbor(s) from "the law" and "justice" (Glaspell 338; Gibbons 41). Minnie Wright and Sade Duplin both respond spontaneously, violently, to abusive relationships—Sade with a shotgun and Minnie with a rope. Moreover, just as Showalter describes Mrs. Hale's and Mrs. Peters's observations as "meaningless to men," so Deputy Carroll's failure "to see and judge clean and dirty plates, slivers of cut pie, wild stitches, and wailing" has "more to do with the fact that he was full-time male than . . . part-time deputy and neither bright nor curious" (Showalter 242; Gibbons 46).

Gibbons's departures from Glaspell's plot, however, figure as significantly as the parallels. Sade Duplin, for instance, initiates Deputy Carroll's investigation of Roy's death, while Minnie Wright sits passively as Mr. Hale—uninvited—searches her home for Wright's body. Minnie, behind bars during the occasion of Glaspell's story, is physically absent as the sheriff and county attorney hunt for clues, but Sade wails at the kitchen table throughout John Carroll's probing. Sade also constructs an elaborate lie, a believable lie concerning Roy's murder ("Sade . . . reported about a rover her husband had run off from prowling about that morning, and in describing the man she was careful to describe a thousand men on the tramp" [45]), whereas Minnie answers Mr. Hale's questions with lines such as, "[Mr. Wright] died of a rope round his neck" and "I didn't wake up"—blunt, worn-down responses that Mr. Hale "didn't see how . . . could be" (327–28). And though Deputy Carroll never once doubts Sade Duplin's integrity, from the start of "A Jury of Her Peers," Mrs. Wright stands condemned, with only a motive needed to set her trial in motion.

Gibbons's chief innovation in revising "A Jury of Her Peers" is salvaging Sade Duplin from the madness to which Minnie Wright falls prey. Minnie seems composed while Lewis Hale questions her—rocking quietly and calling "Come in" at his knock—but bit by bit Mr. Hale de-

scribes a woman "queer" and distracted (327). Compulsively "pleat[ing] her apron," Mrs. Wright "laughs" inappropriately and digresses from simple-sentence responses to mere gestures ("'Why—where is [Wright]?' says I [Hale], not knowing what to say. [Minnie] just pointed upstairs—like this . . ." [327]). After twenty years of marriage and isolation, a woman who "used to wear pretty clothes and be lively" is reduced to a shadow that "just sat there with her hands held together . . . looking down," a speechless psychotic who slips a noose around her husband's neck and fits Gilbert and Gubar's madwoman formula perfectly (332, 328). Sade Duplin, in contrast, keeps her wits. Betty recounts:

> Neighborhood women took turns staying with Sade for weeks and weeks after Roy died. She was afraid to stay in the house alone, which with hindsight isn't surprising. We had all heard, Mean in life, meaner in death. Some nights Sade's companions had to dose her up with double and triple doses of paregoric to get her to sleep. Fear of seeing Roy Duplin or John Carroll either one at her window was more than enough to make Sade lose her reason, but she didn't.
>
> (46–47)

Gibbons bends over backward to assure readers of Mrs. Duplin's recovery. Betty further describes how, after Roy's death, strangers would no doubt "put [Sade] in the category of women who chose a single life, who live in the same house with a cat or a bird or the like all their lives and seem to be so content with everything so still" (47). The cat and bird allusions to "A Jury of Her Peers" are explicit, but Gibbons points to her source only to reconstruct Glaspell's outcome: what symbolizes Minnie's dehumanization represents Sade's improved status.

Furthermore, the tale of a madwoman perpetuated in "A Jury of Her Peers" is displaced and delegitimized by Kaye Gibbons's analogous account. In *Writing Beyond the Ending* Rachel DuPlessis describes narrative displacement as a tactic whereby the reviser, in her remaking of a tale, shifts emphasis "to the other side of the story," a side repressed or "muted" in the original version (108). DuPlessis's second strategy of revision, delegitimation, literally upsets the sequence of the original tale, "put[ting] the last first and the first last" to "rupture conventional morality, politics, and narrative" (108). If in the end of "A Jury of Her Peers" Minnie Wright sits jail-bound, biding time for the asylum, *A Cure for Dreams* restores a "clearer-eyed" Sade to the company of long-lost kin and a home renovated with Roy's hoarded cash (47). Moreover, opposed to Minnie's disoriented responses and wide-eyed gestures, Sade Duplin can talk—skillfully and convincingly—after firing her husband's shotgun; she lies to Sheriff Carroll about the rover, "press[es]" others to take Roy's belongings, and months later protests loudly against a man who deserts his pregnant wife (45, 46, 63). Insofar as *A Cure for Dreams* highlights Sade's coping mechanisms, and Sade's capacity to stay sane and direct John Carroll's investigation, Gibbons offers a fuller picture of the wife/victim/murderer than does Susan Glaspell, thereby enlarging sides of the guilty character which Glaspell's tale stifles. Gibbons also tampers with the sequence of "A Jury of Her Peers" in that she extends Sade's story past Minnie's experience; what occurs after Duplin's death is as crucial to the fifth chapter as the crime itself. More prosperous alone than when married to Roy, Sade "[makes] Roy's room over into a pretty little parlor" and enjoys gifts from her children ("boxes of stockings and sea foam taffy and a damask bed jacket and all sorts of other wonderful things") who never visited while Roy lived (47). Kaye Gibbons appropriates the trappings of Glaspell's story, revises Minnie Wright's situation, and transforms an earlier feminist text's tragedy into Sade Duplin's somewhat tough-to-stomach coup.

A Cure for Dreams revolves on the transforming capacities of talk, from Bridget O'Cadhain's "Jesus, Mary, Joseph! Blessed Virgin, Mother of God!" which signifies Bridget's "oompth" in chartering a starved family across the Atlantic; to Trudy Woodlief's "Tell it!" which encourages Betty's social criticisms; to the midwife tunes Polly Deal sings, which outline proper birthing procedures (9, 10, 89, 168–69). No subject seems insignificant in Gibbons's wielding. From page one, where Marjorie Polly Randolph explains, "talking was my mother's life," to the last sentence, "But I [Marjorie] wasn't sleeping, not for the sounds of the women talking," Gibbons rewrites conventional assumptions of Southern history by offering a distinctly female perspective of events in a small North Carolina town in the twenties, thirties, and forties. If, as linguist Deborah Tannen posits, our lives are a "series of conversations," we do well to follow Lottie Davies's rule of thumb in judging speech: "Listen and hear. . . . keep your ears open in a room with men and women" (Tannen 13; Gibbons 34–35). Certainly the women in *A Cure for Dreams* are strengthened rather than oppressed by words, with characters such as Lottie Davies and Sade Duplin serving as champions of linguistic know-how.

Note

1. The French feminists Monique Wittig and Hélène Cixous, for instance, emphasize women writers' marginality before the androcentric word; see Wittig's *Les Guérillères* (Trans. David Le Vay [New York: Avon, 1973]) and Cixous's "The Laugh of the Medusa" (Trans. Keith Cohen and Paula Cohen, *Signs* 1 [1976]: 875–93). American feminists, though typically skeptical of l'écriture féminine, also rage against notions of writing as an essentially male enterprise; Gilbert and Gubar blast "male metaphors of literary creation" with cynical cunning, asking, "Is a pen a metaphorical Penis?" (*The Madwoman in the Attic* [New Haven: Yale UP, 1984] 7). And Ann Rosalind Jones suspects that "conventional narrative techniques, as well as grammar and syntax, imply the unified viewpoint and mastery of outer reality that men have claimed for themselves" ("Writing the Body: Toward an Understanding of L'Écriture Féminine'" in *Feminist Literary Theory: A Reader*, ed. Mary Eagleton [Oxford: Basil Blackwell, 1986]

229). For a thorough treatment of questions concerning gender and language, see Patricia Yaeger's *Honey-Mad Women: Emancipatory Strategies in Women's Writing*. My essay, in fact, was largely conceived in response to Yaeger's challenge that we "multiply the paradigms available to the feminist critic" in describing "what goes on in women's writing" (239).

Works Cited

Benstock, Shari. "Letters: *The Post Card* in the Epistolary Genre." *Textualizing the Feminine: On the Limits of Genre.* Norman: U of Oklahoma P, 1991. 86–122.

DuPlessis, Rachel Blau. *Writing Beyond the Ending.* Bloomington: Indiana UP, 1985.

Eagleton, Mary, ed. "Women and Literary Production." *Feminist Literary Theory: A Reader.* Oxford: Basil Blackwell, 1986. 40–46.

Gibbons, Kaye. *A Cure for Dreams.* Chapel Hill: Algonquin, 1991.

Glaspell, Susan. "A Jury of Her Peers." *American Women Writers.* Ed. Eileen Barrett and Mary Cullinan. New York: St. Martin's P, 1992. 324–40.

Showalter, Elaine. "Piecing and Writing." *The Poetics of Gender.* Ed. Nancy K. Miller. New York: Columbia UP, 1986. 222–47.

Tannen, Deborah. *You Just Don't Understand: Women and Men in Conversation.* New York: Ballantine, 1990.

Wallace, Marybeth Sutton. "Reaping Words: Gibbons Brings Words to Fruition." *Evening Telegram* [Rocky Mount, NC] 23 Nov. 1990: 8+.

Yaeger, Patricia. *Honey-Mad Women: Emancipatory Strategies in Women's Writing.* New York: Columbia UP, 1988.

Kate Kellaway (review date 2 June 1996)

SOURCE: A review of *Sights Unseen,* in *London Observer,* June 2, 1996, p. 16.

[In the following review, Kellaway complains that there is not enough material in Gibbons's Sights Unseen *to sustain an entire novel.]*

Kaye Gibbons is a young American writer and [*Sights Unseen*] is her fifth book. It is a portrait of a manic depressive mother, by her daughter, and it reads like autobiography.

Madness may be a dramatic subject for fiction but it can also be a closed door, so that although the focus of this novel is on Maggie Barnes and the details of her breakdowns, she stays foreign, unknowable to her daughter and to the reader. There is a sense that if it were possible to climb into the madness more, to let us experience something of what Maggie Barnes was going through or to attempt to understand her psyche, the novel would have more depth. As it is, Maggie seems like a pastel version of a Tennessee Williams character who depends not on the kindness of strangers but on her brutish father-in-law (a tartar with the rest of his family). We seldom hear from Maggie directly—there is little dialogue. At first, the novel seems like a sensitively written freak show: Mother and her latest stunts.

But it improves and it is perhaps not surprising that the description of electric shock treatment is one of the best passages in the book. It is exceptionally well done: careful, horrified but not sensational and, most importantly, it is as close to Maggie Barnes as we are going to get. Equally good is the account of her changed appearance in hospital (the shock of an unbecoming hairstyle which seems to sum up the whole of her awkward, amnesiac new self) and the slow convalescence that follows treatment. It is also affecting and convincing that the daughter should hold on with such tenacity to the hope that, one day, her mother might become a real mother.

Kaye Gibbons writes with great facility and poise but there is not enough material here to sustain a novel (even if it contains enough lunacy to wreck several lives). *Sights Unseen* is itself an elegant straitjacket.

Nancy Lewis (essay date 1997)

SOURCE: "Kaye Gibbons: Her Full-Time Women," in *Southern Writers at Century's End,* edited by Jeffrey J. Folks and James A. Perkins, University Press of Kentucky, 1997, pp. 112-22.

[*In the following essay, Lewis praises Gibbons's characterization in her novels and discusses some of Gibbons's memorable heroines.*]

"I think the Southerner is a talker by nature," said Eudora Welty in an interview twenty years ago, "but not only a talker—we are used to an audience. We are used to a listener and that does something to our narrative style" (*Conversations* 94).

Storytelling is a Southern tradition. In local stores, on porch steps, the storyteller has had an audience of family and neighbors, and through generations of storytelling, much of local custom, character, and mores has been retained. Southern writers are proud of their past and of their literary heritage. In a changed and changing South, writing from an increasingly confused and complex background of shifting social scene, they've held on hard to their roots and maintained their distinctiveness. Despite the merging of the cultures of the North and the South, Walker Percy said in 1972, "perhaps it is still possible to characterize the South as having a tradition which is more oriented toward history, toward the family, toward storytelling and toward tragedy" (Welty, *Conversations* 95).

Contemporary Southern writers of fiction have been criticized for ignoring changes in the evolving South, the urbanization, the homogenization, and the dissolution of family—that element on which so much Southern writing has leaned. They have been admonished for continuing to exploit the rural scene and presenting a disingenuous family image. In 1989, in a piece in *The Nashville Scene* titled "When Is Southern Literature Going to Get Real?" the author finds current writers Jill McCorkle, Bobbie Ann Mason, and others dated and unrealistic. He teases them for holding fast to an outdated perspective. But indeed there's been good reason for the Southern writer to keep a particular nostalgia and pride in the few regional differences that were strong enough to survive the outcome of the Civil War and the nationalism that followed. Though there's no longer the rural isolation of the past, there is a legacy of speech and custom, and the family bloodline still flows. But as Eudora Welty says, "now there are so many layers of life, so many blurrings, so many homogenous things together that you have to send a taproot down perhaps deeper" (*Conversations* 105).

There is a present flowering of Southern writers, perhaps a third generation Southern Literary Renascence that would include Allan Gurganus, Jill McCorkle, Randall Garrett Kenan, Lee Smith, and Gail Godwin. Among this third generation is Kaye Gibbons, a writer who has written five remarkable novels in ten years: *Ellen Foster* was published in 1987, followed by *A Virtuous Woman, A Cure for Dreams,* and in 1993, *Charms for the Easy Life.* A fifth novel, *Sights Unseen,* was published in the fall of 1995: the story of a girl growing up with a mother who lives on the edge of madness. As in her other novels, Gibbons develops her characters with affection and humor, and, allowing us to share their intimate emotions, makes us feel an almost proprietary sympathy with them. With a vernacular authenticity that leads us to believe she didn't need to do her homework, she has presented us with stories and characters most definitely real, uncontrived, and of their time. She has given us, in particular, some memorable women.

From the frontier days, Southern women have shouldered rugged responsibilities. Since men are "generally a bad and incompetent unobservant pack," women have tended to turn to each other for help, for good company, and for general local information. In *A Cure for Dreams,* even while favorable signs in prospective suitors are being looked for, "all this information was traded freely between women with daughters, like meringue secrets or geranium cuttings."

Kaye Gibbons creates women with backbone. We see them as an unspoken community, for they recognize the needs and strengths they have in common and perforce. They are experienced in "the areas of loneliness, abandonment, betrayal, and other furious pursuits" (214), as the narrator of

Charms for the Easy Life observes in her mother and grandmother. We come to know them as individuals, learning self-reliance the hard way, facing misfortune with ingenuity and grit. As Gibbons shows us in *A Cure for Dreams,* they never "glorify in tribulation" (6), but rather seek a way out or a way to cope.

Ellen Foster, in the novel with that title, is the first of Kaye Gibbons's heroines, and she is eleven years old. The straightforward first-person narrative, dramatic for what she's telling us, never garish in the telling, is a story of pain and abuse, a recounting of her meeting with one harrowing situation after another, but it's told by a survivor. From the first pages, opening with the line "When I was little I would think of ways to kill my daddy" (1), we realize that Ellen is a remarkable, spunky little girl. Because her voice rings so true and because she's so clearheaded and honest and so funny to boot, we have absolute faith that she will find a way out of her troubles.

Ellen's brutal, drunken father is accountable for the suicide of her invalid mother. Orphaned soon after by his death from drink, Ellen must find a way of life for herself. Always practical, she realizes that in order to survive she must find herself a family. So she resolutely searches until at last she finds the right one, a kindly foster family from which she takes her last name. From the blessed comfort of her new home, where she tells us "I had me a egg sandwich for breakfast, mayonnaise on both sides. And I may fix me another one for lunch" (2), we are taken through her trials and are increasingly drawn to this plucky heroine.

After her father's death and a brief, happy stay with a sympathetic art teacher, she's placed by the court with her "mama's mama," a demented old woman who blames Ellen for her daughter's death. Having been through the heart-wrenching trauma of seeing her mother die, Ellen is then witness to her grandmother's death. She describes these two events to us in her own vivid but unembellished words. As she lies beside her mother, who has taken a fatal number of pills, she says "My heart can be the one that beats. And hers has stopped" (10). Staying with her declining grandmother, she's determined to keep the vindictive old woman alive. "I tried to make her keep breathing and when she stopped I blew air in her like I should have. She did not live but at least I did not slip into a dream beside her. I just stood by the bed and looked at her dead with her face pleasant now to trick Jesus" (79–80).

For a while she lives with her aunt and cousin, a spoiled and trivial pair who exclude her from their closely woven lives. She sees them clearly for what they are and knowing she's unwanted tells herself she'll treat their home as if it were a hotel. "If a girl was staying at my house that I did not want there, I certainly would be pleased as punch if she announced one night at supper that you will only be seeing me at meal times unless we happen to pass each other on the way to the toilet" (96).

Ellen is sensible and smart. She's smart enough to recognize the absurdity of the school psychologist's questions during their weekly sessions. Exasperated, she says "I do not plan to discuss chickenshit with you" (89). She's smart enough to search out the new mama she needs. "I looked her over plenty good too before I decided she was a keeper" (95).

And, in one of the most poignant parts of the story, her intelligence leads her to become aware of the racial prejudice she'd harbored in her relationship with her black friend, Starletta. In the early days, even though she likes Starletta and is grateful for her family's kindness, she cannot bring herself to eat with them. "No matter how good it looks to you it is still a colored biscuit" (32). By the end of the story, she realizes from her own experiences that racism led her to feel superior. Starletta has come to spend the weekend with Ellen and her new family. Resting together before supper, Ellen muses, "I always thought I was special because I was white. . . . When I thought about you I always felt glad for myself. And now I don't know why. I really don't" (125).

Kaye Gibbons's accomplishment in creating this totally believable and endearing character was an earnest of things to come. She showed us in her first novel that she has the writer's gift Eudora Welty talks of: "A writer's got to be able to live inside all characters: male, female, old, young. To live inside any other person is the jump."

Writing about Katherine Anne Porter's Miranda stories, Gibbons says that Porter's language "pulls the reader vertically towards submerged meanings and horizontally backward through time and memories." In all her novels, Gibbons shows a deft hand in juggling past and present, and in her second novel, *A Virtuous Woman,* we see how artful she is. Here there are two narrators: Ruby, who is dying of lung cancer, and her husband, Jack Stokes. In their plain language, the alternating narrative tells their story, before and after Ruby's death. Through Ruby's voice, as she prepares to die, and Jack's as he mourns her, we get to know them, their views of themselves and of each other. Through each voice recalling the same scenes, their sweet love story unfolds. We're caught up in the most important moments of their lives and the people central to them—a memorable cast of characters including a handful of really nasty ones. The proverb given us in the epigraph proclaims that the price of a virtuous woman is far above rubies. Ruby is indeed priceless. "Strength and dignity are her clothing" (Proverbs 31:10–25).

She is four months dead when the novel opens, and Jack tells us he's already finished the food she prepared and froze for him in her last months, the gesture of a strong as well as a virtuous woman: "I can't do much" (7), she tells us in her fragile state, "but I can do something. There's not a whole lot a woman can do from the grave" (7). Like other women in Kaye Gibbons's novels, she survived hard times by her own strength. "I know now," she tells us, "that this world is built up on strong women, built up and kept up by them, too, them kneeling, stooping, pulling, bending and rising up when they need to go and do what needs to be done" (13).

Jack, a childlike man with a sweet nature who introduces himself always as "Blinking Jack Ernest Stokes—stokes the fire, stokes the stove, stokes the fiery furnace of hell!" (3) is forty, twice Ruby's age, when they marry. Their love, based on a need for one another, deepens during a happy though childless marriage. Ruby knows she's "every bit of his experience" but she herself has already suffered from a disastrous match. We learn that at eighteen, babied by her fairly prosperous family, "lonesome and bored to tears" (25), she elopes with one of her father's migrant workers, a shiftless and surly man who degrades her and finally dies after a knife fight. During that brief marriage, Ruby works as a housemaid for the family who has hired her husband as a farm laborer. Here, where she is both prized and despised as coming from a higher social class than theirs, we meet the other characters central to the story. Tiny Fran, one of Gibbons's few unpleasant women, is the daughter of the household. Fat, pregnant, and unmarried when we meet her, spoiled and "mad at the whole world" (43), she is married off to one of her father's tenant farmers who takes her in exchange for the promise of forty-eight acres of good land. Her illegitimate son is a monstrous creation, a malicious rapist and woman beater who hangs Ruby's mule. The other child, neglected by Tiny Fran, turns to Ruby and Jack for nurturing, and becomes a treasure in their childless marriage.

The narrators are sympathetic people. We are attracted to them and touched by their hardships. They are plain country people; their speech rings of rural North Carolina, their metaphor is of the familiar. They are "versed in country things," as Frost puts it. Jack's mama, he says, "was a tough, hard woman, skin like a cat's tongue" (15). Tiny Fran, "getting into her feedsack of a bathing suit must've been like cramming mud into a glove" (100). Softened by love, Jack says, "I knew the sound of Ruby crying for babies the way I know a robin's call, the same way I know the sparrow's" (103).

Gibbons's characters have their own verbal idiosyncrasies, but much of their talk is regional folk speech familiar to anyone who has lived in the South, especially the rural South. Gibbons accustoms us early on to the cadences, peculiar rhythms, phrases, and provincialisms of her characters. The phrase "used to" replaces "once" or "at one time"; Jack says "used to he used to go sit at the store" (81) and "used to I wouldn't turn my hand over for green peas" (3). "Might could" or "might would" is often used instead of "might be able"; "I might could try for this girl" (20); "she might would could've joined the 4H" (62). We hear Jack say, "I was so tired I thought I might liable not to be able to . . ." (79) and "It wasn't anybody else there I gave a happy hurrah about" (80).

Her characters' speech is in no way contrived. It is natural and right. "When it comes to hearing and replicating the way people speak, Kaye Gibbons has perfect pitch," writes Anne Tyler on the cover of *A Cure for Dreams,* and other reviewers have noted her infallible ear. It is the voices of her characters that make them come alive.

A Cure for Dreams weaves a complex pattern of relationships, but the firm structure and the intimacy of scene and characters keep it within our grasp. We're quickly pulled into the lives of four generations of women, closely bonded by blood and by the very fact of their being women. Here, stronger than ever, is a feeling of party spirit and freemasonry.

Women's voices reverberate in all of Kaye Gibbons's novels and on the opening page of *A Cure for Dreams,* Marjorie, the first narrator, introduces us to her mother, Betty Davies Randolph, who has recently "died in a chair talking, chattering like a string-pull doll" (1). Marjorie says, "I had spent my life listening to her, sometimes all day, which often was my pleasure during snow and long rains—Talking was my mother's life" (1).

We hear Betty's voice comfortably narrating the family history to Marjorie, beginning with her grandmother, Bridget O'Cadhain, who, with her family, had come from Galway to Kentucky, to start farm life. Bridget's daughter, Lottie, tired of her meager surroundings, "perched on ready, hoping for a marriage proposal" (10), at sixteen marries a Welsh Quaker, Charles Davies, and they move to North Carolina. Charles is an ambitious man whose life becomes more and more obsessively centered on work in his farm and gristmill. He had expected his bride to share in the labor, but Lottie was not given to that traditional female involvement; she had married him for "love and rest" (13) and longed for babies. By the time Betty is born, Lottie has grown indifferent to Charles, and with no more babies coming, mother and daughter become increasingly close companions, sharing a life that hardly includes the driven husband.

Life at home being less than satisfactory, Lottie's energies, which are real and formidable, go into finding her own community, with little Betty always at her side, "her goal being to organize a gang of women for a habitual social hour" (30). These are lively meetings, full of gossip, politics, and gambling (this she tries to hide from Charles, who "hated gambling or anything at all involving the luck of the draw" [32]), and here we meet the women of Milk Farm Road. Betty tells us that her mother "remade herself into the Queen Bee, more or less organizing life through knowing everything" (100). She knows every household inside out and she dispenses help and advice to the point of officiousness, the justification for meddling being "anytime somebody's not looking after themselves it becomes your business" (97). But she is sagacious, sound, and of good heart, and her intimate and thorough familiarity with these neighbor women enables her to help them in extraordinary circumstances. She "knew the varying pitches of wives' wails" (43), and in one instance by hearing the cry of a woman whose husband has been murdered and by closely observing the domestic scene, she finds clues—a pie with one piece cut, a row of uncharacteristically messy stitches in a quilt the woman is making, the absence of burrs or dandelion seedwings from her cotton stockings—which lead her to deduce that the deed was done by the woman herself. Since the deputy sheriff investigating the crime has missed all these details and since the husband "was such a sonofabitch" (46), it's clear to Lottie that his wife had ample and justifiable reason to rid herself of a thoroughly bad lot.

Lottie is capable of keeping her own business to herself, of protecting herself from the nosiness of others. Her husband, Charles, undone in the Depression years by his failing farm and unsatisfied obsession with success, walks into the river and drowns himself. When a curious neighbor asks her how he was found, she replies, "Charles was discovered upside down, straight upside down on his head with the river rocks on either side, like bookends" (83). To satisfy the inquisitive questions of her Kentucky relatives, she creates a moving story of her husband losing his life while pulling a tramp from the path of a speeding train.

Strong as is her attachment to her mother, young Betty hankers to leave the confining boundaries of Milk Farm Road and see more of the world. She's encouraged by Trudy Woodlief, an exotic newcomer from Baton Rouge, introduced to us "with one leg high up on a bureau, smoking a cigarette and shaving her legs with lotion and a straight razor" (56). Trudy counsels Betty to leave her mother and Milk Farm Road, if that's what she wants, or to stop whining. Betty does have a try at the outside world. She gets as far as Richmond, Virginia, where an unhappy love affair sends her back home. Here on Milk Farm Road she marries and stays and talks. The last line of the novel is her daughter Marjorie's infant dream-memory of the moments after her birth. "But I wasn't sleeping, not for the sound of the women talking" (171).

Gibbons is increasingly adroit at handling time and place. In the stretch of years covered in *A Cure for Dreams,* there is no leap or disconnection; the conversational narrative transports us effortlessly from present to past and back again; the anecdotal style elucidates the past and introduces secondary characters.

Backgrounds become progressively more distinct in the novels, but though stage and scene are given in more detail, they are given only as needed for the development of the protagonists. Physical descriptions are spare—an occasional glance of green eyes, fresh lavender plaited into a braid of hair, a new dress with a row of lace at the throat—but each character is as vivid as if marked by a cicatrix.

In *Ellen Foster,* where the narrative is intensely inward, the time and place of the story are relatively unimportant. Landmarks have been sketched in to help us follow Ellen's journey from her unhappy parents' house to the clean brick house which is her home with her new mama and family and the setting for her new life. On the way to church, we pass houses and barns; then after going through "colored town," we see white houses and yards, but our concentration is on what happens to the small central figure.

In the works that follow we're made more aware of background (fields, farms, rural landscape, the houses on Milk Farm Road), and of the times when events take place. In *A Cure for Dreams,* "homes were in the grip of Mr. Hoover and his Depression" (30). *Charms for the Easy Life* brings us into the Second World War, when our heroines volunteer in a veterans' hospital, and we're given background details such as jitterbugging being outlawed on the Duke campus ("not so much for moral reasons as because of the numbers of students landing in the infirmary with dislocated shoulders" [199]).

These particulars are not gratuitous or unimportant. We need them for the development of the stories and characters. Perhaps it is the Southern storyteller's inherited practice of honing and editing to please the listener's ear that has given Kaye Gibbons her skill in economy and structure. Even in *Ellen Foster,* she avoids the mistake made so often by writers of putting into their first novels everything they've ever seen, heard, or observed. Gibbons is never wasteful or extravagant. Her characters are always in prime focus: above all, the women and the voices of those women.

Admittedly there are some sympathetic men in these novels, and when a good man does show up he's recognized as such and appreciated with good grace. Jack Stokes in *A Virtuous Woman* has great appeal; Charlie Nutter, a figure in *Charms for the Easy Life,* is a winner; and we have every reason to believe that Margaret, the narrator of the latter story, has chosen well in Tom Hawkings. (He is approved by Margaret's grandmother, Charlie Kate, one of Kaye Gibbons's most astute protagonists.) But on the whole, men are an inferior breed. Ellen Foster's daddy was "a mistake for a person" (49). Men are represented as an unpromising lot, just by their nature, as we see in the deputy sheriff in *A Cure for Dreams,* whose ineptitude "had more to do with the fact that he was a full-time male than it did with the fact that he was merely part-time deputy and neither bright nor curious" (46).

Intelligence and curiosity are, on the other hand, qualities we find in all Gibbons's central women figures, who are certainly reflections of herself, for as Eudora Welty remarks in *One Writer's Beginnings*: "of course any writer is in part all of his characters. How otherwise would they be known to him, occur to him, become what they are?" (101).

These women, like their creator, are smart, alert, and literate, and their literary interests and intellectual curiosity are made to seem as credible as their speech. Ellen Foster tells us: "I told the library teacher I wanted to read everything of some count so she made me a list. That was two years ago and I'm up to the Brontë sisters now" (9). She is excited by the bookmobile, and she spends secret hours with the little plastic microscope she bought and presented to herself for Christmas. Enthralled with what she sees on the slides, she feels she "could stay excited looking at live specimens day in and day out" (104). In *A Cure for Dreams,* the narrator, Betty, "had hit the first grade running and moved right on through like I was born to go to school" (51). Margaret, in *Charms for the Easy Life,* spends much of her time in the two years after high school reading Sophocles, Euripides, Homer, and Aeschylus. It is her grandmother Charlie Kate's wonderful intelligence, as well as her healing powers and charismatic nature, that draws Margaret to her. "I became fascinated with her mind, enamored of her muscular soul" (46).

Charms for the Easy Life presents us with three generations of smart, strong-willed women: Margaret, the narrator; her mother, Sophia; and Sophia's mother, Charlie Kate, a character I'd match against any of the heroines I've admired in recent years. They are a vivid threesome, linked by blood and by their passionate natures. In the case of Charlie Kate and Sophia, the bond is made stronger when the men they have unwisely chosen, one way or another, leave them.

Charlie Kate, at twenty an accomplished and popular midwife, marries a man nowhere near her in spirit or intelligence and in 1910, moves with him and their daughter, Sophia, to Raleigh, North Carolina, where she becomes a curer of ills and a campaigner for good health and hygiene. When her husband leaves her, she has already established a successful practice "with sick people coming forth like the loaves and the fishes" (22). Sophia is her constant companion until she too marries a man far beneath her, handsome but a cad. Their child, Margaret, realizes, when her father dies, that it is not much of a loss. "I didn't think I'd have less of a life with him gone. I know my mother and I would have more" (49). Charlie Kate, who had so disapproved her daughter's bad choice in marrying that she refused to set foot in their house until begged to, on his death moves in with daughter and granddaughter, and their life together is the heart of the story. They are possessed of indomitable spirit and very much aware of their strength as women. As Margaret tells us, "If my grandmother could've populated the world, all the people would've been women" (93).

Charlie Kate's reputation as a self-made doctor continues to grow. Her genius is recognized by licensed medical doctors as well as by her patients, and she's proud of the fact that her fame has reached as far as the Outer Banks, where a leper hears of her healing accomplishments and walks a hundred miles to seek her help.

On her visits to the sick, Sophia and Margaret are her assistants, helping with every kind of grizzly operation; while at home, their daily life is occupied with voracious reading. "When a good book was in the house, the place fairly vibrated" (116). They approach reading with the vigor and passion with which they tackle everything. Margaret tells us that Charlie Kate "would sit for hours and contemplate the disappearance of the opening narrator in *Madame Bovary* with the same intensity with which she would line up a patient's symptoms and then labor over a diagnosis" (117). We don't wonder that Margaret can't bear the thought of leaving home to attend one of the fine colleges her school principal has proposed for her.

Charlie Kate is part of a tradition in the South of women healers whose cures and prescriptions are passed down from one generation to the next. In reading about North Carolina folkways and folk medicine, I've discovered that in some cases a certain amount of wizardry would seem to make the prescription questionable. A great deal of common sense, however, is usually behind these cures, plus intelligence and practicality. In a widely used volume called *Domestic Medicine, or Poor Man's Friend,* published in 1830 in Knoxville, Tennessee, the author, John C. Gunn, thanked God for having "stored our mountains, fields, and meadows with simples [medicinal plants] for healing our diseases" (15). Practical sense and economic necessity suggested the use of things at hand in the kitchen or garden, so remedies included local wild and cultivated plants, herbs, barks, and animals. One learns that sassafras bark or root thins the blood and prevents chills and fevers. Sage or horehound tea is good for general sickness, including colds, and bloodroot soaked in whiskey is used for liver trouble.

In her early days of healing, Charlie Kate refers to Gunn's medical manual and continues to increase her knowledge by keeping up to date with legitimate medical practitioners. "She refused to cross over the line from natural medicine into black magic, although, in many cases, if she had not combined useless folk remedies with treatments she judged to be therapeutic, her uneducated and overly superstitious patients would not have trusted her" (47). But although she's disdainful of voodoo and quackery and shows rationality and wisdom in her dealings with her patients, her prize possession is the charm given to her years ago by a lynching victim whom she had cut down and revived from near death. It is "the hind foot of a white graveyard rabbit caught at midnight, under the full moon, by a cross-eyed Negro woman who had been married seven times" (19). This is the talisman Charlie Kate has saved so many years and presents to her granddaughter, Margaret, to give to the man she loves (hence the book's title, *Charms for the Easy Life*).

The force behind all good writers remains the urgency to communicate. Doris Betts has said, "I write because I have stories I don't want to die with." Certainly one feels, reading Kaye Gibbons, that her stories had to be told, her characters born. One recognizes her unfailing ear, her dazzling control of the passage of time. However, in the increasing rewards of rereading, a conscious probing fails to reveal the sleight of hand that produced these works: the translation of her talents from the inside of her head to the printed page remains a mystery. Even gazing hard at a painting by Vermeer, it's difficult to believe that these seemingly life-size portraits are contained within a canvas scarcely twelve inches square. With similar wizardry, Gibbons, in a condensed number of pages, sweeps us into the lives of her ordinary people, and they become living and three dimensional as she creates for us not only their present world but the past that has made them what they are.

Eudora Welty, in *One Writer's Beginnings,* says,

> It is our inward journey that leads us through time—forward or back, seldom in a straight line, most often spiraling. Each of us is moving, changing, with respect to others. As we discover, we remember: remembering, we discover: and most intensely do we experience this when our separate journeys converge. Our living experience at those meeting points is one of the charged dramatic fields of fiction.

> [102]

It is the expression of Kaye Gibbons's inward journey that helps to explain the distinctive accomplishments of her fiction.

Kathryn McKee (essay date Summer 1997)

SOURCE: "Simply Talking: Women and Language in Kaye Gibbons's *A Cure for Dreams,*" in *Southern Quarterly,* Vol. 35, No. 4, Summer, 1997, pp. 97-106.

[*In the following essay, McKee analyzes the uniquely feminine language in Gibbons's* A Cure for Dreams *and the way that language binds the female characters to a community of women.*]

Not coincidentally, the final word of Kaye Gibbons's third novel *A Cure for Dreams* (1991), is "talking." Pairing that word with the work's first one, "simply," reveals the primary activity of the novel—simply talking. The talkers in this case are the women of small-town North Carolina who take pleasure in the art of conversation and discover in language a power otherwise inaccessible to them as women in pre-World War II America. For the female characters of Gibbons's novel, words bind generations, not just as members of the same family or as citizens of the same small town, but as women. Gibbons offers an intriguing variation on the stereotypical assumption that southerners and women enjoy conversation. She departs in her fiction from an emphasis on language as the transmitter of history and the vehicle for storytelling in order to make conversation and its implications for female community the main thrust of her novel. For Gibbons's women, the desire and the ability to converse meaningfully about daily living are the conveyances between generations, the defining attributes that bind the novel's females into an indissoluble community and give voice and credence to the "domestic ritual" that Ann Romines discusses in her study *The Home Plot.* Language additionally provides the women with a balm for the dreams they relinquished in order to assume their culturally mandated roles.

Yet Gibbons's characters, like Janie in Zora Neale Hurston's *Their Eyes Were Watching God,* discover far more powerful uses for language than solace. Particularly significant is their discovery of the transforming power of language. Language becomes the tool by which these women manipulate the information they give to male char-

acters and by which they shape the realities they otherwise find unbearable. They discover community in conversation, then, but power in the multi-faceted semantics of words. The use of first-person narration, offered not by one, but by three interwoven female voices, is also an important feature of Gibbons's novel, particularly in light of Joanne S. Frye's insightful discussion of the "subversive 'I'" in her study *Living Stories, Telling Lives.* The reader may presume the narrative form of *A Cure for Dreams* to be a record of spoken discourse recalled by the narrator; quotation marks enclose the body of the novel, a fact that necessarily calls the reliability of the text into question at certain crucial junctures. The speaker is Betty Davies Randolph, who cannot tell the story of her own life without the voice of her mother, Lottie, literally intruding onto the page in the form of italicized commentary. Similarly, letters written by Marjorie Polly Randolph, Betty's daughter, frame the central narrative. Thus the voices of three generations conspire to tell the tale of women who find the most satisfying moments of their lives in literal and spiritual conversation with one another. Frye maintains that a "female narrator-protagonist" resists both the cultural and the generic definition of acceptable femininity when she speaks and acts for herself. The protagonist-narrator signals to the reader (who may also approach the text with traditional expectations) that she is capable of change, that she is still in the process of development and thus traditional plot resolutions may not conform to the unfolding of her particular story (64ff.). First-person narration, then, lends power to both the individual and the communal female voices in this text, allowing those voices to tell their own stories, stories about the intricacies of female interaction.

Each of Gibbons's novels incorporates at least one female center of consciousness, and, in fact, she often renders them solely from that perspective. But *A Cure for Dreams,* more forcefully so than any of Gibbons's other works, addresses the issue of female community juxtaposed against the simultaneous development of the individual female voice. Gibbons's exploration of the complex interaction between women makes her text a powerful document in charting a decidedly female approach to the use of language. Hélène Cixous's observation that "there's *tactility* in the feminine text, there's touch, and this touch passes through the ear" (54) lends added significance to the emphasis on orality and aurality in Gibbons's narrative. Not only does she tap into the southern cultural emphasis on oral storytelling, but she also delves into a more far-reaching examination of both the positive and negative aspects of the spoken exchanges and the silences that characterize women's discourse in general—all in one thin volume, ostensibly about three women in rural North Carolina.

In focusing her novel on female discourse, Gibbons distinguishes her work both from the fiction written by the forefathers of the southern renascence and from the writing produced by her southern literary contemporaries. For Gibbons, the inheritance passed from generation to generation is not a reverential remembrance of the past, the pervasive echo of a defeated South heard, for instance, by the genteel upper classes of Faulkner's fiction. Nor do her characters allow their introspection to consume them and thus dangerously blur the distinctions between a past and a present world, as do the characters of Faulkner, Robert Penn Warren or Walker Percy. Even in a later, female-centered text like Lee Smith's *Fair and Tender Ladies,* the significance attached to storytelling is its function as a transmitter of factual material from the past: family history that links one generation to the next and survives orally. While Alice Walker, in a story like "Everyday Use," does focus her examination on female intergenerational relations, she too emphasizes the communication of family memories and inherited practical skills. Maggie does not need the quilts themselves to be able to recall her grandmother; she has learned the art of quilting and that ability connects her to preceding generations of women. For Gibbons's characters, however, the primary function of conversation is not the retelling of the past, although certainly the novel does recount one of the central character's growth to adulthood. For Gibbons's women, conversation has a value in and of itself because it lends them a voice. Historical events like the Great Depression and World War II serve simply as personal markers along the road to each woman's acquisition of an increasingly clearer and more articulate voice. The purpose of that voice is not to equip women for participation in the male-dominated discourse that undeniably continues to structure their physical worlds. Rather their acquisition of voice allows them to talk to one another, and from that communion they draw the strength necessary both to exist within and to circumvent the confines of patriarchal dominion. Thus the legacy passed from woman to woman does not depend on language as the medium for recounting particular events or for transferring the ability to perform particular skills. The legacy is simply talking.

From the perspective of the novel's female characters, the males of *A Cure for Dreams* err in brandishing language as a sign of authority rather than selectively and intelligently employing it as a means of power. Betty's grandfather bursts briefly into the early narrative; he proves memorable chiefly for his alcoholic and daily demands that one of his daughters cook him "a goddamn egg" upon request (8). Although he usually gets his wish, Betty's grandmother berates him so when she learns of his behavior that the kitchen disintegrates into an arena for a shouting match. Betty can well understand why her mother was "perched on ready" to escape all members of the family, regardless of gender (10). The blustering of other men in the text meets with equally limited results. When Betty is twelve, she becomes ill, and the doctor patronizingly dismisses her symptoms as "more or less popular female complaints" until the severity of Betty's illness disproves his diagnosis (22–23). Finally, Roy Duplin, arguably the least sympathetic male in the text, bellows regularly and authoritatively for his wife, Sade—until she stifles his verbal ragings with a gunshot. She probably kills him, Betty speculates, "in the midst of his yapping at her" (45). "Yap-

ping" signals neither verbal felicity nor verbal power but instead reveals an inability to harness the potential of the spoken word.

Other male characters in the novel talk not too loudly or too harshly, but simply too much, reducing their speech to nothing more than the repetition of meaningless words and phrases. Porter, the shopkeeper, repeats the same worn-out explanations about his credit policy to Trudy Woodlief, the lower-class single mother from Louisiana, who finally responds by releasing her band of dirty, scavenging children on the store "like pool balls" (65); they extend to themselves the "credit" their mother so desperately needs. Betty's first romance, with the suave Virginian named Stanton, ends when she discovers his drug dependency. When she walks away from him in the hospital, he can only call out "Hey, girlie! Come back, girlie!" (131). He reduces himself to little more than a stereotypical catcaller with no personal connection to the target of his appeals. As in the case of those who speak with the bullying voice of authority, these men find their ability to use language stunted.

The only man who seems capable of interweaving power and authority in discourse is Betty's father, Charles. After all, he entices Lottie away from her homeland with words she recalls as "*sound[ing] reasonable and true*" (7). But although much that Charles tells Lottie might be true, very little about Charles's married life with Lottie turns out to be reasonable, at least from her point of view. Their love fades quickly, driven out by his churlishness and her refusal to concede to it. Yet Charles knows how to torment his wife simply by uttering the right combination of words. He consistently refers to the summer of 1932 as "the time she let [Betty] get sick"; Betty once "actually saw her [mother] put a hand out for balance" upon hearing the words (25). Yet even Charles's power wanes as his litany of complaints about the economic woes of the Depression outdistances any real suffering experienced by the family. Eventually Betty reports that she and her mother "even talked over his voice about the most trifling of things" (71–72). Poised on the brink of what Betty later recognizes as his unreason, Charles never realizes how completely the power of language has escaped him. Although, as Lucinda MacKethan observes in *Daughters of Time,* "Southern daughters were the creations and inheritors of a culture which in part defined and perpetuated itself by their silence" (5), Lottie teaches Betty to speak. Her father Charles is the representative cultural male who fails to acknowledge the validity of any female voice other than one that mechanically responds to his wishes. Consequently the women talk to each other; Charles talks to himself.

The females in Gibbons's text are the characters who appreciate and utilize the power of language. Lottie learns from her own mother, Bridget, that women have the power to utilize language on their own terms. An Irish immigrant, Bridget refuses to learn English. Despite the fact that her native land cannot provide sustenance for her family, she clings ferociously to the native language that has always ordered her life. Similarly, her descendants Lottie and Betty privilege their own discourse over Charles's, and in so doing privilege their concerns, even the trivial ones, over the voice of economic despair permeating Depression-weary America. Thus they create a world, a reality, of their own in contradistinction to the patriarchally defined one in which they must typically operate. By doing so they neither delude themselves with a false reality nor retreat in weakness from a reality that intimidates them. Rather the women create an alternative reality that is simply more meaningful for them. Lottie's connection to her husband's financial affairs has always been a remote one; he is the financial controller, although she clearly finds means of circumventing his authority (cleaning out his pockets in search of loose bills and change, for instance). The hardships of the Depression era unquestionably affected most Americans. But the female Americans of this novel have a different relationship to the crisis than their male counterparts. Lottie and Betty do not oversee a business. They have made no investments and a bank book does not define the parameters of their real daily world. The boundaries of their reality the women establish for themselves; their language both reflects and empowers their choices.

Women also use language to manipulate the reality perceived by the men of the novel. Occasionally they simply lie. The cycle in which Lottie swears to Charles that she has given up playing cards, only to have him later hear tales of her winnings, for instance, repeats itself several times. Yet when Lottie actually convinces her husband that chintz costs less than gingham and that she saves the family money with her prudent fabric choices, she does more than speak falsely about a single episode. She manipulates her husband's understanding of cloth, but more importantly, she shapes his understanding of her. She figuratively cuts and sews from the material a self she wants Charles to see, a self who will pacify his unreasonable nature and pave for her the path of least resistance in preserving the lifestyle she desires. Likewise, in circulating fictional accounts of the social diseases carried by the woman Roy Duplin adulterously romances, Lottie manipulates not just Roy's actions, but also his perceptions of them. The wayward Roy returns to his troubled home, and Betty learns another lesson from her mother about the power of the spoken—or in this case the whispered—word.

Lottie briefly turns the transforming power of language inward upon her own marriage as well. She most intriguingly exercises the reality-shaping power of words when she completely appropriates her dead husband's existence. Back in her native Kentucky, forced by her family to recount the circumstances of her husband's death, Lottie uses words to transform his suicide into a hero-like rescue of a vagrant from the train tracks. In fact, Charles Davies jumped to his death in what Betty characterizes as "a more particularly selfish act than usual" (81). Thus Lottie briefly glimpses a different life for herself. Yet she remains unmistakably aware of the gulf separating this imaginary world from her real one.

The impulse to manipulate perception with language is complicating from the reader's viewpoint; he or she admittedly encounters a potentially unreliable version of reality rendered by the narrative's storytellers. Lottie and Betty conclude, for example, that the family is not as destitute as the undeniably taciturn Charles maintains they are. But in the panic of the Great Depression, how far can the reader fault the houschold's primary breadwinner for exercising extreme caution? Is it really so ridiculously cruel of him to refuse to spend rationed gas on a driving expedition to window-shop? As his financial woes accelerate, imaginary or genuinely life-threatening, Charles retreats even further from his family and from any human contact. Betty herself observes: "My father had no friends accumulated" (69). From an early age, Betty has essentially adopted her mother's attitudes and mannerisms in dealing with her father, slipping out of the room in her mother's wake when Lottie exits in anger. Thus as Betty brands her father's suicide a supremely selfish act, the reader must wonder how intimately either Betty or her mother even know the man anymore. Also questionable is Betty's assertion that she would "have died for him to talk to me my entire life" (78). Yet Lottie tells her daughter: you *"cried whenever he picked you up"* (15). Whether Lottie works here to mold her daughter's impression of Charles or actually recalls the truth remains unclear. Regardless, Betty records a telling early impression of her father: she and her mother were home "chitter-chattering when he came in from work. When the door closed behind him, I thought, He's come home to ruin our day. . . . This was my first original thought of my father" (15). But that suspicion is really not so original. Her thought likely parallels the one that consistently springs to Lottie's mind. Neither father nor daughter seems to have actively pursued meaningful conversation with the other. Charles recognizes the daughter as a miniature rendering of the mother; Betty perceives her father as the force that threatens her bond with her mother. Thus she moves toward the female community from which her mother draws sustenance, and she learns there the manipulative power of spoken discourse.

The bond between Lottie and Betty transcends any other relationships they formulate, even spousal ones. That tie draws its significance from talking, the very activity that Charles interrupts when he returns home. Betty surmises that her father had so frequently brushed her mother aside that "she had learned to keep her hands to herself with him, which is, I'm sure, why she held my hand fairly continuously" (71). Betty returns gladly the pressure of her grasp. Yet as she clings to Betty's hand, Lottie is seldom silent. That fact is also potentially dangerous, in this case for the development of Betty's individual voice, a voice that can both articulate her independently formulated views and participate in a communal chorus. Interestingly, Mary Field Belenky et al. found in their study, *Women's Ways of Knowing,* "that women repeatedly used the metaphor of voice to depict their intellectual and ethical development; and that the development of a sense of voice, mind, and self were intricately intertwined" (18). Gibbons pins a similar metaphoric significance to women's literal voice in

A Cure for Dreams; Betty's discovery of her ability to speak for herself parallels her movement into articulate womanhood. Yet throughout most of the text Lottie's assertiveness threatens to eclipse her daughter's individuality. She has, for example, created in part Betty's awkward relationship with her father. Lottie encourages Betty to marry Herman before he goes off to war, even going so far as to appropriate Betty's voice completely and actually compose the letter Betty "writes" to him after first learning of his intention to join the Navy. Chief among Herman's attributes, at least from Lottie's perspective, is the fact that his departure will allow mother and daughter to maintain their current routine in the same house. The wedding shower gifts Betty receives are to be incorporated into the joint household the women share. And when Betty is uncertain about how to respond to her new mother-in-law's suggestion that she bake something for Herman's voyage, Lottie literally speaks for her. In that reply, Lottie significantly shapes the role of wife her daughter will anticipate. Betty remembers that Lottie "told Herman's mother that cooking for enlisted men was not my pleasure" (153). Lottie's language literally and repeatedly penetrates the text in the form of italicized passages that overtake Betty's own observations, and the intermingling of their voices typifies this mother-daughter relationship.

Yet the reader can finally recognize each storyteller's voice, despite Lottie's insistent domination of Betty's fledgling impulses to speak. Betty periodically asserts herself in defiance of her mother's wishes (her sojourn in Richmond, for instance) and occasionally even engages her mother in heated debate. Significantly, Betty passes into independent womanhood during the birth of her daughter, Marjorie. In these moments Betty's guide is no longer her mother. It is instead Polly, a mother figure of a different race and class. Polly counsels against sending for Lottie because she has seen too many young women "look for their mama to tell them when they're supposed to hurt and stop hurting. And I think that you as much as anybody needs to do this one thing this time without Miss Lottie" (167). Thus Betty crosses the threshold to motherhood without the literal presence of her own mother, but she is better able to fill her new role because she has established the pain of childbirth in her own experience, rather than through the filter of her mother. Betty names her child in the language she now commands; thus she both appropriates the historically male task of naming and does so without Lottie, her tutor in language acquisition. Betty calls the baby "Marjorie Polly" after the black woman who delivers her, rather than naming her after Lottie. Yet the child's legacy is the same.

That legacy constitutes automatic membership in the physical and spiritual female community from which the women of the novel draw their greatest strength. The circle of women at the novel's core does not consist simply of Lottie and Betty, but broadens to incorporate both a regular gathering of females at Porter's store and the larger surrounding female community. What Lottie instigated as a social gathering becomes a support network of card-playing women; "information was traded freely . . . like meringue secrets or geranium cuttings," particularly "between women with daughters," who are the glad recipients of tidbits about the male residents of this small town (53). Polly's presence in the novel, like that of Trudy Woodlief, further signals that Gibbons's subject in *A Cure for Dreams* is not any particular mother-daughter relationship. It is rather an expansive community of women bound by their similarities. The women Lottie forms into a group, for example, are initially daunted by Trudy Woodlief's unorthodox behavior, but they engineer the solution to her difficulty in buying food; they offer Sade Duplin unspoken support in the face of her husband's alcoholic ragings; and they stand firm behind the economic roller coaster that becomes Amanda Bethune's life. At the center of this operation is Lottie, whose intention, Betty surmises, "was to leave [her husband] without leaving him" (29). Her refuge becomes female companionship with her daughter and with the women of the literal and emotional community in which she lives. After Betty's death, Marjorie observes: "talking was my mother's life" (2). Lottie, her daughter Betty and her granddaughter Marjorie all value similarly not just the pleasure of conversation, but also the life-sustaining force of simply talking. Thus Gibbons and her characters issue direct challenge to a commonplace disdain for "women's talk" traditionally expressed by both men and women and linked to the assumption that the subjects historically predominant in exchanges between women— "concern for the everyday, the practical, and the interpersonal"—are somehow merely trivial fact-trading (Belenky et al. 17). Conversation is the force Gibbons's characters alternately use to shape reality and to stave it off; it is their consolation in the wake of failed dreams, and it is the most enduring gift they give to one another. Talking remains Betty's life. Spoken words, transferred to written ones, preserve her story. Further, by achieving and then using her own voice, Betty lends herself authenticity outside of male rhetoric and outside of what Frye calls "the femininity text," the typical male construction of female experience (3). Lottie herself has endowed Betty and Marjorie with the desire for that authenticity by serving as an illustration of the powerfully articulate woman.

The tellers of this narrative likewise demonstrate that talking alone is not enough to build a community. Talking is only half of an exchange that requires listening as well, the activity that lends talking its significance. Part of what makes language powerful in *A Cure for Dreams* is its function in creating dialogue and creating listeners horizontally among the central characters of the novel and vertically from one generation of those characters to the next. Likewise the reader may hear in the conversation of these fictional women what Romines calls "an essential rhythm of most women's lives"—the rhythm of the domestic world. Romines concludes that "when readers encounter a literature that acknowledges that rhythm and its complex traditions and imperatives, they find themselves drawing from their own lives and histories in unaccustomed ways" (15). Listening, then, is a skill to be cultivated and practiced with regularity, by the characters and especially by the reader, who likewise listens to the stories retold in the narrative. In one of her letters to Betty in Richmond, Lottie encourages her to return home because Polly *"talks continuously and I need somebody here to help me listen to her"* (132). Years of listening to her mother make Betty well-suited both to perform that task and to value a sense of community inspired by the interplay of talking and listening.

Lottie also teaches Betty how to hear the undertones of male language correctly. Often, Betty learns, the most important information lies in what men fail to say; absences in male language can be revelatory to women, especially when the male speaker is unaware of what he is actually communicating. Lottie demonstrates the importance of a single spoken (or not spoken) word—a woman's name—in detecting the nature of male/female relationships. The most loving marriages, Lottie asserts, are those in which the man calls his wife by name. Later, in analyzing her attachment to Stanton, Betty comes to the all-important revelation that Stanton never uses her name. And she walks away from him, hearing in his silence the future he promises. Stanton can only guess at her reasons for leaving.

Thus the women of *A Cure for Dreams* essentially speak and hear a different language than the novel's male characters. That female language both relies on and transcends the literal spoken word. When the sheriff comes to fetch Lottie at a birthday party, Betty recalls "all those women, including myself and the hundred-year-old lady, staring, trying to make out his lips" (40). Immersed in their own community and their own conversation, the women struggle to process the sheriff's intrusion, to reconnect to the world from which he comes and to understand its message. As Betty feared her father's intrusion on the conversation between her mother and herself, so the sheriff spoils the day with news of Roy Duplin's untimely demise. But the sheriff never understands what really happened to Roy, largely because the officer is, in Betty's words, a "full-time male" (46). Lottie pieces together the facts of Sade's crime, relying on her eye for detail in assessing household trivia, but relying most definitively on the truth she hears in Sade's wailing cry. To Lottie's practiced ear, Sade confesses to murder; to the sheriff her admission of guilt remains indecipherable because she utters it in a language that he not only cannot understand, but that he cannot even hear.

The women of this novel just as often communicate in a sort of nonverbal language. Sade and Lottie never mention the fact that Lottie quietly fixes Sade's uneven stitching on the night she kills her husband, yet certainly sending for Lottie on that evening is Sade's tacit request for the help she receives. Later, when a young boy is killed in her father's mill, Betty perceives the depth of her mother's anger in her silence rather than in her conversation; Betty recalls never having "heard her [mother] so quiet and still" (73). After Lottie essentially baits the neighbor's dogs to attack Charles as her retaliation for his hardheartedness, she tells Betty "without telling [her] how pleased she was

with herself" (75). The women never literally discuss the night's events. Conversely, attempting nonverbal communication between sexes proves unsuccessful. Lottie recalls that she had thought marrying Charles *"would be as plain as spoken words, that I was saying without actually saying, I'm marrying you for love and rest"* (13). Charles believes he detects acquiescence in his new wife's silence, acceptance of the life based on physical labor that he spreads out before her like a quilt of possibilities. It is their first misunderstanding, but it is the same misunderstanding that they wrestle with daily for the extent of their married lives. Lottie learns to make sure she and her husband always disagree verbally.

Intriguingly, the female use of both spoken language and silence in *A Cure for Dreams* echoes backward in literary time to another text. Susan Glaspell's "Trifles" (1916), that likewise illustrates the peculiar ability of women to understand one another.[1] In her discussion of metafiction, Gayle Greene observes that "weaving literary allusions into their narratives structurally and thematically, [female authors] problematize 'intertextuality' and enlist it to suggest that experience is structured by the stories we inherit" (19). Glaspell's play about two women who become complicit to murder by their silence resonates powerfully in Gibbons's narrative and may reveal that in addition to being a storyteller, Gibbons is a listener as well. In each work, female characters deduce that a dead man's wife is also his murderer, and they do so by observing the innuendoes of household living from a female perspective. The male characters bypass these details, unable to understand the vital connection in Glaspell's work between an empty birdcage and years of abuse and neglect or the link in Gibbons's story between a sliver of pie and a lifetime of waiting and disappointment. Gibbons even has Lottie restore Sade's ragged stitching to uniformity, just as Mrs. Hale rectifies Mrs. Wright's erratic sewing in the earlier narrative; both guilty women were working on quilts when their characteristically neat stitching became jagged. And in both instances, silence characterizes the ultimate communication between the novel's female characters who understand without ever uttering a word that responsibility for the crime will go unclaimed. They will never affix blame to the guilty wife, and the male characters will likely never add up enough household details to reach the conclusion so patently obvious to the female observers.

Gibbons's echo of Glaspell is likewise silent—she makes no direct reference to the earlier text. Yet the submerged parallels between the works speak volumes about a persistent conviction that men and women see and hear the world differently, that women communicate in a sort of spoken and unspoken language that males finally cannot access. Gibbons's inheritance of Glaspell's story molds her own; Gibbons's text likewise shapes the reader's understanding of female voice. Silence, so long imposed by an institutionalized male authority like the sheriff, is an equally powerful tool when women choose to use it, and thus female characters in both texts communicate just as effectively when they bypass verbal exchange. Gibbons again signals the expansive nature of her subject. She is concerned not merely with a single family or a particular situation, but with illustrating how women learn from one another to tell the stories of themselves by first understanding the tales they hear and thereby inherit from other women. Gibbons's use of Glaspell's text, if intentional, is her direct inheritance, just as Marjorie's is the stories she has heard from her mother and grandmother. If unintentional, the echo of the earlier story constitutes an affirmation that female characters and the female writers who create them often share a similar vision.

Despite Gibbons's exploration of nonverbal communication, Lottie's hope that marriage will be "as plain as spoken words" returns the reader to an important narrative emphasis on the qualities of orality and aurality—the novel exhibits a clear emphasis on the spoken rather than the written word, on hearing rather than on reading. Betty finds her mother's handwriting practically indecipherable because "the words for all the letters looped and whirled back on themselves" (26). Lottie and her daughter write frequently while Betty is away in Richmond, but Betty observes that doing so is "never the same" as talking (125). Betty finally and completely undermines the power of written language by composing a letter to her mother stating her intention to remain in the city, mailing it and then promptly packing her possessions and returning home. The written word does not bind her. Betty has always associated the power of language not with written discourse, but with oral discourse. Betty recalls that when she announced her intention to leave town, she "felt a great deal of power saying this" (114). Her own experiences, particularly in marriage, taught Lottie to harness the power of language verbally. Betty again follows her mother's directive.

The scene of Marjorie's birth at the novel's close further underscores this emphasis on orality. Polly punctuates her continual chatter following Marjorie's birth with chanted rhymes. She thereby exercises first the child's sense of sound, even before that of sight, since Polly puts drops in the baby's eyes as part of the ritual she chronicles in rhyme. Polly also shapes the baby's head "like a ball of dough" and by analogy molds her intellect for participation in the community of women to which she has been born. But the most significant instruction Polly gives the new mother is to keep Marjorie out of the wind because the ears "are the most important parts of a baby" (170). Clearly this child's ears are well-protected, as indicated by the emphasis on hearing in the novel's closing passages. Marjorie writes that her *"first true memory is sound. All sorts of sounds above my cradle. . . . faint and loud and then shrill. Then, Hush! She's sleeping. . . . But I wasn't sleeping, not for the sounds of the women talking"* (171). Thus the child who begins life as a listener grows into a woman who both talks and listens in this narrative woven out of the voices of three storytellers and ordered by the language of a fourth, Gibbons herself. Marjorie's written words frame the text that records the story of her mother's life while simultaneously telling her grandmother's story and indirectly recording her own. Interestingly both Mar-

jorie's and Lottie's words appear literally in italics, suggesting figuratively that the women speak a similar language that spans generations.

Community through conversation, then, is the gift one generation bestows on the next, given and accepted freely in the feminine sense as described by Hélène Cixous in her distinction between the gift and the proper. Cixous describes as well the contrasting male impulse to resist gift-giving in the face of an insistent emphasis on the exchange of property and on being free of debt, literal or emotional. For the women of Gibbons's novel there is no physical exchange. Rather the female characters illustrate the very sense of exchange—of giving freely with an equally rewarding return. Their gift to one another is talking and listening and consequently creating a sense of community that sustains them in the world of male property, the world where, at least in early twentieth-century America, they could seldom bargain successfully.

Admittedly, the reader and the women of the narrative discover that the linguistic community built by the female characters has the potential to be both a negative force in their lives and an ultimately powerless one when confronted by a reality that remains structured by patriarchal oppression. Lottie must leave behind her mother's loud condemnation of her father in order to learn how to speak for herself; similarly Betty finally has to be separated physically from her mother in order to gain her own voice. Gibbons's women do sometimes allow their language to eclipse the voices of other women or they employ language in a characteristically male flourish of force. Lottie, for example, determinedly maintains that her daughter is healthy in spiteful refutation of her husband's accusations, and as a result seriously endangers her child's health. And Sade Duplin, despite the support offered her by her female friends, must finally free herself, not through language, but by use of murderous force. Thus a patriarchally ordered society is the backdrop against which these women necessarily define themselves; in its midst, they strain to hear one another and sometimes they fail. And while that failure may limit the power of the female community Gibbons portrays, it does not finally call into question that community so much as it helps readers to understand its complex nature and the forces that define it. Gibbons offers, then, not just an affirmation of the voices women use to speak to one another; she offers too an exploration of the inherent difficulties in acquiring a voice that sounds different from the culturally dominant one. Sometimes women mimic men and brandish language. Sometimes they become enamored with their own newly claimed voices and forget to listen. Sometimes they doubt the power of their community and feel forced to seek restitution in the violent manner Sade does. The community of women itself continues to exist, however, characterized by the conversation that propels it. The power of female language is not infallible, but it does offer to those who speak and hear it a power through communion otherwise unavailable to them.

In a southern culture based heavily on oral storytelling, Marjorie Polly Randolph does what her mother and her grandmother did not do—utilize the written text as a way to preserve the spoken word. In so doing she does not undermine the value of sound; rather she heightens it by letting her foremothers tell their own stories in their own words. In fact, Marjorie's recording of the stories she has heard orally is the climax of *A Cure for Dreams*. The paramount narrative moment is not Marjorie's marriage nor is it the birth of her child. Marjorie and Gibbons foil the expectations of "the femininity text" by incorporating traditional elements of it and then demonstrating that events like Marjorie's birth play a vital function in a larger accomplishment—the acquisition of an individual voice and of an audience that can both hear and appreciate it. A single voice, Frye maintains, clamors powerlessly against "the femininity text." Representation of social reality "can only be claimed in a voice among other voices, a female 'I' speaking to other women and building shared perspectives as mutual outsiders to the dominant culture" (60). Those shared perspectives are the foundation for the novel's real subject: the community of women that it literally describes and the struggles of its members to acquire an authentic voice allowing them both to speak individually and to blend with the chorus of female voices that is the text of *A Cure for Dreams*. Finally, Gibbons broadens the arc of language's power beyond the women of the novel to touch a wide range of contemporary readers, who likewise hear in its cadences and lacuna the echo of community.

Notes

Since the time that I wrote and submitted this essay, two similar treatments of *A Cure for Dreams* have come to my attention: Tonita Branan's "Women and 'The Gift for Gab': Revisionary Strategies in *A Cure for Dreams*," *Southern Literary Journal* 26.2 (1994) 91–101, and Linda Tate's *A Southern Weave of Women* (1994) 195–204. Both offer detailed and insightful treatments of the intertextuality between Gibbons's novel and Susan Glaspell's *Trifles* and share my assumption that the female characters of *A Cure for Dreams* do not so much appropriate male language as they create a decidedly female way of communicating in verbal and written form. My reading of *A Cure for Dreams* adds to their discussions by offering a more detailed examination of the novels's male characters and an expanded treatment of the interplay between characters' individual voices and the communal voice they combine to create.

1. Glaspell later rewrote her play *Trifles* as a short story called "Jury of Her Peers," first published in 1917. My thanks to my colleague Karen A. Weyler for drawing my attention to the similarities between that story and *A Cure for Dreams*.

Works Cited

Belenky, Mary Field et al. *Women's Ways of Knowing: The Development of Self, Voice, and Mind.* New York: Basic Books, 1986.

Cixous, Hélène. "Castration or Decapitation?" Trans. Annette Kuhn. *Signs* 7.1 (1981): 41–55.

Frye, Joanne S. *Living Stories, Telling Lives: Women and the Novel in Contemporary Experience.* Ann Arbor: U of Michigan P, 1986.

Gibbons, Kaye. *A Cure for Dreams.* Chapel Hill, NC: Algonquin, 1991.

Glaspell, Susan. *Plays.* Boston: Small, Maynard & Company, 1920.

Greene, Gayle. *Changing the Story: Feminist Fiction and the Tradition.* Bloomington: Indiana UP, 1991.

MacKethan, Lucinda. *Daughters of Time: Creating Woman's Voice in Southern Story.* Athens: U of Georgia P, 1990.

Romines, Ann. *The Home Plot: Women, Writing and Domestic Ritual.* Amherst: U of Massachusetts P, 1992.

Giavanna Munafo (essay date 1998)

SOURCE: "'Colored Biscuits': Reconstructing Whiteness and the Boundaries of 'Home' in Kaye Gibbons's *Ellen Foster*," in *Women, America, and Movement,* edited by Susan L. Roberson, University of Missouri Press, 1998, pp. 38-61.

[*In the following essay, Munafo discusses Ellen's changing attitudes toward racial differences in Gibbons's* Ellen Foster *and the implications Ellen's attitude has on the novel as an antiracist text.*]

> Whether they are able to enact it as a lived practice or not, many white folks active in anti-racist struggle today are able to acknowledge that all whites (as well as everyone else within white supremacist culture) have learned to over-value "whiteness" even as they simultaneously learn to devalue blackness. They understand the need, at least intellectually, to alter their thinking. Central to this process of unlearning white supremacist attitudes and values is the deconstruction of the category "whiteness."
>
> —bell hooks, *Black Looks: Race and Representation*

> There's a truth that I am desperate to make you understand: race is not the same as family. In fact, "race" betrays family, if family does not betray "race."
>
> —Mab Segrest, *Memoir of a Race Traitor*

Ellen Foster tracks the plight of a young female protagonist besieged by an alcoholic, abusive father and the pressures of economic as well as emotional privation. The novel opens by turning expectations regarding domesticity and familial relations upside down. Gibbons's astonishing first line—"When I was little I would think of ways to kill my daddy"—bludgeons the daddy's-little-girl prototype so dear to portraits of idealized families. The text works against the fine grain of highly palatable but distorted visions of domestic life and family dynamics. As Veronica Makowski claims, "*Ellen Foster* is Gibbons's attempt to rewrite the saga of the American hero by changing 'him' to 'her' and to rewrite the southern female bildungsroman by changing its privileged, sheltered, upper-class heroine to a poor, abused outcast." In addition, unlike much recent work of the "new South,"[1] Gibbons's first novel makes racial identity and American racism central concerns. *Ellen Foster* displays the racial exigency of concepts like "home" and "family" and reveals that race, and specifically racism, have been erased from the scene in primer-esque editions of the American Dream.

While engaging in explicit and compelling examinations of blackness, Gibbons also conducts a sustained interrogation of the whiteness typically exempted from consideration in investigations of race (where race typically means any race other than white). For the economically and emotionally impoverished Ellen Foster, whiteness constitutes her one saving grace, the privilege that makes her better than nothing and separates her from her black school friend Starletta's brand of marginality. The line demarcating black from white is starkly drawn by Ellen's family where racial and economic liminality destabilize home life. Ellen's father makes what little money they have by selling liquor to the black men with whom he associates—a transgression of the color line that Ellen's maternal grandmother accents by repeatedly hurling the epithet "nigger" at her white son-in-law. Thus, Gibbons establishes the major tensions underlying Ellen's domestic and familial world as both complex and incendiary.

Ellen's mother's death sets the girl's quest in motion, leaving her alone with a father whose alcoholic brutality turns to incestuous assault. Ellen's struggle to escape this dangerous and demoralizing home life leads her into a journey both psychic and material: she must simultaneously reconstruct the figurative and literal dimensions of "home." The stories that Ellen relates chart this journey, which includes significant encounters with six different homes: her school friend Starletta's, where she finds a haven when her father first attacks her; her aunt Betsy's, where her pursuit of long-term asylum results in a comforting but brief two-day hiatus; her sympathetic art teacher's, where school officials, having discovered physical evidence of abuse, temporarily house her; her grandmother's, where the state, after terminating her father's custody and removing her from the art teacher's home, places her; her co-worker Mavis's, where, while living with her grandmother, she spies on scenes of domestic stability; and her aunt Nadine's, where, after her grandmother dies, she stays until being thrown out on Christmas Eve.

During this last, miserable leg of her journey, Ellen asks her cousin about "that woman with all the girls lined up by her" in the church pew and learns that "they are the Foster family and that lady would take in anything from orphans to stray cats" (98–99). Desperate for a home that offers the kind of order and contentment she reads in this scene, Ellen immediately determines to become a member of the "Foster family." Her misreading of descriptor for family name underscores Gibbons's persistent antagonism toward naturalized conceptions of "family." When Ellen does become a member of the town's foster home, she begins signing her school papers "Ellen Foster," inscribing both her childish naïveté and one of the novel's most pressing concerns.

Gibbons insists that familial and domestic reconstitution are both necessary and possible. The location of the foster home, "way on the other side of school," at first renders it out of reach, while its context renders it off-limits: as her cousin puts it, the Fosters live "between the nigger church and Porter's store" (114). This place, Ellen's ultimate home, is sandwiched, that is, between the very racial difference and economic exchange that the housing practices of Ellen's maternal family and white community obsessively disavow. Nonetheless, Ellen trudges the full, cold distance and tells the woman who answers the door, "I mean to be here" (115). Here, at the final turning point in Ellen's narrative, Gibbons depicts a woman-child who's taken her life by the reins, in part out of necessity, in part out of the will to change.

Although the novel accents the import of Ellen's material triumphs (managing to eat enough, dress adequately, save money, and, ultimately, find a new home), a far less tangible achievement—the attempt to reconstruct her own whiteness—crowns her development. Ellen must endeavor to reconstitute her own lived experience of white female racial identity, engendering, as much as possible, a white female self capable of interrupting complicity in white supremacy.

COMPLICITY AND RESISTANCE

Gibbons figures her young white protagonist's search for home and family as continuous with and dependent upon her attempts to revise the racial, and sexual, ideologies they underwrite. Ellen's inheritance includes the assumption of an essential difference between white people and black people, and it insures that she will approach even the most mundane aspects of daily life engaged in practices that maintain and bolster white racial superiority. When she refuses to eat a biscuit her black friend Starletta offers her because it is a "colored biscuit," Ellen reifies the essential difference between these worlds, echoing white supremacy's double-edged habit of insuring its authority and, at the same time, its invisibility via normative status.

"Biscuits," for Ellen, remain part and parcel of her domestic and familial world—an implicitly white terrain—and become "colored biscuits" once removed from that context. Her assignment of the racial marker "colored" exposes the unspoken, unmarked qualifier always already attendant, in Ellen's world, to "biscuits": white. In her study of contemporary American white women's experiences of and relations to racial identity, Ruth Frankenberg explores the process by which "whiteness comes to be an unmarked or neutral category, whereas other cultures are specifically marked 'cultural.'" Her interviewees tend to understand whiteness as no culture, formless, and invisible ("bland" and "blah"), and their attempts to particularize this nothingness consistently summon comparisons "based on color, the linking of white culture with white objects—clichéd white bread and mayonnaise" (199).[2] Taking the tendency of these white women to liken themselves to white bread as one marker of white, female racial identity, Ellen's designation of the biscuit Starletta offers her as "colored," like her refusal to eat it, embodies the ideological boundaries that arise out of white racial anxiety. The color line excludes and polices other and otherness in order to bolster a whiteness that threatens to dissipate into nothingness.

Gibbons's narrative traces Ellen's progress along a route of increasing racial consciousness, moving from her specification of the biscuits Starletta's mother makes as "colored" (and, therefore, inedible to her) and her comment that the sweater Starletta's mother and father give her "does not look colored at all" (and, therefore, can be worn by her), to her recognition that such distinctions denigrate by measuring against implicit white normativity and superiority (32). Gibbons registers this change explicitly; near the end of the novel, Ellen asks her "new Mamma" to "make a fuss over how pretty Starletta is. But not the kind of fuss that says you sure are pretty to be colored. The kind that says you sure are pretty and that is all. The other way does not count" (123). While, on the one hand, this "conversion" can appear contrived, Gibbons aggressively critiques the exploitive aspect of Ellen's relationship to the novel's black families and characters. In so doing, she exposes the complex of resistance and complicity inherent in her young white protagonist's nascent antiracism.

Gibbons inevitably scripts both her heroine's subversive resistance and her inescapable complicity.[3] The novel opens with Ellen's confession that, in the past, she imagined her father's death. The form that this confession takes reveals the dynamics of both racial division and of the gendered domestic order in which Ellen flounders. "When they [the rescue squad] come in the house," fantasizes Ellen, "I'm all in a state of shock and just don't know how to act what with two colored boys heaving my dead daddy onto a roller cot" (1). In the world of her imagination, as in the everyday world of her actual life, Ellen's precarious racial, sexual, and domestic situations converge. The phrase "colored boys" at once summons the battles of the civil rights movement and their failure in this small, rural community, while Ellen's vigilance against transgressions of the color line rings out in the semantics of a racialized "they" entering her domestic space. Further, the moment of trespass figured here elucidates Ellen's sexual vulnerability.

This vulnerability surfaces more explicitly later in the novel, but Gibbons introduces it in this portrait of Ellen surrounded by men who have invaded her home (a domestic space traditionally gendered female and representative of the female body) and who, literally, support the man who, we later learn, exercises his masculine authority as

well as his parental privilege by sexually assaulting her. In the logic of dreams, Ellen's fantasy figures both the wish of her father's death fulfilled and the condensation and displacement of her attendant anxieties.[4] The reverie Ellen entertains here—and with which Gibbons chooses to open the novel—condenses fears of both maternal and paternal abandonment, of domestic instability, of racial disorder, and of sexual vulnerability into a complex image of trespass and invasion. Following the lead of a racist community and culture, Ellen displaces these anxieties, figuring them, not as the products of her mother's disability and father's malfeasance, but as the result of a volatile color line. Further, the rhetoric of black men "coming" in her "house," as she puts it, lends to the scene the specter of sexual and racial trespass made one. This confluence—accented by summoning the especially incendiary interracial coupling of a white woman and a black man—establishes the narrative's insistence on the contingency of Ellen's sexual and racial negotiations. It is in the context of Ellen's struggle to achieve domestic and familial stability that Gibbons most powerfully demonstrates this contingency.

Ellen buys into the equation her grandmother posits between depravity and blackness. Attempting to salvage some shred of paternal affinity, the child lays the blame for her father's criminality and cruelty on his affiliation with blackness. Thus, instead of figuring the attendants of her fantasy as allies—insofar as they remove her abusive father—she imagines them as agents of disruption and as threats to her own racial and sexual purity.

Still on the first page of the novel, Gibbons stresses the impact Ellen's father's actual death has upon the status of their home. "Next thing I know," Ellen tells us, "he's in the ground and the house is rented out to a family of four" (1). Ellen has no home to call her own. Immediately following this recollection, as the narrative shifts to the present, we learn that her home situation has, since then, radically changed:

> I live in a clean brick house. . . . Two years ago I did not have much of anything. Not that I live in the lap of luxury now but I am proud for the schoolbus to pick me up here every morning. My stylish well-groomed self standing in the front yard with the grass green and the hedge bushes square.
>
> (2)

Gibbons stresses the significance of superficial control of the domestic environment, often turning Ellen's attention to the pleasures of such control. The fact that, in her new home, "[e]verything matches" and "is all so neat and clean" enthralls Ellen (5). She embraces order as a corrective to disorder and espouses cleanliness as a corrective to filth, both literally and metaphorically.

Ellen's materialistic impulses derive from both actual neediness and what Gibbons exposes as a familial and cultural consumerism. The novel explores the impact and limitations of the latter while documenting the extent and implications of the former. Dressed warmly in winter, with regularly washed hair, Ellen cherishes the emblems of care and nurturance her foster home provides, truly amazed, after so much deprivation, that, after eating an egg sandwich with "mayonnaise on both sides" for breakfast, she can actually choose to fix herself another for lunch (2). Thus provisioned with a glimpse of Ellen's present-tense, orderly, and stable domestic situation, we lurch quickly back and forth with Ellen as she recalls the journey she has taken, beginning with its inception in flight from her violent, abusive biological home.

"Shaking Itself to Death": Hearth and Home Undone

Gibbons provides a parable of parenting, one that Ellen relies upon after her mother's death, to gauge prospective "new mamas":

> When the beans were ready to eat she would let me help pick. Weeds do not bear fruit. She would give me a example of a bean that is grown to hold in one hand while I picked with the other. If I was not sure if a particular bean was at the right stage I could hold up my example of a bean to that bean in question and know.
>
> (49)

Providing her with the tools to judge ripe from unripe, good from bad, Ellen's mother laid down a path for her daughter to follow in life. As Ellen says, "I just worked the trail my mama left," and her struggle to find a home and a new mama continue this effort to reconstruct the "one season" of her mother's wellness during which she enjoyed such nurturance and care (49).

The model her mother provides contains lessons as much about fighting cultural and, consequently, racial turf wars as about discerning ripe from unripe. As in her subsequent novels, Gibbons recounts the plight of a white woman who "marries down" and incurs the wrath and rejection of her wealthy family. The physical and emotional deterioration such displacement induces contributes to Ellen's eventual homelessness. While Gibbon's attention merely skims the mother's story, it reveals how her choices shape Ellen's life. Ellen inherits from her mother the impulse to transgress restrictive social codes. Crossing the class line, in this case, entails crossing the color line, however unwittingly. For when Ellen's mother marries across class lines she enters a world where the color line so determinedly policed in her community of birth wavers and shifts erratically. Without the complementary schism of radical economic disparity, racial divisions become far more unruly and, in some ways, far more threatening.

While Gibbons's portrait of Ellen's father and his "colored buddies" suggests some measure of interracial congeniality, the author situates this integrationist cameo in the context of commercial exchange, alcoholism, and sexual violence (25). "Missah Bill," as they call him, sells liquor to the black men with whom he drinks to excess. As the retention of formal address indicates, even among drinking buddies the distinction between white supplier and black consumer remains. On the other hand, the homosocial bonding in which Ellen's father and his black companions engage finds its support in shared socioeconomic alienation (one source of his retreat into alcoholism) and the compensatory sexual dominance they assume and enact. Ellen, whose racist essentialism rings out in her reference to the "pack of colored men" from whom she hides, tells us she "always walked in wide circles around [her father]"—a marking of distance from both his sexual rapacity and his racial transgressiveness (25). The novel scrutinizes Ellen's predicament and responses, charting the complex relations between racial, economic, and sexual ideologies and practices. Gibbons's portrait of Ellen as sexual prey and of the racial and economic contexts out of which her situation arises initiate Ellen's quest for a new home and family and her corresponding struggle to reconfigure her own racial and sexual positioning.

Ellen is "just about ripe" according to one of her daddy's "colored" friends who cautions, "[y]ou gots to git em when they is still soff when you mashum" (37). Like a sweet potato, Ellen is to be harvested and mashed for consumption.[5] Sensing danger, she hides in the closet and explains,

> What else do you do when your house is run over by colored men drinking whiskey and singing and your daddy is worse than them all put together?
>
> You pray to God they forget about you and the sweet young things that are soff when you mashum and how good it feels when she is pressed up by you. You get out before one can wake up from being passed out on the floor. You get out before they start to dream about the honey pie and the sugar plums.
>
> (37)

Venturing out from her hiding place, Ellen attempts to escape from the house, but her flight is interrupted by her father's drunken sexual assault. Gibbons shapes Ellen's narrative here so that the past-tense experience and the present-tense relating of it merge: "Get away from me he does not listen to me but touches his hands harder on me" (38). Breaking from him, she races away from the abuse her home has come to represent and towards Starletta's house, toward, as she says, "the smoke coming out of the chimney against the night sky" (38).

This paradigmatic image of hearth and home, writ large against the night sky, beckons Ellen away from her "natural" home and toward a newly reconstituted one. She runs, in part, from the blackness signified by her father and his buddies—the racial difference that essentialist white supremacy equates with both lasciviousness and violence. This is not to say that her father and his cohorts are not lascivious and violent, but the novel displays the fallacy of an implicit connection between such "evil" and race, literal blackness. Significantly, Ellen runs from one "black" scene to another here, from blackness as evil to blackness as haven. The former frighteningly threatens to undermine her whiteness (marker of both racial and sexual "purity"), while the latter provides both the necessary reification of that whiteness and a context in which to begin reevaluating it.

As the narrative progresses, Ellen's concept of "home" and all of that term's seemingly immutable qualities undergo gradual but, ultimately, radical revision. While her indoctrination into whiteness has taught her that her father's association with black men constitutes his evilness, she discovers that he is "worse than them all put together" and that his "evil" retreats "back into his self" (38). If her home consists of him, she concludes, it cannot house her any longer.

Gibbons closes the scene of Ellen's flight with the child wondering "what the world has come to," and, indeed, her world has come to pieces in ways both tragic and, at the same time, potentially fruitful. Against the supposed fixity of domestic order Gibbons asserts its fragility and constructedness. Describing the general state of affairs in her home at the time of her mother's death, Ellen says, "[e]verything was so wrong like somebody had knocked something loose and my family was shaking itself to death. Some wild ride broke and the one in charge strolled off and let us spin and shake and fly off the rail" (2). On the verge of disillusionment, Ellen both appeals to a higher power and registers its absence; she believes in the cosmic glue that supposedly binds families together while, at the same time, she knows that no such "natural" bonds exist in her family.

Similarly, in flight from her biological home and toward the smoking chimney that signifies haven, Ellen reports, "I gather my head and all that is spinning and flying out from me" (38). This image of barely contained disintegration—which suggests how profoundly Ellen's sense of self depends upon the state of her domestic and familial relations—closes the chapter. Acutely aware that "the one in charge" has jumped ship, Ellen attempts to take the wheel, as it were, and keep her life from "shaking itself to death."

POLICING BLOODLINES

Willing to stay at Starletta's house only one night, Ellen turns to her mother's sister, Betsy, for shelter from her father's abuse. In selecting this new home, Ellen resorts to a set of acceptable criteria heavy on superficial elements and sadly light on more sustaining ones: a bathtub is important, as is a "nice house," one with "flowers growed all up on the mailbox" (40–41). Superficial comforts abound at Aunt Betsy's; they shop and buy Ellen a dress and "more little things than [she] can think of," like "a pair of gloves with a sequin cat sewed across the hands" that she "cannot play in" but "are good to look at" (41). Gibbons further stresses the feebleness of the visit's emotional substance: Ellen entertains herself by bathing, "[l]ooking in dresser drawers," and "[f]ingering the what-nots," while her aunt "spends right much time on the couch looking at magazines with stars in them" (41). Fresh from her father's abusive hold, Aunt Betsy's plush consumerism pampers Ellen's sorely bruised sensibilities.

However, Ellen eventually comes to deride Betsy's consumerism. Having just delivered the news of Betsy's mother's death, Ellen responds to her aunt's "so near Christmas" scathingly: "I was dying my own self," she explains, "to tell her well Betsy why don't you just see if the undertaking driver will stop and let you shop a minute on the way to the grave?" (90). The contrast between Ellen's initial embrace and eventual rejection of Betsy's consumer-driven, superficial existence mimics the contrast between her original insistence, vis-à-vis her black coworker Mavis's family, that she "only wanted one [a home] white and with a little more money" and her ultimate realization that economic and racial demarcations cannot insure domestic and familial stability or happiness (67). Betsy's whiteness and her economic stability, at least as much as her aunthood, preselect her as appropriate guardian, just as blackness and poverty render Starletta's family inappropriate—despite Betsy's blatant insensitivity to Ellen's situation and Starletta's family's explicitly rendered concern for her well-being and its readiness to intervene. Ellen's formulation of an acceptable home as "white and with a little more money" (more, that is, than the impoverished homes of the black families she encounters) reflects both the racial homogeneity of "family" and an overdetermined correlation between racial identity and economic status.

Ellen's foray into Betsy's posh domesticity is short-lived, and she returns to her own home reluctantly, determined to evade her father's attempts to "grab and swat" (43). But, despite Ellen's heroic stab at self-protection and her persistent effort to stay "home," school officials discover physical evidence of abuse and initiate Ellen's next series of relocations. Ultimately, the school's intervention results in a court decision that grants her grandmother legal custody, placing Ellen once more, and more permanently, in the care of her maternal family.

Ellen immediately becomes the target of the hatred her grandmother, until now, had reserved for her son-in-law. Class anxiety compels her to label Ellen's daddy "nigger and trash"—his life is marred by business failure, rowdiness, and alcoholism, all marks, when coexistent, of the downward mobility Ellen's mother married into despite (or specifically *to* spite) her mother's wishes. Economic hardship, emotional excess, and substance abuse come to distinguish rich from poor not because these conditions and behaviors are exclusively or even disproportionately the province of the latter, but, rather, because the authority of the former results in part from projecting such destabilizing threats onto the economic and racial others against whom it defines itself.

Although the child strongly resembles her mother (Mavis, significantly, affirms this resemblance [65]), her grandmother insists that she favors her scoundrel father. When Ellen's father dies, her grandmother tells her "make sure you cry more than you did for your mama," legislating through her matriarchal (and economic) authority Ellen's affiliation with paternal (and alienation from maternal) ancestry (69). Holding Ellen responsible for her mother's daughterly infractions, the vindictive woman sends Ellen out to work in the fields. Ellen reports, "I used to play in the fields with Starletta and watch her mama and daddy chop but I never figured it would be me one day"—a subtle but unmistakable glossing of the separate racial spheres overwhelmingly maintained in Ellen's world and reinscribed by her grandmother (63). Ellen's white skin does not spare her field labor because her grandmother equates the girl's previous associations with black people (her father's buddies and her school friend Starletta) with a transgression of the color line so radical it renders Ellen a "nigger," just like her father.

Each gesture further reinforces the separation the woman desperately seeks to impose between herself and the embodiment of her daughter's transgression. Translating class difference into racial difference magnifies its distance from the white self—magnifies, in other words, its otherness—to insure the stability of white, upper-class identity. This attempt to consolidate whiteness is perhaps most obvious when her grandmother ascribes to Ellen the racist clichés attached to black female sexuality. "You laid up all in that house with your daddy's buddies. I'm surprised you don't have some little nigger baby hanging off your titty," she derisively tells Ellen (78). In this last, specifically gendered, maneuver of disassociation, Gibbons's portrait of the old, white mistress summons the not-so-subtle role female sexual "purity" plays in the struggle to define and bolster white racial identity. Constructed in accordance with racist ideology, white women's racial identity—like black women's—finds expression in explicitly sexual terms.

Shut up in a museumlike "torture chamber" of isolationism, Ellen imagines her grandmother's insistence that she is no longer white made literal. Projecting her own racial anxieties and desires onto a handy proxy, she fantasizes "turning [her] buddy Starletta loose" to "have a rampage in one room and out the other" among her grandmother's "what-nots" and "costly items" (62). Unlike the accessories of life with Aunt Betsy, the objects that populate Ellen's new quarters fail to pacify her neediness, even on first encounter. Alienated from use-value and collected as a means of self-aggrandizement, the elaborately turned furniture and ancient vases Ellen curiously ponders enjoy a protectedness only exceeded by that which envelopes her grandmother's own carefully guarded status. "I'll break your little hand if you touch that vase," she warns Ellen, who attests to the seriousness of the threat by confessing that it made her "think how a broke hand might feel" (62).

Ellen's vision of riotous racial other wreaking havoc in the heart of white domestic civility underscores Ellen's ability and willingness to trade in racist clichés, especially under duress regarding her own unstable racial and sexual identity. On the other, the displacement of her own desires in this projection onto Starletta at the same time articulates Ellen's identification with her friend, and it underwrites Ellen's incipient reconfiguring of "home" as not showplace but habitat. Rather than painting the Starletta of

Ellen's fantasy rampage "savage," Gibbons's consistently antagonist rendering of Ellen's familial domains figures her disruptive potential as an advantageous, even necessary, corrective. The fact that Ellen imagines her desire fulfilled by Starletta (instead of imagining herself demolishing her grandmother's moneyed, white, female preserve) registers her recognition that the space is racialized, that its sanctity engenders its whiteness and vice versa.

Gibbons similarly interrogates the disjunction between the state's investment in white bloodlines and Ellen's experience of her own biological family when, after the grandmother's death, Aunt Nadine inherits guardianship of the girl. Prior to this state-engineered arrangement, Ellen's only narrated encounter with Nadine takes place in the aftermath of Ellen's mother's death, and Gibbons's portrait of their interaction then provides a telling context for the familial fiasco occasioned by Ellen's eventual placement in Nadine's home. Ellen's initial observations of her mother's sister stress the workings of the color line, exposing both Ellen's own reliance upon racist commonplaces and her aunt's obsessive racial anxiety. Ineptness, a quality Ellen disdains, summons things black when Ellen considers her aunt's inability to efficiently and calmly manage her own sister's funeral. The girl complains that "[Nadine] could not organize a two-car colored funeral so she has herself all worked up over this affair" (14). At the same time, she registers the ludicrousness of Nadine's racial paranoia, explaining, "[w]e have to drive through colored town to get to the [funeral]. . . . My aunt is so glad to be out of colored town. She unlocks her car door because now she feels safe" (19). Both party to and critical of such racial vigilance, Ellen catalogs its preponderance in the world of her family and community.

Nadine's fear of entering "black" spaces signals the vulnerability historically rendered fundamental to the very category "white woman." As Vron Ware demonstrates in *Beyond the Pale,* oppressive ideologies of both race and gender traffic in images like this one of a white woman whose physical proximity to racial others spells racial and sexual danger.[6] Ellen's ruminations about her aunt's profession, which arise as the funeral caravan makes its way through "colored town," emphasize this dangerous proximity. Ellen describes Nadine's fawning attitude toward the undertaker, explicitly noting the connection between such deference and Nadine's "job":

> My aunt is entertaining the smiling man. That is her part-time job. When she is not redecorating or shopping with Dora she demonstrates food slicers in your home.
>
> She will bring her plastic machine into your living room and set the whole business up on a card table. After everybody plays two or three made-up games she lets you in on the Convenience Secret of the Century. She will tell you how much it would run you in the store. If the smiling man has a wife he can expect my aunt and her machine in his living room sometime soon.

(17)

The gendered economy charted here has particular implications regarding domestic and familial frameworks. Women prepare the family's food, but men control the means by which that work can be accomplished. Thus, Nadine must broker the "Convenience Secret of the Century" through men to women. In much the same way that children's material requirements and accessories must both appeal to children themselves and to their parents, wives compose Nadine's target market while husbands are the ultimate consumer. Her job entails, as Ellen notes, entertaining men, cajoling them into the wide-spirited gesture of providing their wives with tools to lighten the burdens of domestic labor. Ellen's description of Nadine's job relies upon the popular, euphemistic rhetoric of prostitution ("entertaining men"), a correspondence that underscores the sexualized nature of her position in men's homes. As in both Ellen's original home and her Aunt Betsy's (where Gibbons stresses the ornamentalism of women's activities), subservience characterizes wives' relations to husbands, women's relationships to men—female self-interest remains routed through male desire.

Continuing her reverie regarding Nadine's occupation, Ellen links it to the racial anxiety and color line surveillance apparent in Nadine's locking and unlocking of her car door. Passing out of "colored town" and into white neighborhoods, Ellen comments, "[o]h and wouldn't she like to be inside one of these white houses peeling cucumbers in a snap! And she will tell you about how everybody got his money and especially about the doctors. All they do is cheat, gamble, and run around" (19). Nadine's eagerness (as intuited or projected by Ellen) to enter the white domestic space of the houses they pass contrasts markedly with her fear of being removed from the safety of her automobile and exposed to the perceived danger of "colored" neighborhoods. The car figures Nadine's own person/world: locked and inaccessible in response to racial difference, unlocked and accessible in response to racial homogeneity. The sexual connotations of Nadine's locked and unlocked personal space—particularly in the context of the sexualized rhetoric that describes her job—reinforce the intimately related racial ones.

In rejecting black individuals and homes as unfit for even commercial exchange, Nadine reinforces her own racial privilege while disarming the threat of identification posed by the fact that both she and the black communities/individuals she disdains are the objects of white male exploitation. Perhaps even more threatening are the potential sexual and gender-based alliances suggested by the hypothetical incursions into interracial domestic/commercial exchange Nadine so adamantly disavows. "Entertaining" a "smiling [black] man" while engaging in the sisterhood of wives generates a nightmare of miscegenistic affiliation.

The contradiction Gibbons displays here—between Nadine's projection of sexual license onto racial others and her willingness to trade on her own sexuality in commerce with white men—is a central one. White supremacy allows and encourages Nadine to disavow her own libidinal

agency in the service of maintaining distinct boundaries between white and nonwhite, pure and impure. White women, in particular, must remain "locked" against a perceived threat to both their whiteness and their supposed chastity. This mechanism obscures the fact that, at the same time, sexism fixes Nadine as sexualized object in relation to men and male-dominated culture. Thus she can both endorse the myth of black hypersexuality (in locking herself off from blackness as an expression of her own sexual and racial purity) and, paradoxically, exploit her own sexuality to negotiate a space in the economic terrain controlled by white men (by unlocking herself to prospective white male customers). This contradiction results directly from the authorizing function whiteness serves in relation to the category "woman."

Having barely initiated her quest for domestic and familial reconstruction, Ellen registers not the complexities of Nadine's racist machinations, but the simple fact of their intrusive, insipid presence. Indeed, as noted, Ellen's own white supremacist inheritance encourages her to participate in Nadine's racist orientation even as she chronicles its obtrusiveness. Later in her journey, however, when Ellen must live with Nadine, she has already encountered the stifling xenophobia of her grandmother's home as well as the alternative domestic and familial models resident in the homes of Starletta, Julia and Roy, and Mavis.

Ellen's brief stay with Aunt Nadine and cousin Dora, and especially the dreadfully disappointing and painful Christmas she spends with them, propels her into the foster care system. At this point in the novel, Gibbons's two alternating narratives converge: the predominantly unhappy story of the events that lead up to Ellen's ultimate rejection of her "natural" family (told in past tense) and the predominantly happy story of her life as a member of the "Foster family" (told in present tense). Gibbons accents the centrality of the racial dynamics operating in the foster home Ellen embraces. Recollections of life at Nadine's interrupt immediate, joyous preparations for Starletta's visit to the "Foster" home, until the narratives collapse into one at the point of Ellen's defection from her family and initiation into a newly constituted foster family. Significantly, while Starletta's visit promises, for Ellen, to resolve all inequities ("then we will all be straight," she says), her "family" Christmas underscores the divisiveness dominating the space demarcated by Ellen's family ties (100).

Like Aunt Betsy, Aunt Nadine proves to be her mother's daughter, a woman consumed by shopping and blind to the tragic circumstances of her niece's life. At Christmas she showers her daughter, Dora, with every gift the child desires, and more, while presenting Ellen, the prototypical poor relation, with one packet of art paper. Her excuse—that Ellen is "so peculiar and hard to buy for"—suggests the more rudimentary motivation for her thoughtlessness: Nadine conceives of Ellen not as a member of her family, not even as another member of her chosen community, but as that which is "peculiar." The grandmother's habit of magnifying the distance between herself and Ellen persists in Nadine's treatment of her ward. Framed by Ellen's eagerness to make Starletta's visit a milestone of bridge-building (afterward she hopes to feel that "the two of us are even"), this familial betrayal ends with Ellen's final severing of conventional family ties (100). When Nadine threatens to evict Ellen from her home on Christmas, the girl flees and presents herself to her "new mama," the woman she's identified in church as a potentially appropriate mother.

In framing Ellen's ultimate break from blood ties with her endeavor to forge a meaningful and lasting connection with Starletta, Gibbons emphasizes Ellen's need to bridge racial divisions as an integral part of the process of home-building she embarks upon as a member of the "Foster" family. This family exists in curious relation to the notions of "family" that Ellen has experienced as so constraining. At once a family and not a family, Ellen's foster home provides many of the elements she deems necessary to an acceptable home, yet it allows for reconstruction, revision, and experimentation. Although she is "not sure if it has ever been done before," Ellen asks permission for her black friend to visit for the weekend (85). And, although none of the biological family members with whom she's lived would permit this blurring of the color line on their property, Ellen's "new mama" says, "sure Starletta can come stay with us" and even offers to "whip up" some hand-towels with an *S* embroidered on them for their guest (99, 100). The fact that her new family welcomes Starletta overjoys Ellen, who deems this revision of "home" ground-breaking, comparing it to declarations of war and the miracle of birth (99).

Gibbons traces the development of Ellen's relation to Starletta, a relation that moves from condescension and proprietariness ("she was mine") to respect and recognition. Starletta takes "a hunk [of birthday cake] with the N part out of [Ellen's] name"—a scriptural exchange that suggests the larger exchange taking place, one in which Ellen begins to substitute humane, empathetic identification for white supremacist distortions. Starletta ingests the *N* from Ellen's name, and the embroidered *S* from Starletta's name remains with Ellen.

THE COLORED PATH

Gibbons specifically locates a conglomerate model of acceptable domesticity in three extrafamilial homes, and she accents their freedom from cruelty and abuse. Significantly, she also stresses these homes' liminal positions vis-à-vis dominant modes of consumer exchange, as well as their relative remove from white supremacist patriarchy. Two of these homes belong to black characters who, as a direct result of racial exploitation, inhabit the extreme low end of the economic terrain charted by the novel. The third home belongs to a markedly eccentric white couple who debunk arbitrary racial as well as sexual divisions (welcoming Starletta into their home and reversing typical gender roles) while waging a battle against the marketplace by growing their own produce organically. Among other things, Ellen learns not that black families are good and white families are bad but, rather, that just as blackness itself does not signal evil, whiteness itself does not signal benevolence, or even sufficiency. While the novel trades, at times, in stereotypes (the black family, especially mother, as source of nurturance and care for the white child) and perpetuates servant/served models of relation between black and white communities or individuals, Gibbons persistently undermines whiteness's claims to authority and ultimately figures Ellen's development as affirming only insofar as it incorporates a resistance to white supremacist ideologies regarding her own identity and its familial and cultural contexts.

Ellen's journey both begins and ends by seeking Starletta. Gibbons opens the chapter following Ellen's father's first sexual assault with Ellen negotiating the terms of her lodging with Starletta's mother. The woman refuses payment and takes the traumatized child into her bed for the night, but Ellen's concern for maintaining racial boundaries compels her to sleep in her coat on top of the covers. Thus, she "cannot say [she] officially slept in the bed" (39). However, when she gets up the next morning, Ellen reports, "I was surprised because it did not feel like I had slept in a colored house" (39). While her experience insists that the terms of essentialist racial differences are inadequate, Ellen remains firmly situated within a sociocultural system that makes access to alternative terms both difficult and threatening. Nonetheless, Ellen intuits that Starletta's home might be a safer, more comforting environment than her own, despite the former's lack of what her white family and world had always identified as necessary prerequisites to acceptable domesticity: running water, private quarters, spotless floorboards. While Ellen continues to subordinate Starletta and her family, relying on the marker "colored" to distinguish their home and community from her own, her experience undermines this practice little by little.

Ellen's encounters with her biological family vitiate any residual faith in blood ties the girl may have harbored after her mother's death and father's abusiveness. Her placements in and observations of extrafamilial homes encourage Ellen to envision "home" beyond the boundaries of "natural" family ties. Ellen's familial experiences equip her to identify elements she does not wish to include in the home she seeks to reconfigure, and her extrafamilial experiences (with Starletta's family, Julia and Roy, and Mavis's home) enable her to identify elements she considers essential to that reconfiguration.

Only willing to seek refuge at Starletta's for occasional brief periods and expelled from her Aunt Betsy's, Ellen remains at home until, as noted, school officials intervene. They place her fate in the hands of the courts and arrange for Ellen to stay with her art teacher, Julia, and Julia's husband, Roy, until custody decisions can be made. This arrangement suits Ellen, who, when told that her teachers "had decided what to do with [her]," responds with relief, "It is about time. . . . Yes Lord it is about time" (45).

Soon thereafter, when her father invades the school-grounds, exposing himself and yelling that he will "pay for it"—"it" presumably referring to sexual access to his daughter—Julia comforts Ellen and adds, "let's go home" (54). Gibbons stresses that Ellen does consider her teacher's house her *home*: she begins Ellen's next account, "When we got home . . ." (55).

But Gibbons quickly interrupts this amenable domestic arrangement with the news that the court has decided to place Ellen back with her family (55). "I do not believe it," Ellen comments, adding, "It sounds crazy to me because the three of us could pass for a family on the street" (55). Ellen gauges the acceptability of familial relation, at least in part, corporeally. In Starletta's family, for example, she would stick out like the proverbial sore thumb—because of her whiteness. Such a unit decidedly would not "pass for a family on the street." The court, on the other hand, has its own criteria. It upholds the white family as "society's cornerstone," rejecting extrafamilial claims to parental relation (56).

Julia and Roy provide the care and parenting of an appropriate family for Ellen, but Gibbons exposes the ways the state intervenes to police reconstructed families in accordance with its own economic and racial agendas. Julia and Roy, ex-hippie artists and organic farmers in the post-civil-rights-movement South, cannot prevail in their bid for the child against her grandmother's Old South, monied gentility. While Ellen's virulently racist grandmother runs a plantation-like spread, houses black field laborers in "shacks," and "[does] not pay them doodly-squat," Julia and Roy graciously welcome Starletta into their home to celebrate Ellen's birthday (21, 66). Their response to Ellen's friendship with Starletta contrasts markedly with that of Ellen's other teachers who make quite plain that a "colored" friend "would not do" (44). Additionally, Julia and Roy eschew arbitrary gender-driven divisions of labor, Julia holding down a job and Roy remaining home to "do his thing"—garden, cook, and perform housework (48).

Additionally, Gibbons accents the correlation between Ellen's experiences gardening with Julia and Roy and her experiences gardening with her deceased mother. Indeed, it is only while working in the garden with them that Ellen recalls the single happy memory she harbors—the way her mama "liked to work in the cool of the morning" and how she worked the garden trail her mama left (49). It is during her stay with Julia and Roy that Ellen first converts the telling and retelling of that "one season" of happiness (a fantasy) into a reenactment of such pleasure and well-being (a reality). When the child welfare agency selects the aged, solitary blood kin over the eager couple as Ellen's new family, it interrupts this process of regeneration, effectively foreclosing the curative process Gibbons emphatically associates with growing seasons and garden paths. The agency's decision also authorizes the xenophobic dimensions of Ellen's biological family and rejects an alternatively fluid and inclusive familial model. The state re-places Ellen in a "home" constructed on the very

grounds of white supremacy and exploitation, hence the thickness of (white) blood wins out.

Ellen observes that the judge—in positing her family as part of "society's cornerstone"—"had us all mixed up with a different group of folks," since her family "never was a Roman pillar but is and always has been a crumbly old brick" (56). Gibbons summons the Eurocentric formula for white purity and supremacy: Greek and Roman civilizations as conglomerate figure for civilization itself, a figuring that invariably measures white superiority against the "uncivilized" cultures of darker peoples. As Ellen's white racial defenses soften, the court attempts to bolster them. Ellen must struggle not only against the indoctrination of her childhood, which enforced white supremacy as her racial privilege (the messages she received from her mother's family, as from the school system and the culture in which it thrived, that blacks "would not do" and that her father's "evil" resulted from his association with blacks), but also against legal and political institutions determined to uphold the color line by insisting upon the inviolability of white bloodlines.

Firmly ensconced within the acceptable bounds of her grandmother's home, Ellen nonetheless discovers a route beyond its racist borders. It is from the vantage point of institutionally enforced familial membership that Ellen initiates her self-consciously articulated quest for an acceptable, not necessarily biological, home and family. Gibbons continues to make racial identity central to Ellen's attempted reconfiguration of these structures. Desperate for companionship and care, Ellen develops an apprenticeship with Mavis, one of the black women with whom she works in the fields while living with her grandmother. Mavis affirms Ellen's resemblance to her deceased mother, enabling the child to resist her grandmother's insistent equating of Ellen with her father. Significantly, her relationship with Mavis enables Ellen to claim her maternal inheritance while struggling to unlearn the racism of her familial and cultural environments.

Working in the fields with Mavis—like working in the garden with Julia and Roy—reinvents Ellen's one season of happiness in the garden with her mother. Mavis, like Ellen's mother, lays down a path for Ellen to follow, and Ellen, in turn, works the trail Mavis leaves just as she worked her mother's trail. The rows of the fields mimic the paths and trails, both literal and figurative, so prominent throughout the novel. Here, too, Gibbons weaves narratives of familial reconstruction with narratives of racial reconfiguration. The "path" upon which Ellen embarks during her field-work summer becomes the path that leads to her newly constituted vision of the home she desires.

Drawn to the life outside her grandmother's pallid mansion, the child eases her hunger for meaningful, loving family ties by observing Mavis's family at day's end. Ellen, retaining her habit of marking racial difference with the prefix "colored," discovers the "colored path" toward home:

While I was eavesdropping at the colored house I started a list of all that a family should have. Of course there is the mama and the daddy but if one has to be missing then it is OK if the one left can count for two. But not just anybody can count for more then his or her self.

While I watched Mavis and her family I thought I would bust open if I did not get one of them for my own self. Back then I had not figured out how to go about getting one but I had a feeling it could be got.

(67)

The process of denaturalizing family ties essential to Ellen's quest for a new home involves her reconceptualization of home as something one might "get" as opposed to something one simply has. Additionally, as Ellen comes to realize that the models of home available within her extended family do not meet her requirements, she must negotiate the color line, which insists that "colored house[s]" provide not models but antimodels of white homes.

Indeed, Ellen's report (just before moving from her grandmother's house to Nadine's) that "this time this would *not* be home" emerges specifically in the context of the distance, both literal and figurative, from Nadine's to what Ellen has come to call the "colored path" toward "home" (emphasis added, 94). Ellen relinquishes the tenets of "natural" family ties and, consequently, as she puts it, "do[es] not have to feel sad about being here [at Nadine's] in the middle of a place so far from the house at the end of the colored path" (94). The path to which Ellen refers here is, in actuality, the path from her grandmother's estate to the houses of the field laborers with whom Ellen worked all summer. Preparing to leave her grandmother's, Ellen explains,

I knew I had found a little something on that colored path that I could not name but I said to myself to mark down what you saw tonight because it might come in handy. You mark down how they laugh and how they tell the toddler babies, you better watch out fo them steps. They steep! Mark all that down and see if you can figure out what made you take that trip every night. Then when you are by yourself one day the list you kept might make some sense and then you will know that this is the list you would take to a store if they made such a store and say to the man behind the counter give me this and this and this. And he would hand you back a home.

(93–94)

Ellen's conception of the world remains firmly situated within a consumerist rhetoric and logic, and her reliance on the marker "colored" to distinguish one world from another persists. At the same time, the "colored path" and the lessons at its end provide Ellen with a model essential to the progress of her domestic and familial quest, a quest that entails critique of and antagonism toward these very tendencies. A continuation of the "path" laid down by her mother's lessons apropos discerning ripe from unripe, good from bad, the "colored path" comprises both the ma-

terial means of access to a specific house, Mavis's, and the ideological process of reconstruction Ellen must undergo to achieve the "home" she lacks. Ellen arrives at Nadine's painfully conscious of the fact that her chosen path—the "colored path"—leads elsewhere.

Ellen self-consciously identifies domestic and familial characteristics in direct defiance of both the spoken and the unspoken racial boundaries excluding Starletta's and Mavis's homes from those culturally sanctioned as models or substitutes for her own. It is significant that Julia and Roy's home similarly provides Ellen with crucial exposure to and insight into alternative models, contributing to the conglomerate picture she incrementally sketches of a reconfigured home and family. Gibbons situates Ellen's whiteness as at once inscribed by white supremacist familial and cultural forms and practices and as susceptible to revision.

In closing, the novel equivocates. But does this equivocation derive from Gibbons giving with one hand what she takes away with another or, instead, from constraints that may be inherent in white antiracist fiction? Ellen's indoctrination into white supremacist ideology insures that when she looks at Starletta she sees a stereotype of a "little black girl." Ellen even admits that Starletta "never has said much good or bad to me" (84). The novel can be faulted for this portrait and for its habit of making black characters and homes serviceable vis-à-vis Ellen's tragic tale and heroic advances. But insofar as it reveals the machinations of whiteness that are responsible for this kind of marginalization, Gibbons's novel, far from taking white centrality for granted, persistently strives to undermine it. The narrative struggle is one insistent upon "making room for" Starletta's story. Nonetheless, Starletta remains a narrative absence, a gap. This problem is one built into the very fabric of Gibbons's novelistic challenge here—the entire tale is told from the perspective of an abused, outcast little girl whose ability to empathize with or imagine the subjectivities of others is necessarily constrained. Aside from Ellen, no other character in *Ellen Foster* moves beyond type into fictive personhood. But, importantly, Gibbons makes special claims for Starletta and for Ellen's ability to move beyond the very restrictions at issue here.

Interestingly, while Gibbons makes little or no effort to develop Starletta's character beyond Ellen's caricature-ish portrait, the author admits to having considered and then abandoned the possibility. Discussing the origins of *Ellen Foster*, Gibbons explains that she "began writing a poem from the viewpoint of the black girl who becomes Ellen's best friend, but the story gradually metamorphosed into a novel." In the same interview, she also mentions that, when she began a subsequent novel, *Charms for the Easy Life,* she had planned to continue the story of the black midwife introduced in *A Cure for Dreams,* but decided that the midwife character in *Charms* "should be white, not black, as originally conceived."[7] The tension apparent in Gibbons's account between the desire to tell a black tale, as it were, and the drive to interrogate white racial identity may be at the heart of *Ellen Foster*'s final uneasiness. In the end Ellen's "triumph"—embodied, as the text insists, in her relation to Starletta—rings slightly tinny.

When Ellen acknowledges that she "came a long way to get here," her "here" is both physical domestic space (the foster home) and ideological space (125). Gibbons's closing emphasis on Ellen's relationship to Starletta and to black people more generally privileges interracial (black/white) resolutions over intraracial (white/white) ones. But because Gibbons has not established adequate grounds for a truly mutual interaction between Ellen and Starletta, Ellen's imagined reunion wherein she and Starletta will finally be "even" is more wishful thinking than likely outcome (100). This problem arises, not because Gibbons mistakes her novel's "real" concern for race relations (as reviewer Ralph C. Wood claims), but because the race relations at the very heart of *Ellen Foster* have as much to do with the way "'race' betrays family" in Ellen's biological family as they have to do with interracial alliances.[8]

Because the novel ends with a protracted reverie about Starletta, Gibbons signals to us that here is the "here" to which Ellen has traveled all along. Forty pages sooner, however, Ellen's conception of what family and race, including whiteness, mean and do not mean crystallizes:

> I wonder to myself am I the same girl who would not drink after Starletta two years ago or eat a colored biscuit when I was starved?
>
> It is the same girl but I am old now I know it is not the germs you cannot see that slide off her lips and on to a glass then to your white lips that will hurt you or turn you colored. What you had better worry about though is the people you know and trusted they would be like you because you were all made in the same batch. You need to look over your shoulder at the one who is in charge of holding you up and see if that is a knife he has in his hand. And it might not be a colored hand. But it is a knife.
>
> (85)

These thoughts prompt Ellen to muse, "Sometimes I even think I was cut out to be colored and I got bleached and sent to the wrong bunch of folks" (85). As at novel's end, Ellen gropes toward her "here," a destination whose physical manifestation she has discovered in her foster home but whose less material dimensions she will continue to explore and reimagine armed with potentially transformative experiences and realizations. Skin color does not determine character. Being from the "same batch" does not insure against cruelty and abandonment. Violence between family members is far more likely than violence between strangers. The myth of the deranged racial other is a smoke screen used to obscure the real story of domestic violence and sexual abuse in white homes. White womanhood, when sculpted in response to imagined black male sexual aggression, is both deformed and disabled—convinced that the enemy lies in wait outside, white women are made helpless against the enemy among them. Here lies the fer-

tile ground Ellen has both stumbled upon and determinedly sifted as the basis for her continued growth.

Kaye Gibbon's first novel may not, as its conclusion so much strives to imply, heal the divisions between Ellen and Starletta (or between Ellen's and Starletta's worlds), because these divisions have been made both palpable and hardy by history, culture, and personal trauma. Nonetheless, *Ellen Foster* reveals the ways in which ordained domestic and familial models are intimately wed to economics of race and gender that, in American culture now as historically, are made and maintained in the service of white supremacist patriarchy. Ellen's physical and conceptual dislocation from her "real" home and family enables her ultimate relocation, both literal and ideological, in a home and family where the possibility of resisting those economics constitutes her real triumph.

Notes

1. Kaye Gibbons, *Ellen Foster* (New York: Vintage Books, 1987), 1. Subsequent citations will be made parenthetically in the text. Veronica Makowski, "'The Only Hard Part Was the Food': Recipes for Self-Nurture in Kaye Gibbons's Novels," *Southern Quarterly* 30 (Winter-Spring 1992): 103; Pearl K. Bell, "Southern Discomfort," *The New Republic* 198 (February 29, 1988): 40.

2. Ruth Frankenberg, *White Women, Race Matters: The Social Construction of Whiteness* (Minneapolis: University of Minnesota Press, 1993), 197, 199.

3. I am indebted to Caroline Rody here, whose analysis of another white, female, antiracist narrative, *Wide Sargasso Sea*, suggestively addresses this point. Concerned with the contours of what she calls "daughterist" literature, Rody explores white feminist and antiracist or anticolonialist revolt against systems of white supremacist patrimony. See her "Burning Down the House: The Revisionary Paradigm of Jean Rhys's *Wide Sargasso Sea*," in *Famous Last Words: Changes in Gender and Narrative Closure*, ed. Alison Booth (Charlottesville: University Press of Virginia, 1993).

4. See Sigmund Freud, *On Dreams* (London: W. W. Norton, 1952), 76.

5. I owe the sweet potato comparison to Angela Gilchrist, a student in the seminar on Toni Morrison's novels I taught at the University of Virginia during the spring of 1994.

6. Vron Ware, *Beyond the Pale: White Women, Racism, and History* (New York: Verso, 1992).

7. Kaye Gibbons, interview by Bob Summer, in *Publishers Weekly* 240 (February 8, 1993), 60, 61.

8. Ralph C. Wood, "Gumption and Grace in the Novels of Kaye Gibbons," *The Christian Century* 109 (September 23–30, 1992): 843; Mab Segrest, *Memoir of a Race Traitor* (Boston: South End Press, 1992), 102.

Jane Fisher (review date 2-9 January 1999)

SOURCE: A review of *On the Occasion of My Last Afternoon,* in *America,* Vol. 180, No. 1, January 2-9, 1999, pp. 17-8.

[*In the following review, Fisher discusses Gibbons's* On the Occasion of My Last Afternoon *in terms of its relationship with the author's other works.*]

During her brief career, Kaye Gibbons has earned an impressive number of literary and popular honors—awards and grants from the American Academy and Institute of Arts and Letters, the Ernest Hemingway Foundation and the National Endowment of the Arts, as well as the tribute of having two novels featured by Oprah Winfrey's Book Club. This wide acclaim stems from her ability to find comedy in tragedy and moral beauty in ugliness. All of her novels draw life from her unflinching honesty, her foregrounding of hatred and violence and their destructive consequences.

Many of Gibbons's novels employ first-person narrators disempowered in some way—through childhood (*Ellen Foster, Sights Unseen*), economic hardship or social class (*Ellen Foster, A Virtuous Woman*) and gender and historical circumstance, as in her most recent novel [*On the Occasion of My Last Afternoon*]. Disempowered, yes, but not blinded, since her narrators perceive their imperfect worlds clearly and seek solace only in truth, which, almost miraculously, leads to love.

Her novels typically begin with a sympathetic narrator or character who faces injustice early on but finds healing in a perfect parent figure (for even her married couples rely on parent-child roles). I suspect that Gibbons' major appeal as a novelist lies in her linking of unrelenting truth with the transformative power of unconditional love.

In *On the Occasion of My Last Afternoon,* Gibbons departs from earlier works in several important ways. First, this is a historical novel, set mainly between 1842 and 1865 in Virginia and North Carolina. Its first-person narrator, Emma Garnet Tate Lowell, reconstructs the main events of her life on her last day. And what a life it has been. Born to a tyrannical father and a saintly mother on a thriving James River plantation, Emma marries an altruistic physician from a prominent Boston family and spends most of the war nursing wounded soldiers in Raleigh, N.C. After the war and her husband's death, she continues to work for liberal social causes in the Reconstruction South.

Gibbons' decision to center the novel on Emma's last day has both positive and negative effects, giving *On the Occasion of My Last Afternoon* a sense of biographical closure but a lack of narrative suspense, due mainly to the depiction of a life already completed, which dispenses with the openness and sense of future possibilities so often found in her works.

Gibbons' revelation of the ways in which the antebellum South depended on an intricate structure of lies is an interesting approach to the period. In choosing to write a Civil War novel, Gibbons, whose strength lies in characterization rather than overt action, private satisfaction rather than public achievement, engages one of the most daunting genres in American literature, developed with greater skill by William Faulkner, Toni Morrison and most recently Charles Frazier, her fellow North Carolinian.

Yet by relating various family disputes to the larger battles of the Civil War, Gibbons has given her novel unexpected vitality, especially in the second half, reminding her reader that not all upper-class, white, slave-owning women were comfortable with slavery. Emma's moral voice, if sometimes bordering on the sentimental, much like that found in Louisa May Alcott's *Little Women,* never reaches the pitch of Scarlett O'Hara's narcissistic whine in Margaret Mitchell's *Gone With the Wind.*

As an imaginative historical character, Emma seems almost too good to be true, both in the breadth of her experience and her lack of racial prejudice. Part of what makes Gibbons's first novel *Ellen Foster* so engaging is the narrator's admission of her racial prejudice, which allows her to work to make periodic adjustments, much as Huck Finn does in relation to Jim in Twain's *Huckleberry Finn.* Gibbons works hard in *On the Occasion of My Last Afternoon* to make Emma's relative lack of racism believable both through her close relationship with Clarice, a free black woman who acts as Emma's surrogate mother, and her early hatred of her father, who lied about killing a slave. Emma confesses that she is not completely free of the slave-holders' taint of lying.

Emma struggles against her villainous father, the gory Civil War hospital and the conservative atmosphere of the antebellum and Reconstruction South that would limit the sphere of her activity to the home, though her major battle—learning to tell the truth—seems to have taken place before the novel begins, and the reader must look carefully for traces of it.

On the Occasion of My Last Afternoon, a lively and readable novel, becomes more interesting when read in conjunction with Gibbons's other novels or against the background of the ongoing American obsession with race, status and truth.

Kristina K. Groover (essay date Spring 1999)

SOURCE: "Re-visioning the Wilderness: *Adventures of Huckleberry Finn* and *Ellen Foster,*" in *Southern Quarterly,* Vol. 37, Nos. 3-4, Spring, 1999, pp. 187-97.

[*In the following essay, Groover contrasts the quests in Gibbons's* Ellen Foster *and Mark Twain's* Huckleberry Finn.]

> *Persons attempting to find a motive in this narrative will be prosecuted; persons attempting to find a moral*

in it will be banished; persons attempting to find a plot in it will be shot.

—Author's note [*Adventures of Huckleberry Finn*]

Mark Twain's disclaimer notwithstanding, Huck Finn's journey down the Mississippi is linked—by motive, moral, and plot—with a pervasive tradition in American mythology and literature: the notion that quest, the lone journey into the wilderness, forms the quintessential American experience. In his 1954 work *The American Adam,* R. W. B. Lewis describes the protagonist at the center of this myth as "a figure of heroic innocence and vast potentialities, poised at the start of a new history" (1); he is "happily bereft of ancestry, untouched and undefiled by the usual inheritances of family and race; an individual standing alone, self-reliant and self-propelling" (5). Within this myth, maturation and self-discovery are defined by a linear journey in which the protagonist gains increasing levels of autonomy and separation from family and community. As Huck Finn embarks on his journey, he leaves behind not only his abusive father, but the Widow Douglass, school, church, and all other social forces which threaten to "sivilize" him.

Despite the universality which its central position in American literature implies, a quest tradition defined by flight from family and community into an untamed wilderness is a tradition which pointedly excludes women. As Nina Baym points out, only men in American society have historically had the mobility required to produce a "believable flight into the wilderness" (72). Women within this tradition are cast not as questing heroes, but as the domestic conservators whom the heroic Adam must flee. Mythic heroes from Natty Bumppo to Nick Adams leave behind mothers, wives, sisters, and lovers as they embark on solitary quests in search of self-knowledge and truth. This paradigm of the American literary hero as a lone adventurer is less illustrative of "the uniquely American," Baym argues, than of "what is alleged to be the universal male psyche" (79). Indeed, the Adamic myth finds corroboration in studies of male and female psychological development which suggest that maturing males in American culture learn to value individuation, separation, and linear movement, while girls and young women learn to value affiliation and community.[1]

Women's exclusion from the quest tradition is particularly important when considering the quest plot as not merely an adventure story, but as the central paradigm for spiritual experience in the American literary tradition. As his name implies, the American Adam's roots are not only literary and historical, but spiritual as well. Early Puritan texts depict the literal sojourn in the New England wilderness as a spiritual descent into the wilderness of the soul. In the mid-nineteenth century, when Puritanism no longer dominated the imaginations of most American writers, a pervasive concern with soul, spirit, and metaphysical experience continued to mark the writings of the Transcendentalists and their inheritors. And, despite the break with tradition that distinguishes much twentieth-century American literature, many works from the modernist canon depict crowded but spiritually void urban landscapes which reveal the intersection between the physical and the spiritual, the literal and the psychic to be found in the wilderness quest. Texts throughout the American canon depict the quest as a spiritual journey, a search for transcendence and meaning beyond the temporal world. If female characters are excluded from quest—the central paradigm for spiritual experience in American literary tradition—are they also excluded from the realm of spirituality? Or do texts by American women authors offer alternative patterns for spiritual seeking?

Mark Twain's *Adventures of Huckleberry Finn* and Kaye Gibbons's ***Ellen Foster*** offer a prototype for examining the revision of the quest myth by American women writers. Both Huck and Ellen are children without protection in a threatening adult world; they are motherless, and are victimized by abusive fathers. Both are from southern, rural backgrounds and struggle with the racism of their communities. Finally, both texts are shaped by the quest motif, although the shapes and the goals of the journeys they depict are quite different. Huck Finn, like other Adamic heroes in the canonical literature, flees the restrictions imposed by home and family in order to seek freedom on the great river. The Mississippi River valley, described in Edenic terms, becomes a mythic wilderness in which Huck wrestles with his community's hypocrisy. His journey is not only a physical escape from society's strictures, but the struggle to transcend his community's values and to act on his own innate sense of morality. When he returns, reluctantly, to his community, it is only for a brief time: in order to maintain his integrity as the questing American hero, he must "light out for the Territory" rather than become "sivilized." While Jim's freedom at the end of *Adventures of Huckleberry Finn* is a literal release from the bondage of slavery, Huck's is a spiritual and psychic freedom from the entrapment represented by society.

For Ellen Foster, however, homelessness represents not freedom, but spiritual oblivion. Although she does embark on a quest, it is not the canonical hero's linear flight *from* home and the restrictions it imposes, but a circular journey *to* home and its promise of physical and spiritual nurturance. From the safety of her new home, Ellen declares that "even when I laid out flat and still my legs felt like they were walking again. But I would not move ever from there" (120). For Ellen Foster, home is not a source of entrapment, but a sacred space which represents the fulfillment of all desire.

While, traditionally, domestic themes have served as the invisible backdrop for "important" action in American literature, recent studies such as Ann Romines's *The Home Plot* (1992) and Helen Fiddyment Levy's *Fiction of the Home Place* (1993) have identified "domestic fiction" as an important literary form during both the nineteenth and twentieth centuries. Many of these domestic texts not only convey distinctive values and traditions associated with domesticity, they also critique the spiritual quest motif, subordinating it to a female-defined spirituality centered in the home. For these novelists, home serves not merely as the seat of traditional Christian piety, as in many sentimental domestic novels of the mid-nineteenth century, but as its own source of spiritual truth. In these texts, the routine, cyclical tasks of caring for children, doing housework, and tending gardens take place within a distinctly female version of mythic time.[2] Characters in these works experience a fluidity between the spiritual and temporal worlds, locating spiritual truth in home and community rather than in the solitude of a wilderness quest. By portraying home as sacred, these texts deconstruct conventional dualisms between spirit and body, heaven and earth, God and human.

Domestic work, in literature as in life, is a paradox: it carries little prestige, is low-paid or unpaid, and is, by its very nature, undone nearly as quickly as it is completed; yet it is also the work without which, as Virginia Woolf writes in *A Room of One's Own*, "those seas would be unsailed and those fertile lands a desert" (116). While traditional male activity is linear and quest-oriented, domestic activity is by its very nature cyclical and repetitive. Domestic work is, in Romines's terms, a "sacramental activity" which perpetuates both the physical and the spiritual well-being of a household (6). Its cyclical nature approximates women's experience of time as cyclical rather than linear, and its close association with the well-being of household members reflects women's concern with relationship and community. When it functions to preserve and sustain life against a harsh external world, domestic ritual has transcendent power, blurring the distinction between earthly and spiritual life.

Both *Adventures of Huckleberry Finn* and **Ellen Foster** open with scenes of domestic life gone wrong. The first line of **Ellen Foster** both evokes and fractures the incantatory "once upon a time" of myth: "When I was little," eleven-year-old Ellen reflects, "I would think of ways to kill my daddy" (1). The child who dreams of killing her own father signifies a distortion of natural order brought about by violence, neglect, and incest. In keeping with mythic tradition, Ellen views the distortion of her family life as having supernatural significance, her fractured domestic life serving as a symptom of spiritual disorder. Raised by an alcoholic father and a sickly and ineffectual mother, she describes her family's deterioration in apocalyptic terms which contrast sharply with her usually pragmatic language and tone: "Everything was so wrong like somebody had knocked something loose and the one in charge strolled off and let us spin and shake and fly off the rail" (2). For Ellen, her family's degeneration is a cosmic event suggesting abandonment by "the one in charge." Similarly, the relatives who fail to protect her are not merely uncaring, they are personifications of evil. "She had some power," Ellen says of her hateful maternal grandmother. "Without saying one word she could make my bones shake and I would think of ghost houses and skeletons rattling in all the closets. Her power was the sucking kind that takes your good sense and leaves you limp like a old zombie" (68).

Huckleberry Finn, too, is a victim of his father's neglect and abuse. Pap Finn, like Ellen Foster's father, "drank his own self to death," but not before kidnapping his son, beating him, and leaving him locked up day and night in a riverside cabin. In *Huckleberry Finn*, however, domestic concerns move quickly to the margins of the quest story. As he takes to the river with Jim, Huck flees not only his father's abuse, but the Widow Douglass's attempts to "sivilize" him. As he plans the escape from his father's cabin, Huck muses, "I didn't want to go back to the widow's any more and be so cramped up and sivilized, as they called it. . . . I reckoned I would walk off with the gun and some lines, and take to the woods when I ran away. I guessed I wouldn't stay in one place, but just tramp right across the country, mostly night times, and hunt and fish to keep alive, and so get so far away that the old man nor the widow couldn't ever find me any more" (23). Huck revels not in the safety and protection of the Widow's home, but in his freedom. After two months on his own, Huck confesses that "I didn't see how I'd ever got to like it so well at the widow's, where you had to wash, and eat on a plate, and comb up, and go to bed and get up regular . . ." (22). In Mark Twain's text, home is thus constructed as a place that the questing hero longs to escape.

For Huck Finn, spiritual transcendence is found not in the home, but in the wilderness of the great river, far from the interference of civilization. Huck describes life on the river in Edenic terms: in the morning he and Jim "set down on the sandy bottom and watched the daylight come. Not a sound, anywheres—perfectly still—just like the whole world was asleep" (99); at night, "Sometimes we'd have the whole river to ourselves for the longest time" (100). Although Huck, like Ellen Foster, is an intensely practical figure, he nonetheless finds in the wilderness setting a transcendent sense of peace and freedom which precipitates a rare moment of speculation about the nature of the universe: "We had the sky, up there, all speckled with stars, and we used to lay on our backs and look up at them, and discuss about whether they was made, or only just happened . . ." (101).

Significantly, it is only when Huck and Jim occasionally disembark and encounter people from riverside towns that their quest is threatened. The innocence of the questing American hero confronted with a corrupt civilization is illustrated most poignantly in Huck's encounter with the Grangerfords, who welcome Huck into their home when a steamboat runs over the raft in a fog and forces him ashore. Initially, Huck admires both the Grangerford family and their comfortable home, which seems richly luxurious to him. He is shocked, however, by the senselessness of the Grangerfords' long-time feud with the Shepherdsons, none of whom can remember "what the row was about in the first place" (92). When he observes a shoot-out between the two families in which Buck, a boy his own age, is killed, Huck is horrified: "It made me so sick I most fell out of the tree. . . . I wished I hadn't ever come ashore that night, to see such things" (97–98). Mark Twain thus represents family and community life—even in the guise of the seemingly kind and generous Grangerfords—as dangerous and duplicitous, at odds with the heroic quest and with Huck's innate sense of morality. When Huck flees back to the wilderness—to the raft and to Jim—his troubles subside: "We said there warn't no home like a raft, after all. Other places do seem so cramped up and smothery, but a raft don't. You feel mighty free and easy and comfortable on a raft" (99). While home is a stifling and even corrupting influence, the wilderness offers freedom and transcendence beyond the "sivilized" world.

For Ellen Foster, however, the domestic realm does not suffocate, but rather sustains and preserves life. When her mother is ill, Ellen cleans the house and fixes the meals, disdaining her father for his failure to provide care. She describes activities such as gardening with her mother in Biblical terms: "my mama . . . liked to work in the cool of the morning. She nursed all the plants and put even the weeds she pulled up in little piles along the rows. . . . Weeds do not bear fruit" (49). Even after her mother's death, Ellen's few memories of domestic happiness serve as parables, stories which provide life lessons for a child without a mother to guide her:

> I know I have made being in the garden with her into a regular event but she was really only well like that for one season.
>
> You see if you tell yourself the same tale over and over again enough times then the tellings become separate stories and you will generally fool yourself into forgetting you only started with one solitary season out of your life.
>
> That is how I do it.
>
> (49)

Preserved in Ellen's memory, domestic practices serve a spiritual role, providing guidance and connecting the living and the dead.

Living essentially alone except for her father's occasional drunken visits, Ellen, like Huck Finn, is a child free from parental restrictions. Unlike Huck, who revels in his freedom, however, Ellen strives to duplicate a "normal" family life for herself. Following her mother's example, she compensates for her lack of a home and family by "mothering" herself while she waits for a new home. Alone, she plays "family," cutting out pictures of a man, a woman, and children and outfitting them with cut-out domestic comforts from the Sears catalog. When she joins the Girl Scouts, Ellen plays the role of her own parent, "sign[ing] my daddy's initials saying I had made a handicraft or wrapped a ankle or whatever the badge called for" (27). While Huck and Jim shed even the restriction of clothing while living on the raft, Ellen comforts herself by wearing bits of her mother's clothing under her own dresses. And, while Huck Finn pulls fish from the river and steals melons from gardens, Ellen chooses the food that most resembles, for her, a proper meal: "I found the best deal was the plate froze with food already on it. A meat, two vegetables, and a dab of dessert" (25). While Ellen can repli-

cate the domestic trappings of a real home, however, she knows that its essence lies not in material things, but in maternal love. Taking control of her own destiny, Ellen defines the goal of her quest in domestic terms: "I decided that if I quit wasting time I could be happy as anybody else in the future. . . . And that is what I did. That is why I think I am somebody now because I said by damn this is how it is going to be and before I knew it I had a new mama" (95).

In the course of their quests, both Huck and Ellen reject conventional religion as ineffectual at best and hypocritical at worst. Living at the Widow's house, Huck exposes the falsity of Miss Watson's religious platitudes:

> She told me to pray every day, and whatever I asked for I would get it. But it warn't so. I tried it. Once I got a fish-line, but no hooks. It warn't no good to me without hooks. I tried for the hooks three or four times, but somehow I couldn't make it work. By-and-by, I asked Miss Watson to try for me, but she said I was a fool. She never told me why, and I couldn't make it out no way.
>
> (11)

Even while admiring the Grangerfords, Huck recognizes their duplicity as they sit in church with guns held between their knees, then talk admiringly afterward of the preacher's sermon on brotherly love. Ellen, similarly, recognizes the hypocrisy of traditional religion in the blundering, superficial minister who performs her mother's funeral service:

> I do not know this preacher. He says that even though he did not know my mama he feels like he knew her well because he has met us and we are all so nice. It does not bother him that what he said does not make good sense.
>
> And what else are you going to say when the Bible comes flat out and says killing yourself is flinging God's gift back into his face and He will not forgive you for it ever? The preacher leaves that out and goes straight to the green valleys and the streets of silver and gold.
>
> (20)

For Ellen, the easy platitudes of conventional religion provide neither help nor comfort. When she learns that her new mama receives financial support from a local congregation, she accepts her obligations pragmatically: "You go in that church and act genuine. Even if you think what he has to say that week is horse manure or even if you believe it is a lie you sit there and be still. Worse could happen than for you to sit for an hour. You could be where you came from" (56).

Living with her new mama, Ellen finds that real fulfillment comes not during church, but afterward, in her new home. Ellen confesses that she stays "starved" all through the service, waiting for the real nourishment that comes afterward: "When or if you come to my house now after church you will smell all the things that have been simmering on low. It has been waiting for me and me for it" (58). As important as the physical nourishment of Sunday dinner is the spiritual nourishment gained through the ritual of preparing food for the coming week, a communal activity that is at the heart of Ellen's new domestic life:

> Everything we do almost on Sundays has to do with food. When we finish the meal on hand it is time to prepare chicken salad, ham salad, bread, three bean soup, or what have you for that week's lunch boxes. . . .
>
> Everybody like me, Stella, Francis, my new mama, Jo Jo, but not the baby are involved in this Sunday cooking. . . .
>
> Today it is bread and soup. It does not sound like much but it is hardy and I like to show it off in the lunchroom when all the other people have a measly tray of this or that.
>
> (58)

In comparison to the Sunday dinner and rich domestic ritual that follows the service, churchgoing is an empty tradition.

As ineffectual as the church as a source of healing is the school psychologist with whom Ellen meets weekly. The psychologist's inscrutable questions, his accusations of defensiveness and twisting of Ellen's words "like a miracle into exactly what he wanted me to say" make it impossible for her to tell the truth about her life. "I do not plan to discuss chickenshit with you," she tells him definitively on her final visit. "I might be confused sometimes in my head but it is not something you need to talk about. Before you can talk you have to line it all up in order and I had rather just let it swirl around until I am too tired to think" (89). In order to recover from her past, Ellen requires not the professional care of a minister or psychologist, but the loving care found in the home. "[T]here have been more than a plenty days," Ellen says of her new mama, "when she has put both my hands in hers and said if we relax and breathe slow together I can slow down shaking. And it always works" (121). Her new mama's "cure" for Ellen's troubles lies in such nurturing activities as washing Ellen's hair ("I feel her long fingers on my head and pray that it takes a long time for me to be clean," Ellen confesses), sewing and cooking for her, and including her in the communal activities of the household (36). Through domestic ritual and maternal love, this foster mother nurtures not only Ellen, but all of her girls. "You don't need to see through the walls here to know when my new mama is alone with one of her girls telling them about how to be strong or rubbing their backs," Ellen reports. "You can imagine it easy if it has happened to you" (121). In Kaye Gibbons's fictional world, healing of both body and spirit is found in the home.

As she establishes family and domestic life as sources of transcendence, Gibbons redefines home and family. Like Pap Finn, Ellen's own relatives threaten her safety rather than protecting and nurturing her. After her mother's death, Ellen's father fails to provide for her most basic needs, neglecting either to feed her or to pay the power bill. When her father and his friends make their sporadic raids on the kitchen, Ellen is affronted at this invasion of her domestic space: "Who said they could come in my house and have a free-for-all?" she wonders. "Who said they could be here?" (37). Ellen's other relatives also prove inadequate at providing care. Ellen describes the few days she spends with her Aunt Betsy as a scene of domestic bliss:

> All afternoon and night and on into the next day is like magic. I do not think of anything but the flowers on the sheets and the bubbles in the bath water.
>
> This is the life.
>
> (41)

Unlike Huck, who finds such trappings "smothery," Ellen is supremely happy amidst these domestic comforts. While Aunt Betsy is happy enough to have Ellen spend a weekend with her, however, she has no intention of becoming a surrogate mother. When the court places Ellen with her maternal grandmother, her unsuitability as a mother figure is signified by Ellen's description of her house as a "museum" full of "what-nots" that she is forbidden to touch. Even the meals her grandmother serves illustrate the gulf between the two. On most days, Ellen comes home to find a plate left for her in the kitchen. On Sundays, however, when she and her grandmother share the dinner table, "we both picked at our little individual chickens or turkeys and did not talk" (66). Compared to the communal tradition that accompanies meal preparation at her new mama's house, meal time in her grandmother's home reflects the absence of a true family life.

While Ellen is taken in grudgingly by her own relatives, she is lovingly embraced by a variety of alternative families. When her father sexually abuses her, Ellen flees not into the wilderness, as Huck Finn does in fleeing from his own abusive father, but to a loving home: that of her friend, Starletta. From her own lonely home, Ellen has often watched the smoke rising from Starletta's chimney, musing that "[y]ou know it is a warm fire where the smoke starts" (29). When her father assaults her, Ellen instinctively runs "down the road to Starletta. Now to the smoke coming out of the chimney against the night sky I run" (38). When she is placed in a temporary home with her art teacher and her husband, Ellen observes longingly that "the three of us could pass for a family on the street" (55). In contrast to Ellen's "real" family, Julia and Roy allow her to be a child for the first time in her life:

> She said it was good I loosened up. We would run around and she would tell me to let it all hang out. Let your hair down good golly Miss Molly let it all hang out. Go with the flow, she would say. Make up a tune and throw in some words and go with the flow.
>
> I had no idea people could live like that.
>
> (47)

While such alternative families prove far better at meeting Ellen's needs than does her own family, however, the court insists that she be placed with her own relatives, again signifying the ineffectiveness of institutions in providing care. "What do you do when the judge talks about the family society's cornerstone but you know yours was never a Roman pillar but is and always has been crumbly old brick?" Ellen wonders. "He had us all mixed up with a different group of folks" (56). Her forced return to her nightmarish relatives recalls Huck Finn's similar plight at the hands of another well-meaning but uninformed judge: "The judge and the widow went to law to get the court to take me away from him and let one of them be my guardian; but it was a new judge that had just come, and he didn't know the old man; so he said courts mustn't interfere and separate families if they could help it; said he'd druther not take a child away from its father" (19–20). While Ellen persists in her search for family, however, redefining family in the process, Huck rejects the very notion of family. At the end of his adventure, when Tom Sawyer's Aunt Sally vows to adopt and "sivilize" Huck, he balks: "I can't stand it. I been there before" (245). While domesticity threatens to encroach on Huck's freedom as long as he remains within reach of the Widow Douglass and Aunt Sally, beyond the Mississippi River valley lies the seemingly endless wilderness of the Territory, with its seductive promise of quest, freedom, and adventure.

Ellen's desperate quest for a home and family gradually leads her to question the racism she has inherited from her community. Although she seeks shelter from her father at Starletta's house, Ellen refuses to eat any of the food Starletta's mother prepares; wary of staying in a "colored house," she sleeps, fully dressed, on top of the covers. Reflecting her community's bigotry, she worries, "As fond as I am of all three of them I do not think I could drink after them. I try to see what Starletta leaves on the lip of a bottle but I have never seen anything with the naked eye. If something is that small it is bound to get into your system and do some damage" (29–30). While she is living with her grandmother, Ellen is cared for by Mavis, a black servant who tells her stories of her mother's girlhood and shields her from her grandmother's cruelty. Each evening, Ellen walks to Mavis's house to watch her and her family. Seeing their care for one another, Ellen begins to reconsider her own understanding of family:

> I started a list of all that a family should have. Of course there is the mama and the daddy but if one has to be missing then it is OK if the one left can count for two . . .
>
> While I watched Mavis and her family I thought I would bust open if I did not get one of them for my own self soon. Back then I had not figured out how to go about getting one but I had a feeling it could be got.
>
> (67)

As she gains experience with her own neglectful family and with the outsiders who care for her, Ellen gradually reconsiders the meaning of family:

> I am old now I know it is not the germs you cannot see that slide off her lips and on to a glass then to your white lips that will hurt you or turn you colored. What you had better worry about though is the people you know and trusted they would be like you because you were all made in the same batch. You need to look over your shoulder at the one who is in charge of holding you up and see if that is a knife he has in his hand. And it might not be a colored hand. But it is a knife. . . .
>
> When I stayed with my mama's mama I made a list of all that I wanted my family to be and I put down white and have running water.
>
> Now it makes me ashamed to think I said that.
>
> (85)

In redefining family, Gibbons suggests that blood ties cannot always be trusted to "[hold] you up." Far from creating a despairing picture of family, Gibbons merely widens her focus, finding love and support for her heroine from sources that the rural southern community rejects. Ellen finds the love that sustains her only when she abandons both her community's prejudices and its restrictive definition of family.

Huck Finn, too, must reject his community's prejudices in order to fulfill his quest. Although Huck lives on the margins of his community, he has internalized its bigotry: he acknowledges that Jim "had an uncommon level head, for a nigger" (65) but claims that "you can't learn a nigger to argue" (68); and, when he ascertains Jim's grief over being parted from his family, Huck muses wonderingly, "I do believe he cared just as much for his people as white people does for their'n. It don't seem natural, but I reckon it's so" (131). Through his physical journey, Huck literally leaves behind Miss Watson, the Grangerfords, and the duke and dauphin—who, Huck declares, make him "ashamed of the human race" (137)—as representatives of society's restrictiveness, hypocrisy, and racism. He only fulfills his spiritual quest, however, when he also rejects the moral values his society embodies by allowing Jim to share his flight to freedom. Although he is shocked and ashamed to find himself a "nigger-stealer," Huck bravely resolves to "go to hell" if he must in order to help his friend. The plight of the runaway slave is thus cast in terms of the Adamic myth: Jim, like Huck, must leave family and community behind to find freedom.

In a revision of the quest tradition, Ellen resolves her relationship with Starletta not by sharing a flight to freedom, but by sharing her home. Equally as important as the physical nurturance her new mama offers Ellen is her unhesitating welcome for Starletta:

> My new mama says sure Starletta can come stay with us . . .
>
> Have you ever felt like you could cry because you know you just heard the most important thing anybody in the world could have spoke at that second? . . . All that mattered in my world at that second was my new

mama and the sound of yes in my ears oh yes Starletta is welcome here.

(99)

Ellen's preparation for Starletta's arrival is a series of domestic rituals: she cleans the house, has her new mama embroider Starletta's initials on a set of towels, and gives instructions about the supper menu. When Starletta arrives, Ellen shares with her her favorite activity: lying on the bed in her room, waiting for dinner. "I will lay here too and wait for supper beside a girl that every rule in the book says I should not have in my house much less laid still and sleeping beside me," Ellen muses. "I came a long way to get here but when you think about it real hard you will see that old Starletta came even farther" (125–26). The fulfillment of Ellen's quest is thus located both in home and in family—a family defined neither by blood ties nor by race, but by love and care.

The conclusion of each text highlights Twain's and Gibbons's differing versions of the spiritual quest fulfilled. At the end of his journey, Huck "light[s] out for the Territory," thus signifying that the hero's quest can only be fulfilled in the flight from home and community. Ellen Foster's journey, however, is one she is happy to abandon when she arrives at her new mama's home: "I have laid in my bed many many days since that first afternoon I heard her in the kitchen and I am always as glad to rest as I was then" (120). Ellen signifies her integration into this domestic life by signing her school papers with a new name:

> That may not be the name God or my mama gave me but that is my name now. Ellen Foster. . . . Before I even met Stella or Jo Jo or the rest of them I heard they were the Foster family. Then I moved in the house and met everybody and figured it was OK to make my name like theirs. Something told me I might have to change it legal or at church but I was hoping I could slide by the law and folks would think I came by the name natural after a while.
>
> (88)

In choosing her name, Ellen again rejects the authority of both the courts and the church. Her new name signifies instead the authority of her own experience: no longer alone in the world, nor the daughter of an abusive father, she belongs to a loving home of her own choosing.

The quest myth that dominates the American literary canon, shaped by male psychology and male social position, reflects both the desire for separation and the freedom to choose autonomy from home, family, and community. As Baym suggests, this paradigm illuminates a central American myth regarding the relationship of the individual to society:

> The myth narrates a confrontation of the American individual, the pure American self divorced from specific social circumstances, with the promise offered by the idea of America. The promise is the deeply romantic one that in this new land, untrammeled by history and

social accident, a person will be able to achieve complete self-definition. Behind this promise is the assurance that individuals come before society, that they exist in some meaningful sense prior to, and apart from, societies in which they happen to find themselves. The myth also holds that, as something artificial and secondary to human nature, society exerts an unmitigatedly destructive pressure on individuality.

(71)

Although female characters are largely excluded from this quest tradition, however, they are not excluded from spiritual experience in literary texts.[3] In *Ellen Foster,* Kaye Gibbons revises the spiritual quest paradigm by suggesting that transcendent experience may be located not only in an uninhabited wilderness, but in the midst of family and community. In Gibbons's text, the flight from home is an exhausting and terrifying journey; home, by contrast, offers both physical and spiritual safety. By treating home as sacred space, *Ellen Foster*—as well as numerous texts by Willa Cather, Harriette Arnow, Eudora Welty, Ellen Glasgow, Alice Walker, Gloria Naylor, and others—redefines spirituality based on women's experience of domestic life and their valuing of affiliation and community. Female characters in these works seek transcendence not in male myths of freedom and wilderness, but in the familiar terrain of women's domestic lives.

Notes

1. See Gilligan, *In a Different Voice: Psychological Theory and Women's Development,* and Chodorow, *The Reproduction of Mothering: Psychoanalysis and the Study of Gender.* For a discussion of masculinity as the norm in the psychological theories of Freud, Piaget, Erikson, Kohlberg, and other researchers, see Gilligan, chapter 1, "Woman's Place in Man's Life Cycle." In *Toward a New Psychology of Women,* Jean Baker Miller argues that the very idea of male separation is a myth which gains its power not through its truth, but through its prescriptive quality: "Few men ever attain such self-sufficiency, as every woman knows. They are usually supported by numbers of wives, mistresses, mothers, daughters, secretaries, nurses, and others. . . . Thus, there is reason to question whether this model accurately reflects men's lives. Its goals, however, are held out for all, and are seen as the preconditions for mental health" (437).

2. Scholars in a number of disciplines have commented on women's experience of time as cyclical rather than linear, often in connection with their experience of domesticity. In *The Sacred and the Feminine: Toward a Theology of Housework,* theologian Kathryn Allen Rabuzzi writes, "Though we know better, we often act as though linear, quantifiable time (associated with questing) were given in nature. . . . Though our subjective experiences of time vary, nonetheless we tend to assume that there is some sort of temporal sequence 'out there,' apart from ourselves. This kind of time that we assume is 'out there' we describe as historic, meaning that it is progressive

and nonrepeatable, having a forward motion like the flow of a river . . . it is useful to see how a rough distinction between linear and mythic time reflects differences in traditional masculine and feminine time experiences. Women's housebound time is typically characterized by amorphousness or circularity or both . . ." (145–46). In *Tapestries of Life: Women's Work, Women's Consciousness, and the Meaning of Daily Experience,* Bettina Aptheker describes women's lives as "fragmented and dispersed," "episodic," . . . "they are often determined by events outside of women's control. . . . Women are continually interrupted" (39). In *The Reproduction of Mothering,* sociologist Nancy Chodorow writes that women's domestic activities have a "nonbounded quality. They consist, as countless housewives can attest and as women poets, novelists, and feminist theorists have described, of diffuse obligations . . . the work of maintenance and reproduction is characterized by its repetitive and routine continuity, and does not involve a specified sequence of progression" (179).

3. In *Women and Spirituality,* Carol Ochs points out that the concept of spiritual quest as a flight from domestic and communal life pervades Western theology as well as psychology and literature: "The image of the journey permeates the classics of Western spirituality. The notion of a journey with a well-marked itinerary permeates psychology as well . . . both presuppose a linear progression with later stages that are valued more highly than earlier ones. . . . The adoption of the journey model carries with it the view that part of our life has value and meaning only insofar as it contributes to the goal of the journey. Living in itself is not considered intrinsically valuable—the only value is in the goal we supposedly long to achieve" (24). This emphasis on quest in patriarchal theology has resulted in a "landscape of the sacred" in which, theologian Elizabeth Dodson Gray writes, only "[a] few places, a few people, a few occasions are seen to concentrate and to embody the holy . . . The only moments in time which become hallowed by an aura of holiness are those which involve these places, these people, these texts and these acts. The rest of life is perceived as a vast desert of the mundane, the unholy" (2).

While traditional Western theology tends to view sacred experience as separate from ordinary, earthly experience, feminist theology emphasizes the presence of the sacred embodied in earthly experience. Feminist theology views personal experience not as trivial or mundane, but as an authoritative source of spiritual revelation. Unlike patriarchal theology, which establishes a few places and activities as realms of the sacred, feminist theology locates the sacred in ordinary experience. The root of theology, feminist theologian Rosemary Ruether writes in *Sexism and God-Talk,* is "codified collective human experience . . . Experience includes experience of the divine, experience of oneself, and experience of the

community and the world, in an interacting dialectic" (12). Traditional theologies, however, have dismissed those who create their own religious myths as heretics. "Theologians are ignorant of what every anthropologist knows," Naomi Goldenberg writes, "—i.e., that the forms of our thought derive from the forms of our culture" (115). Feminist theologians are thus distinctive in recognizing what Ruether terms "codified, collective human experience" as an authoritative source of spiritual truth. The fact that the kinds of experiences that have been "collected" and "codified" in Western culture have been almost exclusively male, however, has resulted in a male-centered theology. If women's daily lives are radically different from those of men, then their perceptions of divinity and transcendence will be shaped by those experiences, emerging as a distinctively female spirituality.

Works Cited

Aptheker, Bettina. *Tapestries of Life: Women's Work, Women's Consciousness, and the Meaning of Daily Experience.* Amherst: U of Massachusetts P, 1989.

Baym, Nina. "Melodramas of Beset Manhood: How Theories of American Fiction Exclude Women Authors." *The New Feminist Criticism: Essays on Women, Literature, and Theory.* Ed. Elaine Showalter. New York: Pantheon, 1985. 63–80.

Chodorow, Nancy. *The Reproduction of Mothering: Psychoanalysis and the Sociology of Gender.* Berkeley: U of California P, 1978.

Gibbons, Kaye. *Ellen Foster.* 1987. New York: Vintage, 1990.

Gilligan, Carol. *In a Different Voice: Psychological Theory and Women's Development.* Cambridge: Harvard UP, 1982.

Goldenberg, Naomi. *Changing of the Gods: Feminism and the End of Traditional Religions.* Boston: Beacon P, 1979.

Gray, Elizabeth Dodson. *Sacred Dimensions of Women's Experience.* Wellesley: Roundtable P, 1988.

Levy, Helen Fiddyment. *Fiction of the Home Place: Jewett, Cather, Glasow, Porter, Welty, and Naylor.* Jackson: UP of Mississippi, 1993.

Lewis, R. W. B. *The American Adam: Innocence, Tragedy and Tradition in the Nineteenth Century.* Chicago: U of Chicago P, 1955.

Miller, Jean Baker. *Toward a New Psychology of Women.* Boston: Beacon P, 1976.

Ochs, Carol. *Women and Spirituality.* Totowa, NJ: Rowman and Allanheld, 1983.

Rabuzzi, Kathryn Allen. *The Sacred and the Feminine: Toward a Theology of Housework.* New York: Seabury P, 1982.

Romines, Ann. *The Home Plot: Women, Writing, and Domestic Ritual.* Amherst: U of Massachusetts P, 1992.

Ruether, Rosemary. *Sexism and God-Talk: Toward a Feminist Theology.* Boston: Beacon P, 1983

Twain, Mark [Samuel Clemens]. *Adventures of Huckleberry Finn.* Ed. Henry Nash Smith. Boston: Houghton, 1958.

Woolf, Virginia. *A Room of One's Own.* San Diego: Harcourt, 1929.

Sharon Monteith (essay date April 1999)

SOURCE: "Between Girls: Kaye Gibbons' *Ellen Foster* and Friendship as a Monologic Formulation," in *Journal of American Studies,* Vol. 33, No. 1, April, 1999, pp. 45-64.

[*In the following essay, Monteith studies how the structure of Gibbons's* Ellen Foster *as a monologue affects the presentation of the relationship between Ellen and Starletta, demonstrating how Ellen's first-person narration essentially robs Starletta of her own voice in the novel.*]

I

In the work of contemporary writers who explore the racial and social geography of growing up in the American South, fleeting encounters between white and black girls abound but enduring friendships prove to be more problematic to represent.[1] In *Ellen Foster* (1987), Ellen and Starletta's association stretches across the novel whereas, most frequently in fictions, the points at which black and white women converge and relate tend to be brief and transient, as in Toni Morrison's *Beloved* (1987) where a heavily pregnant and fugitive Sethe is aided by poor white Amy; or in Thulani Davis's *1959* (1992) where the brief kindness of a white woman is remembered as a significant, if fleeting gesture. I wish to raise questions about the ways in which cross-racial childhood relationships are represented formally and aesthetically. There is often an understandable but troubling literary–critical impasse whereby black girls are contained within the first-person narrations of white protagonists which, whilst explicating the connection between the girls, risk engulfing or subsuming the black "best friend." I shall examine the ways in which this may be the inevitable result of the *Bildungsroman* form and consider how the representation of the cross-racial friendship at the heart of *Ellen Foster* is modified in direct correspondence to the novel's structuring.

Landscapes of childhood are received rather than chosen, and contemporary writers often explore the ways in which the young black and white girls gravitate towards friendships with each other but become victims of the structuring of the Southern societies the novels seek to reflect. Their roles are important as markers of the boundaries Southern society sought to maintain and to stabilize via

childhood identity formation under racial segregation. Ruth Frankenberg's recent study sees the "social geographies of race" as the organizing principle of the childhoods of the white American women she interviews for whom unofficial demarcations according to race still persisted, wherever and whenever they grew up. This is an examination of racial geography which refers to the "racial and ethnic mapping of a landscape in physical terms, and enables also a beginning sense of the conceptual mapping of self and other with respect to race operating in white women's lives."[2]

This facet of Southern culture in particular fascinates writers; there are a number of autobiographies and memoirs in which writers explore childhood friendships within the crucible of race and segregation. Lynn Bloom has described race as that "touchy subject . . . that permeates twentieth-century southern childhood autobiographies and distinguishes them, as a group, from other American childhood autobiographies."[3] The "touchy subject" is also inescapable in fictions that seek to testify to and explore the searing effect racial division could have on young girls in the South. There is a marked propensity in fiction and film to fix representations of cross-racial relationships of all types in earlier decades when social roles were fixed and black characters had little space to manoeuvre outside an established paradigmatic formulation (white child/black nurse; white mistress/black domestic; white employer/black chauffeur).[4]

The meeting between a white girl and a black girl in contemporary fiction is frequently represented as a profound and meaningful encounter, an epiphany. It is this propensity that seems to underpin most fictional delineations of cross-racial childhood associations. Dorothy Allison, in *Bastard Out of Carolina* (1992), and Nanci Kincaid, in *Crossing Blood* (1994), each delineate Southern landscapes of childhood and pursue the idea of cross-racial relationships as transgressive.[5] For their young white girl protagonists, meeting with a young black girl constitutes an epiphanic moment, a moment that carries much in terms of the text's meanings as it illuminates the white girl's progress towards adult understanding. Meaningful as the affiliation may be, however, such a relationship cannot and does not endure in either novel. In *Ellen Foster,* Kaye Gibbons relies upon such binary oppositions in order to explore in a more developed way the relationship between Ellen and Starletta. Starletta is Ellen Foster's only friend, but she is firmly fixed as auxiliary to Ellen since Ellen is driven by an intensely personal quest to re-establish family and order in her life. The reader is appalled by the situation Ellen finds herself in, compelled to follow her quest to find a new and safe home for herself, and admires the pragmatic determination with which she intends to achieve her ends. This is the basis of the reader's engagement with Ellen's personal narrative. In her monologue, she recognizes how the adult world will judge her association with her black friend and she begins, consciously and systematically, to differentiate herself from Starletta at every turn. Disorder has ruled Ellen's life; her family falls apart, her home becomes unsafe as her drunken father lurches around it, so Ellen concerns herself with order and cleanliness and fixes Starletta as her opposite in order to judge what those characteristics might be. Starletta is inextricably linked into the dialectic of order and cleanliness versus disorder and dirt that preoccupies Ellen. Her first comment on seeing Starletta in the church at her mother's funeral focuses in on this most precisely: "I see Starletta and she looks clean" is immediately followed by the statement "Starletta and her mama both eat dirt."[6] Her observations bespeak a social conditioning, according to Southern design, whereby poor white people learned to differentiate themselves at any and every level from poor black people.

In contemporary fiction, white girls are frequently fascinated with their black counterparts and pursue connections with them even under the strictures of segregation and even when rebuffed. But the constraints placed upon cross-racial childhood friendships are perhaps best exemplified in the much earlier autobiographical writings of Lillian Smith (1897–1966) who interrogated the ideological apparatus that tried to ensure that friendships that crossed "the color line" would be dissolved when the girls reached the threshold of adulthood and introduction into their appropriately different places in Southern societies. In 1943, before the Fellowship of Southern Churchmen, Lillian Smith spoke out against racial segregation and exposed the detrimental impact of post-Reconstruction controls upon black and white children. She spoke of her own childhood in the 1900s specifically, but also of systems still in effect at the time of her speech:

> No colored child in our country, however protected within the family, is being given today what his personality needs in order to mature fully and richly. No white child, under the segregation pattern, North or South, can be free of arrogance, hardness of heart, blindness to human needs. The bitter and inescapable fact is that our children in America, white and colored, are growing distorted, twisted personalities within the frame of this segregation which our fears and frustrations have imposed upon them.[7]

Smith spoke out forcefully against the "frame of segregation" in her speeches, and much of her autobiographical *Killers of the Dream* (1949) is dedicated to explicating and exposing the false sanctity of white skin that was inculcated into children in the Georgia of her youth.[8] One incident in particular that Smith "forgot" for more than thirty years is wrenched into comprehension. It concerns a little white girl who is discovered living in "Colored Town" and is removed by the white townsfolk, with the aid of the town marshal, from a black family who are deemed "ignorant and dirty and sick-looking colored folks," and who must have kidnapped her. She goes to live with young Lillian's family and the two become firm friends until it is realized that, despite her white skin, Janie is "colored" and must be returned. She will not be allowed over to play, and the dictate that "white and colored people do not live together" is played out to emotional effect in both girls' lives; Lillian feels guilty at having broken a clear social

taboo by sharing her bed and her friendship with a girl who she discovers is black. She shuns her:

> And like a slow poison, it began to seep through me: *I was white. She was colored. We must not be together. It was bad to be together. Though you ate with your nurse when you were little, it was bad to eat with any colored person after that.*[9]

Young Lillian and Janie share an intimacy that is subsequently shattered and distorted and even obliterated from Lillian's memory in the need to adhere to the racial geography of her day.[10]

The girls have engaged in a border crossing which, if it is allowed to continue, will destabilize and disrupt the map of social relations for which they are to be prepared. The episode Smith recounts is especially powerful in its playing out of the "rules" and the "frame" of segregation. After the social structure was legally dismantled, it remained the case that it was deemed reasonable, even natural, that black and white children should play together pre-school. It was the onset of adolescence which marked the point after which their intimacy should be dissolved.[11] This "sorting," entrusted to the institutional jurisprudence of schools, proved insidious but effective and largely unassailable. The girls are manoeuvred out of particular friendships as a result of the inflexibility of racial and social biases.

It is, indeed, striking that white writers who have deemed cross-racial childhood connections significant, in that they have chosen to represent them in their fictions, have simultaneously often left the black girl unvoiced and inactive in the encounter. One writer who does explore a relationship in which both parties strive to be vocal and actively equal participants is Susan Richards Shreve in *A Country of Strangers* (1990). A short consideration of this novel may help to quantify exactly how it is that the friendship in **Ellen Foster** remains stifled and trapped within its structure. It may also serve to illuminate the fact that, whether couched in a monologic or dialogic framework, interracial childhood friendships typically do not endure beyond childhood in contemporary fictions, whatever their form. The two novels are structured very differently, but the problems that arise in maintaining a cross-racial friendship beyond childhood association are present in each. Shreve locates a childhood friendship as one interracial connection amidst many, but she features it centrally; in fact, it is the closest the novel comes to positing a successful cross-racial alliance.

Kate and Prudential meet in Northern Virginia in 1942, and their encounters are mediated through a third-person omniscient narrator who assesses each character's motives and feelings, whereas, in Gibbons' novel, Ellen may only assess her own. The girls' relationship begins in unequivocal aggression and antagonism and Shreve retains a startlingly clear image of their differences, whilst manoeuvring Kate and Prudential towards recognition of the elements that connect their lives. Kate immediately detects Prudential's hatred of her as representative of "white girls."

The hatred is translated into a succinct and memorable incident in which Prudential, feeling a profound urge to spit at Kate, decides to urinate on her instead. She pees from way up in an elm tree, "a long thin stream, straight as a pencil through the branches. Bulls eyes on top of her silky hair."[12] It is, in the scuffle that follows, Kate who spits in Prudential's face. Prudential describes this fight as a "conversation" and it is represented as the most honest exchange that the girls can muster in the first instance. Prudential is thirteen, pregnant by her father and angry. Only when Kate is abused at school by a boy who forces her head towards his erection, and she spontaneously confides the incident to Prudential, is their friendship "sealed." Prudential does not reciprocate with her own experience of abuse, but her shocked "I had no idea that kind of misfortune could happen to a white girl" (p. 111) belies her conditioning, historical and cultural. The white girl may have similar problems.

The girls are edged into contiguous and unforeseen symmetry: "Their bodies touched along the arms and thighs, their bony knees aligned as if such order in presentation were intentional" (p. 110). Shreve patterns their commonality into each evocation of their daily lives in an interracial household in which they are the only members to overlook difference in favour of cohesion: they lunch together, sit closely side by side, and exchange secrets, except for the one alluding to the father of Prudential's baby. Their circumstances are not the same, but their desire to be friends is mutual, for much of the novel. It has been said of Shreve's work in general that, "When her characters are not making grand gestures or being quietly introspective, they are usually talking with each other, most often interpreting and evaluating each other's lives."[13] This general tendency is significantly abridged in the case of Kate and Prudential's reciprocity in that actions figure more than words; just as their first fight was a "conversation," so they go on to demonstrate their mutual support in deeds and actions. Kate buys Prudential a dress as a mark of appreciation and Prudential fights Kate's battle with the schoolboy oppressor on her behalf, exacting revenge in a secondhand retaliation for her own as well as her friend's sexual distress. On only one occasion, and very untypically, does Prudential underline their equitable camaraderie in words: "It's like we were born together, halved out of the same eggshell" (p. 129); the image serves to conjure up the fragility and precariousness of an association such as theirs in rural Virginia in the 1940s. Their friendship gradually slips over into a memory, and the depths they plumbed over Kate's problems are never repeated and so a wall of silence is quietly but significantly erected between them by the close of the novel.

Kate and Prudential exemplify a spirited endeavour to elicit honesty and comfort from a cross-racial childhood friendship, but theirs barely persists beyond the age of thirteen. However, a writer may choose to structure her novel—as *Bildungsroman* or melodrama, through a dominant central character and voice, or in short narrative passages or scenes that coalesce as an exploration of relationships—the outcome tends to be the same when one focuses directly on the cross-racial childhood relationship. Very few withstand social or indeed personal pressures or remain as close, if they persist at all beyond adolescence, as they clearly had the potential to be in childhood. In *Meridian* (1976), set in the aftermath of the Civil Rights Movement and which engages with lost hopes and failed coalitions, Alice Walker has Meridian's grandmother declare that in all her life she has "never known a white woman she liked after the age of twelve."[14] In fact, writers do not tend to push much beyond the onset of adolescence, fixing the girls within a framework that reinscribes the repeated breakdown of cross-racial friendships or never allows them to become truly dialogic encounters in the first place.

II

In *Ellen Foster,* Kaye Gibbons inscribes the girls' social experiences as racially different, their futures as ultimately separate, and their friendships as almost impossible to maintain. The structuring of the text separates the girls and keeps them separate, despite their friendship. Black girls are often framed and constrained within the white protagonists' first-person narratives in *Bildungsromans* or biographical novels; and this form of narration, typically featuring a single narrating voice, fixes the black girl as auxiliary, as an emblem to signify a stage (or stages) in the white protagonist's personal development and rites of passage. The first-person narrated *Bildungsroman,* described by Richard Gray as one of the South's "familiar regional narrative types and structures," is also a monologic form that silences other voices that might otherwise disrupt the monologue or deviate from its flow.[15] The *Bildungsroman* has, of course, also been judged one of the most bourgeois of novelistic forms; classically realist, it privileges the individual, eponymous in this case, her psychology, and her character to the extent that Catherine Belsey has stated that "character, unified and coherent, *is* the source of action."[16] Kaye Gibbons unfixes some of the conventions of the form in her depiction of a poor white girl whose class and language clearly set her outside of a bourgeois formulation.

Nevertheless, the *Bildungsroman* structure envelops the speaking protagonist in a kind of impermeable membrane and functions to divert the reader's attention away from characters who are positioned on the outside. This means that the black friend is not recognized with a space for speech as she could be in a heteroglossic text in which more than one social discourse is represented. It is not the emphasis on Ellen's development that is disturbing, but the inclusion of Starletta as an apparently major spur, whilst rendering her mute and muted in the novel in all circumstances. She never becomes a speaking subject. This results in the aporia, or internal contradiction, in the text, that I read as the gap between the friendship, clearly present in the novel, and the organization of the novel as a monologue which severely limits the representation of that friendship.

The disjunction between white and black characters in a text that can be read as based on an axis of friendship constitutes what I shall call a "fault line" in the text. This fault line splinters the friendship, since the friendship is ultimately only the casing or framework according to which the content of the text may be said to operate. Potential difficulties arise in fiction about women, as well as in feminist praxis, as a result of epistemological standpoints intrinsic in different "feminist" positions. Cross-racial co-operation, apparently of representative importance in contemporary feminist thought, and to the novel under discussion here, risks being undermined by set literary structures and paradigms deployed in the construction of black characters and in representations of black voices that inevitably function to segregate or "other" them, even to silence them completely. Gibbons creates a white girl whose epistemology derives from segregated situations but for whom even a radical ideological breakthrough of the kind she undergoes in the novel is contained within a narrative structure that, whilst it necessarily privileges her, denies agency to the "other" character on the friendship axis, Starletta. No matter what Ellen may think *or* feel about her friend at the end of the novel, the monologue form cannot disclose the voice or "I" of Starletta since Ellen is the only developed subject of the text and it is her evolving consciousness that prevails.

It is generally the case that Kaye Gibbons writes novels in the form of first-person monologues since her intention is to create Southern women characters who will appear to tell their own stories. She has indicated that she begins

> her conceptualization of a work with character and voice, not with plot and abstract ideas . . . In her writing, interior experience is more important than surface experience, and language is the important interpretative mechanism for bringing that to the reader, even concerning memories of surface experience.[17]

For "surface experience" I understand social actions and interactions, and the "abstract ideas" mentioned here I read as political as well as philosophical and existential considerations. In this her first novel, it is particularly the case that details of region and society receive attention only so far as Ellen chooses to articulate her child's understanding of wider issues. Ultimately, whatever does or does not transpire in the novel is circumscribed by Ellen, as Gibbons has her rationalize herself as an autonomous and coherent self. This is clear from the sheer number of times that Ellen repeats the phrase "my own self" so central to her idiom and idiolect. Her monologue is the self-analysis that her child psychologist tries unsuccessfully every Tuesday at school to extract from her. In this way, Gibbons leaves little room for the interactions, dramatic confrontations, and emotional and violent exchanges that may be enacted in a more melodramatic text.

Ellen Foster is a self-celebratory monologue in the voice of a child who has not yet fully discovered that human experience is necessarily dialogic and collaboratory. Ellen's monologue has, to employ Bakhtinian terms, a "centripetal" and a "monologic" imperative and force in which Starletta's silence is as necessary as it is disquieting. It is

hard for Ellen to consider anyone else in any depth whilst she is in the process of self-formation, as is indicated when she takes the name Foster, a new name (the reader is never made aware of her family name). Ellen mistakes the term "foster family" for the family name of her "new mama" and appropriates it as a signal of her wish to cut the ties with her old life and with a "worn-out" name in order to make herself anew. The link she preserves with Starletta is really the sole connection she actively seeks to maintain with her old lifestyle; Starletta is her chosen and designated "other."

Ellen begins to reconcile herself to her *own* illogicalities in the way that Elizabeth Abel has discussed in another context when she notes that to (re)construct a friend is to (re)view the self so that the friend acts as an alter ego that "refines and clarifies the narrator's self-image."[18] In the final pages of the novel, Gibbons dramatizes the complex negotiations of racial social geography in which Ellen is involved, but solely in terms of Ellen's character. Starletta is sidelined even in the final pages and her silence remains unsatisfactory. Gibbons has implied that she was unaware of this factor until she got to the end of the book and "realized she hadn't talked." Significantly, though, rather than interrogate the motivation behind this feature of the text, and its effects, as Ellen Douglas does openly in *Can't Quit You Baby* (1988), Gibbons provides a get-out that legitimates as it disclaims:

> I said, "Kaye, you've got to say why this girl has not said a word and I said, well she stutters and doesn't like to talk." I took care of that real quickly.[19]

Shirley M. Jordan, interviewing Gibbons, does not pursue the issue, but effectively disabling Starletta, disempowering an already disempowered character, does not "take care" of the discomfort and disappointment this reader feels in having Starletta simply act as a silent witness and accomplice to Ellen's most forceful engagement with life. In Ellen, Gibbons creates a character whose strength, vitality, and creative good sense go some considerable way towards undermining a tenacious image of a "poor white" girl as hopeless, but her creation of Ellen's black counterpart is all the more disappointing as a result. Starletta remains a plot function in spite of Gibbons's general engagement with issues of race and representation in her work.[20]

A more theoretical focus on the constitution of the subject is described by Tzvetan Todorov in his elaboration of Bakhtin's aesthetic of otherness. For Bakhtin, self-consciousness as consciousness of self can only be realized "through another and with another's help," for:

> every internal experience occurs on the border, it comes across another, and this essence resides in this intense encounter . . . Man has no internal sovereign territory; he is all and always on the boundary; looking within himself, he looks *in the eyes of the other or through the eyes of the other.*[21]

These ideas include the condition of self-existence as reliant on the other, so that existence becomes dialogical in principle. Bakhtin is interested in the writer or artist's relation to the characters he or she creates, but here I foreground the interrelationship between characters in an application of Bakhtin's ideas, in order to clarify how a novel that *ostensibly* values the mutuality and interdependency of friendship can nevertheless remain monologic in form by denying dialogue. In Bakhtinian terms:

> Ultimately monologism denies that there exists outside of it another consciousness, with the same rights, and capable of responding on an equal footing, another and equal *I* . . . The monologue is accomplished and deaf to the other's response; it does not await it and does not grant it any *decisive* force. Monologue makes do without the other; that is why to some extent it objectivizes all reality. Monologue pretends to be the *last word.*[22]

Extrapolating from Bakhtin, I would argue that a monologic outlook dominates *Ellen Foster*; not simply as a result of Gibbons's own acknowledgement that Starletta's voice was of no particular concern, but as evidenced in the formal structuring of the novel itself. Starletta is finally little more than a device circumscribed by a monologic textual exploration of the protagonist. In his application of Bakhtinian ideas to popular cultural products that apparently seek to promote white and black racial harmony in America, Robert Stam points out the dangers of "pseudopolyphonic" discourses whereby certain voices are disempowered because they are marginalized, so that the "dialogue" that takes place is really between a voiced individual and a "puppet-like entity that has already been forced to make crucial compromises."[23]

In many ways, Starletta is the puppet in the text, whose reality is objectivized. Starletta figures only as a component in a series of elements in Ellen's life that she is trying to fix in some order. The picaresque quality of their encounters as nodal points in a linear model bears this out. The construction of Starletta's character and of her silence comes perilously close to the construction of African-American characters as foils in an "American" literary tradition as noted by Toni Morrison, and by Ralph Ellison before her. If Starletta's silence is read as accommodation, she becomes an accommodating black presence in the novel. In *Playing in the Dark,* Morrison describes black characters operating as a "control group" in a white American literary experiment and in the formation of white American national culture. Her idea can be extended in an analysis of the black characters in Gibbons's novel as they operate in Ellen's reformulation of her personal identity. For Morrison:

> Africanism is the vehicle by which the American self knows itself as not enslaved, but free; not repulsive, but desirable; not helpless, but licensed and powerful; not history-less, but historical; not damned but innocent; not a blind accident of evolution, but a progressive fulfilment of destiny.[24]

Morrison discusses nineteenth- and early twentieth-century texts as the language of her analogies indicates; ideas of individualism and freedom were inextricable from those of oppression and slavery, but *Ellen Foster* has frequently been compared with *Huckleberry Finn,* and its philosophy is distinctly Emersonian. Ellen's idiosyncratic first-person narrative commentary is replete with Southern speech patterns reminiscent of Huck's, and the motif of self-reliance so strong in Twain's novel is clearly present in Gibbons's, from the epigraph from "Self-Reliance" to the end of the novel. Both Huck and Ellen escape alcoholic and abusive fathers and are orphaned but, whereas Huck "suffered" the informal maternalism of the Widow Douglas and Aunt Sally, Ellen is immediately tied into the decisions of Court Welfare hearings and regular monitoring by an educational psychologist. Despite the obvious differences in context, the course Ellen is set upon in the novel involves her primarily in a progressive articulation of her own identity, and Starletta is, like Jim for Huck, the only other character present throughout the text who services this end. Gibbons is clearly aware of the American literary tradition, most clearly explicated by Leslie Fiedler, in which African Americans and Native Americans have functioned as subordinate and peripheral "sidekicks" to white individualistic protagonists. In *Ellen Foster,* she retains the basis of this binary intact as she negotiates such a relationship for her protagonist.

III

In *Ellen Foster,* the speaking protagonist records the period of her childhood in which she begins to identify herself as separate from her parents and as an active force in shaping both her environment and her future in the contemporary South. Starletta, her black friend, is the only character featured throughout the text who remains a constant presence despite the changes in Ellen's life. Ellen's mother's suicide precipitates Ellen's advance into the wider world, and Starletta is present at Ellen's mother's funeral at the beginning of the book; she is the first and the only person from Ellen's former life to visit once Ellen has established herself in a new foster home. But Ellen's efforts to lift herself out of what she understands to have been an ill-starred start in life quickly become indivisible from what she deems the clearest means of demonstrating herself to be a young lady of clean habits and reasonable, moderate behaviour: she sets herself directly against what she deems to be the "standards" of the black members of the Southern community in which she resides. Not only does Ellen seek to restore what order and routine she experienced whilst her mother was alive, she also embarks upon a related quest to ascertain her individual needs. Simultaneously, she discovers that she and Starletta are united by more than what divides them, and she wishes to maintain their connection in the new life she is in the process of mapping for herself: "I feel like she grew behind my back and when I think about her now I want to press my hands to her to stop her from growing into a time she will not want to play" (p. 97). This realization is slow in coming, but it forms the trajectory of what is clearly a friendship plot. Prior to this discovery, the novel is punctuated by scenes in which Ellen expresses her wish to fit herself into quite conventional images of girlhood. With the intention to become a Girl Scout, Ellen signals her desire for a new and widely acceptable image. Her full school uniform is a source of pride and satisfaction as it marks her out as a "good" student.

Much of the time Ellen is groping towards a new identity, even though she couches her intentions in highly conformist terms, and her narration is cluttered with concerns about the impression she makes on others. Ellen invests time and effort in herself, as made manifest in her attention to clothes and the outward presentation of self, but her determination to reassert herself in this way does not leave much time to devote to her own psychological recovery from the traumas that beset her, or to consider the meaning of her friendship with Starletta. This would involve considerable self-scrutiny and Ellen's unceasing and, at times, breathless monologue belies a concerted effort to be outwardly self-confident rather than inwardly self-searching. Her bid to create a coherent sense of self, the express goal of the *Bildungsroman* form, excludes a more open and problematic engagement with the facets of her character that are not immediately assimilable into this particular discourse of the self.

Ellen's prejudices and judgements about black people are disclosed along with her other feelings: Starletta is her friend but she will not eat in Starletta's home nor will she drink from the family's utensils, despite having decided that they live "regular"—her shorthand for "like white folks." Her joy at the Christmas present she receives from them is redoubled with "Oh my God it is a sweater. I like it so much. I do not tell a story when I say it does not look colored at all" (p. 38). These and other indicators clarify the chasm that separates her own place in society from Starletta's, despite the way this directly contradicts her personal experiences. Ellen feels that her most safe and comfortable retreat is the black family's home. She escapes there on the occasion when her drunken father mistakes her for her dead mother in the dark and she sleeps there in security, the like of which she has never experienced at home or when forced to stay with her own grandmother.

Initially, I felt that Gibbons might be working to create a different effect—or misprision—in her codification of race relations from that created in much previous American literature where the white protagonist is mirrored or shadowed by a black companion. The reader is encouraged in the belief that Ellen's sharp and pragmatic self-reliance is her most valuable asset. For the most part, she demonstrates an uncanny ability to slice through hypocrisy and etiquette and to catch people in a few words, as can be seen in her debunking of psychoanalysis and the court system. She disdains the child psychologist's tentative explanations that she may be suffering from "identity problems" following the traumas of her early life: "I hate to tell him he's wrong because you can tell it took him a long time to make up his ideas. And the worst part is I can see he believes them" (p. 103). Similarly, the studied homilies of the judge who presides over the case for Ellen's guardian-

ship are recognized for what they are; Ellen astutely reconciles the illogicality of his decisions in such a way as to preserve herself from the full force of their impact on her life:

> What do you do when the judge talks about the family society's cornerstone but you know yours was never a Roman pillar but is and always has been crumbly old brick? I was in my seat frustrated like when my teacher makes a mistake on the chalkboard and it will not do any good to tell her because so quick she can erase it all and on to the next problem.

> He had us all mixed up with a different group of folks.

> (p. 66)

Despite such perspicacity, Gibbons shows that the social etiquette of race relations is much more difficult for Ellen to penetrate. She has Ellen revise her assumptions and come to understand that the criteria she employed to judge a black family as inferior was mistaken. But, finally, I do not think that the codification of the primary relationship differs significantly from paradigmatic depictions in earlier novels. In fact, Ellen refers to Starletta as "the baby" for much of this novel and describes her as "hers," almost as a doll might be hers to keep and to love. Starletta is a kind of talisman for Ellen, certainly a touchstone in the sense of a comfortable place that she can return to at points on her journey of self-discovery and in her monologue. Each time the two meet there are examples of Ellen's tendency to feel that she may "own" her black "buddy": at the cinema, "Starletta was the only colored girl at the movies and she was mine" (p. 60); on the bus, "I need to tell the driver first thing that I'll be having a extra passenger on board this afternoon. She'll be getting off at my house. She's colored but don't act like you notice. And she'll be sitting right up front with me. And she'll be getting off at my house" (p. 142).

There are other black characters who are minimally drawn and who form part of Ellen's environment. Initially, they seem simply auxiliary figures playing "bit parts" but they come to serve most importantly as an alternative locus for Ellen's desires for home and security. Starletta's parents are only an extension of Starletta, unnamed and described solely in terms of what they do for Ellen. They are a collective presence, but when Ellen goes to live with her grandmother and is set to work in her cotton fields, she meets Mavis, one of the cotton pickers, and she spies on black homes and communal homelife from the bottom of "colored lane" with a half-acknowledged loneliness and envy. Her homelessness is the key to Ellen's mire of conflicting emotions, her psychological and existential predicament, the predicament she refuses to confront beyond her pragmatic assessment of her own needs. She comes to know Mavis who protects her from the heavier work and who confides that Ellen's mother was her childhood friend and that she knew her "good as I know my own self" (p. 76). Although the pairing of the young white girl and older black woman lasts only a short while, it would seem to have a specific bearing on Ellen's reassessment of her own position with regard to Starletta, and Ellen's dawning apprehension that a "home" is of limited value if unsupported by wider social affiliations that can help to make it a shared space rather than a lonely sanctuary.

By the end of the novel, Ellen feels the need to "straighten out" things between herself and Starletta so they can become "even friends" within the space of her new home, but this "evening out" does not include the need for dialogue with her friend since Starletta's speech is never represented. Ellen does begin to seek physical intimacy with her friend rather than disdain it, "I wonder if Starletta would let me take a bath with her" (p. 141) and she sings her name inside her head all morning looking forward to Starletta's weekend sleep-over. The language certainly registers love and desire, but Starletta is clearly the *object* of Ellen's affections. Ellen, Gibbons makes clear, is awakening to the wonderment and significance of a friendship from which she has derived comfort whilst denying its full import in her world, and in so doing she begins to desegregate her mind and her understanding but fails to dismantle the strategies of containment via which she has embodied Starletta. Consequently, there would seem to be a tension between the form of *Bildungsroman* and the idea of representing a cross-racial friendship within it, particularly when, for her author, Ellen is "a child who thinks first and then feels."[25]

Ellen makes what she affirms is a revolutionary gesture and statement about her friend; she has Starletta to stay in her home as a special guest when "every rule in the book says I should not have her in my house, much less laid still and sleeping by me" (p. 146). The novel ends on a clear note of social reconciliation, but it is primarily Ellen's reconciliation with her "own self" *via* Starletta, in a confession that facilitates an advance in Ellen's independent assessment of her life and her future but that does not permit response or debate:

> Starletta I always thought I was special because I was white and when I thought about you being colored I said to myself it sure is a shame Starletta's colored. I sure would hate to be that way. . . . now I remember that they changed that rule. So it does not make any sense for me to feel like I'm breaking the law . . . if they could fight a war over how I'm supposed to think about her then I'm obligated to do it. It seems like the decent thing to do.
>
> (p. 146)

The attitudinal shift has come about as a result of the accumulated experiences of living in a biracial community that Ellen undergoes in this picaresque tale; staying the night in Starletta's home and picking cotton in her grandmother's fields, for example. The reader is also reminded, during Ellen's "confession," of Huck's "crisis of conscience" over slavery and over whether he should inform Miss Watson of the whereabouts of "her runaway nigger," Jim. Where Huck confounds his sin with not upholding the codes of slavocracy, Ellen harbours no such paradoxical contradistinctions but, lightly ironic, Gibbons has Ellen

luxuriate in the magnanimity and munificence that "integration" with Starletta brings to her sense of self by having her draw on the Civil War and on Civil Rights history to create an "ending" in the manner of the "old stories" (and *Huckleberry Finn* may be one of them) that Ellen loves to read. This is dryly done, but it nevertheless conforms to the convention of narrative "closure" that one expects in a classic realist format where the protagonist's maturation and self-discovery is "the end" and this "ending" forecloses on any further or deeper interaction with others.

It is disappointing, therefore, that despite the threshold of ideological understanding the character may be said to reach by the end of this *Bildungsroman,* and her belated acknowledgement that this is largely as a result of her friend, she still cannot see the importance of listening to Starletta, finding out what she thinks and might wish to say. In this I would disagree with Jay Clayton who reads **Ellen Foster** as a narrative of racial reconciliation and who asserts that "the plot culminates in Ellen's *successful* efforts to make amends for former slights to her best friend" (my emphasis).[26] Clayton implies that the novel plays out its utopian possibilities, whereas I would argue that they are left unfulfilled and that the ending remains far too ambiguous to be a culmination of all the ideas raised by the plot.

Arguably, Starletta remains silent because the "text" to be read is Ellen herself and the textual lacunae in the representation of Starletta are the inevitable result of structuring the novel according to the principles of the *Bildungsroman* which serves, on the one hand, to emphasize and, on the other, to retreat from what I have termed the "friendship plot" or the "friendship axis" in **Ellen Foster.** The friendship is plotted along an axis, the line about which the figure of Ellen may be understood to revolve. The novel is plotted around the friendship that helps to co-ordinate the trajectory of Ellen's life and progress and this draws on the sense of alliance present in some definitions of the word "axis." A friendship axis is clearly present and can be traced specifically via a series of nodal points in the girls' relationship that structure the writing as a developing friendship for Ellen: a Christmas spent together, shopping together, a visit to the cinema, and Starletta's visits to two of Ellen's foster homes. They go to the same school and, although in different classes, their connection is maintained, largely it seems because Ellen makes no particular friends in her own homeroom as Starletta does in hers. The childhood friendship operates strategically to point up the relationships between institutions like school and the Girl Scouts, small-town life and family life, that are such socially powerful forces against which the crises of friendship contend. This is especially the case for an interracial friendship when, for example, there is no integrated, or segregated, Girl Scout group for Starletta to attend.

Gibbons leaves Ellen Foster on the threshold of a new phase of development, but the subordination of Starletta in the text does not offer much in the way of hope for sisterly connection. If one wishes to detect hope for the association, nevertheless, it may be present in the way in which Ellen has come to realize that Starletta has an existence independent of her; she has her own friends and ideas and she may decide to drift away from their association, something Ellen intends to try to prevent by becoming an "even friend":

> something tells me inside that one of these days soon she will forget me. So I have to make a big very big good time with her that she will not forget . . . I know for a fact that I would not ever forget her but you can never be sure about how somebody else thinks about you except if they beat it into your head. At least that is how I am worried about Starletta who never has said much good or bad to me but before long I will have to know I am in her head like she is in mine. It is good to have a friend like her.

(p. 99)

This passage is unusual in a novel that focuses so exclusively on the protagonist; it shows Ellen as she begins to appreciate that Starletta acts independently outside and apart from herself, but it also remains typical in its self-involved emphasis on Ellen's own fears, observations, and needs. Ellen remains consistent in her utilization of Starletta as a standard against which she may measure her own progress; so even her invitation to Starletta to stay in her new home acts as a celebration of how far *she* has progressed or of how far *her* world may be differentiated from Starletta's, "she would think back on me and how she stayed in the white house all night with Ellen" (p. 99).

She says quite a lot towards the end of her monologue about her dawning understanding of the social order that kept her prejudices and assumptions in place and about the possibilities for a more open acknowledgement of differences across race. Certainly, Ellen has learned some important lessons about where she fits and where she may choose to place herself within a Southern scheme of social relations but, as the novel closes, she is resting comfortably in the image she has fashioned of her own magnanimity in reconciling her "new" carefully integrated self with Starletta. Finally, individualism overrides the friendship plot in **Ellen Foster.** The friendship plot informs the composition of the text but only so far as it helps to situate a "self-made" American individual on the threshold of a new phase in life.

The cross-racial childhood friendship in Southern literature about girls is a palimpsest wherein the complexities of race and gender may be collapsed into a single unitary relationship when the complexities begin to intersect with the young girls' lives. This is not to say that each representation is a social protest or reformist in some sense (Belva Plain's *Crescent City* (1984), for example, is clearly neither[27]) but rather that the history of segregation restricts representations of a childhood friendship that seek to incorporate realism in their form or credibility in their content. Toni Morrison has said that there is always some-

thing "more interesting at stake than a clear resolution in a novel" and, unlike Jay Clayton who feels there is a sense of culmination at the end of **Ellen Foster,** I believe that important ambiguities remain.[28] It is left ambiguous as to whether Ellen's developing self should finally be understood as essentially self-reliant or whether her sense of identity owes much more to group experience and to a salient cross-racial friendship. Such ambiguities are the crux of Ellen's monologue and of her story.

Notes

1. This article is a revision of the paper "Between Girls: Cross-racial Childhood Friendships in Contemporary Southern Narratives" delivered at the Society for the Study of Southern Literature 1996 Conference, 11–13 April 1996, Richmond, Virginia.

2. Ruth Frankenberg, "Growing up White: Racism and the Social Geography of Childhood," *Feminist Review,* 45 (Autumn 1993), 54–55.

3. Lynn Z. Bloom, "Coming of Age in the Segregated South: Autobiographies of Twentieth-Century Childhoods, Black and White," in J. Bill Berry, ed., *Home Ground: Southern Autobiography* (Columbia and London: University of Missouri Press, 1991), 113.

4. Examples include *Corinna, Corinna* (dir. Jessie Nelson, 1994) set in the 1950s which examines cross-racial relationships predominantly through the white child/black nurse formulation; *The Long Walk Home* (dir. Richard Pearce, 1990) in which the white mistress/black domestic relationship features in Alabama in the 1950s, and *Driving Miss Daisy* (dir. Bruce Beresford, 1989) in which a "friendship" between an elderly Jewish lady and her elderly black chauffeur is played out in Atlanta over twenty-five years.

5. Nanci Kincaid, *Crossing Blood* (New York: Avon Books, 1994). Dorothy Allison, *Bastard Out of Carolina* (London: Flamingo, 1993).

6. Kaye Gibbons, *Ellen Foster* (London: Jonathan Cape, 1988), 22. Subsequent references will be included in the text. Most reviewers have assumed the novel takes place in rural Nash County, North Carolina, the area in which Gibbons herself grew up, but particulars of place are not specified in the monologue.

7. Lillian Smith, "Children and Color" in Michelle Cliff, ed., *The Winner Names the Age: A Collection of Writings by Lilian Smith* (New York: W. W. Norton and Co., 1978), 30.

8. Joel Kovel would appear to support Smith's ideas: "if we are to study the existence in culture of a fantasy creation such as racism, it is to the infantile roots of mental experience that we must first turn." See *White Racism: A Psychohistory* (London: Free Association Books, 1988), 251. It is also important to note that Lillian Smith's name still features as the

title of an annual Southern literary award that goes to the work that most powerfully and successfully interlaces black and white identity issues in the South.

9. Lillian Smith, *Killers of the Dream* (New York: W. W. Norton and Co., 1949), 29. Smith's mining of her memories is echoed by Melton McLaurin, *Separate Pasts: Growing up White in the Segregated South* (Athens: University of Georgia Press, 1987), in his description of spitting after putting a football pump in his mouth that had been in the mouth of his black friend, Bobo. At this point in his narrative, McLaurin becomes aware of his acculturated belief that he and Bobo belonged to "two fundamentally different worlds and that society demanded that we each stay in the world designated for us" despite years of shared play, 27–41.

10. In *The Temple of My Familiar* (London: Penguin, 1990) Alice Walker also creates a situation where Fanny, a black woman who grew up in Georgia, repressed the memory of her white playmate Tanya. It is only through therapy that she regains this memory which she had suppressed after the shock of being hit by Tanya's grandmother for kissing her little white granddaughter.

11. This "sorting" is a significant feature of a system that is examined by the Nebraskan Tillie Olsen in the short story "O Yes" (1956) in *Tell Me A Riddle* (New York: Laurel, 1979), 48–71. It is also noted by the white interviewees who reconstruct their childhoods in Ruth Frankenberg, *The Social Construction of Whiteness: White Women Race Matters* (London: Routledge, 1993). Tangentially, they remember that black childhood friends were "'tracked' into vocational and remedial classes in high school" and they lost contact with them after this point (p. 79).

12. Susan Richards Shreve, *A Country of Strangers* (London: Sceptre, 1990), 66. Subsequent references will be included in the text.

13. Katherine C. Hodgin in Joseph M. Flora and Robert Bain, eds., *Contemporary Fiction Writers of the South: A Bio-Bibliographical Sourcebook* (Westport, Conn.: Greenwood Press, 1993), 411.

14. Alice Walker, *Meridian* (London: The Women's Press, 1982), 105.

15. Richard Gray, *Writing the South: Ideas of an American Region* (Cambridge University Press, 1986), 234.

16. Catherine Belsey, *Critical Practice* (London and New York: Methuen, 1980), 73. My italics.

17. Julian Mason, "Kaye Gibbons [1960–]" in Flora and Bain, 161.

18. Elizabeth Abel, "(E)Merging Identities: The Dynamics of Female Friendship in Contemporary Fiction by Women," in *Signs: Journal of Women in Culture and Society*, 6: 3 (1981), 423.

19. Kaye Gibbons in Shirley M. Jordan ed., *Broken Silences: Interviews with Black and White Women Writers* (New Brunswick: Rutgers University Press, 1993), 78.

20. In *A Virtuous Woman* (1989), for example, Gibbons explores marriage and bereavement, and also the role and stereotype of the black housekeeper and how her white employer's leisure is incumbent upon the black woman's skills as well as her economically inferior position.

21. Mikhail Bakhtin as quoted in Tzvetan Todorov, *Mikhail Bakhtin: The Dialogical Principle* (Minneapolis: University of Minnesota Press, 1984), 95–96.

22. Ibid., 107.

23. Robert Stam, *Subversive Pleasures: Bakhtin, Cultural Criticism and Film* (Baltimore and London: The Johns Hopkins University Press, 1989), 232.

24. Toni Morrison, *Playing in the Dark: Whiteness and the Literary Imagination* (Cambridge, Mass. and London: Harvard University Press, 1992), 52. For a more detailed reading, see my "Writing for Revision," *new formations: a journal of culture/theory/ politics,* 20 (Summer 1993), 173–180.

25. Kaye Gibbons in Jordan, p. 78.

26. Jay Clayton, *The Pleasures of Babel: Contemporary American Literature and Theory* (New York and Oxford: Oxford University Press, 1993), 140. Clayton only considers *Ellen Foster* in passing but, in an otherwise illuminating and important study, he misreads the example on which he bases his argument. He has it that Ellen *visits* Mavis and her family and so begins to articulate what a family may be and what it should contain, whereas in the text Ellen is only *spying* on the black families who live on the edge of her grandmother's plantation, so her assessment of a family unit is much more a projection of her own desires than an empirical experience of a particular black household.

27. Belva Plain, *Crescent City* (London: HarperCollins, 1993) A popular writer of historical romances, Plain sees the dramatic potential of New Orleans in the period from the 1830s to the Civil War. She "goes South" in one of her many novels and reinscribes motifs that owe much to *Gone With The Wind* in a romantic and sentimental story. The black child, Fanny, is an adjunct to the white child, Miriam, and a foil for her, little else.

28. Toni Morrison in interview with Nellie McKay as quoted in Jan Furman, *Toni Morrison's Fiction* (Columbia: University of South Carolina Press, 1996), 42.

FURTHER READING

Criticism

Bellante, Carl and John. "Janowitz and Gibbons: Feminist Fatales." *Bloomsbury Review* 13 (May, 1993) 13.

> The Bellantes assert that Gibbons's *A Cure for Dreams* and Tama Janowitz's *The Male Cross-Dresser Support Group* both fall short of their artistic aims.

Dodd, Susan. "A Sentimental Education." *Washington Post Book World* 28 (12 July 1998): 9.

> Dodd praises the fairy-tale aspects of Gibbons's *On the Occasion of My Last Afternoon.*

Wolcott, James. "Crazy for You." *New Yorker* 71 (21 August 1995): 115-16.

> Wolcott discusses the difficulty Gibbons had in writing *Sights Unseen,* which needed seven rewrites to complete the work.

Additional coverage of Gibbons's life and career is contained in the following sources published by the Gale Group: *Authors and Artists for Young Adults,* **Vol. 34;** *Contemporary Authors,* **Vol. 151;** *Contemporary Authors New Revision Series,* **Vol. 75;** *Contemporary Southern Writers; DISCovering Authors 3.0; DISCovering Authors Modules: Popular Fiction and Genre Authors; Major 20th-Century Writers,* **Edition 2;** *Novels for Students,* **Vol. 3;** *Something About the Author,* **Vol. 117; and** *Literature Resource Center.*

Susan Gubar
1944-

(Full name Susan David Gubar) American editor and literary critic.

The following entry presents an overview of Gubar's career through 2000.

INTRODUCTION

A distinguished professor of English at Indiana University, Gubar is a leading feminist literary critic who has principally and frequently collaborated with Sandra Gilbert, another esteemed critic and professor, to produce innovative works of criticism revealing the characteristics of a distinctly female literary tradition and style. The pair co-edited *The Madwoman in the Attic* (1979), which literary scholars worldwide have acknowledged as a seminal work of American feminist studies. With accessible prose and intelligent argumentation, this groundbreaking work challenges the authority of the Western literary canon on the basis of its nearly complete exclusion of women writers, introducing as well the idea of "anxiety of authorship" as a fundamental condition of women writers, particularly those of the nineteenth century. Gubar and Gilbert have also jointly edited the *Norton Anthology of Literature by Women* (1985), which is the first collection to gather a varied range of women's writings in English from the fourteenth century to the present. Besides co-authoring other feminist studies and an original satirical piece with Gilbert, Gubar has produced literary criticism with other scholars and has also published two studies as an individual author, *Racechanges: White Skin, Black Face in American Culture* (1997) and *Critical Condition: Feminism at the Turn of the Century* (2000). While critics have generally hailed *The Madwoman in the Attic* as a landmark work of both feminist studies and literary scholarship, the study has also provoked hostility from some scholars who have denounced its middle-class, white, heterosexual perspective. Such critical responses to this and subsequent works by Gubar and Gilbert have promoted the growth of an increasingly diversified body of scholarship on women's literary experiences.

BIOGRAPHICAL INFORMATION

Born in 1944, Gubar attended Queens College of the City University of New York, where she earned a bachelor's degree in 1965. She received a master's degree from the University of Michigan in 1968 and a doctorate from the University of Iowa in 1972. The following year Gubar

joined the English faculty at Indiana University, where she met and quickly befriended Gilbert. Together, they launched their successful collaborative venture in feminist studies with the publication of *Shakespeare's Sisters* (1979), a collection of critical essays on women poets written from a decidedly feminist viewpoint. That same year, Gubar and Gilbert published the critically acclaimed work that catapulted them to national prominence, *The Madwoman in the Attic,* which received a nomination for the National Book Critics Award for outstanding book criticism in 1979. As critical debate about their ideas escalated during the early 1980s, academic publishers W. W. Norton & Company approached Gubar and Gilbert with a project idea that resulted in *The Norton Anthology of Literature by Women,* for which Gubar was named Woman of the Year in 1986 by *Ms.* magazine. Gubar next collaborated with Gilbert on the ambitious three-volume study *No Man's Land* (1988, 1989, 1994), which defines literary modernism in terms of gender warfare for possession of literary authority. Meanwhile, Gubar co-edited with other scholars the essay collections *For Adult Users Only* (1989) and *English Inside and Out* (1992), which deal with violence in pornography and the place of women literary critics within the largely male-dominated discipline, respectively. In 1995, Gubar and Gilbert published *Masterpiece Theatre,* a satire on university life, and *Mothersongs,* a collection of poetry written by, for, and about mothers and motherhood. Since then, Gubar has authored two books on her own, *Racechanges,* a critical examination of cross-racial and transsexual imagery in various media, and *Critical Condition,* a collection of essays evaluating the status of feminist studies at the turn of twentieth century. Gubar has continued to teach English at Indiana University and to lecture extensively, frequently accompanied by Gilbert.

MAJOR WORKS

A study of women writers in the nineteenth century, *The Madwoman in the Attic* describes several key developments in the history of women's writing. Through close biographical and textual readings of the works of female novelists—ranging from Jane Austen, Charlotte and Emily Brontë, and Mary Shelley to George Eliot and Emily Dickinson—this work traces the evolution of a distinctly feminine narrative style that developed in reaction to the male-dominated literary discourse that prevailed at the time in which these authors wrote. According to the study's thesis, because nineteenth-century women writers were forced to write within limits dictated by a patriarchal literary tradition that equated the pen with the penis, women writers were largely viewed as trespassers in a male domain and either condemned as unfeminine or ridiculed as "lady novelists" and "female poetasters." Gubar and Gilbert argue that women writers grew both afraid that they lacked the ability to express themselves artistically and angry that pervasive patriarchal attitudes toward women trapped them in such a position. In short, *The Madwoman in the Attic* demonstrates that by channeling those emotions and experiences into language, nineteenth-century women writers developed not only a uniquely feminine style, but also a language that subverts patriarchal ideology. *The Norton Anthology of Literature by Women* (Gubar and Gilbert's next work) is an encyclopedic collection of writings by women in English, chronologically arranged from the fourteenth century to the mid-1980s, including selections by minority, working-class, commonwealth, and lesbian women. The introduction to this volume reiterates the existence of a female literary tradition, while the selected works detail the evolution of female styles and subjects within that tradition. *No Man's Land,* a three-volume collaborative effort with Gilbert, posits that the radical departures that characterize modernism originate not only from social, political, and economic factors but also from gender or sexual conflicts. This work thematically outlines the further evolution of women's literature from the late Victorian period through contemporary times by arguing that the tenets of literary modernism were designed to advance patriarchal attitudes in reaction to increasing numbers of published female authors in the early part of the twentieth century. Comprised of volumes titled *The War of the Words* (1988), *Sexchanges* (1989), and *Letters from the Front* (1994), this series addresses such themes as the violence against women's efforts to subvert patriarchal culture, the influence of imperialism, the suffrage movement, and the significance of the shift in feminist literary techniques between the 1930s and 1990s. *Racechanges,* Gubar's first book-length solo work, examines the importance of cross-cultural identification between whites and blacks in matters of authorship and creativity, adapting techniques that explore the influence of gender in literary arts to racial dimensions of writing. A reflection of as much as an assessment of the contemporary status of feminist literary thought, the essays collected in *Critical Conditions* concern a range of conflicts and divisions spawned by the academic discipline of feminist studies itself, from its infancy in the early 1980s through the next generation.

CRITICAL RECEPTION

When *The Madwoman in the Attic* appeared in 1979, the field of feminist studies as an academic discipline was yet to be recognized in the American university curriculum. Many critics concede that Gubar and Gilbert's pioneering work of literary criticism has not only contributed to that discipline but has also spurred the establishment of and defined the parameters for feminist scholarship as a viable academic pursuit in the United States. Hailed as a breakthrough in literary studies, *The Madwoman in the Attic* is widely regarded as a touchstone in the study of the female literary imagination. Some critics, however, have qualified

their praise for *The Madwoman in the Attic.* A few have objected to many of its assertions, claiming that they are premised upon reductive, distorted, anachronistic, or ideologically-driven readings of certain texts; others have detected a specifically white, middle-class, heterosexual bias throughout the work. Similarly, some critics have faulted Gubar and Gilbert's work in *The Norton Anthology of Literature by Women* for a perceptible preference for modern and contemporary writers. Others have suggested that the pair bent their scholarship to political ends and that they chose works fitting their theories rather than the best works representing particular authors. Although minority groups are well represented in the volume, some critics complained that the collection's scarcity of pre-eighteenth-century writers tends to emphasize the accomplishments of professional authors at the expense of other forms of female literary expression, such as letters and diaries. However, most scholars have applauded Gubar and Gilbert's efforts in *The Norton Anthology of Literature by Women,* widely referring to the collection as a gauge for evaluating women writers's literary achievements within a written tradition, but also citing it as evidence of an earlier literary feminism. A majority of literary scholars have agreed that Gubar and Gilbert's body of criticism has cast a new light on literature by showing thematic and stylistic affinities between the works of female writers from similar and dissimilar cultures and eras. Likewise, many feminist critics have credited the pair with inspiring the proliferation of feminist scholarship—both pro and con—during the closing decades of the twentieth century, particularly owing to Gubar and Gilbert's insistence that women's writings constitute a distinct tradition that traces a matrilineal evolution of language at odds with a dominant patriarchal culture. Since the publication of *The War of Words,* however, critics have become more and more stringent in their assessments of Gubar's collaborations with Gilbert.

PRINCIPAL WORKS

Shakespeare's Sisters [editor, with Sandra M. Gilbert] (criticism) 1979

The Madwoman in the Attic: A Study of Women and the Nineteenth-Century Literary Imagination [with Gilbert] (criticism) 1979

The Norton Anthology of Literature by Women: The Tradition in English [editor, with Gilbert] (criticism) 1985

No Man's Land: The Place of the Woman Writer in the Twentieth-Century, Volume 1: The War of the Words [with Gilbert] (criticism) 1988

For Adult Users Only: The Dilemma of Violent Pornography [editor with Joan Hoff] (criticism) 1989

No Man's Land: The Place of the Woman Writer in the Twentieth-Century, Volume 2: Sexchanges [with Gilbert] (criticism) 1989

English Inside and Out: The Places of Literary Criticism [editor with Jonathan Kamholtz] (criticism) 1992

CRITICISM

Carolyn G. Heilbrun (essay date 25 November 1979)

SOURCE: "The Return of the Repressed," in *Washington Post Book World,* Vol. 9, No. 16, November 25, 1979, pp. 4, 6.

[*In the following essay, Heilbrun praises* The Madwoman in the Attic *as a major work of feminist critical theory.*]

The pens of authorship have not only been, until the 19th century, entirely in the hands of men: the pen has also been male, a part of the male anatomy. Women could possess it only as a monstrosity. With the beginning of the 19th century, this attitude, taken less obviously for granted, began to be stated: Gerard Manly Hopkins called the artist's creative gift a male gift, a male quality. Jane Austen, Anthony Burgess latterly remarked, "lacks a strong male thrust." Women who wrote, therefore, became by that act anomalous creatures.

Nor was this all. Woman had no story of her own; men have always told her this, and woman has believed it. She must be either silent and angelic or, rebelling, try to tell her story and become monstrous. The woman writer's battle had been, therefore, not so much against the male reading of society, as against the male reading of *her*.

As women now labor to create a tradition for themselves in which female stories are possible, the need for a profound study of women writers and of the female literary imagination has become apparent: feminists need not only examples of their despair and enforced passivity, they need a theory to explain the cause of that despair and to establish a base for the rebellion against it. Professors Gilbert and Gubar have now given us such a study. It is imperative reading not only for feminists, but for any scholar, particularly of the 19th century, who thinks he or she has understood the great novels of that time.

As a creature "penned by man," the authors tell us, woman has been penned in and penned up. As woman began her

"journey through the looking glass toward literary autonomy," her choices were few. The story of Snow White neatly embodies these choices. Like Snow White, woman may be passive, worshipped in a glass coffin or, like the stepmother, she may tell her own story. Gilbert and Gubar show how women authors, by projecting their rebellious impulses not onto their heroines, but onto mad or monstrous women, like Bertha in *Jane Eyre*, have dramatized their own desperate divisions. These monstrous women act out the subversive, if unconscious, impulses every woman feels before the patriarchy.

If a lovely young girl like Austen's Catherine Morland believes she can become the heroine of her own life story, the author of herself, she discovers, no less than Frankenstein's monster (another female creation), that she is an actor only in someone else's plot. As Charlotte Bronte was to observe, "the good woman is . . . half doll, half angel; the bad woman almost a fiend."

The great dazzle of this book arises from its analysis of female texts. Consistently, the authors are able to show how the true vision of women's destiny lies hidden beneath the surface story. Women's great literature, the sort everywhere studied by grad students, is a palimpsest, and the picture the artist painted with her soul lies beneath the surface colors, has long so lain, waiting to be revealed.

Let me speak plainly. This book's importance lies partly in its awareness that women will starve in silence until new stories are created which confer on them their own power of storymaking. But its major contribution is its careful development of theory and of a reading of literature which needs no excuses before the proud and closed male establishment. This work must come as a revelation to all readers, not least of all those male scholars who will be unable to ignore it in their own work. Gilbert and Gubar have written a pivotal book, one of those after which we will never think the same again.

The Madwoman in the Attic is long and expensive and worth every penny, although one hopes soon for a paperback edition. Gilbert and Gubar, have not, of course, sprung full blown from nowhere. In addition to their own brilliance, this book reflects the work of many scholars of both sexes; it is particularly encouraging that much of its analysis incorporates what other women scholars have expressed, or adumbrated. At last, feminist criticism, no longer capable of being called a fad, is clearly and coherently mapped out.

Woman has always known the costly destructiveness of anger; as she has raged to escape from male houses and male texts, she has known the cost to herself and has rewritten the male plots, especially Milton's, taking for herself the role of devil. Allowing the doubles in her writing the violence she could not allow herself or her heroines, woman has revised male genres to record her own story in disguise. Like the mythic Ariadne, woman has known the way through the labyrinth for men, but has been unable herself to escape. Now, women novelists and poets, no longer alternatively either scorned as feminine or put down as deficient in femininity, may begin to use their skills for their own, and not male, purposes. *The Madwoman in the Attic*, by revealing the past, will profoundly alter the present, making it possible, at last, for woman writers to create their own texts.

Rosemary Dinnage (essay date 20 December 1979)

SOURCE: "Re-creating Eve," in *New York Review of Books,* Vol. XXVI, No. 20, December 20, 1979, pp. 6, 8.

[*In the following essay, Dinnage agrees with Gubar and Gilbert's views regarding the frustrations of nineteenth-century women as authors, but nevertheless asserts that they "insensitively" force "nineteenth-century attitudes into twentieth-century molds."*]

Women's situation, Charlotte Brontë wrote, involves "evils—deep-rooted in the foundation of the social system—which no efforts of ours can touch: of which we cannot complain; of which it is advisable not too often to think." Sandra M. Gilbert and Susan Gubar's closely argued interpretation of nineteenth-century women's writing is concerned to show that, even in writers such as Brontë who were openly concerned with the "woman question," pent-up frustration over the evils of which it was best not to think produced images of rage and violence: vicious doubles of submissive heroines, saboteurs of conventional stereotypes, coded messages between innocuous lines. Mad Mrs. Rochester, creeping from the attic to tear and burn, stands for them all.

Though ultimately, I believe, Gilbert and Gubar belittle their women subjects by ignoring their generosity and detachment, by representing them—as they particularly wished not to be—as women before writers, and by imposing a twentieth-century gloss on nineteenth-century imaginations, they have an important subject to explore. They are equipped (if one accepts the bias produced by ignoring male writers and most male critics) with a scholarly knowledge of the period, including its obscure corners—*Frankenstein, Aurora Leigh*, Maria Edgeworth, Jane Austen's juvenilia—and they ingeniously bring in myth and fairy tale to support their arguments.

Lilith, Snow White, Beth March; the angel in the house, Salome, Swift's sullied Celia; the Blessed Damozel, Medusa, Cinderella; Amelia Sedley and Becky Sharp; the witch and the nun, stepmother and fairy princess, mermaid and Virgin Mary: as women are the first gratifiers and punishers in all our lives, so they reappear in the imagination for ever after in opposed images of goodness and badness. In the nineteenth century the split reached its most grotesque proportions: the spotless Victorian lady, in London, lived in a city of 6,000 brothels. Thackeray's repellent image, quoted by Gilbert and Gubar, condenses the angel and the monster into one:

In describing this siren, singing and smiling, coaxing and cajoling, the author, with modest pride, asks his readers all around, has he once forgotten the laws of politeness, and showed the monster's hideous tail above water? No! Those who like may peep down under waves that are pretty transparent, and see it writhing and twirling, diabolically hideous and slimy, flapping amongst bones, or curling around corpses; but above the water line, I ask, has not everything been proper, agreeable, and decorous . . . ?

Gilbert and Gubar argue that women's conception of themselves as writers has been deeply overshadowed by this ambivalence, by the lack of an appropriate model, and the threat of monstrous unwomanliness; if, with a part of themselves, women writers endorsed the ideal of woman as modest and self-abnegating (and I think they did so more often than the twentieth century or Gilbert and Gubar imagine), it was in conflict with the part that, just by writing, defied the unforgettable reply of the Poet Laureate Robert Southey to Charlotte Brontë: "Literature cannot be the business of a woman's life, and it ought not to be. The more she is engaged in her proper duties, the less leisure will she have for it, even as an accomplishment and a recreation." The options open, in their writing, therefore, ranged from violence to irony and from deliberate to unconscious. Brontë was an honest woman, but what are we to make of her reply to Southey?

I had not ventured to hope for such a reply; so considerate in its tone, so noble in its spirit. . . . You kindly allow me to write poetry for its own sake, provided I leave undone nothing which I ought to do. . . . In the evenings, I confess, I do think, but I never trouble any one else with my thoughts. I carefully avoid any appearance of pre-occupation and eccentricity, which might lead those I live amongst to suspect the nature of my pursuits. . . . I trust I shall never more feel ambitious to see my name in print; if the wish should rise I'll look at Southey's letter, and suppress it.

Southey, commended her "receiving admonition" so "considerately and kindly." We must, I think, make the imaginative leap necessary to see the letter, as Mrs. Gaskell did, as written quite without irony (though fortunately soon disregarded). The position of Victorian females not only had moral nourishment in it but great histrionic appeal.

But the lilies festered. Gilbert and Gubar, quoting Emily Dickinson's "infection in the sentence breeds," postulate a tradition of anxiety and confusion passed down to women writers, and link it with "the vapours," with anorexic, wasting heroines, with Emily Dickinson's agoraphobia, and above all with claustrophobia, recurrent images of women trapped in stuffy parlors, gothic mansions, isolated attics. Certainly the world that their interpretation recreates is a suffocating one, without humor or light or mutuality, and breeding a thousand ugly and distorted forms of female rage; if not violent, as in the Brontës' books, then cunningly subversive as in Jane Austen's.

But is it the world of women's novels themselves? Often, comparing Gilbert and Gubar's interpretations with the texts, one finds nineteenth-century attitudes insensitively forced into twentieth-century molds. They feel very free to decide when their authors do and do not mean what they say; when the latter endorse, for instance, conventional virtues, married love, or religious faith, they assume them to be consciously or unconsciously falsifying; where they conform to twentieth-century assumptions they find them honest. This is a dangerous practice, as we know from psychoanalytical literary criticism; here it reduces rather than enhances the dignity of the writers discussed. Where Gilbert and Gubar find pessimism and rancor one often finds, on the page, an actual relish for the otherness of masculinity, a fair-mindedness about the relations between the sexes. Because these writers lived closer to the imagination than to rational argument they often did fuse the "angelic passivity" / "Satanic revenge" dichotomy. "I am so glad," wrote George Eliot, "there are thousands of good people in the world who have very decided opinions and are fond of working hard to enforce them—I like to feel and think everything and do nothing, a pool of the 'deep contemplative' kind."

But they *should*, we now feel, have been as embattled and anxious as Gilbert and Gubar find them. If they were not always so, can we be misreading the context? Perhaps we are unable to imagine how, in an age with fewer illusions than ours about controlling nature, submission to inscrutable Providence was everyone's rationalization; women's task, certainly, but they knew it as part of a joint endeavor in which they were a significant part of the pattern. "Our wills are ours, to make them thine"; every period provides its formula to keep despair in check. Or are we perhaps prevented from seeing childbearing, and its relation to women's status, through the eyes of previous centuries? Gilbert and Gubar, in the context of *Wuthering Heights*, talk of women's "horror of being . . . reduced to a tool of the life process"—a recently invented horror; and it is new, too, to have to see birth as a kind of selfish environmental pollution like dropping beer cans. There may have been, in the days of high infant mortality, a deeper implicit respect for the "tools of the life process" than we can now imagine.

In any case, when these fictions go beyond sex hostility it is because, simply, the stronger the imaginative power, the wider and more objective the sympathy; Gilbert and Gubar's critique works better with minor novels than with major ones. The authors refer back often, for instance, to the dark shadow of *Paradise Lost*—to Virginia Woolf's criticism in her journals of its "aloofness and impersonality," to Dorothea Casaubon as amanuensis to Miltonic father/husband, to Shirley Keeldar's "His brain was right; how was his heart?"—and interpret some of the novels' plots as female reworkings of the Genesis myth; this is perhaps ingenious in the case of *Frankenstein*, but *Wuthering Heights*' satanic tension seems to belong to a different, self-sufficient world. *Villette* is indeed a novel of despair, in which submission is almost parodied, as concentration-camp inmates took over the behavior of their guards. We feel Lucy Snowe's very calm to be poisonous with an-

ger—though it is worth noticing that in her bitter essay on "Human Justice" (not "Human Nature" as Gilbert and Gubar say) Lucy represents justice not as masculine but as a cruel slatternly woman, like the wet-nurses Victorian babies depended on, or the mother who deserted Brontë so early. Gilbert and Gubar are also acute about the more florid fantasies of *Jane Eyre*; but they maltreat *Shirley*. They pinpoint ambivalence and masochism in *The Mill on the Floss*, but fail with *Middlemarch*.

An obvious instance is their view of the marriage of Tertius and Rosamond Lydgate in that book. Eliot sets this unhappy partnership beside the equally incongruous one of Dorothea and Edward Casaubon; both Dorothea and Tertius are shown to have embarked on these disasters through a combination of idealism and foolishness, and both must suffer for their choice and be schooled in generosity toward their partners. Dorothea does, as Gilbert and Gubar show, experience Casaubon in images of coldness and sterility, and chafe desperately against a "nightmare of a life in which every energy was arrested by dread." But Eliot equally shows Lydgate's suffering, hurt and ignored by a wife unable to love: beautiful Rosamond is as enclosed, as frozen as the aging Casaubon. Like him, she is both timid and self-satisfied, entirely engrossed in her own interests; Lydgate is an appendage, not a person, to her, just as Dorothea is only a convenience for Casaubon. Like Casaubon, Rosamond is incapable of an original thought; she finds Lydgate's doctoring "not a nice profession, dear," and is made anxious and stubborn by the discovery that he has any ideas that differ from hers.

This is the conventional reading, and Eliot makes it absolutely plain. No one is blamed but, simply, we like the generous, energetic, straightforward Dorothea and Tertius better than their stunted partners. It is a balanced enough picture of the difficulty, for everyone, of seeing clearly and acting generously. Gilbert and Gubar's reading of both the women as victims, both the husbands as oppressors, simply denies the sympathy and subtlety of the book.

What Eliot makes clear is that Dorothea and Lydgate are strong characters who painfully learn—learning being the point for characters in nineteenth-century fiction—some compassion for their weaker partners. Rosamond learns salutary lessons too, but it is her husband who pays for his mistake of rashly hoping for a compliant angel, for the rest of his life: "Lydgate had accepted his narrowed lot with sad resignation. He had chosen this fragile creature, and had taken the burthen of her life upon his arms. He must walk as he could, carrying that burthen pitifully." Casaubon, equally, is a fragile creature for whom Dorothea has to recognize responsibility. When she struggles with her rage and overcomes it with mercy, she is rewarded by seeing plainly his loneliness and timid affection, and feels "something like the thankfulness that might well up in us if we had narrowly escaped hurting a lamed creature." To call, as Gilbert and Gubar do, this choice of hers "repression" (which is an unconscious defense, not a moral decision) is to make nonsense of what George Eliot has made so clear.

Shirley, too, is at times mutilated by one-sided interpretations. "Brontë's heroines are so circumscribed by their gender that they cannot act at all," say the authors, but in fact the action, both for the two "heroines" and two "heroes," is to find a workable solution to the problem of women and men coexisting affectionately; an evenhanded combat is played out by opponents who enjoy each other. Shirley and Caroline are benign female doubles, the one softer than she likes to appear, the other tougher. Caroline's odious uncle—"These women are incomprehensible"—represents the view that good relations between the sexes are impossible. All marriages, at bottom, are unhappy, all husbands and wives "yoke-fellows," "fellow-sufferers." But "If two people like each other, why shouldn't they consent to live together?" asks Caroline; and she and Shirley thrash the question out, distinguish good and bad behavior from sex roles:

> "We know that this man has been a kind son, that he is a kind brother: will any one dare to tell me that he will not be a kind husband?"

> "My uncle would affirm it unhesitatingly. 'He will be sick of you in a month,' he would say."

> "Mrs. Pryor would seriously intimate the same."

> "Miss Yorke and Miss Mann would darkly suggest ditto."

But—

> "When they *are* good, they are the lords of the creation. . . . Indisputably, a great, good, handsome man is the first of created things."

> "Above us?"

> "I would scorn to contend for empire with him,—I would scorn it. Shall my left hand dispute for precedence with my right?—shall my heart quarrel with my pulse?—shall my veins be jealous of the blood which fills them?"

Before the marriages at the end, all four characters have learned lessons: Robert has been chastened, Caroline fortified, Louis—the poor tutor, male equivalent of Jane Eyre—learned to put love before pride and property, and "Captain" Shirley tamed, in a delightfully erotic game of submission to her tutor (who is in turn supported by her: "I thought I should have to support her and it is she who has made me strong"). The two women clear-sightedly *like* their chosen men—"I do like his face—I do like his aspect—I do like him so much! Better than any of these shuffling curates, for instance—better than anybody; bonnie Robert!" and the regard is mutual—"It delights my eye to look on her: she suits me. . . ." The four have struggled with the problem that the sexes must have differences in order to attract each other, and come up with excellent compromises. The remarkable thing is that there is honesty, not repression; amicable erotic teasing, not festering hostility; and the marriages at the end, far from being "unreal," "ridiculous fantasy," and "a fairy tale," as Gilbert and Gubar assert, have been well worked for.

Gilbert and Gubar, with Brontë's use of stone as an image of masculine lovelessness in mind, see the setting of Robert's proposal—by a stone wall and fragment of a cross—as a deliberate suggestion of the barrenness of marriage. But, as with other images they interpret throughout the book, there is a different meaning that they ignore: in Yorkshire the outcropping stone seems the very image of strength and constancy, and Charlotte Brontë uses it in this sense, not only in Rochester's "brow of rock" and Louis's "great sand-buried stone head" but in the tremendous metaphor in her preface to *Wuthering Heights*—"a granite block on a solitary moor . . . there it stands colossal, dark, and frowning, half-statue, half-rock. . . ." The very use of "Moore" as the brothers' surname is a use of the Brontës' central image of timeless and austere sustenance.

Shirley's vision, of the true Eve which she opposes to Milton's is of "a woman-Titan. . . . She reclines her bosom on the ridge of Stilbro' Moor; her mighty hands are joined beneath it. So kneeling, face to face she speaks with God." The male and female images coalesce. Gilbert and Gubar's aim is also to reconstruct an Eve, a mother-artist "whom patriarchal poetics dismembered." Indeed they do open up a new dimension in these works, and one will always see them differently. But "we must dissect in order to murder" the fetid angel in the house, they say, and their Eve is not re-created without further dismemberment.

Nina Auerbach (essay date Summer 1980)

SOURCE: "The Madwoman in the Attic," in *Victorian Studies,* Vol. 23, No. 4, Summer, 1980, pp. 505–07.

[In the following essay, Auerbach commends Guber and Gilbert's "liberated" readings of nineteenth-century women writers in The Madwoman in the Attic.]

Feminist criticism seemed to spring alive in the 1970s when Kate Millett's *Sexual Politics* smashed into patriarchal myths about womanhood; it is fitting that *The Madwoman in the Attic* should finish out the decade by recomposing this mythology in feminist terms. Sandra M. Gilbert and Susan Gubar's rich compendium of the images, fears, and dreams of power that haunted nineteenth-century woman writers is a definitive, if not totally consistent, study of the mythos of subversion out of which the woman's tradition arose.

The Madwoman in the Attic begins by indicting an overweening patriarchal culture that imposed Otherness on its women by forcing on them the twin myths of angel and monster. Though Gilbert and Gubar seem at first to share Virginia Woolf's gallant intention of killing both the angel in the house and the monster out of it, their book suggests that they are half in love with their antagonists' projections; their composite paradigm, the madwoman in the attic, is a haunting figure who blends angel and monster in a new, unforgettable shape that is woman's own.

Just as Gilbert and Gubar find conventional male images behind the incendiary force of *Jane Eyre*, so they elaborate upon Harold Bloom's Oedipal paradigm of literary criticism to define a woman's art that rises in wounded resistance from the assault of the male pen/penis. The heart of their book is a feminization of William Blake's myth of Albion, whereby the giant form of a single woman artist, Gertrude Stein's "mother of us all," writes first like Jane Austen in pseudoangelic code, then "falls" into the Gothic/Satanic mode with Charlotte and Emily Brontë and Mary Shelley, then dizzily withdraws from the searing patriarchal sun into the convoluted feints and personae of George Eliot and Emily Dickinson. Though this myth rests on assumptions that do not always make historical sense, it does reconstruct the traditional canon of woman writers in a resonant way.

Many individual readings, particularly the long central section on Charlotte Brontë, will be familiar to feminist critics already saturated in the nineteenth-century woman's tradition; in general, ***The Madwoman in the Attic*** is less a revolutionary manifesto than a bible of revolution, giving definitive form to the collective work of a decade. Gilbert/Gubar (who for the purpose of this review exist as one corporate giant form) admittedly build on the work of Ellen Moers and Elaine Showalter; but whereas Moers and Showalter presented themselves as literary historians, restoring the "lost Atlantis" of the woman's tradition to the continent of English literature, Gilbert/Gubar is a sibylline persona, reweaving the threads of a timeless tapestry.

Moreover, while Moers and Showalter stressed the masked strength of their hidden continent, Gilbert/Gubar present us with a community of radical anxiety, blended by the dis/ease engendered by the male pen/penis. Their writing madwoman reverses Edmund Wilson's paradigm, for the bow of her ambition strikes open the wound oppression generates: "the pulse of ambition seems itself to be an impulse of disease, the harbinger of a wound, or at least a headache" (p. 330). Their free woman is one who can break out of male authorization to tell her own story, but the art discussed is radically maimed. The book's central aim is to translate the coded essence of an essentially duplicitous canon, and it yearns implicitly for a literary atmosphere which would allow a Jane Austen or an Emily Dickinson to speak out, free from wiles and disguises. But the critic in me doubts whether Austen or Dickinson should have put their cards on the table. A wound does regenerate into a perfectly apposite bow, and I wonder whether a less oppressed art would be a more memorable legacy.

Like the madwoman in the attic herself, then, this book has the flaws inherent in its strength. For one thing, though much literary criticism ignores history, Gilbert/Gubar defy it. Thus, they argue less by amassing evidence than by weaving a pastiche whereby one woman artist speaks for all in a timeless world. It is brilliantly suggestive to cite Emily Dickinson as a gloss on Mary Shelley, Sylvia Plath as a spokeswoman for Emily Brontë's Catherine, May Sarton as an image of George Eliot's female Gothic, but it

also disturbs me in its blurring of individual contours. For me, the choric method within which the argument takes shape works best when some documented kinship is available; for example, a brilliant discussion of "Milton's cook" places Emily Brontë's Nelly Dean by citing Charlotte's distilled portrait of Emily in *Shirley*, as the sister artists combine to slay Milton's bogey and restore the primacy of the first woman. The family bond here is literal and essential. Elsewhere in the book, I feared the reconstruction of a corporate womanhood as undifferentiated as the angels and monsters Gilbert/Gubar began by wanting to slay.

Similarly, the book posits a patriarchal oppressor who is more gargantuan than any I have met, in the nineteenth century or our own. It begins with a rhetorical question that does not stay for an answer: "Is a pen a metaphorical penis?" (p. 3). "Well, no," I mumbled, but the book galloped off without my qualifications, assuming a universal conspiracy between writing and patriarchy and ignoring an equally timeless and, for me, even more oppressive metaphorical equation between literary creativity and childbirth. Throughout the book, Gilbert/Gubar seem to me too quick to erect a giant straw penis to explain the shapes of woman's art, thereby reverting to Virginia Woolf's stinging definition of woman's primal role: "reflecting the figure of man at twice its natural size."

Thus, while I think it is a brilliant idea to discuss the impact of Milton's misogyny on woman's art, the book entangles *Frankenstein* and *Wuthering Heights* so deeply in *Paradise Lost* as almost to rob these great novels of autonomous life, ignoring Milton's similar impact on canonical works by men, such as *Tom Jones* and *Great Expectations*. While it is indisputable that repression and resistance are the germs of woman's art, too much deconstructive power may be conceded here to a spectral antagonist, too little to the restorative creations of the artist herself.

There is a more perplexing way in which giant hand of man rests on this book. Male myths about womanhood which many of us have found dubiously compelling buttress the authors' own mythology with no analysis of their validity in a woman's pantheon. The first quotation in the book evokes George MacDonald's femme fatale, Lilith, and Dante Gabriel Rossetti's outsize Astarte Syriaca illustrates the introductory quest for a feminist poetics. In fact, all six of the prefatory illustrations are paintings by men; in a book that strains toward isolating the undiluted female voice, we need a discussion of the status of these male images. At one point, the authors conclude a fervent discussion of woman's need to free herself from the prison of character in a male-conceived plot by citing Chaucer's wife of Bath as if she too were writing the book; a later discussion of the female hell of *Wuthering Heights* is supported by Robert Graves's *The White Goddess*. One recurrent motif rests upon a dashing feminist interpretation of Snow White, a tale which many feminist folklorists deplore. While I admire the authors' boldness in appropriating traditional male stereotypes of womanhood, I miss an attempt to place them. Few feminist readers will grant

Graves's white goddess the imaginative integrity of the madwoman in the attic without some impulse toward demystification. Here and elsewhere, patriarchal structures are granted a power they do not seem to have earned.

But one of the strengths of this strong and massive book is its intensification of the reader's urgency to break free and tell her own story. The impact and excitement of the demands it makes, the questions it asks, and the readings it establishes transcend its sometimes shaky methods and generalizations. Many readers will probably approach a book of this length and density by reading around in it piecemeal at need, and the individual readings are always compelling and definitive: never again can Mary Shelley be seen as the domestic angel to Percy's Prometheus, Jane Austen and George Eliot as the obedient dolls of patriarchy who inflict sense and renunciation on their rebellious readers, or Charlotte Brontë as patriarchy's flattering scapegoat, the frustrated spinster who longs only for a mate. Though like the authors they write about, in abstaining from attacking their male antagonists directly, not deigning even to cite traditional critics, Gilbert and Gubar have won the battle of the books: the madwoman has been unleashed from her hiding place, and the rage and power cloaked in the woman's tradition are out of the attic at last. Such a jubilant achievement assures us that woman writers of the nineteenth century can never again be adored and patronized in the old way.

Patricia Meyer Spacks (essay date Winter 1980)

SOURCE: "New Questions," in *Yale Review*, Vol. 69, No. 2, Winter, 1980, pp. 266–70.

[*In the following essay, Meyer Spacks appreciates the boldness and importance of Gubar and Gilbert's feminist readings of literature, however she argues that the dogmatism of their ideological commitment causes them to distort the literature they interpret in* The Madwoman in the Attic.]

New questions generate new answers, new focus refracts new light. Sometimes ideology provides the crucial focus: Marxism, psychoanalysis, structuralism, now feminism. Feminist criticism has flourished with increasing vitality in the last decade, demonstrating ever more surely its validity as a mode of inquiry and of assertion. *The Madwoman in the Attic*, scholarly, authoritative, and imaginative, reinterprets a large body of literature in a fashion that demands and creates serious attention. Nineteenth-century fiction and poetry will never look quite the same again.

Sandra Gilbert and Susan Gubar know precisely what questions they wish to ask. "What does it mean to be a woman writer in a culture whose fundamental definitions of literary authority are . . . both overtly and covertly patriarchal? If the vexed and vexing polarities of angel and monster, sweet dumb Snow White and fierce mad Queen, are major images literary tradition offers women, how does such imagery influence the ways in which women attempt the pen? . . . Does the Queen try to sound like the King . . . ? Or does she 'talk back' to him?" In an effort to resolve such problems about female voices, female images, they range over nineteenth-century fiction and poetry, mainly but not entirely English, with excursions back into seventeenth-and eighteenth-century poetry and prose and with reference to men as well as women writers. Jane Austen, Mary Shelley, Emily and Charlotte Brontë, George Eliot, Christina Rossetti, and Emily Dickinson supply central texts for investigation, but the authors skillfully interweave allusions to other works. They also demonstrate their command of a large body of criticism, and they articulate their own "feminist poetics." They have written, in short, a strikingly ambitious book.

Ambitious, and in many respects impressive. Gilbert and Gubar confront Harold Bloom, responding to his male mythology of precursors and swervings and anxieties not merely with anger but with a valuable transformation of terms. Given the patriarchal tradition, they argue, women authors cannot experience the "anxiety of influence." The "strong precursors" not only embody alien natures themselves, they seek to reduce the woman to stereotypical angel or monster, to deprive her of creative selfhood. She feels, therefore, a more radical "anxiety of authorship," troubled by her separation from the line of precursors, fearful that "the act of writing will isolate or destroy her," fearful even that true creativity cannot belong to her. She struggles not against the influence of her male predecessors but against their restrictive definitions of her, which threaten to deprive her of power and even of full humanity. Her characteristic solution, these critics believe, depends on disguise, on the construction of "works whose surface designs conceal or obscure deeper, less accessible (and less socially acceptable) levels of meaning." Thus the woman writer manages simultaneously to conform to and subvert patriarchal standards.

Gilbert and Gubar try to penetrate beneath the surface in order to locate the subversive energies of female literary depths. They find such energies expressing themselves in recurrent patterns: rewritings of *Paradise Lost*, for example; parodic structures of allusion; ambiguous evocations of monstrosity and madness. Through such recurrences they (and their readers) discover unexpected connections. *Wuthering Heights* turns out to resemble "Goblin Market" not in its play with the supernatural but in its fundamental reversal of Milton's myth; Mary Shelley as writer reveals affinities with Dorothea Brooke as character. The readings of individual works often produce startling and persuasive insights. Victor Frankenstein, we learn, has a female as well as a male aspect, resembling not only Adam but Eve, not only Satan but Sin. Catherine Earnshaw, in *Wuthering Heights*, terrified by what she sees in the mirror, struggles to recapture a "true lost self," destroyed partly by the image of the fine lady she has become. The symbolic identification of witch and nun in *Villette* expresses the impossibility of escape for women; if, like Lucy Snowe, they avoid becoming witch or nun, they suffer haunting by both.

Isolated from their context, such summarized readings may sound thin or strained; in the critical setting this study provides, they reverberate richly. The force of *The Madwoman in the Attic* derives from its wholeness, its insistence on a total vision, its own radical subversion of Bloomian theory. Although the detailed interpretations of texts offer their own rewards, such interpretations function more importantly as contributions to a new mode of literary history and criticism. Gilbert and Gubar display their skills as readers and as scholars, but their commitment means more to them than their skills. Their book demands response to that commitment.

As a guide to critical inquiry, however, the commitment has its troubling aspects. To say that new questions engender new responses implies that the shape of questions determines that of answers: new shapes, necessarily; but perhaps distortions. Take, for example, the extended treatment of Jane Austen. A third of the way through the first of two chapters on Austen, Gilbert and Gubar cavalierly dismiss the claims of other critics in order to assert their own. "Austen demystifies the literature she has read" not for the reasons assigned by Mary Lascelles, Marvin Mudrick, or Marilyn Butler, "but because she seeks to illustrate how such fictions are the alien creations of writers who contribute to the enfeebling of women." This categorical assertion does not appear to emerge from readings of the texts; on the contrary, it determines those readings. *Northanger Abbey* thus describes a girl "entrapped in a series of monstrous fictions which deprive her of primacy." By means of other fictions, *Emma* leads its heroine to utter submission and to identification with Jane Fairfax "in her realization of her own powerlessness." Elizabeth Bennet's refusal to answer Lady Catherine (*Pride and Prejudice*) testifies to her diminishment, as does her effort not to laugh too soon at Darcy. All these young women surrender their self-sufficiency and responsibility to adopt humiliating strategies of apparent submission by which alone they can succeed.

Generations of readers, male and female, have responded to Elizabeth's defiance of Lady Catherine's bullying as triumph, not defeat, and have seen her restraint of the impulse to ridicule as an enlarged capacity to function without the defensive mockery she has learned from her father. Catherine Morland appears to have far more "primacy" at the end of *Northanger Abbey* than at its beginning, freed of her own enfeebling fantasies and of the gullibility which makes her subject to the fantasies of others. The interpretations of Austen here offered, in other words, however ingenious, contradict the direct experience most readers have of the books. Gilbert and Gubar might argue the naïveté or the patriarchal corruption of those who deny their claims; yet literary texts possess their own authority. One must take seriously the emotional effect *Pride and Prejudice* has on its large audience—and one must worry about a critical procedure which ignores or denies that effect.

The Madwoman in the Attic in its interpretations sometimes neglects textual evidence for dogmatic assertions of essentially political "intuition." Aunt Norris, in *Mansfield Park*, we are told, should be forgiven her moral failures because of her harsh circumstances. Living on a small fixed income, she must resort to flattery, the critics suggest, as her only means of gaining pleasure. Moreover, she indulges the Bertram daughters "in part out of genuine affection and loyalty." Little in the novel's language supports this statement; moreover, the writers ignore Aunt Norris's real cruelty to Fanny, as though "flattery" represented her most serious failing. Emily Dickinson's wearing of white "announces that she herself incarnates the paradox of the Victorian woman poet—the Self disguised as the Other, the creative subject impersonating the fictionalized object—and as such she herself enacts the enigma that she perceives at the heart of her culture, just as Melville's 'albino Whale' embodies the enigma nineteenth-century culture saw in nature." Anything can mean anything, one begins dizzily to feel. When young Catherine Earnshaw complains of Hindley and his wife "kissing and talking nonsense by the hour—foolish palaver we should be ashamed of," Gilbert and Gubar conclude, with no textual substantiation, that "she understands, perhaps for the first time, the sexual nature" of the adult relationship. Catherine's "self-deceptive decision to marry Edgar" requires no moral response from the reader because she has no choice: "Given the patriarchal nature of culture, women must fall—that is, they are already fallen because doomed to fall."

Everywhere, in short, these authors find evidence for the oppression of women which they initially posited: their answers precede their questions. And despite the splendid readings (notably of "Snow White" and *Frankenstein*), the provocative linkages and comparisons (Emily Dickinson and Walt Whitman, for a particularly striking instance), the care for detail as well as pattern—despite all these virtues, and despite the skill, intelligence, and energy of the authors, one must feel reservations about *The Madwoman in the Attic*. Exemplifying the large claims that feminist criticism now can make, it does not altogether support those claims. To inquire why a writer's femaleness matters, what specifically it means, can sharply illuminate familiar works. Such questions generate the most meaningful results when posed with genuine openness and answered on the basis of close attention to the text. So asked, so answered, they avoid the weaknesses of this study, where apparent complexity of interpretation often reduces itself to the reiteration of female misery, and the special focus of the inquiry on occasion obscures a novelist's or a poet's true power. The imaginative boldness of *The Madwoman in the Attic*, inseparable from its ideology, unquestionably demands attention for this book. Its brilliant vision and its intermittent blindness derive alike from the commitment which informs it, a commitment which has here generated sharp perception and commanding generalization but which, given more flexibility in its literary application, might produce criticism less marred by astigmatism.

Rosemary Ashton (essay date 8 August 1980)

SOURCE: "The Strongly Female Tradition," in *Times Literary Supplement,* No. 4,037, August 8, 1980, p. 901.

[*In the following essay, Ashton argues that the feminist thesis in* The Madwoman in the Attic *is unconvincing.*]

"Is a pen a metaphorical penis?" ask the authors of this study [*The Madwoman in the Attic*]. If it is, "with what organ can females generate texts?" Both questions are put rhetorically. Indeed, how could they be answered without exposing the paradox at the basis of the "feminist poetics" the authors wish to construct? On the one hand, they aim to show how women have been cabined, cribbed, confined, kept "mute" in a patriarchal society which requires sewing and submission from its women while men "father" or "author" texts, wielding the exclusive power of the pen/penis. On the other, it is part of ntion to account for female authorship, that contradiction in the terms in which they set their study. Hence the title of the book, a reference to the "mad double" who subverts the apparently docile adherence of the female writer to a "male" tradition.

That the authors are under some strain in this task is apparent from the first chapter, in which they deal with Anne Finch, Countess of Winchelsea, who, according to them, was "cut off from generative energy, in a dark and wintry world" and was yet a poet, and therefore—though the authors do not say so—in one important sense not cut off. In order to establish fully the repressiveness of the tradition, they stress "the curious passivity with which Fiuch responded (or pretended to respond) to male expectations and designs", ignoring, except for that glance in brackets, the irony and wit which bespeak her power as an author. Perhaps the real subject of the book ought to be "the centuries-long silence of so many women who must have had talents comparable to Finch's", but of course that is no subject.

The problem remains intractable. This is a purposefully written book essentially without a thesis. In its ambitious attempt to place its authors—Jane Austen. Mary Shelley, Emily and Charlotte Brontë, George Eliot and Emily Dickinson—in a "female tradition", it sends readers in contrary directions without providing a Penelope to lead them through the maze of threads. The authors write of George Eliot:

> Although until quite recently she has been viewed almost exclusively in terms of male literary history, Eliot shows in "The Lifted Veil" that she is part of a strong female tradition: her self-conscious relatedness to other women writers, her critique of male literary conventions, her interest in clairvoyance and telepathy, her schizophrenic sense of fragmentation . . . place Eliot in a tradition that still survives today.

In what sense is the "female tradition" here "strong"? "The Lifted Veil" may yield interesting psychological material about George Eliot, but it is not one of her strongest works. One wonders what is gained by focusing on the female strength of this story at the expense of the works belonging to "male literary history", such as *Middlemarch* and *Daniel Deronda*. Certainly our expectations of "feminist" insights into *Middlemarch* are disappointed: the section on this novel is little more than a repetition of previous criticism. Of *Daniel Deronda* very little is said. Moreover, many of their comments on George Eliot could apply equally to male authors. Sterne offered a "critique of male literary conventions." Bulwer and Browning were interested in clairvoyance. Dickens in images of confinement, and so on.

Some of what the authors say of George Eliot is suggestive:

> Perhaps even her placing of her novels in pre-industrial historical settings can be related to her nostalgia for a time when women's work was important to the maintenance of the human community. In any case, Eliot's troubled movement from Evangelical self-denial to a religion of humanity is only one index of the juggling she had constantly to perform between her identification with male culture and her undeniable consciousness of her self as a woman.

Here is a proper tentativeness about the part such considerations may have played in George Eliot's career. Mostly, however, the authors attempt a bold inclusiveness. Not content with assessing Mary Shelley's "retelling" of *Paradise Lost* in *Frankenstein*, they seek to make further sexist points:

> Animal and misshapen, these emblems of self-loathing [in Sylvia Plath's "In Plaster"] must have descended at least in part from the distended body of Mary Shelley's darkly parodic Eve/Sin/Monster, whose enormity betokens not only the enormity of Victor Frankenstein's crime and Satan's bulk but also the distensions or deformities of pregnancy and the Swiftian sexual nausea expressed in Lemuei Gulliver's horrified description of a Brobdignagian breast, a passage Mary Shelley no doubt studied along with the rest of *Gulliver's Travels* when she read the book in 1816, shortly before beginning *Frankenstein*.

This passage is one of many in which logic is stretched. A common syntactical formula is:

> Thus if all women writers, metaphorical orphans in a patriarchal culture, seek literary answers to the questions "How are we fal'n, / Fal'n by mistaken rules . . . ?" motherless orphans like Mary Shelley and Emily Brontë almost seem to seek literal answers to that question, so passionately do their novels enact distinctive female literary obsessions.

The reader is not offered the freedom to dissent from a) (that "all women writers . . . seek literary answers . . .") but pushed on to accept b) ("Mary Shelley and Emily Brontë almost seem to seek literal answers . . ."). What, by the way, does "literal" mean here?

The strain is apparent, too, in the mixing of metaphors. A sentence like "Authored by a male. God and by a godlike male, killed into a perfect image of herself, the woman writer's self-contemplation may be said to have begun with a searching glance into the mirror of the male-inscribed literary text" is so overreaching as paradoxically to fall short of accessible argument. For 650 pages these indefatigable authors exhaust the reader with such formidable but unconvincing rhetoric. Is this their conscious revenge for centuries of enforced female muteness? Much energy and scholarship lie behind this book, yet its importance is minimal. The authors claim in their preface to have been "surprised" that they had "found what began to seem a distinctively female tradition." It is hard not to suspect that they found just what they were looking for, and equally hard to give acceptance to their "findings."

Annette Kolodny (review date March 1980)

SOURCE: A review of *The Madwoman in the Attic,* in *American Literature,* Vol. 52, No. 1, March, 1980, pp. 128–32.

[*In the following review, Kolodny praises* The Madwoman in the Attic *for opening up a new way to read women writers, but regrets that the authors, despite their fine chapter on Emily Dickinson, do not distinguish between British and American conditions of authorship for women.*]

Following upon a richly detailed anatomy of the ways in which women in general have found themselves "enclosed in the architecture of an overwhelmingly male-dominated society," and would-be women writers, in particular, have discovered themselves "constricted and restricted by the Palaces of Art and Houses of Fiction male writers authored" (p. xi), Sandra M. Gilbert and Susan Gubar observe that, despite all obstacles, "by the end of the eighteenth century . . . women were not only writing, they were conceiving fictional worlds in which patriarchal images and conventions were severely, radically revised" (p. 44). To delineate what they perceive as "a common, female impulse to struggle free from social and literary confinement through strategic redefinitions of self, art, and society" (p. xii), and thereby account for the artistic development of those "nineteenth-century women writers who found viable ways of circumventing" (p. 72) the encumbrances of what Gertrude Stein called the "patriarchal poetry" of our literary inheritance, Gilbert and Gubar set themselves the formidable task of constructing "a feminist poetics" (p. 17).

A healthy corrective to the habit of explaining away women's writing as the irregularity in an otherwise regular design, *The Madwoman in the Attic* quite literally *excavates* the imputed "'oddity' of women's writing" (p. 73) to discover the underlying coherence of an art designed "both to express and to camouflage" (p. 81). Swerving "from the central sequences of male literary history," according to

Gilbert and Gubar, women writers "achieved essential authority by telling their own stories," *but*—and this is the key—they did so "by following Emily Dickinson's famous (and characteristically female) advice to 'Tell all the Truth but tell it slant—In short," they conclude,

> like the twentieth-century American poet, H. D., who declared her aesthetic strategy by entitling one of her novels *Palimpsest,* women from Jane Austen and Mary Shelley to Emily Bronte and Emily Dickinson produced literary works that are in some sense palimpsestic, works whose surface designs conceal or obscure deeper, less accessible (and less socially acceptable) levels of meaning. Thus these authors managed the difficult task of achieving true female literary authority by simultaneously conforming to and subverting patriarchal literary standards.
>
> (p. 73)

The readings that result from Gilbert's and Gubar's skillful joint peeling away of the layers of that palimpsest are nothing short of breathtaking, uncovering—in even the best known of these texts—shapes and strategies we had never really seen before.

What may prove troublesome to the readers of this journal is the book's imbalanced and sometimes indiscriminate yoking together of American and British materials. For, despite numerous references to and, in some instances, even extended discussions of Anne Bradstreet, Margaret Fuller, Harriet Beecher Stowe, Louisa May Alcott, Kate Chopin, and Charlotte Perkins Gilman, among others, the only American to whom a full chapter is devoted is Emily Dickinson. As a result, the "feminist poetics" developed here is developed largely out of British sources; and that inevitably raises the crucial question as to whether the conditions of authorship were contemporaneously identical for women in England and America. Certainly, their social, economic, and political contexts were not. And while it cannot be denied that the works of the English "satirists of the eighteenth century," with their "virulent visions" of what Gilbert and Gubar call "the female monster" (p. 30), were greedily imported to American shores, moving periodicals like *The Ladies Magazine* to declare, in 1792, that, where women writers are concerned, "we admire them more as authors than esteem them as women," it is also the case that that same century saw the publication of Parts I and II of Charles Brockden Brown's treatise on female equality, *Alcuin,* and heard Susannah Rowson's young charges annually recite her decidedly egalitarian maxim, "It would be absurd to imagine that talents or virtue were confined to sex or station."

The issue becomes even more confused in the decades following the Revolution and on into the first half of the nineteenth century when, for reasons of patriotic pride, American writers sought to divorce themselves from slavish adherence to contemporary European—especially British—models; their aim, instead, was to develop an indigenously "American" literature. It might even be argued that, during the first half of the nineteenth century, American authors, generally, suffered before the dominance of the enormously rich European literary inheritance the same kind of "inferiorization" which Gilbert and Gubar attribute to eighteenth-and nineteenth-century women writers' response to a past rich with maledesigned literary forms. If this can be admitted, then it must also be the case that American women writers entered upon the revisionary stage of literary history with a role somewhat different from that assumed by their English counterparts. For, like their sisters across the sea, denied both classical education and genuine societal encouragement to authorship, American women, too, experienced a profound alienation from the inherited Great Tradition; but, unlike them, they also shared with their American brothers a nagging distrust of any desire to wholly participate in such continuities. Whether this sense of double removal—by virtue of both sex and nationality—from dominant literary traditions proved an added burden or offered an unforeseen liberation, only a comprehensive study focused primarily on American women writers could assess. But that kind of study is neither promised nor offered here. Still, the lack of attention to questions of national differences does tend to weaken—but never vitiate—the persuasiveness of their analyses of American authors.

Happily, however, it does not seriously diminish either the power or the originality of the chapter on Emily Dickinson. Placing Dickinson within the context of contemporary fiction by and about women—as explored in the preceding chapters—and thus relating her life and work to "the proliferation of fictional Victorian women in white," Gilbert and Gubar discover in Dickinson's poses an "acting out both [of] her reading and its implications" (p. 621) which permitted this "apparently timid, even . . . neurotically withdrawn" (p. 582) young woman to escape "the Requirements of Victorian reality by assuming the eccentricities of Victorian fiction" (p. 621). "The fantasies of guilt and anger" that were expressed in the writings of her female contemporaries "were literally enacted by Dickinson in her own life, her own being," they argue:

> Where George Eliot and Christina Rossetti wrote about angels of destruction and renunciation, Emily Dickinson herself became such an angel. Where Charlotte Bronte projected her anxieties into images of orphan children, Emily Dickinson herself enacted the part of a child. Where almost all late eighteenth-and nineteenth-century women writers from Maria Edgeworth in *Castle Rackrent* to Charlotte Bronte in *Jane Eyre*, Emily Bronte in *Wuthering Heights*, and George Eliot in *Middlemarch*, secreted bitter self-portraits of madwomen in the attics of their novels, Emily Dickinson herself became a madwoman—became . . . both ironically a madwoman (a deliberate impersonation of a madwoman) and truly a madwoman (a helpless agoraphobic, trapped in a room in her father's house).
>
> (p. 583)

By seriously attending—as no male critic ever has—to the iconic significance of Dickinson's ubiquitous white dress, Gilbert and Gubar are able to trace for us "a series of characters" informing both the life and the poetry. "Impersonating simultaneously a 'little maid' in white, a dead woman in white, and a ghost in white," they show how "Dickinson split herself into a series of incubae, haunting not just her father's house but her own mind." And "the ambiguities and discontinuities implicit in her white dress became," they conclude, "as much signs of her own psychic fragmentation as of her society's multiple (and conflicting) demands upon women" (pp. 621–22).

Neither all Americanists nor all feminist scholars will feel equally satisfied with the readings of particular poems generated by such a context; and Americanists, in particular, may note the omission of other factors influential upon Dickinson's language and imagery, including, most obviously, her acquaintance with the meeting-house and the familiar vernacular of New England Calvinism. Nonetheless, Gilbert and Gubar make a persuasive case for examining "Dickinson's reading of fiction, especially fiction by women," as relevant to her poetry, and they clearly demonstrate how much has been lost in the earlier critical disposition to dismiss "her self-dramatization as 'mere' girlish posing" or to ignore "the magnitude of the problem Dickinson had to solve as a *woman* poet" (pp. 583–84).

Precisely these emphases make *The Madwoman in the Attic* an indispensable addition to every Americanist's bookshelf, taking its place beside Ann Douglas' *The Feminization of American Culture*, Nina Baym's *Woman's Fiction*, and Emily Stipes Watts's *The Poetry of American Women from 1632–1945*, as at least a partial approach, and a necessary building-block towards a fully comprehensive rewriting of women's literary history in the United States. Fluently written, with every page attesting to the "exhilaration" of a successful collaboration (p. xiii), *The Madwoman in the Attic* is also essential reading for anyone who wants to grasp the key questions motivating feminist literary criticism as it is currently practiced in the American academy. For, whether or not one finally assents to the Gilbert and Gubar model for "understanding the dynamics of female literary response to male literary assertion and coercion" (p. xii), there can be no doubt that it represents a bold new step in understanding what it means "to be a woman writer in a culture whose fundamental definitions of literary authority are . . . overtly and covertly patriarchal" (p. 45).

Valerie Miner (essay date 11 February 1980)

SOURCE: "Those Proper Ladies Writing in the Attic," in *Christian Science Monitor*, Vol. 72, No. 54, February 11, 1980, p. B12.

[*In the following review, Miner praises* The Madwoman in the Attic *for "uncovering a discernible female imagination."*]

The grand success of this study is that it stimulates us to re-read those books by proper ladies from the 19th century. As Sandra M. Gilbert and Susan Gubar reconsider each work, they introduce us to *The Madwoman in the Attic*, the author's double, hiding in the seams of her writing, reflecting her anxiety and rage.

Gilbert and Gubar shatter the images of Jane Austen as the timid parlor mouse, the Brontës as contented rural lasses. George Eliot as the ugly, mannish scourge: ". . . almost all late 18th and 19th century women writers from Maria Edgeworth in 'Castle Rackrent' to Charlotte Brontë in 'Jane Eyre.' Emily Brontë in 'Wuthering Heights,' and George Eliot in 'Middlemarch,' secreted bitter self-portraits of madwomen in the attics of their novels. . . ." These "madwomen," according to the authors, railed about the sexual double standard, the domestic entrapment of women and other feminist issues.

"Feminist" is an approach taken by these two scholars without apology, despite the notable risk to their critical credentials in the male academic establishment. Gilbert and Gubar, associate professors of English literature at the University of California, Davis, and Indiana University respectively, insist on assessing art within the context of sexual politics.

The Madwoman in the Attic discusses female literature as a response and a contrast to "male writing." For instance, Miltonian morality loomed large in the consciences of Victorian women: they were carefully schooled in his themes of incest, woman's evil power man's godliness. But by use of the "madwoman" and other palimpsests, they were able to refute and reinterpret his mandates.

If novelists wrote about "madwomen" to express their feminism, the authors suggest, female poets became "madwomen" because the barriers to lyric poetry were almost impermeable. They cite Emily Dickinson's poems as offering both the ironic impersonation of the madwoman and the realistic reflection of Dickinson's genuine eccentricities: "Dickinson's life itself, in other words, became a kind of novel or narrative poem, in which, through an extraordinarily complex series of maneuvers, aided by costumes that came inevitably to hand, this inventive poet enacted and eventually resolved both her own anxieties about her art and her anger at female subordination."

"I'm Nobody! Who are you?" asked Dickinson. "How dreary—to be—Somebody— / How public—like a Frog— / To tell one's name—the livelong June— / To an admiring Bog!"

Thanks to Gilbert and Gubar, the admiring Bog grows larger. We return to the writing of these 19th-century women with renewed curiosity, with intimations of a discernible female imagination.

Phoebe Pettingell (essay date 25 February 1980)

SOURCE: "A Prey to Madness," in *New Leader,* Vol LXIII, No. 4, February 25, 1980, pp. 16–17.

[In the following essay, Pettingell expresses ambivalence towards The Madwoman in the Attic, *seeing it as intelligently insightful but marred by "questionable theorizing," and "simplistic" feminist "jargon."]*

What nightmare inspired a quiet teenage mother to create *Frankenstein*? Was it necessary for the Brontë sisters and Mary Ann Evans to publish under masculine pseudonyms? Why did Emily Dickinson choose to immure herself in her parents' house all her life and write poems in secret, when she might have exercised her vivacious talents on the world at large? Do the violent images all these writers employ have a common denominator in their experience as women?

These questions are addressed in a radical new study, *The Madwoman in the Attic: The Woman Writer and the Nineteenth-Century Literary Imagination,* by feminist critics Sandra M. Gilbert and Susan Gubar. As their central postulate they assert that the female imagination differs significantly from the male. And because the woman writer is treated as an interloper in that male club called the English Literary Tradition, they argue, to the extent that her work is not merely imitative it has to be subversive. Outwardly "one of the boys," she clandestinely foments rebellion against their values and revises their mythology. "Even the most apparently conservative and decorous women writers obsessively create fiercely independent characters who seek to destroy all the patriarchal structures which both their authors and their authors' submissive heroines seem to accept as inevitable." They must be careful, however, to disguise their feminine perspective as a masculine one, for to be caught rebelling would be fatal: The male archangels who guard the Miltonic literary bastion would cast the offenders into the outer darkness of "lady novelists" and "female poetasters." Yet ignorance or denial of the female imagination, Gilbert and Gubar insist, has hitherto prevented an authoritative interpretation of their subjects' works—a lack they seek to remedy in this volume.

The madwoman referred to in the title is Bertha Rochester of Charlotte Brontë's *Jane Eyre*. Though her husband denies her existence and locks her in the attic, she eludes her keeper at night to haunt the sleeping members of his household like the spirit of Darkness. Gilbert and Gubar perceptively demonstrate that rather than the stock Gothic bogy critics have usually seen, Bertha is really the character all women fear to become—"intemperate and unchaste," as Mr. Rochester describes her, aggressive to the point of murderous half-beast/half witch. He contrasts the demure Jane Eyre, his "good fairy," with this demon, but Jane knows the anger she was capable of during her repressive childhood and is afraid that in the role of Rochester's mistress she might be driven to lose her control and find herself taking Bertha's place in the attic. Jane and Bertha are, in a sense, doubles. The madwoman can also be seen as a fictional release for the dark, repressed side of Charlotte Brontë's life, straining against unendurable frustrations.

The authors trace their twin preoccupations with confinement and monstrosity through the novels of Jane Austen,

Mary Shelley, Emily Brontë, and George Eliot. Noting that Austen might at first seem an outsider to this company, they contend that her writing, too, is a "cover story" that conceals resentment. Her heroines defend themselves against male gibes about woman's proverbial inconstancy and flightiness with their only weapon, wit, although Austen, in the role of Fate, often comes to their aid before book's end by humbling their powerful opponents. "Men have every advantage in telling their own story," remarks Anne Eliott during one barbed exchange in *Persuasion*. "The pen has been in their hands." Women, she dryly adds, "live at home, quiet, confined, and our feelings prey on us."

Milton, the grim patriarch of Romanticism and something of a misogynist, forced his daughters to read Latin and Greek aloud to him in his blindness, a task the girls bitterly objected to because they could not understand the languages. Gilbert and Gubar liken 19th-century women writers to Milton's daughters trying to cast off their yoke: Mary Shelley rewrote his creation story in *Frankenstein*; Emily Brontë reversed the values of his heaven and hell in *Wuthering Heights*; and George Eliot criticized the ambiguous results of compelling dutiful sacrifices.

But all these women paid the price of suffering from the classical anxiety of rebellious children: Wishing to be accepted on their own terms, they needed at the same time to be approved of on Milton's. This double-bind, in which the very aggressive powers required to create are reckoned unwomanly, drives women to write with *repressed* violence. It was a reading of *Paradise Lost*, our critics infer, that gave Mary Shelley her famous nightmare. In the resulting novel, she subverts the Miltonic order: When Frankenstein peruses that epic, he is convinced that he is the is "the new Adam"; simultaneously he fulfills many of the roles Milton assigned to the put-upon Eve. As for the Brontës and George Eliot, they hid behind masculine names because they worried that their subject matter might be thought unfeminine.

The American poet Emily Dickinson, a devout admirer of these female English novelists, was so impressed by the figure of the madwoman in the attic that she decided to take the role upon herself. Dressed ever in white, she kept to her room, writing "half-cracked" notes or poems to people she refused to see. This persona was deliberately cultivated, Gilbert and Gubar insist, because so long as she knew that others thought her crazy, she did not need to worry about the unorthodoxy of her verse; madness was a pose that gave her artistic freedom. "When what her world called 'sanity' threatened, she steadied her hold on [madness] . . . in which she imagined fierce flights of escape like the one Milton's Eve takes."

The close textual readings Gilbert and Gubar give the novels are often insightful and valuable. Moreover, the critics display scholarly responsibility in not forcing their material to fit their argument. They do not attempt to portray their authors as modern feminists, or suggest that they were attempting to overthrow their societies; these novelists, after all, were conservative about most everything except their art. Gubar's perceptions about Jane Austen are delicate and, ultimately, poignant. Gilbert's study of Milton's ambiguous influence on Mary Shelley and Emily Brontë is brilliant and original. Her portrait of Charlotte Brontë burns with an emotional conviction very much in the spirit of that passionate writer's work.

George Eliot presents more of a problem. Her themes are not so succinct and her complex personality is harder to capture. It is too bad that so much space is wasted on "The Lifted Veil," a Gothic story of little merit that is being given too much attention by critics after years of deserved neglect. Still, Gubar offers fascinating insights into the influence of the American feminists Margaret Fuller and Harriet Beecher Stowe on Eliot. The English novelist praised Fuller's sense of "the Nemesis lurking in the vices of the oppressed." While she found this quality lacking in Stowe's fiction, *Uncle Tom's Cabin* served to bolster her faith in "the possibility of a uniquely female tradition in literature characterized by love rather than anger." Thus Eliot meted out strong punishments to her characters, yet allowed her heroines to develop "resources that transform the vindictive noose of the author's revengeful plot into a kind of lifeline held out to other creatures threading their way through the labyrinth" of an unhappy and imperfect world.

In contrast to the largely persuasive mid-section of ***The Madwoman in the Attic***, the theoretical introduction and the two chapters on women poets at the end are shrill and combative. Out come the feminist bludgeons ("patriarchal society") coupled merrily with the Freudian (pens equal penises). Gilbert and Grubar claim that their theory of the "anxiety of female authorship" was inspired by Harold Bloom's "anxiety of influence." "For our purposes," they announce sententiously, "Bloom's historical construct is useful not only because it helps identify and define the psychosexual context in which so much Western literature was authored, but also because it can help us distinguish the anxiety and achievements of female writers from those of male writers." They fail to realize, though, that Bloom's is not a theory of social influence; it holds that human nature would dictate the same literary pattern under any conditions. Gilbert and Gubar appear to believe that "society" was responsible for the schizophrenia of the 19th-century woman writer, just as they think that Freud's theories are "an analysis of patriarchal society" rather than a statement about basic human nature. They are reminiscent of the Marxist critics who are convinced that if society were changed, our attitudes would alter as well.

The real inspiration for this book seems not to be Harold Bloom but Virginia Woolf, whose *A Room of One's Own* the authors quote reverently on innumerable occasions. Unfortunately, Gilbert and Gubar mistake her aphorisms for profundity; where Woolf trips lightly, they galumph. (Even if Woolf took the ideas presented in that essay as seriously as her disciples do, her treatment of them was superficial.) Dubious judgment is evident as well in the treatment of poetry. Elizabeth Barrett Browning's tedious "Aurora Leigh" is defended because these critics like its "message." Because they have no ear for Emily Dickinson's nuance, their readings make her into one of the worst poets of all time!

I wanted this book to be better than it is, for Gilbert and Gubar have seized on a powerful image and some strong ideas. Alas, their combination of the original and the rigid gives **The Madwoman in the Attic**, like many of its subjects, a schizophrenic personality. It is a pity that so much intelligence and insight should give way to questionable theorizing and simplistic jargon.

Louise Bernikow (review date February 1980)

SOURCE: A review of *The Madwoman in the Attic,* in *Ms.,* Vol. 8, No. 8, February, 1980, p. 39.

[*In the following review, Bernikow admires the way Gubar and Gilbert support their arguments in* The Madwoman in the Attic.]

[**The Madwoman in the Attic**] is long, rich, and brilliant. Sandra M. Gilbert and Susan Gubar, their voices blended, the seams mended, write as one, and that one sees deeply into literature. They shed light on the relationship between 19th-century women living imprisoned in men's houses and female writers of the time imprisoned in masculine texts. They look closely, anatomizing the work of Jane Austen, the Brontës, George Eliot, and Emily Dickinson.

The authors have a big picture: the effect of life on art, archetypes of the female imagination, the meaning of recurrent images of enclosure and madwomen in attics. And they have infinite detail: close reading of Charlotte Brontë's novels, a chapter for each; careful treading through Dickinson's poems. These readings are subtle, entwined—take time to read, return to the original, read again. On Brontë's *Villette*, especially, they open doors. The section on "white" imagery in Dickinson's life and poems takes off like a jazz riff. White, they begin, frequently represents white heat and polar cold. Both. They spin this thread of thinking, stop, spin another.

Many feminists have been waiting for someone to counter Freudian critic Harold Bloom's "anxiety of influence" theory of literature. Against his theory of how (male) writers enact struggles with their literary fathers in order to create, Gubar and Gilbert posit an "anxiety of authorship" to describe what happens to women writers. They speak of "dis-ease" and "infection in the sentence" as the literary manifestations of female anxiety. This is a piercingly articulate chapter, provocative and hearty.

Having **The Madwoman in the Attic** at hand is like having a good friend nearby. She is enormously well read, sharp, visionary in what she sees when she reads a book.

You love to talk with her. You thank her for what she shows you; you always come back to her; count on her insights; and you like her enormously.

Margaret Miller (review date 1981)

SOURCE: "Angels and Monsters of Feminist Fiction," in *Virginia Quarterly Review,* Vol. 57, No. 2, Spring, 1981, pp. 358–61.

[*In the following review, Miller contends that in* The Madwoman in the Attic *Gubar and Gilbert are more successful when applying their theories to certain authors, such as Charlotte Bronte, than when they critique George Eliot or Jane Austen.*]

It is unquestionably true that **Madwoman in the Attic** is an ambitious and substantial work of criticism and scholarship. It offers important feminist rereadings of many of the major texts by women writers in the 19th century. In it, Gilbert and Gubar demonstrate an impressive command not only of the primary texts but also of the biographies, letters, juvenilia, and criticism of the writers covered; the range of allusion goes beyond the 19th century to include 17th- and 18th-century literature, as well as myth, fairy tale, psychoanalytic literature, and literary theory. The book provides more than a series of illuminating readings: these readings arise out of a general theory about the problems faced by the female literary subculture in the 19th century and about the techniques which evolved among women writers to deal with these problems.

Gilbert and Gubar begin with the assumption that 19th-century women writers had a different relationship with their literary predecessors than their brothers had. The woman writer, before being able to move on to self-definition, had to struggle with the two "paradigmatic polarities" (p. 76), angel or monster, in terms of which she was defined by male writers and which were so alien to her sense of herself as a woman and as a writer. In creating versions of the self in her fiction, therefore, with the help of her female precursors she radically revised those conventions. Monsters appear, yes, but they are madwomen, burning down the patriarchal mansion. Angels show up as well, but strangely afflicted with anorexia, agoraphobia, claustrophobia, aphasia, and amnesia. Moreover, the angel and the monster seem strangely related, the madwoman acting out the subversive impulses of the good heroine and, as the authors would have it, of her creator. Further, since those impulses cannot be expressed directly by any woman who wants the approval of her culture, she writes conventional novels or poetry with concealed levels of meaning, "palimpsestic" works "whose surface designs conceal or obscure deeper, less accessible (and less socially acceptable) levels of meaning" (p. 73).

Given their interest in male predecessors, it is not surprising that a section of the book is concerned with that great

Nobodaddy among male writers, Milton. The authors' expressed concern with Milton is in his effect on creative women, not in what he may have intended by his portrayal of females (both Eve and Sin) in *Paradise Lost*. Nevertheless, that distinction is lost when the authors offer their feminist reading of the epic rather than focusing on the articulated distress of women writers from Wollstonecraft on about his portrayal of Eve. This reading of Milton forms the background for the analysis of two other works which they consider responses to *Paradise Lost: Frankenstein*, which articulates Shelley's acquiescence in Milton's cosmology, and *Wuthering Heights*, an attempt to rewrite the epic "*so as to make it a more accurate mirror of female experience*" (p. 220; italics theirs). The choice of *Frankenstein* seems reasonable enough, given the prominent references to Milton in that book, and their reading is a valuable extension of the work done recently by Ellen Moers and others to see it as a text written by a woman. *Wuthering Heights* seems at first an irritatingly eccentric choice, as they themselves admit; despite the weakness of the connection, however, their focus on the heaven/hell imagery in the book turns out to be extremely fruitful.

This book originated from work Gilbert and Gubar did on Charlotte Brontë, on whom each of them has previously published articles. Brontë, more than any other novelist in the 19th century, has received attention from feminist critics, primarily because of the passionate rebelliousness that has so disturbed critics as different as Miss Rigby and Virginia Woolf. The section on Brontë is the strongest in the book: without being redundant, they build on recent feminist perceptions about her work, which in Brontë's case have surely provided explanations of puzzling or disturbing elements that have been ignored by conventional criticism. The endings of her novels are a primary focus; when a novel like *Shirley* concludes with the prospective bridegroom saying that his bride "gnaws her chain," a radical dissatisfaction with the conventional happy ending and with what marriage meant in reality to women might reasonably be inferred. Their discussion of the significance of Bertha Mason in *Jane Eyre* (who provided the title for their book) is particularly good: they see her as the embodiment of Jane's anger, which far more than her sexuality disturbed Victorian critics. Their treatment of *Villette* focuses on the even more oblique ways in which Lucy's repressed rage at being perhaps the most deprived heroine in English fiction is displayed: through imagery, through the unreliable narration, through her use of other female characters—nuns, young girls, witches—to represent aspects of her self, and so on.

The chapters devoted to the more conservative Jane Austen and George Eliot are not as convincing as the one on Brontë. In them, despite many good insights, we see some of the characteristic weaknesses of the book, which surface occasionally in the best chapters as well. Here the tendency to focus on minor works as keys to the major fiction becomes irritating: Eliot's "Lifted Veil" is given a strained reading and assigned too much importance in indicating characteristic attitudes in Eliot's major fiction.

Gilbert and Gubar share with some other modern feminist critics a tendency to regard female characters as victims, no matter how clearly the writer places them in an unfavorable light. Both Austen and Eliot give short shrift to female characters who do not manage to live according to a rigorous moral code in spite of the evident restrictions on their lives and training, and very few readers perceive, as Gilbert and Gubar do, any secret sympathy from these writers for characters like Mrs. Norris in *Mansfield Park* or Rosamond in *Middlemarch*. The authors also have a tendency to assert points that are then treated as proven or are supported by muddled reasoning: in the Austen section, for instance, the assertion that bitchy women "enact impulses that make them doubles not only for the heroines but for their author as well" (p. 170) seems more counterintuitive than it does with Brontë and surely calls for some cogent defense. Their case is by its very nature hard to prove—secret, oblique meanings in a text are harder to argue for convincingly than obvious ones—but the jaggedness of Brontë's fictional surface gives them a better toehold than the smooth, authoritative polish of Eliot's and, especially, Austen's.

The book concludes with a section on Emily Dickinson, nicely prepared for by a discussion of several English poets, most notably Elizabeth Barrett Browning and Christina Rossetti. In Dickinson they see the conflicts and symbols they have been tracing embodied not just in her poetry but also in her life. Emily Dickinson the angel, dressed in white; Emily Dickinson the madwoman, the agoraphobic afraid to leave her father's house: it is an intriguing view and provides us with a thread by which to find our way through the poetry of that very puzzling artist.

Madwoman in the Attic is probably the most ambitious and comprehensive book of feminist literary criticism yet written, and as such it is to be reckoned with. It provides us with a fresh look at the major female texts of the 19th century, and if it occasionally seems wrong-headed, it is never inconsequential. No one interested in the 19th century or in women writers can afford to overlook it.

Penny Boumelha (review date August 1982)

SOURCE: A review of *The Madwoman in the Attic*, in *Review of English Studies*, Vol. 33, No. 131, August, 1982, pp. 345–47.

[*In the following excerpt, Boumelha stresses Harold Bloom's methodological influence on* The Madwoman in the Attic.]

. . . [In *The Madwoman in the Attic*,] Gilbert and Gubar take their methodological point of departure from Harold Bloom's parables of the anxiety of influence—a theory which has on occasion been attacked as patriarchal, but which they commend for making central and explicit the male dominance of Western literary history that is naturalized and allowed to remain unspoken in most other accounts. ***The Madwoman in the Attic*** attempts to supplement that theoretical work with an account of the traditions of women's writing, traditions established as such writing struggles to make a space for itself within (or beside) Bloom's Oedipal scenario of the strong male poets. The woman writer, they argue, must confront not only the anxiety of influence which she shares with the male writer, but also a primary and potentially crippling 'anxiety of authorship', as she seeks among the works of her female precursors the enabling legitimation of her own act of defiance. Faced with the choice between becoming a 'lady writer' (with all the trivialization that that condescending and circumscribing phrase implies) or a male mimic, she enters through her texts into a dialogue with those precursors, from which she learns to seek out strategies for the subversion of the patriarchal traditions.

After a theoretical exposition, the larger part of ***The Madwoman in the Attic*** is given over to a detailed examination of that dialogue and those strategies. Gilbert and Gubar persuasively demonstrate elements of a conscious tradition within women's writing by drawing out recurrent narrative paradigms (such as the Fall), female figures (like Snow White or Lilith), and images (among them the activities of sewing and mirroring, and the 'women's diseases' of anorexia and agoraphobia). To set against this tradition, they examine some ways in which women's fictions have undermined the authoritative male texts. Jane Austen's novels are made to reveal how parody and silence can subvert what appears to be the most submissively conventional of structures; while in Charlotte Brontë's fiction, a self-division verging on self-hatred brings forth the image of Bertha Mason which gives Gilbert and Gubar their title, and which exemplifies the projection of the destructive potentialities of sexuality, rage, and revenge on to a demonic *alter ego*; George Eliot, on the other hand, adopts a masculine persona which enables her to enforce retributive narrative resolutions upon the rebellious impulses that threaten the coherence of her texts. Other, and rather less satisfactory, chapters chart the relation of Mary Shelley and Emily Brontë to the Miltonic version of Eden and the Fall, and examine the work of nineteenth-century women poets.

Bloom is very evidently the precursor of this book, in the preference for visionary authors and Gothic sub-texts, in the serious (solemn?) use of puns and metaphor, and in the occasionally questionable use of biographical material. Though it is over-long and sometimes over-detailed, ***The Madwoman in the Attic*** is a remarkable and valuable examination of the significance and modulations of gender as an ideological determination of women's writing. Sometimes, however, the concentration on gender has the effect of confining women authors in a prison of sex which seems to be outside all other social forces, and the result can be reductive. After all, Eliot's difficult and unstable migration between the roles of Romantic visionary and Victorian sage, for example, cannot wholly be ascribed to the subversion of her masculine persona by an inescapable aware-

ness of her own womanhood. To present it as such is to elide all those other ideological determinants—such as the conflict between Evangelical Christianity and moralizing rationalism—that enter into the conjuncture of her texts. . . .

David Porter (essay date March 1984)

SOURCE: "Dickinson's Readers," in *New England Quarterly*, Vol. 57, No. 1, March, 1984, pp. 106–10.

[*In the following excerpt, Porter discusses* The Madwoman in the Attic *in an essay reviewing feminist reading strategies used to interpret Emily Dickinson's poetry.*]

Seven recent studies of Emily Dickinson seek the crucial thing that is missing from her life and work: a center that will finally arrest the freeplay of inference about the poet's reclusive existence and her large aggregation of brief poems. All but two of these critical works approach Dickinson from an acute feminist angle. The remaining two attempt to find coherence in the manuscript books that the poet put together, systematically and then sporadically, over a period of twenty years, beginning when she was twenty-seven. The persistence of this itch to make sense of Dickinson inevitably raises a basic question about critical validation: how many myths and countermyths can the poet, who called herself a "backwoodsman," inhabit simultaneously?

Feminist criticism, asserting as its first principle that sexual identity and art are inseparable, is essentially biographical and socially based. Its central *topos* for the nineteenth century is a patriarchal social structure against which women writers, by overt or covert means, rebelled. The critical objective is to find the terms by which that agenda of subversion, the "subtext," was encoded in the writing and the hierarchy of power, with its inequality of gender relationships, betrayed. As a basic strategy, feminist criticism tends to split off the writer's motivation from the rest of the literary experience and to overlook what is idiosyncratic as expression and fortuitous as art.

But a poem is two things at the same instant: something said and something made. The making bears on what it is that can be said, and this transaction probably cannot be overlooked if literary criticism is to remain not only critical but literary. Thus feminist criticism, as its single most significant and welcome challenge, has sharpened the need for new thinking about the central concern of poetics, that is, what makes a verbal message a work of art.

The feminist ideology as it applies to Emily Dickinson holds that she withdrew into her father's house deliberately to do her writing and to reject the society that stifled her because she was a woman and because she wrote. Selections from her poems as well as passages from the letters are used to make an autobiographical account. Such critical purposefulness sometimes necessitates an uncritical view of the poems so as to include the most banal of them. Out of this program, a drama emerges in which Dickinson, by one strategy or another, from poor syntax to feigned madness, sustained herself.

That view of self-dramatization links the essays collected in Suzanne Juhasz's *Feminist Critics Read Emily Dickinson*. The premise, as outlined in Juhasz's introduction, is that the poet's art "is an extension and manifestation of her specific biographical, psychological, cultural situation" and that "Dickinson's actions make sense." The essays range, with varying perceptiveness, over the poet's metaphorical transformations, her themes of masculinity, love, and childhood, and her language.

Adalaide Morris's even-handed essay on Dickinson's love for men and for women, based on the three "Master" letters and similar poems and the poems and notes she sent to her sister-in-law Susan, shows "the extravagance of Dickinson's commitments" and concludes that "she hesitated to choose any one habit of loving." The unsustainable assumption, however, is that the 276 poems sent to Susan were actually written for her. Barbara A.C. Mossberg argues too narrowly that the poet was "a career child" whose "obsessive use of the little girl persona" reflects "the lack of society's esteem for and encouragement of her mental abilities." In a metaphorical *tour de force*, Sandra M. Gilbert, presenting a variation on her portrait of Dickinson in *The Madwoman in the Attic* (coauthored with Susan Gubar), asserts that the poet by "a process of self-mythologizing" managed to "recreate herself-and-her-life as a single, emblematic text" in which she exploited "the constraints of nineteenth-century womanhood so as to transform and transcend them." Evidently outperforming Oscar Wilde, the poet put her creative genius into her life as well as her art. Gilbert's metaphors of transformation abound; for example, she regards Dickinson's white dress first as "an empty page on which in invisible ink this theatrical poet quite consciously wrote a letter to the world" and then, because of its colorless color, as similar to Melville's Moby-Dick.

Three essays examine Dickinson's language. Joanne Feit Diehl skillfully illuminates the poet's originality, seeing her setting her linguistic complexities against the world's "barrenness of circumstance." Diehl's generalization concerning "misunderstanding" by those Dickinson "hoped would recognize and nurture her genius," however, is incorrect in view of our knowledge of the importunities over the years of editors, Helen Hunt Jackson, and others. Margaret Homans, in the most sophisticated of the essays, proposes that Dickinson developed a new kind of expression that breaks down the gender hierarchy embedded in language. In arguing that the poet initiated a "critique of the dualistic structure of language and of metaphor," that is, that she upset rhetorical habits responsible for hierarchization, Homans has made Dickinson, of all dread things, a deconstructionist! Cristanne Miller's essay presents a similar, simplified argument that Dickinson "manifests her (female) poetic freedom in undermining traditional patterns of language." A typical disruption is said to occur in the phrase "How many times these low feet staggered," where the poet, Miller states unconvincingly, means "flaming poetic feet" that stagger thought.

The best written of the essays is by Joanne A. Dobson, who seeks to define "that elusive masculine form" that haunts the poetry and, like Albert Gelpi in his essay in *Shakespeare's Sisters*, concludes that it is "an enduring archetype lodged deep within her psychic makeup," a "dimly perceived 'masculine' self . . . that had long been deprived in the 'real' world of recognition and expression." Karl Keller's breezy essay entitled "Notes on Sleeping with Emily Dickinson" asserts in a campy reflection of the Gilbert thesis that Dickinson's life "was show biz." Deliberately outrageous, he explains that there are "those who are in on her, and there are those who aren't" and asks "Are there those genders who get her code . . . and those genders who don't?" Keller is good on Dickinson's cryptic nature, but he misses the syllabic constraint in her lines that made her muddle her language, and he chooses to misread, for example, a simple poem about flowers as Dickinson's idea about the mixed pleasures of sleeping with a man. One wonders what he might have done with the line "Make this Bed with Awe" had he known that this was her nickname for her brother Austin!

In the background of the Juhasz essays is the assertive theatrical parable from Gilbert and Gubar's *The Madwoman in the Attic* that transforms the poet's life into fiction. The book's vast premise is that nineteenth-century women writers in England and America "almost obsessively create characters who enact their own, covert authorial anger." Adopting Virginia Woolf (in particular her story of Judith Shakespeare, the mythic sister of William) and a simplified Harold Bloom as presiding spirits, Gilbert and Gubar construct the myth into which Dickinson is fitted: "while the woman novelist may evade . . . her authorial anxieties by writing *about* madwomen and other demonic doubles . . . the woman poet must literally *become* a madwoman." Dickinson's "inner novel" shows her, always dressed in white, enacting a little maid, a fierce virgin, a nun, a bride, a madwoman, a dead woman, an empress, and a gnome. "Dickinson's life itself," they write, "became a kind of novel or narrative poem" in which, aided by costumes, she acted out "her anxieties about her art and her anger at female subordination."

The strategy of exposition depends often on rhetorical sleight of hand—one thing "suggests" another, certain actions "for all practical purposes" become others—as in the phrase "in some sense," which attempts to tie down a balloon of generalization: "indeed, almost all nineteenth-century women were in some sense imprisoned in men's houses." There is more metaphorical freeplay: "In a sense," the authors write, "we might say that as a private spider artist Dickinson employs her yarn of pearl to resolve her quarrelsomely fragmented public selves—the nun and the gnome, the virgin and the empress—into a single woman pearly white." Of Dickinson's disclaimer that her poems were confessional, the authors blur the distinction the poet made between fiction and reality: "Even if the poet's 'I' . . . is a 'supposed person,' the intensity of her dangerous impersonation of this creature may cause her to take her own metaphors literally, enact her themes herself."

Imaginative in its staging, *The Madwoman in the Attic* succeeds by its stolidly thematic method in transforming each woman writer into an ideological model enacting "the paradigmatic female story," a portrayal of women writers' "raging desire to escape male houses and male texts. . . ."

Phyllis Rose (essay date August 1985)

SOURCE: "Women Writers and Feminist Critics," in *Atlantic*, Vol. 256, No. 2, August, 1985, pp. 88–91.

[*In the following essay, Rose praises Gubar and Gilbert's literary analyses in* The Norton Anthology of Literature by Women, *but is concerned about the effect of establishing a female literary canonon on future women writers.*]

At more than 2,000 pages and over two pounds, [*The Norton Anthology of Literature by Women*] is not in any sense to be taken lightly. Intended as a textbook for courses in women's literature, it is likely to be widely used, because of the prestige of its editors, Sandra M. Gilbert and Susan Gubar, in the field of women's studies, and because of the prestige of the Norton anthology series in university literature departments. Our daughters and granddaughters will lug this book home on vacations from college. With what baggage will it freight their minds?

Happily, it should convince them that writing is not an activity alien to women. From Julian of Norwich and Margery Kempe in the Middle Ages to Alice Walker and Leslie Marmon Silko, women have produced a large and varied body of writing in English. This anthology includes close to a hundred and fifty authors, from many countries. The numbers are smaller the further back one goes, but the surprises are greater. In the fifteenth century Margery Kempe wrote about being tempted to commit adultery by a man who refused her when she consented. In the seventeenth century Aphra Behn wrote a poem about male impotence, called "The Disappointment." It's also good to know that women can write dazzlingly about nothing at all—like the dying Alice James, who described the seductive moment when she felt herself "floated for the first time into the deep sea of divine *cessation.*"

The burden that Gilbert and Gubar have imposed on women of the future is the burden of a tradition—a nurturant tradition. It used to be that women writers, working in silence, exile, and cunning, sought out other women writers to admire. Virginia Woolf wrote about Dorothy Wordsworth and Christina Rossetti, among others, and these essays helped her "self-definition as a woman writer," Gilbert and Gubar say. "For if women *had* written, and

written successfully, women *could* write." To Virginia Woolf and her successors, the female literary past was, according to Gilbert and Gubar, "empowering rather than intimidating." Now that the female literary past has been enshrined in this gigantic anthology, the observation that it has been empowering in the past becomes a moral imperative for the future. Finding and loving our literary ancestors is no longer a secret pleasure and private solace but a filial duty.

In editorial comments throughout the book Gilbert and Gubar present a female tradition of support and encouragement, a literature "empowered by female community." Eudora Welty's debt to Katherine Anne Porter is noted, as is Elizabeth Bishop's loyalty to her "major female literary mentor," Marianne Moore. Not for women is the kind of literary past Harold Bloom describes, which creates anxiety and provokes rebellion. Not for women is a literary history filled with conflict and marked by aggressive self-definition. Whereas little boys, even wimpy little boy writers, are allowed to hate their literary fathers and have their rebellions, little girls, even rebellious little girl writers, are expected to be good and love their literary mothers.

This anthology takes the model of a women's therapy group and extends it over time and space to art: women join hands across the ages to enhance their self-definition as women writers and to help one another create. Some writers don't want to belong to such a group. Because the editors have been so inclusive, because they apologize for having been "unable to represent such increasingly self-aware movements as those currently being pioneered by Chicanas and Italian-American women," one wonders at their omissions. A few I noticed among contemporary writers (of whom sixty-one are included): Ann Beattie, Anne Tyler, Joan Didion, Susan Sontag, Renata Adler, Annie Dillard, Cynthia Ozick. The suspicion arises that at least one or two of these individual talents declined to make one with The Tradition in English. In her lifetime, as Gilbert and Gubar tell us, Elizabeth Bishop refused to let her work be included in collections of women's writings. Her executor allows it now.

Why might a woman writer prefer not to be a Woman Writer? Perhaps for the same reason a frog dislikes to be used as a demonstration of the nervous system. It's afraid that might be all there is to life. A tension, a potential conflict, exists between women writers who sometimes do not want to be thought of as Women Writers or, indeed, even as women, and feminist literary critics who need them to be their material. The conflict of interest is, I think, insufficiently acknowledged. The male tradition, which has never assumed that writers, editors, and critics all have a common interest simply on the grounds of gender, seems to me in this case at any rate the more humane.

"Literature by women" is in fact a controversial category, not self-evidently valid like "English literature" or "American literature." Who could imagine refusing to be included in *The Norton Anthology of English Literature*? Who, on the other hand, could take seriously a *Norton Anthology of Literature by Men*? The editors dodge this important issue and in doing so render the anthology covertly polemical.

The more feminist the writers, the more comfortable the editors seem to feel about including them. Susan Griffin, represented by one poem, is praised for being "consistently productive and persistently feminist in her writing," whereas excuses must be made for Denise Levertov: "Though she does not define herself as a feminist, her poetry frequently expresses a distinctively female perspective on the world, celebrating the values of nature and nurture." So a hierarchy is established: women who write, Women Writers, who have a distinctively female perspective and celebrate values that Gilbert and Gubar consider female (like nature and nurture), and self-consciously feminist writers. But in that case, where are the important feminist nonfiction writers of recent times? Where are Betty Friedan, Susan Brownmiller, Germaine Greer, Gloria Steinem? The book is too political for a good anthology of literature and yet it is not an anthology of feminist writings. Despite the editors' conviction that the texts they've included, "at the very least, suggest the contours of the canon into which readers will be able to assimilate the works of many other women authors," the grounds for their choices are unclear.

Certainly this is a democratic anthology—truly great writers get little more representation that the merely interesting. It is best read as a collection of works about women's experience rather than as a collection of great works by women. Fair enough. Why shouldn't content occasionally be allowed to take precedence over form? The emphasis on female perspective leads to the inclusion of some wonderful pieces—for example, Ursula Le Guin's "Sur," a story about an imaginary expedition to the South Pole in 1909 by a group of South American women who think, "If Captain Scott can do it, why can't we?" They make it to the pole but find the event anticlimactic. It's a delightful parable about the female preference for affiliation over achievement. And there's the rub. The story has been selected to make a point about female nature. So has story after story, poem after poem. Occasionally, an effect other than that of didacticism is produced. An excerpt from Anaïs Nin's diary about the attraction between her and June Miller overcomes the deadly pointedness of the anthology. Presumably, the passage has been selected to illustrate erotic attraction between women, but the passage wins. It *is* erotic.

True, if you want the red-hot experience of literature, you do not go to a Norton Anthology. It is a teaching tool, not to be faulted for not being Palgrave's *Golden Treasury*. Still, the amount of apparatus, as opposed to art, in this volume is appalling. The literature scarcely has a chance. The editors seem to pick the shortest piece by each writer and then engulf it in a critical essay that leaves no question of how you should respond. Isak Dinesen is represented by "The Blank Page," perhaps the briefest story she wrote. Jean Rhys, a great story-writer, is given only two

pages to prove herself, and barely can. One story serves to represent—or misrepresent—Eudora Welty, Tillie Olsen, Carson McCullers, Muriel Spark, Doris Lessing, Willa Cather, Sarah Orne Jewett, and Grace Paley, among others. So you come to depend on the critical essay. How would you know that Dorothy Parker was funny if the editors didn't tell you so, and didn't quote, in the headnote, Parker's quip "Brevity is the soul of Lingerie"? You'd never know it on the basis of her story "You Were Perfectly Fine," one of her most mannered and dated—but one of her shortest.

Sometimes the literature seems positively to exist so that Gilbert and Gubar may write about its author. Alice Dunbar-Nelson is represented by a twenty-one-line poem and discussed in a considerably longer essay, which tells about her work in behalf of civil rights and world peace (black women are excused from the insistent pressure to join hands with other women—questions of race are allowed to take precedence over those of gender) and also about her marriages to the poet Paul Laurence Dunbar and then to the publisher of the *Wilmington Advocate*.

Indeed, *The Norton Anthology of Literature by Women* is marked by a courtesy to husbands that we never see toward wives in predominantly male anthologies. Joyce Carol Oates, we are told, is married to "the scholar Raymond Smith." Ursula Le Guin met her husband, "the historian Charles A. Le Guin," when she was studying in Paris on a Fulbright. Margaret Drabble married an actor and began writing backstage, when she was pregnant. The domestic details are welcome, of course, as gossip always is, and in some ways useful. They suggest a context of domesticity for women's writing in which every act of creativity becomes a miracle. But sometimes the notations are ludicrous: "The daughter of Isidore and Nan Gordimer, she attended . . ." And sometimes they are misleading: "The mother of two children, Paley captures . . ." Would anyone think of saying, "The father of ten children, Dickens captures . . ."? It privileges experience over art (as does this entire anthology), suggesting that there is a necessary connection between the experience of mothering and the ability to render it in art.

Gigantism afflicts new fields; modesty comes with endurance. *The Norton Anthology of Literature by Women* cannot resist, in its historical introductions, presenting much of human history anew. The rule seems to be that no proper name can go unexplained; the assumption, that the reader knows nothing and must learn all from this anthology. Thus, on one page we have "the poet-suffragist Alice Meynell," "the colonial apologist Rudyard Kipling," the "activist-feminist writers Charlotte Perkins Gilman and Crystal Eastman," and "the Viennese psychoanalyst Sigmund Freud (1856–1939)." Some selections seem to exist to be footnoted, so that essential information may be perpetuated. One of these is Dorothy Parker's poem "Song of One of the Girls," which names many great women in history and permits explanations like "Sappho was a Greek lyric poet of the seventh century B.C." and "Madame Récamier (1777–1849) was a French beauty and friend of Madame de Staël." It is the kind of thing you give to girls to make them proud of being female, like The Great Women of History Cut-Out Book.

Mind-numbing generalizations are endemic to this sort of anthology. They seem more egregious here, because *The Norton Anthology of Literature by Women* might have limited itself. Instead, in order to talk about the flowering of women's literature in the twentieth century, the editors feel they must recount the rise to power of "Benito Mussolini, *Il Duce* ('the leader')" and of "Adolph Hitler, the so-called *Fuehrer* ('leader')." We must know that bomber pilots in the Second World War were more alienated from their victims than those in the First World War. We must know about DNA and ICBMs as well as IUDs.

This kind of writing generates its own connections. American writers went to Paris in the twenties not because it was cheap to live there but "because the new availability and speed of steamships, railroads, and motorcars had made longrange travel easy." Blacks, Chicanos, Puerto Ricans, "and other disadvantaged groups" move into the decaying cities of America. Members of the white middle class sit in the suburbs watching *Ozzie and Harriet*. They develop an ethic of togetherness, maturity, and adjustment. The Southern Gothic writers come along to depict immaturity and perversity. Movements sweep across the pages in waves of abstraction. Everything fits. But it has been an effort. Sometimes one's heart goes out to the editors, who have taken on so much. "Charting the movements of twentieth-century writers, painters, and musicians," they confess, "can be dizzying." Sometimes one's heart goes out to the student who must stay awake through prose like this: "To complicate matters further, the new researches of anthropologists and archeologists led to a kind of cultural relativism that fostered skepticism about the nature of human society itself." It seems a lot to ask of the reader, to encompass both the great sweep of twentieth-century history and the marital history of Alice Dunbar-Nelson.

The critical introductions in *The Norton Anthology of Literature by Women* are better—indeed, they are awesome—when they address themselves more narrowly to women's literature and women in literature. The editors provide a brilliant interpretation of *Frankenstein*, in which both Frankenstein the creator and his creation, the lonely outcast monster, are seen as images of female experience. They are excellent at describing the female angle in various writers' work—Le Guin's anthropological interest in gender, Muriel Spark's interest in communities of women. They refreshingly bring together Daisy Buchanan and Brett Ashley as flappers, and see the flapper as an image of the destructive power of women, an expression of male fear. They provide a welcome account of fifties male writing from a female point of view, an account that speculates that Second World War pinups led to a fetishizing of female body parts in the writing of Henry Miller. They zero in with deadly accuracy on male literary sexism, both that of writers, like Norman Mailer, who commit acts of ag-

gression against their female characters and that of critics like William Gass, who criticizes women writers for lacking "that blood congested genital drive which energizes every great style."

Read as a polemic, *The Norton Anthology of Literature by Women* constitutes the best extended piece of writing there is on literature by and about women. Gilbert and Gubar have amassed more information about women writers than exists in any other document. They have unlocked what Carolyn Kizer calls "the world's best-kept secret:/ Merely the private lives of one-half of humanity." For finding lines like that, one should be grateful to them. Along with much that is sweet and much that is useful, however, they have thrust into the book bags of the future the ambivalent gift of a female tradition wrapped in a seventies-style political sentimentality that insists we should love one another because we are all in it together. And as an anthology of literature, this one weighs on the spirit like a two-pound balloon.

Laura Shapiro with Sandra Gilbert and Susan Gubar (interview date January 1986)

SOURCE: "Gilbert and Gubar," in *Ms. Magazine,* Vol. 14, No. 7, January, 1986, p. 59.

[*In the following interview by Shapiro, Gubar and Gilbert discuss their work together, and the strategies they used in compiling* The Norton Anthology of Literature by Women.]

Sandra Gilbert and Susan Gubar met in an elevator 13 years ago, and by the time it arrived at the fourth floor, an extraordinary partnership had gotten off the ground as well. Gilbert, professor of English at Princeton, and Gubar, professor of English at Indiana University, have collaborated on some of the most invigorating work to date in a field they helped to establish: the study of literature by women. Their first book, *The Madwoman in the Attic* (1979), examined the means and metaphors by which women writers in the 19th century defied what Emily Dickinson called "the House Without the Door," the edifice of personal and artistic constraint built up around literary women. Le Anne Schreiber, writing in *The New York Times Book Review*, said Gilbert and Gubar had offered "the first persuasive case for the existence of a distinctly female imagination."

But it's their second book, published last spring, that seems destined to turn "Gilbert and Gubar" into campus shorthand all over the country. To that brick-and-board bookshelf that holds the Norton Anthologies of English and American Literature in thousands of dormitory rooms, a new volume has been added: *The Norton Anthology of Literature by Women*. A monumental work spanning six centuries and all the English-speaking countries, the newest Norton is more than a treasure trove: it constitutes a historic first step toward redefining the canon of great literature. With this anthology, Gilbert and Gubar have not only given voice to an amazing range of authors, but enabled us to hear those individual voices as part of a female tradition, even as we recognize the stylistic or thematic traditions they may share with men.

These days Gilbert and Gubar are working on a sequel to *The Madwoman in the Attic,* to be titled *No Man's Land: The Place of the Woman Writer in the Twentieth-Century*. With jobs and families keeping them half a continent apart, they depend on travel and telephone to get much of their work accomplished; and when they're together, judging from this interview, they do a lot of laughing and shouting and interrupting each other. They also listen to each other, so intently you'd think one had never heard the other speak her mind before. Perhaps this—and a tremendous appreciation for each other's jokes—keeps their collaboration one of the healthiest and most productive imaginable.

[*Shapiro:*] *How did the two of you get together?*

[Gubar:] We were asked to team-teach—

[Gilbert:] We weren't *asked* to team-teach—

[Gubar:] We—

[Gilbert:] Once upon a time, in 1973, I got into an elevator in Ballantine Hall at Indiana University—

[Gubar:] And I was already in the elevator—

[Gilbert:] Going to the fourth floor. And I said, you must be Susan Gubar. Because we had both just been hired. So we got to know each other, we spent a lot of time—

[Gubar:] Complaining about the fact that the phone never rang unless it was long distance.

[Gilbert:] So we decided to call each other.

[Gubar:] So we got together, and we began talking.

[Gilbert:] It was very strange. I worked in modern British literature, and I used to go around saying, in what I thought was a very feminist way, that because I was a woman didn't mean I would have to work on women. In fact I would show my feminist strength and independence by working on men, which was obviously a superior thing to do. But something was happening to me. Just before I got the job at Indiana, I was working on a book about death and I started reading about Emily Brontë. And I found that I really was just interested in the Brontës. Susan in the meantime was also interested in the Brontës. You were working on *Villette*—

[Gubar:] But before that I was teaching 18th-century literature, which is what I had been trained in, and I was pregnant. I was teaching Swift and Pope. And I remember that as I was getting larger in the pregnancy, the course started to revolve around images of monstrous women in

Pope and Swift. I was seeing all these horrible images—nursing mothers and monstrous women, stupid, fat, horrible madwomen—but I had not understood that there was a connection between my alienation from the literature and my own body.

[Gilbert:] And the other thing that happened was that my youngest daughter, who was then about eight, was reading *Little Women*. So I reread *Little Women*. Then she started reading *Jane Eyre*, and I reread *Jane Eyre* with her, and we used to talk about it. And I started developing all kinds of theories about *Little Women* and *Jane Eyre*. So I think we were both ready for some kind of conversion experience, but we neither of us were conscious of the fact.

[Gubar:] It's not just that we hadn't thought about it, it was that when we went to graduate school [in the sixties] and when we went to conferences later, and when we were hired, there was no such category as women's literature or feminist criticism. So when we started teaching our course, which was called *"The Madwoman in the Attic,"* we didn't know where we were going.

[Gilbert:] We had read Mary Shelley and Emily Dickinson and Virginia Woolf and Charlotte Brontë, but we had never read them all together like this. So we had to call each other up on the phone every night and scream for hours.

[Gubar:] "Another image of enclosure and escape!" "Another madwoman!"

[Gilbert:] We were just totally overwhelmed.

Was that when you wrote **The Madwoman in the Attic***?*

[Gubar:] We started to work on the book in 1975, exactly when Sandra went to Davis [University of California], and we were physically separated by miles and miles of the continent.

[Gilbert:] And that's when it began—the phone bills and the mail, the planes.

How did you divide up the work?

[Gubar:] It was clear that the poets were for Sandra. She's a poet and she was getting the poets. Austen I had always loved, so I got Jane Austen.

[Gilbert:] I didn't feel much of an affinity for George Eliot, and she liked George Eliot a lot better, so she was going to get George Eliot. Interestingly, that's where our differences were productive, because we knew we were going to have to sit down and work out a mutually agreeable stance toward the problem of George Eliot.

[Gubar:] With the Brontës, it was obvious that you were going to get *Wuthering Heights*. You had always loved the book and taught it, and I had always been interested in *Villette*.

[Gilbert:] And I got *Frankenstein*, which was nice.

Are your writing styles similar?

[Gubar:] Oh, not at all. We have horrible disagreements about "moreovers"—

[Gilbert:] And "howevers," and I will not say who is on which side of that.

[Gubar:] One person very much likes to sprinkle transitionary words, and the other person likes to take them out. There are a lot of disagreements, but usually we feel that they go somewhere, they make the prose more interesting.

[Gilbert:] Also, increasingly in recent years we do write together very much more than we used to. In working on the sequel to **Madwoman,** there are something like five enormous chapters in the opening sections, and we've been writing every word together.

You mean one of you sits at the typewriter and the other leans over her shoulder?

[Gilbert:] We each have a notebook, and we both write the same words in the notebook. We sit there with our notebooks, and we—

[Gubar:] And we talk.

[Gilbert:] We have done a little bit of working on a word processor with one of us typing but it's—

[Gubar:] It's not as easy to write.

[Gilbert:] Sometimes it helps, if we get blocked. But then, sometimes we get blocked at the word processor and we go back to the notebook, and sit by the fire, and have a drink, and write in our notebooks.

Do you ever feel you're losing your separate intellectual identities?

[Gilbert:] I think we have separate ideas. Don't you think so?

[Gubar:] Yes, I think we do. Sometimes there is a desire to go and give a paper on your own, that does remind you that you are a separate intellect. And I think we try very hard to keep that up. Most of the articles that we publish are separately written.

[Gilbert:] And we can distinguish between ideas that we think are ours—this is *our* position on such-and-such, and it's usually been very carefully worked out together—and something *I* am writing.

Whose idea was it to have an anthology of literature by women—yours or Norton's?

[Gubar:] We proposed it. They wanted to do some "market research"—whether or not there would be a long-range textbook use, how many courses there are in women's studies, how many courses in women's literature—and they did some of that before they gave us a contract.

Did Norton give you any special directives on style or content?

[Gubar:] We very much decided to go to Norton for the book and do it as a Norton anthology, in Nortonian style, with the critical apparatus and the headnotes and all. That was our decision, because we felt it would be a way of legitimizing women's literature.

[Gilbert:] The Nortons *are* the standard anthologies, and to call the book the **Norton Anthology of Literature by Women** is to perform a sort of canonizing or certifying gesture.

What was it like to put together that huge volume?

[Gilbert:] It was an enormous amount of work in rather a short time—I think we took three years on the project. We went through hundreds and hundreds of books, everywhere we went we were schlepping enormous boxes of books, and we would read through the complete works of these people. Some of it was very hard to find; we could only get it in rare book rooms. And we'd go through bibliographies, magazines—we found the Margaret Drabble story in a magazine; it had never been published in book form. And people would tell us about things—that was wonderful, we were very grateful to them.

[Gubar:] The secretarial assistant to our editor at Norton was very interested in Canadian literature, and she made us a list, which included the poems by Margaret Atwood we ended up using. They were very recent, and we hadn't come across them. She also turned us on to Alice Munro. And the wives of our colleagues would give us ideas. People who had done a great deal of work on a particular figure would just put books in the mail for us.

[Gilbert:] We took great pleasure and delight in choosing some people. Jane Lead was a wonderful 17th-century mystic—there are only about four volumes of her work available in the whole country, so it was a particular pleasure to publish some of it. And Rebecca Cox Jackson—she came to our attention late, in an essay by Alice Walker. We were constantly revising and negotiating, because there are women writers whose works are just now being excavated.

[Gubar:] Sandra was lecturing at Oberlin, and two people there got in touch with her. They had discovered Elizabeth Drew Stoddard, a 19th-century short story writer whose work was almost unknown. So she got in very late—we just lucked out. Another time, I was reading an essay about Lorraine Hansberry by Adrienne Rich and she mentioned two feminist essays Hansberry had written, before there was any talk of feminism. I contacted her literary executor, and we came up with this selection. Of course she's never thought of in these terms—everyone thinks of *A*

Raisin in the Sun—but it's a strong feminist statement, very tongue-in-cheek, called "In Defense of the Equality of Men."

You've been criticized for applying feminist standards rather than literary ones in the selection process.

[Gubar:] We were very aware of the fact that there is a kind of sanctified feminist canon, and that we had to represent those figures who are always taught and who are always looked to; but there is also a canon of, quote, great work, and we had to consider that, too. And we were always thinking about representation from various perspectives—lesbian writers, black women writers, working-class women writers, immigrant women writers. We were also very concerned to include writers like Elizabeth Bishop, who did not place themselves in either a feminist or a female tradition, but who were great writers.

[Gilbert:] Obviously, women are conscious of being women, in the same way that anybody who is in a particular cultural situation is conscious of being in that situation. I mean it would be very odd indeed to have an anthology of American literature in which you didn't include texts by Americans who discussed their American-ness. When Emerson writes "The American Scholar," you put it in an anthology of American literature because it is a statement by a major figure about how he feels as an *American* writer. So naturally there are going to be women who talk about being women, and that's a crucial part of the tradition, but we didn't want to *just* include things like that. I don't think the selection process was politicized. I think that after a while we became conscious of certain themes that seemed to recur, but you would want to do that in any anthology.

[Gubar:] If we had two poems, and one seemed to be more focused on the issue of being a woman, we tended to use it, *if* it was typical of the work. But of course never when it would misrepresent someone. We wouldn't do that at the price of distorting a literary reputation or oeuvre. If Marianne Moore wrote about animals, we were going to choose poems about animals.

[Gilbert:] But besides writing about all the metaphysical questions of men, women really do write about the problems and pleasures of growing up female. We found themes of women's friendships, the effect of reading upon women, the effect of their lack of access to education, and especially what that meant to them as writers. There was the theme of mothers, and mothering, and daughters. And of course there were changes over time—the issue of women's work, for instance, became increasingly important in the 20th century and it wasn't at all in the 18th. The poet Anne Finch called it "the dull manage of a servile house."

One reviewer said the critical apparatus—the introductions and headnotes—outweighed the texts, and that you put too much emphasis on biographical and social detail.

[Gubar:] We try to give a lot more information about the fabric of a woman's life, what it felt like to her, her relationship to her husband, her children—and interestingly, this has been taken as a sort of feminine fall into domestic trivia. Aren't we just as good as men? Why don't we just deal with them as intellectuals, why do we have to descend to these petty domestic little details about marriages and children? Our point would be the exact opposite—why don't we approach male literary history too from these, quote, petty domestic issues, which are so interesting and, after all, shape the way art gets produced?

[Gilbert:] Our task in writing those period introductions was overwhelming. We had to cover both Britain and America, and we had to introduce students to the so-called mainstream literary and social history of the period—that is, the male-dominated history—and then we had to explain how women's lives were affected by or, indeed, influenced that mainstream history We began to see connections between texts and times that we probably had not seen quite so clearly before.

[Gubar:] But I think there's something else going on. When there was no canon, and women writers were not available, we could all agree that this was wrong and that women writers should be studied. Now we're in a stage where we're producing a canon. And there's going to be more disagreement about who should be in, who should be out. I think ultimately it's going to be healthy.

[Gilbert:] But I think there are women critics who would always have felt that you shouldn't define a woman's tradition, that women really are part of the mainstream. There's no question that a number of women writers are afraid that to identify themselves as women writers is somehow trivializing. That in itself shows there are problems for women writers, if to be called a woman writer is to be put down. But as a writer myself, I understand that you don't want somebody telling you that you have to consciously write as part of a certain tradition and that you have to write about certain subjects—your imagination has to feel completely free.

How has the book been received on campuses? What do you think its effect will be?

[Gilbert:] Norton sent out little cards with the desk copies, to ask people what they thought of the book, and all the comment cards that we've gotten back have been absolutely enthusiastic.

[Gubar:] And the letters and notes and newspaper reviews have been fantastic.

[Gilbert:] Courses that really explore women's literary history in depth have not existed before because there has been no book that you could use. We know this is the first time so many genres, so many women, so many periods, and so many countries have been brought together, and we know it's not definitive. It's very preliminary—but it will help us to understand the richness of our literary heritage.

[Gubar:] I agree with Sandra that it's tentative, but having it allows us to trace a historical process that was invisible before. This is a kind of gathering together of voices that will allow us to hear each individual voice in a new way.

[Gilbert:] I hope students will be able to see that the literary history in the mainstream anthologies is not the whole story. Particularly for young women students who are beginning to write themselves, we hope this will be heartening.

[Gubar:] We created the book in part to encourage courses on gender and literature, so that students—both undergraduates and graduates—can begin thinking of literary creativity and history in this new way. But of course we're haunted by the omissions—all the writers we couldn't include because of space limitations.

So you have to look at this canon you've created and think about how, down through the ages, nobody will read all the people you've left out?

[Gilbert:] Well, one way to look at it is not to think about the ages. You think about the second edition.

Denis Donoghue (essay date 10 March 1986)

SOURCE: "A Criticism of One's Own," in *New Republic*, Vol. 194, No. 10, March 10, 1986, pp. 30–4.

[*In the following essay, Donoghue examines several feminist critics, and observes that feminist criticism is often reductionist and politically motivated. Donoghue maintains that* The Norton Anthology of Literature by Women *adversely affects feminist criticism because of Gubar and Gilbert's selection of works in the collection.*]

I have been reading a good deal of feminist criticism and scholarship. Not all of it—I am sure to have missed many books and essays I should have read. But I have made an attempt to see what has been happening in feminist criticism since 1970, when Kate Millett's *Sexual Politics*, the book usually taken as having started the feminist field by provoking sentiments and passions in its favor, was published. The main problem I have encountered is not the multiplicity of books and essays in the field. That is merely a quantitative matter, endemic in every area of scholarship: Who can keep up with anything these days? The difficulty, rather, is to determine what the present context of feeling is.

The Annual Report for 1984 of the American Literature Section of the Modern Language Association, for instance—but is it an "instance," and of what?—includes Annette Kolodny's claim that "in the wake of all the new information about the literary production of women, Blacks, Native Americans, ethnic minorities, and gays and lesbians; and with new ways of analyzing popular fiction, non-canonical genres, and working-class writings, all prior

literary histories are rendered partial, inadequate, and obsolete." In the same report, compiled by Donald Yannella, Professor Marianne DeKoven evidently holds "that women have the same claim as men to having 'invented' modernism in America," and cites as evidence three fictions by women: Charlotte Perkins Gilman's "The Yellow Wallpaper" (1891), Kate Chopin's *The Awakening* (1899), and Gertrude Stein's *The Lives* (1903–6). She also claims that there is "an official version of modernism," as in Hugh Kenner's *A Homemade World*, which defines it (these are DeKoven's words, not Kenner's) as "a revolted flight, by means of the 'fabulously artificed,' Dedalian wings of male technology, from the primary horror of female (pro)creativity." I'm not sure whether these sentiments, which seem wild to me, accurately indicate the context of feminist criticism or some bizarre hyperbole; a real fury in the words, or willed turbulence worked up for the occasion.

But there are some tangible episodes, one of which is especially significant. On April 28, 1985, the novelist Gail Godwin reviewed the new *Norton Anthology of Literature by Women* for the *New York Times Book Review*. Her account of the book was quietly severe. She disapproved of the editors' "stated desire to document and connect female literary experience rather than present a showcase of the most distinguished writing by women in English from Julian of Norwich in the 14th century to the present day." The *Norton Anthology,* she maintained, forced "the individual female talent to lie on the Procrustean fainting-couch of a 'dis-eased' tradition."

Godwin's review angered several well-known feminist critics, including Elaine Showalter, Alicia Ostriker, Carolyn Heilbrun, Nina Auerbach, Myra Jehlen, Nancy K. Miller, and Catharine R. Stimpson. They accused her of denying "the existence of a female literary tradition" (Ostriker). In her reply, Godwin went a step further than her review: she "mourned the authors who were slighted in the *Anthology* by having their most trivial or least representative works selected because these works helped the editors establish a sisterhood of themes and images they felt ran through most women's writing."

It was an interesting moment of telegrams and anger, but the critical issue was not well defined. Godwin made it clear that she wanted to see in a *Norton Anthology of Literature by Women* an ample selection of the best writing in English by women writers, to demonstrate once if not for all that women have written well and continue to write well. The criteria she silently appealed to were those generally accepted in literary criticism; criteria by which it is agreed, for instance, that Yeats's "Among School Children" is a much better poem than his "The Lake Isle of Innisfree." But she failed to make clear that the criteria adopted by the Norton editors in this anthology are not critical at all. They are political and sociological. The literary merit of the items chosen is not a major consideration for the editors. They are concerned to document the range of experience—and the resultant constraints and anxieties—peculiar to women. George Eliot's minor poem "Brother and Sister" was chosen because "it explores the same sibling relationship she had placed at the center of her semi-autobiographical *The Mill on the Floss*." It is evident that "explores" in that sentence suppresses every critical or qualitative consideration; it sets aside the questions of crucial concern to literary criticism in favor of documentary value and thematic relevance.

If literary criticism were to have its way, *The Norton Anthology of Literature by Women* would be a textbook in sociology rather than in literature. But literary criticism has so often failed to define its way, so often failed to know what its way is, that one more failure won't amount to a scandal. It is common practice for courses in literature to roam into considerations of history, nationality, theology, and indeed sociology. Courses on "the English Novel" are rarely confined to a strict account of forms and genres. But teachers keep their consciences reasonably clear by choosing the best novels; or at least the novels that seem to be the best, according to the criteria of critical discrimination. True, these criteria are rarely defined, and teachers often rely upon a conventional or habitual notion of their deliverances. I suppose most teachers have a general sense of critical discrimination, like a passport; they don't carry it around, but they could produce it if they had to.

But the distinctive mark of the *Norton Anthology* is that it does not even pretend to select its material according to the criteria of literary criticism. Just as historians and sociologists choose their documents without reference to literary merit, the Norton editors have assembled documentary evidence to support a case against men—or against the world. The fact that some of the items chosen are also works of literary merit is a coincidence, however congenial. The *Anthology* would make a good textbook in a course in sociology called "Women and Their Fate." It is flagrantly misleading as a selection of literature by women.

It is my understanding that feminist criticism has two agendas. The first is the larger one: it can be found in Jacques Derrida's several polemics culminating in his *Éperons: Les Styles de Nietzsche*; in Luce Irigaray's *Speculum de l'autre femme* (1974) and *Ce Sexe qui n'en est pas un* (1977); and nearer home, in the Derridean essays by Gayatri Chakravorty Spivak and other critics. The agenda says that there is no discourse but masculine discourse, that women are trapped in a syntax that is phallocratic and phallogocentric. As a result, women are condemned either to adopt the masculine discourse that leaves them essentially unexpressed, or to engage in a masquerade by which they mime the masculine syntax and take upon themselves, speciously of course, the signs of presence and power. It is the fate of women, therefore, to gratify their masters. The paradigm of this fate is the faked orgasm.

I allude to this agenda so far as I can understand it. Many feminists would claim that by physiological definition I can't understand it. So I quote a passage from *Ce Sexe qui n'en est pas un* to let Irigaray speak in her own words,

though it is crucial to the agenda that no woman has her own words. I give the passage in English, but the French is to me just as opaque:

> I am a woman. I am a being sexualized as feminine. I am sexualized female. The motivation of my work lies in the impossibility of articulating such a statement; in the fact that its utterance is in some way senseless, inappropriate, indecent. Either because *woman* is never the attribute of the verb *to be* nor *sexualized female* a quality of *being*, or because *am a woman* is not predicated of *I*, or because *I am sexualized* excludes the feminine gender. In other words, the articulation of the reality of my sex is impossible in discourse, and for a structural, eidetic reason. My sex is removed, at least as the property of a subject, from the predicative mechanism that assures discursive coherence. I can thus speak intelligently as sexualized male (whether I recognize this or not) or as asexualized. Otherwise, I shall succumb to the illogicality that is proverbially attributed to women. All the statements I make are thus either borrowed from a model that leaves my sex aside . . . or else my utterances are unintelligible according to the code in force.

Now, virtually every modern writer has claimed that the words available to him or to her are somehow wrong. It could be argued that Irigaray has said what she wants to say not only in words but "in other words." Or that men don't feel themselves released from what T. S. Eliot called "the intolerable wrestle with words." But even if we grant—who are the "we" who grant?—that Irigaray's complaint is valid, it is not clear what the same "we" can do to satisfy it, or even to mitigate it. The agenda amounts to an imputation of Original Sin, except that the official Original Sin was ascribed to the whole human race and this one is confined to men.

The charge is so omnivorous, moreover, that no particular man need feel intimidated by it. It reminds me of Hannah Arendt's account of "the banality of evil," an accusation so grand that it left every individual free to go about his or her business. Am I really guilty of the allegedly phallogocentric enforcement of meaning in discourse? When did I commit the crime? Besides, if a new discourse were to be devised, vaginacentric rather than phallogocentric, a "fault" would remain, wouldn't it? And presumably the whole revisionist process would have to be undertaken again, this time in favor of men. (To be fair to Derrida, he wouldn't want a mere change of center, the Mother displacing the Father; he wants to dislodge every center by an endless play of signifiers.)

So what is to be done to placate Irigaray? The gestures that several critics have made seem to me further examples of patronage. If Jonathan Culler, Terry Eagleton, and Fredric Jameson refer to the reader as "she" rather than the conventional "he," what purpose is served? I have no answer. I have read several essays that argue that women should keep to their own company, pursuing the possibilities of sisterhood and planning eventually to make a separatist difference. But I don't know the status of this suggestion in feminist rhetoric as a whole.

It may be the case that the first agenda is strictly women's work, and that the best a man can do is keep out of their way. Irigaray is determined to ensure that speech about women is not to be taken as "a recuperation of the feminine within a logic that maintains it in repression, censorship, nonrecognition." I'm not sure what she means, unless she thinks that this recuperation would only be yet another instance of repressive tolerance (Marcuse's phrase), the strategy by which a man's world expands to make room for women and merrily proceeds upon its powerful way. To prevent this from happening, Irigaray proposes, as she says, to jam the theoretical machinery. Instead of trying to construct a logic of the feminine that would still take the "ontotheologic" of masculine discourse as its model, she would aim to disrupt every discourse.

I assume she sees her work as the Luddite phase of feminism. But she also sees herself, more conventionally, as revising Freud's phallocratic psychoanalysis, a job already in the hands of Karen Horney, Melanie Klein, Marie Bonaparte, and other critics. In America the most "reasonable" place for such revisionists is in Deconstruction, which undertakes to reveal discourse as sovereign predicate of the Father. Presumably this project satisfies not only women who resent phallogocentric power, but men who profess to be ashamed of possessing it. The fact that the project seems to me largely specious, and indeed "in bad faith," is an old quarrel by now.

The second agenda of feminist criticism is smaller, and far more tangible. Women want a bigger slice of the cake, but not a transfigured cake. In practice, this entails readier access to publishers, fellowships, and grants; affirmative action in their favor in the professions; more space and time at the M.L.A. conventions; steadier promotion in the universities; more magazines devoted to feminist issues; women's studies in the curriculum of universities and colleges. The demands on this agenda are now, I gather, universally accepted. They have been implicit in feminist sentiment since Mary Wollstonecraft's *A Vindication of the Rights of Women* (1792) and Margaret Fuller's *Women in the Nineteenth Century* (1855), their motto Fuller's: "Let them be sea-captains, if you will." Or rather: "if they will."

Immense progress has been made on the second agenda. There are dozens of magazines given over entirely to women. Columbia University Press has announced the publication of a new series of books on "gender and culture." The editors are Carolyn Heilbrun and Nancy K. Miller, and the first batch includes Nina Auerbach's *Romantic Imprisonment* and Naomi Schor's *Breaking the Chain: Women, Theory, and French Realist Fiction.* Discourse may still be as Irigaray describes it, but it has not reduced women to silence or to forms of expression that are self-evidently frustrating.

The most obvious merit of feminist criticism is that it has drawn attention to writers and writings that have been neglected. The **Norton Anthology** prints, complete, Chopin's *The Awakening*, Toni Morrison's *The Bluest Eye*, and (hardly a neglected work) *Jane Eyre*. Other feminist essays make strong cases for Rebecca Harding Davis's *Life in the Iron Mills* and Alice James's *Diary*. (It wouldn't worry me, by the way, if I were asked to pay just as much attention to Alice's diary as to her brother Henry's *Notes of a Son and Brother*.)

But the question of literary merit, as distinct from sociological interest, is rarely raised by feminist critics. When it is, the argument is desperate. We are to believe that literary criteria are incorrigibly man-made values, and are compromised by the power they enforce. Lillian S. Robinson at least faces the issue of merit and value in one of the best essays in *The New Feminist Criticism*:

> Is the canon and hence the syllabus based on it to be regarded as the compendium of excellence or as the record of cultural history? For there comes a point when the proponent of making the canon recognize the achievement of both sexes has to put up or shut up; either a given woman writer is good enough to replace some male writer on the prescribed reading list or she is not. If she is not, then either she should replace him anyway, in the name of telling the truth about the culture, or she should not, in the (unexamined) name of excellence. . . . It is ironic that in American literature, where attacks on the male tradition have been most bitter and the reclamation of women writers so spectacular, the appeal has still been only to pluralism, generosity, and guilt. It is populism with the politics of populism.

The only swipe in that passage is the reference to "the (unexamined) name of excellence." The alternative to pluralism is the examined name of excellence; anything less is disgraceful. As for her last sentence, the appeal she refers to is populism without the name of populism—that is, sociology. But Robinson is right. If a feminist critic wants to dislodge a male writer and install a woman writer in his place in the curriculum, she should make a case for her on literary grounds that she would herself choose and expound; or insist on installing her anyway, as Robinson says, "in the name of telling the truth about the culture." But she should not fudge the issue.

It is also a distinct merit that feminist critics and scholars are compelling attention to forgotten or ignored moments in the past. Carroll Smith-Rosenberg's *Disorderly Conduct* is exemplary in this regard. Its theme is "the nature and the origins of the separate world of nineteenth-century women." Smith-Rosenberg's methods are taken mainly from anthropology (Mary Douglas, Victor Turner) and semiology (Roland Barthes). Her documentary materials are gathered for the light they cast upon mothers and daughters, friendship between women, marriage, menstruation, menopause, the New Woman, androgyny, the New York Female Moral Reform Society, prostitution, women in the Second Great Awakening, the American Medical Association and its attitude toward abortion. I can't imagine that an American historian would have studied these moments and issues with such concentration if a context of feminist criticism were not already available to take account of them.

But the context sometimes produces lurid results. Nina Auerbach could have written her essays on 19th-century fiction and poetry even if an official feminism had never existed. But she would not have pressed or pushed her perceptions if extreme feminist motives had not claimed her allegiance. I don't find anything distinctively feminist in her account of the separation of the sexes in *Dombey and Son*, but this passage from her essay on the Brownings has the feminist ring to it:

> Having survived a poet who made epic claims for herself, Robert Browning perpetuated her voice by turning it into his own; he "married" Elizabeth Barrett one more time when he appropriated her after her death, weaving her declarations into the corrosive fabric of his dramatic monologues. According to Irvine and Honan, she had found from the first something sinister in his ability to read her: "She had been frightened of him at first. She felt he had a power over her, that he could read her thoughts as he might read a newspaper." This initial ability to read Elizabeth ripened into an ability to write her and finally, with love and reverence, to silence her.

I don't find this persuasive. The paradigm seems to have preceded the need of it; it has an air of applied romance. The springs of Browning's poetry are to be sought in his relation to Shelley in particular, and to several other voices offering him a poetic strategy. Elizabeth's voice was one of those, but a minor one. The feminist drama of a man's possession, co-option, and final, loving suppression of a woman seems to have provoked Auerbach into finding it exemplified, however implausibly, in Robert and Elizabeth.

Auerbach also seems to me to claim as distinctively feminist perceptions notions that in fact have long been commonplace. Her essays on Jane Austen, for instance, don't amount to a radical revision of the standard sense of Austen's novels that has been current since D. W. Harding published, many years ago, an essay called "Regulated Hatred," in which he argued that Austen's artistic problem was to find a form and a style that would enable her to settle her account with a society she in great part hated.

"The task of feminist critics," according to Elaine Showalter, "is to find a new language, a new way of reading that can integrate our intelligence and our experience, our reason and our suffering, our skepticism and our vision." The task "should not be confined to women," though she confines it to women in *The New Feminist Criticism*. Studying "woman as reader," she calls for a feminist critique, "a historically grounded inquiry that probes the ideological assumptions of literary phenomena." For "woman as writer," Showalter proposes a "gynocriticism" that concerns itself with "the psychodynamics of female creativity; linguistics and the problem of a female language; the trajectory of the individual or collective female literary career; literary history; and, of course, studies of particular writers and works."

That sounds like a full day's work. In practice, however, feminist critics have much reduced the range of their literary interests. Many of their essays are, so far as critical theory arises, regressive. I have read feminist essays that study the characterization of Emilia in *Othello* as if L. C. Knights had not shown the penury of such questions 50 years ago (in his famous essay "How Many Children Had Lady Macbeth?"). Was Jane Austen opposed to marriage? Did she dislike children? What did she think of motherhood? Did Shakespeare restrict women to a narrow range of emotions? Did Yeats patronize Maud Gonne and other women? These are wretched questions, even if they are excused as marking a primitive stage in the development of a more interesting feminist criticism.

Indeed, feminist criticism at its present stage seems to me to be a libel upon women. The questions it asks are insultingly reductive. The situation is very odd: feminist critics are selling their literature short while promoting it at every turn. Promotion belongs to the history of advertising, but not less to the history (with its drifts and turns) of political sentiment. Where women should beware women—that is, where women writers should refuse the embrace of feminist critics—is in their implication that a woman writer can only transcribe the experience she has been given, and cannot imagine experience other than her own. Feminist critics have matronized their writers; they have set them a list of themes, motifs, and situations amounting to one physiologically ordained predicament, and told them that it is their destiny to annotate it. A woman writer is supposed to be merely an amanuensis of her fate. For her, there is one story and one story only.

So I was pleased when Brigid Brophy protested, in the *Times Literary Supplement* on July 26, 1985, that many feminist critics forget that there are writers "whose imagination is fired by what they have not experienced, Shakespeares who create *Romeo and Juliet* out of not visiting Verona and *Antony and Cleopatra* out of never setting eyes on the Nile." If feminist critics libel women, they also, in the same reductive spirit, deny the imagination.

Specifically, they deny women the imaginative power that Bakhtin calls "dialogic." His distinction between monologic and dialogic imagination is one of the most valued references in contemporary criticism. The writer with monologic vision insists that every thought gravitates to him as a sign of his power, a power he exerts unremittingly throughout his composition, controlling every ostensibly different point of view. The dialogic vision projects "a plurality of independent and unmerged voices and consciousness, a genuine polyphony of fully valid voices." What occurs (Bakhtin takes Dostoyevsky as his example) "is not a multitude of characters and fates in a single objective world, illuminated by a single authorial consciousness; rather a plurality of consciousness, with equal rights and each with its own world, combine but are not merged in the unity of the event." It is evident that feminist criticism denies women writers dialogic imagination; it consigns women to their fate, and recognizes them only when they transcribe their fatality.

What now? The smaller agenda is well in hand. Since it presents itself as a matter of politics and sociology, our institutions know how to deal with its demands, reducing the number of telegrams and appeasing the anger. Women's studies are a new area of growth in university departments, and welcome mainly for that reason. At the end of the *Oresteia,* the avenging Furies have been transformed into the benign Eumenides, a change of disposition that authorities can indeed bring about by observing the propriety of discourse. Nothing as fundamental as a change of heart is required. As for Luce Irigaray and the large agenda: I can't see anything happening there. A change of heart wouldn't be enough to effect the transfiguration she demands.

Elizabeth Boyd Thompson (review date Winter 1988)

SOURCE: A review of *No Man's Land: The Place of the Woman Writer in the Twentieth-Century, Volume 1: The War of the Words,* in *Modern Fiction Studies,* Vol. 34, No. 4, Winter, 1988, pp. 747–49.

[*In the following review, Thompson writes that Volume one of* No Man's Land *lacks intellectual rigor and a "solid theoretical basis."*]

The publicity sheet accompanying the review copy of *No Man's Land* quotes Joyce Carol Oates, Carolyn Heilbrun, Elaine Showalter, and J. Hillis Miller in fulsome praise of Sandra Gilbert and Susan Gubar's sequel to *The Madwoman in the Attic*. Oates calls *No Man's Land* "fast, funny, profound in its theoretical assertions, and deliciously irreverent in its asides." Heilbrun finds it "exciting and ground-breaking." Showalter extols the "ambitious range, scholarly passion, and intellectual panache" of the authors. Miller (the token male?) credits Gilbert and Gubar with rewriting "the history of modernism." These comments have, of course, been taken out of context, selected from, we must assume, longer, more detailed prepublication reviews, and we must grant the possibility that these prestigious critics might have tempered their praise at some point in a longer assessment of the work. That said, I must beg to differ with these worthies.

Not that I disagree entirely. I too find *No Man's Land* "fast" and "funny"; but "fast and loose" more accurately describes the book's theoretical assertions. In fact, my major objection to this book is that it lacks a solid theoretical basis; it leaves too many assumptions unexamined, too many terms undefined. The omnipresent puns and self-conscious word play are precious and intrusive, contributing neither insight into the texts engaged nor a healthy sense of ironic balance to the argument. The range is certainly "ambitious," but there is no depth of perception or analysis to match. On one level Miller's assertion that Gilbert and Gubar "rewrite the history of modernism" is entirely accurate; how accurately they rewrite it is another question altogether.

A quick look at Chapter Five, "Sexual Linguistics: Women's Sentence, Men's Sentencing," will help to bring some of my objections into focus. This chapter attempts "to integrate the divergent forces of power, language, and meaning" by examining the "relationship between sexual difference and the symbolic contract in an effort to trace the permutations of the modern battle over language and secondarily to place recent ideas about sexual linguistics in a larger historical context." ("Symbolic contract" is Julia Kristeva's term. According to Kristeva, "Sexual difference . . . is translated by and translates a difference in the relationship of subjects to the symbolic contract which *is* the social contract. . . .") Precisely what this shadowy, pseudolinguistic relationship might actually signify is unclear, unless Gilbert and Gubar's assertion that "from Fielding's Mrs. Slipslop to Sheridan's Mrs. Malaprop, such verbose creatures dramatize the idea that the more pretensions women have to learning the less they know" might be considered a concrete example. The problem is that the same "linguistic anatomy" might just as well be applied to a number of male characters. Such an application in no way denies the possibility of an undercurrent of misogyny in these female characterizations; it does, however, call into question the validity of Gilbert and Gubar's rather one-sided theories of sexual linguistics. The more serious problem for me is that buried under the puns, the jargon, and the theoretical deadwood are two excellent critics who are wasting their time being shop-front feminists. Simplifying and politicizing intellectual and literary history is not rewriting it. And simplification often fails to confront the most damaging, because least obvious, dangers of patriarchy. They can do better—and have.

Julie Abraham (review date 2 July 1988)

SOURCE: "Modern Romancers," in *Nation,* Vol. 247, No. 1, July 2, 1988, pp. 27–8.

[*In the following review of* No Man's Land: The War of the Words, *Abraham objects to Gubar and Gilbert's attempts to validate women's literature by placing it in the mainstream of twentieth-century critical categories.*]

Feminist literary criticism can still be a marginal enterprise in an intellectual universe that also contains William Bennett, Allan Bloom and Gertrude Himmelfarb. But in the almost twenty years since Kate Millett's *Sexual Politics* helped to inaugurate the field, feminist criticism has also prospered: It now has its own establishment, its own mainstream and margins.

One of the key works in the process of consolidation was Sandra M. Gilbert and Susan Gubar's 1979 study, *The Madwoman in the Attic: The Woman Writer and the Nineteenth-Century Literary Imagination*. They synthesized a decade of feminist analyses and applied the result to the recognized nineteenth-century stars—Jane Austen, the Brontës, George Eliot and Emily Dickinson—while also rewriting Harold Bloom's account of literary history as a fatherson contest to incorporate struggles between fathers and daughters. This established their penchant for the large formulation, their position within the feminist critical establishment and their role as purveyors of feminist critical assumptions beyond its ranks. All these elements were confirmed by their editorship of the 1985 *Norton Anthology of Literature by Women*, itself a major commercial sign of the impact of feminist criticism on the teaching of literature in the United States.

Gilbert and Gubar present their latest effort, *The War of the Words*, as the theoretical introduction to a three-volume successor to the *Madwoman*, titled *No Man's Land: The Place of the Woman Writer in the Twentieth-Century*. This work will be completed by two volumes of close textual readings, one due later this year and the other in 1989. Their subtitle, with its implication that there is such a character as "the woman writer," indicates in advance that they still aspire to the definitive statement on a grand scale, to the repeat achievement of a critical if not a popular blockbuster.

While mainstream critics of twentieth-century literature are still responding to the challenge of feminist criticism by adding Virginia Woolf but talking about E. M. Forster, in *The War of the Words* Gilbert and Gubar have brought forward a host of women writers who don't even make it to the footnotes of *The Pound Era*. They have produced an eminently readable study just when academic criticism is courting the abstruse in order to reassure itself of its own significance. They talk about novels, stories, poems and plays instead of other critics and critical works. They use "minor" and shorter works to make major points, marshaling their sources in bulk—there are no revolutionary theories based on one novel by Balzac, or *Great Expectations* and a Conrad novella. And they frequently bypass the conventional designations of period and style that often, for example, inhibit serious discussions of the realists writing when modernism was in flower.

But, in order perhaps to insure accessibility, they have chosen to tell us a story, a narrative history of twentieth-century literature they begin as far back as 1848, with the Brontës, and bring up to 1987. And, in order perhaps to deal with the range of the material they are covering, they have chosen the most traditional story for women, the only story women were supposed to figure in before the experiments of twentieth-century literature, a story of their relations to men. Gilbert and Gubar "conflate and collate" the lives and works of individual male and female writers to create "one possible metastory, a story of stories about gender strife," a "history of [hetero]sexual battle." These writers are divided into couples as well as camps: "James and Wharton, Yeats and Lady Gregory, Hemingway and Stein, Lawrence and Mansfield (or H. D.), Wells and West (or Richardson), Eliot and Woolf, Graves and Riding, Miller and Nin." The terms change over the course of the story, for example from "stern Victorian husbands and their maddened wives" to "turn-of-the-century misogynists and rebellious suffragists," and later "mid-century he-men and ambitious independent women." At different times dif-

ferent sides claim victory: "At the height of the modernist era . . . both sexes by and large agreed that women were winning, while postmodernist male and female writers, working in the 1940s and 1950s, reimagined masculine victory." But the women writers and their works are continually placed in literary history in terms of their relation to male writers and their works. Our heroines cannot be seen to contemplate any other aspect of their existence. Gilbert and Gubar have in effect given us a nineteenth-century novel about twentieth-century women's writing.

Although they argue that the major change that occurred in literary history in the course of the shift into the twentieth century was that women writers could now have literary foremothers as well as father, they attempt to explain the relations between the new generations of women writers in terms of a version of Freud's "family romance." Women writers are described as "oscillating between" literary mother and father figures, and so female or male peers, in a schema in which women's relations to each other are always still mediated by a father figure, so that Gilbert and Gubar can maintain their heterosexual focus.

The history of Anglo-American literary criticism also becomes part of the battle. In their chapter on "Tradition and the Female Talent," the authors discuss the politics of literary criticism and in particular of canon formation, suggesting that

> the emergence of modern male literary discourse, exemplified by theoretical and canon-forming works like "Tradition and the Individual Talent," *The ABC of Reading* (1934), *Seven Types of Ambiguity* (1930), and *The Well-Wrought Urn* (1947), can be seen as an attempt to construct *his* story of a literary history in which women play no part.

Even contemporary Lacanian revisions of Freud and "French Feminist theory" can be absorbed into this motif. Jacques Lacan becomes a descendant of Tennyson, Gilbert and Sullivan, Eliot and Pound, incorporated into the discussion of male misogyny and attacks on women's writing. Meanwhile, the writings of the proponents of "écriture féminine" are merged with those of some 1970s U.S. feminists and retrospectively placed in a line of resistance that goes back to Virginia Woolf.

But the battle of the sexes seems an odd narrative framework to choose when one of the distinctive characteristics of twentieth-century women's writing, as Rachel Blau DuPlessis has argued, is its challenge of the male-female romance plot. Virginia Woolf observed in 1927:

> We long sometimes to escape from the incessant, the remorseless analysis of falling into love and falling out of love, of what Tom feels for Judith and Judith does or does not altogether feel for Tom. We long for some more impersonal relationship. We long for ideas, for dreams, for imaginations, for poetry.

Exchanging individual stories for a "metastory," or love for hostility, does not diminish Gilbert and Gubar's familiar emphasis on Tom and Judith. Their record of conflict between the sexes emphasizes male-female differences, obscuring a history of literary experimentation with gender boundaries and stereotypes that they themselves have discussed in earlier essays. It also neutralizes and contains the unprecedented literary presence of lesbians and gay men. Lesbian writers, editors and patrons—including Woolf, Sylvia Beach, Margaret Anderson, May Sarton— were responsible not only for much of the writing Gilbert and Gubar discuss but also for the publication and promotion of works by straight and gay women and men, from Marianne Moore's first book of poetry to James Joyce's *Ulysses*. Also, during the first part of this century, the "lesbian" functioned as the sign of the modern, in the work of writers as disparate as D. H. Lawrence and Radclyffe Hall, Proust and F. Scott Fitzgerald. As Gertrude Stein declared, "I so naturally had my part in killing the nineteenth century and killing it dead," and she was not referring to the lessons she gave Hemingway.

What Gilbert and Gubar's battle of the sexes does, however, is insure that their account of twentieth-century women's writing is firmly anchored to mainstream histories of twentieth-century literature and the assumptions on which those histories are based. The *War of the Words*' discussion of "modernism" reveals the limits this imposes. Gilbert and Gubar use the term in two different ways. In part it serves as a historical marker for literature produced after the turn of the century and during the interwar period. At the same time, they discuss modernism in more familiar terms as a specific "high culture" phenomenon. Gilbert and Gubar argue that this modernism must be seen as a response to the threatening "rise of the female imagination" as well as to such already recognized nineteenth-and early twentieth-century crises as "the industrial revolution . . . the fall of God" and the Great War. But their argument depends on upholding (even though now self-consciously) the traditional delineation of literary modernism as the product of Eliot, Pound and Joyce, "a men's club," as they observe. They cannot pursue the possibility that modernism was also created by the female imaginations of Woolf, Stein, Dorothy Richardson or Djuna Barnes. They cannot ask what "modernism" was or might have been.

Similarly, despite their charges about the politics of canon formation and their own violations of convention in attempting to include women at all, Gilbert and Gubar do not question the principle of the canon. In their preface they ask simply, "What exactly *is* the canon of twentieth-century literature by women, given that increasing numbers of women have entered the literary marketplace in the last one hundred years and that so many reputations are still in flux?"

Based on the principle of hierarchy implicit in the idea of the canon, their efforts to be inclusive are inevitably constrained. As they work to develop a women's canon parallel to the men's, they incorporate examples of the work of women writers from a "black tradition" or a "science fiction tradition"—Ann Petry, James Tiptree Jr. (Alice B.

Sheldon). But these appear as amplifications of arguments based on an implicit mainstream—white, heterosexual women who produce contemporary realist or experimental work. Meanwhile, false parallels are constructed by the designation of black, science fiction or lesbian traditions as subsets within a canon of twentieth-century women's writing. There are obviously greater differences than similarities in the relations of black, lesbian or science fiction writers to their particular "traditions." The historical experiences such traditions refer to are widely divergent, and the relation of the writing in question to any more conventionally canonical culture varies greatly.

Waving their standard in the battle of the sexes, Gilbert and Gubar have produced the kind of feminist work that looks most threatening. They rework the terrain of male writers' hostility to women that Kate Millett established, some old favorites making a reappearance beside new entrants to the lists: D. H. Lawrence's phallic politics, Hemingway's lament for Francis Macomber, and Mailer's Rojack, for example, are now accompanied by stories by Henry James and Aldous Huxley, poems by Thomas Hardy, Robert Lowell, Ted Hughes, and T. S. Eliot's *Sweeney Agonistes* proposing, "Any man has to, needs to, wants to / Once in a lifetime, do a girl in." But the woman reviewing male abuse of women is, after all, the feminist of conventional literary and political imagination. This feminism is paradoxically much easier to assimilate than more complex feminisms with other concerns. Gilbert and Gubar have taken their overall title, *No Man's Land*, from the language of World War I trench warfare—battles in which both armies were male. "No man's land" was a place where, if there were no men, there was no one. This seems to be the anxiety at the center of their new work, but some feminist criticism has moved beyond the need to define "the place of the woman writer" in a male territory in order to insure that someone is really there. If Gilbert and Gubar's approach is the result of a desire to mainstream feminist concerns, *The War of the Words*, in its reduction of both the complexities of its subject and of feminist perspectives, provides an object lesson in the dangers of that goal.

But it seems that Gilbert and Gubar's relation to feminism in *The War of the Words* is rather nervous overall. Feminist scholarship in the 1980s has included a range of attempts to place the contemporary women's movement in its historical context. Gilbert and Gubar also attempt to contextualize second-wave feminism, but do so in a cultural balancing act that pairs feminism with "masculinism" and "misandry" with "misogyny," regardless of the differing values of those terms. Feminism becomes one result of the "sex antagonism" they record. Their balance between "masculinist" and "feminist" is established in the service of ideals of "aesthetic excellence," "great literature," "effective works of art" and "creativity," which are explicitly distanced from "doctrinaire politics" and "ideology," leaving Gilbert and Gubar on the side of "great literature" and superior to "ideology." This looks like an attempt to locate themselves above and beyond a history in which feminists struggle and, as feminism tells us, ideology is inescapable. It points us back in the direction of the "great tradition" that feminist critics began by challenging.

In *The War of the Words*, Sandra Gilbert and Susan Gubar present mainstream literary criticism with a wealth of material it prefers to ignore and a new version of an old story. But so far, *No Man's Land* feels like retrenchment practiced on material that demands daring. Is this postfeminist criticism, and if so, can we afford it?

Jenny Turner (essay date 1 April 1988)

SOURCE: "Very Much Afraid of Virginia Woolf," in *New Statesman,* Vol. 115, No. 2975, April 1, 1988, pp. 24–5.

[*In the following essay, Turner examines the literary and social contexts of the gender conflict presented in* No Man's Land: The War of the Words.]

Hitting London in 1908, Ezra Pound looked forward to a career of ramming imagism's "phallic direction" right into the city's "great passive vulva."

His good friend William Carlos William's long poem "Paterson" was padded out and/or enriched with letters quoted verbatim, without permission, from Marcia Nardi, an ex-lover and herself a fine but struggling poet. These letters refer hysterically to private matters and to Williams' "complete damning of my creative capacities."

Today Pound, and even more Williams, are still looked up to for pointing ways away from Eliot-type mystification and into the concrete, into spoken language, poetry as industry, as technic, as Tool. Sandra Gilbert and Susan Gubar see this as part of a great masculinist war effort to colonise the flourishing "mother tongues" of modern vernacular culture and so keep *patrio sermo*—the word of the father—in the style to which it is accustomed. Once said, so obvious.

Gilbert and Gubar's last collaboration was *The Madwoman in the Attic* (1979), which explored patterns of "enclosure and escape, maddened doubles as asocial surrogates for docile selves, metaphors of discomfort . . . along with obsessive depictions of diseases like anorexia, agoraphobia and claustrophobia" in the works of the famous woman writing in 19th century England and North America. This one undertakes the enormous task of working out how feminities fit in to the Anglo-American canon of literary modernism.

The thesis is basically that the grinding liturgies of decline and renewal which gave Pound, Williams, Joyce such creative energy were set going by men anxious at seeing women flooding the public sphere. The damned muse won't sit still and then she starts answering back.

Strategies for coping with this monstrous dispossession were varied but never accommodationist. It is easy to read this book as a bestiary of peevish "no-men" and the stupid sexpots-stroke-omphalosses of all evil they constructed, as codpieces, for protection and glorification of their own. On the one side we have Fisher King, Leopold Bloom, a poet with "dugs" on like Eliot's Tiresias. On the other, tidily seeping orifice piles like Molly Bloom, or liberated evil blue meanies like Lawrence's Gudrun (who, you may recall, liked killing rabbits).

This strand of the argument is given resonance by Gilbert and Gubar's interest in and development of Harold Bloom (US literary critic; no relation of Molly)'s 1973 allegory of poetic misprision. Bloom's "anxiety of influence" reads "strong poets" as locked in primal struggle with their literary pre-cursors for the right to bear the father's word. In tone it is very Adam and God on the Sistine Chapel roof. But the irony of its stature next to little modern men beetling about does add a ring to, say, Lawrence's hideous atavism or Eliot's attempts to wrest a great tradition back for himself.

We will have to wait for volumes two and three of this study to see fully how feminine works transform the myth. In the meantime, Gilbert and Gubar's run some data on how women responded to the great cosmic slagging match and offer what is, however psychoanalytically suspect, a virtuoso reading of Virginia Woolf's critical essays. Long before she was a novelist, Woolf worked hard as the first serious researcher and chronicler of the female tradition from which she wanted to come. Gilbert and Gubar suggest she was also remarkable in being about the first woman writer decisively to overcome a masculinity complex. She was modern enough, and courageous enough, to need no male trappings, no pseudonym, no George Sand suit, no Gertrude Stein gruffness to write. But, no matter what Adrienne Rich says, this wasn't easy or unambivalent.

The writer confronting her possible foremothers is beside herself with anxiety and envy. She is guilty to know their pain yet glories in it. She wants to whisk their mantles from them yet wants to give them her own, yet secretly fears neither can be as good as a man's.

This dimension to Woolf's investigations can be seen in a 1924 essay called "Indiscretions: 'Never Seek To Tell Thy Love, Love That Never Told Can Be'—But One's feelings for Some Writers Outrun All Prudence." The author-to-be is tiptoeing up on a harem, we "tremble slightly as we approach the curtain and catch glimpses of women behind it and even hear ripples of laughter . . ." The voyeurism expresses the daughter's distance from past writers, her entanglement, her desire to rip the veil that can't be ripped. I wonder how Woolf would feel if she could see today's identically structured invocations of the dead, if she could read the countless poems and essays apostrophising her as adopted mother, or view her imagined genitalia served up for devotion at Judy Chicago's *Dinner Party.*

The War of the Words is very Ivy League in its length (another two volumes to go: the promise of infinite bequests), in its combination of clever close readings with voluminous research done by research assistants, in being all tied up in an alfresco allegorical bow at the expense of socio-historical realism. There is little sense of real social worlds, of the textures of public and private lives, of how public spheres develop not as concepts but institutions.

The modern movement was made up of little magazines, bigger ones, revolutions in ways of understanding sexuality, class, work, the world, the travel and communications industries, so many factors. So drawn onto the plane of myth, the authors miss distinctions between public and private words, conscious propaganda and the dynamic works—never as schematic as they'd like to think—of the unconscious in jokes, slips, dreams and artworks. They don't discuss the coming of feminism as a political option and, therefore, the fact that many women—Isak Dinesen, for example—consciously opted to be anti-feminist. Such details may not alter the basic structures much, but they enrich the ways we see women—and men—in their social and literary existences.

Anne Herrmann (review date Fall 1989)

SOURCE: A review of *No Man's Land, Volume 1: The War of the Words* and *No Man's Land, Volume 2: Sexchanges,* in *Criticism: A Quarterly for Literature and the Arts,* Vol. 31, No. 4, Fall, 1989, pp. 507–12.

[*In the following review of volumes one and two of* No Man's Land—The War of the Words *and* Sexchanges—*Herrmann argues that Gubar and Gilbert have "abandoned" the notion of the separate literary tradition for women, which they had offered in* The Madwoman in the Attic, *and devalue lesbian writers, especially Gertrude Stein.*]

I remember walking down a tree-lined street in New Haven, between the library and a small, set-back bookstore, when a fellow graduate student rushed up to me to announce that the first "feminist poetics" had arrived. No longer would the French have a monopoly on discourses that addressed the intersection of literary theory and gender. No longer would members of clandestine reading groups seek out unpublished manuscripts that made such discourses available to those unfortunate few who only read English. No longer would every seminar paper on feminist criticism require a rationale. The year was 1979 and the "poetics" was Gilbert and Gubar's *The Madwoman in the Attic: The Woman Writer and the Nineteenth-Century Literary Imagination*.

Ten years later I find myself reviewing the first two volumes of the sequel to that "poetics." Ten years is a long time to wait and a long time to sustain the same project, especially in a field as transformational and transformed as

feminist criticism. Gone is the exhilaration and trepidation of the "first," perhaps because Gilbert and Gubar's edition of *The Norton Anthology of Women Writers: The Tradition in English* has stolen the limelight. Perhaps because so much of the material in *No Man's Land* is already familiar, having been published elsewhere. Perhaps because Shari Benstock's encyclopedic survey of the modernist women (at least those who made it to *Women of the Left Bank*) has already appeared (1986). It is not a sense of "belatedness" (the apprehension underlying Harold Bloom's theory of the "anxiety of influence") that one is left with at the end of almost 800 pages. Rather, it is a sense that even though the co-authors "had to rethink everything we had ever been taught about twentieth-century literature," that rethinking does not include the category of Literature nor the project of a literary history.

While *The Madwoman in the Attic* attempted to construct a distinctly female literary tradition in the nineteenth century, *No Man's Land* focuses on the "social, literary and linguistic interactions of men and women from the middle of the nineteenth century to the present." Gilbert and Gubar have abandonned both the (feminist literary critical) notion of a separate literary tradition and the (literary historical) notion of periodization strictly by century. Instead they have retained the spatial metaphor, substituting the figure of female confinement and escape borrowed from *Jane Eyre* with a soldier's description of the trenches from World War I, subsequently borrowed as trope by numerous writers. The self-division of the woman writer has been replaced with the war between the sexes. An internalized conflict between the author and her enraged double has given way to the externalized conflict between an impotent and hostile "no-man" and an anxious because potent New Woman over primacy in the literary marketplace. The pen, which was once a metaphoric penis, has become a metaphoric pistol.

The first volume, *The War of the Words*, offers "an overview" of literary production from 1850 to 1980 in the United States and England by means of stories and poems which are read allegorically in order to reiterate *ad infinitum* the meta-story of the sexual battle. The second volume, *Sexchanges*, focuses on the period between 1880 and 1930 and analyses fewer texts in greater detail, with entire chapters devoted to Kate Chopin, Edith Wharton and Willa Cather. The assumption of the second volume draws on that of the first: "the sexes battle because sex roles change, but, when the sexes battle, sex itself (that is, eroticism) changes." Because the second volume treats "eccentric subjects" like "necrophilia, parthenogenesis and transvestism," and because some of its topics are not only "eccentric but painful," such as imperialist xenophobia, lesbianism and the Great War, the authors feel the need to include a disclaimer: "About such disturbing material, all we can finally say is, Reader, we felt we had to write it, but please don't kill the messenger." Still hearing the echoes of Bronte's heroine, it doesn't take long to realize that the repressed double, not the Creole but the lesbian writer, has moved out of the attic and into the closet.

The "anxiety of authorship" which named the conflict for nineteenth century women writers between accepting and rejecting a literary tradition based on paternal authority in the absence of literary foremothers has been replaced by the "female affiliation complex." The source is still Freud ("Female Sexuality"), the woman writer is still a literary daughter and her story is still told as a family romance:

> If we translate this model of female psychosexual development into a map of literary paths, we can see that, whether the female artist turns to what Freud would judge a normative renunciation of her desire for a literary mother to the tradition of the father, whether in what Freud might see as a frigid rejection of both allegiances she attempts to extricate herself altogether from her own aesthetic ambitions, or whether in a move that Freud might define as "defiant" and "homosexual" she claims the maternal tradition as her own, she has at last to struggle with what we would provisionally define as a complicated *female affiliation complex.*
>
> (Vol. I, p. 168)

But given the fact that there is only one metastory, namely the battle of the sexes, how many of these paths will be not just described, but valorized (using terms like "normative" and "homosexual")? In Freud's own words, the three options are asexuality (the woman gives up on her "masculine proclivities" because boys are better at them), homosexuality (she forms a "masculinity complex" by refusing to give them up) and heterosexuality (the masculine is the love object rather than the source of identification). On the one hand this set of relations between the feminine and the masculine is much more complicated than the simple binarism of the battle. On the other hand, given the metaphor of (hetero) sexual conflict (for Gilbert and Gubar as well as for Freud) the only legitimate battle and/or sex is with men. On some basic level, the two sets of paths are not even comparable, given that Freud never mentions the maternal or the relations between women.

If the nineteenth century was characterized by a powerful father-daughter paradigm, the twentieth is marked by "anxiety and exuberance" over finally having, not a mother, but a choice of literary parentage. Literary foremothers produce as much if not more ambivalence than fathers once did. Rather than "influence" from outside, there is now a choice. And because there is a choice, women writers can decide with whom to affiliate (although one cannot choose not to affiliate). And having chosen, they become linked (once again) to a genealogy with its own "quasi-familial inevitability." Should one choose the mother,

> the literary daughter finds herself in a double bind. If she simply admires her aesthetic foremother, she is diminished by the originatory power she locates in that ancestress; but, if she struggles to attain the power she identifies with the mother's autonomy, she must confront . . . the peril of the mother's position in patriarchy, the loss of male emotional approval paradoxically associated with male approbation—as well as the intimacy with the mother that would accompany daughterly subordination.
>
> (Vol. I, p. 195)

In other words, the relation to the mother, and thus to other women, is not the solution either. Although Gilbert and Gubar suggest that the "monolithic pattern" of an earlier women's literary history has been displaced by a "variety of patterns," it is clear that the same patterns keep repeating themselves. The one who wins the battle is the one who keeps it going longest and the author who claims that distinction is Edith Wharton.

The chapter entitled "Angel of Devastation: Edith Wharton on the Arts of the Enslaved" is truly exceptional. Like Gilbert and Gubar, Wharton addresses the same issues "book after book, story after story," namely *The subject creature. The arts of the enslaved.* In other words, she provides "a feminist analysis of the construction of 'femininity.'" But presumably unlike her co-critics, she repudiated both the "bonds of sisterhood" (of a woman's separate sphere) and the "shoulder to shoulder feminist solidarity" (adopted by the New Woman). Instead, she was nicknamed "John" and expressed more concern for what she would wear than for what she had written before her first meeting with Henry James. What distinguishes this chapter is that contradiction has replaced dualism, a search for "Herland" (the utopian alternative to "No Man's Land") has given way to an analysis of patriarchal gender formations (at least for the leisure class of the Gilded Age) and revealing social ills is seen as a separate enterprise from curing them. Wharton was not a feminist but she can be read as offering a feminist analysis of gender relations which ultimately indicts men for the formation and perpetuation of the leisure class. In spite or because of her "ferocious irony" she offers no alternative for the feminine except "contact with the stronger masculine individuality." She was both a "man's woman" and a "self-made man" and within that contradiction one finds the most complex rendition of "sexchanges," not as redemption but as critique.

At the same time Wharton's depiction of sexual arrangements can do nothing but repeat itself, finding variations only in the multitudinous character formations and plot structures of her novels and short stories. Because there is no solution, the battle must go on: "For though this writer was never consciously to align herself with the female camp in the battle of the sexes, her secret feelings toward men, even toward men she loved, were often, and not surprisingly, at least subtly hostile." This statement makes explicit the fundamental paradox of patriarchal gender relations and thus of Gilbert and Gubar's argument. Like the plot of a popular romance, the point is not to avoid or settle the dispute but to keep it going in the name of love for the purpose of marriage. What makes Wharton additionally attractive is that female rage once again undergoes repression and reappears in the subtext, in this case, the ghost story. There Wharton can safely imagine turning on her master by portraying the erotically illicit.

A similar attempt to rewrite eroticism on the part of lesbian writers encounters a quite different critical reception. Even though the chapter "'She Meant What I Said': Lesbian Double Talk" ends with the statement that its subject matter has been the "first, fully self-conscious generation of lesbian writers," the authors nevertheless choose as their analytic categories the loneliness of the lesbian in heterosexual society and thus of the lesbian writer in literary history, an aesthetic of mutuality or "double talk" that can turn collaboration into collusion, and a principle of pain which seems to persist in same-sex relations, primarily because these relationships so isolate the lovers that each one must constantly fear the loss of a separate identity. "Perpetual, ontological expatriation" becomes the plight of those who live in the "supposedly native land which is heterosexuality." The real danger is not the "no man's land of sex" but the attempt on the part of any woman writer to create "her own land" and thus put into question not only the "female affiliation complex," but the very notion of a literary history: "In their attempts to write new and strange words that evade the territorial battles between literary men and women, the lesbian expatriates looked back to an ancient, almost mythic literary history or forward to the total annihilation of literary history." In either case, not to the kind of literary history that Gilbert and Gubar want to construct. Here the chief offender is Gertrude Stein.

The reading of Stein is the least successful in the entire two volumes. At one point the co-critics go so far as to begin a paragraph: "While a number of readers have felt victimized by Stein's impenetrable sentences or resentful about their failure to makes sense of her nonsense, even the responses of her admirers identify her authorial audacity with male mastery." (A footnote corroborating the first point of view refers the reader to a male critic whose book appeared in 1958). Certainly Gilbert and Gubar include themselves among "a number of readers" and their main complaint about Stein has to do with the fact that she created "her own land," put herself at its center and from there engaged in a "self-authorizing aesthetics" that exploited not only Alice, but continues to exploit us as readers. Neither a utopian "Herland" nor a battle of the sexes, Alice simply cannot be portrayed as the enraged but repressed dark double of Gertrude nor can Gertrude be described as an anxious and thus hostile "no-man." Instead (in Gilbert and Gubar's emplotment) Alice becomes the author of *The Autobiography of Alice B. Toklas* which she gives to Gertrude as a subversive gift by producing the only readable Stein.

Since even Gilbert and Gubar complain that Stein herself is always the central focus of any treatment of her work, it might be useful to consider what the stakes are, besides lifestyle. Worse than being manly in the most masculinist way, Stein puts into question three fundamental principles underlying the project of *No Man's Land*: she refuses predecessors, thus rejecting the "female affiliation complex"; she engages in an "aesthetics of solipsism," thus undermining the very notion of Literature; and she turns collaboration into collusion, thus challenging the premises of co-authorship ("We feel this book is fully collaborative," Gilbert and Gubar write in their introduction). Paraphras-

ing their own words: Stein claims all literary history as her own; she refuses to produce representational works; she rejects the notion of revision; and she creates only for herself. What could be more frustrating, more anxiety-provoking, more antithetical for two critics who want to create their own (definitive) literary history based on representational works required to substantiate a meta-story, having done so for over ten years in the hope of reaching the entire community of literary critics? Stein's worst crime is that she turns words into weapons, not against men, but against women readers, and not because her topics might be "eccentric and painful," but because there are none that lend themselves to recuperation by Gilbert and Gubar's history. Her textual/sexual strategies make us re-think everything, not just "twentieth century literature."

From Freud's point of view (according to Gilbert and Gubar) "the 'masculinity complex' could be carried no further." For Gilbert and Gubar, "The father had been turned into a fat-her" (based on the insights of six year old Molly Gubar). Perhaps an even more fundamental anxiety lies at the heart of their project, a fear of the female body which in its "excess" usurps the position of the father and/or abuses the role of the mother. In an otherwise interesting and provocative discussion of Olive Schreiner's *The Story of an African Farm*, one finds the following statement: "If Tant' Sannie is the only mother figure on the farm, we can understand the dilemma she poses by crystallizing it into the sentence, There is no mother and she is huge." Both of these sentences, in their aphoristic brevity, in their focus on fatness, in their concern with the parental, point to issues that can't be dealt with simply by including a chapter on lesbian writers or by suggesting that daughters can choose with whom to affiliate. They reflect an unquestioning attachment to the family romance, to Freudian discourses on sexuality, and to quotable quips. What, then, one might ask, has feminism done for anyone besides the publishing industry?

The point is not to reveal and revel in the unexplored anxieties of Gilbert and Gubar. The point is that a feminist criticism which thought that the daughter would be better off having a choice of parentage than an "anxiety of no-authorship," must eventually recognize that some choices are more valued than others and that choosing peaceful co-existence with a woman can be more threatening than engaging in battle with a man. More importantly, the privileging of analytic paradigms like the "battle of the sexes" not only laments but produces forms of epistemic violence by categorically excluding lesbian writers who can then only be included as nostalgic, lonely expatriates. The move from the attic to a "no man's land" has proven perhaps more advantageous for the modern woman writer than for the feminist literary critic. The fact that there are no men or men with "no-manhood" means that there might be women who embody those attributes once thought to be inherently masculine.

Elizabeth Boyd Thompson (review date Winter 1989)

SOURCE: A review of *No Man's Land: The Place of the Woman Writer in the Twentieth-Century, Volume 2: Sexchanges* in *Modern Fiction Studies,* Vol. 35, No. 4, Winter 1989, pp. 867–68.

[*In the following excerpt, Boyd calls* Sexchanges—*volume two of* No Man's Land—*a better book than the series' first volume,* The War of the Words; *but holds that* Sexchanges *is still full of unexamined assumptions.*]

According to Carolyn Heilbrun, "*No Man's Land* challenges the very basis of interpretation for a whole period. The study of modernism will never be the same." I hope she is right. For although I often doubt the success of Sandra M. Gilbert and Susan Gubar's challenge, I certainly applaud their attempt. *Sexchanges* returns to many of the issues presented in *The War of the Words* (the first volume of the three volume series), notably "the relationship between female dreams of a powerful Herland and male fears of a debilitating no man's land" and "the discrepancy between men's hostility toward what they perceived as threatening female autonomy and women's anxiety about what they saw as the fragility or even the fictionality of such autonomy." This book also elaborates a number of themes mentioned but not treated in depth in the first volume: "the sexual imagery associated with imperialism and its decline, with the intensified consumerism of Gilded Age America, and with the opening as well as the closing of the American frontier"; "the evolution of turn-of-the-century and modernist women's revisionary mythic and religious ideas"; "the relationship of the feminist and free love movements to the female imagination"; "the emergence of a lesbian literary tradition"; and "the asymmetrical impact of the Great War on men and women."

However, the "principal focus" of the book is on "changing definitions of sex and sex roles as they evolve through three phases." Gilbert and Gubar identify these phases as: "the repudiation of the Victorian ideology of femininity that marked both feminism and fantasy during what we might call the overturning of the century; the antiutopian skepticism that characterized the thought of such writers as Edith Wharton and Willa Cather . . . ; the virtually apocalyptic engendering of the new for both literary men and literary women that was, at least in part, fostered by the fin de siècle formation of a visible lesbian community, even more shockingly triggered by the traumas of World War I, and perhaps most radically shaped by an unprecedented confrontation (by both sexes) with the artifice of gender and its consequent discontents."

In spite of the emphasis on literary men and women, this book leans more toward social than literary history. And as such, the treatment of the effect of World War One on British women (Chapter Seven, "Soldier's Heart: Literary Men, Literary Women, and the Great War") is far and away the most interesting chapter in the book. Gilbert and Gubar argue that the absence of men in society and the

economy during the war "fostered the formation of a metaphorical country not unlike the queendom Charlotte Perkins Gilman called Herland." Sharp divisions between the men on the firing line and the women in the factories were underscored by recruitment posters the subtext of which was often "dulce et decorum est, pro *matria* mori," and the aftermath of the war that had done so much to further women's liberation found women facing a backlash of misogyny, evoked by the nightmare of the trenches.

This is a better book than *War of the Words* in a number of ways. The theoretical basis is still shaky, based on too many unexamined assumptions, but the style is clearer, and the puns and self-conscious word play are under better control, and consequently more effective. With such an all-encompassing agenda, it is little wonder that Gilbert and Gubar often merely skim the surface. Overall, it is an inconsistent work in which flashes of brilliance alternate with flabby overstatement and flimsy generalizations. In spite of its flaws, it is a good read, especially for those interested in social history. . . .

Kathleen Blake (review date July 1989)

SOURCE: A review of *No Man's Land: The War of the Words,* in *Journal of English and Germanic Philology,* Vol. 88, No. 3, July, 1989, pp. 454–57.

[*In the following review of the first volume of* No Man's Land, *Blake contends Gubar and Gilbert ought more strongly to have stressed their argument that patriarchal forms are not embedded in language.*]

Sandra M. Gilbert and Susan Gubar have followed up their *Madwoman in the Attic* with a "Daughter of Madwoman" as powerful as its progenitor. *No Man's Land* is the first volume in a projected three-volume series. It gives the grounding and grand scheme of literary history that recasts Modernism and Postmodernism as episodes in the gender agon initiated by the nineteenth-century rise of women and women writers. Gilbert and Gubar here extend their historical range to the twentieth century and treat male as well as female authors, exhibiting a greater historicism and theoretical self-awareness than in *Madwoman*. And while still with a basis in Freud, they present a critique of Freud and Freudian revisions, and their feminist manifestations.

Still frequently referring to Harold Bloom, whose Freud-based "anxiety of influence" helped them formulate their idea of the "anxiety of authorship" of nineteenth-century women writers, Gilbert and Gubar stress a twentieth-century rivalry that is not so much Oedipal as a sibling rivalry between the sexes in a period when women were moving beyond their initial anxiety about writing at all and into full-fledged contention with men. The first pair of chapters offers literary responses to the new aspirations and achievements of women in books by both men and women that represent a heightened battle of the sexes. The next pair of chapters covers the battle of the sexes over literary heritage, the last over claims to language itself.

In a still-Freudian fashion Gilbert and Gubar associate sexual and artistic energy and associate both with aggression and its release. But the aggressive outweighs the erotic. From the title on, *No Man's Land* concerns sexual war. Sometimes the terms of the erotic seem almost expendable, introduced in deference to Freudian theory.

But deference to Freud is not the hallmark of this book, for it gives us a Freud and Freudian theory "haunted by history." Gilbert and Gubar premise their work on the possibility of some meaningful access to historical knowledge and a corollary access to knowledge of authors. They hold that "challenges to history and authorship, radically anti-patriarchal as they may seem, ultimately erase the reality of gendered human experience" (p. xiv).

They consider Freud's theories to be in large measure constructed as reaction-formations to the emergence of feminism and new claims and accomplishments by women. Freud knew what the femininity of the future might look like, and he inclined to deplore it, as is tellingly shown by a letter he wrote sometime after translating John Stuart Mill's *Subjection of Women*. Thus, castration anxiety looks like the theory of a man increasingly aware of threats to male prerogative, penis envy like the theory of a man who might wish that women felt more of it. Freud theorized a female sexuality unfavorable to sublimation, for instance, in the form of artistic creativity; he did so facing an historic upswing in the number of artists who were women.

In reaction to new womanhood, Freud is, in fact, a characteristic male Modernist, according to Gilbert and Gubar's central conception. His psychological theory is haunted by the same history as that haunting twentieth-century literature. Gilbert and Gubar acknowledge the pressures that have been held to shape the period in standard accounts— the loss of faith, Darwinian visions of nature, the new psychology, the discontents of industrial civilization, the great war—all inaugurating an age of anxiety. But they characterize the period as also and above all an age of sexual anxiety. This has been overlooked because "few recent historians have grasped the profundity of the social metamorphosis brought about by the 'new woman'" (p. 21). And yet all the other anxieties can be seen as variants and feeders of the sexual one. Manhood, the culture of patriarchy, was challenged by the new woman at a time when it lost god the father, and lost man as ancestor and gained the monkey, when it contemplated the patricidal Oedipus complex, when it saw captains of industry confronted by unfilial workers, when a male generation was decimated in the trenches. Thereafter manhood lost jobs in the Depression, family pride of place in the mid-century era of momism, and first-sex standing in the second wave of feminism since the 1970s.

No Man's Land begins with Ted Hughes's "Lovesong"— "His words were occupying armies / Her laughs were an

assassins attempts"—and circles back to Sylvia Plath's poems of vengeful female victory, "Lady Lazarus" and "Daddy." Throughout, Gilbert and Gubar deploy representative figures and intertexts. And their study is sweepingly comprehensive. Sometimes it briefly changes the light by which we view a work; sometimes it goes into brilliantly disturbing detail. After these first chapters on the sex war represented in texts, the heat of battle seems to intensify in the middle chapters on competing male and female claims to be heirs of literary history. Gilbert and Gubar present male writers as hard driven by Nathaniel Hawthorne's "damned mob of scribbling [and publishing, popular, and money-making] women" to insist on the masculinity of the great tradition. In literature and in life they show male defensiveness over female literary success, rivalries with literary women, and usurpation of their work. Most interesting is the construction of a "literary history that denies the reality of women writers" (p. 153), especially by Eliot in "Tradition and the Individual Talent" and "The Wasteland," and by many others as well.

Women must all the more fend off doubts and affirm the reality of women writers. Gilbert and Gubar trace a relationship of affiliation between many women writers and their female precursors. If inheritance from foremothers is less assured than from forefathers, it is less automatic, and both demands and makes possible a more active choosing of the ancestral lines that count. While in the nineteenth century women suffered anxiety about being authors at all within a male literary tradition, in the twentieth century they increasingly sought a female tradition. This mitigated the anxiety of authorship and even offered a certain advantage as it loosed women from the anxiety of influence that still burdened men. Women were heirs of a less overwhelming great tradition, less belated, freer to form their own affiliations with the female past.

All this is argued through an enormous range of examples too long to list. The sheer number of women writers referred to is impressive evidence of the burgeoning of writing by women since the nineteenth century, and of the need for this book. Gilbert and Gubar give all this writing a place in literary history, and challenge our conception of that history in order to accommodate it. Their work takes part in the battle between the sexes over literary history that it analyzes.

In their last chapter they treat the rival claims of the sexes to be makers of language. Again they may be said to take sides, but here the line they draw falls not only between women and men but between themselves and neo-Freudian theorists of language, and between their own Anglo-American feminism and the French feminist camp.

At stake is whether language is a "materna lingua" or "patrius sermo," a mother tongue or phallologos. Gilbert and Gubar stress male fears of losing linguistic control, especially an "anxiety of the vernacular." Losing much of the gender privilege of education in classical and learned languages, men faced the rising power of ordinary language that gave them no special fluency compared to women. Gilbert and Gubar discuss the low status of the mother tongue with reference only to its sexual association. Their book does little to correlate sexual terms with socioeconomic-educational-class terms of analysis. This might certainly be done in the case of the vernacular, which is the language of the nonelite, including but not limited to women.

Male efforts to recapture an elite language appear in difficulty, abstraction, obscurity of style. The examples include not only Stéphane Mallarmé and James Joyce but Jacques Derrida. Gilbert and Gubar show women writers usurping and parodying male high language. Gertrude Stein makes English itself into a foreign tongue. H. D.'s punning is linguistically high-handed. And women also enjoy more exuberance than "vertigo of the vernacular" than men. Gilbert and Gubar might credit male writers such as Joyce with a certain amount of reveling in the linguistically low as well as the high. Throughout, they treat the male case with understanding, but, it must be said, the female case with more. The neuter only could be neutral according to their view of sex antagonism, so that they seem as fair as can be expected.

The main assertions of this chapter are that "the female subject is not necessarily alienated from the words she writes and speaks," and further that there is an "astonishing priority of that mother tongue which is common to both men and women" (pp. 229, 266). To argue these points Gilbert and Gubar must counter the neo-Freudian language theory of Jacques Lacan, disclaim phallogocentrism, dissociate language acquisition from the Oedipus complex, so concerned with relations with the father, and locate it earlier in relations with the mother who "in many cultures . . . feeds the child words even as she furnishes her or him with food" (p. 264). In certain funny, punny displays of their own linguistic power, Gilbert and Gubar call for a recognition of grandmatology, and they let it be known that "Mom is not mum."

They should have extended this whole discussion, for it is one of their most important. They have distanced themselves from Freudian theory enough to stand against its most influential current revision. And since that revision has influenced a whole camp of feminist theory, they stand against that, too. They oppose Julia Kristeva and the French feminism that holds that the Name of the Father is inscribed in language itself. Gilbert and Gubar do not consider women's oppression to be that primal. And their book presents us with a female volubility, a record of publication, an honor roll of powerful women authors sufficient to have helped shape the literary history of the whole period, and to cast in doubt any Freudian or feminist theory of language that makes it out to be a father and not a mother tongue.

Terry Castle (essay date 2 June 1989)

SOURCE: "Pursuing the Amazonian Dream," in *Times Literary Supplement,* June 2, 1989, pp. 607–08.

[*In the following essay,* Castle *discusses* Sexchanges, *and reviews Gubar and Gilbert's argument that men's deaths have sparked women's creativity.*]

In **Sexchanges,** the latest instalment of **No Man's Land,** their ambitious multi-volume study of woman writers of the twentieth century, the feminist critics Sandra Gilbert and Susan Gubar edge, not without anxiety, towards a disturbing yet suggestive theory of the female imagination: that women's creativity is unleashed, if not powerfully excited, by the deaths of men. Describing the tremendous outpouring of women's writing during and after the First World War, they draw a fearsome yet compelling conclusion: that the spectacle of collective male agony and vastation—the abrupt removal of an entire generation of brothers, sons, and lovers—provided a subterranean psychological liberation for women writers. Even while Virginia Woolf, Vera Brittain, Edith Wharton and Katherine Mansfield mourned the devastation wrought by the war, observe Gilbert and Gubar, their fictional and autobiographical works expressed a latent realization "even at the height of the conflict, that not only their society but also their art had been subtly strengthened."

> Vera Brittain noted that when her fiancé, Roland, was killed, "his mother began to write, in semi-fictional form, a memoir of his life," and added that she herself was "filled with longing to write a book about Roland." And in *A Son at the Front*, an admiring tale of an artist-father whose art is mysteriously revitalized by the death of his soldier son, Edith Wharton offered an encoded description of a similar transformation of a dead man into an enlivening muse.

Similarly "enlivening" effects were felt among women poets. In an extreme case, as in the gruesomely jingoistic verse of Jessie Pope quoted by Nosheen Khan in *Women's Poetry of the First World War*, an unconscious delight in the drama of male maiming and destruction seems almost palpable. Witness Pope's ghoulish urging of the troops off to war in "The Call" ("Who's for the trench— / Are you, my laddie?") or her jolly refusal, in "The One-Legged Soldier", to feel sorry for men who've had their legs blown off. "Though one shank may be wooden", she cheerfully intones, "There's a kick left in the good'un." Other women, such as the American-born poet Mary Borden, wrote more bitterly of male suffering, yet even here, in the most eloquent anti-war verse, one senses a subliminal freeing up, as though the ordeal of the loved one were also functioning as a powerful licence, an enabling event, imbuing the female poet's voice with new and unprecedented authority.

Gilbert and Gubar, it must be said, seem ill at ease with the notion of a "dead man" at the heart of female creativity. In their preface they apologize, rather nervously, for the dead-man-as-muse idea. "Our analysis of the asymmetrical responses of literary men and literary women to the Great War that haunts modern memory inevitably uncovers a distressing sexual competition which seems to have allowed at least some women to profit from male pain." Reflecting on this "disturbing material", they conclude self-protectively, "Reader, we felt we had to write it, but please don't kill the messenger."

The ambivalence is understandable. It is indeed unsettling to discover that certain kinds of creativity may be enhanced by the displaced fulfilment of hostile, even murderous wishes. Yet once acknowledged, the notion that women writers throughout history have been inspired by a subliminal desire to take the place of men is not so easily dismissed. Given the age-old cultural taboo against female self-expression, a woman can only begin to write, it seems, by activating in herself some fantasy of usurpation: some dream of rivalling or supplanting that man (real or symbolic) who flaunts his power over her. For Gilbert and Gubar, women's writing has, from its beginnings, obsessively revealed a hidden aggressive wish—for revenge against masculine authority, for a silencing of the male voice, for some utopian space from which men or their books have been *removed*. In women's literature of the late nineteenth and early twentieth centuries—in the writings of Charlotte Perkins Gilman, Olive Schreiner, Willa Cather, Kate Chopin, Edith Wharton, Gertrude Stein and Djuna Barnes—the wish manifested itself, they argue, in the recurrent figuring of what they call a "Herland" or "No Man's Land": an imaginative landscape in which men are absent or irrelevant and women live happily on without them.

One could say that feminist literary critics are just now beginning to discover what misogynists have known all along. In earlier centuries, as Janet Todd reminds us in her useful survey of eighteenth-century English women's writing, *The Sign of Angellica*, male writers realized precisely what antagonistic impulses might be at work when women took up the pen. "In former times", wrote Samuel Johnson in 1753, "the pen, like the sword, was considered as consigned by nature to the hands of men. . . . The revolution of years has now produced a generation of Amazons of the pen, who with the spirit of their predecessors have set masculine tyranny at defiance." At least since the eighteenth century—when women first entered the literary market-place in large numbers—the problem for women writers has been how to come to terms with the aggressive (if disguised) "Amazonian" wish legislating their own creative acts.

In [Janet] Todd's account [*The Sign of Angelica: Women, Writing, and Fiction 1660–1800*] the psychic freedom of the first professional women writers gives way in subsequent generations to increasing diffidence and self-suppression. In the works and careers of late seventeenth and early eighteenth-century women the urge to compete with men seems relatively uncensored: Todd writes engagingly of the "naughty triumvirate" of Aphra Behn, Delarivier Manley and Eliza Haywood—each of whom enjoyed doing battle with male rivals and inventing stories in which female characters triumphed blatantly over feckless fathers and lovers. She is also good on the rebellious "empress-mongering" of Margaret Cavendish, the eccentric Duchess of Newcastle, who signed her works "Margaret the First" and proudly imagined herself the ruler of a new gynocentric universe. In a characteristically uninhibited gesture, the fantastical duchess disrupted a meeting of the all-male Royal Society by appearing in an over-the-top mixture of male and female clothing and "an immense petticoat requiring six maids for support."

Later in the eighteenth century, however, as masculine antipathy to the new class of "scribbling women" grew, women writers increasingly veiled their competitive impulses. Todd describes the intensifying pressure on women to conform to what were perceived as acceptably feminine styles of authorship—to exempt from their writing any trace of self-promotion, wit, scurrilousness, or anti-male critique. By the end of the eighteenth century, most women writers had more or less resigned themselves to the genteel model of female authorship: sentimental novels, conduct books and educational tracts flowed from their pens in a polite, inoffensive burble. A writer like Mary Wollstonecraft, whose work preserved something of the forthright utopianism (and rhetorical violence) of the earlier women writers, found herself treated as a pariah.

The aggressive energy informing female authorship surfaced obliquely of course—in feats of productivity (the pious Hannan More published over a hundred works) and in subversive deformations of established plots and genres. In many early novels by women, for example, the conventional happy ending—the marriage of the heroine—more often appears as a species of subtle torture: Burney's beleaguered heroines (as Todd notes) totter into matrimony "like invalids entering an asylum." Certain genres likewise provided a covert psychological outlet for women writers. As the excellent new volume of essays *Writing the Female Voice*, edited by Elizabeth C. Goldsmith, suggests, the epistolary novel was from its beginnings associated with residual female power and challenges to patriarchal authority. By masquerading as "private" writing, letter fiction allowed women to "write the female voice" in a relatively unconstrained way and to elaborate, once again, undercover dreams of social and erotic resistance.

The theme of covert resistance is central to Nancy K. Miller's exciting new book of feminist literary theory, *Subject to Change*. Miller (whose last book *The Heroine's Text* dealt with the sexual plots of French eighteenth-century fiction) has some claim to being considered the most interesting and thoughtful critic now working on the history of women's writing. (Along with Jane Gallop, she is also one of the wittiest.) The subtitle "Reading feminist writing" is significant: like Gilbert and Gubar, Miller is concerned with the transgressive aspects of female creativity and the ways in which women's texts since the seventeenth century, particularly in France, have incorporated an ongoing "poetics of dissent"—an alternative vision of literature and its production.

A women writer becomes a feminist writer, according to Miller, when her work exhibits (in however veiled a fashion) a "signature" of gender. To discover in women's writing the "marks of a producing subject" the critic must engage in a process which Miller, happily reclaiming a once-suspect term, dubs "overreading." Overreading is the search for that "icon or emblem within the fiction itself that obliquely figures the symbolic and material process entailed in becoming a (woman) writer." In Miller's most important historical example, Madame de Lafayette's *La Princesse de Clèves*, the charismatic sign of female authority is the figure of the pavilion—that space to which the heroine retreats after her decision not to marry the Duc de Nemours. By refusing "male sexuality as a plot", writes Miller, the princess (along with her creator) also refuses the patriarchal plot of literature itself. The feminized space of the pavilion can be read both as "the iconography of a desire for a revision of story, and in particular as a revision of closure" and as a sign of Lafayette's own resistance to the cultural taboo against female self-expression. Later French women writers—Graffigny, Staël, Sand and Colette—obsessively rewrite Lafayette's "refusal of love" scenario, returning explicitly to the pavilion as a figure for female artistic autonomy. In George Sand's *Valentine*, for example, the heroine, avoiding the consummation of her marriage to a count, retreats with a male admirer to a *folie* on the edge of her husband's country estate and embarks on a painting career. In this "transformation of an essentially frivolous place . . . into a scene of artistic and intellectual production", writes Miller, one may detect both "a feminist appropriation of the pastoral matrix" and the "anguished alibi of the woman [Sand] who would justify her passage to writing."

Is Miller's "signature" yet another version of the competitive wish at the heart of women's writing? Interestingly enough, Miller's own appropriations of critical authority seem linked to a half-conscious triumph over a (dead) male mentor. In a number of essays in *Subject to Change*, Miller, as if motivated by a repetition compulsion, returns several times to Roland Barthes's famous essay "The Death of the Author" precisely in order to assail Barthes for being indifferent to the issue of gender:

> The postmodernist decision that the Author is Dead and the subject along with him does not, I will argue, necessarily hold for women, and prematurely forecloses the question of agency for them. Because women have not had the same historical relation of identity to origin, institution, production that men have had, they have not, I think (collectively) felt burdened by *too much* Self, Ego, Cogito, etc. Because the female subject has juridically been excluded from the polis, hence decentred, "disoriginated," deinstitutionalized, etc., her relation to integrity and textuality, desire and authority, displays structurally important differences from that universal position.

Women intellectuals, of course, have always been fascinated by Barthes; the loving *hommage à Roland* has been a staple in women's recent critical writing from Susan Sontag to Helen Vendler. And Miller, in her own way, loves him too, acknowledging with affection the "seductive" influence that Barthes's playful theorizing has had on her own work. Miller's extravagant, ingratiating style is Barthesian in inspiration; likewise her elegant attention to literature's "pleasures, dangers, zones, and codes of reference." At the same time, however, Barthes operates here, as the blurb ambiguously has it, as a "famously Dead Author"—the dead male muse—whose absence from the scene allows Miller room for her own very powerful assertions of difference. The rebellious psychodynamics of women's writing thus reinscribe themselves in the subliminal spaces of feminist criticism.

After the brilliant coruscations of Miller's work, Tess Cosslett's far more conventional book *Woman to Woman: Female friendship in Victorian fiction* seems tame. Cosslett's central thesis is not exactly inflammatory: female friendship in nineteenth-century women's fiction, she argues, is contained within "a male—female romance structure" where it functions "to assimilate the women to conventional roles, and to bring about the male—female resolution." Women's friendships uphold patriarchal order: through a bond with another woman (who may be very different in personality, status, or aspirations) the Victorian heroine "comes to terms" with those problematic aspects of herself which must be resolved before she can be safely married off to a man. Thus the independent heroine may come "to recognize her sexuality through her contact with a 'fallen women'" or the fallen woman may be "reclaimed for respectability by her 'pure' sister." In readings of Eliot, Charlotte Brontë, Barrett Browning and several lesser writers, Cosslett pursues the same claustrophobic argument with little modification: that far from being a radical assertion of female solidarity, the typical Victorian fictional women's friendship is merely a temporary stage in a larger cultural "parable" of female repression and confinement. The reader must avoid, above all, interpreting such friendship subversively, as displaced lesbian desire: nineteenth-century women writers, says Cosslett, "negotiated" with contemporary conservative ideology "and 'lesbian' was not a concept available to them."

In this questionable assertion, one senses the critic in retreat from the radical potentialities of her own subject. Yet it is perhaps not fair to blame Cosslett alone for a failure of nerve. While feminist critics have begun to explore the competitive urges activating women's writing—the Amazonian dream of usurping male authority—they have been reluctant to connect this separatist fantasizing with any explicitly lesbian poetics. Gilbert and Gubar, it is true, embark on such a project in the last chapters of *Sexchanges*, where they discuss at some length the lives and works of various lesbian modernists after the First World War. They cite Renée Vivien's droll assertion that men represent the "unaesthetic par excellence" and Woolf's nostalgic plaint that "only on Lesbos" did women possess the ideal conditions for creativity.

Yet even here one senses a lingering anxiety—manifest most strikingly in the curiously intense attack that Gilbert and Gubar wage on Gertrude Stein, the undisputed Penthesileia of modern women's letters. They are hostile to Stein's public and private acts of "male impersonation" and sympathize with Alice B. Toklas, consigned (as they see it) to the thankless role of wife to a pseudo-male genius. On no evidence to speak of they hint that Alice, not the macho Gertrude, really wrote *The Autobiography of Alice B. Toklas*. This odd Steinbashing seems significant: Stein may indeed pose a limit case for heterosexual feminists. Stein's dream of repossessing masculine power was shockingly visible, not only in the spectacular high butch drama of her physical presence (and in her unsentimental dealings with male rivals like her brother Leo and Ernest Hemingway) but in the sheer transgressiveness of her writing, in which she strove both to reinvent English prose and to commemorate her sexual love for another woman. We still barely know how to read her—either her dislocations of language or her dislocations of power. And though Gilbert and Gubar might disagree, precisely because Stein lived out her wish for mastery in a less censored way than any woman writer before or since, she remains, still, our most truthful and intransigent image of feminist literary authority.

Celia Patterson (review date Spring 1989)

SOURCE: A review of *No Man's Land, Volume 2: Sexchanges,* in *Tulsa Studies in Women's Literature,* Vol. 8, No. 1, Spring, 1989, pp. 128–30.

[*In the following review of* Sexchanges, *Patterson explores Gubar and Gilbert's emphasis on World War I as a cause and metaphor for the sexual struggle between men and women at the beginning of the twentieth century.*]

Sexchanges explores revisions of gender that occurred in society and were reflected in literature from the 1880s through the 1930s. As in their first volume (1988), in volume two Gilbert and Gubar continue to associate sexual difference with sexual antagonism, although they focus here on the antagonism specifically related to redefinitions of gender and sexuality: "the sexes battle because sex roles change, but, when the sexes battle, sex itself (that is, eroticism) changes" (p. xi).

The book begins with an analysis of Rider Haggard's *She* (1887). The heroine, *She-who-must-be-obeyed*, is "a monstrously passionate woman with angelic charm" (p. 6) that no man can resist, the matriarchal ruler of an African kingdom, the possessor of the secret of immortality, all of which make her particularly threatening to the male who has been sent to destroy her. Her misrule is ended when she is annihilated by a "phallic pillar of fire" (p. 46), a denouement that resolves the problem of female power and restores patriarchal authority, thus alleviating male anxiety over the rising autonomy of the New Woman in the second half of the nineteenth century.

This apocalyptic destruction of the heroine sets the standard for the great male hostility toward female power that Gilbert and Gubar extract from every male text they analyze. Male perception of increasing female power as a threat is not matched, however, by female perception of the "fragility or even the fictionality" (p. xii) of that power. This "asymmetry" (an asymmetry that Gilbert and Gubar christen "the MLA syndrome," "given the ambivalent responses to the visibility of women in our own largest professional organization," p. 50) sets the measure for comparisons throughout the volume. In the literary battle between the sexes, the male strategy is to win by destroying the enemy; the female strategy is to win "without directly engaging in combat" (p. 50). Sometimes a female author's tactics of avoiding the enemy involve either the heroine's chosen self-destruction or her unavoidable destruction due to natural and cultural constraints placed on her eroticism. Sometimes a heroine is saved by repudiating eroticism, like the women in Charlotte Perkins Gilman's *Herland* who reproduce through parthenogenesis. Sometimes female desire is ignored altogether or found "unsayable" (p. 168), as in works by Edith Wharton and Willa Cather who concentrate on analyzing the social aspects of the American version of "feminization and its discontents" (p. 120).

As the literary battle of the sexes moved into the modernist period, female authors began to imagine successful alternatives to the gender definitions that constrained their desire. Eschewing "the fatality of heterosexuality" (p. 193), the lesbian expatriates in Paris in the early part of the twentieth century devoted themselves to "reinventing gender" (p. 213) in life and in literature. Alienated from both male and female literary traditions, they developed the aesthetic strategy of collaboration, constructing "a literary tradition out of what they had: each other" (p. 222). (This strategy has been recuperated by Gilbert and Gubar through their own collaboration as feminist critics alienated from male critical traditions.) Many female modernists also engaged in cross-dressing, in their lives as well as in their texts, as a means of redressing gender difference and as a metaphor for transcending biological sexuality. Regarding costumes as selves (that is, as psychological identities) and selves as costumes, they changed both with equal ease, thus subverting the idea of categorical gender difference altogether, the source of that antagonism Gilbert and Gubar implicitly identify as the basis for sexual battles.

Undoubtedly chapter 7, "'Soldier's Heart': Literary Men, Literary Women, and the Great War" (reprinted here from *Signs,* 8, No. 3 [1983]) will serve as the "heart" of all three volumes. The Great War provides the title for their work, "no man's land," the strip of land between opposing trenches that no man could inhabit. The war also seems to be the source of their consistently militaristic rhetoric and serves as a paradigm for their theme, the battle of the sexes. They rewrite the history of the war, representing it not so much as a struggle between the Central and the Allied Powers as a struggle between male and female powers, "*as if* the Great War itself were primarily a climactic episode in a battle of the sexes that had already been raging for years" (p. 260, emphasis mine). The "unmanning terrors of combat" (p. 260) turned men into "no-men" "not men" (p. 260), while women assumed positions of power on the homefront—taking the jobs the men left behind—or served at the front as nurses and ambulance drivers with passive and dependent male patients, so reversing the normal social order. While men fell, women rose, much (contend Gilbert and Gubar) to women's satisfaction. Understandably women appreciated, even celebrated, the higher wages, the autonomy, the positions of power, the sense of participating in history that the war provided many women for the first time; unfortunately men often perceived women's attitudes toward their new power as ghoulish, depicting their female characters as vampires "who feed on wounds and are fertilized by blood" (p. 262). Gilbert and Gubar seem to concur in this opinion in their analysis of both male and female texts of the period, positing a female "sexual glee" in contrast to a male "sexual gloom" (p. 264). The proposition is a disturbing one. No wonder they ask for mercy in their preface: "Reader, we felt we had to write it, but please don't kill the messenger" (p. xvii).

Pamela L. Caughie (essay date Spring 1989)

SOURCE: "The (En)gendering of Literary History," in *Tulsa Studies in Women's Literature,* Vol. 8, No. 1, Spring 1989, pp. 111–20.

[*In the following essay, Caughie contrasts Gubar and Gilbert's* The War of Words—*which explains modernism as a male reaction against the appearance of women writers*—*with Michael H. Levinson's* A Genealogy of Modernism: A Study of English Literary Doctrine 1908–1922.]

> *Engender*: 1. Of the male parent: To beget; "Thanne sholde he take a yong wyf and a feir / On which he myghte engendre hym an heir" (*The Merchant's Tale,* 28–29); 2. Of the female parent: To conceive, bear; "O Error, soon conceived, / Thou never coms't unto a happy birth, / But kill'st the mother that engend'red thee!"
>
> (*Julius Caesar,* V, iii, 70–72)

The making of the modern has become a critical preoccupation in recent works, both as a *subject* (how modernism was made by its practitioners) and as an *ideology* (how modernism has been and will be made by literary historians). Various books, such as Robert Kiely's collection, *Modernism Reconsidered* (Harvard, 1983), Alice Jardine's *Gynesis: Configurations of Woman and Modernity* (Cornell, 1985), Perry Meisel's *The Myth of the Modern* (Yale, 1987), and Sydney Janet Kaplan's forthcoming *Katherine Mansfield and the Origins of Modernist Fiction,* focus on different writers, isolate different time periods, read different texts, and as a result, construct divergent explanations for the engendering of literary modernism. If I single out Levenson's *Genealogy* and Gilbert and Gubar's

No Man's Land, it is because their asymmetry clearly sets the stakes in these efforts to make modernism. The former book painstakingly sets forth the conflicting forces that converged to form a particular strain of canonical modernism; the latter book provocatively challenges the very grounds of that argument.

The titles of these two works display their differences: Levenson's approach is temporal, Gilbert and Gubar's, spatial; Levenson covers a mere fourteen years, Gilbert and Gubar well over a century. The title of my review, taken (with parentheses added) from Gilbert and Gubar, and my headnote, adapted from the *OED*, specify their different emphases. For Levenson, the engendering of literary modernism, or one line of it, takes the form of a "recognizable lineage" among Hulme, Ford, Pound, Lewis, and Eliot. Excluding women from his study and ending with Eliot as the "heir of English modernism" (p. x), his understanding of *engender* would seem to be "of the male parent." In contrast, Gilbert and Gubar's understanding of *engender* stresses not the heir but the error of such accounts as Levenson's that "kill'st the mother," whether by neglecting a matrilinear development or by idealizing the mother as muse. Their book is a gendering of literary history, which for them means seeing what has long been discussed in terms of a generational conflict as masking "a more profound sexual-literary struggle" (p. 126), the battle of the sexes that is their metaphor throughout. They use *engender* in the second sense, "of the female parent," not only in their fourth chapter on "The Female Affiliation Complex," but also in their argument that women have been the bearers of literary modernism. The difference between these two books, then, could be said to boil down to the difference between the two definitions of *engender*: fathering and mothering. Levenson analyzes literary history as something made, in this case, by a few key men (p. x); Gilbert and Gubar analyze the history that has made us (p. xiii), the woman's cause and its historical ramifications.

Michael Levenson's book is, in his words, "a study in literary transition" (p. x). Levenson traces in detail the "minute changes" in modernist theory and practice over a short period of time, mainly the years 1908 to 1914, changes in thinking that have been seen as contradictions or confusions in light of the postwar period of "consolidation" from 1915 to 1922. Beginning with a reading of Conrad's *The Nigger of the "Narcissus"* in the first two chapters, Levenson identifies contradictory tendencies in modernist writing: toward precise physical description (realism) and toward the depths of consciousness (subjectivism). Placed in the context of Arnold, Pater, and Huxley, Conrad's novel reveals the "ideological crisis" of modernism, the conflict between *physis* and *psyche*, objectivity and subjectivity, authority and the individual. It is the changing shape of this crisis, and the critical confusion it has led to, that Levenson explores throughout. The next three chapters place Hulme, Ford, and Pound in the context of the subjectivist tradition from Arnold and Pater to Conrad and James in order to show that far from turning away from romanticist individualism, modernist Impressionism, Imagism, and Vorticism were at this time intensely, even aggressively, individualistic, only later to be read by their practitioners as anti-individualist. Levenson's point: "modernism was individualist before it was anti-individualist, anti-traditional before it was traditional, inclined to anarchism before it was inclined to authoritarianism" (p. 79).

The remaining four chapters account for this change, tracing Hulme's movement from romanticism to classicism and then to abstractionism, as well as Pound's movement, through Eliot's influence, from an assertion of the artist's self-sufficiency to an emphasis on control and traditional authority, from imagism and free verse to controlled and complex poetry. It is Eliot, Levenson says, who sought "to revise and reorder the prevailing modernist ideas, to free them of contradiction, to provide for them an adequate theoretical base" (p. 159). In doing so, "Eliot systematically undermined a series of formerly dominant concepts: sincerity, simplicity, freedom, expression, emotion" (p. 159), thereby winning modernism a place in the established literary order it had so long opposed. Thus Eliot's importance for Levenson's study: he revised the early oppositions into a new equilibrium and consolidated opposing tendencies between individualism and tradition (pp. 186, 219). Eliot is the heir to modernism not because he inherited it but because he made it. Without him, this genealogy could not have been written.

"Genealogy," writes Foucault in "Nietzsche, Genealogy, History," "requires patience and a knowledge of details, and it depends on a vast accumulation of source material. . . . It opposes itself to the search for 'origins.'"[1] Genealogy, he continues, focuses on contradictions and on the changes in a word, like *modernism*, not on its continuity. It is in this sense that Levenson's study is a genealogy, not a search for a father or for origins, Levenson says, but for "relative contributions" (p. 104); an insistence not on the continuity of a movement but on its instability (p. 187). It is his "relentless erudition," his refusal of "metahistorical" explanation, and his attention to "the myriad events" through which the concept of modernism was formed (Foucault, p. 81) that makes Levenson's book valuable. The lineage Levenson traces "shows the heterogeneity of what was imagined as consistent with itself" (Foucault, p. 82). For these reasons, Levenson's is an excellent study in genealogy, restoring, as he says, the intricacy to a literary period too often treated as a piece.

Yet Levenson's study diverges from Foucault's genealogy in two important ways. The first has to do with the type of history each writes: Foucault's work is social history, Levenson's is intellectual history. The second has to do with the end of historical investigation. "As it is wrong to search for descent in an uninterrupted continuity," Foucault writes, and Levenson would agree, "we should avoid thinking of emergence as the final term of historical development" (p. 83). Ending with Eliot as the heir and unifier of modernism suggests such a final term, a culmination that, as Foucault reminds us, is merely an episode "in a series

of subjugations" (p. 83). Emergence, then, is not the closing off of a struggle but "a place of confrontation" (p. 84), a "non-place" (p. 85), a no man's land. It is at this place that Gilbert and Gubar enter, revealing the kind of thing that can be subjugated in a genealogy such as Levenson's. If, as Levenson shows, the "retreat to a sceptical individualism" in Ford and Hulme was "a retreat from mass culture, widening democracy, and . . . an encroaching scientific materialism" (p. 61), Gilbert and Gubar argue that such a retreat was also, and primarily, a retreat from woman and the steady encroachment of women on the literary marketplace. And further, the difficult position of the male writers Levenson discusses, who attack the cultural authority on which their literary authority depends, points to the asymmetry of male and female modernists' responses to such cultural changes.

Because their spatial metaphor takes us into that no-place of literary struggle, Gilbert and Gubar give us less a genealogy (despite their focus on female affiliation and literary foremothers in chapter 4) than a metahistory, "a story of stories about gender strife": "In our view, the history of the sexual battle that we shall relate here is one of the major tales that begins to emerge from the apparent chaos of history, and it is a tale told differently over time and formulated differently by men and women" (p. xiv). Their story begins with a reading of Tennyson's *The Princess* published in 1847. Significantly, this is the year before the Seneca Falls Conference, which Karen Offen has recently cited as a commonly accepted beginning of American feminism.[2] Gilbert and Gubar's point is that the rise of feminism in the late nineteenth century along with women's increasing influence in the literary market—as writers, editors, publishers, and patrons—brought on the battle of the sexes and prepared for the advent of modernism. Tennyson's poem turns the anxiety of influence or generational conflict so often seen as the source of modernism into a sexual anxiety. In Ida's rebellion, Tennyson brings together aesthetic romanticism (forefathers) and political revolution (feminism) so that the "imaginative autonomy, sexual freedom, and political revolution" (p. 12) associated with romanticism are connoted feminine. Thus, the repudiation of artistic freedom and revolutionary aesthetics that Levenson traces in writers such as Babbitt, Hulme, Pound, and Eliot is for Gilbert and Gubar a reaction against "feminist demands" and "female power" (p. 12).

Their first chapter sets up the line of attack pursued through particular skirmishes waged throughout the book: women and men "engendered words and works" in response to the sexual antagonisms and anxiety brought on by the rise of feminism and the fall of the Victorian "lady," and thus modernism is "differently inflected" for men and women writers (p. xii). Focusing on the social and personal conflicts of the turn-of-the-century, Gilbert and Gubar present such sexual anxiety as the motivation behind modernism, "fueling the innovations of the avant garde in order to ward off the onslaughts of women" (p. 131). While the first two chapters present men's and women's different responses to the appearance of women on the social and literary scene, the third and fourth chapters present their asymmetrical responses to their female literary precursors of the nineteenth century. Finally, the fifth chapter, "Sexual Linguistics: Women's Sentence, Men's Sentencing" (a version of their 1985 *New Literary History* article), treats the battle of the sexes as a battle for linguistic primacy (p. 228) and shows how the different responses to literary mothers and the mother tongue inspired different kinds of linguistic fantasies in men's and women's texts.

A paragraph from Gilbert and Gubar's third chapter, "Tradition and the Female Talent: Modernism and Masculinism," summarizes their argument well:

> Thus when we focus not only on women's increasingly successful struggle for autonomy in the years from, say, 1880 to 1920, but also on their increasingly successful production of literary texts throughout the nineteenth and twentieth centuries, we find ourselves confronting an entirely different modernism. And it is a modernism constructed not just against the grain of Victorian male precursors, not just in the shadow of a shattered God, but as an integral part of a complex response to *female* precursors and contemporaries. Indeed, it is possible to hypothesize that a reaction-formation against the rise of literary women became not just a theme in modernist writing but a motive for modernism.
>
> (p. 156)

Set alongside a passage from Levenson's text, the differences are telling:

> Why egoism at this moment? . . . it is worth reiterating a suggestion raised in connection with Ford Madox Ford: namely that the coincident pressures of mass culture and technical culture put an unbearable strain on the culture of liberalism. . . . In the face of working-class militancy, religious and philosophic scepticism, scientific technology and the popular press, there was a tendency—especially among the artists and intellectuals—to withdraw into individual subjectivity as a refuge for threatened values.
>
> (p. 68)

A comparison of these passages clearly reveals that what Levenson discusses in terms of a cultural crisis giving rise to modernism (e.g., the loss of faith, the rise of technology, the spread of democracy) Gilbert and Gubar argue must be reexamined in conjunction with the profound change that occurred in the relations between the sexes from the mid-nineteenth century on. Thus, their focus on women is more than an analysis of sexual differences in writing, more than an argument for a counter canon of female modernism: it means no less than a paradigm shift in our thinking about literary history. One need not accept Gilbert and Gubar's basic premise—that the battle of the sexes is the motive force behind modernism—to see how significant their scholarship is for our construction of literary history, canons, and curriculums. Where Levenson seeks to restore modernity to history, Gilbert and Gubar

seek to restore women to modernity, and thus to social and literary history. As Susan Friedman puts it, the "man's 'case' (history) becomes the ground of the woman's 'cause.'"[3]

My emphasis on engendering along male and female lines, then, brings these books into strong relief, but at the risk of a reductive generalization. Seeing these two books only as patrilinear and matrilinear modernisms suggests that they represent two strains of modernism. They do not. And it is this very important point that may well be obscured by both books, in Gilbert and Gubar's insistence on sexual oppositions, as if men and women writers did not share interests and strategies, as well as in Levenson's division of modernism into "lines" of development, as if Woolf (omitted from this particular genealogy) could not be discussed along with Conrad and Eliot. Instead of male and female modernism or different lines of development, their different emphases should show us what's at stake in the making of literary history. As examples of the stakes in these histories, as well as the insights each book has to offer us, I want to focus on their different explanations of the same phenomena: namely, the great figure, Futurism, and T. S. Eliot.

Levenson explains what Ford called "the passing of the great figure" in terms of the modernists' "hostility toward the established order" (looking to the past, that is) conjoined with a loss of what Woolf called a "common belief": "[Ford] possesses no comprehensive vision, no moral authority, no proposals for reform. The great Victorian figure implied the possibility of a coherent and encompassing point of view—not the partial glimpse of the specialist, but the wide and comprehensive vision of a moral prophet. In a democratic and technological society, argued Ford, such figures were obsolete and unwanted . . ." (p. 52). But if, as Wyndham Lewis wrote, there was "no mature authority," it was due less, Gilbert and Gubar say, to the loss of an ideology than to the influx of women into the literary market, less to hostility toward male predecessors than to hostility toward female contemporaries: "Where the male precursor had had an acquiescent mother-muse, his heir now confronted rebellious ancestresses and ambitious female peers, literary women whose very existence called the concept of the willing muse into question" (p. 130).

Their presentations of the role of Futurism in modernist thought also reveal the different explanations produced by different starting points. Gilbert and Gubar see Marinetti's Futurism as characteristic of male modernists' hostility and violence. Futurism captured the attention of such modernists as Lewis and Lawrence, they argue, because "it captures the aggressiveness with which many men in England and America responded to feminist incursions" (p. 22). Quoting Marinetti to show the link between "male militarism and misogyny," they insist: "The militarist impulse that impelled the Futurists' glorification of war did not just help fuel a war that would occur in the near future; it also indirectly enacted and reflected the war between the sexes that was already being waged" (pp. 22–23).[4] According to Levenson, the early modernists, such as Hulme, Lewis, and Pound, rejected Futurism, except as it called for revolution in art and rebellion against the past: "They rejected the cult of technology, speed and machinery, the wilful lawlessness of Futurist pictorial composition and the poetic principle of 'words at liberty.' Futurism, as we shall see, became an important polemical adversary, and much of English modernist doctrine was defined in opposition to its principles" (p. 77).

But perhaps the most telling difference between these books lies in their treatment of Eliot. Levenson too has his war, "The War Among the Moderns," discussed in his penultimate chapter. Here Levenson focuses on the efforts of Pound and Eliot to counter the dissemination of modernist techniques and thereby to consolidate what Perry Meisel calls "the myth of the modern." One skirmish occurs between Pound and Amy Lowell over the name of Imagism. When Lowell was planning her collection, *Some Imagist Poets*, Pound feared that Lowell would appropriate the name "Imagism" and thus weaken the movement by undermining its coherent identity (p. 147) and its "elite nature" (p. 148).[5] The dispute was mirrored two years later in Eliot's review of *The New Poetry: An Anthology* edited by Harriet Monroe and Alice Corbin Henderson. In this review, Eliot takes issue with Monroe and Henderson's definition of literary modernism, opposing their "ideal of absolute simplicity and sincerity" with "the exercise . . . of intelligence" and their promotion of self-expression with an argument for "selection, suppression, control and order" (pp. 158–59). These attacks on Imagism and *vers libre*, Levenson says, were motivated by the need to distinguish the spurious from the genuine modernism (p. 154), much as early modernists needed to distinguish their innovations from their predecessors' poetry. Where early modernists proclaimed their freedom from traditional poetic standards, Eliot now proclaimed the need for such standards in order to defend modernism against freedom (and democratization) in art, for with such freedom came a loss of modernism's position as cultural vanguard. That is, a difficult and rigorous poetry was necessary to keep modernism in the hands of an elite, a point Gilbert and Gubar also make (p. 152). Eliot, like Pound, feared "the dissemination of literary method [would] work toward its vulgarization" (Levenson, p. 154). That vulgarization was mockingly termed "Amygism."

Levenson's war already intimates the lines of Gilbert and Gubar's battle. His examples call attention to the sexual politics bound up with this aesthetic conflict. But as important as the personal conflict between men and women (Pound, Eliot; Lowell, Monroe, Henderson) are the sexual connotations of this war against mass culture. For Gilbert and Gubar, this vulgarization is the vernacular, or the mother tongue feared by men. Women are in league with the materialism, the masses, the mediocrity threatening modernism. That is, such reassertion of control as Eliot and Pound exercise is an attempt to reclaim a *patrius sermo* and "to regain the mastery lost when male artists were

forced by history [with the rise of literacy, the spread of democracy, the entrance of women into the universities] to operate within the degrading confines of the vernacular mother tongue" (p. 259). The dense, hard, classical poetry often associated with modernism is a direct response to the democratization and dissemination of a literary method, but, Gilbert and Gubar argue, this dissemination, as well as the simplicity, sincerity, and freedom promoted by early modernists, is the result of women's role in the literary scene, and thus hard verse is a defensive reaction of men to their loss of literary authority.

Where Levenson focuses on the aesthetic conflict and the cultural politics in the making of modernism, Gilbert and Gubar focus on the personal conflicts and the sexual politics. If Eliot created for modernism a place in the established literary canon, he did so not just by providing it with a "stable literary doctrine," as Levenson says (p. 219), but by constructing a story of literary history "in which women played no part" (Gilbert and Gubar, p. 154). Eliot's turn to the metaphysical poets, his establishment of an ideal order in "Tradition and the Individual Talent," and his longing for an ideal past before the dissociation of sensibility set in, all work, Gilbert and Gubar note, to erase "the history associated with the entrance of women into the marketplace" (p. 154), a history that Levenson does not treat. *The Waste Land*, as Joyce quipped, "ends [the] idea of poetry for ladies" (p. 156) not just because it promotes a "masculine aesthetics of hard, abstract, learned verse" (p. 154), as Gilbert and Gubar say, but because the consolidation of modernism it represents effectively excludes women writers.

"How did male reactions [to women's presence in the literary market] inflect the engendering of literary history in the twentieth century?" Gilbert and Gubar ask (p. 129). Levenson's genealogy presents one answer to that question. "Eliot, who has become prominent recently, will *continue to be so*," Levenson asserts, "since he came to exemplify English modernism, since he presided over the changes in its definition and presentation, and since he wrote its most celebrated work. In a significant sense, he inherited the mantle of the London avant-garde, and it is our task to see what he made of the legacy" (p. 167, my emphasis). And it is Gilbert and Gubar's task to dismantle that legacy.

The motivation behind and the contribution of Gilbert and Gubar's book become quite apparent when read in the context of Levenson's. Read by itself, however, the book displays many problems: its militaristic rhetoric and its overgeneralizations can be irritating; its readings of selected passages neglect their larger textual contexts; its insistence on sexual oppositions obscures complexities; and its flagrant repetition makes this reader fear two more volumes. Read by itself, Levenson's study is a clear and complex discussion (which also, however, begets a maddening tendency to overexplain each and every digression) of the engendering of modernism. Read along with Gilbert and Gubar, its indebtedness to Eliot's version of literary history makes Levenson's study an act of affiliation, "the act of taking a son" (*OED*). Indeed, the child (literary historian) is father of the man (modernist doctrinaire). Both works reveal to varying extents a kind of circularity: Levenson's story tracing, not questioning, the literary history established by its own culmination, Eliot; Gilbert and Gubar's story telling a tale of sexual combat that their own rhetoric and examples presuppose.

There is no victor in this battle, unless it is the reader who learns the divergent ways modernism can be made. Where Gilbert and Gubar caution against privileging cultural and intellectual crises at the expense of social and sexual upheavals, Levenson cautions against privileging one metastory at the expense of ideational complexities and individual differences. Levenson subverts the very dualisms that structure Gilbert and Gubar's argument, showing how such oppositions are misplaced contrasts and tracing, in the words of George Eliot, "the suppressed transitions which unite all contrasts" (p. ix). Yet Gilbert and Gubar may well undermine the ground of Levenson's study, showing the extent to which Levenson is the heir of Eliot. As Levenson shows how modernism was made anew by a poet who comes to it late, so Gilbert and Gubar show how literary history will be made anew by feminist critics and historians belatedly entering the field.

Notes

1. Michel Foucault, *The Foucault Reader*, ed. Paul Rabinow (New York: Pantheon Books, 1984), p. 76. Subsequent references will appear parenthetically in the text.

2. Karen Offen, "Defining Feminism: A Comparative Historical Approach," *Signs*, 14 (Autumn 1988), 123. Dates signify. Gilbert and Gubar's beginning date coincides with the rise of feminism in America; Levenson's, as he points out, with the arrival of Pound in London. Gilbert and Gubar's study has no ending date, for the battle of the sexes is still being waged; Levenson ends in 1922 because in that year *The Waste Land, Ulysses,* and Yeats's *Later Poems* were published, marking the highpoint of modernism. Levenson significantly overlooks Woolf's *Jacob's Room* and Mansfield's *In the Garden Party* published as well in 1922, just as he overlooks Mansfield's arrival in London in the same year as Pound. But likewise, Gilbert and Gubar overlook important writers publishing, or trying to publish, in the 1840s, such as Feuerbach, Stirner, and Marx and Engels, whom Levenson discusses.

3. Susan Stanford Friedman, "Texts in the Trenches," *The Women's Review of Books*, 5, July 1988, 14.

4. The gender qualifier in the phrase "male militarism" is important since Gilbert and Gubar champion female militancy and aggression throughout. In chapter 2, "Fighting for Life: The Women's Cause," they begin by blaming male acts of aggression for inaugurating the battle of the sexes (p. 65) and thereby *obliging* women to engage in sexual combat (p. 66). Such "asymmetry," they argue, justifies in women's writing a violence they repudiate in men's.

5. While Levenson may seem to miss an important sexual difference here—the male (Pound's) insistence on proprietary rights, the female (Lowell's) insistence on wider dissemination—he goes on to point to "a small historical irony" that counters such a simple sexual opposition: "A year later, after the publication of *Some Imagist Poets,* Imagism became vastly fashionable in the United States, and Lowell was confronted with the circumstance that had tormented Pound, the loss of literary identity in the wash of imitators. Fearing that she might lose control of the movement, she herself considered copyrighting the name 'Imagist,'" something she had earlier told Pound he couldn't do (p. 148).

Elizabeth Rosdeitcher with Sandra M. Gilbert and Susan Gubar (interview date 1989)

SOURCE: "An Interview with Sandra M. Gilbert and Susan Gubar," in *Critical Texts: A Review of Theory and Criticism,* Vol. 6, No. 1, 1989, pp. 17–38.

[*In the following interview conducted by Rosdeitcher, Gubar and Gilbert discuss a variety of topics such as their work, women writers, feminist criticism, their critics, and their writing partnership.*]

[*Rosdeitcher:*] *I'd like to begin with a discussion of* **The Madwoman in the Attic***, which has come to be regarded as one of the founding texts of American feminist criticism. What did you feel were the most pressing issues it raised at the time of its publication?*

[Gubar:] Well, Sandra and I began thinking about *The Madwoman* in 1974, and as we were working on it a generation of feminist literary critics had begun to emerge, working primarily on issues of images of women in male literature and then on the recovery of the neglected or misread female literary tradition. The best example of the first category, images of women in male-authored literature, would be something like *Sexual Politics* by Kate Millett, which came out quite early.

In the second category, as we were writing, we were reading Ellen Moers's *Literary Women*, Pat Spacks's *Female Imagination*, and then Elaine Showalter's book, *A Literature of Their Own*. Both of those projects, images of women and the recovery of neglected or misread women, were obviously part of the impetus for the writing of *The Madwoman in the Attic*; that is, we were looking at texts by women from Jane Austen through George Eliot, Elizabeth Barrett Browning, Christina Rossetti, and Emily Dickinson in order to understand them as a response to male-authored images of women in Victorian literature.

At the same time, we were also fascinated by theories of literary history which seemed skewed by issues of gender that were not fully articulated, that were hidden inside, let's say, Harold Bloom's idea about the anxiety of influence. So finally we were trying not only to recover a neglected tradition, not only to read books that we thought were fascinating by linking them to each other and to a set of common themes or strategies—say, doubling or schizophrenia, disease, imprisonment—but also to figure out the dynamics of literary influence for women, and that was how we arrived at the concept of the "anxiety of authorship." We wanted to understand what it meant for the nineteenth-century woman writer to grapple with a predominantly male literary inheritance. How did that effort instill feelings of anxiety that then led her to subvert the conventions of genres she inherited because they were male-defined?

[Gilbert:] While everything that Susan says is absolutely true—especially in what I guess we'd all consider a "professional sense"—I'd like to add something more personal about how I, and I guess both of us, *experienced* our work on **The Madwoman**. We had never actually planned to write a book together; in fact, what happened was that we taught a course together in response to a need expressed to us at Indiana University in the fall of 1974. The department thought there should be courses on, of all things, *women* writers—and Susan and I discovered we were both interested in that subject. We got together and made up a syllabus, rather naively, out of all the books by women writers we felt we wanted to reread (or, indeed, to *read*, carefully, for the first time). Neither of us was trained in that field (which was in any case not then considered a "field"). I had specialized in modern British literature; Susan in eighteenth-century prose fiction. But I had just been rereading *Little Women, Jane Eyre*, and *Wuthering Heights* with my youngest child, then nine years old (a girl). And I thought I could, suddenly, see all kinds of mysterious and somewhat mystifying connections among these works. Susan, as I recall, was planning to write something about *Villette*. So we welcomed the chance to teach the course, although both of us, as I also remember, were fairly ignorant about what would now be called feminist theory. We'd read Simone de Beauvoir, Betty Friedan, and Kate Millett, but not much else. Most of the other stuff came out after we'd started writing the book.

After some struggle (I wanted at first to call the course "Upstairs/Downstairs," in honor of the TV program that was then popular), we compromised on a different title: **The Madwoman in the Attic.** I think that was because, after doing all this reading with my daughter Susanna, I had become fascinated by the figure of Bertha Mason Rochester, the infamous attic-bound first wife in *Jane Eyre*. I had vague, quite inchoate feelings that she had something to do with, on the one hand, Jo March (in *Little Women*) and, on the other hand, Heathcliff (in *Wuthering Heights*). I had odd ideas about doubles, but I couldn't have explained much more than this. I was really a poet and a critic of poetry, just beginning to learn how to read and analyze fiction!

But when Susan and I started to teach the course something magical happened. *All* the books—novels, poems, short stories, even essays—seemed to have significant relationships to each other. Thematic, stylistic, all kinds of connections. Neither of us, I should say, had ever studied any of these works in such a (female) context. I can say for myself, indeed, that I'd never *studied* most of them at all. In eight years of college and graduate school, I'd only read a few books by women—for example, Jane Austen's *Emma*, Virginia Woolf's *Mrs. Dalloway*, Emily Brontë's *Wuthering Heights*, a few Dickinson poems—that was pretty much it! And those works had been defined, conventionally, in terms of the history of the novel, the history of modernism, the Victorian tradition, or the American Renaissance. So, suddenly rereading them, along with other works, in this remarkably new way was utterly transformative. Susan and I used to call each other almost every night, literally screaming with excitement about the connections we saw. There *was*, we suddenly understood, what is now identified as a "female literary tradition"—a tradition that crosses all the usual geographic, generic, and historical boundaries. It was after that intellectual metamorphosis, as I recall, that we understood we wanted to write a book. More specifically, we were *seized* by the idea that we had to write a book about this. And it was then, too, that we began to read, with great passion, all the terrific criticism then beginning to appear—that is, works such as the ones Susan has mentioned: Moers' and Spacks's books, Judy Fetterley's *The Resisting Reader*, all of Elaine Showalter's work, and so forth.

In what way do you see women transforming male genres?

[Gilbert:] I'm not sure that I understand exactly what you mean by "male genres." Genres that are inherently or essentially *male*? Genres for the most part constructed by male writers? On the assumption that you mean the latter (since I don't think there are any such things as inherently masculine genres), I'd say that women sometimes feel alienated from certain literary forms that reflect a particular kind of male psychosexual development, forms that emphasize, for example, a "homosocial bonding" (to use a phrase Eve Sedgwick has popularized) with male-dominated tradition. I'm thinking of the pastoral elegy, the epic, the verse tragedy, all of which, in one way or another, represent the western literary tradition to itself, as it were—justifying God's ways to "man," offering the poet a consoling way of confronting mortality through visions of aesthetic resurrection, and so forth. These are modes in which, as we found in working on the **Norton Anthology of Literature by Women**, women writers only very infrequently write, either because (and we're not sure of the answer here) they don't *need* to, or they *can't*.

Compare Emily Dickinson with Walt Whitman, for instance. This odd couple founded American poetry as we now know it, its mother and father, and they have a lot more in common: they were radical innovators, artistic revolutionaries, brilliant performers of the self in a culture that hardly knew how to respond to what appeared to be their profoundly idiosyncratic texts. Yet while Dickinson seems in many ways linguistically and generically isolated from the art of her precursors (she almost always writes in what John Crowe Ransom called "folk meter"—that is, in the prosodic form of the Protestant hymnal—and never attempts difficult "classical" genres), Whitman alludes (for instance, in "When Lilacs Last in the Dooryard Bloom'd") to the pastoral elegy and (in "Out of the Cradle") to the standard Romantic poem of initiation (e.g., Wordsworth's "Intimations Ode") as well as, arguably (in "Song of Myself"), to such a quasi-epic as *The Prelude*. But this isn't to say that Dickinson is inferior to Whitman, or that Whitman is less "original" than Dickinson. Merely to say that they are strikingly different in their relationship to hegemonic (that is, male-created) genres.

[Gubar:] Well, but to a certain extent when you are dealing, let's say, with the history of the novel and you are facing the traditions established by male authors like Smollett, Fielding, Richardson, then the nineteenth-century woman writer might feel that she is confronted by conventions that need to be altered for her to experience her anger at those very scripts, her sense of discomfort. In her juvenilia, for example, Jane Austen parodied the sentimental epistolary novel most famously deployed by Richardson. And we dealt with that revisionary impulse, Sandra did, in her discussion of *Frankenstein* as a revision and a critique of Milton's *Paradise Lost*. When you think about Lucy Snowe in *Villette*, you can see the way in which Brontë is trying to come to terms with literary traditions linked to the Lucy of Wordsworth's famous poems, traditions related to the silencing of the heroine whose death really becomes a kind of impetus for the male poet, almost a source of inspiration. So the question of women resisting or reshaping what is inherited is a very important one.

I wonder if you could discuss the reception of The Madwoman, *how you think it has affected later works of criticism?*

[Gubar:] Well, **The Madwoman** was a lucky book because it received a very wonderful review in *The New York Times*, and it was then the runner up for the Pulitzer Prize and, I think, the National Book Critics Circle Award, so it got a lot of attention, much of it very good.

It received some critical reviews, one by Mary Jacobus in *Signs* that asked important questions about our conceptualization of historical change and the monolithic figure of the madwoman. So I would say the critical reviews were serious ones and posed important problems that we then went on to grapple with in later works. But for the most part that book has gotten the best reviews of anything we've published.

[Gilbert:] Yes, true. It *was* a lucky book, and we *did* learn a lot from skeptical reviews. But to be frank, I'd have to say that such a rapid success was in a way problematic for us. It has certainly meant a lot of anxiety about the "sequel," which is what our latest work, the three-volume *No*

Man's Land, supposedly is. Can one suffer from an anxiety of (one's *own*) influencing? I think perhaps we do, and have. I think that precisely because **The Madwoman** did elaborate a kind of monolithic "plot"—a plot for nineteenth-century (and earlier) women's literature that I believe we both still see in such work—we feared that we might be expected to, perhaps we *ought* to, come up with a comparable "plot" for feminism-and-modernism. But as you know, if you've been reading the successive volumes of **No Man's Land**, we feel that the plot becomes far more complicated in a post-suffrage, post-women-in-the-professions era; in fact, the plot has now become *plots*.

In some ways, your critical strategies seem to differ between **Madwoman in the Attic** *and* **No Man's Land**. *In* **The Madwoman** *you describe the mapping of a female literary history as not only the project of twentieth-century feminist critics but also of the nineteenth-century women's literature you discuss. You seem to participate in the task their works imply by telling "the story of the woman artist who enters the cavern of her own mind and finds there the scattered leaves not only of her own power but of the tradition which might have generated that power" (98). When in the twentieth century the relationship between women writers and their female precursors becomes more complex, partly because such precursors are known, your own assessment about what constitutes an empowering strategy seems different. In your chapter, "Sexual Linguistics," for example, you suggest that the revision of theories about women's relation to language is a common strategy of feminist texts including your own. Does this difference reflect a change in your own critical assumptions? Did your reading of twentieth-century writers elicit a change in these assumptions?*

[Gilbert:] I don't think our critical assumptions, such as they are—and they're fairly pragmatic—have changed significantly. I think we're still working as literary/cultural historians, albeit fairly newfangled ones. But to the extent that we find the Bloomian/Freudian model of literary psycho-history an appealing one—which needs nevertheless to be radically revised by feminist critics—we've had to factor in a whole set of profoundly new phenomena: the *visibility* of female precursors for both female and male writers; the entrance of women into the literary marketplace; the asymmetries of male and female history in the last century or so—of, that is, a history in which middle-class white women on, as we like to say, "both sides of the Atlantic," have increasingly gained public power while their male contemporaries have lost many of their great expectations, etcetera, etcetera. And that's why, as I just remarked, the "plot" of **The Madwoman**, such as it was, has become a complex of "plots."

[Gubar:] I'm not sure that our critical assumptions haven't changed. Putting together the **Norton Anthology of Literature by Women** impressed on both of us, I suspect, the diversity of women's literary accomplishments in the twentieth century. That book intervened between **The Madwoman** and the first volume of **No Man's Land**. Also, as Sandra has just suggested, we've begun focusing on the interactions of men and women in an historical age when literary women did have scribbling sibling rivalries with their male contemporaries. So, for example, we study modernism in *The War of the Words* not only in terms of the anxiety of a rising middle class, the Great War, the dark Satanic mills of industrialization, and the death of God, but also in terms of male anxiety about women's prominence in the literary marketplace. We're not arguing that those other factors aren't important—clearly they are—but that there was yet another anxiety for such writers as Joyce, Eliot, Lawrence, and Hemingway: a sexual anxiety fostered by the powerful female matrilineage established in the nineteenth century.

At the same time, we are now beginning to think that in the twentieth century, the woman writer facing a female literary past, seeing very visible female precursors like Jane Austen, the Brontës, and George Eliot, had to come to terms with her relationship to her female precursors. To what extent does that matrilineage become empowering because it establishes models for female creativity? To what extent does it foster a sense of belatedness, the feeling among twentieth-century literary women that they are no longer in a position of primacy as pioneers? Also is there therefore a sense of a kind of rivalry with the past? If the nature of the past is one of disease, of anger, of isolation, what does it mean to become a woman writer in the twentieth century? These are the ideas with which we grappled when we wrote the chapter in *The War of the Words* on "The Female Affiliation Complex."

So you suggest that women writers are in fact ambivalent about this inheritance?

[Gubar:] We had originally thought that it would be very empowering. Our first idea was that in the nineteenth century the woman writer had no female precursors.

[Gilbert:] And so, as Elizabeth Barrett Browning said, "England has had many learned ladies, but where are the poetesses? I look everywhere for grandmothers and find none." In other words, for nineteenth-century women writers, we felt, the very concept of a literary matrilineage was sort of a turn-on. You can certainly see this in some of Emily Dickinson's writings about Barrett Browning—for instance, in the poem that begins "I think I was enchanted / When first a sombre Girl— / I read that Foreign Lady—." And you can obviously see it, too, in the Barrett Browning remark I just quoted. And yet, and yet . . .

[Gubar:] So we assumed that in the twentieth century when literary women looked back and found literary mothers and grandmothers they would be ecstatic. But what we found was something much more complex, something much more problematic.

[Gilbert:] We found, in fact, something that does suggest rivalry as well as reverence. Or anyway something that suggests a kind of nervousness about ancestresses. If Char-

lotte Brontë was, as Virginia Woolf thinks (and says in *A Room of One's Own*), a powerfully originatory figure, what does that mean for her granddaughters? Can they share in her imaginative strength, or did she use it all up, use up the genre, the audience, the metaphors, the language? And if they *can* share her strength, does that mean they must also share her pain?

To what extent do you think all female writers are engaged in coming to terms with a specifically female literary past?

[Gubar:] Oh, I think they are up to the present day. Margaret Drabble asks, how happy was Emma when she married Mr. Knightly? Did she enjoy being in bed with him? Margaret Atwood rewrites *Jane Eyre* in *Lady Oracle*, and Erica Jong frequently laments the fact that there is no female Chaucer, that her ancestresses from Emily Dickinson through Virginia Woolf were severe or suicidal. This is an issue that is very perplexing still today. When Adrienne Rich confronts Emily Dickinson, she does write a lyrical essay celebrating "Vesuvius At Home," but she also composes a poem about Emily Dickinson in which she suggests that Dickinson had it out "on her own premises" in part because she was a "woman, masculine/in single-mindedness," a woman her mentor considered "half-cracked."

[Gilbert:] And similarly both Sylvia Plath and Anne Sexton worry about "whining and quailing" like Edna St. Vincent Millay or Sara Teasdale. They worry, that is, about seeming to be "lady poets" or "poetesses." Yet even while they suffer from these anxieties, each in her own way pays homage to female precursors. Plath says of Virginia Woolf that "her books make mine possible" and Anne Sexton writes a beautiful tribute to Plath, after Plath's suicide. In the same mode, Elizabeth Bishop complains in a letter that art is art and gender gender, but composes her inspiring and inspired "Invitation to Miss Marianne Moore." All these mixed messages and the ambiguities they represent are brilliantly summarized, by the way, in Caryl Churchill's play *Top Girls*, where a group of celebrated women from history and literature meet at a dinner party and reveal both the triumphs and the tribulations of the female past.

Are you saying that you no longer focus on the *madwoman or on* the *tradition in English, but on multiple responses to crucial historical events?*

[Gilbert:] Yes, I guess that's one thing we're saying. Throughout the twentieth century, as women have increasingly moved into the public sphere, our history has become ever more complicated. The battle of the sexes that we described in volume I of *No Man's Land, The War of the Words*, necessarily required a whole range of strategies from participants on both sides, male and female, and it also fostered enormous sociocultural changes—which, in volume 2 of this series, we've called "sex changes." And those changes meant that some of the women we're studying in volume 3, *Letters from the Front*, are so conscious of the artifice of gender that they become, in effect, what we've called "female female impersonators." I'm thinking, for example, of Edna Millay, who posed as a kind of weary, witty *femme fatale*, and of Marianne Moore, who posed as a sardonic, school-marmish "old maid"—and also, ultimately, as a female George Washington Crossing the Delaware. But you could make a comparable argument about H. D. or even more recent writers, like Plath and Jong. And of course at the same time, male writers—a number of them equally conscious of the arbitrariness of sex roles—are resorting to strategies of their own, often strategies involving theories of self and mask, personality and costume.

[Gubar:] Yes, that's why there's a chapter in *Sexchanges*, on literary responses to the Great War, a chapter on transvestism (in the writings of both male and female modernists), and another on the emergence for the first time of a consciously defined lesbian literary community. Renée Vivien writes quite differently from Amy Lowell or Gertrude Stein, but all three were attempting to establish a new kind of poetry, one that could speak the desires of homosexual women who felt themselves to be alienated both from patriarchal literary conventions and from a female tradition that excluded or marginalized them.

In relation to the battle of the sexes that Sandra just mentioned, by the way, we're not arguing that Zora Neale Hurston solved the problem of literary daughterhood in the same way that Virginia Woolf did. Or the same way that Susan Glaspell did. But twentieth-century literary women often grappled with similar difficulties; for example, Hurston's "Sweat," Woolf's legend about Professor Von X, and Glaspell's "Trifles" all deal with women's response to an escalation in sex-antagonism.

How do you perceive the relationship between strategies of feminist criticism and those of other oppressed groups such as black or third-world critics?

[Gubar:] Well, whenever I go out on the road to give lectures and I meet people interested in black literary criticism, I'm struck by how similar the endeavors are. But I'm also very aware that the metaphorical identification between white women and blacks has occasioned a number of slippages.

Let me begin with the first point, the commonality of the enterprises. It seems to me that black literary critics, like feminist critics, are concerned with recalcitrant and vexing images in literature—in the black literary tradition, the minstrel, the Uncle Tom, the Jezebel, the Topsy figure. Both feminist critics and black studies scholars seek to excavate lost or neglected traditions by recovering texts frequently out of print, unavailable, or untaught. Methodologically, too, there are similar emphases on personal reactions to texts that are read for their ideological significance. Of course black feminist literary criticism—by people like Mary Helen Washington, Deborah McDowell, and Barbara Christian—seeks to negotiate between both critical enterprises.

On the other hand, anyone who has done any work on suffrage history knows that there is a long tradition of somehow equating white women metaphorically with blacks. It goes way back to Stanton and Anthony if not before, when they talked about the way the woman and the Negro, as they say, have been denied a name, voting privileges, property rights, legal power, and so forth. And you can see in the suffrage movement that this analogy sometimes allowed white women to argue in competition with the claims of abolitionists, or later, civil rights activists, that white women somehow should take precedence over blacks. The result is what one critic has called a debilitating competition of victimization between blacks and women.

[Gilbert:] I would like to interject here that there is an interesting basic problem which supports the notion of "commonality" even while it subverts that concept. I mean the idea of "otherness," which has been used for centuries in patriarchal western culture (and no doubt in many other societies too) to define both sexual *and* racial "others" as inferiors, outlanders, barbarians. Certainly throughout the imperialist nineteenth century, in both Britain and the United States, women and the colonized, women and slaves or blacks, were at least in part equated, even while male leaders claimed that women who were "ladies" must be somehow saved or protected from the potential depredations of the colonized (mutinous Indians, for example) or of, say, recently freed slaves. Despite a lot of genteel ideology, in other words, and a lot of heated rhetoric, these groups *were* analogically linked to each other. Almost through a kind of social homeopathy, I'd say. Sander Gilman has done some very interesting work on this, as has Lewis Wurgaft, but there's much more to be done, focusing on writers from Cooper to Haggard, from Kipling to Twain.

[Gubar:] And I think that when you approach black literary history from a feminist point of view, you arrive at some interesting results too. I recently drafted a chapter for volume three, *Letters from the Front*, on the Harlem Renaissance and women novelists, specifically Jessie Fauset, Nella Larsen, and Zora Neale Hurston, and it seems to me that these women are responding to the issues of feminism, but in a different way from their white contemporaries. It also seems to me that literary history in the black tradition may not be as male-dominated, or not in the same way. From the very inception (as far as we can tell) of black literary history, with Phillis Wheatley all the way through Frances E. W. Harper and Pauline Hopkins to more contemporary times, black literary women were very prominent in the Afro-American tradition. Of course, literacy was frequently denied both male and female slaves in the South. And so the dynamics of literary influence function somewhat differently.

[Gilbert:] In fact, if we look at contemporary writing in the United States, it's clear that many of our most powerful current writers are black women: Toni Morrison, Paule Marshall, Alice Walker, Toni Cade Bambara, Gayl Jones,

Gloria Naylor. And then look at the other marvelous writers who are from ethnic minorities: Louise Erdrich, Maxine Hong Kingston, Linda Hogan, Leslie Marmon Silko, and on and on. Does what we consider "marginality" really foster empowerment? If so, only for women? For both sexes but in different ways? These are issues that obviously need study.

What do you take to be the relationship between sexual and racial identities?

[Gubar:] The female novelist I am working on—Fauset, Larsen, and Hurston—are all concerned with that problem; that is, how do you come to terms with racist and sexist or misogynist images? I think that each one answers this question differently. Fauset has been faulted by contemporary black feminist critics for being a kind of ladylike, decorous anti-feminist, but I suspect that her novels have not yet been fully understood or appreciated. For Fauset, black women have a responsibility to reconstruct black manhood precisely because of the onslaughts of a society dedicated to mythologizing black male sexuality in such a way as to justify lynching.

[Gilbert:] Perhaps we should also add here the obvious point that in a racist society, members of an oppressed racial minority are almost always at an even greater economic and social risk than people of the dominant group—i.e. women—who are subordinated or oppressed because of their gender. Is it necessary to say this? Clearly a white "lady" of a certain class, despite all the constraints of the "pedestal," has privileges that her working-class black counterpart doesn't have. Alice James had access, after all, to luxuries that certainly weren't available to Harriet E. Adams Wilson, the author of *Our Nig!*

I'd like to go on to how you use psychoanalysis in your work. One critic of **No Man's Land** *suggests that in your telling of the "one metastory of gender strife," you foreground the patriarchal structure of the Freudian "family romance." Although it is clear that you seek to historicize Freud's work by pointing out that he, too, was responding to threats of increasing female power and changing concepts of femininity, how do you negotiate between your critique of Freud and your uses of his theories?*

[Gilbert:] I'd begin by saying that we are inclined to use Freud in much the way that such other feminist/psychoanalytic critics as Juliet Mitchell and Jacqueline Rose do. Our Freud, in other words, is a Freud mediated through, on the one hand, Lacan (who makes Freud literary/linguistic) and, on the other hand, through, well, let's say, Foucault—that is, through a study of the ideology of institutions that interrogates the assumptions of so-called "theory" as rigorously as it questions any other social or cultural precepts. But since I don't want to seem merely to be repeating the lessons of the masters, let me reiterate how much we've learned from feminists like Mitchell and Rose. What I think they demonstrate to us is both the accuracy of Freud's *de*scriptions and the fallibil-

ity of his *pre*scriptions. This is the course I know we tried to follow—negotiating between description and prescription—throughout the most quasi-psychoanalytic of our chapters, which I guess would be chapter two of *The Madwoman* and chapters three and four of *The War of the Words*. Freud's genius was that he looked through the flesh of the patriarchal family and saw its bones. But (to pursue the metaphor, in which I'm now entrapped), since he himself lived under the skin of the family romance, or *it* lived in his blood, he had fundamentally to acquiesce in its imperatives even while, with his characteristic pessimism, he analyzed them.

[Gubar:] Let me just add that we see the affiliation complex for the woman writer in the twentieth century following the stages of evolution that Freud maps out in the growing girl; that is, for Freud, the healthy girl solves the Oedipal dilemma by translating her desire for the mother to her desire for the father. That would be the literary woman, we argue, who turns toward male literary history in her definition of herself as a writer. And then, Freud says, the "immature" woman who renounces the father suffers from frigidity, and we discuss the renunciation of aesthetic desire in the female literary tradition. Finally, we analyze what Freud sees as another immature move, when the girl remains trapped in her relationship with the mother, as an affiliation of the woman writer with her matrilineal past.

One of the things we're doing, then, is revising Freud's valuations. What he sees as a regressive move, that is, the girl's attachment to the mother, we see as a healthy effort on the part of the woman writer to come to terms with her literary grandmothers. At the same time, we question Freud's notion that the growing girl (or by extension the female artist) sticks to one path. A given woman writer can fit into all three categories, can position herself in various works in different stances toward the past. It is surely significant that Freud was writing at the time when the patriarchal family was breaking down, because he was writing about structures that were changing but that were also deeply recalcitrant: the family, the child, the mother, and the father. To the extent that he tried to explain how babies become boys and girls, he provided a vocabulary, if nothing else, for coming to terms with the engendering of identity and creativity.

How do you respond to the problem raised by some critics that this vocabulary itself inscribes and perpetuates patriarchal relations?

[Gilbert:] I don't think it needs to. Description isn't prescription. Analysis is, in fact, the opposite of ideology. It seems to me that we can only escape the dynamics that shape us if we are conscious of them, as in the old statement about those who don't know history being condemned to repeat it. Maybe we could say that those who don't know *family* history are condemned to repeat it.

[Gubar:] Analysis the antithesis of ideology? We'll get it for that! Well, again I would move towards the women writers themselves and what they say about this. Maybe a useful example here would be someone like H. D. H. D. went through an analysis with Freud after she had been mentored by proponents of what she viewed as a great patrilineage, people like Lawrence, Aldington, and Pound. What H. D. does in the middle of her career is she stops publishing poetry. After writing a number of poems about the hostility and competition of her male contemporaries, she renounces poetic desire. And at that moment, in her fiction and translations, she begins searching for models of female creativity, turns, in what Freud himself told her was a regressive move, to the recovery of the mother, the Minoan-Mycenaean civilization behind patriarchal culture, and she writes *Trilogy*, a poem about her own aesthetic resurrection and about the recovery of the goddess. It seems that there you see a woman coming to terms with Freud personally and poetically in a way that inspires her to write a book-length poem.

[Gilbert:] Or, from another direction, Virginia Woolf might be said to have come differently to terms with the Freudian family romance in, say, *To the Lighthouse* (even though she doesn't seem even to have read Freud at the time she wrote that novel). What will happen to the daughters—the blood daughters and the spiritual daughters, Lily Briscoe and, maybe, Minta Doyle—when Mrs. Ramsay, the archetypal mother, dies? Is there life after the family romance has disintegrated, and, if so, what is that life? What is the *new*? If you remember the last section of *To the Lighthouse*, you will recall, I imagine, that the shape of the new isn't very clear to the Ramsay daughters, who don't know what to send to the lighthouse keeper, or to Lily, who is only comfortable with Mr. Ramsay after their conversation alights on "the blessed island of good boots." Yet it seems to me that it is, precisely, the dissolution of a Freudian structure on which Woolf meditates here.

And from another direction still, look at how useful Freudian paradigms are for examining the entrapment of Sylvia Plath (or her fictive speaker) in "Daddy"'s "black shoe," where she can neither breathe nor "achoo." What happens when the family romance lingers, and malingers, well into the middle of our own era? If we don't recognize it, don't know how caged we are in those old bones, how can we struggle free of it?

[Gubar:] Yes. By studying the patriarchal family we're not seeking to perpetuate it. Isn't it a kind of fiction in America today anyway? I mean does it exist? I don't know if there are many.

[Gilbert:] I'm afraid that I think there are lots. Lots of patriarchal families. Indeed, even if the patriarchal family is a fiction, it's a *real* one—and one that women all too often have to struggle to maintain, perhaps precisely *because* it's fictive. Don't you think that's what we're writing about now?

[Gubar:] The powers of supreme fictions—yes, that's what has always concerned not only us as literary critics but

many feminist theorists of psychosexual development. When Adrienne Rich writes "Compulsory Heterosexuality," she too, oddly enough, is beginning to deal with issues raised not only by Nancy Chodorow, but by Freud. Both Chodorow and Kim Chernin examine women's psychological stages of development by confronting and reshaping Freudian paradigms in general and his idea of the pre-Oedipal in particular.

In your work you make use of Freud's notion of Oedipal and pre-Oedipal phases to explain the social construction of identity in patriarchal culture. You maintain that in the pre-Oedipal stage a subject is as yet unmarked by the social determinants of identity such as race and gender, and you support this idea with readings of female modernists. One example occurs in Hurston's Their Eyes Were Watching God *in which Janie is not conscious of being black until the age of six when she sees a photograph of herself; in Willa Cather's novel* The Professor's House *you find Cather postulating the existence of a "prepatriarchal self" in the professor. Could you elaborate your conception of this presocial identity and its value to your work?*

[Gilbert:] Pre-Oedipal is very trendy right now, isn't it? I can't help remembering a remark Coppelia Kahn—who is a wonderful psychoanalytic critic—made at a conference I once attended: "Sell Oedipal, buy pre-Oedipal!" But seriously folks . . .

[Gubar:] I think these ideas, promulgated very differently by Hurston and Cather, have to do with fantasies of the presexual self. I would not read them as psychosexual theories exactly. It seems to me that the nausea Cather feels about gender in *The Professor's House*, about outmoded modes of femininity and about patriarchal roles that are debilitating to men, is countered by the fantasy of a presexual self. You see that fantasy quite frequently in the works of women writers; the notion, for instance in Katherine Mansfield, that the child is in touch—because she has not gone through this terrible fall into gender—with some ontological fullness that's almost gynandrous. Sandra explored this in her chapter on *Wuthering Heights*. The young Cathy, before she is bitten by the bulldog, before she is put into the crinoline, wounded, and placed in a parlor, this Cathy feels linked to Heathcliff and not split up, not feminized or entrapped in some kind of a role. This utopian yearning in women's literature reflects the longing for the child's self which represents a self before gender, a paradise lost.

I think though, in terms of our own theories, that you are really referring to a notion we propounded in the last chapter of ***The War of the Words***, "Sexual Linguistics." There what we were trying to counter was the idea that language in itself is necessarily, quintessentially patriarchal. We were discussing some women's sense that the language we have inherited is confining because it is male-dominated. And yet, many literary women feel that they are entitled to a primary relationship to language, that they are not necessarily alienated from language.

[Gilbert:] Basically, in our chapter (and our earlier essay) on "Sexual Linguistics," we were trying to come to terms with Julia Kristeva's argument that the "social contract" is inextricably entangled with the "symbolic contract." Working out of Lacanian assumptions, Kristeva has claimed that the child is inducted into society, through the Oedipus complex, at the same moment when she or he is initiated into language; hence, girl children, "always already" (as the saying goes) marginalized in patriarchal culture/society, are always already excluded from some sort of primary access to language, whose syntax is a sort of "guarantee" of sociocultural hierarchies. We tried to demonstrate in our chapter that this isn't necessarily so. First, we tried to do this by situating current feminist concepts of a "woman's language" in a *history* of female *and* male linguistic fantasies—a kind of utopian linguistics or a series of linguistic utopias that go back pretty far and that certainly characterize literary modernism in England, the United States, and France.

Then, we questioned the idea that the child's *linguistic* socialization has to occur at the same moment as her/his basic acculturation. Babies start learning language very early—as we know because we're both mothers. In Freudian or Lacanian terms, they start talking even before they enter the so-called "Oedipus." And in most societies and families they learn language from their mothers (or from a female care-giver), not from—or not directly from—"patriarchs," even when their moms are ostensibly functioning as "agents of patriarchy." The mother, as we should all remember, has enormous verbal power. So speaking pragmatically, empirically, it seems really possible to question the conflation of the "social contract" (which does tell the child who and what he or she is, structurally, in a culture that subordinates women and girls) with the "symbolic contract" (which tells the child that she or he has to speak in order to *be*).

You have been criticized by such critics as Mary Jacobus and Toril Moi as maintaining an essentialist theory of gender. Since you explicitly state throughout your work that gender is a social construct, this criticism perhaps reflects a difference in the way you conceptualize gender. How would you describe that difference between your own concept of gender and that of your critics?

[Gubar:] Well, I would begin by thinking about both the political and historical implications of what I take to be Mary Jacobus's and Toril Moi's point. They seem to be working on the assumptions established by such people as Jacques Derrida and Roland Barthes that there is no subject, that we can all enjoy ourselves on the free-play ground of the signifier, that the author is dead, that there is a kind of interplay between signs that means that meaning is indecipherable. And it seems to me that one needs to think about the political ramifications of such assumptions. The best response I have heard was by Henry Louis Gates, who said, "Isn't it interesting that there is no subject just at that moment when blacks and women are entering the academy." What does that do for us? What does that do *to* us?

[Gilbert:] The "feminine," according to some of these theorists—and I'm approximately quoting one of that group—is not what some critics "quite banally understand" as any work signed by a woman. In other words (and we find this in the writings of Cixous and Kristeva as well), in the view of such thinkers lots of male writers are better at "inscribing" what's called "the feminine" than many women are. But what does this notion mean about "the feminine"? What, then, *is* "the feminine"? Alas, "the feminine" here seems not to have anything to do with any sort of experiential reality (and I understand that the word "reality" is a problematic signifier pointing to a tenuous concept), but rather with a whole set of stereotypes: the unconscious, darkness, rebelliousness, fluidity, etc. etc. Ah, the wonderful, watery "feminine"! It seems to leak and gush through the writings of Joyce, Artaud, Bataille. Whereas George Eliot and Jane Austen and Charlotte Brontë—and probably Margaret Drabble and Margaret Atwood and Toni Morrison—are a bunch of linear, binary-haunted *men*.

I think I'm saying that in this particular definition—the one that dissolves authors into linguistic fields and assumes that any notion of history is identical with "essentialism"—"the feminine" is anything that you want it to be. Anything that you desire. The wildness, the disruption, the fantastic language about which you've been dreaming. (I guess you can see how this fits in with the fantasy of a utopian language that we were discussing earlier!) Never mind what Adrienne Rich talks about as the "absorbed drudging" author (forgive me for using such a word as *author*) crouched at her desk. If the little marks made by her pen as it traces free-playing signifiers don't come out just the way you, the feminist critic, want them to, well then they're not "feminine."

[Gubar:] Of course, the older I get the more convinced I am that gender constructs are transformed over time, that they are radically different in different societal and cultural contexts, but that they are extraordinarily resilient. And they resurface over and over again. I would say this about racial constructs as well. Ideas about gender, about the nature of masculinity, the nature of femininity, do transform themselves in different periods but they are extremely powerful. By talking about the free-play of the signifier, one is defusing that power as it is experienced in women's lives. Elaine Showalter speaks about women critics feeling on their pulses what they are writing about when she talks about an experiential base to feminist criticism, and I think there's some truth to that.

So gender constructs are less fluid than some critics suggest?

[Gilbert:] It seems to me that they are differently fluid, and I think that's what Susan was just saying. They're *historically* fluid: obviously Victoria Woodhull, the nineteenth-century free love advocate, was responding to a very different social context from the one in which Gloria Steinem, or Helen Gurley Brown, finds herself. Sexual liberation, as we understand the concept, meant in nineteenth-century America something very different from what it means today. As did "the feminine." And "the feminine" meant something rather different for James Joyce than what it probably means for Hélène Cixous or Mary Jacobus or Toril Moi. I think history, insofar as we can understand it, or can understand parts of it, aspects of it, is so subtly nuanced that we have to be awfully careful not to see in it merely the shapes of our desire. Although, of course, we'll always see those too!

[Gubar:] We spoke about the desire for gender fluidity as it appears in images of the child, and we also trace it in the icon of the cross-dresser, the androgyne. I think the desire for sexual fluidity in a book like *Orlando* is absolutely clear. But even that novel was written out of Woolf's consciousness that women have found it difficult to achieve rooms of their own, or 500 pounds a year. I think the desire for gender fluidity is an important utopian yearning and is reflected in the work of Moi and Jacobus and Nelly Furman and many other people. But I'm not convinced that gender fluidity is an everyday reality.

Given your sense that the author's signature is, as you say, inflected in her or his work, how do you perceive the role of men in feminism?

[Gubar:] Well, I think that the difference between **The Madwoman**—to get back to your earlier question—and **No Man's Land**, in part, is a move away from isolating the female literary tradition and a move toward understanding the interactions in the twentieth century between male and female literary traditions and figures. What does modernism have to do with a crisis in masculinity and anxiety about the "no man"? Our interest in that question means that we focus now not only on definitions of femininity, but on evolving definitions of masculinity. Clearly this is an important subject for male critics too. I think many male critics today—one thinks of Terry Eagleton, and, alas, one also thinks of Frank Lentricchia—are using ideas about the engendering of literary history that were developed by feminist critics. And for the most part I think that's a healthy and important development in feminist thinking. I get worried when it's combative or appropriative.

[Gilbert:] Or, worse still, when it's patronizing. As in a certain kind of "more feminist than thou" stance, in which the male critic assumes that now *he* has entered the field he can instruct these poor benighted women in how they ought to go about their work. Not that we don't think that we feminist critics can sometimes be, in our own embattled way, *matronizing*. But at the very least, conflicts among feminist critics (and I think of the issues you just raised about Moi and Jacobus) are, like disputes among Afro-American critics, in some sense family quarrels, and family quarrels among people who understand themselves to have been marginalized for all too long. It is crucial to us that we can now take our work seriously enough to fight about it. But there's something odd, something dis-

tasteful, something *suspect*, about the position of a critic who claims to dispute our conclusions because he understands all our assumptions without having, as it were, inhabited our premises!

Could you elaborate some of the problems? In what way do you find Lentricchia's use of feminism, for instance, particularly suspect?

[Gubar:]. Well, in an interview published in this very journal, Professor Lentricchia does something which he also did in an earlier attack on **The Madwoman**. It seems to me that he wages the kind of rhetorical war of words that I think we've been tracing in the pages of **No Man's Land**. He says in the interview that feminists come to him and say, "We don't like Gilbert and Gubar either, but we don't piss on our generals in public." Now, I wouldn't expect anyone to say that to me, but actually I wouldn't expect them to say it to anybody. Now, maybe that's naive of me.

[Gilbert:] No, no, certainly not. Think about it, after all. There's a certain implicit, or maybe explicit, sexism here. I mean, can you really imagine a woman saying that? Wouldn't it be pretty hard, and fairly embarrassing, for a woman to "piss on her general" in public? Anatomically, that is? So maybe, for all his ostensible "feminism," Lentricchia is revealing his hidden assumptions: about hierarchy (generals), and pissing (in public, standing up?). Susan, we've been saying that anatomy isn't destiny; but what if it is? What if we feminists *can't* piss on our generals in public? What if our genitals determine the way we deal with our generals?

[Gubar:] Still, I don't think Lentricchia represents the vast majority of male critics in this country. I think that a number of men are producing important books, including the one that Alice Jardine did with Paul Smith, *Men in Feminism*, which includes fascinating essays by people like Robert Scholes and Stephen Heath. So I wouldn't see Lentricchia's positioning of himself as paradigmatic, and furthermore, he takes that combative role with men, too. So it might just be his problem.

[Gilbert:] Oh, I agree. Jonathan Culler, Larry Lipking, Uli Knoepflmacher—we can all name a number of men who are doing interesting work in gender studies. But I find it significant that I want to call it "gender studies." In some part of myself, I'm really political enough to want to continue seeing feminism as a *women's* movement. We must all understand the inflections, imperatives, dynamics, of gender—in our culture, our society, our literature. But feminism is originally, and specifically, about addressing and redressing what Mary Wollstonecraft once called "the wrongs of women." Let's not forget that. I'm agreeing, in other words, with a fundamental point that my colleague Elaine Showalter made in her essay on "Critical Cross-Dressing."

As a final question, I'd like to ask you about your collaboration. It is tempting to see this as another facet of a specifically feminist strategy. How do you regard your collaboration?

[Gilbert:] I think that what I tried to say earlier about the personal origins of *The Madwoman* has a lot to do with the origins of our collaboration, too. Just as *The Madwoman* didn't come out of a willed, intentional, intellectual experience but rather out of an idea that really seized us, so our collaboration wasn't the result of a conscious political decision. It was something exciting and fascinating that happened to us, the way the book did. We taught a class together, we got a set of ideas together. Quite without forethought, we had what I've sometimes called a "conversion experience." One autumn the scales fell from our eyes in Bloomington, Indiana, just as the leaves were falling from the trees. We understood that there *was* what we had never been taught there was: a female literary tradition! And since we had figured it out together, we had to write about it together. And the fact that the collaboration worked, is still working, had and does continue to have something to do with what is now called "feminist process." But not with intentional political process. Rather, with the notion that the political (or the poetical) is the personal. I'd say we *felt* our ideas, at that point, with a passion that could only lead to friendship.

[Gubar:] I know that people do speak to us after lectures or write to us about the collaboration because they view it as an ideological decision, a commitment that decenters authority, decentralizes the author, and represents a kind of communality or partnership which they see as feminist. But I have to say for us, as Sandra just did, that it was not embarked upon for any political or ideological reason, and I think it would be pretty dangerous for someone to collaborate with someone else for those purposes because I think collaboration involves a kind of interchange that has to be based upon personal affection and camaraderie. For me, it's different and luckier than writing alone, and it's a great pleasure.

The one way it does conform, for me, to those political ideas has to do with some of the critiques you've mentioned from Jacobus through Moi to Lentricchia. It's very daunting to get the kind of criticism that we get. All of those people you've mentioned feel that they are more radical than we are. But we get it from the other side, too. We just encountered an article written by Jeffrey Hart, who claims that the *Norton Anthology of Literature by Women* "enshrines works whose inclusion is not literary quality but resentment." And who argues that Sandra and I are radical militants who are destroying the excellence of the humanistic inheritance that should be represented through, basically, Chaucer, Shakespeare, Milton and Wordsworth. To the extent that we are attacked by ultraconservatives as well as radicals who don't think we're "feminist enough," collaboration really is a solace because it's easier to laugh with someone else. And you can reassure each other that at least you think what you're doing is important and what you believe in.

[Gilbert:] True. Sometimes I feel that—given the Scylla and Charybdis out there, from a Lentricchia who feels that our feminist colleagues should "piss on their generals" to

a Jeffrey Hart who sees us as destroying Western Civilization—collaboration is a very special solace. I mean, collaboration is an existential pleasure. It's like having someone else around to hold your hand while you leap into the abyss. How often does *that* happen, after all?

Katherine Fishburn (review date Spring 1989)

SOURCE: A review of *No Man's Land, Volume 1: The War of the Words,* in *Studies in the Novel,* Vol. 21, No. 1, Spring, 1989, pp. 104–07.

[*In the following review, Fishburn praises Gubar and Gilbert for their explication of modernism in* The War of the Words, *the first volume in their* No Man's Land *series.*]

What was modernism anyway? What were its origins? What distinguishes the work of the female modernists from that of the male modernists? These are the basic questions underlying volume one of Sandra M. Gilbert and Susan Gubar's projected three-volume series *No Man's Land: The Place of the Woman Writer in the Twentieth-Century*. In this volume, *The War of the Words*, they "offer an overview of social, literary, and linguistic interactions between men and women from the middle of the nineteenth century to the present" (p. xii). In the second and third volumes, *Sexchanges* and *Letters from the Front*, they plan to examine the literature of the period in more detail, including the feminist modernism of Virginia Woolf and the postmodern feminism of Sylvia Plath.

Ten years ago Gilbert and Gubar burst into critical prominence with the publication of *The Madwoman in the Attic* (Yale, 1979), their highly acclaimed study of nineteenth-century women's fiction and poetry. Not only did *The Madwoman in the Attic* provide feminist scholars with a convenient catch-phrase, more seriously it helped to lay the foundations of American feminist critical theory and forced critics to rethink the literature of an entire century. What *Madwoman* did for criticism of the nineteenth century, *No Man's Land* promises to do for that of the twentieth. As their title suggests, the metaphor Gilbert and Gubar have chosen is that of war—the war between the sexes that seared the modern period, making monsters of women and martyrs of men, the same war that is being bitterly fought today in the pages of critical theory. For the battle they wage in this war of the words, Gilbert and Gubar have come fully armed with passionate conviction, mother wit, and multitudinous examples. In short, *No Man's Land* is a delightfully worthy entrant on the critical field of battle, certain to inspire vigorous debate wherever it is read.

In tracing the origins of modernism, Gilbert and Gubar do not entirely dismiss the traditional explanations for its rise (Darwin, Freud, World War One), but they do insist on the importance of the profound social changes "brought about by the 'new women' and, in particular, by their struggle for the vote" (p. 21). For the men, it was a time of almost debilitating anxiety, occasioned not just by the uncertainties of war but also the stunning entry of women as serious competitors into the economic and literary marketplaces. This anxiety found expression in the abundance of "maimed, unmanned, victimized characters," which according to Gilbert and Gubar, were "obsessively created by early twentieth-century literary men" (p. 36). And because "modernist texts describe explicitly sexual duels between characters who tend to incarnate female voracity and male impotence" (p. 35), Gilbert and Gubar argue that these victimized men function as more than traditional "metaphors of metaphysical angst" (p. 36). These victimized men, in fact, represent a widespread and quite specific fear of women. Even where the texts "do not explicitly deal with sexual battles," it is nonetheless clear that "men feared they were losing such contests" since "[i]mages of impotence recur with unnerving frequency in the most canonical male modernist novels and poems" (p. 35). A representative example of this tendency, of course, is T. S. Eliot's "The Love Song of J. Alfred Prufrock," which was originally titled "Prufrock Among the Women" and which in its final form "emphasizes the ways in which the absurdly self-conscious modern male intellectual is rendered impotent by, and in, the company of women" (pp. 31–32). That the male modernists felt particularly threatened by literary women is also clear from James Joyce's confident prediction that *The Waste Land* would end the "idea of poetry for ladies" (p. 156).

As the century progressed, literary men found various ways to defend themselves against women. One strategy was to weaken women by feminizing them; ironically enough, "just as more and more women were getting paid for using their brains, more and more men represented them in novels, plays, and poems as nothing but bodies"— bodies subdued and regulated by men (p. 47). In short, the penis became "a therapeutic instrument in the domestication of desire," which "was always on the verge of turning into a penis as pistol, an instrument of rape and revenge" (p. 48). Other strategies Gilbert and Gubar identify involved "mythologizing women to align them with dread prototypes; fictionalizing them to dramatize their destructive influence; slandering them in essays, memoirs, and poems; prescribing alternative ambitions for them; appropriating their words in order to usurp or trivialize their language; and ignoring or evading their achievements in critical texts" (p. 149). Of all these, the most significant seems to have been the attempt the avant grade male writers made to "define their artistic integrity in opposition to either the literary incompetence or the aesthetic hysteria they associated with women" (p. 157). Was male modernism, in other words, an inspired phobic response to the growing power of women? Was it a brilliant offensive campaign to transform "the *materna lingua* into a powerful new kind of *patrius sermo*" (p. 253), a language women could not speak? Gilbert and Gubar seem to think so. Indeed, they work from the controversial hypothesis that "a reaction-formation against the rise of literary women be-

came not just a theme in modernist writing but a *motive for modernism*" (p. 156; emphasis added).

But what of the women themselves? What were they up to? Noting that the period "is differently inflected for male and female writers" (p. xii), Gilbert and Gubar found that women "often felt even more imperiled than men did by the sexual combat in which they were obliged to engage" (p. 66). Though it is true that many women suffered from feelings of "guilt" and "vulnerability," still others "felt empowered" by their sex's advancement; as a result, "the female half of the dialogue is considerably more complicated than the male" (p. 66). But as powerful as they might have felt themselves, many women writers could only "imagine female victory" through such indirect means as "duplicity and subterfuge or through providential circumstance" (p. 66). Or they simply emasculated the male characters, a solution that brought victory but very little satisfaction, since "[t]riumph over an unworthy, diminished, or disabled opponent may feel like exploitation of his misfortune" (p. 90). Although some women managed to fight the trend and create truly powerful female protagonists, it was a limited insurrection soon contained by other women's terrible need to punish their own heroines. What we would regard today as "a healthy impulse to depict women actively fighting their male opponents" (p. 100), turn-of-the-century writers saw as a "horrifying necessity, born of escalating male bellicosity and inexorably leading to female defeat" (p. 101). These earlier texts are so "punitive" toward strong women, Gilbert and Gubar reason that their authors had "internalized just the horror at independent womanhood which marks the writings of literary men from Faulkner to Wylie" (p. 101).

Not only did women writers feel ambivalent toward their own heroines, they felt ambivalent toward their female ancestors, vacillating between feelings of prideful joy and fearful anxiety. Unlike women of the nineteenth century, twentieth-century women have been faced with choosing between "their matrilineage and their patrilineage in an arduous process of self-definition" (p. 169). Because women are faced with "a bewildering multiplicity of stances toward the past," Gilbert and Gubar suggest that women have had "to struggle with . . . a complicated female affiliation complex" (p. 168). This "paradigm of ambivalent affiliation [is] a construct which dramatizes women's intertwined attitudes of anxiety and exuberance about creativity" (p. 170). In other words, though women writers revere their female precursors, they are "also haunted and daunted by the autonomy of these figures" (p. 195). The ambivalence arises, Gilbert and Gubar suspect, because "the love women writers send forward into the past is, in patriarchal culture, inexorably contaminated by mingled feelings of rivalry and anxiety" (p. 195).

While I find their model (based on Freud's model of the family) theoretically persuasive, I am not sure I can agree with their conclusion that having a female history "may not be quite so advantageous as some feminists have traditionally supposed" (p. 196). I cannot help but think, for example, that Alice Walker speaks for most twentieth-century women writers when she describes the joy and self-affirmation she felt upon discovering the work of Zora Neale Hurston ("Saving the Life that is Your Own: The Importance of Models in the Artist's Life," *In Search of Our Mothers' Gardens: Womanist Prose* [New York: Harvest, 1984]). Is Gilbert and Gubar's theory of a female affiliation complex, therefore, a projection of what they themselves have experienced in reverse? In other words, could it be, as a colleague of mine from VPI has suggested, that Gilbert and Gubar themselves have been caught up as critics in the receiving end of this ambivalence? Are the newest feminist critics "haunted and daunted" by these two (too) powerful foremothers?

Whatever the answer to these speculations might be, I find in Gilbert and Gubar's own work evidence of some ambivalence regarding the theories they propose. Most of this ambivalence occurs in the book's final chapter, "Sexual Linguistics: Women's Sentence, Men's Sentencing." Although I found here some of the most exciting and appealing ideas in the entire book, Gilbert and Gubar, strangely enough, seem almost reluctant to claim them as their own. Arguing that James Joyce's puns represent "not a linguistic *jouissance* rebelliously disrupting the decorum of the text, but a linguistic *puissance* fortifying the writer's sentences," for example, they then apply their thesis to Jacques Derrida but do so almost unwillingly: "*Provisionally, tentatively*," they write, "we would suggest that a similar maneuver may be at the heart of what Geoffrey Hartman calls Derridadaism, in particular at the heart of an otherwise opaque exercise like Derrida's *Glas*" (pp. 260–61; emphasis added). In a related passage, they introduce yet another challenge to male thinking through the odd device of calling their own ideas into question: "*if any of our speculations have any validity*," they write, "we must also ask whether the whole structure of 'hierarchized' oppositions that some of us have thought essentially patriarchal has been historically erected as a massive defense against the deep throat of the mother and the astonishing priority of that mother tongue which is common to both men and women" (p. 266; emphasis added). No fan myself of Jacques Lacan, I find Gilbert and Gubar's insistence on the priority of the mother tongue a compelling alternative to his Law of the Father. For this reason, I am puzzled by the rhetorical hesitancy in these passages. I realize the theories they challenge are both popular and powerful—but that is all the more reason for Gilbert and Gubar to be as intrepid here as they are elsewhere in the book.

In fact, for me, much of the pleasure of *No Man's Land* comes from the authors' profanation of the sacred ground of twentieth-century literature. Clearly, they too take pleasure in desecrating the father's gods, graves, and scholars as in their contention that Hemingway and Fitzgerald regarded the Louvre as a "penile colony" (p. 36); their description of Norman Mailer's Stanley Rojack as a "Ruta-rooter" (p. 53); and their transformation of Derrida's *Grammatology* into a "grandmatology" (p. 239); and so

on. Though their outrageous punning will surely offend many (as in their tasteless reference to Gertrude Stein as a "fat-her" [p. 188]), this humor is not without purpose. Mikhail Bakhtin reminds us in *The Dialogic Imagination*, for example, that laughter "demolishes fear and piety before an object . . . thus clearing the ground for an absolutely free investigation of it" (Austin: U. of Texas Press, 1981; p. 23). And so it is here: Gilbert and Gubar's feminist humor is both liberating and empowering, permitting us, in Bakhtin's words, to "finger" modernism "on all sides . . . dismember it, lay it bare and expose it" (Bakhtin, p. 23). Nor is humor their only weapon. For, as their attacks on Hemingway, Fitzgerald, Eliot, Lawrence, Graves, etc., suggest, these postmodern women warriors certainly have, in Mary Daly's words, the "courage to blaspheme" (*Gyn/Ecology: The Metaethics of Radical Feminism* [Boston: Beacon Press, 1978] p. 264). Why, then, do they fight so cautiously to have their own ideas accepted?

Whatever the reason, they show a similar caution when they respond to the theories of the French feminists. In the following example, they are speculating about what Virginia Woolf meant by the phrase a "woman's sentence": "Provisionally, we want to suggest that Woolf used what was essentially a *fantasy* about a utopian linguistic structure . . . to define (and perhaps disguise) her desire to revise not woman's language but woman's relation to language" (p. 230). This strikes me, as does much of the above, as an eminently reasonable interpretation and a practical way out of what often become the labyrinths of linguistic theory. It is not the last word on a female language, but it gives us a great deal to think about.

Though the book's impact is somewhat lessened by the hesitancy evident in the final chapter, overall it remains a powerful vehicle for interrogating our most deeply held convictions about modernism. For this reason alone, it would be worth reading. the woman's need of man" (p. 41) and of Austen she writes "a subtler reading of Jane's fiction shows how consistently she queries and even reverses the agreed social assumptions" (p. 44). I cannot help but think that when Miles refers to Brontë and Austen in this way she undermines the stature of two of our greatest (women) writers. She also seems to contradict herself in her final chapter. On page 204 she criticizes the "sheer parochialism of much women's writing" because of its "narrow concentration upon the minutiae of women's lives, the emphasis on domestic difficulties and sexual sorrows"; then on page 206 she claims that "any denial of the validity of women's lives and experience—any denial—is inescapably the same old misogyny rising up from the primeval swamp, whether expressed by a man, or as frequently happens, a woman."

In conclusion I feel impelled to comment on certain errors and omissions in both *The Female Form* and *No Man's Land*. Although they are not major problems, they seem to suggest a pattern. For some reason, Miles is under the impression that Rita Mae Brown is a black woman (p. 110) and that Maya Angelou's autobiography *I Know Why the Caged Bird Sings* is a novel (p. 104). For their part, Gilbert and Gubar think Richard Wright's book is called *A Native Son* and Zora Neale Hurston's heroine is named Janie Crawford *Killocks* Starks Woods (p. 238). Though these are admittedly minor mistakes, I cannot help but be troubled by the fact that in one way or another they all involve blacks. I am also troubled by Gilbert and Gubar's subtitle, ***The Place of the Woman Writer in the Twentieth-Century,*** when what they mean is the place of the *Anglo-American* woman writer. Miles, in referring to Maxine Hong Kingston's *The Woman Warrior*, observes that: "Female *Angst* and alienation from the all-pervading structures of male domination are expressed with no less anguish in the 'advanced' world" (p. 126). As far as I am concerned, when Miles puts the word *advanced* in inverted commas here, she does nothing to correct or eliminate the cultural slam implied in her comparison.

These mistakes and oversights ruin neither book for me (though for other reasons I find them much more problematical in Miles' book than in Gilbert and Gubar's), but I interpret them as a disturbing indication of the continuing ethnocentricity of white western feminists. It is perhaps no wonder that Alice Walker prefers the concept of "Womanist," when three such notable feminist scholars inadvertently duplicate the same kind of critical narrowness they have set out to correct.

Katherine Fishburn (review date Winter 1990)

SOURCE: A review of *No Man's Land, Volume 2: Sexchanges,* in *Studies in the Novel*, Vol. 22, No. 4, Winter 1990, pp. 472–76.

[*In the following review, Fishburn praises* Sexchanges *for the vastness of the authors' scholarship, and the depth and originality of their insights. Fishburn argues, however, that the book is intellectually flat.*]

In this, [*Sexchanges*] the second volume of their projected three-volume series ***No Man's Land,*** Sandra Gilbert and Susan Gubar resume their ambitiously comprehensive revisioning of modernism. As they did in the previous volume, ***The War of the Words*** (1988), Gilbert and Gubar work here from the premise that the originating motives that lay behind the rise of literary modernism can be best explained by the sweeping changes in the status of women that occurred at the end of the nineteenth century. The importance of Gilbert and Gubar's attempt to redefine the material causes of Anglo-American modernism as an issue of gender cannot be overstated as the authors seek to "locate the text in its sociocultural context," believing as they do that "the concepts 'female' and 'male' are inextricably enmeshed in the materiality and mythology of history, which has also . . . almost always been experienced as gendered" (p. xvi). They focus, therefore, on the "changing definitions of sex and sex roles as they evolve through

three phases: the repudiation or revision of the Victorian ideology of femininity that marked both feminism and fantasy during what we might call the overturning of the century; the antiutopian skepticism that characterized the thought of such writers as Edith Wharton and Willa Cather, who dramatized their discontent with what they saw as a crippling but inexorable feminization of women; the virtually apocalyptic engendering of the new for both literary men and literary women that was, at least in part, fostered by the fin de siècle formation of a visible lesbian community, even more shockingly triggered by the traumas of World War I, and perhaps most radically shaped by an unprecedented confrontation (by both sexes) with the artifice of gender and its consequent discontents" (p. xii).

Sandra Gilbert and Susan Gubar open *Sexchanges* with an irreverent and audaciously overdetermined reading of Rider Haggard's *She* as a paradigmatic example of "the century's bestselling, masculinist mythology" (p. 5), in which they argue that the novel's enormous popularity was a result of the era's sexchanges, "the feared 'recessional' of the British empire, the intensified development of such fields as anthropology and embryology, and the rise of a host of alternative theologies" (p. 7). The novel's "rolling pillar of Life" they read not only as a Freudian penis but also as "a Lacanian phallus, a fiery signifier whose eternal thundering return speaks the inexorability of the patriarchal law She has violated in Her Satanically overreaching ambition" (p. 20). That is, "it becomes, in a sense, the pillar of society, an incarnate sign of the covenant among men (and between men and a symbolic Father) that is the founding gesture of patriarchal culture" (p. 20). "Finally, therefore, naked and ecstatic, in all the pride of Her femaleness, She must be fucked to death by the 'unalterable law' of the Father" (p. 21). This Gallopean (Galloping?) verbal performance represents Gilbert and Gubar at their most outrageous—and, I would argue, their most effective, for who, after encountering this Lacanian phallus in the pages of *Sexchanges*, will ever be able to read *She* again without thinking of It?

Earlier versions of this chapter, like many others in *Sexchanges*, have previously appeared in print as individual essays. I myself was originally moved to read Haggard's novel, as a matter of fact, after reading Sandra Gilbert's "Rider Haggard's Heart of Darkness" which appeared in *Coordinates: Placing Science Fiction and Fantasy* alongside Susan Gubar's **"She in Herland: Feminism as Fantasy"** (edited by George Slusser et al. [Carbondale: Southern Illinois University Press, 1983], pp. 124–49). Whether my response is one Gilbert herself would have wanted is, of course, an altogether different matter!

As successful as Gilbert (and Gubar)'s overdetermined reading of Rider Haggard is, however, most of *Sexchanges* is actually devoted to what Nancy K. Miller would call "overreadings" of several well-known women's texts ("Arachnologies: The Woman, The Text, and the Critic," *The Poetics of Gender*, ed. Nancy K. Miller [New York: Columbia University Press, 1986], pp. 270–95). In response to the ideas of Roland Barthes in *S/Z*, Miller defines overreading as a practice that "involves reading women's writing not 'as if it had already been read,' but as if it had never been read, *as if* for the first time. Overreading also involves a focus on the moments in the narrative which by their representation of writing itself might be said to figure the production of the female artist" (p. 274). "Only the subject who is both self-possessed and possesses access to the library of the already read," Miller argues, "has the luxury of flirting with the escape from identity" (p. 274)—a critique of postmodernism that Gilbert and Gubar make themselves when they acknowledge in the preface to *Sexchanges* that "although poststructuralist feminists rightly view 'female' and 'male' as arbitrary constructs, some refuse to acknowledge the possibility that these powerful constructs inexorably make and mark the products of the imagination" (p. xv). "When we ourselves use the words 'woman' and 'man,' 'female' and 'male,' 'feminine' and 'masculine,' therefore, we are always deploying what we, too, understand as artificial, socially determined signifiers. But we are also always using these terms both to explore their changing resonances and to examine the ways in which such changes in meaning affected the lives and art of the writers we have chosen to study" (p. xvi).

In any event, putting the questions of postmodernism aside for a moment, the overreadings of women's texts that Gilbert and Gubar perform in *Sexchanges* constitute the most valuable aspects of their own text.

I was delighted, for example, by their overreading of Kate Chopin's *The Awakening*, which they treat as the "liberation and celebration of female desire" (p. 94), "a female fiction which both draws upon and revises fin-de-siècle hedonism to propose a feminist myth of Aphrodite/Venus as an alternative to the patriarchal western myth of Jesus" (p. 96). "Edna's last swim," they read not as symbolic of her impending suicide and death but as a metaphor of "resurrection, a sort of pagan female Good Friday that promises an Aphroditean Easter. In fact, because of the way it is presented, Edna's supposed suicide enacts not a refusal to accept the limitations of reality but a subversive questioning of the limitations of both reality and 'realism'" (p. 109).

Though Gilbert and Gubar's discussion of Willa Cather is (quite openly) indebted to Sharon O'Brien's work, I also found it useful in understanding what they call Cather's "critique of erotic desire" (p. 170).

And I was particularly interested in their handling of Gertrude Stein whom they credit with "obliterating literary history altogether" (p. 223). For Gilbert and Gubar, Stein was a "man of genius" (p. 223) who brazenly "refused all predecessors" (p. 238). Respectful of Stein's intellect and her influence on modernism, Gilbert and Gubar nonetheless frankly admit they find most of her work "boringly incomprehensible and self-serving" (p. 245) and accuse her of promoting a "self-authorizing aesthetics of solipsism"

(p. 248). "Stein presented herself as a demonic anti-God," they argue, "who unmakes significance in her non-literature and thereby reduces all of literary history to a history of naive signification. In fact, the very autonomy Stein achieved in her marriage with Alice helped her turn her words into weapons which rob her readers of their ability to comprehend" (p. 249). Though Gilbert and Gubar are in little danger of losing professional credibility by making these kinds of deconstructive claims, it is refreshing to encounter an example of such critical candor.

In a book that is full of provocative readings, Gilbert and Gubar save their most provocative reading for their interpretation of the lesbian relationship between Alice B. Toklas and Gertrude Stein. "Usurping *Alice's* persona, appropriating *Alice's* voice," they argue, "*Stein* presents herself as an unappreciated, isolated pioneer, and she thereby turns collaboration into collusion: living, listening, and telling do transform one into the other, but the result is a kind of cannibalism, as *Stein* makes *Alice* into a character of her own devising who, in turn, certifies *Stein* as the genius who will usher in the twentieth century" (p. 251; emphases added). Is Gilbert and Gubar's use of "Alice" and "Stein" intentional in this passage? That is, are they calling attention to Alice's subordinate status by using her first name and Stein's last name? Or are they perpetuating the unequal division of power they deplore? In any event, they end with a zinger of a question themselves, a question that haunts me: "Is it possible that Alice B. Toklas actually wrote *The Autobiography of Alice B. Toklas*?" (p. 252).

I would add but one more question. Why in a discussion of collaboration between women, do Gilbert and Gubar, themselves the late twentieth-century's most famous and successful feminist collaborators, not mention their own working relationship at this point in the book? Surely their own more equitable intellectual arrangement must have had some bearing on their ability to decode the auto(bio)graphy of Alice B. Toklas and Gertrude Stein.

Though clearly there is much to learn from and admire in *Sexchanges*, I must admit that I find myself wishing for more attention to the work of other recent theorists. It is true that Gilbert and Gubar do occasionally mention DuPlessis, Kristeva, Lacan, and Cixous, but I still think their work could be further enriched by the ideas of Michel Foucault, Roland Barthes, Alison M. Jaggar, Mary Jacobus, Monique Wittig, Rita Felski, Susan Bordo, and Nancy Fraser, to mention just a few. While I appreciate the vast amount of time that must be spent in reading the primary sources for a project of this magnitude, I do find the absence of these other theorists deeply disappointing and somewhat puzzling.

Even more puzzling is Gilbert and Gubar's oversight when it comes to naming Rachel Blau DuPlessis's seminal work on feminist narrative. In their discussion of Kate Chopin, Gilbert and Gubar suggest that Edna's final journey is "toward a genre that intends to propose new realities for women by providing new mythic paradigms through which women's lives can be understood" (p. 110). As I read this, I could not help but think of DuPlessis's description of prototypes in *Writing Beyond the Ending: Narrative Strategies of Twentieth-Century Women Writers* and wondering why Gilbert and Gubar haven't placed their ideas into her well-known framework. Women's new myths, DuPlessis suggests, "replace archetypes with prototypes. They do not investigate moments of eternal recurrence, but rather break with the idea of an essentially unchanging reality" (p. 133). "A prototype is not a binding, timeless pattern," DuPlessis continues, "but one critically open to the possibility, even the necessity, of its transformation. Thinking in terms of prototypes historicizes myth" (p. 134).

DuPlessis, influenced herself by Louis Althusser, also argues that "narrative structures and subjects are like working apparatuses of ideology, factories for the 'natural' and 'fantastic' meanings by which we live" (p. 3). Conversely, "[a]ny social convention is like a 'script,' which suggests sequences of action and response, the meaning we give these, and ways of organizing experience by choices, emphases, priorities" (p. 2). In their reading of *The Awakening,* Gilbert and Gubar claim that Edna Pontellier "finds herself incapable of proposing any serious plot alternatives" (p. 107). "As Edna eventually realizes, even such a fiction betrays desire into the banalities of conventional romance, so that ultimately her dinner party in chapter thirty is the best, the most authentically self-defining, 'story' she can tell" (p. 108). Are these readings, in their emphasis on plots and stories, similar to what DuPlessis argues (and what Foucault might argue) or are they to be understood only as metaphoric word play? What relationship between language (discourse/scripts/narrative) and subjectivity are Gilbert and Gubar proposing here?

I have the same questions about their discussion of Wharton who, they argue, is capable of imagining only minimal societal change; Wharton's "imaginings of change or at least of (momentary) freedom from institutions that may be changeless, are almost always mediated through allusions to what is literally or figuratively *unsayable*: through evocations of what is illicit, what is secret, what is silent; through representations of what does not 'fit' into ordinary language or conventional systems of signification" (p. 157; emphasis in original). Gilbert and Gubar hypothesize that Wharton was only able to solve the problem of trying to name the unnameable by writing in a minor genre. For them, "the paradox of saying the unsayable, of speaking the unspeakable, infuses and energizes the very genre of the ghost story" (p. 159). But, again I ask, what is the view of subjectivity and textuality that they are working from in this discussion?

Ironically throughout a book they have self-consciously called *Sexchanges* rather than addressing the material origins of the gendered differences they insist on, Gilbert and Gubar seem content to discuss their consequences and transmutations. In chapter eight, for example, they discuss "Cross-Dressing and Re-Dressing: Transvestism as Meta-

phor." Instead of taking this opportunity to investigate the dialectical relationship between gendered subjectivity and society or that between biological sexuality and society (as Alison Jaggar does in *Feminist Politics and Human Nature* [1983, rpt. Totowa, NJ: Rowman and Littlefield, 1988]), Gilbert and Gubar focus on the metaphoric issue of transvestism. What they argue has its merits and certainly its fascinations (prurient and otherwise), but they never really grapple with the fundamental issues the way Jaggar does. When women cross-dressed, according to Gilbert and Gubar, they were "defying the conflation of sex roles and sex organs that many of their male contemporaries sought to reinforce" (p. 327). But where do our co-authors stand on this issue? Do they agree with Jaggar that "nothing is natural in human social life" (p. 112) or do they accept some kind of sexual essentialism or biological determination? What is their politics? Are they, in Jaggar's terms, liberal feminists, radical feminists, socialist feminists, or none of the above? They so insist on gender differences in this series that I begin to wonder if they are not (unwittingly perhaps) reinforcing Cixous's dualistic phallologocentric metaphor: man/woman. Some linguistic dualism is certainly reinforced by their unexplained use of such outmoded terms as "prophetess" (p. 63), "victress" (p. 147), "ancestresses" (p. 178), and "creatrix" (p. 204). If this is a joke, I don't get it. And if it's not, I don't understand it any better. Are the authoresses of *Sexchanges* to be similarly identified?

In short, what Gilbert and Gubar seem to be presenting as self-evident truths, such as the notion of gendered subjectivity and the relationship between texts and their sociocultural contexts, the theorists that I cited above have more successfully problematized. Because Gilbert and Gubar have not undertaken to problematize these issues nor the relationship between texts and subjectivity, their own work—as witty and challenging as it can be—maintains a kind of intellectual flatness. But in their defence, let me repeat what I said in my review of *No Man's Land*: after Gilbert and Gubar, our understanding of Anglo-American literary modernism will certainly never again be the same. Let me also acknowledge the vast amount of material that has gone into this series. As always, their knowledge of literary texts is nothing short of amazing, and so is the scope of their historical scholarship (though they do get one detail wrong: Amelia Bloomer did not invent bloomers, as they claim—she only wore them and thus quite inadvertently gave them her name; bloomers were invented by Elizabeth Smith Miller). The absence of other theoretical perspectives is by no means a fatal flaw, but it does weaken an otherwise impressive achievement.

Chandra Mukerji (review date July 1990)

SOURCE: "The Fate of Women Writers," in *Contemporary Sociology,* Vol. 19, No. 4, July, 1990, pp. 511–13.

[*In the following review, Mukerji discusses the theoretical propositions of volumes one and two of* No Man's Land *by discussing the two works in relation to Gaye Tuchman's book* Edging Women Out.]

There are two quite distinct traditions of feminist studies, one in the social sciences and the other in the humanities. The former looks at women in the world, acting, thinking, and responding to a social and natural environment dominated by males. The latter looks at human cultural forms, from literature and film to scientific epistemology, to consider gender and consciousness—the ways in which women are conceptualized, dreamed of, hoped for, and compared to men (by both women and men, albeit in different ways).

The books under review here, Gaye Tuchman's *Edging Women Out* and Gilbert and Gubar's **No Man's Land, Volumes 1 and 2** represent the best of the work from both traditions. Together they highlight the virtues (even the necessity) of each type of analysis for understanding the lives of women and womanhood (as a cultural category). Ironically, they also indicate the partial and perhaps even misleading understandings of women we develop by focusing exclusively on either one of these types of analysis. But they also make clear how large and complex a problem understanding gender and culture must necessarily be. Thus they make sense of the partialing out of this analysis to diverse groups of researchers with their own specialties.

Making a comparison between the books is a little tricky. Each looks at women and English-language literature, but Tuchman focuses on the last half of the nineteenth century, while Gilbert and Gubar focus on the early part of the twentieth century. Still, the processes that they document are linked: they show a strong response to (mainly a rejection of) female power in the world of literature, one in institutional terms, and the other in the imagery and language of the writers who established literary modernism.

Tuchman centers her analysis around materials from the archives of the Macmillan publishing firm in London. She uses primarily aggregate data from the archives (publication lists, readers' reports, and lists of readers assigned to manuscripts, among other things) to ground her contention that women novelists, who had dominated English-language novels in the early nineteenth century, were being displaced by men by the end of that century. From 1840 until World War I, women authors were regularly submitting about twice as many manuscripts for publication as their male counterparts, and from the 1840s through the 1890s their books were more likely to be accepted for publication than books by male authors. But by the turn of the century more men were submitting books, and books by male authors had a greater chance of publication.

Tuchman explains this phenomenon in terms derived from the sociology of occupations. She notes that it is not at all unusual for occupations dominated by women to be "invaded" by men when they become lucrative or powerful enough to attract men. This pattern is an example of what she calls the "empty field phenomenon." The group occupying the field is socially so insignificant that the field seems (to powerful groups) empty, and available for colonization. This, according to Tuchman, is what happened with novel writing. She contends that men were generally not interested in writing novels before 1840 because novelists made little money and received minimal prestige for their efforts. But the market for novels increased dramatically, and respected literary men began to write novels, so male authors began to see cultural and economic possibilities in the form. As they entered into novel writing they changed the novel's form and redefined the novelist as a new kind of artist-writer. In so doing, they assured a rupture with the women novelists who had dominated the field earlier in the century. Their work became the "other" against which the new art was defined.

Tuchman argues that this takeover of the novel was not the result of men's coming along and more or less by accident writing more and better novels. Men could make these occupational inroads in part because male writers dominated poetry and the other prestigious forms of literature (both fiction and nonfiction) and hence could bring reputations from their other work. More importantly, the primary decision makers in publishing houses (publishers and publishers' readers) were men who shared a distaste for "feminine" writing and contempt for the intellectual capabilities and aesthetic standards of female readers.

In making this argument, Tuchman stays close to her data (in the tradition of occupational research). She quotes the snide comments made about women writers and readers by the men who judged the manuscripts. She is very careful to protect herself from charges of exaggerating gender bias in the analysis. But she pays a price for this. Tuchman provides no data on the historical context in which this reorganization of novel writing took place, so she does not look at broader changes in gender relations in the period that might have affected the opinions of publishers about gender and writing. The limited ambitions for the analysis help to keep it a solidly empirical study, but leave it with only a partial explanation of the shift that Tuchman wants to explain.

Gilbert and Gubar provide us with much of the rest of the story. They try to understand how gender relations were being reorganized around the turn of the century by the struggle for women's suffrage and its institutional concomitants (such as new educational opportunities for women). They argue that these changes put strains on gender identities and led to an escalation of "the battle of the sexes." Gender worries became central to literary struggles in the period, affecting the shift toward modernism (which Gilbert and Gubar associate with a male obsession with conflictual gender relations and uneasy, ambiguous gender identities). The literature by men in this period was filled with hostilities toward "women scribblers" on the one hand, and toward powerful women figures or female institutions on the other. Male writers were anything but uniform in their ideas about the consequences of greater emancipation of women; some supported greater autonomy for women, but many more associated female power with destruction of the male. These men drew women as both victims and victimizers, sources of corruption and of mindless lust; they also treated women as the source of cultural banality and the degradation of literature. In spite of their differences, almost all men imagined the power of women to be both formidable and worrying.

Twentieth-century women writers also addressed gender conflicts and identity in their writings. While their male colleagues exaggerated female power and its consequences, they were more sober. Some shared with men many of the tenets of modernism—particularly a distaste for female "scribblers who degraded the novel. But while they may have felt contempt for some women, they were less sanguine about the virtues of male authority. In addition, a substantial number of women used their writing to project feminist fantasies of female autonomy, power, and sexuality.

Gender not only entered into the themes and imagery in the writing by both women and men in the period, it also shaped language. As Gilbert and Gubar note, such usages as "mother tongues" and "muscular language" were made problematic by gender warfare. Some women started searching for ways to position and use language outside patriarchy, while some men, such as Joyce, looked to esoteric language use as the source for gender-based authority in language.

Gilbert and Gubar present and discuss these differences in male and female consciousness among writers in quite sociological terms, considering aggregate qualities of gender groups. But the analysis addresses only minimally the questions of class that complicated gender relationships (the lesbian/feminist voices were often from upper-class women and threatened most intensively the identities of new writers of lower-class origins). The authors also ignore the institutional arrangements in book publishing that affected the relative power of male and female writers—the sort of thing that Tuchman makes so clear. But Gilbert and Gubar's books together with Tuchman's provide a marvelous view of the complexities of gender relations and literature around the turn of the century.

Eve Kosofsky Sedgwick (review date September 1990)

SOURCE: A review of *No Man's Land, Volume 1: The War of Words,* in *English Language Notes,* Vol. 28, No. 1, September, 1990, pp. 73–7.

[*In the following review of* The War of Words, *Sedgwick praises Gubar and Gilbert's discussion of conflicts between women, but faults the writers for apparent homophobic slips regarding men.*]

In his nightclub act, Michael Feinstein has a rather strange song about what happens when women stick together:

> Shall we join the ladies?
> I mean *really* join the ladies
> And make one great big lady? Whaddaya say—Queen Kong![1]

Sandra M. Gilbert and Susan Gubar (who, whatever the pleasures of their durable, celebrated collaboration, must get tired of being conflated into one great big lady) have written in *The War of the Words* an exploration of the relations between and among women, even more than of the relations between women and men. The most interesting section of the book reflects on "the multiple binds in which the twentieth-century woman writer feels herself to be caught when she confronts the new reality of her female literary inheritance." First, the authors explain,

> she sees the pain her precursors experienced and wishes to renounce it. . . . In addition, though, she acknowledges the power her precursors achieved and worries that she may not be able to equal it. . . . Finally, however, she fears the consequences of both renunciation and rivalry: to renounce her precursors' pain or to refuse to try to rival them may be to relinquish the originatory authority their achievements represent. . . .

(198–9)

In addition to helping us ask more acutely about the particular novelty of the twentieth-century woman writer's situation, this angle of inquiry makes it possible and necessary to ask about the relation that *The War of the Words* itself establishes between, on the one hand, the two twentieth-century women who have authored it and, on the other, the women precursors to whose work it attends. Gilbert and Gubar argue persuasively that what they call the female "affiliation complex" is better suited to the trope of the adoptive than of the biological family; and it is easy to see the imperatives of the "affiliation complex" behind their own project:

> By looking *at* the precursor, the female inheritor distances herself from her foremother's struggle while at the same time participating vicariously in the primal moment of composition. . . . By looking *for*—seeking out, choosing, and thus achieving a kind of power over—precursors, the twentieth-century woman writer eases the burden of what Harold Bloom has called the "anxiety of influence." . . .

(199)

Each of the many strategies by which women writers approach the "affiliation complex" has strengths and liabilities. The authors show, for instance, that the "passionate dialogue" by which Virginia Woolf individualized and dramatized her female precursors also, in some ways, risked trivializing them: "As she transforms these precursors into characters in search of an author named Virginia Woolf, the author of *A Room of One's Own* often verges upon caricature. Moreover, concentrating on their bodies rather than upon their books, she frequently seems to be evading a serious consideration of texts whose power might make her tremble" (204).

The relational strategy adopted in this book is different from Woolf's: its highly synthetic form, as much as its feminist intent, involves it in a project, not of individuating, but of joining the ladies. Feinstein's airily hallucinatory song suggests the reconstitutive violence the authors perform here on their precursors: "I move we join those darling daughters / I mean join them to each other / and make one great huge mother." Focusing on texts and de-emphasizing particular authorial bodies (with a few exceptions, including quite an ugly discussion of Gertrude Stein's size), the book also, far more than *The Madwoman in the Attic*, de-emphasizes the particularity of individual authors, in favor of a focus on experiences, strategies, thematics that many are seen to have shared. Individual texts are subject to the same treatment: it is the rare reading, here, that is sustained for more than a paragraph or two, and the reader balances the loss in sharpness against a gain in breadth when brief readings of multiple texts are joined into argument through a kind of molecular aggregation.

> As we have seen, from Charlotte Brontë's Bertha Mason Rochester and Mary Wilkins Freeman's Old Woman Magoun to Rebecca West's Evadne Silverton, Carson McCullers's Miss Amelia Evans, and Joanna Russ's Jael, women characters created by women writers have repeatedly drafted themselves into what Sylvia Townsend Warner called 'the great civil war' between men and women. . . . Some years after such thinkers as Simone de Beauvoir, Betty Friedan, and Kate Millett had begun to reinvent the women's movement, James Tiptree, Jr.—elsewhere the author of fantasies about female autonomy—recorded in "The Screwfly Solution" (1977) a terrifying vision of a femicidal Holocaust. And to return to Sylvia Plath. . . .

> (118–9)

This technique seems to combine authorial diffidence (the idea that a mosaic of allusion to and quotation from precursor-women makes an argument stronger than could the authorial voice itself) with what one might also perceive as a certain aggression of accretion. The creation for, and at the same time *out of*, women writers of a relatively undifferentiated, somewhat utopian mass of female commonality, may evoke in the woman writer who reads such passages anxiety at the same time as solidarity.

One of the casualties of this approach is the analysis—at best, fragile and hard-won in contemporary feminism—of the ways in which women may differ from and indeed oppress one another along dimensions that are not reducible to the sameness of their gender. In one particularly striking example, the authors of this book quote a passage from Ann Petry about her black heroine's murderous rage against

> "Jim [her husband] and the slender girl she'd found him with; . . . the insult in the moist-eyed glances of white men on the subway; . . . the unconcealed hostility in the eyes of white women. . . . [and] the white world which thrust black people into a walled enclosure."[2]

When Gilbert and Gubar paraphrase Petry's passage, however, the explicit involvement of women black and white

in the oppressions described in it simply disappears. "What emerges from this passage is an explanation of the black woman's position at the bottom of the social ladder": she is "oppressed by both white and black *men*" "because the black *man* is unmanned by the white *man* [and] needs to exert special mastery over 'his' woman" (103–4, emphasis added). Predictably, then, although the disadvantaged racial and economic status of black or poor women writers is treated throughout this book as a relevant factor in their gender construction, the privileged or exploitive status of white or economically comfortable women is not. And the U.S. history that the authors treat as relevant to their gender argument does not include the history of domestic race or class relations.

Across the differentials between women—basically generational ones—that it is interested in, however, the book makes it newly possible to construct some fine and useful maps. Joining the gentlemen, on the other hand, in the substantial sections of this book dealing with male writers, seems a far less discriminant undertaking. The fact that some form of misogyny is detectable in many or most male writers seems to mean that there are no differences between men worthy of feminist analytical attention. One might have thought, for instance, given that "compulsory heterosexuality" is one of the forces described here as shaping women's positions and identities, that it could make some difference that the period under discussion was marked by sudden, radical rupture in the history of male homo/heterosexual definition, including the formation of (men's as well as women's) homosexual and gay identities, and the foundation of the first (male-centered) movements for homosexual rights. But these developments are not so much as mentioned. Oscar Wilde, to name one signal figure of this history, appears only as "the son of a woman poet, the editor of *Women's World* and the author of an . . . essay on 'English Poetesses'" (144)—just one more man with a negative opinion of some women writers. (At that, he fares better than William Burroughs; neither Burroughs' sexuality *nor his writing* is mentioned, only—did you guess?—the fact that, "as if literalizing" a quoted poem by someone else, but also as if literalizing everything else about men in the book, he accidentally killed his wife [52].) There is a brief discussion of Tennessee Williams and Allen Ginsberg as figures with a consciously oblique relation to compulsory heterosexuality (50–52). Aside from them, however, a man in this book can only be either a he-man or what the authors call, in the joke of their title and in frequent, often apparently homophobic usages thereafter, a "no-man"—a would-be he-man who, for a variety of reasons (effeminacy, cuckoldry, lack of heterosexual desire, all treated as involuntary and demeaning), isn't up to his job of dominating women and therefore feels "threatened" by them.

I don't after all, however, get the feeling that this book is very interested in men writers. The undifferentiating sections on men seem (as the authors might put it) "belated" in relation to germinal feminist works like Kate Millett's

Sexual Politics. This book's central, more enlivening project and contribution is to show that joining the ladies need not require the fiction that our feelings about each other can be simple or uniform. As is likely to happen when women stick together, the result, if glutinous, is also often jolly.

Notes

1. From "Shall We Join the Ladies," written by Marshall Barer and David Ross (Williamson Music, ASCAP); recorded on "Michael Feinstein Live at the Algonquin."

2. P. 103; from Ann Petry, *The Street* (New York: Pyramid, 1961), pp. 266–67.

Helen Carr (review date 7 October 1994)

SOURCE: "Battle Stations," in *New Statesman and Society,* Vol. 7, No. 323, October 7, 1994, pp. 45–6.

[*In the following review of the three volumes of* No Man's Land, *Carr faults Gilbert and Gubar for reductionist and strained readings of the texts they present.*]

The phrase "No Man's Land" is a curiously negative and undecided image for women's writing. For the most striking characteristic of a No Man's Land is surely emptiness. Yet if the 1,200 odd pages in the three volumes of this account were to prove nothing else, they make clear that the 20th century is full of women writers.

Gibert and Gubar, both senior US academics, themselves seem to be hunkering down in the trenches. *No Man's Land* is conscientious but confused, painstaking but perplexed. It has nothing like the panache and drive of their landmark account of 19th-century women's writing, *The Madwoman in the Attic* (1979), published in the heady early days of feminist literary criticism, when women were women and a man's place was in the wrong. Now that it is necessary to talk about the mutability and fictiveness of gender roles, and men come not only as patriarchs but as homosexuals, Jews and blacks, everything is less easily resolved.

In that earlier book, Gilbert and Gubar argued that the central metaphors by which to understand the 19th-century woman writer—and by which the writers understood themselves—were those of entrapment and escape. That meant entrapment in the patriarchal home, in the patriarchal House of Fiction, in patriarchal womanhood, and escape into self-definition and the discovery of an alternative identity through the act of writing.

Perhaps because it was not simply a work of criticism but an existential *Bildungsroman* in its own right, the book proved immensely liberating for a whole generation of women students. But it has been much criticised: for its neglect of all forms of oppression other than gender, for its theoretical thinness, for the sheer excess in its depiction of the "anxiety of authorship" these women suffered. After all, by the 19th century, writing was established as one of the few ways a middle-class woman could earn money, and very good money some of them earned.

These critiques have clearly fuelled a degree of "anxiety of authorship" in *No Man's Land* itself, though the concessions are fairly limited. The three volumes have again been organised around a central metaphor, this time that of the sexwar. *The Madwoman in the Attic*, they say, recorded the period of female resistence; *No Man's Land* that of female rebelliousness. The rise of the New Woman and the erosion of Victorian definitions of femininity produced a misogynistic backlash, a battle to keep women off male territory, and caused the modernist movement itself. The first volume, *The War of Words*, was an overview from Tennyson to the present and the second, *Sexchanges*, went as far as the interwar years. *Letters from the Front*, the final volume, takes up the story there.

It discusses, among others, Virginia Woolf. Marianne Moore, Edna St Vincent Millay, Zora Neale Hurston, Jesse Faucet, H D and Sylvia Plath. One virtue of this long battle-song is that it brings into view lesser-known writers as well as more established names. But much of the critical account is a relentlessly reductive or strained reading of texts to wrench out images of violence and prove their point.

Nor is it easy to be convinced that Marianne Moore (who after all worked with Native Americans) objected to colonialism only because it was patriarchal, or that it was solely because fascism was "a form of masculinism" that literary women opposed it. Misogyny and masculinism in male modernist writing does need further analysis, and the New Woman did provoke a backlash, but to describe our war-torn century simply as a war between the sexes raises more problems than it solves.

Gilbert and Gubar can make their metaphor work only when they fiercely prioritise gender difference. When they move into discussions of homosexuality or race, as they now feel impelled to do, it is clear that the troops refuse to divide neatly into two sides. They resolutely set their faces against any kind of "so-called post-structuralist" theory that might give them a subtler way of examining the violence and instability of power. Their argument that modernism is differently inflected for male and female writers must be right, but those texts will also be inflected by a range of other differences—not least money and class, factors quite ignored here. All the same, this packed history helps to make clear the rich and varied contribution made by women writers to the modernist movement, something hardly acknowledged when the first volume appeared seven years ago.

Ann Ardis (review date Fall 1995)

SOURCE: A review of *No Man's Land, Volume 3: Letters from the Front*, in *Tulsa Studies in Women's Literature*, Vol. 14, No. 2, Fall, 1995, pp. 366–69.

[In the following excerpt, Ardis praises Letters from the Front, *but objects to its scanty coverage of the Harlem Renaissance and of black writers in general.]*

. . . . As Gillian Beer has noted, the third and final volume of Sandra Gilbert and Susan Gubar's *No Man's Land: The Place of the Woman Writer in the Twentieth-Century* is disappointingly anglocentric.[1] Because both [Michael A.] North and [Laura] Doyle argue so convincingly for the historical inseparability of white modernism and the Harlem Renaissance, reading *Letters from the Front* in tandem with [North's] *The Dialect of Modernism* and [Doyle's] *Bordering on the Body* makes Gilbert and Gubar's treatment of the latter seem thin. Unlike North's and Doyle's pairing of black and white texts, the chapter on feminism and the Harlem Renaissance and the briefer discussions of black writers in chapters seven and eight do not adequately counterbalance the remaining chapters' focus on either one or a pair of white writers (Woolf, Edna St. Vincent Millay, Marianne Moore, H. D., Sylvia Plath). Nonetheless, there is much of value in this enormous study. In and of itself, the vastness of this project is exhilarating, a testimony both to what two scholars and a bevy of research assistants can achieve through collaboration, and a bracing alternative to the claustrophobia induced by close reading after close reading of either canonical or noncanonical texts.[2] Gilbert and Gubar's broad-brushed thematic approach has its drawbacks, of course. For careful historical contextualization, one must perforce look elsewhere—to *The Dialect of Modernism*, to Sydney Janet Kaplan's *Katherine Mansfield and the Origins of Modernist Fiction* (1991), or to Carolyn Steedman's *Childhood, Class, and Culture in Britain: Margaret McMillan, 1860–1931* (1990), for example. But, as in the first two volumes of *No Man's Land*, Gilbert and Gubar's work here continues quite usefully to point up the "act[s] of affiliation" by means of which other scholars have told stories about the making of modernism without acknowledging the gendering of that history.[3]

My one criticism of *Letters from the Front* is different from though tangentially related to Beer's. Early on in this study, Gilbert and Gubar's invocation of Joan de la Riviere's psychoanalytic work on masquerades of femininity suggests their rejection of—or at least a serious rethinking of—the feminist essentialism and the monolithic plotting of "woman's life" for which their earlier work has been criticized. Indeed, their final chapter begins with an explicit reference to the ways in which *Letters from the Front* differs in its feminist methodology from their earliest collaborative project, *Madwoman in the Attic*. Noting how they "dramatized the dilemma" (p. 305) of nineteenth-century women writers through the story of Snow White in that study, they chart a different course for themselves as well as for twentieth-century writers in "The Further Adventures of Snow White: Feminism, Modernism, and the Family Plot":

> [A]s we now conclude *No Man's Land*, we feel we have been reviewing so many new and different plots—all of them explored in various ways by twentieth-century women writers—that it is no longer possible to propose a monolithic "tale" about the female imagination. What had been a single tradition has become many traditions, as women's spheres have widened and the certainties of men's worlds have crumbled.
>
> (p. 360)

Notwithstanding this opening gambit, however, this final chapter's witty, Scherezhade-like retellings of Snow White climax on a discordantly monologic note of praise for the "emergence of the child-poem in the female literary tradition" as a "major transformation" in the situation of twentieth-century women writers (p. 402). The final retelling of Snow White's story centers on biological maternity and gives biological mothers and daughters exclusive rights to the "forest" of new stories that Gilbert and Gubar imagine as the future of women's writing:

> *There was a good Queen who pricked her finger with a needle, watched blood fall on the snow, gave birth to a girl-child named Snow White, and lived to raise her. And sometimes when this Queen looked into the mirror of her mind, she passed in her thoughts through the looking glass into the forest of stories so new that only she and her daughter could tell them.*
>
> (p. 403, italics in original)

Why retell Snow White as a story about a biological mother's relationship with her daughter? Why describe the future of women's writing as the exclusive property of women and their biological daughters? In light of the many and varied masquerades of femininity and masculinity surveyed in *Letters from the Front*, this final, and supposedly utopian, version of Snow White seems both retrograde and exclusionary—a throwback to the biological (and hence racial) paradigm of motherhood that Laura Doyle would like to believe we have already jettisoned.

But perhaps I am overreacting to the conclusion of *Letters from the Front*. It is entirely possible that "Further Adventures of Snow White" should *not* be read as the conclusion of a book-length argument—and as such, should *not* be criticized for falling short of the project marked out elsewhere in this study. Instead, perhaps it should be treated as a performance piece, as an occasional essay whose inconsistency with other materials in this volume is a consequence of this being a collection of collaborative writings produced and gathered together over a period of time. The latter approach would certainly produce a more generous reading of this chapter. It would respect the dialogism of collaborative feminist scholarship explored in recent issues of *Tulsa Studies*. And it would also honor both the vampiness of these "mirror" critics[4] and the sense of *No Man's Land* being an exercise in feminist literary history that, as William Cain suggested recently, "cannot really be brought to a close" in spite of its ostensible completion with **Letters from the Front**. "In their future work, Gilbert and Gubar themselves will no doubt add to, qualify, and complicate the story that this three-volume history recounts," Cain suggests in his introduction to *Making Feminist Literary History: The Literary Scholarship of Sandra M. Gilbert and Susan Gubar* (1994).[5] A comment Nina Auerbach made in 1980 about **Madwoman in the Attic** supports Cain's point in its relevance, fifteen years later, to **Letters from the Front**: "one of the strengths of this strong and massive book is its intensification of the reader's urgency to break free and tell her own story." A "book of this length and density" can quite happily be read "piecemeal at need."[6]

Notes

1. Gillian Beer, "Dispersed as We Are," *Times Literary Supplement*, 30 June 1995, p. 7. She means this in two respects: their discussion of women writers is not as global as their title might suggest; and they neglect British writers such as Sylvia Townsend Warner, Angela Carter, and Jeannette Winterson who are more familiar to British readers than to Americans.

2. For an important reminder of the blindness that accompanies the insights of close reading as an interpretive strategy, see Peter Rabinowitz's "Canons and Close Reading," in *Falling into Theory: Conflicting Views on Reading Literature*, ed. David Richter (Boston: St. Martin's, 1994), pp. 218–22. Doyle's study is the one that feels claustrophobically focused on six texts by contrast with North's as well as Gilbert and Gubar's.

3. This is Pamela Caughie's point in "The (En)gendering of Literary History," *Tulsa Studies in Women's Literature*, 8, No. 1 (1989), 119. William Cain concurs in his introduction to *Making Literary History: The Literary Scholarship of Sandra M. Gilbert and Susan Gubar* (New York and London: Garland Publishing, 1994): "Perhaps the major achievement of feminist theory and criticism—to which Gilbert and Gubar have made a major contribution—has been the deconstruction of modernism. This involves not only the critique and revision of the history of literary modernism, but also the dismantling of the history of all literary periods that the modernist generation of critics, scholars, and men-of-letters enshrined in books and embedded in classrooms in colleges and universities" (p. xliv).

4. I am borrowing, and collapsing, Gilbert and Gubar's own distinction between French poststructuralist feminist criticism and Anglo-American work, as used in "The Mirror and the Vamp: Reflections on Feminist Criticism." Originally published in *The Future of Literary Theory*, ed. Ralph Cohen (New York: Routledge, 1988), this essay is reprinted in Cain, *Making Feminist History*, pp. 3–36.

5. Cain, p. xxxviii.

6. Nina Auerbach, Review of *Madwoman in the Attic, Victorian Studies*, 23, No. 4 (1980), 506.

Roberta Rubenstein (essay date Spring 1995)

SOURCE: "Altering the Critical Landscape," in *Belles Lettres,* Vol. 10, No. 2, Spring, 1995, pp. 30–31.

[*In the following essay surveying Gubar and Gilbert's work in* The Madwoman in the Attic *and the three volumes of* No Man's Land, *Rubenstein lauds the studies, calling them a "landmark of feminist literary criticism."*]

Sometimes it seems as if Sandra Gilbert and Susan Gubar have read every significant text of fiction, poetry, and drama (as well as a few less significant ones) authored by a woman. In their ambitious and influential project of reconsidering the literary writing of women over two centuries, Gilbert and Gubar have fundamentally altered the critical landscape and assumptions about women's writing. The four-volume work that has resulted from their remarkable collaboration over nearly two decades has earned its place as a landmark of feminist literary criticism—indeed, of literary scholarship—produced during our era.

In the first volume, **The Madwoman in the Attic: The Woman Writer and the Nineteenth-Century Literary Imagination** (1979), Gilbert and Gubar began with the provocative question, "Is a pen a metaphorical penis?" and proceeded to expose the hidden stories beneath the "cover stories" in 19th-century texts by women; the madwoman of Charlotte Brontë's *Jane Eyre* was transported from her marginal location in Mr. Rochester's attic into the central chamber of female consciousness. The succeeding three-volume study, **No Man's Land: The Place of the Woman Writer in the Twentieth-Century** (which culminates with this final segment), delivers with equal brilliance a series of readings that demonstrates the interpenetrating influences of war, gender redefinitions, and the literary imagination. Dauntlessly addressing major critical questions ranging from the shape of the literary canon to the significance of particular literary texts and historical events, the authors have forged new interpretive links between social and literary history and literary analysis.

In **The War of the Words** (1988), Gilbert and Gubar theorize that modernism, the significant literary movement of the early 20th-century, "is differently inflected for male and female writers" because of the "distinctive social and cultural changes to which it responds." The rise of feminism in the late 19th century produced a "sexual antagonism" that in turn fueled a battle of the sexes, expressed both socially and literarily for several decades thereafter. **Sexchanges** (1989) focuses specifically on the sexual experimentations and altered definitions of the erotic that such antagonisms generated. As the authors so felicitously phrase it (in one of many lively wordplays), "the sexes battle because sex roles change, but, when the sexes battle, sex itself (that it, eroticism) changes."

The concluding volume, *Letters from the Front* (1994), extends the encompassing metaphor of battle and war as the defining terms for understanding women's "letters" or literary expressions, from the cultural "front" in this century. The authors emphasize works primarily by "representative women writers who . . . seem to have . . . access to the repository of myths and images, injunctions and contradictions, which registers the psychological effects of social change." The authors' central premises are the overarching influence of war(s), the ubiquity of impersonation, and the artifice of gender itself as a social construct.

Two corollary preoccupations weave together Gilbert and Gubar's masterful critical syntheses and interpretations of Virginia Woolf, Jessie Fauset, Nella Larsen, H. D. (Hilda Doolittle), Sylvia Plath, and others. The first is that history becomes "gendered" through women writers' dramatizations of the difference public (male) and private (female) events. The second is that these writers express, within their frequently experimental texts, their struggles not only to articulate but also to *survive* the difficult transition from the "old" to the "new," whether conceptualized as history, gender roles, literary text, or self.

In the opening chapter, the authors highlight the ongoing dialectic in Virginia Woolf's works between "official" and "unofficial" history, as well as that between "the demise of the old and the birth of the new." Elaborating on a theme sounded in *Sexchanges* (in which such preoccupations as masquerade and transvestism operate as central visual expressions of destabilized gender roles), the authors consider the disjunctions between *self* and *self-presentation* in writers who feel compelled to become, in the interests of their art, what Gilbert and Gubar term "female female impersonators." Thus, the body of the work is linked to the body of the poet herself: Edna St. Vincent Millay and Marianne Moore emerge from these pages less as dilettante poets than as writers who created masks for themselves to establish "spaces from which they could question many of the conventions of their culture." They influenced a later generation of poets—Sylvia Plath, Adrienne Rich, and Anne Sexton—to regard the poetic persona as a self-conscious mask that could be intentionally manipulated. However, Moore and Millay themselves became trapped in the very disguises they constructed. Mimicry served an even more essential purpose for African-American women writers of the Harlem Renaissance, as well as for their inwardly divided characters. Struggling against the double oppressions of gender and race, female characters created by Jessie Fauset and Nella Larsen retreat into impersonation and "passing" as the only ways to "shuttle between yes and no, to play at being the New Woman a racist culture never [let] them be."

Although literature produced during the "Great War" expressed a profound inquiry, registered through the texts of both female and male writers, into gender definitions and assumptions, World War II brought renewed sexual polarization on both cultural and literary fronts. Additionally, the links between sex, the weaponry of war, and death are encapsulated in a variety of cultural artifacts and terms: women enshrined in soldiers' "pin-up girl" posters or labeled sexual "bombshells," "male bonding" (except for homosexuality, which was vilified), and the emergence of the "he-man." Thus, mid-century female poets faced a much sharper set of cultural and social restrictions concerning writing and being. Sylvia Plath is a pivotal figure in the project of re-establishing "the new" once again; Gilbert and Gubar locate Plath centrally in mid-century by tracing her literary lineage backward to the modernists (Lawrence, Woolf, Yeats) and forward to the generation of poets whom she directly influenced (Rich, Sexton, Levertov).

A dark counterpoint in the gender wars emerges in the mid-century narratives of threatened virility by such male writers as Joseph Heller, John Barth, Kurt Vonnegut, and Norman Mailer. Wittily revising Simone de Beauvoir's crucial observation about the social sources of female identity, Gilbert and Gubar observe that, for a number of male writers in mid-century, "one is not born a man; one does not become a man; one pretends to be a man." The authors also discuss narratives by contemporary female writers from Doris Lessing to Margaret Atwood and others who have added to the literature of gender and cultural critique.

There are many more splendid insights than cannot be suggested in a review of this length. But I cannot close without mentioning the brilliant concluding chapter of this study. In *The Madwoman in the Attic*, Gilbert and Gubar revise the fairy tale of "Snow White" to expose the hidden gender messages they discerned in the queen's looking glass. Now, 15 years later, they explode the story to illustrate the multiple ways in which not simply gender but also narrative, feminist (and other) literary criticism and cultural pluralism have evolved during this century—and even during the years encompassed by their critical enterprise. In "The Further Adventures of Snow White: Feminism, Modernism, and the Family Plot," the authors reprise the major cultural and literary metamorphoses that they have so illuminatingly traced throughout the several volumes. If the 19th century permitted a paradigmatic "real story"—a "family romance" that fixed the parameters of female experience—the 20th century, the authors suggest, is too complex and fluid to yield a single paradigm. Rather, the plot has dissolved into multiple, contradictory scenarios. The "Ur-story" of Snow White unfolds to provide a witty smorgasbord of narrative variations and options, a series of "choose your own adventure" scripts ranging from nontraditional gender possibilities to "alternate modes of eroticism," from parodies of Woolf and other canonical writers to denouements that imitate Lacanian analyses or conveniently deconstruct themselves.

Moreover, since the once-inexorable opposition between writing and motherhood has also been dissolved, the competition between Snow White and her stepmother has lost much of its explanatory power. "How, then, would this newly born mother-writer tell the old story of 'Snow White'?" Sandra Gilbert and Susan Gubar ask. I won't spoil their masterstroke by revealing here how they answer the question with their own new and affirmative ending—both to Snow White's story and to their engaging revision of our evolving collective narrative.

Kathleen Blake (review date October 1995)

SOURCE: A review of *Sexchanges*, in *Journal of English and Germanic Philology*, Vol. 94, No. 4, October, 1995, pp. 591–96.

[*In the following review, Blake examines the role of the femme fatale in* Sexchanges.]

The second volume of this three-volume project confirms the distinction, authority, and style of Sandra Gilbert and Susan Gubar as commentators on British and American literature of the twentieth century, and the role of women in shaping it. This major study of modernism worthily follows Gilbert and Gubar's *The Madwoman in the Attic* and *The Norton Anthology of Literature by Women*, which have made so large a difference in our understanding of nineteenth-century literature by women, and so extended our range of exposure to writings by women from previous centuries to the present.

Sexchanges carries forward the ideas of Volume 1 of *No Man's Land*, giving more time to close readings of texts, and somewhat more to those of women than men, such as Olive Schreiner, Charlotte Perkins Gilman, Edith Wharton, Willa Cather, Gertrude Stein, Djuna Barnes, and Virginia Woolf. But there is still a strong contextualization of the meanings of the works of both sexes for each other. This is because, contrary to an idea of modernism as masculine—committed to originality, hence phallic (Pound), the grand thesis here is the formation of modernism in the dawning of feminism that opened awareness of female powers of origination and cast much male originality into competition or reaction. Thus the *relation* of male and female is central to modernism, and it is to be understood as an intensified battle of the sexes producing an accelerated pace of sexchanges.

New Womanhood, dreaming of Herland, raised the specter of No Man's Land for men, often driving them to retrenchment. But on the woman's side Gilbert and Gubar call our attention not to a triumphant Amazon but to an equivocal femme fatale. No Man's Land is land lost but not clearly gained, and it makes an apt setting for Gilbert's and Gubar's conception of modernism. It is true that on this military scene the femme fatale may not quite seem to fit; yet it is with this figure that the book begins. Chapter by chapter she is less or more in view but continues to be important, for she illustrates an idea of what is "damaged or

damaging" (p. 148) in women's role. She is no idealized adversary to man, not unscathed by her long history of subordination nor purely and righteously scathing as she rises up against it. Her experience has been fatal enough to make her fatal to men and to herself in certain ways. Certainly, in their preface Gilbert and Gubar note the optimism and hopes for a new relation of the sexes expressed by a number of writers of the turn of the century. And through the book, change for the good is glimpsed, more often by women than men. But meeting such visions are male fears and hostilities and female anxieties, involving weaknesses and culpabilities. The material is "disturbing." Gilbert and Gubar hint that they bring bad news: "All we can finally say is, Reader, we felt we had to write it, but please don't kill the messenger" (p. xvii).

The femme fatale of Chapter 1 is Rider Haggard's *She*. She is other (Egyptian), primal, ancient, powerful, learned in old wisdom and close to metaphysical secrets, sexual and deadly, also burdened and tormented. She is She-Who-Must-Be-Obeyed and threatens to take over the earth; to men and Britons She is She-Who-Must-Be-Destroyed. This is done in a phallic manner involving a "pillar of Life" not to be missed by Gilbert and Gubar, with their keen eye for sexual imagery, and counterpointed to the grotesquely feminine-domestic method of "hotpotting" used by Her subjects to decapitate/castrate intruding men (by putting red hot earthen pots over their heads). For a frame of reference for Haggard's femme fatale Gilbert and Gubar give us La Gioconda, La Belle Dame Sans Merci, Lamia, Moneta, Geraldine, Venus, Astarte, Helen, Cleopatra, Faustine, Dolores, Sappho, Lucy Westenra, the White Worm, Lilith, and Salome, amongst other female figures positioned at the heart of darkness. Ease with a huge scope of literary reference lends interest and authority to the book. And with this goes powerful historical framing, often reinforced through details from the author's personal experience. Thus *She* is placed amidst a matrix of late nineteenth-century associations: with the new powers and claims of women; new research into the biology of ovulation and the anthropology of matriarchy; imperial dominions threatening to escape and even reverse the direction of domination; and recovered exotic and esoteric religious lore—foreign in source and the domain of female spiritualists at home—all of which might challenge male-imperial-Christian confidence.

One might suppose the femme fatale to be the special conjuration of anxious men, a figure to be overcome as in Haggard's yarn. But Gilbert and Gubar present her as an important figure for women as well. In Chapter 2, Lyndall of Schreiner's *Story of An African Farm* is a variant, "for while men like Haggard viewed the New Woman as *femme fatal* to men, Schreiner presents the New Woman's feminism as a fatality that will eventually kill *her*" (p. 53). They make use of Schreiner's feminist critique of women's training to the role of "sex parasite" in *Women and Labour*. In their reading of *The Story of An African Farm* there is damage all around: "The parasite drains life from the independent organisms on which she feeds and thereby reduces men to instrumentality while simultaneously diminishing her own chance of autonomous survival" (p. 60). Indeed, the feminist protagonist who condemns a parasitical way of life only does the worse job of it after finding that she doesn't manage to live by her own resources very well either.

The tormented self-destructiveness of the femme fatale also comes to the fore in Chapter 4, where we see through Wharton's Lily Bart of *The House of Mirth* that "it is fatal to be a femme fatale" (p. 140). Wharton seems to ask what will happen to a sex parasite with nothing to feed on. Gilbert and Gubar show that Lily, though not really a feminist, lacks conviction in carrying out the parasitical female role and lets slip chances on the marriage market. Further, men in this and others of Wharton's novels are curiously lacking as hosts for the parasite. It is not only that they do not propose, but that the best of them seem to have little to offer, already to be weak, drained. As No Men they are unsustaining hosts before the parasite has found a means of support in herself. This is a fatale situation, especially for the femme, and Lily, like Lyndall, dies.

It is May Welland of *The Age of Innocence* whom Gilbert and Gubar call "damaged or damaging." She is not the expected image of the femme fatale. In her case purity and innocence are her means for ruthlessly hanging on to her husband, despite his love for another woman. But purity and innocence are elements of blankness trained into her as a woman (a lady), so that it is by the damage she has suffered that she does damage. Gilbert and Gubar characterize Wharton herself in terms that evoke the femme fatale, disdainful of the feminine arts she also practices, fashionably "dressed to kill" (p. 136), implacable in her books and out of them against ladies and feminists, men and No Men, an all around "Angel of Devastation" in James's phrase that gives the chapter its title.

For Gilbert and Gubar other women writers are less focused on fatality. The most clearly utopian work they discuss is Gilman's *Herland*, where all is well for women without men. They recognize how much Cather sees in girlhood, reclaiming the stories of frontier girls from oblivion in the saga of the West, and embodying in girls a "mythic America" (p. 184). They read Chopin's *The Awakening* in a strikingly positive manner. Rather than interpreting the novel's end in suicidal terms, they understand it to affirm some second coming of Aphrodite, as an alternative to a patriarchal Jesus. Edna Pontellier swims out to sea as a celebrant of some erotic faith.

Gilbert and Gubar are true to broadly Freudian premises recognizable in their work since **The Madwoman in the Attic** in weighing eros and anger heavily on the plus side for women and women's literature, and they are on the lookout for the return of the repressed as "erotic defiance" (p. 165). So it comes as no surprise that they are unenthusiastic about the small role of sexuality or rebellion in *Herland*, enthusiastic about Aphrodite in *The Awakening*, eager to give credit to Wharton, despite the negativism in

her novels, for getting some unsayable good things said (subtextually) in her ghost stories about jouissance and defiance, and sorry that Cather stops short with glorifying girlhood before the emergence of eroticism. In fact, the word "fatal" reenters with regard to Cather. Her "fatal attraction to a renunciation of passion" is said to have posed "her greatest literary problem" (p. 205). That renunciation of desire must mean renunciation of aesthetic desire is—rather thinly—argued with reference to Cather's story "Before Breakfast."

A kind of desire that Gilbert and Gubar pay less attention to is material appetite, that is, for things rather than sex. Literary criticism seldom does acknowledge this, other than as lamentable greed. Actually feminists may be just the ones to open up to a less dismissive attitude, for material inequality has been a very important part of the subjection of women over the centuries, and material progress seems very much to the point. In fact, Chapter 7 on the literature of the Great War makes a great deal of women's satisfaction in the jobs and money they gained when men left for the front. It notes that there could even be a profit motive for marriage in light of the chance for war-widows' compensation. One reason "We Enjoyed the War" (in the memoir by this name by Iris Barry) was that "we were all getting rich, or richer" (p. 273). This wide-ranging and eye-opening chapter covers the benefits accruing to women in economic terms, as well as in opportunities for new kinds of work, experience, and adventure, in sexual liberation, and eventually in the vote, while men suffered death, dismemberment, demoralization, depersonalization, displacement, disillusionment, psychic disinheritance, and unmanning in the No Man's Land of the trenches. With awareness of how much material good may mean to women, Gilbert and Gubar might have shown more understanding of Lily Bart's hunger for the jewels, clothes, rooms, furniture, houses. Perhaps Wharton herself found release or gratification of desire, not only through covert expressions of erotic defiance, but through overt enjoyment of affluence, in her deluxe travels, her clothes, her houses. Her first full-length work, *The Decoration of Houses*, sounds interesting in this respect, and might have been more than mentioned. In a similar manner Gilbert and Gubar might have attended to Cather's portrayals of girls who manage to grow up not so badly as economic successes. The immigrant girls who go from farmwork to town domestic service so as to help pay off their families' land debt and to fund new investments in farm equipment, and then marry the sons of family operations similarly well capitalized "are today managing big farms and fine families of their own; their children are better off than the children of the town women they used to serve" (*My Antonia*, Bk. II, sect. ix). Also worth greater consideration would be the rise of Antonia's friends the hired girls Tiny Soderball and Lena Lingard through successes at business and investment on their own. They end up well-to-do in San Francisco. Fatality does not hang so heavily on them.

Not that Gilbert and Gubar always force the point about fatality. Some chapters—as on Chopin—radiate a positive viewpoint, while others—as on the Great War—are exuberant on women's gains, though very sensitive to men's account of the toll taken on them. A fine example is the comparison of "The Waste Land" and *Mrs. Dalloway*, according to which both take inspiration from the figure of a dead good soldier—Eliot's fallen friend Jean Verdenal to whom the *Prufrock* volume was dedicated and Woolf's character of the shellshocked veteran and suicide Septimus Smith. But each work makes the figure function differently, in one as muse of a male wasteland, in the other as muse of reaffirmation and a woman's party.

With the chapters on lesbian writers and on cross-dressing the image of the femme fatale comes back into view. Certainly gay gaiety is acknowledged in Barnes's *Ladies' Almanack*, and festivity in Woolf's account of Orlando's many sex-changes. Independence from men that does not mean renunciation of passion—this carries credit for critics who hold Aphrodite in high regard; after all, Sappho has Aphrodite for her patron goddess (p. 113). Also salutary is the co-identifying and collaborative mode of the lesbian, both as lover and as writer. Gilbert and Gubar give sustained analysis to the sharing, boundary-blurring, and "double-talking" of identity represented by Barnes and Stein in lesbian love. They also point to the sense of collaboration with the literary past made possible by the lesbian writer's relation to Sappho. Renée Vivien and H. D. find advantage in the very fragmentariness of Sappho's legacy: "The modern woman could write 'for' and 'as' Sappho and thereby invent a classical inheritance of her own" (p. 225).

At the same time all is not so well. The lesbian carried some fatality in the popular mind of the period, and Gilbert and Gubar cite historians of lesbianism to show a "morbidification" of perceived "inversion" and perversity" fostered even by studies aiming to be purely scientific, or sympathetic (p. 216). Radclyffe Hall makes the lesbian a figure of tragic loneliness. Vivien features a tormented and tormenting Sappho, with an air of voluptuous evil familiar from Baudelaire and Swinburne, Satanic, a "lesbian femme fatale" (p. 227). Not too far from this is the woman in men's clothes as painted by Romaine Brooks: marked, outcast, joyless, the femme fatale crossdressed as Byronic hero with seductive glamour. Amy Lowell and Marguerite Yourcenar associate Sappho with "the anguish of a fated, if not fatal, eroticism' (p. 235). And while Gilbert and Gubar indicate what is of value in lesbian co-identification and collaboration, much of the chapter exposes the dangers involved.

Thus *Nightwood* probes identity problems when the same-sex lover seems so much oneself that to lose her is to lose oneself. Dependency and selfishness can be part of this love. In the long section on Stein and Toklas, Stein's role as "Alice's Phallus"—husband-baby-genius-special person served by wife-mother—appears egotistical and sexist enough. Gilbert and Gubar see Stein's hard-to-read writing as aggressively asserting independence from any literary tradition or bounds of language, and in a way that is masculine—if we agree that unmaking is an even more masculine gesture than making. And they present it as self-serving writing that means more to the writer than the reader. However, for them, *The Autobiography of Alice B. Toklas* makes a break. It explores the interdynamics between masculine and feminine roles and in a manner of presentation that not only cultivates more relationship with the reader but is collaborative in authorship, so that it is hard to know where Stein leaves off and Toklas begins. Still, for Gilbert and Gubar, co-identification and collaboration like this prompt thoughts of usurpation, appropriation, even some sort of cannibalism, "as Stein makes Alice into a character of her own devising, who, in turn, certifies Stein as the genius" (p. 251).

In its title, "Cross-Dressing and Re-Dressing," the last chapter raises the issue of "redress," some compensation to emerge from modernist sexchanges in *No Man's Land.* Surely there are gains seen, here as in the rest of the book. For instance, if Barnes's cross-dressing, transsexual Robin Vote seems to reach so far beyond male-female norms as to appear subhuman, she also appears mythic and sanctifying. But *Sexchanges* does not end so positively. We are told that recent deconstructions of gender identity as propounded by men like Derrida may not serve women. Gilbert and Gubar briefly consider the tricky question of whether feminism might require some conception of a gender "essence" if it is to have any constituency or cause. If modernism presents an escalated battle of the sexes, how are we to measure the outcome if there are no men or women left? For a postmodern conclusion Gilbert and Gubar instance Caryl Churchill's play *Cloud Nine.* "When the old roles dissolve the new ones are just as absurd and pathetic" in this sexchanging romp through a "wasted London," an "unreal city" (pp. 375–76). A study that begins with the femme fatale ends invoking "The Waste Land." We see no win and no redress. We do see power, fascination, risk, transfiguration, beauty, and terror as women—damaged and damaging—have entered modernism and helped make it.

Elaine Showalter (review date 14 June 1996)

SOURCE: "Miss Marple at the MLA," in *Times Literary Supplement,* No. 4,863, June 14, 1996, p. 9.

[*In the following review, Showalter praises the satire of* Masterpiece Theatre, *but finds much of it already dated.*]

I was in the audience in 1989 when Sandra Gilbert and Susan Gubar gave a dramatic reading of Act One of their literary satire, *Masterpiece Theatre,* at the Modern Language Association's annual conference. Their spirited performance was rapturously received by a ball-room full of professors and graduate students, battered by attacks from the Right and grateful for a few minutes of laughter in the gruelling four-day professional marathon. The rumour in the corridors was that Gilbert and Gubar were getting phone calls from literary theorists insulted because they had not been parodied. That frail commodity, academic reputation, depends on publicity, on being what literary critics as well as Hollywood moguls call "a player."

But ah, the vanity of human wishes, and the fleetingness of fame! Nothing dates like satire, and perhaps academic satire most of all. It's not that the culture wars of the 1980s are over today, but that they are being fought on different terrain. William Bennett, then the scourge of the humanities, has moved on to edit bestselling anthologies on virtue, and to decry gangsta rap, talk shows and film violence. Lynne Cheney, then the conservative Director of the National Endowment of the Humanities, is now out of office and out of the headlines, while a terminal NEH is being phased out. Like many of the entertainers and celebrities Gilbert and Gubar mention—Madonna, Imelda Marcos, Michael Jackson—many of the academic superstars of *Masterpiece Theatre* are no longer chart-toppers, or have reinvented themselves in new guises. Thus this contribution to the culture wars already seems dated, and readers will need to consult the annotated cast of characters at the end to figure out some of the jokes.

Masterpiece Theatre is a three-part melodrama about the abduction and attempted murder of a nameless Text, and the subsequent efforts of an international cast of villainous neo-conservatives, hypocritical Marxists and poststructuralists, greedy capitalists, academic traditionalists, computer hackers and pop-culture barbarians, to wipe it out, while the idealistic young assistant professor, Jane Marple, and her cohort of Third World women novelists, eager undergraduates and feminist sages (Carolyn Heilbrun, Ursula LeGuin and Toni Morrison) unsuccessfully try to save it. The plot begins in the United States, where professors from Harvard and Duke, and cynical Republican politicos are squabbling about the literary canon and political correctness, while industrial powers like Exxon are polluting the environment. It moves on to London and Paris, where various Oxford dons, post-colonial jet-setters and Parisian theorists mingle and chatter in the British Museum pub or in three-star Left Bank restaurants, while Rupert Murdoch's tabloids scream "THATCHER CLOSES POLYS. TELLS PROFS TO SCRAM!" It ends at an international writers' conference in New York, where egomaniacs such as Norman Mailer, Camille Paglia and Kathy Acker mug for the cameras, while Literature is blasted out of existence by Hypertext.

In their introduction, Gilbert and Gubar describe themselves as part of academia's "excluded middle", annoyed by the paradoxes and blind spots of both Right and Left in the culture wars. As Jane Marple proclaims at the end, "You were all to blame. Some of you wanted money, some political power, some professional advancement, some philosophical hegemony, some language games, some just general destruction."

This is a heavy didactic agenda for satire, and Gilbert and Gubar are further weighed down by their decision to weave lengthy quotations from their large cast of real protagonists into the script. While some of these do bear parody (like George Bush's musings on gun control—"when you see somebody go berserk, and get a weapon and go in and murder people, of course, it troubles me"), many are cold as yesterday's mashed potatoes. There is not much amusement to be garnered from Julia Kristeva's disquisitions on the way the semiotic *chora* behaves, or Fredric Jameson's views on the late capitalist social order. These scenes, with their emphasis on the contradiction between the Marxist rhetoric and the champagne tastes of some critical celebrities, also risk endorsing the anti-intellectual clichés of the envious and lazy.

Gilbert and Gubar are funniest and most effective, however, when they unleash their own considerable wit, as in recalling their "salad-bar days" as SG1 and SG2 on the lecture circuit, or describing a red-faced Jesse Helms, crying to the Lord to "find that text and strike it down. . . . It's better dead than read." At its best, *Masterpiece Theatre* conveys the Alice-in-Wonderland absurdity of *fin-de-siècle* academic life, as well as its disagreements and deep fears. "Will the humanities, and in particular, the profession of English, endure as a recognizable discipline, transform itself, or slide toward extinction in the future world of letters? Will the future even include a world of letters?" *Masterpiece Theatre* suggests that whatever the academic future holds, it will always be fertile ground for satire.

Kathleen Blake (review date April 1996)

SOURCE: A review of *No Man's Land, Volume 3: Letters from the Front,* in *Journal of English and Germanic Philology,* Vol. 95, No. 2, April, 1996, pp. 269–71.

[*In the following review of* Letters from the Front, *the third volume of* No Man's Land, *Blake commends the monumental scope of the collection.*]

After reviewing the prior two volumes of *No Man's Land* the reviewer reaches number three, impressed but tired after close to 1,200 pages of Gilbert and Gubar's critical coverage. Volume 3 is not only monumentally piled on top of Volumes 1 and 2 but on top of the earlier big book *The Madwoman in the Attic* on nineteenth-century women's writing and *The Norton Anthology of Literature by Women*, surveying centuries. A huge history and inventory of texts and a huge contribution to feminist literary criticism culminate here with Gilbert and Gubar unfazed and unflagging. The reviewer recovers her wind in a short review. The object is to end, and at the end is appreciation.

Letters from the Front redeploys the tropes of the prior books. We have the nineteenth-century madwoman's anger let loose in the battle of the sexes that shapes modernism and postmodernism. An instance is the chapter on H. D.'s struggle to define herself and her artistry against the influence of Ezra Pound, D. H. Lawrence, and Sigmund Freud.

World War II gives rise to a chapter on a literature of war. Gilbert and Gubar describe a lower-morale World War II than we might expect when it comes to the war between men and women. Instead of freeing women into new roles as the authors claim (in Volume 2) was the case in World War I, this war is a Blitz on Women. Sources of demoralization are the resurgence of male dominance in fascism, male bonding among soldiers, and the fusing of imagery of sex and death in popular culture, with women cast as threatening whores or betraying girls he left behind him. Among these hostilities Muriel Rukeyser, Katherine Anne Porter, and Sylvia Plath identify women with Jews as victims, while others from Marianne Moore to Stevie Smith cannot enjoy good faith in doing so, feeling not free from being "smug goys" themselves.

Part of the military trope is that of the no man's land—which gives the trilogy its title. No man's land is the contested space between the sexes not yet definitively claimed on either side. Chapters on Female Female Impersonators and Male Male Impersonators explore such an unstable minefield of provisional and projected sex roles. The no man was never exemplified so thoroughly before as in the antiheroes of Joseph Heller, Philip Roth, Kurt Vonnegut, Roald Dahl, Stanley Elkin, Vladimir Nabokov, and others. These figures make identities and careers of their masculine insecurities. The no woman or female female impersonator is explored via Edna St. Vincent Millay and Marianne Moore, who don self-consciously artificial images of womanliness as the "It-girl of the hour" or the spinster schoolteacher and then critically examine what it is to wear "this garment that I may not doff."

A doubled self-impersonation is seen in the chapter on Feminism and the Harlem Renaissance, where black women writers such as Jessie Redmon Fauset, Nella Larsen, and Zora Neale Hurston depict the problems of female female impersonate and, in Marjorie Garber's phrase, the "black face in blackface," or New Woman and New Negro roles in conflict. The black woman may be drawn to impersonate womanliness to strengthen the culturally emasculated black no man in his male role.

Through these struggles in no man's land, Charlotte Perkins Gilman's utopian Herland of Volume 2 has not yet been attained. Familiar from Volume 2 are female threats to men in the figure of the femme fatale. The femme fatale vividly reappears in the chapter on Plath where in "Herr God, Herr Lucifer" a "flaming red-haired revenant threatens a resurrection of the feminine that will explode the old order by destroying the powers of the patriarchal enemies" (p. 300). But on balance women remain the ones at greater risk. Ann Jellicoe, Mary McCarthy, and Muriel Spark suggest that women are hardly made more secure by male insecurities. Their "heroines protect themselves against men whose entrapment in the masculinity complex poses as grave a threat to women as did traditional patriarchal forms of domination" (p. 345–46).

There are some ways out of the war that Gilbert and Gubar have noted before: opting out of heterosexuality by frigid-ity (H. D.) or homosexuality (Adrienne Rich); devolution from human to animal identity (Moore); spiritual transcendence or sanctification (H. D., Hurston). Of course, many would say the ultimate way out is suicide (Plath). Shakespeare's sister has been writing a lot throughout the twentieth century (and she put pen to plenty of paper in the nineteenth), but after all of *No Man's Land* (and *Madwoman*) Gilbert and Gubar seem to share Virginia Woolf's sense of difficulty in writing a "Chapter on the Future" (for *Orlando*), and it is especially hard to project a happy ending.

They try though. It has got to be better than that the literary battle between men and women brings us to the battle between women and women in warring feminist literary-critical camps (p. 375). For all their tropes of battle—and they lack great interest in non-hostilities—they are blithe writers, pouring forth so much with energy and style, troping and also punning playfully to the end of their magnum opus. The story of Snow White makes a comeback from *Madwoman* in a funny series of retellings. The story can end with the triumph of Snow White and the Queen over the Prince or vice versa; it can end with a free-love laying down of arms between the sexes; it can end with sex role transformations and Snow White and Queen in each other's arms; or with identity-free impersonations all around: "Forget your transcendental signifiers! . . . 'I'm nobody, who are you? Are you nobody too?'" (p. 367).

But Gilbert and Gubar have a favorite ending. For it they hark back to their view of Plath as having found something better than suicide, having found herself as a creator of poetry and life, a mother poet. They refuse to see Plath in grim terms and insist on her profound affirmation in *Ariel*. They love it when the girl's premonition that "I am a genius of a writer" is realized as she became a mother. This suits their faith from Volume 1 in language as not necessarily phallogocentric but a "mother tongue." They applaud Plath's initiation of a tradition of "mother poets," Rich, Anne Sexton, Denise Levertov, Diane Wakoski, an instance of female literary affiliation in contrast to the embattlement of literary relations between the sexes traced since *Madwoman*. So the book ends happily (and punningly) with the "mater-iality" of fine works mothered by procreative creativity. Snow White's mother doesn't have to die, to give up doing other things to bear a child. She and her child live and tell stories.

This is an ending in narrative terms like the rhetorical questions in argument that we have seen before, say in a passage on Woolf: "The battle of the sexes is not over . . . Yet that battle might bear fruit in what new life, what new creature? An ambivalent women artist like Lily Briscoe? A wild child like Mrs. Manresa? A new Woman who is, in conventional terms, no woman, like Miss La Trobe . . . ? Or a new being of all sexes and none, like Orlando?" (p. 55). It is an ending by shift of tropes from war to birth. But Gilbert and Gubar's long account of the war makes it hard to imagine new births that are not into it.

Gayle Pemberton (review date 13 July 1997)

SOURCE: "Minstrels and their Masks," in *Washington Post Book World,* Vol. 27, No. 28, July 13, 1997, p. 4.

[*In the following review, Pemberton praises Gubar's* Racechanges *as a work which contributes to the ability to "envision a post-racist society."*]

Anyone looking for an easy application of Susan Gubar's findings in *Racechanges: White Skin, Black Face in American Culture* can travel to a white high school. Look at the dress, hairstyles, hear the music and a considerable amount of slang, watch the high-fives and other gestures of the students to discover racechanges, or whites passing as blacks. Racechanging is "meant to suggest the traversing of racial boundaries, racial imitation or impersonation, cross-racial mimicry or mutability, white posing as black or black passing as white, pan-racial mutuality." Such a broad spectrum of racial theorizing, performance and attitude provides the framework for Gubar's exploration of literature, art, photography, psychology and a host of other topics: The task is an enormous one, in which Gubar effectively demonstrates, on the one hand, just how obdurate and tenacious are categories of race in the United States and Europe and, on the other, how these categories are porous, inconsistent and capricious. Youth culture is always an easy mark; understanding the dynamics of racechange in its more persistent and pervasive adult forms is something else. Gubar amasses a formidable amount of scholarship to do just that.

We are all victims of a dualism that divides the world into various pairs like good and evil, black and white. Gubar uses blackface as a metaphor for defining the ways in which blackness and whiteness have been socially constructed. The grotesque makeup and speech, the gestures and gyrations of minstrels in the 19th century are examples of whites animating vicious and highly concocted stereotypes of black people. Drawing upon this heritage, early American movies went further in establishing a litany of images of black inferiority that are alive and well today. What *Racechanges* does best is to illuminate the complexities of blackface for blacks and for whites. According to Gubar, "many racechange performances teach a cruel lesson to black audiences: When you repeatedly see yourself falsely depicted, you have no sense of your right to be in the world, or, indeed, you gain a conviction that you cannot, do not, should not exist." The white in blackface dramatizes the notion that whiteness is fundamentally colorless, its existence predicated upon the necessity of "the subordinated black body."

Racechanges examines the usual suspects in discussions of whites in blackface—from movies like "The Birth of a Nation," "The Jazz Singer" and "Imitation of Life"; to the literary inventions of Kate Chopin, William Faulkner, John Berryman and Norman Mailer; to white patrons of the Harlem Renaissance like Nancy Cunard and Carl Van Vechten. Gubar invigorates this list with arresting visual images and commentary on artists like Picasso and Robert Colescott; Robert Mapplethorpe's photography; black artists in black-face, real and figurative, like the legendary Bert Williams or "Bojangles" Robinson. "To adopt minstrelsy is to collude in one's own fetishization; but to relinquish efforts to adapt it is to lose completely a cultural past appropriated by whites," is one conundrum. Perhaps the most dramatic illustration of this is a sequence of three photographs of Paul Robeson: as Phi Beta Kappa graduate of Rutgers, to harlequin-clothed character in the play "Voodoo," to angry savage of the same play, looking more like a child in the middle of a tantrum than a menacing adversary.

Susan Gubar, Distinguished Professor of English at Indiana University, has been for many years identified with feminist literary scholarship, most notably in her coauthorship, with Sandra Gilbert, of *The Madwoman in the Attic* and *No Man's Land*, studies of women writers. That Gubar would next enter into a scholarly inquiry on race and gender is logical. *Racechanges* benefits from its recognition that race is a highly gendered topic and that much white thinking about race "fetishizes black men even as it effectively obliterates the existence of black women." Nonetheless, she admits to having been "blind" to the racial implications of some of her previous work. This is an important admission, particularly at a time when many white scholars have discovered race for the very first time.

Gubar succeeds in avoiding "the aridity of academic jargon," but *Racechanges* still requires a sophistication not regularly associated with Virginia Woolfs "common reader," the author's targeted audience. It should be read as a companion piece to the works of those scholars whose insights buttress this work, among them Patricia J. Williams, bell hooks, Frantz Fanon, Ronald Takaki, Michael Rogin, Eric Lott, Rey Chow, Leslie Fiedler, Ann Douglas and Toni Morrison.

"The liberating potential of racechanging iconography is only now being tapped in various performances, mediations, films, and art works that use cross-racial imagery to enact or envision post-racist ways of being and perceiving," Gubar writes. To even envision a post-racist society is contingent upon understanding the offensive, dense and wildly contradictory nature of our racist past and present. *Racechanges* should be encouragement enough for readers to begin that task.

Suzanne Juhasz (review date Winter 1997)

SOURCE: A review of *No Man's Land, Volume 3: Letters from the Front,* in *Signs: Journal of Women in Culture and Society,* Vol. 22, No. 2, Winter, 1997, p. 458.

[*In the following review, Juhasz discusses* Letters from the Front, *volume three of* No Man's Land, *and comments on the "constructed" nature of gender in the study of literature.*]

Letters from the Front is the conclusion to Sandra M. Gilbert and Susan Gubar's ambitious and wide-ranging three-volume study of the place of the woman writer in the twentieth century, itself a sequel to their landmark work on the woman writer in the nineteenth century, *The Madwoman in the Attic*. (1) As they have moved through the centuries, with gender as the lens for observing literature in its relation to culture (and vice versa), they have read, and written about, just about everything. Their ability to elucidate such diverse material with wisdom and wit is by now legendary. Along the way, "everything" has of necessity involved them in the major changes in conceptual and philosophical approaches to their topic that have taken place over the past fifteen years. Reading *No Man's Land,* one moves from modernism to postmodernism. The final volume, especially, even as it includes theory as a significant site of women's writing, employs the insights of social constructionism to twentieth-century writing and shows how the writers of fiction and poetry produce that ideology.

The work as a whole looks at what happens to gender arrangements when, under historical and cultural pressures, their assumed God-given stability is questioned. The late nineteenth-century rise of feminism and the subsequent fall of Victorian concepts of "femininity" set in motion, Gilbert and Gubar contend, a war of the sexes (a battle about sex, sexuality, and gender) that played out across the century and resulted in, among other things, the literary modernisms that women and men have variously produced. They show how male hostility toward a perceived threatening female autonomy moves ultimately into angry confusions about the nature of masculinity as well as femininity. For women, anxiety about the fragility of even such fictional autonomy, along with hope for the destruction of old sexual rules and the redemptive construction of new social roles—that is, the idea of women's community, literary tradition, and psychic space, "the dream of Herland"—becomes an awareness of the artifice of gender itself. The concept of "female-female impersonation" shows women as writers both playing with and interrogating "femininity"—using it as a masquerade, as performance, defensively and with a recognition of the power inherent in the ability to construct an identity rather than inherit one.

Letters from the Front moves from the end of World War I to the present, focusing particularly on World War II and the manner in which the battle of the sexes is at once intensified and dispersed, so that there is no longer division between a war ground and a "home front." It includes characteristically astute studies of Virginia Woolf; poets from Edna St. Vincent Millay, Marianne Moore, and H. D. through Sylvia Plath, Anne Sexton, and Adrienne Rich to contemporary poets; Harlem Renaissance writers like Jessie Fauset, Nella Larsen, and Zora Neale Hurston; literary reactions to World War II; comic fictions by both men and women of the 1960s and 1970s; and feminist critics from Simone de Beauvoir to Mary Daly. The ability to cast their vision so widely is a strength that Gilbert and Gubar, above all contemporary literary critics, possess—but it also creates a problem. In order to cover so much, in order to maintain coherent reasoning, they do not (perhaps they do not want to?) reveal the intricacies and contradic-

tions of the texts they study. Their look at particular works often charts a single-minded course that serves primarily to advance the more general argument.

In this final volume, the authors are particularly concerned with the future. When gender is not a given but a construct, what new world might be possible? For "despite the fictive nature of femininity and masculinity, men and women continue to recycle farcical but intransigent gender assignments" (354). By and large, the authors show the struggle to imagine a future that continues to elude embodiment. They show as well the confusion and bemusion evoked by a "cultural pluralism that makes definitive denouements virtually inconceivable" (361).

The volume does not, however, end with hands raised in dismay over the artifice of identity and the multiple and increasingly fictive plots thus engendered. Rather, it focuses on the one remaining "fact" of (female) maternity, and on a new literary genre, mother writing, to show how procreativity combines with creativity to produce a narrative of which the woman can see herself as independent author. The writer speaking to her child addresses "a future she can now imagine shaping, as she herself has been shaped by a past she reimagines as empowering rather than debilitating" (402). This insight, shared by other recent theorists of "maternal subjectivity," is deeply important; to the extent that all women are not mothers, however, this particular power is necessarily limited.

I would suggest an additional approach to the future, one that concerns ways in which *No Man's Land* addresses demographic variables of sexual orientation, race, and ethnicity. For example, rather than understanding lesbianism as either a separate and peculiar experience (with its own chapter in *Sexchanges*), or as one in a list of fictive roles that can be played by a woman—"femme fatale, New Woman, mother-woman, warrior woman, feminized woman, no-woman, female female impersonator, goddess, lesbian, sextoid" (368), one might see how recent reconstructions of homosexuality inform and transform constructions of heterosexuality as well. In *No Man's Land* heterosexuality is the unquestioned normative gender arrangement at the center of the prevailing sex wars. The discourse centers on "men" versus "women," whether fictive or non, thereby reiterating the hegemony of traditional categories. But if gender and sexuality can be defined by all their forms, including homosexuality and heterosexuality, and by a multitude of ethnic expressions, their pluralism may well facilitate a paradigm shift that moves beyond patriarchal dualism.

Gwen Bergner (review date Winter 1998)

SOURCE: A review of *Racechanges: White Skin, Black Face in American Culture,* in *Modern Fiction Studies,* No. 4, Winter, 1998, pp. 1073–75.

[*In the following review, Bergner appreciates the broad scope and ethical concern of* Racechanges.]

Comprehensive in scope, Susan Gubar's *Racechanges: White Skin, Black Face in American Culture* explores the psychological and ideological implications of cross-racial mimicry in twentieth-century culture. This wide-ranging study of film, literature, and visual arts examines an impressively large number of artifacts that are by now standard objects of cultural studies of race in America, including films such as *The Birth of a Nation, The Jazz Singer*, and *Blonde Venus*; literary works by Carl Van Vechten, Nancy Cunard, Zora Neale Hurston, and Ernest Hemingway; and photographs and paintings by Man Ray, Robert Mapplethorpe, and Pablo Picasso—to name a few. *Racechanges* also discusses in fruitful ways some lesser-studied works such as the paintings of Robert Colescott, the drawings of Richard Bruce Nugent, the fiction of Saul Bellow, the poetry of Anne Spencer, and the conceptual art of Adrian Piper. Gubar collects these varied and numerous cultural texts under the rubric "racechanges," a term which is "meant to suggest the traversing of race boundaries, racial imitation or impersonation, cross-racial mimicry or mutability, white posing as black or black passing as white, pan-racial mutuality." Gubar explains that such racial impersonations permeate not only our popular culture—from nineteenth-century minstrelsy to Vanilla Ice—but also our intimate daily lives; she cites a man who speaks "'black talk'" to his dog and her own daughter who used to address Gubar by mimicking the words of her mother's African-American childhood friend, Theresa: "'I loves ye, honey. But you're de WRONG color.'" Although these idiosyncratic "racechanges" are usually hidden by whites—who consider them degrading to black people—they are integral to daily life and indicative of the ways in which white identity is "predicated on black Others." In a formulation that recalls Eric Lott's groundbreaking study of minstrelsy, Gubar sets out to investigate the fear and loathing, desire and envy of such impersonations.

Ambitious in scope and broad in methodology, *Racechanges* will be most useful for the general audience to which it is addressed: "To some scholarly readers, [. . .] my speculations may seem grounded in subjects too diverse, while to others they will seem undertheorized. I took both these risks quite consciously in an effort to enliven my topic for [. . .] 'the common reader.'" Those specializing in African American and race studies will be familiar with many of the book's findings from the work of such scholars as Michael Rogin, Eric Lott, Eric Sundquist, and Toni Morrison. However, specialists and non-specialists alike will be drawn to the numerous illustrations—reproductions of film stills, paintings, and photographs. Especially compelling are the color plates of Robert Colescott's ironic and parodic paintings such as *George Washington Carver Crossing the Delaware* and his revision of Van Gogh's *The Potato Eaters* titled *Eat Dem Taters*. Gubar's reading of Colescott's *Shirley Temple Black and Bill Robinson White* (in which a black Shirley Temple and white Bill Robinson traipse down a garden path) is especially astute: "Shirley Temple does not appear simply darkened, Bojangles simply lightened in skin tone. Instead, racial transformation eroticizes the couple, draining away their innocence and infusing them with a vaguely perverse ribaldry. Why does the prancing Robinson White seem to be leering at the equally coquettish and rather hefty Temple Black? Does their berry picking hint at the saying 'the darker the berry the sweeter the juice'?" Gubar goes on to elaborate the painting's implications for the sexualizing of black girl children and the simultaneous emasculating and making-virile of black men.

Gubar's attentiveness to the representation of men, women, whites, and blacks in the visual art of Colescott and others signals her intent to theorize the intersections of race and gender as a corrective to her earlier work on gender which, as she acknowledges, had ignored issues of race. The chapter titled "Psychopathologies of Black Envy" is unusually even handed in its analysis of the dynamics of inter-racial desire—masculine and feminine, heterosexual and homo-erotic. Returning to the subject of women, Gubar breaks new critical ground with "What Will the Mixed Child Deliver," a chapter on the significance of mothers giving birth to children of a different race or color than themselves.

Gubar is not embarrassed to admit that she is concerned, at base, with an ethical question: "How can white people understand or sympathize with African Americans without distorting or usurping their perspective?" Resisting a simplistic answer, *Racechanges* nonetheless demonstrates the question's relevance and urgency.

Anne Stavney (review date Spring 1999)

SOURCE: A review of *Racechanges: White Skin, Black Face in American Culture,* in *Tulsa Studies in Women's Literature,* Vol. 18, No. 1, Spring, 1999, pp. 124–25.

[*In the following review, Stavney lauds* Racechanges *as a useful study examining the ideas of "whiteness" and "blackness" in American culture.*]

In *Racechanges: White Skin, Black Face in American Culture,* Susan Gubar examines instances of cross-racial mimicry and mutability in twentieth-century film, literature, journalism, painting, photography, and plastic art. Asserting the centrality of what she terms "racechange" to modern and postmodern American culture, Gubar maintains that performances of racial imitation or impersonation provide a means of measuring "altering societal attitudes of race and representation" (p. 10). Such impersonation can be a strategy of the disempowered—as demonstrated by narratives of white-to-black racechange that educate a "white" character and by extension a white audience about American racism. Racial imitation can also function as a method to disempower the other by usurping the other's place, wresting authority and symbolic power, and thereby devaluing blackness and establishing whiteness as the norm. Gubar emphasizes in her introduction and in subsequent chapters that no single effect can be said to emanate from racechange. It is a "trope that embodies the slipperiness of metamorphosis in its adoptions or adaptations as well as in its historical evolution" (p. 41). The project sets out to delineate the multiple dimensions—psychological, aesthetical, and ethical—of cross-racial mimicry and imagery in twentieth-century American culture.

Because the nineteenth-century minstrel stage functioned as a precursor to Hollywood screen images of blackface, the study contends in its early chapters that the birth of the American film industry was predicated "upon the death of [the] African American" (p. 65). Films such as *The Birth of a Nation* (1915) and *The Jazz Singer* (1927) allowed a white audience to assure themselves of black inferiority. In the context of this recurring "spirit-murder at the movies" and in other popular culture, African American artists of the early twentieth century found it especially difficult to locate effective strategies for countering the destructive effects of white supremacist logic. Should one vilify whiteness or glorify blackness in order to subvert racist stereotypes? Some literary and graphic texts of the Harlem Renaissance associate whiteness with nothingness; some associate blackness with fullness of being; still others neither delegitimize whites nor legitimize blacks but seek to challenge hegemonic stories of black racial origins that functioned to subordinate Africans in America. *Racechanges* also studies proponents of modernism who attempted a racial ventriloquism they associated with linguistic experimentation (chapter 4); portraits of black male genitalia created by white male and female artists (chapter 5); and the figure of the unexpectedly colored infant or mixed-race child that resurfaces in twentieth-century fiction (chapter 6). The closing chapter shifts from analyzing the motives of racechange to its effects. Though it has historically served racist ends, Gubar contends that cross-racial performance has a liberating potential that is only now being realized. Performance artist Sandra Bernhard, playwright George C. Wolfe, and portraitist Iké Udé are examples of racial impersonators who "neither abandon [their] origins nor pass into the other group's world" and in so doing create "a new (volatile and not necessarily unified) racial category" (p. 249). These "trans-racial transgressions" put the lie to racial classification and assumptions of a coherent racial self that undergird denials of black subjectivity and humanity.

Gubar's best work is in demonstrating the multiple and intricate ways in which notions of racial superiority and inferiority are reinscribed, interrogated, and challenged by cultural production. The study joins others by Robert Toll, Eric Lott, Michael Rogin, and Toni Morrison in analyzing white impersonations of blackness that until recently have been merely dismissed as unacceptable, indefensible, and "racist." Yet such a label should not obligate the end of critical conversation. For as Gubar convincingly explains, it is in understanding the means and methods by which white supremacist ideology circulates in American culture that we may envision and enact "postracist ways of being and perceiving" (p. 241). The strength of Gubar's study is,

however, an index to its chief weakness. Its interpretative frame—to elucidate the "traversing of racial boundaries, racial imitation or impersonation, cross-racial mimicry or mutability, white posing as black or black posing as white, pan-racial mutuality" (p. 5)—makes her extremely sensitive not only to racial but also to gender and sexual references, as well as to the dynamics of cultural production and consumption. The trope of racechange, however, proves too elastic and all-inclusive to convince; it tends to lose explanatory power because it encompasses too much. Overwhelmed by examples of racial impersonation, *Racechanges* remains undertheorized, and most specialist readers will be left wanting a more cogent model of what racechange includes *and* excludes. Gubar acknowledges this possible outcome in the preface, contending that she purposely avoids "the aridity of academic jargon" because she intends her study for "the common reader" (p. xviii). It is unlikely, however, that discussion of "mimetic mimicry," "the gothic effects of scapegoating inflicted on the Other," or the "misogyny enacted through the figure of the black penis-not-a-phallus" will prove easily accessible or compelling to the nonspecialist (pp. 79, 105). Nevertheless, *Racechanges* continues and usefully complicates the study of "whiteness" and "blackness" in American culture, and future scholarship can develop and deepen the analysis of racial impersonation that Gubar and others have begun.

Scott Heller (essay date 17 December 1999)

SOURCE: "The Book That Created a Canon: *Madwoman in the Attic* Turns 20," in *Chronicle of Higher Education*, Vol. 46, December 17, 1999, p. A20.

[*In the following essay marking the twentieth anniversary of the publication of* The Madwoman in the Attic, *Heller reviews the history of the book's influence on students, teachers, and scholarship.*]

The story of feminist literary criticism can be told through the fortunes of *The Madwoman in the Attic*, the classic argument for a women's literary tradition by Sandra M. Gilbert and Susan Gubar.

Upon its publication in 1979, the big, ambitious volume, subtitled *The Woman Writer and the Nineteenth-Century Literary Imagination*, vaulted its authors into the front ranks of their field. They went on to write a three-book sequel on the 20th century, and to edit a sweeping anthology that fashioned a canon of women's writing throughout the ages. Gilbert-and-Gubar, pronounced as if one word, became shorthand for one kind of feminist scholarship. And ever so rapidly, that shorthand went from compliment to complaint, as critics on both the right and the left accused them of reducing complicated issues to a battle between women and men.

Madwoman, still the two scholars' most famous book, has sold more than 70,000 copies, remaining in print since

Yale University Press first published it. The 20th anniversary is prompting the press to release a special edition, with a new introduction by the authors. In a session at the Modern Language Association conference this month, colleagues and disciples will sum up the book's impact, especially in the classroom. "Students at various levels can work with it," explains William B. Thesing, a professor of English at the University of South Carolina, who organized the session. "Feminist criticism after Gilbert and Gubar is really much more difficult for students—it's jargon-ridden and sometimes antagonistic," he adds.

"It's been so powerful that it doesn't have to be explicitly cited—it's simply in the air," says Susan Fraiman, an associate professor of English at the University of Virginia. At the M.L.A., she plans to summon back the moment of the book's release, to remind younger scholars "how audacious, original, and even profane" the book was for its time.

Jennifer DeVere Brody was a high-school senior when she read a glowing review in *The New York Times Book Review*. She asked for *Madwoman* as a Christmas present, devoured it, and decided to enroll in Vassar College, the rare campus where a student could major in Victorian studies. She's now an associate professor of English at George Washington University.

Paging through her well-worn 1983 copy, she calls *Madwoman* "very much a book of its time."

"It's a monumental book, not only in size but in scope," says Ms. Brody, who now teaches it to another generation of undergraduates.

Scholars were not the only ones to notice. Widely reviewed in newspapers and magazines, *Madwoman* was a finalist for both the Pulitzer Prize and the National Book Award. Today, it's unusual for a feminist book to make such a splash. "Feminist criticism now doesn't feel as vital," says Ms. Gubar, a professor of English and women's studies at Indiana University. "That saddens me."

In 1973, Ms. Gubar was a young assistant professor new to the Midwest when she discovered a kindred spirit in Ms. Gilbert, a new associate professor at Indiana. Neither was trained as a Victorianist, but they shared a passion for the works of the Bronte sisters, George Eliot, and Jane Austen, among others.

Women were badly outnumbered in a department that the professors recall as stuffy and uncongenial. "When I arrived, an older professor handed me his syllabus and asked me to type it, assuming I was a secretary," says Ms. Gubar.

Yet feminism was in the air, if not in the classroom.

"There was a strong urgency to live feminist lives," Ms. Gubar recalls. "But there certainly was nothing called feminist criticism at the time."

In 1974, the professors team-taught a course, an accelerated seminar that allowed Ms. Gilbert more time to commute to her family in California, where her husband taught at the University of California at Davis. Instead of situating a woman writer in her period, they argued for a distinct women's literary tradition, and therefore included Jane Austen and Sylvia Plath on the same syllabus.

The various books were connected, the scholars argued, by the ways their authors struggled to express women's experiences in a patriarchal society. The prototypical figure was Bertha Mason, a spectral presence in *Jane Eyre*. Bertha turns out to be the imprisoned wife of the hero, Rochester, and late in the novel burns down his mansion. To the scholars, Bertha was a kind of double for Jane herself, able to express the passions that the well-mannered governess could not. She was one of many such female figures literally or metaphorically imprisoned, and aching to break free, in books by women writers.

Five years later, the syllabus for that course became the 700-page *Madwoman*. "It's incredible to me now that we wrote that big a book so fast," adds Ms. Gilbert. "We were ourselves on fire."

They were no longer in the same department, however. After only a year at Indiana, Ms. Gilbert returned West, where she got her own professorial appointment at Davis. Despite being separated by miles, teaching duties, and their responsibilities as mothers, the scholars continued to write together for the next two decades.

Indeed, only in 1997 did Ms. Gubar publish her first book as a lone author, *Racechanges: White Skin, Black Face in American Culture.* Ms. Gilbert, a poet as well as a critic, was the president of the M.L.A. in 1996. Most recently, she published *Wrongful Death: A Medical Tragedy,* an account of how her 61-year-old husband inexplicably died during routine surgery.

That tragedy has taken the scholars in different professional directions. Ms. Gilbert is working on a study of elegies. Ms. Gubar remains an active voice in the debates within feminism. *Critical Condition: Feminism at the Turn of the Century,* a collection of her recent essays, is due out by the end of the year. It includes **"What Ails Feminist Criticism?,"** a 1998 article that caused a stir when first published in the journal *Critical Inquiry*.

Because Ms. Gilbert is on leave in Paris, she won't be at this month's M.L.A. conference, and Ms. Gubar decided not to appear at the *Madwoman* panel without her. After a decade of lecturing in tandem around the world, they find themselves together less often. But last August, they did share the stage at a conference of Victorian-studies scholars at the University of California at Santa Cruz. They delivered their remarks as a dialogue, which is how they frame the introduction to the anniversary edition of *Madwoman*. As an authorial pair, Gilbert and Gubar have not published together for most of this decade, save for *Masterpiece Theatre: An Academic Melodrama,* a comic jibe at their critics.

And critics they have. "Gilbert and Gubar have paid a price for their accomplishments, and have been roughly indicted in tones of voice that are seldom employed for male scholars of comparable importance," notes William E. Cain, a professor of English at Wellesley College, in his introduction to *Making Feminist History: The Literary Scholarship of Sandra M. Gilbert and Susan Gubar.*

Many scholars willing to open the canon to women authors still resist the feminist insistence that a writer's gender is crucial to her work, Mr. Cain points out. "The notion of women who write, read, or teach as *women* strikes antifeminists as special-interest criticism, as cheerleading and propaganda," he writes.

Yet for Gilbert and Gubar, later generations of feminists have been among their steadiest critics. They accuse the professors of speaking too broadly, and ignoring distinctions among women of different races, classes, and nationalities.

From the first sentence on, however, *Madwoman* wasn't going to be a measured literary study. "Is the pen a metaphorical penis?" the authors asked. The first hundred pages establish their argument for a distinctly "feminist poetics," challenging Harold Bloom's famous postulation that all writers toil under the "anxiety of influence." Women writers don't have forebears to write against; rather, *Madwoman* argued, they suffer from the "anxiety of authorship" in a culture that doesn't deem them worthy of taking up the pen at all.

The authors advanced their claim in chapters on Jane Austen, Mary Shelley, George Eliot, and Emily Dickinson, as well as in close readings of several books by Charlotte Bronte. Despite its fame, the analysis of *Jane Eyre* is actually comparatively brief.

While the book divided reviewers, it quickly became the kind of opus that demanded a reaction. Some who didn't buy the thesis praised the close readings. And some who admired the ambition didn't like the way every novel was shoehorned into an overarching feminist argument.

Over time, the climate changed. "We were being accused of sins that in those early days we knew not of," writes Ms. Gilbert in the new edition.

Poststructuralism challenged the notion that there was anything "essential" at all about women or women's writing. And attention to race complicated matters further. "We were cast as establishment puppets just too dumb to notice that we wrote from a position of middle-class, white, heterosexual privilege," Ms. Gilbert notes.

Madwoman "had this incredibly synthetic view," explains Beth Newman, an associate professor of English at Southern Methodist University. "It didn't take long before other people started pointing out just how partial their view was."

Among the most famous retorts came from Gayatri Chakravorty Spivak, the postcolonial theorist at Columbia University. In a widely circulated 1985 essay, she pointed out a crucial blind spot in the critics' depiction of Bertha Mason in *Madwoman*: Ignoring that Bertha was a Creole Jamaican, the authors leave out of their account the ways that British imperialism and racism afforded privileges to white women. In Ms. Spivak's rendering, Bertha's attic stands in for the marginalized third world.

"That turned their approach upside down," recalls Ms. Newman, who has edited a critical companion to *Jane Eyre* for Bedford Books. "It pointed out the whole book was really about 19th-century middle-class white women." Other aspects of their argument began to seem quaint as well. "For feminist critics, circa 1979, it made women's anger seem invigorating," says Ms. Newman. "Yet that did have a tendency to end in the romanticization of madness."

In the new edition, Ms. Gilbert agrees that the press for more exact analysis is a sign of strength within feminist criticism. "But such nuance may be precisely what we couldn't afford at a time when it was enough suddenly to see that there could be a new way of seeing," she notes.

Today's feminist literary critics, raised on Gilbert and Gubar, have very different aims and methods.

Ms. Brody of George Washington, who read *Madwoman* in high school, did her graduate training in the era of cultural studies. As a result, she doesn't want to give novels—let alone novels by women—a special place in her analysis of the Victorian era. In *Impossible Purities: Blackness, Femininity, and Victorian Culture* Ms. Brody discusses plays, paintings, and minstrel songs, as well as novels, to explore how depictions of black femininity shore up the superiority of white Englishness.

None of the novels in *Madwoman* figures in her work. "What keeps Victorian studies white," says Ms. Brody, "is the focus on the novel."

While her book has been well-received (and gets a plug in the new edition of *Madwoman*), a study like Ms. Brody's can never hope to gain the kind of audience that Gilbert and Gubar enjoyed during the best moments of the last 20 years. Their ambition, their passion, and their timing are hard to replicate in today's hyper-professional academic culture. Feminist literary critics are fighting smaller, more localized battles, using specialized language, and are less connected to struggles beyond the ivory tower.

Ms. Gubar continues to issue reminders of what once was and what still could be. Over the last few years, she has given a paper at various meetings called **"Who Killed Feminist Criticism?"** When she published the paper in *Critical Inquiry* in 1998, she softened the title to **"What Ails Feminist Criticism?"** But her tone remains angry and wounded, as she struggles to get beyond generational disputes and to imagine "some hope for recovery," a feminism that addresses "the here and now."

Robyn Wiegman, an associate professor of women's studies and English at the University of California at Irvine, answered back in the journal this year, labeling Ms. Gubar's article "a lament for the lost status of the literary." She contends that literary and cultural theory have made feminism more sophisticated, and healthier, than Ms. Gubar believes.

Ms. Wiegman still teaches the introduction to *Madwoman* in the rare classes she teaches on criticism. "You could teach the history of feminist literary criticism by teaching that book and the conversations that came out of it," she says.

Among those lessons: Critical fashions move more quickly than ever. "There's so little in literary criticism that doesn't feel like a period piece 10 years later," adds Ms. Newman. "That's more a statement about the profession than anything."

Susan E. Rogers (review date August 1999)

SOURCE: A review of *Racechanges: White Skin, Black Face in American Culture* in *Journal of American Studies*, Vol. 33, No. 2, August 1999, pp. 368–69.

[*In the following review, Rogers lauds the seriousness of Gubar's approach to her subject in* Racechanges.]

From Fred Astaire and Virginia Woolf in black face to Josephine Baker in black face and Dick Gregory in white face; from Whoopi Goldberg in a milk bath to a Pears soap advert depicting a black child's skin washed milk-white; and from Man Ray's photograph *Noire et Blanche* (1926) to Jean-Paul Darriau's sculpture *Red, Blond, Black and Olive* (1980) the pictorial images in Susan Gubar's *Racechanges* engage the reader in a series of inquiries before a word of text has been read. The critical analysis which accompanies the book's numerous and astounding illustrations does not disappoint. Gubar presents an intensely thought provoking investigation of the cultural space inhabited by artists, writers and entertainers whose work, intentionally or not, challenges the notion of a fixed opposition between black and white. Her writing refuses to shy away from the complex perspectives that such a project demands, but, rather, attests to the ambiguity and shifting nature of representations of blackness and whiteness, to what she early on outlines as the suggestive meanings embraced by the term racechange: "the traversing of race boundaries, racial imitation or impersonation, cross racial mimicry or mutability . . . pan racial mutuality."

Each of the five main chapters addresses a specific, but not necessarily isolated, manifestation of racechange. The second and third chapters work well in conjunction, the former exploring white to black racechange in films and television, while the latter goes on to examine black artists' reclamations of such impersonations as well as their narratives about the origins of white justifications of black inferiority. Gubar is commendably attentive to both the liberating and reductive potential of such processes. Chapter four explores linguistic ventriloquism, in writings of the modernist era onwards, and the desire it reveals for white writers to at once adulate and erase blackness. This awareness of white cross-racial longing, of white artists' simultaneous "figuring and disfiguring" of blackness, as well as the dilemmas this creates for blacks trying to reclaim white masquerades, is one of the study's strengths. The final two chapters highlight perhaps the most disconcerting aspects of racechange, firstly with an exploration of the connections between perceived sexual deviance and racechange and then with an examination of cultural depictions of mixed-race children.

Despite the potential Gubar's discussion offers to focus on the playfully subversive aspects of racechange, her concern is with the serious and deep-rooted anxieties that it reveals. Throughout a text characterised by sensitivity to paradox, Gubar remains keenly attuned both to the recalcitrant racist assumptions that so often permeate acts of racechange and to the subversive possibilities that exist on the boundaries of racial impersonation. Ultimately and provocatively she holds out for the radical potential of transracial personas to "enact or envision postracist ways of being and perceiving."

Maureen T. Reddy (essay date June 2000)

SOURCE: "A Critic's Work Is Never Done," in *Women's Review of Books*, Vol. 17, No. 9, June, 2000, p. 17.

[*In the following review of* Critical Conditions, *Reddy pays tribute to Gubar's pioneering feminist criticism.*]

Retrospectively, we can all trace epochs in our lives, moments when everything changed. It is more difficult to recognize those moments in the present tense; but I remember knowing I was living through such an epoch-change in my own life in 1979 as I read Sandra Gilbert and Susan Gubar's co-authored *The Madwoman in the Attic: The Woman Writer and the Nineteenth-Century Literary Imagination*. I was a beginning graduate student in English, planning to focus on Victorian fiction; I had read most of the feminist literary criticism then in print (amazing now that it once was possible to do such a thing!) and knew that I wanted to contribute to that field, but was uncertain about what exactly I might do.

Slogging through the scads of non-feminist criticism assigned in my classes, I was increasingly disheartened by its prevailing tone of superiority, its competitive mode, its lack of relation to the world outside itself. Reading Gilbert and Gubar was exhilarating: there was real passion in their work, a clear sense of more at stake than their own academic careers, a collaborative sensibility totally at odds with the usual solitariness evident in literary criticism. Even when I strongly disagreed with particular insights, scribbling objections in the margins of the book, I felt a powerful sense of connection with the co-authors. *Madwoman* was, in short, an amazing inspiration.

I begin with this bit of personal history in order, first, to pay tribute to Susan Gubar and also to try to give some sense of how important her work (both alone and with Sandra Gilbert) has been. But lest this opening give the impression that Susan Gubar is some sort of icon of the past glory of feminist criticism, I want to make clear that her reputation does not rest on *Madwoman* alone, but has been built and sustained on numerous works published since then, including the co-edited *Norton Anthology of Literature by Women*. This new book, *Critical Condition*, extends her already considerable reach and is another kind of inspiration, as in it she engages with new feminist critical methods and problems.

But *Critical Condition* is also sometimes disheartening, for, despite her critical acuity, Gubar occasionally missteps rather seriously. For example, the book's subtitle—*Feminism at the Turn of the Century*—misleads: Gubar's seven essays are not about feminism *per se* but about one branch of feminism, the academic variety. This qualification strikes me as a significant one, but one not sufficiently acknowledged in the book. Gubar's essays analyze particular women artists, poets, novelists, dramatists and writers of non-fiction; the underlying subject is academic feminism, particularly feminist literary criticism from the 1970s to the present—a topic related to but not the same as "feminism," as any feminist outside of academia would immediately note, perhaps with some asperity. Although the introduction to the book relates the world outside the academy to the narrower concerns of the essays, both the subtitle and the essays themselves elide the distinction. A reader approaching the book expecting a survey of feminism at the present moment will be disappointed.

That said, I think the essays have considerable appeal outside the academy, and most definitely beyond the boundaries of literature departments. Gubar's diagnosis of feminism's "critical condition" stresses her ambivalence: her "sense of being poised between causes for regret and for celebration." Feminist studies' condition, she argues, "has itself become critical because of a number of heated disputes that have put its proponents at odds."

We could, of course, extend that claim to feminism in general. Gubar sees current feminist theory as largely irrelevant to life. Too often, she notes, we in specialized fields of study find ourselves speaking only to ourselves, and none too clearly at that. There is a "societal importance" to feminists making their writing lucid, accessible to and usable by women outside disciplinary or even interdisciplinary networks. Gubar evidently sees literature as a possible meeting ground for academic and non-academic feminists. In an essay called "Lesbian Studies 101 (As Taught by Creative Writers)," she argues that "poems and stories can bridge the gap between women outside the academy and theorists inside universities seeking to illuminate lesbian lives and loves," a claim that could easily be extended to other areas of illumination.

Gubar's own readings—of Jeannette Winterson's "The Poetics of Sex," Faith Ringgold's story quilts, Anna Deavere Smith's *Fires in the Mirror*, Mary Wollstonecraft's *A Vindication of the Rights of Woman*, Marilyn Hacker's "Ballad of Ladies Lost and Found," Adrian Piper's *My Calling (Card)* among others—are luminous, perceptive and accessible. They show Gubar at her absolute best while also demonstrating why feminist criticism matters.

The first essay in the book, **"Women Artists and Contemporary Racechanges,"** analyzes some complicated, difficult works by several Black women artists whose subject is the endless complexity of race and gender, their intertwining and their resistance to easy (or even hard) formulaic conclusions. This essay, among the strongest in the book, includes the most convincing reading I have seen of Faith Ringgold's disturbing "We Came to America" quilt. This quilt shows a Black Statue of Liberty in the foreground, holding a naked Black child; in the background a ship—a slave ship?—burns, while in the center Black figures struggle in a roiling, seemingly bloody sea. Gubar links this to Ringgold's larger body of work, pointing out that the quilt works as a "sort of shorthand on the detriments of twentieth-century racial paradigms" and going on to address what she calls Ringgold's characteristic "emphasis on cultural-miscegenation." Illustrations in beautiful, vibrant color of four of Ringgold's quilts accompany the essay.

Gubar explores the ways in which Ringgold, Anna Deavere Smith and Adrian Piper challenge common constructions of race and gender in their art, using "the commonplace gap between phenotype (a type distinguished by visual characteristics) and genotype (a type distinguished by hereditary traits) to frustrate conventional racial lexicons." At the end, she turns her analysis back on itself, acknowledging the self-contradictory nature of her enterprise: trying to examine works that undermine racial binaries yet focusing only on works by self-identified women of color seems to reinforce precisely those binaries. Gubar rightly admits that her quandary "reflects a current impasse in feminist thinking, namely, the need to employ identity categories for the purposes of political agency versus the fictiveness of those categories as displayed by poststructuralist and and postcolonial theorists."

Unfortunately, not all of the essays are as successful or as productively thought-provoking as ""**Women Artists and Contemporary Racechanges.**" The essay I find weakest is **"What Ails Feminist Criticism?"** which some readers may know already from its first appearance in *Critical Inquiry* in 1998. Here Gubar traces a brief history of three decades of feminist criticism, identifying four different phases, then focuses on what she sees as the "maladies" of the current phase. In sum, she concludes that feminist literary criticism and theory suffer from "a bad case of critical anorexia" brought on by the twin forces of "racialized identity politics" that make "women" mean "only a very particularized kind of woman" and of poststructuralist insistence that "women" is a fiction.

Gubar is not as generous nor as insightful a reader of certain theorists as she is of creative artists, and the entire essay seems one long, excessively one-sided complaint against bell hooks, Chandra Mohanty, Hazel Carby, Gayatri Spivak and Judith Butler. Although she begins this complaint by describing her targets as "brilliant scholars," their brilliance gets lost in the assault on their ideas and writing styles. The tone often seems aggrieved, as Gubar bewails a "barrage of diatribes directed at white feminists" and claims that in the 1980s "white feminists began to feel beleaguered by blatantly imperative efforts to right the wrong of black female instrumentality."

As Gubar sees it, critiques of white feminist work essentialized white women, ignored exceptions and fundamentally, were simply too censorious. I disagree, and am troubled by this hurt and angry response to what strikes me as the necessary and righteous anger of feminists of color. While I have no *prima facie* objection to complaints—in fact, I often quite enjoy complaining myself—this essay and its thematic twin, "The Graying of Professor Erma Bombeck," both subvert their own arguments by what I see as insufficient nuance, and seem curiously at odds with both the tone and the substance of other essays.

One recurring theme in this collection is Gubar's concern about the reproduction of feminism. Quoting Sylvia Plath, she asks, "Will the hive survive?"—will feminist scholarship continue or will a new generation have to start all over again? As Gubar points out, successors mean a future, and she most certainly wants a future for feminist criticism. *Critical Condition* concludes with **"A Chapter on the Future,"** in which Gubar draws on the responses of a diverse group of feminist critics and theorists to a questionnaire she sent them. She asked forty feminist critics—what she calls "an unscientifically selected cohort group"—ten questions about their hopes for the future of feminist criticism and their views of its major accomplishments. The words Gubar herself wants to speak to the next generation of feminist critics are hopeful and cautionary at once, reminding them of how much has already been accomplished but also of how much still needs to be done.

I don't think that Gubar needs worry much about successors: she already has them, and they know there is a lot still to be done. The combination of hope and caution in *Critical Condition*, the excitement about new critical approaches (such as critical race theory) and the sadness and anger about the overthrow of other methods (such as those that assume "woman" is an unproblematic and useful category) suggest that she herself is one of her own successors. That is, she has done a great deal, and it is clear that she plans to do still more.

Lorna Sage (essay date 17 March 2000)

SOURCE: "Learning New Titles," in *Times Literary Supplement*, No. 5,059, March 17, 2000, p. 26.

[*In the following essay, Sage praises* Critical Conditions *and Gubar's ability to remain committed to explicating the varieties of feminist criticism which have developed since the publication of* The Madwoman in the Attic.]

Recent statistics in the United States have apparently revealed that fewer women are being murdered by their husbands, not because there's less misogyny abroad but because there's less marriage. This is a good example of the way in which there have been enormous changes in the patterns of people's lives, which seem only loosely or mockingly related to what we projected. No wonder the postmodern picture of the individual as a passive construction of occult power at large seems plausible. Susan Gubar, looking at the relation between what 1970s feminist teachers and scholars wanted, and what has actually happened, is caught in a similar paradox; there are more women students, teachers, women's-studies programmes in universities, particularly in the Humanities, than anyone would have dreamed, but there is less and less common ground on what women mean.

Some of the reasons for this are obvious. Feminist academics first got jobs, and tenure, in significant numbers "at exactly the moment when the profession itself came under intense pressure to downsize." The result was that competition, the pressure to publish, and the need to distance yourself from your predecessors in the name of originality, were all savagely increased. Susan Gubar describes the situation—"fissures . . . between women of different ranks, between older and younger women, between women within traditional departments and those in multidisciplinary programmes . . .", and so on—with exemplary restraint and even humour. She deliberately doesn't extend the grim picture, as she might well have, to point out that the very consciousness-raising that brought so many more women and previously excluded minorities into higher education itself led to the rationing. Women in women's-studies programmes came up against the limits of official inclusiveness with particular force. It is no accident that the kind of post-structuralist theory that Gubar feels most ill at ease with is very well equipped to explain how exclusion works and how divisions proliferate. Though a lot of it is notoriously obscurely expressed, its accounts of endlessly deferred meaning and compromised agency uncannily resemble the real world, or at least the real academic world, that oxymoron. Theory promises to give you symbolic capital, in other words, the only kind most of us are going to accumulate much of. Privilege your powerlessness is one of its messages.

If Gubar avoids this kind of careless fighting talk, it is because she is intellectually and temperamentally disposed, despite all, to read the situation constructively. The form of *Critical Condition*—a collection of essays—means she doesn't have to produce an authoritative overview of the whole story. You can piece it together, though: first, the phase (Kate Millett's *Sexual Politics*, 1969) of showing how women were characterized in male-dominated histories and stories; second, the building of female traditions (as in her own **The Madwoman in the Attic,** in 1979, written with Sandra M. Gilbert); third, African-American and lesbian identity politics (speaking "as a . . ."); then with queer theory and postcolonial theory in the 1990s "those very terms . . . themselves underwent a sort of spectacular unravelling." And here we are, back to square one, with the best work in the field addressing itself to "the perplexity of women's fractured, divided, multiplied and contradictory modes of identification."

So where next? Some have given up on the whole game of identifying. Elaine Showalter is quoted as saying "I don't care what the latest development is in feminist theory or gender theory. It's completely irrelevant to me." Gubar, though, reads this as an understandable reaction to the kind of raw hostility that has become a feature of relations among feminist critics. She herself has, as she tells us, fought to resist cynicism, and the pieces that manage to digress from the question of "What Ails Feminist Criticism" show that she has struggled to good effect. The essay on the reflections on race and colour in the work of visual artists like Faith Ringgold is subtle, funny and heartfelt; and the analysis of the work of Marilyn Hacker, Jeannette Winterson and Rebecca Brown, in which Gubar finds a "metalesbian" message is very smart. Though there is something a bit odd about the implication that you need visionary sapphic abilities "to leap over historical facticity." Can't heterosexual writers do the daring illusions any longer? Perhaps Gubar is just being a good reader, showing she can learn new tricks herself. That is what she does in the book's potentially most interesting piece, **"Eating the Bread of Affliction",** about teasing out the relations between her Jewishness and her feminism, when she reflects on the impact of African-American Studies:

> After black scholars convinced feminist thinkers about the importance of race, identity politics provided a vocabulary for Jewish women to take seriously their own hyphenated identities.

True to form, however, she wants to point to the Jew as one of modernism's most representative outsiders, whose fortunes she and Sandra Gilbert partly traced in their mammoth **No Man's Land.** There is some fascinating work to be done on American feminism's links with Jewish immigrant and diaspora culture, and un-American Activities, only hinted at here.

But at the same time, this gently personal piece marks a retreat. "Has 'What is to be done?' been replaced by 'Who am I?'" she asks, and the answer must be partly yes. Not entirely, though, for the paradoxical reason that—judging from her tone—she is indeed a kind of Jewish Mom in the quarrelsome household of academe. She can't retire into herself, can't bring herself not to interfere. Her determination is her most powerful argument for continuing to search

for common ground, or at least new ways of disagreeing, since fractures and fault-lines are not going to go away. Any overview is a grand-scale act of will and ingenuity, but it is an act, something you do, not something you are.

Academic women edit texts, do archival research, write literary biographies, teach writing and review books, as well as engage in the "mind-numbing battles" that Susan Gubar deplores. There is room to live intellectually, in other words, without having to compete over who's more marginal than whom. And there is even a book to be written on the perverse pleasures of claustrophobia for academic anchoresses that she is altogether too caring to contemplate.

Dana D. Nelson (review date Spring 2000)

SOURCE: A review of *Racechanges: White Skin, Black Face in American Culture,* in *Journal of Women in Culture and Society,* Vol. 25, No. 3, Spring, 2000, p. 912.

[*In the following review, Nelson suggests that* Racechanges *is weakened because its conceptualization of race is "ahistorical and transcultural."*]

Susan Gubar prefaces her book **Racechanges: White Skin, Black Face in American Culture** with an unsettling catalog of examples drawn from middle-class, mostly academic whites' "confessions" to habitual modes of blackface minstrelsy. They range from secret imitations of Stepin Fetchit to jive-talking by dog-owners, practices that whites save for moments of domestic intimacy. This is the Africanism of the white bourgeoisie, the (beloved) heart of (imagined) darkness that Toni Morrison defined in *Playing in the Dark.*[1] Gubar asserts that such moments, as well as the more public ones she also analyzes in the book, while having "little to do with actual changes in melanin and sometimes even less to do with real African Americans," serve usefully to "illuminate the psychology of whites who have evolved through a series of oppositional identities predicated on black Others" (xv). But Gubar soon specifies her focus somewhat more generally than her preliminary examples and her title signal: her book is less interested in white appropriations of "blackness" for the psychological maintenance of white supremacy than it is in "transracial performances" (xviii)—which trouble race as cross-dressing troubles gender—and in the "importance of cross-racial patterns of imagery" (xvi).

Racechanges is typical of Gubar's energetic and wide-ranging academic style. Beginning with a quick analysis of an ancient Janiform vessel, one side featuring what U.S. viewers today would think of as a "white" woman's face and the other that of a "black" woman, Gubar admits that "conceptualizations of race have not remained static" since the vase was made in 510 B.C., yet she insists on the paradigmatic value of the vase for understanding race in contemporary U.S. culture. "Reading the vase now," she argues, "demonstrates how configurations of corporeal traits contributed to a black/white divide that paradoxically provoked in people on each side of it various transgressive maneuvers, much as has the arranging of the world into male and female" (5). Anticipating scholars who will find her subjects "too diverse" Gubar provides examples of the transgressive maneuvers she calls "racechanges" with wide appeal to a "common reader" (xviii). Instances include Ellen Craft in her gender-and race-changed escape from slavery; Edouard Manet's 1863 painting *Olympia*; Virginia Woolf's Dreadnought caper; the performances of Josephine Baker; Bing Crosby's 1942 movie *Holiday Inn*; Richard Pryor and Gene Wilder in *Silver Streak*; Michael Jackson's much-discussed "whiten[ing] and westerniz[ing of] all his features" (20); and Robert Mapplethorpe's "Man in a Polyester Suit" (1980) and Ike Ude's signifying response to it (1995).

The book is best in its chapter on "Psychopathologies of Black Envy" (5). There, Gubar argues that white men's blackface performances register not just homoerotic love and cultural/political/economic theft but also "an uncanny, different kind of masculinism, an excessively physical masculinism stripped of traditional patriarchal privilege" (174–75). The book's weakest aspects are Gubar's inability to decide whether "race" is biological or cultural (oddly, given her reliance on poststructuralism to conceptualize "racechange" she suggests the answer is both [14]); her frequent assumption of a white readership as well as a unified white social consciousness (e.g., "Yet because we have become a society more aware of how insulting such impersonations can be, the time for studying racial imitations has now begun," [40]); and her attempt to explain "racechange" in U.S. culture through an apparatus that is ahistorical (510 B.C. to 1998), transcultural (British, French, and U.S. cultures), and broadly bilateral. The study's breadth actually despecifies "race" within U.S. culture, offering the impression that while there might be minor variations, "race" has functioned as a "black/white" issue across cultures and epochs. And white Gubar points out the uneven reciprocity of racechange between whites and blacks in the United States (she admits even to having been "alarmed" by it [241]), the sheer weight of her analysis—for instance, her introductory fascination with Michael Jackson—actually blunts the force of her ruminations on the dissymmetry of "racechange." . . .

K. Anthony Appiah (essay date 27 April 2000)

SOURCE: "Battle of the *Bien-Pensant*," in *New York Review of Books*, Vol. 47, No. 7, April 27, 2000, p. 42.

[*In the following essay, Appiah discusses the tensions and divisions among academic feminist theorists as they are reflected in* Critical Conditions.]

1.

Academic moralism is one of the oldest traditions of the university, which began, after all, as an ecclesiastical insti-

tution whose students were mostly destined to be members of the clergy. In the early part of the twentieth century, the ethical voice in the American university was to be heard from the philosophy department as well as the divinity school, both of which were dominated by varieties of Protestantism. When William James or John Dewey spoke to the educated public on the conduct or meaning of life, they were only doing their job. They were not-so-terribly secular clerics, whose voices were heard alongside—occasionally even above—those of the official priesthood.

Sometime before the mid-century, however, professional philosophy in America became more centrally preoccupied with questions in epistemology and metaphysics, which were of less obvious relevance for their lay fellow citizens: the most influential figures in American philosophy in the decades after the Second World War were philosophers—some native, like W. V. O. Quine, some immigrant, like Rudolf Carnap—whose work was dauntingly technical and, by and large, not addressed to the moral life.[1] In becoming national and then international, the university had had also to become less sectarian and more secular; and so, as a result, the withdrawal of the philosophers from ethical questions left a gap that could no longer be filled by the divinity school. Questions of public ethical concern were increasingly the subject of the social sciences. But psychologists, sociologists, and economists often proclaimed their "value neutrality." (That was, to a degree, what made their pronouncements credible: they offered guides to living in the guise of technical, objective, scientific information.) And so when someone had to speak up for values the literature faculty increasingly took up the slack.

It did not always do so comfortably. As the literary scholar John Guillory has observed, modern English departments represent the confluence of two nineteenth-century traditions: belles-lettres and philology. The scientific aspirations of the latter discipline gave rise to an emphasis on interpretative method and theoretical speculation. That focus on literature's mechanics—the medium rather than the message—now goes by the name of "literary theory." But these theorists never had the field to themselves; the spirit of moralism in academic literary criticism has a long pedigree in twentieth-century America, ranging across the continent, and alphabet, from Irving Babbit to Yvor Winters. And in the postwar period, as the United States assumed more confidently its global leadership, a professor of English like Lionel Trilling could speak for American values, for liberalism and democracy, and find them embedded, already waiting for us, in the high literary canon. The tone was that of a (progressive) gentleman's club; the signature color was tweed.

Today's academic moralism in the humanities sounds rather different. In the Sixties and Seventies of the last century, the liberation movements of blacks, women, and homosexuals often found their voice in literary work; this social fervor crossed the threshold of the English department just as the numbers of blacks, women, and open homosexuals increased at universities that had once been citadels of white and male privilege. The genteel cadences of old did not survive the resulting culture wars, for the liberationists aimed to dismantle the ethical consensus that earlier critics had assumed: Trilling's magisterial "we," once meant to conjure a moral community, came to be deplored as a blithe "exclusion of difference." "Essentialism" began as a word for criticizing anyone who assumed that all X's shared the same characteristics. And so, at the turn of the Eighties, the word was first used against nationalists of various sorts and women. There were black and Jewish essentialists, feminist essentialists, lesbian essentialists.

At the same time, in an ironic twist, "essentialist humanism" became a key term of opprobrium, an accusation flung at anyone who did not insist that society had created important differences between men and women, black and white, gay and straight, rich and poor, or who did not accept that those differences undermined the assumption of a shared humanity in the humanities. Now you could be an essentialist both for saying that people were different and for saying that they were the same. The result was to change not just the subject matter but the rhetorical tenor of academic criticism. Trilling, though he might have rejected William K. Wimsatt's approach to literature—which was text-centered and showed no interest in the author's psychological processes—would not for this reason have thought Wimsatt wicked. But if African-American literary criticism was an adjunct of Black Liberation—which, as a matter of dignity and justice, was obviously a business of the highest moral importance—then academic disagreements could easily spill over into conflicts more vulgarly political; and the dissemination of intellectual error might not only undermine the movement, it might also reflect bad character.

Of course, it wasn't the liberation movements that made literary study contentious. When Harold Bloom urged us to trace literary influences not as the transmission of tradition, the cultivation of a precious heritage, but as an Oedipal struggle of the sons against the fathers, his Freudian allegory was offered as an account of relations among poets. But one might be forgiven for suspecting that the idea came not from communing with the souls of Wordsworth and Blake but from Bloom's own experience of the struggle for existence in the groves of academe. Shelley may not have been battling Milton, but Harold Bloom, the author of *Shelley's Mythmaking*, was certainly battling Earl Wasserman, the author of *Shelley: A Critical Reading*. Individuality in scholarship, as in life, begins with defining yourself both within and against a tradition. What the new context added was the increasing moralization of the process of definition. Since academic generations always define themselves by resisting the interpretations of their predecessors, the moralization of intellectual differences (this is not just a point about the English department) was bound to lead to trouble.[2]

As you will have noticed, the alliance of liberation movements and literary study hasn't made criticism politically

potent or politics critically informed: the revival of Zora Neale Hurston hasn't altered wage inequities; nor is her name one to conjure with in the primaries even of her native Florida. But this alliance did bring the conduct of literary scholars under minute "political" scrutiny, at least in the classroom, the conference, and the critical essay. It has raised the heat of literary debate, without always shedding more light. And the feminist shibboleth that the personal is the political—or perhaps one ought to say a particular construal of that shibboleth—has made the personal conduct of critics fair game for interpretation and "critique."

I once attended a conference on postcolonial criticism at which one of the speakers mistakenly addressed a young African professor as a graduate student and then left the conference early to catch a plane home. Both of these things were surely, at worst, lapses of manners: and yet the incident led to the publication of densely theoretical, fiercely denunciatory essays among the speaker's fellow third world, poststructural, and Marxian theorists. It isn't easy, in such a setting, to distinguish the *ad feminam* from the substantive objection. Literature may not be, as Matthew Arnold thought, the "criticism of life," but literary scholarship is, often enough, the criticism of critics.

2.

In 1979, Professors Sandra Gilbert and Susan Gubar published *The Madwoman in the Attic: The Woman Writer and the Nineteenth-Century Literary Imagination*, a work that shaped profoundly the then burgeoning field of feminist literary scholarship.[3] Ever since, this book has appeared regularly on reading lists in courses in departments of English around the country. It was not a work of high theory, but one of literary interpretation and textual recovery: it discussed a wide selection of nineteenth-century novelists and their critical reception, among them Kate Chopin, Edith Wharton, Willa Cather, and Gertrude Stein. Some of them, such as Edith Wharton, were criticized for their criticism of the work of other women writers. Beginning in 1988, Gilbert and Gubar published three further volumes that continued this work into the twentieth century; and, in 1985, they published the first edition of *The Norton Anthology of Literature by Women: The Tradition in English*, a work that helped shape, willy-nilly, a canon of women's writing for the next generation of students of English.

These books were feminist in aim, intention, and self-description. And part of their literary energy came from the fact that they were envisaged as part of the project of combating patriarchy and building a new feminist consciousness, especially for the young women in the classes where they were (and are) so widely used. In their 1979 opus, Susan Gubar and Sandra Gilbert castigated Harold Bloom for the ostensibly masculine bias of his account of literary relations—a man might attack his literary paterfamilias, but the literary relations among women, we were assured, were far more supportive. Far from seeking to overthrow their literary forebears, women writers were seeking a literary community; and the enemy was patriarchy, not their foremothers.

Despite their own experience of successful feminist collaboration, the response to their scholarly undertaking hardly confirmed this happy conviction. In later years, Susan Gubar writes, she has found herself (as part of "that curious entity called 'Gilbert and Gubar'") lambasted by various "insurgent" critics for various purported sins: she was "essentialist," didn't sufficiently acknowledge black women or lesbians, failed to keep pace with high theory—the list was no doubt long. (For example, it was pointed out that "Gilbert and Gubar" had made nothing of the fact that the madwoman in the attic of their title—Bertha Mason in Charlotte Brontë's *Jane Eyre*—was a Jamaican Creole.) To judge from her new book, *Critical Condition: Feminism at the Turn of the Century*, the experience has been demoralizing. The field of feminist criticism—a field she did much to establish—is now, she tells us, cluttered with alienating jargon and riven by divisive identity politics.

Critical Condition has its origins in an episode that is sketched—I use this word advisedly—in the book's introduction. At some time (she does not say when) Professor Gubar was "a candidate for a senior position at a school to remain nameless." Informed by the chairman of the department that there was a risk that her appointment would be opposed by some of his more conservative senior colleagues—and assuming, as one gathers, that she could count on the support of the younger feminists—she gave a talk entitled **"Who Killed Feminist Criticism?"** in which she referred to some of the ideas of the critics who had attacked her. The talk, she tells us, cost her the job. And the opposition came not from the right but from the left. The visiting feminist progressive found herself condemned, astonishingly, as a troglodyte, perhaps even a racist. When she arrived she was Kate Millett; when she departed, John Rocker.

A final version of this talk is printed toward the end of the book as **"What Ails Feminist Criticism?"** (Dr. Gubar has, on sober reflection, taken the unusual step of moving the patient from the morgue back to the ICU.) She admits that the original paper was "probably written in too bellicose a manner." But if it was anything like the essay in this volume, it was its subject, not its tone, that was bound to cause trouble, and for at least two reasons. First, in considering feminist criticism, she objected (as she puts it here in the introduction) to "what Toni Morrison calls 'the calcified language of the academy.'" This confirmed the opinion of those who thought her insufficiently theoretical; since, if you object to academic language, it is often assumed that this is because you—unlike your more savvy colleagues—have a hard time understanding it.

But worse was to come; for Gubar also criticized "certain sponsors of African-American, postcolonial, and poststructuralist studies" for "subverting the term 'woman' that feminism needs to assure its political agency."[4] That is,

she argued (to uncalcify the language a bit) that often, in the struggle for justice, what you need to insist on is not what divides women but what they have in common. Since what divides women, as she argued, was insistence on their differences, she could be pigeonholed by her critics with those essentialists who are allegedly hostile to women of color and lesbians. The effect of her remarks was thus only to confirm the worst suspicions of her detractors. A quondam insurgent critic fell victim to a new insurgency.

What Gubar had done was to respond to the major criticisms of her earlier work in the natural way: by attacking the works of her critics. The effect was only to inflame them. Given the new moralism, this led not just to vigorous disagreement but also to assaults upon her character. She did not give up: she read versions of the paper on several other occasions around the country and finally published it (in 1998) in *Critical Inquiry*, which is about the most visible journal in literary studies. After the response she reports, this was either courageous persistence or evidence of masochism.

Clearly Susan Gubar believes that her dogged criticism of the new insurgency has left her with a reputation (if only in some *soi-disant bien-pensant*—or at least *soi-pensant bien-disant*—quarters) as an essentialist and a reactionary. So her new book is both apology and apologia—or, to put it another way, it is an act of what's known, on Madison Avenue, as "positioning." The opening chapters feature sympathetic discussions of African-American art (the quilts of Faith Ringgold, the conceptual art of Adrian Piper, the performances of Anna Deavere Smith); lesbian literature (the poetry of Marilyn Hacker and the "astonishingly diverse productions" of Jeannette Winterson); and her discovery of her own "inner ethnic" as she explores the relations of Judaism and feminism.

Each of these essays is a concession to "difference": to the recognition that women are, after all, not all the same. If, as the critics alleged, when "Gilbert and Gubar" wrote "woman" what they had unconsciously assumed was a female heterosexual of the white middle classes, then displaying the range of her interest in women who were neither straight nor white would seem to be a suitable act of clarification, if not atonement. At the very least, as Professor Gubar writes in the book's introduction, she hopes that her "positive engagement with the insights of African-American, postcolonial, and poststructuralist thinkers in what are now the opening chapters" will "free me from the allegation that I had dismissed or calumniated their labors." This book is driven by something other than the ordinary academic worry that one might be in error; it is, so to speak, Susan Gubar's soul, not her mind, that seems to be up for judgment.

Well, I, for one, am happy to acknowledge the essential goodness of Professor Gubar's soul.[5] The question is why she has ended up having to defend herself before a tribunal that is largely unseen and unnamed. Discriminating between what is and isn't worthwhile is the purpose of intellectual judgment. Why, then, could she not criticize her critics without having her character impugned? The answer is, in part, that the intertwining of academic and social agendas has given rise to an outlandish rhetorical inflation, a storming-of-the-Bastille bombast brought to bear on theoretical niceties. Individuals get taken for kinds: a particular third world literary feminist theorist comes to represent all women of color. Not teaching Jeannette Winterson is taken to mean excluding her from the canon, which is easily inflated into excluding lesbians from it; and soon we have unqualified talk of the "exclusion" of lesbians—or gays or blacks—which sounds as though you're keeping them out of the class, or the university, or running them out of the neighborhood. This is indeed moralism; but it is moralism run amok.

There is, to be sure, an argument lurking in the background here: it is that literal exclusion somehow stems from literary exclusion. Or, to speak more precisely, that much of the oppression in the world is the result of speaking and writing and thinking about people in the wrong way. If all men thought about women in the right way, fewer men would beat up their wives. I believe this is a truth, even a truism. But there remains a difference between thinking ill of a black woman's critical writings and thinking ill of her or of all black women. And there is yet a further distinction between thinking or speaking ill of people and beating them up. The point is that not every intellectual error about women—or blacks or lesbians—is as harmful as every other. Once you conflate errors of these different orders, you end up dissipating energy in pointless skirmishes while the vital battles are being lost all around you.

In her introduction, Susan Gubar worries that many women undergraduates today "do not define feminism as equity for women or an awareness of the social construction of gender or reproductive control or political agitation for the ending of sexual violence." Presumably these young women would be happy to identify with feminism if they did define it as "equity for women" and the like; and one is therefore inclined to ask why they do not. Professor Gubar suggests that at least part of the explanation has to do with the nature of recent feminist debates: what she describes as "mind-numbing battles in which so-called social constructionists faulted so-called essentialists for their naive totalizing, feminists of color blamed white scholars for their racism, lesbian critics accused straight thinkers of homophobia." Perhaps, if academic disputation looks to her students as it does to Professor Gubar, being a feminist doesn't seem like much fun.[6]

Neither, I suspect, does being a literary critic. In the last few decades, as countless cultural theories have jostled and collided, as the concept of literature itself has been relentlessly "interrogated," academic criticism—which is to say, literary scholarship and interpretation for its own sake and its own satisfactions—has lost a sense of cultural purpose. Accordingly, critics have increasingly turned to writing about each other. ("Garbage is garbage," a well-known philosopher used to say, "but the history of garbage is scholarship.") This soon becomes something of a tar pit: Susan Gubar's new book is, in no small part, criticism about criticism of criticism. Which, I suppose, means that what you're now reading is criticism of criticism about criticism of criticism. I'm sorry: it's just the spirit of the times.

Susan Gubar, it must be said, is clearly interested in literature as well as committed to political feminism. The book she's produced, however, tells us less about literature than about the social tensions in her profession at the end of the twentieth century. There is even a chapter, entitled "The Graying of Professor Erma Bombeck," devoted in part to discussing the personal and professional relations of older and younger women scholars. Such matters, I have come to feel, are probably better handled by practitioners than by critics of narrative: one finishes her book convinced that the most interesting version of *l'affaire Gubar* would be a novel by David Lodge, or Molly Hite.[7] (Or Philip Roth, whose forthcoming novel, *The Human Stain*, has much to say about the literary academy today.)

And, despite the generality of the reference to feminism in the book's subtitle, it is actually largely about literary feminism within the academy; which is, as Susan Gubar says in her introduction, "less an activist, more a scholarly enterprise." A review of her book is not, therefore, the place to discuss whether feminism outside the literary academy is dead, let alone ailing. But so far as the literary academy goes, my sense is that the heyday of the sort of Mau-Mauing to which Professor Gubar was subjected has passed, not just in feminist debates but also in those about race and sexuality as well. "Identity politics" has fallen into bad odor, at least among many members of university faculties (which does not guarantee, of course, that you recognize it when you do it yourself). Theory for its own sake, too, has lost some of its luster, another small victory for the spirit of belles-lettres in its apparently endless struggle with philology. Indeed, *mirabile dictu*, there are more and more literary critics—feminist and otherwise— who actually devote themselves to . . . literature. Susan Gubar's field may well be in a "critical condition," but there are signs that it is on the mend.

Notes

1. This process is described and lamented in Cornel West's *American Evasion of Philosophy* (University of Wisconsin Press, 1989). It's perhaps worth observing that, with John Rawls's *A Theory of Justice* (Harvard University Press, 1979), ethics once more assumed a place of honor in professional American philosophy, and that philosophers of distinction have increasingly addressed not only moral theory—which can be as dense and difficult as the most abstruse metaphysics—but also practical ethics.

2. The struggle to overthrow the theories of one's predecessors is central, if in very different ways, to the natural sciences as well—at least, if either Karl Pop-

per or Thomas Kuhn (who agree in this, if in little else) is to be believed. But what is at stake is not usually moralized in the natural sciences.

3. Reviewed in these pages by Helen Vendler. See *The New York Review*, May 31, 1990.

4. It is, in this context, a none-too-subtle reframing of the original talk—which did not mention Morrison—to put the first complaint into the mouth of the best-known living black woman writer.

5. This is probably the place to admit that her first chapter has an epigraph from an essay of mine; though, alas, the suggestions she quotes were glossed by me—in a phrase she does not cite—as "the proposals of a banal postmodernism."

6. It occurs to me that if these young women accept what Susan Gubar sees as feminism's goals, while rejecting the label, this might be accounted not a defeat but a victory.

7. This is something Gilbert and Gubar plainly know: their main joint work of the 1990s was *Masterpiece Theatre: An Academic Melodrama* (Rutgers University Press, 1995).

FURTHER READING

Criticism

Beer, Gillian. "Dispersed As We Are." *Times Literary Supplement*, No. 4,813 (30 June 1995): 6–7.

Beer praises the "prodigious achievement" of the three volumes of *No Man's Land*, but notes several shortcomings in the works of method, style, and scope.

Frank, Katherine. A review of *The Madwoman in the Attic*, by Susan Gubar and Sandra Gilbert. *Philological Quarterly* 59, No. 3 (Summer, 1980) 381–83.

Frank calls *The Madwoman in the Attic* indispensable, and asserts that the book will reform the way audiences will read women authors.

Norris, Margot. A review of *No Man's Land*, by Susan Gubar and Sandra Gilbert. *Comparative Literature* 43, No. 2 (Spring, 1991): 199–201.

Norris argues that volume one of *No Man's Land* is an unconvincing study because Gubar and Gilbert are reductionist and narrow in their scholarship.

Additional coverage of Gubar's life and career is available in the following sources published by the Gale Group: *Contemporary Authors,* **Vol. 108;** *Contemporary Authors New Revision Series,* **Vols. 45 and 70;** *Feminist Writers*; *Major 20th-Century Writers*; **and** *Literature Resource Center.*

Janette Turner Hospital
1942-

(Also has written under pseudonym Alex Juniper) Australian novelist and short story writer.

The following entry presents an overview of Hospital's career through 1997. For further information on her life and works, see *CLC*, Volume 42.

INTRODUCTION

Australian native Hospital is recognized for the sumptuous, complex, highly descriptive language of her fiction. Hospital, who considers herself an "unintentional nomad," has lived in Australia, Canada, the United States, Great Britain, France, and India—all places that have left indelible marks on her psyche and on her writing. Her favorite characters are those who live on the fringes of society, such as prostitutes, drug dealers, and street people of all descriptions. Best known for her novels *Borderline* (1985) and *The Last Magician* (1992) and her short story collection *Isobars* (1990), Hospital's work lends eloquent voice to the effects of displacement on humanity and vividly describes conflicts between culture and gender.

BIOGRAPHICAL INFORMATION

Born in Melbourne, Australia, Hospital moved with her family to Brisbane when she was seven. Her parents, Adrian and Elsie Turner, were deeply religious people who belonged to an evangelical, fundamentalist sect of the Pentecostal faith and who read the King James Bible nightly around the dinner table. The world outside their home, however, was working-class Australia, which was typically anti-authoritarian and anti-religious. Consequently, from the beginning of her life, Hospital found herself negotiating diverse cultures and feeling like an outsider—themes that would later come to dominate her writing. Hospital received a B.A. from the University of Queensland in 1966. While at college, she taught high school English in Brisbane from 1963 to 1966. In 1965 she married Clifford G. Hospital, a scholar of comparative religion and a specialist in Sanskrit. She and her husband left Australia, and from 1967 through 1971, she worked at Harvard University as a librarian. In 1973 Hospital received an M.A. from Queen's University in Kingston, Ontario. A scholar of medieval literature, much of her writing includes allusions to authors such as Dante Alighieri. Hospital went on to teach English at both St. Lawrence College and Queen's University from 1973 to 1982. She accepted appointments as writer-in-residence at the Massachusetts Institute of Tech-

nology during 1985, 1986, 1987, and 1989; the University of Ottawa in 1987; the University of Sydney and La Trobe University in Melbourne, Australia, in 1989; Boston University in 1991; and the University of East Anglia, England, in 1996. Hospital returned to La Trobe University as an adjunct professor of English from 1990 to 1993. She also lived in India while her husband was on sabbatical in 1977. This experience inspired her first novel, *The Ivory Swing* (1982), which received the Seal First Novel Award from Seal Books. She was awarded the Atlantic First Citation in 1978 from *Atlantic Monthly,* and received another Citation from the magazine in 1982 for her short story, "Waiting." Hospital's first collection of short stories, *Dislocations* (1986), received the CDC Literary Prize and, in 1988, the Fellowship of Australian Writers Award. In 1989 her novel *Charade* (1988) was awarded the Torgi Award from the Canadian Association for the Blind and the Australian National Book Council Award. *The Last Magician,* was considered for the prestigious Booker Prize in 1992. Hospital has also written a mystery novel, *A Very Proper Death* (1990), under the pseudonym Alex Juniper. Hospital remains an international itinerant, living in Australia, North America, and Europe during different parts of the year.

MAJOR WORKS

Before Hospital was a novelist, she was an honored short story writer, and she continues to work in this genre. The stories in her first collection, *Dislocations,* explore the fragmentary elements of contemporary life and show characters of many nationalities responding to upheaval as an opportunity for growth. The final story in the collection, "After Long Absence," shows the protagonist trying to return to her family despite her resentment for having been raised a Jehovah's Witness, for which she was ostracized by other children. In the end, she is unable to compromise and learns that she is truly homeless, even in the midst of her parents and siblings. In Hospital's second collection, *Isobars,* the characters exist in a limbo between past and present and are often haunted by ghosts. In "A Little Night Music," a male passenger on an airline flight continually apologizes to his nervous female seatmate, who had barely missed a previous flight that was destroyed by an explosion. After the plane lands, she sees the man's picture in a newspaper and discovers that he was the ghost of the terrorist who bombed the ill-fated flight and perished with all aboard. "The Last of the Hapsburgs," another piece featuring a ghostly presence, focuses on the theme of dislocation. The title characters are the surviving members of a Jewish family that persevered through the Holocaust. They are endlessly jeered in the parochial area of Queensland where they live. On Friday nights, they gather and listen to the violin played by the ghost of their eldest son, who perished in a concentration camp. Hospital's first novel, *The Ivory Swing,* grew from her experiences living in India with her husband. Through observing the marginalized position of a widowed woman in a wealthy Indian household, Hospital examines several cultural paradoxes and the effects they have on all the characters involved. In *The Tiger in the Pit* (1983), Hospital presents a family drama around the arrangement of an anniversary celebration. (The title is taken from a T. S. Eliot poem and also alludes to the novel's cantankerous patriarch.) The story is told through different points of view that juxtapose the perceptions of the family members and their tangled personal histories. *Borderline,* the novel that established Hospital as a major writer, again explores one of her recurring themes—dislocation. While waiting to cross the border between the United States and Canada, Felicity and her companion discover an illegal immigrant from El Salvador. On impulse, they rescue the immigrant from the freezer van where she is hidden and take her to a remote cottage in Quebec. The remainder of the book focuses on the woman's subsequent disappearance and her would-be rescuers' attempts to repair the harm they caused. *Borderline* functions not only as a thriller, but also as an examination of both personal and political boundaries.

Charade, Hospital's next novel, attempts to link the world's cultures and the wonders of the physical world to a human search for origins. The plot weaves together allusions to Scherherazade's *One Thousand and One Nights,* Werner Heisenberg's uncertainty principle, and the Australian search for roots and identity; all in the context of the protagonist's year-long affair with a physicist at the Massachusetts Institute of Technology and her search for the father she never knew. *The Last Magician* is a novel of alternative realities, replete with medieval symbolism. The novel is set primarily in Australia, and is peopled with outsiders living on the fringes of society. Hospital follows the lives of four childhood friends who, partly as the result of a terrifying shared secret, have evolved into adults that deal with the past in vastly different ways. Set in a fictive Sydney, the novel exposes this shared secret and the impact it has on her characters' lives. Hospital uses these revelations to comment on the contrast between rich and poor in first-world countries and human beings' perceptions of reality. *Oyster* (1996), her latest novel, is set in the remotest part of the Australian Outback, a place called Outer Maroo. Far from the stereotype of wilderness tales with noble pioneers bringing civilization to the savages, *Oyster* is filled with questionable characters and acts of violence. In the novel, Outer Maroo consciously cuts itself off from all communication outside its borders in an attempt to erase the world's memory of it. Everyone in the town has been implicated in the mistreatment of slave laborers who once mined precious opals. The entire population of Outer Maroo continues to benefit financially from the ill-gotten profits and they now have a vested interest in keeping the truth a secret.

CRITICAL RECEPTION

Hospital's work has been praised for its lush language that, despite its complexity, manages to maintain an airy quality. Many critics consider her to be an expatriate Australian writer (a label that Hospital disdains) who is at her best when her work is set in Australia. However, some reviews note that American readers may find Hospital's work somewhat challenging due to its profusion of unfamiliar Australian place names. Additionally, her novels, most notably *The Last Magician,* have been criticized for being difficult reads and for attempting to cover too much material, whether through plot, theme, or characterization. Hospital is esteemed by many reviewers as a "prose stylist," whose fertile imagination and imagery reveal a serious author unafraid to take chances with profound themes. Still, there are critics who argue that Hospital's work is often hampered by an overuse of literary allusions, ambiguous conclusions, and difficult plot lines that tend to limit her audience.

PRINCIPAL WORKS

The Ivory Swing (novel) 1982
The Tiger in the Tiger Pit (novel) 1983
Borderline (novel) 1985
Dislocations (short stories) 1986
Charades (novel) 1988
Isobars (short stories) 1990
A Very Proper Death [as Alex Juniper] (novel) 1990
The Last Magician (novel) 1992
Collected Stories: 1970-1995 (short stories) 1995
Oyster (novel) 1996

CRITICISM

John Bemrose (review date 6 March 1989)

SOURCE: "Just Being Alive," in *Macleans,* March 6, 1989, p. 62.

[*In the following review, Bemrose concludes that* Charades *is "an uneven achievement." While praising Hospital's vivid writing and incorporation of science themes, Bemrose finds shortcomings in the novel's evasive cleverness.*]

Oscar Wilde's words—"Truth is rarely pure and never simple"—could stand as an epigraph for Janette Turner Hospital's fourth novel, *Charades,* a book that is as much mind-tease as story, as much about what did not happen as what did. Hospital has seemed on the verge of writing such a novel for some time. Ever since the Australian-born writer burst onto the Canadian literary scene with *The Ivory Swing,* which won the Seal first-novel award for 1982, her richly inventive, highly intuitive prose has strained to escape beyond the borders of ordinary perceptions and narrative style. Now, with the example of certain Latin American and European writers before her, Hospital has broken through into her own convoluted and fascinating fictional wonderland, where truth is something to pursue but never quite catch.

Hospital's heroine, Charade Ryan, is a young, footloose Australian woman whose global wanderings are driven by an intense desire to assemble the known fragments of her past into some kind of meaningful picture. Above all, she wants to find her father, Nicholas Truman, a philandering university lecturer from England who years earlier had a fling with Charade's mother, Bea. As the novel opens, Charade's search has brought her to the Massachusetts Institute of Technology—the Cambridge university where Hospital herself is currently in her fourth term as writer in residence. There, Charade has an affair with a brilliant professor of theoretical physics, Koenig. Most of the novel consists of their pillow talk as Charade, who seems to prefer conversation to making love, spins out various possible versions of her past to the bemused physicist.

There is something desperate about Charade. It soon becomes clear that she is a compulsive talker who must keep the words flowing in order to feel real. "If I stop talking," she tells Koenig, "I'll vanish like camphor." And for all her avowals that she is looking for the truth, there is something evasive in her monologues, too, as if perhaps the real truth about her life were something that she would rather avoid. She discovers it anyway: at the end of the novel, she finally stumbles onto some traumatic revelations about her birth. And while the information may not be what she was looking for, at least it offers some clues as to why Charade is so driven and unhappy.

Charade's desperation lends the book an aura of feverish brilliance. And her intellectual curiosity allows Hospital to make the bravest and most complex use of scientific theory in a novel since John Updike's *Roger's Version.* In Koenig's explanations of his work, Charade finds a tenuous justification for the elusive, paradoxical quality that reality has for her. Koenig tells her how, in science, two researchers will often come up with contradictory yet mathematically demonstrable results. Such situations led Koenig to call the possibility of knowing anything for certain "a useful fraud."

Charades is a compendium of such frauds, some more useful—or entertaining—than others. Charade tells several highly contrasting versions of how she came to be. At times, she seems to disappear altogether while her story flows from the viewpoint of other characters, including her bawdy, lower-class mother—whom Charade labels "The Slut of the Tamborine Rain Forest"—and Bea's more reserved, scholarly girlfriend, Katherine Sussex. The two carry on a running rivalry over Nicholas, who in turn is hopelessly bound to a beautiful but highly neurotic Holocaust survivor. As the narrative moves through and around those characters, the effect is at once disorienting and exciting, rather like participating in a magic trick with a masterful magician.

Yet, for all its sleight of hand, *Charades* is an uneven achievement. At times, Hospital's cleverness seems to be a smoke screen hiding an absence of anything important to say. Part of the problem is that Charade's exchanges with Koenig become a series of predictable gestures and attitudes. As well, Hospital, like her own heroine, frequently dances away from an anecdote before its narrative impact has been solidly established. Still, many incidents—particularly those evoking childhood—are as vibrant and compelling as the Australian landscape in which they are set. Katherine recalls how, one day on a school outing, she climbed a mountain by herself and experienced a moment of ecstasy. "She had a sense of herself as a solar whiteness," Hospital writes, "without shape, without limits in time or space, pulsing with a kind of exaltation whose only analogue might be the dramatic rush of wind at the rainy edge of a cyclone." It is in such passages, in such language, that *Charades* reaches beyond mere intellectual brilliance and touches something of the paradoxical quality of being alive.

Valerie Miner (review date 23 April 1989)

SOURCE: "The 1,001 Australian Nights," in *Los Angeles Times Book Review,* April 23, 1989, pp. 3, 7.

[*In the following review, Miner offers a positive assessment of* Charades.]

Many Americans will read this wildly imaginative novel as a contemporary version of "1,001 Nights" or as an attempt to reconcile the *Angst* of our post-Nazi Holocaust, pre-nuclear holocaust era by understanding scientific theories. Indeed, Janette Turner Hospital's stunning fourth novel is a resurrection of Scherherazade as well as an extrapolation of Heisenberg's uncertainty principle. It reads even more provocatively as an Australian odyssey of self-determination.

Charades opens in a dimly lit office at MIT. Prof. Koenig looks up from his article on theoretical physics to find a young woman reading over his shoulder. The beautiful, irreverent visitor from Oz compliments his writing and introduces herself as the friend of someone he does not remember. Is he dreaming? Is Charade, he wonders, simply a metaphor for his guilt about his former wife?

Thus begin the 366—not 1,001—nights of a mysterious love affair between the quixotic traveler and the spiritually threadbare middle-aged academic. Their pasts intersect in peripheral, yet significant ways. Their relationship emerges in antipodean mirror images. Only by talking obsessively, night after night, can Charade unknot the painful secrets of her parentage. The listening sustains Koenig enough so that he can turn from his safe academic abstractions, begin to confront his own past and imagine a personal future.

Charade speaks with classic Australian self-deprecatory brashness. She inherits an Anglo-Celtic schizophrenia, assuming one set of legacies from the English upper class and another from the Irish convict class. Her loving, earthy mother represents the essence of home: In fact she was born on January 26, Australia Day. Her father is absent, foreign, ephemeral. Her own name is both symbolic—for she does not know what part of herself is real—and homophonous—because in the abbreviated Australian vernacular (*mossies, barbies, journos*)—Scherherazade could well be clipped to Charade. Like many young Australians, she travels widely, casting nets for her identity and discovering, at least, who she is not.

The various British Empire cousins bear more than a touch of parody. Charade's English relatives are caricatures of pathetic pretention. Canada is portrayed as a respite for the sensible and timid Aunt Kay. The United States is personified by a sympathetic, but clueless mid-life professor who takes himself too seriously. Australia is young, vibrant, a wee bit dazzled by the Northern Hemisphere but ultimately enlightened about the richness of its own culture.

Charade is reared in the Tambourine Rain Forest, near the east coast (barrier reef) of Australia. ". . . my mum would stare and shake her head. Never seen anything like it, she would say. There were always brothers and sisters, older and younger, falling all over one another and me. It was a small and noisy place, a fibro shack with lizards on the walls, and racks and holes that were hung with sacks of spiders' eggs. But I would wedge myself into a corner, two sides protected, cross-legged on the floor, a book propped open on my knees, and I wouldn't even deign to acknowledge the company."

During her erratic, tender affair with Koenig, Charade explains that she is working at odd jobs around the world while searching for her father. Originally, a coincidence draws her together with the physicist. Later, she learns he was born the same year as her father and that his wife bears marked similarities to her mother. The incest metaphor is played out on many levels.

This is not a linear narrative. Reading the novel is rather like scrambling for keys through an untidy desk. You discover a lost letter, a misplaced message, an unfinished task, a whole life to which keys are an incidental distraction. Hospital writes with luminous wit and ripe sensuality about the sublime and the wretched. The most powerful scenes border on taboo:

"When I was six or seven, she says, I found a dead man in the rain forest and I kept him as a pet. He was my secret. I suppose he was a swaggie. . . . And his smell had its hooks into me. . . . Every day I held a handkerchief over

my nose and mouth and watched the ants: the way they embroidered him and covered him with soft brown bunting. Birds spoke to him, and perhaps it was their beaks that punctured his purple balloon-skin. . . . And then he began to deflate, at first quickly with little shudders . . . , but after that slowly, silkily, peacefully, like a glove as a hand withdraws. Each day he was thinner and flatter. I liked him better then, because his smell had escaped from him, bubbling away between the ferns. When he was clean and white inside his muddy clothes, when he smelled as sweet and yeasty as moss, I put flowers in his eyes. You can be my father, I told him."

The novel is also a seductive intellectual exercise in which Charade tries to comprehend her life in the context of Koenig's scientific explanations about chance and probability. "And I subscribe, generally speaking, to the Copenhagen view," Koenig says, leaving the lectern of the bedpost and pacing back and forth from dresser to door. "I think Bohr and Heisenberg won that argument over against Einstein; I think it's past denying. The imprecision of all perception. The observer, by imposing a particular set of questions, also predetermines the answers he will find."

Charade's "particular set of questions" is evoked by the very names of her friends and relatives. Father is Nicholas—"St. Nick"—Truman—"true man." Mother is. Bea—"Queen Bee," whose nature is simply to "be" with her brood of multifathered children in the forest. And the heart of her search is the elusive Verity, in whom lies a strange, important truth.

It is a measure of Hospital's lush talent that none of this seems contrived. She takes the reader on an exuberant tour of quantum physics, Middle Eastern mythology, the comparative cultural legacies of British imperialism and still leaves you caring about her characters. What happens to Charade and Koenig together and apart is left appropriately open. All you know is that they are both the better for their idiosyncratic affair and temporarily at opposite ends of the Earth.

Edith Pearlman (review date October 1991)

SOURCE: A review of *Isobars*, in *Boston Review*, Vol. XVI, No. 5, October, 1991, pp. 27-8.

[*In the following review, Pearlman offers a tempered assessment of* Isobars, *which she finds challenging and vivid, but also confusing and indulgent.*]

The title story begins the collection. Maybe it shouldn't. **"Isobars,"** subtitled **"A Fugue on Memory,"** is a difficult piece of work. It borrows its form from the musical fugue: statement and counterstatement. This unlinear method of telling demands collaboration from the reader who has idly selected the book from the New Fiction table. He may put it down again, confused. The writer makes free with place names unfamiliar to an American: names like Ringwood and Ballarat. (Most of the stories take place in Australia.) The heroine of **"Isobars"** enters in a burst of wordplay as M: "for Made in Melbourne, maid in Melbourne, for memory itself." Next she turns into Em, then Emily. Emily grows up to be a writer, so we can assume that she's a stand-in for Janette Turner Hospital, anticly renaming herself. (The above break is not a misprint. Transitions in this story are made not with words but with typography, within sentences, in an apparent effort to replicate in prose the meteorologist's isobar, an imaginary line on a map connecting places of equal pressure.)

Not an easy story at all. In it Janette Turner Hospital reveals her quirkiness. But she reveals also her strengths. Emily walks with her two grandfathers on the shore of a lake: "With a grandfather at each side like charms at her wrists, Emily flexes her toes, she sinks her bare feet into gurgling mud." We are quickly allied with this child, who makes her bewildered way through the swirls of memory, of events variously interpreted, of cruel episodes—a drowning, a stabbing. Thoreau enters, doing a comic turn. An odd narrative indeed, but a compelling one. By the last paragraph—

> I'll be back, the blade whispers (a sleazy sound, cold as steel against pliant skin). In dream after dream, I'll be back.

—we too feel the knife at our throats.

And then, after this demanding beginning, what indulgences await! Stories throb with incident, erupt with personalities. The method is still fugal—themes stated and restated, time moving in circles. An episode in the present foreshadows one in the past. Characters walk modestly into and out of the action and only later flare into consequence. Motifs—a gold coin, a bicycle—appear flatly and then reappear with hyper-real intensity. Ms. Hospital is master of her technique.

"Uncle Seaborn" tells of a posthumous sibling—a boy born a few weeks after the death of his infant older brother. He feels a disastrously strong affinity for that never-known brother. A generation later their nephew yearns to be part of their lost lives. The waves call to all three. **"Bondi"**— it's the name of a beach; water is everywhere in Janette Hospital's world—introduces us to two young women, cousins, brought up within the same pious sect. In the beginning one is bad and one is good. Their roles don't reverse as we might expect; instead they helicly twist.

"Eggshell Expressway" brilliantly exposes the life of a fifteen-year-old prostitute hooked on angel dust. We become part of the hectic fantasies of one of her customers; we understand through expert interior monologue the girl's passion for the drug; we wince at her suffering at the hands of her pimp, cruelty that seems all the more vicious because the prostitute herself doesn't wince. In **"The Last of the Hapsburgs"** a spinster school teacher in the outback develops a liking for one of her students, a girl born late in life to a pair of maddened survivors of the Holocaust.

The spinster teacher seems at first to be an eccentric letter-writing virgin belonging to an earlier literary tradition: a stock character, though rendered with Ms. Hospital's usual lush precision. But Lucia Davenport is not conventional; she is having a bouncy affair with the local policeman. The girl she likes is gawky, tongue-tied, embarrassed about her loony parents, unaware that she is a beauty in the making. She too seems stock. And so we are not surprised by the teacher's promise to this promising girl: "You'll win scholarships, Rebecca. To university. You'll escape from here."

But we are brought up short by the response.

"Rebecca stopped then, turning, swaying in the haze. 'But this is where we've escaped to,' she said."

Hospital's dialogue is insistent, funny, accurate. Nobody sounds like anybody else. Not a description is slack. An adulterer, just out of bed, "stumbled into the ropey noose of sheets." A headstrong young woman waiting to have her fortune told begins to tat: "fingers flying, a cream silk streamer of crochet snaking out of her hands, twitching, growing, curling under the sofa like some live nervy creature." A boy dives into a lake and discovers a drowned church; "he looked through the rose window and saw a phosphorescent glow, then kept plummeting to the soft Gothic arch. The nave was full of green radiance."

In work as abundant as this there are inevitable excesses. There are punny titles (in **"The Loss of Faith,"** Faith is a woman), occasional portentous abstractions, and all those damned place names. These last can be slyly evocative, though; sliding from British to Aboriginal, they hint at the variety of the Continent. "People began driving out from Townsville and Ayr and Home Hill, from Charters Towers and Collinsville, and from any number of smaller salt-of-North Queensland towns: Thalanga, Mungunburra, Millaroo, Mingela."

The author is as various as the names—a conscious artist who uses metaphor, simile, and alliteration; French and blasphemy; scripture and song.

Nancy Engbretsen Schaumburger (review date Winter 1991-92)

SOURCE: "What Do Men Really Want?," in *Belles Lettres*, Vol. 7, No. 2, Winter, 1991-92, pp. 18-19.

[In the following review, Schaumburger offers a positive assessment of Isobars.*]*

As a fervent admirer of Janette Turner Hospital's first collection of stories, **Dislocations,** I must reluctantly admit to a twinge of disappointment with her latest, **Isobars.** Perhaps it is because of the author's—as yet—unsure handling of the elements some reviewers have likened to magic realism, but that seems to me more akin to the metaphysical twists in Muriel Spark's fiction. Yet, Hospital deserves commendation for embarking on such a complex, promising artistic experiment, even if it does not always succeed.

Isobars are imaginary lines on a weather map connecting places of equal barometric pressure. Similarly, all of Hospital's characters are torn between past and present, between their Australian homeland and long-ago relationships that they have postponed resolving and their location now (often cities in the United States and Canada). In short, they exist *between* the connections or, to put it another way, they are all haunted (sometimes literally).

The grim title story is a "fugue" on many memories—from Thoreau's to a five-year-old girl's—about grieving mothers, drowned children, murdered women, raped women. **"Isobars"** suggests that we must choose between safe indifference to the persistent violence of men against women and children or "march to a different drummer" and pay the price of involvement, possibly death. All the characters are surrounded by primal bodies of water from Walden Pond to the Pacific Ocean. These watery depths and uneasy memories reinforce Hospital's theme that human things change with geologic slowness, if at all.

One of her most teasing, effective stories, **"A Little Night Music,"** concerns a white-knuckled flight from London to Singapore of people who are mostly originally scheduled passengers of a previous plane, blown to bits by a terrorist bomb. Lucy has taken Valium and whiskey to lessen her fear of lightning striking twice. A late-boarding male passenger sits next to her. As they listen to "Concert Above the Clouds," they occasionally bump each other and soon fall into a brief, passionate embrace. His only communication, repeatedly, is "I'm sorry." Lucy lapses into a terrifying dream of tunnels and the other passenger with a lantern. When she awakens, he has vanished; the stewardess never saw him. His photograph, though, is in the morning paper. He is a well-known terrorist who exploded with his victims on the missed flight. Is Lucy hallucinating or has she been on a trip to heaven and hell with a ghostly guide?

Another experiment, this one a sex farce and entirely successful, is **"The Chameleon Condition."** It concerns a child-like man named Adam, whose complicated philandering leads to a nervous disease in which his whole body embarrassingly changes color from nausea green to remorseful yellow. Finally, poetic justice reduces him to desperation by means of a dream of the three women he has most disappointed cheerfully playing cards in a warm, glass-enclosed room; he stands outside, invisible to them all, despite turning feverish rainbows of color.

Another Adam, in the tragicomic **"The Loss of Faith,"** thinks he sees his Australian ex-wife, Faith, on a New York subway on the day she dies. The adult daughter who "forgave him least" calls with the news and, separately, they have the identical memory of a happy family day at the beach, complete with Adam smelling surf and experi-

encing innocence. He too dreams of a time when "not a thing has gone wrong yet." The crux of this quirky story of paradise lost, though, is the astute, tired conclusion of the young Smith alumna whom Adam beds as he shakily confesses his sins: "The love life of male intellectuals . . . continues to be a quest for the perfect listener." How true, we nod wryly, and how sad.

Men in Hospital's stories tend to be recognizable types, barbarians or babies, seeking salvation through women. **"I Saw Three Ships"** features an elderly, alcoholic, guilt-ridden veteran who sits on a chilly beach waiting for a mysterious, beautiful girl to make her regular appearance. In language suggestive of "Kubla Khan," he perceives her as the angel of his redemption. Like the Smith alumna, she too listens, and she unknowingly brings grace to the veteran with her mermaid-singing on Christmas Day.

"Here and Now," the last and best of this collection, focuses on the meeting of mutual solace between Walter, a ninety-year-old scholar, and his fifty-year-old colleague Alison, both longing for Australia at a Canadian college party. He lost a son in Australia years ago, she just lost her mother; both are grieving for a gentler, simpler time. Walter, an exceptional man with an arresting manner like that of the Ancient Mariner, tells an anecdote about the unexpected kindness of Australians in an epidemic of beached whales; they formed a bucket-brigade and kept the creatures alive with great tenderness. Alison asks when this remarkable event in his Methuselah-like life occurred, and he replies, inspired, "Here and now!" One wishes it were only so.

Hospital performs a virtuoso-like turn in this slim collection. Her work is deepening, taking risks, and often triumphing. One looks forward with pleasurable curiosity to her next effort.

Janette Turner Hospital with Missy Daniel (interview date 14 September 1992)

SOURCE: "Janette Turner Hospital: The Australian Writer Finds Inspiration for Her Fiction in Her Own 'Dislocated' Life," in *Publishers Weekly,* September 14, 1992, pp. 80-1.

[*In the following interview, Hospital discusses* The Last Magician *and the influence of place and personal experience on her fiction.*]

Janette Turner Hospital is, simply put, a natural Scheherazade.

It's not just that she saw in Scheherazade, who told tales to save her life, "the perfect narrative framework" for her 1989 novel *Charades.* It's that the primitive force of her fiction, its command of the sensuous as well as the spiritual, leads a reader of her five novels and two collections of stories to believe that she, too, is telling tales to stave something off, to "negotiate" her own life. In *The Last*

Magician, her newest novel, published this month by Holt, Hospital explores the secrets of the Queensland rain forest as well as life in the demimonde "quarry" of Sydney, Australia, the country of her birth, and she uses a hooker who quotes Milton and a Chinese-Australian photographer who quotes Lao-Tze to tell a harsh and desperate tale about what she identifies as "the murky underside of respectability."

"Various establishment systems—the law, the academic world, the literary world—are put on trial and found severely wanting," she says of her new novel, while sitting on the deck at her home in Kingston, Ontario. The house sits in a thickly wooded spot where the St. Lawrence River meets Lake Ontario, at the point where the magnificent Thousand Islands begin to dot the river. "But it's wider than that. I locate the quarry, a metaphor for the underside of the city, in Sydney, but I don't mean it to be specifically Sydney or even specifically Australia. It's really about the underside of Western society."

Hospital was born in Melbourne and grew up in Brisbane. A small, blond dynamo of a woman who will turn 50 later this year, she left Australia for the U.S. in 1967 together with her husband, Cliff, a comparative religion scholar whose specialty is Sanskrit and who now teaches at Queens University in Kingston, Ontario. And so began a nomadic life that has led her to Boston and Cambridge, to India, London, Los Angeles, Canada, Australia and back again. She has taught writing at MIT and Boston University as well as in Ottawa, Sydney, and Monash, and now she spends half of every year teaching at La Trobe University in Melbourne.

Hospitals first novel, *The Ivory Swing,* received Canada's prestigious Seal Award in 1982; it was issued here the following year. *The Tiger in the Tiger Pit* (1984) and *Borderline* (1985) confirmed her talent and her prolificity. All three were published by Dutton and reprinted by Bantam. Bantam published her fourth, *Charades,* in both hardcover and paperback, and Louisiana State University Press issued two volumes of stories, *Dislocations* (1988) and *Isobars* (1991).

The Last Magician is Hospital's first book with agent Molly Friedrich, and her first with Holt and editor Marian Wood, whom Hospital describes as "an immensely alert and intelligent reader. She also has an absolutely extraordinary photographic memory. I really want an editor who I feel has deep empathy with the manuscript and with me," she explains. "When I bleed she bleeds—and it's always been 'she' with me. I've never had a male editor." Her longtime Canadian editor is Ellen Seligman at McClelland and Stewart. In London it's Lynn Knight at Virago, and in Australia it's Rosanne Fitzgibbons at the University of Queensland Press. *The Last Magician* received keen reviews in England, and was reported to be "widely tipped" for the Booker Prize.

"The fact that I was mugged once in inner-city Boston, and then went to live in inner-city Sydney while teaching

at the university there, also had a big bearing on the shape the novel took," Hospital reveals. "I talked to male and female street prostitutes and street kids, and sat on the steps of soup kitchens for the homeless and talked to people there. The story I kept hearing again and again was that among their regular clients were people whose faces they saw in the newspapers—politicians, judges, lawyers, and cops—and that paradox fascinated me. Law keepers, the guardians of law, order and morality, consort all the time with the lawbreakers—that was what I wanted to explore."

"The world is thick with messages, . . . crowded with absences," observes Hospital, who traces both views in this novel. Many of the other themes familiar to readers of her earlier work will be found again in *The Last Magician.* There are people who disappear, people who are dislocated, people in transit, people who cross borders, people who can't speak. There is the potency of place, particularly the lush and wanton Australian rain forest. There are preoccupations with judgment, power, atonement, revelations, love and memory. There are old wounds, absences, secrets, silences, and open endings. We all inherit plots and then ride them like treadmills, as Hospital has written elsewhere.

But the theme of being silenced, of being without a voice, is especially powerful in the new novel. "That's always been of interest to me in my writing—to give a voice to the people who don't have one in the normal media channels or in literature. But I also felt in a rather scary way that I was writing about my own silencing, which was just engulfing me. I was writing about my own experience as an intellectual and literary figure in Australia. It certainly has to be said that Australia's not a nurturing environment either for intellectual or literary women, and in fact it often sets out to be incredibly destructive.

"I didn't think I'd be able to finish the book. I had to make little deals with myself, trick myself into finishing it. I knew there were going to be terrible penalties for saying the things I wanted to say about the hostility of authority systems. I felt that when I finished I'd probably never write again. It was the first time ever that I finished a novel and was not already in the space of the next one. But I've reached the stage now where I'm yearning to write some stories that were brewing in Australia, especially about my trips through the outback. It's a good sign."

Hospital has written one mystery novel, *A Very Proper Death,* published under the pseudonym Alex Juniper by Random House in Canada and by Scribners in the U.S. But *The Last Magician,* she says, is also "an intricate murder mystery. The last magician is the one who outmagics all the others, who's in possession of the truth, who removes all the illusions. He's a photographer who simply monitors, records and stores things, which I think is a metaphor for the artist. He doesn't always know the significance of a photograph when he takes it, and in fact the murder is solved 20 years after it took place, from a photograph, from the retroactive significance that a viewer realizes years later." But there's more than one murder mystery to this novel, and the solution to the second is not nearly so incontrovertible as the first.

The story's ending is genuinely ambiguous. "Right from my very first novel I have always had open endings," Hospital acknowledges. "In **Borderline** I wanted to make the reader feel the real horror, the trauma of refugees who never know for sure if their loved ones are dead or alive. But it is very much the basic experience of my much-dislocated life that relationships end, and years later open again. There is no such thing as a final chord until the last final chord, until we die."

But the opening chord of **The Last Magician** is emphatic. It is a clear allusion to Dante's *Inferno,* and so it should come as no surprise that Hospital is also a scholar of medieval literature. She says she was "electrified on multiple levels" five years ago when she saw some photographs by Sebastio Salgado in the *New York Times* of the Serra Pelada gold mine in Brazil—thousands of peasant slaves swarming up and down the steep sides of a huge pit, like a vision of hell. "It seemed like a Bosch canvas, it was so arrestingly horrific. And it resonated with my inner landscape of nightmares and night terrors after being mugged. But I am also steeped in Dante, and the image of the pit immediately made me think of Botticelli's drawings of the Inferno. It was two portrayals of the same scene, one in the 15th century and one in the 20th century. It's not that I really thought it out. I just knew from the kind of humming I got in my head and the vibrations in my body that all of this had something to do with a novel. But I had no idea what, or where I was going to set it.

"Then I went off to teach in Sydney and lived on a street on the cusp between being semi-slum and being gentrified. One end was burned out, boarded up, abandoned buildings lived in by squatters and derelicts—'derros' in Australian slang. Kids lived in the basements and on the sidewalks. They lived in the subway station, which was tunneled into the rock cliffs in the ravines [beneath the city.] I felt I was somehow moving in the landscape of these photographs and the Botticelli drawings. By that time the ferment level in my mind was quite high. I was zipping back and forth as I constantly do when I'm in Australia, from Brisbane to Sydney and back to the rain forest, putting it all together."

"Ideas and subjects just grab me by the scruff of the neck. I get the abstract central conception of the novel first, and a vivid sense of place and locale comes early on. Then the characters, and last of all the plot. It's just something I simply discover. Once I've got my central conception, my place, my characters, I set out, and I literally don't know where I'm going. I find out when I've written the novel what's going to happen."

In Hospital's imagined world the powerful emotions and events of childhood are often played off against those of adulthood, and **The Last Magician** is no exception. Asked about the moving, terrifying childhood games and taunts that enter into the narrative, Hospital confesses, "I lived opposite a cutting in the railway line both in Melbourne and in Brisbane, and we played daredevil games as kids. We used to lie on the tracks, and the boy next door always claimed that if you would lie parallel, inside them, the train could pass over you. I suppose there are certain little fragments, splinters of yourself, that do get into characters," she allows.

"I suppose I remember the past so well because in primary school I was, by imposed necessity, a loner"—she came from an intensely conservative and fundamentalist religious family—" so you become a very acute observer. You're always trying to translate to yourself what's going on, and you play things over in your mind, trying to figure out their meaning, because it's all foreign to you, trying to learn behaviors, what other kids do. You become a very close and sharp observer. Then, too, when you're wrenched from and geographically dislocated from your past, you have an intense motivation to hang onto it, to recall it. Plus there's just loss. I miss the Queensland rain forest so much. You hang onto the images of the things you pine for."

But Hospital is adamantly not an expatriate writer. "That's a label other people put onto you," she says. "There's the whole issue of nationality. I'm constantly being asked to account for this—'Do you consider yourself an Australian writer? A Canadian writer?' I am just someone whose life has been exceedingly nomadic, but unintentionally so. I am deeply and viscerally attached particularly to Brisbane, also to this spot in Kingston, to Boston, to a village in South India—all these places leave permanent grooves in my life, and they matter to me. The countries that vilify their writers who leave, and regard it as a species of treason if you go—Australia, India, Canada, Ireland—it's a sign of postcolonial cringe. England and America, countries that have a strong enough sense of themselves, never do it and don't feel threatened, but the colonies do."

One way to handle the pain of life, of course, is to write. "That's why it's so difficult to write," Hospital admits. "It's so painful to reactivate the old pains; it's a risky thing to do for one's own well-being. But these things lurk. They catch you off guard, and their potency is not lessened for lying dormant. And the safest way to deal with them is in coded form, in as labyrinthine and transposed a way as possible. You try to let the pain seep away."

For this passionately Australian writer who has shown that she has the straight-out gift for telling a story, perhaps even the silences, in the end, will speak.

Richard Eder (review date 20 September 1992)

SOURCE: "Down Underworld," in *Los Angeles Times Book Review,* September 20, 1992, pp. 3, 12.

[*In the following review, Eder offers a generally favorable assessment of* The Last Magician, *though he finds fault in the novel's slow and disorienting start.*]

To get to the Australian rain forest from downtown Brisbane, you take Ann Street, go right on George to Roma Street, and follow the northwest artery as it successively becomes Kelvin Grove Road, Enoggera Road and Samford Road. After an hour or so, "you will cross that indistinct and provisional line where the city of Greater Brisbane could perhaps be said to end, and primordial time could be said to begin."

Thus, in this opening passage of her Gothic mystery-tale of contemporary evil [*The Last Magician*], Janette Turner Hospital connects the matter-of-fact everyday world with the realm of the mythic. It is as if "The Divine Comedy" started by listing the bus transfers Dante had to make to reach the middle of his life's road and the dark wood where he begins his visit to Hell.

The Last Magician refers to Dante repeatedly. In the swirling montage of images that make up its first part and color the more coherent narrative that eventually emerges, there is the recurring vision of a vortex of damnation. There are references to an old engraved illustration of the descending circles in the Inferno, and to a recent photograph of a Brazilian gold mine where the brutalized workers struggle on swaying ladders from one level to the next. Throughout, there is the central symbol of the Quarry: a metastasizing underworld of wretchedness—part realistic and part allegorical—that Hospital sets in catacombs below the sunny prosperity of Sydney, where much of the action takes place.

The author writes in a densely mannered style, and often with powerful beauty. We need the beauty because, for a long time, very little is clear. Lucy, the narrator, collapses in a London cinema when she sees an art film made by Charlie, whom she knew several years earlier in Sydney, and who suddenly disappeared. There were other disappearances, that of Lucy's lover Gabriel among them. Certain shots in the film rip open a scar of tormented memories and, beyond that, a seam of mystery and evil that goes back two generations. Lucy flies immediately to Sydney to take up the quest—the one halted by Charlie's and Gabriel's disappearance.

At first we get scrambled fragments of story and characters. There is a pervading sense of universal sickness, a piercing note of denunciation, and striking images that seem to know their places but refuse to reveal them to us. It is as if Hospital were running her own film in fast-rewind, showing everything on the screen but allowing it no pattern. The rewind is not fast enough; it takes nearly 150 pages, and by that time, a reader's intention to seek may succumb to the author's intention to hide.

What has been hidden and hinted at so demandingly, though, emerges as a story of high tension and terrifying allure. It begins as dangerous games among five children on a farm outside Brisbane 40 years ago. One of the boys, Robby Gray, is rich and cowardly; one of the girls, Cat, is dirt-poor and fearless. There is Cat's little brother, Willy,

who is slow-witted and whom she fiercely protects. The other two—Catherine and Charlie—are willing captives to Cat's untamed vitality.

So is Robby, but in a sick and twisted fashion. By birth and family position, he should be king of the mountain, but he is scared of mountains. He loves Cat as the others do, but to him, love means power and possession. In a loathsome and brutal way, he exercises his power, and the innocent Willy is accidentally killed as a result. When the authorities act, Robby's family standing shields him, and Cat is sent to reform school. Her wild spirit labels her incorrigible, and pushes her to repeated efforts to escape. Finally, it leads her to take to the streets as a prostitute; to disappear—in the book's thematic image—into the Quarry.

Robby grows up to become Robertson Gray; sleek, assured, a judge, and a powerful member of the Establishment in Sydney. Catherine and Charlie, haunted by the memory of Cat and of what was done to her, grow up trying to come to terms with what they know. They become lovers, then split up and go abroad. She returns from London after a few years and becomes a prominent TV interviewer. He stays in New York as a photographer. Photography provides *The Last Magician* with one of its major themes and with the engine of its plot. The ability of the camera to catch what even the photographer doesn't know is there—"to let me see what I have seen," as Charlie puts it—instill in him the conviction that he can recover the past and bring Gray to account.

Charlie returns to Sydney in the late 1980s, 25 years after he left it. His quest is soon joined by Gabriel, Gray's estranged son. Lucy, Gabriel's lover, becomes their witness and the book's narrator. The quest is for Cat—there are some shadowy suggestions that she may be working the Sydney underworld—but it becomes something much broader.

Hospital's theme is corruption; specifically, the corruption of power. It is a power that, under the pretext of order and social necessity, maintains itself comfortably on top of a cesspool. When necessary, it will use any violent means to secure itself. Gray personifies the corruption as he has since childhood. He is on top and Cat is in the Quarry.

Or, as it turns out, not. Before the book ends, in a pattern suggesting the downward spirals of Dantean Hell, we read of other crimes. When Gray is in his 30s, Cat gets on a trolley car he is riding with his first wife and little Gabriel. That night, Gray comes home all bloody; the next day, he leaves his wife. Years later, the bones of a young woman, scored by stab marks, are found wedged under a rock in the rapids where Gray, Cat and the others once played. Charlie's and Gabriel's disappearance follows warnings that prominent people in Sydney want them to stop their quest. And when Lucy, who had fled, returns to Sydney to take up this quest once more, she finds a photograph that seems to link Gray to the vanishings.

Hospital wields her story and characters with the larger-than-life bravura of an Expressionist allegory. Everything is deliberately too much. Both Gabriel and Lucy represent a younger generation determined to breach the gulf between privilege and the Quarry. Gabriel—not very convincingly—has become a muckraking investigator of his father's world even before Charlie conveniently finds him. Lucy, even less convincingly, was a brilliant student, and when Charlie meets her, she is having a postgraduate cultural and social experience by working in a high-society brothel. She mixes raunchy street talk with quotations from Milton.

Gray is loathsome all the way through. Even his cuff links and the way he eats oysters at fashionable dinner parties are loathsome. His third wife—a deconstructionist feminist who is mean to the hired help; I expect Hospital is settling scores—matches him.

Hospital's magnifications and simplifications can be jarring, even silly, particularly before we get some hold on the outsized story her outsized methods are revealing. Yet even at her most arbitrary, the author is never careless or coarse. Her writing has perfect pitch; at its wildest, it retains a golden refinement. So do her themes, for all their odd twists. She takes many risks and most of them work; the one that doesn't is our long wandering through the dark wood of her initial montage, and the long time it may take us before we can trust her there. Good she is, but she's not Virgil.

Jonathan Coe (review date 24 September 1992)

SOURCE: "Syndey's Inferno," in *London Review of Books,* September 24, 1992, p. 22.

[*In the following review of* The Last Magician, *Coe finds fault in the novel's unconvincing narrator and gratuitous literary allusions.*]

Mess is one of the distinguishing features of Janette Turner Hospital's writing, but also one of its abiding themes: and part of the reader's difficulty has always been to decide how much of the mess is intention, and how much miscalculation. The characters in *Borderline,* her 1985 novel which has many formal similarities with *The Last Magician* (including an obsession with Dante), are all engaged in transgressing boundaries, whether willingly or not, and the title story of her collection *Isobars* makes explicit its preoccupation with 'ideas of order' imposed upon a messy and shifting reality. Lines drawn on a map, she wrote in that story, are 'talismanic' and represent 'the magical thinking of quantitative and rational people'. Her latest novel gives this notion an urgent political twist, by supposing that the 'ideas of order' entertained by our governing classes are equally talismanic, and that their regulating power is in fact just as illusory as the power of isobars to make sense of 'the sloshing flood of time and space'. From the perspective of a smart garden party overlooking Sydney harbour, the line separating order (of which Hospital

disapproves, because it's authoritarian) from chaos (of which she approves, because it's human) is called sharply into question: 'Where else,' her narrator asks, 'is the membrane between manicured lawn and quarry so wafer thin?' The 'quarry' referred to here is a nightmarish warren into which Sydney's underclass has been driven: Hospital likes to describe it in terms of Dante's hellish circles, its outer regions consisting of seedy pubs and bars, its innermost recesses taking the form of hideaways beneath railway tunnels and tube lines. Somewhere inside this labyrinth there is a woman called Cat, and the search to find her keeps the plot's engine ticking over, although the narrator is certainly in no hurry to let us know why it should be so important. Eventually we learn of a childhood trauma. A quartet of friends indulge in a dangerous game which goes tragically wrong. When the blame is laid, unjustly, on Cat, she is sent away to reform school and from that day onward can never be persuaded to speak. One of the participants and chief witnesses to the injustice, a young prig called Robinson Gray, keeps quiet about his part in it and grows up to be a distinguished judge even while the secret continues to burn away inside him. The other two children, one called (confusingly) Catherine and the other a Chinese Australian by the name of Charlie Chang, spend the rest of their horrified lives trying to make contact with Cat, tracing her fleeting appearances through strip joints, prisons and police files in Sydney and Brisbane.

Chang finally makes a career out of photography—which makes him the 'last magician' of the title—and his photographs become one of the key devices through which the narrative gets filtered. Their quizzical, open-eyed, receptive viewpoint is the one which the book clearly endorses, and an implicit contrast is set up with Robinson Gray's sinister, furtive power-mongering. One flashback to their school debating society finds them on opposite sides. The subject is 'Triage' (which is the bête noire of the whole novel)—the theory that 'in times of crisis or natural disaster, it is legitimate, in the interests of a stable society, and for the greater good of the majority, for the authorities to establish a system of priorities; that is, it is legitimate to ask, *If all cannot be saved, who then should be saved?*' Gray proposes the motion, Chang opposes it, and the headmaster judges Gray the winner for successfully arguing that 'the ability to be intelligently "cruel" when the occasion demands is the hallmark of enduring civilisations.' This is a bald statement of the attitude *The Last Magician* sets out to rail against, and which it shows to be fixed in the psyche of the power-hungry as immovably as the rituals of a children's game.

The novel's polemic, then, is loud and forthright: but there's a good deal of apparatus to dismantle before we can arrive at it. The narrator of these events is Lucy, a call-girl turned TV researcher, who is a generation younger than the traumatised quartet but becomes a close friend of both Charlie and Catherine, as well as having an affair with Robinson Gray's son, Gabriel. This makes for a peculiar narrative perspective: at once distanced from the action by the intervention of a third person, we are also brought uncomfortably close to it by virtue of her intense emotional involvement. Hospital used this effect in **Borderline,** where the narrator was a piano tuner called Jean-Marc whose life only occasionally intersected with those of the protagonists. The problem with such an approach is that it makes enormous demands on the character in question: the voice and the range of sympathies must be much more than usually flexible. And in some ways Lucy fits the bill. She's a one-time private schoolgirl who sheds her snobbish attitudes following a youthful encounter at a railway station with another girl who spits at her for being a 'prissy little fancy-pants cunt'. The ease with which she discards her former identity derives from her gift for 'shapeshifting' ('from time to time, I find myself inside the skin of other people'), and we get a graphic illustration of this when, on the same day and the same railway platform, a middle-aged woman exposes herself to the assembled crowd and Lucy suddenly finds that she identifies with her vividly, so that 'through some unimaginable, unconscionable error, she is exposed, without underwear, to a mob'.

Despite all the hard work she has put into giving her a plausible history, though, Hospital continues to ask too much of her narrator. Doubts about Lucy arise quite early in the novel, when she takes a ferry across the harbour to Manly and finds herself being chatted up by a sleazeball. Her peppering of the subsequent conversation with literary and artistic references may, I suppose, be a ploy to deter his advances: more likely, it's the author's way of smuggling in the allusive baggage which she feels (mistakenly) will give the novel resonance. These awkwardly colloquial manoeuvrings ('You ever read the Russian novelists?' 'You heard of Titian?') do nothing except guarantee the sacrifice of credibility on the altar of a pointless intertextuality. Lucy describes herself, at one point, as having 'an inconveniently busy and sceptical mind'. But this is disingenuous, because the busy-ness of her mind is nothing if not convenient for the author, enabling her to drop in those all-important gestures towards Dante ('You know what else it reminds me of? . . . Dante's Inferno. The Botticelli drawings. Have you seen them?'), and even a few references to art movies—always thrown off, of course, with the same note of assumed vagueness ('like one of those European movies . . . something by that Italian director', 'like someone in a mournful intellectual movie . . . one of those slow bleak things by that Japanese bloke'). By turning her into such a compulsive name-dropper, Hospital makes it increasingly difficult for us to believe in Lucy's stated preference for low-life company over Sydney's literati. In the scene at the posh garden party she makes a beeline for the barman, saying that 'I do feel at home with the people who tap off beer and dole out icecubes for the cocktail crowd': but why should this be, if what she really wants to talk about is Browning and De Sica? By now we might well feel that Lucy's shape-shifting, her chameleonic crossing of borders, is essentially a function of the various uses which the author intends to put her to, so that the decision to interpose her

between the reader and some of the novel's most significant events can only dilute their impact.

Luckily this is not a fatal flaw, since the most powerful passages in the book—the scenes describing the all-important childhood incident—are presented without too much of Lucy's mediating presence. Hospital seems a little nervous that these passages are going to strike people as lurid, because she allows herself some moments of overt self-justification in which she makes sarcastic calls for a literature of 'modesty and social decorum . . . a literature that is unassertive, limpid, economical and lean' (all of which **The Last Magician** is most certainly not). Such tactics are still considered tricksy and newfangled by some readers (and critics), who perhaps forget that the privilege of authorial self-criticism dates back at least to the introductory chapters of *Tom Jones*. In Hospital's case, they are, all the same, unnecessary: few novelists have written with such authority about childish passions and the influence they carry over into what passes for adulthood. It isn't only the reader's relief at being allowed to bask in the waters of realism after the necessary thorniness of the earlier sections: more importantly, Hospital's imagination takes fire at this point, and the descriptions of Cat, Charlie, Robinson and Catherine as they pass from idyllic play at Cedar Creek Falls to disaster and recrimination are filled—as befits a novel of this title—with a dark and terrible magic. Other affecting touches are less insistently signalled, such as the unobtrusively devastating moment when the six-year-old Gabriel realises the depth of contempt his father feels for his mother, as he watches him cutting in on a newspaper reporter to save him the wasted effort of seeking his wife's opinion on anything. The leaps of sympathy which Hospital performs at times like this make her more overtly adventurous techniques seem laboured: it's ironic, really, that they should turn out to be the most memorable features of a novel which professes such vigorous disdain for 'modest late 20th-century social realism'.

Diane Turbide (review date 5 October 1992)

SOURCE: "Circles of Hell," in *Macleans,* October 5, 1992, p. 66.

[*In the following review, Turbide offers a positive assessment of* The Last Magician.]

When Janette Turner Hospital described her new novel to an audience of booksellers in Toronto in July, she linked her dense, lush writing style to the rain forest in Queensland, Australia, where she grew up. "The rain forest is nature at its most baroque," said the internationally acclaimed writer, 50, now based in Kingston, Ont. "My prose reflects that." As in much of her earlier work, Hospital's fifth and most ambitious novel, **The Last Magician,** possesses a narrative as twisting and tangled as jungle undergrowth. Part mystery, part philosophical exploration, it tells an intricate tale of sexual obsession, corruption and murder. But its essence is an emotionally charged meditation on loss and absence, on time and memory, on the head's ability to deny what the heart knows. Lucy, the book's main narrator, struggles to make sense of old, unresolved traumas, trying, writes the author, "to salvage the future and predict the changeable past."

The Last Magician extends some of the concerns that have marked Hospital's prize-winning earlier works. Her four previous novels and two short-story collections are packed with imagery of black holes, borders and chasms—danger spots on the psychological or physical terrain. Her characters are sensitive people living on the edge. They are often rootless, straddling respectable society and a symbiotically linked netherworld of violence.

In *The Last Magician,* Hospital takes those ideas to a new and richly satisfying level. At the heart of the story is a horrifying childhood death that took place decades ago and continues to haunt four people. One of them is Charlie Chang, a Chinese-Australian photographer and experimental film-maker through whose eyes the death is re-enacted. In the past, he is among a group of children who play a dangerous game of chicken on railway tracks. The most recklessly brave is Cat, a tomboyish waif from the wrong side of town whose independent spirit fascinates and disturbs the others. "The trouble with Cat's kind of power is that there are people who develop a passion to break it," observes Charlie, who worships her. The ones who try to break her are private-school boys, including Robinson Gray, who both loves and fears Cat. One day, the railway game goes too far, and tragedy follows.

In a masterful scene that depicts how the wheels of society run roughshod over the powerless, the authorities find Cat responsible while the real perpetrators escape. She is sent to reform school, an event that begins a long cycle of imprisonment, escape and self-destruction as a stripper and prostitute. The others lose track of her. Charlie flees to New York City, while Robinson marries, has a son, Gabriel, and becomes a respected judge.

It is Gabriel and his lover, Lucy, the prostitute-narrator, who set things in motion again. Gabriel is on his own quest to find Cat; an accidental meeting on a streetcar between his parents and Cat when he was six changed his life irrevocably. "The riddle kept eating him," Hospital writes of Gabriel's confusion about Cat's role. "He was ravenous."

Eventually, Gabriel and Charlie collaborate to find Cat. Their search takes them to the quarry, an underground system of caves and tunnels near Sydney, which has been claimed by squatters, pimps, prostitutes and drug addicts—and which Hospital compares to Dante's Inferno. And by linking it to the city's establishment—especially the lawyers, judges, and policemen who frequent it as customers—Hospital creates an unforgettable image of the pervasiveness of violence and the equally strong desire to ignore

it. "The quarry is leaking into the city, and the city is seeping quarrywards," she writes. "Everyone knows this, but everyone denies it."

Hospital pushes at the borders of conventional narrative, retracing the same ground from different points of view and superimposing new layers of interpretation. Her technique is close to Charlie's photographic method, which she describes as "mutational collage." Charlie's photos, which Lucy deconstructs in detail, ultimately provide the clues to what happened to Cat. When Lucy asks the powerfully intuitive Charlie, the magician of the title, why he takes so many pictures, he responds, "So that I will see what I have seen." His enigmatic explanation suggests that things the conscious mind suppresses are important.

Richly allusive, *The Last Magician*'s plot sometimes threatens to disappear amid all the literary sleight of hand. But the sensuousness of the prose—and the unforgettable image of the quarry—more than compensate. Hospital's new book provides ample evidence that she has some impressive tricks up her sleeve.

Louis K. MacKendrick (review date Winter 1992-93)

SOURCE: "Clever By Far," in *Essays on Canadian Writing,* No. 48, Winter, 1992-93, pp. 55-9.

[*In the following review, MacKendrick provides an analysis of the characters and themes in* Isobars, *concluding that the volume is "a distinctive, accomplished, and completely engaging collection."*]

The great majority of the 18 stories in Janette Turner Hospital's *Isobars* have an Australian setting. Those few with a North American locale seem more predictable and even lugubrious; they are flatter in style and more linear, altogether less apt to fracture time and voice in their narration. In short, they are less lyric in manner, less playful—for most of those stories of the Land Down Under have their own particular lightness of being and even, if the word is not cross-examined, luminosity. They range from the conventional to the refreshingly peculiar, from the sombre to the transcendental. Many are singularly stylish. A pallid recital of plot elements would be a self-defeating exercise, given Hospital's cheerful, even cheeky predilection for employing narrative and temporal slips and dislocations in her story lines: the classical unities are sometimes observed only in their complete breach. A quick perusal, then, of some of *Isobars*'s interesting and attractive features.

The title story, subtitled **"A Fugue on Memory,"** initially links meteorological plotting with its imaginative/creative counterpart. This is a kind of punning wit that Hospital frequently manifests, even indulges, in this collection. The story's events are linked by bodies of water, as one action is perceived and interpreted from differing viewpoints at different times. Furthermore, actions and times are conflated, for "An isobar is an imaginary line connecting places of equal pressure on a map" (33). This is a remarkable fiction, as much for its technique as for its arresting content: the words *brutal, subtle, insidious, murderous, suggestive, sly, rationalizing,* and *obscure* would not be out of place in any attempt to describe the feeling, the manner, and the narrative of this story. More directly, and more figuratively, at times some of these stories seem to echo particular techniques, or characters, or situations, along varying lines of narrative pressure: they employ what E. M. Forster described as "rhythm" in his *Aspects of the Novel* (1927)—repetition plus variation.

The collection opens with **"The Mango Tree,"** one of a clutch of stories dealing with sometimes eccentric family relationships. The story has a not completely comfortable focus on the religious beliefs of the narrator's family, and on the narrator's separation from his family's religious insistence in his secular world. He has recognized "the kind of holy innocence that can inflict appalling damage" (11), and the coexistent polarities of anger and love are richly evident. This is not a typical Hospital fiction, for she does not often write the same story. There may be repeated situations, modes, characters, relationships, and even peculiarities of style, but these exist in a usually satisfactory number of permutations and combinations. This said, **"The Second Coming of Come-by-Chance,"** a story filled with mock-religious terminology, is about a formerly drowned town that resurfaces in a drought, preceded by the reappearance of the Anglican church. However, there are gaps in the sequence of events, or in what appear to be events— was there a rape, and, if so, was it committed by aborigines or policemen? Even the title contains a deliberate pun on its carnal and religious connotations. The narrative perspective begins in irony, or with cheerily offhand and contrary humour; thereafter it veers to the fantastical, and then into pathos and darker imaginings, only to end with the superior and dismissive tone of a journalistic editorial.

Other family stories include **"Morgan Morgan,"** about a narrator's extravagant Welsh grandfather who comes to stand for the truths contained in fabrications, fictions, and wishes. **"Bondi"** looks at two female cousins, one a free-spirited, touchingly "bad" girl—restless, daring, provocative. But the story has one moment of delicious comedy, an affray on a beach described in exaggeratedly epical and quasi-medieval terms—this in a narrative that ends soberly with heavy implications about the loss of innocence (not necessarily in youth) and the intrusion of the world's hedonistic ugliness. In **"The Bloody Past, The Wandering Future"** a family's particular themes, its adherences, are traced through several generations: this appears to be one of Hospital's favourite narrative strategies. In **"Uncle Seaborn,"** we are told that "the past conferred meaning" (61): the theme is another relative constant in such family fictions. Here, however, we are given a practical demonstration of it. It is not a lip-service theme, an abstraction at the centre—Hospital's stories are usually too unsettled, unsettling, kinetic, mobile, to permit such settlement and convenience. This story also belongs to several genera-

tions: it portrays the family's sustaining, life-and-death relationship with the sea, with one of their dead, and with their inherited treasures. Here, too, are touches of the mystical or, more properly, the supernatural—not an unfamiliar element in *Isobars.*

"A Little Night Music" is a completely conventional ghost story about terrorism and an airline disaster. However, due to Hospital's custom of ranging from the traditional to the eccentric within an identifiable type of story, **"Eggshell Expressway"** is passing strange. It, too, is a ghost story, but one with a strongly sexual component and a compelling cast: an addicted teenaged hooker, her pimp, a dead and obsessed judge. To these dramatis personae Hospital adds puns ("Lisa who wears her habit like a nun" [142]); a wonderfully explicit and beautifully comic scene of fellation; sadistic lashings; other raw and brutal details; and a compelling description of a black, hedonistic, irresistible pit of desire, satisfaction, and suicide, to create a story that holds many pleasures and horrid delights.

A ghost also appears at the outset of **"The Loss of Faith."** The author's impulse here would seem to have been sheerly parabolic, though the fictional license is not necessarily exercised. Adam's first wife, Faith, dies, but she is not the only woman in his life: the light and meaningless part of the story is his compulsive recitation to a waitress he has picked up. This is in dramatic contrast to an earlier scene, in which Adam, Faith, and their daughter (who will later, as an adult, feel hostility toward her father) spend their time together on a beach, a scene that is stunning in its pastoral niceness. The story has a curious mixture of pathos and puns, as well as sentimentality and manifestations of revenge. Adam's Marist education means that "the world was always thick with symbol" (162), symbol that the reader, through Adam, will perceive, if he or she is willing to accept the author's prompting. The story is confused, or intruded upon, by the narrative point of view; there are temporal slips; there is a great deal of structural equilibrium beneath its deceptive, less-than-innocent narrative surface.

Elsewhere, a fantasy is balanced by its denial. **"The Chameleon Condition"** is a curious alloy of reality and dream, or nightmare. Its male protagonist changes colours. He is Adam; his current lover, preceded by two wives, is Eve; he is reactionary, isolated, and, even in his dream, excluded. The story has elements of parable about it, and metaphorical and hallucinatory associations. Its serious matter dwells uneasily with its initial, basically comic premise: in the throes of moonlit sexual delight, "His legs were bright blue with gratification. Blue as a peacock's feather. Blue as Krishna when the milkmaids licked him with their thousand tongues" (114). In contrast, in **"The Last of the Hapsburgs"** an old-maidish, unsatisfied schoolteacher, who appears sly and superior in the letters she writes to her sister, is dramatically and rudely disabused of the romantic fantasies and fictions she creates about several of her pupils. In effect, she is temporarily exposed and privately punished for escaping her own inhibitions. The story is suffused with patronizing, and later uncompromisingly vulgar, ironies.

It may not be completely apparent that some of Hospital's stories—those that generally seem to take few if any liberties with narrative arrangement—centre on preoccupied, obsessed, or compulsive characters. In **"Dear Amnesty,"** a woman graphically takes on what she imagines to be the physical suffering of the victim she adopts; she cannot relinquish this identification, nor can she keep herself from writing letters to Amnesty International. In **"Queen of Pentacles, Nine of Swords,"** a mordant and cynical Native woman is seemingly compelled by her baser nature. She holds no illusions about her social and economic position as an outsider, and believes her life to be predetermined by tarot-card readings. She is ruled by reason and superstition, and is as much drawn to aggressive overachievement and dramatic upward mobility as she is to prostitution. This woman is an intriguingly contradictory individual; her story is, in the favourable sense of the word, compelling.

"I Saw Three Ships," the final story in the collection, traces a delightful seaboard May-December platonic romance. Old Gabe, chiding himself for his foolishness, thinks the girl he meets on the beach "belonged in a different dimension" (91). Hospital makes an excellent analogy here: Gabe "hobbled to meet her like a broken toy, overwound" (90). The teenaged enchantress, who seems to have an obsessive concern for the enraptured oldster, is named, appropriately, Angela, and she heals the guilt Gabe feels about the conflict between his aged condition and his new romantic foolishness. She gives meaning to his solitary existence, and he thinks only about her mystery and radiance. The story—set in a practical world of pain, a world that occasionally shows traces of enchantment—is of a visitation; it is singularly touching, and again demonstrates Hospital's versatility.

Many of the stories in *Isobars* possess a great deal of self-conscious charm, sometimes to the extent that they become self-conscious performances. Reading them, we can often sense and appreciate the author's winsomeness, her consciousness of stylistic preening, and the careful lusciousness of her images. There is a cleverness in Hospital's arrangements, and often a sophisticated wittiness, even a delight, in her narrative tone. We acknowledge that the trick is smoothly and inoffensively turned. Hospital's work is sprightly, assured, coherent, and controlled: there are no apparent lapses in voice, or tone, or perspective, or intensity. These stories deliver the persuasive illusion of casual and familiar confidence, as their voices move comfortably within their narrative boundaries. Characters are economically drawn and wonderfully human—quite an achievement given Hospital's narrative riffs and sometimes eccentric associations. In short, *Isobars* is a distinctive, accomplished, and completely engaging collection.

Erin McGraw (review date Winter 1993)

SOURCE: "Styles and Variations," in *Georgia Review*, Vol. XLVI, No. 4, Winter, 1993, pp. 802-13.

[*In the following excerpt, McGraw comments on trends in prose style in recent fiction and offers positive assessment of* Isobars.]

Those who live by a highly developed and elaborated style die by that same style. Recent fiction has begun to reassert an interest in style—that is, in storytelling in such a way that the reader is aware of method as well as material—but it's a thin line that separates a style exercised to its full potential from one that is pushed over the edge into parody. (Of this, there are few better examples than late Hemingway.) A writer who is concerned with particular devices and writerly tics spends a lot of time fretting. Is this one simile too many? Is this the parenthetical aside, the footnote, or the interior monologue that will finally capsize credibility or exhaust the reader's patience? Fiction that moves away from or exaggerates conventional idioms is fiction with a curl in the middle of its forehead—when it's good it's very good, and when it's bad it's horrid. Whether a particular set of narrative devices is as ornamented as William Goyen's or as stripped down as Donald Barthelme's, as soon as those devices stop enhancing the story's movement they start impeding it and irritating the reader. But when a highly developed style is carried off, it's exciting to read, a bravura performance: the writing shimmies across tightropes to the delight of the audience, who didn't think it could be done.

Writers and publishers have moved past the short-declarative-sentence lockstep that characterized most of the eighties, and attention to well-crafted, highly individuated voices has become modish. Fiction's house these days is roomy enough to contain the lapidary prose of Michael Chabon or the baroque barrages of Martin Amis, right next door to Toni Morrison's fierce lyricism, Alice Munro's disciplined meditations, and T. C. Boyle's gonzo lit. . . .

Janette Turner Hospital's prose is as luxurious and flamboyant as a peacock. It is self-consciously gorgeous, and its use of repeated rhythms and piled-up dependent clauses can have the soothing, near-mesmerizing quality of a chant. Hospital's style reflects her content, since her stories return again and again to issues of otherworldliness—the half-heard echoes of ancestors, or mysterious forces that tie her characters to strangers and ram their fates together. Because the call of the emerging voices of memory and guilt rises so high, her characters have to fight all the time to keep a grip on the everyday.

To give bulk and credence to her vision, which could so easily degenerate into third-rate, woozy mysticism—half-digested Jung mated with *Picnic at Hanging Rock*—Hospital's narrative prose is exotic and inflated, full of unlikely couplings. "Before the avocadoes and kiwi fruit and mangoes, back in the time of the sugarcane, Wednesday afternoons used to roll in with a dreadful humid regularity," she writes in **"The Last of the Hapsburgs,"** the second story in her fine collection, *Isobars.* The sentence begins with a figure that recalls myth and fairy tale ("Before the avocadoes . . . back in the time . . ."), but the interesting element here is that the sense of mythic proportion is not dispelled when we come to the humor of those dreadful, humid, regular Wednesdays. The narrator is allowing some wit, but the language is still slightly formal, not out of keeping with the kiwis.

Instead of propping up showy language in order to knock it down, as [Dev] Hathaway does by revealing such lushness to be disproportionate and comic, Hospital's world *is* stubbornly mythic, and style helps to create it. One character muses about *"gryphons rampant* and *fields azure* blooming in her waking thoughts"; another, in his cups, "sucks in his cheeks and pinches his lips to show contempt for these words falling out like junk from an overstuffed closet." Such thoughts aspire to a noble level that has little to do with common conversation.

Hospital doesn't content herself with lofty diction or idiosyncratic descriptions to pull us in. Paragraphs spelunk into the psyches of her characters and bring up fragments of buried history, one shard at a time. But plunging into the headlong lives of characters can be frustrating; readers have to trust that it will all make sense eventually. In **"Uncle Seaborn"** a man sifts through his parents' effects, then telephones his family on another continent:

> "We miss you," his wife and children said. "We love you."
>
> "I can't hear you," he panicked. The surf of static again, the whispering, hissing, wave-washing, word-washing, the line going dead. The tyranny of distance, he thought. The ocean wins every time.
>
> In the next drawer he found Uncle Seaborn's gold half-sovereign and felt elation, then fear, then elation.

Or, from **"Eggshell Expressway"**:

> "A tawdry set-up." He's weeping now. "Taking advantage. Meanwhile the real marksmen (who knows how many?) are everywhere: the toll booth, Circular Quay, the Law Courts, every doorway in King's Cross, the expressway underpass, oh yes, the underpass, that surprises you, doesn't it? You'd be sick at what goes on in that labyrinth, that slime-pit, that sewer-maze, that—
> . . . They got him," he moans. "They got him." He sees the skull burst like an eggshell, blood all over the expressway.

The dropped hints, the inferences, the unexpected violence and circularity—all of these devices are employed to tease readers along. The stories move in circles, and the questions posed are not the standard ones of narrative—*What's going to happen next?*—but instead the questions of psychology: *Why does she keep bringing that up? What does the underpass have to do with anything?*

Hospital works out a tricky balance, burying traditional, causal narrative underneath obliqueness and allusion. The balance can slip and become coy (in **"Eggshell Expressway"** and in **"Dear Amnesty,"** an uncharacteristically predictable tale in which the body of a devoted Amnesty International letter-writer takes on the suffering of the woman she's hoping to free), or never quite break forward into clarity (**"Isobars"**). Given how much of her material inclines toward the fey, however, Hospital uses style as a means to supply greater credence to the compulsions and illusions that rule her characters.

Her best stories—**"The Last of the Hapsburgs," "The Second Coming of Come-by-Chance," "Queen of Pentacles, Nine of Swords"**—are wonderful, thick and exotic. They create a world filled with doors that open onto other doors, where several versions of the truth are likely and the boundaries that fence off surreality break down. It's a testimony to Hospital's authority that after reading this book filled with infidelity, violence, and tormented sex of various sorts—three stories out of fifteen have to do with prostitutes, two are about rape, and **"The Last of the Hapsburgs"** ends with an act of filthy violation by a group of boys toward their aging female teacher and two girl students—a reader can come away thinking about the author's language.

Nancy Engbretsen Schaumburger (review date Spring 1993)

SOURCE: "Rich and Strange," in *Belles Lettres,* Vol. 8, No. 3, Spring, 1993, p. 8.

[*In the following review, Schaumburger praises the intellectual rewards of* The Last Magician *but finds shortcomings in the novel's expansive range and underdeveloped characters.*]

The heroine of Janette Turner Hospital's novel *Charades* (1989) is told that she has a first-class "grab-bag mind," full of arcane, unrelated, brain-teasing oddments of information. If you, too, delight in such intellectual quirkiness, you will applaud this Australian-born writer's latest effort, *The Last Magician.* Highly innovative and daring, this sensuous novel is bursting with images and ideas both rich and strange.

Most of its characters—or at least the seekers among them—seem to be walking almanacs of curious lore. They are obsessed with the case of a most significant person missing from their lives, who has probably been murdered. The detective elements in the plot do not appear by accident; Hospital is also the author of a successful crime thriller, *A Very Proper Death,* under the charming pseudonym of Alex Juniper.

Charlie Chang, as the Australian-Chinese hero of this title calls himself, is a photographer and filmmaker of tricky, disturbing symbolic effects. He is also the manager of a posh Sydney restaurant/whorehouse aptly named the Inferno, which employs Lucy/Lucia, the narrator, a Milton-quoting prostitute who has made a different "choice in cages," a temporary detour from the normal world, to acquire the forbidden knowledge of the "secret cupboard under the stairs." Catharine, a TV documentary interviewer, and Robbie, a high-ranking judge, often dine there; Catharine eventually interviews Lucy and hires her as an assistant, while Robbie periodically slips off from his current wife to the perverted world upstairs.

Charlie, Catharine, and Robbie share a dark childhood secret: their wild Queensland friend, Cat, who lured them all into dangerous games on the railroad tracks, finally became a victim herself. Robbie first prevented Cat from saving her retarded brother from an oncoming train, then told the sheriff (while Charlie and Catharine remained silent) that Cat had caused the boy's death. As a result, Cat entered a downward path from reform school to prostitution, prison, and occasional demonic reappearances in her old chums' lives.

Charlie joins forces with Gabriel, Robbie's estranged drifter son, who works at the Inferno, to track down the long-missing Cat; they are convinced that she holds the key to several unresolved dilemmas of identity and culpability. In their quest for clues, they descend nightly into the Quarry, the criminal underbelly of Sydney.

The Quarry becomes the leading symbol of the novel: teeming subterranean dope dens and other Bosch-like scenes of horror that sometimes extend as far as the earth below suburban gardens. Visitors include not only the desperate and the damned, but also the haunted, like Charlie and Gabriel, and even such ultrarespectable figures on the evening news as Judge Robinson "Robbie" Gray. Charlie and Gabriel appear to die in a knife fight. And it remains for Lucy to assemble the crucial bits of information necessary to solve the murder(s). Lucy and Catharine remain the sole survivors of the far-reaching consequences of Cat's fateful childhood.

This ambitious novel weighs the consequences of crime and punishment, memory and remorse, collective guilt, and other societal issues. The novel's scope is immense, perhaps one reason why it falters. Ultimately, a novelist must convince the reader that her characters are real. We must learn to care about them. In this feat Hospital falls short. Despite this, there are many intellectual pleasures in *The Last Magician,* so indulge yourself and look forward to this prolific author's next offering.

One quibble: *The Last Magician* is ill-served by the murky, almost pornographic cover art, which I hope Hospital's publishers will replace.

Times Literary Supplement (review date 29 October 1993)

SOURCE: A review of *The Ivory Swing,* in *Times Literary Supplement,* October 29, 1993, p. 22.

[*In the following review, the critic offers a favorable assessment of* The Ivory Swing.]

Readers who enjoyed Janette Turner Hospital's most recent novel, *The Last Magician* (1992), will take delight in *The Ivory Swing,* which was originally published in 1982. It tells the story of Juliet, an academic's wife who with her family is transplanted from the stultifying small-town atmosphere of a provincial Canadian university to the isolation of a South Indian village. Living for a year on the estates of Shivaraman Nair, a wealthy farmer and ostentatious patron of the arts, Juliet, her husband David and their two children are expected to acknowledge and respect the strictures of the high-caste household.

For Juliet, already half-inclined to rebellion by the frustrations of her domestic life, the situation proves intolerable. It is further complicated by the family's involvement with Yashoda, a widowed relative of the Nairs, who also occupies a house on the estates. Half-westernized by travel and education, Yashoda refuses to follow the requirements of her *dharma,* the seclusion proper to widowhood. She seeks freedom, comfort and, ultimately, protection from David and Juliet, who discover that their easy liberalism is inadequate to deal with the moral and emotional complexities of orthodoxy. Juliet is unable to view Yashoda's position dispassionately because of her own impulse to identify with the trapped and the oppressed; in making this connection, she comes to realize how much freedom she has, but how ambivalently she regards it. For David, Yashoda represents an appeal to his sexuality and masculinity that he can neither reject nor understand.

The story is worked out with extraordinary delicacy and precision, never scoring easy hits and always demanding our interpretive effort. In particular, the relationship between Juliet and the child servant Prabhakaran provides an elegant and moving demonstration of the paradoxes of liberty and imprisonment. By focusing on the specific, Turner Hospital invests it with great depth, and creates a drama that delivers much that is important and universal.

Ray Willbands (review date Winter 1994)

SOURCE: A review of *The Last Magician,* in *World Literature Today,* Vol. 68, No. 1, Winter 1994, pp. 209–10.

[*In the following review, Willbands offers a positive assessment of* The Last Magician.]

Janette Turner Hospital's seventh work of fiction [*The Last Magician*] is set in Brisbane, at the edge of the Queensland rain forest, in Sydney, and briefly in New York. It is a very contemporary pondering of the nature of reality, time, disorder, and power, with a repeated reference to chaos theory and the possibility of falling through cracks in to a parallel universe, a dark reality of underworld horror.

The novel concerns two generations, with Cat, Catherine, Charlie, and Robbie in the first, and Robbie's son Gabriel and his girlfriend, the narrator Lucy, in the second. The first generation grows up in Brisbane, attending school, playing "chicken" on railroad tracks, swimming nude in a rain-forest waterfall pool. Cat, part heroine, part Circe, is a willful, mesmerizing girl from the lower class who is catapulted from her adoring middle-class friends into reform school and into prostitution. Though she disappears into the underworld of Brisbane and later Sydney, a world described in terms of Dante's *Inferno* and called "the quarry," Cat is always present in the memory of her friends and is in fact a kind of psychopomp leading them again and again from their world of comfortable reality to remember and to face over and over the hellish world of violence, murder, drugs, poverty, and sexual depravity that is only a scratch or a slip beneath the surface of the ordinary world. Charlie records reality as a photographer and is fascinated by the denizens of "the quarry"; Catherine moves about the world making film documentaries and is never beyond the provocation of Cat to show the dark side of life; Robbie, the villain in the novel, moves to Sydney and prescribes law as a judge, although of all the characters he is most in need of judgment.

The momentum in the novel comes through the activities of Lucy and Gabriel, the second-generation Cat-addicts, drawn to her and to her world by their need to see through illusion and to encounter the dark truth that she represents. The central mystery of the novel involves the whereabouts of Cat, the question of whether she remains alive, the power she still has to motivate and control the major characters who have in some way touched her.

The Last Magician is ambitious and timely. Ugly alternative realities press themselves on us from every side, and the notion of an enveloping underworld is credible. In terms of prose style, though sometimes succumbing to literary cliché, Hospital is more often seductive and amazing. However, the problems I have with her novel are several: the story is repetitive, the same ground covered again and again; the magnetic nature of the willful Cat is insisted upon, as is the universal importance of the story itself. But finally, Hospital's story is magical. Beware. While it may be medicinal, even chic, to romp in postmodern violence and ugliness, the experience is not pleasant, nor is it meant to be. Enter Turner's world at your own risk, and be sure you won't forget it.

David Callahan (review date Spring 1996)

SOURCE: "Acting in the Public Sphere and the Politics of Memory in Janette Turner Hospital," in *Tulsa Studies in Women's Literature,* Vol. 15, No. 1, Spring, 1996, pp. 73–81.

[*In the following essay, Callahan describes Hospital's body of work as "unsettling and satisfying at the same time."*]

Janette Turner Hospital's work self-consciously privileges sites and moments of tension in which the operations of memory and its reconstructions are placed in question. At

the beginning of *The Last Magician* (1992), to take one of many possible examples, the narrator pauses in her facile insertion of the beginning of Dante's *Inferno* as a positioning reference for her story when she realizes that: "In the middle of darkness, I came to the black fact that there *was* no straight way—no way on, no way out."[1] These middles, these locations between two sides or borders, provide fulcrums that problematize both sides, both possible directions, and that thus render identity as always already displaced. But there is much more to Turner Hospital's work than what is, after all, a fashionable displacement. Typical Turner Hospital characters also exist in limbo between cultures and tend to contest both personal and cultural resolutions to the questions these tensions articulate. Add to this Turner Hospital's constant concern with the double binds in which women are situated, and we have both a subtly modulated and fiercely committed examination of the consequences and practices attendant upon contemporary anxieties about cultural and gendered dislocation.[2] In this process one of the most significant borders, perhaps the most significant of these interfaces that leak into one another, is one of the less obvious ones: that of the relation between public accountability and responsibility and the representations of memory (with all their attendant ontological problems) that the personal search for displaced meaning and compromised origins in Turner Hospital's work dramatizes.

The search for stable points of memory and thus for sources of personal identity, so intense and troubling in her fiction, is constantly destabilized by the pressure of the public sphere (understood in a general sense and not in the more restricted, eighteenth-century sense with which Habermas made the phrase famous) and by the urgency of accepting responsibility in it. This does not mean that in her work Turner Hospital privileges the private over the public, that she sees the quest for identity as needing to battle against the intrusions of the public in neo-Romantic vein. In *Borderline* (1985) the principal characters are imagined by the narrator to be attempting, to some extent, to evade or excuse intervening against the grain. Both Felicity and Gus feel themselves slipping out of their "real" lives and dragged into widening public circles as they become involved in the attempt of the Salvadoreans to cross the U.S.A.-Canada border. Despite the problems they have with this, I think it is clear that we are positioned as readers to approve of their involvement, partly by way of moral positioning and partly by way of narrative involvement; that is, we want this narrative to continue and for this we need them to be involved. However, it is noticeable that this reading of the characters' commitment is constructed for us by the withdrawn and self-absorbed narrator, Jean-Marc, who will discover, ironically, that his constructions are in fact interventions of his own, and more, that they are pleasurable.

In *The Last Magician* there is a more explicit narratorial appeal to the need to face up to both a social and a personal violence literally underlying our every action. In *The Last Magician* the complicities of the private with the public are assumed and tracked from the beginning by both Lucy and Charlie Chang, reporters on others' lives as television journalist and film-maker, and their occupations are seen to form a continuum with their roles as prostitute and photographer of the quarry (the underworld on which public life feeds and through which it defines its value). In both cases their roles as institutionalized participant-voyeurs, as it were, foreground the gaps between other people's public faces and their unguarded selves, with the clear suggestion that private aggrandizements and power plays intrude too much into the public sphere, not vice versa. The book thus seems to be a sustained appeal to the need to face up to how private and public violence inflect each other, more specifically how the erasure of the other operates on a multitude of levels, from the operation of public triage (sorting out social hierarchies according to "quality"—as perceived by those sections of society that have the power to assert their hierarchies) to the homogenizing priorities of childhood.

As for Proust, with whom Turner Hospital has important similarities, the investigation of the appropriations and effacements of memory and the painful search for origins are ultimately a political project, however personal they may appear on the surface. The establishment of the nature of agency and its always already (re)constructed nature becomes imperative in Turner Hospital's work, but without the consoling certainties of personal identity, cultural affirmation, or received truths. On the track of lost time, and recalling a related quest in Proust's *In Search of Lost Time,* in Marcel's words, "what we have not had to decipher, to elucidate by our own efforts, what was clear before we looked at it, is not ours."[3] Memory may slither all over the place but that is how we hook ourselves into events, that is how they become events for us. In the search for our own origins there is no disinterested position from which to proceed, but that interestedness becomes or rather brings into view what is value for us and thus where our responsibilities lie.

This intersection of what we might call hermeneutic and moral concerns leads to a triple displacement at the heart of Turner Hospital's work: (1) on the first level there is the sense of ontological displacement that arises from the inevitable interestedness of memory and from its constant coming up against other memories, other versions—"'Bea's difficult,' Charade says. 'It's hardest with someone who's too close. Bea's a patchwork. I'd have to cobble her together from other people's talk . . . I'd be very unreliable on Bea'";[4] (2) on the second level there is the displacement from one's personal history that this awareness entails and, implicated in this, the realization that the attempt to reconstruct or gain access to that past itself becomes a part of the identity the reconstruction is trying to piece together; (3) on the third level there is the displacement from public event and from the possibilities of public responsibility and intervention that these apparent foreclosures of certain meaning and value seem to posit.

Turner Hospital, in dialogue with these questions, comes down clearly on the side of the necessity of engagement, not just stressing the need actively to intervene but also enforcing the realization that any position, any putative avoidance of action, is also to intervene, so that there is no not intervening. This being the case, we are engaged in a constant moral positioning of ourselves, whether we believe we are or not. Practice is always related to value. Beyond, however, this relatively standard contemporary hermeneutic understanding, it seems apparent that in her fiction there are ways of acting that are good, valuable, right, and that Turner Hospital shows the moral force, indeed responsibility, of what we might call a feminist postmodernism: that is, a postmodernism aware of the fragmented nature of identity, of the (necessary) fiction of the subject position, of the ludic nature of the fictional combinations of these fragments we constantly engage in, but a postmodernism that is prepared to assume the possibility, even the necessity, of some form of seriousness and engagement.

Turner Hospital's work is of interest because of the dynamic and troubling ways in which she vivifies the conflicts and paradoxes inherent in these issues. Almost programmatically, she has worked her way, in her novels, through a testing of their propositions in the messy areas of (to simplify): intercultural constraints and conflicts (*The Ivory Swing,* 1982), family history and family histories (*The Tiger in the Tiger Pit,* 1983), the interfaces or borders between the personal and the political (*Borderline,* 1985), speculation about the nature of creation and reality and the implication these things might have for representing identity and responsibility (*Charades,* 1989), and, to some extent, the recapitulation and intensification of many of these issues in *The Last Magician* (1992). Within her short stories the focus tends to be even sharper, especially when dealing with the representations of memory and mechanisms of cultural constancy, which condition dealings between different cultures or subcultures.

In Turner Hospital's first novel, *The Ivory Swing,* the central scenario of the novel is the woman's attempt to approach the alien culture that surrounds her. But the mere attempt to appreciate and understand also acts upon this world and in this world. At question are the possibilities of agency for women in a world where those possibilities have been circumscribed by men in such a way that acting comes to be constructed as transgressing. Turner Hospital appears to favor the first of the two fundamental political choices outlined by, for example, Marcelle Marini, in "From Minority Creation to Universal Creation":

> is feminist action itself a transitory action destined to make society and culture *really mixed* spaces for the first time in history? Or is it a matter of constructing for the future a society and culture rigorously parallel and foreign to those of men?[5]

In her intervention in this sociocultural process, however, Turner Hospital begins with representations of female development stunted and rendered impossible by the social boundaries that prevent both Juliet and Yashoda from developing along lines they perceive as desirable and, to a certain extent, by their complicity in models of powerlessness. She does not subscribe to what, in Jane Marcus's words, is an "essentialist critical stance [that] absolves the female from guilt, complicity and responsibility."[6] In *The Ivory Swing* the action consists of restating the problems, establishing Turner Hospital's understanding of the multiple double binds under which women operate—a restatement that I find mostly convincing, although not everybody does. Graham Huggan suggests that the novel is in fact "seriously flawed, mismanaged to the extent that [it] ends up by reinforcing the very prejudices [it] sets out to undermine."[7] I find the implicit suggestion in Huggan's article that the anxieties of grappling with cultural stereotypes can be circumvented by not presenting a character or characters who internalize these stereotypes to prefigure some sort of sanitization of the problems.

In *Borderline* and *Charades,* however, although such restating is also present, Turner Hospital moves on from this to representations of women acting, succeeding, creating their own spaces and understandings of events, possessing power. That is, in Sally Robinson's summary position in *Engendering the Subject,* women's self-representation

> proceeds by a double movement: simultaneously *against* normative constructions of Woman that are continually produced by hegemonic discourses and social practices, and *toward* new forms of representation that disrupt these normative constructions.[8]

In the development of women's agency in her work, moreover, Turner Hospital is not one to represent women as triumphantly usurping power and intervening heroically in the creation of this mixed society. Her heroines are as mixed as the society in whose creation they are stages, and the sphere in which this mixedness is most apparent is that interface between representation (here memory) and action.

Taking three crucial moments in her fiction, then, I would like to look first at *Charades,* in which we are led through a maze of investigations into representing the universe, or creation, and into reconstructing Charade's life, or creation. In this twinned process it often appears throughout the novel that reality depends upon the operations of memory in some absolute way: "I can do what I like with the past; it is easy as plasticene; it only exists now and then," thinks Katherine, close friend of Charade's mother and one of the novel's central characters (p. 141). The novel cunningly leads us into the pasts of the characters in such a way that the malleability of the past seems more than proven, until suddenly we are confronted with something that has been just outside of range, unsuspected, until this moment—the characters' relation to a historical event with a powerful and troubling relation to the nature of memory: the Holocaust. Koenig—the physicist, Charade's lover, and principle male character in the book—mentions a name, and spinning into Charade's "aunt" Katherine's head comes a newspaper poster: "Did Six Million Die? Holocaust a Hoax, Zundel says. More survivors give testimony today" (p. 183). The fashionably plasticene nature of the past does not seem so glib now, and the re-

sponsibility to get it right comes into focus. Memory is further contextualized by responsibility moreover to a very public sphere and, typically, a sphere in which the representations by one culture of another culture—Germans of Jews—originated the problem. Although the representation of the Holocaust may not be separable from its reality, the latter has an existence that we have the duty to represent in a way that problematizes, to say the least, any claims for the plasticene nature of memory and reality. As Sue Gillett says in an article on this novel, Koenig's

> own experience of the trial, however, forces him to realize that mimesis does not operate in a neutral space and cannot, alone, ensure credibility. . . . Truth is not inherent in the object itself, but needs the imaginative sympathy of the onlooker in order to exist. Without that sympathy, without the meeting of subject and object, correspondence can find no support.[9]

Truth, then, cannot exist without our intervening on its behalf, and this leads us to the second moment in Turner Hospital's work I wish to consider. In *Borderline* we encounter a character reporting a narrative in which other characters appear to be the principal protagonists. What is the point of this narrator? Obviously, Turner Hospital's New York editor wondered too, and Turner Hospital had to plead in a letter: "I cannot emphasize too much that J-M's [Jean-Marc's] chapters are *anything but* trimmings added to the main plot line."[10] The interposition of this narrator appears to allow both for reflecting upon the central issues of truth, of saying right, of doing right, of bearing witness, and of intervening, and for dramatizing, in Barbara Johnson's words on *Billy Budd,* that "gaps in cognition, far from being mere absences, take on the performative power of true acts."[11] Jean-Marc battles with that "imaginative sympathy of the onlooker," as he tells us that "truth must be tempered because mere accuracy was false."[12] In this way he "began by guarding not only against error, but against the spirit of error" (p. 189).

To what extent are we prepared to take this at face value? The answer is that we are prepared to let Jean-Marc invent practically anything as long as we get our story, as long as we get it in terms with which we are familiar. Moreover, as Turner Hospital relates,[13] readers tend to deny that Felicity dies just as Jean-Marc does, even though he provides enough evidence for us to accept that this has happened and even though Turner Hospital thought she had written enough to convince us that Felicity had indeed died, been murdered. Among the many possible resonances of this narratorial relationship, one is pertinent to our purpose: it is not possible not to intervene, not possible not to assume responsibility. Even the distanced piano tuner cannot avoid imaginative sympathy or an awareness of the pleasures and dangers of intervening, that is, of the pleasures and dangers of wielding responsibility (which recalls the blind piano tuner, Jean-Yves, in Angela Carter's "The Bloody Chamber" (1979); putatively unseeing and ineffectual, he nevertheless denies his ineffectuality and intervenes just at the crucial moment to save the threatened woman from death).[14] As Jean-Marc proceeds with his narrative, he comes increasingly to realize the attractions it holds and ironically reproduces to some extent what he perceives to be the megalomania of his painter father. He approaches an understanding of, finally, in Deborah Bowen's words on Janette Turner Hospital, "the image's representation of the past as a magical site of potential transfiguration."[15] In this way the novel carries out a simultaneous representation of two public interventions: that of Felicity and Gus helping someone they do not know in the face of danger and death, and that of Jean-Marc reconstructing this to the point where he understands that the personal realm he thought he inhabited is not enough.

The third episode is Gabriel's anguishing memory of his father engaged in inserting himself into history and public event, in *The Last Magician.* Both central characters in the novel's consideration of the circulation of power in society, Gabriel's father serves as the principle agent of the suppression of difference, while Gabriel is both an investigator of his father's power, and of the hidden machinations of the powerful in general, as well as one of his father's principle victims. Gabriel's father, later to become Judge Robinson Gray,[16] has observed a neighbor getting into the paper on the occasion of the phasing out of Brisbane's trams. Intensely jealous, he deliberately stages an appearance on a tram so as to build up his public profile, and, as he practices on his son the preceding day before uttering it (supposedly off the cuff) to a reporter, he claims: "The present crosses the Great Divide and descends into history" (p. 149). While he has apparently been raiding the books in his library to come up with inspiration for what he is going to say to the (tipped-off) reporter, there is a further intratextual allusion here in the use of "descends." Gabriel's father intends it to sound portentous, intends it to refer to an important geographico-cultural site for Australians—the Great Dividing Range—but it also brings to mind the Dantean network in the novel, the underworld of the lost and damned, called the "quarry" (after the famous photograph by Sebastião Salgado of Brazilian *garimpeiros* quarrying for gold in a vast mud pit), so that in this novel of undermining levels Robinson Gray undermines himself by relating his history, or his History, to a descent, to the underworld.

Wanting to be a part of History, of public event, he damns himself both in terms of the novel's dynamics of allusion and in terms of his son's perception of him. In this attempt to insert himself into public awareness, Gabriel perceives his father's inauthentic nature, that the public sphere for him is not a realm of public concern but rather of self-aggrandizement. This episode becomes extremely complex and important in the development of the novel, but for my purposes here I merely wish to indicate Turner Hospital's insistent attacks on the appropriation of the public sphere for the aggrandizements of personal power and her determination that we should see this appropriation as such. History is not plasticene, any more than is personal memory, and whatever our difficulties of representationality, our responsibility to history remains firmly delineated in her fiction. The public sphere must not be allowed to be appropriated by liars, cheats, and oppressors.

With these brief core samples from Turner Hospital's fiction I have wished to suggest that her fiction bears witness to a tough-minded confrontation both of contemporary understandings of reality as constructed and of the embattled nature of responsibility to event and representation. Nonetheless, while her fiction may be tough-minded, and while Turner Hospital loads the narrative dice in favor of committed intervention, the destabilizing of identity witnessed in her work through her examination of the operations of memory and cultural displacement renders the basis for such action highly problematical. We have her word for it that, for example, in *Borderline* one of Turner Hospital's primary concerns was "the essential unreality, for us in the safe and insulated North American middle class . . . of many real and verifiable and quite horrific events which go on daily all around us in the world."[17] Yet clear answers as to how the equally strongly delineated argument in her work that a relation between the always already displaced nature of memory and subject position, on the one hand, and public responsibility, on the other hand, may be articulated or hermeneutically tidied up do not seem forthcoming. Slightly rephrasing Michael Ryan, "displaceability is born at the same moment as natural [responsibility]. There is no moment prior to the possibility of displacement when [responsibilities] are purely natural."[18] Janette Turner Hospital's understanding of the negotiations this difficulty involves is perhaps why her work is so unsettling and satisfying at the same time, at least to this reader, and her further grapplings with the politics of memory eagerly awaited.

Notes

1. Janette Turner Hospital, *The Last Magician* (London: Virago, 1992), p. 3. Further references will be cited in the text.

2. See my "Janette Turner Hospital and the Discourse of Displacement," in *(Inter)national Dimensions of World Literature in English,* ed. W. Zach (Tübingen: G. Narr, 1996), pp. 335–40.

3. Marcel Proust, *Time Regained,* Vol. XII of *Remembrance of Things Past,* trans. Andreas Mayor (London: Chatto and Windus, 1970), p. 241. I prefer to refer to this book as *In Search of Lost Time,* as it has finally appeared in the version, unfortunately unavailable to me, translated by C. K. Scott Moncrieff, Terence Kilmartin, and D. J. Enright (London: Chatto and Windus, 1992).

4. Turner Hospital, *Charades* (London: Virago, 1990), pp. 221–22. Further references will be cited in the text.

5. Marcelle Marini, "From Minority Creation to Universal Creation," *NLH,* 24 (1993), 228.

6. Jane Marcus, "Alibis and Legends: The Ethics of Elsewhereness, Gender and Estrangement," in *Women's Writing in Exile,* ed. Mary Lynn Broe and Angela Ingram (Chapel Hill: University of North Carolina Press, 1989), p. 272.

7. Graham Huggan, "Orientalism Reconfirmed? Stereotypes of East-West Encounter in Janette Turner Hospital's *The Ivory Swing* and Yvon Rivard's *Les Silences du Corbeau*," *Canadian Literature,* 132 (Spring 1992), 46.

8. Sally Robinson, *Engendering the Subject: Gender and Self-Representation in Contemporary Women's Fiction* (Albany: SUNY Press, 1991), p. 11.

9. Sue Gillett, "*Charades*: Searching for Father Time: Memory and the Uncertainty Principle," *New Literatures Review,* 21 (Summer 1991), 71.

10. Turner Hospital, "Letter to a New York Editor," *Meanjin* [Melbourne, Australia], 47 (1988), 563.

11. Barbara Johnson, *The Critical Difference: Essays in the Contemporary Rhetoric of Reading* (Baltimore: Johns Hopkins University Press, 1980), p. 108.

12. Turner Hospital, *Borderline* (London: Virago, 1990), p. 189. Further references will be cited in the text.

13. See Turner Hospital, "Letter to a New York Editor."

14. Angela Carter, "The Bloody Chamber," in *The Bloody Chamber and Other Stories* (Harmondsworth: Penguin, 1981), pp. 7–52.

15. Deborah Bowen, "Borderline Magic: Janette Turner Hospital and Transfiguration by Photography," *Studies in Canadian Literature/Etudes de la littérature canadienne,* 16 (1991), 195.

16. Turner Hospital has a fascination with judges, invariably male, those arbiters of laws whose flaws trouble her, whose flaws suggest the tenuous and rotten basis of the social contracts by which we bind ourselves.

17. Turner Hospital, "Letter to a New York Editor," 560.

18. Michael Ryan, "Deconstruction and Social Theory: The Case of Liberalism," in *Displacement: Derrida and After,* ed. Mark Krupnick (Bloomington: Indiana University Press, 1983), p. 159.

Selina Samuels (essay date Summer 1996)

SOURCE: "Dislocation and Memory in the Short Stories of Janette Turner Hospital," in *Journal of Modern Literature,* Vol. 20, No. 1, Summer, 1996, pp. 85-95.

[*In the following essay, Samuels examines the Australian settings, themes of dislocation and exile, and interrelated aspects of past, place, and national identity in Hospital's short fiction, particularly in light of Hospital's Australian origins and expatriate perspective.*]

In the eponymous first story in the collection entitled *Isobars,*[1] Janette Turner Hospital describes the convolution of time and place, the region of memory: "These particular isobars connect points where the pressure of memory ex-

erts an equivalent force" (p. 1). Hospital's "isobars," in which memory is cyclical and identity is entangled in evocations of place, contain moments of crisis and illumination that blur the distinction between past and present. The major concerns of Hospital's short stories in the collections *Dislocations*[2] and *Isobars* are distinctive of the short story form and of expatriate fiction: fragmentation and isolation, transitoriness and dislocation. The word "dislocation" indicates the significance of place, of location, in Hospital's short stories. Her ambivalence toward place is reflected in the way in which she moves among countries in her stories—Australia, India, Canada, the United States—and in the dislocation felt by her characters, who are consistently described as inhabiting the peripheries of society. Hospital often evokes place in the form of a representation of "home," which is located in memories: the memories of Hospital's characters and of the writer herself. Hospital left Brisbane in 1967, and, after living in the United States, Canada, India, and London, she now divides her time among Canada, Australia, and Boston and is best described as an expatriate writer. Despite this—and the fact that her work is probably better known in North America than in Australia—she must be considered an Australian writer, not only because she was born in Melbourne, but because her short stories reveal her implicit connection to the places of her childhood, and especially to Queensland.

Although Janette Turner Hospital locates her stories in several countries, those stories that are set in Australia are, in my view, her most effective. This perception may be the inevitable romanticism of an expatriate Australian reading the writing of an expatriate Australian, but, nevertheless, it is certainly true that she defines place and its effect on personal identity most clearly in her Australian stories. In a review of *Isobars,* Dennis Danvers maintains that Hospital's best stories are those that concentrate more on the story itself than on the ideas behind it.[3] I would add that her most successful stories are those that place story within a tangible context and by doing so emphasize the emotive over the cerebral. This emotive quality is frequently positioned in the use of memory, and the idea of the past is entwined with her literary recreations of her own childhood. It is not surprising that the number of stories about Australia increases in Hospital's second collection, nor that her two most recent novels, *Charades* (1988) and *The Last Magician* (1992), indicate an artistic return to Australia. It seems, particularly in *Isobars,* that the writer's memory is reflected in the memories of her characters, some of whom remember their pasts in Australia while living in another part of the world. Many of the stories in both collections, most notably **"The Bloody Past, The Wandering Future"** and **"After Long Absence,"** are clearly autobiographical.

Hospital's tendency to romanticize the past and past place is, I believe, an inevitable aspect of the fiction of the exile or expatriate. The experiences of the exile and the expatriate are not the same: the expatriate is voluntarily detached from his or her original homeland, while the exile is banished and unable to return, inevitably producing a more fervent yearning for home.[4] Often, however, expatriation becomes, over a course of years, a form of cultural or emotional exile, and both conditions promote a sense of dislocation and romanticism of the past. As Andrew Gurr notes, "The expatriate seeks to identify or create a cultural history and therefore a cultural identity which is necessarily based on the past."[5] Hospital has a tendency to create—to adapt a phrase from Salman Rushdie—Australias of the mind.[6] Her emphasis on memory in her fiction, her identity as an expatriate living in both Canada and Australia, and the wandering identities of so many of her characters, all contribute to the schematic approach which she adopts in her descriptions of place. The notion of exile for Australian writers has always been bound up with representations of the land: for the colonial outcasts from Britain, Australia was a place of exile, a "threat to be mastered, an object to be possessed, an Other to be incorporated into or appropriated by the self."[7] Furthermore, I would suggest that the position of Australia has tended to be perceived by Australian writers as one of cultural exile from the metropolis. As Diana Brydon and Helen Tiffin maintain, "all Australians, black and white, still suffer from the 'cultural cringe' induced by the complex of imperial fictions."[8] It is significant that in **"Isobars,"** which functions as Hospital's explication of her work, her discussion of memory centers on location: Melbourne, India, Canada, Brisbane. These locations appear to dissolve into one another as the water of the pond in the park in Melbourne where she played as a child becomes the Arabian Sea in southern India, which in turn freezes to become a Canadian lake in winter. Memory is circular, and memory is place. The narrative moves arbitrarily between Melbourne and Brisbane; indeed, Melbourne becomes Brisbane in the memory of the writer. Hospital writes, "they are one circle now, rampart, the ring of accusers, prison wall, ghetto, all the same circle" (*Isobars,* p. 7). These moments of confluence in memory and image are isobars, and such moments are the essence of Hospital's short stories.

Modern short stories are characterized by their fragmentation and lack of resolution. This is in part a result of the form itself, with its emphasis on a single moment, a significant experience: Nadine Gordimer's "flash of fireflies."[9] I would suggest that this fragmentation, along with the sense of isolation which Frank O'Connor has identified[10] and which so many of Hospital's characters share, is also characteristic of writing from the margins of society. O'Connor has suggested that the short story flourishes in an incompletely developed culture such as a regional culture, or, presumably, a postcolonial culture, lacking total social cohesion. As Clare Hanson notes, "The short story seems to be the mode preferred by those writers who are not writing from within a fixed and stable cultural framework."[11] This is descriptive of the experiences of writers who write from the frontiers, such as writers from postcolonial cultures, and, of course, female writers. It is also descriptive of Janette Turner Hospital's characters and their relationship to place. Just as notions of exile for Australian

writers have been bound up in representations of the land, the portrayal of Australian location and landscape has been central to evocations of Australian identity. Thus, Hospital writes from within an Australian tradition. The desire to create a national identity, for example, is reflected in the development of the Australian short story from Henry Lawson's popular images of outback survival, images which persisted in national literature until the publication in 1955 of Patrick White's *The Tree of Man,* which challenged the accepted portraits of Australia and altered the course of Australian literature.[12] As Kay Schaffer notes, "the land is the terrain on and against which both Australian men and women symbolically measure their identity."[13] Hospital's short fiction, proceeding from a disjointed, displaced notion of location towards an apparent acceptance of identity, albeit an ambiguous one, expresses a re-creation and exploration of such images of Australia.

In her concentration on members of postcolonial cultures who look to the centers, moving away from parochial homelands, Hospital discusses not only the difficulties of describing experience and relating present experience to that of the past, but also the problematic nature of place within time.[14] This emphasis takes the form in some stories of a detached description of the Indian Community in Canada, a large and ghettorized Diaspora;[15] **"Happy Diwali,"** from *Dislocations,* and **"Queen of Pentacles, Nine of Swords,"** from *Isobars,* describe this community. The notion of transitoriness is expressed in Hospital's wandering and displaced academics, situated in American or Canadian universities, but remembering their homes in Australia. In **"To Be Discontinued,"** Katharine stands on a Canadian campus and remembers the University of Queensland, moving out of one place and into another that is her past, remembering the smell of magnolia and jasmine, the sensual lush atmosphere of Queensland, contrasted with the cold sterility of Lake Ontario. For many of Hospital's characters, memory appears to transform time utterly, telescoping the past into the present and removing all sense of linearity. Edward Said describes the collision of past and present as a feature of the literature of exile: "For an exile, habits of life, expression or activity in the new environment inevitably occur against the memory of these things in another environment. Thus, both the new and the old environments are vivid, actual, occurring together contrapuntally."[16] In **"The Loss of Faith,"** an expatriate Australian academic and sexual philanderer sees his first wife, the Faith of the title, on the subway in New York on the day on which she dies in Sydney. This vision is tied up in his sense of national identity, which has been blurred after many years in America and many marriages. In Adam's memory, people and place are inextricably linked, and the death of his first wife, so far away, throws his past and the location of it into sharp relief. The emphasis in this story, and indeed throughout *Isobars,* is on the power of memory to evoke place and on the significance of location—and, of course, dislocation—in the creation of individual identity.

The inescapable nature of the past, and of the writer's own past, is indicated by Hospital's pungent descriptions of

Australia, descriptions that are less formulaic than her portrayals of the sterile academic environment of Canada and the United States. However, Hospital's concern is the mythical and symbolic force of place as the repository of memory, and to some extent her portrayals of Sydney and Brisbane are schematic. Prefiguring her most recent novel, **The Last Magician,** Sydney is a city of corruption and cheap sexual thrills. In **"Bondi,"** Sydney's most famous beach is the location of voyeurism and racial battles. Amid the bare breasts and skimpy briefs, "the peacock parade on its mating route between towels and bodies" (**Isobars,** p. 73), a battle breaks out between the white beachgoers and the "wogs," revealing the ugliness at the heart of Bondi hedonism, an ugliness that Hospital tends to identify with Sydney itself.

> *It's wogs! The wogs started it. They were bothering a white girl, they threw sand in a white lady's face, they kicked a football right into a little kid's head, a little white kid, he's got concussion.* Theories fly as fast as punches, as thick as blood. *Go get'em, send the buggers back where they bloody came from.*
>
> (p. 75)

Walking on the beach in the early morning of the following day, the protagonist's reverie is shattered when she steps on a hypodermic syringe, and looking around her she surveys the beach: the "vision splendid" of "hundreds of condoms and hypodermics" (p. 81). Sydney is Hospital's image of the polluted paradise, a corrupted colony defiled by the urgency of addiction and the loss of identity. The hypocrisy of Australia's biggest city is expressed in **"Eggshell Expressway,"** in which a judge who is almost fanatically obsessed by his desire to clean up the "expressway underpass," "that labyrinth, that slime-pit, that sewer-maze" (p. 107), visits a prostitute who allows him the thrill of crossing the boundaries, the dotted lines, the fortification lines between the underpass and "civilization." His final betrayal by the prostitute's pimp is inevitable: the judge is an aging Prince Hal who fails to escape in time, as self-destructive and subterranean as are those who inhabit the underpass. Hospital's image of Sydney is effective but stylized, indicating her preoccupation with the symbolic significance of place.

Brisbane is the parochial land of the writer's youth, where memories of difference and ostracism emit from the mango tree outside the kitchen window. In **"The Bloody Past, The Wandering Future,"** Hospital describes the role that Brisbane plays in the narrator's—and presumably her own—life, the city to which her great-grandfather escaped from Eastbourne and from his wife and child, establishing a train of events that made Brisbane "home." The narrator's memories catch her unawares; they are her "visitants" (p. 183); she may be looking at the St. Lawrence river, but it is the Brisbane River that she sees, flooding like her memories, the fear of the loss of Brisbane to the water and mud drawing her to return.

> As for us, my expatriate husband and myself, the mere thought of Brisbane almost ceasing to be did something

to us. We couldn't afford it, but we had to go home—come home—that summer; the *northern* summer, that is—though it was a mild and sweet-smelling winter in Brisbane, and the wattles were in bloom along the river.

> (p. 185)

In her memories, Brisbane is quaint and colonial, the 1953 coronation celebrated with fervor and festivity, the city festooned with colored bunting, watched on television sets in shop windows because no one had her own television set. The ambivalence of Hospital's attitude to Brisbane and to her past is highlighted in this story. After only two generations in Australia, the narrator's father says of Brisbane: "'This is the place where we belong. . . . You'll always belong here. And your children. And your children's children'" (pp. 187–88). But at the end of the story, she remembers walking with her grandfather in a park and looking at the statue of Persephone. She is weeping because she misses her mother, her grandfather tells her: "'She misses her mother Demeter. And she wants to go back. Whichever world she's in, she always misses the other one and wants to go back'" (p. 189).

Hospital contrasts the gentle sentimentality of her evocations of Brisbane with the descriptions of northern Queensland, marginalized and lost, a geographical "Other." In some of her most powerful stories, such as **"You Gave Me Hyacinths," "The Last of the Hapsburgs,"** and **"The Second Coming of Come-by-Chance,"** the protagonist is an outsider within a peripheral community, a teacher in a small town in far north Queensland. In **"The Last of the Hapsburgs,"** the second story in **Isobars,** Miss Davenport is in exile, teaching in a school in Port Douglas. Her displacement in this parochial environment is expressed by her identification with two of her students who are also outsiders, Hazel, who is Aboriginal and therefore representative of a colonized culture displaced in its own land, and Rebecca, whose parents are Jewish and survivors of the Holocaust. The description of Rebecca's family, nicknamed "the Last of the Hapsburgs" by the hostile and insensitive locals, indicates poignantly the discordance of place. They are rumored to live in a castle in the Daintree Forest, and to be, of course, "as rich as Midas" (p. 15). Miss Davenport discovers, however, when invited home for *shabbas,* a ritual alien to the dense rainforest of Queensland, that the Weiss home is more like a farmhouse out of the Black Forest and that they are terribly poor. As they speak of Mendelssohn and literature over dinner, it seems bizarre to Miss Davenport that they have chosen such a place in which to escape the demons of the past. But they have not escaped. Rebecca's parents still listen to Leo, Mr. Weiss' oldest son, play the violin, although he was killed in the Holocaust. The presence of the past and its horrors so pervade the house in the Daintree that Miss Davenport also hears Leo play:

> *And then,* she wrote to Ida, *I don't know how to explain this, but I heard it too. I definitely began to hear a violin. At first it was so faint that I thought I was hearing the echo of Mr Weiss's hope, but then it was*

Mendelssohn, unmistakably. The first movement of the violin concerto. When it ended, Mr Weiss was crying.

(pp. 21–22)

Miss Davenport, herself an exile from some unnamed scandal, encourages Rebecca to apply for scholarships, to escape from Port Douglas and its suffocating insignificance, but Rebecca replies, "'But this is where we've escaped to'" (p. 23). In an attempt to forge some sort of bond between them and between themselves and their environment, Miss Davenport invites the girls to swim with her in the gorge, but it is an experiment that fails. Their escape to the coolness and seclusion of the pool is shattered by the arrival of a group of five boys, who subject them to terrible humiliation, commenting on their naked bodies, stealing their clothes, and finally defecating into the pool. For Hospital, Queensland is not only a place of escape, but also one of entrapment.

In **"The Second Coming of Come-by-Chance,"** Hospital tells the rather surreal tale of a town in Northern Queensland that emerges as the lake in which it had been submerged evaporates during a particularly fierce drought. The excitement surrounding the resurfacing of this town is reminiscent of gold fever, but there is some ambiguity about the nature of Come-by-Chance; although everyone at the site can see the emerging buildings, no trace of them shows up in photographs. Hospital juxtaposes the eerie nature of this situation with her satire of the portentous interpretations of politicians and religious spokespeople, who pompously associate this remarkable occurrence with the imminent election in Queensland ("Come-by-Chance became symbol and rallying cry for a lost way of life, a simpler cleaner time, which each political party vowed to restore"—*Isobars,* p. 43) or the imminent second coming, depending on political and religious affiliations. The appearance of Adeline Capper, however, shatters the satirical style of the story, as she returns to Come-by-Chance after many years in a form of emotional exile. Adeline had been the teacher at the local school, a common Hospital outsider who made the mistake of importing progressive ideas into a blinkered society. The re-emergence of the town comes to symbolize the re-emergence of Adeline's past, her suppressed nightmares. Indeed, Adeline thinks of the town as the place where the victims of nightmares are trapped, "[a]nd they can never leave" (p. 43). The truth which Adeline denied so long ago, and which even now haunts her, must be exposed as Come-by-Chance emerges into the harsh drought-stricken landscape: years earlier, walking home from visiting an Aboriginal family, an unconventional and even subversive act in itself, Adeline was offered a lift by local policemen and then raped by them, the rape blamed on the one would ever believe the truth shatter her: "She thinks: I will never know for sure again if night is night and day is day, what is dream or not-dream" (p. 48). Her terrifying insight into the arbitrary nature of truth and of experience is mirrored by the mysterious re-appearance of Come-by-Chance, which may or may not be a mirage. Does it exist, or have we created it as an image of collective past, collective guilt, like Adeline's guilt at her complicity in the wrongful conviction of the Aboriginal men of her rape? "At times one has to ask oneself," writes a reporter for the Melbourne newspaper *Age,* "if Queensland is our own Gothic invention, a kind of morality play, the Bosch canvas of the Australian psyche, a sort of perpetual *memento mori* that points to the frailty of the skein of civilisation reaching out so tentatively from our southern cities" (p. 50). He continues:

> To return to Sydney or Melbourne and write of the primitive violence, the yobbo mentality, the mystics, the pathetic old woman generating lurid and gratuitous confessions, the general sense of mass hallucination . . . to speak of this is to risk charges of sensationalism. And indeed, after mere days back in the real world, one has the sense of emerging from a drugged and aberrant condition.
>
> One has to ask oneself: Does Queensland actually exist?
>
> And one has to conclude: I think not.
>
> Queensland is a primitive state of mind from which the great majority of us, mercifully, have long since evolved. And Come-by-Chance is a dream within a nightmare, the hysteric's utopia, the city of Robespierre, Stalin, Jim Jones, the vision of purity from which history recoils.

(p. 50)

This description of Queensland from a southern journalist reveals clearly the inevitable separatism that takes place in large countries. Rejecting the possibilities of an homogenous national consciousness, Australians constitute their identities through comparison: Sydney with Melbourne, New South Wales with Queensland, the mainland with Tasmania. Thea Astley, a Queensland writer, maintains that the portrayal of Queensland is "all in the antitheses. The contrasts. The contradictions."[17] This passage is also reminiscent of the colonial representations of Australia and other exotic locations as "other": primitive, difficult to accept, alien. This is, of course, comparable to Edward Said's argument in *Orientalism,* which exposes the imperial strategy of control through the creation and perpetuation of the construction of the Oriental as Other.[18] Here, Hospital makes a rather sardonic reference to Conrad's *Heart of Darkness,* with Queensland as the repository of colonial fears, the aberrant other, the "hallucination" at the heart of the civilized colonized world. Such a place is, naturally, as seductive as it is terrifying, and Hospital's descriptions of the landscape reveal the literary conventions from which she is writing, constituting Queensland as recognizable exotica:

> Summer comes hot and steamy with the heavy smell of raw sugar to the north—east coast of Australia. The cane pushes through the rotting window blinds and grows into the cracks and corners of the mind. It ripens in the heart at night, and its crushed sweetness drips into dreams. I have woken brushing from my eyelids the silky plumes that burst up into harvest time. And I have stood smoke—blackened as the cane fires licked the night sky, and kicked my way through the charred

stubble after the men have slashed at the naked stalks and sent them churning through the mill.

("**You Gave Me Hyacinths,**" *Dislocations,* p. 23)

Such passages reveal a paradoxical tendency within Hospital's writing: to romanticize a landscape that exists in her memory rather than in her present experience and to write for a foreign market. She frequently characterizes Queensland as the exotic frontier of civilization, only superficially tamed, a portrait that I believe is self-consciously designed to appeal to readers to whom Australia is the end of the universe and recognizable only for boomerangs and Crocodile Dundee. The language that she uses is predictably literary, but perhaps this is the only language available to her. As Brydon and Tiffin note in the recent *Decolonising Fictions,* for the majority of writers in Australia there is no alternative to English, and the challenge for these writers is to make English their own and "make it register the specifics of their own experiences."[19] Perhaps, as Miss Davenport realizes in "**The Last of the Hapsburgs,**" there is not existing language to describe such surroundings as these:

Surf rises from her ankles to her knees. *Sing me North Queensland,* it lisps with its slickering tongues.

I can't, she laments, hoisting up her skirt. *I can't.*

She would need a different sort of alphabet, a chlorophyll, a solar one.

The place will not fit into *words.*

(pp. 11–12)

Similarly, Adeline Capper, escaping from Come-by-Chance to Melbourne, discovers that she cannot communicate in the civilized, cultured, and—to her—meaningless words of that southern city: "She was mute. The same hollow alphabet. No. Hollower. She could not acquire the knack of words that floated so weightlessly. She fled back to Queensland. She dreamed of alphabets that sent down deep webbing roots" (*Isobars,* p. 48). The lack of respect for language is itself a form of paralyzing isolation, a reinforcement of a peripheral consciousness, a colonization. In both stories, Hospital portrays the characters' powerlessness in terms of their relationships towards language and of the irrelevance of the available words to their experiences. In his study of the short story writers of Canada and New Zealand, W. H. New argues that the writers from the fragments of European culture (and few places can be more fragmented and isolated than far north Queensland), developing disparately, are faced with the dilemma of the nature and manner of expression: ". . . as the writers in the new societies attempted to make literature out of their own experience they faced three problems of story-telling: whose story to tell, whom to tell it to, how to tell it."[20] As the short story reflects the fragmentation of modern consciousness, it also lends itself to the expression of the vision of those outside the mainstream culture and language.

Adeline cannot find the language to speak the truth and denounce her attackers. Words have become a form of at-

tack and are identified with the rape: ". . . she can remember only grass and ants and the shapes of words. The words themselves are jagged, they hurt her skin" (*Isobars,* p. 46). The language of the boys who terrorize Miss Davenport, Rebecca, and Hazel in the pool in "**The Last of the Hapsburgs**" is a weapon: unanswerable and mysterious, defiling, brutal, revealing the lack of power of the women. "The acts of men, even when they are boys, Miss Davenport thought, are shouts that rip open the signs that try to contain them. We have no access to a language of such noisiness. Our voices are micemutter, silly whispers" (*Isobars,* p. 27). Just as Miss Davenport and Adeline can use only the language conferred upon them, preventing them from ever accurately expressing their experiences, Hospital is trapped by a language that cannot conceive of the fact of northern Queensland, refuting its logic, questioning its existence. Her tendency to mythologize, then, is a form of emotional shorthand, a poignant evocation of a place that mystifies and beckons, a mingling of confusion, and a need to return.[21]

I have concentrated on Hospital's Australian stories not only to indicate the emphasis on place within memory, but also to illustrate the way in which the memory of the reader may function within the story. The question I have asked myself while reading these stories is whether my preference for Hospital's stories about Australia is due to the fact that I am filling the gaps of the narrative with my own memories. Hospital's stories concentrate on the moment of "instantaneous perception,"[22] in which the past is implicit, but vague and emotive, relying on absence and silence. David Miall suggests that the elliptical nature of the modern short story requires the reader constantly to reinterpret his or her knowledge, oscillating between the building and the breaking of illusions. The reader resorts to an emotional response, to prediction and anticipation, to fill the gaps and thus reconstitute the story.[23] Eudora Welty would argue that this engages the reader's memory, reconfiguring the story according to remembered experience.[24] The poignancy of remembered place is implicit in the creation of the archetypal image of the isolated wanderer, Ulysses or Odysseus. "Home" is a powerful image and is made more powerful by the reader's placing her or himself within the narrative, locating a personal image of "home," the place from which one has escaped but for which one will eternally yearn. Memory and dislocation are therefore mingled. My identification with Hospital's stories is perhaps more specific than that of readers who were not born in Australia (although her descriptions of my home, Sydney, are not particularly romantic or welcoming), but the notions of memory and displacement that pervade her stories are universal.

"**After Long Absence**" is the final story in Hospital's first collection of short stories, *Dislocations.* In this story, the narrator, a writer, returns to her parents' home in Brisbane, seeking some undefined resolution or catharsis. Despite the time she has spent away from her family, she characterizes her relationship with her parents as "the same old roller-coaster of anger and love" (*Dislocations,* p. 203).

She has rejected their strict religious outlook on life and still resents her upbringing as a Jehovah's Witness and the ostracism which it entailed. Her father prefigures the reconciliation that she craves by allowing his wine glass to be filled at a lunch with her friends, and even taking polite sips from the glass, an act of compromise and love that she finds herself unable to mirror. Asked to read the Bible at a family dinner, she refuses, although she knows, "[i]t cannot be a concession anywhere near as great as my father's two sips of wine—a costly self-damning act" (p. 210). Her inability to compromise or to forgive horrifies and shames her, but it teaches her something very important: she cannot go home. Her epiphany is not a celebration of her return, but an accentuation of her homelessness and displacement, even in the midst of her family.

The final story in *Isobars,* "Here and Now," concerns an academic, Alison, in Ontario, who receives a phone call from Brisbane telling her that her mother has died. The flood of memories that this news produces causes location to collide: Lake Ontario becomes the Brisbane River, and she realizes her displacement from either vision. The time difference between Canada and Australia enhances the confusion surrounding place. Looking at both places at once, "the frozen loop of a Queensland river," Alison realizes that her mother "died in the early hours of tomorrow morning" (*Isobars,* p. 176). The relationship between past and present is reflected in the ninety-year-old Walter's memory of whales beached on the east coast of Australia, a memory that appears to him to be a vital description of the present:

> . . . the people of the coast are forming water lines, passing buckets, keeping them wet and alive. One by one, they are being dragged back to the water and towed out to sea. Wonderful people, the Australians. I walk along the beaches, you know, and watch. . . . It was because of the whales that I sent my son out there, after the war. He never came back.
>
> (pp. 174–75)

The fluidity of time, of memory, and of location in this story contrast with the rigid delineation between past and present in "After Long Absence." At the end of "Here and Now," Alison realizes that she must return to Brisbane, to her past, which is also her present: "Tomorrow, Alison thinks, I will fly all the way back to the beginning" (*Isobars,* p. 177). Janette Turner Hospital's two collections of short stories, both concerned with memory and with the contrapuntal relationship between location and dislocation, chart a movement from a sense of the ambiguity and transitoriness of place to an almost intoxicated desire to return.

Notes

1. Janette Turner Hospital, *Isobars* (University of Queensland Press, 1990). All subsequent quotations from this edition will be included parenthetically in the text.

2. Janette Turner Hospital, *Dislocations* (University of Queensland Press, 1986). All subsequent quotations from this edition will be included parenthetically in the text.

3. Dennis Danvers, Review of *Isobars, Antipode,* V (1991), p. 148.

4. Andrew Gurr quotes an article by Mary McCarthy to this effect, "Exiles, Expatriates and Internal Emigres," *The Listener,* LXXXVI (1971), pp. 705–08, in *Writers in Exile* (The Harvester Press, 1981), p. 18.

5. *Writers in Exile,* p. 23.

6. Salman Rushdie, *Imaginary Homelands* (Granta/Penguin, 1991). Rushdie writes of Indian expatriate literature: "Exiles or emigrants or expatriates are haunted by some sense of loss, some urge to reclaim, to look back, even at the risk of being mutated into pillars of salt. But if we do look back, we must do so in the knowledge—which gives rise to profound uncertainties—that our physical alienation from India almost inevitably means that we will not be capable of reclaiming precisely the thing that was lost; that we will, in short, create fictions, not actual cities or villages, but invisible ones, imaginary homelands, Indias of the mind" (p. 10).

7. Kay Schaffer, "Women and the Bush: Australian National Identity and Representations of the Feminine," *Antipodes,* III (1989), p. 8.

8. Diana Brydon and Helen Tiffin, *Decolonizing Fictions* (Dangaroo Press, 1993), p. 50.

9. In "The Flash of the Fireflies," *Short Story Theories,* ed. Charles May (Ohio University Press, 1976), pp. 179–80.

10. Frank O'Connor, *The Lonely Voice: A Study of the Short Story* (The World Publishing Co., 1963).

11. Clare Hanson, *Short Stories and Short Fictions 1880–1980* (Macmillan Press, 1985), p. 12.

12. I am indebted for this idea to Professor Brian Matthews, Head of the Institute of Commonwealth Studies in London.

13. Schaeffer, p. 9.

14. Valerie Shaw, in *The Short Story: A Critical Introduction* (Longman, 1983), analyzes the vital issue of transitoriness in representations of place, representations that are of particular importance in the writing of exiles and expatriates.

15. These stories are reminiscent of Bharati Mukherjee's stories about the Indian ghettoes in Canada, in her collection *Darkness.*

16. Edward Said, "Reflections on Exile," in *Out There: Marginalization and Contemporary Culture,* R. Ferguson, *et al,* eds. (MIT Press, 1990), p. 366.

17. Thea Astley, "Being a Queenslander: A Form of Literary and Geographical Conceit," *Southerly,* XXXVI (1976), p. 263.

18. Edward Said, *Orientalism* (Penguin, 1991).

19. Brydon and Tiffin, p. 30.

20. W. H. New, "Dreams of Speech and Violence," *The Art of the Short Story in Canada and New Zealand,* (University of Toronto Press, 1987), p. 22.

21. The short story form, characterized as much by what is omitted as by what is stated, is well suited to those writers whose relationship to the world is constituted by boundaries, powerlessness, silence. As New writes in reference to Katherine Mansfield's "The Bay": "language is power; language is male; male language cannot express female understanding; therefore a female using male language acquires a power only to the degree she becomes a male surrogate; but a surrogate maleness produces only a surrogate power, neither of them real; therefore language does not represent power or reality for a female; except that in reality the system that equates power with male language still exists" (p. 216).

22. This is an expression used by Jean Pickering in "Time and the Short Story," in *Re-reading the Short Story,* Clare Hanson, ed. (Macmillan Press, 1989), p. 47.

23. David Miall, "Text and Affect: A Model of Story Understanding," in *Re-reading the Short Story,* p. 10.

24. Eudora Welty, "The Reading and Writing of Short Stories," in *May,* p. 171.

Ruth Brandon (review date 4 October 1996)

SOURCE: "Desert Hearts," in *New Statesman,* October 4, 1996, p. 45.

[*In the following review, Brandon offers a positive assessment of* Oyster.]

If you want to write novels these days, the old white Commonwealth is the place to be born. There's a sweep and poetic confidence in the work of a Rushdie, a Malouf, or in the Newfoundland of Annie Proulx, that leaves most English novels looking tame and parochial. Janette Turner Hospital (born in Australia, living in Canada) is up there with the very best.

Oyster is about demagoguery, mass hysteria and the closed communities in which they flourish. To the Queensland opal-mining townlet of Outer Maroo, lost in the western outback, comes the mysterious and charismatic Oyster. He, too, is drawn by opals, but also by the prospect of power. He sets himself up as leader of a millennial community just outside town. Young people in search of a better life drift in there. Oyster is their god and their prophet; he has them in his thrall; they become his creatures.

The townsfolk fear and distrust all foreigners. Why? What are they hiding? Oyster's Reef, his community, vanishes.

What happened to it? Who is Oyster and what is the secret of his power? The catalyst for the showdown is the arrival in town of Nick and Sarah, each of whom has lost a child to Oyster's Reef.

There is no exit from either Outer Maroo or Oyster's Reef; no point of contact with the outside world. Under these circumstances notions of reality become relative. The distorted seems normal, the mad becomes sane.

The barren, drought-stricken wilderness of Outer Maroo is a fair approximation of Hell; Oyster's community, when it first begins, seems like a sort of Heaven. But the tragic end is never in question.

We follow with bated breath the steps to Armageddon. The reader is further hooked, and disbelief suspended, because we, too, have no point of comparison. To most of us the Queensland outback is as alien as Mars, and about as extreme in both climate and landscape.

Oyster is cunningly constructed: told from different viewpoints, it moves forwards and backwards in time. Its tight plotting and ventriloquial characterisation gives it the grip of a thriller. But it manages to overcome the main pitfall of such tales: can the ending, with all its necessary unravellings, avoid anticlimax? The answer is that if, as here, your story is based upon mood and character rather than intricacies of plot, it can.

Oyster has other virtues. Its language is sensuous and poetic, disproving the general rule that you can have language (Rushdie, Amis) or engagement (Rendell) but not both. Its psychology is sub-fie. And it achieves the mysterious freedoms of magic realism without succumbing to the tiresome cop-out of failing to answer the questions you've raised.

In short, *Oyster* triumphantly walks a tricky tightrope. One result is that even the smallest lapses jar. Occasionally the language gets too carried away or the symbolism is too rawly visible. And can any book still quote *Alice in Wonderland* and live? These are cavils. This is a wonderful book that deserves to sell millions.

Peter Robb (review date 6 March 1997)

SOURCE: "Roasted," in *London Review of Books,* March 6, 1997, p. 26.

[*In the following review of* Oyster, *Robb finds shortcomings in the novel's heavy-handed profundity and improbable plot and characters.*]

Ten or so years ago I stayed with a friend who was a senior doctor in Queensland's largest hospital, the Royal Brisbane. Most weekends he was on call to attend emergencies in remote inland areas by medical service plane or helicopter. The trips sometimes generated their own emergencies, since the helicopter pilot was a Vietnam veteran with a need for extreme situations and ready to create them when they didn't come naturally. Other times, in a 24-hour absence he'd fly thousands of miles in a small plane to a point due west and back, to airlift a terminal case from some tiny near-desert settlement like the one where Janette Turner Hospital's new novel is set. One Monday my friend came back from one such dot on the map with what remained of a man who seemed to have been beaten to death, or near it, by more than one person. The victim had been an outsider, someone who'd turned up in town a few months earlier and got a job in the local pub. The story of his accidental fall was corroborated by everyone in the town and made no sense at all of his injuries. The man died, I believe, and that was the end of it. After reading **Oyster** I remembered this and wondered whether any account of the man's fate reached his friends or family, if he had any.

Oyster is about the strangers and drifters who turn up in such outback places and people them. Outer Maroo is delineated by real geographical co-ordinates and a mass of meteorological and mineralogical data, but doesn't itself appear on the maps. This is not simply a question of its being fictional: its fictional inhabitants have gone to some lengths to erase their town from the records. One of the strangers in the novel is a woman called Miss Rover, a schoolteacher who's been kicked to death and fed to a feral pig for voicing unmentionable truths, but who remains a central presence, a voice and a memory in what follows. Janette Turner Hospital's premise of an outback town where such things might happen is all too-likely, and you wonder why she works so hard at giving verisimilitude to an unlikely plot, piling on the information and following up her story with a bibliography of half a dozen titles.

Outer Maroo is an ordinary drought-stricken outback settlement, socially riven between the boozers and the fundamentalist wowsers, with a history of usurpation and massacre in its relations with the aboriginal Murris. What makes it special, apart from the preternaturally large looming of the Living Word Gospel Hall, is its hidden opal wealth. Four years before the week that constitutes the foreground of the story, a charismatic stranger has walked into town, clad in loose white garments and carrying a rifle. He has curls, a beard, intense and disturbing milky-blue eyes and a golden body. He talks like a religious huckster but the locals are mesmerised by the splendid opals he shows them. Soon they're in business together, mining, polishing, selling. Oyster, the charlatan, runs his opal mine out of town as a millenarian religious commune, importing ingenuous young back-packers as labour. They become his prisoners and slaves. Their cards and letters home never leave town. Small planes fly in secretly from Singapore to remove the gems. The whole community is implicated, from the big graziers to the woman at the store. Everyone is making money, except the back-packers slaving underground, bearing the cult leader's children and doing the things cultists do. In town and at the mine, those who know too much and those who want to leave, die. Outer Maroo writes itself off the map.

It's too good and too bad to last, and three years later, for slightly obscure reasons, Oyster and his back-packers all die underground in an explosion and fire that the cult leader himself may have caused. A year later, a man from Melbourne and a woman from Boston arrive in Outer Maroo looking for their lost children. They meet up with Mercy and Jess, two of the three female witnesses at the centre of the story, and give the final prod that sets off a series of events which culminate in another, and definitive, apocalyptic fire.

In its telling, the story darts about and attitudinises and seems a lot more complex in the early pages than it turns out to be by the end: the outline takes some picking out through the dust kicked up by the author's heels. Sorting out what happened when, and whose sensibilities it's being refracted through, is heavy-going at first, but the bravura display of the early pages, however tiresome, is necessary to establish that Outer Maroo is a Place of the Mind, and 'all of those who find the place are lost.' Outer Maroo 'is thick with coded messages, but the messages are legible only to those who can read the secretive earth'. This requires a tipping of the bush-hat to aboriginal culture, though the Murris have moved out for the duration of the story, apart from Ethel, who 'sits there, cross-legged in the red dust at the edge of the bora rings, smiling to herself . . . putting the scattered rocks back where they belong, filling gaps in the circles and centuries'. **Oyster** makes highly questionable use of the ancient aboriginal communings imputed to the token Ethel over her smoking gidgee leaves. It also entails a great deal of rumination on climate and geography, since 'this disturbing story is sometimes fragmented and dispersed by shifting filaments of moisture in the upper air, and by variable atmospheric densities, and by rifts in time . . . the facts may seem to float loose in a sequence of their own devising.'

The trouble with these ruminations is that they get in the way of the story. Early on, Jess the barmaid, whose CV is pure proletarian violence, is starting to make a record of events. She takes up her pen at the height of the climactic blaze that's roasting everyone in town except for her and Ethel and an old opal miner. A tiny group, fate unknown behind the smoke, is making a dash for Brisbane and freedom in a stolen Land Rover. This is major drama. A change of wind and our threesome in town may be incinerated too. And what does the eager reader get? Jess's untimely meditations on the art of fiction:

> I write because what else is there to do? I write against time. I write against the whim of the fire. If the flames pass over us, I would like a record at least, to survive. This is a sort of primitive magic I'm engaged in, I recognise that, and I'm well aware that whatever I get written won't last as long as the bora rings, but at least it will huddle safely under Cretaceous layers older than the first firestick . . . perhaps my writing will be stranger than runes.

After further reflections on the nature of time and history ('time does not run in a straight line and never has. It is a capillary system, mapped outwards from whichever pulse point the observer occupies')—while the corrupted population of Outer Maroo is being devoured by the flames—Jess lays down her pen and leaps into the opal miner's cot with him, 'everything a blur of skin, legs, cock, cunt, breasts, buttocks . . . we feast on each other.' Her mind, however, is already on other things: 'Beginnings astonish me, the way they can rise out of ashes; and as for histories of lovers, they're outrageous. They're like folk tales, they're like fantasies, with the embarkation points of the two protagonists so often incongruous and the crossing of their paths so random; not to mention the question of their ruthlessness . . .' Jess, like Mercy and Miss Rover, is an incorrigible conceptualiser. Their habit of cerebration is sometimes what gets them into trouble, but mostly they just rabbit on and on for the sake of it, their thoughts indistinguishable from the author's. You soon feel that cerebration is the point, and the whole rather silly affair of the cult and the opals and the tyranny of silence and the dozens of people burnt alive is a pretext for a string of *aperçus.* Pulled between the story's violence and its obtrusive recording consciousness, *Oyster* wants to have it both ways. It reads like an awful lot of other novels, the award-winning kind, of the last decade or so. Joan Didion floats into view—her manner, if not her anorexic vigour.

Roasted people are a substantial novelty in Turner Hospital's writing. *Oyster* bears the marks of a radical discontent, a resolve to break out of the writers' workshop ghetto, to cut loose from sensitive souls with time on their hands, to lift off through the realm of the minor award into the mainstream and maybe a major motion picture. In a big, gutsy way Turner Hospital has struck out beyond the black stump for an international readership and taken on the brutal man's world of the Australian outback, its open spaces and closed minds—all colour, movement and apocalyptic fire. With its sinister stranger in town, *Oyster* is a throwback to the American Western. The scene is very film-set Western, too: the single dusty street with the store, the pub and the Gospel Hall facing off and everyone always on hand for the key showdowns.

The cast makes sense as action movie material. There's nothing open-ended about these neatly tied bundles of attributes. Old fossicker Major Miner never appears without a mention of the fall of Singapore, his defining experience, or concerned parent Nick without a reference to growing up Greek in Australia, which is his. The grazier's wife, Dorothy Godwin, is a kleptomaniac, the burnt-out pastor, Charles Given, has lost his faith and his books, the walk-on Pete Burnett is basically a decent bloke, the stepmother Sarah an American Jewish intellectual, the barmaid Jess silent and warmly sturdy. Oyster of the yeasty groin and fluttering white garments is a cipher. Peripheral figures utter a kind of computer-generated demotic and nobody grows or changes or surprises, not even crucial Mercy Given, who's really a double act with her mentor, the 'transferred' schoolteacher Susannah Rover. The late Miss Rover exists mainly in Mercy's memory, where her spunky

truth-telling seems so arch and knowing that you come to understand why the inhabitants of Outer Maroo did away with her.

Oyster is more about the place than the people, and while a silly story is a silly story, the determination to get down something of the look and the feel of Outer Maroo is more than a cinematic come-on. The anxiety lurking behind the showing-off and the millennial flourishes in this book has been around ever since Australian writing started taking itself seriously, at least since Patrick White announced his intention to 'people the great Australian emptiness' with his works. The writer's fear seems to be that in and for themselves these places and these people lack interest—that only an ungainly effort of the will can turn this matter into respectable fiction. Whence the great kitsch structures of White's novels of the Fifties and early Sixties, those parts of his books that now seem so dated and inessential, the dragging-in of religion and spirituality to give 'meaning'. Something similar happened with the painters, Sidney Nolan and Arthur Boyd, plonking allegorical figures in their Australian bush, inventing mythologies; but they managed it more lightly and more wittily than the writers. Turner Hospital's own anxieties in *Oyster* seem to lie closer to the surface. Outer Maroo is as assertively 'real' as its R. M. Williams boots, its Fourex beer and Toyota 4WDs. What it might be like to live there, however, with the drought, the heat and the isolation, but without cult deaths, dirty money and imported hysteria, is an order of reality quite missing here.

Turner Hospital is the author of forty-odd short, sharp and shapely stories, a lot of them set in the unpromising terrain of the anglophone university network of conferences, visiting professorships, and writer's residencies, especially in Canada, where she now lives for much of the time. They work the vein of memory, displacement, nostalgia, jolted by brief encounters and tiny unsettling experiences. Many adhere closely to the known facts of Turner Hospital's career. The voice in these stories is assured, at home in its limited milieu of faculty angst, and they have the great strength of achieving their effects in a brief compass. Reading them after *Oyster* makes you thankful that Jane Austen, hitting her limits in *Mansfield Park,* never decided to go for broke with an epic of slavery, sex and religion on Sir Thomas's Antiguan plantations.

Carolyn Bliss (review date Autumn 1997)

SOURCE: A review of *Oyster,* in *World Literature Today,* Vol. 71, No. 4, Autumn, 1997, p. 861.

[*In the following review of* Oyster, *Bliss finds fault in the novel's melodramatic plot and trite forebodings.*]

Australian-born writer Janette Turner Hospital's sixth and latest novel [*Oyster*] is an old-fashioned page-turner which offers up an intriguing mystery but finally fails to deliver either the anticipated shocks or revelations. Set in the Queensland outback village of Outer Maroo, a settlement so deliberately off the map that "anyone who finds this place is lost," the novel concerns the doomsday cult of a self-styled and shady messiah named Oyster and the effect of his communal opal-mining enterprise on the initially bemused but increasingly uneasy townspeople. In this place where people go to be nowhere—to be out of reach of loved ones, the law, and the government—Oyster and his wide-eyed groupies at first seem to belong as naturally as the perennial drought and the suffocating smell of death which accompanies it. But Oyster and his operations begin to pose a series of threats, especially as his community threatens to outnumber that of Outer Maroo. Finally, something must be done by someone. But by whom? Was the catastrophe precipitated by nervous economic interests within the opal-mining industry or its back-alley adjuncts? By disgruntled or terrified townspeople? By Oyster's rivals for spiritual authority among the leaders of what passes for orthodox religion in the town? Or was it perhaps Oyster himself, nudging the chosen few in the direction of the promised land? These questions, and their accompanying issues of culpability, are revisited with dangerous insistence by two newcomers—relatives of long-missing members of Oyster's cult—who arrive demanding answers. In confronting them, the town must of course confront its dark complicity in Oyster's designs.

Many of these themes will be familiar to readers of Hospital. The issue of moral responsibility has consumed her since her first, award-winning novel, *The Ivory Swing.* The combination of this concern with pronounced plotline and elements of the mystery-thriller genre will be remembered from *Borderline,* as will the preference for bestowing allegorical names on central female characters. In *Borderline* it was Felicity; in *Oyster* it is Mercy Given, who naturally survives the Jonestown (or is it Waco?) style holocaust at Oyster's camp. Finally, the theme of chronologically and geographically displaced people searching for where home might be and what it might demand of them recalls the stories of *Dislocations,* as well as much of Hospital's other work. Stylistic markers from Hospital's earlier texts are present as well. Examples are the use of the extended conceit and experimentation with point of view, which emerges here as an uneasy and unpredictable shifting between first and third persons.

Autobiographical echoes can also be heard. Of course, a woman who sees herself as a reluctant nomad and who divides her time among North America, Europe, and Australia would be preoccupied with issues of belonging and its costs. Of course, a woman who had been mugged at knife point would take note of ad hoc violence and the omnipresence of evil.

Finally, however, *Oyster* seems weakened by too much melodrama and too banal a message. As evidence of melodrama, let me cite the death of Susannah Rover, roving, noisy, and worst of all nosy schoolteacher imported from outside, who is kicked to death and thrown down a mine

shaft where her corpse can be consumed by a feral pig, trapped there for the purpose. As evidence that the message is at least too broad and entirely unsurprising, let me quote the character who articulates it. Near the end of the novel, Sarah (mother of dead cult member Amy) reflects, "Extremism is everywhere. . . . There's no safe place." Dutifully, the novel demonstrates extremism in faith and faithlessness, love and hate, selfishness and self-sacrifice, greed and generosity, weather, environment, and character.

Perhaps as millennial fervor heats up, a fervor sometimes not unlike Oyster's, we need to hear this sort of warning. I doubt, however, that *Oyster* is its most effective vehicle. Read the novel for its evocation of an unforgettable place and for its compelling story. Don't read it for its insights on human nature or religion run amok.

FURTHER READING

Criticism

Armstrong, Judith. "Some Local Dantes." *Overland* 147 (Winter 1997): 83-5.
> A review essay including brief discussion of *Oyster.*

Burgin, Richard. "The Quest for the Perfect Listener." *New York Times Book Review* (29 September 1991): 18.
> A review of *Isobars.*

Callahan, David. "Becoming Different in the Work of Janette Turner Hospital." *Ariel* 28, No. 2 (April, 1997): 23-34.
> Callahan examines the presentation and intersection of opposing social, sexual, and cultural perspectives in Hospital's fiction. Callahan asserts that Hospital's work reveals the author's conscious effort to confront problematic aspects of "otherness" and to convey the multifaceted experience of difference and marginalization.

Ellis, Markman. "In the Back of the Outback." *Times Literary Supplement* (13 September 1996): 22.
> Ellis offers a positive assessment of *Oyster,* though notes that the novel's literary sophistication lends "a sense of self-indulgence."

Hower, Edward. "She Lived By Theft and By Enchantment." *New York Times Book Review* (13 September 1992): 15.
> A review of *The Last Magician.*

Huggan, Graham. "Orientalism Reconfirmed?" *Canadian Literature* 132 (Spring 1992): 44-56.
> Includes analysis of *The Ivory Swing,* Hospital's postcolonial Canadian perspective, and aspects of the "East-West encounter" motif in the novel.

Loewinsohn, Ron. "Daddy: Sometimes a Particle, Sometimes a Wave." *New York Times Book Review* (12 March 1989): 14.

> A review of *Charades.*

McNeil, Jean. "Witches' Brew." *Women's Review of Books* X, No. 4 (January, 1993): 14.

> In this review of *The Last Magician,* McNeil commends Hospital's sophisticated literary constructs and highly-charged prose, but concludes that the novel's intellectual and moral concerns are ill-supported by its characters.

Neild, Elizabeth. "Disjointed Lives." *Women's Review of Books* VI, Nos. 10-11 (July, 1989): 34-5.

> Neild provides favorable readings of Hospital's themes, characters, and narrative style in *Borderlines, Dislocations,* and *Charades.*

Peck, Dale. "Way Outback." *New York Times Book Review* (22 March 1998): 11.

> A review of *Oyster.*

Skow, John. "Lost in the Wilderness." *Time* (6 April 1998): 77.

> A positive review of *Oyster.*

Thompson, Barbara. Review of *Dislocations,* by Janette Turner Hospital. *New York Times Book Review* (25 December 1988): 9.

> A review of *Dislocations.*

Additional coverage of Hospital's life and career is contained in the following sources published by the Gale Group: *Contemporary Authors,* **Vol. 108; and** *Contemporary Authors New Revision Series,* **Vol. 48;** *Contemporary Novelists;* **and** *Literature Resource Center.*

Tama Janowitz
1957-

American novelist, short story writer, journalist, and children's writer.

The following entry presents an overview of Janowitz's career through 1996. For further information on her life and works, see *CLC,* Volume 43.

INTRODUCTION

Both reproached and lauded for her bold depictions of late twentieth-century American society, Janowitz is a best-selling novelist who also became a celebrity in the worlds of fashion, art, and advertising in the 1980s and early 1990s. At one time, Janowitz was the subject of tremendous media exposure due to her association with the New York City art scene, which centered around pop art guru Andy Warhol. Critics have also identified her as part of a "literary brat pack" that includes novelists Jay McInerney, Bret Easton Ellis, and Douglas Coupland. Janowitz claims Henry James, Edith Wharton, and Vladimir Nabokov among her major influences, but her literary style encompasses a wide range of references; from the broad English farces of Evelyn Waugh to comic strips and the impact of television on modern culture. Janowitz specializes in making bold characterizations of mainstream pop culture and uses sharp satire to capture the "poses and pretentions" of the upper-class Manhattan art world.

BIOGRAPHICAL INFORMATION

Although a long-time resident of New York City, Janowitz was born in San Francisco, California; the daughter of Julian Frederick Janowitz, a psychiatrist, and Phyllis Winer, a poet and professor. Her childhood was marked by a liberal parenting style and her parents' divorce. Janowitz studied at several different institutions including Barnard College, Hollins College, Yale University School of Drama, and Columbia University. After college, she settled in New York and worked as a freelance journalist, a model, an assistant art director, and a writer-in-residence. Janowitz first began writing fiction during her college years. She completed *American Dad* (1981), her first published novel, several years after college while working in the New York fashion and art world. Her first critical success was *Slaves of New York* (1986), a collection of short stories which inspired an 1989 film by Ismail Merchant and James Ivory (in which Janowitz also appeared). *A Cannibal in Manhattan* (1987), an earlier work, was released by Janowitz's publisher immediately following the success of *Slaves of*

New York. Janowitz developed strong ties with the New York art scene, and especially with her close friend, Andy Warhol. Warhol's creative marketing approach and post-modern sensibilities were qualities that influenced Janowitz in her formative professional years. Employing Warhol's trademark technique of "visualization" (where an individual constantly imagines oneself as successful in order to achieve success), Janowitz boldly pursued her celebrity status as she participated in the decadent lifestyle embraced by many young affluent New Yorkers during the 1980s. In 1992, Janowitz married Tim Hunt, the curator of the Andy Warhol estate.

MAJOR WORKS

American Dad focuses on the life of a young man named Earl Przepasnick and his handling of his parents' divorce. Earl's relationships with his father, his psychiatrist, and his mother, are autobiographical in nature and reflective of several events in Janowitz's youth. *Slaves of New York* is a collection of twenty-two short stories inspired by Janowitz's experiences living in Manhattan and her relations to the New York City art world. Several of the stories center on a young jewelry maker named Eleanor and her artist boyfriend, Stash. Another prominent character is Marley Mantello, a self-assured painter who dreams of becoming a success. The stories exhibit an abundance of humor that helps mask a deep underlying darkness. This style is also prevalent in *A Cannibal in Manhattan*, whose main character, Mgungu Yabba Mgungu, is a young man brought to New York from a South Seas island by a wealthy socialite. Mgungu quickly encounters the barbarity of civilized life, and the novel, through its central metaphor, provides commentary on the culture of consumer capitalism. Janowitz exploits the Shakespearean conceit of "gender in disguise" in *The Male Cross-Dresser Support Group* (1992), which centers around Pamela Trowel (who sells advertising for *Hunter's World* magazine) and her befriending of a nine-year-old street urchin. Gender themes are also woven into *By the Shores of Gitchee Gumee* (1996), a story based on the poetry of Henry Wadsworth Longfellow. The novel focuses on Maud Slivenowicz, a nineteen-year-old who lives with her family in a trailer by the polluted shores of Lake Superior. Janowitz explores issues central to post-feminist thought through her portrayal of Maud and her sister, Marietta. Susan Bolotin referred to the novel as "a picaresque satire of twentieth-century America." Janowitz returned to her usual New York setting in her 1999 novel, *A Certain Age*. The city's social climbers and their cocktail-party circuit are again reexamined, this time with the focus on an unmarried woman in her thirties and her ruthless quest for a wealthy, well-connected husband. In April 2001, Janowitz collaborated with illustrator Tracy Dockray on the children's book, *Hear That?*, which centers around a mother playing a listening game with her young son.

CRITICAL RECEPTION

Although her first novel, *American Dad,* was widely ignored by critics, Janowitz's second work, *Slaves of New York,* became an international best-seller that immediately thrust her into the media spotlight. Readers were drawn to her dark sense of humor and her vivid, engaging descriptions of the ethics behind New York's avant-garde art scene. Critics, however, did not respond so favorably as the general public. Although some reviewers praised her bold prose style (Alice H. G. Phillips said that Janowitz "observes everything with a sharp eye but with a New York bohemian's true affection for her world"), many critics took issue with Janowitz's tendency to stress style over substance. They criticized Janowitz for her exhaustive descriptions of pop culture minutiae and for her thinly-veiled allusions to high-society gossip. Raymond Sokolov called *Slaves* a "slovenly collection" with "restlessly indistinct" prose, labelling Janowitz "a writer for nonreaders." *Slaves of New York* has endured as Janowitz's best reviewed work, although her follow-up novels have remained popular with readers across the country. When asked in an *Esquire* interview how she felt about the negative critical response to her work, Janowitz commented: "My feelings are hurt

. . . and you feel like, oh how could you say this, but it doesn't bother me that much because what can you do, you're writing the best book you can. And the other side of me feels glad that they trashed it because mostly the books that I don't like are the ones getting the lovely reviews." Hailed as a "marketing artist" by the *New York Times,* Janowitz is a writer whose fiction has drawn close scrutiny, and whose work has been hailed as a vivid and telling rendition of American postmodern urban life.

PRINCIPAL WORKS

American Dad (novel) 1981
*Slaves of New York (short stories) 1986
A Cannibal in Manhattan (novel) 1987
The Male Cross-Dresser Support Group (novel) 1992
By the Shores of Gitchee Gumee (novel) 1996
A Certain Age (novel) 1999
Hear That? (juvenilia) 2001

*This work was adapted for the film *Slaves of New York* (1989), with a screenplay written by Janowitz, who also appeared in the film.

CRITICISM

Raymond Sokolov (review date 22 July 1986)

SOURCE: "New Girl in Town," in *Wall Street Journal,* July 22, 1986, Vol. CCVIII, No. 15, p. 28.

[*In the following excerpt Sokolov objects to the substance of Janowitz's prose in* Slaves of New York.]

Uptown in the shabby genteel offices of *The New Yorker* they have been waiting at least a decade for the aged editor William Shawn to step down. At age 80, he has become a laughingstock, devoting his once-distinguished, once-amusing magazine to n-part screeds on staple grains and vanished airplanes, indulging an old man's whim for young women writers of dubious (literary) virtue.

The latest of these Shawn-genues is Tama Janowitz, whose stories mostly chronicle clothes-conscious young women caught up in the current Manhattan art-and-club scene. Ms. Janowitz is in a position to know about her subject. In her real life, she is the queen of the art mob, goes to parties on the arm of Andy Warhol, has her picture on the cover of *New York* magazine, and now she lies exposed, down to her most unmentionable fiction, in *Slaves of New York.*

Should you happen to be swept up in the Janowitz craze to the point of actually opening this slovenly collection, you will discover a cast of characters ranging from pathetic Eleanor, slave of her boyfriend Stash, to that self-proclaimed saint and genius, the painter Marley Mantello. Do not look to them for depth (or even shallow) of character. What you get is what you see walking around the artburbs of Manhattan, in the store windows and bars of SoHo, Tribeca and the Lower East Side.

Ms. Janowitz is trying to report on the scene from the ambivalent position of an unenthusiastic participant. There is nothing intrinsically wrong with this posture. It could work, but fiction is carried on through language, and Ms. Janowitz is not in control of the only one she's got.

She is, for instance, a bit shaky in the area of English vocabulary.

The always-tedious Marley returns to his apartment and discovers a smelly "curled black pile on top of the messy bed-clothes" and concludes that "some animal had performed its ablutions" there.

This passage cannot be taken literally. To perform ablutions is to wash, to wash the body or to cleanse a wine chalice in church. Since washing, in either sense, is not what Marley supposes the intruding animal did on his bed, the Janowitz reader has to make a choice: Either Ms. Janowitz doesn't know what "ablutions" means or she wants us to think that Marley doesn't. There's no way of telling, because Ms. Janowitz's prose is so restlessly indistinct that you never know how to take it. Now she is ironic. Now she does a parody of stiff, formal speech. Now she is spewing out a surreal list of dishes on a menu.

This account exaggerates the case, but not greatly. Some of the stories, the ones touched by the editorial caress of Mr. Shawn, are cleanly written in their fatigued, affectless way. But now that this collection lets us see Ms. Janowitz whole, we can see her for the art-world figment that she is, a writer for nonreaders. Without the still-potent imprimatur of *The New Yorker,* she would never have attained such high visibility.

This is why it matters so much what happens to *The New Yorker.* It is the only strong force for potential good left on our literary landscape. The rest is publicity or trend. But *The New Yorker* can still bring the general reader together with the serious writer, or could if it wanted. The worrisome thing is that the influence built up over decades is ebbing in the uncertain atmosphere of the Shawnian twilight.

Alice H. G. Phillips (review date 12 December 1986)

SOURCE: "From the Hip," in *Times Literary Supplement,* December 12, 1986, p. 1409.

[*The following review provides a brief synopsis of* Slaves of New York *and comments on the book's range of characters and themes.*]

From its opening tale, related flamboyantly by a rich girl turned prostitute, to its final case history of a modern sado-masochistic relationship, Tama Janowitz's first collection of short stories [*Slaves of New York*] is designed to attract the attention of the young and the trendy. But then, almost all of its characters are New York artists, art dealers, designers or models with reputations to make and high rents to pay; *they* know that catching the eye of the right people is what sells paintings or ideas—or whatever it is you're selling.

Janowitz keeps her balance on the tilted game board. She observes everything with a sharp eye but with a New York bohemian's true affection for her world, and applies her mischievous sense of humour to its artworks ("flatulent balloons"), personalities ("furious elves and fairies, in twentieth-century disguise") and social events:

> One artist . . . made strange movements with his mouth like a kissing gourami. One artist was so famous he refused to sit with the rest of us; he had his own private table on the balcony, where he was seated with a famous French movie actress. The one sitting across from me was quite drunk. . . . While he was talking to someone he picked up a full ashtray . . . and emptied it under the table.

Janowitz alternates various odd storytellers and the hip narrator of the case histories with two main narrators who are perfect comic creations. Seven of the twenty-two stories are told by Eleanor, an insecure jewellery designer months behind the latest fashions. Five others are narrated by the epic painter Marley Mantello, who plans to erect his own frescoed chapel next to the Vatican, when he gets financial backing, and says things like, "my feeling is, in the future we will have real heroes. Like me." Eleanor is cowed by the arty people she knows and acutely aware of her own marginality, whereas Marley is certain he is a genius; together, they make up a balanced person.

As we witness Eleanor's and Marley's small daily humiliations and follow them around the city on their erratic quests for love, artistic immortality and a decent place to live, we begin to like them. Eleanor's jewellery starts to appear in glossy magazines; she scrapes up the courage—and the cash—to leave her possessive but marriage-shy boyfriend and rent her own bedsit, in which she throws a party almost but not completely spoiled for her by her anxieties. Marley is terrorized by an enormous New York tomcat, is evicted from his flat, and is more wounded than he admits when his best friend tells him his paintings are "like a lot of stuff done in the early seventies"—the deadliest insult in the art forum of the 1980s.

The collection's only real excursion outside Manhattan is to London. Eleanor nostalgically recalls the year she spent as a student in London; her mother's old acquaintance Lord Simeon, a professor at London University, invites her to lunch *tête à tête* in his tower, is terribly charming and eccentric in the face of her youthful American boorishness, promises to ring her soon and cook his special curry for her, and promptly forgets her. Eleanor is haunted by the memory of the glass case in his college which usually contained the body of the founder, Jeremy Bentham; the case was empty because the corpse was being held for ransom by a rugby team from a rival college.

Michael Dibdin (review date 5 February 1987)

SOURCE: "Ghosts in the Machine," in *London Review of Books,* February 5, 1987, pp. 12-13.

[*In the following review, Dibdin discusses Janowitz's thematic concerns in the novel* Slaves of New York.]

How do you like to be approached by a strange work of fiction? Do you prefer a hearty handshake ('Call me Ishmael'), a more discursive line ('All happy families are alike'), or a low-key manner ('For a long time I used to go to bed early')? What about this, for example?

> After I became a prostitute, I had to deal with penises of every imaginable shape and size. Some large, others quite shrivelled and pendulous of testicle. Some blue-veined and reeking of Stilton, some miserly.

The narrator is a Jewish princess who took up her trade 'when my job as script girl for a German-produced movie to be filmed in Venezuela fell through'; her pimp, Bob, had been a doctoral candidate in philosophy and American literature at the University of Massachusetts; their Avenue A walk-up is littered with empty syringes, douche bags, whips, garrottes, and packages of half-eaten junk food. 'As far as his role went', Bob 'could have cared less', but 'I felt that . . . I was growing intellectually as well as emotionally. Bob was both sadist and masochist to me; for him I was madonna and whore. Life with him was never dull.'

The lead story in **Slaves of New York** reads like a come-on for a quite different book, featuring a cast of hip mutants strong on style, heavy sex and drugs, and 'caring less'. Such a book would no doubt be successful: more so, perhaps, than the one Tama Janowitz has written, which may explain why her publishers have pushed it out front. But seekers after cheap thrills are going to be disappointed. Sex and violence are almost eerily absent from **Slaves,** and so far from 'caring less', the characters who haunt its pages care obsessively about everything and nothing.

The bulk of the 22 stories are first-person narratives. Only in two of the others, **'Snow-ball'** and **'The New Acquaintances,'** is the author on something like top form, while the rest range from slight jests (**'You and the Boss,'** a swipe at the Bruce Springsteen myth) through stylised anecdotes (the two **'Case Histories'**) to a fable about a symbiotic relationship (**'Kurt and Natasha'**). While there is much to admire here, the tone is often tiresomely arch and there is a sense of arbitrariness which disappears the

moment Tama Janowitz slips into the fluid and treacherous mode where she is completely at home.

Most of these monologues are narrated by two characters, Eleanor and Marley Mantello, forming two discontinuous story-lines, like a soap-opera with half the episodes missing. We first meet Eleanor as one of the 'slaves' of the title. Art Buchwald tried to debunk *Last Tango in Paris* by joking that it was about the difficulties of finding accommodation to rent in the French capital. In **Slaves** that gag becomes a bottom-line reality. 'There're hundreds of women,' Eleanor warns a girlfriend who is thinking of moving to New York. 'And all the men are gay or are in the slave class themselves. Your only solution is to get rich, so you can get an apartment and then you can have your own slave. He would be poor but amenable.' Eleanor is in her late twenties and living with Stash, an artist who is 'authoritative and permissive, all at the same time. In other words, I can do whatever I want, as long as it's something he approves of.' But the alternative is bleak: an apartment on 14th Street at $1500 a month is 'a real find' even if you have to install the toilet and fixtures yourself. So for now Eleanor cooks, shops and cleans for Stash, walks his dog and deals with his moods: 'sometimes I felt as if I were the sole member of the Bomb Squad: I had to defuse Stash.' But it's his apartment, and since the jewellery she makes—'shellacked sea horses, plastic James Bond-doll earrings'—is not successful, her choice is between living with Stash on his terms and going home to her mother. 'If ever I get some kind of job security and/or marital security, I'm going to join the feminist movement,' Eleanor vows. In the end she gets a job and moves out, but finds herself 'in the same mess, only in a different neighbourhood'.

Like Eleanor, Marley Mantello—a manic-depressive artist and self-styled 'genius'—is at an age when drawing cheques on the future becomes more difficult. But there the similarity ends. 'I would have numbered myself in with the rest of humanity, only I was one step above it: by that I mean I was an artist, which redeemed me.' Even less successful than Stash, Marley cherishes grandiose dreams of building a 'Chapel of Jesus Christ as a Woman' next to the Vatican, but meanwhile starves on canned Chef Boy-ar-dee sauce and is evicted from his unheated apartment. He is also tormented by anxiety—'Was I well enough to get up today? Did my stomach hurt? Was an unhealed cut on my finger a sign of cancer?'—and chilly draughts from the ruthless jungle world he perceives all around. His only defence is his ego, which he keeps inflated to lunatic proportions while subjecting his fellow artists to a mordant line in criticism: 'he was basically a smart guy, basically talented. But the basically that I'm speaking of is basically mediocre.' His paintings mythologise reality—Ulysses as a failed Forties artist in a denim jacket and blue jeans, Penelope living in a Cape Cod beach house—and this vision extends itself to the people around him: 'gods and pixies' who have 'forgotten their true selves and are out trying to make a buck and win influential friends'. His comic potential is heightened by a stilted and rhetorical tone of voice

('Say not so!') but Janowitz's control ensures that the comedy never gets too safe. The concluding pages of **'Life in the Pre-Cambrian Era,'** for example, show a mind on the brink of madness. Marley's work starts to sell, but our enduring image of him remains that fixed by Eleanor, watching his drunken behaviour at a baseball game: 'out in left field, staggering around in circles'.

The way in which this image operates as both detail and metaphor is typical of the skill with which Tama Janowitz avoids the risk of anecdotalism. *Slaves* might easily have degenerated into a heap of gimmicky tales about wacky artist-folk, a Post-Modern *Scènes de la Vie de Bohème*, Biff cartoons filmed by Paul Morrissey. Despite the odd in-joke (one character 'refused to travel above 14th Street, claiming that it led to mental decay') this never looks likely to happen, thanks to Janowitz's success in making her subject-matter thematic: her characters create a bewildering range of 'art objects', but first and foremost they create themselves. For this is a world where 'essentialism' is a dirty word, as the narrator of **'Engagements'** discovers in her 'Poetics of Gender' colloquium. 'Fixed identities' are out: 'to speak of identity is to speak of racism'; 'post-gendered subjectivities' and 'the notion of the subject in progress' are in. The same notion is expressed in more homely form by Eleanor's mother, who 'had always told me I could be anyone I chose', while another character takes this to its logical conclusion: 'everything that happens to you is because you want it to.' Hence the greater stability of the first-person narratives in *Slaves*. In a world where you cannot 'speak of identity', the pronoun of identity is paradoxically privileged because of its very ambiguity: I say 'I', but so do you.

Sartre once told a questioner: 'Obviously I do not mean that whenever I choose between a millefeuille and a chocolate éclair I choose in anguish.' But that kitsch anguish is the air that these New Yorkers breathe. What to wear? Who to see? What to say? It's easier to stay home:

> I found fun very traumatising, difficult even. In some ways it was more fun not to have fun. To me, having fun was almost identical to feeling anxious. I thought I preferred to sit at home by myself, depressed.

Everything demands a choice. Even one's appearance is not 'fixed'. Told about a surgeon who will 'trade work for paintings', one artist replies: 'In that case, I'd like to have my whole self redone. But not my hair.' Nor is who you are in any way determined by what you do: 'Most of the people I knew were doing one thing but considered themselves to be something else: all the waitresses I knew were really actresses, all the xeroxers . . . were really novelists, all the receptionists were artists. There were enough examples of . . . receptionists who went on to become famous artists that the receptionists felt it was okay to call themselves artists.' Any talk of one's background is strictly taboo:

> 'I always meant to ask you—where are you from?' I say. 'Originally.' 'Where am I from?' she says. 'Where

am I from? What kind of question is that?' Is my question in terrible taste, or is she crazy?

Eleanor has no business asking such questions—she should be deciphering the signals people send about their choices. Unfortunately she is not very good at that, either. In **'Patterns'** she falls victim to the stratagems of a gay fashion designer, who, typically, claims to dislike 'any kind of game-playing'. Eleanor agrees: '"I've never been able to figure out the rules." Wilfredo said he could appreciate this quality in me.' Even when it is clear that she has been used, Eleanor finds it hard to believe: 'I felt so adamant that Wilfredo and I were meant to be together.' A similar sense of rightness also deceives Cora in **'Engagements,'** when she learns that her dream apartment has been rented: 'That was my apartment. It *felt* like my apartment.' Feelings are not to be trusted out there in the semantic jungle.

Nevertheless, nostalgia for fixed roles and identities remains strong; the jungle bristles with animal life. Besides owning dogs which are treated with greater consideration than people, the characters in *Slaves* are compared with horses, llamas, beavers, panthers, salamanders, lizards, lions, gibbons, vixens, hornets, fawns, elephants, moose, orang-utangs, octopuses, gorillas, goats, rats, rattlesnakes, monkeys and mice in a frantic attempt to pin them down. As Eleanor reflects, 'I had seen those *National Geographic* wild-life specials on TV . . . animals met each other, performed some little courting dance, and mated for life. They knew exactly what to do; they relied on instinctive behaviour that had not given their parents and grandparents any problems either.' For humans, on the other hand, even eating is problematic. Tama Janowitz conveys the full shuddering recoil from food we have all felt as children, that panicky cry: 'You expect me to put *that* in my mouth?' Japanese restaurateurs in particular will not be voting her Ms Popularity this year, and devotees of tinned ham should also stay away. Food is often offered aggressively, in a ritual of domination and submission, notably when Marley is obliged to eat a huge breakfast prepared by 'plump collector Chuck Dade Dolger', having been warned by his dealer Ginger that 'he's going to think you're a wimp if you don't eat very much.' The story is called **'Turkey Talk'**: Chuck and Marley don't talk turkey, they just gabble. But when Ginger offers a comment she is silenced: 'These are men talking, Ginger.' Marley doesn't mind people criticising his work 'because I had a simple way of dealing with it—I didn't listen.' The air is thick with messages, but everyone is transmitting and no one receiving. When Eleanor telephones home her mother interrupts her so that she can listen to two other voices on the line, inaudible to Eleanor, whose conversation is clearly more interesting to her than what her daughter has to say.

Despite the very real humour of the book, the underlying tone remains dark. This is not the bland affluent suburban West Coast world of *The Serial*, where anything goes and nothing matters. The machine these ghosts inhabit is a fruit machine: it pays out. At a party a stranger asks Eleanor about her relationship with Stash:

'Is he rich?' she said . . .

'No,' I said.

'Are you?'

'No.'

'Well, why would you go out with him?' she said.

Eleanor has no answer to that, but later, when a drunken male friend tells her, 'You shouldn't act so desperate,' she snaps back, 'I consider life itself to be an act of desperation,' and even the ebullient Marley is finally reduced to a numbed tone as he recounts his sister's pointless death. Like Stevie Smith, Tama Janowitz is aware that 'being comical does not ameliorate the desperation.' The narrator of *Novel on Yellow Paper* refers to the 'talking voice that runs on, and the thoughts that come'. Eleanor comments: 'Well, once again I am silently rambling on. I have to reel myself back in like a fish.' In both cases, the self-deprecation is an essential element in a perfectly achieved tone of voice. The opening lines of a book can be deceptive; what really matters is whether the writer can find and maintain the appropriate tone. There is some unevenness in this collection, but in the best stories Tama Janowitz passes that test triumphantly.

In **'Who's on first?'** an impromptu baseball game is effortlessly exploited as an extended metaphor for the oddly cosy, self-regarding world of *Slaves*: a world where everybody knows everybody, usually carnally; where adults behave like children and a five-year-old is the only one who knows what is going on, where nothing is predictable, not even failure. Eleanor wants to play, but is afraid of disgracing herself. When she arrives at the field she feels 'like some actress who's walked on the movie set without her script. Obviously I don't belong.' She is tempted not to play but to make her escape: 'But the thought of stepping out from under the carbon-arc lamps of the imaginary world, a place brighter than day into the blackness that falls immediately beyond, fills me with terror.'

Sonia Pilcer (review date 18 October 1987)

SOURCE: "Pre-Literate in Manhattan," in *Los Angeles Times Book Review,* October 18, 1987, p. 10.

[*In the following review, Pilcer briefly considers several thematic implications of* A Cannibal in Manhattan.]

Perhaps you've seen her Amaretto ads. The most visible of a highly publicized group of young writers who have been hailed "the literary brat pack," Tama Janowitz has brand recognition. Her new book [*A Cannibal in Manhattan.*] has been launched with the breathless hype usually reserved for rock acts.

Despite the off-putting title, I was ready to be entertained by her deadpan humor and offbeat characters.

Unfortunately, Janowitz fails to find a voice for Mgungu Yabba Mgungu, as she did for her down-town *Slave* denizens. "I am nothing more than a savage," says Mgungu. "I don't understand even the simplest theories of electricity." Yet this cannibal does know his American brand names as well as the city's hottest clubs.

One hopes that Mgungu might be given some original observations to chew on. Instead, we are served such whopping platitudes as, "A life in the United States. How was I to know what people said or did is not the same at all as what they mean?"

The book itself features a photo scrapbook straight out of fanzinedom, including Janowitz and friends cavorting as the characters, complete with makeup and hair-stylist credits. I guess the hottest shot is of a wizened Andy Warhol, portraying *Cannibal* museum curator Parker Janius. Throughout, the pages are peppered with drawings of skulls and other exotica.

Ballpoint through his nose, Mgungu is a savage dressed up with nowhere to go but the cover of *Time* magazine. After all, cannibals should get their 15 minutes of fame too. The other characters are blatant stereotypes including heiress Maria Fishburn, played by *Interview*'s Paige Powell, rock star Kent Gable, Parker Junius, pizza parlor Joe and a few others who listlessly manipulate poor Mgungu.

It could even be said that Mgungu's naive tone reflects his creator, who told *Paper,* a downtown magazine, "It was really just me trying to be this man. To me society is a big con. I never quite figured out the skills to get along in society."

Finally, what we have is a portrait of greed: a publisher who will package a best-selling author's juvenilia and a promising writer who doesn't know the difference. Could Mgungu be an allegory for Janowitz's cynical exposure in American media?

Peter Reading (review date 4-10 March 1988)

SOURCE: "Into the Faded Air, the Torpid," in *Times Literary Supplement,* No. 4,431, March 4-10, 1988, p. 245.

[*In the following review, Reading discusses the texts and subtexts of* A Cannibal in Manhattan.]

To the South Pacific island of New Burnt Norton, home of the sometime cannibalistic, almost extinct Lesser Pimbas, comes nubile New York billion-heiress Maria Fishburn—ostensibly to teach algebra to the hapless natives under the auspices of the Peace Corps, but really because she fancies the tribe's president-elect, five-foot purple-skinned Mgungu Yabba Mgungu, having seen his picture on the front of the *National Geographic* years earlier and fallen in love with him. Maria dispatches her prize back to the States. The ensuing culture-shock, recorded in Mgungu's idiosyncratic first-person English, is the subject of Tama Janowitz's amusing picaresque fiction [*A Cannibal in Manhattan.*]

The noble savage serves, of course, to accentuate the real absurdity, viciousness and debasement of the sophisticated civilization into which he is deposited. With somewhat forced ingenuousness the quondam cannibal plods a well-worn itinerary through the disaster zone of modern urban social and psychotic mess. The satirical sallies include a jab at piety ("Oh, Jackie Kennedy Onassis, I prayed, suddenly turning to religion in a time of need"), a memorably funny encounter with a recalcitrant airborne jakes and a gnashing of teeth at the vagaries of airline cuisine ("a very hard roll, soggy in the center and topped with tiny seeds like gnats, while within were some curious greasy strands of meat").

The flavour is of mild Waugh fare. The curator of the Museum of Primitive Cultures has invited Mgungu to participate in an International Dance Festival—"The Polynesian girls' troupe has done nothing but pick up men since they got over here. The Whirling Dervishes have refused to come out of their room for three days unless I send up a goat for them to sacrifice." And the more urbane culture of the Whitney is sent up as our savage critic ponders the confusing exhibits of blank canvas, tar and feathers, a dead chicken, smashed pottery and an alarm clock—the lauded representatives of contemporary Fine Art.

There's an element, too, of black mischief, when, in a bout of inadvertent atavistic anthropophagy, the hero eats barbecued bits of his newly-espoused Maria. By now he's involved with the underworld and the landscape has hardened to the gritty, grot-strewn grey areas of the city. Maria, evidently involved in junk-traffic (and having been, in part at least, attracted to the islander by his knowledge of a unique New Burnt Norton narcotic), has been wasted by her seedy pals.

Indeed, *A Cannibal in Manhattan* is at its best when dealing with the seedy. The cartography of garbage-and-stray-dog waste land is impeccable. Mgungu's sojourn with the winos is funny, compassionate and productive of a humane Dickensian character-sketch—Daddyo, a Vietnam veteran whose costume incorporates a defunct television cabinet and whose demise is unexpectedly affecting.

A swatch of photographs with spoof captions may at first appear to enhance the "reality" of the New York and New Burnt Norton backgrounds, but is ultimately no more than a sham *avant-garde* detraction; nor is there much to justify cluttering the pages with irrelevant mediocre graphic design doodles.

Elizabeth Kaye (essay date November 1988)

SOURCE: "Fifteen Minutes over Soho," in *Esquire,* November, 1988, pp. 170-84.

[*In the following essay, Kaye presents a detailed portrait of Janowitz's personal life, commenting on her professional milieu and various critical attitudes toward her work.*]

From the back she looks like a stick figure drawn by a child. From any angle, she clearly aspires to be both a rebel and a waif. Her abundant hair has been likened to a bird's nest, a furry wigwam, a lion's mane. It is going gray at the temples.

Had she had less distinctive hair, her life might have been quite different. The hair has been useful in furthering the career of a writer whose most notable creation has proven to be herself.

Wherever she goes, people stare at her. Those ignorant of who she is can tell that she is Someone. As much as she solicits attention, obtaining it seems to unnerve her and to reduce her to a state that is both zoned out and out of control. Her face goes dead, her eyes roll upward, her head bobs from side to side. When she smiles, her face changes. Her smile is sweet and sometimes wistful. It lightens and softens her face and disappears in an instant.

Her eyes are lined with black, brightened by blue contact lenses. She says she wears tinted lenses because they are easier to find if one drops out, though that is probably not the only reason. Her skin is whitened with Germaine Monteil makeup, her lips reddened with lipstick that she reapplies even when she doesn't need to. "If I could get it down," she says, "I'd look like one of those Warhol silkscreen portraits where it's all mouth and then eyes."

She looks better without makeup but she doesn't think so.

There Is No Peter Parker

Tama has just agreed to be portrayed in a Marvel comic. The thought of this makes her smile. She always smiles when she contemplates doing something that will upset people. "I love to upset people," she says, "I don't know why."

Now she chews a piece of Care Free gum while the episode she'll appear in is detailed by the editor of *Spider-Man.*

"Peter Parker, who is Spider-Man, has written a book," he explains, "and he'll be going on the talk shows and you'll be on the talk shows with him."

"I don't want to go on the talk shows," says Tama. "I thought I was going to get to be in the comic book."

"This is *in* the comic book," the man tells her. "There is no Peter Parker. There is no Spider-Man. These are all characters."

Tama laughs. Her laugh sounds like a small bird gasping for air. Then she says, "Do you use many other authors?"

As it happens, Tom Wolfe was a Marvel comic character in 1968, though Tama is surely, as she puts it, "the first Princeton fellow to be in a Marvel comic."

She regards it as "fun and goofy." Her publicist regards it as "just totally Tama." Others are apt to regard it as one more in a growing list of activities that would seem to qualify Tama for tenure only on *Hollywood Squares.*

"Like, being in a Marvel comic or any of that stuff, I know it's going to drive people crazy," she says, "and I do get upset when they act horrified and nasty and it does hurt my feelings and make me feel bad but I can't help it and I can't stop myself from wanting to upset them more. And then people go, like, 'Well, who does she think she is? Her fifteen minutes are going to run out pretty soon.'"

Paging Mr. So and So

The apogee of Tama's brief and controversial career came lately, with her involvement in the movie ***Slaves of New York.*** To the degree that she views herself as Cinderella—which is considerable—the making of this movie has been her pumpkin. Every afternoon, she goes to the set, mostly to hang out. Before filming started she never knew what to do with herself each day when she had finished writing. She would become bored, fretful, lonely; she has no hobbies. Now, when people ask her about the movie, she tells them, "I don't know what I'll do when its over."

The movie began shooting in April 1988. In addition to a place to go in the afternoon, writing the script has given Tama several other things she always wanted: a collaborative project, the ability to get credit cards at last, and, potentially, a craft to fall back on if she can no longer get published. It has also given her the friendship of the producer Ismail Merchant and the director James Ivory, two elegant and accomplished men. "So now I'm like working with these guys," says Tama.

In early spring, she accompanied Merchant and Ivory to Los Angeles, where they held auditions. "It was the most fun thing I ever sat through. I mean, like there I was in the Beverly Hills Hotel and everything and you'd hear, 'Paging Mr. So and So.'"

As all writers do, she wants to feel that her work is loved, that she is loved for her work. This has eluded her among literary people. With Merchant and Ivory she had found it. "I mean it's just been overwhelming," she says. "They're completely respectful of me. They had me out to their house in the country, they had me out to dinners. I've never been treated like this before where I felt like people were interested in my feelings and liked me."

Ivory appears to be an unlikely collaborator for Tama Janowitz. He wears well-pressed khaki pants, has neatly combed silver hair, and looks like a man who could afford a large yacht but would consider it more tasteful to own a small one. He seems out of place on this movie set in a building in TriBeCa, where a messy room with graffiti-covered walls replicates the disarray of a downtown artist's apartment.

During a break, Ivory comes over to Tama to talk about some rewrites. She smiles and chews her gum faster. Ivory tells her, "That scene is nine pages. The whole script is 121 pages. We can't have such a monstrously heavy scene, so give it a rethink." Tama nods earnestly, repeatedly, her mouth slightly open. She takes a pen out of her purse and gnaws on it.

"Now," says Ivory, "what does the scene need to tell us?" He speaks with the slightly forced joviality of a teacher who is trying not to intimidate a frightened pupil. Rapidly, he enumerates the scene's four salient points, ticking them off one by one on his fingers. Tama nods, keeps chewing on the pen, decides to take notes, fumbles in her purse for a piece of paper. She settles for an opened envelope.

One of the actors watches her. Tama thinks he's cute, but she's heard he chases all the extras, and she's concluded he's trouble. Still, she keeps looking at him.

She prefers to have a boyfriend but usually doesn't. When she does, it ends badly. Her recent affair with a wealthy Texan fell apart after six months when she asked, "Where is this going?" and he said, "No place." Shortly after that he married a salesgirl from Woolworth's.

Tama used to suspect that her love affairs were disasters because she didn't like men. She's changed her mind.

"The truth is I just love men," she says. "I think men are so great. I mean, they add excitement. You know, I mean, the men want to hang around with the men, and the women want to go out with the men—we're all like anxious to be with the men. I'm just as guilty of it as the next person."

For most of her adult life she's lived alone. She's tired of it.

She's So Much Smarter

Her closest friend is her mother. They talk on the phone several times each day. Phyllis Janowitz has red hair as thick as Tama's, a quiet voice, and a guileless manner. She is a respected poet who teaches at Cornell University. She spent the first part of her working life as a wife, a mother, and a dietician.

"I feel like she's better than I am," says Tama. "I feel like she's so much smarter and her poetry's fantastic and she's better looking and like I'm just a watered-down version of what she would have been if she'd lived in a time when women didn't have restrictions placed on them."

"She always says that," her mother says. "It makes me feel good. But I don't believe it."

The Sixties Came Along

Tama's father is a neo-Freudian psychiatrist. She was three when he finished his residency at the Langley Porter Psychiatric Institute in San Francisco. She was five when he moved his family to Amherst, Massachusetts.

Early on, it was apparent that Tama loved to read and draw. Her parents neither encouraged nor discouraged her. "I really believed," her mother says, "that you're born to do something and that you're the only one who knows it." She was no more directive about when to go to sleep or what to wear. "I don't think I told her to do anything," she says. "I guess the Sixties came along."

Her father was equally permissive. "He didn't mind if I went into his room," says Tama, "and read his Playboys. The only thing you had to be careful of was not making noise when he was seeing patients."

When Tama was eight her parents decided to take her and her younger brother to Esalen for a year. But Esalen was not open to children. "My parents couldn't believe it," says Tama. "They said, 'Esalen is supposed to be this free place and the people are naked and it's beautiful and they won't let children go there? What kind of double standard is that?' So we never made it to Esalen."

I'll Finally Have a Friend

Tama viewed her mother as "a poet in a dream world." She viewed her father as "more rooted in the concrete." This might have been a good combination for a marriage; as things turned out, it wasn't.

Tama was ten when her parents divorced. They were the only divorced couple in the neighborhood. Tama's friends were told by their parents that she was a bad influence and that they should not play with her. Tama was lonely and frightened. She became closer to her mother.

Her mother was suffering, too, and late at night she confided in Tama. She told her about her own loneliness, her own fears. She told her about her frustrations with work. Tama was too young to have any advice to offer. Instead, she would listen, ask questions, try to console her. "She's so kind," says her mother. "I think I'd be dead if it wasn't for her. I couldn't really live without her."

"And it's funny, but even before she was born, I thought, when she's grown, I'll finally have a friend."

American Dad

After the divorce it seemed to Tama that her father always had a new wife or girlfriend that she did not like. She did not think that they liked her either. "Some did," her father recalls, "some didn't."

Of more concern to Tama was her father's opinion of her. Her mother always maintained that he, too, disliked her. "The only explanation that we've ever come up with," she says now, "is that Tama reminds him of me. And he never accepted her. He always made her feel like she was a no-good bitch."

"It was never true," says Dr. Janowitz, "that I did not care for Tama. That's something Phyllis did to her. She used Tama as an ally and tried to convince her that I was the enemy of both of them. And I guess she did."

Tama's sense that her father held her in contempt is one of the few things about herself that she does not like to discuss. "I'm sure it affected me a lot," she says flatly, "and I'm positive it gave me a lot of motivation to prove myself. Whatever."

When Tama was twenty-three her first book was published. It was called **American Dad.** At the time she told an interviewer, "My father is a bastard but I've resolved that issue." The book told the story of a disagreeable, overbearing, oversexed neo-Freudian psychiatrist who accidentally kills the narrator's poet mother. "Well . . ." says Phyllis Janowitz, "of course it's totally fiction."

Ultimately, Tama's attitude toward her father became far more generous than her mother's. "But I'm not my mother," she says. "I'm the child."

White Rats and Rabbits

Phyllis Janowitz supported her children on grants she won for her poetry. Money was always scarce. They never went to movies. They had a television, but it had bad reception. For entertainment they played cards and went to the library.

At home, they read a lot but rarely talked about what they read. "We just switched books," says Tama. They always read during dinner. The pages were smudged with spaghetti sauce, little darkenings from London broil, butter from baked potatoes. Tama and her brother did the cooking.

Their tiny house was filled with plants. Tama raised white rats and rabbits in the basement. Occasionally the phone would ring, but nobody answered it.

This Bleak Town

"The time when it was the worst for me," says Tama, "was when I was about fifteen and my mother would take me with her when she went to get her unemployment check. It was like in this bleak town where steelworkers were unemployed and there were signs for jobs at Arby's and we'd wait in line with people covered with mud and dirt. We'd wait a really long time. I found it really depressing."

One day, her mother discovered that a magazine had accepted two of her poems when she received a check for $200. "I was prancing around the living room," says Phyllis Janowitz. "I was just so high. I think anything a parent gets a lot of joy out of has got to make a big difference to a kid, and I'm sure that gave her the idea that the rewards for writing—even though they're not apparent for a long time—when they come it's fantastic. . . . She had seen me so miserable and depressed and always at my worst and then to see me so happy."

"God knows what it did to her."

PEOPLE BEING NICE TO ME

It is Tama's birthday. She is thirty-one years old. Her friend Paige Powell, the advertising director of *Interview* magazine and one of Andy Warhol's closest friends, is giving her a party.

Tama became friends with Paige and Warhol in the summer of 1984, after Tama's cousin, who worked at *Interview* told Paige that Tama was going through a bad time in the wake of an ended love affair. Paige had a blind date that night and asked Tama to come along. Warhol heard about the date, thought it sounded interesting, and also went. "And that," says Tama, "was the beginning of it."

Once a week they convened at Cafe Luxembourg, the Ritz, Cafe Roma, Il Cantinori, Le Cirque. Paige recalls Tama saying, "This is so special to me to go out, to get all dressed up and look forward to something." She had begun to define her persona as an orphan in an evening gown.

Tama came to regard Warhol with the worshipfulness she now bestows on Merchant and Ivory. He was another man old enough to be her father who treated her kindly. She thinks of Warhol often when she goes out and especially when she is at Texarkana, a restaurant they often went to together and where her birthday party is now taking place.

She arrives early, wearing a pink Mongolian lamb coat, black stockings, a fitted black top, and a yellow spandex miniskirt.

Greeting her guests, Tama chews gum, drinks a beer, plays with her hair. Often she says, "I have no friends." At other times she says, "I have as many people I could call in the middle of the night as anyone else." The most important of these is Paige, one of the few people, besides her mother, with whom Tama is at ease. In the weeks after Warhol died, Paige was unable to function. Tama moved in with her, took care of her, tended to literally hundreds of queries and requests that Paige could not deal with. In those weeks, Paige saw that Tama has more sense and substance than her patient-on-a-day-pass manner suggests. She may also have learned that unlike most people, who reveal their craziness only to those closest to them, Tama shows only those closest to her that she is actually sane.

Soon Tama is seated in the center of a long table, opening her gifts. She is flanked by her neighbor Jerry Mack, who works at CBS, her two male cousins, her publicist at Crown, and the dress designer Nicole Miller, who was once part of the Warhol circle. She keeps saying, "I'm not used to people being nice to me." This is something she often says.

Stephen Sprouse arrives with Debbie Harry. Both are dressed in black. Sprouse gives Tama a green minidress he designed and once lent her to wear on *Late Night with David Letterman.*

Tama hurries to the bathroom to put on the dress. She leaves her miniskirt in the bathroom. When it is returned to her it is folded into fourths and is smaller than a napkin.

Throughout the evening Tama disappears often to renew her lipstick and comb her hair. For dinner, she orders a stuffed green chili and salmon. She eats much faster than everyone else.

By 1:00 she decides to go to the set, where they will be shooting throughout the night. The party ends. She puts on her pink lamb coat. The coat is very short and very fluffy. Beneath it her legs look even longer and thinner than usual. She steps out quickly into the chilly night air.

She is as famous as she ever fantasized being, the embodiment of the exotic creature she hoped to become. She hurries down the street, driven by restlessness, energy, and complex cravings.

As she has always been, she is fixed on her destination.

HER WHOLE IDEA

She began writing short stories at Barnard. She had arrived there with a trunk on which she and her mother had pasted wallpaper embossed with naked ladies. The trunk was packed with jeans, sweaters, a ruffled purple dress from the Salvation Army, and a long-sleeved gold lamé tube top.

She no longer remembers what her first stories were about. She remembers only that people were shocked by them. "That," says her mother, "was her whole idea."

"I would read my stories in class and the other women would be so horrified and the teacher would like go, 'Oh, God, what has she brought in now?' It was like all these people were responding to my stories." This seems to be the point at which her literary ambitions were born.

SOMEONE WHO CAN'T WRITE YET

After college, she worried that she could not make a living. She did what educated people sometimes do in that situation. She went back to college. She won a fellowship at Hollins College in Virginia. She went there thinking, "Well, in a year I'll find out if I can write." By the end of that year she had written **American Dad.** She sold a section to *The Paris Review.* She sold the entire novel to Putnam.

It was, she said shortly after its publication, "not the most perfectly written book. But . . . it has the raw energy of someone who can't write yet." This perception did not go unshared. *The New York Times Book Review* said the book's "fine comedic inventiveness" was "consistently undermined by the lack of grace—and, even more so, precision." On the other hand, says Tama, "I didn't expect to get reviewed in the *Times*. That was like wonderful in itself."

Putnam did not publicize *American Dad.* It was barely distributed and sold fewer than a thousand copies. She wrote a second book, *A Cannibal in Manhattan.* Putnam rejected it. So did all the other publishers to whom her agent sent it. She wrote a third novel, *Memoirs of a Megalomaniac.* No one wanted that either. She kept writing. She fantasized about being famous. In her fantasies everybody knew her name, wanted to know her, liked her.

She had been raised on grants and academic handouts; now she lived on them: first a fellowship at the Fine Arts Work Center in Provincetown, then $12,500 from the National Endowment for the Arts. She moved back to New York, found an apartment, bought a plywood platform bed and a ten-dollar typewriter table. She began a fourth novel.

She finished the book. She couldn't get it published. She applied for more grants, and got them. She worked all day. At night, she watched people dining in restaurants on Columbus Avenue. "It was just this feeling like here's all these people and I can't get through to anybody."

Always the Girlfriend

She took to wandering around downtown Manhattan. On many nights there were art openings. She discovered that anyone could go to them. At each opening, there were stacks of invitations to more openings. It was 1982, the beginning of what she calls "the East Village thing."

There were parties, new clubs, new galleries. There were dealers poised to cash in. Newly rich artists who would later be lucky to sell a canvas for $300 held forth on the hazards of being a genius.

She moved in with an artist who had once been an assistant to Warhol. He paid the rent, she bought the groceries and cooked him elaborate dinners. At night they went to the Disneyworld of downtown clubs, Area. Tama wore purple lipstick and a leather jacket and was too shy to talk to anyone. "She was always meek," Paige Powell recalls, "and always the girlfriend."

Every morning she wrote five pages. She completed a fifth novel. When it didn't sell, she thought, "I can't spend another year doing this." She decided to write short stories. Those she could finish in three days to three months. She could send them to magazines and get a response quickly. At the very least, she says, it would "speed up the rejection process."

A Passive Young Woman

She had been writing stories for three months when an editor at *The New Yorker* called and said they wanted to

publish **"The Slaves in New York"** a story about a passive young woman who has difficulty making a living, frequents the downtown club scene, and cooks elaborate dinners for her unpleasant artist boyfriend. The story ran in the December 31, 1984, issue. It was followed by three more stories about the same characters. Suddenly, it seemed as if everyone was reading them. "It's fun," Andy Warhol said of Tama's work, "to read about people you know disguised under other names." Tama's boyfriend didn't think so.

It was not long before she had moved out of his apartment into a ten-by-thirteen-foot apartment of her own. She hung a four-by-six painting of herself on the wall. She kept writing. She had come to believe in "visualization." She used it often: she pictured herself on a talk show, she pictured her name on the best-seller list, her face on a magazine cover. She pictured herself in the company of glamorous people.

A Second Shot

In the summer of 1985, Crown Publishers signed a deal with Tama for a book of short stories. They paid $4,000 for a cardboard box filled with her work. Tama desperately wanted the book to sell. "I had written the other book, and it didn't do a damn thing because nobody knew me and they didn't promote it. So then I was broke for five years and I couldn't get a damn book published. Finally I get a second shot at publishing a book. I was determined I wasn't going to go through that ever again."

This portended that she would have to do something a bit more radical than sit at home, visualizing fame.

She had just begun her friendship with Andy Warhol. Looking at Warhol, Tama would think, "Here's this person who goes out every night and the press always writes about him. They never say nice things, but it doesn't bother him."

Looking at Warhol, gossip columnist Richard Johnson believes, "Tama got an idea about how to make herself famous. And she copied him, and it worked."

It Becomes Its Own Animal

On December 18, 1985, six months before *Slaves of New York* was published, the New York *Daily News* ran the following item: "Fiction writer Tama Janowitz was seen with Snap artist Patrick McMullan at the BeBop Cafe, Kamikaze, TNR, Area, and the Saint in one night. 'I hear great lines and think—how can I work that into a story?' she says."

McMullan took pictures for *Details* and *New York Talk,* magazines that covered the downtown scene. There was something going on downtown every night, and McMullan was always invited. Tama met him in November 1985 and began going around with him.

He took many pictures of her and made sure they were published. He introduced her to the columnists who had helped girls of the moment like Dianne Brill and Lisa E. become, in Daniel Boorstin's phrase, "famous for being well known."

"Although with Tama there was a little more substance," says McMullan, "because she had an actual book coming out."

She also had a black beauty mark pasted on her cheek, a gold leather jacket covered with graffiti, a penchant for making charmingly self-effacing statements in a voice that sounded like Judy Holliday on Thorazine. Soon, each time she went out, she was written about. "Then a lot of times when I didn't go out they'd mention that I'd been there. I mean, it takes over itself, it becomes its own animal."

What Shoves It Up There

The implicit message of Tama's publicity campaign on her own behalf was not lost on Crown's publicity department. "Tama was willing to do anything," her publicist, Susan Magrino, says now, "short of, you know, compromising."

Soon Tama and two friends pinned banners reading **Slaves of New York** across their chests. They marched into the Four Seasons at lunchtime. They handed out book excerpts. This incident was approvingly detailed in a *New York* magazine cover story about Tama. Tama posed for the cover picture in a meat locker, alluring in a low-cut black dress and airbrushed cleavage. After that Susan Magrino's job became easier. All that summer Tama was interviewed by writers of soft features. Items appeared whenever she had a book signing or went to the parties at which she was now a welcome addition. "When you combine beauty, intelligence, and humor," asks her socialite friend R. Couri Hay, "doesn't that spell good guest?"

With each interview and appearance, Tama further refined her image. At first, she had presented herself as a fashionable underdog. Now she upped the ante on both halves of that equation, achieving a persona that was unspeakably hip and pathetically beleaguered. She wore black leather and a leopard-skin belt. She was quoted as saying, "Life is incredibly difficult."

In midsummer she became the star of the first "literary video." This was Crown's designation for a four-minute commercial to be aired on Showtime and HBO, using MTV techniques to sell books to people who don't read. It showed Tama walking through Manhattan's meat-packing district in an evening dress, Tama at dinner with Andy Warhol, Tama discoursing about the "raw energy" of her work, dressed in clothes borrowed for the occasion from Betsey Johnson. Only the absence of genuine wit kept it from achieving the director's stated intention. This was to portray Tama as "a Gracie Allen of the Eighties." The video got her booked on the *Today Show*.

Soon, she was telling David Letterman and Joan Rivers the same stories about the transvestites outside her apart-ment. Soon, she was smiling prettily on *Good Morning America* while editor Gordon Lish intoned that if self-promotion was all right for Hemingway and Twain it was all right for Tama Janowitz. Within the literary establishment there didn't seem to be many others who thought so. But the literary establishment was not essential to the realization of Crown's dreams for Tama, who was, in the words of Susan Magrino, "too fabulous to be wasted on the book pages."

Slaves of New York made *The New York Times* best-seller list in mid-August 1986. It peaked at number fifteen. "It was never going to do something like number three," says Tama, "because like *penis* was in the first paragraph so it wasn't Book of the Month Club and that's what shoves it up there."

I Mean, How Could They Do That?

In Tama's closet are two cardboard boxes filled with clippings. They contain articles from the *Chicago Sun-Times*; *The Chronicle-Herald* of Halifax, Nova Scotia; *The Milwaukee Journal*; the *Press Democrat* of Santa Rosa, California; and dozens of other newspapers. The clippings show that **Slaves of New York** made the best-seller list in every major city in the United States. They also show that Tama's publicity campaign in her own behalf became distasteful to the journalists she was trying to charm. "Citizens," reads an article Tama clipped from *The Boston Globe* at the time her video was released, "it's gone too far."

This perception was pervasive. It did her little good with critics when **A Cannibal in Manhattan,** a book she had completed some years earlier, was reworked and published in the fall of 1987. Her editor, Betty Prashker, was disappointed when Tama brought it to her. "I had hoped it would be more like **Slaves,**" she says. "We talked about it. We discussed it, and this was what she wanted to do."

Tama's cardboard boxes contain dozens of reviews of **Cannibal.** They are far less favorable than the lukewarm reviews she received for **Slaves of New York.** "Tama Janowitz," James Wolcott wrote in *Vanity Fair,* "has her own pinup fantasies. Publicity is her satin sheet." The book, wrote Michiko Kakutani in *The New York Times,* was essentially "the jottings of an untalented arriviste."

"My feelings are hurt," she says of these critiques, "and you feel like, oh how could you say this, but it doesn't bother me that much because what can you do, you're writing the best book you can. And the other side of me feels glad that they trashed it because mostly the books that I don't like are the ones getting the lovely reviews."

Tama also kept a copy of the most vehement attack against her. It was published in *The New Yorker,* the sine qua non of her success. "All that this novel is about," wrote Terrence Rafferty, "is a writer feeding greedily on her own reputation."

Rafferty also discussed Tama's work in **Slaves.** Most of the book was written, he said, "in the glib, soothing voice of a sitcom." "It was weird," says Tama, "like it was weird. I mean how could they trash the same stories they themselves had published? At the same time, when somebody's going on being so irate you're sort of flattered to have that kind of vitriol, and the fact that they're like screaming does give me sort of a thrill."

I'M JUST AS MISERABLE AS THE NEXT PERSON

Tama is at a book signing attended by twenty-three young authors. Ten of them are women. Tama is the only one who does not need to wear her name tag, and she is not wearing it. The signing is being held at the Scribner's bookstore on Fifth Avenue. Tama has been placed in one of the most prominent spots, on the landing at the top of the staircase. Several other female authors look up and glare at her.

Before she became successful, she avoided the literary world. The gossip made her feel competitive and failed. She did not like hearing about someone's $50,000 advance or about who got invited to the PEN convention in Italy. Now she claims such conversation bores her, that she prefers the company of "regular people," that literary types make her nervous and uneasy. "Like, I admire Saul Bellow," she says, "but what the hell am I going to sit around talking to him about?"

She has few connections to other writers, in literary terms or otherwise. "She's disliked," one New York editor says, "by anyone who feels they haven't gotten the attention they deserve and that Tama's getting more than she's entitled to."

And there is another reason young authors dislike her. "Tama is the first Warhol writer," Bret Easton Ellis says. "Her attitude about the literary establishment is very Warhol. People feel that that aesthetic shouldn't intrude on the so-called serious literary world."

Other young writers feel that her work is not good and that their work is not being taken seriously because of her public behavior. Whenever Tama is talked about, Ellis says, "those ads always come up."

The ads, for Amaretto and Rose's Lime Juice, first appeared in June 1987. The latter paid Tama, who wanted to buy an apartment, around $10,000 to stand on Arthur Schlesinger Jr.'s desk while Annie Leibovitz took their picture.

"It sounded fun," says Tama. "I mean, if a serious writer is supposed to be somebody who sits at home with little glasses, I mean forget it, I'll put on a tutu and go out to a nightclub. I mean, why can't I be a serious writer and still do the other stuff? It's like you're supposed to be one thing or the other, but you aren't supposed to mix them."

Sometimes she says of other people's reaction to her, "But I don't care what they think. Why should I? Who are they? Are they my friends?"

At other times she says, "The truth is, they're just jealous of me. Now, why that should be I don't know. I'm just as miserable as the next person."

And there are times when she says, "Maybe I did care what they thought in the beginning. But it seems as if the less you care the easier it is."

Ellis believes that at this point, if Tama doesn't care it's just as well. "Those people," he says, "don't want her now."

I LIKE GUM VERY MUCH

And so it is an isolated Tama who signs books, her hair, as usual, in her face, her jaws, as usual, worrying a hunk of Care Free gum.

A short young man walks up to her table. He wears jeans and a black Members Only jacket. He has flat, unhappy eyes. He tells Tama that he wishes he, too, were a famous writer. "But I don't have the motivation. I've been co-managing a soul group, but I work in retail." He places a crumpled brown paper bag in front of her. Tama opens it. It contains dozens of little packages of Chiclets, two to a box. "They aren't going to explode or something, are they?" asks Tama. He shakes his head. "I'll eat one if you want," she says. "I like gum very much."

The young man has watched Tama from a distance in the two years since she became a public figure. In October he placed an ad in *The Village Voice* that read: "I'd like to meet you." "But I didn't put a box number on it," he says, "so I didn't get an answer." Now he gives Tama his card. He asks her how her movie is going. Tama tells him what she has told everyone all evening. "I don't know what I'll do," she says, "when it's done."

THE BEST WEEK OF MY LIFE

Every night, Tama goes to see the dailies. One night, Sam [not his real name], the actor she thinks is cute but trouble, asks her to have a drink with him and some of the other guys. The next night the two of them go off together for a drink at Cafe Luxembourg.

In the next week, they attend a party at M.K. for Nick Rhodes and a birthday party at M.K. for Elizabeth Ray, whom Tama identifies as "this woman from like a Washington scandal."

They spend a weekend at the house in Quiogue that Tama shares with Paige; they have a barbecue with a few other people in Tama's garden. They also have several discussions about where they will live once Tama sells her place in New York and Sam sells his house in Los Angeles and they move in together. By the end of the week, Tama says she can feel "the edges of my personality dissolving." To spend more time with Sam, she abandons her usual routine of writing five pages a day of a new novel.

"This was the best week of my life," she says. "One goddamn rare moment. I know it won't last. The movie will end. The guy may not be interested in me. The book I'm working on may be a piece of garbage I have to throw away. But I never had everything before. This week I have everything. It's scary. Andy used to say that thing about the fifteen minutes of fame. If you get fifteen minutes of happiness that's the big deal. And this is my fifteen minutes."

You Know, Love

The night after the movie finishes shooting, there is a wrap party for the cast and crew. The party is on a boat that sails from a yacht club on the West Side and goes up and down the Hudson. Tama arrives in a red Chinese sheath she bought in Chinatown for forty dollars and had shortened into a minidress. "Everything was set," she says, "for like nostalgia and sentiment."

It turns out that Sam is in a terrible mood. Tama follows him around the boat asking, "What's the matter?" He doesn't answer. She keeps asking. He won't tell her. She asks again. He disappears. Tama goes around the boat asking other people if they've seen him. Then she sits down at a table and cries.

After the boat docks, some members of the cast and crew invite her to a club. She goes home to wait by the phone. At 2:00 A.M. she gives up, walks over to the Cafe Luxembourg, has a drink, and tells her troubles to the maître d'. He is very sympathetic. He saw Sam when they came in together on their first date the week before. He thought Sam was very handsome.

Sam calls in the morning. "It was like a once-in-a-lifetime evening," she tells him, "and you ruined it for me." He apologizes. Tama has never had a man apologize to her before. She had planned never to see him again. Now, in a quandary, she sounds like a character in one of her stories.

"Every time you get a success," she says, "if you're with a guy they can't take it, they find a way to fuck it up for you. Time after time after time. And when I've been alone it's just not the same fun as when you can share it with somebody. I mean, what's the use about getting a big prize or a big reading or a big celebration when you don't have somebody to share it with? You know, you're walking around with some other element that's missing, which is, you know, love. So you can have your big prize but you're alone and when you're with somebody they're going to wreck it for you. That's the only way it's been with me."

"But God help you if they ever have a big award or a prize if you behave like that, believe me there's somebody who's younger, who's pretty, who's not threatening, and they'll be with her in one minute, the turn-around time is so short for these guys. I mean, I sit around here feeling blue for a long time. A year. I mean, I don't know how long it takes me to get over it."

"And, okay, you say to yourself, I don't want to have low self-esteem. I'm not ever going to be the richest, the youngest, the prettiest thing, but I'll make myself into an interesting person with an interesting life and all it adds up to is they're so threatened by you that they end up with the salesgirl from, you know, Woolworth's, or a person who's weeping all the time and maybe she's going to go to law school and maybe she's going to go to medical school and maybe she's going to be an actress and maybe she doesn't really know what she's going to do but can you loan her $200 she's getting evicted from her apartment. *That's* the one they go off with."

"I just can't seem to . . . I don't know. I don't want to be alone and I can't be putting up with that crap all the time. I see very strong women and they manage to somehow manipulate the guy and keep him in line and he behaves himself. I don't have that in me. I'm too busy just watching them in action and I forget that I'm supposed to say—whatever you're supposed to say to train somebody. I don't know how to train somebody."

It's Probably Not Going to Work Out

A week after the wrap party, Tama goes downtown to what was once the production office for **Slaves of New York.** The desks are empty. The bulletin boards are bare. Tama is here to pick up a painting of a spinach can that was used in the movie.

She and Sam spent the weekend together before he went back to L.A. Now she misses him and thinks maybe it would have been easier if she hadn't seen him again.

It turns out there's a woman living in his house, a legal secretary. Tama isn't sure if she's a tenant or a girlfriend. Last night he called and she suggested that he come to New York and move into her apartment.

"And he goes, 'I can't because my furniture would get scratched if there were tenants in here and I can't let that happen.'"

"I mean, I want somebody who's so crazy about me they can't live without me. If they don't want to come live with me because their furniture might get scratched, it's probably not going to work out."

There are a few people in one of the offices. Someone tells her that the painting was delivered to her apartment earlier in the day. With nothing left to do, she says goodbye.

"These people work on movies all the time," she says as she walks down the hall, "so they're used to this intense coming together and then now we can get rid of each other and we'll go on to our next experience. But I'm not going to have that." She steps into the elevator. "I wouldn't have come back down here," she says, "if it weren't for the painting."

When Tama gets home she finds the painting waiting for her and she finds a message on her answering machine. "I'm calling to ask," a male voice says, "if the Marvel comic was delivered." The little smile comes over her face. She rushes to the mail-box. It isn't there. She calls the man back. He tells her there's been a mistake, they'll send it first thing the next morning. The prospect of seeing it cheers her. Real life is hard, but it's fun to be a cartoon.

Julie Salamon (review date 19 October 1992)

SOURCE: A review of *The Male Cross-Dresser Support Group,* in *Wall Street Journal,* Vol. 220, October 19, 1992, p. A12.

[*In the following brief excerpt, Salamon praises portions of* The Male Cross-Dresser Support Group *for its wit and intelligence.*]

Tama Janowitz has solved the casting problem for her latest novel, *The Male Cross-Dresser Support Group.* She has written and directed a film version, conceived as a promotional gimmick.

Without having seen the film but having read the book, I strongly recommend the film. It's only 40 seconds long, an appropriate amount of time to spend with Ms. Janowitz's ruminations about her heroine's periods, her electrolysis, her hair and—I'm not kidding—ethics and morality in the late 20th century.

This time Ms. Janowitz's main character is a charmless creature named Pamela, who finds salvation for her dreary existence by taking unofficial custody of a young boy and taking him on the road. For Pamela and Ms. Janowitz life is one absurdist joke after another, strung together by the author's philosophizing.

For instance: "To find a head in the road might be a quirk of fate, but to find a head in the road and then to stumble upon the scene of one's father and stepmother's demise— obviously some larger psychosis or neurosis is involved. But hey, so what? I mean, who the hell actually cares? Life is short and psychoanalysis is long. In the end the only cure is death. In the meantime, as my mother always told me, the main point of existence was to have fun and grow as a human being."

With Ms. Janowitz, insipid memories are always being sparked by unbelievable events. Yet here and there some real intelligence and wit emerge. So one suspects it's deliberate. She wants to be the Proust for pinheads.

Tom Shone (review date 14 November 1992)

SOURCE: "Eight Million Characters in Search of an Author," in *Spectator,* November 14, 1992, pp. 39-40.

[*In the following review, Shone contemplates the humorous aspects of Janowitz's style.*]

Eighties junk fiction is showing its paunch. 'The ancient tallow of fast food' hangs around Tama Janowitz's new novel [*The Male Cross-Dresser Support Group*]. The most frequently used adjective in the book? Greasy. The pizza her heroine eats at the start: 'A spot of grease glistened in the centre'. The lamb chops she remembers eating as a child: 'greasy, gristly'. The hamburger on page 72: 'greasy'. The hair of the schmuck on page 205: 'filthy, greasy, unwashed'. Even the trees on the sidewalk have 'greasy leaves'.

A male writer might at this point have attempted to extrapolate from the grunge some general theory of urban decrepitude (think of the work to which mucus is put by Martin Amis, or the existential mileage Easton Ellis gets out of human innards). Janowitz's pleasant 300-page gossip is blissfully free of such vanities. 'Yeeauuck' would seem to be the sum of its satirical take on the world, and much the better it is for it too.

Pamela Trowell is a typical Janowitz creation: a low-rent bundle of bangles and bravado, discount-chic and urban neuroses, eking out an existence somewhere near the bottom of the fashion chain—receiving last year's hand-me-downs from her boss's wife—and living in a flat which, when on the one occasion it was burgled, actually got tidier. What's more, there's a rather ominous yellow slime on her bathroom floor.

It is one of many such accretions in the book—globules, gelatin, goo, gel, globs, gloop, glue, gunk, and, of course, grease abound, and that's just the Gs—all of which seem to lead like slug trails back to the countless men who line up so obediently for Janowitz's character assassinations: 'Bronc' Newman, art director of the magazine where Pamela works, who takes her to a peep show to see a disappointing bout of human/pig sex; a cabbie who prostrates himself at her feet in order to lick them; her craven boss, whose wife only likes to have sex with a paper bag over her head, and who wants a go at being dominated himself; and sex pest Alby, 'my own personal lunatic,' who trails Pamela, begging hand jobs under café tables.

Only Abdhul, a young street waif of unknown age and parentage who tags her home one night from a pizza parlour and whom she subsequently takes under her wing, offers any respite from the spinelessness. The sex pests pile up. Pamela gets sacked from the office. The bathroom stain gets larger. And so it is with Abdhul that Pamela finds herself fleeing New York to her father's country retreat, gathering with her as she goes an affenpinscher puppy, a frog, and a human head.

That the reader is happy to tag along with such calculated absurdities is largely down to Janowitz's narrative tone. Like some Barbie doll gone to seed, Pamela's *schtick* is engagingly dippy. Getting the sack she finds time for a *schpiel* about testicles and figs, while nothing seems to shake her core belief that having your leg mounted by a dog is the funniest thing that can happen to a girl, while being stuck in a loo without any loo paper the most nightmarish.

Janowitz's humour has that pleasingly raddled logic of a drunkenly told shaggy dog story, which gives you reservations about recommending it. The eccentricities can, for instance, become over-rehearsed, and over-reliant on sitcom-style résumés like:

> I've lost my job and I'm kidnapping a child to go and find out if my father and his wife are dead or alive, and you're wondering what to serve at a dinner party?

The lathering of zaniness also tends to obliterate the difference between her characters. Which Marshall scholar has a gay brother and an insane sister? Is it her father, the marijuana-smoking gynaecologist? Or was it her ex-friend Patty, the one who once went to a peep house with a tiny African transvestite, possibly a pygmy? Or is it just the woman who sells them the affenpinscher puppy, one of whose husbands was a Grand Prix racing driver? These mini-histories float curiously free of the characters to whom they are attached, and, since their relevance is discrete and not cumulative, don't add much to the novel's overall structure.

'There are eight million stories in the naked city' maintained the opening credits of the TV show, 'and this is one of them.' Janowitz, however, wants to tell them all, and all at once. Having read the result, her collection of eccentrics might have been much happier if released into their natural environment, a collection of short stories. Which isn't to say that even as they are, they are not at times both funny and engaging.

Elizabeth Young (essay date 1992)

SOURCE: "Library of the Ultravixens: The Lost Phallus—Where *did* I Put It?—in the works of Tama Janowitz, Mary Gaitskill, and Catherine Texier," in *Shopping in Space*, edited by Elizabeth Young and Graham Caveney, Atlantic Monthly Press and Serpent's Tail, 1992, pp. 142-93.

[*In the following essay, Young discusses Janowitz's oeuvre within the framework of postmodern feminist theory.*]

"Slipping through the stitch of virtue, Into crime"

(Djuna Barnes, *The Book of Repulsive Women*)*

I. BOHEMIANS AND BAD GIRLS

It is the 1950s and our heroine is sitting in the kitchen. Outside, a bomb-shelter broods in the backyard. She is watching her mother who, in a flowered pinny and turban is doing a hundred things at once: mixing the Bisto gravy, worming the cat, sudsing the smalls, dashing away with a smoothing iron, all because she's W.O.M.A.N. Her daughter's never going to grow up like that . . . In a trice she's become a pouting, blonde dolly-bird in a crochet minidress, bowling down the King's Road in a pink sports car. Next, she's in a kitchen, hopelessly stirring mung beans in some rustic commune, bra-less and unencumbered in trailing cheese-cloth. Another click and she's up at the barricades screaming for abortion on demand, wages for housework and lesbian rights. This year she's wearing dungarees and leather and has a crewcut. Suddenly she's gone again. She re-appears striding on impossible stilettos through a hushed, open-plan office. Her make-up is discreet, her hair streaked, her suit expensive; she exudes power. She has terrific legs. Then she's back in a kitchen again, as big as a loft. It *is* a loft. She clutches a winsome child dressed in overly interesting jeans and she's doing a hundred things at once. She looks confused. We've come a long way haven't we, baby? And it's all been so *quick*. All these common, iconic, representations of women with all the pressures they embody, can have flashed past our heroine before she has even reached middle age. They are indicative of the cultural schizophrenia that has engulfed women as they try to appease a contradictory pantheon of contemporary imperatives. The impossibility of internalizing such seismic social change within a short period has led to a cluster of warring responses within literature, feminism and feminist literary theory.

The books discussed in this chapter were all published during the 1980s. To a very large extent, they ignore the feminist movement, at least in any overt way. It became fashionable at this time to, post-haste, proclaim post-feminism, as if troublesome and cataclysmic social change had been assimilated as smoothly as Jello. The success of writers such as Tama Janowitz and Mary Gaitskill, whose fiction certainly avoided any strident feminism, seemed to confirm the emergence of a more sophisticated (more rational? better-tempered?) type of woman whose books would mercifully appeal to all readers, regardless of gender.

Such easy assessments avoided consideration of a number of issues essential to any analysis of the novels, the most obvious being that none of these books could have been written without the experience of feminism and the freedoms, particularly sexual freedoms, that such experience had granted the authors. There was no denying that these new texts resembled not at all the large number of overtly feminist Anglo-American novels whose content was already so predictable as to invite parody. We've all read them: books that pullulate with fluids, books brimming with childbirth and menarche, abortion and menopause. These were books that tried to break the silence and cram centuries of female experience into a few short years of writing, books whose plots frequently celebrated the discovery of lesbian love and lore and that had awful titles like *Women Are Bloody Wonderful*. A few years of this and nobody wanted to pick up a "feminist" novel, let alone write one.

The reasons for so many of these books being vaguely disappointing lay deep within the pragmatic, utilitarian politics of the Anglo-American feminists. England, in particular, with its empirical traditions, had a profound, traditional mistrust of theory and abstract thought which English feminists unwittingly perpetuated without seeing it for what it was—one of the classist aspects of the English patriarchy dedicated to impeding thinking and education in society at large. French feminists, versed in the tradition of European thought, were much more open to theory. During the first decade of post-war feminism they were deeply influenced by Jacques Lacan's thinking on psychoanalysis and his belief that the moment of Oedipal crisis and repression of desire for the mother is synonymous with our acquisition of language and entry into the Symbolic Order, our acceptance of the Law of the Father.

Many French feminists became concerned with what they termed *"l'écriture féminine."* This aligned an attempt to locate within literature the unconscious, repressed desires of the pre-Oedipal period along with the Deconstructionist theories of Jacques Derrida and their emphasis on the instability of meaning in language. French philosopher Julia Kristeva had seen conventional social meaning as encoded in language to be the underlying structure supporting all our social and cultural institutions. She had suggested that the fragmentation of meaning in the pre-modernist work of Lautréamont, Mallarmé and other Symbolists posed a revolutionary challenge to the social order by virtue of its delineation of the immensely powerful and arbitrary rhythms of the unconscious. Kristeva hoped that women writers would be able to dislocate language and patriarchal conventions by a similar use of the "spasmodic force" of the unconscious, further powered by their close gender identification with the powerful, pre-literate pre-Oedipal mother-figure. It was indeed from this area that the most influential and avowedly feminist literature emerged, primarily in the work of Monique Witting and Hélène Cixous. One could not hope to re-create in textual form what Lacan called the "Imaginary", the infant period when there is no perceived separation from the mother; this being pre-Oedipal, pre-linguistic, any attempt to do so would result in psychotic gibberish. However in *l'écriture féminine,* one could, as Cixous puts it "work on the difference",[1] that is strive to undermine the dominant phallocentric logic of language, oppose the "binary oppositions" between the masculine and the feminine that exist in language and stress an open-ended textuality that would resist "closure" or resolution. Cixous was much influenced by the work of Derrida who maintains that meaning can only be located through the "free play of the signifier", or rather that meaning is always potential, always deferred as we pass from signifier to signifier in language without there being the possibility of a "transcendental signified", an ending or closure. There are few parallels with these writings and theories amongst English feminist novelists apart from in the work of Nicole Ward Jouve, herself French by birth, and Christine Brooke-Rose.

L'écriture féminine resists biologism—that is the Anglo-American feminist emphasis on women as real, biological entities who can only hope to change their status by opposing patriarchy in all its historical and political manifestations. Instead, the French theorists foreground language to the point of gender-fluidity, by stressing the textuality

of sex and thus not excluding certain male texts from the *"féminine."* Julia Kristeva asserts that it is not biological difference that determines feminist potential but ourselves as "subject in process": "our identities in life are constantly brought into question, brought to trial, over-ruled."[2] Identity itself is endlessly unstable, endlessly open to change. Kristeva has attempted to align feminism and the avant-garde in an androgynous challenge to the very discourses that make such positions possible. Her project is one of subversion from within, re-defining *"différence"* (which in French denotes both difference and deferral), within the multiplicity and heterogeneity of textuality itself. She feels that the woman and the artist, the feminist and the avant-garde can all converge and dissolve in a deviance that is writing. They would seek to trangress the boundaries of which they speak and in doing so expose those boundaries for what they are—the product of phallocentric discourse and of women's relation to patriarchal culture. Incidentally anarchic, they would ceaselessly deconstruct the discourse they work within and constantly strive to write what cannot be written. Many of these theories are somewhat utopian and often deeply irritating to Anglo-American feminists who cannot see much gender fluidity or polymorphous perversity down the supermarket. Even the French theorists themselves were unable to agree on multiple points of psycho-analysis, class and race privilege, literary representation and the patriarchal implications of theory itself.

The schism between the pragmatic "biologist" politics of Anglo-American feminisms and the language theory of the French groups is further complicated by the "crisis of legitimation", in Jean-François Lyotard's phrase, within post-modernism itself; the erosion of the Symbolic Order and a loss of faith generally, in what Lacan calls the Law of the Father. The various strands within feminism—the theoretical and the fictional, the political and the linguistic—can be seen as mirroring the cultural schizophrenia that has engulfed us. But for the woman writer—imprisoned of necessity within her language—the act of demanding access to discourse still means a submission to the phallocentrist masculine that constitutes the language of the Symbolic Order. On the other hand, to refuse discourse, fictional or otherwise, merely re-inscribes women as the signifiers of mystery, silent, "unspoken." How to work within male discourse while defying it? How to stand outside its voices without assuming the role of female "essence"? For the woman writer there are a multiplicity of problems within these trajectories.

The novels in question, those of Tama Janowitz, Mary Gaitskill and Catherine Texier are neither straightforwardly feminist and celebratory of the women's movement nor do they reflect French literary theory. They do not "work on the difference"; they make little attempt to undermine phallocentrism, nor do they show any profound commitment towards defusing the bottom-line binary oppositions of male/female within language. They are neither literary experimentations that aim towards an open-ended non-oppositional textuality nor feminisms presented within "ordinary" narrative forms. Are they "post-feminist", post-feminism being the convenient mirage that was foisted upon us during the eighties, along with another chimera, that shy woodland creature, the New Man? Feminism had all been so *worthy,* so *earnest.* Wasn't it a mite *passé*? Human nature doesn't change much, does it? This impulse to turn down the bellowing biologism and re-appear in bustiers and fish-net stockings was more than understandable but reductive in literary terms for women writers. Feminism *did* exist. Language theory *had* developed and a disinclination to engage with either left these American novelists in a curious limbo where most of their work, however sensitive and intelligent, could not really evolve from being entertainments into the disruptive vitalities of art.

The novels in question actually display many of the impulses charted by feminist theory: the urge towards androgyny wherein women reject the dichotomies between masculine and feminine as being, in Kristeva's term, purely "metaphysical"; the desire for union with the Lost Mother of Oedipal theory. Desire is encoded within language and the authoritative act of writing, the "claiming of space" is always expressive of powerful, erotic impulses. If desire and language are synonymous, writing is symptomatic of desire that *doubles back* and *underwrites* or impersonates itself and is then doubly emphasized within the impulsive "ejaculations" of creative text. Women writers incurious about the phallocentrism of the language they assume will tend to re-enact, in unconscious form, the moment of their entry into desire and language at the Oedipal crux, the point at which they locate their phallic lack. In these novels we see, like shadows beyond the text, all the elements of the original drama. ("Doesn't every narrative lead back to Oedipus?" writes Roland Barthes. "Isn't storytelling always a way of searching for one's origin, speaking one's conflicts with the Law, entering into the dialectic of tenderness and hatred?")[3] We see the loss of the phallus, the emergence of desire, the search for the Other, the seductive girl-child, the many Fathers—the Good, the Bad and the Indifferent—and the development of their role as love-object. We note the longing to recreate symbiotic union with the pre-Oedipal Mother, that monstrous, magical figure who contains both Masculine and Feminine; we observe the wounds of the castration complex. Although basic Freudian theory has been spectacularly developed and challenged, notably by Lacan and Luce Irigaray, nevertheless much feminist textual theory is still concerned with the way in which conventional Freudian theory writes out women, condemns them to absence, to being deviations from the male norm, to be forever defined in negative terms as forms of nothingness or no-importance; passive as opposed to the male active, dark as opposed to light, fluidic, emotional, mysterious—emblematic of the unconscious. Thus, in claiming language the woman writer assumes a formidable task and must literally write herself into being.

The chaoticism of women's literature after feminism can be further explained by the urge, the desperate need to "catch up" in a pitifully short time. While much hitherto neglected women's writing from the past was excavated and published, contemporary women novelists had to contend simultaneously with the past and the present. They had to deal with the weight of literary history, they had to re-assess their own, frequently male, literary influences and they had to grapple with all the cultural imperatives of postmodern society. They had to try and form both new identities and new literatures in the teeth of great blasts of feminist theory. It was a formidable task and thus hardly surprising that instant, skimpy "traditions" emerged.

One of these was the American "Bad Girl" writer. These were writers who seemed to have taken every cliché about American womanhood from a century of fiction—they would be fiery, independent, free-spirited, uninhibited—and forced them juicily through the mill of post-war sexual liberation to produce a literary Cosmo girl. The original was probably Erica Jong with *Fear of Flying,* swiftly joined by Lisa Alther and *Kinflicks.*[4] In their work such writers focused on the women who had opened their hearts and legs to the counter-culture in the sixties, and trilled on through feminism and all varieties of sexual experimentation into burgeoning eighties privilege and success. They were bountiful, orgasmic, lip-glossed Amazons. The heroine of a late Jong novel, *Any Woman's Blues,* is the neo-autobiographical figure of Isadora Wing, ragingly concupiscent, complete with chic divorce, goy toy-boy and designer daughter. Jong still wrote like a Hall-mark card. Lisa Alther's heroine in a late book, *Bedrock,* cloyingly confides that, "Hormones had always been her drug of choice."[5] These women gave the impression that nothing would ever stop their fictional heroines; they would soon be picking out low-cut winding sheets and stretching mottled arms from the grave for one last grab of cock. They would presumably, in Joe Orton's phrase, be buried in a "Y-shaped coffin."[6] These writers were selling sex. The books had nothing to do with feminism and were, in fact, positively degrading to women. They promoted a rampant sexual consumerism, set impossible standards of wealth and allure and re-inforced the sexist image of women as hormonal harpies who could never drag their thoughts above the pelvis.

It has to be admitted that the writers under consideration, Tama Janowitz, Mary Gaitskill and Catherine Texier, all belong to this Bad Girl "tradition." They may have weighed in with a chic downtown version and a nihilistic punk allure but the books are still lewd, lustful and explicit, with a genteel veneer of high seriousness and, as such, comprise a publisher's wet dream. If, in addition, the writer presented an attractive package, was youngish, personable and gave good interview, the marketing machine went into overdrive. This contains a sinister implication for women writers who do not conform to this marketing ideal and may consequently be doomed to media neglect. The writers under consideration here are all attractive women and the considerable material and status awards of their choosing to write almost exclusively about sex has to be taken into consideration. Is such writing little more than an astute career move? This is the "Madonna" debate. Can women criticize other women who use their sexuality in an autonomous fashion to become rich and powerful? Surely their rise is a triumph of feminism? Or do they merely perpetuate degrading sexist stereotypes?

Some women now consider that, during the eighties, far from being able to settle permanently into the workplace and consolidate the advances of feminism, women were being subtly undermined by media campaigns that eroded their frail confidence. Susan Faludi, author of *Backlash: The Undeclared War Against Women* considers that neurosis-inducing, glossy chat-show glop about New Men, co-dependency, baby-hunger and Women Who Love Too Much was deliberately intended to destabilize the new-found strength of the single, independent, self-determined woman. But were women really so fragile that they fell into a swoon of anxiety over nonsensical psychobabble? Certainly, during the eighties all types of pre-feminist behaviour from flirting to falsies were once again legitimized and even fashionable. In the eighties, sisterhood was Doubtful, Bitchiness was back. It is interesting to observe however that while the novels in question may avoid straight down-the-line feminism, neither do they tend towards any of the other eighties feminine extremes of power-shopping, ruthless ambition and bitchy back-bite. They all foreground friendship between women and are in general very warm and loving towards their own sex. It seems as though the female character who appears most frequently in these fictions—the bohemian artist and downtown clubber—was totally absent both from the dour-dressing Dworkin dyke set or the power-dressing of the uptown rich bitch. And indeed was it not always so? One of the most notable absences in literature was precisely that of the bohemian woman artist and the work of Mary Gaitskill in particular went a long way towards re-(ad)dressing this issue.

II.

Tama Janowitz was the first of the "New Wave" women writers to impinge on British consciousness. Here in England we were shielded from the worst of the media circus that surrounded her burgeoning career but we got the message. She was hip, sophisticated. She knew Andy Warhol and Jean-Michel Basquiat! She looked great with her black, tangled, just-risen-from-a love-nest mane of hair, carmine pout and tight-clinched waist. This was no drab, mouthy dyke who was going to go all dismal and angry on talk shows. Janowitz was Lifestyle incarnate—you could be cute and intellectual and celebrated and rich all at once and still have credibility. What more could any woman ever want? In the face of all this the quality of her writing seemed hardly to count. In England, *Slaves of New York* was the first of her books to be published and sold well although critics tended to dismiss it as lightweight trendy New York pap. In fact Janowitz was a serious, thoughtful writer who didn't really deserve much of the image-linked nonsense that surrounded her and precluded her books being read with any real care. However,

her first three novels together comprise something of a cautionary tale in terms of postmodern literature.

American Dad, published originally in 1981, was a fairly traditional first novel, although instantly hailed by reviewers as being "new-wave" and "postmodern." It is obviously the work of a careful, considered young writer with a thorough grounding in literature. It is a traditional coming-of-age novel concerning the transformation of character, a *Bildungsroman,* and chiefly remarkable for Janowitz's choice of a male narrator and protagonist. It is relatively rare for a woman writer to adopt the male voice and particularly so at the time this novel was written when there was so much emphasis on the nature of women's experience. In assuming literary discourse at all women become, in theoretical terms, bisexual and it is rare for them to go further and claim the male voice in its entirety. (Kathy Acker is a notable exception.) Janowitz does not use the male persona here to deliver any sarcastic feminist critique of men. Her portrayal of Earl Przepasnick is a gentle and sympathetic one as if she had merely transposed many of her own adolescent memories—as one does in a first novel—into a male body without any particular reflection on the obsession with gender difference that had seized the rest of the Western world. This apparent reluctance to emphasize gender nevertheless comprises a statement of its own. It frees Janowitz from any of the constraints of representing a world newly imbued with feminism which would have been unavoidable with a female narrator. At the same time it allows her to usurp a very male tradition of American fiction—the sprawling *Look Homeward Angel* summation of youth and adolescence, the small-town look at life in a big country—and by very dint of her, as author, being female, to turn it subtly to her own ends. In a period when, despite all the demands for equality, the two sexes seemed more violently at odds that they had ever been, Janowitz's choice of narrator is brave and seems like a quiet plea for a more humanist, less divisive socio-sexual agenda.

American Dad is a dense and detailed book, written in the safe past tense of childhood. It opens climactically with a murder, a maiming and the memory of a divorce, although these are all swiftly revealed to be incidents which came about arbitrarily, or accidentally. They foreground the thematic thrust of the book which is a description of the lives of children whose parents were caught up in the turbulent cross-currents of the sixties. Such parents, vulnerable and more like children themselves, were unable to bequeath to their offspring the illusions of stability and order that had sustained earlier generations. Earl makes this clear when he says: "He was my father. He should grow up and act like one."[7] The lives of such parents swirled with chaos, divorce, extra-marital partnerships and terrible uncertainties. This enables Janowitz to implicitly deconstruct the traditional coming-of-age novel, which achieves resolution when the hero is able to reach a maturity which makes peace with, and approximates to, the values of the parental generation as in, for example *The Catcher in the Rye* or *To Kill a Mockingbird.* For the children in *American Dad,* however, the question is whether they will be able to survive at all or reach maturity in anything other than a psychologically fragmented state. In this respect they are more akin to Joel in Truman Capote's *Other Voices, Other Rooms,* who had no parents at all and was thus completely at the mercy of random influences. This is the central paradox of *American Dad*; the parents are very much present, very much loved but at the same time they are absent in the sense of being able to pass on coherent values to their offspring. Janowitz proves unable to investigate fully all the implications of this scenario; once Earl reaches adolescence she becomes more interested in detailing the lurid surfaces of contemporary society in the manner typical of her later work and the book loses its original impetus.

The first part of the book describes the childhood of Earl and Bobo Przepasnick after their parents, Robert and Mavis, decide to get a divorce. Robert is a sensual, bearded dope-smoking psychiatrist who occupies a curiously interstitial point in American history; his instincts are those of a backwoodsman, a frontiersman. He learns "to live off the land, fry day-lily bulbs and blossoms, spear frogs, brew tea from sassafras leaves."[8] At the same time these traditional American urges, far from dating him, unite him with the sixties trends towards self-sufficiency and a rejection of overt consumerism. Earl calls him "Paul Bunyan, Abraham Lincoln, Hunter S. Thompson rolled into one", further clarifying the point.[9] In many respects he is a milder version of the demented father in Paul Theroux's *The Mosquito Coast,* who implodes under the contradictions of past and present American realities. Robert similarly claims to be "a man of the future—higher on the evolutionary scale than the rest of society."[10] "It's going to take a while for the rest of mankind to catch up with him," says his son.[11] The mother, Mavis, is eccentric, confused and pitiable. A talented poet, she is constantly defeated by the exigencies of the world. It is clear that both parents have been wrecked on the tides of time; their perception embodies an older world whilst their daily lives are lived amongst the slippages of the new one.

By the time Earl is twelve, the parents are divorced and he has met other young casualties of the divorce wars—sex-crazed six-year-olds, children stoned on LSD or given hash brownies to calm them.[12] As Earl and Bobo get older, Earl comes to understand that the divorce was "the end of Bobo." Before it, Earl says, Bobo was "a fine person, a thoughtful person, but he was a sane person." The divorce "shocked him into a kind of reality that he might not otherwise have experienced. It stopped him completely from suffering an artistic sensibility, it prevented him from being a weirdo of any sort. He was a thoroughly American boy."[13] The inference is that the cataclysmic trauma of divorce or some similar fragmentation of past tradition is now necessary if children are to be "normal" and able to cope with present-day reality—not that this normality, in Earl's view, is to be recommended: it is the opposite of "sane." This establishes a complex interplay of binary oppositions, between the "artistic sensibility" and "normal-

ity" in both the old and new worlds. The "All-American" sensibility, once the "natural" product of security and tradition and an edenic past, has always been despised by the aesthetic "artistic" sensibility. Nowadays however, it takes a wrenching "unnatural" event to produce that "All-American", seemingly natural "normality." The divorce, Earl concludes was "probably the best thing that could have happened" to Bobo. He "became normal."[14]

The first part of *American Dad* is a mature work with its reflections on time, schism and the family. What is interesting about the book and, indeed, about Janowitz's work in general is the way in which, as Earl grows up and into the "present" and she concentrates increasingly on this "present" in this and later work, the whole tenor of the writing becomes increasingly "immature" as if traditional maturity, responsibility and understanding were qualities quite useless in apprehending contemporary reality. By the time Janowitz comes face to face with her self and her own milieu in *A Cannibal in Manhattan* her work is positively infantile in its short-sightedness and self-gratification. This, while not, I think, wholly deliberate underlines truisms about the infantilization of the individual in consumer society and the cravings for instant gratification. These lie in such opposition to the very act of writing which by its nature constantly defers meaning as well as deferring reward in a material sense that any attempt to combine the consumer ecstasy of the "endless present" in which we live with fictional form not only implodes "traditional" fiction but requires exceptional control of new forms if the writer is not to slip into a whining mimesis of the immature urges s/he portrays.

After Earl leaves his parental homes he finds it impossible to live up to the heroic image of his father he still retains. The rest of the book chronicles Earl's relationship with various girlfriends in college and abroad, relationships in which he takes a meek, supplicatory role entirely at odds with the images of men prevalent at the time as bullying sexist beasts. Janowitz finally collides with her future subject matter—the observation of strange urban tribes—when Earl meets an American "milky chocolate" model with "raspberry-coloured electrocuted hair" and blue lips.[15] We are nearly in *Slaves of New York* country. Earl finally loses his virginity to this sweet-natured giantess with the room-temperature IQ. The novel rather desperately attempts a traditional ending when Earl achieves manhood by having a baby—called Robert—with another girlfriend, the aristocratic English Elmira. Earl's father is seriously wounded when chopping down trees, trees having been earlier represented in the book as an image of age, history and tradition. The wounding of the "King", the Father, allows Earl to achieve adulthood and to make his peace with the elder Robert. Despite woundings, schisms, the chopping-down of the past, family tradition will struggle on in the form of Earl's new little family, a tradition that has been totally changed and yet, in its essential biological bondings, remains unchanging.

All that remains to be said of *American Dad* is that it performs textually and thematically in a traditional way while seeking out elements of the contemporaneous that co-exist uneasily with the *Bildungsroman* tradition. Janowitz is in transition between the past and the present in fiction as she writes the book. Janowitz also demonstrates a strong interest in anthropology, in cannibal tribes and in adopting anthropology to urban life, Earl speaks of his adventures as "sacred and religious rituals of the highest order . . . food for thought for anthropologists in every land and clime"[16] and this interest in urban "tribes" informs Janowitz's subsequent work. Lastly **American Dad** is an exercise in double consciousness. As a male, Earl can engage in Oedipal struggle with his father and emerge victorious in the traditional way by begetting a son. However this psychic battlefield is subtly informed by Janowitz's understanding of men as being far more vulnerable and "feminine" than they might have appeared had the author been male.

Simultaneously, the act of projecting imaginatively into the male voice is bounded for the reader by the knowledge that the female author has, in life, no such solutions as are available to Earl within the Oedipal crisis. Ironically this triumphant engagement with Oedipality is only accessible to Janowitz through the adoption of a male narrator, a male persona. She is able to use fictional language as illusion to "masquerade" as a man and to cloak gender difference whilst, subliminally, as a woman she re-enacts her own Oedipal struggle by her emergence into "public" written text. The novel is both fluid and uncertain in its combination of traditional "male" and "female" qualities. It is simultaneously dense *and* tentative as the author attempts to resolve the double-consciousness or multiple voicing inherent in its creation.

Janowitz moved decisively into the postmodern with *Slaves of New York.* This was her most successful book and is comprised of a number of brief vignettes of downtown New York life. Many of these had already appeared in magazines including the *New Yorker, Interview* and *Mississippi Review.*

The vignettes in *Slaves of New York* often move into the present, or historic present tense so beloved of postmodern novelists. This has always served several functions. It denotes the "endless present" of consumer culture where linear time and appropriate cause and effect have been blasted away by drug use, chaos theory and media blitz. It mirrors the moral and intellectual flexibility required for survival in a multi-textured, frequently nonsensical and paradoxical environment. It also forces the readers to engage with the novelist's "now", to involve them as closely with events as language will allow. In providing no past-tense "safe distance" it drags the reader into the literary equivalent of co-counselling.

Presentations of urban life at their most flat and affectless approach the imagistic condition of poetry or abstract art and are even more resistant to analysis and theory in that they are not founded in emotion. Janowitz is in general too quirky and critical to achieve this blandness but despite this, and despite considerable literary ingenuity, it be-

comes increasingly clear that she is not always wholly in control of her material.

For example, the first piece in the book, entitled **"Modern Saint 271,"** describes the experiences of a prostitute. The contemporary call-girl is a figure that appears not only in Janowitz's work but also in that of Gaitskill and Texier and at first their intentions seem clear. As women writing about these all-too familiar male fantasy figures, they demystify and clarify them, banishing forever any connotations of seamy, exotic sleaze and ludicrous tart-with-a-heart/madonna-whore projections and replacing them with human beings. (One cannot but recall Alice Munro's complaint about "the figure of an idiotic, saintly whore": "Men who made books and movies seemed to have a fondness for this figure, though Rose noticed they would clean her up. They cheated, she thought . . ."[17] Actually, in a different way Janowitz, Gaitskill and Texier "clean her up" too by substituting the nice middle-class girl with intellectual interests, paying her way through college perhaps. Although this incarnation is often far closer to contemporary reality than to the numberless sentimental male imaginings, it is still of course approximate. However streetwise the New York writers are, they all remain nice, educated middle-class kids—I mean, they're not Iceberg Slim, the street-smart black author of the classic memoir *Pimp.* Still Janowitz's portrayal of a prostitute's life does not seek to shield the reader. Her description of the penises encountered by her call-girl is right on the ball, so to speak. "Some blue-veined and reeking of Stilton, some miserly. Some crabbed, enchanted, dusted with pearls . . ."[18] This accentuates the tone of the piece which hovers between a repulsive, squalid factuality and a gentle dreaminess, all qualities which are profoundly welded together in the personality of the prostitute, her life, past and present and her relationship with her pimp. This latter is notably tender and sensitive, banishing all clichés of pimpdom; the intellectual Bob "with his long, graceful hands, his silky mustache, his interesting theories of life and death"[19] is sweetly ineffectual as a pimp although he sensibly comforts her with drugs. "He would softly tie up my arm and inject me with a little heroin."[20] The tender cadences of such sentences which seem to shed soft cloudy halo-lights on the two characters fit admirably with Janowitz's designation of the prostitute as a "modern saint", a phrase which is only barely ironic. This gentleness also foregrounds the girl's own quasi-religious belief that she "was like a social worker for lepers" and that "As in the convent, life is not easy."[21] This holiness, this saintliness, coupled with all the descriptions of the ugly litter that surrounds fiscal sex, raises the whole piece to the level of religious kitsch wherein the sublime must co-exist with mundane sentiment. As a complex evocation of an imaginative modern sexuality the piece destabilizes fixed notions surrounding sexuality, prostitution and religion whilst simultaneously undermining its own assertions with a gentle kitschy gloss. However, there is another more ominous textual reading which lies within the literary evocation of sex for sale. The author, by concentrating so blatantly on sex in the first story of the book, is herself offering sex for sale, in the book. As with the first sentence of Catherine Texier's *Panic Blood* and its insistence on "cunt" these writers are proferring sex, in some form, to the readers, sex which will "sell" the books. Doesn't it always? In this respect, and we must consider that they are using the language of the patriarchy, Texier's book "opens" with, or like, a "cunt" and Janowitz blends authorial voice with the voice of a prostitute, thus immediately "displaying" the text, in invitation, as sexual. This instant sexualization of the text presents the text itself as slut, to be "penetrated" by the reader. The very softness and gentleness of the text itself here, its "female" qualities render it all the more pleasurable as an erotic invitation and there is something questionable here in these authors' insistence on sexual matters. If, in Roland Barthes's analysis, all texts "flirt" with the reader, these precipitately embrace the readers and drag them into bed. No one could ever mistake Kathy Acker's sexual explicitness in language for a seductive invitation but Janowitz, Gaitskill and Texier are offering a very seductive, non-aggressive sexual enjoyment within the "body" of the text of young, beautiful, middle-class intellectuals/authors—or call-girls.

Slaves of New York takes us on a tour of New York City in the eighties, "dust and grit tossed feverishly in the massive canyons between the skyscrapers."[22] Everyone dreams of a better, more creative life. "All the waitresses I knew were really actresses, all the Xeroxers in the Xerox place were really novelists, all the receptionists were artists."[23] Although these vignettes can function as individual stories, many of the characters are linked from one to the other, comprising a sort of novella. There are other, separate pieces too.

In one, **"You and the Boss,"** Janowitz executes a clever pastiche of a style of star-crazed writing sometimes found in fanzines. I have a near identical piece—at least in style—written, in all seriousness, some twenty-odd years ago, by a girl who spent a day with Jim Morrison. Janowitz uses the form to rubbish both the "legend" of a pop star, in this case Bruce Springsteen, and the clone-like qualities of a star's girlfriends. It is very funny. In "real life" of course, Bruce proves to be "larger than life." In fact, "Bruce is the size of a monster . . . his body might take up an entire billboard." Bruce eats "a dozen eggs, meatballs, spaghetti and pizza" for breakfast (all solid blue-collar food) and, worst of all, "He sings while he eats."[24] His home is furnished with the common touch—terminal tack—and so on. In another piece, **"Engagements,"** Janowitz takes a clever swipe at post-structuralist critical discourse. Her heroine attends a Women's Studies Course at Yale but when she re-reads her notes which include the line "A gendered identity 99% of the time is built onto a person who has a sex", they sound to her "as if they had been written in a foreign language."[25] She gives some more examples, which haven't quite degenerated into such gibberish and decides that this language "gracefully circled a subject without ever landing to make a point",[26] which is fair enough I suppose. As this also makes the point that Janowitz herself is perfectly familiar

with these terms one might be tempted to ask why she makes relatively little of them in her writing and to consider the fact that were she more feminist/more experimental in language she would certainly not have been so successful—or at least not so quickly or so dramatically. But something about Janowitz seems to convey a genuine sweetness and precludes sinister accusations of calculation.

Some of Janowitz's concerns in *Slaves of New York* are all too familiar from other New York novels; the surreal street-life, the traditional flash of Trash Aesthetic as she describes one heroine's fascination with those tasteless but irresistible offers one finds in junk magazines—"Pegasus pendant with genuine ruby and swirl of faux diamonds"![27]—and inevitably that hideous eighties food obsession. This latter ranges from the parodic, as in Ellis's work ("eggplant-chocolate-chip icecream") to the everyday middle-class New Yorker diet: "Cornish game hen with orange glaze, curried rice, asparagus . . . or fettucine Alfredo with aragula salad . . ."[28] This is probably the worst aspect of New York novels of that period, trapping the English reader in a combination of *Guardian Weekend* and a Foodie convention.

There is also in Janowitz's fiction a subterranean feminist awareness, adroitly twisted to comic effect in the text: "You don't know why you spend half your life trying to scrub your body free from essential oils and the other half smearing stuff onto it."[29] She goes in for a rather endearing faux-naivety too, distancing herself further from her heroines; one of whom, contemplating a vast range of airplane food muses: "It must be difficult to raise the chickens, lettuce and so forth so far off the ground."[30]

Overall the stories that describe a particular circle of art-world characters are probably the least effective; they have an unwitting, inbuilt paradox in that Janowitz cannot decide if these characters are lovable, madcap, zany kooks or thoroughly unpleasant and inadequate human beings. It was this particular indecision that doomed the Ismail Merchant/James Ivory film-of-the-book (although the clothes were good). Eleanor, the central figure, is the one most exempt from this troubling uncertainty. Although she is a loopy jewellery-maker who produces "shellacked seahorses, plastic James Bond-doll earrings",[31] that kind of thing, she is both innocent, vulnerable and victimized. Janowitz probably means the others to embody a fine literary ambiguity but in this she is unsuccessful and merely returns the reader again and again to the central paradox of their unlikeability. Eleanor's lover, artist Stashua Stosz, is a disagreeable bully and another artist, Marley Mantello, purveyor of neo-classical themes—"The God of Baseball playing a game of billiards with Bacchus"[32], for example—is a self-professed genius, and well-nigh unbearable. Art dealer Victor is not much better. Janowitz undoubtedly intends a satire on the art world and its self-serving lunacies. There is an artist "who paints traumatic situations"—a rape, a car accident—in a medium he "invented himself . . . ground bones and blood acquired from garbage pails outside the meat market." Another "environmental" artist is "moving heaps of mud from one part of Montana to another" and yet another wants "to cover the Golden Gate Bridge in Band-Aids."³³ Janowitz's satiric intentions are severely undercut by her own obvious affection for and interest in contemporary art, a dichotomy that permeates the characters who are simultaneously, and impossibly, supposed to combine crass self-interest and blunted affect with finer feelings and profound sensitivities. Not that the two aspects are inimical in one personality, far from it, merely that Janowitz fails to animate the potential. Although she attempts to raise significant points, as when avid collector Chuck feeds the hungry Marley Mantello a humungous breakfast, a scenario that suggests correspondences between art, creativity, hunger and desire, she fails to develop them. Ultimately we have more shopping-list fiction—fashion, style, quirky sexual detail, consumer jokes—whose most profound statement seems to be that life doesn't live up to advertising. No one is demanding the improbable resolution or the metaphors of her first book but trivia, even if grounded in common emotional conflict, remains trivia.

Janowitz chose to further pursue the role of quasi-anthropologist to the urban nomad in *Slaves of New York.* For example, she writes of men: "When I went out with them it was only to study them further as if they were natural history museum exhibits."³⁴ In her subsequent book, *A Cannibal in Manhattan,* that particular approach is carried in a cutesy way to its logical extreme. The project must have seemed both ambitious and impeccably postmodern. A noble savage would be transported suddenly to New York City. Unencumbered by Western perceptions and preconceptions he would faithfully record the rites and rituals of this eccentric new culture. From within his innocent voice Janowitz would be able to satirically re-present the entire urban hive in all its cross-pollinated absurdities. Simultaneously she would test the boundaries of the novel itself by providing a photographic "record" of her hero's decline and fall. The reader, aware of the jokey nature of this photographic "documentation" wherein the author's friends impersonate the book's characters, would knowingly collude in the fictionalized artifice and double-bluff. All aspects of the book, from epigraph to index, would self-reflexively participate in this ironic game, questioning and blurring the edges of what actually comprises a book. Furthermore the reader would be excluded as much as included in the joke for the true "story", that of Janowitz's inter-action with her peer-group, would lurk beyond his reach and establish that the reader has no right-of-access nor chance ever to fully decode an author's meaning. It was a bold idea but could only ever have worked through an incredible feat of authorial projection and sustained imagination. The entire concept was initially hobbled by the fact of Janowitz herself possessing a wholly Western set of perceptions and the consequent difficulties of simultaneously referring to and denying this. Although she tries to locate the entire enterprise in the realm of the absurd by using an epigraph from Lewis Carroll's writing, the problem needs a more ingenious solution. Critics and readers also proved intransigent and were puzzled by an enterprise which, for all its subterranean sophistication, struck them as being overtly naive, confused and possibly even racist.

Everything was wrong with the book. Dedicated to Andy Warhol, its inner focus was on Janowitz's private life and friendships. This was less experimental than élitist and readers reacted accordingly. When, in 1928, Djuna Barnes entertained her friends with caricatures and gossip in *The Ladies Almanack,* she had the sense to publish and distribute it privately to interested parties.

Mgungu is an uncivilized savage from, of all places, "New Burnt Norton." (We are forced to note, tiredly, that the author is well read.) He is rescued by one Maria Fishburn, heir to a Great New York family. They are obviously supposed to belong to what used to be called "Our Crowd."³⁵ This smug expression was used to collectively describe the enormously rich Jewish families in New York (Guggenheim, Seligman, Gimbel, Loeb) who rose to power in the early part of this century. The "Our Crowd" now in the novel is actually Andy Warhol and his art-world henchpersons. For example, the "photographs" of Maria Fishburn are pictures of Paige Powell, Warhol-circus stalwart and *Slaves of New York* film starlet. Mgungu is a knowing modern "savage", a professional "savage" who trades on the commodities exchange with money from the Feed the Infants Federation and knocks up shoddy artefacts for tourists. Maria brings him to New York for a Dance Festival at the Museum of Primitive Cultures, curator Parker Junius (photograph of Andy Warhol). Mgungu goes to a nightclub, meets an improbable Cockney rock star and a lovable delicatessen owner (photograph of Brigid Berlin, old Warhol trouper), Maria marries Mgungu but she is in the clutches of master criminal Reynar Lopato whose main interest lies in Mgungu's ability to concoct a powerful narcotic known as Joy Paul Guilford. Maria now gets the recipe. Lopato fraternizes with a dwarf called Mikhail, plainly modelled on Truman Capote. Capote's ghostly presence further underlines the café society parameters of the novel. Maria is killed and Mgungu, set up by Lopato, unknowingly consumes his murdered bride. Lopato intends to distribute Joy Paul Guilford and appropriate Maria's fortune. As a well-known public "cannibal", Mgungu is an obvious suspect in her death. He goes on the run amongst the homeless on the streets and ends up in prison.

It would be possible, if unprofitable, to pursue the play of intended meanings throughout the book. There is the theme of the innocent abroad, misled by greedy, shifty New Yorkers and their lawyers. There are correspondences between "civilized" and "savage" behaviour and dense multi-textured attempts to locate primal forces in behaviour. The whole book is a turgid satire on modern manners and emits a steady low-grade fog of heavy-handed farce. It is carelessly written and often nonsensical in no very illuminating way—Mgungu's primitive home has patches of "couscous fur"³⁶ stitched to the walls. Mgungu's language is in simplistic grammatical disarray: "The time did pass"; "the wind was howling very fierce."³⁷

Although undoubtedly good-natured the novel does not cohere on any level. The photographs of friends dressed up and credited in the index make an embarrassed voyeur of the reader, excluded from the in-jokes. As a sub-textual commentary on Andy Warhol and his world it might be of interest to the most demented Warholian acolytes—others might as well read his diaries, or a good biography. Like the Aykroyd/Belushi film *The Blues Brothers*, **A Cannibal in Manhattan** is a private album whose delicate clues to international gossip render it ultimately more inaccessible. As in the case of that particular film, it may amuse those who are heavily drugged—on Joy Paul Guilford perhaps. The final coy references to styling and designers in the acknowledgements make it more than ever a casualty of eighties greed, vanity and the tendency to believe in shallow public myths. It is as much doomed to date as the fashionable world it covertly flashes at us like a stripper granting a swift, pitying peep to a particularly frustrated and under-privileged audience.

Janowitz is not an untalented author but her grip on postmodernist fiction has so far proved shaky and it seems inevitable that she will have to reconsider her intentions. Although many people found **A Cannibal in Manhattan** more or less repellent it may be that, for a time, she was just another Andy Warhol victim (they should have had a Helpline) who succumbed to his whispers of "You're so great! You're a star! You can do anything you want!" ("He always played the evil fairy," claimed an associate.[38]

Janowitz's progression from serious young *littérateur* to high society darling contains an unwitting commentary on such a dizzying social ascent; as in the case of Truman Capote, the higher she rose, the more her writing deteriorated.

Notes

*Djuna Barnes, "Seen from the 'L'" in *The Book of Repulsive Women* (New York, 1915).

I am grateful to Graham Caveney for his assistance with the theory in the first part of this chapter.

1. *Revue des Sciences Humaines,* no. 168: 480. I am indebted to Toril Moi's *Sexual/Textual Politics* (New York: Methuen, 1985) for much of this analysis of contemporary French feminism.

2. Julia Kristeva, "A Question of Subjectivity," *Women's Review,* 12 October 1986, 19.

3. Roland Barthes, *The Pleasure of the Text,* trans. Richard Miller (New York: Hill & Wang, 1975), 47.

4. Erica Jong, *Fear of Flying* (New York: Signet, 1974); Lisa Alther, *Kinflicks* (New York: Signet, 1977).

5. Erica Jong, *Any Woman's Blues* (New York: Perennial Library, 1991); Lisa Alther, Bedrock (New York: Knopf, 1990).

6. Joe Orton, "What the Butler Saw" in *The Complete Plays* (New York: Grove, 1977).

7. Tama Janowitz, *American Dad* (New York: Crown, 1981), 52.

8. Ibid., 31.

9. Ibid., 127.

10. Ibid., 36.

11. Ibid., 37.

12. Ibid., 44-45.

13. Ibid., 83.

14. Ibid.

15. Ibid., 208.

16. Ibid., 210.

17. Alice Munro, *The Beggar Maid (Stories of Flo and Rose)* (New York: Vintage, 1991), 28.

18. Tama Janowitz, *Slaves of New York* (New York: Washington Square Press, 1987), 1.

19. Ibid., 3.

20. Ibid., 2.

21. Ibid., 2, 6.

22. Ibid., 5.

23. Ibid., 125.

24. Ibid., 37.

25. Ibid., 23.

26. Ibid., 24.

27. Ibid., 28.

28. Ibid., 8.

29. Ibid., 58, 59.

30. Ibid., 59.

31. Ibid., 7.

32. Ibid., 45.

33. Ibid., 92, 115

34. Ibid., 28.

35. Stephen Birmingham, *Our Crowd* (New York: Harper & Row, 1967).

36. Tama Janowitz, *A Cannibal in Manhattan* (New York: Washington Square Press, 1988), 19.

37. Ibid., 55.

38. *Vanity Fair* (April 1992): 143.

Susan Bolotin (review date 20 October 1996)

SOURCE: "Hiawatha Goes Hollywood," in *New York Times Book Review,* Vol. 101, October 20, 1996, p. 13.

[*In the following review Bolotin provides a summary of the plot of* By the Shores of Gitchee Gumee.]

The creative muse manifests itself in many forms. Even Henry Wadsworth Longfellow's "Song of Hiawatha" has provided its share of inspiration, albeit mostly to parodists. But one has to wonder what it was about the famous narrative poem that got Tama Janowitz's juices going. Could it have been the notion of an innocent culture heading for its inevitable destruction, or the image of the magnificent Hiawatha revenging the sins perpetrated against his mother? Was it simply the stupefying tom-tom cadence? As my kids would say: Whatever. Or as I would say: No matter why you decide to set a novel by the shores of Gitchee Gumee, you may get soaked.

By the Shores of Gitchee Gumee, Ms. Janowitz's latest novel, is a picaresque satire of 20th-century America. The heroine, Maud Slivenowicz, 19, is one of five children living in a decrepit trailer near the now-polluted Gitchee Gumee (nuclear waste, don't you know?) with their kooky mother, Evangeline. (It might be time for Ms. Janowitz to discuss this Longfellow thing with someone.) Maud, whose favorite pastime is citing bizarre examples from "The Sex Life of the Animals"—"Did you know the blood fluke lives in a state of permanent copulation, inside a chicken?" she asks one new acquaintance—is on a big-game hunt for the right man to claim her virginity. Her sister, Marietta, is likewise obsessed with men and sex, but her literary taste runs to "Hiawatha," which she quotes without even giving a person proper warning. The boys in the family fill their time fixing cars and dreaming of Hollywood stardom (the eldest), writing bad poetry and music (the next) and cooking (the youngest).

Though each child was born from a different, usually vaguely recalled liaison, they are all blessed with a striking handsomeness and what I'm sure Ms. Janowitz thinks of as a winning innocence. I found them uniformly uninviting and dull. But, as my kids would say: Whatever. Or as I would say: Oy. (That's not a totally gratuitous Yiddishism: one of the Slivenowicz dogs is named Trayf.)

Anyway, after a string of unbelievable events, the Slivenowicz trailer rolls into the lake. One of Evangeline's boyfriends, on the lam, kidnaps the culinarily inclined youngest, who is perhaps his son, as well as Maud and her oldest brother, Pierce (the one whose fantasies run toward Bel Air mansions). The kids outsmart the crook, escape and head for Los Angeles. Along the way, they steal cars, food and money; they bilk and abandon people who try to help them.

This is supposed to be witty, as is Maud's ability to persuade the studly though retarded Pierce to prostitute himself (and I'm not speaking metaphorically). "He's going to first see if you want to go back to his place. You don't. . . . You say you have an appointment, but indicate that alley in back. . . . Get a newspaper first, or something, if you want some distraction."

Awful. And it goes on like that until the family is reunited in southern California, where Evangeline announces that she's pregnant with her sixth child, this time courtesy of a turkey baster (she's decided to try lesbianism). The entire Malibu community, rivaling the Slivenowiczes in silliness, falls for Pierce's pretty face, while Maud falls for Fred. (Trust me, you don't need to know who Fred is.) And so on, and so on, until I found myself wondering how I could ever have thought of "Hiawatha" as anything but brief.

When Longfellow died, he was the most famous poet in the English-speaking world. Over the generations since, his talents have been reconsidered, with "Hiawatha" most frequently cited as an example of his shallowness. Blessedly, Ms. Janowitz still has time to dig herself a deeper pond.

Tamsin Todd (review date 20 October 1996)

SOURCE: "This is the Forest Primeval," in *Washington Post Book World,* October 20, 1996, p. 6.

[*In the following review, Todd addresses issues of Janowitz's style and theme while providing a summary of* By the Shores of Gitchee Gumee.]

Here's a bright gem of a book—literally. The jacket lettering is done in electric-blue and lime-green; a neon-yellow hairless dog is freakily emblazoned mid-page; and in the background are surreally rolling bubble-gum-pink clouds, which, if you remember, also featured prominently on the cover of Douglas Coupland's *Generation X.*

Which reference is confusing, because the distinctive landscape Tama Janowitz explores in her fiction doesn't have much to do with Coupland's frighteningly candid cultural snapshots. Sure, there are disaffected characters in TamaLand and references to pop culture and lots of funky retro clothing. But in general TamaLand is an upbeat place. Often (as in Janowitz's *Slaves of New York* and *The Male Cross-Dresser Support Group*) TamaLand is Manhattan, seen through the eyes of vaguely arty types: painters on the make, hat designers, staffers at obscure magazines. They live downtown, dress excellently, chat glibly, act quirkily, and know they're ultrahip and getting hipper all the time.

By the Shores of Gitchee Gumee is set in Longfellow country, but don't be fooled. Substitute trees for sidewalks, trailers for skyscrapers, and you're back in familiar territory. Inhabiting this version of TamaLand are the Slivenowiczes: mother Evangeline and her five children. These include the acid-tongued 19-year-old narrator, Maud, whose pastimes include reading *The Encyclopedia of Poultry* and discussing the mating patterns of octopi and other invertebrates; her Longfellow-reciting sister, Marietta; and their precocious 6-year-old brother, Leopold, who cooks for the family and says things like, "I can be a flirt, but basically I have no intention of being deflowered." The Slivenowiczes live in the only trailer in a defunct trailer park near the town of Nokomis, which is 100 miles from the nearest mall, has a pizza joint staffed by a convicted child molester and a brand-new library without any books, where the librarian reads *Candide* during children's hour. Other characters include a born-again retired UPS stockholder, an English lord named Simon Halkett, who suffers predictably from boarding-school trauma; and a detoxed periodontist, who shares his supply of nitrous oxide with the Slivenowicz clan.

The first half of the novel takes place in Nokomis, where one of Evangeline's ex-lovers (a motorcycle-riding criminal who might be Leopold's father) holes up in the library and has a standoff with the FBI. The second half tracks the penniless Slivenowiczes' bizarre adventures as they wind across the country towards L.A., where they hope to make brother Pierce a movie star. What drives the novel is the speed of Janowitz's prose and the frantic weirdness of the scenes. Besides the standoff at the Nokomis library, there's a wheelchair chase, several carjackings, a kidnapping, and lots of farcical seduction scenes. The organization is episodic, and moving from chapter to chapter feels a bit like wandering around an amusement park: You go quickly from ride to ride, staying at each one just long enough to get a quick thrill, and then you're on to something new.

Janowitz's prose is popcorn-light, interspersed with moments of incisive satirical observation. A supermarket is "nice and cool" with the "faint aroma of decayed meat and rotting vegetables." In a hotel lobby Maud peruses brochures: "A place called Butterfly World housed more than five hundred different kinds of butterflies and their larvae. An ad for the Weeki-Wacki Lounge and Supper Club said the lounge had been in operation since 1957. Real Polynesian performers danced nightly, and there was a photograph of a Mexican waiter holding up a suckling pig on a platter in front of philodendron."

But all too often the writing is over the top. Metaphors are heavy-handed, as in this description of Simon: "He looked like an ethereal tuberculosis patient who wrote poetry on a mountaintop during the First World War." Maud's voice is more absurd than funny. One moment she's considering a career in prostitution, the next she's sounding like a Jane Austen heroine: "I wish I were dead. What's going to become of me? My own mother doesn't even like me. I have no money, no connections, no talents, I live in a trailer that isn't even good enough to be called a Winnebago."

Clearly this novel is a satire—of dysfunctional families, discount malls, fast food, freeway culture, L.A. movie culture, Florida retiree culture, trailer park culture and much,

much more. In the best satires we recognize something of ourselves; but here everything is so frantic and disjointed that it all seems slightly unreal, like the hairless dog on the jacket. In TamaLand you get to gape at lots of strange people. You speed all over the place and you get few thrills. Sometimes violent things happen, but no one gets hurt. Everything is slick and neony. At the end of the day you leave feeling pleasant, a little lightheaded, a little queasy, and also a little bit empty.

FURTHER READING

Criticism

Bellante, John and Bellante, Carl. "Janowitz and Gobbins: Feminist Fatales." *The Bloomsbury Review* (May/June 1993): 13.
    Examines the "male-bashing" post-feminist strain in Janowitz's *The Male Cross-Dresser Support Group.*

Bradham, Margaret. "Familial Failings." *Times Literary Supplement* (12-18 May 1989): 518.
    Contains a brief synopsis and commentary on *American Dad.*

Driscoll, F. Paul. "Going to the Opera with Tama Janowitz." *Opera News* (November 1996): 26, 28-9, 65.
    A conversation with commentary between Driscoll and Janowitz that draws parallels between operatic texts and scenarios and Janowitz's fiction.

Janowitz, Tama with John and Carl Bellante. "A Chic, Cheeky Chat with Tama Janowitz." *The Bloomsbury Review* (May/June 1993): 13-14, 20.
    In this interview, John and Carl Bellante discuss with Janowitz the craft of writing and the role of the author's personal life in her fictional works.

Lehman, David. "Two Divine Decadents." *Newsweek* (7 September 1987): 72.
    A comparative review of novels by Janowitz and Bret Easton-Ellis.

Plunket, Robert. "Hello, Cruel World." *New York Times Book Review* 97 (30 August 1992): 3.
    In this review of *The Male Cross-Dresser Support Group,* Plunket addresses the narrative voice used in the novel.

Sikes, Gini. "How Long Can Tama's 15 Minutes Last?" *Mademoiselle* 96, No. 4 (April, 1989): 102, 104, 276.
    Sikes incorporates interview fragments into an assessment of Janowitz's career.

Additional coverage of Janowitz's life and career is contained in the following sources published by the Gale Group: *Contemporary Authors,* **Vol. 106;** *Contemporary Authors New Revision Series,* **Vols. 52 and 89;** *Contemporary Novelists;* *Contemporary Popular Writers;* *Discovering Authors Modules: Popular Fiction and Genre Authors Modules;* **and** *Literature Resource Center.*

Francis King
1923-

(Full name Francis Henry King; has also written under the pseudonym Frank Cauldwell) Swiss-born English novelist, nonfiction and short story writer, and poet.

The following entry provides an overview of King's career from 1985 through 1997. For further information on his life and works, see *CLC*, Volumes 8 and 53.

INTRODUCTION

King is an award-winning author of over forty works that include novels, novellas, short story collections, nonfiction, and poetry. Known primarily for his fiction, King focuses more on people than events and his writing frequently includes sharp portrayals of characters finding themselves in different areas of the world. Sometimes referred to as a "dark" writer, King employs satire, humor, and perversity to explore his characters' eccentricities as well as the pain and fragility that lie beneath them.

BIOGRAPHICAL INFORMATION

King was born in Adelboden, Switzerland in 1923. He spent his childhood in India until age eight, when he was sent to an English boarding school. As a young man, King became a pacifist, avoiding World War II, and chose instead to work the land and study at Balliol College in Oxford. While he was at Oxford, King published three novels and various poems. In 1951, he joined the British Council, serving in Italy, Greece, Finland, Egypt, and Japan. King returned to England years later and worked as a reviewer and drama critic. He went on to hold professional positions as president and vice president of the English branch of the International Association of Poets, Playwrights, Editors, Essayists, and Novelists (PEN), and president of International PEN. He also cofounded the Writers' Action Group. The people and places encountered during his travels had a lasting impact on King, and his writings continually draw on his experiences as an expatriate and foreigner.

MAJOR WORKS

King's works include fictionalized accounts of his childhood, his life during the war years, his mother's life, his experiences in postwar Florence, his travels while employed at the British Council, and his life in Brighton after "retiring" from the council. Family relationships and sexual

identity are two of the most prominent and consistent themes in his work. Several of King's early novels so openly addressed homosexuality that many critics during the 1950s refused to mention them. In fact, the homosexual subject matter in *The Firewalkers* (1955, reissued in 1985) forced King to find a new publisher. In this novel set in Athens, the narrator interacts with the elderly and eccentric Colonel Grecos. King uses a similar story structure in *Punishments* (1989), *Secret Lives* (1991), *The One and Only* (1994), *Ash on an Old Man's Sleeve* (1996), and *Dead Letters* (1997). In each work, a chance meeting between two men (often from different countries) is a catalyst for major and lasting changes in their lives. *Punishments* deals with the hardships encountered by Michael Gregg, who becomes enamored of German man during a student trip to Germany in 1948. In the highly praised *Secret Lives,* the plot centers around Sir Brian Cobean and his relationship with a Japanese boy, Osamu, who is fleeing an arranged marriage. When Sir Brian dies of AIDS, Osamu must explain to the world why he and he alone will receive Brian's estate. *The One and Only* examines themes of jealousy and obsession, feelings which arise when the protagonist Mervyn meets Robert, a man who is in love with Mervyn's mother. When Robert is shunned in favor of another man, he manipulates Mervyn's feeling toward his mother, who neglected him as a child. Robert and Mervyn's shared rage leads to their own sexual relationship and Mervyn eventually kills his mother. Years later, Robert writes a manuscript that details the crime extensively and Mervyn is desperate to keep it from being published. In *Ash on an Old Man's Sleeve,* sixty-nine-year-old Elliot Baker becomes infatuated with a wealthy, young police officer in Havana. As the two men travel through Cuba together, Baker's obsession with the officer makes him reflect on the theme of religious and sexual suppression. An Australian named Steve and an Italian aristocrat are at the center of King's *Dead Letters.* They meet by chance in Sicily, form a relationship, and the aristocrat becomes increasingly dependent on Steve. Abuse in Steve's past prevents him from being able to love; however, the Italian is still able to draw inspiration from him. One of King's most successful and critically praised novellas, *Frozen Music* (1987), is a fictional account of King's life in India. The narrator, Rupert, looks back on a trip taken with his father to India. During the trip Rupert is forced to come to terms with his mother's death and to accept the reality of a vastly changed country. *The Woman Who Was God* (1988) follows the path of Mrs. St. Just as she travels to Africa to investigate the disappearance of her son, presumably at the hands of a religious sect. As she searches for the truth, Mrs. St. Just becomes obsessed with reconciling her unwieldy preconceptions with what she observes firsthand. In *Visiting Cards* (1990) and *The Ant Colony* (1991), King makes clever use of location and satire. *Visiting Cards* is a campy, almost over-the-top narrative about Amos Kingsley, a little-known travel writer who has accidentally become president of the fictional World Association of Authors. At the Association's latest conference in Malindi, meetings are unproductive, writers are taken prisoner, wives become unfaithful, and a dwarf naval officer begs to display his exhibitionist tendencies. *The Ant Colony,* set in Florence, satirically explores the relationship between the worldly Iris and the frumpy Jack, while also commenting on the lives of British Institute instructors. King's autobiography, *Yesterday Came Suddenly* (1993) makes extensive use of reconstructed dialogues with several people, giving the book an anecdotal flavor that renders it readable and entertaining.

CRITICAL RECEPTION

Although his novels are well regarded, King is primarily known for his mastery of the short fiction and novella forms. David Profumo writes that the "pressures of the shorter genre . . . make so incisive his descriptions of psychology and place." Some critics find King's prose loose and overwritten. Others describe his writing style as detached, commenting that he sometimes fails to elicit reader sympathy. King admits to a pessimistic world-view, but disagrees in part with critics who call his work dark.

Commenting on the darker themes in his work, King has stated that "it is a darkness illuminated (I hope) by acts of decency, generosity and valor." King has also been faulted for implausible plotlines and for including too many characters in his work. Many of his detractors concede, however, that the King canon is rich with keen observation and deep insights into his characters' emotional lives. His blunt, straightforward prose is regarded as one of his main strengths, and critics judge his ability to portray the intricacies of human behavior as one of his most effective tools. Critic Martin Seymour-Smith asserts that King is "one of the best writers of fiction [that] England possesses."

PRINCIPAL WORKS

*The Firewalkers: A Memoir [as Frank Cauldwell] (novel) 1955

Act of Darkness (novel) 1982

My Sister and Myself: The Diaries of J. R. Ackerley [editor] (nonfiction) 1982

Frozen Music (novella) 1987

The Woman Who Was God (novel) 1988

Punishments (novel) 1989

Visiting Cards (novel) 1990

**Florence: A Literary Companion (nonfiction) 1991

The Ant Colony (novel) 1991

Secret Lives: Three Novellas [contributions by Francis King, Tom Wakefield, and Patrick Gale] (novella) 1991

Yesterday Came Suddenly (autobiography) 1993

The One and Only (novel) 1994

A Hand at the Shutter (short stories) 1996

Ash on an Old Man's Sleeve (novel) 1996

Dead Letters (novel) 1997

*Reissued in 1985 under Francis King.

**Part of John Murray's Literary Companion series

CRITICISM

Stephen Everson (review date 12 April 1985)

SOURCE: A review of *The Firewalkers,* in *New Statesman & Society,* April 12, 1985, p. 26.

[*In the following review of* The Firewalkers, *Everson comments favorably on the novel's writing and on the character Cedric. He warns readers that although the novel was reissued in the Gay Modern Classics series, it does not treat homosexuality as a subject.*]

The Firewalkers was first published in 1956 under the pseudonym 'Frank Cauldwell' after the British Council had given Francis King the choice of publishing it under his own name or remaining in their employ. This autobiographical novel describes the young narrator's encounters with Greece and with elderly eccentric Colonel Grecos. At the centre of the book, touchingly described, is the platonic but devoted relationship between Grecos and another misfit, the staggeringly ugly German youth Götz.

In his new introduction Francis King describes the 'exhilarating sense of liberation' he experienced as a 'prim young man' setting foot in Athens. *The Firewalkers* is very much a young man's novel, but, despite his liberation, a young man who remains rather serious. Grecos is an absurd as well as a magnanimous figure and King's affection for him blunts the humorous edge of the writing, which can hover a little uneasily between irony and sentiment. Nevertheless, the social and diplomatic community in Athens gives King scope for some nicely judged vignettes and he finds a welcome sharpness in his observation of Cedric, the rich, promiscuous and queeny expatriate Englishman.

The Gay Modern Classics series has provided some welcome re-issues, but the danger in labelling a book like *The Firewalkers* a 'gay classic' is that it will be judged in the wrong way, *as a gay novel*. It is not. Homosexuality is certainly treated in the novel—and in a refreshingly unselfconscious way—but it is by no means the book's subject or even a major part of it. To read it as a gay book is to misjudge it from the start. That said, it is pleasant to have *The Firewalkers* in print again, especially as it appears under the author's real name for the first time.

David Profumo (review date 29 August 1987)

SOURCE: "Mischief That Is Past," in *Spectator*, August 29, 1987, pp. 28–9.

[*In the following review of* Frozen Music, *Profumo asserts that although King's prose is looser here than in his short stories, the narrated novella succeeds in its exploration of a father and son coming to terms with the past.*]

'I promised my mother I should never use that wretched word "novella"', wrote Dorothy Parker, and for many readers the term does seem to be a taxonomical cop-out for something that is 'entre chien et loup'. When Hutchinson launched its novella series, in which *Frozen Music* is the latest offering, it was good to see a new platform available for what is essentially the bonzai novel, more leisurely than the long short story, yet compact enough to be held in the imagination of a single entity.

In stylistic terms, *Frozen Music* has more affinity with Mr King's novels than with the stories that are perhaps his finest achievements; the pressures of the shorter genre, that make so incisive his descriptions of psychology and place, here give way to a looser prose that is even occasionally slack. What shines through, nonetheless, is the author's sure touch with the tensions and disappointments of life.

The three-layered story is narrated by Rupert Ramsden—the blurb writer knows him as Julian—a man recalling in his late fifties the fraught pilgrimage he made back to India some decades previously in the company of his father, Philip, and his young Finnish step-mother, Kirsti. They visit the vicinity of Balram, where Rupert's mother died when he was a child, and through its interplay of memory and geography the book charts the painful resolution of earlier traumas in a way that proves most unsettling.

Although the ultimate focus of the trip is the now overgrown cemetery where his first wife lies, Philip struggles along the way to rediscover the India that he once knew. His old-world courtesy, and his policy of taking the line of least resistance, blinker his appreciation of the changes that have intervened; as the saga opens, he will not recognise the new topography of the modern Balram, a place soiled with industrial sprawl and the squalor of 'bidonville' slumlands, and maintains as they drive into it that they have taken a 'wrong turning, something like that'.

This might be the motto to sum up his life. As his sniffy and often fastidious son gradually comes to terms with his own memories of the area it transpires that the mother who was dying from consumption was also being comforted by a young Canadian doctor, and this earlier deception is finally mirrored in the emotional imbroglio between Kirsti and Rupert when his father is also taken ill in one of the seedy hotels where they come to reside.

The title of this novella derives from one of the several unfinished studies on which the narrator's father has been working for years. All that Rupert knows is that it is about architecture (one of the loves of his amateur career in the world of books) but as the new India is experienced it becomes clear that the whole process of the frozen past is being thawed out for both father and son. Remembered details of his childhood quicken in the heat of the situation, and the memory of the past is seen as 'the cruellest of all betrayals'.

But this cruelty—something at which Mr King excels—is finally wrenched round to create a perspective in which, for all its surprises, his characters seem to have arrived at an equilibrium. There is more than one act of darkness here, and in the end it makes for a book, novel or novella, that is as disconcerting as anything one has come to expect from one of our foremost observers of the friction that seems to be part and parcel of what we call love.

Martin Seymour-Smith (review date 27 March 1988)

SOURCE: "A Death in India," in *Washington Post Book World*, March 27, 1988, p. 10.

[*In the following review, Seymour-Smith praises the structure and depth of* Frozen Music.]

There is some confusion about the nature of fictions that are too short to call novels but too long to call short stories. There are *novellas, Novelle, novelettes*—and even *récits,* André Gide's invention. The *novella,* which we are used to from Boccaccio, was simply a short prose narrative. The *Novelle,* more self-consciously developed by Goethe at a time when the short story as known to us had hardly been conceived as a form, and then by other Germans such as Kleist and Storm, is more complex, but is often marked by an "unexpected turn" or a climax preceded by an outline masterly in its compactness (as may be seen in the best tales of the unjustly forgotten German writer Paul Heyse, who won the Nobel Prize in 1910).

The form has always been a risky one, because the most brilliant examples tend to eclipse the rest. In these days writers tend to call anything that falls between the two stools of the story and the novel, simply so far as length is concerned, a "novella": while it is always a mistake to be too academic, some attention to what the Germans were actually trying to achieve might be salutary. This unusually good example by Francis King demonstrates why: the successes of good authors are frequently to be found embedded in the basic critical concepts, since criticism was once founded on the example of literature rather than (as now) the other way round.

Francis King, although underrated, has certainly earned the title of a modern master, and is one of the best writers of fiction England possesses. He has written 19 novels and six story collections and is equally distinguished in both forms. *The Custom House, The Last of the Pleasure Gardens,* and, in particular, *A Domestic Animal,* with its brilliantly morbid, shrewd and finally deeply compassionate study in unreciprocated homosexual love and jealousy, are all novels of high achievement, and have been acknowledged as such. His best stories are models of economy, exercises in truth to life such as stories, after all—even if this is a cliché—ought to be. He has been thought of as a pessimistic and even depressing writer, but has not been given his due for the breadth of his tolerance and compassion. There is no substantial study of his work. This is both a loss and a scandal.

In *Frozen Music* King goes back to India, the setting of his memorable second novel, *Never Again.* By deceptively simple means he achieves subtlety, and the kind of broad irony demanded by Gide for short fictions. The narrator gives a retrospective account of his return to India in the company of his father and the latter's new young Finnish wife. From the context of this account he goes back even further, to the time of his childhood and the premature death of his mother from tuberculosis—a death which has always puzzled and distressed him. Ungenerously, even meanly, he finds his father a stupid old bore. But when we arrive at the present, which we do fleetingly, we understand very differently.

This, besides being a rewarding work in itself, ought to be a lesson to younger novelists. Certainly we see pessimism

and world-weariness in the narrator's descriptions of the dirt and falsity of the India of the 1950s. But are these the author's feelings? We ought, too, to note that the narrator's sourness and hatred of his surroundings is mechanical: each time he makes an unpleasant judgment, the true circumstances correct him. All this is exquisitely understated, and amounts to short fiction as it should be written.

Philip Glazebrook (review date 23 April 1988)

SOURCE: "The Sport of a Mad Mother," in *Spectator,* April 23, 1988, pp. 31–2.

[*In the following review of* The Woman Who Was God, *Glazebrook asserts that King includes too much detail and too many fleeting characters in his novel. However, Glazebrook does praise King's well-constructed narrative.*]

There is a relief in putting yourself into the hands of so accomplished a constructor of fiction as Francis King, which encourages you to suspend disbelief, suspend too to some extent the critical organs, and allow credulity a long rein. You accept that the novelist in the pages of his book may claim to be God, creating a real world. So, if at the finish you find that your credibility, or naivety, has been manipulated, as it was in my case with **The Woman Who Was God,** you feel a little sore. I detected in my notes for this review a huffish tone (now eliminated, I hope) which would not reflect my admiration for the professionalism with which I had been taken for a ride by Mr King.

The novel's protagonist is a dimmish, drabbish woman possessed by the belief that her only son's death in a quasi-religious 'community' in Africa was not an accident. Unable to impose this obsessive idea on her ex-husband, or on the authorities—the official outward world composed of the interlocking trivia which prevents its disintegration—she resolves to travel to Africa to impose on the very scene of the event a version of that event which will not tear such a hole in the interlocking trivia which comprises her own interior world as to cause her own disintegration. She sets out to alter the reality which does not fit in with her preconceptions; and (the author assures us in the book's last line) she succeeds. Truth is no match for obsession.

Mr King has conceived the idea of writing a novel from the subjective viewpoint of this woman whose mental instability, known to her friends and evident to observers, is not revealed to the reader, who is gulled into taking her views seriously. The irony of this trick played upon his credulity only becomes clear to the reader when he has finished the book—hence my pique—but, more important, the point and direction of much of the matter in the book is not evident (or was not evident to me) save in retrospect. Take for instance this passage:

> At a meeting of the WI, when old Mrs Perrott, always
> out of touch because of the distance of her dilapidated,

thatched cottage from the village, suggested that 'that nice Mrs St Just' should be asked to join the sub-committee for the summer fête, the vicar's wife said in a hushed voice, almost as though Ruth might be outside the door listening: 'Oh, I hardly think . . . not at the moment . . . ,' and everyone silently nodded.

In retrospect I see that I might have gathered from this paragraph that Ruth was bonkers and everyone knew it; but, in reading the passage, I have to confess to impatience with what seemed an excess of detail about people and circumstances—old Mrs Perrott, the summer fête—which we never hear of again.

Altogether, in my unenlightened state, the narrative seemed to me at times excessively prolix and clogged with detail, every object and person weighted down with epithets. Though respectfully alert, as Mr King's reader is bound to be, I was looking for conventional direction-posts, and I did not see in the merciless accumulation of trivia the haunted, confused, threatening world that presses in upon a demented woman. I began to tire of characters who came in through one door, were minutely described in both appearance and background, only to disappear through another door forever. Fortunately I had my wits about me when the significant character at last burst into Mrs St Just's cabin on an African ferry. Dave is a journalist who wants to be a novelist: wants to be, that is, not a reporter of facts but an inventor of them, like a madwoman or God. He abets her. It is his newspaper article that hatches out her obsession into a cockatrice of mischief with the power to invade the real world, and to overturn the 'community'.

The 'community's' motto is Aleister Crowley's apothegm, 'Do what you will is the whole of the law'. The notion of such moral laxity, as applied to her son, is what has most horrified Mrs St Just. Here too is a difficulty for the reader, who sees, when he is at last shown the 'community', that Crowley's dictum has led only to the usual sorry perversions of the Sunday papers, not at all to the 'strange, terrible things' that so darken and appal poor Mrs St Just's mind. Not privy to her dementia, the reader will not feel his flesh creep with horror, as hers does, at the notion of a white baby being raised by blacks in an African village, even if the child is the physical result of an incestuous relationship.

Such difficulties (which will perhaps not beset a more percipient reader at all) Mr King has brought on himself by the form he has chosen for his novel. I must not carp, or sound peevish. Seen in retrospect, Mr King's control of character and situation is thoroughly efficient—early in the book he shows us a predatory youth scrounging sustenance in a café, and shows us in masterly fashion how Mrs St Just dominates his aggression—and we may be confident that the effects produced are those intended. Now and again the heart of some matter is touched in a few words, so that we see the universal under the particular (I would cite the wretched woman trying to imagine her son normal and happy among friends, and finding it

impossible: 'the realisation of that impossibility,' says Mr King, 'filled her with sadness'). Then there is the felicity of images: watching an incident which hints at vices she dreads, Mrs St Just 'felt knowledge glide into her, as slithery and venomous as a snake'. And then there is a down-at-heel Greek shipping-clerk who is called, I am glad to say, Taki. All these skills and congruities I enjoyed, and I found too that the atmosphere of the 'community' in its old slaving-station had worked into my mind (though readers familiar with Sri Aurobindo's ashram at Pondicherry, similarly ruled by a woman known as 'Mother', may find the two places run together in their thoughts).

Mr King has constructed a novel which is cunningly planned and skilfully executed: my cavil is that its shapeliness is only apparent to me in retrospect, when the tendency of what has seemed supererogatory may be appreciated.

Wendy Lesser (review date 27 November 1988)

SOURCE: "The Haunter and the Haunted," in *Washington Post Book World,* November 27, 1988, pp. 6–7.

[*In the following review of* The Woman Who Was God, *Lesser criticizes what she perceives as King's lack of empathy for his characters, especially Ruth St. Just, and maintains that the too-clever plot does not allow readers to know or identify with Ruth.*]

There's something disconcertingly wrong with Francis King's latest novel, but throughout most of **The Woman Who Was God** it's hard to put your finger on exactly what the problem is. Every time you think you've found a flaw, the novel justifies it by placing it in the context of the main character's thoughts. For instance, when we get a sentence like "The waves lisp in the luminous crescent of the beach, as they sweep in and then fold one over the other," we think we've caught King in the act of over-writing—until we learn a page later that this sentence, like the rest of the short opening chapter, actually belongs to the character's vision: "She has imagined it as a novelist might have imagined it."

The novel is cleverly written, but that very cleverness in the end proves to be its undoing. However, to begin with we are sucked in by the rather suspenseful plot. The "she" of the quotation given above is Ruth St. Just, whose only son has mysteriously perished on an island off the African coast, in a compound ruled over by one Madame Vilmorin. This lady-guru is called "Mother" by all her disciples, and King allows us to believe for most of the novel that she is the "woman" of the title. St. Just—British, divorced, a fading beauty, a somewhat impractical owner of a not-very-successful restaurant in the Cotswolds—gets no support for her suspicions from either her ex-husband or the British Foreign Office. She therefore resolves to sell her restaurant, travel alone to French-speaking Africa, and find out for herself what happened to her son. Most of the novel is an account of her journey and her eventual discoveries mainly as seen through her perceptions.

There are exceptions, however, to this point of view. Early on, for instance, we get a Foreign Office employee looking out his London window at her and thinking, "Tire-some woman!" And throughout the novel King interjects little foreshadowing messages, such as "Ruth was to get used to ancient servants being called 'the boy,'" or "Unlike most of her dreams, it was not one that she forgot on waking or, indeed ever forgot." Who is telling us these things, if not Ruth? Are they meant to shake our impression that hers is in fact the perceiving sensibility of the novel? Are they intended to create a feeling of impending doom? Or are they merely Francis King's attempt to have it both ways—to pretend to be inside his main character and at the same time show us he knows more than she does?

The real problem with the novel is that it utterly lacks empathy. In a satire like Tom Wolfe's *Bonfire of the Vanities* such an absence may not be particularly noticeable (though I noticed it and disliked it even there). But in a novel that's ostensibly about personal loss and grief the lack of feeling is a major hole in the fabric.

At one point Ruth thinks about a reporter's article on her "case": "Sad, lonely, bewildered, bereaved, frustrated: well, yes, no doubt she was all those things, but she did not like him to call her them in print." But it is King who really commits that journalistic error; it is he who seems to think he can convey this woman without identifying with her. That flaw becomes most noticeable in our utter lack of sadness about the lost son. Granted, we never knew him. But neither did we know the kidnapped little girl in Ian McEwan's *The Child in Time,* yet McEwan's novel is a wrenching, moving, terrifying portrait of a father confronting the loss of his child.

The Woman Who Was God, on the other hand, is a cold, calculated and, finally, unsuccessful effort to entrap the reader in a woman's anxieties. As a few throwaway remarks suggest (Ruth gets off the airplane in Africa, "the last of the passengers but for a mother with two small, fractiously bleating children"), this author doesn't even *like* children as a class; he's certainly unable to make us understand why a parent would mourn the loss of one of them.

King's excuse (this is a novel built around such booby-trap excuses) might be that it is Ruth, and not himself, who lacks feeling. But the problem is really the other way around. In King's vision, the characters have no integrity or existence of their own; they exist only to play a part in his pathologically clever plot. This book might well have been called *The Author Who Was God*—but in that case it would have made atheists of us all.

Nicholas Lezard (review date 3 June 1989)

SOURCE: "A Dark and Troubling Business," in *Spectator,* June 3, 1989, pp. 34–5.

[*In the following review of* Punishments, *Lezard claims that the novel's principal drawback is its simplistic plot, but that this simplicity is made up for by the depth of the Michael Gregg character and by King's refusal to provide the reader with clear answers.*]

These days, we look at prolific authors as at mothers of unviably large families (when will they get fed up? *We* are); except, really, for Francis King. He is a very professional writer, one of the last who does not rely on producing rubbish to sustain his output. This is his 21st novel. His subject-matter takes him everywhere, but his surprises are psychological; Mr King is not someone you would go to for shockingly inventive prose.

> There was the leaden sky and there was the flat, interminable plain with its ruined houses and factories and its fractured trees and stunted bushes, all looking as though they'd been drawn in sepia with a clumsy brush.

The adjectives cuddle up to the nouns like faithful old dogs. He is a novelist who seems quite happy with the English language just the way it is.

That does not mean he likes people the way they are, or, better perhaps, his people are at their best when they don't like the way they are *Act of Darkness* was dedicated to the begetter of 'that rarest of things, an act of totally disinterested kindness'; here Mr King focuses on disinterested unkindness. Michael Gregg, the narrator of *Punishments,* encloses his story in a four-page-long (two at each end) and contemporary parenthesis of acutely observed domestic disaffection which a less competent or confident writer would have dragged out to four or five times the length. The rest is his account of a summer trip, with a gang of reasonably well-meaning fellow-students, to the ruined Germany of 1948: increasing international understanding, reconciliation with the new generation and all that.

His host is a tall, impossibly handsome, blond German called Jurgen, given to wearing very short shorts and driving all the girls—and, it turns out, at least one of the boys—wild. Jurgen, of course, more or less breaks Michael's heart; Michael ends up married to one of his fellow-students but remains haunted by the experience etc.

The temptation to categorise the homoeroticism in Mr King's novels as special pleading (I am thinking, particularly, of Cyril, the irritating fake in *Voices in an Empty Room*) can at least partly be put down to one's own embarrassment in encountering the subject. Here the attraction Michael feels for the German boy, and their shocking, but discreetly described liaisons, make up the centre of the book and are not affectedly-placed causes for frissons of disgust or delight: the book very definitely does not portray homosexuality as a desirable alternative to heterosexuality. Whatever Mr King is, he is not an apologist: he knows that sex is a dark and deeply troubling business. In fact, the question of homosexuality is not really the question at all. (A good way of recovering the sense of disquiet that used to accompany even the most banal sexual matters is to swap one sex for another. Rather like the way Proust was dimly alleged to have created his female characters: by writing them as men and then changing their names, only here it is the other way round.) The greatest success of *Punishments* is that it finds an excellent objective correlative for the uneasy relationship between Britain and Germany after the war, as well as one for the uncomfortable state of the perpetually confused loyalties of postadolescence. It goes without saying that the author gets a nuance and a verbal tick down so well that that one starts wanting to kick certain characters out of intentionally achieved irritation.

It is sometimes said that Mr King's novels are really expanded short stories, and whether that is true or not elsewhere, it is a technique that serves him well here. What he misses in the way of the broad sweep and tangled plot he catches by the intimate knowledge of his narrator's point of view and the frustrating, epiphanic near-insight of a story simply told, but unable to come up with any neat answers. This, and its central mystery (which you can find out for yourselves) might suggest that he is not doing his intellect justice (E. M. Forster, both *A Passage to India* and *Maurice,* is there in the background, somewhere). But what I think they really suggest is Mr King's continuing mastery of the subtle balancing act between our need and our reluctance for explanation.

Betty Abel (review date July 1989)

SOURCE: A review of *Punishments,* in *Contemporary Review,* July, 1989, p. 45.

[*In the following review of* Punishments, *Abel briefly describes what she feels are the two "punishments" found in the novel.*]

Punishments by Francis King is a subtle, thoughtfully planned novel in which a strong under-stated theme underlies the plot. A young medical student, Michael, recounts his experiences during a journey to Germany almost immediately after the second world war, in the company of a number of other English university students. They are to stay in the homes of German undergraduates. Theirs is a voyage of reconciliation and Michael later calls it a journey 'into a knowledge of others—and, more important, into a knowledge of myself'. His narrative is set between two brief passages dated 1981, although the experiences which he describes, with hindsight, occurred in 1948.

The account of his falling reluctantly but unmistakeably in love with an attractive, even seductive, young man, Jurgen, who leads most of their expeditions to bombed and ruined cities like Dresden and, more significantly, Rosenheim reveals that Michael is finding out much about himself which he had never previously suspected. Subsequently he marries Sally, one of the other English students, but not until he has realised that the encounter between himself and his former 'enemy' turned lover has left behind ruins other than those of towns and buildings. The confrontation, culminating in a trip to the erstwhile beautiful town of Rosenheim, between the English and their German counterparts, all innocent but nevertheless resenting one another under the surface courtesies, brings about an abrupt end to Michael's association with the forceful Jurgen who vanishes, leaving his infatuated lover a 'dry, disintegrating husk'. It is Sally who comforts and restores him, for she alone of them all understands that 'one of the best ways to punish people is to show them what they really are'.

Beneath the manifold activities of a traditional summer school—lectures, seminars, swimming parties and picnics in the woods—Michael plays out his drama on two levels, one the psychological plane and the other a history of the generations and inherited notions of national identities. The 'punishments' are similarly two-fold. The first lies in the knowledge that these few weeks have scarred, even wounded him in a way that will affect him all his life; they have bequeathed a complex, haunting set of motives that are just as irredeemable as those felt by his German hosts. The other shows him that the role of self-congratulatory, 'forgiving' benefactors ill becomes the English students, even as that of 'penitent', if also cynical, stance mars their German co-evals. This intelligent and moving book is highly recommended reading.

Toby Fitton (review date 15 June 1990)

SOURCE: "*Botni* for All," in *Times Literary Supplement,* June 15, 1990, p. 653.

[*In the following review of* Visiting Cards, *Fitton praises the novel, despite his questions about its unlikely premise.*]

Visiting Cards, a jocose novel about the conference procedures of a World Association of Authors (WAA), by a former world president of PEN, contains much salutary sending-up of the scheming (and screwing) that seems to accompany worthy international gatherings. The *donnée* may appear all too familiar; the writers' conference novel, or memoir, may even be a symptom of writer's block. In the practised hands of Francis King, however, some liveliness is imparted to well-worn themes and a pleasant enough tale emerges from rather unpromising material.

Amos Kingsley, a minor travel writer more deserving of the Royal Literary Fund than the Order of the British Empire, finds himself, in his mid-forties, nominated for high office in the international writers' guild. The Japanese vote has mistakenly inverted his name (geddit?), but although originally a compromise candidate he proves himself just the compromiser the organization needs. Kingsley has a talent for moderation and becomes a skilful drafter of accommodating resolutions, always preaching cool when all about him are losing theirs. In spite of his instinct for the workable compromise, a promotion that to begin with seemed like a first-class freebie on the international circuit soon leaves him longing for the obscurity he was proud to have started from.

He arrives for the conference in Malindi, a vaguely oriental country famous for its purgative national dish, *botni,* the effects of which conveniently punctuate the story. Kingsley's comfortably proportioned wife is provoked by the climate (and the diet) into tantalizing infidelities, while he is left yearning for a Japanese delegate whose shopping bags contain less of oriental promise than of giggling little verses dedicated to President Amos himself. The perennial *congressistes* make their appearance: a plaid-trousered American soft-pornographer, an insistent Scandinavian bitch VIP, a Costa Rican giving cabaret impressions of Charlie Chaplin—and so on. Perennial congress issues—confrontations urgently requiring resolutions, or meetings on "literatures in languages of lesser currency"—seem somehow more important than freeing a handful of local writers in prison, the problem that furnishes *Visiting Cards* with its tenuous plot. The situation is saved largely by a *Wunderkind* Goanese fixer of an International Secretary.

In spite of Kingsley's ingrained silliness, which retains "Gosh", "Lordy" and even "Golliwogs" as his favourite expletives, all turns out quite well for him in the end. His *ingénu* virtue (and his marriage) remain intact in spite of international tensions ("one vote only, please, from the Suisse Romande") on the conference platform. There are the mandatory hangovers, even a bit of mandatory congress slapstick when he slips across the ballroom floor into a bowl of *botni*. This is lowlier stuff than one would expect of Francis King, though his confection has some moments of alarming plausibility. No doubt in his real-life period of high international office he has actually—perhaps often—come across a dwarf Malindian naval officer who insists on an introduction that will enable him to demonstrate to the Queen of England his special talent for imitating the war speeches of Winston Churchill.

Mark Illis (review date 16 June 1990)

SOURCE: "The PEN Is Mightier Than the Word," in *Spectator,* June 16, 1990, p. 54.

[*In the following review of* Visiting Cards, *Illis notes that there is a serious side to King's comic novel.*]

Francis King, former President of PEN International, has written a novel about the President of WAA, the World Association of Authors. Given that this fictional President is called Amos Kingsley, and that two early and fleeting characters are called Gabriel Lopez Martinez and Fukushima Kazuo, the novel at first looks like an extended literary in-joke. This is deceptive. The world in which WAA exists is not a satirical construct in which members of PEN, and others, are intended to spot themselves. It is, almost, the real world, the world in which Kingsley Amis exists. It is in fact central to the plot that he exists, because Amos only becomes President because he is mistaken for Amis.

It is hard to be sure which of the two would be less suitable for the job. Amis would at least know how to stand up for himself. Amos, however, is neatly characterised early on, when standing at a urinal beside a macho American author:

> [He] continued to urinate in the nervous spurts which always afflicted him when not alone at this task.

One of Amos's problems is his nervousness. He finds it hard to express himself freely, to impose his ideas, which are a little wishy-washy but undoubtedly humane, on rebellious delegates. Amos has several other problems. He finds it difficult to say no. This is how he comes to write a preface for the collected works of an author he has never heard of, who turns out to have been a Nazi. It is also how he finds that he has promised to inform the Queen of a man from Malindi who gives a remarkable impression of Winston Churchill. These are his minor problems. He has two major problems. The first is that he is facing a revolt within WAA, because he has brought a conference to Malindi while that country is holding three writers as political prisoners. The second is that his wife, a 'beautiful giantess', is unfaithful and that he, while occasionally attracted to other women, never has any luck with them.

The novel enjoyably resolves all of these problems. International literary conferences in which 'screwing, boozing and bitching' are major activities are David Lodge territory, but this book is more reminiscent of Malcolm Bradbury's *Cuts*. It is short, entertaining and determinedly topical, although, like *Cuts,* it is not as topical as it might wish, since one of the conference resolutions is to call for the release of Nelson Mandela. It is what tends to be dismissively called a confection, implying something tasty but insubstantial, and probably unhealthy. It is certainly lightweight, but the form is very effective for pinpointing human frailty. Amos speaks with uncharacteristic cogency for a page and a half on the subject of self-righteousness, condemning the hypocritical, self-serving moral stances of certain delegates:

> So now I beg you—put aside your own feelings of moral superiority and moral outrage and self-righteousness and just think, think solely, of the three men whom . . . I visited yesterday in their prison.

It is an argument for pragmatism, for doing the most effective thing, which may well also be the most discreet thing, and it is inevitable that it sounds like King's unfiltered voice giving it. In this comic novel it takes a kidnapping and a series of fictions developing out of it to resolve all of Amos's problems, but King is also giving a more serious response to the more serious problems.

Paul Binding (review date 7 June 1991)

SOURCE: "Internal Combustion," in *New Statesman & Society,* June 7, 1991, p. 44.

[*In the following review of* The Ant Colony, *Binding finds honesty and objectivity in King's satirical novel about the British Institute in Florence at the end of World War II.*]

To Florence, not long after the end of the second world war, two young people come to teach English at the British Institute: Iris Crediton, who arrives with a whole string of connections (her mother was a famous pianist, well-known in Florentine expatriate circles), and Jack Prentice (his very surname significant), from a workingclass northern family with no social pull anywhere.

They contrast in other ways: pretty Iris has a natural sense of style and a flair for languages, both of which serve her well as life opens up beyond the institute; Jack, clever though he is, and a natural scholar, is defeated by the Italian language. As for style, he won't forsake the scuffed brown shoes, Harris tweed jacket, and shapeless grey flannels that proclaim him everywhere as English. But the reader sees that, at a deeper level, they share other more important qualities. Among these, a lack of experience (both of them are virgins) takes second place to a gentle sense of duty and, dictating this, an inclusive kindness.

Kindness is certainly much needed, and at a premium, in the British colony of Florence, which has sometimes simultaneously both lived off and patronised Italian society. The war having so recently ended, the shadow of Mussolini is everywhere. A good number of those trying to keep up old, elegant ways, and thoroughly looking down on all who haven't known them, had accommodated themselves, with varying degrees of enthusiasm, to the "bullfrog" and his regime. Pre-eminent among these is the perverse queen of the colony, Isabella Lambreni, with a collaborationist past, who intimately links its members to one another.

Nor is kindness much more in evidence in the world of the institute itself (which, of course, has always one eye upon the Florentine beau monde). Bitchier even than its greater counterpart, it is animated by gossip and by the preservation of classfeuds imported from England. English snobbery being what it is, Jack suffers more than Iris from the cruelty of its tittle-tattle, and a principal reason for our sympathy for her is her defence of him in the face of it.

Yet it must not be suggested that Francis King is doing anything so simple or limited as offering a satiric portrait of an out-of-touch, incestuous community, for his interest in the individuality of his people, in their uniqueness combined with their comparative helplessness against social, economic and cultural forces precludes easy judgment and demands understanding.

Hugely rich, camp, idle Ivor Luce, who takes such a shine to Jack Prentice, has, superficially, little admirable about him; but numberless small touches in his evolving portrait confer on him dignity, even a nobility of nature. Giles Conquest, director of studies, would seem a sorry figure with his literary delusions and infidelities. Yet, how moving his breakdown is, and his salvation by a (well-evoked) dog! And, conversely, Iris's discovery of what she can accept, because of the strength of her sexual desire, is chilling, alarming—only we are made to suspend tempting censoriousness.

Francis King is a "pure" novelist, who, faced with the complexity of people and their inter-relations, denies himself any idiosyncracies of style or opinion in their presentation. The result of his sacrifice is a novel (this is one of his very finest) of great subtlety and a humane richness.

Lorna Sage (review date 7 June 1991)

SOURCE: "Name-Droppers," in *Times Literary Supplement,* June 7, 1991, p. 22.

[*In the following review of* The Ant Colony, *Sage examines King's treatment of his characters, especially Jack and Iris.*]

Export the English if you want to have a good look at them, their absurdities and anxieties thrown into high relief against a foreign backdrop. It is the formula of Forster's *A Room With a View* and Woolf's *The Voyage Out* (in her exasperated début she transported them as far as South America), and countless novels before and since. Francis King's **The Ant Colony** is back on Forster territory, in Florence, just after the end of the war, where rubble is still piled round the Ponte Vecchio and the expatriate community is reassembling and dusting off the anecdotes—"What was it that Norman Douglas had said to him?" They are avid for "new blood", which duly arrives in the form of innocent Jack (Yorkshire and Oxford, but much more Yorkshire) and Iris (upper-middle class, ex-ATS) who turn up to teach English at the Institute.

The education of Jack and Iris at the hands of "the colony" is of course the theme. Their separate adventures provide a guided tour of the Florence of camp tradition, mapped-out not in paintings or palaces of Florentines, but in these *personaggi* who have superimposed their own network of intrigue and gossip on the city. Some are grandly penniless, like Audrey Heaton, who scrapes a living on advances for unwritten books, reviews for the *TLS* (a touch implausible, that) and dunning richer friends, while she tends the shrine of her dead lesbian lover Johnnie. Others are wealthy, like Ivor Luce, who is also nearly young by the colony's standards, and who contemplates Jack ("A butch piece. With possibilities. Definitely") in vampiric anticipation. Ivor urges Jack to "behave like an Italian", but that's not exactly what he means: going native here is a matter of becoming one of the characters in the play of sex and patronage; learning the language means acquiring a fund of voyeuristic stories about Edith Wharton, D. H. Lawrence, Aldous Huxley, Reggie Turner, Willie Maugham and "Percy Lubbock in Lerici." And possibly adding your own contribution, canonized in whispers.

King, who was in Florence in the 1940s, has fun with his name-dropping characters, while carefully not dropping any names himself. He is disposed to be forgiving, at this distance: their snobbishness and their self-consciousness and seedy glamour do conceal some small pearls of wisdom, along the lines that moral black and white do not make up the whole spectrum. In one or two corners of the plot there is even room for pathos—particularly in the treatment of ancient Harry Archer, a failed painter tended in his decline by sixteen-year-old Franco who, according to the gossip, is a thief, but in fact sells himself in the Loggia and to save the old man's dignity pretends that the money comes from peddling Harry's shaky handiwork. Vice and violence take place off-stage, so that good humour can, on the whole, prevail. If you don't look too closely, what you see is a community of eccentrics.

Jack does rather better than Iris. Though on the face of it he's a great deal more gauche and vulnerable, those, it turns out, are his saving qualities. Yorkshire innocence survives unscathed (he loses his virginity to a brisk and obliging English nanny, who's very definitely not a member of the charmed circle), only his rough edges are smoothed by the disappointed but gallant Ivor. Moreover, browsing among the bookstalls, he comes on a copy of Coventry Patmore, and, we're told, "It was that volume which was fortuitously to propel him in the direction in which his career as a redbrick academic was eventually to meander." (The syntax itself at moments takes on a leisurely, rootless flavour.) Jack is a lucky Jim, but Iris—precisely because she has connections and introductions galore in the colony—loses her innocence rather more thoroughly, thus illustrating the old fictional adage that men's sexual lives are educational episodes, while women take theirs personally. So in a sense the plot is as "period" as the setting. The darker implications serve mainly to spice the comedy, however. The only seriously wicked characters, and the only seriously good ones for that matter, aren't English in any case: the English, it seems, are saved for niceness and nastiness. King's Florence is a busy limbo where this version of the national character can flourish without encountering any resistance: he mocks his colonists, but colludes with them too, so that their world becomes the closed system implied in the title, comfortably pickled.

Mark Illis (review date 8 June 1991)

SOURCE: "Expatriates Gossiping in Florence," in *Spectator,* June 8, 1991, p. 36.

[*In the following review of* The Ant Colony, *Illis writes that despite the many likeable characters in the novel, the story is not compelling.*]

The English novel is regularly accused of being too quiet, too polite and too safe. It is often described in negative terms: it is unadventurous or unambitious. Francis King has written novels, such as *Act of Darkness,* to which none of these adjectives apply. They are all, however, appropriate in the case of *The Ant Colony.*

Jack, a young, diffident, working-class virgin, and Iris the 'classy' titled daughter of a famous mother, and also a virgin, arrive in Florence to teach English after the war. They spend a year acquiring experience and then leave, sadder and wiser. The circle they inhabit is the expatriate colony, which has the usual characteristics of expatriate communities: it is gossipy, bitchy, and disconsolate, there is a lot of sex of different varieties, and there is a suffocating sense of futility in the air. Its members are like tourists who have stayed too long, and run out of things to do and sights to see. They watch each other. 'Here', says one of them, 'all private lives are public ones.'

The novel moves slowly around a large cast of characters, many of them engaging, some of them sketchy, transferring its attention from Jack to Iris and back again. Jack pines for Iris, and makes a half-hearted pass at her, but in fact they do not see very much of each other over the year. At first everyone but them seems to be having an active sex-life, lesbian, gay or heterosexual, and they miss innuendos, mistake sexualities or overhear orgasmic cries without realising what they are. Iris, however, begins to spend her time with Dale Somers, a gigolo with a weakness for violence. He introduces her to sex. Jack, often lonely, spends his time with Ivor Luce, a middle-aged aesthete who would like to perform a similar service. Ivor eyes him before meeting him in a library: 'A butch piece. With possibilities. Definitely.' This is a refreshing voice disrupting the pervading languid tone of the novel, but it quickly becomes more subdued, and their friendship is purely platonic. Jack has to wait until almost the end of the novel before his inevitable deflowering. He is eventually seduced after a liberating swim by a convenient tourist who first had sex when she was 13. Francis King discreetly leaves the room, or the beach, before any of his characters start to make love. It might be more appropriate in some cases to stay there for the gory details. It seems odd to desert his characters when they are having experiences crucial to their development.

The characters around Jack and Iris slip and slide in their feelings for each other, sometimes in mid-conversation. A smile of 'extraordinary warmth' interrupts cold dislike. A wife despises and then pities and forgives her husband. People seem to be in the wrong relationships, feeling neither love nor hate for each other. They irritate each other but do not arouse passions. A man, losing his mistress, out of love with his wife and children, transfers all his affections to a stray dog he has rescued from being put down. The ones who come off well are the older ones, who retain their dignity, show bravery in small, unostentatious ways and are, above all, kind. These characters are likeable, but likeable characters are not enough to make this a satisfying novel. *The Ant Colony* does not seem to have quite made up its mind. It approaches, but never reaches, the sparkling, sophisticated malice of Mapp and Lucia, while it hints at a darker side which is never explored. Ian McEwan's *The Innocent,* as its title suggests, has a very similar hero, and **The Ant Colony** might have benefited from some dramatic happening to disturb the well-drawn but slightly staid picture it presents. There are a suicide and a broken nose at the end, but both are subordinated to a nostalgic mood of departure, which dominates the final chapters, and seems in retrospect to have dominated the whole story.

Richard Davenport-Hines (review date 2 August 1991)

SOURCE: "Only the Lonely," in *Times Literary Supplement,* August 2, 1991, p. 19.

[*In the following review of* Secret Lives: Three Novellas, *Davenport-Hines judges King's novella, a tale of emotional isolation, as the strongest in the collection, which also includes novellas by Tom Wakefield and Patrick Gale.*]

By far the most arresting of the three novellas in this collection is that by Francis King [*Secret Lives*] which gives the volume its title. This tells the story of a poor Japanese painter named Osamu who comes to London to escape a forced marriage, and becomes the houseboy and lover of a QC, Sir Brian Cobean. The latter is an elegant, persuasive, ruthless, stealthy homosexual who has ruined his wife's life and lives in the grandeur of Holland Park. He falls ill with pneumonia, loses weight, tells his family he has leukaemia, eventually dies of meningitis. Osamu nurses Brian, holds him as he dies, then faces the cold, stilted family and friends who seem never to have suspected the secret life of the dead man.

King's story has a chilling authenticity that makes the reader feel still and icy. Every sentence is beautifully crafted, but with no show of fine writing which would be out of place in such a story. It is a tale of emotional isolation, written (perhaps too easily) from the standpoint of Osamu as victim. But the real sufferer is Brian, and his isolation is almost too terrible to imagine. His military background, his fellow Benchers at the Temple, his own self-contempt have driven him to an extremity in which his life is separated from his feelings. Like other secretive people he fears that without secrets he will lose control of his life. He lives always in a panic of discovery, his polished overglaze a tragic deception. Denying even the nature of his mortal illnesses, Brian lives and dies in a state of lonely, ruthless fright. His predicament is unforgettable.

Tom Wakefield's "The Other Way" is the weakest part of the collection. It is a wistful study of a fat, awkward, gaudy spinster called Brenda who wins a package holiday to Tunisia and befriends a lonely gay male nurse. The story has some attractive moments, a strong ending and its message of self-reliance comes across convincingly; but its action depends on both Brenda and the nurse talking aloud to themselves in monologues which can be overheard by sympathetic strangers. Life is not like that. There are clichés, such as beaches strewn by lager louts, with used condoms and the scene which Wakefield intends as the most repellent moment of Brenda's holiday is both predictable and unsuccessful. The sight, on a beach, of a man's churning buttocks as he and his girlfriend indulge in what Australian teenagers call cement-mixing is not as unpleasant as Wakefield pretends, and certainly it cannot justify the heavy message of panic and estrangement with which he loads it.

Patrick Gale's "Caesar's Wife" is a cheerier and more consistent piece of writing. Its narrator, Mary, is a bright, witty woman working as a senior editor in publishing. For many years she has enjoyed an affair with a rich industrialist, but this is disrupted by the sudden death of his wife. A comedy of manners ensues as Mary tries to resist his proposals of marriage. Although Gale's characterization is not particularly original, the dialogue is sharp and the overall effect entertaining. He also tries a few literary tricks which are all the more successful for not being too ambitious.

There are several consonances between these three novellas. Like one of the authors handled by Mary, their writing has "an air of poised depression"; but the similarities extend beyond style to content. Many of their most sympathetic characters—Brenda, Osamu, and Josh in Gale's story, for example—are people whose parents had bad or non-existent sex lives, children who grew up with no sense of the possibility of successful union or integration with other people. They recognize the potential for grief in monogamy, shy away from the compromises that are required of couples, settle for their integrity alone. The sanest people, these three novellas seem to suggest, are those who respond to people who are attracted to them. Submit without hope or rancour, even to deceptive, self-deceiving Holland Park smoothies.

Paul Binding (review date 23 August 1991)

SOURCE: "Coexistences," in *New Statesman & Society,* August 23, 1991, p. 19.

[*In the following review of* Secret Lives: Three Novellas, *Binding praises King's title novella for its portrayal of characters carrying burdensome secrets and of a man dying of AIDS.*]

In conversation with Professor Barbara Hardy for the *European Gay Review,* Francis King observed that the novella "is not an English genre. It was developed in France and Russia as a concentrated form for narratives of sexual passion." He cites Prevost's *Manon Lascaut* and Turgenev's *First Love.* Now he has followed his own masterly contribution to this un-English genre *Frozen Music,* with ***Secret Lives,*** the title-novella of a triptych, the other two being by Tom Wakefield and Patrick Gale, both already known for their explorations of the heart.

King's title suggests the theme that gives the book its unity: the intimacy, more properly the secrecy, consequent on obsessive passion. For passion, paradoxically, makes us collude with convention, to which it would seem, in its disregard of reason, to be opposed. Our terror that the love-object will be taken from us renders us anxious to appease authority and honour all its shibboleths.

Tom Wakefield's novella seems superficially less concerned with passion than its successors. Brenda, a fat and almost comically tall woman, is a compulsive competition-entrant. She wins a holiday in North Africa, where, bored, afraid and confused, she flees her ghastly camp to cohabit with a fellow-Briton, Leslie, who broods on his own unsatisfactory love life (gay, it turns out). As the two come closer, we learn through a beautifully done confession of the animating passion of this passionless-seeming woman: her mother, with whom she shared so much, and whose treatment by her father has conditioned her.

In Patrick Gale's first-person contribution, Mary is the mistress for one night each week of a famous tycoon. When the tycoon's wife dies, she has to re-appraise this long relationship and prepare to expose what has been carefully hidden. But another secret in the novella is the narrator's feelings for the tycoon's gay son, a handicapped young man who is also a publishing colleague. Camp, spiteful, affectionate, imaginative, Josh most movingly counterpoints the central duo.

King's ***Secret Lives,*** in its intensity and subtlety one of his finest productions, makes overt that conflict that hugged passion sets up. Does one betray it the more by conforming to the world's cruel demands in order to preserve it, or by translating it into terms comprehensible to all which inevitably change and diminish it? Sir Brian Cobean, a distinguished QC, keeps his relationship with a young Japanese, Osamu, secret from everybody. Osamu seems content with this background existence, accepting as Brian's right a social life (including, we understand, a sexual one) exclusive of himself.

Brian grows ill—with Aids, we gradually and appalledly realise. At his death, Osamu, sole beneficiary of his estate, decides that he must let the world know, in the most quietly dramatic manner possible, the truth of their relationship. Francis King's novella haunts the mind with its portraits of people carrying the burdens of emotional situations they can't admit. It also must stand as one of the most sensitive accounts to date of the anguish inflicted by Aids.

What seems to me English in the execution of this un-English form is its strong sense of interconnecting social worlds, and this goes for Tom Wakefield and Patrick Gale as well. Brenda's life as a teacher and Mary's as an editor

enhance the delineations of private stress, not just by giving them a context, but by emphasising the baffling coexistences in all our lives.

Penelope Lively (review date 4 September 1993)

SOURCE: "Places and Friends He Still Can Recall," in *Spectator,* September 4, 1993, p. 26.

[*In the following review of* Yesterday Came Suddenly, *Lively commends King's memoir, which she feels is an engaging and moving work, in large part because of King's use of anecdotes and lengthy dialogue segments.*]

Autobiography comes in many guises—as stern narrative, as expiation, as justification, as smokescreen. Francis King is an accomplished *raconteur* and it is in this style that he has chosen to write his—a sequence of anecdotes by means of which the great array of people with whom he has been associated trip in and out of the pages. The result is [***Yesterday Came Suddenly,***] a book which is always entertaining and sometimes moving. It is a book about others quite as much as it is about the author, which is appropriate, since clearly Francis King's consuming interest is in the quirky behaviour of other people—just as well, for a novelist. He notes that someone once observed that he loved his friends for their faults—a point which is evident indeed as one reads of the egotism of Olivia Manning or the perversities of L. P. Hartley or of Joe Ackerley. Though it should be said that all such portraits are as affectionate as they are candid. Malice is reserved for the few who really got up the author's nose: Lindsay of Balliol, a hapless British Council representative, C. P. Snow ('. . . a Baked Alaska—sweet, warm and gungy on the outside, hard and cold within').

Francis King spent his early childhood in India and was then sent to England as a 'remittance child' at the age of nine, just like Kipling, by whose harrowing story *Baa Baa Black Sheep* he had already been unnerved. In the event, he was never treated in any way like Kipling was, but he cites vividly the feeling of being an 'extra' in other people's homes and attributes to that experience his subsequent tendency to please and placate. The account of childhood and of his family is in many ways the most attractive part of the book. Especially strong is Francis King's honest and perceptive view of his loving but ambivalent relationship with his mother, who lived to a great age and remained always a central figure in his life.

It has been a life very much on the move: Italy, Greece, Finland, Japan. Francis King went overseas for the British Council at the time when the Council attracted colourful and maverick figures as much as or rather than career officials. The Council may have lost out on efficiency, but it was vastly enriched. He began with the British Institute in Florence soon after the war, from which period spring chatty and anecdotal descriptions of expatriate Florentine society centred around such as Harold Acton and Bernard Berenson which set the tone for the rest of the book. From then on we are in the thick of it—Francis King seems to have known everyone you've ever heard of (and a fair number that you haven't)—and the names hurtle forth upon each other's heels: Angus Wilson, Edith Evans, Merlina Mercouri, Harold Nicolson, Louis MacNeice, Somerset Maugham, Anthony Blunt . . . there is no end to it. And if at points this unstoppable catalogue has a whiff of *Jennifer's Diary,* the writing certainly does not. Francis King seems to be endowed with the gift of total recall (or else with an unusually rich archive of diaries and notes)—flicking back through the autobiography you realise that it is as richly spattered with dialogue as a novel.

The second half of the book is taken up with the author's years back in England, having left the Council, living first in Brighton and then in London—packed years in which he writes most of his novels and short stories, does theatre reviewing, and weathers a libel action, the account of which will have many another novelist breaking out in a cold sweat and anxiously reconsidering their own latest typescript. Needing information for literary purposes about the life-style of Brighton deckchair attendants, he puts an ad in the local paper and thus meets the young man who is to become his lover and companion of the next 20 years, and of whose death from Aids he gives an unflinching and acutely painful account. His beloved mother dies also, and he himself encounters cancer. The last section of the book is both brave and sad, and takes the reader back to the author's own comment at the beginning, that at times he feels 'as if life were a matter of picking one's way over the thinnest crust of earth above a sleeping volcano'.

Public events are curiously absent—except for a flurry of international involvement when the author is International Chairman of PEN (a sprightly account of this, and various people's hash settled). I would have liked a little pruning of the parade of personalities in favour of more appraisal of the countries in which he lived. And, especially, it would have been illuminating to hear more of the author's reaction to an entirely changed climate of opinion about homosexuality. For today's young, the pre-Wolfenden days when sex between consenting adult males was an indictable offence must seem like the Stone Age. Francis King has surprisingly little to say about this, except for the comment that an increased toleration made possible for him intense and valued friendships with women. But the revolution in opinion seems to me such a significant one that it would have been enlightening to hear more about it from someone centrally involved.

These are relatively minor carps. This is an autobiography with all the appeal of a compelling novel, and no doubt right now those of the large cast of characters who are still around will be busy letting the author know what they feel about their roles.

Penelope Fitzgerald (review date 5 September 1993)

SOURCE: "Words Break the Pain Barrier," in *London Observer,* September 5, 1993, p. 53.

[*In the following review of* Yesterday Came Suddenly, *Fitzgerald summarizes King's autobiography, commenting on its story-like quality and on King's modesty in relation to his achievements.*]

Francis King, the brilliant and distinguished novelist, poet, critic, travel-writer and biographer, turns out also to have been a successful Brighton landlady (his own definition), short-order cook and agricultural labourer. These experiences have led to 'an attitude of profound, if resigned, pessimism about the world. I do not expect people to behave consistently well, and my observation is that few of them do.' But he has to admit—he could hardly help it—to his own tolerance and compassion.

He is at the same time open-hearted and inexplicable, generous and alarmingly precise. His epigraph is from 'I Look into my Glass', in which Hardy regrets that he ought to have outlived sensual emotion, but never has.

His father was in the Indian police, and he was brought up as a child of the last days of the Raj. He was sent to Shrewsbury, became a pacifist and did his National Service as a conscientious objector, working on two farms and a commune.

As an Oxford undergraduate, he published his first three novels. On his first visit to Venice in a long vacation, 'I was seduced (there is no other word for it) by a gondolier'. He joined the British Council, with assignments in Italy, Greece, Egypt, Finland and Japan, and the pattern of his life seemed set. And yet in 1966, when he was 43, he cut short his career and came back to England to support himself as a novelist.

In Kyoto he had been content, and 'just as I could have opted for an academic career instead of the British Council, and for a domestic life with children and grandchildren, instead of a sexually unorthodox one, so now I could have passed the rest of my years in Japan, instead of at home'. He was haunted, as most of us are, by the path not taken. But he had committed himself to an uncertain, colourful, emotionally adventurous existence, which, however, he was to lead with all the decency, punctuality, sense of family loyalty, orderliness and capacity for hard work to which he has been brought up. This contrast is one of the most attractive features of the book.

Yesterday Came Suddenly, like Francis King's novels, is intensely, almost painfully, true to what his senses record, but also to what other people feel and the curious ways in which they express it. When his father died, for instance, his house-master, 'a decent, unemotional, inarticulate man', sent for him and in his embarrassment offered him a cigarette from the silver box in the study, then hastily moved it away again.

Anthony Burgess and his first wife 'would lurch into the room, arms round each other, faces glistening, hair bedraggled, as though, victims of a shipwreck, they had just emerged from a turbulent sea. By the end of the evening both of them were often hardly coherent. Yet there was something extraordinarily touching about their dependence on each other.'

The middle section of the book expands, not into gossip so much as into brief lives, as memory calls back an exceptional number of friends. King has always been attracted to difficult women and hard cases, and the reader has the opportunity to attend Ivy Compton-Burnett's strange nursery tea-parties, to argue with Melina Mercouri (who 'might have been the captain of a Greek caique bawling out a sailor ordered to wash down the decks'), and sit through an affectionate evening with Somerset Maugham, who 'looked as though at any moment he might crumble into dust'.

He is too judicious to be taken in—he refuses to accept that either E. M. Forster or L. P. Hartley was 'a sweet old thing'—although he perhaps thinks Edmund Blunden rather simpler than he was, and does not quite sound the depths of Louis MacNeice's unhappiness. Meanwhile, we can only be grateful to him for sharing these superbly clear and beguiling memories, and possibly for concealing some of them.

Very few autobiographers can have said so little about their own successes. King does mention the Writers' Action Group, of which he was a cofounder, and which battled for the Public Lending Right, but he says almost nothing about his CBE, or about his *Yorkshire Post* award for *Act of Darkness*. His international presidency of PEN is treated—particularly his stand-off with a battered Norman Mailer—in terms of high comedy. 'The sole real achievement of my Presidency', he says, was the establishment of a PEN centre in the then Soviet Union. He was in severe pain at the time from a recent cancer operation, which was fortunately made better rather than worse by caviare and vodka.

The truth is that *Yesterday Came Suddenly* has been designed from beginning to end as a story, not so much of a career as of love and friendship. Its true weight falls at the end with the death from Aids of David Atkin, Francis King's lover and companion, in 1988. King, the novelist of separation and loss, ends his book with a description of the pain and guilt of his own bereavement. This must have been a difficult chapter to write. The one compensation is that he never feels happier, he says, than when he is writing, even though 'it might have been better for me and for those close to me if it had not been so'.

Jonathan Keates (review date 8 October 1993)

SOURCE: "Wasp at Large," in *Times Literary Supplement*, October 8, 1993, p. 30.

[*In the following review of* Yesterday Came Suddenly, *Keates praises King's "busy, populous chronicle of a literary life."*]

The boy Francis King tasted "a brine-like salt" on his father's forehead when, reluctantly, or at any rate unspontaneously, he kissed him goodnight. The taste, his autobiography's Proustian memory spur, turned out to be a malign portent of disease and death, and it is the presence of these two elements, spectral or all too palpable, which lends a melancholy consistency to [*Yesterday Came Suddenly,* a] busy populous chronicle of a literary life.

A remittance child, like Kipling's Punch in "Baa Baa Black Sheep", he was shipped home from India to be shuffled between aunts and uncles; the Kings, radical Bohemians who lunched him at Rules and talked to him like a grownup, and the Reads, gushing, ribald, philistine and supremely practical. The comparative cheerfulness of this boyhood in exile confounds expectation as much as his apparent serenity at Shrewsbury where he felt mingled indignation and pleasure at discovering "King is the house tart" scribbled on a lavatory door, and worshipped his fagmaster, Bagott, who later (inevitably, one is tempted to suppose) shot himself on the eve of marriage.

King's vinegary, no-nonsense attitude to himself when young means he gives short shrift to his undergraduate pacifism, and is scarcely more charitable towards the prankster and smart alec be became on his return to Oxford, refreshed after a tumultuous initiatory sexual fling with a Venetian gondolier, having published two novels and begun contributing the sort of *Listener* review in which Elizabeth Bowen could be dismissed as "a high-class sobsister, the intellectual's Godfrey Winn."

The happiest, or least troubled portion of the career mapped out here was spent as a teacher for the British Council. From a Britain of shrivelled aid budgets and reduced international influence, we look back with an envious sourness at the fortunate author, "seeing life" against exotically arranged backdrops, in that old-fashioned mode which combines an acceptable measure of domestic bohemianism, a strong dash of café society, and fruitful liaisons with local boys of suitable intelligence and principle.

Meanwhile, the *sommités littéraires* made anecdotal landfall. In Athens, Louis MacNeice, officially entitled "Fun.O" (Functional Officer), was emphatically no fun at all, while Maurice Bowra, whose trousers King tugged off with some difficulty in a hospital operating-theatre after a motoring accident, became positively Neronic in self-esteem: "When I saw that bloody great juggernaut coming straight at us, I remember my last thought was 'My God, what a loss to English culture!'" In Kyoto, Joe Ackerley, his air ticket having been thoughtfully provided by Morgan Forster, became the author's Man Who Came To Dinner, spoiling his Akita dogs rotten, swilling his ruinously expensive Beefeater and satanically playing him off against James Kirkup, towards whose studied *japonnaiseries* and "creative" autobiography King exercises what might be termed a waspish indulgence.

The same mingling of tones, acidulated and compassionate, typifies his approach, elsewhere in the book, to those he befriends either during his British Council years or as a working novelist and reviewer. His strongest suit as a writer has always lain in tracing the incalculable outlines of a relationship, and the most absorbing moments of **Yesterday Came Suddenly** all involve the resilience or sudden implosion of friendships and love affairs, little hard-edged dramas of acceptance or betrayal.

If the names sometimes bunch too thickly (the incident involving Daphne du Maurier staring at an ashtray, for example, might have fallen a harmless victim to the blue pencil), it is worth waiting for them to thin out in front of extended portraits such as those of Ivy Compton-Burnett and Olivia Manning, drawn in the indelible colours of exasperated affection.

"It is better to be drunk with loss", the former tells him, "and to beat the ground than to let the deeper things gradually escape." At two crucial points, the sound of Francis King beating the ground helps to focus and discipline the narrative One is the death, at the age of 102, of his mother, a woman whose power over her family was asserted through a lifetime's submission to their needs, this event leaves him in a state of anguished incredulity. The other is the loss through AIDS of his lover, David Atkin, whose gallantry under fire, as it were, is evoked without the least hint of maudlin exaggeration.

Both in the innocence of its discursiveness, which assumes that the reader can always make time to linger over what the writer has to say, and in its author's candid self-presentation as something of a punctilious fusspot, this book recalls certain of the more pleasurable literary memoirs of the nineteenth century, books such as Thomas Adolphus Trollope's *What I Remember* or Cyrus Redding's *Fifty Years' Recollections*. The genre is fast disappearing, and, in what may be one of its last and most accomplished examples, we should enjoy it while there is still time.

Patricia Beer (review date 16 December 1993)

SOURCE: "Memories Are Made of This," in *London Review of Books*, December 16, 1993, pp. 22–3.

[*In reviewing King's* Yesterday Came Suddenly *alongside Giles Gordon's* Aren't We Due a Royalty Statement? *and William Trevor's* Excursions in the Real World, *Beer concludes that King's "detached" prose style serves* Yesterday Came Suddenly *well.*]

I was well into Giles Gordon's *Aren't We Due a Royalty Statement?* before I noticed that other readers were taking the book seriously, often to the point of denunciation. Up to then I had been assuming that it had set out to be an ingenious spoof, a sort of hoax or parody which had failed to make its intentions thoroughly clear, and that was nothing to be censorious about. But all leg-pullers have to declare themselves eventually otherwise there would be no point, and as I read on it dawned on me that Gordon was not going to declare any such thing. But there is so much to support my original impression that I have still not been able entirely to give up the idea that the book *is* a spoof.

There is a kind of innocent absurdity about it which belongs to the very nature of a good spoof. To begin with, having firmly introduced his book as an autobiography, Gordon puts on a consistent act of not being able to remember a thing, which in the circumstances seems a 'smidgen', as he would say, foolish. He cannot recall the name of the funeral parlour where Tennessee Williams lay in state nor can he remember the venue ('some pub in Fleet Street') where he was to meet Gore Vidal. Probably it had been so with us had we been there, but we might not have thought it necessary to say so, especially if, like Gordon himself, we had not in the event bothered to visit the funeral parlous or actually speak to the live celebrity. The motif of forgetfulness is heard throughout the book. Gordon held an umbrella over Judi Dench on her way 'to I think it was Heal's in Tottenham Court Road'. He made some changes to an article by Ronald Harwood but as to what they were: 'I really can't remember.' This motif could be a useful technical device in another context but in this case it can only be a motive: to cut the great and famous down to size.

It is difficult to catch the intended tone of this book partly because Gordon presents himself as essentially a man with a keen sense of humour, and you never know where you are with people like that. He laughs in the wrong place at a friend's poetry reading. He giggles at names like Rees-Mogg, and splits his sides at the list of those who supported Count Tolstoy (ha ha) in the recent painful court case: Prince Dmitri Galitzine, for instance, and Princess Tatiana Metternich (ho ho). He finds his jokes good enough to repeat, like the one about Sue Townsend: 'creator of Adrian but no mole'. Confronted with such a merry madcap I see that I have no sense of humour at all, and am rather glad about it. On the other hand, in reading this book, I must be missing a lot of jokes. When Gordon speaks of other writers, 'including he who was to become Lord Archer', and a little later tells us that he was employed to teach Prince Andrew to write *grammatically,* I am at a loss. I feel there must be a joke in there somewhere.

Of course it is a perfectly acceptable ploy for a writer to be deliberately silly but I simply cannot decide whether or not this is what Giles Gordon is doing. When he speaks of syllabics as 'a briefly fashionable, and easy, way of writing verse by counting syllables' is he (I am assuming he knows better) being naughtily provocative or is he inventing a comic pig-ignorant character, the Alf Garnett of the world of literature? When he reveals how 'Prince Harry even let my baby daughter Lucy sit on his horse' is he lampooning people who talk like that, or is he talking like that? And then there is the mystery of his sneering. He mocks the writer of the farming column in Private Eye who, he says, 'eager to reveal his pseudonymous identity at one of their parties, introduces himself as Old Muckspreader'. (A natural and friendly thing to do, I would have thought.) Does he forget, or is it meant to be funny, that he himself is extremely eager to make sure that we all know about his own contributions to the *Eye*?

Any autobiographer who has a well-defined role, even at a lowish level, in any particular environment can reasonably be expected to give an interesting and informative account of it. We really can learn a lot from Giles Gordon about the British literary scene of the present and the recent past. The facts are there, rather too many of them sometimes: his article, as it must be called, on PLR, which is embedded in the text, contains material which deserves to be known but could more easily be acquired from a reference book. Length rather than depth is his object and many of those who would read the book might expect the latter and not need the former. It would make a splendid present for a visiting Martian. Gordon deigns to remember enough to provide a great many personalities to look out for—or to mention, should they have died. He gives an accurate portrayal, for instance, of Edith Sitwell and her ill-bred public manners. But here comes a drawback. He makes no real suggestion as to the quality of her work or the possibility that it might be good enough to counterbalance her arrogant rudeness. I do not think for a moment that it was but some do and an alien might and should be given a chance. Gordon's portraits, of course, have to be highly selective as to detail; but his choice in this respect is often unsure. Having described, quite relevantly, Arnold Goodman as 'physically a dauntingly large and hairy man', he adds that there was a Goodman brother who 'was smaller in stature'. Now I come to think of it, though, that might interest an alien.

Francis King, in his autobiography ***Yesterday Came Suddenly,*** writes as straightforwardly as he has always done. Every so often in the course of his long career as a novelist critics have spoken of the detachment of his style, nearly all of them meaning it as a compliment. For most of his formative years and on into middle age, King was an expatriate, born in Switzerland, spending his early boyhood in India, and in manhood working for the British Council in Italy, Greece, Finland and Japan successively. This long exile—and most of it, the British Council part, was voluntary—would affect anyone's prose style, unless of course it was the other way round, the temperament behind the prose style being the prime mover. It is significant that when he said, half-jokingly, that he felt so much at home in Japan he must in a previous existence have been Japanese, an English friend commented that it was a pity he hadn't remembered more of the language. When in 1966, at the age of 43, he returned to England he made Brighton, where he settled for some time, sound just like a foreign country, where they do things differently and you have to try to learn the language but not get too involved.

Detachment in an autobiography is a mixed blessing, but the calmness of King's style is rather welcome when he is speaking of both his own homosexuality and that of the men he met while working abroad. There were a great many. Indeed the reader's first impression is likely to be that the British Council in the Forties and Fifties was, by way of its staff, visiting celebrities and general contacts, only a few citizens short of a latterday Sodom. This turns out to be not quite true; a closer reading shows that in fact gays were numerically outmatched—just—by staid heterosexual husbands. It is a question of treatment. King almost invariably describes the married couples as kind—a word he cruelly overworks—and not much else. His presentation of the homosexuals, on the other hand, is lively and explicit. He refers to a respected member of the teaching staff as 'an inveterate cottager', and recounts how he arranged for Anthony Blunt, who was giving a lecture tour for the Council in Greece, to meet and assess young men ('That one's rather jolly,' 'I rather like that one over there') and sometimes paid them on his behalf, a part of the proceedings about which Blunt displayed great delicacy.

He has nothing detailed or penetrating to say about the politics of the countries he lived in while working abroad, many of which were going through periods of desperate re-adjustment. He can give harrowingly vivid descriptions of the squalor that war had brought to many of the towns and cities he knew, but his accounts of governmental politics tend to be cursory. His attention is caught by people. He may not explore their minds and hearts but he sees the full surface.

Back in England he soon assembled and carefully cultivated a kind of floating salon of compatriots, of both genders and varying sexual tastes, most of them known writers such as J. R. Ackerley, Ivy Compton-Burnett, L. P. Hartley. They were nearly all middle-class, by birth or advancement, and middle-aged, and as by now they are nearly all dead as well, the series of spirited portraits which forms much of the later part of King's book has an intriguing tone which is both racy and funereal. He has already told us that he likes his women friends to be difficult and in London there seems to have been no lack of choice. The sketch of Olivia Manning is one of the best. He presents her irritating, often unpleasant vagaries with something like affection.

It is part of King's technique that when he has something nasty to say he quotes somebody else as saying it: a device that is several years older than Methuselah but still seems to work. He relates that when at a British Council gathering a newcomer asked if Ronald Bottrall was handsome, Roger Hinks replied: 'Well, that all depends on whether you're attracted by men with eyes on the tops of their heads.' It was perhaps rather unwise of King, after that, to include a photograph of Bottrall which shows his eyes to have been in the normal human place. But the inclusion was probably an oversight for King would certainly not set out to discredit one of Hinks's sallies, which he admired excessively, as he did those of Maurice Bowra. His appreciative quotation of their spiteful and meaningless quips seems to indicate that he mistook inaccurate bitchiness for wit.

King's book is mercifully free of the pretence of amnesia which Giles Gordon flaunted and which has been creeping up on the reading public for some time. Penelope Mortimer's parade of forgetfulness, for example, in her recent biography *About Time Too,* knows so few bounds that the only fair comment can be *Private Eye*'s: 'Every time she says she can't remember something the reader simply thinks then why on earth am I paying you to say so?' Francis King permits himself the occasional admission of failure to recall, yes, but not all this disingenuous forgetting.

Knowing as we do that the authors of the three autobiographies under review all write or have written fiction, are all living in England, and have covered much the same period of time, we might expect them to have something in common when they turn to fact. We should be wrong. A tinker, a tailor and a soldier, living in various centuries, might well have more in common when it came to writing their life stories. It could be said, I suppose, that Giles Gordon and Francis King, though very dissimilar, stand in much the same part of the field, but no one could deny that William Trevor in *Excursions in the Real World* is somewhere else, in a world that seems more real then theirs.

In the first place his use of memory, or perhaps one should say his relationship with it, sets him apart. He does not pretend to remember and, more significantly, he does not pretend to forget. He accepts that in this book he must renounce invention. It is an anthology of memories rather than a straightforward narrative but it begins traditionally: 'My earliest memories are of County Cork.' The chapters are arranged in more or less chronological order. In his introduction he turns the whole enterprise over to memory, explaining that this faculty alone has chosen the real people he depicts here; in an excellent clause he describes them as those 'who for one reason or another have remained snagged in the memory'. Later in the introduction he states his approach very clearly by identifying himself as 'the figure whose memory has been tapped in order to provide these forays from the territory of fiction into that of reality as it was'.

I think it is not fanciful to see this voluntary passivity expressed in Trevor's syntax. He certainly uses the passive tense or an intransitive verb much more frequently than he does in his fiction. In the schoolroom 'poster paint was produced,' 'errors and aberrations were corrected.' On holiday abroad, 'postcards are written.' And—best example of all—in Venetian churches, lire drop into ecclesiastical boxes'; look, no hands.

Of course, as Trevor says himself, 'in any record of personal fascinations and enthusiasms, the recorder cannot remain entirely in the shadows,' and this is certainly true in his case. Not all his fine qualities as a writer of fiction can come through into the new territory of fact—not all fiction's techniques are appropriate to autobiography—but many do. One of them is what might be called, if it were not too dull a word, decorum. After the outpourings of biographers who insist on deluging us with more than we wish to know, his delicacy is telling. It enables him to deal with sensitive material—the harrowing deterioration of his parents' marriage, for example—with no loss of eloquence.

Memory could, and presumably did, put forward many important names for him to drop if he wished, but he markedly has not used them. Any writer in search of lost time can exercise his right of veto. Almost the only authors Trevor speaks of are Somerville and Ross; they are allotted a four-page chapter and one of Lucy Willis's engaging illustrations. He never met Ross; she died before he was born. He might just have met Somerville who lived on to be 91, but he says nothing of it here. Trevor's memory of them must be attached to something they were or did in their prime, something which made an impression on him later. Perhaps, for him, they represented the fraught theme of Anglo-Irishness whose implications were made even more complicated, one imagines, by the fact that Trevor, too, was a Protestant. Somerville and Ross, daughters of the Ascendancy, considered themselves to be totally Irish, whereas the Irish they wrote about with such patronising mirth did not consider them to be Irish at all. This situation might well snag in Trevor's memory, though he writes temperately.

One of the most real of the 'real people' whom Trevor presents is Miss Quirke, the girl who 'had been found in a farmhouse at Oola, a few miles from Tipperary, where she'd been vaguely waiting for something to happen'. She was employed to teach William Trevor and his brother at their home before they went to boarding-school; she taught a stimulating hotchpotch of skills and information, not much of it apparently suited to the immediate needs of untravelled schoolboys, like the names of Parisian streets and the history of the electric chair in America. Looking back, Trevor says that 'learning was never again to be as calm or as agreeable as it was in that upstairs room with Miss Quirke'; and the boys half-suspected this at the time. It is a delightful description; the tone made me think of the 'lovely Miss' of D. J. Enright's schooldays as he evokes her in his poem 'And two good things As with many of Trevor's fictional characters, Miss Quirke is mysterious, at first because she is seen through the eyes of young boys but at the end because the adult author asks: 'Did she simply slip back into the County Tipperary landscape?' Although we are in the real world we feel uneasily that that is exactly what happened. After all she was 'found' there.

Now that this new book has told us so many of the facts of Trevor's life, we can see how time has worked with memory to create episodes and situations in his fiction. In the story 'Matilda's England', for example, surely his distress at the disintegration of his parents' once happy marriage has surfaced in the feelings of the child Matilda, whose glad though not fully conscious awareness of the harmony her parents enjoyed is broken for ever when her father is killed in the war. Trevor's ability to represent the passing of time is as keen as ever in this new world. Social mores process in front of us. A man kisses a strange girl: 'she'd have slapped his face in the Fifties and taken him to court in the Nineties, but in the Sixties . . . everybody laughed.' His dexterity in passing from today to fifty years ago is as marked as it has ever been. In the way we all take through the dark wood William Trevor is one of the few who can look round at the past without bumping into a tree.

Gregory Woods (review date 23 September 1994)

SOURCE: "Criminal Connections," in *Times Literary Supplement,* September 23, 1994, p. 22.

[*In the following review of* The One and Only, *Woods criticizes what he views as overwritten passages, but states that the story is "well told" and unique.*]

The past comes back to haunt you. It does in fiction, at least. One does not need a large-scale obsessive, like Proust, to demonstrate how heavily the structure of the novel itself has come to rely on this banal idea. Comeuppance is the key.

The narrator and protagonist of Francis King's [*One and Only*], Mervyn Frost, is sent the typescript of an old school friend's autobiography and finds, to his dismay, that an appalling episode in his own past—which led to his being institutionalized—is described there in full detail, with identities barely disguised. Bob, the friend, will not edit these revelations from his book until a certain price has been paid.

The novel alternates its account of the circumstances leading up to the past crime with Mervyn's reactions to having his sins raked up again. Three of his relationships are pivotal: those with each of his parents, and his one-sided love affair with Bob. All three are conveyed in some depth, with Mervyn's love for his father and lack of love for his mother being particularly clearly and plausibly delineated. His love and hatred for Bob, confused in his own mind, are justifiably less lucid.

Francis King has published more than twenty novels. Long ago, his career reached that condition of reliability which prompts critics to call a writer "distinguished." Beyond that, there does not seem to be a firm consensus on his status. His gay readers will have respectful memories of the early novels which dealt with homosexuality so sanely in such neurotic times. One thinks not only of the books which came out in the 1950s, such as *The Man on the Rock,* but also of later examples like *A Domestic Animal,*

which appeared on the very cusp of Gay Liberation but managed to satisfy pre- and post-liberationist readers alike. King's quality has been variable. It may be that we have Graham Greene to blame for the fact that so many English novelists waste so much of their time writing "entertainments" between their more thoughtful books. It would be hard otherwise to account for the fact that a fine novelist like King will occasionally produce a wretched potboiler like *Visiting Cards.*

Although *The One and Only* is better than that book, there are moments of clumsiness, particularly in the obtrusive hooks at the ends of some chapters: "What none of them even guessed was that one day I would be someone of whom Gladbury"—his old school—"would be ashamed." At times, the narrative is over-explicit: "What she really hated, I am sure, was the idea of having to entertain a number of dull people (as she would see them) scarcely known to her." the redundant parenthetical phrase only looks like a flaw because the book as a whole is so short and the story otherwise so economically told. As in Christopher Isherwood's novels, the blandness of the narrative voice throws up the occasional embarrassing banality: "My life, like a cavernous room, has been full of such echoes, ricocheting back and forth, back and forth. I often wonder if in other people's lives the same thing happens." The crime itself, when it comes, virtually evaporates before one has registered its monstrosity—presumably because the narrator, who perpetrates it, cannot bear to dwell on the details.

At its weakest points, *The One and Only* gives a slight impression of a hoary old yarn: repressed queer with insufferable, suffocating mother, meets and mates with sinister, detached friend, with murderous consequences. It is a measure of King's considerable skill that he leaves the reader with the sense of a tale well told—and a tale we had not heard before.

Charles Godfrey-Faussett (review date 29 March 1996)

SOURCE: A review of *Ash on an Old Man's Sleeve,* in *Times Literary Supplement,* March 29, 1996, p. 22.

[*In the following review of* Ash on an Old Man's Sleeve, *Godfrey-Faussett objects to the novel's "confessional style" and to its forced imagery.*]

With [*Ash on an Old Man's Sleeve*] Francis King juggles the epithets in the aphorism attributed to William Lecky that "sensuality is the vice of young men and old nations." The "ash" of the title doesn't only get on the narrator's sleeve but also up his nose, as a brief encounter with cocaine launches his Cuban holiday in a way he never expected. He writes: "my head, so far from resembling some sealed, over-crowded storeroom, was now a vast, open arena, full of light and air." When he reports a failed bag-snatch by a small boy, he meets Eneas, a handsome young police officer. The book is a recollected account of Elliot Baker's inner life, as homosexual infatuation, culture shock and drugs rearrange his sixty-nine-year-old public-school self-image.

The story derives much of its impetus from Baker's acute awareness in Havana of his isolated but privileged position; not solely because of his white skin and hard currency but also because of Eneas's companionship and the insight it affords him into officialdom under Castro. A retired civil servant himself, he avoids mentioning in the police station that he writes biographies, because "I remembered that in countries like Cuba the authorities tend to be suspicious of writers." His more than biographical interest in Eneas (who takes a week off to be with him) adds salt to his observations on the country's beleaguered and oppressive regime.

King projects his narrator as a sensitive and enquiring man, the soul of probity who, none the less, cannot help enjoying the special relationship with a young man that conditions in Cuba afford him. While he quite clearly despises a promiscuous Yorkshire communist staying at his hotel, there is something precious about his own guilty conscience. The novel's confessional style might excuse some of the clumsiness of the writing ("It was years since I had run, really run. But now I ran."), but it cannot account for the literary posturing or the contrived imagery: the Colombian coke-dealer speaks English "and yes, with a slight lisp, as though each word were a pip that kept getting stuck to his teeth or his lips as he tried to spit it out", and the paintwork on his Oldsmobile apparently looks like the skin of a bruised pear. Most irritatingly, such symbolism is then pressed into the service of an artificial symmetry in the telling of the tale.

The narrative is also hampered by Baker's repeated reflective questioning, which only pays off when he accompanies Eneas on a climactic and dangerous trip into the interior in order to witness the anniversary of a miraculous manifestation of the Virgin. When he is forced to stay overnight by a police raid, it is fortunate that we are accustomed to our narrator's equivocations. It makes King's comparison between the effects of expediently suppressing either faith or sexuality much more easy to swallow. Baker is not even sure whether it was necessarily the narcotics that had affected him so vigorously on his arrival in Havana. Equally, he is prepared to put the miracle down to mass hallucination brought on by the local water. In the mountain village, at some cost to himself, he finally sees the fulfilment of his homoerotic fantasy and of the villagers' primitive religious belief as springing from the same deep source.

William Scammell (review date 30 March 1996)

SOURCE: "Love in a Hot Climate," in *Spectator,* March 30, 1996, p. 29.

[*In the following review of* Ash on an Old Man's Sleeve, *Scammell praises the novel's treatment of sexuality.*]

[In Francis King's novel, *Ash on an Old Man's Sleeve,*] Elliott Baker arrives in the 'hot, dark, mysterious' city of Havana, a valetudinarian of fixed habits and declining powers, more accustomed to watching his step for cracked paving-stones than sniffing 'that strange fermentation of the air' which greets his traveller's enquiring nose. 'You want a good time?' he is asked on his first morning by a couple of prostitutes. 'Of course I wanted a good time. Who doesn't want a good time? But I didn't want a good time with either of them'.

To his own amazement this ex-civil servant and part-time biographer finds himself accepting another offer soon after, and happily snorting cocaine in the back of an old American car. After a short sleep at the hotel he wakes up feeling only 50 instead of 69, and ready for anything. When his carrier bag is snatched by a young boy he is able to give chase, and when later he meets Eneas De León, the 'extraordinarily beautiful young man' who is the police officer assigned to the case, he responds by striking up a friendship and ultimately falling in love with him.

Eneas, a body-builder and ex-stevedore, turns out to be the son of a doctor, but one who disappointed his father by neglecting his studies. A trip to Hemingway's house, now a museum, is foiled by Cuban inefficiency so they go to the beach instead, where Eneas shows off his muscles and flirts with the girls, while Baker is badgered by touts. Cuba's awful poverty, and its inhabitants' permanent hunger for a better life, form a backdrop to the events that follow.

One evening Baker looks up a dyspeptic Dutch gay called Raoul, to whom he has an introduction, and is warned: 'Cuba is not a good place for homos . . . Be careful, my friend, be very careful.' No less a figure than El Commandante himself has proscribed homosexuality as 'a bourgeois perversion', even though he, Raoul, has personally buggered many of his soldiers in this very room. He offers to arrange some 'safe sex' for his guest, which is politely declined (though in a later episode Baker finds himself reversing that decision).

The friendship with Eneas grows apace, Baker treating the childlike young man to a great many presents, and it culminates in a weird trip to a remote village to visit a church where children have reputedly seen a vision of the Virgin Mary. A livid storm blows up; a dog hurls itself at the car, the young carrier-bag thief turns out to be an altar-boy. (We're somewhere between Lowry's volcano, the Marabar caves, and Greeneland.) During a long and melodramatic evening they duly witness a miracle: three children actually appear to fly in the caves, like birds, and the head of a statue of the Virgin moves and speaks. Baker is told later that it gave a message of hope:

> In October El Commandante would die, would die by an act of violence. Then everything would change, everything would be better . . . The Virgin would never break her promise.

Communist policemen break up the remnants of the service. Baker and Eneas spend the night at the local priest's house, sharing a big old-fashioned bed, and a sexual miracle follows the religious one:

> In comparison with innumerable other nights spent with innumerable other people in the course of a promiscuous and much-travelled life, I found the lovemaking which followed abrupt, hurried, clumsy, crude. And yet, with total truthfulness, I can say 'That was the best' . . . I lay in the dark. I felt an extraordinary energy and a happiness no less extraordinary. *'Milagro,'* Diego had said of what happened with the children. This was another miracle, smaller, yes, but a miracle nonetheless. It was as though a withered branch had suddenly put forth flowers.

When he tries to repeat their caresses in the morning, Baker is angrily rebuffed. After their return to Havana Eneas disappears, and Baker spends a miserable time searching for his lost happiness, still nursing the 'disorientation' of 'having fallen in love so totally, so irrationally, so unexpectedly, at so advanced an age'. None of his questions finds an answer. The apparent miracle, Eneas's arrest or flight, Cuba's mysterious brand of 'African' Christianity, buzz in his head like flies. Someone tells him he is just 'a silly old foreign queen' who should know better than to get mixed up with a disappointed young man and a paranoid government. Beaten up and robbed, he finally takes the plane home, still puzzling over his good and bad fortune.

It's rather a four-square and old-fashioned sort of a novel, from the allusive title to the habit of filling in each character's appearance and history from the first moment of his or her appearance on the page. The verbal repetitions—note that triple 'good time' in as many sentences, in the quotation above—give it an air of precise innocence; the economy of means reminded me a little of Anita Brookner. The subtext worries away at bisexuality. The topsoil is content to nourish whatever takes root. In an age of idiom-mongering and neon street-cred the view of sex as an old-fashioned miracle, rather than as an excuse for more verbal humping comes as something of a pleasant shock.

Sarah A. Smith (review date 6 December 1996)

SOURCE: "People of a Certain Age," in *Times Literary Supplement,* December 6, 1996, p. 22.

[*In the following review of* A Hand at the Shutter, *Smith comments on King's "sly" storytelling and on the brave female characters found in this collection of stories.*]

A Hand at the Shutter brings together sixteen of Francis King's stories, half of them already published in journals and anthologies, written over a period of thirteen years. Elegant, well-bred stories, ranging in location from Maida Vale to Slovenia, Buenos Aires to Japan, they form a varied, subtly challenging collection which confirms the author's creative longevity. King focuses on characters of a

certain age and class and places them in circumstances fraught with emotional significance. Thus, "Sukie" ends with an elderly visiting lecturer, desperate to believe in the tears of the prostitute he has rejected—"That could not be acting, could not!" Elsewhere, obsession, loneliness and frustration provide the themes for some sharply observed portraits.

At first sight, the stories seem technically competent but slight in terms of plot and apparent intent. Certainly anyone looking for conventional narrative satisfaction and an easily extractable meaning would be disappointed in King's work. But he is a sly story-teller. Uncertainty, even implausibility, lie at the heart of works such as the recent story, "The Web", which sees middle-class Liz take up with a fraudulent beggar, first sexually and then professionally. Even his seemingly straightforward comic tale, "The Cloven Hoof", unsettles the reader with its mischievous symbolism, while, in the bleak account of "The Tradesman", Death only calls for Mrs Masterman after meals-on-wheels and the hairdresser have already been.

King dares his characters, especially his female characters, into acts of outrage, whether sleeping with a waiter or simply helping an unstable and now law-breaking neighbour. Normally cautions, self-conscious figures thrill to the danger of action without thought, as emotion takes over from dignity. This is a world in which humiliation is inevitable, love unattainable and rebellion a release, in which a wife can leave her neurotic husband and then feel embarrassed: "She did not want to put into precise words that she was jealous not of another woman, of his work, or of a hobby, but of something as abstract as time. It would sound so foolish." Characters are sometimes nudged towards tragicomedy. Do we laugh or cringe over Lauris, a mother so madly possessive that she is jealous of her daughter's budgerigar? Does "Panama", one of the best pieces in the collection, end in irony or poignancy? The stories themselves are coolly open-ended.

There is a recognizable King cast of characters here: the asthmatic, the spinster with her pet dog or cat, and the ageing homosexual with his eye on the waiters. Those familiar with the author's other work will be able to spot some of his minor personal preferences in this collection: a fascination with hot countries and foreign cultures, an admiration for clean finger-nails and large teeth and an equal dislike of undercooked steaks. A neurotic distaste for the next-door neighbours also runs through the book. King's previous novel, *Ash on an Old Man's Sleeve,* opens with the invocation "Surprise me!," and goes on to do just that, after a few pages, describing its seventy-year-old protagonist snorting cocaine in a park at midnight. *A Hand at the Shutter,* Francis King's forty-second book and his seventh collection of short stories, does not hold many surprises. But it offers graceful prose and works which stretch the form and the reader alike, leaving both improved by the exercise.

Tim Haigh (review date 24 October 1997)

SOURCE: "Sicilian Overtures," in *Times Literary Supplement,* October 24, 1997, p. 25.

[*In the following review of* Dead Letters, *Haigh takes issue with the main plot, which concerns Prince Stefano and Steve's relationship.*]

There is a tradition of novels whose power resides in allusiveness and suggestion rather than story-telling. It is as part of this tradition that Francis King intends *Dead Letters.* His aim is to indicate, rather than to tell, to leave things in the shadows or off-stage, rather than to expose them to the glare of sunlight; or, like a De Chirico painting, to give them the mythic resonance of a train in the distance.

The plot is unremarkable. In the 1970s, an Australian on his European trip meets a faded Italian aristocrat in Sicily and accepts his hospitality. The Australian stays longer than he meant to, partly because of the chance to restore the Prince's ancient Bugatti, and partly because the Prince comes to rely on him. But he chafes under the obligation, so he moves on.

Beneath this simple structure lies a whole range of issues. Prince Stefano has no children, and, like his crumbling ancestral home, his line is coming to an ignominious end. Steve, the mechanic, comes from an unhappy background with an abusive father, and he has difficulty loving anybody. The Prince has been writing a book for years, and Steve's presence galvanizes him into finishing it. It subsequently becomes an important work. (Steve sees a movie version of it back home in Australia, and he receives a letter from an academic asking for his recollections of Prince Stefano.) These are the shadows which King throws, filling them out with a host of minor events: a family retainer is killed by the Mafia, Steve repairs a vacuum cleaner for a friend of Stefano's wife, a louche playwright interrupts an agreeable lunch in a restaurant.

More problematic is whether King brings it all off. We can read between the lines, but is there really anything there? We never learn anything about Prince Stefano's book. The novel draws on Lampedusa's life, but in an uncertain and unresolved way. We never know what it is about Steve that changes everything for the Prince. Several times he murmurs that there is much he would like to say, but he cannot bring himself to do so. Then he has a stroke and is unable to say anything. Only after his death can he speak. He sends the boy a handful of postcards bearing gnomic observations, a one-hand-clapping conversation which adds up to an oblique declaration of love. It is not clear whether this love is sexual—Steve is beautiful, but he is not otherwise a very interesting young man—or just a longing for youth and vigour as contrasted with his own decline.

The major theme of the novel is the tension between love and obligation. Steve discovers that he did, after all, love Prince Stefano, and he later wishes he could feel more for his own family. In the end, King's sensibility is simply too delicate. In his reluctance to pin down the details, he has simply let them go. Several times, the Prince almost touches Steve, but draws back. Bringing that issue to a head, or revealing how Steve helped the Prince's book, might have given *Dead Letters* the focus it needed.

FURTHER READING

Criticism

McDadd, Susanne. "Francis King: An Interview." *Pen* (Autumn 1989): 24-25.

McDadd interviews King, focusing on his life and various works.

Mellors, John. "Waves and Echoes: The Novels and Stories of Francis King." *London Magazine* 15, (December 1975–January 1976): 74–82.

Mellors offers a critical assessment of King's work, concluding that *The Custom House, The Waves Behind the Boat,* and *The Japanese Umbrella* are his "most impressive achievements."

Williamson, Malcolm. "Lechers on world peace." *Observer* (London), No. 10365 (10 June 1990): 54.

Williamson offers a positive review of *Visiting Cards.*

How to Use This Index

The main references

> **Calvino, Italo**
> 1923-1985 .... **CLC 5, 8, 11, 22, 33, 39,**
> **73; SSC 3**

list all author entries in the following Gale Literary Criticism series:

BLC = *Black Literature Criticism*
CLC = *Contemporary Literary Criticism*
CLR = *Children's Literature Review*
CMLC = *Classical and Medieval Literature Criticism*
DA = *DISCovering Authors*
DAB = *DISCovering Authors: British*
DAC = *DISCovering Authors: Canadian*
DAM = *DISCovering Authors: Modules*
      DRAM: *Dramatists Module;* *MST:* *Most-Studied Authors Module;*
      MULT: *Multicultural Authors Module;* *NOV:* *Novelists Module;*
      POET: *Poets Module;* *POP:* *Popular Fiction and Genre Authors Module*
DC = *Drama Criticism*
HLC = *Hispanic Literature Criticism*
LC = *Literature Criticism from 1400 to 1800*
NCLC = *Nineteenth-Century Literature Criticism*
NNAL = *Native North American Literature*
PC = *Poetry Criticism*
SSC = *Short Story Criticism*
TCLC = *Twentieth-Century Literary Criticism*
WLC = *World Literature Criticism, 1500 to the Present*

The cross-references

> See also CANR 23; CA 85-88;
> obituary CA116

list all author entries in the following Gale biographical and literary sources:

AAYA = *Authors & Artists for Young Adults*
AITN = *Authors in the News*
BEST = *Bestsellers*
BW = *Black Writers*
CA = *Contemporary Authors*
CAAS = *Contemporary Authors Autobiography Series*
CABS = *Contemporary Authors Bibliographical Series*
CANR = *Contemporary Authors New Revision Series*
CAP = *Contemporary Authors Permanent Series*
CDALB = *Concise Dictionary of American Literary Biography*
CDBLB = *Concise Dictionary of British Literary Biography*
DLB = *Dictionary of Literary Biography*
DLBD = *Dictionary of Literary Biography Documentary Series*
DLBY = *Dictionary of Literary Biography Yearbook*
HW = *Hispanic Writers*
JRDA = *Junior DISCovering Authors*
MAICYA = *Major Authors and Illustrators for Children and Young Adults*
MTCW = *Major 20th-Century Writers*
SAAS = *Something about the Author Autobiography Series*
SATA = *Something about the Author*
YABC = *Yesterday's Authors of Books for Children*

Literary Criticism Series
Cumulative Author Index

Andreae, Johann V(alentin)
  1586-1654 .... **LC 32**
  See also DLB 164
Andress, Lesley
  See Sanders, Lawrence
Andrewes, Lancelot 1555-1626 .... **LC 5**
  See also DLB 151, 172
Andrews, Cicily Fairfield
  See West, Rebecca
Andrews, Elton V.
  See Pohl, Frederik
Andric, Ivo 1892-1975 .... **CLC 8**
  See also AW 36; CA 81-84; 57-60; CANR
  43, 60; DLB 147; MTCW 1
Androvar
  See Prado (Calvo), Pedro
Angelique, Pierre
  See Bataille, Georges
Angell, Roger 1920- .... **CLC 26**
  See also CA 57-60; CANR 13, 44, 70; DLB
  171, 185
Angelou, Maya 1928- .... **CLC 12, 35, 64, 77;**
  BLC 1; DA; DAB; DAC; DAM MST,
  MULT, POET, POP; PC 32
  See also AAYA 7, 20; AMWS 4; BEST; BW
  2, 3; CA 65-68; CANR 19, 42, 65;
  CDALBS; CLR 53; DA3; DLB 38;
  MTCW 1, 2; SATA 49
Anna Comnena 1083-1153 .... **CMLC 25**
Annunzio, Gabriele d'
  See D'Annunzio, Gabriele
Anodos
  See Coleridge, Mary E(lizabeth)
Anon, Charles Robert
  See Pessoa, Fernando (Antonio Nogueira)
Anouilh, Jean (Marie Lucien Pierre)
  1910-1987 .... **CLC 1, 3, 8, 13, 40, 50;**
  DAM DRAM; DC 8
  See also CA 17-20R; 123; CANR 32;
  MTCW 1, 2
Anthony, Florence
  See Ai
Anthony, John
  See Ciardi, John (Anthony)
Anthony, Peter
  See Shaffer, Anthony (Joshua); Shaffer, Pe-
  ter (Levin)
Anthony, Piers 1934- .... **CLC 35; DAM POP**
  See also AAYA 11; BEST; CA 21-24R;
  CANR 28, 56, 73; DLB 8; MTCW 1, 2;
  SAAS 22; SATA 84
Antoine, Marc
  See Proust, (Valentin-Louis-George-Eugene-
)Marcel
Antoninus, Brother
  See Everson, William (Oliver)
Antoninus, Marcus Aurelius
  121-180 .... **CMLC 45**
Antonioni, Michelangelo 1912- .... **CLC 20,**
  144
  See also CA 73-76; CANR 45, 77
Antschel, Paul 1920-1970
  See Celan, Paul
  See also CA 85-88; CANR 33, 61; MTCW
  1
Anzaldua, Gloria (Evanjelina) 1942-
  See also CA 175; DLB 122; HLCS 1
Apess, William 1798-1839(?) .... **NCLC 73;**
  DAM MULT
  See also DLB 175; NNAL
Apollinaire, Guillaume 1880-1918 .... **PC 7**
  See also AW 3, 8, 51; CA 152; DAM POET;
  MTCW 1
Appelfeld, Aharon 1932- .... **CLC 23, 47**
  See also AW 42; CA 112; 133; CANR 86;
  CWW 2
Apple, Max (Isaac) 1941- .... **CLC 9, 33**
  See also CA 81-84; CANR 19, 54; DLB
  130

Appleman, Philip (Dean) 1926- .... **CLC 51**
  See also CA 13-16R; CAAS 18; CANR 6,
  29, 56
Appleton, Lawrence
  See Lovecraft, H(oward) P(hillips)
Apteryx
  See Eliot, T(homas) S(tearns)
Apuleius, (Lucius Madaurensis)
  125(?)-175(?) .... **CMLC 1**
  See also DLB 211
Aquin, Hubert 1929-1977 .... **CLC 15**
  See also CA 105; DLB 53
Aquinas, Thomas 1224(?)-1274 ..... **CMLC 33**
  See also DLB 115
Aragon, Louis 1897-1982 .. **CLC 3, 22; DAM**
  NOV, POET
  See also CA 69-72; 108; CANR 28, 71;
  DLB 72; GLL 2; MTCW 1, 2
Arany, Janos 1817-1882 .... **NCLC 34**
Aranyos, Kakay 1847-1910
  See Mikszath, Kalman
Arbuthnot, John 1667-1735 .... **LC 1**
  See also DLB 101
Archer, Herbert Winslow
  See Mencken, H(enry) L(ouis)
Archer, Jeffrey (Howard) 1940- ...... **CLC 28;**
  DAM POP
  See also AAYA 16; BEST 89:3; CA 77-80;
  CANR 22, 52, 95; DA3; INT CANR-22
Archer, Jules 1915- .... **CLC 12**
  See also CA 9-12R; CANR 6, 69; SAAS 5;
  SATA 4, 85
Archer, Lee
  See Ellison, Harlan (Jay)
Archilochus c. 7th cent. B.C.- .... **CMLC 44**
  See also DLB 176
Arden, John 1930- .... **CLC 6, 13, 15; DAM**
  DRAM
  See also BRWS 2; CA 13-16R; CAAS 4;
  CANR 31, 65, 67; DLB 13; MTCW 1
Arenas, Reinaldo 1943-1990 . **CLC 41; DAM**
  MULT; HLC 1
  See also CA 124; 128; 133; CANR 73; DLB
  145; GLL 2; HW 1; MTCW 1
Arendt, Hannah 1906-1975 .... **CLC 66, 98**
  See also CA 17-20R; 61-64; CANR 26, 60;
  DLB 242; MTCW 1, 2
Aretino, Pietro 1492-1556 .... **LC 12**
Arghezi, Tudor .... **CLC 80**
  See also Theodorescu, Ion N.
  See also CA 167; DLB 220
Arguedas, Jose Maria 1911-1969 .... **CLC 10,**
  18; HLCS 1
  See also CA 89-92; CANR 73; DLB 113;
  HW 1
Argueta, Manlio 1936- .... **CLC 31**
  See also CA 131; CANR 73; CWW 2; DLB
  145; HW 1
Arias, Ron(ald Francis) 1941-
  See also CA 131; CANR 81; DAM MULT;
  DLB 82; HLC 1; HW 1, 2; MTCW 2
Ariosto, Ludovico 1474-1533 .... **LC 6**
Aristides
  See Epstein, Joseph
Aristophanes 450B.C.-385B.C. .... **CMLC 4;**
  DA; DAB; DAC; DAM DRAM, MST;
  DC 2
  See also BEST; DA3; DLB 176
Aristotle 384B.C.-322B.C. .... **CMLC 31; DA;**
  DAB; DAC; DAM MST
  See also BEST; DA3; DLB 176
Arlt, Roberto (Godofredo Christophersen)
  1900-1942
  See also AW 29; CA 123; 131; CANR 67;
  DAM MULT; HLC 1; HW 1, 2
Armah, Ayi Kwei 1939- .... **CLC 5, 33, 136;**
  BLC 1; DAM MULT, POET
  See also BW 1; CA 61-64; CANR 21, 64;
  DLB 117; MTCW 1

Armatrading, Joan 1950- .... **CLC 17**
  See also CA 114; 186
Arnette, Robert
  See Silverberg, Robert
Arnim, Achim von (Ludwig Joachim von
  Arnim) 1781-1831 .... **NCLC 5**
  See also AW 29; DLB 90
Arnim, Bettina von 1785-1859 .... **NCLC 38**
  See also DLB 90
Arnold, Matthew 1822-1888 ..... **NCLC 6, 29,**
  89; DA; DAB; DAC; DAM MST,
  POET; PC 5
  See also CDBLB 1832-1890; DLB 32, 57
Arnold, Thomas 1795-1842 .... **NCLC 18**
  See also DLB 55
Arnow, Harriette (Louisa) Simpson
  1908-1986 .... **CLC 2, 7, 18**
  See also CA 9-12R; 118; CANR 14; DLB
  6; MTCW 1, 2; SATA 42; SATA-Obit 47
Arouet, Francois-Marie
  See Voltaire
Arp, Hans
  See Arp, Jean
Arp, Jean 1887-1966 .... **CLC 5**
  See also CA 81-84; 25-28R; CANR 42, 77
Arrabal
  See Arrabal, Fernando
Arrabal, Fernando 1932- ... **CLC 2, 9, 18, 58**
  See also CA 9-12R; CANR 15
Arreola, Juan Jose 1918-
  See also AW 38; CA 113; 131; CANR 81;
  DAM MULT; DLB 113; HLC 1; HW 1, 2
Arrian c. 89(?)-c. 155(?) .... **CMLC 43**
  See also DLB 176
Arrick, Fran .... **CLC 30**
  See also Gaberman, Judie Angell
Artaud, Antonin (Marie Joseph)
  1896-1948 .... **DC 14**
  See also AW 3, 36; CA 104; 149; DAM
  DRAM; DA3; MTCW 1
Arthur, Ruth M(abel) 1905-1979 ..... **CLC 12**
  See also CA 9-12R; 85-88; CANR 4; SATA
  7, 26
Arundel, Honor (Morfydd)
  1919-1973 .... **CLC 17**
  See also CA 21-22; 41-44R; CAP 2; CLR
  35; SATA 4; SATA-Obit 24
Arzner, Dorothy 1900-1979 .... **CLC 98**
Ash, Shalom
  See Asch, Sholem
Ashbery, John (Lawrence) 1927- .. **CLC 2, 3,**
  4, 6, 9, 13, 15, 25, 41, 77, 125; DAM
  POET; PC 26
  See also Berry, Jonas
  See also AMWS 3; CA 5-8R; CANR 9, 37,
  66; DA3; DLB 5, 165; DLBY 81; INT
  CANR-9; MTCW 1, 2
Ashdown, Clifford
  See Freeman, R(ichard) Austin
Ashe, Gordon
  See Creasey, John
Ashton-Warner, Sylvia (Constance)
  1908-1984 .... **CLC 19**
  See also CA 69-72; 112; CANR 29; MTCW
  1, 2
Asimov, Isaac 1920-1992 ..... **CLC 1, 3, 9, 19,**
  26, 76, 92; DAM POP
  See also AAYA 13; BEST; CA 1-4R; 137;
  CANR 2, 19, 36, 60; CLR 12; DA3; DLB
  8; DLBY 92; INT CANR-19; JRDA;
  MAICYA; MTCW 1, 2; SATA 1, 26, 74;
  SCFW 2
Assis, Joaquim Maria Machado de
  See Machado de Assis, Joaquim Maria
Astley, Thea (Beatrice May) 1925- .. **CLC 41**
  See also CA 65-68; CANR 11, 43, 78
Aston, James
  See White, T(erence) H(anbury)

See also AMWS 2; BW 2, 3; CA 21-24R;
CABS 3; CANR 27, 38, 61; CDALB
1941-1968; DA3; DLB 5, 7, 16, 38;
DLBD 8; MTCW 1, 2

Barbauld, Anna Laetitia
1743-1825 .... **NCLC 50**
See also DLB 107, 109, 142, 158

Barber, Benjamin R. 1939- .... **CLC 141**
See also CA 29-32R; CANR 12, 32, 64

Barbera, Jack (Vincent) 1945- .... **CLC 44**
See also CA 110; CANR 45

Barbey d'Aurevilly, Jules Amedee
1808-1889 .... **NCLC 1**
See also AW 17; DLB 119

Barbour, John c. 1316-1395 .... **CMLC 33**
See also DLB 146

Barclay, Bill
See Moorcock, Michael (John)

Barclay, William Ewert
See Moorcock, Michael (John)

Barfoot, Joan 1946- .... **CLC 18**
See also CA 105

Barham, Richard Harris
1788-1845 .... **NCLC 77**
See also DLB 159

Barker, Clive 1952- ...... **CLC 52; DAM POP**
See also AAYA 10; BEST 90:3; CA 121;
129; CANR 71; DA3; INT 129; MTCW
1, 2

Barker, George Granville
1913-1991 .... **CLC 8, 48; DAM POET**
See also CA 9-12R; 135; CANR 7, 38; DLB
20; MTCW 1

Barker, Harley Granville
See Granville-Barker, Harley
See also DLB 10

Barker, Howard 1946- .... **CLC 37**
See also CA 102; DLB 13, 233

Barker, Jane 1652-1732 .... **LC 42**

Barker, Pat(ricia) 1943- .... **CLC 32, 94**
See also BRWS 4; CA 117; 122; CANR 50;
INT 122

Barlow, Joel 1754-1812 .... **NCLC 23**
See also AMWS 2; DLB 37

Barnard, Mary (Ethel) 1909- .... **CLC 48**
See also CA 21-22; CAP 2

Barnes, Djuna 1892-1982 .... **CLC 3, 4, 8, 11,
29, 127**
See also Steptoe, Lydia
See also AMWS 3; AW 3; CA 9-12R; 107;
CANR 16, 55; DLB 4, 9, 45; GLL 1;
MTCW 1, 2

Barnes, Julian (Patrick) 1946- .... **CLC 42,
141; DAB**
See also BRWS 4; CA 102; CANR 19, 54;
DLB 194; DLBY 93; MTCW 1

Barnes, Peter 1931- .... **CLC 5, 56**
See also CA 65-68; CAAS 12; CANR 33,
34, 64; DLB 13, 233; MTCW 1

Barnes, William 1801-1886 .... **NCLC 75**
See also DLB 32

Baroja (y Nessi), Pio 1872-1956
See also AW 8; CA 104; HLC 1

Baron, David
See Pinter, Harold

Baron Corvo
See Rolfe, Frederick (William Serafino Austin Lewis Mary)

Barondess, Sue K(aufman)
1926-1977 .... **CLC 8**
See also Kaufman, Sue
See also CA 1-4R; 69-72; CANR 1

Baron de Teive
See Pessoa, Fernando (Antonio Nogueira)

Baroness Von S.
See Zangwill, Israel

Barreto, Afonso Henrique de Lima
See Lima Barreto, Afonso Henrique de

Barrett, Michele .... **CLC 65**

Barrett, (Roger) Syd 1946- .... **CLC 35**

Barrett, William (Christopher)
1913-1992 .... **CLC 27**
See also CA 13-16R; 139; CANR 11, 67;
INT CANR-11

Barrington, Michael
See Moorcock, Michael (John)

Barrol, Grady
See Bograd, Larry

Barry, Mike
See Malzberg, Barry N(athaniel)

Barry, Philip 1896-1949 .... **TCLC 11**
See Schwarz-Bart, Andre

Bart, Andre Schwarz
See Schwarz-Bart, Andre

Barth, John (Simmons) 1930- ... **CLC 1, 2, 3,
5, 7, 9, 10, 14, 27, 51, 89; DAM NOV**
See also AITN 1, 2; AW 6; CA 1-4R; CABS
1; CANR 5, 23, 49, 64; DLB 2, 227;
MTCW 1

Barthelme, Donald 1931-1989 ... **CLC 1, 2, 3,
5, 6, 8, 13, 23, 46, 59, 115; DAM NOV**
See also AMWS 4; AW 3; CA 21-24R; 129;
CANR 20, 58; DA3; DLB 2, 234; DLBY
80, 89; MTCW 1, 2; SATA 7; SATA-Obit
62

Barthelme, Frederick 1943- ...... **CLC 36, 117**
See also CA 114; 122; CANR 77; DLBY
85; INT 122

Barthes, Roland (Gerard)
1915-1980 .... **CLC 24, 83**
See also CA 130; 97-100; CANR 66;
MTCW 1, 2

Barzun, Jacques (Martin) 1907- ..... **CLC 51,
145**
See also CA 61-64; CANR 22, 95

Bashevis, Isaac
See Singer, Isaac Bashevis

Bashkirtseff, Marie 1859-1884 .... **NCLC 27**

Bashō, Matsuo
See Matsuo Bashō

Basil of Caesaria c. 330-379 .... **CMLC 35**

Bass, Kingsley B., Jr.
See Bullins, Ed

Bass, Rick 1958- .... **CLC 79, 143**
See also CA 126; CANR 53, 93; DLB 212

Bassani, Giorgio 1916-2000 .... **CLC 9**
See also CA 65-68; 190; CANR 33; CWW
2; DLB 128, 177; MTCW 1

Bastian, Ann .... **CLC 70**

Bastos, Augusto (Antonio) Roa
See Roa Bastos, Augusto (Antonio)

Bataille, Georges 1897-1962 .... **CLC 29**
See also CA 101; 89-92

Bates, H(erbert) E(rnest)
1905-1974 ... **CLC 46; DAB; DAM POP**
See also AW 7; CA 93-96; 45-48; CANR
34; DA3; DLB 162, 191; MTCW 1, 2

Bauchart
See Camus, Albert

Baudelaire, Charles 1821-1867 . **NCLC 6, 29,
55; DA; DAB; DAC; DAM MST,
POET; PC 1**
See also AW 18; BEST; DA3

Baudrillard, Jean 1929- .... **CLC 60**

Baum, Louis F.
See Baum, L(yman) Frank

Baumbach, Jonathan 1933- .... **CLC 6, 23**
See also CA 13-16R; CAAS 5; CANR 12,
66; DLBY 80; INT CANR-12; MTCW 1

Bausch, Richard (Carl) 1945- .... **CLC 51**
See also AMWS 7; CA 101; CAAS 14;
CANR 43, 61, 87; DLB 130

Baxter, Charles (Morley) 1947- .... **CLC 45,
78; DAM POP**
See also CA 57-60; CANR 40, 64; DLB
130; MTCW 2

Baxter, George Owen
See Faust, Frederick (Schiller)

Baxter, James K(eir) 1926-1972 .... **CLC 14**
See also CA 77-80

Baxter, John
See Hunt, E(verette) Howard, (Jr.)

Bayer, Sylvia
See Glassco, John

Beagle, Peter S(oyer) 1939- .... **CLC 7, 104**
See also BEST; CA 9-12R; CANR 4, 51,
73; DA3; DLBY 80; INT CANR-4;
MTCW 1; SATA 60

Bean, Normal
See Burroughs, Edgar Rice

Beardsley, Aubrey 1872-1898 .... **NCLC 6**

Beattie, Ann 1947- ..... **CLC 8, 13, 18, 40, 63;
DAM NOV, POP**
See also AMWS 5; AW 9; BEST 90:2; CA
81-84; CANR 53, 73; DA3; DLBY 82;
MTCW 1, 2

Beattie, James 1735-1803 .... **NCLC 25**
See also DLB 109

Beauchamp, Kathleen Mansfield 1888-1923
See Mansfield, Katherine
See also CA 104; 134; DA; DAC; DAM
MST; DA3; MTCW 2

Beaumarchais, Pierre-Augustin Caron de
1732-1799 . **LC 61; DAM DRAM; DC 4**

Beaumont, Francis 1584(?)-1616 .... **LC 33;
DC 6**
See also CDBLB Before 1660; DLB 58, 121

**Beauvoir, Simone (Lucie Ernestine Marie
Bertrand) de** 1908-1986 .... **CLC 1, 2, 4,
8, 14, 31, 44, 50, 71, 124; DA; DAB;
DAC; DAM MST, NOV**
See also AW 35; BEST; CA 9-12R; 118;
CANR 28, 61; DA3; DLB 72; DLBY 86;
MTCW 1, 2

Becker, Jurek 1937-1997 .... **CLC 7, 19**
See also CA 85-88; 157; CANR 60; CWW
2; DLB 75

Becker, Walter 1950- .... **CLC 26**

Beckett, Samuel (Barclay)
1906-1989 .. **CLC 1, 2, 3, 4, 6, 9, 10, 11,
14, 18, 29, 57, 59, 83; DA; DAB; DAC;
DAM DRAM, MST, NOV**
See also AW 16; BEST; BRWS 1; CA 5-8R;
130; CANR 33, 61; CDBLB 1945-1960;
DA3; DLB 13, 15, 233; DLBY 90;
MTCW 1, 2

Beckford, William 1760-1844 .... **NCLC 16**
See also DLB 39,213

Beckman, Gunnel 1910- .... **CLC 26**
See also CA 33-36R; CANR 15; CLR 25;
MAICYA; SAAS 9; SATA 6

Becque, Henri 1837-1899 .... **NCLC 3**
See also DLB 192

Becquer, Gustavo Adolfo 1836-1870
See also DAM MULT; HLCS 1

Beddoes, Thomas Lovell
1803-1849 .... **NCLC 3; DC 15**
See also DLB 96

Bede c. 673-735 .... **CMLC 20**
See also DLB 146

Bedford, Donald F.
See Fearing, Kenneth (Flexner)

Beecher, Catharine Esther
1800-1878 .... **NCLC 30**
See also DLB 1

Beecher, John 1904-1980 .... **CLC 6**
See also AITN 1; CA 5-8R; 105; CANR 8

Beer, Johann 1655-1700 .... **LC 5**
See also DLB 168

Beer, Patricia 1924- .... **CLC 58**
See also CA 61-64; 183; CANR 13, 46;
DLB 40

Beerbohm, Max
See Beerbohm, (Henry) Max(imilian)
See also BRWS 2

Beg, Shemus
See Stephens, James

Bettelheim, Bruno 1903-1990 .... **CLC 79**
  See also CA 81-84; 131; CANR 23, 61;
  DA3; MTCW 1, 2

Betts, Doris (Waugh) 1932- ...... **CLC 3, 6, 28**
  See also AW 45; CA 13-16R; CANR 9, 66,
  77; DLBY 82; INT CANR-9

Bevan, Alistair
  See Roberts, Keith (John Kingston)

Bey, Pilaff
  See Douglas, (George) Norman

Bickerstaff, Isaac
  See Swift, Jonathan

Bidart, Frank 1939- .... **CLC 33**
  See also CA 140

Bienek, Horst 1930- .... **CLC 7, 11**
  See also CA 73-76; DLB 75

Billings, Josh
  See Shaw, Henry Wheeler

Billington, (Lady) Rachel (Mary)
  1942- .... **CLC 43**
  See also AITN 2; CA 33-36R; CANR 44

Binyon, T(imothy) J(ohn) 1936- .... **CLC 34**
  See also CA 111; CANR 28

Bion 335B.C.-245B.C. .... **CMLC 39**

Bioy Casares, Adolfo 1914-1999 ... **CLC 4, 8,
  13, 88; DAM MULT; HLC 1**
  See Miranda, Javier; Sacastru, Martin
  See also AW 17; CA 29-32R; 177; CANR
  19, 43, 66; DLB 113; HW 1, 2; MTCW 1,
  2

Birch, Allison .... **CLC 65**

Bird, Cordwainer
  See Ellison, Harlan (Jay)

Bird, Robert Montgomery
  1806-1854 .... **NCLC 1**
  See also DLB 202

Birkerts, Sven 1951- .... **CLC 116**
  See also CA 128; 133; 176; CAAE 176;
  CAAS 29; INT 133

Birney, (Alfred) Earle 1904-1995 .. **CLC 1, 4,
  6, 11; DAC; DAM MST, POET**
  See also CA 1-4R; CANR 5, 20; DLB 88;
  MTCW 1

Biruni, al 973-1048(?) .... **CMLC 28**

Bishop, Elizabeth 1911-1979 ..... **CLC 1, 4, 9,
  13, 15, 32; DA; DAC; DAM MST,
  POET; PC 3**
  See also AMWS 1; CA 5-8R; 89-92; CABS
  2; CANR 26, 61; CDALB 1968-1988;
  DA3; DLB 5, 169; GLL 2; MTCW 1, 2;
  SATA-Obit 24

Bishop, John 1935- .... **CLC 10**
  See also CA 105

Bissett, Bill 1939- .... **CLC 18; PC 14**
  See also CA 69-72; CAAS 19; CANR 15;
  CCA 1; DLB 53; MTCW 1

Bissoondath, Neil (Devindra)
  1955- .... **CLC 120; DAC**
  See also CA 136

Bitov, Andrei (Georgievich) 1937- ... **CLC 57**
  See also CA 142

Biyidi, Alexandre 1932-
  See Beti, Mongo
  See also BW 1, 3; CA 114; 124; CANR 81;
  DA3; MTCW 1, 2

Bjarme, Brynjolf
  See Ibsen, Henrik (Johan)

Black, Robert
  See Holdstock, Robert P.

Blackburn, Paul 1926-1971 .... **CLC 9, 43**
  See also CA 81-84; 33-36R; CANR 34;
  DLB 16; DLBY 81

Black Hobart
  See Sanders, (James) Ed(ward)

Blacklin, Malcolm
  See Chambers, Aidan

Blackmur, R(ichard) P(almer)
  1904-1965 .... **CLC 2, 24**
  See also AMWS 2; CA 11-12; 25-28R;
  CANR 71; CAP 1; DLB 63

Black Tarantula
  See Acker, Kathy

Blackwood, Caroline 1931-1996 .... **CLC 6, 9,
  100**
  See also CA 85-88; 151; CANR 32, 61, 65;
  DLB 14, 207; MTCW 1

Blade, Alexander
  See Hamilton, Edmond; Silverberg, Robert

Blaga, Lucian 1895-1961 .... **CLC 75**
  See also CA 157; DLB 220

Blair, Eric (Arthur) 1903-1950
  See Orwell, George
  See also CA 104; 132; DA; DAB; DAC;
  DAM MST, NOV; DA3; MTCW 1, 2;
  SATA 29

Blair, Hugh 1718-1800 .... **NCLC 75**

Blais, Marie-Claire 1939- .... **CLC 2, 4, 6, 13,
  22; DAC; DAM MST**
  See also CA 21-24R; CAAS 4; CANR 38,
  75, 93; DLB 53; MTCW 1, 2

Blaise, Clark 1940- .... **CLC 29**
  See also AITN 2; CA 53-56; CAAS 3;
  CANR 5, 66; DLB 53

Blake, Fairley
  See De Voto, Bernard (Augustine)

Blake, Nicholas
  See Day Lewis, C(ecil)
  See also DLB 77

Blake, William 1757-1827 .... **NCLC 13, 37,
  57; DA; DAB; DAC; DAM MST,
  POET; PC 12**
  See also CDBLB 1789-1832; CLR 52;
  DA3; DLB 93, 163; MAICYA; SATA 30

Blanchot, Maurice 1907- .... **CLC 135**
  See also CA 117; 144; DLB 72

Blatty, William Peter 1928- .... **CLC 2; DAM
  POP**
  See also CA 5-8R; CANR 9

Bleeck, Oliver
  See Thomas, Ross (Elmore)

Blessing, Lee 1949- .... **CLC 54**

Blight, Rose
  See Greer, Germaine

Blish, James (Benjamin) 1921-1975 . **CLC 14**
  See also CA 1-4R; 57-60; CANR 3; DLB
  8; MTCW 1; SATA 66; SCFW 2

Bliss, Reginald
  See Wells, H(erbert) G(eorge)

Blixen, Karen (Christentze Dinesen)
  1885-1962
  See Dinesen, Isak
  See also CA 25-28; CANR 22, 50; CAP 2;
  DA3; MTCW 1, 2; SATA 44

Bloch, Robert (Albert) 1917-1994 .... **CLC 33**
  See also AAYA 29; CA 5-8R, 179; 146;
  CAAE 179; CAAS 20; CANR 5, 78;
  DA3; DLB 44; INT CANR-5; MTCW 1;
  SATA 12; SATA-Obit 82

Blok, Alexander (Alexandrovich)
  1880-1921 .... **PC 21**
  See also AW 5; CA 104; 183

Blom, Jan
  See Breytenbach, Breyten

Bloom, Harold 1930- .... **CLC 24, 103**
  See also CA 13-16R; CANR 39, 75, 92;
  DLB 67; MTCW 1

Bloomfield, Aurelius
  See Bourne, Randolph S(illiman)

Blount, Roy (Alton), Jr. 1941- .... **CLC 38**
  See also CA 53-56; CANR 10, 28, 61; INT
  CANR-28; MTCW 1, 2

Blume, Judy (Sussman) 1938- .. **CLC 12, 30;
  DAM NOV, POP**
  See also AAYA 3, 26; CA 29-32R; CANR
  13, 37, 66; CLR 2, 15, 69; DA3; DLB 52;
  JRDA; MAICYA; MTCW 1, 2; SATA 2,
  31, 79

Blunden, Edmund (Charles)
  1896-1974 .... **CLC 2, 56**
  See also CA 17-18; 45-48; CANR 54; CAP
  2; DLB 20, 100, 155; MTCW 1

Bly, Robert (Elwood) 1926- .... **CLC 1, 2, 5,
  10, 15, 38, 128; DAM POET**
  See also AMWS 4; CA 5-8R; CANR 41,
  73; DA3; DLB 5; MTCW 1, 2

Bobette
  See Simenon, Georges (Jacques Christian)

Boccaccio, Giovanni 1313-1375 .... **CMLC 13**
  See also AW 10

Bochco, Steven 1943- .... **CLC 35**
  See also AAYA 11; CA 124; 138

Bodel, Jean 1167(?)-1210 .... **CMLC 28**

Bodker, Cecil 1927- .... **CLC 21**
  See also CA 73-76; CANR 13, 44; CLR 23;
  MAICYA; SATA 14

Boell, Heinrich (Theodor)
  1917-1985 ..... **CLC 2, 3, 6, 9, 11, 15, 27,
  32, 72; DA; DAB; DAC; DAM MST,
  NOV**
  See also AW 23; BEST; CA 21-24R; 116;
  CANR 24; DA3; DLB 69; DLBY 85;
  MTCW 1, 2

Boerne, Alfred
  See Doeblin, Alfred

Boethius 480(?)-524(?) .... **CMLC 15**
  See also DLB 115

Boff, Leonardo (Genezio Darci)
  1938- .... **CLC 70; DAM MULT; HLC 1**
  See also CA 150; HW 2

Bogan, Louise 1897-1970 .... **CLC 4, 39, 46,
  93; DAM POET; PC 12**
  See also AMWS 3; CA 73-76; 25-28R;
  CANR 33, 82; DLB 45, 169; MTCW 1, 2

Bogarde, Dirk
  See Van Den Bogarde, Derek Jules Gaspard
  Ulric Niven

Bogosian, Eric 1953- .... **CLC 45, 141**
  See also CA 138

Bograd, Larry 1953- .... **CLC 35**
  See also CA 93-96; CANR 57; SAAS 21;
  SATA 33, 89

Boiardo, Matteo Maria 1441-1494 .... **LC 6**

Boileau-Despreaux, Nicolas 1636-1711 . **LC 3**

Boland, Eavan (Aisling) 1944- .. **CLC 40, 67,
  113; DAM POET**
  See also BRWS 5; CA 143; CANR 61; DLB
  40; MTCW 2

Böll, Heinrich
  See Boell, Heinrich (Theodor)

Bolt, Lee
  See Faust, Frederick (Schiller)

Bolt, Robert (Oxton) 1924-1995 ...... **CLC 14;
  DAM DRAM**
  See also CA 17-20R; 147; CANR 35, 67;
  DLB 13, 233; MTCW 1

Bombal, Maria Luisa 1910-1980
  See also AW 37; CA 127; CANR 72; HLCS
  1; HW 1

Bombet, Louis-Alexandre-Cesar
  See Stendhal

Bomkauf
  See Kaufman, Bob (Garnell)

Bonaventura .... **NCLC 35**
  See also DLB 90

Bond, Edward 1934- .... **CLC 4, 6, 13, 23;
  DAM DRAM**
  See also BRWS 1; CA 25-28R; CANR 38,
  67; DLB 13; MTCW 1

Campbell, Joseph 1904-1987 .... **CLC 69**
   See also AAYA 3; BEST 89:2; CA 1-4R;
   124; CANR 3, 28, 61; DA3; MTCW 1, 2
Campbell, Maria 1940- .... **CLC 85; DAC**
   See also CA 102; CANR 54; CCA 1; NNAL
Campbell, (John) Ramsey 1946- ...... **CLC 42**
   See also CA 57-60; CANR 7; INT CANR-7
Campbell, Thomas 1777-1844 .... **NCLC 19**
   See also DLB 93; 144
Campbell, William 1858(?)-1918
   See Campbell, Wilfred
   See also CA 106; DLB 92
Campion, Jane .... **CLC 95**
   See also AAYA 33; CA 138; CANR 87
Camus, Albert 1913-1960 ...... **CLC 1, 2, 4, 9,**
   11, 14, 32, 63, 69, 124; DA; DAB;
   DAC; DAM DRAM, MST, NOV; DC 2
   See also AAYA 36; AW 4; BEST; CA 89-
   92; DA3; DLB 72; MTCW 1, 2
Canby, Vincent 1924-2000 .... **CLC 13**
   See also CA 81-84
Cancale
   See Desnos, Robert
Canetti, Elias 1905-1994 .. **CLC 3, 14, 25, 75,**
   86
   See also CA 21-24R; 146; CANR 23, 61,
   79; CWW 2; DA3; DLB 85, 124; MTCW
   1, 2
Canfield, Dorothea F.
   See Fisher, Dorothy (Frances) Canfield
Canfield, Dorothea Frances
   See Fisher, Dorothy (Frances) Canfield
Canfield, Dorothy
   See Fisher, Dorothy (Frances) Canfield
Canin, Ethan 1960- .... **CLC 55**
   See also CA 131; 135
Cannon, Curt
   See Hunter, Evan
Cao, Lan 1961- .... **CLC 109**
   See also CA 165
Cape, Judith
   See Page, P(atricia) K(athleen)
   See also CCA 1
Capek, Karel 1890-1938 .... **DC 1**
   See also AW 36; BEST; CA 104; 140; DA;
   DAB; DAC; DAM DRAM, MST, NOV;
   DA3; MTCW 1; SCFW 2
Capellanus, Andreas fl. c. 1185- ... **CMLC 45**
   See also DLB 208
Capote, Truman 1924-1984 . **CLC 1, 3, 8, 13,**
   19, 34, 38, 58; DA; DAB; DAC; DAM
   MST, NOV, POP
   See also AMWS 3; AW 2; BEST; CA 5-8R;
   113; CANR 18, 62; CDALB 1941-1968;
   DA3; DLB 2, 185, 227; DLBY 80, 84;
   GLL 1; MTCW 1, 2; SATA 91
Capra, Frank 1897-1991 .... **CLC 16**
   See also CA 61-64; 135
Caputo, Philip 1941- .... **CLC 32**
   See also BEST; CA 73-76; CANR 40
Card, Orson Scott 1951- ..... **CLC 44, 47, 50;**
   DAM POP
   See also AAYA 11; BEST; CA 102; CANR
   27, 47, 73; DA3; INT CANR-27; MTCW
   1, 2; SATA 83
Cardenal, Ernesto 1925- .... **CLC 31; DAM**
   MULT, POET; HLC 1; PC 22
   See also CA 49-52; CANR 2, 32, 66; CWW
   2; HW 1, 2; MTCW 1, 2
Carew, Thomas 1595(?)-1640 . **LC 13; PC 29**
   See also DLB 126
Carey, Ernestine Gilbreth 1908- ...... **CLC 17**
   See also CA 5-8R; CANR 71; SATA 2
Carey, Peter 1943- .... **CLC 40, 55, 96**
   See also CA 123; 127; CANR 53, 76; INT
   127; MTCW 1, 2; SATA 94
Carleton, William 1794-1869 .... **NCLC 3**
   See also DLB 159

Carlisle, Henry (Coffin) 1926- .... **CLC 33**
   See also CA 13-16R; CANR 15, 85
Carlsen, Chris
   See Holdstock, Robert P.
Carlson, Ron(ald F.) 1947- .... **CLC 54**
   See also CA 105; CAAE 189; CANR 27
Carlyle, Thomas 1795-1881 .... **NCLC 22, 70;**
   DA; DAB; DAC; DAM MST
   See also CDBLB 1789-1832; DLB 55; 144
Carpenter, Don(ald Richard)
   1931-1995 .... **CLC 41**
   See also CA 45-48; 149; CANR 1, 71
Carpentier (y Valmont), Alejo
   1904-1980 ..... **CLC 8, 11, 38, 110; DAM**
   MULT; HLC 1
   See also AW 35; CA 65-68; 97-100; CANR
   11, 70; DLB 113; HW 1, 2
Carr, Caleb 1955(?)- .... **CLC 86**
   See also CA 147; CANR 73; DA3
Carr, John Dickson 1906-1977 .... **CLC 3**
   See also Fairbairn, Roger
   See also CA 49-52; 69-72; CANR 3, 33,
   60; MTCW 1, 2
Carr, Philippa
   See Hibbert, Eleanor Alice Burford
Carr, Virginia Spencer 1929- .... **CLC 34**
   See also CA 61-64; DLB 111
Carrere, Emmanuel 1957- .... **CLC 89**
Carrier, Roch 1937- .... **CLC 13, 78; DAC;**
   DAM MST
   See also CA 130; CANR 61; CCA 1; DLB
   53; SATA 105
Carroll, James P. 1943(?)- .... **CLC 38**
   See also CA 81-84; CANR 73; MTCW 1
Carroll, Jim 1951- .... **CLC 35, 143**
   See also AAYA 17; CA 45-48; CANR 42
Carroll, Lewis .... **NCLC 2, 53; PC 18**
   See also Dodgson, Charles Lutwidge
   See also AAYA 39; BEST; CDBLB 1832-
   1890; CLR 2, 18; DLB 18, 163, 178;
   DLBY 98; JRDA
Carroll, Paul Vincent 1900-1968 ...... **CLC 10**
   See also CA 9-12R; 25-28R; DLB 10
Carruth, Hayden 1921- ..... **CLC 4, 7, 10, 18,**
   84; PC 10
   See also CA 9-12R; CANR 4, 38, 59; DLB
   5, 165; INT CANR-4; MTCW 1, 2; SATA
   47
Carson, Rachel Louise 1907-1964 ... **CLC 71;**
   DAM POP
   See also CA 77-80; CANR 35; DA3;
   MTCW 1, 2; SATA 23
Carter, Angela (Olive) 1940-1992 ...... **CLC 5,**
   41, 76
   See also AW 4; BRWS 3; CA 53-56; 136;
   CANR 12, 36, 61; DA3; DLB 14, 207;
   MTCW 1, 2; SATA 66; SATA-Obit 70
Carter, Nick
   See Smith, Martin Cruz
Carver, Raymond 1938-1988 ..... **CLC 22, 36,**
   53, 55, 126; DAM NOV
   See also AMWS 3; AW 2; CA 33-36R; 126;
   CANR 17, 34, 61; DA3; DLB 130; DLBY
   84, 88; MTCW 1, 2
Cary, Elizabeth, Lady Falkland
   1585-1639 .... **LC 30**
Casanova de Seingalt, Giovanni Jacopo
   1725-1798 .... **LC 13**
Casares, Adolfo Bioy
   See Bioy Casares, Adolfo
Casey, John (Dudley) 1939- .... **CLC 59**
   See also BEST 90:2; CA 69-72; CANR 23
Casey, Michael 1947- .... **CLC 2**
   See also CA 65-68; DLB 5
Casey, Patrick
   See Thurman, Wallace (Henry)
Casey, Warren (Peter) 1935-1988 .... **CLC 12**
   See also CA 101; 127; INT 101

Casona, Alejandro .... **CLC 49**
   See also Alvarez, Alejandro Rodriguez
Cassavetes, John 1929-1989 .... **CLC 20**
   See also CA 85-88; 127; CANR 82
Cassian, Nina 1924- .... **PC 17**
   See also CWW 2
Cassill, R(onald) V(erlin) 1919- ... **CLC 4, 23**
   See also CA 9-12R; CAAS 1; CANR 7, 45;
   DLB 6
Cassiodorus, Flavius Magnus c. 490(?)-c.
   583(?) .... **CMLC 43**
Cassity, (Allen) Turner 1929- .... **CLC 6, 42**
   See also CA 17-20R; CAAS 8; CANR 11;
   DLB 105
Castaneda, Carlos (Cesar Aranha)
   1931(?)-1998 .... **CLC 12, 119**
   See also CA 25-28R; CANR 32, 66; HW 1;
   MTCW 1
Castedo, Elena 1937- .... **CLC 65**
   See also CA 132
Castedo-Ellerman, Elena
   See Castedo, Elena
Castellanos, Rosario 1925-1974 .... **CLC 66;**
   DAM MULT; HLC 1
   See also AW 39; CA 131; 53-56; CANR
   58; DLB 113; HW 1; MTCW 1
Castelvetro, Lodovico 1505-1571 .... **LC 12**
Castiglione, Baldassare 1478-1529 ...... **LC 12**
Castiglione, Baldesar
   See Castiglione, Baldassare
Castle, Robert
   See Hamilton, Edmond
Castro (Ruz), Fidel 1926(?)-
   See also CA 110; 129; CANR 81; DAM
   MULT; HLC 1; HW 2
Castro, Guillen de 1569-1631 .... **LC 19**
Castro, Rosalia de 1837-1885 ... **NCLC 3, 78;**
   DAM MULT
Cather, Willa
   See Cather, Willa Sibert
   See also AW 2
Catherine, Saint 1347-1380 .... **CMLC 27**
Cato, Marcus Porcius
   234B.C.-149B.C. .... **CMLC 21**
   See also DLB 211
Catton, (Charles) Bruce 1899-1978 . **CLC 35**
   See also AITN 1; CA 5-8R; 81-84; CANR
   7, 74; DLB 17; SATA 2; SATA-Obit 24
Catullus c. 84B.C.-c. 54B.C. .... **CMLC 18**
   See also DLB 211
Cauldwell, Frank
   See King, Francis (Henry)
Caunitz, William J. 1933-1996 .... **CLC 34**
   See also BEST 89:3; CA 125; 130; 152;
   CANR 73; INT 130
Causley, Charles (Stanley) 1917- .... **CLC 7**
   See also CA 9-12R; CANR 5, 35, 94; CLR
   30; DLB 27; MTCW 1; SATA 3, 66
Caute, (John) David 1936- .... **CLC 29; DAM**
   NOV
   See also CA 1-4R; CAAS 4; CANR 1, 33,
   64; DLB 14, 231
Cavallo, Evelyn
   See Spark, Muriel (Sarah)
Cavanna, Betty .... **CLC 12**
   See also Harrison, Elizabeth Cavanna
   See also JRDA; MAICYA; SAAS 4; SATA
   1, 30
Cavendish, Margaret Lucas
   1623-1673 .... **LC 30**
   See also DLB 131
Caxton, William 1421(?)-1491(?) .... **LC 17**
   See also DLB 170
Cayer, D. M.
   See Duffy, Maureen
Cayrol, Jean 1911- .... **CLC 11**
   See also CA 89-92; DLB 83

Christie, Agatha (Mary Clarissa)
1890-1976 .... **CLC 1, 6, 8, 12, 39, 48, 110; DAB; DAC; DAM NOV**
See also AAYA 9; AITN 1, 2; BEST; BRWS 2; CA 17-20R; 61-64; CANR 10, 37; CD-BLB 1914-1945; DA3; DLB 13, 77; MTCW 1, 2; SATA 36

Christie, (Ann) Philippa
See Pearce, Philippa
See also CA 5-8R; CANR 4

Christine de Pizan 1365(?)-1431(?) .... **LC 9**
See also DLB 208

Chubb, Elmer
See Masters, Edgar Lee

Chulkov, Mikhail Dmitrievich
1743-1792 .... **LC 2**
See also DLB 150

Churchill, Caryl 1938- .... **CLC 31, 55; DC 5**
See also BRWS 4; CA 102; CANR 22, 46; DLB 13; MTCW 1

Churchill, Charles 1731-1764 .... **LC 3**
See also DLB 109

Chute, Carolyn 1947- .... **CLC 39**
See also CA 123

Ciardi, John (Anthony) 1916-1986 . **CLC 10, 40, 44, 129; DAM POET**
See also CA 5-8R; 118; CAAS 2; CANR 5, 33; CLR 19; DLB 5; DLBY 86; INT CANR-5; MAICYA; MTCW 1, 2; SAAS 26; SATA 1, 65; SATA-Obit 46

Cibber, Colley 1671-1757 .... **LC 66**
See also DLB 84

Cicero, Marcus Tullius
106B.C.-43B.C. .... **CMLC 3**
See also DLB 211

Cimino, Michael 1943- .... **CLC 16**
See also CA 105

Cioran, E(mil) M. 1911-1995 .... **CLC 64**
See also CA 25-28R; 149; CANR 91; DLB 220

Cisneros, Sandra 1954- . **CLC 69, 118; DAM MULT; HLC 1**
See also AAYA 9; AMWS 7; AW 3; BEST; CA 131; CANR 64; DA3; DLB 122, 152; HW 1, 2; MTCW 2

Cixous, Hélène 1937- .... **CLC 92**
See also CA 126; CANR 55; CWW 2; DLB 83, 242; MTCW 1, 2

Clair, Rene .... **CLC 20**
See also Chomette, Rene Lucien

Clampitt, Amy 1920-1994 .... **CLC 32; PC 19**
See also CA 110; 146; CANR 29, 79; DLB 105

Clancy, Thomas L., Jr. 1947-
See Clancy, Tom
See also CA 125; 131; CANR 62; DA3; DLB 227; INT 131; MTCW 1, 2

Clancy, Tom .... **CLC 45, 112; DAM NOV, POP**
See also Clancy, Thomas L., Jr.
See also AAYA 9; BEST 89:1, 90:1; MTCW 2

Clare, John 1793-1864 ... **NCLC 9, 86; DAB; DAM POET; PC 23**
See also DLB 55, 96

Clarin
See Alas (y Urena), Leopoldo (Enrique Garcia)

Clark, Al C.
See Goines, Donald

Clark, (Robert) Brian 1932- .... **CLC 29**
See also CA 41-44R; CANR 67

Clark, Curt
See Westlake, Donald E(dwin)

Clark, Eleanor 1913-1996 .... **CLC 5, 19**
See also CA 9-12R; 151; CANR 41; DLB 6

Clark, J. P.
See Clark Bekedermo, J(ohnson) P(epper)
See also DLB 117

Clark, John Pepper
See Clark Bekedermo, J(ohnson) P(epper)

Clark, M. R.
See Clark, Mavis Thorpe

Clark, Mavis Thorpe 1909- .... **CLC 12**
See also CA 57-60; CANR 8, 37; CLR 30; MAICYA; SAAS 5; SATA 8, 74

Clark, Walter Van Tilburg
1909-1971 .... **CLC 28**
See also CA 9-12R; 33-36R; CANR 63; DLB 9, 206; SATA 8

Clark Bekedermo, J(ohnson) P(epper)
1935- .. **CLC 38; BLC 1; DAM DRAM, MULT; DC 5**
See also Clark, J. P.; Clark, John Pepper
See also BW 1; CA 65-68; CANR 16, 72; MTCW 1

Clarke, Arthur C(harles) 1917- .... **CLC 1, 4, 13, 18, 35, 136; DAM POP**
See also AAYA 4, 33; AW 4; BEST; CA 1-4R; CANR 2, 28, 55, 74; DA3; JRDA; MAICYA; MTCW 1, 2; SATA 13, 70, 115

Clarke, Austin 1896-1974 ... **CLC 6, 9; DAM POET**
See also CA 29-32; 49-52; CAP 2; DLB 10, 20

Clarke, Austin C(hesterfield) 1934- .. **CLC 8, 53; BLC 1; DAC; DAM MULT**
See also AW 45; BW 1; CA 25-28R; CAAS 16; CANR 14, 32, 68; DLB 53, 125

Clarke, Gillian 1937- .... **CLC 61**
See also CA 106; DLB 40

Clarke, Marcus (Andrew Hislop)
1846-1881 .... **NCLC 19**
See also DLB 230

Clarke, Shirley 1925-1997 .... **CLC 16**
See also CA 189

Clash, The
See Headon, (Nicky) Topper; Jones, Mick; Simonon, Paul; Strummer, Joe

Claudius, Matthias 1740-1815 .... **NCLC 75**
See also DLB 97

Clavell, James (duMaresq)
1925-1994 .. **CLC 6, 25, 87; DAM NOV, POP**
See also CA 25-28R; 146; CANR 26, 48; DA3; MTCW 1, 2

Clayman, Gregory .... **CLC 65**

Cleaver, (Leroy) Eldridge
1935-1998 . **CLC 30, 119; BLC 1; DAM MULT**
See also BEST; BW 1, 3; CA 21-24R; 167; CANR 16, 75; DA3; MTCW 2

Cleese, John (Marwood) 1939- .... **CLC 21**
See also Monty Python
See also CA 112; 116; CANR 35; MTCW 1

Cleishbotham, Jebediah
See Scott, Walter

Cleland, John 1710-1789 .... **LC 2, 48**
See also DLB 39

Clemens, Samuel Langhorne 1835-1910
See Twain, Mark
See also BEST 2; CA 104; 135; CDALB 1865-1917; DA; DAB; DAC; DAM MST, NOV; DA3; DLB 11, 12, 23, 64, 74, 186, 189; JRDA; MAICYA; SATA 100

Clement of Alexandria
150(?)-215(?) .... **CMLC 41**

Cleophil
See Congreve, William

Clerihew, E.
See Bentley, E(dmund) C(lerihew)

Clerk, N. W.
See Lewis, C(live) S(taples)

Cliff, Jimmy .... **CLC 21**
See also Chambers, James

Cliff, Michelle 1946- .... **CLC 120; BLCS**
See also BW 2; CA 116; CANR 39, 72; DLB 157; GLL 2

Clifton, (Thelma) Lucille 1936- .... **CLC 19, 66; BLC 1; DAM MULT, POET; PC 17**
See also BW 2, 3; CA 49-52; CANR 2, 24, 42, 76, 97; CLR 5; DA3; DLB 5, 41; MAICYA; MTCW 1, 2; SATA 20, 69

Clinton, Dirk
See Silverberg, Robert

Clough, Arthur Hugh 1819-1861 ... **NCLC 27**
See also DLB 32

Clutha, Janet Paterson Frame 1924-
See Frame, Janet
See also CA 1-4R; CANR 2, 36, 76; MTCW 1, 2; SATA 119

Clyne, Terence
See Blatty, William Peter

Cobalt, Martin
See Mayne, William (James Carter)

Cobbett, William 1763-1835 .... **NCLC 49**
See also DLB 43, 107, 158

Coburn, D(onald) L(ee) 1938- .... **CLC 10**
See also CA 89-92

Cocteau, Jean (Maurice Eugene Clement)
1889-1963 .... **CLC 1, 8, 15, 16, 43; DA; DAB; DAC; DAM DRAM, MST, NOV**
See also BEST; CA 25-28; CANR 40; CAP 2; DA3; DLB 65; MTCW 1, 2

Codrescu, Andrei 1946- .... **CLC 46, 121; DAM POET**
See also CA 33-36R; CAAS 19; CANR 13, 34, 53, 76; DA3; MTCW 2

Coe, Max
See Bourne, Randolph S(illiman)

Coe, Tucker
See Westlake, Donald E(dwin)

Coen, Ethan 1958- .... **CLC 108**
See also CA 126; CANR 85

Coen, Joel 1955- .... **CLC 108**
See also CA 126

The Coen Brothers
See Coen, Ethan; Coen, Joel

Coetzee, J(ohn) M(ichael) 1940- ...... **CLC 23, 33, 66, 117; DAM NOV**
See also AAYA 37; CA 77-80; CANR 41, 54, 74; DA3; DLB 225; MTCW 1, 2

Coffey, Brian
See Koontz, Dean R(ay)

Cohen, Arthur A(llen) 1928-1986 ...... **CLC 7, 31**
See also CA 1-4R; 120; CANR 1, 17, 42; DLB 28

Cohen, Leonard (Norman) 1934- ...... **CLC 3, 38; DAC; DAM MST**
See also CA 21-24R; CANR 14, 69; DLB 53; MTCW 1

Cohen, Matt(hew) 1942-1999 .... **CLC 19; DAC**
See also CA 61-64; 187; CAAS 18; CANR 40; DLB 53

Cohen-Solal, Annie 19(?)- .... **CLC 50**

Colegate, Isabel 1931- .... **CLC 36**
See also CA 17-20R; CANR 8, 22, 74; DLB 14, 231; INT CANR-22; MTCW 1

Coleman, Emmett
See Reed, Ishmael

Coleridge, Hartley 1796-1849 .... **NCLC 90**
See also DLB 96

Coleridge, M. E.
See Coleridge, Mary E(lizabeth)

Coleridge, Samuel Taylor
1772-1834 . **NCLC 9, 54, 99; DA; DAB; DAC; DAM MST, POET; PC 11**
See also CDBLB 1789-1832; DA3; DLB 93, 107

Coleridge, Sara 1802-1852 .... **NCLC 31**
See also DLB 199

Coles, Don 1928- .... **CLC 46**
See also CA 115; CANR 38

Demosthenes 384B.C.-322B.C. ...... **CMLC 13**
  See also DLB 176
de Natale, Francine
  See Malzberg, Barry N(athaniel)
de Navarre, Marguerite 1492-1549 ..... **LC 61**
Denby, Edwin (Orr) 1903-1983 .... **CLC 48**
  See also CA 138; 110
Denis, Julio
  See Cortazar, Julio
Denmark, Harrison
  See Zelazny, Roger (Joseph)
Dennis, John 1658-1734 .... **LC 11**
  See also DLB 101
Dennis, Nigel (Forbes) 1912-1989 ...... **CLC 8**
  See also CA 25-28R; 129; DLB 13, 15, 233;
  MTCW 1
De Palma, Brian (Russell) 1940- ...... **CLC 20**
  See also CA 109
De Quincey, Thomas 1785-1859 ..... **NCLC 4,
  87**
  See also CDBLB 1789-1832; DLB 110; 144
Deren, Eleanora 1917(?)-1961
  See Deren, Maya
  See also CA 111
Deren, Maya .... **CLC 16, 102**
  See also Deren, Eleanora
Derleth, August (William)
  1909-1971 .... **CLC 31**
  See also CA 1-4R; 29-32R; CANR 4; DLB
  9; DLBD 17; SATA 5
de Routisie, Albert
  See Aragon, Louis
Derrida, Jacques 1930- .... **CLC 24, 87**
  See also CA 124; 127; CANR 76; DLB 242;
  MTCW 1
Derry Down Derry
  See Lear, Edward
Dersonnes, Jacques
  See Simenon, Georges (Jacques Christian)
Desai, Anita 1937- ..... **CLC 19, 37, 97; DAB;
  DAM NOV**
  See also BRWS 5; CA 81-84; CANR 33,
  53, 95; DA3; MTCW 1, 2; SATA 63
Desai, Kiran 1971- .... **CLC 119**
  See also CA 171
de Saint-Luc, Jean
  See Glassco, John
de Saint Roman, Arnaud
  See Aragon, Louis
Desbordes-Valmore, Marceline
  1786-1859 .... **NCLC 97**
  See also DLB 217
Descartes, Rene 1596-1650 .... **LC 20, 35**
De Sica, Vittorio 1901(?)-1974 .... **CLC 20**
  See also CA 117
Destouches, Louis-Ferdinand
  1894-1961 .... **CLC 9, 15**
  See also Celine, Louis-Ferdinand
  See also CA 85-88; CANR 28; MTCW 1
de Tolignac, Gaston
  See Griffith, D(avid Lewelyn) W(ark)
Deutsch, Babette 1895-1982 .... **CLC 18**
  See also CA 1-4R; 108; CANR 4, 79; DLB
  45; SATA 1; SATA-Obit 33
Devenant, William 1606-1649 .... **LC 13**
De Vries, Peter 1910-1993 ..... **CLC 1, 2, 3, 7,
  10, 28, 46; DAM NOV**
  See also CA 17-20R; 142; CANR 41; DLB
  6; DLBY 82; MTCW 1, 2
Dexter, John
  See Bradley, Marion Zimmer
  See also GLL 1
Dexter, Martin
  See Faust, Frederick (Schiller)
  See also AW 2
Dexter, Pete 1943- .. **CLC 34, 55; DAM POP**
  See also BEST 89:2; CA 127; 131; INT 131;
  MTCW 1

Diamano, Silmang
  See Senghor, Leopold Sedar
Diamond, Neil 1941- .... **CLC 30**
  See also CA 108
Diaz del Castillo, Bernal 1496-1584 .. **LC 31;
  HLCS 1**
di Bassetto, Corno
  See Shaw, George Bernard
Dick, Philip K(indred) 1928-1982 ... **CLC 10,
  30, 72; DAM NOV, POP**
  See also AAYA 24; CA 49-52; 106; CANR
  2, 16; DA3; DLB 8; MTCW 1, 2
Dickens, Charles (John Huffam)
  1812-1870 .... **NCLC 3, 8, 18, 26, 37, 50,
  86; DA; DAB; DAC; DAM MST, NOV**
  See also AAYA 23; CDBLB 1832-1890;
  DA3; DLB 21, 55, 70, 159, 166; JRDA;
  MAICYA; SATA 15
Dickey, James (Lafayette)
  1923-1997 .... **CLC 1, 2, 4, 7, 10, 15, 47,
  109; DAM NOV, POET, POP**
  See also AITN 1, 2; AMWS 4; CA 9-12R;
  156; CABS 2; CANR 10, 48, 61; CDALB
  1968-1988; DA3; DLB 5, 193; DLBD 7;
  DLBY 82, 93, 96, 97, 98; INT CANR-10;
  MTCW 1, 2
Dickey, William 1928-1994 .... **CLC 3, 28**
  See also CA 9-12R; 145; CANR 24, 79;
  DLB 5
Dickinson, Charles 1951- .... **CLC 49**
  See also CA 128
Dickinson, Emily (Elizabeth)
  1830-1886 ..... **NCLC 21, 77; DA; DAB;
  DAC; DAM MST, POET; PC 1**
  See also AAYA 22; CDALB 1865-1917;
  DA3; DLB 1; SATA 29
Dickinson, Peter (Malcolm) 1927- .. **CLC 12,
  35**
  See also AAYA 9; CA 41-44R; CANR 31,
  58, 88; CLR 29; DLB 87, 161; JRDA;
  MAICYA; SATA 5, 62, 95
Dickson, Carr
  See Carr, John Dickson
Dickson, Carter
  See Carr, John Dickson
Diderot, Denis 1713-1784 .... **LC 26**
Didion, Joan 1934- .... **CLC 1, 3, 8, 14, 32,
  129; DAM NOV**
  See also AITN 1; AMWS 4; AW 2; CA
  5-8R; CANR 14, 52, 76; CDALB 1968-
  1988; DA3; DLB 2, 173, 185; DLBY 81,
  86; MTCW 1, 2
Dietrich, Robert
  See Hunt, E(verette) Howard, (Jr.)
Difusa, Pati
  See Almodovar, Pedro
Dillard, Annie 1945- .. **CLC 9, 60, 115; DAM
  NOV**
  See also AAYA 6; AMWS 6; CA 49-52;
  CANR 3, 43, 62, 90; DA3; DLBY 80;
  MTCW 1, 2; SATA 10
Dillard, R(ichard) H(enry) W(ilde)
  1937- .... **CLC 5**
  See also CA 21-24R; CAAS 7; CANR 10;
  DLB 5
Dillon, Eilis 1920-1994 .... **CLC 17**
  See also BEST; CA 9-12R, 182; 147; CAAE
  182; CAAS 3; CANR 4, 38, 78; CLR 26;
  MAICYA; SATA 2, 74; SATA-Essay 105;
  SATA-Obit 83
Dimont, Penelope
  See Mortimer, Penelope (Ruth)
Dinesen, Isak .... **CLC 10, 29, 95**
  See also Blixen, Karen (Christentze
  Dinesen)
  See also AW 6; MTCW 1
Ding Ling .... **CLC 68**
  See also Chiang, Pin-chin

Diphusa, Patty
  See Almodovar, Pedro
Disch, Thomas M(ichael) 1940- ... **CLC 7, 36**
  See also AAYA 17; CA 21-24R; CAAS 4;
  CANR 17, 36, 54, 89; CLR 18; DA3;
  DLB 8; MAICYA; MTCW 1, 2; SAAS
  15; SATA 92
Disch, Tom
  See Disch, Thomas M(ichael)
d'Isly, Georges
  See Simenon, Georges (Jacques Christian)
Disraeli, Benjamin 1804-1881 ... **NCLC 2, 39,
  79**
  See also DLB 21, 55
Ditcum, Steve
  See Crumb, R(obert)
Dixon, Paige
  See Corcoran, Barbara
Dixon, Stephen 1936- .... **CLC 52**
  See also AW 16; CA 89-92; CANR 17, 40,
  54, 91; DLB 130
Doak, Annie
  See Dillard, Annie
Dobell, Sydney Thompson
  1824-1874 .... **NCLC 43**
  See also DLB 32
Doblin, Alfred
  See Doeblin, Alfred
  See also AW 13
Dobrolyubov, Nikolai Alexandrovich
  1836-1861 .... **NCLC 5**
Dobyns, Stephen 1941- .... **CLC 37**
  See also CA 45-48; CANR 2, 18
Doctorow, E(dgar) L(aurence)
  1931- .... **CLC 6, 11, 15, 18, 37, 44, 65,
  113; DAM NOV, POP**
  See also AAYA 22; AITN 2; AMWS 4;
  BEST 89:3; CA 45-48; CANR 2, 33, 51,
  76, 97; CDALB 1968-1988; DA3; DLB
  2, 28, 173; DLBY 80; MTCW 1, 2
Dodgson, Charles Lutwidge 1832-1898
  See Carroll, Lewis
  See also BEST 2; CLR 2; DA; DAB; DAC;
  DAM MST, NOV, POET; DA3; MAI-
  CYA; SATA 100
Dodson, Owen (Vincent)
  1914-1983 .... **CLC 79; BLC 1; DAM
  MULT**
  See also BW 1; CA 65-68; 110; CANR 24;
  DLB 76
Doeblin, Alfred 1878-1957
  See Doblin, Alfred
  See also AW 13; CA 110; 141; DLB 66
Doerr, Harriet 1910- .... **CLC 34**
  See also CA 117; 122; CANR 47; INT 122
Domecq, H(onorio Bustos)
  See Bioy Casares, Adolfo
Domecq, H(onorio) Bustos
  See Bioy Casares, Adolfo; Borges, Jorge
  Luis
Domini, Rey
  See Lorde, Audre (Geraldine)
  See also GLL 1
Dominique
  See Proust, (Valentin-Louis-George-Eugene-
)Marcel
Don, A
  See Stephen, SirLeslie
Donaldson, Stephen R. 1947- .. **CLC 46, 138;
  DAM POP**
  See also AAYA 36; CA 89-92; CANR 13,
  55; INT CANR-13; SATA 121
Donleavy, J(ames) P(atrick) 1926- .... **CLC 1,
  4, 6, 10, 45**
  See also AITN 2; CA 9-12R; CANR 24, 49,
  62, 80; DLB 6, 173; INT CANR-24;
  MTCW 1, 2

Dunn, Douglas (Eaglesham) 1942- .... **CLC 6, 40**
See also CA 45-48; CANR 2, 33; DLB 40; MTCW 1

Dunn, Katherine (Karen) 1945- .... **CLC 71**
See also CA 33-36R; CANR 72; MTCW 1

Dunn, Stephen 1939- .... **CLC 36**
See also CA 33-36R; CANR 12, 48, 53; DLB 105

Dunne, John Gregory 1932- .... **CLC 28**
See also CA 25-28R; CANR 14, 50; DLBY 80

Dunsany, Edward John Moreton Drax Plunkett 1878-1957
See Dunsany, Lord
See also CA 104; 148; DLB 10; MTCW 1

du Perry, Jean
See Simenon, Georges (Jacques Christian)

Durang, Christopher (Ferdinand) 1949- .... **CLC 27, 38**
See also CA 105; CANR 50, 76; MTCW 1

Duras, Marguerite 1914-1996 . **CLC 3, 6, 11, 20, 34, 40, 68, 100**
See also AW 40; CA 25-28R; 151; CANR 50; CWW 2; DLB 83; MTCW 1, 2

Durban, (Rosa) Pam 1947- .... **CLC 39**
See also CA 123

Durcan, Paul 1944- .... **CLC 43, 70; DAM POET**
See also CA 134

Durrell, Lawrence (George) 1912-1990 .... **CLC 1, 4, 6, 8, 13, 27, 41; DAM NOV**
See also BRWS 1; CA 9-12R; 132; CANR 40, 77; CDBLB 1945-1960; DLB 15, 27, 204; DLBY 90; MTCW 1, 2

Dürrenmatt, Friedrich
See Duerrenmatt, Friedrich

Dutt, Toru 1856-1877 .... **NCLC 29**
See also DLB 240

Dwight, Timothy 1752-1817 .... **NCLC 13**
See also DLB 37

Dworkin, Andrea 1946- .... **CLC 43, 123**
See also CA 77-80; CAAS 21; CANR 16, 39, 76, 96; GLL 1; INT CANR-16; MTCW 1, 2

Dwyer, Deanna
See Koontz, Dean R(ay)

Dwyer, K. R.
See Koontz, Dean R(ay)

Dwyer, Thomas A. 1923- .... **CLC 114**
See also CA 115

Dybek, Stuart 1942- .... **CLC 114**
See also CA 97-100; CANR 39; DLB 130

Dye, Richard
See De Voto, Bernard (Augustine)

Dylan, Bob 1941- .... **CLC 3, 4, 6, 12, 77**
See also CA 41-44R; DLB 16

Dyson, John 1943- .... **CLC 70**
See also CA 144

E. V. L.
See Lucas, E(dward) V(errall)

Eagleton, Terence (Francis) 1943- .. **CLC 63, 132**
See also CA 57-60; CANR 7, 23, 68; DLB 242; MTCW 1, 2

Eagleton, Terry
See Eagleton, Terence (Francis)

Early, Jack
See Scoppettone, Sandra
See also GLL 1

East, Michael
See West, Morris L(anglo)

Eastaway, Edward
See Thomas, (Philip) Edward

Eastlake, William (Derry) 1917-1997 .... **CLC 8**
See also AW 2; CA 5-8R; 158; CAAS 1; CANR 5, 63; DLB 6, 206; INT CANR-5

Eberhart, Richard (Ghormley) 1904- .. **CLC 3, 11, 19, 56; DAM POET**
See also CA 1-4R; CANR 2; CDALB 1941-1968; DLB 48; MTCW 1

Eberstadt, Fernanda 1960- .... **CLC 39**
See also CA 136; CANR 69

Echegaray (y Eizaguirre), Jose (Maria Waldo) 1832-1916
See also AW 4; CA 104; CANR 32; HLCS 1; HW 1; MTCW 1

Echeverria, (Jose) Esteban (Antonino) 1805-1851 .... **NCLC 18**

Echo
See Proust, (Valentin-Louis-George-Eugene-)Marcel

Eckert, Allan W. 1931- .... **CLC 17**
See also AAYA 18; CA 13-16R; CANR 14, 45; INT CANR-14; SAAS 21; SATA 29, 91; SATA-Brief 27

Eckhart, Meister 1260(?)-1327(?) ... **CMLC 9**
See also DLB 115

Eckmar, F. R.
See de Hartog, Jan

Eco, Umberto 1932- .... **CLC 28, 60, 142; DAM NOV, POP**
See also BEST 90:1; CA 77-80; CANR 12, 33, 55; CWW 2; DA3; DLB 196, 242; MTCW 1, 2

Edel, (Joseph) Leon 1907-1997 .. **CLC 29, 34**
See also CA 1-4R; 161; CANR 1, 22; DLB 103; INT CANR-22

Eden, Emily 1797-1869 .... **NCLC 10**

Edgar, David 1948- .. **CLC 42; DAM DRAM**
See also CA 57-60; CANR 12, 61; DLB 13, 233; MTCW 1

Edgerton, Clyde (Carlyle) 1944- ...... **CLC 39**
See also AAYA 17; BEST; CA 118; 134; CANR 64; INT 134

Edgeworth, Maria 1768-1849 .... **NCLC 1, 51**
See also BRWS 3; DLB 116, 159, 163; SATA 21

Edmonds, Paul
See Kuttner, Henry

Edmonds, Walter D(umaux) 1903-1998 .... **CLC 35**
See also CA 5-8R; CANR 2; DLB 9; MAI-CYA; SAAS 4; SATA 1, 27; SATA-Obit 99

Edmondson, Wallace
See Ellison, Harlan (Jay)

Edson, Russell .... **CLC 13**
See also CA 33-36R

Edwards, Bronwen Elizabeth
See Rose, Wendy

Edwards, G(erald) B(asil) 1899-1976 .... **CLC 25**
See also CA 110

Edwards, Gus 1939- .... **CLC 43**
See also CA 108; INT 108

Edwards, Jonathan 1703-1758 .... **LC 7, 54; DA; DAC; DAM MST**
See also DLB 24

Efron, Marina Ivanovna Tsvetaeva
See Tsvetaeva (Efron), Marina (Ivanovna)

Ehle, John (Marsden, Jr.) 1925- ...... **CLC 27**
See also CA 9-12R

Ehrenbourg, Ilya (Grigoryevich)
See Ehrenburg, Ilya (Grigoryevich)

Ehrenburg, Ilya (Grigoryevich) 1891-1967 .... **CLC 18, 34, 62**
See also CA 102; 25-28R

Ehrenburg, Ilyo (Grigoryevich)
See Ehrenburg, Ilya (Grigoryevich)

Ehrenreich, Barbara 1941- .... **CLC 110**
See also BEST 90:4; CA 73-76; CANR 16, 37, 62; MTCW 1, 2

Eich, Guenter 1907-1972 .... **CLC 15**
See also CA 111; 93-96; DLB 69, 124

Eichendorff, Joseph Freiherr von 1788-1857 .... **NCLC 8**
See also DLB 90

Eigner, Larry .... **CLC 9**
See also Eigner, Laurence (Joel)
See also CAAS 23; DLB 5

Eigner, Laurence (Joel) 1927-1996
See Eigner, Larry
See also CA 9-12R; 151; CANR 6, 84; DLB 193

Eiseley, Loren Corey 1907-1977 .... **CLC 7**
See also AAYA 5; CA 1-4R; 73-76; CANR 6; DLBD 17

Eisenstadt, Jill 1963- .... **CLC 50**
See also CA 140

Eisner, Simon
See Kornbluth, C(yril) M.

Ekeloef, (Bengt) Gunnar 1907-1968 ... **CLC 27; DAM POET; PC 23**
See also CA 123; 25-28R

Ekelöf, (Bengt) Gunnar
See Ekeloef, (Bengt) Gunnar

Ekwensi, C. O. D.
See Ekwensi, Cyprian (Odiatu Duaka)

Ekwensi, Cyprian (Odiatu Duaka) 1921- ... **CLC 4; BLC 1; DAM MULT**
See also BW 2, 3; CA 29-32R; CANR 18, 42, 74; DLB 117; MTCW 1, 2; SATA 66

Elaine ....
See Leverson, Ada
See also AW 18

El Crummo
See Crumb, R(obert)

Elder, Lonne III 1931-1996 .... **DC 8**
See also BLC 1; BW 1, 3; CA 81-84; 152; CANR 25; DAM MULT; DLB 7, 38, 44

Eleanor of Aquitaine 1122-1204 ... **CMLC 39**

Elia
See Lamb, Charles

Eliade, Mircea 1907-1986 .... **CLC 19**
See also CA 65-68; 119; CANR 30, 62; DLB 220; MTCW 1

Eliot, A. D.
See Jewett, (Theodora) Sarah Orne

Eliot, Alice
See Jewett, (Theodora) Sarah Orne

Eliot, Dan
See Silverberg, Robert

Eliot, George 1819-1880 ...... **NCLC 4, 13, 23, 41, 49, 89; DA; DAB; DAC; DAM MST, NOV; PC 20**
See also AW 8; BEST; CDBLB 1832-1890; DA3; DLB 21, 35, 55

Eliot, John 1604-1690 .... **LC 5**
See also DLB 24

Eliot, T(homas) S(tearns) 1888-1965 ...... **CLC 1, 2, 3, 6, 9, 10, 13, 15, 24, 34, 41, 55, 57, 113; DA; DAB; DAC; DAM DRAM, MST, POET; PC 5, 31**
See also AAYA 28; CA 5-8R; 25-28R; CANR 41; CDALB 1929-1941; DA3; DLB 7, 10, 45, 63; DLBY 88; MTCW 1, 2

Elkin, Stanley L(awrence) 1930-1995 .. **CLC 4, 6, 9, 14, 27, 51, 91; DAM NOV, POP**
See also AMWS 6; AW 12; CA 9-12R; 148; CANR 8, 46; DLB 2, 28; DLBY 80; INT CANR-8; MTCW 1, 2

Elledge, Scott .... **CLC 34**

Elliot, Don
See Silverberg, Robert

Elliott, Don
See Silverberg, Robert

Elliott, George P(aul) 1918-1980 .... **CLC 2**
See also CA 1-4R; 97-100; CANR 2

Elliott, Janice 1931-1995 .... **CLC 47**
See also CA 13-16R; CANR 8, 29, 84; DLB
14; SATA 119
Elliott, Sumner Locke 1917-1991 ..... **CLC 38**
See also CA 5-8R; 134; CANR 2, 21
Elliott, William
See Bradbury, Ray (Douglas)
Ellis, A. E. .... **CLC 7**
Ellis, Alice Thomas .... **CLC 40**
See also Haycraft, Anna (Margaret)
See also DLB 194; MTCW 1
Ellis, Bret Easton 1964- ..... **CLC 39, 71, 117;**
DAM POP
See also AAYA 2; CA 118; 123; CANR 51,
74; DA3; INT 123; MTCW 1
Ellis, Landon
See Ellison, Harlan (Jay)
Ellis, Trey 1962- .... **CLC 55**
See also CA 146; CANR 92
Ellison, Harlan (Jay) 1934- ... **CLC 1, 13, 42,**
139; DAM POP
See also AAYA 29; CA 5-8R; CANR 5, 46;
DLB 8; INT CANR-5; MTCW 1, 2;
SCFW 2
Ellison, Ralph (Waldo) 1914-1994 .... **CLC 1,**
3, 11, 54, 86, 114; BLC 1; DA; DAB;
DAC; DAM MST, MULT, NOV
See also AAYA 19; AMWS 2; AW 1, 11;
BEST; BW 1, 3; CA 9-12R; 145; CANR
24, 53; CDALB 1941-1968; DA3; DLB
2, 76, 227; DLBY 94; MTCW 1, 2
Ellmann, Lucy (Elizabeth) 1956- ..... **CLC 61**
See also CA 128
Ellmann, Richard (David)
1918-1987 .... **CLC 50**
See also BEST 89:2; CA 1-4R; 122; CANR
2, 28, 61; DLB 103; DLBY 87; MTCW
1, 2
Elman, Richard (Martin)
1934-1997 .... **CLC 19**
See also CA 17-20R; 163; CAAS 3; CANR
47
Elron
See Hubbard, L(afayette) Ron(ald)
Elyot, Sir Thomas 1490(?)-1546 .... **LC 11**
Elytis, Odysseus 1911-1996 .... **CLC 15, 49,**
100; DAM POET; PC 21
See also Alepoudelis, Odysseus
See also CA 102; 151; CANR 94; CWW 2;
MTCW 1, 2
Emecheta, (Florence Onye) Buchi
1944- .. **CLC 14, 48, 128; BLC 2; DAM**
MULT
See also BW 2, 3; CA 81-84; CANR 27,
81; DA3; DLB 117; MTCW 1, 2; SATA
66
Emerson, Mary Moody
1774-1863 .... **NCLC 66**
Emerson, Ralph Waldo 1803-1882 . **NCLC 1,**
38, 98; DA; DAB; DAC; DAM MST,
POET; PC 18
See also CDALB 1640-1865; DA3; DLB 1,
59, 73, 223
Eminescu, Mihail 1850-1889 .... **NCLC 33**
Empson, William 1906-1984 ... **CLC 3, 8, 19,**
33, 34
See also BRWS 2; CA 17-20R; 112; CANR
31, 61; DLB 20; MTCW 1, 2
Enchi, Fumiko (Ueda) 1905-1986 ..... **CLC 31**
See also CA 129; 121; DLB 182
Ende, Michael (Andreas Helmuth)
1929-1995 .... **CLC 31**
See also CA 118; 124; 149; CANR 36; CLR
14; DLB 75; MAICYA; SATA 61; SATA-
Brief 42; SATA-Obit 86
Endo, Shusaku 1923-1996 ..... **CLC 7, 14, 19,**
54, 99; DAM NOV
See also CA 29-32R; 153; CANR 21, 54;
DA3; DLB 182; MTCW 1, 2

Engel, Marian 1933-1985 .... **CLC 36**
See also CA 25-28R; CANR 12; DLB 53;
INT CANR-12
Engelhardt, Frederick
See Hubbard, L(afayette) Ron(ald)
Engels, Friedrich 1820-1895 .... **NCLC 85**
See also DLB 129
Enright, D(ennis) J(oseph) 1920- .. **CLC 4, 8,**
31
See also CA 1-4R; CANR 1, 42, 83; DLB
27; SATA 25
Enzensberger, Hans Magnus
1929- .... **CLC 43; PC 28**
See also CA 116; 119
Ephron, Nora 1941- .... **CLC 17, 31**
See also AAYA 35; AITN 2; CA 65-68;
CANR 12, 39, 83
Epicurus 341B.C.-270B.C. .... **CMLC 21**
See also DLB 176
Epsilon
See Betjeman, John
Epstein, Daniel Mark 1948- .... **CLC 7**
See also CA 49-52; CANR 2, 53, 90
Epstein, Jacob 1956- .... **CLC 19**
See also CA 114
Epstein, Joseph 1937- .... **CLC 39**
See also CA 112; 119; CANR 50, 65
Epstein, Leslie 1938- .... **CLC 27**
See also CA 73-76; CAAS 12; CANR 23,
69
Equiano, Olaudah 1745(?)-1797 .... **LC 16;**
BLC 2; DAM MULT
See also DLB 37, 50
Erasmus, Desiderius 1469(?)-1536 ...... **LC 16**
Erdman, Paul E(mil) 1932- .... **CLC 25**
See also AITN 1; CA 61-64; CANR 13, 43,
84
Erdrich, Louise 1954- .... **CLC 39, 54, 120;**
DAM MULT, NOV, POP
See also AAYA 10; AMWS 4; AW 2; BEST
89:1; CA 114; CANR 41, 62; CDALBS;
DA3; DLB 152, 175, 206; MTCW 1;
NNAL; SATA 94
Erenburg, Ilya (Grigoryevich)
See Ehrenburg, Ilya (Grigoryevich)
Erickson, Stephen Michael 1950-
See Erickson, Steve
See also CA 129
Erickson, Steve .... **CLC 64**
See also Erickson, Stephen Michael
See also CANR 60, 68
Ericson, Walter
See Fast, Howard (Melvin)
Eriksson, Buntel
See Bergman, (Ernst) Ingmar
Ernaux, Annie 1940- .... **CLC 88**
See also CA 147; CANR 93
Eschenbach, Wolfram von
See Wolfram von Eschenbach
Eseki, Bruno
See Mphahlele, Ezekiel
Eshleman, Clayton 1935- .... **CLC 7**
See also CA 33-36R; CAAS 6; CANR 93;
DLB 5
Espriella, Don Manuel Alvarez
See Southey, Robert
Espriu, Salvador 1913-1985 .... **CLC 9**
See also CA 154; 115; DLB 134
Espronceda, Jose de 1808-1842 ..... **NCLC 39**
Esquivel, Laura 1951(?)- ... **CLC 141; HLCS**
1
See also AAYA 29; CA 143; CANR 68;
DA3; MTCW 1
Esse, James
See Stephens, James
Esterbrook, Tom
See Hubbard, L(afayette) Ron(ald)

Estleman, Loren D. 1952- ..... **CLC 48; DAM**
NOV, POP
See also AAYA 27; CA 85-88; CANR 27,
74; DA3; DLB 226; INT CANR-27;
MTCW 1, 2
Euclid 306B.C.-283B.C. .... **CMLC 25**
Eugenides, Jeffrey 1960(?)- .... **CLC 81**
See also CA 144
Euripides c. 485B.C.-406B.C. .... **CMLC 23;**
DA; DAB; DAC; DAM DRAM, MST;
DC 4
See also BEST; DA3; DLB 176
Evan, Evin
See Faust, Frederick (Schiller)
Evans, Evan
See Faust, Frederick (Schiller)
See also AW 2
Evans, Marian
See Eliot, George
Evans, Mary Ann
See Eliot, George
Evarts, Esther
See Benson, Sally
Everett, Percival
See Everett, Percival L.
Everett, Percival L. 1956- .... **CLC 57**
See also Everett, Percival
See also BW 2; CA 129; CANR 94
Everson, R(onald) G(ilmour)
1903-1992 .... **CLC 27**
See also CA 17-20R; DLB 88
Everson, William (Oliver)
1912-1994 .... **CLC 1, 5, 14**
See also CA 9-12R; 145; CANR 20; DLB
212; MTCW 1
Evtushenko, Evgenii Aleksandrovich
See Yevtushenko, Yevgeny (Alexandrovich)
Ewart, Gavin (Buchanan)
1916-1995 .... **CLC 13, 46**
See also CA 89-92; 150; CANR 17, 46;
DLB 40; MTCW 1
Ewing, Frederick R.
See Sturgeon, Theodore (Hamilton)
Exley, Frederick (Earl) 1929-1992 .... **CLC 6,**
11
See also AITN 2; CA 81-84; 138; DLB 143;
DLBY 81
Eynhardt, Guillermo
See Quiroga, Horacio (Sylvestre)
Ezekiel, Nissim 1924- .... **CLC 61**
See also CA 61-64
Ezekiel, Tish O'Dowd 1943- .... **CLC 34**
See also CA 129
Fadeyev, A.
See Bulgya, Alexander Alexandrovich
Fadeyev, Alexander
See Bulgya, Alexander Alexandrovich
See also AW 53
Fagen, Donald 1948- .... **CLC 26**
Fainzilberg, Ilya Arnoldovich 1897-1937
See Ilf, Ilya
See also CA 120; 165
Fair, Ronald L. 1932- .... **CLC 18**
See also BW 1; CA 69-72; CANR 25; DLB
33
Fairbairn, Roger
See Carr, John Dickson
Fairbairns, Zoe (Ann) 1948- .... **CLC 32**
See also CA 103; CANR 21, 85
Fairman, Paul W. 1916-1977
See Queen, Ellery
See also CA 114
Falco, Gian
See Papini, Giovanni
Falconer, James
See Kirkup, James
Falconer, Kenneth
See Kornbluth, C(yril) M.

Friedman, B(ernard) H(arper)
1926- .... **CLC 7**
See also CA 1-4R; CANR 3, 48

Friedman, Bruce Jay 1930- ...... **CLC 3, 5, 56**
See also CA 9-12R; CANR 25, 52; DLB 2, 28; INT CANR-25

Friel, Brian 1929- .... **CLC 5, 42, 59, 115; DC 8**
See also BRWS 5; CA 21-24R; CANR 33, 69; DLB 13; MTCW 1

Friis-Baastad, Babbis Ellinor
1921-1970 .... **CLC 12**
See also CA 17-20R; 134; SATA 7

Frisch, Max (Rudolf) 1911-1991 ... **CLC 3, 9, 14, 18, 32, 44; DAM DRAM, NOV**
See also CA 85-88; 134; CANR 32, 74; DLB 69, 124; MTCW 1, 2

Fromentin, Eugene (Samuel Auguste)
1820-1876 .... **NCLC 10**
See also DLB 123

Frost, Frederick
See Faust, Frederick (Schiller)
See also AW 2

Frost, Robert (Lee) 1874-1963 .. **CLC 1, 3, 4, 9, 10, 13, 15, 26, 34, 44; DA; DAB; DAC; DAM MST, POET; PC 1**
See also AAYA 21; CA 89-92; CANR 33; CDALB 1917-1929; CLR 67; DA3; DLB 54; DLBD 7; MTCW 1, 2; SATA 14

Froude, James Anthony
1818-1894 .... **NCLC 43**
See also DLB 18, 57, 144

Froy, Herald
See Waterhouse, Keith (Spencer)

Fry, Christopher 1907- .... **CLC 2, 10, 14; DAM DRAM**
See also BRWS 3; CA 17-20R; CAAS 23; CANR 9, 30, 74; DLB 13; MTCW 1, 2; SATA 66

Frye, (Herman) Northrop
1912-1991 .... **CLC 24, 70**
See also CA 5-8R; 133; CANR 8, 37; DLB 67, 68; MTCW 1, 2

Fuchs, Daniel 1909-1993 .... **CLC 8, 22**
See also CA 81-84; 142; CAAS 5; CANR 40; DLB 9, 26, 28; DLBY 93

Fuchs, Daniel 1934- .... **CLC 34**
See also CA 37-40R; CANR 14, 48

Fuentes, Carlos 1928- .. **CLC 3, 8, 10, 13, 22, 41, 60, 113; DA; DAB; DAC; DAM MST, MULT, NOV; HLC 1**
See also AAYA 4; AITN 2; AW 24; BEST; CA 69-72; CANR 10, 32, 68; CWW 2; DA3; DLB 113; HW 1, 2; MTCW 1, 2

Fuentes, Gregorio Lopez y
See Lopez y Fuentes, Gregorio

Fuertes, Gloria 1918-1998 .... **PC 27**
See also CA 178, 180; DLB 108; HW 2; SATA 115

Fugard, (Harold) Athol 1932- . **CLC 5, 9, 14, 25, 40, 80; DAM DRAM; DC 3**
See also AAYA 17; CA 85-88; CANR 32, 54; DLB 225; MTCW 1

Fugard, Sheila 1932- .... **CLC 48**
See also CA 125

Fukuyama, Francis 1952- .... **CLC 131**
See also CA 140; CANR 72

Fuller, Charles (H., Jr.) 1939- .... **CLC 25; BLC 2; DAM DRAM, MULT; DC 1**
See also BW 2; CA 108; 112; CANR 87; DLB 38; INT 112; MTCW 1

Fuller, John (Leopold) 1937- .... **CLC 62**
See also CA 21-24R; CANR 9, 44; DLB 40

Fuller, Margaret
See Ossoli, Sarah Margaret (Fuller marchesa d')
See also AMWS 2

Fuller, Roy (Broadbent) 1912-1991 ... **CLC 4, 28**
See also CA 5-8R; 135; CAAS 10; CANR 53, 83; DLB 15, 20; SATA 87

Fuller, Sarah Margaret
See Ossoli, Sarah Margaret (Fuller marchesa d')

Fulton, Alice 1952- .... **CLC 52**
See also CA 116; CANR 57, 88; DLB 193

Fuson, Robert H(enderson) 1927- .... **CLC 70**
See also CA 89-92

Fussell, Paul 1924- .... **CLC 74**
See also BEST 90:1; CA 17-20R; CANR 8, 21, 35, 69; INT CANR-21; MTCW 1, 2

Gaboriau, Emile 1835-1873 .... **NCLC 14**

Gadda, Carlo Emilio 1893-1973 .... **CLC 11**
See also CA 89-92; DLB 177

Gaddis, William 1922-1998 ... **CLC 1, 3, 6, 8, 10, 19, 43, 86**
See also AMWS 4; CA 17-20R; 172; CANR 21, 48; DLB 2; MTCW 1, 2

Gage, Walter
See Inge, William (Motter)

Gaines, Ernest J(ames) 1933- ...... **CLC 3, 11, 18, 86; BLC 2; DAM MULT**
See also AAYA 18; AITN 1; AW 5; BEST; BW 2, 3; CA 9-12R; CANR 6, 24, 42, 75; CDALB 1968-1988; CLR 62; DA3; DLB 2, 33, 152; DLBY 80; MTCW 1, 2; SATA 86

Gaitskill, Mary 1954- .... **CLC 69**
See also CA 128; CANR 61

Galdos, Benito Perez
See Perez Galdos, Benito

Galeano, Eduardo (Hughes) 1940- . **CLC 72; HLCS 1**
See also CA 29-32R; CANR 13, 32; HW 1

Galiano, Juan Valera y Alcala
See Valera y Alcala-Galiano, Juan

Galilei, Galileo 1564-1642 .... **LC 45**

Gallagher, Tess 1943- ...... **CLC 18, 63; DAM POET; PC 9**
See also CA 106; DLB 212

Gallant, Mavis 1922- .. **CLC 7, 18, 38; DAC; DAM MST**
See also AW 5; CA 69-72; CANR 29, 69; CCA 1; DLB 53; MTCW 1, 2

Gallant, Roy A(rthur) 1924- .... **CLC 17**
See also CA 5-8R; CANR 4, 29, 54; CLR 30; MAICYA; SATA 4, 68, 110

Gallico, Paul (William) 1897-1976 ..... **CLC 2**
See also AITN 1; CA 5-8R; 69-72; CANR 23; DLB 9, 171; MAICYA; SATA 13

Gallo, Max Louis 1932- .... **CLC 95**
See also CA 85-88

Gallois, Lucien
See Desnos, Robert

Gallup, Ralph
See Whitemore, Hugh (John)

Galt, John 1779-1839 .... **NCLC 1**
See also DLB 99, 116, 159

Galvin, James 1951- .... **CLC 38**
See also CA 108; CANR 26

Gandhi, M. K.
See Gandhi, Mohandas Karamchand

Gandhi, Mahatma
See Gandhi, Mohandas Karamchand

Gann, Ernest Kellogg 1910-1991 ..... **CLC 23**
See also AITN 1; CA 1-4R; 136; CANR 1, 83

Garber, Eric 1943(?)-
See Holleran, Andrew
See also CANR 89

Garcia, Cristina 1958- .... **CLC 76**
See also CA 141; CANR 73; HW 2

García Lorca, Federico 1898-1936 .... **DC 2**
See also Lorca, Federico García

See also AW 1, 7, 49; BEST; CA 104; 131; CANR 81; DA; DAB; DAC; DAM DRAM, MST, MULT, POET; DA3; DLB 108; HLC 2; HW 1, 2; MTCW 1, 2

García Márquez, Gabriel (Jose)
1928- .... **CLC 2, 3, 8, 10, 15, 27, 47, 55, 68; DA; DAB; DAC; DAM MST, MULT, NOV, POP; HLC 1**
See also AAYA 3, 33; AW 1, 6; BEST; CA 33-36R; CANR 10, 28, 50, 75, 82; DA3; DLB 113; HW 1, 2; MTCW 1, 2

Garcilaso de la Vega, El Inca 1503-1536
See also HLCS 1

Gard, Janice
See Latham, Jean Lee

Gard, Roger Martin du
See Martin du Gard, Roger

Gardam, Jane 1928- .... **CLC 43**
See also BEST; CA 49-52; CANR 2, 18, 33, 54; CLR 12; DLB 14, 161, 231; MAICYA; MTCW 1; SAAS 9; SATA 39, 76; SATA-Brief 28

Gardner, Herb(ert) 1934- .... **CLC 44**
See also CA 149

Gardner, John (Champlin), Jr.
1933-1982 ...... **CLC 2, 3, 5, 7, 8, 10, 18, 28, 34; DAM NOV, POP**
See also AITN 1; AMWS 5; AW 8; CA 65-68; 107; CANR 33, 73; CDALBS; DA3; DLB 2; DLBY 82; MTCW 1; SATA 40; SATA-Obit 31

Gardner, John (Edmund) 1926- ...... **CLC 30; DAM POP**
See also CA 103; CANR 15, 69; MTCW 1

Gardner, Miriam
See Bradley, Marion Zimmer
See also GLL 1

Gardner, Noel
See Kuttner, Henry

Gardons, S. S.
See Snodgrass, W(illiam) D(e Witt)

Garfield, Leon 1921-1996 .... **CLC 12**
See also AAYA 8; BEST; CA 17-20R; 152; CANR 38, 41, 78; CLR 21; DLB 161; JRDA; MAICYA; SATA 1, 32, 76; SATA-Obit 90

Garner, Alan 1934- ..... **CLC 17; DAB; DAM POP**
See also AAYA 18; BEST; CA 73-76; 178; CAAE 178; CANR 15, 64; CLR 20; DLB 161; MAICYA; MTCW 1, 2; SATA 18, 69; SATA-Essay 108

Garner, Hugh 1913-1979 .... **CLC 13**
See also Warwick, Jarvis
See also CA 69-72; CANR 31; CCA 1; DLB 68

Garnett, David 1892-1981 .... **CLC 3**
See also CA 5-8R; 103; CANR 17, 79; DLB 34; MTCW 2

Garos, Stephanie
See Katz, Steve

Garrett, George (Palmer) 1929- .. **CLC 3, 11, 51**
See also AMWS 7; AW 30; CA 1-4R; CAAS 5; CANR 1, 42, 67; DLB 2, 5, 130, 152; DLBY 83

Garrick, David 1717-1779 .... **LC 15; DAM DRAM**
See also DLB 84

Garrigue, Jean 1914-1972 .... **CLC 2, 8**
See also CA 5-8R; 37-40R; CANR 20

Garrison, Frederick
See Sinclair, Upton (Beall)

Garro, Elena 1920(?)-1998
See also CA 131; 169; CWW 2; DLB 145; HLCS 1; HW 1

Garth, Will
See Hamilton, Edmond; Kuttner, Henry

Gary, Romain .... CLC 25
  See also Kacew, Romain
  See also DLB 83
Gascar, Pierre .... CLC 11
  See also Fournier, Pierre
Gascoyne, David (Emery) 1916- .... CLC 45
  See also CA 65-68; CANR 10, 28, 54; DLB
  20; MTCW 1
Gaskell, Elizabeth Cleghorn
  1810-1865 .... NCLC 5, 70, 97; DAB;
  DAM MST
  See also AW 25; CDBLB 1832-1890; DLB
  21, 144, 159
Gass, William H(oward) 1924- . CLC 1, 2, 8,
  11, 15, 39, 132
  See also AMWS 6; AW 12; CA 17-20R;
  CANR 30, 71; DLB 2, 227; MTCW 1, 2
Gassendi, Pierre 1592-1655 .... LC 54
Gasset, Jose Ortega y
  See Ortega y Gasset, Jose
Gates, Henry Louis, Jr. 1950- .... CLC 65;
  BLCS; DAM MULT
  See also BW 2, 3; CA 109; CANR 25, 53,
  75; DA3; DLB 67; MTCW 1
Gautier, Theophile 1811-1872 .. NCLC 1, 59;
  DAM POET; PC 18
  See also AW 20; DLB 119
Gawsworth, John
  See Bates, H(erbert) E(rnest)
Gay, John 1685-1732 .. LC 49; DAM DRAM
  See also DLB 84, 95
Gay, Oliver
  See Gogarty, Oliver St. John
Gaye, Marvin (Penze) 1939-1984 ..... CLC 26
  See also CA 112
Gébler, Carlo (Ernest) 1954- .... CLC 39
  See also CA 119; 133; CANR 96
Gee, Maggie (Mary) 1948- .... CLC 57
  See also CA 130; DLB 207
Gee, Maurice (Gough) 1931- .... CLC 29
  See also CA 97-100; CANR 67; CLR 56;
  SATA 46, 101
Gelbart, Larry (Simon) 1928- .... CLC 21, 61
  See also Gelbart, Larry
  See also CA 73-76; CANR 45, 94
Gelbart, Larry 1928-
  See Gelbart, Larry (Simon)
Gelber, Jack 1932- .... CLC 1, 6, 14, 79
  See also CA 1-4R; CANR 2; DLB 7, 228
Gellhorn, Martha (Ellis)
  1908-1998 .... CLC 14, 60
  See also CA 77-80; 164; CANR 44; DLBY
  82, 98
Genet, Jean 1910-1986 .. CLC 1, 2, 5, 10, 14,
  44, 46; DAM DRAM
  See also CA 13-16R; CANR 18; DA3; DLB
  72; DLBY 86; GLL 1; MTCW 1, 2
Gent, Peter 1942- .... CLC 29
  See also AITN 1; CA 89-92; DLBY 82
Gentlewoman in New England, A
  See Bradstreet, Anne
Gentlewoman in Those Parts, A
  See Bradstreet, Anne
Geoffrey of Monmouth c.
  1100-1155 .... CMLC 44
  See also DLB 146
George, Jean Craighead 1919- .... CLC 35
  See also AAYA 8; BEST; CA 5-8R; CANR
  25; CLR 1; DLB 52; JRDA; MAICYA;
  SATA 2, 68
Georges, Georges Martin
  See Simenon, Georges (Jacques Christian)
Gerhardi, William Alexander
  See Gerhardie, William Alexander
Gerhardie, William Alexander
  1895-1977 .... CLC 5
  See also CA 25-28R; 73-76; CANR 18;
  DLB 36

Gerstler, Amy 1956- .... CLC 70
  See also CA 146
Gertler, T. .... CLC 134
  See also CA 116; 121
Ghalib .... NCLC 39, 78
  See also Ghalib, Hsadullah Khan
Ghalib, Hsadullah Khan 1797-1869
  See Ghalib
  See also DAM POET
Ghelderode, Michel de 1898-1962 ..... CLC 6,
  11; DAM DRAM; DC 15
  See also CA 85-88; CANR 40, 77
Ghiselin, Brewster 1903- .... CLC 23
  See also CA 13-16R; CAAS 10; CANR 13
Ghose, Zulfikar 1935- .... CLC 42
  See also CA 65-68; CANR 67
Ghosh, Amitav 1956- .... CLC 44
  See also CA 147; CANR 80
Gibb, Lee
  See Waterhouse, Keith (Spencer)
Gibbons, Kaye 1960- .... CLC 50, 88, 145;
  DAM POP
  See also AAYA 34; CA 151; CANR 75;
  DA3; MTCW 1; SATA 117
Gibran, Kahlil 1883-1931 .... PC 9
  See also AW 1, 9; CA 104; 150; DAM
  POET, POP; DA3; MTCW 2
Gibran, Khalil
  See Gibran, Kahlil
Gibson, William 1914- .. CLC 23; DA; DAB;
  DAC; DAM DRAM, MST
  See also BEST; CA 9-12R; CANR 9, 42,
  75; DLB 7; MTCW 1; SATA 66; SCFW 2
Gibson, William (Ford) 1948- ... CLC 39, 63;
  DAM POP
  See also AAYA 12; CA 126; 133; CANR
  52, 90; DA3; MTCW 1
Gifford, Barry (Colby) 1946- .... CLC 34
  See also CA 65-68; CANR 9, 30, 40, 90
Gilbert, Frank
  See De Voto, Bernard (Augustine)
Gilbreth, Frank B., Jr. 1911-2001 .... CLC 17
  See also CA 9-12R; SATA 2
Gilchrist, Ellen 1935- .... CLC 34, 48, 143;
  DAM POP
  See also AW 9; CA 113; 116; CANR 41,
  61; DLB 130; MTCW 1, 2
Giles, Molly 1942- .... CLC 39
  See also CA 126
Gill, Patrick
  See Creasey, John
Gillette, Douglas .... CLC 70
Gilliam, Terry (Vance) 1940- .... CLC 21, 141
  See also Monty Python
  See also AAYA 19; CA 108; 113; CANR
  35; INT 113
Gillian, Jerry
  See Gilliam, Terry (Vance)
Gilliatt, Penelope (Ann Douglass)
  1932-1993 .... CLC 2, 10, 13, 53
  See also AITN 2; CA 13-16R; 141; CANR
  49; DLB 14
Gilmour, David 1949- .... CLC 35
  See also CA 138, 147
Gilpin, William 1724-1804 .... NCLC 30
Gilray, J. D.
  See Mencken, H(enry) L(ouis)
Gilroy, Frank D(aniel) 1925- .... CLC 2
  See also CA 81-84; CANR 32, 64, 86; DLB
  7
Gilstrap, John 1957(?)- .... CLC 99
  See also CA 160

Ginsberg, Allen 1926-1997 .... CLC 1, 2, 3, 4,
  6, 13, 36, 69, 109; DA; DAB; DAC;
  DAM MST, POET; PC 4
  See also AAYA 33; AITN 1; AMWS 2; CA
  1-4R; 157; CANR 2, 41, 63, 95; CDALB
  1941-1968; DA3; DLB 5, 16, 169; GLL
  1; MTCW 1, 2
Ginzburg, Eugenia .... CLC 59
Ginzburg, Natalia 1916-1991 .... CLC 5, 11,
  54, 70
  See also CA 85-88; 135; CANR 33; DLB
  177; MTCW 1, 2
Giono, Jean 1895-1970 .... CLC 4, 11
  See also CA 45-48; 29-32R; CANR 2, 35;
  DLB 72; MTCW 1
Giovanni, Nikki 1943- .... CLC 2, 4, 19, 64,
  117; BLC 2; DA; DAB; DAC; DAM
  MST, MULT, POET; PC 19
  See also AAYA 22; AITN 1; BEST; BW 2,
  3; CA 29-32R; CAAS 6; CANR 18, 41,
  60, 91; CDALBS; CLR 6; DA3; DLB 5,
  41; INT CANR-18; MAICYA; MTCW 1,
  2; SATA 24, 107
Giovene, Andrea 1904- .... CLC 7
  See also CA 85-88
Gippius, Zinaida (Nikolayevna) 1869-1945
  See Hippius, Zinaida
  See also CA 106
Gironella, Jose Maria 1917- .... CLC 11
  See also CA 101
Giurlani, Aldo
  See Palazzeschi, Aldo
Glanville, Brian (Lester) 1931- .... CLC 6
  See also CA 5-8R; CAAS 9; CANR 3, 70;
  DLB 15, 139; SATA 42
Glaspell, Susan 1882(?)-1948 .... DC 10
  See also AMWS 3; AW 2; BEST 2; CA 110;
  154; DLB 7, 9, 78, 228
Glassco, John 1909-1981 .... CLC 9
  See also CA 13-16R; 102; CANR 15; DLB
  68
Glasscock, Amnesia
  See Steinbeck, John (Ernst)
Glasser, Ronald J. 1940(?)- .... CLC 37
Glassman, Joyce
  See Johnson, Joyce
Glendinning, Victoria 1937- .... CLC 50
  See also CA 120; 127; CANR 59, 89; DLB
  155
Glissant, Edouard 1928- . CLC 10, 68; DAM
  MULT
  See also CA 153; CWW 2
Gloag, Julian 1930- .... CLC 40
  See also AITN 1; CA 65-68; CANR 10, 70
Glowacki, Aleksander
  See Prus, Boleslaw
Gluck, Louise (Elisabeth) 1943- .. CLC 7, 22,
  44, 81; DAM POET; PC 16
  See also AMWS 5; CA 33-36R; CANR 40,
  69; DA3; DLB 5; MTCW 2
Gobineau, Joseph Arthur (Comte) de
  1816-1882 .... NCLC 17
  See also DLB 123
Godard, Jean-Luc 1930- .... CLC 20
  See also CA 93-96
Godden, (Margaret) Rumer
  1907-1998 .... CLC 53
  See also AAYA 6; CA 5-8R; 172; CANR 4,
  27, 36, 55, 80; CLR 20; DLB 161; MAI-
  CYA; SAAS 12; SATA 3, 36; SATA-Obit
  109
Godoy Alcayaga, Lucila 1899-1957 ..... PC 32
  See also Mistral, Gabriela
  See also AW 2; BW 2; CA 104; 131; CANR
  81; DAM MULT; HLC 2; HW 1, 2;
  MTCW 1, 2

Godwin, Gail (Kathleen) 1937- ..... **CLC 5, 8, 22, 31, 69, 125; DAM POP**
See also CA 29-32R; CANR 15, 43, 69; DA3; DLB 6, 234; INT CANR-15; MTCW 1, 2

Godwin, William 1756-1836 .... **NCLC 14**
See also CDBLB 1789-1832; DLB 39, 104, 142, 158, 163

Goebbels, Josef
See Goebbels, (Paul) Joseph

Goebbels, Joseph Paul
See Goebbels, (Paul) Joseph

Goethe, Johann Wolfgang von 1749-1832 ...... **NCLC 4, 22, 34, 90; DA; DAB; DAC; DAM DRAM, MST, POET; PC 5**
See also AW 38; BEST; DA3; DLB 94

Gogol, Nikolai (Vasilyevich) 1809-1852 . **NCLC 5, 15, 31; DA; DAB; DAC; DAM DRAM, MST; DC 1**
See also AW 7; BEST; DLB 198

Goines, Donald 1937(?)-1974 . **CLC 80; BLC 2; DAM MULT, POP**
See also AITN 1; BW 1, 3; CA 124; 114; CANR 82; DA3; DLB 33

Gold, Herbert 1924- .... **CLC 4, 7, 14, 42**
See also CA 9-12R; CANR 17, 45; DLB 2; DLBY 81

Goldbarth, Albert 1948- .... **CLC 5, 38**
See also CA 53-56; CANR 6, 40; DLB 120

Goldberg, Anatol 1910-1982 .... **CLC 34**
See also CA 131; 117

Goldemberg, Isaac 1945- .... **CLC 52**
See also CA 69-72; CAAS 12; CANR 11, 32; HW 1

Golding, William (Gerald) 1911-1993 ..... **CLC 1, 2, 3, 8, 10, 17, 27, 58, 81; DA; DAB; DAC; DAM MST, NOV**
See also AAYA 5; BEST; BRWS 1; CA 5-8R; 141; CANR 13, 33, 54; CDBLB 1945-1960; DA3; DLB 15, 100; MTCW 1, 2

Goldman, Francisco 1954- .... **CLC 76**
See also CA 162

Goldman, William (W.) 1931- ...... **CLC 1, 48**
See also CA 9-12R; CANR 29, 69; DLB 44; IDFW 3

Goldmann, Lucien 1913-1970 .... **CLC 24**
See also CA 25-28; CAP 2

Goldoni, Carlo 1707-1793 .... **LC 4; DAM DRAM**

Goldsberry, Steven 1949- .... **CLC 34**
See also CA 131

Goldsmith, Oliver 1730-1774 . **LC 2, 48; DA; DAB; DAC; DAM DRAM, MST, NOV, POET; DC 8**
See also BEST; CDBLB 1660-1789; DLB 39, 89, 104, 109, 142; SATA 26

Goldsmith, Peter
See Priestley, J(ohn) B(oynton)

Gombrowicz, Witold 1904-1969 .... **CLC 4, 7, 11, 49; DAM DRAM**
See also CA 19-20; 25-28R; CAP 2

Gomez de la Serna, Ramon 1888-1963 .... **CLC 9**
See also CA 153; 116; CANR 79; HW 1, 2

Goncharov, Ivan Alexandrovich 1812-1891 .... **NCLC 1, 63**
See also DLB 238

Goncourt, Edmond (Louis Antoine Huot) de 1822-1896 .... **NCLC 7**
See also DLB 123

Goncourt, Jules (Alfred Huot) de 1830-1870 .... **NCLC 7**
See also DLB 123

Gontier, Fernande 19(?)- .... **CLC 50**

Goodman, Paul 1911-1972 ..... **CLC 1, 2, 4, 7**
See also CA 19-20; 37-40R; CANR 34; CAP 2; DLB 130; MTCW 1

Gordimer, Nadine 1923- ...... **CLC 3, 5, 7, 10, 18, 33, 51, 70, 123; DA; DAB; DAC; DAM MST, NOV**
See also AAYA 39; AW 2; BEST; BRWS 2; CA 5-8R; CANR 3, 28, 56, 88; DA3; DLB 225; INT CANR-28; MTCW 1, 2

Gordon, Adam Lindsay 1833-1870 .... **NCLC 21**
See also DLB 230

Gordon, Caroline 1895-1981 . **CLC 6, 13, 29, 83**
See also AW 15; CA 11-12; 103; CANR 36; CAP 1; DLB 4, 9, 102; DLBD 17; DLBY 81; MTCW 1, 2

Gordon, Charles William 1860-1937
See Connor, Ralph
See also CA 109

Gordon, Mary (Catherine) 1949- .... **CLC 13, 22, 128**
See also AMWS 4; CA 102; CANR 44, 92; DLB 6; DLBY 81; INT 102; MTCW 1

Gordon, N. J.
See Bosman, Herman Charles

Gordon, Sol 1923- .... **CLC 26**
See also CA 53-56; CANR 4; SATA 11

Gordone, Charles 1925-1995 .... **CLC 1, 4; DAM DRAM; DC 8**
See also BW 1, 3; CA 93-96; 180; 150; CAAE 180; CANR 55; DLB 7; INT 93-96; MTCW 1

Gore, Catherine 1800-1861 .... **NCLC 65**
See also DLB 116

Gorenko, Anna Andreevna
See Akhmatova, Anna

Goryan, Sirak
See Saroyan, William

Gotlieb, Phyllis Fay (Bloom) 1926- .. **CLC 18**
See also CA 13-16R; CANR 7; DLB 88

Gottesman, S. D.
See Kornbluth, C(yril) M.; Pohl, Frederik

Gottfried von Strassburg fl. c. 1170-1215 .... **CMLC 10**
See also DLB 138

Gould, Lois .... **CLC 4, 10**
See also CA 77-80; CANR 29; MTCW 1

Govier, Katherine 1948- .... **CLC 51**
See also CA 101; CANR 18, 40; CCA 1

Goyen, (Charles) William 1915-1983 .... **CLC 5, 8, 14, 40**
See also AITN 2; CA 5-8R; 110; CANR 6, 71; DLB 2; DLBY 83; INT CANR-6

Goytisolo, Juan 1931- .... **CLC 5, 10, 23, 133; DAM MULT; HLC 1**
See also CA 85-88; CANR 32, 61; CWW 2; GLL 2; HW 1, 2; MTCW 1, 2

Gozzano, Guido 1883-1916 .... **PC 10**
See also CA 154; DLB 114

Gozzi, (Conte) Carlo 1720-1806 .... **NCLC 23**

Grabbe, Christian Dietrich 1801-1836 .... **NCLC 2**
See also DLB 133

Grace, Patricia Frances 1937- .... **CLC 56**
See also CA 176

Gracian y Morales, Baltasar 1601-1658 .... **LC 15**

Gracq, Julien .... **CLC 11, 48**
See also Poirier, Louis
See also CWW 2; DLB 83

Grade, Chaim 1910-1982 .... **CLC 10**
See also CA 93-96; 107

Graduate of Oxford, A
See Ruskin, John

Grafton, Garth
See Duncan, Sara Jeannette

Graham, John
See Phillips, David Graham

Graham, Jorie 1951- .... **CLC 48, 118**
See also CA 111; CANR 63; DLB 120

Graham, R(obert) B(ontine) Cunninghame
See Cunninghame Graham, Robert (Gallnigad) Bontine
See also DLB 98, 135, 174

Graham, Robert
See Haldeman, Joe (William)

Graham, Tom
See Lewis, (Harry) Sinclair

Graham, W(illiam) S(idney) 1918-1986 .... **CLC 29**
See also CA 73-76; 118; DLB 20

Graham, Winston (Mawdsley) 1910- .... **CLC 23**
See also CA 49-52; CANR 2, 22, 45, 66; DLB 77

Granger, Darius John
See Marlowe, Stephen

Granin, Daniil .... **CLC 59**

Granovsky, Timofei Nikolaevich 1813-1855 .... **NCLC 75**
See also DLB 198

Grant, Skeeter
See Spiegelman, Art

Granzotto, Gianni
See Granzotto, Giovanni Battista

Granzotto, Giovanni Battista 1914-1985 .... **CLC 70**
See also CA 166

Grass, Guenter (Wilhelm) 1927- ... **CLC 1, 2, 4, 6, 11, 15, 22, 32, 49, 88; DA; DAB; DAC; DAM MST, NOV**
See also BEST; CA 13-16R; CANR 20, 75, 93; DA3; DLB 75, 124; MTCW 1, 2

Gratton, Thomas
See Hulme, T(homas) E(rnest)

Grau, Shirley Ann 1929- .... **CLC 4, 9**
See also AW 15; CA 89-92; CANR 22, 69; DLB 2; INT CANR-22; MTCW 1

Gravel, Fern
See Hall, James Norman

Graver, Elizabeth 1964- .... **CLC 70**
See also CA 135; CANR 71

Graves, Richard Perceval 1895-1985 .... **CLC 44**
See also CA 65-68; CANR 9, 26, 51

Graves, Robert (von Ranke) 1895-1985 .. **CLC 1, 2, 6, 11, 39, 44, 45; DAB; DAC; DAM MST, POET; PC 6**
See also CA 5-8R; 117; CANR 5, 36; CD-BLB 1914-1945; DA3; DLB 20, 100, 191; DLBD 18; DLBY 85; MTCW 1, 2; SATA 45

Graves, Valerie
See Bradley, Marion Zimmer

Gray, Alasdair (James) 1934- .... **CLC 41**
See also CA 126; CANR 47, 69; DLB 194; INT 126; MTCW 1, 2

Gray, Amlin 1946- .... **CLC 29**
See also CA 138

Gray, Francine du Plessix 1930- ..... **CLC 22; DAM NOV**
See also BEST 90:3; CA 61-64; CAAS 2; CANR 11, 33, 75, 81; INT CANR-11; MTCW 1, 2

Gray, Simon (James Holliday) 1936- .... **CLC 9, 14, 36**
See also AITN 1; CA 21-24R; CAAS 3; CANR 32, 69; DLB 13; MTCW 1

Gray, Spalding 1941- ..... **CLC 49, 112; DAM POP; DC 7**
See also CA 128; CANR 74; MTCW 2

Gray, Thomas 1716-1771 ... **LC 4, 40; DA; DAB; DAC; DAM MST; PC 2**
See also CDBLB 1660-1789; DA3; DLB 109

Guthrie, Woody .... **CLC 35**
See also Guthrie, Woodrow Wilson
Gutierrez Najera, Manuel 1859-1895
See also HLCS 2
Guy, Rosa (Cuthbert) 1928- .... **CLC 26**
See also AAYA 4, 37; BEST; BW 2; CA
17-20R; CANR 14, 34, 83; CLR 13; DLB
33; JRDA; MAICYA; SATA 14, 62
Gwendolyn
See Bennett, (Enoch) Arnold
H. D. .... **CLC 3, 8, 14, 31, 34, 73; PC 5**
See also Doolittle, Hilda
H. de V.
See Buchan, John
Haavikko, Paavo Juhani 1931- .. **CLC 18, 34**
See also CA 106
Habbema, Koos
See Heijermans, Herman
Habermas, Juergen 1929- .... **CLC 104**
See also CA 109; CANR 85; DLB 242
Habermas, Jürgen
See Habermas, Juergen
Hacker, Marilyn 1942- ...... **CLC 5, 9, 23, 72,**
91; DAM POET
See also CA 77-80; CANR 68; DLB 120;
GLL 2
Hafiz c. 1326-1389 .... **CMLC 34**
Hafiz c. 1326-1389(?) .... **CMLC 34**
Hagiosy, L.
See Larbaud, Valery (Nicolas)
Hagiwara, Sakutaro 1886-1942 .... **PC 18**
See also AW 60
Haig, Fenil
See Ford, Ford Madox
Haig-Brown, Roderick (Langmere)
1908-1976 .... **CLC 21**
See also CA 5-8R; 69-72; CANR 4, 38, 83;
CLR 31; DLB 88; MAICYA; SATA 12
Hailey, Arthur 1920- ..... **CLC 5; DAM NOV,**
POP
See also AITN 2; BEST 90:3; CA 1-4R;
CANR 2, 36, 75; CCA 1; DLB 88; DLBY
82; MTCW 1, 2
Hailey, Elizabeth Forsythe 1938- ..... **CLC 40**
See also CA 93-96; CAAE 188; CAAS 1;
CANR 15, 48; INT CANR-15
Haines, John (Meade) 1924- .... **CLC 58**
See also CA 17-20R; CANR 13, 34; DLB
212
Hakluyt, Richard 1552-1616 .... **LC 31**
Haldeman, Joe (William) 1943- .... **CLC 61**
See also Graham, Robert
See also AAYA 38; CA 53-56, 179; CAAE
179; CAAS 25; CANR 6, 70, 72; DLB 8;
INT CANR-6; SCFW 2
Hale, Sarah Josepha (Buell)
1788-1879 .... **NCLC 75**
See also DLB 1, 42, 73
Haley, Alex(ander Murray Palmer)
1921-1992 . **CLC 8, 12, 76; BLC 2; DA;**
DAB; DAC; DAM MST, MULT, POP
See also AAYA 26; BW 2, 3; CA 77-80;
136; CANR 61; CDALBS; DA3; DLB 38;
MTCW 1, 2
Haliburton, Thomas Chandler
1796-1865 .... **NCLC 15**
See also DLB 11, 99
Hall, Donald (Andrew, Jr.) 1928- ...... **CLC 1,**
13, 37, 59; DAM POET
See also CA 5-8R; CAAS 7; CANR 2, 44,
64; DLB 5; MTCW 1; SATA 23, 97
Hall, Frederic Sauser
See Sauser-Hall, Frederic
Hall, James
See Kuttner, Henry
Hall, Radclyffe 1880-1943
See Hall, (Marguerite) Radclyffe
See also MTCW 2

Hall, Rodney 1935- .... **CLC 51**
See also CA 109; CANR 69
Halleck, Fitz-Greene 1790-1867 .... **NCLC 47**
See also DLB 3
Halliday, Michael
See Creasey, John
Halpern, Daniel 1945- .... **CLC 14**
See also CA 33-36R; CANR 93
Hamburger, Michael (Peter Leopold)
1924- .... **CLC 5, 14**
See also CA 5-8R; CAAS 4; CANR 2, 47;
DLB 27
Hamill, Pete 1935- .... **CLC 10**
See also CA 25-28R; CANR 18, 71
Hamilton, Alexander
1755(?)-1804 .... **NCLC 49**
See also DLB 37
Hamilton, Clive
See Lewis, C(live) S(taples)
Hamilton, Edmond 1904-1977 .... **CLC 1**
See also CA 1-4R; CANR 3, 84; DLB 8;
SATA 118
Hamilton, Eugene (Jacob) Lee
See Lee-Hamilton, Eugene (Jacob)
Hamilton, Franklin
See Silverberg, Robert
Hamilton, Gail
See Corcoran, Barbara
Hamilton, Mollie
See Kaye, M(ary) M(argaret)
Hamilton, (Anthony Walter) Patrick
1904-1962 .... **CLC 51**
See also CA 176; 113; DLB 191
Hamilton, Virginia 1936- ...... **CLC 26; DAM**
MULT
See also AAYA 2, 21; BEST; BW 2, 3; CA
25-28R; CANR 20, 37, 73; CLR 1, 11,
40; DLB 33, 52; INT CANR-20; JRDA;
MAICYA; MTCW 1, 2; SATA 4, 56, 79
Hammett, (Samuel) Dashiell
1894-1961 .... **CLC 3, 5, 10, 19, 47**
See also AITN 1; AMWS 4; AW 17; CA
81-84; CANR 42; CDALB 1929-1941;
DA3; DLB 226; DLBD 6; DLBY 96;
MTCW 1, 2
Hammon, Jupiter 1720(?)-1800(?) . **NCLC 5;**
BLC 2; DAM MULT, POET; PC 16
See also DLB 31, 50
Hammond, Keith
See Kuttner, Henry
Hamner, Earl (Henry), Jr. 1923- ...... **CLC 12**
See also AITN 2; CA 73-76; DLB 6
Hampton, Christopher (James)
1946- .... **CLC 4**
See also CA 25-28R; DLB 13; MTCW 1
Handke, Peter 1942- .... **CLC 5, 8, 10, 15, 38,**
134; DAM DRAM, NOV
See also CA 77-80; CANR 33, 75; CWW
2; DLB 85, 124; MTCW 1, 2
Hanley, James 1901-1985 ..... **CLC 3, 5, 8, 13**
See also CA 73-76; 117; CANR 36; DLB
191; MTCW 1
Hannah, Barry 1942- .... **CLC 23, 38, 90**
See also CA 108; 110; CANR 43, 68; DLB
6, 234; INT CA-110; MTCW 1
Hannon, Ezra
See Hunter, Evan
Hansberry, Lorraine (Vivian)
1930-1965 ..... **CLC 17, 62; BLC 2; DA;**
DAB; DAC; DAM DRAM, MST,
MULT; DC 2
See also AAYA 25; AMWS 4; BW 1, 3; CA
109; 25-28R; CABS 3; CANR 58;
CDALB 1941-1968; DA3; DLB 7, 38;
MTCW 1, 2
Hansen, Joseph 1923- .... **CLC 38**
See also Brock, Rose; Colton, James
See also CA 29-32R; CAAS 17; CANR 16,
44, 66; DLB 226; GLL 1; INT CANR-16

Hansen and Philipson eds. .... **CLC 65**
Hanson, Kenneth O(stlin) 1922- .... **CLC 13**
See also CA 53-56; CANR 7
Hardwick, Elizabeth (Bruce)
1916- .... **CLC 13; DAM NOV**
See also AMWS 3; CA 5-8R; CANR 3, 32,
70; DA3; DLB 6; MTCW 1, 2
Hardy, Thomas 1840-1928 .... **PC 8**
See also AW 4, 10, 18, 32, 48, 53, 72;
BEST; CA 104; 123; CDBLB 1890-1914;
DA; DAB; DAC; DAM MST, NOV,
POET; DA3; DLB 18, 19, 135; MTCW 1,
2
Hare, David 1947- .... **CLC 29, 58, 136**
See also BRWS 4; CA 97-100; CANR 39,
91; DLB 13; MTCW 1
Harewood, John
See Van Druten, John (William)
Harford, Henry
See Hudson, W(illiam) H(enry)
Hargrave, Leonie
See Disch, Thomas M(ichael)
Harjo, Joy 1951- ...... **CLC 83; DAM MULT;**
PC 27
See also CA 114; CANR 35, 67, 91; DLB
120, 175; MTCW 2; NNAL
Harlan, Louis R(udolph) 1922- .... **CLC 34**
See also CA 21-24R; CANR 25, 55, 80
Harling, Robert 1951(?)- .... **CLC 53**
See also CA 147
Harmon, William (Ruth) 1938- .... **CLC 38**
See also CA 33-36R; CANR 14, 32, 35;
SATA 65
Harper, F. E. W.
See Harper, Frances Ellen Watkins
Harper, Frances E. W.
See Harper, Frances Ellen Watkins
Harper, Frances E. Watkins
See Harper, Frances Ellen Watkins
Harper, Frances Ellen
See Harper, Frances Ellen Watkins
Harper, Frances Ellen Watkins
1825-1911 .... **PC 21**
See also AW 14; BLC 2; BW 1, 3; CA 111;
125; CANR 79; DAM MULT, POET;
DLB 50, 221
Harper, Michael S(teven) 1938- ... **CLC 7, 22**
See also BW 1; CA 33-36R; CANR 24;
DLB 41
Harper, Mrs. F. E. W.
See Harper, Frances Ellen Watkins
Harris, Christie (Lucy) Irwin
1907- .... **CLC 12**
See also CA 5-8R; CANR 6, 83; CLR 47;
DLB 88; JRDA; MAICYA; SAAS 10;
SATA 6, 74; SATA-Essay 116
Harris, George Washington
1814-1869 .... **NCLC 23**
See also DLB 3, 11
Harris, John (Wyndham Parkes Lucas)
Beynon 1903-1969
See Wyndham, John
See also CA 102; 89-92; CANR 84; SATA
118
Harris, MacDonald .... **CLC 9**
See also Heiney, Donald (William)
Harris, Mark 1922- .... **CLC 19**
See also CA 5-8R; CAAS 3; CANR 2, 55,
83; DLB 2; DLBY 80
Harris, Norman .... **CLC 65**
Harris, (Theodore) Wilson 1921- ..... **CLC 25**
See also BW 2, 3; CA 65-68; CAAS 16;
CANR 11, 27, 69; DLB 117; MTCW 1
Harrison, Barbara Grizzuti 1934- . **CLC 144**
See also CA 77-80; CANR 15, 48; INT
CANR-15

Henry, Patrick 1736-1799 .... **LC 25**

Henryson, Robert 1430(?)-1506(?) ...... **LC 20**
See also DLB 146

Henry VIII 1491-1547 .... **LC 10**
See also DLB 132

Henschke, Alfred
See Klabund

Hentoff, Nat(han Irving) 1925- .... **CLC 26**
See also AAYA 4; CA 1-4R; CAAS 6;
CANR 5, 25, 77; CLR 1, 52; INT CANR-
25; JRDA; MAICYA; SATA 42, 69;
SATA-Brief 27

Heppenstall, (John) Rayner
1911-1981 .... **CLC 10**
See also CA 1-4R; 103; CANR 29

Heraclitus c. 540B.C.-c. 450B.C. ... **CMLC 22**
See also DLB 176

Herbert, Frank (Patrick)
1920-1986 .... **CLC 12, 23, 35, 44, 85;
DAM POP**
See also AAYA 21; BEST; CA 53-56; 118;
CANR 5, 43; CDALBS; DLB 8; INT
CANR-5; MTCW 1, 2; SATA 9, 37;
SATA-Obit 47; SCFW 2

Herbert, George 1593-1633 ..... **LC 24; DAB;
DAM POET; PC 4**
See also CDBLB Before 1660; DLB 126

Herbert, Zbigniew 1924-1998 ..... **CLC 9, 43;
DAM POET**
See also CA 89-92; 169; CANR 36, 74;
CWW 2; DLB 232; MTCW 1

Herbst, Josephine (Frey)
1897-1969 .... **CLC 34**
See also CA 5-8R; 25-28R; DLB 9

Herder, Johann Gottfried von
1744-1803 .... **NCLC 8**
See also DLB 97

Heredia, Jose Maria 1803-1839
See also HLCS 2

Herlihy, James Leo 1927-1993 .... **CLC 6**
See also CA 1-4R; 143; CANR 2

Hermogenes fl. c. 175- .... **CMLC 6**

Hernandez, Jose 1834-1886 .... **NCLC 17**

Herodotus c. 484B.C.-429B.C. .... **CMLC 17**
See also DLB 176

Herrick, Robert 1591-1674 .... **LC 13; DA;
DAB; DAC; DAM MST, POP; PC 9**
See also DLB 126

Herring, Guilles
See Somerville, Edith

Herriot, James 1916-1995 ...... **CLC 12; DAM POP**
See also Wight, James Alfred
See also AAYA 1; CA 148; CANR 40;
MTCW 2; SATA 86

Herris, Violet
See Hunt, Violet

Herrmann, Dorothy 1941- .... **CLC 44**
See also CA 107

Herrmann, Taffy
See Herrmann, Dorothy

Hersey, John (Richard) 1914-1993 .... **CLC 1,
2, 7, 9, 40, 81, 97; DAM POP**
See also AAYA 29; CA 17-20R; 140; CANR
33; CDALBS; DLB 6, 185; MTCW 1, 2;
SATA 25; SATA-Obit 76

Herzen, Aleksandr Ivanovich
1812-1870 .... **NCLC 10, 61**

Herzog, Werner 1942- .... **CLC 16**
See also CA 89-92

Hesiod c. 8th cent. B.C.- .... **CMLC 5**
See also DLB 176

Hesse, Hermann 1877-1962 ... **CLC 1, 2, 3, 6,
11, 17, 25, 69; DA; DAB; DAC; DAM
MST, NOV**
See also AW 9; BEST; CA 17-18; CAP 2;
DA3; DLB 66; MTCW 1, 2; SATA 50

Hewes, Cady
See De Voto, Bernard (Augustine)

Heyen, William 1940- .... **CLC 13, 18**
See also CA 33-36R; CAAS 9; DLB 5

Heyerdahl, Thor 1914- .... **CLC 26**
See also CA 5-8R; CANR 5, 22, 66, 73;
MTCW 1, 2; SATA 2, 52

Heym, Stefan 1913- .... **CLC 41**
See also CA 9-12R; CANR 4; CWW 2;
DLB 69

Heywood, John 1497-1580 .... **LC 65**

Hibbert, Eleanor Alice Burford
1906-1993 .... **CLC 7; DAM POP**
See also BEST 90:4; CA 17-20R; 140;
CANR 9, 28, 59; MTCW 2; SATA 2;
SATA-Obit 74

Higgins, George V(incent)
1939-1999 .... **CLC 4, 7, 10, 18**
See also CA 77-80; 186; CAAS 5; CANR
17, 51, 89, 96; DLB 2; DLBY 81, 98; INT
CANR-17; MTCW 1

Higgonet, Margaret ed. .... **CLC 65**

Highet, Helen
See MacInnes, Helen (Clark)

Highsmith, (Mary) Patricia
1921-1995 .... **CLC 2, 4, 14, 42, 102;
DAM NOV, POP**
See also Morgan, Claire
See also BRWS 5; CA 1-4R; 147; CANR 1,
20, 48, 62; DA3; MTCW 1, 2

Highwater, Jamake (Mamake)
1942(?)- .... **CLC 12**
See also AAYA 7; CA 65-68; CAAS 7;
CANR 10, 34, 84; CLR 17; DLB 52;
DLBY 85; JRDA; MAICYA; SATA 32,
69; SATA-Brief 30

Highway, Tomson 1951- .... **CLC 92; DAC;
DAM MULT**
See also CA 151; CANR 75; CCA 1;
MTCW 2; NNAL

Hijuelos, Oscar 1951- .... **CLC 65; DAM
MULT, POP; HLC 1**
See also AAYA 25; BEST 90:1; CA 123;
CANR 50, 75; DA3; DLB 145; HW 1, 2;
MTCW 2

Hikmet, Nazim 1902(?)-1963 .... **CLC 40**
See also CA 141; 93-96

Hildegard von Bingen 1098-1179 . **CMLC 20**
See also DLB 148

Hildesheimer, Wolfgang 1916-1991 .. **CLC 49**
See also CA 101; 135; DLB 69, 124

Hill, Geoffrey (William) 1932- ...... **CLC 5, 8,
18, 45; DAM POET**
See also BRWS 5; CA 81-84; CANR 21,
89; CDBLB 1960 to Present; DLB 40;
MTCW 1

Hill, George Roy 1921- .... **CLC 26**
See also CA 110; 122

Hill, John
See Koontz, Dean R(ay)

Hill, Susan (Elizabeth) 1942- .... **CLC 4, 113;
DAB; DAM MST, NOV**
See also CA 33-36R; CANR 29, 69; DLB
14, 139; MTCW 1

Hillard, Asa G. III .... **CLC 70**

Hillerman, Tony 1925- . **CLC 62; DAM POP**
See also AAYA 40; AW 2; BEST; CA 29-
32R; CANR 21, 42, 65, 97; DA3; DLB
206; SATA 6

Hilliard, Noel (Harvey) 1929-1996 ... **CLC 15**
See also CA 9-12R; CANR 7, 69

Hillis, Rick 1956- .... **CLC 66**
See also CA 134

Himes, Chester (Bomar) 1909-1984 .. **CLC 2,
4, 7, 18, 58, 108; BLC 2; DAM MULT**
See also BW 2; CA 25-28R; 114; CANR
22, 89; DLB 2, 76, 143, 226; MTCW 1, 2

Hinde, Thomas .... **CLC 6, 11**
See also Chitty, Thomas Willes

Hine, (William) Daryl 1936- .... **CLC 15**
See also CA 1-4R; CAAS 15; CANR 1, 20;
DLB 60

Hinkson, Katharine Tynan
See Tynan, Katharine

Hinojosa(-Smith), Rolando (R.) 1929-
See also CA 131; CAAS 16; CANR 62;
DAM MULT; DLB 82; HLC 1; HW 1, 2;
MTCW 2

Hinton, S(usan) E(loise) 1950- .... **CLC 30,
111; DA; DAB; DAC; DAM MST,
NOV**
See also AAYA 2, 33; CA 81-84; CANR
32, 62, 92; CDALBS; CLR 3, 23; DA3;
JRDA; MAICYA; MTCW 1, 2; SATA 19,
58, 115

Hiraoka, Kimitake 1925-1970
See Mishima, Yukio
See also CA 97-100; 29-32R; DAM DRAM;
DA3; MTCW 1, 2

Hirsch, E(ric) D(onald), Jr. 1928- .... **CLC 79**
See also CA 25-28R; CANR 27, 51; DLB
67; INT CANR-27; MTCW 1

Hirsch, Edward 1950- .... **CLC 31, 50**
See also CA 104; CANR 20, 42; DLB 120

Hitchcock, Alfred (Joseph)
1899-1980 .... **CLC 16**
See also AAYA 22; CA 159; 97-100; SATA
27; SATA-Obit 24

Hoagland, Edward 1932- .... **CLC 28**
See also AW 2; CA 1-4R; CANR 2, 31, 57;
DLB 6; SATA 51

Hoban, Russell (Conwell) 1925- . **CLC 7, 25;
DAM NOV**
See also CA 5-8R; CANR 23, 37, 66; CLR
3, 69; DLB 52; MAICYA; MTCW 1, 2;
SATA 1, 40, 78

Hobbes, Thomas 1588-1679 .... **LC 36**
See also DLB 151

Hobbs, Perry
See Blackmur, R(ichard) P(almer)

Hobson, Laura Z(ametkin)
1900-1986 .... **CLC 7, 25**
See also Field, Peter
See also CA 17-20R; 118; CANR 55; DLB
28; SATA 52

Hoch, Edward D(entinger) 1930-
See Queen, Ellery
See also CA 29-32R; CANR 11, 27, 51, 97

Hochhuth, Rolf 1931- .. **CLC 4, 11, 18; DAM
DRAM**
See also CA 5-8R; CANR 33, 75; CWW 2;
DLB 124; MTCW 1, 2

Hochman, Sandra 1936- .... **CLC 3, 8**
See also CA 5-8R; DLB 5

Hochwaelder, Fritz 1911-1986 .... **CLC 36;
DAM DRAM**
See also CA 29-32R; 120; CANR 42;
MTCW 1

Hochwalder, Fritz
See Hochwaelder, Fritz

Hocking, Mary (Eunice) 1921- .... **CLC 13**
See also CA 101; CANR 18, 40

Hodgins, Jack 1938- .... **CLC 23**
See also CA 93-96; DLB 60

Hoeg, Peter 1957- .... **CLC 95**
See also CA 151; CANR 75; DA3; MTCW
2

Hoffman, Alice 1952- ... **CLC 51; DAM NOV**
See also AAYA 37; CA 77-80; CANR 34,
66; MTCW 1, 2

Hoffman, Daniel (Gerard) 1923- . **CLC 6, 13,
23**
See also CA 1-4R; CANR 4; DLB 5

Hoffman, Stanley 1944- .... **CLC 5**
See also CA 77-80

Hoffman, William 1925- .... **CLC 141**
See also CA 21-24R; CANR 9; DLB 234

Hughes, Ted 1930-1998 . **CLC 2, 4, 9, 14, 37, 119; DAB; DAC; PC 7**
See also Hughes, Edward James
See also BEST; BRWS 1; CA 1-4R; 171; CANR 1, 33, 66; CLR 3; DLB 40, 161; MAICYA; MTCW 1, 2; SATA 49; SATA-Brief 27; SATA-Obit 107

Hugo, Richard F(ranklin) 1923-1982 .... **CLC 6, 18, 32; DAM POET**
See also CA 49-52; 108; CANR 3; DLB 5, 206

Hugo, Victor (Marie) 1802-1885 .... **NCLC 3, 10, 21; DA; DAB; DAC; DAM DRAM, MST, NOV, POET; PC 17**
See also AAYA 28; BEST; DA3; DLB 119, 192; SATA 47

Huidobro, Vicente
See Huidobro Fernandez, Vicente Garcia

Hulme, Keri 1947- .... **CLC 39, 130**
See also CA 125; CANR 69; INT 125

Hume, David 1711-1776 .... **LC 7, 56**
See also BRWS 3; DLB 104

Humphrey, William 1924-1997 .... **CLC 45**
See also AW 2; CA 77-80; 160; CANR 68; DLB 212

Humphreys, Emyr Owen 1919- .... **CLC 47**
See also CA 5-8R; CANR 3, 24; DLB 15

Humphreys, Josephine 1945- ..... **CLC 34, 57**
See also CA 121; 127; CANR 97; INT 127

Hungerford, Pixie
See Brinsmead, H(esba) F(ay)

Hunt, E(verette) Howard, (Jr.) 1918- .... **CLC 3**
See also AITN 1; CA 45-48; CANR 2, 47

Hunt, Francesca
See Holland, Isabelle

Hunt, Howard
See Hunt, E(verette) Howard, (Jr.)

Hunt, Kyle
See Creasey, John

Hunt, (James Henry) Leigh 1784-1859 .... **NCLC 1, 70; DAM POET**
See also DLB 96, 110, 144

Hunt, Marsha 1946- .... **CLC 70**
See also BW 2, 3; CA 143; CANR 79

Hunter, E. Waldo
See Sturgeon, Theodore (Hamilton)

Hunter, Evan 1926- .... **CLC 11, 31; DAM POP**
See also AAYA 39; CA 5-8R; CANR 5, 38, 62, 97; DLBY 82; INT CANR-5; MTCW 1; SATA 25

Hunter, Kristin (Eggleston) 1931- .... **CLC 35**
See also AITN 1; BEST; BW 1; CA 13-16R; CANR 13; CLR 3; DLB 33; INT CANR-13; MAICYA; SAAS 10; SATA 12

Hunter, Mary
See Austin, Mary (Hunter)

Hunter, Mollie 1922- .... **CLC 21**
See also McIlwraith, Maureen Mollie Hunter
See also AAYA 13; BEST; CANR 37, 78; CLR 25; DLB 161; JRDA; MAICYA; SAAS 7; SATA 54, 106

Hunter, Robert (?)-1734 .... **LC 7**

Hurston, Zora Neale 1891-1960 .. **CLC 7, 30, 61; BLC 2; DA; DAC; DAM MST, MULT, NOV; DC 12**
See also AAYA 15; AW 1,6,11; BEST; BW 1, 3; CA 85-88; CANR 61; CDALBS; DA3; DLB 51, 86; MTCW 1, 2

Husserl, E. G.
See Husserl, Edmund (Gustav Albrecht)

Huston, John (Marcellus) 1906-1987 .... **CLC 20**
See also CA 73-76; 123; CANR 34; DLB 26

Hustvedt, Siri 1955- .... **CLC 76**
See also CA 137

Hutten, Ulrich von 1488-1523 .... **LC 16**
See also DLB 179

Huxley, Aldous (Leonard) 1894-1963 .... **CLC 1, 3, 4, 5, 8, 11, 18, 35, 79; DA; DAB; DAC; DAM MST, NOV**
See also AAYA 11; AW 39; BEST; CA 85-88; CANR 44; CDBLB 1914-1945; DA3; DLB 36, 100, 162, 195; MTCW 1, 2; SATA 63; SCFW 2

Huxley, T(homas) H(enry) 1825-1895 .... **NCLC 67**
See also DLB 57

Hwang, David Henry 1957- .. **CLC 55; DAM DRAM; DC 4**
See also CA 127; 132; CANR 76; DA3; DLB 212; INT 132; MTCW 2

Hyde, Anthony 1946- .... **CLC 42**
See also Chase, Nicholas
See also CA 136; CCA 1

Hyde, Margaret O(ldroyd) 1917- ..... **CLC 21**
See also CA 1-4R; CANR 1, 36; CLR 23; JRDA; MAICYA; SAAS 8; SATA 1, 42, 76

Hynes, James 1956(?)- .... **CLC 65**
See also CA 164

Hypatia c. 370-415 .... **CMLC 35**

Ian, Janis 1951- .... **CLC 21**
See also CA 105; 187

Ibanez, Vicente Blasco
See Blasco Iba

Ibarbourou, Juana de 1895-1979
See also HLCS 2; HW 1

Ibarguengoitia, Jorge 1928-1983 ...... **CLC 37**
See also CA 124; 113; HW 1

Ibsen, Henrik (Johan) 1828-1906 .... **DC 2**
See also AW 2, 8, 16, 37, 52; BEST; CA 104; 141; DA; DAB; DAC; DAM DRAM, MST; DA3

Ibuse, Masuji 1898-1993 .... **CLC 22**
See also CA 127; 141; DLB 180

Ichikawa, Kon 1915- .... **CLC 20**
See also CA 121

Ichiyo, Higuchi 1872-1896 .... **NCLC 49**

Idle, Eric 1943-2000 .... **CLC 21**
See also Monty Python
See also CA 116; CANR 35, 91

Ignatow, David 1914-1997 .. **CLC 4, 7, 14, 40**
See also CA 9-12R; 162; CAAS 3; CANR 31, 57, 96; DLB 5

Ignotus
See Strachey, (Giles) Lytton

Ihimaera, Witi 1944- .... **CLC 46**
See also CA 77-80

Illyes, Gyula 1902-1983 .... **PC 16**
See also CA 114; 109; DLB 215

Immermann, Karl (Lebrecht) 1796-1840 .... **NCLC 4, 49**
See also DLB 133

Inchbald, Elizabeth 1753-1821 ...... **NCLC 62**
See also DLB 39, 89

Inclan, Ramon (Maria) del Valle
See Valle-Inclan, Ramon (Maria) del

Infante, G(uillermo) Cabrera
See Cabrera Infante, G(uillermo)

Ingalls, Rachel (Holmes) 1940- .... **CLC 42**
See also CA 123; 127

Ingamells, Reginald Charles
See Ingamells, Rex

Inge, William (Motter) 1913-1973 ..... **CLC 1, 8, 19; DAM DRAM**
See also CA 9-12R; CDALB 1941-1968; DA3; DLB 7; MTCW 1, 2

Ingelow, Jean 1820-1897 .... **NCLC 39**
See also DLB 35, 163; SATA 33

Ingram, Willis J.
See Harris, Mark

Innaurato, Albert (F.) 1948(?)- ... **CLC 21, 60**
See also CA 115; 122; CANR 78; INT 122

Innes, Michael
See Stewart, J(ohn) I(nnes) M(ackintosh)

Ionesco, Eugene 1912-1994 ... **CLC 1, 4, 6, 9, 11, 15, 41, 86; DA; DAB; DAC; DAM DRAM, MST; DC 12**
See also BEST; CA 9-12R; 144; CANR 55; CWW 2; DA3; MTCW 1, 2; SATA 7; SATA-Obit 79

Ireland, Patrick
See O'Doherty, Brian

Irenaeus St. 130- .... **CMLC 42**

Iron, Ralph
See Schreiner, Olive (Emilie Albertina)

Irving, John (Winslow) 1942- ... **CLC 13, 23, 38, 112; DAM NOV, POP**
See also AAYA 8; AMWS 6; BEST 89:3; CA 25-28R; CANR 28, 73; DA3; DLB 6; DLBY 82; MTCW 1, 2

Irving, Washington 1783-1859 . **NCLC 2, 19, 95; DA; DAB; DAC; DAM MST**
See also AW 1, 8; BEST; CDALB 1640-1865; DA3; DLB 3, 11, 30, 59, 73, 74, 186

Irwin, P. K.
See Page, P(atricia) K(athleen)

Isaacs, Jorge Ricardo 1837-1895 ... **NCLC 70**

Isaacs, Susan 1943- .... **CLC 32; DAM POP**
See also BEST 89:1; CA 89-92; CANR 20, 41, 65; DA3; INT CANR-20; MTCW 1, 2

Isherwood, Christopher (William Bradshaw) 1904-1986 .. **CLC 1, 9, 11, 14, 44; DAM DRAM, NOV**
See also CA 13-16R; 117; CANR 35, 97; DA3; DLB 15, 195; DLBY 86; MTCW 1, 2

Ishiguro, Kazuo 1954- . **CLC 27, 56, 59, 110; DAM NOV**
See also BEST 90:2; BRWS 4; CA 120; CANR 49, 95; DA3; DLB 194; MTCW 1, 2

Ishikawa, Hakuhin
See Ishikawa, Takuboku

Ishikawa, Takuboku 1886(?)-1912 .... **PC 10**
See also AW 15; CA 113; 153; DAM POET

Iskander, Fazil 1929- .... **CLC 47**
See also CA 102

Isler, Alan (David) 1934- .... **CLC 91**
See also CA 156

Ivan IV 1530-1584 .... **LC 17**

Ivask, Ivar Vidrik 1927-1992 .... **CLC 14**
See also CA 37-40R; 139; CANR 24

Ives, Morgan
See Bradley, Marion Zimmer
See also GLL 1

Izumi Shikibu c. 973-c. 1034 .... **CMLC 33**

J .... **CLC 10, 36, 86; DAM NOV**
See also AW 20; CA 97-100; CANR 36, 50, 74; DA3; DLB 182; DLBY 94; MTCW 1, 2

J. R. S.
See Gogarty, Oliver St. John

Jabran, Kahlil
See Gibran, Kahlil

Jabran, Khalil
See Gibran, Kahlil

Jackson, Daniel
See Wingrove, David (John)

Jackson, Helen Hunt 1830-1885 .... **NCLC 90**
See also DLB 42, 47, 186, 189

Jackson, Jesse 1908-1983 .... **CLC 12**
See also BW 1; CA 25-28R; 109; CANR 27; CLR 28; MAICYA; SATA 2, 29; SATA-Obit 48

Kipling, (Joseph) Rudyard 1865-1936 .. **PC 3**
See also AAYA 32; BEST; CA 105; 120; CANR 33; CDBLB 1890-1914; CLR 39, 65; DA; DAB; DAC; DAM MST, POET; DA3; DLB 19, 34, 141, 156; MAICYA; MTCW 1, 2; SATA 100

Kirkland, Caroline M. 1801-1864 . **NCLC 85**
See also DLB 3, 73, 74; DLBD 13

Kirkup, James 1918- .... **CLC 1**
See also CA 1-4R; CAAS 4; CANR 2; DLB 27; SATA 12

Kirkwood, James 1930(?)-1989 .... **CLC 9**
See also AITN 2; CA 1-4R; 128; CANR 6, 40; GLL 2

Kirshner, Sidney
See Kingsley, Sidney

Kis, Danilo 1935-1989 .... **CLC 57**
See also CA 109; 118; 129; CANR 61; DLB 181; MTCW 1

Kissinger, Henry A(lfred) 1923- ..... **CLC 137**
See also CA 1-4R; CANR 2, 33, 66; MTCW 1

Kivi, Aleksis 1834-1872 .... **NCLC 30**

Kizer, Carolyn (Ashley) 1925- .. **CLC 15, 39, 80; DAM POET**
See also CA 65-68; CAAS 5; CANR 24, 70; DLB 5, 169; MTCW 2

Klappert, Peter 1942- .... **CLC 57**
See also CA 33-36R; DLB 5

Klein, A(braham) M(oses)
1909-1972 . **CLC 19; DAB; DAC; DAM MST**
See also CA 101; 37-40R; DLB 68

Klein, Norma 1938-1989 .... **CLC 30**
See also AAYA 2, 35; BEST; CA 41-44R; 128; CANR 15, 37; CLR 2, 19; INT CANR-15; JRDA; MAICYA; SAAS 1; SATA 7, 57

Klein, T(heodore) E(ibon) D(onald)
1947- .... **CLC 34**
See also CA 119; CANR 44, 75

Kleist, Heinrich von 1777-1811 ...... **NCLC 2, 37; DAM DRAM**
See also AW 22; DLB 90

Klima, Ivan 1931- .... **CLC 56; DAM NOV**
See also CA 25-28R; CANR 17, 50, 91; CWW 2; DLB 232

Klinger, Friedrich Maximilian von
1752-1831 .... **NCLC 1**
See also DLB 94

Klingsor the Magician
See Hartmann, Sadakichi

Klopstock, Friedrich Gottlieb
1724-1803 .... **NCLC 11**
See also DLB 97

Knapp, Caroline 1959- .... **CLC 99**
See also CA 154

Knebel, Fletcher 1911-1993 .... **CLC 14**
See also AITN 1; CA 1-4R; 140; CAAS 3; CANR 1, 36; SATA 36; SATA-Obit 75

Knickerbocker, Diedrich
See Irving, Washington

Knight, Etheridge 1931-1991 . **CLC 40; BLC 2; DAM POET; PC 14**
See also BW 1, 3; CA 21-24R; 133; CANR 23, 82; DLB 41; MTCW 2

Knight, Sarah Kemble 1666-1727 .... **LC 7**
See also DLB 24, 200

Knowles, John 1926- . **CLC 1, 4, 10, 26; DA; DAC; DAM MST, NOV**
See also AAYA 10; BEST; CA 17-20R; CANR 40, 74, 76; CDALB 1968-1988; DLB 6; MTCW 1, 2; SATA 8, 89

Knox, Calvin M.
See Silverberg, Robert

Knox, John c. 1505-1572 .... **LC 37**
See also DLB 132

Knye, Cassandra
See Disch, Thomas M(ichael)

Koch, C(hristopher) J(ohn) 1932- .... **CLC 42**
See also CA 127; CANR 84

Koch, Christopher
See Koch, C(hristopher) J(ohn)

Koch, Kenneth 1925- .... **CLC 5, 8, 44; DAM POET**
See also CA 1-4R; CANR 6, 36, 57, 97; DLB 5; INT CANR-36; MTCW 2; SATA 65

Kochanowski, Jan 1530-1584 .... **LC 10**

Kock, Charles Paul de 1794-1871 . **NCLC 16**

Koda Rohan
See Koda Shigeyuki

Koestler, Arthur 1905-1983 ... **CLC 1, 3, 6, 8, 15, 33**
See also BRWS 1; CA 1-4R; 109; CANR 1, 33; CDBLB 1945-1960; DLBY 83; MTCW 1, 2

Kogawa, Joy Nozomi 1935- ..... **CLC 78, 129; DAC; DAM MST, MULT**
See also CA 101; CANR 19, 62; MTCW 2; SATA 99

Kohout, Pavel 1928- .... **CLC 13**
See also CA 45-48; CANR 3

Koizumi, Yakumo
See Hearn, (Patricio) Lafcadio (Tessima Carlos)

Komunyakaa, Yusef 1947- .... **CLC 86, 94; BLCS**
See also CA 147; CANR 83; DLB 120

Konrad, George
See Konr
See also CWW 2

Konrád, György 1933- .... **CLC 4, 10, 73**
See also Konrad, George
See also CA 85-88; CANR 97; CWW 2; DLB 232

Konwicki, Tadeusz 1926- .... **CLC 8, 28, 54, 117**
See also CA 101; CAAS 9; CANR 39, 59; CWW 2; DLB 232; IDFW 3; MTCW 1

Koontz, Dean R(ay) 1945- .... **CLC 78; DAM NOV, POP**
See also AAYA 9, 31; BEST; CA 108; CANR 19, 36, 52, 95; DA3; MTCW 1; SATA 92

Kopernik, Mikolaj
See Copernicus, Nicolaus

Kopit, Arthur (Lee) 1937- ..... **CLC 1, 18, 33; DAM DRAM**
See also AITN 1; CA 81-84; CABS 3; DLB 7; MTCW 1

Kops, Bernard 1926- .... **CLC 4**
See also CA 5-8R; CANR 84; DLB 13

Korolenko, V. G.
See Korolenko, Vladimir Galaktionovich

Korolenko, Vladimir
See Korolenko, Vladimir Galaktionovich

Korolenko, Vladimir G.
See Korolenko, Vladimir Galaktionovich

Kosinski, Jerzy (Nikodem)
1933-1991 .... **CLC 1, 2, 3, 6, 10, 15, 53, 70; DAM NOV**
See also AMWS 7; CA 17-20R; 134; CANR 9, 46; DA3; DLB 2; DLBY 82; MTCW 1, 2

Kostelanetz, Richard (Cory) 1940- .. **CLC 28**
See also CA 13-16R; CAAS 8; CANR 38, 77

Kotlowitz, Robert 1924- .... **CLC 4**
See also CA 33-36R; CANR 36

Kotzebue, August (Friedrich Ferdinand) von
1761-1819 .... **NCLC 25**
See also DLB 94

Kotzwinkle, William 1938- ..... **CLC 5, 14, 35**
See also BEST; CA 45-48; CANR 3, 44, 84; CLR 6; DLB 173; MAICYA; SATA 24, 70

Kowna, Stancy
See Szymborska, Wislawa

Kozol, Jonathan 1936- .... **CLC 17**
See also CA 61-64; CANR 16, 45, 96

Kozoll, Michael 1940(?)- .... **CLC 35**

Kramer, Kathryn 19(?)- .... **CLC 34**

Kramer, Larry 1935- .. **CLC 42; DAM POP; DC 8**
See also CA 124; 126; CANR 60; GLL 1

Krasicki, Ignacy 1735-1801 .... **NCLC 8**

Krasinski, Zygmunt 1812-1859 .... **NCLC 4**

Kristeva, Julia 1941- .... **CLC 77, 140**
See also CA 154; DLB 242

Kristofferson, Kris 1936- .... **CLC 26**
See also CA 104

Krizanc, John 1956- .... **CLC 57**
See also CA 187

Krleza, Miroslav 1893-1981 .... **CLC 8, 114**
See also CA 97-100; 105; CANR 50; DLB 147

Kroetsch, Robert 1927- . **CLC 5, 23, 57, 132; DAC; DAM POET**
See also CA 17-20R; CANR 8, 38; CCA 1; DLB 53; MTCW 1

Kroetz, Franz
See Kroetz, Franz Xaver

Kroetz, Franz Xaver 1946- .... **CLC 41**
See also CA 130

Kroker, Arthur (W.) 1945- .... **CLC 77**
See also CA 161

Krotkov, Yuri 1917- .... **CLC 19**
See also CA 102

Krumb
See Crumb, R(obert)

Krumgold, Joseph (Quincy)
1908-1980 .... **CLC 12**
See also BEST; CA 9-12R; 101; CANR 7; MAICYA; SATA 1, 48; SATA-Obit 23

Krumwitz
See Crumb, R(obert)

Krutch, Joseph Wood 1893-1970 ..... **CLC 24**
See also CA 1-4R; 25-28R; CANR 4; DLB 63, 206

Krutzch, Gus
See Eliot, T(homas) S(tearns)

Krylov, Ivan Andreevich
1768(?)-1844 .... **NCLC 1**
See also DLB 150

Kubrick, Stanley 1928-1999 .... **CLC 16**
See also AAYA 30; CA 81-84; 177; CANR 33; DLB 26

Kueng, Hans 1928-
See Kung, Hans
See also CA 53-56; CANR 66; MTCW 1, 2

Kumin, Maxine (Winokur) 1925- ..... **CLC 5, 13, 28; DAM POET; PC 15**
See also AITN 2; AMWS 4; CA 1-4R; CAAS 8; CANR 1, 21, 69; DA3; DLB 5; MTCW 1, 2; SATA 12

Kundera, Milan 1929- . **CLC 4, 9, 19, 32, 68, 115, 135; DAM NOV**
See also AAYA 2; AW 10; CA 85-88; CANR 19, 52, 74; CWW 2; DA3; DLB 232; MTCW 1, 2

Kunene, Mazisi (Raymond) 1930- ... **CLC 85**
See also BW 1, 3; CA 125; CANR 81; DLB 117

Kung, Hans .... **CLC 130**
See also Kueng, Hans

Kunitz, Stanley (Jasspon) 1905- .. **CLC 6, 11, 14; PC 19**
See also AMWS 3; CA 41-44R; CANR 26, 57; DA3; DLB 48; INT CANR-26; MTCW 1, 2

Kunze, Reiner 1933- .... **CLC 10**
See also CA 93-96; CWW 2; DLB 75

Kureishi, Hanif 1954(?)- .... **CLC 64, 135**
See also CA 139; DLB 194; GLL 2

Kurosawa, Akira 1910-1998 .... **CLC 16, 119;**
DAM MULT
See also AAYA 11; CA 101; 170; CANR 46
Kushner, Tony 1957(?)- .... **CLC 81; DAM**
DRAM; DC 10
See also CA 144; CANR 74; DA3; DLB
228; GLL 1; MTCW 2
Kuzma, Greg 1944- .... **CLC 7**
See also CA 33-36R; CANR 70
Kyd, Thomas 1558-1594 .... **LC 22; DAM**
DRAM; DC 3
See also DLB 62
Kyprianos, Iossif
See Samarakis, Antonis
La Bruyere, Jean de 1645-1696 .... **LC 17**
Lacan, Jacques (Marie Emile)
1901-1981 .... **CLC 75**
See also CA 121; 104
Laclos, Pierre Ambroise Francois Choderlos
de 1741-1803 .... **NCLC 4, 87**
La Colere, Francois
See Aragon, Louis
Lacolere, Francois
See Aragon, Louis
La Deshabilleuse
See Simenon, Georges (Jacques Christian)
Lady Gregory
See Gregory, Isabella Augusta (Persse)
Lady of Quality, A
See Bagnold, Enid
La Fayette, Marie (Madelaine Pioche de la
Vergne Comtes 1634-1693 .... **LC 2**
Lafayette, Rene
See Hubbard, L(afayette) Ron(ald)
La Fontaine, Jean de 1621-1695 .... **LC 50**
See also MAICYA; SATA 18
Laforgue, Jules 1860-1887 . **NCLC 5, 53; PC**
14
See also AW 20
Lagerkvist, Paer (Fabian)
1891-1974 ...... **CLC 7, 10, 13, 54; DAM**
DRAM, NOV
See also Lagerkvist, Par
See also CA 85-88; 49-52; DA3; MTCW 1,
2
Lagerkvist, Par
See Lagerkvist, Paer (Fabian)
See also AW 12; MTCW 2
Lagerkwist, Pär
See Lagerkvist, Paer (Fabian)
Lagerlof, Selma (Ottiliana Lovisa)
See Lagerloef, Selma (Ottiliana Lovisa)
See also CLR 7; SATA 15
La Guma, (Justin) Alex(ander)
1925-1985 .... **CLC 19; BLCS; DAM**
NOV
See also BW 1, 3; CA 49-52; 118; CANR
25, 81; DLB 117, 225; MTCW 1, 2
Laidlaw, A. K.
See Grieve, C(hristopher) M(urray)
Lainez, Manuel Mujica
See Mujica Lainez, Manuel
See also HW 1
Laing, R(onald) D(avid) 1927-1989 . **CLC 95**
See also CA 107; 129; CANR 34; MTCW 1
Lamartine, Alphonse (Marie Louis Prat) de
1790-1869 . **NCLC 11; DAM POET; PC**
16
Lamb, Charles 1775-1834 ..... **NCLC 10; DA;**
DAB; DAC; DAM MST
See also BEST; CDBLB 1789-1832; DLB
93, 107, 163; SATA 17
Lamb, Lady Caroline 1785-1828 ... **NCLC 38**
See also DLB 116
Lamming, George (William) 1927- ... **CLC 2,**
4, 66, 144; BLC 2; DAM MULT
See also BW 2, 3; CA 85-88; CANR 26,
76; DLB 125; MTCW 1, 2

L'Amour, Louis (Dearborn)
1908-1988 ...... **CLC 25, 55; DAM NOV,**
POP
See also Burns, Tex; Mayo, Jim
See also AAYA 16; AITN 2; BEST 89:2;
CA 1-4R; 125; CANR 3, 25, 40; DA3;
DLB 206; DLBY 80; MTCW 1, 2
Lampman, Archibald 1861-1899 ... **NCLC 25**
See also DLB 92
Lancaster, Bruce 1896-1963 .... **CLC 36**
See also CA 9-10; CANR 70; CAP 1; SATA
9
Lanchester, John .... **CLC 99**
Landau, Mark Alexandrovich
See Aldanov, Mark (Alexandrovich)
Landau-Aldanov, Mark Alexandrovich
See Aldanov, Mark (Alexandrovich)
Landis, Jerry
See Simon, Paul (Frederick)
Landis, John 1950- .... **CLC 26**
See also CA 112; 122
Landolfi, Tommaso 1908-1979 .... **CLC 11, 49**
See also CA 127; 117; DLB 177
Landon, Letitia Elizabeth
1802-1838 .... **NCLC 15**
See also DLB 96
Landor, Walter Savage
1775-1864 .... **NCLC 14**
See also DLB 93, 107
Landwirth, Heinz 1927-
See Lind, Jakov
See also CA 9-12R; CANR 7
Lane, Patrick 1939- ... **CLC 25; DAM POET**
See also CA 97-100; CANR 54; DLB 53;
INT 97-100
Lang, Fritz 1890-1976 .... **CLC 20, 103**
See also CA 77-80; 69-72; CANR 30
Lange, John
See Crichton, (John) Michael
Langer, Elinor 1939- .... **CLC 34**
See also CA 121
Langland, William 1332(?)-1400(?) ... **LC 19;**
DA; DAB; DAC; DAM MST, POET
See also DLB 146
Langstaff, Launcelot
See Irving, Washington
Lanier, Sidney 1842-1881 ..... **NCLC 6; DAM**
POET
See also AMWS 1; DLB 64; DLBD 13;
MAICYA; SATA 18
Lanyer, Aemilia 1569-1645 .... **LC 10, 30**
See also DLB 121
Lao-Tzu
See Lao Tzu
Lao Tzu fl. 6046th cent. B.C.-490 ... **CMLC 7**
Lapine, James (Elliot) 1949- .... **CLC 39**
See also CA 123; 130; CANR 54; INT 130
Lardner, Ring
See Lardner, Ring(gold) W(ilmer)
Lardner, Ring W., Jr.
See Lardner, Ring(gold) W(ilmer)
Laredo, Betty
See Codrescu, Andrei
Larkin, Maia
See Wojciechowska, Maia (Teresa)
Larkin, Philip (Arthur) 1922-1985 ... **CLC 3,**
5, 8, 9, 13, 18, 33, 39, 64; DAB; DAM
MST, POET; PC 21
See also BRWS 1; CA 5-8R; 117; CANR
24, 62; CDBLB 1960 to Present; DA3;
DLB 27; MTCW 1, 2
Larra (y Sanchez de Castro), Mariano Jose
de 1809-1837 .... **NCLC 17**
Larsen, Eric 1941- .... **CLC 55**
See also CA 132

Larsen, Nella 1893-1963 .... **CLC 37; BLC 2;**
DAM MULT
See also BW 1; CA 125; CANR 83; DLB
51
Larson, Charles R(aymond) 1938- ... **CLC 31**
See also CA 53-56; CANR 4
Larson, Jonathan 1961-1996 .... **CLC 99**
See also AAYA 28; CA 156
Las Casas, Bartolome de 1474-1566 ... **LC 31**
Lasch, Christopher 1932-1994 .... **CLC 102**
See also CA 73-76; 144; CANR 25; MTCW
1, 2
Latham, Jean Lee 1902-1995 .... **CLC 12**
See also AITN 1; BEST; CA 5-8R; CANR
7, 84; CLR 50; MAICYA; SATA 2, 68
Latham, Mavis
See Clark, Mavis Thorpe
Lathen, Emma .... **CLC 2**
See also Hennissart, Martha; Latsis, Mary
J(ane)
Lathrop, Francis
See Leiber, Fritz (Reuter, Jr.)
Latsis, Mary J(ane) 1927(?)-1997
See Lathen, Emma
See also CA 85-88; 162
Lattimore, Richmond (Alexander)
1906-1984 .... **CLC 3**
See also CA 1-4R; 112; CANR 1
Laughlin, James 1914-1997 .... **CLC 49**
See also CA 21-24R; 162; CAAS 22; CANR
9, 47; DLB 48; DLBY 96, 97
Laurence, (Jean) Margaret (Wemyss)
1926-1987 . **CLC 3, 6, 13, 50, 62; DAC;**
DAM MST
See also AW 7; CA 5-8R; 121; CANR 33;
DLB 53; MTCW 1, 2; SATA-Obit 50
Laurent, Antoine 1952- .... **CLC 50**
Lauscher, Hermann
See Hesse, Hermann
Lautreamont, Comte de
1846-1870 .... **NCLC 12**
See also AW 14
Laverty, Donald
See Blish, James (Benjamin)
Lavin, Mary 1912-1996 .... **CLC 4, 18, 99**
See also AW 4; CA 9-12R; 151; CANR 33;
DLB 15; MTCW 1
Lavond, Paul Dennis
See Kornbluth, C(yril) M.; Pohl, Frederik
Lawler, Raymond Evenor 1922- .... **CLC 58**
See also CA 103
Lawrence, T(homas) E(dward) 1888-1935
See Dale, Colin
See also AW 18; BRWS 2; CA 115; 167;
DLB 195
Lawrence of Arabia
See Lawrence, T(homas) E(dward)
Lawton, Dennis
See Faust, Frederick (Schiller)
Laxness, Halldor .... **CLC 25**
See also Gudjonsson, Halldor Kiljan
Layamon fl. c. 1200- .... **CMLC 10**
See also DLB 146
Laye, Camara 1928-1980 ... **CLC 4, 38; BLC**
2; DAM MULT
See also BW 1; CA 85-88; 97-100; CANR
25; MTCW 1, 2
Layton, Irving (Peter) 1912- .... **CLC 2, 15;**
DAC; DAM MST, POET
See also CA 1-4R; CANR 2, 33, 43, 66;
DLB 88; MTCW 1, 2
Lazarus, Emma 1849-1887 .... **NCLC 8**
Lazarus, Felix
See Cable, George Washington
Lazarus, Henry
See Slavitt, David R(ytman)
Lea, Joan
See Neufeld, John (Arthur)

Lear, Edward 1812-1888 .... **NCLC 3**
See also CLR 1; DLB 32, 163, 166; MAI-
CYA; SATA 18, 100
Lear, Norman (Milton) 1922- .... **CLC 12**
See also CA 73-76
Leavis, F(rank) R(aymond)
1895-1978 .... **CLC 24**
See also CA 21-24R; 77-80; CANR 44;
DLB 242; MTCW 1, 2
Leavitt, David 1961- ..... **CLC 34; DAM POP**
See also CA 116; 122; CANR 50, 62; DA3;
DLB 130; GLL 1; INT 122; MTCW 2
Lebowitz, Fran(ces Ann) 1951(?)- ... **CLC 11,
36**
See also CA 81-84; CANR 14, 60, 70; INT
CANR-14; MTCW 1
Lebrecht, Peter
See Tieck, (Johann) Ludwig
le Carre, John .... **CLC 3, 5, 9, 15, 28**
See also Cornwell, David (John Moore)
See also BEST 89:4; BRWS 2; CDBLB
1960 to Present; DLB 87; MTCW 2
Le Clezio, J(ean) M(arie) G(ustave)
1940- .... **CLC 31**
See also CA 116; 128; DLB 83
Leconte de Lisle, Charles-Marie-Rene
1818-1894 .... **NCLC 29**
Le Coq, Monsieur
See Simenon, Georges (Jacques Christian)
Leduc, Violette 1907-1972 .... **CLC 22**
See also CA 13-14; 33-36R; CANR 69;
CAP 1; GLL 1
Lee, Andrea 1953- ... **CLC 36; BLC 2; DAM
MULT**
See also BW 1, 3; CA 125; CANR 82
Lee, Andrew
See Auchincloss, Louis (Stanton)
Lee, Chang-rae 1965- .... **CLC 91**
See also CA 148; CANR 89
Lee, Don L. .... **CLC 2**
See also Madhubuti, Haki R.
Lee, George W(ashington)
1894-1976 .... **CLC 52; BLC 2; DAM
MULT**
See also BW 1; CA 125; CANR 83; DLB
51
Lee, (Nelle) Harper 1926- . **CLC 12, 60; DA;
DAB; DAC; DAM MST, NOV**
See also AAYA 13; CA 13-16R; CANR 51;
CDALB 1941-1968; DA3; DLB 6;
MTCW 1, 2; SATA 11
Lee, Helen Elaine 1959(?)- .... **CLC 86**
See also CA 148
Lee, John .... **CLC 70**
Lee, Julian
See Latham, Jean Lee
Lee, Larry
See Lee, Lawrence
Lee, Laurie 1914-1997 .... **CLC 90; DAB;
DAM POP**
See also CA 77-80; 158; CANR 33, 73;
DLB 27; MTCW 1
Lee, Lawrence 1941-1990 .... **CLC 34**
See also CA 131; CANR 43
Lee, Li-Young 1957- .... **PC 24**
See also CA 153; DLB 165
Lee, Manfred B(ennington)
1905-1971 .... **CLC 11**
See also Queen, Ellery
See also CA 1-4R; 29-32R; CANR 2; DLB
137
Lee, Shelton Jackson 1957(?)- .... **CLC 105;
BLCS; DAM MULT**
See also Lee, Spike
See also BW 2, 3; CA 125; CANR 42
Lee, Spike
See Lee, Shelton Jackson
See also AAYA 4, 29

Lee, Stan 1922- .... **CLC 17**
See also AAYA 5; CA 108; 111; INT 111
Lee, Tanith 1947- .... **CLC 46**
See also AAYA 15; BEST; CA 37-40R;
CANR 53; SATA 8, 88
Lee, William
See Burroughs, William S(eward)
See also GLL 1
Lee, Willy
See Burroughs, William S(eward)
See also GLL 1
Leet, Judith 1935- .... **CLC 11**
See also CA 187
Le Fanu, Joseph Sheridan
1814-1873 .... **NCLC 9, 58; DAM POP**
See also DA3; DLB 21, 70, 159, 178
Leffland, Ella 1931- .... **CLC 19**
See also CA 29-32R; CANR 35, 78, 82;
DLBY 84; INT CANR-35; SATA 65
Leger, Alexis
See Leger, (Marie-Rene Auguste) Alexis
Saint-Leger
**Leger, (Marie-Rene Auguste) Alexis
Saint-Leger** 1887-1975 .. **CLC 4, 11, 46;
DAM POET; PC 23**
See also CA 13-16R; 61-64; CANR 43;
MTCW 1
Leger, Saintleger
See Leger, (Marie-Rene Auguste) Alexis
Saint-Leger
Le Guin, Ursula K(roeber) 1929- ..... **CLC 8,
13, 22, 45, 71, 136; DAB; DAC; DAM
MST, POP**
See also AAYA 9, 27; AITN 1; CA 21-24R;
CANR 9, 32, 52, 74; CDALB 1968-1988;
CLR 3, 28; DA3; DLB 8, 52; INT CANR-
32; JRDA; MAICYA; MTCW 1, 2; SATA
4, 52, 99
Lehmann, Rosamond (Nina)
1901-1990 .... **CLC 5**
See also CA 77-80; 131; CANR 8, 73; DLB
15; MTCW 2
Leiber, Fritz (Reuter, Jr.)
1910-1992 .... **CLC 25**
See also CA 45-48; 139; CANR 2, 40, 86;
DLB 8; MTCW 1, 2; SATA 45; SATA-
Obit 73; SCFW 2
Leibniz, Gottfried Wilhelm von
1646-1716 .... **LC 35**
See also DLB 168
Leimbach, Martha 1963-
See Leimbach, Marti
See also CA 130
Leimbach, Marti .... **CLC 65**
See also Leimbach, Martha
Leiris, Michel (Julien) 1901-1990 ..... **CLC 61**
See also CA 119; 128; 132
Leithauser, Brad 1953- .... **CLC 27**
See also CA 107; CANR 27, 81; DLB 120
Lelchuk, Alan 1938- .... **CLC 5**
See also CA 45-48; CAAS 20; CANR 1, 70
Lem, Stanislaw 1921- .... **CLC 8, 15, 40**
See also CA 105; CAAS 1; CANR 32;
CWW 2; MTCW 1; SCFW 2
Lemann, Nancy 1956- .... **CLC 39**
See also CA 118; 136
Lenau, Nikolaus 1802-1850 .... **NCLC 16**
L'Engle, Madeleine (Camp Franklin)
1918- .... **CLC 12; DAM POP**
See also AAYA 28; AITN 2; CA 1-4R;
CANR 3, 21, 39, 66; CLR 1, 14, 57; DA3;
DLB 52; JRDA; MAICYA; MTCW 1, 2;
SAAS 15; SATA 1, 27, 75
Lengyel, Jozsef 1896-1975 .... **CLC 7**
See also CA 85-88; 57-60; CANR 71
Lenin 1870-1924
See Lenin, V. I.
See also CA 121; 168

Lennon, John (Ono) 1940-1980 .. **CLC 12, 35**
See also CA 102; SATA 114
Lennox, Charlotte Ramsay
1729(?)-1804 .... **NCLC 23**
See also DLB 39
Lentricchia, Frank (Jr.) 1940- .... **CLC 34**
See also CA 25-28R; CANR 19
Lenz, Gunter .... **CLC 65**
Lenz, Siegfried 1926- .... **CLC 27**
See also AW 33; CA 89-92; CANR 80;
CWW 2; DLB 75
Leonard, Elmore (John, Jr.) 1925- . **CLC 28,
34, 71, 120; DAM POP**
See also AAYA 22; AITN 1; AW 2; BEST
89:1, 90:4; CA 81-84; CANR 12, 28, 53,
76, 96; DA3; DLB 173, 226; INT CANR-
28; MTCW 1, 2
Leonard, Hugh .... **CLC 19**
See also Byrne, John Keyes
See also DLB 13
Leonov, Leonid (Maximovich)
1899-1994 .... **CLC 92; DAM NOV**
See also CA 129; CANR 74, 76; MTCW 1,
2
Leopardi, Giacomo 1798-1837 .... **NCLC 22**
Le Reveler
See Artaud, Antonin (Marie Joseph)
Lerman, Eleanor 1952- .... **CLC 9**
See also CA 85-88; CANR 69
Lerman, Rhoda 1936- .... **CLC 56**
See also CA 49-52; CANR 70
Lermontov, Mikhail Yuryevich
1814-1841 .... **NCLC 5, 47; PC 18**
See also DLB 205
Lesage, Alain-Rene 1668-1747 .... **LC 2, 28**
Leskov, Nikolai (Semyonovich)
1831-1895 .... **NCLC 25**
See also AW 34
Lesser, Milton
See Marlowe, Stephen
Lessing, Doris (May) 1919- ... **CLC 1, 2, 3, 6,
10, 15, 22, 40, 94; DA; DAB; DAC;
DAM MST, NOV**
See also AW 1; BEST; BRWS 1; CA 9-12R;
CAAS 14; CANR 33, 54, 76; CDBLB
1960 to Present; DA3; DLB 15, 139;
DLBY 85; MTCW 1, 2
Lessing, Gotthold Ephraim 1729-1781 . **LC 8**
See also DLB 97
Lester, Richard 1932- .... **CLC 20**
Levenson, Jay .... **CLC 70**
Lever, Charles (James)
1806-1872 .... **NCLC 23**
See also DLB 21
Leverson, Ada 1865(?)-1936(?)
See Elaine
See also AW 18; CA 117; DLB 153
Levertov, Denise 1923-1997 .. **CLC 1, 2, 3, 5,
8, 15, 28, 66; DAM POET; PC 11**
See also AMWS 3; CA 1-4R; 178; 163;
CAAE 178; CAAS 19; CANR 3, 29, 50;
CDALBS; DLB 5, 165; INT CANR-29;
MTCW 1, 2
Levi, Jonathan .... **CLC 76**
Levi, Peter (Chad Tigar)
1931-2000 .... **CLC 41**
See also CA 5-8R; 187; CANR 34, 80; DLB
40
Levi, Primo 1919-1987 .... **CLC 37, 50**
See also CA 13-16R; 122; CANR
12, 33, 61, 70; DLB 177; MTCW 1, 2
Levin, Ira 1929- .... **CLC 3, 6; DAM POP**
See also CA 21-24R; CANR 17, 44, 74;
DA3; MTCW 1, 2; SATA 66
Levin, Meyer 1905-1981 .... **CLC 7; DAM
POP**
See also AITN 1; CA 9-12R; 104; CANR
15; DLB 9, 28; DLBY 81; SATA 21;
SATA-Obit 27

Marquez, Gabriel (Jose) Garcia
See Garc

Marric, J. J.
See Creasey, John

Marryat, Frederick 1792-1848 .... **NCLC 3**
See also DLB 21, 163

Marsden, James
See Creasey, John

Marsh, (Edith) Ngaio 1899-1982 .... **CLC 7, 53; DAM POP**
See also CA 9-12R; CANR 6, 58; DLB 77; MTCW 1, 2

Marshall, Garry 1934- .... **CLC 17**
See also AAYA 3; CA 111; SATA 60

Marshall, Paule 1929- .. **CLC 27, 72; BLC 3; DAM MULT**
See also AW 3; BW 2, 3; CA 77-80; CANR 25, 73; DA3; DLB 33, 157, 227; MTCW 1, 2

Marshallik
See Zangwill, Israel

Marsten, Richard
See Hunter, Evan

Marston, John 1576-1634 .... **LC 33; DAM DRAM**
See also DLB 58, 172

Martha, Henry
See Harris, Mark

Martí (y Pérez), Jose (Julian) 1853-1895 ...... **NCLC 63; DAM MULT; HLC 2**
See also HW 2

Martial c. 40-c. 104 .... **CMLC 35; PC 10**
See also DLB 211

Martin, Ken
See Hubbard, L(afayette) Ron(ald)

Martin, Richard
See Creasey, John

Martin, Steve 1945- .... **CLC 30**
See also CA 97-100; CANR 30; MTCW 1

Martin, Valerie 1948- .... **CLC 89**
See also BEST 90:2; CA 85-88; CANR 49, 89

Martin, Webber
See Silverberg, Robert

Martindale, Patrick Victor
See White, Patrick (Victor Martindale)

Martineau, Harriet 1802-1876 .... **NCLC 26**
See also BEST 2; DLB 21, 55, 159, 163, 166, 190

Martines, Julia
See O'Faolain, Julia

Martinez, Enrique Gonzalez
See Gonzalez Martinez, Enrique

Martinez, Jacinto Benavente y
See Benavente (y Martinez), Jacinto

Martinez Ruiz, Jose 1873-1967
See Azorin; Ruiz, Jose Martinez
See also CA 93-96; HW 1

Martinsen, Martin
See Follett, Ken(neth Martin)

Martinson, Harry (Edmund) 1904-1978 .... **CLC 14**
See also CA 77-80; CANR 34

Marut, Ret
See Traven, B.

Marut, Robert
See Traven, B.

Marvell, Andrew 1621-1678 .. **LC 4, 43; DA; DAB; DAC; DAM MST, POET; PC 10**
See also CDBLB 1660-1789; DLB 131

Marx, Karl (Heinrich) 1818-1883 . **NCLC 17**
See also DLB 129

Masaoka Tsunenori 1867-1902
See Masaoka, Shiki
See also CA 117

Masefield, John (Edward) 1878-1967 ..... **CLC 11, 47; DAM POET**
See also CA 19-20; 25-28R; CANR 33; CAP 2; CDBLB 1890-1914; DLB 10, 19, 153, 160; MTCW 1, 2; SATA 19

Maso, Carole 19(?)- .... **CLC 44**
See also CA 170; GLL 2

Mason, Bobbie Ann 1940- .... **CLC 28, 43, 82**
See also AAYA 5; AW 3,8; BEST; CA 53-56; CANR 11, 31, 58, 83; CDALBS; DA3; DLB 173; DLBY 87; INT CANR-31; MTCW 1, 2

Mason, Ernst
See Pohl, Frederik

Mason, Hunni B.
See Sternheim, (William Adolf) Carl

Mason, Lee W.
See Malzberg, Barry N(athaniel)

Mason, Nick 1945- .... **CLC 35**

Mason, Tally
See Derleth, August (William)

Mass, Anna .... **CLC 59**

Mass, William
See Gibson, William

Master Lao
See Lao Tzu

Masters, Edgar Lee 1868-1950 .... **PC 1**
See also AMWS 1; AW 2, 25; CA 104; 133; CDALB 1865-1917; DA; DAC; DAM MST, POET; DLB 54; MTCW 1, 2

Masters, Hilary 1928- .... **CLC 48**
See also CA 25-28R; CANR 13, 47, 97

Mastrosimone, William 19(?)- .... **CLC 36**
See also CA 186

Mathe, Albert
See Camus, Albert

Mather, Cotton 1663-1728 .... **LC 38**
See also AMWS 2; CDALB 1640-1865; DLB 24, 30, 140

Mather, Increase 1639-1723 .... **LC 38**
See also DLB 24

Matheson, Richard Burton 1926- .... **CLC 37**
See also AAYA 31; CA 97-100; CANR 88; DLB 8, 44; INT 97-100; SCFW 2

Mathews, Harry 1930- .... **CLC 6, 52**
See also CA 21-24R; CAAS 6; CANR 18, 40

Mathews, John Joseph 1894-1979 .. **CLC 84; DAM MULT**
See also CA 19-20; 142; CANR 45; CAP 2; DLB 175; NNAL

Mathias, Roland (Glyn) 1915- .... **CLC 45**
See also CA 97-100; CANR 19, 41; DLB 27

Matsuo Bashō 1644-1694 .... **LC 62; DAM POET; PC 3**
See also Bashō, Matsuo

Mattheson, Rodney
See Creasey, John

Matthews, Greg 1949- .... **CLC 45**
See also CA 135

Matthews, William (Procter, III) 1942-1997 .... **CLC 40**
See also CA 29-32R; 162; CAAS 18; CANR 12, 57; DLB 5

Matthias, John (Edward) 1941- .... **CLC 9**
See also CA 33-36R; CANR 56

Matthiessen, Peter 1927- ... **CLC 5, 7, 11, 32, 64; DAM NOV**
See also AAYA 6, 40; AMWS 5; BEST 90:4; CA 9-12R; CANR 21, 50, 73; DA3; DLB 6, 173; MTCW 1, 2; SATA 27

Maturin, Charles Robert 1780(?)-1824 .... **NCLC 6**
See also DLB 178

Matute (Ausejo), Ana Maria 1925- .. **CLC 11**
See also CA 89-92; MTCW 1

Maugham, W. S.
See Maugham, W(illiam) Somerset

Maugham, W(illiam) Somerset 1874-1965 ... **CLC 1, 11, 15, 67, 93; DA; DAB; DAC; DAM DRAM, MST, NOV**
See also AW 8; BEST; CA 5-8R; 25-28R; CANR 40; CDBLB 1914-1945; DA3; DLB 10, 36, 77, 100, 162, 195; MTCW 1, 2; SATA 54

Maugham, William Somerset
See Maugham, W(illiam) Somerset

Maupassant, (Henri Rene Albert) Guy de 1850-1893 . **NCLC 1, 42, 83; DA; DAB; DAC; DAM MST**
See also BEST; DA3; DLB 123

Maupin, Armistead 1944- ..... **CLC 95; DAM POP**
See also CA 125; 130; CANR 58; DA3; GLL 1; INT 130; MTCW 2

Maurhut, Richard
See Traven, B.

Mauriac, Claude 1914-1996 .... **CLC 9**
See also CA 89-92; 152; CWW 2; DLB 83

Mauriac, François (Charles) 1885-1970 .... **CLC 4, 9, 56**
See also AW 24; CA 25-28; CAP 2; DLB 65; MTCW 1, 2

Mavor, Osborne Henry 1888-1951
See Bridie, James
See also CA 104

Maxwell, William (Keepers, Jr.) 1908-2000 .... **CLC 19**
See also CA 93-96; 189; CANR 54, 95; DLBY 80; INT 93-96

May, Elaine 1932- .... **CLC 16**
See also CA 124; 142; DLB 44

Mayakovsky, Vladimir
See Mayakovski, Vladimir (Vladimirovich)

Mayhew, Henry 1812-1887 .... **NCLC 31**
See also DLB 18, 55, 190

Mayle, Peter 1939(?)- .... **CLC 89**
See also CA 139; CANR 64

Maynard, Joyce 1953- .... **CLC 23**
See also CA 111; 129; CANR 64

Mayne, William (James Carter) 1928- .... **CLC 12**
See also AAYA 20; BEST; CA 9-12R; CANR 37, 80; CLR 25; JRDA; MAICYA; SAAS 11; SATA 6, 68

Mayo, Jim
See L'Amour, Louis (Dearborn)
See also AW 2

Maysles, Albert 1926- .... **CLC 16**
See also CA 29-32R

Maysles, David 1932- .... **CLC 16**

Mazer, Norma Fox 1931- .... **CLC 26**
See also AAYA 5, 36; BEST; CA 69-72; CANR 12, 32, 66; CLR 23; JRDA; MAICYA; SAAS 1; SATA 24, 67, 105

Mazzini, Guiseppe 1805-1872 .... **NCLC 34**

McAuley, James Phillip 1917-1976 .. **CLC 45**
See also CA 97-100

McBain, Ed
See Hunter, Evan

McBrien, William (Augustine) 1930- .... **CLC 44**
See also CA 107; CANR 90

McCabe, Patrick 1955- .... **CLC 133**
See also CA 130; CANR 50, 90; DLB 194

McCaffrey, Anne (Inez) 1926- .... **CLC 17; DAM NOV, POP**
See also AAYA 6, 34; AITN 2; CA 25-28R; CANR 15, 35, 55, 96; CLR 49; DA3; DLB 8; JRDA; MAICYA; MTCW 1, 2; SAAS 11; SATA 8, 70, 116

McCall, Nathan 1955(?)- .... **CLC 86**
See also BW 3; CA 146; CANR 88

McCann, Arthur
See Campbell, John W(ood, Jr.)

McCann, Edson
See Pohl, Frederik

McCarthy, Charles, Jr. 1933-
See McCarthy, Cormac
See also CANR 42, 69; DAM POP; DA3;
MTCW 2

McCarthy, Cormac .... CLC 4, 57, 59, 101
See also McCarthy, Charles, Jr.
See also AW 2; CA 13-16R; CANR 10;
DLB 6, 143; MTCW 2

McCarthy, Mary (Therese)
1912-1989 ... CLC 1, 3, 5, 14, 24, 39, 59
See also AW 24; CA 5-8R; 129; CANR 16,
50, 64; DA3; DLB 2; DLBY 81; INT
CANR-16; MTCW 1, 2

McCartney, (James) Paul 1942- . CLC 12, 35
See also CA 146

McCauley, Stephen (D.) 1955- .... CLC 50
See also CA 141

McClaren, Peter .... CLC 70

McClure, Michael (Thomas) 1932- ... CLC 6,
10
See also CA 21-24R; CANR 17, 46, 77;
DLB 16

McCorkle, Jill (Collins) 1958- .... CLC 51
See also CA 121; DLB 234; DLBY 87

McCourt, Frank 1930- .... CLC 109
See also CA 157; CANR 97

McCourt, James 1941- .... CLC 5
See also CA 57-60

McCourt, Malachy 1932- .... CLC 119

McCreigh, James
See Pohl, Frederik

McCullers, (Lula) Carson (Smith)
1917-1967 .... CLC 1, 4, 10, 12, 48, 100;
DA; DAB; DAC; DAM MST, NOV
See also AAYA 21; AW 5; BEST; CA 5-8R;
25-28R; CABS 1, 3; CANR 18; CDALB
1941-1968; DA3; DLB 2, 7, 173, 228;
GLL 1; MTCW 1, 2; SATA 27

McCulloch, John Tyler
See Burroughs, Edgar Rice

McCullough, Colleen 1938(?)- .... CLC 27,
107; DAM NOV, POP
See also AAYA 36; CA 81-84; CANR 17,
46, 67; DA3; MTCW 1, 2

McDermott, Alice 1953- .... CLC 90
See also CA 109; CANR 40, 90

McElroy, Joseph 1930- .... CLC 5, 47
See also CA 17-20R

McEwan, Ian (Russell) 1948- .... CLC 13, 66;
DAM NOV
See also BEST 90:4; BRWS 4; CA 61-64;
CANR 14, 41, 69, 87; DLB 14, 194;
MTCW 1, 2

McFadden, David 1940- .... CLC 48
See also CA 104; DLB 60; INT 104

McFarland, Dennis 1950- .... CLC 65
See also CA 165

McGahern, John 1934- .... CLC 5, 9, 48
See also AW 17; CA 17-20R; CANR 29,
68; DLB 14, 231; MTCW 1

McGinley, Patrick (Anthony) 1937- . CLC 41
See also CA 120; 127; CANR 56; INT 127

McGinley, Phyllis 1905-1978 .... CLC 14
See also CA 9-12R; 77-80; CANR 19; DLB
11, 48; SATA 2, 44; SATA-Obit 24

McGinniss, Joe 1942- .... CLC 32
See also AITN 2; BEST 89:2; CA 25-28R;
CANR 26, 70; DLB 185; INT CANR-26

McGivern, Maureen Daly
See Daly, Maureen

McGrath, Patrick 1950- .... CLC 55
See also CA 136; CANR 65; DLB 231

McGrath, Thomas (Matthew)
1916-1990 ..... CLC 28, 59; DAM POET
See also CA 9-12R; 132; CANR 6, 33, 95;
MTCW 1; SATA 41; SATA-Obit 66

McGuane, Thomas (Francis III)
1939- .... CLC 3, 7, 18, 45, 127
See also AITN 2; AW 2; CA 49-52; CANR
5, 24, 49, 94; DLB 2, 212; DLBY 80; INT
CANR-24; MTCW 1

McGuckian, Medbh 1950- .... CLC 48; DAM
POET; PC 27
See also BRWS 5; CA 143; DLB 40

McHale, Tom 1942(?)-1982 .... CLC 3, 5
See also AITN 1; CA 77-80; 106

McIlvanney, William 1936- .... CLC 42
See also CA 25-28R; CANR 61; DLB 14,
207

McIlwraith, Maureen Mollie Hunter
See Hunter, Mollie
See also SATA 2

McInerney, Jay 1955- .... CLC 34, 112; DAM
POP
See also AAYA 18; CA 116; 123; CANR
45, 68; DA3; INT 123; MTCW 2

McIntyre, Vonda N(eel) 1948- .... CLC 18
See also BEST; CA 81-84; CANR 17, 34,
69; MTCW 1

McKay, Claude .... PC 2
See also McKay, Festus Claudius
See also AW 7, 41; BLC 3; DAB; DLB 4,
45, 51, 117; GLL 2

McKay, Festus Claudius 1889-1948
See McKay, Claude
See also BEST; BW 1, 3; CA 104; 124;
CANR 73; DA; DAC; DAM MST, MULT,
NOV, POET; MTCW 1, 2

McKuen, Rod 1933- .... CLC 1, 3
See also AITN 1; CA 41-44R; CANR 40

McLoughlin, R. B.
See Mencken, H(enry) L(ouis)

McLuhan, (Herbert) Marshall
1911-1980 .... CLC 37, 83
See also CA 9-12R; 102; CANR 12, 34, 61;
DLB 88; INT CANR-12; MTCW 1, 2

McMillan, Terry (L.) 1951- .... CLC 50, 61,
112; BLCS; DAM MULT, NOV, POP
See also AAYA 21; BEST; BW 2, 3; CA
140; CANR 60; DA3; MTCW 2

McMurtry, Larry (Jeff) 1936- .. CLC 2, 3, 7,
11, 27, 44, 127; DAM NOV, POP
See also AAYA 15; AITN 2; AMWS 5; AW
2; BEST 89:2; CA 5-8R; CANR 19, 43,
64; CDALB 1968-1988; DA3; DLB 2,
143; DLBY 80, 87; MTCW 1, 2

McNally, T. M. 1961- .... CLC 82

McNally, Terrence 1939- ... CLC 4, 7, 41, 91;
DAM DRAM
See also CA 45-48; CANR 2, 56; DA3;
DLB 7; GLL 1; MTCW 2

McNamer, Deirdre 1950- .... CLC 70

McNeal, Tom .... CLC 119

McNeile, Herman Cyril 1888-1937
See Sapper
See also CA 184; DLB 77

McNickle, (William) D'Arcy
1904-1977 .... CLC 89; DAM MULT
See also CA 9-12R; 85-88; CANR 5, 45;
DLB 175, 212; NNAL; SATA-Obit 22

McPhee, John (Angus) 1931- .... CLC 36
See also AMWS 3; BEST 90:1; CA 65-68;
CANR 20, 46, 64, 69; DLB 185; MTCW
1, 2

McPherson, James Alan 1943- .. CLC 19, 77;
BLCS
See also BW 1, 3; CA 25-28R; CAAS 17;
CANR 24, 74; DLB 38; MTCW 1, 2

McPherson, William (Alexander)
1933- .... CLC 34
See also CA 69-72; CANR 28; INT
CANR-28

McTaggart, J. McT. Ellis
See McTaggart, John McTaggart Ellis

Mead, Margaret 1901-1978 .... CLC 37
See also AITN 1; CA 1-4R; 81-84; CANR
4; DA3; MTCW 1, 2; SATA-Obit 20

Meaker, Marijane (Agnes) 1927-
See Kerr, M. E.
See also BEST; CA 107; CANR 37, 63; INT
107; JRDA; MAICYA; MTCW 1; SATA
20, 61, 99; SATA-Essay 111

Medoff, Mark (Howard) 1940- ... CLC 6, 23;
DAM DRAM
See also AITN 1; CA 53-56; CANR 5; DLB
7; INT CANR-5

Medvedev, P. N.
See Bakhtin, Mikhail Mikhailovich

Meged, Aharon
See Megged, Aharon

Meged, Aron
See Megged, Aharon

Megged, Aharon 1920- .... CLC 9
See also CA 49-52; CAAS 13; CANR 1

Mehta, Ved (Parkash) 1934- .... CLC 37
See also CA 1-4R; CANR 2, 23, 69; MTCW
1

Melanter
See Blackmore, R(ichard) D(oddridge)

Melikow, Loris
See Hofmannsthal, Hugo von

Melmoth, Sebastian
See Wilde, Oscar (Fingal O'Flahertie Wills)

Meltzer, Milton 1915- .... CLC 26
See also AAYA 8; BEST; CA 13-16R;
CANR 38, 92; CLR 13; DLB 61; JRDA;
MAICYA; SAAS 1; SATA 1, 50, 80

Melville, Herman 1819-1891 ..... NCLC 3, 12,
29, 45, 49, 91, 93; DA; DAB; DAC;
DAM MST, NOV
See also AAYA 25; AW 3; BEST; CDALB
1640-1865; DA3; DLB 3, 74; SATA 59

Membreno, Alejandro .... CLC 59

Menander c. 342B.C.-c. 292B.C. ... CMLC 9;
DAM DRAM; DC 3
See also DLB 176

Menchú, Rigoberta 1959-
See also CA 175; HLCS 2

Mendelsohn, Jane 1965- .... CLC 99
See also CA 154; CANR 94

Mercer, David 1928-1980 .... CLC 5; DAM
DRAM
See also CA 9-12R; 102; CANR 23; DLB
13; MTCW 1

Merchant, Paul
See Ellison, Harlan (Jay)

Meredith, William (Morris) 1919- .... CLC 4,
13, 22, 55; DAM POET; PC 28
See also CA 9-12R; CAAS 14; CANR 6,
40; DLB 5

Merimee, Prosper 1803-1870 ..... NCLC 6, 65
See also AW 8; DLB 119, 192

Merkin, Daphne 1954- .... CLC 44
See also CA 123

Merlin, Arthur
See Blish, James (Benjamin)

Merrill, James (Ingram) 1926-1995 .. CLC 2,
3, 6, 8, 13, 18, 34, 91; DAM POET; PC
28
See also AMWS 3; CA 13-16R; 147; CANR
10, 49, 63; DA3; DLB 5, 165; DLBY 85;
INT CANR-10; MTCW 1, 2

Merriman, Alex
See Silverberg, Robert

Merriman, Brian 1747-1805 .... NCLC 70

Merritt, E. B.
See Waddington, Miriam

Merton, Thomas 1915-1968 ..... CLC 1, 3, 11,
34, 83; PC 10
See also CA 5-8R; 25-28R; CANR 22, 53;
DA3; DLB 48; DLBY 81; MTCW 1, 2

Merwin, W(illiam) S(tanley) 1927- ... **CLC 1, 2, 3, 5, 8, 13, 18, 45, 88; DAM POET**
See also AMWS 3; CA 13-16R; CANR 15, 51; DA3; DLB 5, 169; INT CANR-15; MTCW 1, 2

Metcalf, John 1938- .... **CLC 37**
See also AW 43; CA 113; DLB 60

Metcalf, Suzanne
See Baum, L(yman) Frank

Mewshaw, Michael 1943- .... **CLC 9**
See also CA 53-56; CANR 7, 47; DLBY 80

Meyer, Conrad Ferdinand
1825-1905 .... **NCLC 81**
See also DLB 129

Meyer, June
See Jordan, June
See also GLL 2

Meyer, Lynn
See Slavitt, David R(ytman)

Meyer-Meyrink, Gustav 1868-1932
See Meyrink, Gustav
See also CA 117; 190

Meyers, Jeffrey 1939- .... **CLC 39**
See also CA 73-76; CAAE 186; CANR 54; DLB 111

Michaels, Leonard 1933- .... **CLC 6, 25**
See also AW 16; CA 61-64; CANR 21, 62; DLB 130; MTCW 1

Michaux, Henri 1899-1984 .... **CLC 8, 19**
See also CA 85-88; 114

Michelangelo 1475-1564 .... **LC 12**

Michelet, Jules 1798-1874 .... **NCLC 31**

Michener, James A(lbert)
1907(?)-1997 .... **CLC 1, 5, 11, 29, 60, 109; DAM NOV, POP**
See also AAYA 27; AITN 1; BEST 90:1; CA 5-8R; 161; CANR 21, 45, 68; DA3; DLB 6; MTCW 1, 2

Mickiewicz, Adam 1798-1855 .... **NCLC 3**

Middleton, Christopher 1926- .... **CLC 13**
See also CA 13-16R; CANR 29, 54; DLB 40

Middleton, Stanley 1919- .... **CLC 7, 38**
See also CA 25-28R; CAAS 23; CANR 21, 46, 81; DLB 14

Middleton, Thomas 1580-1627 .... **LC 33; DAM DRAM, MST; DC 5**
See also DLB 58

Migueis, Jose Rodrigues 1901- .... **CLC 10**

Miles, Jack .... **CLC 100**

Miles, Josephine (Louise)
1911-1985 .. **CLC 1, 2, 14, 34, 39; DAM POET**
See also CA 1-4R; 116; CANR 2, 55; DLB 48

Militant
See Sandburg, Carl (August)

Mill, John Stuart 1806-1873 .... **NCLC 11, 58**
See also CDBLB 1832-1890; DLB 55, 190

Millar, Kenneth 1915-1983 ... **CLC 14; DAM POP**
See also Macdonald, Ross
See also CA 9-12R; 110; CANR 16, 63; DA3; DLB 2, 226; DLBD 6; DLBY 83; MTCW 1, 2

Millay, E. Vincent
See Millay, Edna St. Vincent

Millay, Edna St. Vincent 1892-1950 ...... **PC 6**
See also Boyd, Nancy
See also AW 4, 49; CA 104; 130; CDALB 1917-1929; DA; DAB; DAC; DAM MST, POET; DA3; DLB 45; MTCW 1, 2

Miller, Arthur 1915- ...... **CLC 1, 2, 6, 10, 15, 26, 47, 78; DA; DAB; DAC; DAM DRAM, MST; DC 1**
See also AAYA 15; AITN 1; BEST 1; CA 1-4R; CABS 3; CANR 2, 30, 54, 76; CDALB 1941-1968; DA3; DLB 7; MTCW 1, 2

Miller, Henry (Valentine)
1891-1980 .... **CLC 1, 2, 4, 9, 14, 43, 84; DA; DAB; DAC; DAM MST, NOV**
See also BEST; CA 9-12R; 97-100; CANR 33, 64; CDALB 1929-1941; DA3; DLB 4, 9; DLBY 80; MTCW 1, 2

Miller, Jason 1939(?)-2001 .... **CLC 2**
See also AITN 1; CA 73-76; DLB 7

Miller, Sue 1943- .... **CLC 44; DAM POP**
See also BEST 90:3; CA 139; CANR 59, 91; DA3; DLB 143

Miller, Walter M(ichael, Jr.)
1923-1996 .... **CLC 4, 30**
See also CA 85-88; DLB 8

Millett, Kate 1934- .... **CLC 67**
See also AITN 1; CA 73-76; CANR 32, 53, 76; DA3; GLL 1; MTCW 1, 2

Millhauser, Steven (Lewis) 1943- .... **CLC 21, 54, 109**
See also CA 110; 111; CANR 63; DA3; DLB 2; INT 111; MTCW 2

Millin, Sarah Gertrude 1889-1968 ... **CLC 49**
See also CA 102; 93-96; DLB 225

Milner, Ron(ald) 1938- .... **CLC 56; BLC 3; DAM MULT**
See also AITN 1; BW 1; CA 73-76; CANR 24, 81; DLB 38; MTCW 1

Milnes, Richard Monckton
1809-1885 .... **NCLC 61**
See also DLB 32, 184

Milosz, Czeslaw 1911- ...... **CLC 5, 11, 22, 31, 56, 82; DAM MST, POET; PC 8**
See also BEST; CA 81-84; CANR 23, 51, 91; CWW 2; DA3; MTCW 1, 2

Milton, John 1608-1674 .... **LC 9, 43; DA; DAB; DAC; DAM MST, POET; PC 19, 29**
See also CDBLB 1660-1789; DA3; DLB 131, 151

Min, Anchee 1957- .... **CLC 86**
See also CA 146; CANR 94

Minehaha, Cornelius
See Wedekind, (Benjamin) Frank(lin)

Miner, Valerie 1947- .... **CLC 40**
See also CA 97-100; CANR 59; GLL 2

Minimo, Duca
See D'Annunzio, Gabriele

Minot, Susan 1956- .... **CLC 44**
See also AMWS 6; CA 134

Minus, Ed 1938- .... **CLC 39**
See also CA 185

Miranda, Javier
See Bioy Casares, Adolfo
See also CWW 2

Miranda, Javier
See Bioy Casares, Adolfo

Misharin, Alexandr .... **CLC 59**

Mishima, Yukio .... **CLC 2, 4, 6, 9, 27; DC 1**
See also Hiraoka, Kimitake
See also AW 5; DLB 182; GLL 1; MTCW 2

Mistral, Gabriela
See Godoy Alcayaga, Lucila

Mistry, Rohinton 1952- .... **CLC 71; DAC**
See also AW 6; CA 141; CANR 86; CCA 1

Mitchell, Clyde
See Ellison, Harlan (Jay); Silverberg, Robert

Mitchell, James Leslie 1901-1935
See Gibbon, Lewis Grassic
See also CA 104; 188; DLB 15

Mitchell, Joni 1943- .... **CLC 12**
See also CA 112; CCA 1

Mitchell, Joseph (Quincy)
1908-1996 .... **CLC 98**
See also CA 77-80; 152; CANR 69; DLB 185; DLBY 96

Mitchell, Peggy
See Mitchell, Margaret (Munnerlyn)

Mitchell, W(illiam) O(rmond)
1914-1998 .. **CLC 25; DAC; DAM MST**
See also CA 77-80; 165; CANR 15, 43; DLB 88

Mitford, Mary Russell 1787-1855 ... **NCLC 4**
See also DLB 110, 116

Mitford, Nancy 1904-1973 .... **CLC 44**
See also CA 9-12R; DLB 191

Mo, Timothy (Peter) 1950(?)- ... **CLC 46, 134**
See also CA 117; DLB 194; MTCW 1

Modarressi, Taghi (M.) 1931- .... **CLC 44**
See also CA 121; 134; INT 134

Modiano, Patrick (Jean) 1945- .... **CLC 18**
See also CA 85-88; CANR 17, 40; CWW 2; DLB 83

Moerck, Paal
See Roelvaag, O(le) E(dvart)

Mohr, Nicholasa 1938- .... **CLC 12; DAM MULT; HLC 2**
See also AAYA 8; BEST; CA 49-52; CANR 1, 32, 64; CLR 22; DLB 145; HW 1, 2; JRDA; SAAS 8; SATA 8, 97; SATA-Essay 113

Mojtabai, A(nn) G(race) 1938- ..... **CLC 5, 9, 15, 29**
See also CA 85-88; CANR 88

Moliere 1622-1673 .... **LC 10, 28, 64; DA; DAB; DAC; DAM DRAM, MST; DC 13**
See also BEST; DA3

Molin, Charles
See Mayne, William (James Carter)

Momaday, N(avarre) Scott 1934- ...... **CLC 2, 19, 85, 95; DA; DAB; DAC; DAM MST, MULT, NOV, POP; PC 25**
See also AAYA 11; AMWS 4; CA 25-28R; CANR 14, 34, 68; CDALBS; DA3; DLB 143, 175; INT CANR-14; MTCW 1, 2; NNAL; SATA 48; SATA-Brief 30

Monette, Paul 1945-1995 .... **CLC 82**
See also CA 139; 147; GLL 1

Monroe, Lyle
See Heinlein, Robert A(nson)

Montagu, Elizabeth 1720-1800 .... **NCLC 7**

Montagu, Mary (Pierrepont) Wortley
1689-1762 .... **LC 9, 57; PC 16**
See also DLB 95, 101

Montagu, W. H.
See Coleridge, Samuel Taylor

Montague, John (Patrick) 1929- ..... **CLC 13, 46**
See also CA 9-12R; CANR 9, 69; DLB 40; MTCW 1

Montaigne, Michel (Eyquem) de
1533-1592 .... **LC 8; DA; DAB; DAC; DAM MST**
See also BEST

Montale, Eugenio 1896-1981 ... **CLC 7, 9, 18; PC 13**
See also CA 17-20R; 104; CANR 30; DLB 114; MTCW 1

Montesquieu, Charles-Louis de Secondat
1689-1755 .... **LC 7**

Montgomery, (Robert) Bruce 1921(?)-1978
See Crispin, Edmund
See also CA 179; 104

Montgomery, Marion H., Jr. 1925- .... **CLC 7**
See also AITN 1; CA 1-4R; CANR 3, 48; DLB 6

Montgomery, Max
See Davenport, Guy (Mattison, Jr.)

Montherlant, Henry (Milon) de
1896-1972 ..... **CLC 8, 19; DAM DRAM**
See also CA 85-88; 37-40R; DLB 72; MTCW 1

Monty Python
See Chapman, Graham; Cleese, John (Marwood); Gilliam, Terry (Vance); Idle, Eric; Jones, Terence Graham Parry; Palin, Michael (Edward)
See also AAYA 7

Moodie, Susanna (Strickland)
1803-1885 .... **NCLC 14**
See also DLB 99

Mooney, Edward 1951-
See Mooney, Ted
See also CA 130

Mooney, Ted .... **CLC 25**
See also Mooney, Edward

Moorcock, Michael (John) 1939- ...... **CLC 5, 27, 58**
See also Bradbury, Edward P.
See also AAYA 26; CA 45-48; CAAS 5; CANR 2, 17, 38, 64; DLB 14, 231; MTCW 1, 2; SATA 93

Moore, Brian 1921-1999 ... **CLC 1, 3, 5, 7, 8, 19, 32, 90; DAB; DAC; DAM MST**
See also Bryan, Michael
See also CA 1-4R; 174; CANR 1, 25, 42, 63; CCA 1; MTCW 1, 2

Moore, Edward
See Muir, Edwin

Moore, Lorrie .... **CLC 39, 45, 68**
See also Moore, Marie Lorena
See also DLB 234

Moore, Marianne (Craig)
1887-1972 .... **CLC 1, 2, 4, 8, 10, 13, 19, 47; DA; DAB; DAC; DAM MST, POET; PC 4**
See also CA 1-4R; 33-36R; CANR 3, 61; CDALB 1929-1941; DA3; DLB 45; DLBD 7; MTCW 1, 2; SATA 20

Moore, Marie Lorena 1957-
See Moore, Lorrie
See also CA 116; CANR 39, 83; DLB 234

Moore, Thomas 1779-1852 .... **NCLC 6**
See also DLB 96, 144

Mora, Pat(ricia) 1942-
See also CA 129; CANR 57, 81; CLR 58; DAM MULT; DLB 209; HLC 2; HW 1, 2; SATA 92

Moraga, Cherrie 1952- .... **CLC 126; DAM MULT**
See also CA 131; CANR 66; DLB 82; GLL 1; HW 1, 2

Morand, Paul 1888-1976 .... **CLC 41**
See also AW 22; CA 184; 69-72; DLB 65

Morante, Elsa 1918-1985 .... **CLC 8, 47**
See also CA 85-88; 117; CANR 35; DLB 177; MTCW 1, 2

Moravia, Alberto .... **CLC 2, 7, 11, 27, 46**
See also Pincherle, Alberto
See also AW 26; DLB 177; MTCW 2

More, Hannah 1745-1833 .... **NCLC 27**
See also DLB 107, 109, 116, 158

More, Henry 1614-1687 .... **LC 9**
See also DLB 126

More, Sir Thomas 1478-1535 .... **LC 10, 32**

Morgan, Berry 1919- .... **CLC 6**
See also CA 49-52; DLB 6

Morgan, Claire
See Highsmith, (Mary) Patricia
See also GLL 1

Morgan, Edwin (George) 1920- .... **CLC 31**
See also CA 5-8R; CANR 3, 43, 90; DLB 27

Morgan, (George) Frederick 1922- .. **CLC 23**
See also CA 17-20R; CANR 21

Morgan, Harriet
See Mencken, H(enry) L(ouis)

Morgan, Jane
See Cooper, James Fenimore

Morgan, Janet 1945- .... **CLC 39**
See also CA 65-68

Morgan, Lady 1776(?)-1859 .... **NCLC 29**
See also DLB 116, 158

Morgan, Robin (Evonne) 1941- .... **CLC 2**
See also CA 69-72; CANR 29, 68; MTCW 1; SATA 80

Morgan, Scott
See Kuttner, Henry

Morgan, Seth 1949(?)-1990 .... **CLC 65**
See also CA 185; 132

Morgenstern, S.
See Goldman, William (W.)

Mori, Rintaro
See Mori Ogai
See also CA 110

Morike, Eduard (Friedrich)
1804-1875 .... **NCLC 10**
See also DLB 133

Moritz, Karl Philipp 1756-1793 .... **LC 2**
See also DLB 94

Morland, Peter Henry
See Faust, Frederick (Schiller)

Morren, Theophil
See Hofmannsthal, Hugo von

Morris, Bill 1952- .... **CLC 76**

Morris, Julian
See West, Morris L(anglo)

Morris, Steveland Judkins 1950(?)-
See Wonder, Stevie
See also CA 111

Morris, William 1834-1896 .... **NCLC 4**
See also CDBLB 1832-1890; DLB 18, 35, 57, 156, 178, 184

Morris, Wright 1910-1998 .. **CLC 1, 3, 7, 18, 37**
See also AW 107; CA 9-12R; 167; CANR 21, 81; DLB 2, 206; DLBY 81; MTCW 1, 2

Morrison, Chloe Anthony Wofford
See Morrison, Toni

Morrison, James Douglas 1943-1971
See Morrison, Jim
See also CA 73-76; CANR 40

Morrison, Jim .... **CLC 17**
See also Morrison, James Douglas

Morrison, Toni 1931- . **CLC 4, 10, 22, 55, 81, 87; BLC 3; DA; DAB; DAC; DAM MST, MULT, NOV, POP**
See also AAYA 1, 22; AMWS 3; AW 5; BEST; BW 2, 3; CA 29-32R; CANR 27, 42, 67; CDALB 1968-1988; DA3; DLB 6, 33, 143; DLBY 81; MTCW 1, 2; SATA 57

Morrison, Van 1945- .... **CLC 21**
See also CA 116; 168

Morrissy, Mary 1958- .... **CLC 99**

Mortimer, John (Clifford) 1923- ..... **CLC 28, 43; DAM DRAM, POP**
See also CA 13-16R; CANR 21, 69; CDBLB 1960 to Present; DA3; DLB 13; INT CANR-21; MTCW 1, 2

Mortimer, Penelope (Ruth)
1918-1999 .... **CLC 5**
See also CA 57-60; 187; CANR 45, 88

Morton, Anthony
See Creasey, John

Mosher, Howard Frank 1943- .... **CLC 62**
See also CA 139; CANR 65

Mosley, Nicholas 1923- .... **CLC 43, 70**
See also CA 69-72; CANR 41, 60; DLB 14, 207

Mosley, Walter 1952- .... **CLC 97; BLCS; DAM MULT, POP**
See also AAYA 17; BW 2; CA 142; CANR 57, 92; DA3; MTCW 2

Moss, Howard 1922-1987 ...... **CLC 7, 14, 45, 50; DAM POET**
See also CA 1-4R; 123; CANR 1, 44; DLB 5

Mossgiel, Rab
See Burns, Robert

Motion, Andrew (Peter) 1952- .... **CLC 47**
See also CA 146; CANR 90; DLB 40

Motley, Willard (Francis)
1912-1965 .... **CLC 18**
See also BW 1; CA 117; 106; CANR 88; DLB 76, 143

Motoori, Norinaga 1730-1801 .... **NCLC 45**

Mott, Michael (Charles Alston)
1930- .... **CLC 15, 34**
See also CA 5-8R; CAAS 7; CANR 7, 29

Mountain Wolf Woman 1884-1960 .. **CLC 92**
See also CA 144; CANR 90; NNAL

Moure, Erin 1955- .... **CLC 88**
See also CA 113; DLB 60

Mowat, Farley (McGill) 1921- .... **CLC 26; DAC; DAM MST**
See also AAYA 1; BEST; CA 1-4R; CANR 4, 24, 42, 68; CLR 20; DLB 68; INT CANR-24; JRDA; MAICYA; MTCW 1, 2; SATA 3, 55

Mowatt, Anna Cora 1819-1870 ..... **NCLC 74**

Moyers, Bill 1934- .... **CLC 74**
See also AITN 2; CA 61-64; CANR 31, 52

Mphahlele, Es'kia
See Mphahlele, Ezekiel
See also AW 11; DLB 125, 225

Mphahlele, Ezekiel 1919- .... **CLC 25, 133; BLC 3; DAM MULT**
See also Mphahlele, Es'kia
See also BW 2, 3; CA 81-84; CANR 26, 76; DA3; DLB 225; MTCW 2; SATA 119

Mrozek, Slawomir 1930- .... **CLC 3, 13**
See also CA 13-16R; CAAS 10; CANR 29; CWW 2; DLB 232; MTCW 1

Mrs. Belloc-Lowndes
See Lowndes, Marie Adelaide (Belloc)

M'Taggart, John M'Taggart Ellis
See McTaggart, John McTaggart Ellis

Mtwa, Percy (?)- .... **CLC 47**

Mueller, Lisel 1924- .... **CLC 13, 51; PC 33**
See also CA 93-96; DLB 105

Mujica Lainez, Manuel 1910-1984 ... **CLC 31**
See also Lainez, Manuel Mujica
See also CA 81-84; 112; CANR 32; HW 1

Mukherjee, Bharati 1940- .... **CLC 53, 115; DAM NOV**
See also AW 7; BEST 89:2; CA 107; CANR 45, 72; DLB 60; MTCW 1, 2

Muldoon, Paul 1951- .... **CLC 32, 72; DAM POET**
See also BRWS 4; CA 113; 129; CANR 52, 91; DLB 40; INT 129

Mulisch, Harry 1927- .... **CLC 42**
See also CA 9-12R; CANR 6, 26, 56

Mull, Martin 1943- .... **CLC 17**
See also CA 105

Muller, Wilhelm .... **NCLC 73**

Mulock, Dinah Maria
See Craik, Dinah Maria (Mulock)

Munford, Robert 1737(?)-1783 .... **LC 5**
See also DLB 31

Mungo, Raymond 1946- .... **CLC 72**
See also CA 49-52; CANR 2

Munro, Alice 1931- .... **CLC 6, 10, 19, 50, 95; DAC; DAM MST, NOV**
See also AITN 2; AW 5; BEST; CA 33-36R; CANR 33, 53, 75; CCA 1; DA3; DLB 53; MTCW 1, 2; SATA 29

Munro, H(ector) H(ugh) 1870-1916
See Saki
See also BEST; CA 104; 130; CDBLB 1890-1914; DA; DAB; DAC; DAM MST, NOV; DA3; DLB 34, 162; MTCW 1, 2

Murdoch, (Jean) Iris 1919-1999 ... **CLC 1, 2, 3, 4, 6, 8, 11, 15, 22, 31, 51; DAB; DAC; DAM MST, NOV**
See also BRWS 1; CA 13-16R; 179; CANR 8, 43, 68; CDBLB 1960 to Present; DA3; DLB 14, 194, 233; INT CANR-8; MTCW 1, 2

Murnau, Friedrich Wilhelm
See Plumpe, Friedrich Wilhelm

Murphy, Richard 1927- .... **CLC 41**
See also BRWS 5; CA 29-32R; DLB 40

Murphy, Sylvia 1937- .... **CLC 34**
See also CA 121

Murphy, Thomas (Bernard) 1935- ... **CLC 51**
See also CA 101

Murray, Albert L. 1916- .... **CLC 73**
See also BW 2; CA 49-52; CANR 26, 52, 78; DLB 38

Murray, Judith Sargent
1751-1820 .... **NCLC 63**
See also DLB 37, 200

Murray, Les(lie) A(llan) 1938- .... **CLC 40; DAM POET**
See also CA 21-24R; CANR 11, 27, 56

Murry, J. Middleton
See Murry, John Middleton

Musgrave, Susan 1951- .... **CLC 13, 54**
See also CA 69-72; CANR 45, 84; CCA 1

Muske, Carol .... **CLC 90**
See also Muske-Dukes, Carol (Anne)

Muske-Dukes, Carol (Anne) 1945-
See Muske, Carol
See also CA 65-68; CANR 32, 70

Musset, (Louis Charles) Alfred de
1810-1857 .... **NCLC 7**
See also DLB 192

My Brother's Brother
See Chekhov, Anton (Pavlovich)

Myers, Walter Dean 1937- ..... **CLC 35; BLC 3; DAM MULT, NOV**
See also AAYA 4, 23; BEST; BW 2; CA 33-36R; CANR 20, 42, 67; CLR 4, 16, 35; DLB 33; INT CANR-20; JRDA; MAICYA; MTCW 2; SAAS 2; SATA 41, 71, 109; SATA-Brief 27

Myers, Walter M.
See Myers, Walter Dean

Myles, Symon
See Follett, Ken(neth Martin)

Nabokov, Vladimir (Vladimirovich)
1899-1977 .... **CLC 1, 2, 3, 6, 8, 11, 15, 23, 44, 46, 64; DA; DAB; DAC; DAM MST, NOV**
See also AW 108; BEST; CA 5-8R; 69-72; CANR 20; CDALB 1941-1968; DA3; DLB 2; DLBD 3; DLBY 80, 91; MTCW 1, 2

Naevius c. 265B.C.-201B.C. .... **CMLC 37**
See also DLB 211

Nagai, Sokichi 1879-1959
See Nagai, Kafu
See also CA 117

Nagy, Laszlo 1925-1978 .... **CLC 7**
See also CA 129; 112

Naipaul, Shiva(dhar Srinivasa)
1945-1985 .... **CLC 32, 39; DAM NOV**
See also CA 110; 112; 116; CANR 33; DA3; DLB 157; DLBY 85; MTCW 1, 2

Naipaul, V(idiadhar) S(urajprasad)
1932- .... **CLC 4, 7, 9, 13, 18, 37, 105; DAB; DAC; DAM MST, NOV**
See also AW 38; BRWS 1; CA 1-4R; CANR 1, 33, 51, 91; CDBLB 1960 to Present; DA3; DLB 125, 204, 206; DLBY 85; MTCW 1, 2

Nakos, Lilika 1899(?)- .... **CLC 29**

Narayan, R(asipuram) K(rishnaswami)
1906-2001 .... **CLC 7, 28, 47, 121; DAM NOV**
See also AW 5; CA 81-84; CANR 33, 61; DA3; MTCW 1, 2; SATA 62

Nash, (Fredric) Ogden 1902-1971 . **CLC 23; DAM POET; PC 21**
See also AW 109; CA 13-14; 29-32R; CANR 34, 61; CAP 1; DLB 11; MAICYA; MTCW 1, 2; SATA 2, 46

Nashe, Thomas 1567-1601(?) .... **LC 41**
See also DLB 167

Nashe, Thomas 1567-1601 .... **LC 41**

Nathan, Daniel
See Dannay, Frederic

Nathan, George Jean 1882-1958
See Hatteras, Owen
See also AW 18; CA 114; 169; DLB 137

Natsume, Kinnosuke 1867-1916
See Natsume, Soseki
See also CA 104

Natti, (Mary) Lee 1919-
See Kingman, Lee
See also CA 5-8R; CANR 2

Naylor, Gloria 1950- .... **CLC 28, 52; BLC 3; DA; DAC; DAM MST, MULT, NOV, POP**
See also AAYA 6, 39; BEST; BW 2, 3; CA 107; CANR 27, 51, 74; DA3; DLB 173; MTCW 1, 2

Neff, Debra .... **CLC 59**

Neihardt, John Gneisenau
1881-1973 .... **CLC 32**
See also CA 13-14; CANR 65; CAP 1; DLB 9, 54

Nekrasov, Nikolai Alekseevich
1821-1878 .... **NCLC 11**

Nelson, Willie 1933- .... **CLC 17**
See also CA 107

Nemerov, Howard (Stanley)
1920-1991 .... **CLC 2, 6, 9, 36; DAM POET; PC 24**
See also CA 1-4R; 134; CABS 2; CANR 1, 27, 53; DLB 5, 6; DLBY 83; INT CANR-27; MTCW 1, 2

Neruda, Pablo 1904-1973 .. **CLC 1, 2, 5, 7, 9, 28, 62; DA; DAB; DAC; DAM MST, MULT, POET; HLC 2; PC 4**
See also CA 19-20; 45-48; CAP 2; DA3; HW 1; MTCW 1, 2

Nerval, Gerard de 1808-1855 ... **NCLC 1, 67; PC 13**
See also AW 18

Nervo, (Jose) Amado (Ruiz de) 1870-1919
See also AW 11; CA 109; 131; HLCS 2; HW 1

Nessi, Pio Baroja y
See Baroja (y Nessi), Pio

Nestroy, Johann 1801-1862 .... **NCLC 42**
See also DLB 133

Netterville, Luke
See O'Grady, Standish (James)

Neufeld, John (Arthur) 1938- .... **CLC 17**
See also AAYA 11; BEST; CA 25-28R; CANR 11, 37, 56; CLR 52; MAICYA; SAAS 3; SATA 6, 81

Neumann, Ferenc
See Moln

Neville, Emily Cheney 1919- .... **CLC 12**
See also BEST; CA 5-8R; CANR 3, 37, 85; JRDA; MAICYA; SAAS 2; SATA 1

Newbound, Bernard Slade 1930-
See Slade, Bernard
See also CA 81-84; CANR 49; DAM DRAM

Newby, P(ercy) H(oward)
1918-1997 .... **CLC 2, 13; DAM NOV**
See also CA 5-8R; 161; CANR 32, 67; DLB 15; MTCW 1

Newlove, Donald 1928- .... **CLC 6**
See also CA 29-32R; CANR 25

Newlove, John (Herbert) 1938- .... **CLC 14**
See also CA 21-24R; CANR 9, 25

Newman, Charles 1938- .... **CLC 2, 8**
See also CA 21-24R; CANR 84

Newman, Edwin (Harold) 1919- ...... **CLC 14**
See also AITN 1; CA 69-72; CANR 5

Newman, John Henry 1801-1890 . **NCLC 38, 99**
See also DLB 18, 32, 55

Newton, (Sir)Isaac 1642-1727 .... **LC 35, 52**

Newton, Suzanne 1936- .... **CLC 35**
See also CA 41-44R; CANR 14; JRDA; SATA 5, 77

New York Dept. of Ed. .... **CLC 70**

Ng, Fae Myenne 1957(?)- .... **CLC 81**
See also CA 146

Ngema, Mbongeni 1955- .... **CLC 57**
See also BW 2; CA 143; CANR 84

Ngugi, James T(hiong'o) .... **CLC 3, 7, 13**
See also Ngugi wa Thiong'o

Ngugi wa Thiong'o 1938- .. **CLC 36; BLC 3; DAM MULT, NOV**
See also Ngugi, James T(hiong'o)
See also BW 2; CA 81-84; CANR 27, 58; DLB 125; MTCW 1, 2

Nichol, B(arrie) P(hillip) 1944-1988 . **CLC 18**
See also CA 53-56; DLB 53; SATA 66

Nichols, John (Treadwell) 1940- .... **CLC 38**
See also AW 2; CA 9-12R; CAAE 190; CAAS 2; CANR 6, 70; DLBY 82

Nichols, Leigh
See Koontz, Dean R(ay)

Nichols, Peter (Richard) 1927- .... **CLC 5, 36, 65**
See also CA 104; CANR 33, 86; DLB 13; MTCW 1

Nicholson, Linda ed. .... **CLC 65**

Nicolas, F. R. E.
See Freeling, Nicolas

Niedecker, Lorine 1903-1970 ..... **CLC 10, 42; DAM POET**
See also CA 25-28; CAP 2; DLB 48

Nievo, Ippolito 1831-1861 .... **NCLC 22**

Nightingale, Anne Redmon 1943-
See Redmon, Anne
See also CA 103

Nik. T. O.
See Annensky, Innokenty (Fyodorovich)

Nin, Anaïs 1903-1977 ..... **CLC 1, 4, 8, 11, 14, 60, 127; DAM NOV, POP**
See also AITN 2; AW 10; CA 13-16R; 69-72; CANR 22, 53; DLB 2, 4, 152; GLL 2; MTCW 1, 2

Nishiwaki, Junzaburo 1894-1982 .... **PC 15**
See also CA 107

Nissenson, Hugh 1933- .... **CLC 4, 9**
See also CA 17-20R; CANR 27; DLB 28

Niven, Larry .... **CLC 8**
See also Niven, Laurence Van Cott
See also AAYA 27; DLB 8; SCFW 2

Niven, Laurence Van Cott 1938-
See Niven, Larry
See also CA 21-24R; CAAS 12; CANR 14, 44, 66; DAM POP; MTCW 1, 2; SATA 95

Nixon, Agnes Eckhardt 1927- .... **CLC 21**
See also CA 110

Nkosi, Lewis 1936- ... **CLC 45; BLC 3; DAM MULT**
See also BW 1, 3; CA 65-68; CANR 27, 81; DLB 157, 225

Oneal, Elizabeth 1934-
See Oneal, Zibby
See also BEST; CA 106; CANR 28, 84;
MAICYA; SATA 30, 82
Oneal, Zibby .... **CLC 30**
See also Oneal, Elizabeth
See also AAYA 5; CLR 13; JRDA
Onetti, Juan Carlos 1909-1994 ... **CLC 7, 10;
DAM MULT, NOV; HLCS 2**
See also AW 23; CA 85-88; 145; CANR 32,
63; DLB 113; HW 1, 2; MTCW 1, 2
O Nuallain, Brian 1911-1966
See O'Brien, Flann
See also CA 21-22; 25-28R; CAP 2; DLB
231
Opie, Amelia 1769-1853 .... **NCLC 65**
See also DLB 116, 159
Oppen, George 1908-1984 ...... **CLC 7, 13, 34**
See also AW 107; CA 13-16R; 113; CANR
8, 82; DLB 5, 165
Opuls, Max
See Ophuls, Max
Origen c. 185-c. 254 .... **CMLC 19**
Orlovitz, Gil 1918-1973 .... **CLC 22**
See also CA 77-80; 45-48; DLB 2, 5
Orris
See Ingelow, Jean
Ortega y Gasset, Jose 1883-1955
See also AW 9; CA 106; 130; DAM MULT;
HLC 2; HW 1, 2; MTCW 1, 2
Ortese, Anna Maria 1914- .... **CLC 89**
See also DLB 177
Ortiz, Simon J(oseph) 1941- . **CLC 45; DAM
MULT, POET; PC 17**
See also AMWS 4; CA 134; CANR 69;
DLB 120, 175; NNAL
Orton, Joe .... **CLC 4, 13, 43; DC 3**
See also Orton, John Kingsley
See also BRWS 5; CDBLB 1960 to Present;
DLB 13; GLL 1; MTCW 2
Orton, John Kingsley 1933-1967
See Orton, Joe
See also CA 85-88; CANR 35, 66; DAM
DRAM; MTCW 1, 2
Osborne, David
See Silverberg, Robert
Osborne, George
See Silverberg, Robert
Osborne, John (James) 1929-1994 .... **CLC 1,
2, 5, 11, 45; DA; DAB; DAC; DAM
DRAM, MST**
See also BEST; BRWS 1; CA 13-16R; 147;
CANR 21, 56; CDBLB 1945-1960; DLB
13; MTCW 1, 2
Osborne, Lawrence 1958- .... **CLC 50**
See also CA 189
Oshima, Nagisa 1932- .... **CLC 20**
See also CA 116; 121; CANR 78
Ossian c. 3rd cent. - .... **CMLC 28**
See also Macpherson, James
Ossoli, Sarah Margaret (Fuller marchesa d')
1810-1850 .... **NCLC 5, 50**
See also Fuller, Margaret; Fuller, Sarah
Margaret
See also CDALB 1640-1865; DLB 1, 59,
73, 183, 223, 239; SATA 25
Ostriker, Alicia (Suskin) 1937- .... **CLC 132**
See also CA 25-28R; CAAS 24; CANR 10,
30, 62; DLB 120
Ostrovsky, Alexander 1823-1886 .. **NCLC 30,
57**
Otero, Blas de 1916-1979 .... **CLC 11**
See also CA 89-92; DLB 134
Otto, Whitney 1955- .... **CLC 70**
See also CA 140
Ousmane, Sembene 1923- ... **CLC 66; BLC 3**
See also Sembene, Ousmane
See also BW 1, 3; CA 117; 125; CANR 81;
CWW 2; MTCW 1

Ovid 43B.C.-17 . **CMLC 7; DAM POET; PC
2**
See also DA3; DLB 211
Owen, Hugh
See Faust, Frederick (Schiller)
Owen, Wilfred (Edward Salter)
1893-1918 .... **PC 19**
See also AW 5, 27; BEST; CA 104; 141;
CDBLB 1914-1945; DA; DAB; DAC;
DAM MST, POET; DLB 20; MTCW 2
Owens, Rochelle 1936- .... **CLC 8**
See also CA 17-20R; CAAS 2; CANR 39
Oz, Amos 1939- ...... **CLC 5, 8, 11, 27, 33, 54;
DAM NOV**
See also CA 53-56; CANR 27, 47, 65;
CWW 2; MTCW 1, 2
Ozick, Cynthia 1928- .... **CLC 3, 7, 28, 62;
DAM NOV, POP**
See also AMWS 5; AW 3; BEST 90:1; CA
17-20R; CANR 23, 58; DA3; DLB 28,
152; DLBY 82; INT CANR-23; MTCW
1, 2
Ozu, Yasujiro 1903-1963 .... **CLC 16**
See also CA 112
Pacheco, C.
See Pessoa, Fernando (Antonio Nogueira)
Pacheco, Jose Emilio 1939-
See also CA 111; 131; CANR 65; DAM
MULT; HLC 2; HW 1, 2
Pa Chin .... **CLC 18**
See also Li Fei-kan
Pack, Robert 1929- .... **CLC 13**
See also CA 1-4R; CANR 3, 44, 82; DLB
5; SATA 118
Padgett, Lewis
See Kuttner, Henry
Padilla (Lorenzo), Heberto
1932-2000 .... **CLC 38**
See also AITN 1; CA 123; 131; 189; HW 1
Page, Jimmy 1944- .... **CLC 12**
Page, Louise 1955- .... **CLC 40**
See also CA 140; CANR 76; DLB 233
Page, P(atricia) K(athleen) 1916- ...... **CLC 7,
18; DAC; DAM MST; PC 12**
See also Cape, Judith
See also CA 53-56; CANR 4, 22, 65; DLB
68; MTCW 1
Page, Stanton
See Fuller, Henry Blake
Page, Stanton
See Fuller, Henry Blake
Pagels, Elaine Hiesey 1943- .... **CLC 104**
See also CA 45-48; CANR 2, 24, 51
Paget, Violet 1856-1935
See Lee, Vernon
See also CA 104; 166; GLL 1
Paget-Lowe, Henry
See Lovecraft, H(oward) P(hillips)
Paglia, Camille (Anna) 1947- .... **CLC 68**
See also CA 140; CANR 72; GLL 2;
MTCW 2
Paige, Richard
See Koontz, Dean R(ay)
Paine, Thomas 1737-1809 .... **NCLC 62**
See also AMWS 1; CDALB 1640-1865;
DLB 31, 43, 73, 158
Pakenham, Antonia
See Fraser, (Lady)Antonia (Pakenham)
Palazzeschi, Aldo 1885-1974 .... **CLC 11**
See also CA 89-92; 53-56; DLB 114
Pales Matos, Luis 1898-
See also HLCS 2; HW 1
Paley, Grace 1922- .... **CLC 4, 6, 37, 140;
DAM POP**
See also AMWS 6; AW 3; CA 25-28R;
CANR 13, 46, 74; DA3; DLB 28; INT
CANR-13; MTCW 1, 2

Palin, Michael (Edward) 1943- .... **CLC 21**
See also Monty Python
See also CA 107; CANR 35; SATA 67
Palliser, Charles 1947- .... **CLC 65**
See also CA 136; CANR 76
Pancake, Breece Dexter 1952-1979
See Pancake, Breece D'J
See also CA 123; 109
Pancake, Breece D'J .... **CLC 29**
See also Pancake, Breece Dexter
See also DLB 130
Panchenko, Nikolai .... **CLC 59**
Panko, Rudy
See Gogol, Nikolai (Vasilyevich)
Papadiamantopoulos, Johannes 1856-1910
See Moreas, Jean
See also CA 117
Paracelsus 1493-1541 .... **LC 14**
See also DLB 179
Parasol, Peter
See Stevens, Wallace
Paretsky, Sara 1947- .. **CLC 135; DAM POP**
See also AAYA 30; BEST 90:3; CA 125;
129; CANR 59, 95; DA3; INT 129
Parfenie, Maria
See Codrescu, Andrei
Parini, Jay (Lee) 1948- .... **CLC 54, 133**
See also CA 97-100; CAAS 16; CANR 32,
87
Park, Jordan
See Kornbluth, C(yril) M.; Pohl, Frederik
Parker, Bert
See Ellison, Harlan (Jay)
Parker, Dorothy (Rothschild)
1893-1967 .... **CLC 15, 68; DAM POET;
PC 28**
See also AW 2; CA 19-20; 25-28R; CAP 2;
DA3; DLB 11, 45, 86; MTCW 1, 2
Parker, Robert B(rown) 1932- .... **CLC 27;
DAM NOV, POP**
See also AAYA 28; BEST 89:4; CA 49-52;
CANR 1, 26, 52, 89; INT CANR-26;
MTCW 1
Parkin, Frank 1940- .... **CLC 43**
See also CA 147
Parkman, Francis, Jr. 1823-1893 .. **NCLC 12**
See also AMWS 2; DLB 1, 30, 186, 235
Parks, Gordon (Alexander Buchanan)
1912- .... **CLC 1, 16; BLC 3; DAM
MULT**
See also AAYA 36; AITN 2; BW 2, 3; CA
41-44R; CANR 26, 66; DA3; DLB 33;
MTCW 2; SATA 8, 108
Parmenides c. 515B.C.-c.
450B.C. .... **CMLC 22**
See also DLB 176
Parnell, Thomas 1679-1718 .... **LC 3**
See also DLB 94
Parra, Nicanor 1914- ...... **CLC 2, 102; DAM
MULT; HLC 2**
See also CA 85-88; CANR 32; CWW 2;
HW 1; MTCW 1
Parra Sanojo, Ana Teresa de la 1890-1936
See also HLCS 2
Parrish, Mary Frances
See Fisher, M(ary) F(rances) K(ennedy)
Parshchikov, Aleksei .... **CLC 59**
Parson
See Coleridge, Samuel Taylor
Parson Lot
See Kingsley, Charles
Parton, Sara Payson Willis
1811-1872 .... **NCLC 86**
See also DLB 43, 74, 239
Partridge, Anthony
See Oppenheim, E(dward) Phillips

Pascal, Blaise 1623-1662 .... **LC 35**

Pasolini, Pier Paolo 1922-1975 .. **CLC 20, 37, 106; PC 17**
   See also CA 93-96; 61-64; CANR 63; DLB 128, 177; MTCW 1

Pasquini
   See Silone, Ignazio

Pastan, Linda (Olenik) 1932- .... **CLC 27; DAM POET**
   See also CA 61-64; CANR 18, 40, 61; DLB 5

Pasternak, Boris (Leonidovich) 1890-1960 .... **CLC 7, 10, 18, 63; DA; DAB; DAC; DAM MST, NOV, POET; PC 6**
   See also AW 31; CA 127; 116; DA3; MTCW 1, 2

Patchen, Kenneth 1911-1972 .. **CLC 1, 2, 18; DAM POET**
   See also CA 1-4R; 33-36R; CANR 3, 35; DLB 16, 48; MTCW 1

Pater, Walter (Horatio) 1839-1894 . **NCLC 7, 90**
   See also CDBLB 1832-1890; DLB 57, 156

Paterson, Katherine (Womeldorf) 1932- .... **CLC 12, 30**
   See also AAYA 1, 31; CA 21-24R; CANR 28, 59; CLR 7, 50; DLB 52; JRDA; MAICYA; MTCW 1; SATA 13, 53, 92

Patmore, Coventry Kersey Dighton 1823-1896 .... **NCLC 9**
   See also DLB 35, 98

Paton, Alan (Stewart) 1903-1988 ...... **CLC 4, 10, 25, 55, 106; DA; DAB; DAC; DAM MST, NOV**
   See also AAYA 26; BEST; BRWS 2; CA 13-16; 125; CANR 22; CAP 1; DA3; DLB 225; DLBD 17; MTCW 1, 2; SATA 11; SATA-Obit 56

Paton Walsh, Gillian 1937- .... **CLC 35**
   See also Walsh, Jill Paton
   See also AAYA 11; BEST; CANR 38, 83; CLR 2, 65; DLB 161; JRDA; MAICYA; SAAS 3; SATA 4, 72, 109

Paton Walsh, Jill
   See Paton Walsh, Gillian

Paulding, James Kirke 1778-1860 ... **NCLC 2**
   See also DLB 3, 59, 74

Paulin, Thomas Neilson 1949-
   See Paulin, Tom
   See also CA 123; 128

Paulin, Tom .... **CLC 37**
   See also Paulin, Thomas Neilson
   See also DLB 40

Pausanias c. 1st cent. - .... **CMLC 36**

Paustovsky, Konstantin (Georgievich) 1892-1968 .... **CLC 40**
   See also CA 93-96; 25-28R

Pavese, Cesare 1908-1950 .... **PC 13**
   See also AW 19; CA 104; 169; DLB 128, 177

Pavic, Milorad 1929- .... **CLC 60**
   See also CA 136; CWW 2; DLB 181

Payne, Alan
   See Jakes, John (William)

Paz, Gil
   See Lugones, Leopoldo

Paz, Octavio 1914-1998 . **CLC 3, 4, 6, 10, 19, 51, 65, 119; DA; DAB; DAC; DAM MST, MULT, POET; HLC 2; PC 1**
   See also BEST; CA 73-76; 165; CANR 32, 65; CWW 2; DA3; DLBY 90, 98; HW 1, 2; MTCW 1, 2

p'Bitek, Okot 1931-1982 .... **CLC 96; BLC 3; DAM MULT**
   See also BW 2, 3; CA 124; 107; CANR 82; DLB 125; MTCW 1, 2

Peacock, Molly 1947- .... **CLC 60**
   See also CA 103; CAAS 21; CANR 52, 84; DLB 120

Peacock, Thomas Love 1785-1866 .... **NCLC 22**
   See also DLB 96, 116

Peake, Mervyn 1911-1968 .... **CLC 7, 54**
   See also CA 5-8R; 25-28R; CANR 3; DLB 15, 160; MTCW 1; SATA 23

Pearce, Philippa .... **CLC 21**
   See also Christie, (Ann) Philippa
   See also CLR 9; DLB 161; MAICYA; SATA 1, 67

Pearl, Eric
   See Elman, Richard (Martin)

Pearson, T(homas) R(eid) 1956- .... **CLC 39**
   See also CA 120; 130; CANR 97; INT 130

Peck, Dale 1967- .... **CLC 81**
   See also CA 146; CANR 72; GLL 2

Peck, John 1941- .... **CLC 3**
   See also CA 49-52; CANR 3

Peck, Richard (Wayne) 1934- .... **CLC 21**
   See also AAYA 1, 24; CA 85-88; CANR 19, 38; CLR 15; INT CANR-19; JRDA; MAICYA; SAAS 2; SATA 18, 55, 97; SATA-Essay 110

Peck, Robert Newton 1928- .... **CLC 17; DA; DAC; DAM MST**
   See also AAYA 3; BEST; CA 81-84, 182; CAAE 182; CANR 31, 63; CLR 45; JRDA; MAICYA; SAAS 1; SATA 21, 62, 111; SATA-Essay 108

Peckinpah, (David) Sam(uel) 1925-1984 .... **CLC 20**
   See also CA 109; 114; CANR 82

Pedersen, Knut 1859-1952
   See Hamsun, Knut
   See also CA 104; 119; CANR 63; MTCW 1, 2

Peeslake, Gaffer
   See Durrell, Lawrence (George)

Pellicer, Carlos 1900(?)-1977
   See also CA 153; 69-72; HLCS 2; HW 1

Pena, Ramon del Valle y
   See Valle-Inclan, Ramon (Maria) del

Pendennis, Arthur Esquir
   See Thackeray, William Makepeace

Penn, William 1644-1718 .... **LC 25**
   See also DLB 24

PEPECE
   See Prado (Calvo), Pedro

Pepys, Samuel 1633-1703 .... **LC 11, 58; DA; DAB; DAC; DAM MST**
   See also BEST; CDBLB 1660-1789; DA3; DLB 101

Percy, Thomas 1729-1811 .... **NCLC 95**
   See also DLB 104

Percy, Walker 1916-1990 .... **CLC 2, 3, 6, 8, 14, 18, 47, 65; DAM NOV, POP**
   See also AMWS 3; CA 1-4R; 131; CANR 1, 23, 64; DA3; DLB 2; DLBY 80, 90; MTCW 1, 2

Perec, Georges 1936-1982 .... **CLC 56, 116**
   See also CA 141; DLB 83

Pereda y Porrua, Jose Maria de
   See Pereda (y Sanchez de Porrua), Jose Maria de

Peregoy, George Weems
   See Mencken, H(enry) L(ouis)

Perelman, S(idney) J(oseph) 1904-1979 .. **CLC 3, 5, 9, 15, 23, 44, 49; DAM DRAM**
   See also AITN 1, 2; AW 32; CA 73-76; 89-92; CANR 18; DLB 11, 44; MTCW 1, 2

Peret, Benjamin 1899-1959 .... **PC 33**
   See also AW 20; CA 117; 186

Peretz, Yitzhok Leibush
   See Peretz, Isaac Loeb

Perez Galdos, Benito 1843-1920
   See also AW 27; CA 125; 153; HLCS 2; HW 1

Peri Rossi, Cristina 1941-
   See also CA 131; CANR 59, 81; DLB 145; HLCS 2; HW 1, 2

Perlata
   See Peret, Benjamin

Perloff, Marjorie G(abrielle) 1931- .... **CLC 137**
   See also CA 57-60; CANR 7, 22, 49

Perrault, Charles 1628-1703 ... **LC 3, 52; DC 12**
   See also MAICYA; SATA 25

Perry, Anne 1938- .... **CLC 126**
   See also CA 101; CANR 22, 50, 84

Perry, Brighton
   See Sherwood, Robert E(mmet)

Perse, St.-John
   See Leger, (Marie-Rene Auguste) Alexis Saint-Leger

Peseenz, Tulio F.
   See Lopez y Fuentes, Gregorio

Pesetsky, Bette 1932- .... **CLC 28**
   See also CA 133; DLB 130

Peshkov, Alexei Maximovich 1868-1936
   See Gorky, Maxim
   See also CA 105; 141; CANR 83; DA; DAC; DAM DRAM, MST, NOV; MTCW 2

Pessoa, Fernando (Antonio Nogueira) 1898-1935 .... **PC 20**
   See also AW 27; CA 125; 183; DAM MULT; HLC 2

Peterkin, Julia Mood 1880-1961 ...... **CLC 31**
   See also CA 102; DLB 9

Peters, Joan K(aren) 1945- .... **CLC 39**
   See also CA 158

Peters, Robert L(ouis) 1924- .... **CLC 7**
   See also CA 13-16R; CAAS 8; DLB 105

Petofi, Sandor 1823-1849 .... **NCLC 21**

Petrakis, Harry Mark 1923- .... **CLC 3**
   See also CA 9-12R; CANR 4, 30, 85

Petrarch 1304-1374 .... **CMLC 20; DAM POET; PC 8**
   See also DA3

Petronius c. 20-66 .... **CMLC 34**
   See also DLB 211

Petry, Ann (Lane) 1908-1997 ... **CLC 1, 7, 18**
   See also BW 1, 3; CA 5-8R; 157; CAAS 6; CANR 4, 46; CLR 12; DLB 76; JRDA; MAICYA; MTCW 1; SATA 5; SATA-Obit 94

Petursson, Halligrimur 1614-1674 .... **LC 8**

Peychinovich
   See Vazov, Ivan (Minchov)

Phaedrus c. 15B.C.-c. 50 .... **CMLC 25**
   See also DLB 211

Philips, Katherine 1632-1664 .... **LC 30**
   See also DLB 131

Philipson, Morris H. 1926- .... **CLC 53**
   See also CA 1-4R; CANR 4

Phillips, Caryl 1958- . **CLC 96; BLCS; DAM MULT**
   See also BRWS 5; BW 2; CA 141; CANR 63; DA3; DLB 157; MTCW 2

Phillips, Jack
   See Sandburg, Carl (August)

Phillips, Jayne Anne 1952- . **CLC 15, 33, 139**
   See also AW 4; CA 101; CANR 24, 50, 96; DLBY 80; INT CANR-24; MTCW 1, 2

Phillips, Richard
   See Dick, Philip K(indred)

Phillips, Robert (Schaeffer) 1938- .... **CLC 28**
   See also CA 17-20R; CAAS 13; CANR 8; DLB 105

Phillips, Ward
   See Lovecraft, H(oward) P(hillips)

Rich, Robert
See Trumbo, Dalton
See also IDFW 3

Richard, Keith .... **CLC 17**
See also Richards, Keith

Richards, David Adams 1950- .... **CLC 59; DAC**
See also CA 93-96; CANR 60; DLB 53

Richards, I(vor) A(rmstrong)
1893-1979 .... **CLC 14, 24**
See also BRWS 2; CA 41-44R; 89-92;
CANR 34, 74; DLB 27; MTCW 2

Richards, Keith 1943-
See Richard, Keith
See also CA 107; CANR 77

Richardson, Anne
See Roiphe, Anne (Richardson)

Richardson (Robertson), Ethel Florence
Lindesay 1870-1946
See Richardson, Henry Handel
See also CA 105; 190; DLB 230

Richardson, John 1796-1852 .... **NCLC 55; DAC**
See also CCA 1; DLB 99

Richardson, Samuel 1689-1761 ...... **LC 1, 44; DA; DAB; DAC; DAM MST, NOV**
See also BEST; CDBLB 1660-1789; DLB 39

Richler, Mordecai 1931-2001 .... **CLC 3, 5, 9, 13, 18, 46, 70; DAC; DAM MST, NOV**
See also AITN 1; CA 65-68; CANR 31, 62;
CCA 1; CLR 17; DLB 53; MAICYA;
MTCW 1, 2; SATA 44, 98; SATA-Brief 27

Richter, Conrad (Michael)
1890-1968 .... **CLC 30**
See also AAYA 21; AW 2; BEST; CA 5-8R;
25-28R; CANR 23; DLB 9, 212; MTCW
1, 2; SATA 3

Ricostranza, Tom
See Ellis, Trey

Ridge, John Rollin 1827-1867 ...... **NCLC 82; DAM MULT**
See also CA 144; DLB 175; NNAL

Ridgeway, Jason
See Marlowe, Stephen

Ridgway, Keith 1965- .... **CLC 119**
See also CA 172

Riding, Laura .... **CLC 3, 7**
See also Jackson, Laura (Riding)

Riefenstahl, Berta Helene Amalia 1902-
See Riefenstahl, Leni
See also CA 108

Riefenstahl, Leni .... **CLC 16**
See also Riefenstahl, Berta Helene Amalia

Riffe, Ernest
See Bergman, (Ernst) Ingmar

Riley, Tex
See Creasey, John

Rilke, Rainer Maria 1875-1926 .... **PC 2**
See also AW 1, 6, 19; CA 104; 132; CANR
62; DAM POET; DA3; DLB 81; MTCW
1, 2

Rimbaud, (Jean Nicolas) Arthur
1854-1891 . **NCLC 4, 35, 82; DA; DAB; DAC; DAM MST, POET; PC 3**
See also DA3

Ringmaster, The
See Mencken, H(enry) L(ouis)

Ringwood, Gwen(dolyn Margaret) Pharis
1910-1984 .... **CLC 48**
See also CA 148; 112; DLB 88

Rio, Michel 19(?)- .... **CLC 43**

Ritsos, Giannes
See Ritsos, Yannis

Ritsos, Yannis 1909-1990 .... **CLC 6, 13, 31**
See also CA 77-80; 133; CANR 39, 61;
MTCW 1

Ritter, Erika 1948(?)- .... **CLC 52**

Rivera, Tomas 1935-1984
See also AW 2; CA 49-52; CANR 32; DLB
82; HLCS 2; HW 1

Rivers, Conrad Kent 1933-1968 .... **CLC 1**
See also BW 1; CA 85-88; DLB 41

Rivers, Elfrida
See Bradley, Marion Zimmer
See also GLL 1

Riverside, John
See Heinlein, Robert A(nson)

Rizal, Jose 1861-1896 .... **NCLC 27**

Roa Bastos, Augusto (Antonio)
1917- .... **CLC 45; DAM MULT; HLC 2**
See also CA 131; DLB 113; HW 1

Robbe-Grillet, Alain 1922- .... **CLC 1, 2, 4, 6, 8, 10, 14, 43, 128**
See also CA 9-12R; CANR 33, 65; DLB
83; MTCW 1, 2

Robbins, Harold 1916-1997 .... **CLC 5; DAM NOV**
See also CA 73-76; 162; CANR 26, 54;
DA3; MTCW 1, 2

Robbins, Thomas Eugene 1936-
See Robbins, Tom
See also CA 81-84; CANR 29, 59, 95;
DAM NOV, POP; DA3; MTCW 1, 2

Robbins, Tom .... **CLC 9, 32, 64**
See also Robbins, Thomas Eugene
See also AAYA 32; BEST 90:3; DLBY 80;
MTCW 2

Robbins, Trina 1938- .... **CLC 21**
See also CA 128

Roberts, Kate 1891-1985 .... **CLC 15**
See also CA 107; 116

Roberts, Keith (John Kingston)
1935-2000 .... **CLC 14**
See also CA 25-28R; CANR 46

Roberts, Michele (Brigitte) 1949- ..... **CLC 48**
See also CA 115; CANR 58; DLB 231

Robertson, Ellis
See Ellison, Harlan (Jay); Silverberg, Robert

Robertson, Thomas William
1829-1871 .... **NCLC 35; DAM DRAM**

Robeson, Kenneth
See Dent, Lester

Robinson, Edwin Arlington 1869-1935 . **PC 1**
See also AW 5, 101; CA 104; 133; CDALB
1865-1917; DA; DAC; DAM MST,
POET; DLB 54; MTCW 1, 2

Robinson, Henry Crabb
1775-1867 .... **NCLC 15**
See also DLB 107

Robinson, Jill 1936- .... **CLC 10**
See also CA 102; INT 102

Robinson, Kim Stanley 1952- .... **CLC 34**
See also AAYA 26; CA 126; SATA 109

Robinson, Lloyd
See Silverberg, Robert

Robinson, Marilynne 1944- .... **CLC 25**
See also CA 116; CANR 80; DLB 206

Robinson, Smokey .... **CLC 21**
See also Robinson, William, Jr.

Robinson, William, Jr. 1940-
See Robinson, Smokey
See also CA 116

Robison, Mary 1949- .... **CLC 42, 98**
See also CA 113; 116; CANR 87; DLB 130;
INT 116

Roddenberry, Eugene Wesley 1921-1991
See Roddenberry, Gene
See also CA 110; 135; CANR 37; SATA 45;
SATA-Obit 69

Roddenberry, Gene .... **CLC 17**
See also Roddenberry, Eugene Wesley
See also AAYA 5; SATA-Obit 69

Rodgers, Mary 1931- .... **CLC 12**
See also CA 49-52; CANR 8, 55, 90; CLR
20; INT CANR-8; JRDA; MAICYA;
SATA 8

Rodgers, W(illiam) R(obert)
1909-1969 .... **CLC 7**
See also CA 85-88; DLB 20

Rodman, Eric
See Silverberg, Robert

Rodman, Howard 1920(?)-1985 .... **CLC 65**
See also CA 118

Rodman, Maia
See Wojciechowska, Maia (Teresa)

Rodo, Jose Enrique 1871(?)-1917
See also CA 178; HLCS 2; HW 2

Rodriguez, Claudio 1934-1999 .... **CLC 10**
See also CA 188; DLB 134

Rodriguez, Richard 1944-
See also CA 110; CANR 66; DAM MULT;
DLB 82; HLC 2; HW 1, 2

Roethke, Theodore (Huebner)
1908-1963 .... **CLC 1, 3, 8, 11, 19, 46, 101; DAM POET; PC 15**
See also CA 81-84; CABS 2; CDALB 1941-
1968; DA3; DLB 5, 206; MTCW 1, 2

Rogers, Samuel 1763-1855 .... **NCLC 69**
See also DLB 93

Rogers, Thomas Hunton 1927- .... **CLC 57**
See also CA 89-92; INT 89-92

Rogin, Gilbert 1929- .... **CLC 18**
See also CA 65-68; CANR 15

Rohan, Koda
See Koda Shigeyuki

Rohlfs, Anna Katharine Green
See Green, Anna Katharine

Rohmer, Eric .... **CLC 16**
See also Scherer, Jean-Marie Maurice

Roiphe, Anne (Richardson) 1935- .. **CLC 3, 9**
See also CA 89-92; CANR 45, 73; DLBY
80; INT 89-92

Rojas, Fernando de 1475-1541 .... **LC 23; HLCS 1**

Rojas, Gonzalo 1917-
See also HLCS 2; HW 2

Rojas, Gonzalo 1917-
See also CA 178; HLCS 2

Rolle, Richard c. 1300-c. 1349 ...... **CMLC 21**
See also DLB 146

Rolvaag, O(le) E(dvart)
See Roelvaag, O(le) E(dvart)

Romain Arnaud, Saint
See Aragon, Louis

Romains, Jules 1885-1972 .... **CLC 7**
See also CA 85-88; CANR 34; DLB 65;
MTCW 1

Ronsard, Pierre de 1524-1585 . **LC 6, 54; PC 11**

Rooke, Leon 1934- . **CLC 25, 34; DAM POP**
See also CA 25-28R; CANR 23, 53; CCA 1

Roper, William 1498-1578 .... **LC 10**

Roquelaure, A. N.
See Rice, Anne

Rosa, Joao Guimaraes 1908-1967 ... **CLC 23; HLCS 1**
See also CA 89-92; DLB 113

Rose, Wendy 1948- .. **CLC 85; DAM MULT; PC 13**
See also CA 53-56; CANR 5, 51; DLB 175;
NNAL; SATA 12

Rosen, R. D.
See Rosen, Richard (Dean)

Rosen, Richard (Dean) 1949- .... **CLC 39**
See also CA 77-80; CANR 62; INT
CANR-30

Rosenblatt, Joe .... **CLC 15**
See also Rosenblatt, Joseph

Rosenblatt, Joseph 1933-
See Rosenblatt, Joe
See also CA 89-92; INT 89-92
Rosenfeld, Samuel
See Tzara, Tristan
Rosenstock, Sami
See Tzara, Tristan
Rosenstock, Samuel
See Tzara, Tristan
Rosenthal, M(acha) L(ouis)
1917-1996 .... **CLC 28**
See also CA 1-4R; 152; CAAS 6; CANR 4,
51; DLB 5; SATA 59
Ross, Barnaby
See Dannay, Frederic
Ross, Bernard L.
See Follett, Ken(neth Martin)
Ross, J. H.
See Lawrence, T(homas) E(dward)
Ross, John Hume
See Lawrence, T(homas) E(dward)
Ross, Martin -1915
See Martin, Violet Florence
See also DLB 135; GLL 2
Ross, (James) Sinclair 1908-1996 ... **CLC 13;
DAC; DAM MST**
See also AW 24; CA 73-76; CANR 81; DLB
88
Rossetti, Christina (Georgina)
1830-1894 . **NCLC 2, 50, 66; DA; DAB;
DAC; DAM MST, POET; PC 7**
See also BEST; DA3; DLB 35, 163, 240;
MAICYA; SATA 20
Rossetti, Dante Gabriel 1828-1882 . **NCLC 4,
77; DA; DAB; DAC; DAM MST,
POET**
See also BEST; CDBLB 1832-1890; DLB
35
Rossner, Judith (Perelman) 1935- . **CLC 6, 9,
29**
See also AITN 2; BEST 90:3; CA 17-20R;
CANR 18, 51, 73; DLB 6; INT CANR-
18; MTCW 1, 2
Rostand, Edmond (Eugene Alexis)
1868-1918 .... **DC 10**
See also AW 6, 37; CA 104; 126; DA; DAB;
DAC; DAM DRAM, MST; DA3; DLB
192; MTCW 1
Roth, Henry 1906-1995 ..... **CLC 2, 6, 11, 104**
See also CA 11-12; 149; CANR 38, 63;
CAP 1; DA3; DLB 28; MTCW 1, 2
Roth, Philip (Milton) 1933- ... **CLC 1, 2, 3, 4,
6, 9, 15, 22, 31, 47, 66, 86, 119; DA;
DAB; DAC; DAM MST, NOV, POP**
See also AMWS 3; AW 26; BEST; CA
1-4R; CANR 1, 22, 36, 55, 89; CDALB
1968-1988; DA3; DLB 2, 28, 173; DLBY
82; MTCW 1, 2
Rothenberg, Jerome 1931- .... **CLC 6, 57**
See also CA 45-48; CANR 1; DLB 5, 193
Rotter, Pat ed. .... **CLC 65**
Rousseau, Jean-Baptiste 1671-1741 ...... **LC 9**
Rousseau, Jean-Jacques 1712-1778 .... **LC 14,
36; DA; DAB; DAC; DAM MST**
See also BEST; DA3
Rovit, Earl (Herbert) 1927- .... **CLC 7**
See also CA 5-8R; CANR 12
Rowe, Elizabeth Singer 1674-1737 ..... **LC 44**
See also DLB 39, 95
Rowe, Nicholas 1674-1718 .... **LC 8**
See also DLB 84
Rowlandson, Mary 1637(?)-1678 .... **LC 66**
See also DLB 24, 200
Rowley, Ames Dorrance
See Lovecraft, H(oward) P(hillips)
Rowling, J(oanne) K. 1966(?)- .... **CLC 137**
See also AAYA 34; CA 173; CLR 66; SATA
109

Rowson, Susanna Haswell
1762(?)-1824 .... **NCLC 5, 69**
See also DLB 37, 200
Roy, Arundhati 1960(?)- .... **CLC 109**
See also CA 163; CANR 90; DLBY 97
Roy, Gabrielle 1909-1983 .... **CLC 10, 14;
DAB; DAC; DAM MST**
See also CA 53-56; 110; CANR 5, 61; CCA
1; DLB 68; MTCW 1; SATA 104
Royko, Mike 1932-1997 .... **CLC 109**
See also CA 89-92; 157; CANR 26
Rozewicz, Tadeusz 1921- ..... **CLC 9, 23, 139;
DAM POET**
See also CA 108; CANR 36, 66; CWW 2;
DA3; DLB 232; MTCW 1, 2
Ruark, Gibbons 1941- .... **CLC 3**
See also CA 33-36R; CAAS 23; CANR 14,
31, 57; DLB 120
Rubens, Bernice (Ruth) 1923- .... **CLC 19, 31**
See also CA 25-28R; CANR 33, 65; DLB
14, 207; MTCW 1
Rubin, Harold
See Robbins, Harold
Rudkin, (James) David 1936- .... **CLC 14**
See also CA 89-92; DLB 13
Rudnik, Raphael 1933- .... **CLC 7**
See also CA 29-32R
Ruffian, M.
See Hasek, Jaroslav (Matej Frantisek)
Ruiz, Jose Martinez .... **CLC 11**
See also Martinez Ruiz, Jose
Rukeyser, Muriel 1913-1980 . **CLC 6, 10, 15,
27; DAM POET; PC 12**
See also AMWS 6; CA 5-8R; 93-96; CANR
26, 60; DA3; DLB 48; GLL 2; MTCW 1,
2; SATA-Obit 22
Rule, Jane (Vance) 1931- .... **CLC 27**
See also CA 25-28R; CAAS 18; CANR 12,
87; DLB 60
Rulfo, Juan 1918-1986 ...... **CLC 8, 80; DAM
MULT; HLC 2**
See also AW 25; CA 85-88; 118; CANR 26;
DLB 113; HW 1, 2; MTCW 1, 2
Rumi, Jalal al-Din 1207-1273 .... **CMLC 20**
Runeberg, Johan 1804-1877 .... **NCLC 41**
Rush, Norman 1933- .... **CLC 44**
See also CA 121; 126; INT 126
Rushdie, (Ahmed) Salman 1947- .... **CLC 23,
31, 55, 100; DAB; DAC; DAM MST,
NOV, POP**
See also BEST; BRWS 4; CA 108; 111;
CANR 33, 56; DA3; DLB 194; INT 111;
MTCW 1, 2
Rushforth, Peter (Scott) 1945- .... **CLC 19**
See also CA 101
Russ, Joanna 1937- .... **CLC 15**
See also CA 5-28R; CANR 11, 31, 65; DLB
8; GLL 1; MTCW 1; SCFW 2
Russell, George William 1867-1935
See Baker, Jean H.
See also CA 104; 153; CDBLB 1890-1914;
DAM POET
Russell, Jeffrey Burton 1934- .... **CLC 70**
See also CA 25-28R; CANR 11, 28, 52
Russell, (Henry) Ken(neth Alfred)
1927- .... **CLC 16**
See also CA 105
Russell, William Martin 1947- .... **CLC 60**
See also CA 164; DLB 233
Ruyslinck, Ward .... **CLC 14**
See also Belser, Reimond Karel Maria de
Ryan, Cornelius (John) 1920-1974 ..... **CLC 7**
See also CA 69-72; 53-56; CANR 38
Ryan, Michael 1946- .... **CLC 65**
See also CA 49-52; DLBY 82
Ryan, Tim
See Dent, Lester

Rybakov, Anatoli (Naumovich)
1911-1998 .... **CLC 23, 53**
See also CA 126; 135; 172; SATA 79;
SATA-Obit 108
Ryder, Jonathan
See Ludlum, Robert
Ryga, George 1932-1987 .... **CLC 14; DAC;
DAM MST**
See also CA 101; 124; CANR 43, 90; CCA
1; DLB 60
S. H.
See Hartmann, Sadakichi
S. S.
See Sassoon, Siegfried (Lorraine)
Sabato, Ernesto (R.) 1911- .... **CLC 10, 23;
DAM MULT; HLC 2**
See also CA 97-100; CANR 32, 65; DLB
145; HW 1, 2; MTCW 1, 2
Sacastru, Martin
See Bioy Casares, Adolfo
See also CWW 2
Sacastru, Martin
See Bioy Casares, Adolfo
Sacher-Masoch, Leopold von
1836(?)-1895 .... **NCLC 31**
Sachs, Marilyn (Stickle) 1927- .... **CLC 35**
See also AAYA 2; CA 17-20R; CANR 13,
47; CLR 2; JRDA; MAICYA; SAAS 2;
SATA 3, 68; SATA-Essay 110
Sachs, Nelly 1891-1970 .... **CLC 14, 98**
See also CA 17-18; 25-28R; CANR 87;
CAP 2; MTCW 2
Sackler, Howard (Oliver)
1929-1982 .... **CLC 14**
See also CA 61-64; 108; CANR 30; DLB 7
Sacks, Oliver (Wolf) 1933- .... **CLC 67**
See also CA 53-56; CANR 28, 50, 76; DA3;
INT CANR-28; MTCW 1, 2
Sadakichi
See Hartmann, Sadakichi
Sade, Donatien Alphonse Francois
1740-1814 .... **NCLC 3, 47**
Sadoff, Ira 1945- .... **CLC 9**
See also CA 53-56; CANR 5, 21; DLB 120
Saetone
See Camus, Albert
Safire, William 1929- .... **CLC 10**
See also CA 17-20R; CANR 31, 54, 91
Sagan, Carl (Edward) 1934-1996 .... **CLC 30,
112**
See also AAYA 2; CA 25-28R; 155; CANR
11, 36, 74; DA3; MTCW 1, 2; SATA 58;
SATA-Obit 94
Sagan, Francoise .... **CLC 3, 6, 9, 17, 36**
See also Quoirez, Francoise
See also CWW 2; DLB 83; MTCW 2
Sahgal, Nayantara (Pandit) 1927- .... **CLC 41**
See also CA 9-12R; CANR 11, 88
Said, Edward W. 1935- .... **CLC 123**
See also CA 21-24R; CANR 45, 74; DLB
67; MTCW 2
Saint, H(arry) F. 1941- .... **CLC 50**
See also CA 127
St. Aubin de Teran, Lisa 1953-
See Teran, Lisa St. Aubin de
See also CA 118; 126; INT 126
Saint Birgitta of Sweden c.
1303-1373 .... **CMLC 24**
Sainte-Beuve, Charles Augustin
1804-1869 .... **NCLC 5**
St. John, David
See Hunt, E(verette) Howard, (Jr.)
Saint-John Perse
See Leger, (Marie-Rene Auguste) Alexis
Saint-Leger

Schulz, Charles M(onroe)
1922-2000 .... **CLC 12**
See also AAYA 39; CA 9-12R; 187; CANR 6; INT CANR-6; SATA 10; SATA-Obit 118

Schumacher, E(rnst) F(riedrich)
1911-1977 .... **CLC 80**
See also CA 81-84; 73-76; CANR 34, 85

Schuyler, James Marcus 1923-1991 .. **CLC 5, 23; DAM POET**
See also CA 101; 134; DLB 5, 169; INT 101

Schwartz, Delmore (David)
1913-1966 ... **CLC 2, 4, 10, 45, 87; PC 8**
See also AMWS 2; CA 17-18; 25-28R; CANR 35; CAP 2; DLB 28, 48; MTCW 1, 2

Schwartz, Ernst
See Ozu, Yasujiro

Schwartz, John Burnham 1965- .... **CLC 59**
See also CA 132

Schwartz, Lynne Sharon 1939- .... **CLC 31**
See also CA 103; CANR 44, 89; MTCW 2

Schwartz, Muriel A.
See Eliot, T(homas) S(tearns)

Schwarz-Bart, Andre 1928- .... **CLC 2, 4**
See also CA 89-92

Schwarz-Bart, Simone 1938- . **CLC 7; BLCS**
See also BW 2; CA 97-100

Sciascia, Leonardo 1921-1989 .. **CLC 8, 9, 41**
See also CA 85-88; 130; CANR 35; DLB 177; MTCW 1

Scoppettone, Sandra 1936- .... **CLC 26**
See Early, Jack
See also AAYA 11; BEST; CA 5-8R; CANR 41, 73; GLL 1; SATA 9, 92

Scorsese, Martin 1942- .... **CLC 20, 89**
See also AAYA 38; CA 110; 114; CANR 46, 85

Scotland, Jay
See Jakes, John (William)

Scott, Evelyn 1893-1963 .... **CLC 43**
See also CA 104; 112; CANR 64; DLB 9, 48

Scott, F(rancis) R(eginald)
1899-1985 .... **CLC 22**
See also CA 101; 114; CANR 87; DLB 88; INT 101

Scott, Frank
See Scott, F(rancis) R(eginald)

Scott, Joan .... **CLC 65**
Scott, Joanna 1960- .... **CLC 50**
See also CA 126; CANR 53, 92

Scott, Paul (Mark) 1920-1978 ...... **CLC 9, 60**
See also BRWS 1; CA 81-84; 77-80; CANR 33; DLB 14, 207; MTCW 1

Scott, Sarah 1723-1795 .... **LC 44**
See also DLB 39

Scott, Walter 1771-1832 . **NCLC 15, 69; DA; DAB; DAC; DAM MST, NOV, POET; PC 13**
See also AAYA 22; BEST; CDBLB 1789-1832; DLB 93, 107, 116, 144, 159

Scribe, (Augustin) Eugene
1791-1861 ..... **NCLC 16; DAM DRAM; DC 5**
See also DLB 192

Scrum, R.
See Crumb, R(obert)

Scudery, Madeleine de 1607-1701 .. **LC 2, 58**

Scum
See Crumb, R(obert)

Scumbag, Little Bobby
See Crumb, R(obert)

Seabrook, John
See Hubbard, L(afayette) Ron(ald)

Sealy, I(rwin) Allan 1951- .... **CLC 55**
See also CA 136

Search, Alexander
See Pessoa, Fernando (Antonio Nogueira)

Sebastian, Lee
See Silverberg, Robert

Sebastian Owl
See Thompson, Hunter S(tockton)

Sebestyen, Ouida 1924- .... **CLC 30**
See also AAYA 8; BEST; CA 107; CANR 40; CLR 17; JRDA; MAICYA; SAAS 10; SATA 39

Secundus, H. Scriblerus
See Fielding, Henry

Sedges, John
See Buck, Pearl S(ydenstricker)

Sedgwick, Catharine Maria
1789-1867 .... **NCLC 19, 98**
See also DLB 1, 74, 239

Seelye, John (Douglas) 1931- .... **CLC 7**
See also AW 2; CA 97-100; CANR 70; INT 97-100

Seferiades, Giorgos Stylianou 1900-1971
See Seferis, George
See also CA 5-8R; 33-36R; CANR 5, 36; MTCW 1

Seferis, George .... **CLC 5, 11**
See also Seferiades, Giorgos Stylianou

Segal, Erich (Wolf) 1937- . **CLC 3, 10; DAM POP**
See also BEST 89:1; CA 25-28R; CANR 20, 36, 65; DLBY 86; INT CANR-20; MTCW 1

Seger, Bob 1945- .... **CLC 35**

Seghers, Anna .... **CLC 7**
See also Radvanyi, Netty
See also DLB 69

Seidel, Frederick (Lewis) 1936- .... **CLC 18**
See also CA 13-16R; CANR 8; DLBY 84

Seifert, Jaroslav 1901-1986 .. **CLC 34, 44, 93**
See also CA 127; DLB 215; MTCW 1, 2

Sei Shonagon c. 966-1017(?) .... **CMLC 6**

Sejour, Victor 1817-1874 .... **DC 10**
See also DLB 50

Sejour Marcou et Ferrand, Juan Victor
See Sejour, Victor

Selby, Hubert, Jr. 1928- .... **CLC 1, 2, 4, 8**
See also AW 20; CA 13-16R; CANR 33, 85; DLB 2, 227

Selzer, Richard 1928- .... **CLC 74**
See also CA 65-68; CANR 14

Sembene, Ousmane
See Ousmane, Sembene
See also CWW 2

Senancour, Etienne Pivert de
1770-1846 .... **NCLC 16**
See also DLB 119

Sender, Ramon (Jose) 1902-1982 ...... **CLC 8; DAM MULT; HLC 2**
See also CA 5-8R; 105; CANR 8; HW 1; MTCW 1

Seneca, Lucius Annaeus c. 4B.C.-c. 65 .... **CMLC 6; DAM DRAM; DC 5**
See also DLB 211

Senghor, Leopold Sedar 1906- .... **CLC 54, 130; BLC 3; DAM MULT, POET; PC 25**
See also BW 2; CA 116; 125; CANR 47, 74; MTCW 1, 2

Senna, Danzy 1970- .... **CLC 119**
See also CA 169

Serling, (Edward) Rod(man)
1924-1975 .... **CLC 30**
See also AAYA 14; AITN 1; CA 162; 57-60; DLB 26

Serna, Ramon Gomez de la
See Gomez de la Serna, Ramon

Serpieres
See Guillevic, (Eugene)

Service, Robert
See Service, Robert W(illiam)
See also DAB; DLB 92

Seth, Vikram 1952- .... **CLC 43, 90; DAM MULT**
See also CA 121; 127; CANR 50, 74; DA3; DLB 120; INT 127; MTCW 2

Seton, Cynthia Propper 1926-1982 .. **CLC 27**
See also CA 5-8R; 108; CANR 7

Seton-Thompson, Ernest
See Seton, Ernest (Evan) Thompson

Settle, Mary Lee 1918- .... **CLC 19, 61**
See also CA 89-92; CAAS 1; CANR 44, 87; DLB 6; INT 89-92

Seuphor, Michel
See Arp, Jean

Sevigne, Marie (de Rabutin-Chantal) Marquise de 1626-1696 .... **LC 11**

Sewall, Samuel 1652-1730 .... **LC 38**
See also DLB 24

Sexton, Anne (Harvey) 1928-1974 ..... **CLC 2, 4, 6, 8, 10, 15, 53, 123; DA; DAB; DAC; DAM MST, POET; PC 2**
See also AMWS 2; BEST; CA 1-4R; 53-56; CABS 2; CANR 3, 36; CDALB 1941-1968; DA3; DLB 5, 169; MTCW 1, 2; SATA 10

Shaara, Jeff 1952- .... **CLC 119**
See also CA 163

Shaara, Michael (Joseph, Jr.)
1929-1988 .... **CLC 15; DAM POP**
See also AITN 1; CA 102; 125; CANR 52, 85; DLBY 83

Shackleton, C. C.
See Aldiss, Brian W(ilson)

Shacochis, Bob .... **CLC 39**
See also Shacochis, Robert G.

Shacochis, Robert G. 1951-
See Shacochis, Bob
See also CA 119; 124; INT 124

Shaffer, Anthony (Joshua) 1926- ..... **CLC 19; DAM DRAM**
See also CA 110; 116; DLB 13

Shaffer, Peter (Levin) 1926- .. **CLC 5, 14, 18, 37, 60; DAB; DAM DRAM, MST; DC 7**
See also BRWS 1; CA 25-28R; CANR 25, 47, 74; CDBLB 1960 to Present; DA3; DLB 13, 233; MTCW 1, 2

Shakey, Bernard
See Young, Neil

Shalamov, Varlam (Tikhonovich)
1907(?)-1982 .... **CLC 18**
See also CA 129; 105

Shamlu, Ahmad 1925-2000 .... **CLC 10**
See also CWW 2

Shammas, Anton 1951- .... **CLC 55**

Shandling, Arline
See Berriault, Gina

Shange, Ntozake 1948- .... **CLC 8, 25, 38, 74, 126; BLC 3; DAM DRAM, MULT; DC 3**
See also AAYA 9; BEST; BW 2; CA 85-88; CABS 3; CANR 27, 48, 74; DA3; DLB 38; MTCW 1, 2

Shanley, John Patrick 1950- .... **CLC 75**
See also CA 128; 133; CANR 83

Shapcott, Thomas W(illiam) 1935- .. **CLC 38**
See also CA 69-72; CANR 49, 83

Shapiro, Jane .... **CLC 76**

Shapiro, Karl (Jay) 1913-2000 ...... **CLC 4, 8, 15, 53; PC 25**
See also AMWS 2; CA 1-4R; 188; CAAS 6; CANR 1, 36, 66; DLB 48; MTCW 1, 2

Sharpe, Thomas Ridley 1928-
See Sharpe, Tom
See also CA 114; 122; CANR 85; DLB 231; INT 122

Stevens, Wallace 1879-1955 .... **PC 6**
  See also AW 3, 12, 45; CA 104; 124;
  CDALB 1929-1941; DA; DAB; DAC;
  DAM MST, POET; DA3; DLB 54;
  MTCW 1, 2

Stevenson, Anne (Katharine) 1933- .. **CLC 7,**
  33
  See also CA 17-20R; CAAS 9; CANR 9,
  33; DLB 40; MTCW 1

Stevenson, Robert Louis (Balfour)
  1850-1894 . **NCLC 5, 14, 63; DA; DAB;**
  DAC; DAM MST, NOV
  See also AAYA 24; CDBLB 1890-1914;
  CLR 10, 11; DA3; DLB 18, 57, 141, 156,
  174; DLBD 13; JRDA; MAICYA; SATA
  100

Stewart, J(ohn) I(nnes) M(ackintosh)
  1906-1994 .... **CLC 7, 14, 32**
  See also CA 85-88; 147; CAAS 3; CANR
  47; MTCW 1, 2

Stewart, Mary (Florence Elinor)
  1916- .... **CLC 7, 35, 117; DAB**
  See also AAYA 29; BEST; CA 1-4R; CANR
  1, 59; SATA 12

Stewart, Mary Rainbow
  See Stewart, Mary (Florence Elinor)

Stifle, June
  See Campbell, Maria

Stifter, Adalbert 1805-1868 .... **NCLC 41**
  See also AW 28; DLB 133

Still, James 1906-2001 .... **CLC 49**
  See also CA 65-68; CAAS 17; CANR 10,
  26; DLB 9; SATA 29

Sting 1951-
  See Sumner, Gordon Matthew
  See also CA 167

Stirling, Arthur
  See Sinclair, Upton (Beall)

Stitt, Milan 1941- .... **CLC 29**
  See also CA 69-72

Stockton, Francis Richard 1834-1902
  See Stockton, Frank R.
  See also CA 108; 137; MAICYA; SATA 44

Stoddard, Charles
  See Kuttner, Henry

Stoker, Abraham 1847-1912
  See Stoker, Bram
  See also CA 105; 150; DA; DAC; DAM
  MST, NOV; DA3; SATA 29

Stolz, Mary (Slattery) 1920- .... **CLC 12**
  See also AAYA 8; AITN 1; BEST; CA 5-8R;
  CANR 13, 41; JRDA; MAICYA; SAAS
  3; SATA 10, 71

Stone, Irving 1903-1989 . **CLC 7; DAM POP**
  See also AITN 1; CA 1-4R; 129; CAAS 3;
  CANR 1, 23; DA3; INT CANR-23;
  MTCW 1, 2; SATA 3; SATA-Obit 64

Stone, Oliver (William) 1946- .... **CLC 73**
  See also AAYA 15; CA 110; CANR 55

Stone, Robert (Anthony) 1937- ... **CLC 5, 23,**
  42
  See also AMWS 5; CA 85-88; CANR 23,
  66, 95; DLB 152; INT CANR-23; MTCW
  1

Stone, Zachary
  See Follett, Ken(neth Martin)

Stoppard, Tom 1937- ... **CLC 1, 3, 4, 5, 8, 15,**
  29, 34, 63, 91; DA; DAB; DAC; DAM
  DRAM, MST; DC 6
  See also BEST; BRWS 1; CA 81-84; CANR
  39, 67; CDBLB 1960 to Present; DA3;
  DLB 13, 233; DLBY 85; MTCW 1, 2

Storey, David (Malcolm) 1933- . **CLC 2, 4, 5,**
  8; DAM DRAM
  See also BRWS 1; CA 81-84; CANR 36;
  DLB 13, 14, 207; MTCW 1

Storm, Hyemeyohsts 1935- ..... **CLC 3; DAM**
  MULT
  See also CA 81-84; CANR 45; NNAL

Storm, (Hans) Theodor (Woldsen)
  1817-1888 .... **NCLC 1**
  See also AW 27; DLB 129

Storni, Alfonsina 1892-1938 .... **PC 33**
  See also AW 5; CA 104; 131; DAM MULT;
  HLC 2; HW 1

Stoughton, William 1631-1701 .... **LC 38**
  See also DLB 24

Stout, Rex (Todhunter) 1886-1975 ..... **CLC 3**
  See also AITN 2; CA 61-64; CANR 71

Stow, (Julian) Randolph 1935- ... **CLC 23, 48**
  See also CA 13-16R; CANR 33; MTCW 1

Stowe, Harriet (Elizabeth) Beecher
  1811-1896 .... **NCLC 3, 50; DA; DAB;**
  DAC; DAM MST, NOV
  See also AMWS 1; BEST; CDALB 1865-
  1917; DA3; DLB 1, 12, 42, 74, 189, 239;
  JRDA; MAICYA

Strabo c. 64B.C.-c. 25 .... **CMLC 37**
  See also DLB 176

Strand, Mark 1934- .... **CLC 6, 18, 41, 71;**
  DAM POET
  See also AMWS 4; CA 21-24R; CANR 40,
  65; DLB 5; SATA 41

Stratton-Porter, Gene(va Grace) 1863-1924
  See Porter, Gene(va Grace) Stratton
  See also CA 137; DLB 221; DLBD 14;
  MAICYA; SATA 15

Straub, Peter (Francis) 1943- . **CLC 28, 107;**
  DAM POP
  See also BEST 89:1; CA 85-88; CANR 28,
  65; DLBY 84; MTCW 1, 2

Strauss, Botho 1944- .... **CLC 22**
  See also CA 157; CWW 2; DLB 124

Streatfeild, (Mary) Noel
  1897(?)-1986 .... **CLC 21**
  See also CA 81-84; 120; CANR 31; CLR
  17; DLB 160; MAICYA; SATA 20; SATA-
  Obit 48

Stribling, T(homas) S(igismund)
  1881-1965 .... **CLC 23**
  See also CA 189; 107; DLB 9

Stringer, David
  See Roberts, Keith (John Kingston)

Strugatskii, Arkadii (Natanovich)
  1925-1991 .... **CLC 27**
  See also CA 106; 135

Strugatskii, Boris (Natanovich)
  1933- .... **CLC 27**
  See also CA 106

Strummer, Joe 1953(?)- .... **CLC 30**

Stryk, Lucien 1924- .... **PC 27**
  See also CA 13-16R; CANR 10, 28, 55

Stuart, Don A.
  See Campbell, John W(ood, Jr.)

Stuart, Ian
  See MacLean, Alistair (Stuart)

Stuart, Jesse (Hilton) 1906-1984 ... **CLC 1, 8,**
  11, 14, 34
  See also AW 31; CA 5-8R; 112; CANR 31;
  DLB 9, 48, 102; DLBY 84; SATA 2;
  SATA-Obit 36

Sturgeon, Theodore (Hamilton)
  1918-1985 .... **CLC 22, 39**
  See also Queen, Ellery
  See also CA 81-84; 116; CANR 32; DLB 8;
  DLBY 85; MTCW 1, 2

Styron, William 1925- .... **CLC 1, 3, 5, 11, 15,**
  60; DAM NOV, POP
  See also AW 25; BEST 90:4; CA 5-8R;
  CANR 6, 33, 74; CDALB 1968-1988;
  DA3; DLB 2, 143; DLBY 80; INT
  CANR-6; MTCW 1, 2

Su, Chien 1884-1918
  See Su Man-shu
  See also CA 123

Suarez Lynch, B.
  See Bioy Casares, Adolfo; Borges, Jorge
  Luis

Suassuna, Ariano Vilar 1927-
  See also CA 178; HLCS 1; HW 2

Suckling, SirJohn 1609-1642 .... **PC 30**
  See also DAM POET; DLB 58, 126

Sue, Eugene 1804-1857 .... **NCLC 1**
  See also DLB 119

Sueskind, Patrick 1949- .... **CLC 44**
  See also Suskind, Patrick

Sukenick, Ronald 1932- .... **CLC 3, 4, 6, 48**
  See also CA 25-28R; CAAS 8; CANR 32,
  89; DLB 173; DLBY 81

Suknaski, Andrew 1942- .... **CLC 19**
  See also CA 101; DLB 53

Sullivan, Vernon
  See Vian, Boris

Summerforest, Ivy B.
  See Kirkup, James

Summers, Andrew James 1942- .... **CLC 26**

Summers, Andy
  See Summers, Andrew James

Summers, Hollis (Spurgeon, Jr.)
  1916- .... **CLC 10**
  See also CA 5-8R; CANR 3; DLB 6

Sumner, Gordon Matthew .... **CLC 26**
  See also Sting

Surtees, Robert Smith 1805-1864 .. **NCLC 14**
  See also DLB 21

Susann, Jacqueline 1921-1974 .... **CLC 3**
  See also AITN 1; CA 65-68; 53-56; MTCW
  1, 2

Su Shih 1036-1101 .... **CMLC 15**

Suskind, Patrick
  See Sueskind, Patrick
  See also CA 145; CWW 2

Sutcliff, Rosemary 1920-1992 .... **CLC 26;**
  DAB; DAC; DAM MST, POP
  See also AAYA 10; BEST; CA 5-8R; 139;
  CANR 37; CLR 1, 37; JRDA; MAICYA;
  SATA 6, 44, 78; SATA-Obit 73

Sutton, Henry
  See Slavitt, David R(ytman)

Suzuki, D. T.
  See Suzuki, Daisetz Teitaro

Suzuki, Daisetz T.
  See Suzuki, Daisetz Teitaro

Suzuki, Teitaro
  See Suzuki, Daisetz Teitaro

Swados, Elizabeth (A.) 1951- .... **CLC 12**
  See also CA 97-100; CANR 49; INT 97-
  100

Swados, Harvey 1920-1972 .... **CLC 5**
  See also CA 5-8R; 37-40R; CANR 6; DLB
  2

Swan, Gladys 1934- .... **CLC 69**
  See also CA 101; CANR 17, 39

Swanson, Logan
  See Matheson, Richard Burton

Swarthout, Glendon (Fred)
  1918-1992 .... **CLC 35**
  See also AW 2; BEST; CA 1-4R; 139;
  CANR 1, 47; SATA 26

Sweet, Sarah C.
  See Jewett, (Theodora) Sarah Orne

Swenson, May 1919-1989 ...... **CLC 4, 14, 61,**
  106; DA; DAB; DAC; DAM MST,
  POET; PC 14
  See also AMWS 4; CA 5-8R; 130; CANR
  36, 61; DLB 5; GLL 2; MTCW 1, 2;
  SATA 15

Swift, Augustus
  See Lovecraft, H(oward) P(hillips)

Swift, Graham (Colin) 1949- ...... **CLC 41, 88**
  See also BRWS 5; CA 117; 122; CANR 46,
  71; DLB 194; MTCW 2

Thomas, D(onald) M(ichael) 1935- . **CLC 13, 22, 31, 132**
See also BRWS 4; CA 61-64; CAAS 11; CANR 17, 45, 75; CDBLB 1960 to Present; DA3; DLB 40, 207; INT CANR-17; MTCW 1, 2

Thomas, Dylan (Marlais) 1914-1953 ..... **PC 2**
See also AW 1, 8, 45, 105; BRWS 1; CA 104; 120; CANR 65; CDBLB 1945-1960; DA; DAB; DAC; DAM DRAM, MST, POET, DA3; DLB 13, 20, 139; MTCW 1, 2; SATA 60

Thomas, Joyce Carol 1938- .... **CLC 35**
See also AAYA 12; BEST; BW 2, 3; CA 113; 116; CANR 48; CLR 19; DLB 33; INT 116; JRDA; MAICYA; MTCW 1, 2; SAAS 7; SATA 40, 78

Thomas, Lewis 1913-1993 .... **CLC 35**
See also CA 85-88; 143; CANR 38, 60; MTCW 1, 2

Thomas, Paul
See Mann, (Paul) Thomas

Thomas, Piri 1928- .... **CLC 17; HLCS 2**
See also CA 73-76; HW 1

Thomas, R(onald) S(tuart) 1913-2000 . **CLC 6, 13, 48; DAB; DAM POET**
See also CA 89-92; 189; CAAS 4; CANR 30; CDBLB 1960 to Present; DLB 27; MTCW 1

Thomas, Ross (Elmore) 1926-1995 .. **CLC 39**
See also CA 33-36R; 150; CANR 22, 63

Thompson, Francis Clegg
See Mencken, H(enry) L(ouis)

Thompson, Hunter S(tockton) 1939- ... **CLC 9, 17, 40, 104; DAM POP**
See also BEST 89:1; CA 17-20R; CANR 23, 46, 74, 77; DA3; DLB 185; MTCW 1, 2

Thompson, James Myers
See Thompson, Jim (Myers)

Thompson, Jim (Myers) 1906-1977(?) .... **CLC 69**
See also CA 140; DLB 226

Thompson, Judith .... **CLC 39**

Thomson, James 1700-1748 ... **LC 16, 29, 40; DAM POET**
See also BRWS 3; DLB 95

Thomson, James 1834-1882 .... **NCLC 18; DAM POET**
See also DLB 35

Thoreau, Henry David 1817-1862 .. **NCLC 7, 21, 61; DA; DAB; DAC; DAM MST; PC 30**
See also BEST; CDALB 1640-1865; DA3; DLB 1, 223

Thorndike, E. L.
See Thorndike, Edward L(ee)

Thornton, Hall
See Silverberg, Robert

Thucydides c. 460B.C.-399B.C. ..... **CMLC 17**
See also DLB 176

Thumboo, Edwin 1933- .... **PC 30**

Thurber, James (Grover) 1894-1961 .... **CLC 5, 11, 25, 125; DA; DAB; DAC; DAM DRAM, MST, NOV**
See also AMWS 1; CA 73-76; CANR 17, 39; CDALB 1929-1941; DA3; DLB 4, 11, 22, 102; MAICYA; MTCW 1, 2; SATA 13

Tibullus c. 54B.C.-c. 18B.C. .... **CMLC 36**
See also DLB 211

Ticheburn, Cheviot
See Ainsworth, William Harrison

Tieck, (Johann) Ludwig 1773-1853 .... **NCLC 5, 46**
See also DLB 90

Tiger, Derry
See Ellison, Harlan (Jay)

Tilghman, Christopher 1948(?)- .... **CLC 65**
See also CA 159

Tillich, Paul (Johannes) 1886-1965 .... **CLC 131**
See also CA 5-8R; 25-28R; CANR 33; MTCW 1, 2

Tillinghast, Richard (Williford) 1940- .... **CLC 29**
See also CA 29-32R; CAAS 23; CANR 26, 51, 96

Timrod, Henry 1828-1867 .... **NCLC 25**
See also DLB 3

Tindall, Gillian (Elizabeth) 1938- ...... **CLC 7**
See also CA 21-24R; CANR 11, 65

Tiptree, James, Jr. .... **CLC 48, 50**
See also Sheldon, Alice Hastings Bradley
See also DLB 8

Titmarsh, Michael Angelo
See Thackeray, William Makepeace

Tocqueville, Alexis (Charles Henri Maurice Clerel 1805-1859 .... **NCLC 7, 63**

Tolkien, J(ohn) R(onald) R(euel) 1892-1973 .. **CLC 1, 2, 3, 8, 12, 38; DA; DAB; DAC; DAM MST, NOV, POP**
See also AAYA 10; AITN 1; BRWS 2; CA 17-18; 45-48; CANR 36; CAP 2; CDBLB 1914-1945; CLR 56; DA3; DLB 15, 160; JRDA; MAICYA; MTCW 1, 2; SATA 2, 32, 100; SATA-Obit 24

Tolson, M. B.
See Tolson, Melvin B(eaunorus)

Tolson, Melvin B(eaunorus) 1898(?)-1966 .... **CLC 36, 105; BLC 3; DAM MULT, POET**
See also BW 1, 3; CA 124; 89-92; CANR 80; DLB 48, 76

Tolstoi, Aleksei Nikolaevich
See Tolstoy, Alexey Nikolaevich

Tolstoy, Count Leo
See Tolstoy, Leo (Nikolaevich)

Tomasi di Lampedusa, Giuseppe 1896-1957
See Lampedusa, Giuseppe (Tomasi) di
See also CA 111

Tomlin, Lily .... **CLC 17**
See also Tomlin, Mary Jean

Tomlin, Mary Jean 1939(?)-
See Tomlin, Lily
See also CA 117

Tomlinson, (Alfred) Charles 1927- .... **CLC 2, 4, 6, 13, 45; DAM POET; PC 17**
See also CA 5-8R; CANR 33; DLB 40

Tonson, Jacob
See Bennett, (Enoch) Arnold

Toole, John Kennedy 1937-1969 ..... **CLC 19, 64**
See also CA 104; DLBY 81; MTCW 2

Toomer, Jean 1892-1967 .... **CLC 1, 4, 13, 22; BLC 3; DAM MULT; PC 7**
See also Pinchback, Eugene; Toomer, Eugene; Toomer, Eugene Pinchback; Toomer, Nathan Jean; Toomer, Nathan Pinchback
See also AMWS 3; AW 5; BEST; BW 1; CA 85-88; CDALB 1917-1929; DA3; DLB 45, 51; MTCW 1, 2

Torley, Luke
See Blish, James (Benjamin)

Tornimparte, Alessandra
See Ginzburg, Natalia

Torre, Raoul della
See Mencken, H(enry) L(ouis)

Torrey, E(dwin) Fuller 1937- .... **CLC 34**
See also CA 119; CANR 71

Torsvan, Ben Traven
See Traven, B.

Torsvan, Benno Traven
See Traven, B.

Torsvan, Berick Traven
See Traven, B.

Torsvan, Berwick Traven
See Traven, B.

Torsvan, Bruno Traven
See Traven, B.

Torsvan, Traven
See Traven, B.

Tourneur, Cyril 1575(?)-1626 .. **LC 66; DAM DRAM**
See also DLB 58

Tournier, Michel (Edouard) 1924- .... **CLC 6, 23, 36, 95**
See also CA 49-52; CANR 3, 36, 74; DLB 83; MTCW 1, 2; SATA 23

Tournimparte, Alessandra
See Ginzburg, Natalia

Towers, Ivar
See Kornbluth, C(yril) M.

Towne, Robert (Burton) 1936(?)- ..... **CLC 87**
See also CA 108; DLB 44; IDFW 3

Townsend, Sue .... **CLC 61**
See also Townsend, Susan Elaine
See also AAYA 28; SATA 55, 93; SATA-Brief 48

Townsend, Susan Elaine 1946-
See Townsend, Sue
See also BEST; CA 119; 127; CANR 65; DAB; DAC; DAM MST; INT 127

Townshend, Peter (Dennis Blandford) 1945- .... **CLC 17, 42**
See also CA 107

Tracy, Don(ald Fiske) 1905-1970(?)
See Queen, Ellery
See also CA 1-4R; 176; CANR 2

Traill, Catharine Parr 1802-1899 .. **NCLC 31**
See also DLB 99

Trakl, Georg 1887-1914 .... **PC 20**
See also AW 5; CA 104; 165; MTCW 2

Transtroemer, Tomas (Goesta) 1931- .... **CLC 52, 65; DAM POET**
See also CA 117; 129; CAAS 17

Transtromer, Tomas Gosta
See Transtroemer, Tomas (Goesta)

Traven, B. 1882(?)-1969 .... **CLC 8, 11**
See also CA 19-20; 25-28R; CAP 2; DLB 9, 56; MTCW 1

Treitel, Jonathan 1959- .... **CLC 70**

Trelawny, Edward John 1792-1881 .... **NCLC 85**
See also DLB 110, 116, 144

Tremain, Rose 1943- .... **CLC 42**
See also CA 97-100; CANR 44, 95; DLB 14

Tremblay, Michel 1942- .... **CLC 29, 102; DAC; DAM MST**
See also CA 116; 128; CCA 1; CWW 2; DLB 60; GLL 1; MTCW 1, 2

Trevanian .... **CLC 29**
See also Whitaker, Rod(ney)

Trevor, Glen
See Hilton, James

Trevor, William .... **CLC 7, 9, 14, 25, 71, 116**
See also Cox, William Trevor
See also AW 10; BRWS 4; DLB 14, 139; MTCW 2

Trifonov, Yuri (Valentinovich) 1925-1981 .... **CLC 45**
See also CA 126; 103; MTCW 1

Trilling, Diana (Rubin) 1905-1996 . **CLC 129**
See also CA 5-8R; 154; CANR 10, 46; INT CANR-10; MTCW 1, 2

Trilling, Lionel 1905-1975 .... **CLC 9, 11, 24**
See also AMWS 3; CA 9-12R; 61-64; CANR 10; DLB 28, 63; INT CANR-10; MTCW 1, 2

Trimball, W. H.
See Mencken, H(enry) L(ouis)

Tristan
See Gomez de la Serna, Ramon

Literary Criticism Series
Cumulative Topic Index

This index lists all topic entries in Gale's *Classical and Medieval Literature Criticism, Contemporary Literary Criticism, Literature Criticism from 1400 to 1800, Nineteenth-Century Literature Criticism,* and *Twentieth-Century Literary Criticism.*

Topic Index

CLC Cumulative Nationality Index

ALBANIAN

Kadare, Ismail **52**

ALGERIAN

Althusser, Louis **106**
Camus, Albert **1, 2, 4, 9, 11, 14, 32, 63, 69, 124**
Cixous, Hélène **92**
Cohen-Solal, Annie **50**

AMERICAN

Abbey, Edward **36, 59**
Abbott, Lee K(ittredge) **48**
Abish, Walter **22**
Abrams, M(eyer) H(oward) **24**
Acker, Kathy **45, 111**
Adams, Alice (Boyd) **6, 13, 46**
Addams, Charles (Samuel) **30**
Adler, C(arole) S(chwerdtfeger) **35**
Adler, Renata **8, 31**
Ai **4, 14, 69**
Aiken, Conrad (Potter) **1, 3, 5, 10, 52**
Albee, Edward (Franklin III) **1, 2, 3, 5, 9, 11, 13, 25, 53, 86, 113**
Alexander, Lloyd (Chudley) **35**
Alexie, Sherman (Joseph Jr.) **96**
Algren, Nelson **4, 10, 33**
Allen, Edward **59**
Allen, Paula Gunn **84**
Allen, Woody **16, 52**
Allison, Dorothy E. **78**
Alta **19**
Alter, Robert B(ernard) **34**
Alther, Lisa **7, 41**
Altman, Robert **16, 116**
Alvarez, Julia **93**
Ambrose, Stephen E(dward) **145**
Ammons, A(rchie) R(andolph) **2, 3, 5, 8, 9, 25, 57, 108**
L'Amour, Louis (Dearborn) **25, 55**
Anaya, Rudolfo A(lfonso) **23**
Anderson, Jon (Victor) **9**
Anderson, Poul (William) **15**
Anderson, Robert (Woodruff) **23**
Angell, Roger **26**
Angelou, Maya **12, 35, 64, 77**
Anthony, Piers **35**
Apple, Max (Isaac) **9, 33**
Appleman, Philip (Dean) **51**
Archer, Jules **12**
Arendt, Hannah **66, 98**
Arnow, Harriette (Louisa) Simpson **2, 7, 18**
Arrick, Fran **30**
Arzner, Dorothy **98**
Ashbery, John (Lawrence) **2, 3, 4, 6, 9, 13, 15, 25, 41, 77, 125**
Asimov, Isaac **1, 3, 9, 19, 26, 76, 92**
Attaway, William (Alexander) **92**
Auchincloss, Louis (Stanton) **4, 6, 9, 18, 45**
Auden, W(ystan) H(ugh) **1, 2, 3, 4, 6, 9, 11, 14, 43, 123**
Auel, Jean M(arie) **31, 107**

Auster, Paul **47, 131**
Bach, Richard (David) **14**
Badanes, Jerome **59**
Baker, Elliott **8**
Baker, Nicholson **61**
Baker, Russell (Wayne) **31**
Bakshi, Ralph **26**
Baldwin, James (Arthur) **1, 2, 3, 4, 5, 8, 13, 15, 17, 42, 50, 67, 90, 127**
Bambara, Toni Cade **19, 88**
Banks, Russell **37, 72**
Baraka, Amiri **1, 2, 3, 5, 10, 14, 33, 115**
Barber, Benjamin R. **141**
Barbera, Jack (Vincent) **44**
Barnard, Mary (Ethel) **48**
Barnes, Djuna **3, 4, 8, 11, 29, 127**
Barondess, Sue K(aufman) **8**
Barrett, William (Christopher) **27**
Barth, John (Simmons) **1, 2, 3, 5, 7, 9, 10, 14, 27, 51, 89**
Barthelme, Donald **1, 2, 3, 5, 6, 8, 13, 23, 46, 59, 115**
Barthelme, Frederick **36, 117**
Barzun, Jacques (Martin) **51, 145**
Bass, Rick **79, 143**
Baumbach, Jonathan **6, 23**
Bausch, Richard (Carl) **51**
Baxter, Charles (Morley) **45, 78**
Beagle, Peter S(oyer) **7, 104**
Beattie, Ann **8, 13, 18, 40, 63**
Becker, Walter **26**
Beecher, John **6**
Begiebing, Robert J(ohn) **70**
Behrman, S(amuel) N(athaniel) **40**
Belitt, Ben **22**
Bell, Madison Smartt **41, 102**
Bell, Marvin (Hartley) **8, 31**
Bellow, Saul **1, 2, 3, 6, 8, 10, 13, 15, 25, 33, 34, 63, 79**
Benary-Isbert, Margot **12**
Benchley, Peter (Bradford) **4, 8**
Benedikt, Michael **4, 14**
Benford, Gregory (Albert) **52**
Bennett, Hal **5**
Bennett, Jay **35**
Benson, Jackson J. **34**
Benson, Sally **17**
Bentley, Eric (Russell) **24**
Berendt, John (Lawrence) **86**
Berger, Melvin H. **12**
Berger, Thomas (Louis) **3, 5, 8, 11, 18, 38**
Bergstein, Eleanor **4**
Bernard, April **59**
Bernstein, Charles **142**
Berriault, Gina **54, 109**
Berrigan, Daniel **4**
Berrigan, Ted **37**
Berry, Chuck **17**
Berry, Wendell (Erdman) **4, 6, 8, 27, 46**
Berryman, John **1, 2, 3, 4, 6, 8, 10, 13, 25, 62**
Bessie, Alvah **23**
Bettelheim, Bruno **79**

Betts, Doris (Waugh) **3, 6, 28**
Bidart, Frank **33**
Birkerts, Sven **116**
Bishop, Elizabeth **1, 4, 9, 13, 15, 32**
Bishop, John **10**
Blackburn, Paul **9, 43**
Blackmur, R(ichard) P(almer) **2, 24**
Blaise, Clark **29**
Blatty, William Peter **2**
Blessing, Lee **54**
Blish, James (Benjamin) **14**
Bloch, Robert (Albert) **33**
Bloom, Harold **24, 103**
Blount, Roy (Alton) Jr. **38**
Blume, Judy (Sussman) **12, 30**
Bly, Robert (Elwood) **1, 2, 5, 10, 15, 38, 128**
Bochco, Steven **35**
Bogan, Louise **4, 39, 46, 93**
Bogosian, Eric **45, 141**
Bograd, Larry **35**
Bonham, Frank **12**
Bontemps, Arna(ud Wendell) **1, 18**
Booth, Philip **23**
Booth, Wayne C(layson) **24**
Bottoms, David **53**
Bourjaily, Vance (Nye) **8, 62**
Bova, Ben(jamin William) **45**
Bowers, Edgar **9**
Bowles, Jane (Sydney) **3, 68**
Bowles, Paul (Frederick) **1, 2, 19, 53**
Boyle, Kay **1, 5, 19, 58, 121**
Boyle, T(homas) Coraghessan **36, 55, 90**
Bradbury, Ray (Douglas) **1, 3, 10, 15, 42, 98**
Bradley, David (Henry) Jr. **23, 118**
Bradley, John Ed(mund Jr.) **55**
Bradley, Marion Zimmer **30**
Bradshaw, John **70**
Brady, Joan **86**
Brammer, William **31**
Brancato, Robin F(idler) **35**
Brand, Millen **7**
Branden, Barbara **44**
Branley, Franklyn M(ansfield) **21**
Brautigan, Richard (Gary) **1, 3, 5, 9, 12, 34, 42**
Braverman, Kate **67**
Brennan, Maeve **5**
Breslin, Jimmy **4, 43**
Bridgers, Sue Ellen **26**
Brin, David **34**
Brodkey, Harold (Roy) **56**
Brodsky, Joseph **4, 6, 13, 36, 100**
Brodsky, Michael (Mark) **19**
Bromell, Henry **5**
Broner, E(sther) M(asserman) **19**
Bronk, William (M.) **10**
Brooks, Cleanth **24, 86, 110**
Brooks, Gwendolyn (Elizabeth) **1, 2, 4, 5, 15, 49, 125**
Brooks, Mel **12**
Brooks, Peter **34**

Nationality Index

CLC-145 Title Index

ISBN 0-7876-4634-2

9 780787 646349